Dictionary of Anonymous and Pseudonymous
English Literature

Dictionary

OF

Anonymous and Pseudonymous English Literature

(SAMUEL HALKETT AND JOHN LAING)

NEW AND ENLARGED EDITION

BY

Dr JAMES KENNEDY

LIBRARIAN, NEW COLLEGE, EDINBURGH

W. A. SMITH AND A. F. JOHNSON

PRINTED BOOKS DEPARTMENT, BRITISH MUSEUM

VOLUME SIX

OLIVER AND BOYD

EDINBURGH: TWEEDDALE COURT

LONDON: 33 PATERNOSTER ROW, E.C.

1932

PRINTED IN GREAT BRITAIN BY
OLIVER AND BOYD LTD., EDINBURGH

PREFATORY NOTE

THE supplement has been brought to as great a state of perfection as the leisure of the editors has allowed, and publishers and editors desire to return thanks to all those who have so kindly assisted with material. First to the many correspondents who have sent information on individual books, frequently from family sources and therefore particularly valuable, because otherwise inaccessible. Secondly to those who have helped in a more comprehensive fashion, and among these in particular to the Rev. Charles R. Gillett for materials from the M'Alpin Collection, the catalogue of which, now complete, is a mine of information for the period with which it deals; to Mr John Grant, bookseller, of Edinburgh, for many notes of MS. attributions on copies which have passed through his stock; to Mr Thomas Warburton of Manchester, Messrs G. Harding of Great Russell Street, London, and Dr Offor, Librarian of Leeds University.

Finally the editors desire to thank their colleagues in the Department of Printed Books for a large amount of correction which has been obtained during the preparation of the new edition of the British Museum Catalogue. Where all have helped, it is invidious to particularise, but they feel under special obligation to Messrs A. G. Macfarlane, H. Sellers, C. B. Oldman, and F. C. Francis, and latterly to Mr F. D. Cooper for many corrections on Americana.

W. A. SMITH
A. F. JOHNSON

WITH a view to the issuing of further supplements to this important book of reference the Publishers would be grateful if Authors, Publishers, Librarians and others interested in Anonymous books, would send full particulars of the errors and omissions they encounter, and also of new books as they are issued, in order that the Dictionary may be kept as up-to-date as possible.

Communications to OLIVER & BOYD LTD., Tweeddale Court, Edinburgh, will be duly acknowledged.

A Dictionary of the
Anonymous and Pseudonymous
Literature of Great Britain

T

T. H. BURN [Thomas Harris Burn] ; in memoriam. [By George E. L. Cotton, Bishop of Calcutta.] 8vo. [*Camb. Univ. Lib.*] N.P. [1864]

TABELLA cibaria ; the bill of fare : a Latin poem, implicitly translated and fully explained in copious and interesting notes relating to the pleasures of gastronomy, and the mysterious art of cookery. [By the Abbé Ange-Denis Macquin.] 4to. [O'Donoghue's *Poets of Ireland*.] London, 1820

TABITHA Smallways, schoolgirl. By Raymond Jacberns [Miss M. Selby Ashe]. 8vo. Pp. 310. London, 1912

TABLE (the) and the turner ; or, which of the two is possessed ? Containing remarks on the pamphlets of Messrs Close, Dibdin, Godfrey, "A physician," etc. etc. ; with certain proposed tests, whereby to ascertain, if possible, whether table-turning and table-talking is or is not diabolical. By an anxious enquirer after truth [David Baxter Langley]. 12mo. Pp. 28. [*Bodl.*] London, 1854

TABLE (a) collected of the yeares of our Lorde God, and of the yeares of the Kynges of Englande, from the fyrst yeare of William the Conquerour, shewyng how the yeares of our Lorde God, and the yeres of the Kynges of England concurre and agree together. . . . [By William Rastell.] 8vo. B. L. [*Brit. Mus.*] Londini, 1561

TABLE for determining the apparent time from observed altitudes of the sun or a star. [By Sir Thomas M. Brisbane, Bart.] 8vo. [*Brit. Mus.*] [Cambray] 1818

TABLE (a) of a decimal system of account. [By Harry Borradaile.] 4to. [*Brit. Mus.*] London, 1853

TABLE (a) of dates for the use of genealogists and antiquaries. [By Thomas Moule.] 8vo. [*Brit. Mus.*] London, 1820

TABLE (a) of redemption shewing at one view in what time the principal and interest of any debt from 3 to 6 per % may be discharged by any fund producing yearly from 3½ to 12 per %, with remarks relating to our publick debts. By T. W. [T. Watkins]. Fol. [*W.*] London, 1717

TABLE (a) of the circles arising from the division of a unit, or any other whole number, by all the integers from 1 to 1024 ; being all the pure decimal quotients that can arise from this source. [By Henry Goodwyn, a brewer in West Smithfield.] 8vo. Pp. v. 118. [*Brit. Mus.*] London, 1823

TABLE (a) of the gold coins of the kings of England. By B. W. [Browne Willis], Esq., a member of the Society of Antiquaries. Fol. [Nichols' *Lit. Anec.* ii. 35.] 1733

TABLE (the) of the Lord. By the author of *The Listener, Christ our example*, etc. [Caroline Fry]. 8vo. London, 1837

TABLE (the) of the road : 2 parts. [By Edward Adderley Stopford, Archdeacon of Meath.] 8vo. [F. Boase's *Mod. Eng. Biog.* vi. col. 632.] London, 1853-56

TABLE of the unity of religion in the school of Nazareth. . . . [By T. Martin.] 12mo. [*Brit. Mus.*] London, 1846

TAB   2   TAC

TABLE (the) talker ; or, brief essays on society and literature. [By Wm. Johnstone.] 12mo. 2 vols. [*Nat. Lib. of Scot.*]   London, 1840

TABLE turning and table talking considered with reference to some pamphlets published by N. S. Godfrey and Edward Gillson. By a Member of the University of Cambridge [Rev. William John Edge]. 12mo. [Green's *Bibl. Somers.* i. 205.]
            Cheltenham, 1853

TABLES and chairs ; a practical guide to economical furnishing. By the author of *How to dress on £15 a year* [Millicent Whiteside Cook]. 8vo. Pp. 153.   London [1876]

TABLES calculated to facilitate business in the tin trade. [By Richard Wellington.] 8vo. [Boase and Courtney's *Bibl. Corn.*]
            Marazion, 1836

TABLES for the four Evangelists, containing: I. The harmony of the Gospels, and their general contents. II. The order and number of Christ's recorded appearances after his resurrection. III. The several passages of the Evangelists, as stated in the harmony. IV. A state of our Lord's discourses, according to the order of time. V. A state of our Lord's parables, according to the order of time. VI. A state of our Lord's miracles, according to the order of time. VII. A view of the places where our Lord sojourned. . . . [By Adam Gib.] 8vo. Pp. 31.
            Edinburgh, 1770
    The second edition was published with the author's name.

TABLES for the Holy Alliance, rhymes on the road, etc. etc. By Thomas Brown, the younger, secretary to the Poco-curante Society, and author of *The Fudge-family* and *The Two-penny post-bag* [Thomas Moore]. New edition. 8vo. Pp. ix. 200.
            London, 1823

TABLES of ancient coins, weights and measures, explain'd and exemplify'd in several dissertations. [By John Arbuthnot, M.D.] 4to. [*D. N. B.* vol. 2, p. 64.]   London, 1727

TABLES of the aberration, annual variation, solar and lunar nutation, in N.P.D. for 40 principal fixed stars for every day of the year 1825, as made use of in the computation of the Greenwich standard catalogue. [By John Pond, F.R.S. Fol. Pp. 122, 6.   N.P. [*c*.1830]

TABLES of the increase or decrease of gold and silver in bars. [By —— Seyfang.] 12mo.   Walworth, 1819

TABLET (the) of Cebes ; or, a picture of human life : a poem, copied from the Greek of Cebes the Theban. By a gentleman of Oxford [T. Powis of St John's College]. 4to. Pp. 23. [*Camb. Univ. Lib.*]   Oxford, 1759

TABLET (the) or moderation of Charles the First martyr ; with an alarum to the subjects of England. [By John Arnway, D.D.] 8vo. Pp. 124. [*Bodl.*]   1649
    Address to the King signed : A. A.

TABLET (the) ; or, picture of real life . . . in a select set of essays, serious and jocose, upon the most interesting subjects . . . [By Peter Shaw.] 8vo. Pp. xx. 371. [*Brit. Mus.*]
            London, 1762
    First issued in 1750 as "The reflector, representing human affairs . . ." *q.v.* These are the same sheets, with a new title-page.

TABLE-TALK ; or, selections from the Ana : containing extracts from the different collections of Ana, French, English, Italian, and German, with bibliographical notices. [By George Moir.] 8vo. Pp. x. 326. [Constable's *Miscellany*, vol. x.]   Edinburgh, 1827

TABOR'S teachings ; or, the veil lifted : a glimpse of Christ's glory and intercourse with his people for ever. By the author of *Heaven our home*, etc. [William Branks, minister in Torphichen]. 8vo. Pp. x. 271. [*Brit. Mus.*]   Edinburgh, 1865

TABULA numerorum quadratorum decies millium . . . A table of ten thousand square numbers. . . . [By John Pell.] Fol. [*Brit. Mus.*]
            London, 1672

TABULÆ linguarum ; tables of nouns and verbs. . . . By H. C. [Henry Clarke]. 12mo. [*D. N. B.* vol. 10, p. 427.]   Manchester, 1793

TABULAR (a) series of decimal quotients for all the proper vulgar fractions, of which, when in their lowest terms, neither the numerator nor the denominator is greater than 1000. [By Henry Goodwyn.] 8vo. Pp. v. 153. [*Camb. Univ. Lib.*]   London, 1823

TACITUS and Bracciolini ; the Annals forged in the XVth century. [By John Wilson Ross.] 8vo. [*Lib. Journ.* iv. 24.]   London, 1878

TACTICAL notes. By X. Y. Z., author of *The Officer's vade mecum* [Capt. Ronald Martin]. 12mo. Pp. 176.
            London, 1915

TACTICAL talks and tramps. By Sextus [William Charles Christie]. For Officers and N.C.O.'s of the Special Reserve and Territorial Force. 8vo. Pp. 80. [*Brit. Mus.*]
            London, [1911]

TACTOMETRIA ; or, the geometry of regulars. By J. W. [J. Wybard]. 8vo. [*Queen's Coll. Cat.* i. 637.]
London, 1650

TAFFI'S masterpiece . . . Being the Muscipula Oxoniensis [of Edward Holdsworth], translated into burlesque verse by a Cantab. 8vo. [*Brit. Mus.*]
London, 1709
Other translations were entitled " Muscipula . . ." and " The Mouse-trap . . ."

TAGHCONIC ; or, letters and legends about our summer home. By Godfrey Greylock [Joseph Edward Adams Smith]. 12mo. [*Brit. Mus.*]
Boston, 1852

TAHTAR (the) tribes. [By John Kitto, D.D.] 12mo. [*G. C. Boase.*]
London, 1848

TAILOR (the) of Gloucester. By Beatrix Potter [Beatrix Heelis]. 16mo. Pp. 85. [*Brit. Mus.*]   London, 1903

TAILOR (the) of Vitré. [A novel.] By May Wynne [Mabel Wynne Knowles]. 8vo. Pp. 320.   London, 1908

TAILS and Ballids. By Barney Bradey [William Theodore Parkes, journalist]. 8vo. [*O'Donoghue's Poets of Ireland.*]
Dublin, 1865

TAILS with a twist. The verses by " Belgian Hare " [Lord Alfred Bruce Douglas] ; the pictures by E. T. Reed. Obl. 8vo. Pp. 72. [*Brit. Mus.*]
London [1898]

TAINT (the) of the City. By Charles Eddy [Charles E. Rose]. 8vo. [*Brit. Mus.*]   London, 1903

TAINTED gold. [A novel.] By Paul Trent [Edward Platt]. 8vo. Pp. 304. [*Brit. Mus.*]   London, 1918

TAKE heed of both extreams ; or, plain and useful cautions against Popery and Presbytery. [By Luke de Beaulieu.] 8vo. [*D. N. B.* vol 4, p. 52.]
London, 1675

TAKE one at night. By Keble Howard [John Keble Bell]. 8vo. Pp. 246. [*Brit. Mus.*]   London, 1919

TAKE your choice ! Representation and respect ; imposition and contempt. Annual Parliaments and liberty, long Parliaments and slavery. [By Major John Cartwright.] 8vo. [*Camb. Univ. Lib.*]   London, 1776

TAKEN at his word. By Tom Cobbleigh [Walter Raymond]. 8vo. [*Brit. Mus.*]
London, 1897

TAKEN at the flood ; a novel. By the author of *Lady Audley's secret*, etc. etc. [Mary Elizabeth Braddon]. 8vo. 3 vols.   London, 1874

TAKEN by force ; a novel. By Kilsyth Stelliers [Wellbourne Summers]. 8vo.
Aberdeen, 1895

TAKEN by the enemy. By Oliver Optic [William Taylor Adams]. 8vo. [Cushing's *Init. and Pseud.*]
Boston, 1890

TAKEN upon trust. By the author of *Recommended to mercy* [Mrs M. C. Houstoun]. Second edition. 8vo. 3 vols.   London, 1863

TAKING (the) of Jerusalem in the first Crusade. [A poem which obtained the Chancellor's Medal for English verse. By William C. Kinglake.] 8vo. [*Camb. Univ. Lib.*]
Cambridge, 1832

TAKING (the) of Newcastle, etc. etc. [Edited by John Trotter Brockett.] 12mo. [*W.*]   Newcastle, 1825
A reprint of " A particular relation of the taking of Newcastle," etc., published at London in 1644. The preface signed : J. T. B.

TAKING (the) of Tiverton, with the castle, church and fort by Sir Th. Fairfax on the Lords-day last Octob. 19, 1645 ; also the several defeats given to Goring by his Excellency, etc. [By John Rushworth ?] 4to. [*W.* ; *Brit. Mus.*]   London, 1645

TAKING (the) of Winchester by the Parliaments forces ; as also the surrend'ring up of the Castle. [A poem.] By I. W. [John Ward]. 4to. [*D. N. B.* vol. 59, p. 321.]   London, 1642

TAKINGS ; or, the life of a Collegian : a poem. [By Thomas Gaspey.] Illustrated by Richard Dagley. 8vo. [*Edin. Univ. Lib.*]   London, 1821

TALBOT and Vernon ; a novel. [By John L. MacConnel.] 12mo. [*Brit. Mus.*]   New York, 1850

TALBURY (the) girls. . . . [A novel.] By Clara Vance [Mrs Mary Denis, *née* Andrews]. 8vo. Pp. 359. [Cushing's *Init. and Pseud.*]   London [1886]

TALE (the). By Joseph Conrad [Joseph Conrad Korzeniowski]. 4to. Pp. 34.
London, private print, 1919

TALE (a) for the Pharisees. By the author of *Dives and Lazarus* [William Gilbert]. 8vo.   London, 1859

TALE (a) in a tub, or a tub lecture as it was delivered by My-heele Mendsoale an inspired Brownist ; and a most upright translator : in a meeting house neere Bedlam, the one and twentieth of December, last, 1641. Written by J. T. [John Taylor, the water-poet]. 4to. [Thomason's *Coll. of Tracts*, i. 49.]   London, 1641

TALE (the) of a Casualty clearing-station. By a Royal Field-leach [Col. F. A. Symons, R.A.M.C.]. 8vo.
Edinburgh, 1917

TALE (the) of a modern genius; or, the miseries of Parnassus: in a series of letters. [By John Fitzgerald Pennie.] 12mo. 3 vols. [Mayo's *Bibl. Dors.* p. 163.] London, 1827
The dedication signed: Sylvaticus.

TALE (the) of a nettle. Written by a person of quality [Jonathan Swift]. Fol. S. sh. [*Camb. Hist. of Eng. Lit.*] Cambridge, 1710

TALE (a) of a tub; written for the universal improvement of mankind: to which is added, An account of a battel between the antient and modern books in St James's Library. [By Jonathan Swift.] The third edition corrected. 8vo. [Arber's *Term. Cat.* iii. 693.] London, 1704

TALE (a) of adventure. By an officer of the United States Army [Sergeant —— Atkins]. 12mo. [*Amer. Cat.*] Philadelphia, 1871

TALE (a) of an old castle. [A novel.] By W. Heimburg [Bertha Behrens]; translated from the German. . . . 12mo. Pp. 185. [Cushing's *Init. and Pseud.*] New York, 1889

TALE (the) of Archais; a romance in verse. By a Gentleman of the University of Cambridge [Aleister Crowley]. 8vo. Pp. viii. 89. [Crowley's *Works*, 1905.] London, 1898

TALE (a) of encumbered estates. By Celticus [Andrew Claiborne]. 8vo. [Kirk's *Supp.*] 1851

TALE (a) of intemperance. By an Observer [Cyril Pearl]. 8vo. Boston, 1839

TALE (a) of Lexington; a national comedy, founded on the opening of the Revolution. [By Samuel B. H. Judah.] 12mo. [Sabin's *Dictionary.*] New York, 1823

TALE (a) of Lulworth . . . drawn up from letters. . . . [By William Henry Chamberlaine.] 8vo. Pp. 27. [*Brit. Mus.*] Bath, 1888

TALE (the) of Mr Tubbs; a story of a knight without armour. By J. E. Buckrose [Mrs Falconer Jameson]. 8vo. Pp. 299. [*Brit. Mus.*] London, 1918

TALE (the) of the Butterhorn; a poem. By Matthew Meek [Richard Ramsay]. 8vo. [O'Donoghue's *Poets of Ireland.*] Belfast, 1811

TALE (a) of the fifteen. By C. E. M. [Constance E. Miller]. 8vo. Pp. 79. London [1883]

TALE (the) of the four white swans. By Fiona Macleod [William Sharp]. 8vo. Pp. 96. Portland, Maine, 1907

TALE (a) of the Great Mutiny. By Vedette [Rev. William Henry Fitchett]. 8vo. [*Lond. Lib. Cat.*] London, 1902

TALE (a) of the Pyrenees (Ramuncho). By Pierre Loti [Captain M. J. Viaud, of the French Navy]; translated from the French. 8vo. London, 1923

TALE (a) of the Revolution, and other sketches. By the author of *Peter Parley's tales* [S. G. Goodrich]. 12mo. [*Brit. Mus.*] Philadelphia, 1845

TALE (the) of the Serpent. By Sundowner [Herbert Tichborne]. 8vo. Pp. x. 282. London, 1902

TALE (the) of the swallow; from the German of H. v. B. [Maria Hedwig von Buelow?]. 8vo. [*Brit. Mus.*] 1884

TALE (a) of the times. By the author of *A gossip's story* [Mrs Jane West]. Dedicated by permission to Mrs Carter. Third edition. 12mo. 3 vols. London, 1803

TALE (a) of the war of 1870. . . . [By Thomas Gregory Smith.] 12mo. [*Brit. Mus.*] London [1871]

TALE (a) of the Western Counties. By George Budock [Sydney Hodges, artist]. 8vo. [Cushing's *Init. and Pseud.*] London [c. 1870]

TALE (a) of three bonnets. [In verse. By Allan Ramsay.] 8vo. Pp. 36. [*Brit. Mus.*] N.P. 1722

TALE (a) of Tucuman, with digressions, English and American. [A poem.] By Junius Redivivus [William Brydges Adams]. 12mo. [*Brit. Mus.*] London, 1831

TALE (a) of two nations. By "Coin" [William Hope Harvey]. 8vo. Pp. 302. Chicago, 1895

TALE-BEARER (the). [A tale.] By Mark Allerton [William Ernest Cameron]. 8vo. Pp. 112. [*Brit. Mus.*] London, 1924

TALENT in tatters; or, some vicissitudes in the life of an English boy. By Hope Wraythe [Miss Edith Hawtrey]. With 8 full-page illustrations. 8vo. Pp. 256. London, 1878

TALENTS improved; or, the philanthropist. By the author of *The miseries of human life* [Rev. James Beresford]. 12mo. [Allibone's *Dict.*] London [c. 1810]
Attributed also to Harriet Corp.

TALENTS (the) of Edmund Kean delineated. [By John W. Cole, dramatist.] 8vo. Pp. 19. [*Brit. Mus.*] London, 1817

TALENTS (the) run mad; or, eighteen hundred and sixteen: a satirical poem, in three dialogues, with notes. By the author of *All the talents* [Eaton Stannard Barrett]. 8vo. Pp. 70. London, 1816

TALEOFATUBODON (the); or, the naturalist and the British Association. By the author of *John justified* [Col. Charles William Grant]. Obl. 4to. [Green's *Bibl. Somers.* i. 502.]
Bath, 1875

TALES. By a Barrister [Frederick Liardet, M.A.]. 8vo. [*Lond. Lib. Cat.*]
London, 1844

TALES. By the author of *Amy Herbert* [Elizabeth M. Sewell]. 8vo. 10 vols. [*Brit. Mus.*] London, 1858-62

TALES about animals. By Peter Parley [Samuel G. Goodrich]. Tenth edition. 16mo. [*Brit. Mus.*] London, 1847

TALES about shipwrecks and disasters at sea. By Peter Parley [George Mogridge]. 8vo. [*Brit. Mus.*]
London, 1847

TALES about temperaments. By John Oliver Hobbes [Mrs Reginald W. Craigie, *née* Pearl T. Richards]. 8vo. Pp. 166. London, 1902

TALES about the United States of America, geographical, political, and historical; with comparative view of other countries. By Peter Parley [George Mogridge]. Third edition. 12mo. Pp. x. 285. London, 1838

TALES about Wales; with a catechism of Welsh history. [By Mrs Eliza C. Campbell]; edited by Captain Basil Hall. 12mo. [*Cardiff Free Lib.*]
London, 1837

TALES and adventures by sea and land; translated from the French of Fouqué [by James Burns, publisher]. 8vo. London, 1847

TALES and adventures for the young. By the author of *Home and its duties*, etc. [Mrs J. Werner Laurie]. 12mo. [*Brit. Mus.*] London [1869]

TALES and illustrations, chiefly intended for young persons. By Charlotte Elizabeth [Mrs Tonna]. Fourth edition. 12mo. 3 vols. Dublin, 1844

TALES and legends. By the authors of *The odd volume*, etc. [the Misses Corbett]. 8vo. 3 vols.
Edinburgh, 1828

TALES and legends of the English lakes and mountains. . . . Compiled by Lorenzo Tuvar [Wilson Armitstead]. 8vo. [Boase's *Mod. Eng. Biog.* i. col. 83.] London [1852]

TALES and sketches. By a cosmopolite [James Lawson]. 12mo. [*Brit. Mus.*]
New York, 1830

TALES and sketches. By a country schoolmaster [William Leggett]. 8vo. [Cushing's *Init. and Pseud.*]
New York, 1829

TALES and sketches [of Findhorn and the Divie district]. By Jacob Ruddiman, A.M., of Marischal College, Aberdeen [William Hay]. 8vo. Pp. 304. [P. J. Anderson's *Aberd. Univ. Bibl.* p. 448.] Edinburgh, 1828

TALES and sketches . . . By the author of *Hope Leslie* [Miss Catherine Maria Sedgwick]. 12mo. [*Brit. Mus.*]
London, 1842

A second series was published in 1844.

TALES and sketches of Christian life in different lands and ages. [By Mrs Elizabeth Charles.] 8vo. [*Brit. Mus.*]
London, 1850

TALES and sketches of Scottish life. [By George Jacque, U.P. minister, Auchterarder.] [R. Inglis.] 1849

TALES and souvenirs of a residence in Europe. By a lady of Virginia [Mrs William Cabell Rives]. 8vo. [Cushing's *Init. and Pseud.*]
Philadelphia, 1842

TALES and traditions of Tenby. [Compiled by George Philip W. Scott.] 8vo. Pp. viii. 160. [*Brit. Mus.*]
Tenby, 1858

TALES by the O'Hara family; containing Crohoore of the bill-hook, The Fetches, and John Doe. [By John Banim.] 12mo. 3 vols.
London, 1825

TALES explanatory of the Sacraments. [By Emily C. Agnew.] 12mo. 2 vols. [*Nat. Lib. of Scot.*] London, 1846

TALES for children. [By Mrs Gertrude Parsons, *née* Hext.] 12mo. [Boase and Courtney's *Bibl. Corn.* ii. 426.]
London, N.D.

TALES for Sunday scholars. By the author of *Clary's confirmation* [F. E. Reade]. 16mo. London [1878]

TALES for the amusement of young persons. [By John Corry.] 12mo. [*D. N. B.* vol. 12, p. 256.]
London, 1802

TALES for the marines . . . By Harry Gringo [Henry Augustus Wise]. 8vo. [Cushing's *Init. and Pseud.*]
Boston, 1855

TALES for Toby. By Ascott Robert Hope [Ascott Robert Hope Moncrieff]. 8vo. London, 1900

TALES for youth; in thirty poems: to which are annexed, historical remarks and moral applications in prose. By the author of *Choice emblems for the improvement of youth* [John Huddlestone Wynne, printer]. Ornamented with cuts, neatly designed and engraved on wood, by Bewick. 12mo. Pp. x. 158. London, 1794

Preface signed: J. H. W.

TALES from a mother-of-pearl basket. By Anatole France [Anatole France Thibault]; translated from the French. 8vo. Pp. 247. New York, 1896

TALES from American history. By the author of *American popular lessons* [Eliza Robbins]. 12mo. 3 vols. [*Brit. Mus.*] New York, 1834

TALES from London life. By Veritas [Alice A. Pitman]. 8vo. London [1890]

TALES from Switzerland. [By Mrs A. Yosy.] 8vo. [*Bodl.*] London, 1822

TALES from the *Bristol Mirror*, 1842. [By Richard Smith.] 8vo. Pp. 246. [Hyett and Bazeley's *Gloucest. Lit.* iii.] Bristol, 1842

TALES from the diary of a Sister of Mercy [Charlotte M. Braeme]. 8vo. London, 1866

TALES from the Odyssey, for boys and girls. By Materfamilias [Mrs C. M. Bell]. 8vo. [*Lib. Journ.* v. 188.] New York, 1880

TALES from the Rabbins and the Koran. [By Alex. Hay Japp, LL.D.] 8vo. London, 1892

TALES from the Western Moors. By Geoffrey Mortimer [Walter M. Gallichan]. 8vo. Pp. 294. [*Brit. Mus.*] London, 1897

TALES from twelve tongues; translated by a British Museum librarian [Henry B. Wilson]. 8vo. Pp. 302. [*Brit. Mus.*] London [1883]

TALES in rhyme, and minor pieces in the Scottish dialect. [By Robert Lochore, shoemaker.] 8vo. [Rogers' *Mod. Scot. Minstrels*, iv. 91.] Glasgow, 1815

TALES in rhyme, for boys. By Old Humphrey [George Mogridge]. 12mo. Pp. 105. London [1851]

TALES in rhyme, for girls. By Old Humphrey [George Mogridge]. 12mo. Pp. 108. London [1851]

TALES in verse for the amusement of leisure hours. [By Thomas Hamilton, 6th Earl of Haddington?] [*D. N. B.* vol. 24, p. 212.] [*c.* 1720]

TALES of a briefless barrister. [By William Pitt Scargill.] 12mo. 3 vols. [*Brit. Mus.*] London, 1829

TALES of a cruel country. By Gerald Cumberland [Fred C. Kenyon]. 8vo. Pp. 336. London, 1919

TALES of a London parish, etc. By the author of *Tales of Kirkbeck*, etc. [Henrietta L. Farrer]. Edited by the Rev. W. J. E. Bennett. 8vo. Pp. x. 321. London, 1851

TALES of a parrot, done into English from a Persian manuscript intitled Tooti Namêh. By a teacher of the Persic, Arabic . . . and English languages [Rev. Benjamin Gerrans]. 8vo. Pp. xvi. 188. [*Brit. Mus.*] London, 1792

TALES of a pilgrim. By the author of *A summer ramble in the North Highlands* [Alexander Sutherland, Lieutenant]. 8vo. Pp. 394. Edinburgh, 1827

TALES of a tar, with characteristic anecdotes. By one of the authors of *The naval sketch book* [William Nugent Glascock]. 12mo. London, 1830

TALES of a terrace. By Heber K. Daniels [—— Farquhar Palliser]. 8vo. [*Brit. Mus.*] London [1895?]

TALES of a traveller. By Geoffrey Crayon, Gentn. [Washington Irving]. Illustrated with original designs. 8vo. Pp. 456. London, 1850

TALES of a voyager to the Arctic Ocean. [By Robert Pierce Gillies.] 12mo. 3 vols. [*Brit. Mus.*] London, 1826
A second series was published in 1829.

TALES of an antiquary; chiefly illustrative of the manners, traditions, and remarkable localities of ancient London. [By Richard Thomson.] 12mo. 3 vols. [*Brit. Mus.*] London, 1828

TALES of an Indian camp. [By James Athearn Jones.] 12mo. 3 vols. [Sabin's *Dictionary*.] London, 1820

TALES of Ardennes. By Derwent Conway [Henry David Inglis]. 8vo. [*Brit. Mus.*] London, 1825

TALES of Chinatown. By Sax Rohmer [Arthur Sarsfield Ward]. 8vo. Pp. 322. [*Who's Who in Lit.*] London, 1922

TALES of college life. By Cuthbert Bede, B.A., author of *Verdant Green*, etc. [Edward Bradley]. 8vo. Pp. 115. London, 1856

TALES of Dunstable Weir. By Zack [Miss Gwendoline Keats]. 8vo. Pp. 307. [*Brit. Mus.*] London, 1901

TALES of fault and feeling. By the author of *Zeal and experience* [Mrs Busk]. 12mo. [*Brit. Mus.*] London, 1825

TALES of hearsay. By Joseph Conrad [Joseph Conrad Korzeniowski]. 8vo. Pp. 288. London, 1925

TALES of humour, gallantry, and romance, selected and translated from the Italian [by John Yonge Ackerman]. 8vo. [Jaggard's *Index*.] London, 1824
The translator's name is also given as —— Southern. [*Brit. Mus.*]

TALES of Ireland. By the author of *Traits and stories of the Irish peasantry* [William Carleton]. 8vo. [S. J. Brown's *Ireland in fiction*.] London, 1834

TALES of Irish life, illustrative of the manners, customs, and condition of the people; with designs by George Cruikshank. [By Michael James Whitty.] 8vo. 2 vols. [*Bodl.*] London, 1824

TALES of Kirkbeck ; or, the parish in the Fells. (First series.) By the author of *Lives of certain Fathers of the Church in the fourth century*, etc. [Henrietta Louisa Farrer]. 8vo. Pp. xii. 270. London, 1848

TALES of magic and meaning. By Alfred Crowquill [Alfred Henry Forrester]. 8vo. [*Camb. Univ. Lib.*] London, 1856

TALES of many climes ; in verse, with notes. By C. C. V. G. [Mrs Dawson Wetherelt]. 12mo. [*O'Donoghue's Poets of Ireland.*] Dublin, 1832

TALES of many lands. By the author of *Tales of the great and brave* [Margaret Fraser Tytler]. 8vo. [*Brit. Mus.*] London, 1839

TALES of martyr times. By the author of *The Spanish brothers* [Deborah Alcock]. 8vo. [*Brit. Mus.*] London, 1872

TALES of military life. By the author of *The military sketch book* [William Maginn, LL.D.]. 12mo. 3 vols. London, 1829

TALES of my country. By the author of *Early recollections* [Selina Bunbury]. 8vo. [*Brit. Mus.*] Dublin, 1833

TALES of my father. [Reminiscences.] By A. M. F. [Alicia Maria Falls]. 8vo. Pp. x. 269. [*Brit. Mus.*] London, 1902

TALES of my grandmother [relating to Ayrshire]. [By Archibald Crawfurd.] 12mo. 2 vols. [Paterson's *Poets of Ayrshire*, p. 334.] Edinburgh, 1825

TALES of my landlord, collected and arranged by Jedediah Cleishbotham, schoolmaster and parish-clerk of Gandercleuch [Sir Walter Scott]. [Vol. I. Black Dwarf. Vols. II. III. IV. Old Mortality.] Third edition. 12mo. 4 vols. Edinburgh, 1817

—— Second series, collected and arranged by Jedediah Cleishbotham, schoolmaster and parish-clerk of Gandercleugh [Sir Walter Scott]. [Containing The Heart of Mid-lothian.] 12mo. 4 vols. Edinburgh, 1818

—— Third series, collected and arranged by Jedediah Cleishbotham, schoolmaster and parish-clerk of Gandercleugh [Sir Walter Scott]. [Containing The Bride of Lammermoor, and A Legend of Montrose.] 12mo. 4 vols. Edinburgh, 1819

—— Fourth and last series, collected and arranged by Jedediah Cleishbotham, schoolmaster and parish-clerk of Gandercleugh [Sir Walter Scott]. [Containing Count Robert of Paris, and Castle Dangerous.] 8vo. 4 vols. Edinburgh, 1832

TALES of my neighbourhood. By the author of *The collegians* [Gerald Griffin]. 12mo. 3 vols. London, 1835

TALES of my time. By the author of *Blue-Stocking Hall* [W. P. Scargill]. 12mo. 3 vols. London, 1829
Ascribed also to Mrs J. C. Loudon. [*Nat. Lib. of Scot.*]

TALES of other days ; with illustrations by George Cruikshank. By J. Y. A. [John Yonge Ackerman]. 8vo. [Olphar Hamst, p. 186.] London, 1830

TALES of passion : Lord Lovel's daughter. The Bohemian. Second love. By the author of *Gilbert Earle* [Francis Barry Boyle St Leger]. 12mo. 3 vols. London, 1829

TALES of Peter Parley [Samuel Griswold Goodrich] about America and Australia. 12mo. London, 1827

TALES of Peter Parley [Samuel Griswold Goodrich] about Europe, Asia, Africa, America, and Oceania. Seventh edition. 12mo. [Allibone's *Dict.*] London, 1828

TALES of real life. By an Officer's widow, author of *Miscellaneous poems* [Mrs Elizabeth Pilfold]. 8vo. [Green's *Bibl. Somers.* i. 408.] Bath [1859]

TALES of sea and land. By the author of *Peter Parley's tales* [Samuel Griswold Goodrich]. 12mo. [*Brit. Mus.*] Philadelphia, 1846

TALES of secret Egypt. By Sax Rohmer [Arthur Sarsfield Ward]. 8vo. Pp. 319. [*Brit. Mus.*] London, 1918

TALES of superstition and chivalry. [Verse. By Anne Bannerman.] 8vo. Pp. 144. [*D. N. B.* vol. 3, p. 139.] London, 1802

TALES of terror. By Dick Donovan [Joyce E. Preston Muddock]. 8vo. Pp. 328. [*Brit. Mus.*] London, 1899

TALES of terror ; with an introductory dialogue. [By Matthew Gregory Lewis.] Second edition. 8vo. Pp. 154. London, 1808

TALES of the Braganza ; or, reminiscences of a voyage. By the author of *The magician priest of Avignon*, etc. [T. H. Usborne]. Second edition. 12mo. Pp. iv. 240. London, 1852

TALES of the century ; or, sketches of the romance of history between the years 1746 and 1846. By John Sobieski and Charles Edward Stuart [John Hay Allan and Charles Stuart Hay Allan]. 12mo. Edinburgh, 1847

TALES of the coast guard. By Lieutenant Warneford, R.N. [Sir William Howard Russell ?]. 8vo. Pp. 230. [Allibone's *Dict.*] London, 1856

TALES of the Colonies ; or, adventures of an Emigrant [in Tasmania ; by Charles Rowcroft, Colonial Magistrate]. 8vo. 3 vols. [*Brit. Mus.*]
London, 1843

TALES of the Cordelier metamorphosed, as narrated in a manuscript from the Borromeo Collection and in the Cordelier Cheval of M. Piron, with translations. [By George Hibbert.] 8vo. Pp. 54. [*W.; Martin's Cat.*]
London, 1821
Etchings by Robert Cruickshank.

TALES of the Crusaders. By the author of *Waverley*, etc. [Sir Walter Scott, Bart.]. [Vols. I., II., The Betrothed ; Vols. III., IV., The Talisman.] 8vo. 4 vols. Edinburgh, 1825

TALES of the dead ; principally translated from the French. [By Mrs Utterson.] 8vo. Pp. viii. 248. [*Bodl.*]
London, 1813

TALES of the devil, from the original gibberish of Professor Lumpwitz, S.U.S. and C.A.C. in the University of Snoringberg [Henry William Bunbury]. 4to. Pp. 56. [*Bodl.*]
Bury St Edmunds, 1801

TALES of the early ages. By the author of *Brambletye House*, etc. [Horace Smith]. 12mo. 3 vols. London, 1832

TALES of the Empire, told round the camp-fire. By Reginald Wray [W. B. Home-Gall]. 8vo. [*Brit. Mus.*]
London, 1901

TALES of the factories [in verse]. By the authoress of *Ellen Fitzarthur* [Catherine Bowles, later Mrs Southey]. 8vo. [*Brit. Mus.*] Edinburgh, 1833

TALES of the fairys ; translated from the French [of M. C. La Mothe]. 12mo. [Arber's *Term Cat.* iii. 123.]
London, 1699

TALES of the first French Revolution ; collected by the author of *Emilia Wyndham* [Mrs Anne Marsh]. 8vo. Pp. 284. London, 1849
These tales are : " Professional visits of le Docteur Noir," " Sealed orders," " Limoëlan," and " The soldier's fortune" ; and form vol. xxxi. of The Parlour Library.

TALES (the) of the Genii ; or, the delightful lessons of Horam, the son of Asmar : faithfully translated from the Persian manuscript, and compared with the French and Spanish editions, published at Paris and Madrid, by Sir Charles Morell, formerly ambassador from the British settlements in India to the Great Mogul [but really by Rev. James Ridley]. 8vo. [Nichols' *Lit. Anec.* ii. 382 ; *Mon. Rev.* xxxi. 478.]
London, 1764

TALES of the good woman. By a doubtful gentleman [James Kirke Paulding]. 12mo. [*Brit. Mus.*]
New York, 1836

TALES of the great and brave. [By Margaret Fraser Tytler.] 8vo. Pp. iv. 328. [*Bodl.*] London, 1838

TALES of the Great St Bernard. [By George Croly, LL.D.] Second edition. 8vo. 3 vols. London, 1829

TALES of the Hermitage . . . [By Mrs Mary Pilkington.] 12mo. Pp. 228. [*Brit. Mus.*] London, 1798

TALES of the Hoy ; interspersed with song, ode, and dialogue. By Peter Pindar, Esq. [John Wolcott, M.D.]. [Part I.] 4to. Pp. iv. 64.
London [1798]

TALES of the manor. By the author of *The private history of the Court of England*, etc. [Mrs S. Green]. 12mo. 2 vols. [*Biog. Dict.* 1816 ; *Brit. Crit.* xxxiii. 95.] London, 1809

TALES of the martyrs ; or, sketches from Church history. [By Annie Field Elsdale.] Second edition. 12mo. [*Lib. Journ.* iv. 137.] London, 1844

TALES of the moor. By Josias Homely [John Bradford] ; containing Reginald Arnolf, Tom Stirlington, etc. 12mo. [*Camb. Univ. Lib.*] London, 1841

TALES of the moors ; or, rainy days in Ross-shire. By the author of *Selwyn in search of a daughter* [Caroline Bowles, afterwards Mrs Southey]. 8vo.
Edinburgh, 1828

TALES of the Munster festivals, containing, Card drawing ; the Half Sir ; and Suil Dhuv, the coiner. By the author of *Holland-tide, or Irish popular tales* [Gerald Griffin]. 12mo. 3 vols.
London, 1827

TALES of the North Riding. By Stephen Yorke [Miss Mary Linskill]. 8vo. 2 vols. [*Brit. Mus.*]
London, 1871

TALES of the North-west ; or, sketches of Indian life and character. By a resident beyond the frontier [William Joseph Snelling]. 8vo. [Cushing's *Init. and Pseud.*] Boston, 1830

TALES of the peerage and the peasantry. [By Mrs Arabella Sullivan.] 12mo. 3 vols. [*Brit. Mus.*] London, 1831

TALES of the schoolroom. By the editor of *The parting gift* [Agnes Strickland]. 12mo. Pp. vii. 188. [*Brit. Mus.*] London [*c.* 1835]
Dedication signed : Z.

TALES of the slave squadron. By Lt. Warneford [Sir William Howard Russell ?]. 8vo. [Allibone's *Dict.*]
London [1860]

TALES of the Solway. By a Gallovidian [J. Aitken]. 8vo. [Mitchell and Cash's *Scot. Topog.*] 8vo.
Dumfries, 1873

TALES of the South of France. [By Miss Frances Mary Peard.] 8vo.
London [*c.* 1860]

TALES of the stumps. By "Tivoli" [Horace William Bleackley]. 8vo. [*Brit. Mus.*]
London, 1901

TALES of the sun. By Lucas Cleeve [Mrs Howard Kingscote, *née* Adelina G. I. Wolff.] 8vo. London [*c.* 1890]

TALES of the trains; being some chapters of railroad romance. By Tilbury Tramp, Queen's Messenger [Charles Lever]. 12mo. [*D. N. B.* vol. 33, p. 139.] London, 1857

TALES of the tripod. By Pertinax Particular [Tobias Watkins]. 8vo.
Baltimore, 1821

TALES of the turf; and rank outsiders. [Poems.] By Hyder Ali [Robert L. Cary, jun.]. 8vo. [*Amer. Cat.*]
Chicago, 1891

TALES of the twelfth and thirteenth centuries; from the French of M. Le Grand. [Translated by John Williamson.] 12mo. 2 vols. [*Gent. Mag.* lxxi. ii. 957 ; *Mon. Rev.* lxxvi. 59.]
London, 1786
Reprinted in 1790 under the title of "Norman tales."

TALES of the wars of our times. By the author of *Recollections of the Peninsula,* etc. [Col. Joseph Moyle Sherer]. 8vo. 2 vols. [Green's *Bibl. Somers.* i, 478,] London, 1829

TALES of the West. By the author of *Letters from the East* [John Carne]. 12mo. 2 vols. [*Brit. Mus.*]
London, 1828

TALES of the wild and the wonderful. [By George Borrow?] 8vo. Pp. x. 356. [Borrow's *Works, ed. Clement Shorter,* 1924.] London, 1825

TALES of the woods and fields ; a second series of *The two old men's tales.* [By Mrs Anne Marsh.] 12mo. 3 vols.
London, 1836

TALES of travel West of the Mississippi. By Solomon Bell [William Joseph Snelling]. 8vo. [Cushing's *Init. and Pseud.*] Boston, 1831

TALES of travels in the north of Europe, including Brook's Travels in Lapland, Conway's Travels in Norway, Sweden, and Denmark, and Granville's Travels in Russia and Poland. By Solomon Bell [William Joseph Snelling]. 8vo. [Cushing's *Init. and Pseud.*] Boston, 1831

TALES of two countries [viz. Russia and Italy]. By Maxim Gorky [Aleksyei Maksimovitch Pyeshkov]. 8vo. Pp. 250. London, 1914

TALES of two people. By Anthony Hope [Sir Anthony Hope Hawkins]. 8vo.
London, 1908

TALES of unrest. By Joseph Conrad [Joseph Conrad Korzeniowski]. 8vo. Pp. 292. London, 1898

TALES of woman. [Edited by Frederick Shoberl. Containing The wife. Helen. The Russian daughter. The mother.] 12mo. 2 vols.
London, 1828

TALES of yore. [A collection of prose translations from French and German ; by William Taylor.] 8vo. 3 vols. [*D. N. B.* vol. 55, p. 476].
London, 1910

TALES old and new. By the author of *On the edge of the storm,* etc. [Margaret Roberts]. 8vo. Pp. 307.
London, 1872

TALES on the Beatitudes. By the author of *Clary's Confirmation,* etc. [Miss Frances E. Reade]. 8vo. [*Brit. Mus.*] London, 1878

TALES, traditions, and antiquities of Leith, with notices of its trade, commerce, etc. [By William Hutchison.] Revised edition, brought down to the year 1865. 8vo. Pp. iv. 380.
Leith, 1865
The first edition, published in 1853, has the author's name.

TALES translated [by Alexander Dow] from the Persian of Inatulla of Delhi. 8vo. 2 vols. [*D. N. B.* vol. 15, p. 383.]
London, 1768

TALISMAN (the), a drama ; a tale of the eleventh century. By the authoress of *St Bernardine* and *Poems by L.— three series* [Catherine Swanwick]. 8vo. [Olphar Hamst, p. 73.] London, 1864

TALISMAN (the) for 1828 (1829, 1830). [Preface signed : Francis Herbert, *i.e.* William Cullen Bryant.] 12mo. 3 vols. [Foley's *Amer. Authors.*]
New York, 1827-29

TALISMAN (the) ; from the Russian of Alexander Pushkin [by George Borrow], with other pieces. 8vo. [Wise's *Bibl. of Borrow.*] St Petersburg, 1835

TALK kindly, but avoid argument. . . . [By Charles King Whipple]. 8vo.
London, 1873

TALK (a) on religion. By C. H. W. [Charles H. Waterhouse]. 8vo.
Vienna [1892]

TALKING (the) horse ; and other tales. By F. Anstey [Thomas Anstey Guthrie]. 8vo. [*Brit. Mus.*] London, 1894

TALKS about the [Civil] War. By Uncle Jesse [C. E. Babb]. 8vo. [Cushing's *Init. and Pseud.*]
Cincinnati, 1875

TALKS on David Livingstone. [Introduction signed : T. R. W. L., *i.e.* Theodore R. W. Lunt]. 4to. Pp. 31. [*Brit. Mus.*]   London, 1920

TALKS with boys and girls ; or, wisdom better than gold. By a layman [Benjamin Barton Comegys]. 8vo. [Kirk's *Supp.*]   Philadelphia, 1878

TALKS with the bairns, about the bairns. By Ruth Elliott [Lillie Peck]. 12mo. Pp. 160. [*Brit. Mus.*] London [1882]

TALKS with the Professor. By the Listener [Walter Grierson]. 8vo. Pp. 189. [*Brit. Mus.*] London [1930] No. 7 of the Outline Library.

TALKS with Uncle Morris ; or, the friend of my boyhood. By Old Humphrey [George Mogridge]. 8vo. Pp. 64. [*Brit. Mus.*]   London [1881]

TALL (the) man of Winton and his wife. . . . By Over Forty [Nathan Green]. 8vo. [Cushing's *Init. and Pseud.*] Nashville, Tennessee, 1872

TALL (a) ship. By "Bartimeus" [Lewis Anselm da Costa Ricci]. 8vo. London, 1918

TALL (the) villa ; a novel. By Lucas Malet [Mrs Mary St Leger Harrison, *née* Kingsley]. 8vo. Pp. 254. London, 1920

TALLAHASSEE (a) girl. [A novel. By Maurice Thompson]. 16mo. [Foley's *Amer. Authors.*] Boston, 1882

TALLEYRAND ; a spectacular play in three acts. By Laurence Pritchard [Mrs Cecil Campbell]. 8vo. Pp. 77. [*Brit. Mus.*]   Bristol [1924]

TALPA ; or, the chronicles of a clay farm : an agricultural fragment. By C. W. H. [Chandos Wren Hoskyns]. 8vo. [*Birm. Cent. Lib.*] London, 1852

TALVI'S [Mrs Therese Albertine Luise Robinson's] History of the colonization of America ; edited by William Hazlitt, Esq. barrister-at-law. 12mo. 2 vols. London, 1851

TAMBURLAINE the Greate ; who, from the state of a shepheard in Scythia, by his rare and wonderfull conquests, became a most puissant and mighty monarque. [By Christopher Marlowe.] 4to. B. L. No pagination. [*Dyce Cat.*]   London, 1605
—— With his impassionate furie, for the death of his lady and loue faire Zenocrate : his forme of exhortation and discipline to his three sonnes, and the manner of his owne death. The second part. [By Christopher Marlowe.] 4to. B. L. No pagination. London, 1606

TAMERLANE and other poems. By a Bostonian [Edgar Allen Poe]. 12mo. [Cushing's *Init. and Pseud.* i. 38.] Boston, 1827

TAMING (the) of Tamzin. [A story for juveniles.] By Esmé Stuart [Amélie Claire Leroy]. 8vo. Pp. 253. [*Who's Who in Lit.*]   London, 1920

TAMMER'S duel. [A story.] By E. Heron [Kate O'Brien and Hesketh Pritchard]. 8vo. Pp. vii. 215. [*Brit. Mus.*]   London, 1898

TAMWORTH (the) reading room ; letters to *The Times* on an address delivered by Sir Robert Peel, Bart., on the establishment of a reading room at Tamworth. By Catholicus [John Henry Newman, D.D.]. 8vo. [*Brit. Mus.*]   London, 1841

TANCRED, a tale ; and other poems. By the author of *Conrad, a tragedy* [Alfred Bunn]. 8vo. Pp. viii. 102. [Green's *Bibl. Somers.* ii. 502.] London, 1819

TANCRED the hero ; and other fairy tales. By Margaret Ormiston [M. O. Curle]. 8vo. Pp. 92. [*Border Mag.* 1923, p. 47.] London, 1920

TANGLED destinies. [A novel.] By Dick Donovan [Joyce Emerson Preston Muddock]. 8vo.   London, 1908

TANGLED (the) skein. [A novel.] By Baroness Orczy [Mrs Montagu Barstow]. 8vo. Pp. 332. London, 1907

TANGLED (a) tale. By Lewis Carroll [Rev. Charles Lutwidge Dodgson]. 8vo.   London, 1885

TANGLED talk ; an essayist's holiday. By T. Talker [William Brighty Rands]. 8vo. [Boase's *Mod. Eng. Biog.* iii. 34.] London, 1864

TANGLED threads. [A novel.] By Esmé Stuart [Miss Amélie Claire Leroy]. 8vo. Pp. 320. [*Who's Who in Lit.*]   London, 1897

TANGLED trinities. By Daniel Woodroffe [Mrs Mary Woods]. 8vo. [*Brit. Mus.*]   London, 1901

TANGLED up in Beulah Land. [A novel.] By J. P. Mowbray [Andrew C. Wheelen]. 8vo. [*Amer. Cat.*] New York, 1902

TANGLEDOM ; enigmas, problems, riddles, and transformations. By Nillor [Charles R. Ballard]. 8vo. [*Amer. Cat.*]   Boston, 1904

TANGLES and corners in Kezzie Driscoll's life. By "Fleeta" [Kate W. Hamilton]. 8vo. [*Amer. Cat.*] Philadelphia, 1883

TANGLES unravelled. By Flora M'Flimsey [Evelyn Kimball Johnson]. 8vo.   New York, 1890

TANIA'S peril ; or, the edge of an abyss ; a Russian story. By Henry Greville [Madame Alice Marie Céleste Fleury Durand]. 8vo. [*Amer. Cat.*] New York, 1891

TANNER (the) boy [viz. Ulysses Grant], and how he became a Lieutenant-General. By Major Penniman [Charles Wheeler Denison]. 8vo. [Cushing's *Init. and Pseud.*] Boston, 1864

TANNHÄUSER ; or, the battle of the bards : a poem. By Neville Temple [Hon. Julian Charles Henry Fane] and Edward Trevor [Edward Robert Bulwer-Lytton]. 8vo. Pp. 117. [Olphar Hamst, p. 124.] London, 1861

TANTALUS. [A novel.] By the author of *The adventures of John Johns* [Frederic Carrel]. 8vo. Pp. 260. [*Brit. Mus.*] London, 1913

TANTE Claire. By the author of *Rob Lindsay and his school* [William Mac-Gillivray, W.S.]. 8vo. [*Brit. Mus.*] Edinburgh, 1906

TANTRA of the great liberation [Maha nirvanatantra] ; a translation from the Sanskrit with introduction and commentary. By Arthur Avalon [Sir John G. Woodroffe, of Calcutta]. 8vo. [*Amer. Journ. of Theology*, Oct. 1910, p. 441.] London, 1913

TAORMINA, and other poems. [By Helen Lowe.] 8vo. Pp. 197. London, 1864

TARANTULA (the) ; or, the dance of fools : a satirical work. . . . By the author of *The rising sun*, etc. [Eaton Stannard Barrett]. 8vo. 2 vols. [*D. N. B.* vol. 3, p. 281.] London, 1809
Ascribed also to Edward Dubois.

TARBUCKET ; or, the humble petition of the Bethel Union Society in the year 1820. By Capsicum [Rev. George Charles Smith]. 8vo. [Cushing's *Init. and Pseud.*] London, 1820

TARDY George. [By George Henry Boker.] 4to. [Foley's *Amer. authors.*] New York, private print, 1865

TARES ; a simple history. By Ricus [Whateley William Ingall]. 4to. Pp. 23. [*Brit. Mus.*] Deal, 1924

TARIES on tour through the Lake District. By J. A. [John Armstrong, printer]. 8vo. [Sinton's *Bibl. of Hawick.*] Hawick [1810?]

TARQUIN the Proud [a tragedy] and other poems. [By Samuel Prout Hill.] 8vo. [*Brit. Mus.*] London, 1843

TARTANVILLE ; the idyll of a northern village. By Catter Thun [Rev. Hugh Mackenzie Campbell]. 8vo. Pp. 162. [Anderson's *Aberd. Univ. Bibl.* p. 500.] Brechin, 1891

TASSO. [A poetical drama.] By Rose Neil [Miss Isabella Harwood]. 8vo. [Cushing's *Init. and Pseud.*] London, 1879

TASSO and Leonora ; the commentaries of Ser Pantaleone degli Gambacorti, Gentleman Usher to the august Madama Leonora D'Este. By the author of *Mary Powell* [Anne Manning, later Mrs Rathbone]. 8vo. [*Brit. Mus.*] London, 1856

TASTE ; an epistle to a young critic. [By John Armstrong, M.D.] 4to. [*D. N. B.* vol. 2, p. 95.] London, 1753

TASTE : an essay . . . [from the French of Charles Rollin]. 8vo. Pp. 54. [*Manch. Free Lib.*] London, 1732

TASTE (a) of the everlasting feast presented in a briefe contemplation of the great that shall be in heaven at the marriage supper of the Lambe ; prepared by E. L. [Edward Lane], minister of the gospell. 4to. [*Brit. Mus.*] London [1670?]

TASTE (the) of the town ; or, a guide to all publick diversions. Viz. I. Of musick, operas, and plays. . . . II. Of poetry, sacred and profane. . . . III. Of dancing, religious and dramatical. . . . IV. Of the mimes, pantomimes and choruses of the antients. . . . V. Of audiences, at our theatrical representations. . . . VI. Of masquerades ; ecclesiastical, political, civil and military. . . . VII. Of the athletic sports of the antients. . . . [By James Ralph.] 8vo. Pp. xxiv. 237. [*D. N. B.* vol. 47, p. 221.] London, 1731
The epistle dedicatory is signed : A. Primcock.
This work appeared first in 1728 with the title " The touchstone, or historical essays . . ." *q.v.*

TATONG, the little slave ; a story of Korea. By Cousin Annie [Annie Maria Barnes]. 8vo. [*Amer. Cat.*] Richmond, Va., 1899

TATTERS. By Beulah [Fanny D. Bates]. 8vo. [Cushing's *Init. and Pseud.*] New York, 1892

TATTINE. By Ruth Ogden [Mrs Frances Otis Ide]. 8vo. [*Amer. Cat.*] New York, 1899

TAUNTON of to-day ; things which a stranger wants to know about the town. . . . [By Reginald Barnicott.] 8vo. [Green's *Bibl. Somers.* iii. 310.] Taunton, 1895

TAVERN anecdotes, and reminiscences of the origin of signs, clubs, coffee-houses, streets, city companies, wards, etc. ; intended as a lounge-book for Londoners and their country cousins. By one of the old school [William West, bookseller]. 8vo. [*D. N. B.* vol. 60, p. 346.] London [1825]
Wrongly attributed to Colin Mackenzie.

TAVERN (the) of the three virtues ;
translated from the original of Saint-
Juirs [*i.e.* René Delorme]. Illustrated.
4to. Pp. xxx. 155. [*Brit. Mus.*]
London [1896]

TAVISTOCKE (the) Naboth proved
Nabal ; an answer to a narrative by
Tho. Larkham in the name of the
church of Tavistocke in Devon. By
F[rancis] G[lanville], D[ig.] P[ol-
wheele], W[alt.] G[odbear], N[ic.]
W[atts], W[illiam] H[ore], etc. 4to.
[*W.* ; Davidson's *Bibl. Devon.* p. 51.]
London, 1658

TAXATIO papalis ; being an account of
the tax-books of the united Church
and court of modern Rome, or of the
Taxæ cancellariæ apostolicæ,and Taxæ
sacræ poenitentiariæ apostolicæ. By
Emancipatus [Rev. Joseph Mendham].
8vo. [*Mendham Collection Cat.* p. 202.]
London, 1825
The second edition, 1836, bears the
author's name.

TAXATION. By an irresponsible taxpayer [the Hon. Mrs Caroline Norton].
8vo. Pp. 34. Private print [*c.* 1840]

TAXATION, 1891-1892. . . . A history.
[By Hubert Haer.] 8vo. Pp. 173.
[*Brit. Mus.*] London, 1892

TAXATION in Ceylon. [By A. M. and
John Ferguson.] 8vo. [*Lond. Lib.
Cat.*] Colombo, 1890

TAXATION no tyranny ; an answer
to the resolutions and address of the
American Congress. [By Samuel
Johnson, LL.D.] Fourth edition. 8vo.
Pp. 91. London, 1774
In collected works (London, 1792), vol.
viii.

TAXES (the) ; a dramatick entertainment. [By Phanuel Bacon.] 8vo.
[*D. N. B.* vol. 2, p. 371.] London, 1757

TAXIDERMIC and other notes. By a
collector [G. H. Hawtayne]. 12mo.
[*Col. Inst. Lib.*]
Georgetown, Demerara, 1884

TAXIDERMY ; or, the art of collect-
ing, preparing and mounting objects
of natural history. [By T. E. Bow-
dich.] 12mo. [*Brit. Mus.*]
London, 1820

TAYLORS physicke has purged the
divel ; or, the divell has got a squirt,
and the simple, seame-rent, thread-
bare Taylor translates it into railing
poetry, and is now soundly cudgelled
for it. By Voluntas Ambulatoria
[Henry Walker ?]. 4to. [*Christie-
Miller Cat.*] [London] 1641
A satire upon John Taylor, the water-poet.

TEA and Toddy. By Leo Ross [David
Anderson Moxey, M.D., Elocutionist].
8vo. [*Brit. Mus.*] Edinburgh, 1878

TEA cultivation in Ceylon ; pruning
and kindred subjects. By " Rustic "
[Edward Hamlin]. Second edition,
revised. 8vo. [*Calc. Imp. Lib.*]
Colombo, 1905

TEACHER'S (the) harvest. By the
Teacher [Mrs E. N. Horton]. 8vo.
[Kirk's *Supp.*] Boston, 1852

TEACHERS (the) of the world unvailed ;
wherein the ground of their ministry
is manifested, both in doctrine and
practice, to be out of the light which
cometh from Christ, in the witchcraft
deceiving the people. . . . Declared
against by G. F. . . . [By George
Fox.] 4to. Pp. 30. [Smith's *Cat.
of Friends' Books*, i. 650.]
London, 1656

TEACHER'S (the) prayer on the morn-
ing of the confirmation of her pupils.
[By Emily Mann.] 12mo.
London [1852]

TEACHING the catechism . . . By
the editor of *The sower* [Francis H.
Drinkwater]. 8vo. Pp. 123. [*Brit.
Mus.*] London, 1924

TEACHING (the) of the "Scotch
sermons" exhibited and examined.
By a layman [Robert Gossip, late of
the *Daily Review*]. 8vo. Pp. 52.
Edinburgh, 1881

TEACHINGS (the) of flowers, historical
and legendary. . . . [By Mrs ——
Paterson, *née* Carruthers.] 8vo.
Belfast, N.D.
Contemporary attestation.

TEACHINGS of the ages. By A. C.
Traveller [Mrs H. K. W. Clark].
8vo. [Kirk's *Supp.*]
San Francisco, 1874

TEACHINGS of the Christmas tree,
for children, young and old ; translated from the German [by Charles
Chorley, newspaper editor]. 8vo.
[Boase and Courtney's *Bibl. Corn.*
p. 1009.] Truro, 1876

TEACHINGS of the Master. By a
disciple [Samuel Halbeart Turner].
8vo. [*Amer. Cat.*] New York, 1868

TEARES of Ireland ; wherein is lively
presented, as in a map, a list of the
unheard cruelties and perfidious
treacheries of bloud-thirsty Jesuits
and the Popish faction. [Preface by
James Cranford.] [*D. N. B.* vol. 13,
p. 16.] 1642

TEARES (the) of the beloved ; or,
the lamentation of Saint John, con-
cerning the death and passion of
Christ Jesus our Saviour. By J. M.
[Jervis (or Gervase) Markham]. 4to.
[*W.* ; Lowndes' *Bibl. Man.*]
London, 1600

TEARES (the) of the Muses. By Ed. Sp. [Edmund Spenser]. 4to. No pagination. London, 1591
Followed by "Virgils Gnat. Long since dedicated to the most noble and excellent Lord; the Earle of Leicester, late deceased," having no separate title-page.

TEARFUL (a) victory; a story for children. By Darley Dale [Miss Francesca M. Steele]. 8vo. Pp. 128. London [1880]

TEARS for the death of Alexander Earle of Dunfermeling. [By John Lyon.] 4to. [Pollard and Redgrave.] Edinburgh, 1622

TEARS (the) of a grateful people; a Hebrew dirge and hymn, chaunted in the Great Synagogue, St James's Pl., Aldgate, on the day of the funeral of King George III. . . . By Hyman Hurwitz, of Highgate: translated by a friend [Samuel Taylor Coleridge]. 8vo. Pp. 13. [Ashley Lib.] London [1820]

TEARS (the) of Alnwick; a pastoral elegy, in memory of the late Duchess of Northumberland. By a student of the Middle Temple [Henry Lucas]. 4to. [Watt's Bibl. Brit.; Mon. Rev. lvi. 68.] London, 1777

TEARS (the) of genius; occasioned by the death of Dr [Oliver] Goldsmith. By Courtney Melmoth [Samuel Jackson Pratt]. 4to. Pp. 32. [Brit. Mus.] London, 1774

TEARS of Granta; a satire addressed to Undergraduates in the University of Cambridge. By an Undergraduate [T. U. Stoney]. 4to. [Bartholomew's Camb. Books.] Cambridge, 1812

TEARS (the) of Jerusalem; or, some short remarks on the dilapidated state of many of our country churches. . . . By S. T. B., a Graduate of Balliol College, Oxford [John Noble Shipton, rector of Othery]. 8vo. [Green's Bibl. Somers. ii. 124.] Bristol, 1820

TEARS (the) of St Margaret; also, odes of condolence to the high and mighty musical directors, on their downfall. . . . By Peter Pindar, Esq. [John Wolcott, M.D.]. 4to. Pp. vi. 47. [D. N. B. vol. 62, p. 293.] London, 1792

TEARS (the) of the Indians . . . written in Spanish by Casaus and made English by J. P. [John Phillips]. 8vo. Pp. 134. [Lowndes' Bibl. Man. p. 1314.] London, 1656

TEARS (the) of Yorkshire for the loss of the Marquis of Rockingham. . . . [By Dr Edward Miller.] 8vo. Pp. 30. [D. N. B. vol. 37, p. 406.] Doncaster [1782]

TEA-TABLE rhymes. By Leicester Romayne [M. P. Guimaraens]. 8vo. [Brit. Mus.] London, 1905

ΤΕΧΝΗ-ΠΟΛΙΜΟΓΑΜΙΑ; or, the marriage of armes and art July 12, 1651: being an accompt of the act at Oxon. to a friend. By R. W. [Robert Whitehall]. 4to. No pagination. London, 1651
"Rob. Whitehall of Merton coll. supposed to be the author."—MS. note by Wood.

TECHNETHYRAMBEIA; or, a poem on Paddy Murphey, under-porter of T[rinity] C[ollege], Dublin. [By Rev. William Dunkin, D.D.]; translated from the original Latin by J. Cowper. 8vo. [O'Donoghue's Poets of Ireland.] Dublin, 1730

TECHNIQUE (the) of the love affair. By a gentlewoman [Doris Langley Moore]. . . . 8vo. Pp. ix. 227. [Brit. Mus.] London [1928]

TECUMSEH of the Shawanoes; a tale of the War of 1812. By Col. H. R. Gordon [Edward Sylvester Ellis]. 8vo. [Amer. Cat.] New York, 1898

TECUMSEH; or, the warrior of the West: a poem in four cantos. . . . By an English officer [Major John Richardson]. 12mo. Pp. viii. 135. [Brit. Mus.] London, 1828

TED Frisco, the tattooed man. [By Robert Andrew Scott Macfie.] 8vo. [Brit. Mus.] Liverpool, 1898

TEDDY and Carrots; two merchants of Newspaper Row. By James Otis [James Otis Kaler]. 12mo. Pp. 225. Boston, 1896

TEDDY Ashton's [C. Allen Clarke's] Lancashire readings and recitations. 8vo. 3 parts. [Brit. Mus.] Blackpool, 1921-24

TEDDY B. and Teddy G., the Roosevelt bears. By Paul Piper [Seymour Eaton]. 4to. [Amer. Cat.] Philadelphia, 1907

TEDDY'S button. By the author of Eric's good news [Miss Amy Le Feuvre]. 8vo. Pp. 119. London, 1895

TEDDY'S ship. [A tale.] By A. B. Romney [A. Beatrice Rambaut]. 8vo. [Brit. Mus.] London, 1899

TEETOTALISM (number two). By J. M. [James Maltman, M.A.]; a book opposing Teetotalism, but advocating the spread of pure Christianity against the curse of drunkenness. 8vo. Edinburgh, 1901

TEKEL; or, Cora Glencoe. By Braganza [H. A. Bragg]. 8vo. [Cushing's Init. and Pseud.] Philadelphia, 1870

TEKEL; thou art weighed in the scales and found wanting; or, the national religion of England brought to the test of Holy Scripture and found everywhere defective and erroneous. By Puto [Henry Bate, surgeon]. 8vo. [*Brit. Mus.*]
London, 1872

ΤΕΚΜΗΡΙΑ μετρικα; symptoms of rhyme, original and translated. [By Rev. Peter Hall, M.A.]. 4to. Pp. 69.
London, 1824

"25 copies printed. Presented by the author to the Bodleian Library. Peter Hall. July 8th. 1826."—MS. note by Hall in the Bodleian copy.

TELEMACHUS; a masque. [By George Graham]: set to music by Phil. Hayes, Bac. Mus. 4to. Pp. 14. [*Bodl.*]
London, 1764

TELESCOPE (the); or, moral views for children. [By Margaret Roberts.] 12mo. [*Gent. Mag.* lxxxv. i. 81.]
London, 1805

TELL mamma. [A tale.] By the author of *A trap to catch a sunbeam* [Mrs Mackarness, *née* Matilda Anne Planché]. 8vo. [*Brit. Mus.*]
London, 1874

TELL me a story. By Ennis Graham [Mrs Mary Molesworth]. 8vo. Pp. 196.
London, 1875

Dedication signed: A. V. G. M.

T E L L your wife. By Clara Vance [Mrs M. Andrews Denison]. 8vo. [Cushing's *Init. and Pseud.*]
New York, 1885

TELL-TALE (the); or, home secrets told by old travellers. By H. Trusta [Mrs Elizabeth Stuart Phelps]. 12mo. [*Brit. Mus.*]
Boston, 1853

TELL-TALE (the); or, sketches of domestic life in the United States. By H. Trusta [Mrs E. S. Phelps] and Grace Greenwood [Sara Jane Lippincott, *née* Clarke]. 16mo. [*Brit. Mus.*]
London [1852]

ΤΕ´ΛΟΣ (τὸ) καὶ τὸ ἔργον. The highest end and chiefest work of a Christian set forth in two plain discourses, concerning the glory of God and our own salvation. By J. W. [Joseph Waite, minister at Sprowton, Suffolk]. 8vo. Pp. 8, 116.
London, 1668

T E M P E R A N C E (a) lecture. [In verse.] By a village curate [Rev. William Glenn, B.A. T.C.D.]. 8vo. [O'Donoghue's *Poets of Ireland.*]
Dublin, 1877

TEMPERANCE rhymes. [By the Rev. William Gaskell.] 8vo. Pp. 79. [Axon's *Gaskell Bibl.*]
London, 1839

TEMPERANCE sermons in St Paul's Cathedral, Metropolitan Tabernacle. . . . Reprinted from the Temperance Record. . . . [By H. J. Ellison and J. P. Chown.] Fol. [*Brit. Mus.*]
London [1870]

TEMPERANCE (the) Shorter Catechism and confession of faith, with unabridged notes. By the author of *The Sabbath on the rock*, etc. [Robert Wilson]. 8vo. Pp. 160. [*Brit. Mus.*]
Glasgow, 1877

TEMPERATE (a) discussion of the causes which have led to the present high price of bread; addressed to the plain sense of the people. [By Charles Long, M.P., Secretary to the Treasury.] Third edition. 8vo. Pp. 45. [*W.*]
London, 1800

TEMPERATE (a) ward-word, to the turbulent and seditious Watch-word of Sir Francis Hastinges, knight, who indevoreth to slander the whole Catholique cause, and all professors thereof, both at home and abrode. . . . By N. D. [Nicolas Doleman, *alias* Father Robert Parsons]. 4to. Pp. 129. [Jones' *Peck*, p. 54.]
[Antwerp] 1599

TEMPEST (the); an opera: taken from Shakespear: as it is performed at the Theatre-Royal in Drury-Lane, the songs from Shakespear, Dryden, etc., the music composed by Mr Smith. [By David Garrick.] 8vo.
London, 1756

TEMPEST-TOSSED; the story of Seejungfer. By the author of *Mademoiselle Mori* [Miss Margaret Roberts]. 8vo. Pp. 319. [*Brit. Mus.*]
London, 1884

TEMPLAR (the) Knights. [By Alexander Walker.] 8vo. [Robertson's *Aberd. Bibl.*]
Aberdeen, 1887

TEMPLARIA; papers relative to the history, privileges, and possessions of the Scotish Knights Templars, and their successors the Knights of St John of Jerusalem. [Collected by James Maidment.] 4to. 4 parts. [*W.*; Martin's *Cat.*]
[Edinburgh] 1828

TEMPLARS (the); an historical novel. [By Peter Leicester.] 12mo. 3 vols.
London, 1830

TEMPLE Bar the city Golgotha; a narrative of the historical occurrences of a criminal character associated with the present Bar. By a member of the Inner Temple [James Holbert Wilson]. 4to. Pp. 68. [*N. and Q.*, April 1870, p. 359.]
London, 1853

TEMPLE (the) knock'd down; or, R——l action. By Peter Pindar [John Wolcot, M.D.]. 8vo. Pp. 27.
London [1814]

15

TEMPLE Melodies; a collection of about two hundred popular tunes adapted to nearly five hundred favorite hymns, selected with special reference to public, social, and private worship. [By Darius E. Jones.] 4to. Pp. 224.
New York, 1856

TEMPLE (the) of corruption; a poem. [By W. Churchill.] 4to. Pp. 23. [*Bodl.*] London, 1770

TEMPLE (the) of dullness; with the humours of Signor Capochio, and Signora Dorinna : a comic opera of two acts, as it is perform'd at the Theatre-Royal in Drury-Lane; the music by Mr Arne. [Attributed to Colley Cibber.] 4to. London, 1745

TEMPLE (the) of fame; a poem, in-scrib'd to Mr Congreve. [By Thomas Yalden, D.D.] 8vo. [Edward Solly, in the *Bibliographer*, vol. 4, p. 93.]
London, 1709

TEMPLE (the) of fame, and other poems. By Ganymede [John Arthur Coupland]. 8vo. Pp. 87. [*Brit. Mus.*] London, 1891

TEMPLE (the) of fire. By Lewis Ramsden [Dr W. Lisle Dowding]. Pp. 360. London, 1905

TEMPLE (the) of Flora. [By Robert John Thornton, M.D.] 4to. [Jackson's *Bibl. of Botany.*] London, 1812

TEMPLE (the) of health; a poetic vision; occasioned by the universal joy expressed on His Majesty's most happy recovery. By a lady [Grace Arthur]. 4to. Pp. 12. London, 1789

TEMPLE (the) of Melekartha. [By Isaac Taylor.] 8vo. 3 vols. [Lowndes' *Bibl. Man.* p. 2583.] London, 1831

TEMPLE (the) of truth; or, the best system of reason, philosophy, virtue, and morals, analytically arranged. [By Charles Edward De Coetlogon.] Second edition. 8vo. [Darling's *Cyclop. Bibl.*] London, 1807

TEMPLE (the) of Venus; a gentle satire on the times. By the author of *The Meretriciad* [Edward Thompson]. 4to. 2 parts. [*D. N. B.* vol. 56, p. 209.]
London, 1863

TEMPLE-OGE (the) ballad. By Philanthropos [Richard Pockrick]. 8vo. [*Brit. Mus.*] Rathfarnham, 1730

TEMPLES (the) of the Orient, and their message in the light of Holy Scripture, Dante's Vision, and Bunyan's Allegory. [By Mrs Elizabeth Anna Gordon.] 8vo. [*Brit. Mus.*]
London, 1902

TEMPLE-STUDENT (the); an epistle to a friend, who had requested the author's opinion of some verses. [By George Keate.] 4to. Pp. 27. [*Gent. Mag.* Sept. 1797, p. 796.] London, 1765

TEMPORA mutantur; or, the great change from 73 to 93, in the travels of [Gilbert Burnet] a professor of theology at Glasgow from the primitive and episcopal loyalty through Italy, Geneva, etc. to the deposing doctrine under Papistico - phanatico - prelatico colours at Salisbury. [By Charles Leslie.] 4to. [*Brit. Mus.*]
London, 1694

TEMPORAL (the) government of the Pope's state. [By Thomas Denham.] 8vo. Pp. 268. [*N. and Q.* 25th Feb. 1860, p. 137.] London, 1788

TEMPORAL (the) interest of North America; showing the causes and cure of the many distractions, wants, poverty, and ill-will to each other, which we are exposed to. . . . By a lover of his country [Joseph Morgan]. 8vo. [Evans' *Amer. Bibl.* ii. 58.]
Philadelphia, 1733

TEMPORAL power; a study in suprem-acy. By Marie Corelli [Caroline Cody]. 8vo. Pp. viii. 587. [*Brit. Mus.*]
London, 1902

TEMPTATION; a novel. By Leigh Cliffe [George Jones]. 12mo. 3 vols. [*Brit. Mus.*] London, 1823

TEMPTATION (the) of Phillip Carr. [A novel.] By May Wynne [Mabel Wynne Knowles]. 8vo. Pp. 312.
London, 1906

TEMPTATION; or, a wife's perils. [By Mrs M. A. Gascoigne.] 12mo. 3 vols. [*Nat. Lib. of Scot.*]
London, 1839

TEN acres enough; a practical experi-ence, showing how a very small farm may . . . keep a very large family. [By Edmund Morris.] 12mo. [Sabin's *Dictionary*.] New York, 1864

TEN books of Homer's Iliades, trans-lated out of French by A. H. [Arthur Hall]. 4to. [*Christie-Miller Cat.*]
London, 1581

TEN centuries of European progress. By Aquarius [Lowis d'Aguilar Jackson]. 8vo. [*Brit. Mus.*] London, 1891

TEN chapters in the life of John Han-cock; now first published since 1789. [By Stephen Higginson.] 8vo. Pp. 68. [Sabin's *Dictionary*.] New York, 1857

TEN days at Monte Carlo, at the Bank's expense. By V. B. [Victor Bethell]. 8vo. [*Brit. Mus.*]
London, 1898

TEN days in Paris; or, notes of a short tour from Manchester in May and June 1854. By Crux [John Harland]. Pp. iv. 98. Manchester, 1854

TEN dollars enough; keeping house well on ten dollars a week. . . . By Catherine Owen [Mrs Helen Nitsch]. 8vo. [*Amer. Cat.*] Boston, 1887

TEN hints addressed to wise men, concerning the dispute which ended . . . in the dismission of Mr [Francis James] Jackson, the British Minister to the United States. [By John Lowell, LL.D.] 8vo. [*Brit. Mus.*]
[Boston, 1809]

TEN lectures on the Martyrs. By P. Allard ; authorised translation by Luigi Cappadelta [Charles Louis Dessonlavy]. 8vo. [*Brit. Mus.*]
London, 1907

TEN letters introductory to College residence. By a Tutor. [Signed : C. D. *i.e.* Charles Daman, M.A.] 8vo. [*Bodl.*]   Oxford, private print, 1848

X LETTERS on the Catholics. *See* Letters on the subject of the Catholics, etc.

TEN letters on the Church and Church establishments. . . . By an Anglo-Canadian [Rev. Adam Townley, D.D.]. 8vo. Pp. 80. [Cushing's *Init. and Pseud.*]   Toronto, 1839

TEN (the) pleasures of marriage. . . . Written by A. Marsh, Typogr. [By Aphra Behn ?] 8vo.   London, 1682
    The second part is entitled, " The confession of the new married couple. . . ."
    See an edition reprinted in London, 1922.

TEN quaeres upon the ten new commandements of the General Council of the Officers of the Armies, Dec. 22, 1659. [By William Prynne.] 4to. Pp. 8. [*Brit. Mus.*]   [London, 1660]

TEN sonnets. [By] W. E. A. A. [William Edward Armitage Axon]. 8vo.
[Manchester, private print] 1887

TEN thousand a-year. [By Samuel Warren.] 8vo. 3 vols. [Courtney's *Secrets*, p. 90.]   Edinburgh, 1841

T E N thousand miles against five thousand ; or, what is the best gauge for the new Indian railways ? [By A. W. Forde.] 8vo. [*Calc. Imp. Lib.*]
Bombay, 1870

TEN thousand miles on a bicycle. By Karl Kron [Lyman Hotchkiss Bagg]. 8vo. Pp. cvii. 799. [Cushing's *Init. and Pseud.*]   New York, 1887

TEN (the) times one record. [By Rev. E. E. Hale.] 4to.   Boston, 1893-5

TEN to seventeen ; a boarding-house diary. By Ingraham Lovell [Mrs Josephine D. D. Bacon]. 8vo. [*Amer. Cat.*]   New York, 1908

TEN (the) ton cutter. By Harry Castlemon [Charles Austin Fosdick]. 12mo. [*Amer. Cat.*]   New York, 1898

TEN years in a lunatic asylum. By Mabel Etchell [Charlotte Phillips]. 8vo. Pp. viii. 368. [*Bodl.*]
London [1868]

TEN years in Anglican orders. By " Viator " [Rev. Johannes Godfrey F. Raupert]. 8vo.   London, 1898

TEN years in London. . . . By the old Bushman [Horace William Wheelwright]. 8vo. [*Reform Club Cat.* p. 415.]   London, 1865

TEN years in Sweden ; being a description of the landscape, climate, domestic life, forests, mines, agriculture, field sports, and fauna of Scandinavia. By "An old Bushman," author of *Bush wanderings in Australia*, etc. [Horace William Wheelwright]. 8vo. [*Brit. Mus.*]
London, 1865

TEN years of imperialism in France [1851-1861] ; impressions of a " Flaneur " [C. B. Derosne]. 8vo. [*Brit. Mus.*]   Edinburgh, 1863
    Ascribed also to General Eber.

TENANT (the) of the Grange. [A novel.] By Morice Gerard [Rev. John Jessop Teague]. 8vo. Pp. 362.
London, 1903

TENANT (the) of Wildfell Hall. By Acton Bell [Ann Brontë]. 12mo. 3 vols.   London, 1848

TENANTS (the) and landlords versus the Free Traders. By Powdavie [Peter Robert Drummond, bookseller]. 8vo. [Boase's *Mod. Eng. Biog.* i. col. 922.]   Perth, 1850

TENANTS (the) of Johnson's Court ; and other tales. By Janet Armytage [Katharine Janet Armytage Axon]. 8vo.   London, 1891

TENDER and true ; a colonial tale. By the author of *Clara Morison* [Catherine Ellen Spence]. 8vo. 2 vols. [*Brit. Mus.*]   London, 1856

TENDER and true ; poems of love. Selected by the editor of *Quiet hours*, etc. [M. W. T. *i.e.* M. W. Tileston]. 16mo. Pp. xi. 180. [*Brit. Mus.*]
Boston, 1882

TENDER (the) passion. [A novel.] By M. E. Francis [Mrs Francis Blundell, *née* Mary E. Sweetman]. 8vo. Pp. 320.   London, 1910

TENDER (a) salutation of perfect love unto the elect of God. . . . [Signed : E. B. *i.e.* Edward Burrough, Society of Friends.] 4to. [Smith's *Cat. of Friends' Books*, i. 365.] London, 1661

TENDRILS. By Reuben [Rev. Robert Stephen Hawker, M.A., vicar of Morwenstowe]. 12mo. Pp. viii. 86. [*Brit. Mus.*]   Cheltenham, 1821

TENDRILS in verse. By one who hath tasted that the Lord is gracious [Ebenezer Palmer, the publisher]. 8vo. Pp. 270.   London, 1856
    The third edition, 1880, gives the author's name.

TENETS (the) of the Buckinghamshire Anabaptists. [By —— Penn, of Cold Aston.] 8vo. Pp. 31. London, 1723

TENNESSEAN (a) abroad ; or, letters from Europe, Africa, and Asia, 1851-52. [By Randal W. M'Gavock.] 8vo. [Cushing's *Init. and Pseud.*]
New York, 1853

TENNESSEE (a) judge ; a novel. By the Arkansaw traveller [Opie P. Read]. 8vo. Pp. 325. Chicago, 1893

TENNYSONIANA ; notes bibliographical and critical on Early poems of Alfred & C. Tennyson. Opinions of contemporary writers. In Memoriam ; various readings, with parallel passages in Shakespeare's Sonnets. Various readings in later poems (1842-1865). Patriotic and minor poems. Allusions to Scripture and to classic authors. The Tennyson portraits. Bibliographical list of Tennyson's volumes and of his contributions to periodical publications. [Preface signed : R. H. S. *i.e.* R. H. Shepperd.] 8vo. Pp. xii. 170. London, 1866

TENNYSON'S fairies, and other stories. By Joaquim Miller [Cincinnatus Hiner Miller]. 12mo. [Cushing's *Init. and Pseud.*] Boston, 1889

TENOR (the) and the boy. [A novel.] By Sarah Grand [Frances Clarke, later Mrs Haldane M'Fall]. 8vo. Pp. 264.
London, 1899

TENTAMEN novum ; proving that Timothy and Titus were diocesan rulers of Ephesus and Crete, by an argument drawn from the time of S. Paul's beseeching Timothy to abide at Ephesus, and leaving Titus at Crete, as it is briefly demonstrated in the annals of Paul, wrote by the most learned prelate Dr Pearson, late Lord Bish. of Chester, with an answer to J. O.'s [Owen's] Plea for scripture-ordination. By T. G. [T. Gripps] E. A. P. 8vo. Pp. 198.
London, 1696

TENTAMEN ; or, an essay towards the history of Whittington, some time Lord Mayor of London. By Vicesimus Blenkinsop, LL.D., F.R.S.A.S.S., etc. [Theodore Edward Hook]. 8vo. Pp. viii. 76. [*D. N. B.* vol. 27, p. 274.]
London, 1820
A satire on Alderman Wood and Queen Caroline, rigidly suppressed.

TENTAMEN theologicum ; or, an attempt to assist the young clergyman in the choice of a subject for his sermon on any Sunday throughout the year. By E. D. [Rev. Edward Davison]. 8vo. [*Brit. Mus.*]
Durham, 1850

TENTH (the) commandment. By Gladys Dudley Hamilton [Marguerite L. Glentworth]. 8vo. Boston, 1902

TENTH (the) epistle of the first book of Horace imitated. [By Edward Burnaby Greene.] 4to. [*Gent. Mag.* lviii. 276 ; *Mon. Rev.* xv. 653.] 1756

TENTH (the) Muse lately sprung up in America ; or, severall poems, compiled with great variety of wit and learning. . . . [By Mrs Anne Bradstreet, *née* Dudley.] 8vo. [*Brit. Mus.*]
London, 1650
The second edition, which appeared at Boston in New England, was the first book by a woman printed in the United States : its title begins, " Several poems compiled with great variety. . . ." See above.

TENTH (the) note of the Church examined, viz. Holiness of life. [By Thomas Tenison, D.D., Vicar of S. Martin's in the Field.] 4to. Pp. 16. [Jones' *Peck*, p. 438.] London, 1687

TENTS (the) of Kedar. By the author of *The Valley of Baca* [Kathleen Mary Smith]. 8vo. London, 1886

TENURE (the) of kings and magistrates ; proving, that it is lawfull, and hath been held so through all ages, for any, who have the power, to call to account a tyrant, or wicked king, and after due conviction, to depose, and put him to death ; if the ordinary magistrate have neglected, or deny'd to doe it. . . . Published now the second time, with some additions. . . . The author J. M. [John Milton]. 4to. Pp. 60. [Masson's *Life of Milton*, iv. 64, 5, *note*.] London, 1650
The first edition was published in 1649.

TEONE ; or, the magic maid : a poem. By Rusco [Mary Ann Smith]. 8vo. [Cushing's *Init. and Pseud.*]
Milwaukee, 1862

TERCENTENARY (the) of Corydon ; a bucolic drama in three acts. By Novus Homo [William John Courthope, of New College, Oxford]. 8vo. Pp. iv. 29. [R. Inglis.] Oxford, 1864

TERENCE in English. By R. B. [Rev. Richard Bernard of Epworth.] 4to. [Green's *Bibl. Somers.* ii. 166.]
London, 1598
Later editions in 1607, 1614, 1641.

TERENCE'S comedys, translated into English [with the Latin on the opposite page], with critical and explanatory notes : to which is prefixed a dissertation on the life and writings of Terence, containing an enquiry into the rise and progress of dramatic poetry in Greece and Rome, with remarks on the comic measure. [By Thomas Cooke.] 12mo. 3 vols. [*W.*]
London, 1734

TERENTIUS; the Andrian, a comedy: attempted in English metre. [By Sir Henry Charles Englefield, Bart.] 8vo. [*W.*; Martin's *Cat.*]   London, 1814

TERIBUS; the ballad of Hornshole and the fight of 1514; adapted to the ancient air [by R. S. Craig, advocate]. 4to. [Sinton's *Bibl. of Hawick.*]
Hawick [*c.* 1896]

TERMES (les) de la Ley; or, certaine difficult and obscure words and terms of the common lawes. [By John or Wm. Rastell.] 12mo. [*Brit. Mus.*]
London, 1629

TERMINAL synchronism of Daniel's two principal periods, two thousand three hundred days, and a time, times, and the dividing of time. By the author of *Daniel's great period of two thousand three hundred days discovered* [Rev. Richard Hastings Graves, Dean of Ardagh]. 8vo. [*Brit. Mus.*]
London, 1858

TERMS of communion agreed upon by the Scots Methodists, but generally known by the specious denomination of the Presbytery of Relief; their own explanation of said terms, with remarks upon both: in a letter from a Presbyterian to his friend in Aberdeen. [By Thomas Bennett, minister of the Antiburgher church, Ceres, Fife.] The third edition, with the addition of the 9th, 10th, and 11th deductions, and the footnote upon deduction 5th. 12mo. Pp. 24. [Struthers' *History of the Relief Church* (1843), p. 571.]
Edinburgh, 1779

TERMS (on) of communion: I. The boundaries of the Church. By the Rev. C. K. P. [Charles Kegan Paul]. 8vo. Pp. 26.   Cambridge, 1861
No. V. of Tracts for priests and people.

TERMS (the) of ministerial and Christian communion imposed on the Church of Scotland by a prevailing party in the General Assembly, in opposition to the great bulk both of office-bearers and private Christians. . . . With an appendix relating to the new pamphlet [by Rev. John Hyndman] call'd, A just view of the constitution of the Church of Scotland, etc. [By John Maclaurin, minister at Glasgow.] 8vo. Pp. xii. 140. [Struthers' *History of the Relief Church*, p. 558.]   Glasgow, 1753

TERRA Australis cognita; or, voyages to the Terra Australis or Southern hemisphere, during the sixteenth, seventeenth and eighteenth centuries. [Based in part on the French work of Charles de Brosses, by John Callander, advocate.] 8vo. 3 vols. [*D. N. B.* vol. 8, p. 255.]   Edinburgh, 1766-78

TERRA pacis; a true testification of the spirituall lande of peace, which is the spirituall lande of promyse. . . . Set-foorth by H. N. [Hendrik Niclas]. Translated out of Base-almayne. 8vo. B. L. [*Brit. Mus.*]
[Amsterdam? 1575]

TERRACE (the) of Mon Desir. By George Afterem [Harold Williams, M.D.]. [*Lib. Journ.* xiii. 230.]
[*c.* 1885]

TERRÆ-FILIUS; or, the secret history of the University of Oxford, in several essays: to which are added, Remarks upon a late book, entitled, University education, by R. Newton, D.D., Principal of Hart-Hall. [By Nicholas Amhurst.] 12mo. 2 vols.
London, 1726
This work appeared originally in fifty numbers, the first of which is dated January 11, 1721. and the last July 6. of the same year.
It was an ancient custom at Oxford, in the public acts, for some person, who was called Terræ Filius, to mount the Rostrum, and divert a large crowd from all parts, with a merry oration, interspersed with secret history, raillery and sarcasm, as the occasions of the times supplied him with matter. Amhurst was expelled from St John's College, Oxford, probably for his whig principles, *hinc illæ lachrymæ;* he made it his business to satirize the University.—*See* Ralph's Case of authors.

TERRÆ-FILIUS; to be continued daily during the Eucænia at Oxford in honour of the Peace, Tuesday, July 5 to Friday, July 8. [By George Colman. 4to. Four numbers.] [*D. N. B.* vol. 11, p. 391.]   Oxford, 1763

TERRIBLE (a) family. [A novel.] By Florence Warden [Florence Alice Price, later Mrs George E. James]. 8vo. Pp. 190.   London [1893]

TERRIBLE (the) mysteries of the Ku-Klux-Klan. By Scalpel, M.D. [Edward H. Dixon]. 8vo. [Cushing's *Init. and Pseud.*]   New York, 1868

TERRIBLE (a) out-cry against the loytering, exalted prelates. . . . By Mr Prinne [or rather by Henry Walker, called the Ironmonger]. 4to. Pp. 6. [*Brit. Mus.*]   1641

TERRIBLE (the) stormy wind and tempest, Nov. 27, 1703; considered, improved, and collected, to be held in everlasting remembrance; to which is added, Fair warning to a careless world. By the author of *The infallible way to contentment* [Abednego Seller]. 4to. [Arber's *Term Cat.* iii. 693.]
London, 1705

TERRIBLE tractoration. *See* Poetical (a) petition . . .

TERROR (the) of the road. [A novel.]
By Vivian Grey [Elliott E. Mills].
8vo. [*Brit. Mus.*]   London, 1906

TERRY Hogan ; an eclogue, lately
discovered in the Library of the Propa-
ganda at Rome, and now first translated
from the Irish. . . . [By Walter Savage
Landor?] 12mo. Pp. 35. [*Brit.
Mus.*]   London, 1836

TESSA Treleven. [A novel.] By Morice
Gerard [John Jessop Teague]. 8vo.
[*Lond. Lib. Cat.*]   London, 1922

TEST (a) case, elucidating who are
Christ's and who are Anti-christ's. . . .
[Signed: W. D. F, *i.e.* William D.
Forsyth.] 8vo. Pp. 78. [*Brit. Mus.*]
                      Littleborough, 1905

TEST (the) of filial duty ; in a series of
letters between Miss Emilia Leonard
and Miss Charlotte Arlington. [By
Sarah Scott.] 12mo. 2 vols. [Brydges'
Cens. Lit. iv. 292 ; *Mon. Rev.* xlvi. 165.]
                      1772

TEST (the) of true godliness ; a sermon
preached at the funeral of Philip
Harris, late of Alston, in the county
of Devon, Esquire, August 10, 1681.
By J. Q., minister of the Gospel [John
Quick]. 4to. [Davidson's *Bibl. Devon.*
p. 167.]   London, 1682

TEST (the) of truth. [By Mary Jane
Graham.] 8vo. [*Brit. Mus.*]
                      London, 1831

TESTAMENTARY counsels. . . . By
a retired solicitor ; carefully revised
by a member of the American Bar
[Simon Greenleaf]. 8vo.
                  Troy, New York, 1845

TESTAMENTARY (the) duty of the
parliament of Scotland, with a view
to the treaty of union now on foot, and
considerably advanced betwixt the two
kingdoms. [By Thomas Spence.] 4to.
                      1707

TESTIMONIE (the) of a true fayth ;
conteyned in a shorte catechisme,
necessary to all families, for the more
knowledge of God, and better bryng-
yng vp of chyldren in his fayth and
feare : gathered and written for the
benefite of Gods well disposed children, by C. S. preacher [Christoph.
Shutte]. 8vo. No pagination. B. L.
[*Bodl.*]   London, 1577

TESTIMONIE (a) of antiquitie, shewing
the auncient fayth in the Church of
England touching the sacrament of
the body and bloude of the Lord here
publikely preached. . . [By Matthew
Parker.] 8vo. [*D. N. B.* vol. 43,
p. 263.]   London [1567 ?]
Also reprinted in 1675 as "A Testimony . . ."

TESTIMONIE (a) of the true Church
of God confirmed as well by the
doctrine as lives of sundry holy men,
both patriarkes, and prophetes, and
also by the Apostles and their true
successours. . . . Translated out of
the French by William Phiston. [By
Simon de Voyon.] 4to. [*Camb. Univ.
Lib.*]   London [*c.* 1580]

TESTIMONIES of different authors,
respecting the colossal statue of Ceres,
placed in the vestibule of the Public
Library at Cambridge, July the first,
1803 ; with a short account of its
removal from Eleusis, November 22,
1801. [By Edward Daniel Clarke,
LL.D.] 8vo. Pp. 25. [*Nat. Lib. of
Scot.*]   Cambridge, 1803

TESTIMONIES (the) of Irenæus, Justin
Martyr, Tertullian, Novatianus, Theophilus, Origen, (who lived in the two
first centuries after Christ was born,
or thereabouts;) as also, of Arnobius,
Lactantius, Eusebius, Hilary, and
Brightman ; concerning that one God,
and the persons of the Holy Trinity :
together with observations on the
same. [By John Biddle.] 8vo. Pp. 86.
[Wallace's *Antitrin. Biog.*]
                      London [*c.* 1650]

TESTIMONIES (the) of several citizens
of Fickleborough, in the kingdom of
Fairy-land, concerning the life and
character of Robert Hush [Sir Robert
Walpole], commonly called, Bob : to
which are prefixed, some memoirs of
the life of Charity Hush, the grandfather, and of Oliver Hush, the father
of the said Bob. [By William Wagstaffe, M.D.] 8vo. Pp. 23.
                      London, 1713

TESTIMONIES to the genius and
memory of Sir Joshua Reynolds. By
the author of *Imperfect hints towards
a new edition of Shakspeare* [Samuel
Felton]. 4to. [Nichols' *Lit. Anec.*
ix. 135.]   London, 1792

TESTIMONIES with respect to the
extent of the death of Christ, as a sacrifice for sin. Compiled by a Sabbath-
School teacher [William Cuninghame,
of Lainshaw]. 8vo. Pp. 24.
                      Glasgow, 1822

TESTIMONY (the) borne by the Coran
to the Jewish and Christian Scriptures.
[Preface signed : W. M. *i.e.* Sir William
Muir, LL.D.] 8vo. Pp. xiv. 127.
                      Allahabad, 1860

TESTIMONY (the) of facts concerning
the continuation of miracles in the
Church. [By R. B. Lusk—the
publisher.] 8vo. Pp. 70. [*Brit. Mus.*]
                      Greenock, 1832
Signed : R. B. L.

TESTIMONY (the) of sceptics to the truth of Christianity; with the evidence of pagan historians, and the confirmation of fulfilled prophecy. By the author of *Heroines of our time* [Joseph Johnson]. 8vo.   London, 1861

TESTIMONY (the) of Scripture in support of the unity and supremacy of God. [By Rev. —— Harrison, Unitarian.] 12mo. [*Brit. Mus.*]
                                        Kendal, 1816

TESTIMONY (a) of the appearance of God. . . . With some reasons why Margaret Hambleton doth deny the Presbyterians of Scotland. [Signed: A. P. *i.e.* Alexander Parker.] 4to. Pp. 8. [*Brit. Mus.*]   N.P. [1658?]

TESTIMONY (the) of "the Christ"; being notes of lectures by F. E. R. [F. E. Raven]. 8vo.   London, 1903

TESTIMONY (the) of the Lord concerning London, witnessed in truth and faithfulnesse, to the consciences of all people, that they may return to the Lord. . . . [Signed: E. B. *i.e.* Edward Burrough.] 4to. [Smith's *Cat. of Friends' Books.*]   London, 1657

TESTIMONY (the) of the spirit of prophecy concerning the true Church at this day; set forth in three parts, at three several times, under the title of Peace and truth, or, the mystery of God laid open, in a discourse upon the fourth and fifth chapters of the Revelation. . . . [By Walter Garrett.] 8vo. [*Bodl.*]   London, 1706-7

TESTIMONY (a) to the true light that lightens every man that cometh into the world. [By] W. B. [W. Bennit]. 4to. [*Brit. Mus.*]   [London] 1688

TESTIMONY to the truth; or, the autobiography of an atheist. [By Alexander Harris.] 8vo. Pp. xvi. 312.   London, 1848
  The fourth edition, with the title a little varied, has the author's name.

TESTING (the) of Olive Vaughan. By Christian Lys [Percy John Brebner]. 8vo. [*Amer. Cat.*]   New York, 1909

TESTING (the) of the torment. . . . By Elsie Jeanette Oxenham [Elsie Jeanette Dunkerley]. 8vo. Pp. 213. [*Brit. Mus.*]   London, 1925

TEXAN (the) rifle-hunter; field sports on the prairie. By "The Ranger" [Capt. —— Flack]. 8vo. [Cushing's *Init. and Pseud.*]   London, 1866

TEXAS, and its late military occupation and evacuation. By an officer of the Army [Captain Edwin D. Phillips]. 8vo. [*Brit. Mus.*]   New York, 1862

TEXAS (a) blue bonnet. [A tale.] By Emilia Elliott [Caroline Emilia Jacobs]. 8vo. [*Amer. Cat.*]   Boston, 1910

TEXAS (the) Revolution. . . . By Probus [David Lee Child]. 8vo. [Cushing's *Init. and Pseud.*]   Washington, 1843

TEXTES of Scripture, chayning the holy Chronicle vntyll the sunne lost his lyght, and the Sonne brake the Serpentes head; dying, rising, and ascending. [The Address to the Christian reader signed: H. B. *i.e.* Hugh Broughton.] 4to. No pagination. B. L. [*Pollard and Redgrave.*]
                                        London, 1591

TEXTS for the times. By Ascott R. Hope [Ascott Robert Hope Moncrieff]. Second edition. 12mo. Pp. 232.
                                        Edinburgh, 1872

TEXTS misquoted and misapplied. By R. C. L. B. [Robert Casper Lee Bevan]. 8vo. [*Brit. Mus.*]   London, 1879

TEXTS of Holy Scripture compared together, relating to the true and real deity of the Son and Holy Ghost. [By John Walrond of Ottery.] 8vo. Pp. 43. [Darling's *Cyclop. Bibl.*]
                                        London, 1720

TEXTS of Scripture suggested to the serious consideration of those who deny the efficacy of the two holy Sacraments, Baptism and the Lord's Supper. . . . By J. H. A. [John Horrocks Ainsworth]. 8vo. Pp. 24. [Sparke's *Bibl. Bolt.* p. 2.]   Bolton, 1848

TEXTS which Papists cite out of the Bible, for the proof of their doctrine concerning the obscurity of the Holy Scriptures, examined. [By Edward Fowler, D.D.] 4to. [*Mendham Collection Cat.* p. 112.]   London, 1688

TEXTUARY (the) and Ritualist; or, Biblical and Liturgical repertory: intended as a help to students of the Bible, and a guide to members of the Church. By a clergyman [Rev. Joseph White Niblock, D.D.]. 12mo. [*W.*]
                                        London, 1835
  11 Nos. No more published.

THACKERAY (the) country. By Lewis Melville [Lewis Samuel Benjamin]. 8vo. Pp. 236. [*Who's Who in Lit.*]
                                        London, 1905

THACKERAY the humourist and the man of letters; the story of his life, including a selection from his characteristic speeches, now for the first time gathered together. By Theodore Taylor, Esq., Membre de la société des gens de lettres [John Camden Hotten]. With photograph from life by Ernest Edwards, B.A., and original illustrations. 8vo. Pp. vii. 223.
                                        London, 1864
  Really by W. Moy Thomas. [*N. and Q.* 9th Jan. 1915.]

THACKERAYANA ; notes and anecdotes, illustrated . . . by William
Makepeace Thackeray. . . . [Compiled
by Joseph Grego.] 8vo. Pp. xx. 492.
[*Brit. Mus.*]   London, 1875

THAIS ; the monk's temptation. By
Anatole France [Jacques Anatole
Thibault] ; translated by A. H. Hall.
8vo. Pp. 179.   London, 1917

THALATTA ; a book for the seaside.
[Edited by Thomas Wentworth
Higginson and Samuel Longfellow.]
12mo. [Foley's *Amer. Authors.*]
                           Boston, 1853

THALATTA ! or, the great commoner ;
a political romance. [By John Skelton.] 8vo.   London, 1862
   The Prefatory note signed : S.

THALIA'S banquet, furnished with an
hundred and odde dishes of newly
devised epigrammes. . . . By H. P.
[Henry Peacham, M.A.]. 12mo.
[*Christie-Miller Cat.*]   London, 1620

THAMA. [A novel.] By Onoto Wat-
anna [Mrs Winifred Eaton Babcock].
8vo.   London, 1910

THAMES (the) angler. By A. W. S.
[Arthur W. Smith] and M. W. H. [M.
W. Hallett]. 12mo. Pp. 62. [West-
wood and Satchell's *Bibl. Pisc.*]
                           London, 1846

THAMES rights and Thames wrongs.
By John Bickerdyke [Charles Henry
Cooke]. 8vo. [*Who's Who in Lit.*]
                           London, 1900

THAMUTA ; the spirit of death ; and
other poems. [By Mary Grace
Cooper.] 8vo. [*Brit. Mus.*]
                           London, 1837

THANKS (the) of an honest clergyman
for Mr Paul's speech at Tybourn, July
the 13th, 1716. [By Arthur Ashley
Sykes.] Third edition. 8vo. [Disney's
Memoir of Sykes, p. xii.]
                           London, 1716
   The Speech was written by Lawrence
Howell.

THANKSGIVING ; and other poems.
By Agatha [Bessie Lawrence]. 8vo.
[*Camb. Univ. Lib.*]   New York, 1880

THANKSGIVING (a) sermon preached
at Christ's Church before the Lords
Justices and Council. By W. L. [W.
Lightburn], D.D. 4to. Pp. 24. [Dix
and Dugan's *Dubl. Books.*]
                           Dublin, 1661

THAT artful vicar. [A novel.] By the
author of *The Member for Paris*
[Eustace Clare Grenville Murray].
8vo. [*Brit. Mus.*]   London, 1879

THAT child. By the author of *The
Atelier du Lys* [Miss Margaret Roberts].
8vo. Pp. 237.   London, 1885

   VOL. VI.

THAT gay deceiver. [A novel.] By
Albert Ross [Linn Boyd Porter]. 8vo.
[*Amer. Cat.*]   New York [*c.* 1890]

THAT girl of mine. [By Maurice
Francis Egan.] 8vo. [*Brit. Mus.*]
                           Philadelphia, 1877

THAT husband of mine. By Clara
Vance [Mrs Mary Andrews Denison].
12mo. [*Amer. Cat.*]   New York, 1885

THAT imp. [A novel.] By John Strange
Winter [Mrs Arthur Stannard, *née*
Henrietta E. V. Palmer]. 12mo.
                           London, 1887

THAT imp Marcella. [A tale.] By
Raymond Jacberns [Miss M. Selby
Ashe]. 8vo. Pp. 316.
                           Edinburgh, 1907

THAT is to say——. [A novel.] By
"Rita" [Mrs W. Desmond Hum-
phreys, *née* Eliza M. J. Gollan]. 8vo.
Pp. 318. [*Brit. Mus.*]   London, 1910

THAT little girl ; a novel. By Curtis
Yorke [Mrs W. S. Richmond Lee].
8vo. Pp. 275.   London, 1901

THAT lover of mine. [By Maurice
Francis Egan.] 8vo.
                           Philadelphia, 1877

THAT Mrs Smith. [A novel.] By
John Strange Winter [Mrs Arthur
Stannard, *née* Henrietta E. V. Palmer].
12mo.   London, 1893

THAT other person. By Averil Beaumont [Mrs Margaret Hunt]. 8vo.
[Cushing's *Init. and Pseud.*]
                           London, 1887

THAT the Bishops in England may and
ought to vote in cases of blood : written
upon occasion of the Earl of Stafford's
case. By a learned pen [Thomas
Barlow, Bishop of Lincoln]. With
some answers to the objections. . . .
Fol. Pp. 16. [*Manch. Free Lib.*]
                           London, 1680
   Another edition, also anonymous (8vo),
was published in the same year under the
title, " The rights of the Bishops to judge
in capital cases in Parliament, cleared. . . ."
[*Brit. Mus.*]

THAT troublesome dog. [A story.]
By Raymond Jacberns [Miss M. Selby
Ashe]. 8vo. Pp. 306. London, 1911

"THAT very Mab." [A novel. By Miss
May Kendall and Andrew Lang.]
12mo. [*Brit. Mus.*]   London, 1885

THAT which hath wings ; a novel of the
day. By Richard Dehan [Clotilde
Graves]. 8vo. Pp. 492. London, 1918

THAT which seems best is worst ; ex-
prest in a paraphrastical transcript of
Juvenal's tenth satyre : together with
the tragicall narration of Virginia's
death, interserted by W. B. [William
Basse or William Barkstead]. 12mo.
[*W.* ; Lowndes' *Bibl. Man.*]
   Imprinted by Felix Kingston, 1617

THAT wife of mine. By the author of *That husband of mine* [Mrs Mary Andrews Denison]. 8vo. Pp. 160. [*Brit. Mus.*]   London [1880]

THATCHER'S (the) wife ; or, an account of Mary Camps. By the author of *The retrospect* [Richard Marks]. Fifth edition. 12mo. Pp. 54. [*Brit. Mus.*]   London, 1820

THAT'S it ; or, plain teaching. By the author of *The reason why, General science* [Robert Kemp Philp]. . . . Illustrated by more than one thousand wood engravings. 8vo. Pp. xiv. 370. [Boase and Courtney's *Bibl. Corn.* ii. 494.]   London, 1860
    Published in twelve monthly parts.

THAUMATURGIA ; or, elucidations of the marvellous. By an Oxonian [Samuel Reynolds Hole]. 12mo. 1835

THAUMATURGUS. [A poem.] By Ryrie Bjolla Padring [Patrick Vincent FitzPatrick]. 8vo. Pp. 137.
                London, 1828

THEALMA and Clearchus ; a pastoral history in smooth and easie verse : written long since by John Chalkhill, Esq., an acquaintant of Edmund Spencer. [Edited by Isaac Walton.] 8vo.   London, 1683

THEATRE (the) ; to be continu'd every Tuesday and Saturday. By Sir John Edgar [Sir Richard Steele]. Fol. [*W.*]   London, 1720
    The first number is dated Saturday, Jan. 2 ; and the last and 27th number, Tuesday, Mar. 29. to Sat. April 2, 1720.

THEATRE (the) and the Church ; or, Gospel truth to be realised. [By Rev. George Edis Webster.] 8vo. [*Brit. Mus.*]   Woodbridge, 1845

THEATRE (the) of Catholiqve and Protestant religion, divided into twelue bookes ; wherein the zealous Catholike may plainelie see, the manifest truth, perspicuitie, euident foundations and demonstrations of the Catholique religion. . . . Written by I. C. student in diuinitie [John Colleton]. 8vo. Pp. 664. [*Bodl.*]   1620

THEATRE (the) of the Greeks, containing, in a compendious form, a great body of information relative to the rise, progress, and exhibition of the drama ; together with an account of dramatic writers from Thespis to Menander : to which is added, a chronology and an appendix, containing critical remarks, by Porson, Elmsley, and others. [By Philip Wentworth Buckham.] 8vo. [*Brit. Mus.*]   Cambridge, 1825

THEATRE (the) of the Greeks ; or, the history, literature, and criticism of the Grecian drama ; with an original treatise [by Rev. J. Tate, of Richmond, Yorkshire] on the principal tragic and comic metres. Second edition. [By John William Donaldson.] 8vo. Pp. x. 489. [*Nat. Lib. of Scot.*]
             Cambridge, 1827

THEATRE (the) of the present war in North America. By A. Y * * * [Arthur Young], Esq. 8vo. [*Brit. Mus.*]   London, 1758

THEATRES (the); a poetical dissection. By Sir Nicholas Nipclose, Baronet. [Wrongly attributed to David Garrick.] Second edition. 4to. Pp. viii. 80.   London, 1772

THEATRIC (the) tourist ; being a genuine collection of correct views, with brief and historical accounts of all the principal provincial theatres in the United Kingdom. [By James Winston.] 4to. [*Brit. Mus.*]
              London, 1805

THEATRICAL anecdotes. By Jacob Harwood [Herman D. J. von Schevichaven]. 12mo. [*N. and Q.* 4th Dec. 1920.]   London, 1882

THEATRICAL (the) candidates ; a musical prelude. [By David Garrick.] [*D. N. B.* vol. 21, p. 23.]
             London, 1775

THEATRICAL entertainments consistent with society, morality, and religion ; in a letter to the author of "The stage the high road to hell" : shewing that writers arguments to be fallacious, his principles enthusiastic, and his authorities (particularly from the ancients) misconstrued and perverted : with a counter-dedication to the Rev. Dr Madan. [By H. Flitcroft.] 8vo. Pp. 32.   London, 1768

THEATRICAL portraits epigrammatically delineated ; wherein the merit and demerit of most of our stage heroes and heroines are excellently painted by some of the best masters ; inscribed to the performers of both theatres. By A. Macaroni [—— Taylor]. 4to. [Watt, *s.v. Theatre ; N. and Q.* 14th Dec. 1861, p. 473.]
             London, 1774

THEATRICAL records ; or, an account of English dramatic authors, and their works. [By Robert Dodsley.] 12mo. Pp. 135, 30.   London, 1756

THEATRICAL (the) Review; or, new companion to the play-house: containing a critical and historical account of every tragedy, comedy, opera, farce, etc., exhibited at the theatres during the last season. . . . By a society of gentlemen independent of managerial influence. [By John Potter.] 12mo. 2 vols. [Lowndes' *Bibl. Man.* p. 2641.] London, 1772
Originally published in a newspaper.

THEATRICAL tears; a poem occasioned by Familiar Epistles to Frederick J——s [Jones], Esq. [Signed: R. N. O. *i.e.* Robert N. Owenson.] 12mo. Pp. 47. [O'Donoghue's *Poets of Ireland.*] Dublin, 1804

THEATRICAL (the) world and the Lord's Day. [By John Gritton.] 8vo. London, 1882

THEATRICALS; an interlude; and other sketches. By the author of *Miss Molly* [Beatrice May Butt]. 8vo. Pp. 384. Edinburgh, 1896

THEAURAUJOHN High-Priest to the Jewes, his disputive challenge to the Universities of Oxford and Cambridge, and the whole Hirarch. of Roms clargical Priests. [By T. Tany.] 8vo. [Thomason's *Coll. of Tracts*, i. 864.] London, 1652

THEBAID (the) of Statius; translated into English verse, with notes and observations, and a dissertation upon the whole, by way of preface. [By William L. Lewis.] 8vo. 2 vols. [*Manch. Free Lib.*] Oxford, 1767

THEEVES, theeves; or, a relation of Sir Iohn Gell's gathering up the rents of the lords and gentlemen of Darbyshire, in gathering up the rents of the lords and gentlemen of that county by pretended authority from the two houses of parliament. [By Peter Heylin, D.D.] 4to. Pp. 9. [*Bodl.*] 1643

THEIR happiest Christmas. [A novel.] By Edna Lyall [Ada Ellen Bayly]. 12mo. London, 1890

THEIR high adventure. [A novel.] By John Oxenham [William Arthur Dunkerley]. 8vo. Pp. 254. London, 1921

THEIR marriage. [A novel.] By Curtis Yorke [Mrs W. S. Richmond Lee]. 8vo. Pp. 316. London, 1908

THEIR marriage bond. By Albert Ross [Linn Boyd Porter]. 8vo. [*Amer. Cat.*] New York [1895]

THEIR only son at war; a drama. By Hugh Bancam [Hugh D. MacNab]. 8vo. Pp. 22. [*Brit. Mus.*] Riverbank, Ont., 1917

THEIR Oxford year. By Barbara Burke [Oona Howard Ball.] 8vo. [*Who's Who in Lit.*] London, 1909

THELGE. [A tale. By H. M. L. Lanark.] 8vo. Pp. 99. London, 1901

THELMA; a society novel. By Marie Corelli [Miss Caroline Mackay, afterwards Cody]. 8vo. 3 vols. [*Brit. Mus.*] London, 1887

THELYPHTHORA; or, a treatise on female ruin, in its causes, effects, consequences, prevention and remedy, considered on the basis of the divine law: under the following heads, viz. marriage, whoredom, and fornication, adultery, polygamy, divorce. . . . [By Rev. Martin Madan.] 8vo. 2 vols. [*D. N. B.* vol. 35, p. 290.] London, 1780

THEMES and translations. By John W. Montclair [John William Weidemeyer]. 8vo. [Cushing's *Init. and Pseud.*] New York, 1867

THEMIS; a satire. [By William Peach.] 8vo. [Crockford's *Cler. Directory.*] London, 1852

THEMISTOCLES; a satire on modern marriage. [By John Moncreiff, author of *Appius.*] 4to. Pp. 16. [*Brit. Mus.*] Edinburgh, 1759

THEMISTOCLES, the lover of his country; a tragedy, as it is acted at the Theatre-Royal in Lincoln's-Inn-Fields. [By Samuel Madden, D.D.] Third edition. 8vo. [Baker's *Biog. Dram.*] London, 1729

THEODORA; an oratorio. [By Thomas Morell, in three parts, and in verse.] Set to music by Mr Handel. 4to. [*Brit. Mus.*] London, 1750

THEODORA; and other stories. By Elizabeth Olmis [Annie Elizabeth Loomis]. 8vo. Philadelphia, 1897

THEODORA; or, the Spanish daughter: a tragedy [in five acts, and in verse. By Sophia Lady Burrell]. 8vo. [*Brit. Mus.*] London, 1800

THEODORE Hook; a sketch, from the *Quarterly Review.* [By John Gibson Lockhart.] 12mo. [*W.*] London, 1852

THEODORE; or, the gamester's progress: a poetic tale. [By Richard Scrafton Sharpe.] 12mo. Pp. 120. London, 1799

THEODOSIUS; or, a solemn admonition to Protestant-dissenters, on the proposed repeal of the Test and Corporation Acts: in which are considered the political and religious characters of Dr P—— [Priestley], Dr Price, Mr Fox, Judge ——, Mr Sheridan, Mr B——, Mr Sawbridge, Mrs F——, etc. [By the Rev. Philip Withers.] 8vo. Pp. 68. London, 1790

THEOGNIS ; a laugh in the cavern of evil. By Catius Junior [Elizabeth R. Torrey]. 8vo.   Boston, 1856

THEOGNIS restitutus ; the personal history of the poet Theognis deduced from an analysis of his existing fragments : a hundred of these fragments translated or paraphrased in English metre are arranged in their proper biographical order with an accompanying commentary ; with a preface in which the suggestion of Mr Clinton, as to the true date of the poet's birth (viz. in Olymp. 59) is confirmed by internal evidence. [By John Hookham Frere.] 4to. Pp. 117. [*Brit. Mus.*]
                                   Malta, 1842

THEOLOGIA mystica ; or, the mystic divinitie of the aeternal invisibles, viz. the archetypous globe, or the original globe. . . . By a Person of Qualitie, J. P. [John Pordage], M.D. 8vo. [*Brit. Mus.*]   London, 1683

THEOLOGIA mystica ; two discourses concerning divine communications to souls duly disposed. I. The antiquity, tradition, and succession of mystical divinity among the Gentiles. . . . II. Of the guidance of the Spirit of God : the doctrine of the H. Scriptures, of the Catholick Church, and of the Church of England in particular, upon a discourse of Sr. Matthew Hale concerning it. [By Edward Stephens.] 8vo. Pp. 14, 78. [Walton's *Biog. of Wm. Law*, p. 637.]   London, 1697
      Part II. has a separate title, and pagination [pp. 40].

THEOLOGICAL (a) dialogue ; containing a defence and justification of Dr John Owen from the forty-two errors charged upon him by Mr Richard Baxter. [By Isaac Chauncy.] 4to. [*D. N. B.* vol. 10, p. 171.]
                                  London, 1684

THEOLOGICAL (a) discourse on the Lamb of God and His enemies. [Signed : R. H. *i.e.* Richard Harvey.] 4to. [*Brit. Mus.*]   London, 1590

THEOLOGICAL (the) influence of the Blessed Virgin on the Apostolical school. By Christianus [Willis Probyn Nevins]. 8vo.   London, 1888

THEOLOGICAL (the) Leaf ; an occasional paper, consisting of tracts and extracts connected with the Oxford controversy. [By Richard Walker, B.D.] Nos. 2. 3. 4. 8vo. Pp. 8, 16. [*Bodl.*]   [Oxford, 1842]

THEOLOGICAL mysteries ; or, Genesis analyzed : being an attempt to show the necessity for a revision and re-translation of the Old Testament. By Zetetes [Thomas Ryan], Worthing. 8vo. Pp. 19.   London, 1864

THEOLOGICAL repository ; consisting of original essays, hints, queries, etc., calculated to promote religious knowledge. [Edited by Dr Joseph Priestley.] 8vo. 6 vols. [*W. ; Lowndes' Brit. Lib.*] London, 1773-88

THEOLOGICAL (a) survey of the human understanding ; intended as an antidote against modern deism. [By Robert Applegarth.] 8vo. Pp. 276.   Salisbury, 1776

THEOLOGICAL (a) systeme upon that presvpposition, that men were before Adam. The first part. [By Isaac Peyrerius.] 8vo.   London, 1655
      Part of a work entitled "Men before Adam," *q.v.*

THEOLOGICAL thoughts on God, the creation, fall and redemption of man ; and on God's dealings with man from the creation to the final consummation of all things. [By William Smith, LL.D.] 8vo. Pp. 394. [*Biog. Dict.* 1816 ; *Brit. Crit.* xxxiii. 389.]
                                   London, 1808

THEOLOGICAL (the) trilemma. . . . By Clericus [Rev. J. H. Pettingell]. 8vo. [Cushing's *Init. and Pseud.*]
                                 New York, 1878

THEOLOGICALL rules, to gvide vs in the vnderstanding and practice of holy Scriptures : two centuries : drawne partly out of Scriptures themselves : partly out of ecclesiastical writers old and new. Also Ænigmata sacra, holy riddles ; or misticall cases and secrets of diuinitie, with their resolutions. Four centuries : the vnfolding whereof layeth open that truth that concerneth saluation. By T. W. preacher of the Word [Thomas Walkington]. 8vo. Pp. 6, 125. [Lowndes' *Bibl. Man.* p. 2814.]   London, 1615
      "Ænigmata sacra" has a separate title and pagination.

THEOLOGICO-PHILOSOPHICAL (a) dissertation concerning worms in all parts of human bodies. [By William Ramesay, M.D.] 8vo.
                                   London, 1727

THEOLOGY (the) and philosophy in Cicero's Somnium Scipionis, explained ; or, a brief attempt to demonstrate, that the Newtonian system is perfectly agreeable to the notions of the wisest ancients : and that mathematical principles are the only sure ones. [By George Horne, D.D., Bishop of Norwich.] 8vo. Pp. 105.
                                   London, 1751

THEOLOGY (the) of linguistics. By A. B. C. [Rev. Alonzo Bowen Chapin, D.D.]. 8vo. [*Brit. Mus.*]
                               Mercersburg, 1853

THEOLOGY of nature and revelation. By an amateur theologian [O. Hutchinson]. 12mo. Pp. 55. [Eddy's *Universalism in America*, ii. 588.]
New York, 1885

THEOLOGY (the) of the Old Testament; or, a Biblical sketch of the religious opinions of the ancient Hebrews . . . By George L. Bauer. [Translated from the German by Philip Harwood.] 8vo. [*Brit. Mus.*]
London, 1838

THEONOMIA; or, divine laws. . . . Addressed to the Evangelical Churches of the Christian world. [Signed : J. B. *i.e.* John Byers.] 8vo. Pp. 24. [*Brit. Mus.*]   Manchester, 1883

THEOPHANIA; or, a scriptural view of the manifestation of the Logos, or pre-existent Messiah : as contradistinguished from angelic personation of the Deity, with which it has been erroneously confounded. . . . By Twinrock Elmlicht, Esq. [Thomas Peter Mitchell]. 12mo. Pp. xxiv. 620.
London, 1857

THEOPHANIA; or, severall modern histories represented by way of romance : and politickly discours'd upon. By an English person of quality [Sir W. Sales]. 4to. [*N. and Q.* Jan. 1852, p. 88.]   London, 1655

THEOPHILA; or, loves sacrifice : a divine poem, written by E. B. Esq. [Edward Benlowes]. Several parts thereof set to fit aires by Mr J. Jenkins. Fol. Pp. 46, 268. [*D. N. B.* vol. 4, p. 226.]   London, 1652

THEOPHILUS and Philander; a dialogue containing remarks on the Rev. Mr M'Dowell's Second Letter to the supposed author of *The Catholic Christian.* [By Rev. John Cameron, M.A., Dunluce.] 12mo. Pp. 38. [*D. N. B.* vol. 8, p. 297.] Belfast, 1772

THEOPHILUS to Gaius ; an epistle : shewing the inexpediency of forms, and reasons for the use of free and unprescribed prayer, in the Protestant dissenting Churches : occasioned by an introductory letter, in the Specimen of a liturgy, etc. [By Caleb Fleming.] 8vo. Pp. 31. [*Bodl.*]   London, 1753
Signed : Theophilus.

THEOPOLIS Americana ; an essay on the Golden Street of the Holy City . . . In a sermon to the General Assembly of the Massachusett-Province in New-England. 7 d. 9 m. 1709. [By Cotton Mather, D.D.] 12mo. Pp. 51. [*Bodl.*]   Boston, 1710

THEOPOLIS ; or, the City of God, New Jerusalem, in opposition to the city of the nations, Great Babylon : being a coment upon Revelation, chaps. xx., xxi., in which the mystery of the two states, worlds, and Kingdoms, Christ's and Antichrist's . . . are particularly unfolded. . . . [By Henry D'Anvers.] 8vo. [*D. N. B.* vol. 14, p. 39 ; Whitley's *Bapt. Bibl.* i. 97].
London, 1672
Other issues of the same year have slight variations in the title.

THEORETICAL astronomy examined and exposed. By "Common Sense" [William Carpenter]. 8vo. [*Brit. Mus.*]
London [1864]

THEORISTS (the) ; a satire. By the author of *Medico - Mastix* [Ralph Schomberg, M.D.]. 4to. [Green's *Bibl. Somers.* i. 509.]   Bath, 1774

THEORY (the) and construction of Hadley's quadrant demonstrated, and also all the necessary directions given for adjusting the glasses and using it for taking the altitudes of the sun, moon and stars, for finding the latitude at sea. Illustrated by copper plate figures. . . . [By G. Wright.] 8vo. Pp. 28. [*W.*]   London [*c.* 1795]

THEORY and practice of chirurgical pharmacy ; comprehending a complete dispensatory for the use of surgeons. . . . [By Robert Dossie.] 8vo. [*Camb. Univ. Lib.*]   London, 1761

THEORY (the) and practice of gardening ; wherein is fully handled all that relates to fine gardens, commonly called pleasure-gardens, as parterres, groves, bowling-greens, etc. . . . Done from the French original [of Antoine Joseph Dezallier D'Argenville] printed at Paris, anno 1709. By John James of Greenwich. 4to. Pp. 10, 218. [*Nat. Lib. of Scot.*]
London, 1712

THEORY of agency ; or, an essay on the nature, source, and extent of moral freedom, . . . [By John Perkins.] 8vo. Pp. 43. [Evans' *Amer. Bibl.* iv. 291.]
Boston, 1771

THEORY (the) of agreeable sensations in which after the laws observed by nature in the distribution of pleasure are discovered, the principles of natural theology and moral philosophy are established. . . . Translated from the French [of Louis Jean Levesque de Pouilly]. 12mo. Pp. 266. [*Quérard; Mon. Rev.* ii. 66.]   [London] 1749

THEORY (the) of chess ; a treatise in which the principles and maxims . . . are explained. [By Peter Pratt.] 8vo. [*Van der Linde* i. 404.] London, 1799

THEORY (the) of dreams ; in which an inquiry is made into the powers and faculties of the human mind, as they are illustrated in the most remarkable dreams recorded in sacred and profane history. [By Robert Gray, Bishop of Bristol, or Dr J. Ferrier.] 12mo. 2 vols. [Lowndes' *Bibl. Man.*] London, 1808

THEORY (the) of evidence. [By Henry, Earl Bathurst.] 8vo. [*European Mag.* xxvi. 159; *Mon. Rev.* xxv. 151.] London, 1761

THEORY (the) of human progression, and natural probability of a reign of justice. [By Patrick Edward Dove.] 8vo. London, 1850

THEORY (the) of money in connection with some of the prominent doctrines of political economy. By a Scotch banker [George Drummond Charles, teller, Royal Bank, Glasgow]. 8vo. Edinburgh, 1868

THEORY (the) of teaching. . . . By a teacher [Mrs Anna Cabot Lowell, *née* Jackson]. 8vo. [Appleton's *Cycl. of Amer. Biog.*] Boston, 1841

THEORY (the) of the consecration of the most holy Eucharist, as exhibited in the Liturgies of the Church of England, and the Episcopal Church of Scotland. . . . By H. H. [Rev. Henry Humble]. 8vo. Pp. 19. [*New Coll. Lib.*] Edinburgh, 1873

THEORY of the Exchanges ; the Bank Charter Act of 1844 ; the abuse of the metallic principle to depreciation. [By Henry Roy, M.D.] 8vo. London, 1864

THEORY (the) of the foreign exchanges. [By Viscount George Joachim Goschen.] 8vo. London, 1861
Later editions bear the author's name.

THEORY of the rights of authors ; translated from the French [of Antoine Augustin Renouard] by L. S. C. [Luther Stearns Cushing]. 8vo. Boston, 1839

THEORY (the) of the syphon plainly and methodically illustrated ; containing, besides the chief properties of the instrument, some new remarks on its use in accounting for reciprocating springs. [By William Cockin.] 8vo. [*Gent. Mag.* June 1801, p. 576 ; *Mon. Rev.* lxvi. 180.] London, 1781

THEORY (the) of vision, or visual language, shewing the immediate presence and providence of a Deity, vindicated and explained. By the author of *Alciphron, or, the minute philosopher* [George Berkeley, D.D., Bishop of Cloyne]. 8vo. Pp. 64. [Berkeley's *Works, ed. Fraser,* i. 369.] London, 1733

THEORY (the), or rationale of ideas, in a letter to a friend. [By Archibald Campbell.] 8vo. Pp. 27. London, 1727
Signed : A. (B.) C. and addressed to S. J. S. B.

THEOSEBIA, or the Churches advocate ; endeavouring the promotion of loyalty to our king, and fidelity to the Episcopal Church. . . . [By Sir Roger L'Estrange.] 4to. Pp. 26. London, 1683

THEOSOPHY and the higher life ; or, spiritual dynamics and the divine and miraculous man. By G. W. [George Wyld, M.D.]. 8vo. London, 1880

ΘΕΟΣΠΛΑΓΧΝΙΣΘΕΙ'Σ ; or, the yernings of Christs bowels towards his languishing friends. By S. M. [Samuel Moore]. 4to. [Thomason's *Coll. of Tracts,* i. 709.] London, 1648

THERAPEUTICS ; or, a new practice of physic. [By Thomas Marryat.] Fourth edition. 4to. [*Brit. Mus.*] Shrewsbury, 1775
The title of the sixth edition reads : " The art of healing ; or, a new practise of physic . . ." 1777. Later editions have the author's name.

THERE being no Gospel for Tithes, how did they become Law ? or, an examination of the title-deeds of the English Church as by Law established, by a plain man [William Cobbett]. Introduced by George Pitt. 8vo. Pp. 112. [Smith's *Cat. of Friends' Books. Supp.* p. 273.] Croydon, 1876
A reprint of Cobbett's " Legacy to Parsons."

THERE is wisdom in silence. [By James Gregory, M.D.] 8vo. Pp. 2. Edinburgh, 1810

THEREBY. [A novel.] By Fayr Madoc [Miss —— Maddock]. 8vo. 2 vols. Edinburgh, 1883

THERESE ; or, the orphan of Geneva : a tale of great interest. By the author of *Fatherless Fanny* [Clara Reeve]. 8vo. [*Brit. Mus.*] London [1844 ?]

THERIAD (the) : an heroi-comic poem with notes. [By Thomas Rodd.] 8vo. [Nichols' *Lit. Illust.* viii. 680.] [London, 1790]
Utopia : penned for Timothy Tiger, Lemuel Leo, and Barachias Bruin, at the sign of the Foaming Boar, Wolf-Street, the North-East corner of Savage-Square.

THERMOPYLÆ; or, repulsed invasion: a tragic drama, in three acts [and in verse. Enlarged from R. Glover's Leonidas by J. P. Roberdean]. 8vo. [*Brit. Mus.*]   London [*c.* 1850]

THESAURUS ecclesiasticus provincialis; or, a survey of the diocese of Exeter. . . . [By the Rev. William Jones.] 4to. Pp. iv. 116.
Exeter, 1782

THESAURUS incantatus; the enchanted treasure, or the spagyric quest of Beroaldus Cosmopolita. [By Arthur Machen.] 8vo. Pp. 64. [*Arthur Machen: a bibliography.*]
London [1888]

THESAURUS medicaminum; a new collection of medical prescriptions, distributed into twelve classes, and accompanied by pharmaceutical and practical remarks. . . . The second edition, with an appendix and other additions. By a member of the London College of Physicians [Richard Pearson, M.D.]. 8vo. Pp. 412. [*Watt's Bibl. Brit.; Mon. Rev.* xviii. 106.]   London, 1794

THESPIS; or, a critical examination into the merits of all the principal performers belonging to Drury-Lane Theatre. [By Hugh Kelly.] 4to. [*Brit. Mus.*]   London, 1766

THETFORD Chalybeate Spa; a poem. By a parishioner of St Peter's [George Bloomfield]. 8vo. [*Brit. Mus.*]
Cambridge, 1820

THETIS and Peleus; or, the chain of roses: a mythological love story told in one act. By the authors of *The Princesses in the tower*, etc. [Frank Talfourd and others]. 12mo. Pp. 21. [*Brit. Mus.*]   London [*c.* 1851]

THEY must needs go, that the Devil drives; or, a whip for traytors. . . . [By Peter Chambers.] 8vo. [Thomason's *Coll. of Tracts*, i. 563.]   London, 1652

THEY who question. [By Miss Sarah Macnaughton.] 8vo. Pp. 349.
London, 1914

THIBAW'S Queen. By Henry Fielding [Henry Fielding Hall]. 8vo. Pp. 302.
London, 1899

THICK and thin seeding, or a new and scientific method of seeding grain. To which is added a description of a certain remedy for hop blight and all plant vermin. By Sigma [Samuel Newington]. 8vo. [*Brit. Mus.*]
London, 1856

THIMBLE (the); an heroi-comical poem, in four cantos. By a gentleman of Oxford [W. Hawkins?]. 4to. [*Brit. Mus.*]   London, 1744

THING (the) which is right. [A novel.] By Lewis Ramsden [A. Lisle Dowding]. 8vo. Pp. 94.
London, 1917

THINGS after death; three chapters on the intermediate state, with thoughts on family burying places, and hints for epitaphs in country churchyards. [By John Miller, late Fellow of Worcester College, Oxford.] 8vo. [*Nat. Lib. of Scot.*]   London, 1848

THINGS as they are. [A political pamphlet. By John Percival, second Earl of Egmont.] 8vo. 2 parts. [*D. N. B.* vol. 44, p. 370.]
London, 1758-61
Attributed also to Owen Ruffhead.

THINGS divine and supernatural conceived by analogy with things natural and human. By the author of *The procedure, extent and limits of human understanding* [Peter Browne, D.D., Bishop of Corke and Rosse]. 8vo. [*Brit. Mus.*]   London, 1733

THINGS generally. By Max Adler [Charles Heber Clark]. 8vo. Pp. 180. [*Who's Who in Lit.*]   London [1902]

THINGS in general; being delineations of persons, places, scenes, circumstances, situations, and occurrences, in the Metropolis and other parts of Britain; with an autobiographical sketch, *in limine*, and a notice touching Edinburgh. By Laurence Longshank, gent. [Robert Mudie]. 8vo. Pp. viii. 294. [Anderson's *Aberd. Univ. Bibl.* p. 444.]   London, 1824

THINGS more excellent. By "Steward" [Isabella A. Baird]. 8vo.
London, 1904

THINGS new and old; for the glory of God and everlasting benefit of all who read and understand them; or, old revelations and prophecies. . . . By a descendant of one of the early Puritan Governors [Albert Welles]. 8vo. Pp. 261.   Portland, Maine, 1845

THINGS new and old in religion, science, and literature. [By John Duns, D.D., and Mrs Margaret Duns.] 8vo. Pp. vi. 364.   London, 1857

THINGS new and old, relative to life; being sermons on different subjects. By T. H. [Thomas Hughes]. 8vo. [*Brit. Mus.*]   London [1871]

THINGS (the) of a child. [An autobiographical sketch.] By M. E. Francis [Mrs Francis Blundell, *née* Margaret E. Sweetman]. 8vo. Pp. 335.
London, 1918

THINGS old and new; being a sequel to *The chronicles of Waltham*. By the author of *The subaltern* [Rev. George Robert Gleig]. Second edition. 8vo. Pp. iv. 196.   London, 1845

THINGS seen in Egypt. By Clive Holland [Charles J. Hankinson]. 12mo. Pp. 254. [*Who's Who in Lit.*]
London, 1907

THINGS seen in Japan. By Clive Holland [Charles J. Hankinson]. 8vo. Pp. 252. [*Who's Who in Lit.*]
London, 1906

THINGS seen in Normandy and Brittany. By Clive Holland [Charles J. Hankinson]. 8vo. [*Who's Who in Lit.*]
London, 1924

THINGS set in a proper light. . . . By an orthodox clergyman of Massachusetts [Rev. Jacob Norton]. 8vo.
Boston, 1814

THINGS set in a proper light; an answer to a noble author's misrepresentations of "Things as they are." [By John Perceval, Earl of Egmont.] 8vo. [*Lond. Lib. Cat. Supp.*]
London, 1758

THINGS that are Cæsar's rendered unto Cæsar, and things that are God's rendered unto God. By . . . M. W. [Morgan Watkins]. 4to. Pp. 30. [*Brit. Mus.*]
[London] 1666

THINGS that cannot be shaken. [By A. B. Wyness.] 8vo. [*Robertson's Aberd. Bibl.*]
Aberdeen, 1890

THINGS that have happened. [A novel.] By Dorothea Gerard [Madame Longarde De Longarde]. 8vo. [*Who's Who in Lit.*]
London, 1899

THINGS that have wings. [By George Mogridge.] 16mo. [*Brit. Mus.*]
London [1851]

THINGS that I doubt ; dedicated to the authors of Essays & reviews, by a doubting disciple [Rev. John Henry Blunt]. 4to. Pp. 8.
Oxford [*c.* 1860]

THINGS (the) that women do. [A novel.] By Florence Warden [Florence Alice Price, later Mrs George E. James]. 8vo. Pp. 320.
London, 1912

THINGS to be thought of. [By Miss Henrietta Wilson.] 12mo. [*D. N. B.* vol. 62, p. 100.]
Edinburgh, 1853

THINGS worth knowing about horses. By Harry Hieover [Charles Bindley]. 8vo. Pp. 266. [*Brit. Mus.*]
London, 1859

THINK before you speak ; or, the three wishes ; from the French of Mme. de Beaumont, by the author of *The peacock at home* [Mrs Catherine Ann Dorset, *née* Turner]. 8vo.
London, 1809

THINK on these things. [By John Abercrombie, M.D.] 12mo. Pp. 36.
Edinburgh, 1839

Republished in *Essays and Tracts* with the author's name.

THINKING (the) few. [A satirical poem, against the Arians. By Rev. Robert Magill.] 8vo. [*O'Donoghue's Poets of Ireland.*]
Belfast, 1828

THINKS - I - TO - MYSELF ; a serio-ludicro, tragico-comico tale, written by Thinks-I-to-myself, who ? [Edward Nares, D.D.] ; to which is added, a preface concerning the author. . . . Ninth edition : embellished with a portrait of the author Thinking-to-himself. 12mo. 2 vols. [*Brit. Mus.*]
London, 1816

THIRD (a) and fourth part of Pegasus ; taught by Bankes his ghost to dance in the Dorick moode, to the tune of Lachrymæ. In two letters from Oxford, July 1. 1648. [By Thomas Pierce of Magdalen College.] 4to. Pp. 6. [*Bodl.*]
1648

Letters signed : Basilius Philomusus. Author's name in the handwriting of Wood.

THIRD (the) and last part of the Address to the free-men and free-holders of the nation. [By Edward Bohun.] 4to. Pp. xxii. 138. [*Bodl.*]
London, 1683

Ascribed also to Sir Roger L'Estrange.

THIRD (the) and last part of the magistracy and government of England vindicated ; with reasons for a general act of indemnity, etc. [By Sir Bartholomew Shower.] 4to. Pp. 8. [*Bodl.*]
[London, 1689 ?]

THIRD (the) book of history ; containing ancient history in connection with ancient geography. . . . By the author of *Peter Parley's Tales* [Samuel Griswold Goodrich.] The third edition. 12mo.
Boston, 1836

THIRD Catholicke letter in answer to the arguing part of Dr Stillingfleet's second letter to Mr G[odden]. By J. S. [John Sergeant]. 4to. [*Jones' Peck*, i. 129.]
London, 1687

THIRD (a) check to antinomianism ; in a letter to [Richard Hill] the author of *Pietas Oxoniensis*. By the Vindicator of Mr Wesley's *Minutes* [John Fletcher]. 12mo. [*Gent. Mag.* lvi. 29 ; *Mon. Rev.* xlvii. 160.]
Bristol, 1772

THIRD (a) collection of trios, duets, single songs and rotas, selected from the authentic MSS. of the author of *Turn fair Clora*, etc. [Henry Harington, M.D.]. Fol. [*Green's Bibl. Somers.* i. 248.]
Bath, 1800

THIRD (a) conversation, between John, a Baptist, and Ebenezer, a Seceder, on the faith of the Gospel; in which the point of difference between them is clearly stated, and the mistakes of the second conversation [by Rev. Archibald M'Lean] corrected. By the author of the first conversation [Thomas M'Crie, D.D.]. 12mo. Pp. 76. [*Life of Dr M'Crie by his son*, p. 39.]
Edinburgh, 1799
Written by Dr M'Crie in concert with the Rev. George Whytock, Dalkeith.

THIRD (a) crack about the Kirk; or, questions for the times, answered by modern reformers. [By Norman M'Leod, D.D.] 8vo. Pp. 16. [*New Coll. Lib.*]   Glasgow, N.D.

THIRD (a) defense of an argument made use of in a letter to Mr Dodwel to prove the immateriality and immortality of the soul. . . . [By Samuel Clarke, D.D.] 8vo.   London, 1708
See also "A second defense . . ."

THIRD (the) Estate. [A story of the French Revolution.] By Marjorie Bowen [Miss Gabrielle Vere Campbell]. 8vo. Pp. 374. London, 1917

THIRD (the) Hampden agitation. [By Arthur P. Stanley, D.D. On the agitation against R. D. Hampden, Bishop of Hereford.] Pp. 8.
London, 1847

THIRD (a) leaf omitted out of the Record report; or, some remarks upon the evidence given by the principal witnesses adverse to the Record Commission; contained in a third letter addressed to a member of Parliament. [By John Bruce, F.S.A.] 8vo. Pp. 20. [*Bodl.*]   London, 1837

THIRD (a) letter concerning toleration; in defense of the argument of the letter concerning toleration, briefly consider'd and answer'd. [By Jonas Proast.] 4to. Pp. 79. [*Bodl.*]
Oxford, 1691

THIRD (a) letter from a gentleman in the country, to his friends in London, upon the subject of the penal laws and tests. [By William Penn?] 4to. [Smith's *Cat. of Friends' Books*, ii. 304.]
London, 1687

THIRD (a) letter for toleration, to the author [Jonas Proast] of the *Third letter concerning toleration*. [By John Locke.] 4to. Pp. 350. [Watt's *Bibl. Brit.*]   London, 1692
Signed : Philanthropus.

THIRD (a) letter to a clergyman in the country, in defence of what was said in the two former, about the entry of the Parliament-writ in the journals of Convocation, and the insertion of a certain clause in the archiepiscopal mandate. [By Dr Francis Atterbury.] 4to. Pp. 22. [*Brit. Mus.*]
London, 1702

THIRD (a) letter to a person of quality, being a vindication of the former, in answer to a late pamphlet intituled A discourse of use of images &c. [By Edward Pelling.] 4to. Pp. 34. [Jones' *Peck*, ii. 428.]   London, 1687

THIRD (a) letter to F. Lewis Sabran, Jesuit; wherein the defence of his challenge concerning invocation of saints, is examined and confuted. [By Edward Gee.] 4to. Pp. 14. [Jones' *Peck*, ii. 411.]   London, 1688

THIRD (a) letter to Lord John Russell, containing some remarks on the ministerial speeches delivered during the late sugar debates; with an appendix, containing copies of the despatches of Sir C. Grey and Lord Harris. By Jacob Omnium [Matthew James Higgins]. 8vo. Pp. 41.
London, 1848

THIRD (a) letter to the author of the Confessional, containing remarks on the three last chapters of that book. [By Gloucester Ridley.] 8vo. [*Brit. Mus.*]   London, 1768

THIRD (a) letter to the editor of the *Edinburgh Weekly Journal*, from Malachi Malagrowther, Esq. [Sir Walter Scott, Bart.] on the proposed change of currency, and other late alterations, as they affect, or are intended to affect, the kingdom of Scotland. 8vo. Pp. 39.
Edinburgh, 1836

THIRD (a) letter to the inhabitants of Whitby; being the conclusion of the whole matter. By a friend of the people [John Watkins]. 12mo. Pp. 36. [Smale's *Whitby Authors*.]
Whitby, 1836

THIRD (a) letter to the people of England on liberty, taxes, and the application of public money. [By John Shebbeare, M.D.] 8vo. Pp. 60. [*W.*]   London, 1756

THIRD letter to the Rev. W. Palmer . . . on Auricular Confession, and the absolute necessity thereof; also the nullity of the Church of England's ordinations, notes, etc. . . . By Vcrax, a Catholic layman [M. D. Talbot]. 8vo. [*Brit. Mus.*]   London, 1841

THIRD (a) letter to the Right Honourable Edmund Burke, Esq., on the subject of the evidence contained in the reports of the select committee of the House of Commons ; with an introductory preface. [By Captain Joseph Price.] 8vo. Pp. 52, 95.
London, 1782 ; reprinted 1783

THIRD (the) Napoleon ; an ode to Alfred Tennyson, Esq. [By Robert Story.] 8vo. Pp. 11. [*Brit. Mus.*]
London, 1854

THIRD (the) note of the Church examined, viz. Duration. [By John Williams, D.D. Bishop of Chichester.] 4to. Pp. 16. [Jones' *Peck*, p. 437.]
London, 1687

THIRD (the) part of a treatise, intituled: Of three conversions of England: conteyninge, an examen of the calendar or catalogue of protestant saints, martyrs and confessors, diuised by John Fox, and prefixed before his volume of Acts and monuments ; with a paralell or comparison thereof to the Catholike Roman calendar, and saints therein conteyned. . . . By N. D. [Nicolas Doleman, *alias* Robert Parsons]. 8vo.   1604

THIRD (the) part of Advice to the painter, concerning the great Turk, Count Teckley, and the forces against them ; the French, the Spaniards, the Dutch, and the English. [By Andrew Marvell.] Fol. Pp. 2.
London, 1684
More probably by Henry Savile. See the note to "Advice to a painter" in the Supplement.

THIRD (the) part of Naked truth ; or, some serious considerations, that are of high concern to the ruling clergy of England, Scotland, or any other Protestant nation. . . . [By Edmund Hickeringill.] Fol. Pp. 44. [*D. N. B.* vol. 26, p. 348.]   London, 1681
See *supra*, "The naked truth."

THIRD (the) part of No protestant plot : with observations on the proceedings upon the bill of indictment against the E. of Shaftesbury: and a brief account of the case of the Earl of Argyle. [By Robert Ferguson.] 4to. Pp. iv. 151. [*D. N. B.* vol. 18, p. 351.]
London, 1682
The first and second parts have been attributed to the Earl of Shaftesbury.

THIRD (a) part of the Caveat against the Whiggs, in a short historical account of their transactions since the Revolution. [By Charles Hornby.] 8vo. Pp. 108. [*Bodl.*] London, 1712

THIRD (the) part of the New Athenians no noble Bereans ; being an answer to the *Athenian Mercury* of the 14th of the 4th month, called June, in behalf of the people called Quakers. [By William Penn.] Fol. [Smith's *Cat. of Friends' Books*, ii. 308.]
London, 1692

THIRD remarks upon an Essay [by John Locke] concerning the human understanding. . . . [By Thomas Burnet, M.A.] 8vo. [*D. N. B.* vol. 7, p. 408.]   London, 1699

THIRD (a) reply to the *Edinburgh Review*, by the author of a Reply to the calumnies of that Review against Oxford [Edward Copleston, D.D.]. 8vo. Pp. 16.   Oxford, 1811

THIRD (a) synopsis ; containing some of the chief arguments for popular election from the sacred Epistles. . . . [By Rev. James Hill, M.A., of Kirkpatrick-Durham.] 12mo. Pp. 32.
Edinburgh, 1734

THIRD (the) tour of Dr Syntax ; in search of a wife : a poem. [By William Combe.] 8vo. Pp. 279. [*D. N. B.* vol. 11, p. 430.]   London, 1821

THIRDE (the) and last part of Connycatching. With the newly devised knauish art of foole-taking. The like cosenages and villenies neuer before discouered. By R. G. [Robert Greene]. 4to. No pagination. B. L. [*Pollard and Redgrave.*]   London, 1592

THIRTEEN essays on the policy of manufacturing in the country. [By Matthew Carey.] 8vo. Pp. 30. [Sabin's *Dict.* iii. 342.]
Philadelphia, 1830

THIRTEEN letters on our social condition, addressed to the editor of the *Sheffield Courant.* [By Thomas Arnold, D.D.] 8vo. Pp. 37. [*Brit. Mus.*]   Sheffield, 1832

THIRTEEN months in the rebel army, 1861-62. By an impressed New Yorker [William G. Stevenson]. 8vo. [Cushing's *Init. and Pseud.*]
New York, 1862

THIRTEENTH (the) chapter to the Romans, vindicated from the abusive senses put upon it. Written by a curate of Salop, and directed to the clergy of that county, and the neighbouring ones of North Wales; to whom the author wisheth patience, moderation, and a good understanding for half an hour. [By William Fleetwood, Bishop of Ely.] 8vo. [*Brit. Mus.*]   London, 1710

THIRTEENTH (the) note of the Church examined, viz.: the confession of adversaries. [By Richard Kidder, M.A., Rector of S. Martin's, Outwich.] 4to. Pp. 24. [Jones' *Peck*, p. 439.]
London, 1687

THIRTY (the) days. By Hubert Wales [William Piggott]. 8vo. Pp. 311. [*Brit. Mus.*] London, 1915

THIRTY letters on the trade of Bristol ; the causes of its decline, and means of its revival. By a Burgess [J. B. Kington]. 8vo. Pp. 346. [Hyett and Bazeley's *Gloucest. Lit.*] Bristol, 1834

THIRTY letters on various subjects. [By William Jackson, of Exeter.] The second edition corrected and improved. 8vo. 2 vols. London, 1784
The third edition, London, 1795, has the author's name.

THIRTY years ; being poems new and old. By the author of *John Halifax, gentleman*, etc. [Dinah Maria Mulock]. 8vo. London, 1880

THIRTY years of foreign policy ; a history of the secretaryships of the Earl of Aberdeen and Viscount Palmerston. By the author of *The Right Hon. B. Disraeli, M.P. a literary and political biography* [Thomas Macknight]. 8vo. Pp. xi. 440. [F. Boase's *Mod. Eng. Biog.*] London, 1855

THIRTY years' view ; or, a history of the working of the American Government for thirty years, from 1820 to 1850 ; chiefly taken from the Congress Debates, the private papers of General Jackson, and the speeches of Ex-Senator Benton. . . . By a Senator of thirty years [Thomas Hart Benton]. 8vo. 2 vols. [*Brit. Mus.*]
New York, 1857

THIRTY-SIX hints to Sportsmen. [By Albany Savile.] 12mo.
Okehampton [1825]

THIRTY-SIX morning prayers. . . . [By Lady Chambers, wife of Sir Robert Chambers, Chief Justice of Bengal.] 4to. London, 1821

THIRTY-SIX plain maxims on the way to live and die in peace ; from the pastor of St Paul's, Haggerstone [Rev. William Stone] to his flock. 12mo. S. sh. [Cushing's *Init. and Pseud.*]
London, 1864

THIRTY-SIX short, plain sermons. By a London suburban minister [Rev. G. Hunt Jackson]. 8vo.
London, 1871

THIRTY-SIX years of seafaring life. By an old Quarter-Master [John Bechervaise]. 8vo. [*Brit. Mus.*]
Portsea, 1839

$30,000 (the) bequest, and other stories. By Mark Twain [Samuel P. Clemens]. 8vo. Pp. viii. 521. London, 1906

THIRTY-TWO years in a House of Mercy. By H. N. [Harriet Nokes]. 8vo. Pp. 96. London, 1895

THIS gallant Caualiero Dicke Bowyer, newly acted. [By William Wayer.] 8vo. No pagination. [*Bodl.*]
London, 1605
The running title is : The historie of the triall of Cheualry.

THIS indenture witnesseth. By Averil Beaumont [Mrs Margaret Hunt]. 8vo. 3 vols. [Cushing's *Init. and Pseud.*]
London, 1875

THIS is an encouragement to all the women's meetings in the world. By G. F. [George Fox]. 8vo. Pp. 96. [Smith's *Cat. of Friends' Books.*]
N.P. 1676

THIS is the myrrour or glasse of healthe, necessary and nedefull for every person to loke in, that will kepe theyr bodye free from the sycknesse of the pestylence, and it sheweth howe the planettes do reygne in euery houre of the day and night, with the natures and exposicions of the XII. sygnes. . . . [By Thomas Moulton.] 8vo. No pagination. B. L. [*Bodl.*]
London [1539 ?]
Other editions have different titles : "This is the glasse of helthe . . .", "Thys is the myrrour . . ." One edition of the same year is not anonymous.

THIS is to all officers and souldiers of the armies in England, Scotland, and Ireland ; and to all magistrates, and them in authority in these nations, and the dominions thereunto appertaining for them to read. [By George Fox.] 4to. Pp. 8. London, 1657
Signed : G. F.

THIS is to the clergy who are the men that goes about to settle religion, as they say, according to the Church of England. . . . [Signed: M. F. *i.e.* Margaret Fell, later Mrs Fox.] 4to. Pp. 8. [Smith's *Cat. of Friends' Books.*] London, 1660

THIS man's dominion : a story of self-will. By Deas Cromarty [Mrs Rob. A. Watson, *née* Sophia Anne Fletcher]. 8vo. London, 1894

THIS son of Vulcan ; a novel. By the authors of *Ready-money Mortiboy*, etc. [Walter Besant and James Rice] 8vo. 3 vols. London, 1876
Preface signed : W. B. [and] J. R.

THIS troublesome world. [A novel.] By the authors of *The Medicine Lady* [Elizabeth Thomas Meade, and another]. 8vo. 3 vols. London, 1893

THIS work-a-day world. By Holme Lee, author of *Sylvan Holt's daughter* [Harriet Parr]. 8vo. 3 vols.
London, 1875

THISTLE (the); a dispassionate examine of the prejudice of Englishmen in general towards the Scotch nation ; and particularly of a late arrogant insult offered to all Scotchmen, by a modern English journalist. In a letter to the author of Old England of Dec. 27, 1746. [By William Murray, Lord Mansfield.] 8vo. [*Brit. Mus.*]
London, 1747

THISTLEDOWN. [Verses.] By E. S. G. S. [E. S. G. Saunders]. 16mo. [*Brit. Mus.*] 1866

THISTLEDOWN ; or, the black witches of the Wild West : a collection of anecdotes of the West country. By Anonymous [Arthur George Pain]. 8vo. [*Brit. Mus.*] Bridgwater, 1909

THISTLES of Mount Cedar. By Ursula Tannerforst [Emily Tilghman]. 8vo. [*Amer. Cat.*]
Philadelphia, 1905

THO. Mori vita et exitus ; or, the history of Sir Thomas More, sometime Lord High Chancellor. Collected out of several authors by J. H. [John Hoddesdon]. 8vo. Pp. 150. [*Lowndes' Bibl. Man.*] London, 1652

THOMAS à Kempis, canon regular of St Augustine's Order, his sermons on the Incarnation and passion of Christ ; translated out of Latin [by Miles Pinkney, *alias* Carre]. 12mo. [*D. N. B.* vol. 9, p. 178.] Paris, 1653

THOMAS against Bennet. . . . [By Rev. Daniel Mayo, M.A.] 8vo. [*D. N. B.* vol. 37, p. 171.]
London, 1702

THOMAS and Sally ; or, the sailor's return : a musical entertainment, as it is performed at the Theatre-Royal in Covent-Garden. [By Isaac Bickerstaffe.] The music composed by Doctor Arne. 8vo. [*Brit. Mus.*]
London, 1761

THOMAS Chalmers, the man ; his times and work. [By Andrew James Symington.] 8vo. [*Lib. Journ.* iii. 380.] Ardrossan, 1878

THOMAS Curry, the pious keelman ; an authentic narrative. [By C. N. Wason.] 8vo. Pp. 28. Newcastle, 1822

THOMAS de Quincey ; his life and writings ; with unpublished correspondence. By H. A. Page [Alex. Hay Japp, LL.D.]. 8vo. 2 vols. [*Lib. Journ.* iii. 380.] London, 1877

THOMAS Gainsborough ; a record of his life and works. . . . By N. d'Anvers [Mrs Nancy R. E. M. Bell, *née* Meugens]. 8vo. Pp. 150. [*Birm. Cent. Lib.*] New York [1897]

THOMAS Grant first Bishop of Southwark. By Grace Ramsay, author of *A woman's trials*, etc. [Kathleen O'Meara]. With two portraits. 8vo. Pp. vi. 491. London, 1874

THOMAS of Reading ; or, the sixe worthy yeomen of the west. Now the sixth time corrected and enlarged by T. D. [Thomas Deloney]. 4to. B. L. [*Pollard and Redgrave.*]
London, 1632

THOMAS Whythorne, an unknown Elizabethan composer. By Peter Warlock [Philip Heseltine]. 8vo. Pp. 11. [*Brit. Mus.*] London [1927]

THOMASINA ; a biography. By the author of *Dorothy*, etc. [Margaret Agnes Colville, later Mrs Paul]. 8vo. 2 vols. [*Brit. Mus.*] London, 1875

THOMSON the Great kild ; or, a perfect narrative of the totall routing of the Levellers neere Wellingborough. . . . [Signed : J. R. *i.e.* John Rushworth.] 4to. [*Brit. Mus.*] London, 1649

THOREAU ; his life and aims. By H. A. Page [Alexander Hay Japp]. 8vo. [*Lib. Journ.* vi. 190.]
Boston, 1877

THORN (a) in her heart. [A novel.] By Bertha M. Clay [Charlotte M. Braeme]. 8vo. Pp. 247.
New York [1889]

THORN (the) in the nest. By Martha Farquharson [Martha Finlay]. 8vo. [Cushing's *Init. and Pseud.*]
New York, 1880

THORNBERRY Abbey, a tale of the Established Church. [By Gertrude Parsons, *née* Hext.] 8vo. Pp. 169. [Boase and Courtney's *Bibl. Corn.* ii. 425.] London, 1846

THORNCLIFFE Hall ; or, why Joel Milford changed his opinion of boys whom he once called "goody-goody fellows." By Francis Forrester [Daniel Wise, D.D.]. 8vo. New York, 1891

THORNEY Hall ; a story of an old family. By Holme Lee, author of *Maude Talbot* [Harriet Parr]. 8vo. [*Lit. Year Book.*] London, 1855

THORN-FALCON hill ; a poem. [By Henry Waugh.] 8vo. [Green's *Bibl. Somers.* iii. 317.] Taunton, 1859

THORNIAD (the) ; a familiar epistle. [By Thomas Crofton Croker.] 8vo. [O'Donoghue's *Poets of Ireland.*]
Cork, 1876

THORNICROFT'S model. By Averil Beaumont, author of *Magdalen Wynyard* [Mrs A. W. Hunt]. 8vo. 3 vols. [*Nat. Lib. of Scot.*]. [London] 1873

THORNS and orange-blossoms; a novel. By Bertha M. Clay [Charlotte M. Braeme]. 8vo. New York, 1884

THORNTON Abbey. [By John Satchell.] 12mo. 3 vols. London, 1806
The second edition, 1814, is not anonymous.

THORN-TREE (the); being a history of thorn worship, of the twelve tribes of Israel, but more especially of the lost tribes and House of David. By Theta, a lineal descendant of the hereditary standard-bearers of Normandy and England, "the Knights of the Swan" [William Thorn]. 8vo. [Olphar Hamst.] London, 1863

THORNY (a) path. By Hesba Stretton, author of *Jessica's first prayer*, etc. [Sarah Smith]. 8vo. Pp. 160. London [1879]

THORPE Regis. By the author of *The rose garden*, etc. [Frances Mary Peard]. 8vo. 2 vols. [*Brit. Mus.*] London, 1874

THOR'S Town and John o' Groat's, in fact and fiction. [By William Campbell.] 4to. Pp. 66. Thurso, 1902

THOSE boys. [A tale.] By Faye Huntington [Mrs Isabella H. Foster]. 8vo. Pp. 64. London [1895]

THOSE children. [A novel.] By Curtis Yorke [Mrs W. S. Richmond Lee]. 8vo. Pp. vi. 308. London, 1896

THOSE difficult years. [A novel.] By Faith Baldwin [Faith Baldwin Cuthrell]. 8vo. Pp. 349. [*Amer. Cat.*] Boston [1925]

THOSE good Normans. [A series of sketches, translated from the French.] By "Gyp" [Gabrielle S. M. de Mirabeau, Comtesse de Martel]. 8vo. Pp. 286. Chicago, 1896

THOSE midsummer fairies. By Baynton Foster [Theodora C. Elmslie]. 8vo. Philadelphia, 1896

THOSE pretty St George girls. By one of the set [Mrs Pierre Lorillard]. 8vo. [*Lib. Journ.* xiv. 59.] Philadelphia, 1883

THOSE Westerton girls. [A novel.] By Florence Warden [Florence Alice Price, later Mrs George E. James]. 8vo. Pp. 111. London, 1891

THOTH; a romance. By the author of *Toxar* [Joseph Shield Nicholson, LL.D., Professor in Edinburgh University]. 8vo. [*Brit. Mus.*] London, 1889

THOU art the man; a novel. By the author of *Lady Audley's secret* [Mary Elizabeth Braddon, later Mrs Maxwell]. 8vo. London, 1894

THOU shalt not. [A novel.] By Albert Ross [Linn Boyd Porter]. 8vo. Pp. 366. [*Brit. Mus.*] New York, 1889

THOU shalt not steal; the school for ingratitude. . . . A comedy in five acts. [By —— Fisher.] 8vo. [*Brit. Mus.*] London [1798]

THOUGHT breezes. . . . [A periodical]; edited by O'Leah [William Heald]. 4to. London, 1898

THOUGHT echoes. [Poems. By Rev. Timothy J. O'Mahony, D.D., D.C.L.] 8vo. [O'Donoghue's *Poets of Ireland*.] Dublin, 1891

THOUGHTFUL hours. By H. L. L., author (in part) of *Hymns from the land of Luther* [Jane L. Borthwick]. 8vo. Pp. vii. 200. [*Brit. Mus.*] London, 1867

THOUGHTLESS (a) seven. By the author of *Probable sons* [Amy Le Feuvre]. 8vo. Pp. 96. New York, 1897

THOUGHTLESS (the) ward. By a lady [Miss Ferguss, of Bugden, Huntingdonshire]. 12mo. [*Gent. Mag.* xciv. 1. 224; *Mon. Rev.* lvii. 319.] London, 1777

THOUGHTLY (the) ones; a novel. By Zack [Miss Gwendoline Keats]. 8vo. London, 1903

THOUGHT-READER'S (a) thoughts; being the impressions and confessions of Stuart Cumberland [Charles Garner, of Oxford]. 8vo. Pp. xi. 326. [*Brit. Mus.*] London, 1888

THOUGHTS about promoting the interest of Christ's Universal Church. [By Rev. Edward Stephens, of Cherington.] 4to. [*Brit. Mus.*] London [*c.* 1700]

THOUGHTS about the city of St Louis; her commerce and manufactures, railroads. . . . [By John Hogan.] 8vo. [Sabin's *Dictionary*.] St Louis, 1854

THOUGHTS among flowers. [By John Kitto, D.D.] 12mo. [*D. N. B.* vol. 31, p. 234.] London [1843]

THOUGHTS and aphorisms from the works of George Sand [Madame A. L. A. Dudevant]. 8vo. Edinburgh, 1911

THOUGHTS and characters; selections from the writings of the author of *The Schönberg-Cotta family* [Mrs Elizabeth Charles]. 8vo. Pp. 503. [*Brit. Mus.*] London [1884]
The title of an earlier edition (1877) begins: "Selections . . ."

C

THOUGHTS and feelings. By Arthur Brooke [John Chalk Claris, editor of the *Kent Herald*]. 12mo. [*Gent. Mag.* March 1866, p. 439.]   London, 1820

THOUGHTS and hints for conservative electors. [By John Miller, M.A., Fellow of Worcester College, Oxford.] 8vo. Pp. 14.   London, 1837

THOUGHTS and memories in verse. By G. C. B. [George Clement Boase, minister in Brighton]. 8vo. Pp. viii. 192. [*Brit. Mus.*]   Brighton, 1876

THOUGHTS and opinions of a statesman [Wilhelm von Humboldt], in a selected series of letters. [Translated by Catherine M. A. Couper and edited by Sir Arthur Helps.] 12mo. Pp. 166.   London, 1849

THOUGHTS and recollections by one of the last century [William Stewart Rose]. 8vo. Pp. vi. 237. [*Brit. Mus.*]   London, 1825

THOUGHTS and stories on tobacco for American lads ; or, Uncle Toby's anti-tobacco advice to his nephew. . . . By Simeon Toby [George Trask]. 12mo. [Cushing's *Init. and Pseud.*]   Boston, 1852

THOUGHTS and suggestions submitted to the consideration of the Society of Friends. By H. B. [Henry Bewley]. 12mo. [Smith's *Cat. of Friends' Books*, i. 118.]   Dublin, private print, 1859

THOUGHTS at seventy-nine. By the author of *Thoughts on devotion*, etc. [John Sheppard]. 8vo. Pp. xx. 200. [Green's *Bibl. Somers.* iii. 242.]   London, 1865
    Dedication signed : J. S.

THOUGHTS by the way. [By W. N. Nash.] 32mo. [*Brit. Mus.*]   Birmingham [1835 ?]

THOUGHTS by the wayside. By the authoress of *Things old and new* [Lucy Emra, later Mrs Croggon]. 8vo. Pp. iv. 111. [*Brit. Mus.*]   Canterbury, 1836

THOUGHTS concerning education. By one of the working classes [Henry Brittain]. 8vo.   Birmingham [1870]

THOUGHTS concerning the Bank, with some facts relating to such establishments in other countries : respectfully submitted to the Honourable the General Assembly of Pennsylvania. By one of their Constituents [Tench Coxe]. 8vo. [Evans' *Amer. Bibl.* vii. 18.]   Philadelphia, 1786

THOUGHTS concerning the origin of power. [By John Wesley.] 12mo. Pp. 12. [*Bodl.*]   Bristol, 1772

THOUGHTS (the) concerning toleration vindicated and enforc'd, in answer to the 12 and 13 pages of a scurrilous pamphlet [by James Ramsay], entituled Toleration's fence removed, etc. [By Sir Archibald Sinclair.] 4to. Pp. 12.   N.P. 1703

THOUGHTS during sickness. By the author of *The doctrine of the cross* and *Devotions for the sick-room* [Robert Brett]. 8vo. Pp. xvi. 132. [*Camb. Univ. Lib.*]   Oxford, 1853
    Dedication signed : R. B.

THOUGHTS for a Convention ; a memorandum on the state of Ireland. By A. E. [George W. Russell]. 8vo. Pp. 31.   Dublin, 1917

THOUGHTS for Christmas. [Signed : J. E. M. *i.e.* Julia Elizabeth Marshall.] 8vo.   N.P. [1895]

THOUGHTS for the age. By the author of *Amy Herbert* [Elizabeth Missing Sewell]. 8vo. Pp. viii. 348.   London, 1870

THOUGHTS for the day. [By Dorothy Anne Thrupp.] 12mo.   London, 1836

THOUGHTS for the holy week for young children. By the author of *Amy Herbert* [Elizabeth Missing Sewell]. 8vo. Pp. vi. 97.   London, 1857

THOUGHTS for the New Year ; the Rector's offering. [By Rev. Gilbert H. Sayres.] 8vo. [Sabin's *Dictionary*.]   Jamaica, 1850

THOUGHTS for the people. . . . [By Gerrit Smith.] 8vo. [Sabin's *Dictionary*.]   Peterboro, New York, 1865

THOUGHTS for the thoughtful. By Old Humphrey [George Mogridge]. Third edition. 12mo. Pp. viii. 280.   London, N.D.

THOUGHTS from a girl's life. [By Miss L. F. M. Phillips.] 8vo.   Oxford, 1870

THOUGHTS from the inner circle. [Poems. By John Alfred Langford, LL.D., H. Latham and W. H.] 8vo. [*Brit. Mus.*]   Birmingham, 1857

THOUGHTS in idle hours ; poems by M. G. C. [Maria Gertrude Cooper]. 8vo. [Green's *Bibl. Somers.*]   Bath, 1870

THOUGHTS in past years. By the author of *The cathedral* [Isaac Williams]. 8vo. [*Brit. Mus.*]   Oxford, 1838

THOUGHTS in rhyme. By an East Anglian [Charles Feist]. [*N. and Q.* 2nd Oct. 1858, p. 278.]   1825

THOUGHTS in the cloister and the crowd. [By Arthur Helps.] 8vo. [*Brit. Mus.*]   London, 1835
    First book written by Sir Arthur Helps.

THOUGHTS in the night ; a poem written in Auvergne. By a Wanderer [Robert Mackenzie Beverley, LL.B.]. 8vo. [*Brit. Mus.*]   London, 1852

THOUGHTS in verse. By E. B. [E. Bibby]. 12mo. [*Brit. Mus.*]
London, 1873

THOUGHTS in verse. By M. W. J. M. [Miss M. W. J. Matthews]. 8vo. Pp. vii. 104. [Dobell's *Private Prints*, p. 114.]   Private print, 1860

THOUGHTS in verse for communion seasons. [By Rev. John Roberts.] 12mo. Pp. 32.   Edinburgh, 1867

THOUGHTS in verse, on private prayer and publick worship. [By Rev. James Ford, M.A.] 8vo. Pp. 56. [Dobell's *Private Prints*, p. 178.]
N.P., private print, 1867

THOUGHTS occasioned by the proceedings on Bristol bridge, and the melancholy consequences, on the awful night of Monday, 30th September, 1793. By a lady [Miss Jane Cave, later Mrs Winscom]. 8vo. Pp. 7. [Hyett and Bazeley's *Bibl. of Gloucest. Lit.* iii. 88.]   Bristol, 1793

THOUGHTS (the) of a country gentleman upon the reading of Dr Sacheverell's Tryal, in a letter to a friend. [By George Smalridge, D.D.] 8vo. [*Brit. Mus.*]   London, 1710

THOUGHTS (the) of a dying man ; a faithful report of matters uttered by many in the last minutes of their lives. . . . [By Cotton Mather.] 12mo. Pp. 47. [G. Brinley's *American Library*.]   Boston, 1697

THOUGHTS of a layman concerning patronage and presentations. [By Andrew Crosbie, advocate.] 8vo. Pp. iv. 52. [*Nat. Lib. of Scot.*]
Edinburgh, 1769

THOUGHTS of a Lincolnshire freeholder on the late address of Sir Gilbert Heathcote, of Normanton-Park, in the county of Rutland, Baronet, to the freeholders of the county of Lincoln. [By Samuel Partridge, M.A.] The fourth edition. 8vo. Pp. 45. [*Bodl.*]
Boston and Spilsby [1796]

THOUGHTS (the) of a member of the Lower House, in relation to a project for restraining and limiting the power of the Crown in the future creation of Peers. [By Sir Robert Walpole, 1st Earl of Orford.] The second edition. 8vo. [*Brit. Mus.*]   London, 1719
See the note to "Some reflections upon a pamphlet . . ."

THOUGHTS of a physician, being the second series of *Evening thoughts*. [By Joseph Bullar, M.D.] 12mo. Pp. iv. 176.   London, 1868

THOUGHTS of a private person, about the justice of the gentlemens undertaking at York, Nov. 1688. [By Thomas Osborne, Earl of Danby, later Duke of Leeds.] 4to.
[London] 1689

THOUGHTS of a Queen. By Carmen Sylva [Elizabeth, Queen of Roumania]. 8vo. Pp. 116.   London, 1901

THOUGHTS of a Tory author concerning the press. [Ascribed to Joseph Addison.] 8vo. Pp. 8. [Lowndes' *Bibl. Man., art. Press.*]
London, 1712

THOUGHTS (the) of a traveller upon our American disputes. [Signed : Viator, *i.e.* Sir William Draper.] 8vo. Pp. iv. 28. [*Edin. Univ. Lib.*]
London, 1774

THOUGHTS (the) of an honest Tory, upon the present proceedings of that party. In a letter to a friend in town. [By Benjamin Hoadly.] 8vo. Pp. 14. [*Brit. Mus.*]   London, 1710

THOUGHTS of an old man of independent mind, though dependent fortune, on the high price of corn. [By Alexander Dalrymple.] 8vo. [*European Mag.* xlii. 422 ; *Mon. Rev.* xxxiv. 214.]   London, 1800

THOUGHTS (the) of God. By the author of *Morning and night watches*, etc. [John Ross Macduff, D.D.] Third edition. 8vo. Pp. 144.
London, 1863

THOUGHTS of great musicians ; from the German of La Mara [Marie Lipsias]. 8vo. Pp. 71. [*Amer. Cat.*]
New York, 1896

THOUGHTS of Patricius. [By R. Geoghegan.] 8vo.   Dublin, 1785

THOUGHTS of peace for the Christian sufferer : a selection of short passages from Scripture. [By Emma Parr.] 16mo. [*Brit. Mus.*]   London, 1840

THOUGHTS of present concernment for the relief of the poor in a scarcity of corn. . . . By a member of the Incorporated Society [David Stephens]. 8vo. Pp. 16. [*Manchester Free Lib.* p. 688.]   Dublin, 1746

THOUGHTS of sunshine in sorrow. . . . [By Ellen St John Hunt.] 8vo. [*Brit. Mus.*]   London, 1862

THOUGHTS on a continuation of the Book of Common Prayer used in the Church of England. By a lay member of that Church [John Stow]. 8vo. 2 vols. [Cushing's *Init. and Pseud.*]
London, 1850-56

THOUGHTS on a parliamentary reform. [By Soame Jenyns.] The second edition. 8vo. Pp. 26. [*Bodl.*]
London, 1784
In Jenyns' collected works, vol. ii.

THOUGHTS on a pebble ; or, a first lesson in geology. [By Gideon Algernon Mantell.] 12mo. [*Brit. Mus.*]
London, 1836

THOUGHTS on affectation, addressed chiefly to young people. [By Althea Fanshawe.] 8vo. Pp. xvi. 296. [*Brit. Mus.*]
1805

THOUGHTS on art, and notes on the Exhibition of the Royal Scottish Academy of 1868. By Veri Vindex [Sir George Reid and John F. White]. 8vo.
Edinburgh, 1868

THOUGHTS on books and reading. [By Josh Bevan Braithwaite.] 12mo. [Smith's *Cat. of Friends' Books, Supp.* p. 67.]
London, 1855

THOUGHTS on Calvinism ; a poem. [By Thomas Taylor.] 12mo. [*Bodl.*]
Northampton, 1831

THOUGHTS on Church matters in the diocese of Oxford. [By Joseph Henry Wilson.] 8vo.
London, 1858

THOUGHTS on civil liberty, on licentiousness, and faction. By the author of *Essays on the characteristics*, etc. [John Brown, D.D.]. 8vo. Pp. 167. [*Bodl.*]
Newcastle upon Tyne, 1765

THOUGHTS on Clubs. By a country cook [J. George Luff]. 8vo.
Hawick, 1899

THOUGHTS on cruelty to animals : with anecdotes on the subject. [By Luke Howard, of Plaistow.] 8vo. [Smith's *Cat. of Friends' Books*, i. 982.]
London, 1821

THOUGHTS on deceit. [By William Pettman.] 8vo. Pp. 40. [*Bodl.*]
Margate, 1806

THOUGHTS on defence, from a Canadian point of view. . . . By a Canadian [William Foster Coffin]. 8vo. Pp. 55. [*Brit. Mus.*]
Montreal, 1870

THOUGHTS on duelling, and the Christian character ; in four letters . . . suggested by three "affairs of honour" which have occurred in modern days between certain British senators. By Gabriel Stickingplaister [Rev. Richard Warner]. 8vo. [Green's *Bibl. Somers*. i. 494.]
Bath, 1840

THOUGHTS on East-India affairs, most humbly submitted at this critical conjuncture, to the consideration of the Legislature and the proprietors of East-India stock. By a quondum servant of the company [John Zephaniah Holwell]. 8vo. Pp. 4, 60.
London, 1784

THOUGHTS on ecclesiastical establishments, particularly the Established Church of Scotland. By a layman [John Gibson, W.S.]. 8vo. Pp. 4, 80. [*Edin. Univ. Lib.*]   Edinburgh, 1832

THOUGHTS on education. By the author of *Britain's Remembrancer* [James Burgh]. 8vo. Pp. 80. [*Brit. Mus.*]
Edinburgh, 1747

THOUGHTS on elocution. [By John Martin.] 12mo. Pp. 36. [*Bodl.*]
London, 1798

THOUGHTS on equal representation. [By Francis Bassett, Lord De Dunstanville.] 8vo. [Boase and Courtney's *Bibl. Corn.* i. 112.]   London, 1783

THOUGHTS on executive justice, with respect to our criminal laws, particularly on the circuits. . . . With an appendix, occasioned by a charge given [by Baron Perryn] to the Grand Jury for the County of Surrey. By a sincere well-wisher to the public [Martin Madan]. The second edition. 8vo. [*Brit. Mus.*]   London, 1785

THOUGHTS on finance and Colonies. By Publius [Samuel B. Williams]. 8vo.
London, 1846

THOUGHTS on general gravitation, and views thence arising as to the state of the universe. [By Alexander Wilson, M.A.] 4to. [*D. N. B.* vol. 62, p. 75.]   London, 1777

THOUGHTS on government ; applicable to the present state of the American Colonies : in a letter from a gentleman [John Adams] to his friend [George Wythe, of Virginia]. 8vo. Pp. 16. [Evans' *Amer. Bibl.* v. 216.]   Philadelphia, 1776

THOUGHTS on habit and discipline. [By Joseph John Gurney.] 8vo. [Smith's *Cat. of Friends' Books*, i. 893.]   London, 1844
The third edition, published in 1845, has the author's name.

THOUGHTS on hunting ; in a series of familiar letters to a friend. [By Peter Beckford.] 4to. Pp. 334. [*Bodl.*]
Sarum, 1781

THOUGHTS on intervention. By a citizen of Pennsylvania [William Bradford Reed]. 8vo. [Cushing's *Init. and Pseud.*]   Philadelphia, 1852

THOUGHTS on Jeremy Bentham ; or, the principle of utility considered in connection with ethical philosophy and criminal jurisprudence. By a member of the Manchester Athenæum [J. P. Culverwell]. 8vo. Pp. 51.
London, 1843

THOUGHTS on labor, capital, currency. By a citizen of Maryland [H. Mankin]. 8vo. [Cushing's *Init. and Pseud.*]
Baltimore, 1864

THOUGHTS on laughter. By a Chancery barrister [Basil Montague]. 12mo. Pp. 68. [*Brit. Mus.*]　　London, 1830

THOUGHTS on life, present and future ; ten sermons. By D. S. [Rev. David Swan]. 12mo.　　　London, 1872

THOUGHTS on life-science. By Benjamin Place [Edward Thring]. 8vo. [*Lib. Journ.* ii. 307.]
London, 1869

THOUGHTS on man in his relation to God and to external nature ; with minor poems. [By John Montgomery, minister of the Free Church, Innerleithen, Peebles.] 8vo. Pp. 168. [*Brit. Mus.*]　　　London, 1852

THOUGHTS on many things. By Francis T. Gompertz. [Edited by J. A. *i.e.* John Andrews, of Wadham College.] 8vo. Pp. 164. [*Brit. Mus.*]
Oxford, 1904

THOUGHTS on martial law, and on the proceedings of general courts-martial. [By Sir Richard Joseph Sullivan.] 4to. [*Brit. Mus.*]
London, 1779

THOUGHTS on medical reform. By a retired practitioner [John Allen]. 8vo. Pp. ii. 32. [*W.*]　　　London, 1833

THOUGHTS on men and things ; a series of essays. By Angelina Gushington [Charles W. Radcliffe-Cooke]. 8vo. [Cushing's *Init. and Pseud.*]
London, 1868

THOUGHTS on mixt communion ; in a letter [signed : Aristobulus, *i.e.* James Turner]. 8vo. [*Brit. Mus.*]
Coventry, 1773

THOUGHTS on modern politics ; a poem upon the Slave trade. [By Rev. Neil Douglas, Dundee.] 8vo. Pp. 248. [*D. N. B.* vol. 15, p. 344.]
London, 1793

THOUGHTS on money, circulation and paper currency. [By Patrick Murray, 5th Lord Elibank.] 8vo. Pp. 33.
Edinburgh, 1768
Author's name in the hand-writing of Dr David Laing.

THOUGHTS on mortality, occasioned by the death of ——. [By Rev. —— Davidson.] 8vo. [*Brit. Mus.*]
Newcastle, 1789

THOUGHTS on Mr [Charles James] Fox's secession for six months. . . . [By Rev. Charles Edward Stewart, Rector of Reed, in Suffolk.] 8vo. [*Lond. Lib. Cat. Supp.*]　London, 1798

THOUGHTS on national defence. [Signed : W. B. *i.e.* Rear-Admiral William Bowles.] 8vo. [*Camb. Univ. Lib.*]　　　　London, 1848

THOUGHTS on national insanity. [By Joseph Towers, LL.D.] 8vo. Pp. 40. [*Gent. Mag.* lxxiii. 1. 355 ; *Mon. Rev.* xxiii. 94.]　　　　London, 1797

THOUGHTS on nature and religion ; or, an apology for the right of private judgment maintained by Michael Servetus in his answer to John Calvin. [By Patrick Blair, M.D., Cork.] 8vo. [*Edin. Univ. Lib.*]　　　N.P. 1774

THOUGHTS on old age ; good words from many minds. By Hesba Stretton [Sarah Smith]. 8vo. Pp. 128.
London, 1906

THOUGHTS on Orkney and Zetland, their antiquities and capabilities of improvement ; with hints towards the formation of a local society for the investigation and promotion of these objects ; to which are annexed extracts from curious manuscripts, together with useful lists. [By Alexander Grant Groat.] 8vo. Pp. 47. [*Brit. Mus.*]
Edinburgh, private print, 1831

THOUGHTS on our acquisitions in the East Indies ; particularly respecting Bengal. [By George Johnstone, M.P., Governor of Florida.] 8vo. [*European Mag.* xlii. 422.]　　　London, 1771

THOUGHTS on our Articles of religion, with respect to their proposed utility to the State. [By Christopher Wyvill.] 4to. [John Jebb's *Works*, iii. 1 ; *Mon. Rev.* xlv. 239.]　　　London, 1771

THOUGHTS on Parliamentary reform. [By Soame Jenyns.] 8vo. [*Brit. Mus.*]　　　　　London, 1784

THOUGHTS on preaching. [By Sidney Hall Fleming.] 8vo. Pp. 19. [*Brit. Mus.*]　　　　Bedford [1872]

THOUGHTS on preaching the gospel to the heathen, and on the cause of the want of success. By a missionary [Anthony Hammond]. 12mo. Pp. 36. [*Brit. Mus.*]　　　Bedale, 1842

THOUGHTS on public trusts. [By William Dawson.] 12mo. [*Brit. Mus.*]
Edinburgh, 1805

THOUGHTS on religion and other subjects, by Monsieur [Blaise] Pascal ; translated from the French [by Basil Kennet]. 8vo. [Arber's *Term Cat.* iii. 389.]　　　　London, 1704

THOUGHTS on religious subjects. [By Neil Smith.] 8vo. [Robertson's *Aberd. Bibl.*]　　　　London, 1867

THOUGHTS on Sandeman's Letters on Hervey's *Theron and Aspasio.* By an old woman [Mrs Anne Dutton]. 8vo. Pp. 54. [Whitley's *Bapt. Bibl.* ii. 216.]　　　　London, 1761

THOUGHTS on some points in our system of judicial procedure. By a lawyer [Frederick Hallard]. 8vo. Pp. 53. [*Nat. Lib. of Scot.*]
Edinburgh, 1858

THOUGHTS on some questions of the day. [By George Dudley Ryder.] 8vo. [*Brit. Mus.*]   London, 1869

THOUGHTS on spiritual ethnology. By Ignotus [John Tindall Harris]. 8vo. Pp. 24. [Smith's *Cat. of Friends' Books, Supp.* p. 179.]   London, 1874

THOUGHTS on subjects connected with India. By an Officer of the Madras Engineers [Captain Samuel Best]. 8vo. Pp. 35.
Private print, 1839

THOUGHTS on taxation. . . . By a commissioner of taxes [Francis Newbery]. 8vo. [*Brit. Mus.* ; *Mon. Rev.* xxvii. 459.]   London, 1798

THOUGHTS on taxation, and a new system of funding, by which the land holder and stock holder, being equally secured, would run the same fortune, and the latter escape the dangerous envy of being considered as a kind of foreigner, unconcerned in the calamities of the country. . . . [By G. P. Towry.] A new edition, with additions. 8vo. Pp. 14.   London, 1785
The author's answer to a letter from a noble Earl, signed : G. P. T * * *

THOUGHTS on the Aberdeen case [of Professor W. Robertson Smith]. By a pre-disruption elder [Benjamin Bell, surgeon]. 8vo.   Edinburgh, 1880

THOUGHTS on the abolition of the slave trade, and civilization of Africa ; with remarks on the African Institution, and an examination of the report of their committee, recommending a general registry of slaves in the British West India islands. [By Joseph Marryatt.] 8vo. Pp. vii. 235. [*Bodl.*]
London, 1816

THOUGHTS on the advancement of academical education in England. [By James Yates.] 8vo. [*Royal Institution Cat.*]   London, 1826
The second edition, 1827, bears the author's name.

THOUGHTS on the best modes of carrying into effect the system of economy recommended in His Majesty's proclamation. [By James Deacon Hume.] 8vo. Pp. xvi. 46.
London, 1801

THOUGHTS on the Book of Common Prayer, used in the Church of England, by a lay member of that Church, compiler of a Biblical catechism, a metrical version of the Bible Psalms, etc. [John Stow]. 8vo. Pp. 272. [*Bodl.*]
London, 1850

THOUGHTS on the building and opening of a district church at Summertown, near Oxford. [Signed : J. B. *i.e.* Rev. John Badcock.] 8vo. [*Brit. Mus.*]   Oxford, 1832

THOUGHTS on the calls and invitations of the Gospel. Republished from the Missionary Magazine, with some additions, by the author. To which is now added, a reply to some animadversions. [By Rev. Archibald Maclean, Baptist minister, Edinburgh.] 8vo. Pp. 43. [Whitley's *Bapt. Bibl.*]
Edinburgh [1797]

THOUGHTS on the cameos and intaglios of antiquity, suggested by a sight and survey of the Blenheim collection. By a lover of the fine arts [Vaughan Thomas, B.D.]. 8vo. Pp. 68. [*Brit. Mus.*]   Oxford, 1847
The first title-page begins Addressed to His Grace, etc. Thoughts etc.

THOUGHTS on the Canticles. By M. E. H. [M. E. Holland]. 8vo. [*Aberd. Pub. Lib.*]   Aberdeen, 1884

THOUGHTS on the case of the local preachers in the Methodist Connexion. By an old local preacher [Vicary Purdy]. 8vo. Pp. 20. [*Brit. Mus.*]
Bristol, 1820

THOUGHTS on the cause of the present discontents. [By Edmund Burke.] 8vo. Pp. 79.
London, printed ; Dublin, reprinted, 1770
In collected works, London 1852, vol. iii.

THOUGHTS on the causes and consequences of the present high price of provisions. [By Soame Jenyns.] 8vo. Pp. 27. [M'Culloch's *Lit. Pol. Econ.* p. 193.]   Dublin, 1768
In collected works, vol. ii.

THOUGHTS on the causes of the present failures. [By William Roscoe.] 8vo.   London, 1793

THOUGHTS on the condition and prospects of popular education in the United States. By a citizen of Pennsylvania [Frederick Adolphus Packard, LL.D.]. 8vo. [Cushing's *Init. and Pseud.*]   Philadelphia, 1836

THOUGHTS on the constitutional power and right of the crown, in the bestowal of places and pensions ; humbly submitted to the attention of the people of England in general, and electors of members of parliament in particular. . . . [By Francis Webb.] 8vo. [Murch's *Dissenters*, p. 327 ; *Mon. Rev.* xlvi. 450 ; *Gent. Mag.* lxxxv. ii. 563.]
London, 1772

THOUGHTS on the currency. . . . By an old merchant [Hon. John Nesmith]. 8vo. [Cushing's *Init. and Pseud.*]
Lowell, 1860

THOUGHTS on the currency, with suggestions for placing it on a new and permanent basis. By a resident in Sunderland [William Anderson]. 8vo. Pp. 16. [*Brit. Mus.*]
Bishopwearmouth, 1847

THOUGHTS on the death of Mr Woodmason's children, destroyed by fire, 18th Jan. 1782. [By Peregrine Branwhite.] 12mo. [*D. N. B.* vol. 6, p. 229.]
London, 1782

THOUGHTS on the dismission of officers, civil or military for their conduct in parliament. [By James Adair.] 8vo. [*Gent. Mag.* Aug. 1798, p. 720; Almon's *Biog. Anec.* i. 83; Watt's *Bibl. Brit.*]
London, 1765

THOUGHTS on the duty of a good citizen, with regard to war and invasion; in a letter from a citizen to his friend. [By Jonas Hanway.] 8vo.
London [1756]

THOUGHTS on the English government; addressed to the quiet good sense of the people of England. Letter I. [By John Reeves.] 8vo. [*Brit. Mus.*]
London, 1795

Letters 2, 3, and 4 by the same author were published in 1799.

THOUGHTS on the Epistle to the Romans, for laymen. By one of them [Samuel Welman]. 8vo. Pp. 112.
London, 1917

THOUGHTS on "the excitement" [relating to Free-masonry] in reply to a letter to the Hon. Edward Everett first published in the National Ægis and Massachusetts Yeoman. [By the Rev. George Allen.] 8vo. [*W.*; [*Brit. Mus.*]
Worcester [Mass.] 1833

THOUGHTS on the extreme misery of the Irish poor. . . . An humble attempt to promote industry and prevent vice. [By Hugh Josiah Hansard.] 4to. [*Brit. Mus.*]
[London, 1784]

THOUGHTS on the farther improvement of aerostation; with a description of machine now constructed. [By Samuel Hoole.] 8vo. [*Book Prices Current*, 1922.]
London, 1785

THOUGHTS on the first rainbow, in connection with certain geological facts. [By William Bateman Byng.] 8vo. [*W.*]
London, 1852

THOUGHTS on the Gospel of Jesus Christ the Son of God [according to Matthew]. By a lay member of the Church of England [John Stow]. 8vo. Pp. 813. [Cushing's *Init. and Pseud.*]
Greenwich, 1846

THOUGHTS on the great circumspection necessary in licensing public alehouses; submitted to the consideration of the gentlemen acting in the commission of the peace throughout England. By a justice of the peace [John Disney, D.D.]. 8vo. Pp. 16.
London, 1776

THOUGHTS on the Holy Spirit and his work. By the author of *Thoughts upon thought* [John G. Hewlett]. 12mo. [*Brit. Mus.*]
London, 1845

THOUGHTS on the importance of religion. [By W. Allen.] 12mo. Pp. 11. [*Brit. Mus.*]
Swansea, 1808

THOUGHTS on the importance of the manners of the great to general society. [By Hannah More.] Eighth edition. 12mo. Pp. 142. [*Gent. Mag.* lviii. 339.]
London, 1790

THOUGHTS on the increasing wealth and national economy of the United States. By Observator [Samuel Blodget]. 8vo. [Cushing's *Init. and Pseud.* ii. 107.]
Washington, 1801

THOUGHTS on the late transactions respecting Falkland's islands. [By Samuel Johnson, LL.D.] The second edition. 8vo. Pp. 75.
London, 1771

In collected works, London 1792, vol. viii.

THOUGHTS on the letter of Buonaparte [to King George III., Dec. 1799] on the pacific principles and last speech of Mr Fox. By a Suffolk freeholder [Rev. Charles Edward Stewart]. 8vo. [*Brit. Mus.*]
London, 1800

THOUGHTS on the life and times of David. By C. H. M. [Charles H. Mackintosh]. 12mo.
[*c.* 1860]

THOUGHTS on the Litany. By a naval officer's orphan daughter [S. M. Heaton]. Edited by the Rev. George Heaton, M.A. of Catherine Hall, Cambridge. . . . 12mo. Pp. viii. 220.
London, 1840

Signed: S. M. H.

THOUGHTS on the mental functions; being an attempt to treat metaphysics as a branch of the physiology of the nervous system. [By John James Waterston.] 8vo.
Edinburgh, 1843

Afterwards included in collected works, with the author's name, edited by Dr John Scott Haldane.

THOUGHTS on the misery of a numerous class of females; particularly addressed to those of their own sex, whom God has entrusted with affluence; for which they must shortly give account. [By Rev. John Walker, Dublin.] 12mo.
Dublin, 1793

THOUGHTS on the national defence. [By Charles Gordon-Lennox, Duke of Richmond.] 8vo. Pp. ii. 141.
London, 1804

THOUGHTS on the naval strength of the British Empire. [By Sir John Sinclair.] Part II. 8vo.
London, 1782
The author's name appears on the title-page of Part I. [*Mon. Rev.* lxvi. 469.]

THOUGHTS on the new and old principles of political obedience. [By George Holford.] 8vo. [*Brit. Mus.*]
London, 1793

THOUGHTS on the origin and nature of government ; occasioned by the late disputes between Great Britain and her American colonies. [By Allan Ramsay, Junr., son of the poet.] 8vo. Pp. 64.   London, 1769

THOUGHTS on the plan for a Magdalen House for repentant prostitutes. . . . [By Jonas Hanway.] 4to. Pp. 59. [*Brit. Mus.*]   London, 1758

THOUGHTS on the popular opinions of eternal punishment, being synonymous with eternal torment. . . . [By Thomas Conolly Cowan.] 12mo. Pp. 64.
London, 1844

THOUGHTS on the preliminary Articles of Peace. By a Kentish clergyman [Rev. Edward Hankin]. 8vo. Pp. 32.
London, 1801

THOUGHTS on the present commercial distress, and on the means to prevent its recurrence. By a merchant [Richard Blanshard]. 8vo. Pp. 23. [*Brit. Mus.*]   London, 1826

THOUGHTS on the present crisis, in a letter from a constituent to his representative [William Peter, M.A., barrister]. 8vo.   London, 1815

THOUGHTS on the present crisis of our domestic affairs. By another lawyer [George Chalmers]. 8vo. [*Brit. Mus.*]
London, 1807

THOUGHTS on the present depressed state of the agricultural interest of this kingdom, and on the rapid increase of the poor-rates ; with observations on Mr Curwen's plan for bettering the condition of the poor. [By Robert Fellowes, D.D.] 8vo. [*Edin. Univ. Lib.*]   London, 1817
Subscribed : A Magistrate.

THOUGHTS on the present position of the Established Churches in England and Scotland, particularly the latter, and how far in some minor matters legislation may be desirable ; a letter addressed to the "Right Hon. E. S. Gordon, M.P. . . ." By an Episcopalian landowner in five Northern parishes [Andrew Steuart, of Auchlunkart]. 8vo. Pp. 68.   Edinburgh, 1875

THOUGHTS on the present prices of provisions, their causes and remedies. By an independent gentleman [John Symmons]. 8vo. [*W.*]
London, 1880

THOUGHTS on the present Rebellion, addressed to all thinking and honest Irishmen. By Eumenes [John Walker]. 8vo. Pp. 16. [*Brit. Mus.*]
Dublin, 1798

THOUGHTS on the present state and prospect of legal discontent. [By Robert Hill Sandys.] 8vo. 9 nos. [*Brit. Mus.*]   London, 1853

THOUGHTS on the present state of affairs. [By Gideon Duncan.] 8vo. Pp. 22.   N.P. [*c.* 1800]
Contemporary attestation of authorship.

THOUGHTS on the present state of affairs with America, and the means of conciliation. [By William Pulteney, Earl of Bath.] 8vo. Pp. 100. [*Bodl.*]
London, 1778

THOUGHTS on the present state of the college of Dublin ; addressed to the gentlemen of the University. [By J. Forsageth, D.D.] 8vo. Pp. 82. [*Bodl.*]   Dublin, 1782
Attributed also to Arthur Browne. [*Camb. Univ. Lib.*]

THOUGHTS on the present system of academic education at the University of Cambridge. By Eubulus [Samuel Butler, D.D., of Shrewsbury]. 8vo. [*Camb. Hist. of Eng. Lit.* vol. 14, p. 594.]
London, 1822

THOUGHTS on the principles of civil government, and their foundation in the law of nature. By S. N. [Thomas Elrington, D.O.]. 8vo. [*D. N. B.* vol. 17, p. 333.]   Dublin, 1793

THOUGHTS on the privileges and power of juries, suggested by the case of James Robertson and Walter Berry, printer and bookseller, Edinburgh. [By James Anderson, LL.D.] 8vo. [*W.*]   Edinburgh, 1793
This pamphlet is signed "Mercator," and is reprinted from *The Bee.*

THOUGHTS on the probable influence of the French Revolution on Great Britain. [By Sir Samuel Romilly.] 8vo. [*D. N. B.* vol. 49, p. 189.]
London, 1790

THOUGHTS on the properties and formation of the different kinds of air ; with remarks on vegetation, pyrophori, heat, caustic salts, mercury, and on the different theories upon air. [By Robert Harrington.] 8vo. [*Mon. Rev.* lxxiv. 449.]   London, 1785

THOUGHTS on the proposed annex-ation of Texas to the United States. . . . [Preface signed: T. S. *i.e.* Theodore Sedgwick.] 8vo. [*Brit. Mus.*]   New York, 1844

THOUGHTS on the proposed change of currency, and other late alterations, as they affect, or are intended to affect, the kingdom of Scotland. [By Sir Walter Scott, Bart.] 8vo. Pp. 60.
Edinburgh, 1826
The first of three letters addressed to the Editor of the *Edinburgh Weekly Journal*, and signed: Malachi Malagrowther.

THOUGHTS on the proposed dissolu-tion of the Cambridge Camden Society, suggested for the consideration of the members. By a member of this Com-mittee [Philip Freeman, M.A.]. 8vo. Pp. 27. [Bartholomew's *Camb. Books.*]
London, 1845

THOUGHTS on the propriety of fixing Easter term. [By Sir Giles Rooke, M.A., Judge of Common Pleas.] 8vo. [*D. N. B.* vol. 49, p. 208.]
London, 1792

THOUGHTS on the prospect of a regicide peace, in a series of letters. [By Edmund Burke.] 8vo. Pp. iv. 131. [*Brit. Mus.*]   London, 1796

THOUGHTS on the Protestant ascend-ency in Ireland; with an appendix. [By James Mason.] 8vo.
London, 1805

THOUGHTS on the providence of God. [By John Shore, 1st Baron Teign-mouth.] 8vo. [*Bodl.*] London, 1834

THOUGHTS on the question of the East suggested by a tour in Turkey, Syria and Egypt. . . . [By George Dawson Damer, M.P.]   London, 1840
Contemporary attestation.

THOUGHTS on the riots at Bir-mingham. By a Welch freeholder [David Jones of Llandovery]. 8vo. Pp. 29.   London, 1791
Attributed also to George Rous.

THOUGHTS on the rise and decline of the polite arts. [By Henry Constantine Jennings.] 8vo. [*Brit. Mus.*]
London [1798]

THOUGHTS on the Sabbath. [By Arthur Knox.] 8vo. Aberdeen, 1882

THOUGHTS on the Scriptural expecta-tions of the Christian Church. By Basilicus [Rev. Lewis Way]. Third edition. 8vo. Pp. 106. [Cushing's *Init. and Pseud.*]   London, 1828

THOUGHTS on the "Seven last words on the Cross." By the author of *Chronicles of the Schönberg-Cotta family* [Elizabeth Rundle, later Mrs Arthur P. Charles]. 12mo.   London, 1887

THOUGHTS on the several regulations necessary to the appointment of an Advocate - General, &c. [By —— Mawhood.] 4to. [*W.*]
London, 1775

THOUGHTS on the singing of psalms and anthems in Churches. [By Rev. William White, D.D.] 8vo.
Philadelphia, 1808

THOUGHTS on the singing of un-authorised hymns in public worship . . . submitted to the consideration of the archbishops and bishops. . . . By one of their brethren [Richard Mant, D.D.]. 8vo.   London, 1835

THOUGHTS on the slavery of the negroes. [By Joseph Woods.] 8vo. [Smith's *Cat. of Friends' Books*, ii. 955.]
London, 1784

THOUGHTS on the state and prospects of Conservatism. . . . By R. S. O. [R. S. Orsler]. 8vo. Pp. 16.
Manchester, 1837

THOUGHTS on the state of the Ameri-can Indians. . . . By a citizen of the United States [Silas Wood]. 8vo. [Cushing's *Init. and Pseud.*]
New York, 1794

THOUGHTS on the state of the country. [By Peter Stuart.] 8vo. Pp. 173. [*Manch. Free Lib.* p. 696.]
London, 1812

THOUGHTS on the State-Church question. By a Protestant Non-conformist [Edward Ash, M.D.]. 8vo. [Cushing's *Init. and Pseud.*]
London, 1861

THOUGHTS on the study of natural history. [By James Lawson Drummond, M.D.] 8vo.   London, 1820

THOUGHTS on the study of prophecy . . . With a few words on the twenty-fourth chapter of St Matthew's Gospel. By a barrister [Peter Frederick O'Malley, Q.C.]. 12mo.
London, 1849

THOUGHTS on the sufferings of Christ. [By W. Giles.] 8vo. Pp. 76. [Whitley's *Bapt. Bibl.*]   1810

THOUGHTS on the theory and practice of the French constitution. By an Englishman [Francis Bassett, Lord De Dunstanville]. 8vo. [*D. N. B.* vol. 3, p. 377.]   London, 1794

THOUGHTS on the times; a poem, with notes. By Leonidas [Harry Wood Smith]. 8vo. Pp. 24. Merthyr, 1860

THOUGHTS on the times, but chiefly on the profligacy of our women, and its causes; addressed to every parent—husband—and modest woman in the three kingdoms. [By Philip Thick-nesse.] 8vo. Pp. v. 200. [Green's *Bibl. Somers.* ii. 512.]   London, 1779
Attributed also to Francis Foster.

THOUGHTS on the war, and on European policy. [By Samuel Lobb.] 8vo. Calcutta, 1870

THOUGHTS on trade and a publick spirit. . . . [By Thomas Baston.] 8vo. Pp. 212. [*Manch. Free Lib.* p. 730.] London, 1716

THOUGHTS on trial by jury in civil causes ; with a view to a reform of the administration of justice in Scotland. In a series of [xv] letters. [By James Grahame.] 8vo. Pp. 70. [*Brit. Mus.*] Edinburgh, 1806

THOUGHTS respecting the origin of treasonable conspiracies and rebellious insurrections. . . . [By John Potter.] 8vo. London, 1803
Writer's own declaration of authorship.

THOUGHTS suggested by Lord Lauderdale's Observations upon the *Edinburgh Review.* [By Henry Brougham, Lord Brougham.] 8vo. Pp. 93. [Thomas's *Bibl. List*, p. 6.] London, 1805

THOUGHTS upon a new coinage of silver . . . as it relates to an alteration in the division of the pound Troy. [By Magens Dorrien Magens.] 8vo. Pp. vi. 104. [*Manch. Free Lib.* p. 441.] London, 1798

THOUGHTS upon liberty. By an Englishman [Rev. John Wesley]. 12mo. Pp. 24. [Osborn's *Method. Lit.* p. 46.] Bristol, 1772

THOUGHTS upon our present situation, with remarks upon the policy of a war with France. [By Sir George Dallas.] 8vo. [*D. N. B.* vol. 13, p. 396.] London, 1793

THOUGHTS upon religion. By Blaise Pascal ; translated from the French [by Basil Kennett, D.D.]. 8vo. [*Brit. Mus.*] London, 1704

THOUGHTS upon the aristocracy of England. By Isaac Tomkins, Gent. [Henry Brougham, Lord Brougham and Vaux]. Sixth edition. 8vo. Pp. 23. [*Quarterly Review*, liii. 540.] London, 1835

THOUGHTS upon the Catholic question, by an Irish Roman Catholic [Anthony Richard Blake]. 8vo. Pp. 85. [*Brit. Mus.*] Dublin, 1828

THOUGHTS upon the four last things : death ; judgment ; heaven ; hell : a poem in four parts. [By Joseph Trapp, D.D.] Fol. 4 parts. [*Bodl.*] London, 1734-35

THOUGHTS upon the political situation of the United States of America, in which that of Massachusetts is more particularly considered. . . . By a native of Boston [Jonathan Jackson, *or* George R. Mïnot, *or* James Sullivan]. 8vo. Pp. 209. [Evans' *Amer. Bibl.* vii. 226.] Worcester, Mass., 1788

THOUGHTS upon the present condition of the stage and upon the construction of a new theatre. [By Frederick Howard, Earl of Carlisle.] 8vo. [*Gent. Mag.* xcv. ii. 370.] London, 1808

THOUGHTS upon the present contest between the Administration and the British Colonies in America, addressed to the merchants. . . . [By William Smith, D.D.] 8vo. Pp. 46. London, 1775

THOUGHTS upon thought ; for young men. In three parts. [By John G. Hewlett.] 8vo. [*Brit. Mus.*] London, 1843

THOUGHTS, verses, and songs. By Claribel [Mrs Charles Barnard, *née* Caroline Arlington]. 8vo. Pp. 314. [O'Donoghue's *Poets of Ireland*, p. 16.] Edinburgh, 1877

THOUGHTS versified. By C. [Anna Caroline Steele]. Pp. 86. [*Brit. Mus.*] Braintree, Mass., 1860

THOUSAND (a) and one notable nativities ; the astrologer's "Who's Who." Compiled by the sub-editor of *Modern Astrology* [Alfred H. Barley]. 8vo. Pp. viii. 116. [*Brit. Mus.*] London, 1911

THOUSAND (a) golden thoughts. . . . By the author of *Language of the eye* [J. Turnley]. First series. 16mo. [*Brit. Mus.*] London, 1860

THOUSAND (a) lines : now first offered to the world we live in. [By Martin Farquhar Tupper.] 12mo. Pp. 60. [*W.*] London, 1845

THOUSAND (a) notable things on various subjects, disclosed from the secrets of nature and art. . . . [By Thomas Lupton.] 12mo. Pp. 262. London, 1793
The first edition, 1660, and other editions were not anonymous.

1000 quaint cuts from books of other days, including amusing illustrations from children's story books. . . . [By Andrew W. Tuer.] 4to. Pp. 170. [*Brit. Mus.*] London [1886]
Signed : A. W. T.

THOUSANDTH (the) and second night. By Frank Heller [Gunnar Serner] ; translated . . . by Edwin Björkman. 8vo. Pp. 333. [*Brit. Mus.*] New York [1925]

THREAD (the) of gold. By the author of *The house of quiet* [Arthur Christopher Benson]. 8vo. [*Brit. Mus.*] London, 1905

THREAD (the) of proof. [A novel.] By Headon Hill [Frank Edward Grainger]. 8vo. Pp. 330. [*Brit. Mus.*]
London, 1912

THREADS and patches on political economy. By Honestas [John George Muir]. 8vo. Pp. xi. 161.
London, 1901

THREATENING letter from Douglas [Andrew Reed] the self-acknowledged author of *No fiction*, to Lefevre [Francis Barnett]. With Lefevre's reply. Second edition. 4to. [*W.*; *Brit. Mus.*]   London, 1822

THREE All-Saints summers, and other teachings of nature. [By Bishop Wm. W. How.] 8vo.   London [1861]

THREE amateur scouts. [A tale.] By Raymond Jacberns [Miss M. Selby Ashe]. 8vo. Pp. 300. London, 1910

THREE autumn days in Perthshire. [By James Brebner.] 12mo. [Mitchell and Cash's *Scot. Topog.*]   Dundee, 1874

THREE (the) barriers : notes on Mr Darwin's *Origin of species.* [By Gilbert Rorison.] 8vo. Pp. 180. [*Brit. Mus.*]
Edinburgh and London, 1861
Preface signed : G. R.

THREE bears and Gwen ; a story for children. By May Wynne [Mabel Wynne Knowles]. 8vo. Pp. 224.
London [1920]

THREE books of occult philosophy, written by Henricus Cornelius Agrippa, of Nettesheim : translated out of the Latin by J. F. [John French, M.D.]. 8vo. Pp. 583. [*D. N. B.* vol. 20, p. 252 ; Ferguson's *Bibl. Chem.* i. 293.]
London, 1651
The translation is wrongly attributed to John Freake.

THREE (the) C.'s ; a co-operative triologue [in verse]. . . . By E. V. N. [Edward Vansittart Neale]. 8vo. [*Brit. Mus.*]   Manchester, 1888

THREE (the) C.'s ; the city surveyor of works, the civic arms. By a citizen [of Bath, *i.e.* Robert Edward Myhill Peach]. 8vo.   Bath, 1888

THREE (the) Cæsars ; sketches by Timon [H. Willats]. 8vo.
London, 1869

THREE (the) chancellors ; or, sketches of the lives of William of Wykeham, William of Waynflete, and Sir Thomas More. [Three biographies first published independently. By Augusta Theodosia Drane.] 8vo. [*Brit. Mus.*]
London, 1860

THREE Christmas eves. By Mignon [Mrs Baseley]. 8vo.
Manchester, 1902

THREE comedies, translated from the Spanish [by Henry, Lord Holland]. 8vo. [*W.*; *Brit. Mus.*] London, 1807

THREE considerations proposed to Mr William Pen, concerning the validity and security of his new Magna Charta for liberty of conscience, by a Baptist [Thomas Comber, D.D.]. 4to. [Smith's *Bibl. Anti-Quak.* pp. 25, 135.]
N.P. 1688
In the Memoirs of the life and writings of Dr Comber, by his great-grandson, it is stated (append. p. 427) that one of the MSS. found among his papers has the title, "Three considerations addressed to W. P. concerning the security of his new Magna Charta for liberty of conscience."

THREE courses and a desert ; comprising three sets of tales, West country, Irish, and legal ; and a melange. [By William Clarke.] With 50 illustrations by George Cruikshank. Fourth edition. 8vo. Pp. 432. [*Brit. Mus.*]
London, 1850

THREE (the) Cruikshanks ; a bibliographical catalogue, describing more than 300 works . . . illustrated by Isaac, George, and Robert Cruikshank. By Frederick Marchmont [Hugh Arthur Torriano]. The introduction by Julian Moore. 8vo.   London, 1897

THREE (the) daughters of night ; a novel. By Derek Vane [Mrs B. Eaton-Back]. 8vo. Pp. 226. [*Lit. Year Book.*]   London, 1897

THREE days at Killarney, with other poems. [By Rev. Charles Hoyle, Overton, Wilts.] 8vo. [*Brit. Mus.*]
London, 1828

THREE (the) days of Wensleydale. By the Wensleydale poet [William G. M. J. Barker]. 8vo. [Kirk's *Supp.*]
London, 1854

THREE (the) death-cries of a perishing Church. From *The Nottingham Review*, with additions and corrections. [By William Howitt.] 12mo. [Smith's *Cat. of Friend's Books*, i. 102.]
Nottingham, 1835

THREE dialogues ; 1. On the nature of religion, 2. Church and State, 3. Ritualism, from Cambridge. . . . [By John Frederick Mortlock.] 8vo. Pp. 15. [Bartholomew's *Cumb. Books.*]
[London] 1868

THREE dialogues between a dean and a curate on the amusements of clergymen and christians in general. By Edward Stillingfleet [William Gilpin]. 8vo. Pp. 224. [Jessel's *Bibl. of playing cards*, p. 110.] London, 1796

The correct title begins "On the amusements of clergymen . . .", *q.v.* in the Supplement.

THREE dialogues concerning liberty. [By Jackson Barwis.] 8vo. Pp. 116. London, 1771

A fourth dialogue concerning liberty has the author's name.

THREE discourses: 1. On the use of books. 2. On the result and effects of study. 3. On the elements of literary taste; delivered at the anniversary meetings of the Library Society at Chichester, Jan. 1800, 1801, 1802. By the President [Thomas Sanden, M.D.]. 8vo. 3 parts. [*N. and Q.* 1st April 1865, p. 269.] London, 1802

The three discourses were published separately in the years in which they were delivered.

THREE discourses on certain symbols used in [Catholic Apostolic] worship; being a practical explanation of their meaning and advantage. [By George E. Boase.] 8vo. Pp. 48. [*Boase's Cat. of Cath. Apost. Works*, p. 6.] Dundee, 1855

Third edition in 1892.

THREE discourses on eternity, and the importance and advantages of looking at eternal things. [By James Orton.] 12mo. [*W.*; *Brit. Mus.*] London [*c.* 1830]

THREE discourses on miracles and miraculous power. [By John Bate Cardale, solicitor.] 8vo. [Kirk's *Supp.*] London, 1856

THREE discourses; one, a defence of private judgment; the second, against the authority of the magistrate over conscience; the third, some considerations concerning the re-uniting of Protestants. The two first translated from the Latin, the third from the French, of Dr Samuel Werenfels, professor of divinity in the University of Bale, in Switzerland. . . . By Phileleutherus Cantabrigiensis [Thomas Herne]. 8vo. [*Brit. Mus.*] London, 1718

THREE dissertations; 1. On the divinity of our Saviour; 2. On the Atonement; 3. On the personality and divinity of the Holy Ghost. By John Isherwood [or rather Rev. Thomas Bancroft, M.A.]. 8vo. Pp. 223. [Sparke's *Bibl. Bolt.* p. 17.] Oxford, private print, 1835

THREE dissertations; one on the characters of Augustus, Horace, and Agrippa . . . by the Abbé de Vertot . . . another on the gallery of Verres, by the Abbé Fraguier . . . a third on the nature, origin, and use of masks in theatrical representations among the ancients, by Mr Boindin. . . . [Translated and edited by George Turnbull, LL.D.] 4to. Pp. xv. 122. [*Brit. Mus.*] London, 1740

THREE dramas. By the authoress of *St Bernardine*, and other poems [Catherine Swanwick]. 8vo. Pp. 208. [Olphar Hamst.] London, 1866

THREE (the) Elizabeths. [By Agnes M. Stewart.] 8vo. [Cushing's *Anon.*] Baltimore [*c.* 1860]

THREE epochs in the life of a woman. . . . By a clergyman's wife [Mrs E. A. Hart, *née* Fanny Wheeler]; dramatised. . . . 8vo. [*Brit. Mus.*] Manchester, 1881

THREE essays. 1. Essay on the new project for a land mint. . . . 2. A second essay concerning the land mint. 3. A scheme proposing a true touchstone for the due trial of a proper Union betwixt Scotland and England, etc. By the author of *The Character of the true publick spirit* [Andrew Brown, M.D., Dolphinton.] 8vo. [*Edin. Univ. Lib.*] Edinburgh, 1706

THREE essays concerning church government, viz. I. An impartial inquiry into the order and government settled by Christ and his apostles in the Church. II. An inquiry into the divine right of Presbytery. III. The Phœnix: or, prelacy revived from the ashes of its funeral, and established upon the same principles and arguments which are made use of against it, by the author of *The funeral of prelacy*. [By Simon Couper, curate at Dunfermline.] 4to. Edinburgh, 1704

THREE essays on important subjects, read at Thearne, in the parish of Beith, at the close of three successive exhibitions of cattle, in 1827, 1828, and 1829. By a cultivator of the ground [Andrew Aitken]. 8vo. Pp. 40. [*New Coll. Lib.*] Beith, 1830

THREE (the) essentials. [A novel.] By Dorothea Gerard [Madame Longarde de Longarde]. 8vo. Pp. 314. London, 1904

THREE experiments of living: within the means; up to the means; beyond the means. [By Mrs Hannah F. Lee.] A new English edition. 8vo. [*W.*; *Brit. Mus.*] London, 1848

THREE (the) Fenian brothers ; or, some scenes in Irish life. By an Irishman [John Hamilton, of St Ernans]. 12mo.
London, 1866

THREE (the) frights and the three beauties ; with the story of Bobinette : sketches of girls' lives. By Sarah Tytler [Henrietta Keddie]. 8vo. Pp. 194.   London [1881]

THREE for a penny ; or, hints for advertisers. By sundry witty persons [rather, by Thomas W. H. Crosland]. 8vo. Pp. 64. [*Brit. Mus.*]
London, 1905

THREE (the) fountains ; a faëry epic of Euboea ; with other verses. By the author of *The afterglow* [George S. Cautley]. 8vo. [*Brit. Mus.*]
London, 1869

THREE (the) friends. . . . By Maria [Maria D. Weston]. 8vo.
Boston, 1849

THREE general epistles to be read in all the congregations of the righteous, who are gathered out of the house of Adam in the fall, into the house of Christ that never fell, to be read amongst them. By G. F. [George Fox]. 4to. Pp. 22.   1664

THREE generations of a godly house ; memorials of the Treacher family. [Signed : A. H. *i.e.* Arthur Hall.] 8vo. Pp. 52. [*Brit. Mus.*]
London, 1896

THREE generations ; the study of a middle-class Scottish family. By Sarah Tytler [Henrietta Keddie]. 8vo.
London, 1911

THREE gifts and other poems. By Keith St John [Mrs Katharine St John Noyes Guion]. 8vo. [*Amer. Cat.*]
Newhaven, Conn., 1905

THREE girls. [A novel.] By John Strange Winter [Mrs Arthur Stannard, *née* Henrietta E. V. Palmer]. 12mo.
London, 1892

THREE (the) graces ; a novel. By the Duchess [Mrs Margaret Argles, later Mrs Hungerford]. 8vo. Pp. 304.
Philadelphia, 1895

THREE (the) grand queries resolved ; shewing the great iniquity and injustice in any one prince, that attempts by war . . . to be sole lord paramount . . . over all other kings, free princes and states. By a gentleman learned in divinity, law and history [John Brydall]. 4to. [*Lincoln's Inn Lib.*]
London, 1707

THREE (the) homes. By Nellie Graham [Mrs Annie Dunning, *née* Ketchum]. 8vo. [Cushing's *Init. and Pseud.*]
Philadelphia, 1863

THREE (the) homes ; a tale for fathers and sons. By F. T. L. Hope [Faintly Trust the Larger Hope, *i.e.* Frederick William Farrar, D.D., Dean of Canterbury]. 8vo. Pp. vii. 389. [*The Academy*, Oct. 1896, p. 239.]
London, 1873

THREE hours after marriage ; a comedy, as it is acted at the Theatre Royal. [By John Gay.] 8vo.
London, 1717
The "Advertisement" concludes in these words :—" I must farther own the assistance I have receiv'd in this piece from two of my friends ; who, tho' they will not allow me the honour of having their names join'd with mine, cannot deprive me of the pleasure of making this acknowledgment."—John Gay. (The friends alluded to are Pope and Arbuthnot.)

THREE (the) houses : the house of prayer ; the house appointed for all living ; the house not made with hands. [By Mrs H. Potter.] 12mo. [*Brit. Mus.*]   Ipswich, 1843

THREE hundred and fifty portions of the Book of Psalms selected from various versions, with a collection of 600 hymns, adapted for public worship. [By the Rev. Josiah Pratt.] 12mo. [Lowndes' *Brit. Lib.* p. 433.]
London, 1829

THREE in Norway. By two of them [James A. Lees and Walter J. Clutterbuck]. Third edition. 8vo. Pp. xii. 307. [*Brit. Mus.*]   London, 1887

THREE Irish glossaries. Carmac's glossary codex A. (from a manuscript in the library of the Royal Irish Academy), O'Davoren's glossary (from a manuscript in the library of the British Museum), and a glossary to the Calendar of Oingus the Culdee (from a manuscript in the library of Trinity College, Dublin). With a preface and index by W. S. [Whitley Stokes]. 8vo. Pp. lxxx. 168. [*Brit. Mus.*]   London, 1862

THREE (the) judgments. By A. H. B. [Alfred H. Burton]. 8vo.
London [1894]

THREE kingdoms made one, by entring covenant with one God. . . . By E. W. [Ezekiah (or Hezekiah) Woodward]. 4to. [*Brit. Mus.*]   London, 1643

THREE (the) kingdomes healing-plaister ; or, the solemne covenant of reformation and defence explained : wherein is shewed the authority, antiquity, and use of an holy covenant : the occasions moving to it, and the ends in doing it, the necessity of it at this time, for diverse reasons herein expressed . . . By G. S. Gent. [George Smith]. 4to. [Gerould's *Sources of Eng. Lit.* 1530.]   London, 1643

THREE (the) ladies of London. By R. W.

    See " A right excellent and famous comedy called . . ."

THREE letters addressed to the editor of the *Quarterly Review*, in which is demonstrated the genuineness of the three heavenly witnesses, 1 John v. 7. By Ben David [John Jones, LL.D.]. 8vo. Pp. 70. [*Gent. Mag.* April 1827, p. 372.]   London, 1825

THREE letters addressed to the readers of Paine's *Age of Reason.* By one of the people called Christians [Jeremiah Waring]. 8vo. [Smith's *Cat. of Friends' Books*, ii. 216].   London, 1797

THREE letters addressed to the Right Hon. Lord Viscount Melbourne and the Right Hon. Sir Robert Peel, Bart. on the present state of parties, urging the necessity of union, and suggesting the means by which it is attainable. By a conservative Whig [Thomas Wallace]. 8vo. Pp. ii. 124.   London, 1835

THREE letters between a clergyman [Rev. John Young, D.D., Hawick] and a layman [Wm. Nicol, merchant at Selkirk] concerning the Testimony [of the Associate Synod], and the obligation of the Covenants upon posterity. [Edited by W. Nicol.] 12mo. Pp. 45.   Edinburgh, 1799

THREE letters concerning systematic taste, exemplified, in the Centaur not fabulous : Laicus's letter of 7th June 1755, *London Evening Post*, and the Bishop of London's second volume of discourses. [By Caleb Fleming.] 8vo. Pp. 58. [*Bodl.*]   London, 1755

THREE letters concerning the present state of Italy ; being a supplement to Dr Burnets letters. [By Gilbert Burnet.] 8vo. [*New Coll. Lib.* p. 129.]   N.P. 1688

THREE letters concerning the state of Italy ; being a supplement to Dr [Gilbert] Burnet's Letters. [By Burnet, from material supplied by H. Sydney and Dr Hutton.] 12mo. [Clarke and Foxcroft's *Life of Burnet.*]   London, 1688

THREE letters, containing remarks on some of the numberless errors and defects in Dugdales Baronage : and occasionally in some other authors. [By Charles Hornby.] 8vo. Pp. 250. [*Gent. Mag.* June 1810, p. 507 ; Aug. 1810, p. 188.]   London, 1738

THREE letters, declaring the strange odd proceedings of Protestant divines when they write against Catholicks. . . . By J. V. C. [John Vincent Cane]. 12mo. [*Brit. Mus.*]   N.P. 1671

THREE letters from a London merchant to a country friend on the late monetary crisis. [By William Ellis.] 8vo. [*Brit. Mus.*]   London, 1866

THREE letters of credit ; and other stories. By " Kim Bilir " [A. H. Scaife]. 8vo. [*Lib. of Col. Inst.* 1905.]   Victoria [B.C.] 1894

THREE letters on military education, addressed to the editor of *The Times.* By Jacob Omnium [M. J. Higgins]. 8vo. Pp. 19.   London, 1855

THREE letters on the policy of England towards the Porte and Mohammed Ali. [By Sir J. Gardner Wilkinson.] 8vo. Pp. 63. [*W.*]   London, 1840

THREE letters relating to the Navy, Gibraltar, and Portmahon, wrote in the year 1747 and 1748, but now first published ; being very applicable to the present time. [By James Lind, M.D.] 8vo. Pp. xxii. 138. [*Lond. Lib. Cat.*]   London, 1757

THREE letters tending to demonstrate how the security of this nation . . . lys in the abolition of the present penal laws and tests. . . . [By William Penn.] 4to. Pp. 27. [*Brit. Mus.*]   London, 1688

THREE letters to Dr Clarke, from a clergyman of the Church of England ; concerning his Scripture-doctrine of the Trinity : with the Doctor's replies. Published by the author of the said Three letters [John Jackson]. 8vo. Pp. 33. [*New Coll. Lib.* p. 180.]   London, 1714

THREE letters to Dr Price, containing remarks on his Observations on the nature of civil liberty, the principles of government, and the justice and policy of the war with America. By a member of Lincoln's Inn, F.R.S., F.S.A. [James Lind]. 8vo. [*Brit. Mus.*]   London, 1776

THREE letters to Lord Brougham, on the execution in Upper Canada, of . . . Lount and Matthews. By a British subject [Sir Francis B. Head, Bart.]. 8vo. [Cushing's *Init. and Pseud.*]   London, 1838

THREE letters to Lord Viscount Howe. With remarks on the attack at Bunker's Hill. The second edition ; to which is added a comparative view of the conduct of Lord Cornwallis and General Howe. [By Israel Mauduit.] 8vo. Pp. 48. [*D. N. B.* vol. 37, p. 83.]   London, 1781

THREE letters to the author of the Confessional. [By Gloucester Ridley, LL.B., and Archbishop Secker.] 8vo. 3 parts. London, 1768
"If instead of reading only the Confessional they (the petitioning clergy) would read together with it Dr Ridley's answers, wherein he was assisted by our late most worthy and most able metropolitan (Secker) they would see the sophistry of the arguments detected," etc.—Bp. Newton's *Memoirs*. See *Gent. Mag.* Nov. 1774, and Jan. 1775 in which they are stated to be almost entirely written by Archbishop Secker.

THREE letters to the editor of the *Cornhill Magazine* on public school education. By Paterfamilias [Matthew James Higgins]. 8vo. [*Brit. Mus.*] London, 1861

THREE letters to the Hebrew nation. By the author of *The Christian*, a poem [Charles Crawford]. 12mo. [*Brit. Mus.*] London, 1817

THREE letters to the members of the present parliament, with a discourse on kings and ministers of state ; to which is prefixed a letter to Sir John Philipps Bart. occasioned by his recess from parliament. [By Caleb D'Anvers, *i.e.* Nicholas Amhurst.] 8vo. Pp. 54. [*Brit. Mus.*] London, 1747

THREE letters written in Spain to D. Francisco Riguelme commanding the third division of the Gallician army. [By Walter Savage Landor.] 8vo. Pp. 31. [Wise and Wheeler's *Bibl. of Landor.*] London, 1809

THREE little kittens. By Comus [Robt. M. Ballantyne]. 4to. [*Cushing's Init. and Pseud.*] London, 1857

THREE little spades. By Amy Lothrop [Anna Bartlett Warner]. 12mo. [*Amer. Cat.*] New York [1868 ?]

THREE martyrs of the nineteenth century [Dr Livingstone, General Gordon, and Bishop Pattison]. By the author of *The Schönberg-Cotta Family* [Mrs Elizabeth Charles]. 8vo. London, 1885

THREE men ; a novel. By Maxim Gorky [Aleksyei Maksimovitch Pyeshkov]; translated by Charles Horne. 8vo. London, 1902

THREE men and Troddles. By R. Andom [Alfred N. Barrett]. 8vo. [*Brit. Mus.*] London, 1916

THREE men of mark. [A novel.] By Sarah Tytler [Miss Henrietta Keddie]. 8vo. Pp. vi. 334. London, 1901

THREE millions ; or, the way of the world. By Oliver Optic [William Taylor Adams]. 8vo. [*Cushing's Init. and Pseud.*] Boston, 1891

THREE (the) monks ! ! ! From the French [of Madame —— Guénard] by H. J. Sarrett. 12mo. 2 vols. [*Brit. Mus.*] London [1803]

THREE months among the moose ; a " Winter's tale " of the northern wilds of Canada. By a military chaplain [Rev. Joshua Fraser]. 8vo. [*Cushing's Init. and Pseud.*] Montreal, 1881

THREE months from home ; notes of a tour. By C. M. [Charles Mackenzie, bookseller in Edinburgh]. 12mo. Pp. 43. Greenock, private print, 1873

THREE months in Egypt ; written for the children. By L. L. A. [Mrs L. L. Adams], author of *A ride on horseback through the Holy Land.* 8vo. [*Brit. Mus.*] Boston, 1877

THREE months' rest at Pau, in the winter and spring of 1859. By John Altrayd Wittitterly [Elizabeth T. Carne]. 8vo. Pp. 267. [Boase and Courtney's *Bibl. Corn.* i. 60.] London, 1860

THREE more letters on the subject of the Catholics, to my brother Abraham, who lives in the country. By Peter Plymley [Sydney Smith]. 8vo. [*Brit. Mus.*] London, 1807

THREE new songs, entituled, I. The artillery recruiting, or a new song in praise of that brave and useful body of men. II. The allies triumph. III. Pride and passion. By W. D. [W. Duncan]. 12mo. Pp. 12. [J. Maidment.] Dundee, 1794

THREE nights in Perthshire ; with a description of the festival of a " Scotch Hairst Kirn " : comprising legendary ballads, etc. In a letter from Percy Yorke, Jr. to J. Twiss, Esq. [By Thomas Atkinson, Junior, bookseller.] 12mo. Pp. 66. [*Letter from the author accompanying the presentation copy to Sir Egerton Brydges, Bart.*] Glasgow, private print, 1821

THREE northern romances, Siegfried, Lohengrin, Undine ; old tales retold by Norley Chester [Emily Underdown] and Richard Wilson. 16mo. Pp. 191. [*Brit. Mus.*] London, 1925

THREE of them. [A novel.] By Maxim Gorky [Aleksyei Maksimovitch Pyeshkov]; translated from the Russian by A. Linden. 8vo. Pp. 391. London, 1905

THREE of us. By Thekla [Mrs Caroline Atherton Mason, *née* Briggs]. 8vo. [*Lib. Journ.* v. 222.] Boston, 1880

THREE (the) Oxonians ; a novel. By Frank Usher [F. U. Waite, of Balliol College, Oxford]. 8vo. 3 vols. London, 1873

THREE (the) partes of commentaries, containing the whole and perfect discourse of the ciuill warres of Fraunce —. With an addition of the cruell murther of the Admirall Chastilion, and diuers other nobles, committed the 24 daye of August Anno 1572. Translated out of. Latine [of Petrus Ramus] into Englishe by Thomas Tymme, minister. 4to. [*W.*; Lowndes' *Bibl. Man.*] London, 1574

The work has been by some attributed to Jean de Serres, and by others to François Hotman.

THREE people. [A tale.] By Pansy [Mrs Alden, *née* Isabella Macdonald]. 8vo. Pp. 308. London, 1901

THREE plays . . . Selindra, Pandora, Ormasdes. [By Sir William Killigrew]. 12mo. London, 1665

First edition. Later editions, with additional plays, bear the author's name.

THREE poems, Mahanaim ; or, strivings with a Saviour ; containing a dialogue betwixt Jesus and an afflicted soul ; Peniel, or, the combatant triumphing, expressing comfort under clouds, and the triumph consummat, or the state of glory. By an experienced admirer of sanctified afflictions [John Wilson, Episcopalian]. 4to. [*Brit. Mus.*]
1706

Attributed also to James Webster.

THREE poems of St Paul's cathedral : viz. the ruins ; the rebuilding ; the choire. [By James Wright]. Fol. Pp. 12. [*D. N. B.* vol. 63, p. 107.] London, 1697

THREE political letters to a noble Lord, concerning liberty and the constitution. . . . [By Thomas Gordon, of Kirkcudbright.] 8vo. [*Brit. Mus.*] London, 1721

THREE praiers, one for the morning, another for the evening ; the third for a sick-man : whereunto is annexed, a godlie letter to a sicke-friend ; and a comfortable speech of a preacher, vpon his death bed. [By Henry Smith.] 8vo. Pp. 30. [*Bodl.*] London, 1591

THREE (the) questions : What am I ? Whence came I ? Whither do I go ? [By Wm. Haig Miller, banker.] 8vo. Pp. vi. 119. [Cushing's *Anon.* p. 672.] London, 1843

THREE rascals. By Raymond Jacberns [Miss M. Selby Ashe]. 8vo. Pp. 216. London, 1903

THREE R —— l bloods ; or, a lame R——t, a darling commander, and a love-sick admiral : a poem. By Peter Pindar, Jun., author of the *R——l lover* [John Agg]. Seventh edition. 8vo. Pp. 27. London, 1812

THREE scouts. By Paul Creyton [John Townsend Trowbridge]. 8vo. [*Amer. Cat.*] New York, 1907

THREE seasonable quæres, proposed to all those cities, counties, and boroughs, whose respective citizens, knights and burgesses have been forcibly excluded, uniustly eiected, and disabled to sit in the Commons house, by those now acting at Westminster. [By William Prynne.] Fol. S. sh. [*Brit. Mus.*] London, 1660

THREE sermons. By a layman [George Hardinge]. 8vo. London, 1813

THREE short discourses on the duty of parents, the Holy Scriptures and the Sabbath. [By John Charlesworth ?] 12mo. [*W.; Brit. Mus.*] Newark, 1787

THREE (the) sisters ; a story translated [by Sir Wm. Domville] from the German. 12mo. Pp. 70. [*Brit. Mus.*] London, private print, 1842

THREE sixteenth-century sketches [of William of Orange, Admiral Coligny, and the Regent Murray]. By Sarah Brook [Caroline Emelia Stephen]. 8vo. Pp. 256. [*Brit. Mus.*] London, 1884

THREE speeches against continuing the army, &c. as they were spoken in the House of Commons the last session of parliament ; to which are added, the reasons given by the Lords, who protested against the bill for punishing mutiny and desertion. The first is by W—— S——, Esq. [William Sheppen]. The second is by E—— J——, Esq. [E. Jeffrys]. The third is by Sir T—— H——, Bart. [Sir Thomas Hanmore]. 8vo. Pp. 46. London, 1718

THREE speeches unspoken in the last session of parliament, and reserved to the second thoughts of this next. [By John Humfrey.] 4to. Pp. 12. London, 1703

A fourth speech is added at the end.

THREE stories and a play. By John Oliver Hobbes [Mrs Reginald Walpole Craigie, *née* Pearl M. T. Richards]. 8vo. London, 1901

THREE sunsets, and other poems. By Lewis Carroll [Rev. Charles L. Dodgson]. 4to. London, 1898

A reprint of poems from *Phantasmagoria, Sylvie and Bruno, The Jabberwock Magazine,* with two fresh poems.

THREE tales for an idle hour. By the author of *The sunbeam* [Cecilia Anne Jones]. 8vo. [*Brit. Mus.*] London, 1867

Signed : C. A. T.

THREE (the) times and a half, and the seven times [mentioned in the Book of Daniel]. By the author of *Essays on the Church* [Robert B. Seeley]. 8vo. Pp. 31. [*Brit. Mus.*]   London, 1881

THREE times three. [A tale.] By Mrs George Archibald [Anna Campbell, later Mrs George Archibald Palmer]. 8vo. [*Amer. Cat.*]   Chicago, 1899

THREE times three ; a story for young people. By "Pansy" [Mrs Isabella (Macdonald) Alden]. 4to.
                            Chicago, 1897

THREE to one ; a comedy, in three acts. [By John Lettsom Elliot.] 8vo. Pp. 83. [*Athen. Lib.*] [London] 1850

THREE tracts of the great medicine of philosophers for humane and metalline bodies. . . . All written in Latin by Eirenæus Philalethes Cosmopolita [George Starkey] ; translated into English. . . . 8vo. 3 parts. [*Brit. Mus.*]   London, 1694

THREE tracts on the corn-trade and corn-laws : viz. 1. A short essay on the corn-trade and corn-laws, containing, a general relation of the present method of carrying on the corn-trade. . . . 2. Considerations on the laws relating to the importation and exportation of corn. . . . 3. A collection of papers relative to the price, exportation, and importation of corn. . . . [By Charles Smith, a miller.] 8vo. [*M'Culloch's Lit. Pol. Econ.* p. 68.]   London, 1766

THREE tracts respecting the conversion and instruction of the free Indians, and negroe slaves in the colonies ; addressed to the venerable Society for propagation of the Gospel in foreign parts. [By William Knox.] 8vo. Pp. 41. [*Bodl.*]   N.P. [1768]

THREE (the) travellers ; a tale [in verse. By Rev. Walter Chamberlaine, M.A., T.C.D.]. 12mo. [O'Donoghue's *Poets of Ireland.*] 12mo.   Dublin, 1733

THREE treatises : the first concerning art ; the second concerning music, painting, and poetry ; the third concerning happiness. By J. H. [James Harris]. 8vo. [Watt's *Bibl. Brit.*]
                            London, 1744

THREE (the) voices of God on the unfermented wine question. By the author of *The Sabbath on the Rock* [Robert Wilson, Glasgow]. 8vo. Pp. 128. [*Brit. Mus.*]   London, 1875

THREE (the) vows ; and other romances at Chatsworth. . . . [By Peter George Patmore.] 8vo. 3 vols. [*Brit. Mus.*]
                            London, 1845
    Another issue has the title " Chatsworth ; or, the romance of a week."

THREE (the) wakings ; with hymns and songs. By the author of *The voice of Christian life in song*, etc. [Mrs Elizabeth Charles]. 8vo. Pp. vi. 194. [*Brit. Mus.*]   London, 1859

THREE weddings. [By Margaret Agnes Colville, later Mrs —— Paul.] 8vo. [Cushing's *Anon.* p. 672.]
                            London, 1870

THREE weeks after marriage ; a comedy, in two acts, as performed at the Theatre-Royal in Covent-Garden. [By Arthur Murphy.] 8vo. [Baker's *Biog. Dram.*]   London, 1776
    Originally produced and published under the title : " What we must all come to."

THREE (the) wishes. [By Mrs Mary E. Gellie.] 12mo. [*Lib. Journ.* iii. 379.]
                            London, 1878

THREE wives. By the author of *Margaret and her bridesmaids*, etc. [Mrs Anne Marsh]. 8vo. 3 vols. [*Brit. Mus.*]   London, 1868

THREE years adventures of a minor in England, Africa, the West Indies, South Carolina, and Georgia. By William Butterworth [Henry Schroeder], engraver. 8vo. [*D. N. B.* vol. 50, p. 441.]   Leeds, 1822

THREE years among the working-classes of the United States during the war. By the author of *The autobiography of a beggar-boy* [James Dawson Burns]. 8vo. [*Brit. Mus.*]
                            London, 1865

THREE years in Europe ; being extracts from letters sent from Europe. By a Hindu [Rames Chandra Datta]. Second edition. 8vo.   Calcutta, 1873
    The third edition, 1890, bears the author's name.

THREE years in field-hospitals of the Army of the Potomac. By Mrs H. [Mrs Anna M. Holstein, *née* Ellis]. 8vo. Pp. 131. [*Brit. Mus.*]
                            Philadelphia, 1867

THREE years in the Pacific ; containing notices of Brazil, Chile, Bolivia, Peru, etc., 1831-34. By an officer of the U.S. Navy [Wm. S. W. Ruschenberger]. 8vo. 2 vols. [*Brit. Mus.*]
                            London, 1835

THREE years' practical experience of a settler in New South Wales ; extracts from letters, 1834-1837. [By James Waugh.] 12mo. [*Sydney Lib.* ii. 167.]
                            Sydney, 1838

THREE years' travels from Moscow over-land to China, through Ustigia, Siriania, Permia, Libiria, Daowr, Great Tartary, etc., to Peking ; containing an exact and particular description of the extent and limits of those countries, and the customs of the barbarous inhabitants. . . . Written by his Excellency E. Ysbrants Ides [Evert Ides], Ambassador from the Czar of Muscovy to the Emperor of China. . . . To which is annexed an accurate description of China, done originally by a Chinese author [Dionysius Kao]. . . . 4to. [Arber's *Term Cat.* iii. 480.]
London, 1705

THREE years with the Duke ; or, Wellington in private life. By an ex-Aide-de-Camp [Lord William Pitt Lennox]. 8vo. [*Brit. Mus.*]
London, 1853

THREE-CORNERED essays. By a middle-aged Englishman [Rev. Frederick Arnold]. 8vo. [*Brit. Mus.*]
London, 1886

THREE-FOLD (a) discourse between three neighbours, Algate, Bishopsgate, and John Heyden, the late cobler of Hounsditch, a professed Brownist. . . . [By John Taylor, the Water-poet.] 4to. London, 1642

THREEFOLD (the) path to peace. By Xena [Janet R. Rees]. 12mo.
London, 1904

THREE'S company. By May Wynne [Mabel Wynne Knowles]. 8vo.
Glasgow [1917]

ΘΡΗΝΩΔΗ ; or, Englands passing-bell. [By Thomas Gilbert.] 4to. [*Wood's Athen. Oxon.* iv. 407.] London, 1679

THRENODIES, sketches, and other verses. By the author of *Thysia* [Morton Luce]. 12mo. [*Brit. Mus.*]
London, 1910

THRESHOLD (the) of Atrides. [Poems.] By George F. Preston [John Byrne Leicester Warren, third Baron de Tabley]. 8vo. [O'Donoghue's *Poets of Ireland.*] London, 1861

THRESHOLDS. [A novel.] By Faith Baldwin [Faith Baldwin Cuthrell]. 8vo. Pp. 284. [*Brit. Mus.*] London [1926]

THRIE (the) tales of the priests of Peblis ; containing many notabill examples and sentences. [Attributed by Pinkerton to David Steill, and by Sibbald to Rolland.] 4to. B. L.
Edinburgh, 1603

THRIFT ; or, hints for cottage housekeeping. By the author of *A trap to catch a sunbeam* [Mrs Henry S. Mackarness]. 12mo. Pp. 32.
London [1855]

THRILLING (a) balloon voyage. By Ranger [Luther L. Holden]. 8vo. [*Cushing's Init. and Pseud.*]
Boston, 1870

THRILLING incidents of the Wars of the United States, comprising the most striking and remarkable events of the Revolution, the French War, the Tripolitan War, etc. By the author of *The Army and Navy of the United States* [Jacob K. Neff]. 8vo. [*Brit. Mus.*] Philadelphia, 1848

THRO' love and war. [A novel.] By Violet Fane [Mary Montgomerie, later Mrs Singleton, afterwards Lady Currie]. 8vo. 5 vols. London, 1886

THROUGH a Dartmoor window. By Beatrice Chase [Olive Katherine Parr]. 8vo. Pp. 284. [*Lit. Who's Who.*]
London, 1915

THROUGH a needle's eye. [A tale of English village - life.] By Hesba Stretton [Sarah Smith]. 8vo. 2 vols.
London, 1870

THROUGH Airedale, from Goole to Malham. By Johnnie Gray [Harry Speight]. 8vo. [*Brit. Mus.*]
London, 1891

THROUGH Algeria. By the author of *Life in Tuscany* [Mabel Sharman Crawford]. 8vo. Pp. 362. [*Lond. Lib. Cat.*] London, 1863
Life in Tuscany (1859) is not anonymous.

THROUGH Connemara in a governess cart. By the authors of *An Irish cousin*, etc. [Edith Œone Somerville and Violet Martin]. 8vo. Pp. 200. [S. J. Brown's *Ireland in Fiction.*]
London, 1893

THROUGH Egypt to Palestine. [By M. E. Beck.] 12mo. [*Birm. Ref. Lib.*] Birmingham, 1873
Another edition, published in the same year, gives the author's name.

THROUGH fire to fortune. [A novel.] By Mrs Alexander [Mrs Alexander Hector, *née* Annie French]. 8vo. Pp. 316. [*Brit. Mus.*] London, 1903

THROUGH flood and flame. [A novel. By Sabine Baring-Gould.] 8vo. 3 vols. [*Brit. Mus.*] London, 1868

THROUGH green glasses. [A novel.] By F. M. Allen [Edmund Downey]. 8vo. Pp. 236. [*Brit. Mus.*]
London, 1888

THROUGH my spectacles. By "Proavia" [Kate Hope]. 8vo. 3 vols. [*Brit. Mus.*] London, 1878

THROUGH night to light. By Norman Stuart [Mrs Bartle Teeling, *née* —— Lane-Clarke]. London [*c.* 1890]

THROUGH patience. By Faye Hunting-
ton [Mrs Isabella H. Foster]. 12mo.
[Cushing's *Init. and Pseud.*]
Philadelphia, 1869

THROUGH rifted clouds ; a novel. By
Annabel Gray [Mrs Annie Cox]. 8vo.
2 vols. [*Lit. Year Book.*]
London, 1891

THROUGH rough waters. [A tale.]
By the author of *The rose garden,
Unawares*, etc. [Miss Frances Mary
Peard]. 8vo.   London, 1878

THROUGH storm and stress. . . . By
Mardale [Richard H. Holme]. 8vo.
[*Brit. Mus.*]   London, 1902

THROUGH the ages ; a psychological
romance. By the author of *The
honeymoon* [the Duke de Medina
Pomar]. 8vo. 3 vols. [*Brit. Mus.*]
London, 1876

THROUGH the crucible. By Claud
Heathcote [James Harwood Panting].
8vo. [*Lit. Who's Who.*]
London, 1898

THROUGH the eye to the heart ; or,
eye-teaching in the Sunday-school.
By Collene Fisk [Rev. Wilbar Fisk
Crofts, B.D.]. 8vo. [*Lib. Journ.* xiv.
59.]   New York, 1873-8

THROUGH the flood ; the story of an
out-of-the-way place. By Esmé Stuart
[Amélie Claire Leroy]. 8vo. Pp. 292.
London, 1892

THROUGH the goal of ill. [By R. J.
Alfred.] 8vo. Pp. viii. 347. [*Brit.
Mus.*]   London [1888]

THROUGH the land of the Aztecs ; or,
life and travel in Mexico. By a
Gringo [Arthur St Hill]. 8vo.
London, 1892

THROUGH the looking-glass ; and
what Alice found there. By Lewis
Carroll [Rev. Charles L. Dodgson].
8vo. [Williams' *Bibl. of L. C.*]
London, 1872

THROUGH the mill ; or, rambles in
Texas. By Rux [Captain Hyacinthe
Daly Devereux]. 8vo. London, 1892

THROUGH the ranks to a commission.
[By Lieut. John Edward Acland-
Troyte.] 8vo. [*Lib. Journ.* vi. 190.]
London, 1881

THROUGH the red-litten windows ;
and the old river house : stories. By
Theodor Hertz-Garten [Mrs —— de
Mattos]. 12mo. Pp. 191. [*Who's
Who in Lit.*]   London, 1892

THROUGH the rough-wind ; a story
of the collieries. By Crona Temple
[Miss Corfield]. 8vo. London, 1880

THROUGH the shadows. By the
author of *Sydney Grey* [Miss Annie
Keary]. 8vo. 3 vols. [*Brit. Mus.*]
London, 1859

THROUGH the turf-smoke ; the love,
lore, and laughter of Old Ireland. By
Mac [Seumas MacManus]. 8vo.
London, 1899

THROUGH to-day. [By M. Elliott.]
8vo.   London, 1892

THROUGH veldt and forest ; an African
story. By Harry Collingwood [William
J. C. Lancaster]. 8vo. [*Brit. Mus.*]
London, 1913

THROUGH winding ways. By Henry
Hayes [Ellen Warner Olney, later
Mrs Kirk]. 8vo. [*Who's Who in
Lit.*]   Philadelphia, 1880

THROUGHOUT the year ; poems old
and new. By Guy Roslyn [Joshua
Hatton]. 12mo. [*Who's Who in Lit.*]
London, 1886

THROW (a) for a throne ; or, the Prince
unmasked. By Chancery Lane, Esq.
[James Edwin Wilson]. 8vo. [*Lib.
Journ.* v. 54.]   London, 1872

THROWN on her own resources ; or,
what girls can do. By Jenny June
[Mrs Jane Cunningham Croly]. 8vo.
[Cushing's *Init. and Pseud.*]
New York, 1891

THROWN on the world. By Bertha
M. Clay [Charlotte M. Braeme]. 12mo.
New York, 1887

THROWN together ; a story. By the
author of *Misunderstood* [Florence
Montgomery]. Second edition. 8vo.
2 vols. [*Brit. Mus.*]   London, 1872

"THRUST out" ; an old legend. By
the author of *Drifted and sifted*, etc.
[Jessie Maclaren]. 8vo. Pp. 336.
[*Nat. Lib. of Scot.*] Edinburgh [1873]

THULE ; or, vertues historie. (Book I.)
By F. R. [Francis Rous]. 4to. [*W.* ;
Lowndes' *Bibl. Man.*]   London, 1598
On Malone's copy in the Bodleian, the
author's name is printed at length.

THUMP'S client. By Charles D. Knight
[Mrs R. L. Gilbert]. 8vo. [Cushing's
Init. and Pseud.]   New York, 1880

THUNDER (the) bird. By B. M.
Bower [Mrs Bertha Muzzy Sinclair].
8vo. Pp. 317. [*Brit. Mus.*]
Boston, 1919

THUNDER from heaven against the
back-sliders and apostates of the
times. By W. A. [William Aspin-
wall]. 8vo. [Thomason's *Coll. of
Tracts*, ii. 109.]   London, 1655

THUNDER from the throne of God
against the temples of idols. [By
Samuel Chidley.] 4to. Pp. 36.
[Thomason's *Coll. of Tracts*, ii. 6.]
[London] 1652

THUNDERBOLT (the). [A novel.]
By George Colmore [Mrs Baillie
Weaver]. 8vo. Pp. 312. [*Who's
Who in Lit.*]   London, 1919

THUNDERER (the) ; a romance of Napoleon and Josephine. By E. Barrington [Mrs L. Adams Beck]. 8vo. Pp. 317. [*Brit. Mus.*]
London, 1927

THURID ; and other poems. By G. E. O. [George Edmund Otis]. 8vo. [Cushing's *Init. and Pseud.*]
Boston, 1874

THURLSTON tales. By the author of *Tales of a voyager to the Arctic ocean* [Robert Pierce Gillies]. 12mo. 3 vols. [*Brit. Mus.*]
London, 1835

THURSO and its neighbourhood. [By D. Coghill.] 8vo. Pp. 88. [Mowat's *Bibl. of Caithness*, p. 51.]
Thurso, 1898

THURTELL'S crime. [A novel.] By Dick Donovan [Joyce E. P. Muddock]. 8vo. Pp. 320.
London, 1906

THWARTED ; or, ducks' eggs in a hen's nest : a village story. By the author of *Misunderstood* [Florence Montgomery]. 8vo. Pp. viii. 255. [*Brit. Mus.*]
London, 1874

THY Kingdom come. [By Julia A. Mathews.] 8vo.
Edinburgh [1868]

THY name is truth. [A novel.] By Sydney Starr [Miss Fanny Gallaher]. 8vo. 3 vols. [S. J. Brown's *Ireland in Fiction.*]
Dublin, 1884

THY neighbor's wife. By Albert Ross [Linn Boyd Porter]. 8vo. Pp. 316.
New York, 1893

THYRA Varrick. [A novel.] By Luke Sharp [Robert Barr]. London, 189—-

THYSIA ; an elegy in forty-five sonnets. [By Morton Luce.] Third edition. 12mo. [*Brit. Mus.*]
London, 1910

TIB. [A novel.] By George Douglas [Mrs George Ferme, of Haddington, *née* Douglas]. 8vo. Pp. 319.
Edinburgh, 1892

TIBER (the) and the Thames ; their associations past and present. [By Edward C. Bruce.] 8vo. [*Brit. Mus.*]
Philadelphia [1876]

TICKLER (the). [A satirical publication ; seven numbers. By Paul Hiffernan, M.D.] 8vo. [*D. N. B.* vol. 26, p. 366.]
Dublin, 1748

TICONDEROGA once more. By B. F. D. [Benjamin Franklin Da Costa, D.D.]. 8vo. [Cushing's *Init. and Pseud.*]
New York, 1870

TIDE (the) of fortune. [A Cromwellian romance.] By Morice Gerard [Rev. John Jessup Teague]. 8vo. Pp. 282. [*Brit. Mus.*]
London, 1916

TIDE (the) of the Moaning Bar. [A tale. By Mrs Frances Hodgson Burnett.] 8vo. [*Brit. Mus.*]
London [1879]

TIDEWAY (the). [A novel.] By Austin Clare [Miss M. W. James]. 8vo. Pp. 388.
London, 1903

TIDEWAY (the). [Fifteen short stories.] By John Ayscough [Monsignor Francis Bickerstaffe-Drew]. 8vo. Pp. 320.
London, 1918

TIDINGS from the East, as promulgated by Daniel the Prophet, 2390 years ago. [By James Wallis.] 8vo. [*Brit. Mus.*]
[London ? 1857]

TIECK'S "Lover of Nature," a tale : translated . . . by John Smith [Henry Swasey M'Kean]. 8vo.
Cambridge, Mass., 1833

TIGER (the) and the insect. By the author of *Helen's babies* [John Habberton]. 8vo.
London, 1902

TIGER-SLAYER (the) ; a tale of the Indian desert. By Gustave Aimard [Olivier Gloux] ; translated from the French by Sir F. C. L. Wraxall. 8vo.
London [1874]

TILBURY Nogo ; or, passages in the life of an unsuccessful man. By the author of *Digby Grand* [George John Whyte Melville]. 12mo. 2 vols. [*Brit. Mus.*]
London, 1854

TIM. [A story. By Howard Overing Sturgis.] 8vo. Pp. 318. [*Brit. Mus.*]
London, 1891

TIM and Tip. . . . By James Otis [James Otis Kaler]. 8vo.
Boston, 1890

TIM Bobbin resurrected. By Teddy Ashton [Charles Allen Clarke]. 8vo. Pp. 48. [*Who's Who in Lit.*]
Blackpool, 1911

TIM Bobbin's [John Collier's] Lancashire dialect and poems, rendered intelligible to general readers by a literal interpretation, and the obsolete words explained by quotations from the most early of the English authors. 8vo. [*W.*]
London, 1828

TIM Bobbin's adventures with the Irishman . . . By M. R. L. [M. R. Lahee]. 8vo. Pp. 55. [*N. and Q.* Feb. 1869, p. 168.]
Manchester, 1860

TIM (the) Bunker papers ; or, Yankee farming. By Timothy Bunker, Esq. [Rev. William Clift]. 8vo. [Cushing's *Init. and Pseud.*]
New York, 1868

TIM Harrison. By Nellie Grahame [Mrs Annie Dunning, *née* Ketchum]. 12mo. [Cushing's *Init. and Pseud.*]
Philadelphia, 1864

TIME ; an elegy. By a student of Marischal College [Robert Alves, M.A.]. 8vo. [*Aberd. Quatercent. Studies*, No. 19, p. 340.]
Aberdeen, 1766

TIME and faith; an inquiry into the data of ecclesiastical history. [By William Edward Hickson.] 8vo. 2 vols. [*D. N. B.* vol. 26, p. 362.]
London, 1857

TIME and the things of time. [By Moses Birnie.] 8vo. [Robertson's *Aberd. Bibl.*]   Aberdeen [*c.* 1850]

TIME and truth reconciling the moral and religious world to Shakespeare; the greatest poet and dramatist, the greatest moral-philosopher and philanthropist, that ever livëd in the tide of times. . . . [By B. S. Naylor.] 12mo. Pp. xii. 232. [*Bodl.*]   London, 1854

TIME (the) bargain; or, Tourmalin's time-cheques. By F. Anstey [Thomas Anstey Guthrie]. 8vo.   Bristol, 1905

TIME bargains tried by the rules of equity, and principles of the civil law. [By Sir David Dalrymple.] 8vo. Pp. 36. [*Nat. Lib. of Scot.*]
London, printed; Edinburgh, reprinted, N.D.

TIME (the) for the publication of banns. [By John Griffiths, M.A.] 8vo. Pp. 8.
[1867]

TIME (the) of Christ's second coming identified with the Day of Judgment. . . . By the author of *Millenarianism indefensible* [Alexander Gardner]. 12mo. [*Brit. Mus.*]   Paisley, 1833

TIME (the) of the end, and other poems. [By Mrs Eddis.] 12mo.
London [1851]

TIME (the) serving Proteus and ambidexter divine uncased to the world; containing the letters of Mr John Dury . . . the first to Joseph Hall, late bishop of Exeter, the second to William Lawd, late Archbishop of Canterbury. . . . [By William Prynne.] 4to. [*Brit. Mus.*]   London, 1650

TIME, the avenger. By the author of *Emilia Wyndham*, etc. [Mrs Anne Marsh, *née* Caldwell]. 8vo. 3 vols. [*D. N. B.* vol. 36, p. 219.]
London, 1851

TIME (a) to weep; or, the reasonableness and necessity of continuing the observation of the xxx day of January in Scotland, as well as England, as a day of solemn humiliation and publick sorrow: a sermon preached in the country. By one of the suffering clergy of the Church of Scotland [William Milne or Mylne]. 8vo. Pp. 35. [*Nat. Lib. of Scot.*]   Edinburgh, 1720

TIME will tell. [A temperance tale.] By N. J. N. [Mrs A. G. Wilson]. 8vo. [*Brit. Mus.*]   Glasgow, 1868

VOL. VI.

TIME-HONOURED Lancaster; historic notes on the ancient borough of Lancaster . . . By Cross Fleury [R. E. K. Rigbye]. 8vo. Pp. xi. 612. [*Brit. Mus.*]   Lancaster, 1891

TIMELY seeking of God urged. By the pastor at Malden [Joseph Emerson]. 8vo.   Boston, 1837

TIMES (the); a drama. By John Daly [John Besemeres, merchant in Calcutta]. 8vo. [Cushing's *Init. and Pseud.*]   London, 1853

TIMES (the); a poem. [By Charles Churchill.] 4to. [*W.*]   London, 1764

TIMES (the): a poem. By an American [Benjamin Church, M.D.]. 4to. Pp. 16. [Evans' *Amer. Bibl.* vol. 4, p. 67.]
[Boston, 1765]

TIMES (the) anatomiz'd in severall characters. By T. F. [Thomas Forde]. 12mo. [*W.*; Lowndes' *Bibl. Man.*]
London, 1647
Wrongly attributed to Thomas Fuller.

TIMES and days; essays in romance and history. By the author of *Auto da fe* [John H. Balfour Browne]. 8vo.
London, 1898

TIMES and places; or, our history. . . . [By Isaac L. Mocatta.] 8vo.
London, 1872

TIMES (the) and the teaching of Jesus the Christ; by the author of *The Great Law* [W. Williamson]. 8vo. Pp. 453.
London, 1912

TIMES (the) on the American War; an historical study. By L. S. [Sir Leslie Stephen]. 8vo.   [*Brit. Mus.*]
London, 1865

TIMES (the); or, the flag of truce. By the white Republican [Hiram Fuller]. 8vo. [Cushing's *Init. and Pseud.*]
Richmond, 1863

TIMES (the); or, the prophecy; a poem. [By George Daniel.] 4to. [Watt's *Bibl. Brit.; Brit. Crit.* xxxviii. 633.]   London, 1811

TIMES (the); or, views of society: a poem, with notes; to which is added an appendix, containing various scenes from four plays, written for Drury Lane Theatre, but ultimately withdrawn . . . [By John Barber.] 8vo. Pp. 207.   London, 1819

TIMES, places, and persons of the Holie Scriptures; otherwise entituled, The general view of the Holy Scriptures. [By Thomas Hayne, M.A.] 4to. [*D. N. B.* vol. 25, p. 300.]
London, 1607

D 2

TIME'S treasure ; or, devout thoughts for every day of the year expressed in verse. [By William Penney, Lord Kinloch.] 8vo. Pp. 283.
Edinburgh, 1862
The second edition, 1863, has the author's name.

TIME'S tunefull Tabor ; being divers diary notes ; selected from the original MS. of Master Camden Crookedstaff [Edwin Roffe] by his trusty friend E. Roffe. 4to. London, 1862
12 copies, privately printed.

TIMMY Top-boots. By H. N. W. B. [Mrs Harriet Newall (Woods) Baker]. 8vo. [Cushing's *Init. and Pseud.*]
Boston, 1870

TIMOLEON ; a tragedy. [By Benjamin Martin or Martyn.] 8vo.
London, 1730
The second edition has the author's name.

TIMON in love : or, the innocent theft : a comedy, taken from Thimon Misanthrope of the Sieur de Lisle ; as it is acted at the Theatre-Royal in Drury-Lane, by his Majesty's servants. [By John Kelly.] 8vo. Pp. 55. [Baker's *Biog. Dram.*] London, 1733

TIMON of Athens ; published with three copperplates. [By Charles Lamb.] 12mo. Pp. 36. [*Ashley Library.*]
London, 1807
Several of Lamb's *Tales from Shakespear* were issued separately without the author's name.

TIMOTHY and Philatheus ; in which the principles and projects of a late whimsical book [by Matthew Tindal] entitled " The Rights of the Christian Church," etc., are fairly stated and answered in their kind. . . . By a layman [William Oldisworth]. 8vo. 3 vols. [Watt's *Bibl. Brit.*]
London, 1709-10

TIMOTHY'S guest ; a story for anybody. By Kate Douglas Wiggin [Mrs George C. Riggs]. 8vo. Pp. 206.
London, 1892

TIM'S sacrifice. By Mignon [Mrs Baseley]. 8vo. Manchester, 1902

TIM'S sister ; or, a word in season. By Mrs Madeline Leslie [Mrs Harriet Newall Baker]. 8vo. [Cushing's *Init. and Pseud.*] Boston [1863]

TIM'S troubles ; or, timid and true. By M. A. Paull [Mrs John Ripley]. 8vo. Pp. 456. [*Who's Who in Lit.*]
London, 1898

TIN (the) duties. [By Sir Charles Lemon, M.A.] 8vo. Pp. 16. [Cushing's *Anon.* p. 674.] London, 1833

TIN (the) trumpet ; or, heads and tales for the wise and waggish ; to which are added, poetical selections by the late Paul Chatfield, M.D. Edited by Jefferson Saunders, Esq. [Written chiefly by Horace and James Smith.] 12mo. 2 vols. [*Brit. Mus.*]
London, 1836

TINNED meats, fish, and fruits ; and how to use them. By the author of *Supper dishes for people with small means* [Emily de Vere Mathew]. 8vo. Pp. 50. [*Brit. Mus.*] Ipswich [1887]

TINNEVELLY (the) missions. [By George E. L. Cotton, D.D. Reprint from the *Calcutta Review.*] 8vo. [*Camb. Univ. Lib.*] Calcutta, 1864

TINTED (the) Venus ; a farcical romance. By F. Anstey [Thomas Anstey Guthrie], author of *Vice versâ*. 8vo. London, 1896

TINTINALOGIA ; or, the art of ringing improved. By T. W. [Thomas White]. 12mo. [*N. and Q.* March 1854, p. 241.] 1668

TINY houses and their builders. By one of the authors of *Poems written for a child* [Mrs Fanny Hart]. 8vo.
London, 1876

TIP Lewis and his lamp. [A story.] By Pansy [Mrs Isabella (Macdonald) Alden]. 8vo. Pp. 256.
London [1891]

TIP-CAT. [A tale.] By the author of *Miss Toosey's mission* [Evelyn Whitaker]. New edition. 8vo. [*Amer. Cat.*] London, 1891

TIPLING (the) philosophers ; a lyrick poem : to which is subjoin'd, a short abstract of their lives and most memorable actions. [By Edward Ward.] 8vo. Pp. 40. London, 1710

TIPTOE. By Katherine Williams [Mrs Laura A. Buck]. 8vo. [Cushing's *Init. and Pseud.*] New York, 1871

TIPTREE Hall farm, Essex. . . . [Signed : R. R. *i.e.* R. Rolton.] 8vo. [*Brit. Mus.*] London [1853]

TIPTREE races ; a comic running poem. By C. C. [Charles Clark], Great Totham, Essex. 8vo. [*Brit. Mus.*]
Maldon, 1833

TIRED Church members. By Amy Lothrop [Anna Bartlett Warner]. 8vo. Pp. 112. [Cushing's *Init. and Pseud.*] New York, 1881

TIROCINIUM : or, an elementary Latin reading book, adapted to *The child's Latin primer*, for the use of preparatory and accidence schools. [By Benjamin Hall Kennedy, D.D.] 12mo. Pp. vi. 96. London, 1848
New edition with the author's name, London, 1855.

'TIS all a farce; a farce. [By John Till Allingham.] 8vo. [Baker's *Biog. Dram.*]   London, 1800

'TIS an old tale, and often told. [By Isabel Goldsmid.] 12mo. [*Nat. Lib. of Scot.*]   London, 1839

'TIS merry when Gossips meet. [By Samuel Rowlands.] 4to. No pagination. [*Pollard and Redgrave.*]   London, 1609
> Running title, "A crew of kind gossips." Other editions were entitled, "Well met gossips . . ." and "A whole crew of kind gossips."

'TIS well it's no worse : a comedy ; as it is performed at the Theatre Royal in Drury-Lane, by His Majesty's servants. [By Isaac Bickerstaffe ; altered from Calderon's *El Escondido y la Tapada*.] 8vo. Pp. ix. 104. [*Brit. Mus.*]   London, 1770

TIT for tat ; a comedy in three acts : performed at the Theatres Royall Hay-market, Drury-Lane, and Covent-Garden, printed under the inspection of James Wrighton, prompter, exactly agreeable to the representation. [By George Colman, the elder.] 8vo. Pp. 49. [Baker's *Biog. Dram.*]   London, 1788

TIT for tat ; for juvenile minds ; with large additions of prose and verse for more mature intellects, in advocacy of peace principles. [By John Harris.] 12mo. Pp. 140.   London, 1853
> See below for an earlier edition entitled "Tit for tat ; original poems . . ."

TIT for tat ; or, a purge for a pill. . . . By Dick Retort [William Cobbett]. 8vo. [Cushing's *Init. and Pseud.*]   Philadelphia, 1796

TIT for tat ; original poems for juvenile minds. By Q. in the corner [John Harris]. 8vo. [Smith's *Cat. of Friends' Books*, i. 99.]   London, 1830

TITAN'S Letter to Milo. [By Albert Williams.] 8vo. [*W.*]   London, N.D.

TITCOMB'S letters to young people, single and married. Timothy Titcomb Esquire [Josiah Gilbert Holland]. Twelfth edition. 8vo. [*Brit. Mus.*]   New York, 1859

TITHES, and the Church which owns them. By Justitia [Charles Joseph Weld-Blundell]. 8vo. [*Lond. Lib. Cat.*]   London, 1894

TITHES indefensible ; or, observations on the origin and effects of tithes, addressed to country gentlemen. [By Thomas Thompson.] 8vo. Pp. 118. [*Bodl.*]   York, 1792

TITHING (a) table ; or, a table of tithes and oblations, according to the ecclesiastical laws and ordinances established in the Church of England. By W. C. [Bishop Carleton]. 4to. [Lowndes' *Bibl. Man.* p. 2687.]   London, 1662

TITLE (the) of a thorough settlement examined ; in answer to Dr [William] Sherlock's Case of the allegiance due to sovereign powers, &c. With an appendix in answer to Dr Sherlock's Vindication. [By Dr Robert Jenkin, Master of St John's College, Cambridge.] 4to. Pp. 6, 80. [*Brit. Mus.*]   London, 1691

TITLE (the) of kings proved to be jure divino ; and also that our royall Soveraign King Charles the Second is the right and lawfull heir to the crown of England, and that the life of his father, Charles the First, was taken away unjustly, contrary to the common-law, statute-law, and all other lawes of England. . . . By W. P. [William Prynne]. Esq. 4to. [*Cat. of the Lond. Inst.*]   London, 1660

TITLE (the) of the family of Shams-ud-Dowlah to the throne of Oude considered. [By General J. Briggs.] 8vo. [*Calc. Imp. Lib.*]   London, 1839

TITLES of honour. (Barons by tenure : Barons by writ.) [Extracted from a manuscript of Sir Thomas Saint George (1686), by Sir C. G. Young.] 8vo. 2 parts. [*Brit. Mus.*]   London, private print, 1864, 60

TITULAR (the) barony of Clavering ; its origin in . . . the Norman house of Clavering authenticated . . . from the public records. [Introduction signed: G. B. M. *i.e.* George Blacker Morgan.] Fol. Pp. vi. 44. [*Brit. Mus.*]   London, private print, 1891

TITUS before Jerusalem ; and other poems. [By Frances A. Garland.] 12mo. [Shum's *Bath Books*, p. 85.]   Bath [1852]

TITUS Lucretius Carus, the Epicurean philosopher, his six books *De Natura Rerum* done into English verse with notes. [By Thomas Creech.] 8vo. Pp. 222, 46. [*Brit. Mus.*]   Oxford, 1682

TITUS Vespasian ; a tragedy. [By John Cleland.] 8vo. [Lowndes' *Bibl. Man.*]   London, 1755
> Though not mentioned on the title-page, this tragedy is followed, with continuous pagination, by "The ladies subscription ; a dramatic performance ; designed for an introduction to a dance."

TIVERTON (the) woolcomber's defence. By one unconcerned, but a friend to liberty [Rev. William Daddo, A.M.]. 4to. [Boase and Courtney's *Bibl. Corn.* i. 102.]   London, 1750

TIVOLI. [A novel.] By E. M. Lauderdale [Mrs G. M. Moore]. 8vo. Pp. 278. [S. J. Brown's *Ireland in Fiction.*]   Cork, 1886

TO ——: I said to you a few months ago: See "Letter on Irish affairs."

TO a lady on her passion for old china. [A poem. By John Gay.] 4to. Pp. 5. [*Brit. Mus.*]   London, 1725

TO a nun confess'd. [A novel.] By Irene Osgood [Mrs Robert Harborough Sherard]. 8vo.   London, 1906

TO a young gentleman in love. [By Matthew Prior.] Fol. S. sh. [*Ashley Library.*]   [London] 1702

TO all kings, princes, rulers, governours, bishops and clergy, that profess Christianity in Christendom; being a distinction between the laws, commandments and ordinances of the higher powers, for the punishment of evil doers, and for the praise of them that do well. . . . By G. F. [George Fox]. 4to. Pp. 27.   London, 1685

TO all magistrates, teachers, schoolmasters, and people in Christendome, who teach your children the way of the heathen, out of their books, in naming the dayes, and months, and times, and observing your feasts, as followeth. . . . [By George Fox.] 4to. Pp. 8.
London, 1660
    Signed: G. F.

TO all people in all Christendom concerning perfect love, pure wisdome and the holy faith, and who they are that banisheth them, and who they are that entertains them; and how Christendome hath not received this love and this faith to edifie and build them. . . . [By George Fox.] 4to. Pp. 8.
N.P., N.D.
    Signed: G. F.

TO all people upon the face of the earth. [Signed: John, *i.e.* John Perrot.] 4to. [*D. N. B.* vol. 45, p. 27.]
London, 1661

TO all that professe Christianity, are these following particulars. Concerning their name of Christians. Loving enemies. The worship in spirit. Gospel-fellow-ship. Their many heads and baptismes. Their many Churches. Their disagreeing about Scriptures interpretation. By G. F. [George Fox]. 4to. Pp. 8.   London, 1661

TO all the faithful brethren born of the immortal seed of the father of life, and sent forth in the great commission, and power of the king of eternal glory, to gather his elect from the winds of the earth, forth of all nations and kindreds where they are scattered; this to you is the word of God. [By William Dewsbury.] 4to. Pp. 8.
London, 1661
    Signed: W. D., and dated from York Castle.

TO all the nations under the whole heavens; and to all those who have ministered the letter, and yet are ignorant, and. haue kept others in the ignorance both of the letter and spirit also: from those people who are despitefully called Quakers, who tremble at the word of God in their hearts. . . . G. F. [George Fox]. 4to. [Smith's *Cat. of Friends' Books*, i. 660.]
London, 1660

TO all the Royallists that suffered for His Majesty [Charles I.]; and to all the rest of the good people of England. The humble Apologie of the English Catholicks. [By Roger Palmer, Earl of Castlemaine.] 12mo. [Gillow's *Bibl. Dict.*]   1666
    Wrongly attributed to Dr R. Pugh.

TO all thē that loue Goddes worde vnfaynedly L. R. wysheth grace. [By William Roy and Jerome Barlowe.] 8vo. [*Pollard and Redgrave.*]
Wesell, 1546

TO all who smoke! A few words in defence of tobacco: or, a plea for the pipe. By "Cavendish" [Samuel Bevan]. 8vo. [Smith's *Cat. of Friends' Books*, i. 262.]   London, 1857

TO, at, and from Berlin. By R. F. H. [Rosa F. Hill]. 8vo. Pp. 155. [*Brit. Mus.*]   London, 1871

TO be or not to be. [A novel.] By Mrs Alexander [Mrs Alexander Hector, *née* Annie French]. 8vo.
London, 1890

TO David Garrick, Esq.; the petition of [the letter] I.; in behalf of herself and her sisters. [By John Hill, M.D.] 8vo. [Cushing's *Anon.* p. 674.]
London, 1759

TO farmers; a short account of the cause of the disease in corn, called by farmers, the blight, the mildew, and the rust. By the Right Hon. Sir Joseph Banks, Bart., K.B. Re-edited with marginal annotations . . . by an agriculturist, F.R.S. and F.S.A. [Sir Thomas Hanmer, Bart.]. 8vo. [*W.*]   London, 1807

TO H.R.H. Prince Edward of Wales ; a poem. By H. W. F. [Henry Francis Wilson]. 8vo. London, 1888

TO Her Most Excellent Maiestie Henrietta Maria, Queen of Great Britain, Dr L's [George Leyburn's] apologie. 4to. No title-page. [Gillow's *Bibl. Dict.*] [Douay, 1660]

TO Her Royal Highness the Princess of Wales, with the tragedy of Cato. Nov. 1714. To Sir Godfrey Kneller, on his picture of the King. [By Joseph Addison.] Fol. Pp. 9. [*Ashley Library.*] London, 1716

TO him that hath. [A novel.] By Ralph Connor [Charles W. Gordon, D.D.]. 8vo. [*Lond. Lib. Cat.*] London, 1922

TO his own master ; a novel. By Alan St Aubyn [Miss Frances Marshall]. 8vo. London, 1898

TO husbands, fathers, and brothers, especially those of the labouring classes ; being a warning against prevailing delusions. . . . By a brother [George Clement Boase]. 8vo. [Boase and Courtney's *Bibl. Corn.* i. 28.] Edinburgh, 1848

TO Lady Horatia Waldegrave on the death of the Duke of Ancaster. [Verses. By Horace Walpole.] 4to. Pp. 3. [*Brit. Mus.*] [Strawberry Hill, 1779]

TO London for the Jubilee [of Queen Victoria]. By Kit [Mrs Katherine B. Coleman]. 8vo. Pp. 154. Toronto, 1897

TO London then and now. 1837, 1897, etc. By Carl Sartor [Charles Taylor]. 8vo. Pp. 87. [*Brit. Mus.*] Partick, 1898

TO love and to be loved. By the author of *I've been thinking* [A. S. Roe]. 8vo. [*Brit. Mus.*] Ipswich, 1855

TO meet the day throughout the Christian year. [By Andrew K. H. Boyd, D.D.] 8vo. London, 1889

TO Mr E. L. on his Majesties dissolving the late parliament at Oxford, March 28, 1681. [By White Kennett, D.D.] [*Bodl.*] 1681

A broadside.

TO Mr Gray, on his Ode. [Verse. By David Garrick.] 4to. Pp. 2. [*Brit. Mus.*] [Strawberry Hill, 1757]

TO my Lady Morton on New-years-day, 1650 ; at the Louver in Paris. [By Edmund Waller.] Fol. S. sh. [*Bodl.*] London, 1661

TO my louynge brethren that is troublyd abowt the popishe aparell, two short and comfortable epistels. [By Anthony Gilby.] 12mo. [*Cumb. Univ. Lib.*] [London, 1566]

TO Parliament. The humble remonstrance of the Company of Stationers. [By Henry Parker.] 4to. [*Brit. Mus.*] London, 1643

TO Poland in war time ; a journey into the East. By Joseph Conrad [Joseph Conrad Korzeniowski]. 8vo. Private print, 1919

TO right the wrong. [A novel.] By Edna Lyall [Ada Ellen Bayly]. 8vo. London, 1894

TO Rome—or the Bible ? A reply to Cardinal Bourne. [By Charles A. Salmond, D.D.] 8vo. Pp. 32. London, 1918

TO set her free. [A novel.] By G. M. Robins [Mrs Louis Baillie-Reynolds]. 8vo. 2 vols. London, 1895

TO Sions lovers ; being a golden egge, to avoid infection ; or, a short step into the doctrine of laying on of hands. . . . [Signed : S. J. *i.e.* Sarah Jones.] 4to. [*Brit. Mus.*] London, 1644

TO Sir Godfrey Kneller at his country seat. [A poem. By Thomas Tickell.] Fol. Pp. 3. [*Brit. Mus.*] London, 1722

TO step aside is human. [A novel.] By Alan Saint Aubyn [Miss Frances Marshall]. 8vo. Pp. vi. 296. [*Brit. Mus.*] London, 1896

TO the agriculturists of North Northumberland ; letter second. By J. S. Donaldson, Esq. [J. S. Darling, W.S.]. 8vo. Berwick, 1836

TO the author [—— Shepherd of Bath chapel] of *Infant Baptism* : dated 1773. [By Mary Gillam.] 8vo. Pp. 4. [*Bodl.*] 1777

TO the beloved and chosen of God in the seed elected, particularly in London and elsewhere, who have seen the day of Christ, and received the message of peace and reconciliation in these last dayes of his glorious appearance. [By Edward Burrough.] 4to. Pp. 8. London, 1660

Signed : E. B.

TO the bitter end ; a novel. By the author of *Lady Audley's secret*, etc. [Mary Elizabeth Braddon, later Mrs John Maxwell]. 8vo. London, 1872

TO the citizens of the United States ; review of the address of the Free Trade Convention. [By Matthew Carey.] 8vo. [Sabin's *Dict.* iii. 342.] [1831]

TO the constituent members of Trinity Chapel. . . . [By John Murray.] 8vo. [Robertson's *Aberd. Bibl.*] [Aberdeen, 1824]

TO the electors of Great Britain ; serious reflections on a dissolution of Parliament. By an elector [Isaac Preston]. 8vo. [*Brit. Mus.*] London, 1784

TO the great and learned among Christians ; the petition of poor Christians . . . with questions . . . to Joseph Priestley. [By Thomas Witherby.] 8vo. [*Lond. Lib. Cat. Supp.*] London, 1793

TO the healing of the sea ; a novel. By Francis H. Hardy [Edward James Cattell]. 8vo. Pp. 301. London, 1900

TO the high and honourable Parliament of England now assembled at Westminster, the humble petitions, serious suggestions, and dutifull expostulations of some moderate and loyall gentlemen, yeomen, and freeholders of the Eastern Association, &c. [By Rev. Nathaniel Ward.] 4to. Pp. 31. [*N. and Q.* 23rd March 1867, p. 237.] 1648

TO the Hundred of Blything. [An address on the subject of the Poor-Law assessment. By J. Jermyn?] 8vo. [*Brit. Mus.*] [Southwold ? 1821 ?]

TO the inhabitants of Berry Pomeroy. [By Rev. W. B. Cosens, vicar of Berry Pomeroy.] [Davidson's *Bibl. Devon.* p. 108.] 1852

TO the Lord Provost of Glasgow, the two following letters are respectfully addressed, on the subject of the organ, which, in the month of August last, was introduced into St Andrews Church, Glasgow ; to which are added, Remarks on the Rev. James Begg's Treatise on the use of organs. [By Alexander Fleming, D.D.] 8vo. Pp. 81. Glasgow, 1808

TO the Lords of the British Parnassus ; a protest [in verse : signed J. H. D.]. By the author of *Albion's fall* [John H. Davies]. 8vo. London, 1885

TO the magistrates, the military, and the yeomanry of Ireland. [By Sir Richard Musgrave, Bart., M.P. for Lismore.] 8vo. [*W.*] Dublin, 1798
Signed : Camillus.

TO the majesty of the people, the Christian-political mouse-trap ! or the world reformed by order, truth and good humour, &c. [By P. Labellière.] 8vo. [*Brit. Mus.*] London, 1789

TO the memory of a lady lately deceased [Mrs Lyttelton, wife to George Lyttelton, Esq., one of the Lords of the Treasury] ; a monody. [By George, Lord Lyttelton.] Fol. Pp. 15. London, 1747

TO the memory of the most renowned Du-Vall ; a pindarick ode. By the author of *Hudibras* [Samuel Butler]. 4to. Pp. 13. [*Brit. Mus.*] London, 1671

TO the most illustrious, John, Earle of Lauderdale, &c. His Majesties High Commissioner for the kingdom of Scotland, His Grace, a congratulatory welcome of an heart-well-wishing quill : Hecatombe. [By Mungo Murray.] Fol. S. sh. [*Nat. Lib. of Scot.*] N.P., N.D.
Signed : M. M.

TO the musicioners, the harpers, the minstrels, the singers, the dancers, the persecutors ; from one who loved dancing and musick as his life . . . [Humphry Smith]. 4to. Pp. 8. [*Brit. Mus.*] London, 1658

TO the no less vertuous than engenious Mrs Mary More ; upon her sending Sir Thomas More's picture (of her own drawing) to the Long Gallery at the public schools in Oxon. R. W. [R. Whithall, of Merton College]. Fol. S. sh. N.P. 1674
Author's name in the Bodleian copy in the handwriting of Wood.

TO the parliament of the Commonwealth of England ; fifty nine particulars laid down for the regulating things, and the taking away of oppressing laws, and oppressors, and to ease the oppressed. By G. F. [George Fox]. 4to. Pp. 23. [Smith's *Cat. of Friends' Books*, i. 658.] London, 1659

TO the patrons of ecclesiastical livings. [By Browne Willis, LL.D.] 4to. Pp. 8. N.P., N.D.

TO the present authority or heads of the nation of England ; this among others in my testimony. . . . [Signed W. S. *i.e.* William Smith, of Besthorp.] 4to. [Smith's *Cat. of Friends' Books*.] London, 1664

TO the Proprietors of East India stock. [A letter, signed : Detector, *i.e.* Nathaniel Brassey Halhed.] 8vo. [*Brit. Mus.*] London, 1783

TO the Protector and Parliament of England. [By George Fox.] 4to. [Smith's *Cat. of Friends' Books*, i. 656.] London, 1659

TO the right high and mightie prince, Iames by the grace of God, King of great Britannie, France, and Irelande. . . . An humble supplication for toleration and libertie to enioy and observe the ordinances of Christ Iesvs. . . . [By Henry Jacob.] 4to. [*Pollard and Redgrave*.] N.P. 1609

TO the Right Honourable James Earl of Perth, Lord Drummond, and Stob-Hall, &c. Lord High Chancellor of his Majesties most ancient kingdom of Scotland ; the congratulatory welcome of an obliged quill. [By Mungo Murray.] Fol. S. sh.   N.P., N.D.

Signed : M. M.

TO the Right Honourable Mr Harley on his first appearing in publick, after the wound given him by Guiscard. [By Joseph Trapp.]   Fol. S. sh. [Watt's *Bibl. Brit.*]   London, 1711

Another edition in the same year bears the author's name.

TO the Right Reverend the Ld. Bishop of Carlisle ; containing a third vindication of Edward the Third ; letter III. [By Thomas Rymer.] 8vo.
London, 1706

TO the Right Reverend the Ld. Bishop of Carlisle ; containing an historical deduction of the alliances between France and Scotland : whereby the pretended old league with Charlemagne is disprov'd : and the true old league is produced and asserted. To which is added, a notable piece of church-history from her Majesty's archives ; never before publish'd ; letter II. [By Thomas Rymer.] 8vo.
London, N.D.

TO the Rockies and beyond ; a summer on the Union Pacific Railroad and its branches. By Alter Ego [Robert E. Strahorn]. 8vo. [*Camb. Univ. Lib.*]
Omaha, 1879

TO the saints in Sion, a song of praise ; together with some short hints, especially in the 2nd part, by way of prophecy, concerning the judgments of God upon the world for their sins, by famine, by the sword, by pestilence, and by fire from heaven : written at Carlisle in Cumberland, about 50 years ago, and now published by consent of the writer. T. S. [Thomas Story]. 8vo. [Smith's *Cat. of Friends' Books*, i. 61 ; ii. 637.]   London, 1740

TO the Society of the Beaux Esprits ; a Pindarik poem. By the author of the late *Satyr against woman* [Robert Gould]. 4to. Pp. 27. [*Brit. Mus.*]
London, 1687

TO the Society of the people called Quakers. [By John Payne.] Fol. [Smith's *Anti-Quak.* p. 353.]
N.P. 1793

Signed : Pacificus.

TO the sons of Gregffydh of Rhys ap Tewdwr, Prince of S. Wales ; a Pindaric ode by [J. Staunton] the author of *St Nicholas Hill.* 4to. Pp. 41. [Dobell's *Private Prints*, p. 171.]
N.P. 1869

TO the suffering seed of royalty, wheresoever tribulated upon the face of the whole earth ; the salutation of your brother under the oppressive yoak of bonds, in Rome-prison of mad-men. John [John Perrot]. 4to. [*D..N. B.* vol. 45, p. 27.]   London, 1661

TO the third generation. By Hope Daring [Miss Anna Johnson]. 8vo.
New York, 1901

TO the Wh[ig]s Nineteen queries, a fair and full answer, by an honest Torie ; purely for the publick good of his country. [By Francis Atterbury.] 12mo. Pp. 16.   London, 1710

TO thee Charls Stuart King of England, am I moved of the Lord to write ; and to thee it is the visitation of his love, through him whose travel hath been for thee, that thy soul may be saved in the day of the Lord, therefore hear that thy soul may live, and thy dayes be prolonged in the house of thy pilgrimage. [By George Bishop.] 4to. Pp. 8. [Smith's *Cat. of Friends' Books.*]
N.P. [1660]

The second half to "C. S. K." signed : J. P.

TO those who suffer ; a few points in theosophical teachings. By Aimée Blech [Lionel Dalsace]. Translated from the French by Fred. Rothwell. 8vo. Pp. 95. [*Brit. Mus.*]
London, 1908

TO trisect any given angle. [Signed : W. H. *i.e.* Wilfrid Hampson.] 4to. 4 parts. [*Brit. Mus.*]   [1912-13]

TOAST (the) ; an heroick poem in four books, written originally in Latin, by Frederick Scheffer : now done into English, and illustrated with notes and observations, by Peregrine O'Donald, Esq. [By William King, LL.D., Principal of St Mary Hall, Oxford.] 4to. Pp. 232. [Martin's *Cat.*]
Dublin printed ; London reprinted, 1736

TOBACCO (the) problem. By Meta Lander [Mrs Margaret Woods Lawrence]. 8vo. [Cushing's *Init. and Pseud.*]   Boston, 1886

TOBACCO (the) question ; physiologically . . . and statistically considered : reprinted from the *Dublin University Magazine.* [By Wm. Edward Armitage Axon.] 8vo. Pp. 13. [*Brit. Mus.*]
Manchester [1871]

TOBACCONIST (the); a comedy of two acts altered from Ben Johnson : acted at the Theatres Royal in the Haymarket and Edinburgh. [By Francis Gentleman.] 8vo. Pp. 4, 50. [Baker's *Biog. Dram.*]   London, 1771

TOBY ; his experiences and opinions. By Ascott R. Hope [Ascott Robert Hope Moncrieff]. 8vo. Pp. 151.
London, 1892

TOBY Tyler ; or, ten weeks with a circus. By James Otis [James Otis Kaler]. sq. 12mo.   New York, 1882

TOCSIN (the); with several minor poems. By a member of the Honourable Society of Lincoln's Inn [Daniel Cabanel]. 4to. [*Gent. Mag.* lxxxv. 1, 144 ; *Brit. Crit.* xxxix. 191.]   1811

TO-DAY ; a satire. By Ernestus [Bertie Ambrosse]. 8vo.   London, 1818

TO-DAY and yesterday ; a satire. [By Sir Henry Lytton Bulwer.] 4to. Pp. 29. [Martin's *Cat.*]   Chiswick, 1824

TO-DAY in Ireland. [By Eyre Evans Crow.] 12mo. 3 vols. [*Camb. Univ. Lib.*]   London, 1825

TO-DAY, to-morrow, and for ever. By Kirkby Burton [Nellie Robinson]. 8vo.   London, 1892

TODDLE Island ; being the diary of Lord Botsford. [A novel. By James Dennis Hird.] 8vo. Pp. 406. [*Brit. Mus.*]   London, 1894

TODDLES'S Highland tour ; being the strange adventures of Richard Toddles and Tom Stepwell during their journey in Scotland. [By Edmund Routledge.] 12mo.   London, 1864

TOILE (a) for two-legged foxes ; wherein their noisome properties, their hunting and vnkenelling, with the duties of the principall hunters and guardians of the spirituall vineyard is liuely discouered, for the comfort of all her Highnesse trustie and true-hearted subjects, and their encouragement against all Popish practises. By J. B. [J. Baxter], Preacher of the word of God. 8vo.   London, 1600

TOILERS in London. By John Law [Miss —— Harkness]. 8vo. [*Lond. Lib. Cat.*]   London, 1889

TOINETTE ; a tale of Southern life. By Henry Churton [Albion W. Tourgée]. 8vo. [Cushing's *Init. and Pseud.*]   New York, 1874

TOINETTE, and other stories. By Barbara Yichton [Lydia Farrington Krause]. 8vo. Pp. 137.
New York, 1897

TOKEN (a) for the children of New England ; or, some examples of children in whom the fear of God was remarkably budding. . . . [By Cotton Mather.] 12mo. Pp. 36. [G. Brinley's *Amer. Lib.*]   Boston, 1700

TOKEN (a) for youth ; containing several advices and directions to children and youth. . . . By J. J. [James Janeway]. 12mo. [*Brit. Mus.*]
London, 1709

TOKEN (a) of Christian love ; or, the fourth gift of Theophilus Philanthropos, student in Physick [Robert Poole, M.D.]. The second edition, greatly enlarg'd. 8vo. Pp. viii. 34. [*D. N. B.* vol. 46, p. 103.]   London, 1740

TOLANDO-PSEUDOLOGO-MASTIX ; or, a curry-comb for a lying coxcomb ; being an answer to a later piece of Mr Toland's, called Hypatia. [By John King, D.D., prebend of York.] 8vo. [*D. N. B.* vol. 31, p. 141.]   London, 1721

T—L—ND'S invitation to Dismal to dine with the Calves-head club ; imitated from Horace, Epist. 5. Lib. 1. [By Jonathan Swift.] Fol. S. sh. [*Camb. Hist. of Eng. Lit.*] N.P. [1712]
Dismal is Daniel Finch, Earl of Nottingham, who was nicknamed the Dismal Orator.

TOLD by the taffrail. By Sundowner [Herbert Tichborne]. 8vo.
London, 1901

TOLD by two. By Marie St Felix [Mrs Jerome Morley Lynch]. 8vo. [*Amer. Cat.*]   Chicago, 1901

TOLD in "Tatt's." By Nathaniel Gubbins [Edward Spencer]. 8vo. [*Who's Who in Lit.*]   London, 1903

TOLD in the twilight ; or, short stories for long evenings. By Sidney Daryl [Douglas Straight]. 8vo. [*Brit. Mus.*]
London, 1867

TOLD on the Pagoda ; tales of Burmah. By Mimosa [Mrs M. Chan-Foon]. 8vo. Pp. 136. [*Who's Who in Lit.*]
London, 1895

TOLERATION Act explained ; an answer to a legal argument on the Toleration Act, shewing that the court of quarter sessions have a judicial function as to the administration of oaths to persons offering themselves for qualification as Protestant dissenting ministers. By a barrister of the Temple [George Wharton Marriott, B.C.L.]. 8vo. Pp. 39. [*Bodl.* ; *Bibliographer*, vol. 5.]   London, 1812

TOLERATION and liberty of conscience considered and proved impractible, impossible, and, even in the opinion of dissenters, sinful and unlawful. [Attributed to Dr John Nalson.] 4to. [*Lincoln's Inn Lib.*]   London, 1685

TOLERATION defended ; or, the letter from a gentleman [James Ramsay] to a member of parliament concerning toleration considered ; with some observes on Mr Meldrum's sermon. [By George Brown, Episcopal Minister.] 4to. Pp. 24. [*Nat. Lib. of Scot.*]
Edinburgh, 1703

TOLERATION disapprov'd and condemn'd by the authority and convincing reasons of I. That wise and learned King James and his Privy-Councill. Anno Reg. 2do. II. The Honourable Commons assembled in this present parliament in their votes &c. Feb. 25. 1662. III. The Presbyterian ministers in the City of London met at Sion-Colledge Decemb. 18. 1645. IV. Twenty eminent divines. . . . [By William Assheton, D.D., of Brasen-Nose College.] 4to. Pp. 78. [*Bodl.*]
Oxford, 1670

TOLERATION discuss'd ; in two dialogues. I. Betwixt a conformist, and a non-conformist ; laying open the impiety, and danger of a general liberty. II. Betwixt a presbyterian, and an independent ; concluding, upon an impartial examination of their respective practises, and opinions, in favour of the independent. [By Sir Roger L'Estrange.] 8vo. [Darling's *Cyclop. Bibl.*] London, 1670

TOLERATION (a) in Scotland no breach of the Union. [By William Strahan, LL.D.] 4to. Pp. 8.
London, 1712

TOLERATION not to be abused ; or, a serious question soberly debated, and resolved upon presbyterian principles : viz. Whether it be adviseable, especially for the presbyterians, either in conscience or prudence, to take advantage from his Majesties late declaration, to deny or rebate their communion with our parochial congregations, and to gather themselves into distinct and separate churches? By one that loves truth and peace [Francis Fullwood, D.D.]. 4to. Pp. 35. [Orme's *Life of Baxter*, ii. 263.] London, 1672

TOLLERATION sent down from heaven to preach ; or, godly religious meetings, and true gospell preachers, praying and preaching, in other places then parish churches and chappels, justified by the highest powers ; and signally owned by testimonies from heaven, ought not to be condemned or forbiden, but rather allowed and tollerated by men upon earth. . . . Written in Glocestershire the begining of the 10th month, 1665. By R. F. [Richard Farnworth]. 4to. Pp. 37.
1665

TOLERATION with its principal objections fully confuted ; or, an answer to a book entitled, Sions groans for her distressed. . . . By H. S. [Henry Savage], D.D., chapl. to His Majesty. 4to. Pp. 81. London, 1663

TOLERATION'S fence removed, the Thoughts [by Sir A. Sinclair] concerning the present state of affairs in so far as they respect a toleration considered, and exposed. Plain dealing with the presbyterians as it is not found, so not to be expected from prelatical pamphleteers ; or, a vindication of a Letter from a gentleman to a member of parliament concerning toleration from all the cavils that have been advanced against it, and the wilfull mistakes about it. [By James Ramsay.] 4to. Pp. 36. [*Nat. Lib. of Scot.*] Edinburgh, 1703

TOLL (the) bar. By J. E. Buckrose [Mrs Falconer Jameson]. 8vo. Pp. 318.
London, 1907

TOLONDRON ; speeches to John Bowle, about his edition of *Don Quixote* : together with some account of Spanish literature. [By Joseph Baretti.] 8vo. [*Gent. Mag.* lviii. ii. 1029.] London, 1786

TOLTEC (the) cup ; a romance. . . . By Nym Crinkle [Andrew C. Wheeler]. 12mo. New York, 1890

TOM Brown at Oxford. By the author of *Tom Brown's school days* [Thomas Hughes, Q.C.]. 8vo. 3 vols.
Cambridge, 1861

TOM Benton's luck. By F. Benton Williams [Herbert Elliott Hamblen]. 8vo. New York, 1898

TOM Brown's school days. By an old boy [Thomas Hughes]. Third edition. 8vo. Pp. viii. 420. Cambridge, 1857

TOM Chips. By Ouno [T. M. Ashworth and another]. 8vo. [Cushing's *Init. and Pseud.*] Philadelphia, 1875

TOM Cladpole's journey to Lunnun, shewing the many difficulties he met with, and how he got safe home at last, told by himself, and written in pure Sussex doggerel by his Uncle Tim ; second edition, to which is added, Tom Cladpole's return, and a portrait of Tom in his travelling costume. [By Richard Tower.] 12mo. Pp. 38. [*W.*] Hailsham [1844 ?]

TOM Crib's Memorial to Congress ; with a preface, notes, and appendix. By one of the Fancy [Thomas Moore]. Second edition. 8vo. Pp. xxxi. 88.
London, 1819

TOM Cringle's letters on practical subjects, suggested by experiences in Bombay. [By William Walker.] 8vo. [*Brit. Mus.*]   Bombay, 1863

TOM Cringle's log. [A novel.] [By Michael Scott.] 8vo. [*Brit. Mus.*]
Paris, 1836

TOM Dawson ; a novel. By Florence Warden [Florence Alice Price, later Mrs George E. James]. 8vo. Pp. 392.
London, 1910

TOM Double return'd out of the country; or, the true picture of a modern Whig, set forth in a second dialogue between Mr Whiglove and Mr Double, at the Rummer tavern in Queen-Street. [By Charles Davenant, LL.D.] 8vo. Pp. 64. [Arber's *Term. Cat.* iii. 693.]
London, 1702

TOM Essence ; or, the modish wife : a comedy, as it is acted at the Dukes Theatre. [By Thomas Rawlins.] 4to. Pp. 67. [Baker's *Biog. Dram.*]
London, 1677

TOM Fox ; or, the revelations of a detective. [By John Bennett.] 8vo. [*Brit. Mus.*]   London, 1860

TOM Genuflex ; or, "life's little day." [A novel.] By Aunt Cherry [Mrs Jane Rowland]. 8vo. Pp. vii. 213.
Whitland, 1901

TOM Knight ; or, true honour from God only. By the author of *The wreck of the Vanguard* [Harriet Carson]. 8vo.
London [1877]

TOM Loseley ; boy. By "Cuthbert" [Rev. John Edwin Copus]. 8vo.
New York, 1906

TOM Moody's tales ; edited [or rather wholly written] by Mark Lemon. 8vo. [*Brit. Mus.*]   London, 1864

TOM of Bedlam's answer to his brother [Benjamin] Hoadly, St Peter's Poor parson, near the Exchange of principles. . . . [By Rev. Luke Milbourne.] 8vo. Pp. 16. [*Brit. Mus.*]   London, 1709

TOM of Bedlam's short answer to his Cozen Tom W—lst—n, occasioned by his late discourses on the miracles of our Saviour. [By Thomas Woolston himself.] 8vo. [*D. N. B.* vol. 62, p. 437.]   London, 1728

TOM Pippin's wedding ; a novel. By the author of *The fight at Dame Europa's school* [Henry William Pullen]. 8vo. Pp. 392.   London [1871]

TOM Punsibi's letter to Dean Swift. [By Thomas Sheridan, D.D.] Fol. S. sh. [*Brit. Mus.*]   [Dublin ?] 1727

TOM Raw, the Griffin ; a burlesque poem, in twelve cantos : illustrated by twenty-five engravings descriptive of the adventures of a cadet in the East India Company's service, from the period of his quitting England to his obtaining a staff situation in India. By a civilian and an officer on the Bengal establishment [Sir Charles D'Oyly]. 8vo. [*Gent. Mag.* Nov. 1845, p. 531.]   London, 1828

TOM Sawyer abroad ; Tom Sawyer, detective ; and other stories. By Mark Twain [Samuel Langhorne Clemens]. 8vo. Pp. 410.
New York, 1896

TOM Tel-troths message and his pens complaint ; a worke not unpleasant to be read nor unprofitable to be followed. Written by Jo. La. [John Lane], gent. 4to. [*Brit. Mus.*]   London, 1600

TOM Thumb ; a tragedy, as it is acted at the theatre in the Hay-market. [By Henry Fielding.] 8vo. Pp. 16. [Baker's *Biog. Dram.*]   London, 1730
The title of a later edition (1731) begins : "The tragedy of tragedies . . ."

TOM Tit ; his sayings and doings. . . . By Ismay Thorn [Edith Caroline Pollock]. 8vo. Pp. 176. [*Brit. Mus.*]
London [1884]

TOM Treddlehoyle's peep at t'Manchester Art Treasures Exhebishon e 1857. [By J. Rogers.] 12mo. [*N. and Q.* Feb. 1869, p. 169.]   Leeds, 1857

TOM, unlimited ; a story for children. By Martin Leach Warborough [Charles Blairfindie Grant Allen]. 8vo. [Courtney's *Secrets*, p. 106.]   London, 1897

TOM Winstone. By Martha James [Martha Claire Douglas]. 8vo.
Boston, 1902

TOMASO'S fortune ; and other stories. By Henry Seton Merriman [Hugh Stowell Scott]. 8vo. Pp. 306. [*Brit. Mus.*]   London, 1904

TOMB (the) of Alexander reviewed ; in eight letters to a friend. By Heraclides [Edward Daniel Clarke]. 8vo. [Cushing's *Init. and Pseud.*]
London, 1806

T O M B E S (the), monuments, and sepulchral inscriptions lately visible in St Paul's Cathedral and St Faith's under it, completely rendred in Latin and English, with several historical discourses on sundry persons intombed therein : a work never yet performed by any author old or new. By P. F. [Payne Fisher], student in antiquities. . . . 4to. [*Upcott.*]   London [1684]
Another edition reads "compiled by Major P. Fisher, student in antiquities," etc.

TOMBO-CHIQUI ; or, the American savage : a dramatic entertainment, in three acts. [By John Cleland.] 8vo. [Baker's *Biog. Dram.*]
London, 1758

TOM-BOY (a) ; or, playing with fire. By Arrah Leigh [Mrs H. C. Hoffmann]. 8vo. Pp. 171. New York [1889]

TOMMIAD (the) ; a biographical fancy, written about the year 1842 [in verse. By George James Finch-Hatton, Earl of Winchelsea and Nottingham]. 8vo. Pp. 56. [*Brit. Mus.*]
London, private print, 1882

TOMMIEBEG (the) shootings ; or, a moor in Scotland. By Thomas Jeans [Rev. Sir James Cameron Lees, D.D.]. 8vo. Edinburgh, 1860

TOMMY and Millie. By Fleeta [Kate W. Hamilton]. 8vo. [*Cushing's Init. and Pseud.*] Philadelphia, 1891

TOMMY Atkins of the Ramchunders. By "Nunquam" [Robert Blatchford]. 8vo. Pp. 284. London [1895]

TOMMY Big-eyes. By the author of *Betsy Lee*, etc. [Thomas Edward Brown]. 8vo. Douglas [1896]

TO-MORROW ? A novel. By Victoria Cross [Miss Vivien Cory]. 8vo. Pp. 308. London, 1910

TOM'S wife, and how he managed her. [By George D. Tallman.] 8vo.
New York, 1877

TON and antiquity ; a comedy, in two acts. [Dedication signed : T. S. *i.e.* Thomas Streatfield.] 8vo. Pp. 41. [*Brit. Mus.*] Oxford [1798]

TONGUE (the) ; or, essays on the uses and abuses of speech. . . . By the author of *The duty of children to their parents* [R. Wright]. 12mo. [*Brit. Mus.*] Wisbech [1805 ?]

TONGVE-COMBAT (a), lately happening betweene two English souldiers in the tilt-boat at Grauesend, the one going to serue the King of Spaine, the other to serue the States Generall of the Vnited Provinces ; wherein the cause, course, and continuance of those warres, is debated, and declared. [By Thomas Scott.] 4to. [*Pollard and Redgrave.*] London, 1623
Ascribed also to Henry Hexham. [*Brit. Mus.*]

TO-NIGHT at eight ; comedies and comediettas. By A. X. [Fannie Aymar Mathews]. 8vo.
Chicago, 1889

TONS of money ; a farce in three acts. By Will Evans and Valentine [Arthur Valentine Peachey]. 8vo. Pp. 85. [*Brit. Mus.*] London [1927]

TONY and his harp. By H. N. W. B. [Mrs Harriet Newell (Woods) Baker]. 8vo. [Cushing's *Init. and Pseud.*]
Boston, 1870

TONY and Puss ; translated from the French of P. J. Stahl [Pierre Jules Hetzel]. 4to. London, 1870

TONY Butler. [A novel. By Charles James Lever.] 8vo. 3 vols. [*Brit. Mus.*] Edinburgh, 1865
Originally published in *Blackwood's Magazine.*

TONY Lumpkin in town ; a farce. . . . [By John O'Keeffe, dramatist.] 8vo. [Baker's *Biog. Dram.*] London, 1778

TONY'S Chums ; a tale of a summer holiday. By May Wynne [Mabel Wynne Knowles]. 8vo.
London [1915]

TOO clever by half ; or, the Harroways. By the Mofussilite [John Lang]. 8vo. [*N. and Q.* Oct. 1869, p. 373.] 1853

TOO late repented. By Mrs Forrester [Mrs —— Bridges]. 8vo. Pp. 295.
Philadelphia, 1895

TOO much alone ; a novel. By F. G. Trafford [Mrs Charlotte E. L. Riddell, *née* Cowan]. 8vo. 3 vols. [*Brit. Mus.*] London, 1860

TOO soon ; a study of a girl's heart. By the author of *Patty*, etc. [Katherine S. Macquoid]. 8vo. 3 vols.
London, 1873

TOOTHED gearing ; a practical handbook. . . . By a Foreman Pattern Maker [Joseph Gregory Hornor]. 8vo. Pp. viii. 208. [*Brit. Mus.*] 1892
Preface signed : J. H.

TOPICKS in the laws of England ; containing media, apt for argument, and resolution of law cases : also an exposition of severall words, not touched by former glossaries. [By John Clayton, of the Inner Temple.] 8vo. Pp. 16, 138. [*Bodl.*]
London, 1646
Dedication signed : J. C.

TOPO ; a tale about English children in Italy. By G. E. Brunefille [Lady Colin Campbell, *née* Gertrude Elizabeth Blood]. 8vo. [*Brit. Mus.*]
London, 1878

TOPOGRAPH ; or, pedestrian's companion to the byeways within nine miles of Devonport and Plymouth, favourite walks of N. T. C. [Noel Thomas Carrington]. 12mo.
Devonport, 1833

TOPOGRAPHER (the) ; containing a variety of original articles, illustrative of the local history and antiquities of England, particularly on the history and description of ancient and eminent seats and stiles of architecture. . . . [By Sir Sam. E. Brydges and the Rev. Stebbing Shaw.] 8vo. 5 vols. [*Brit. Mus.*] London, 1789-1821

TOPOGRAPHER (the) ; numb. 1. for March 1821. [Edited by Sir T. Phillips.] 8vo. [*W.*]
[Middle Hill], private print, 1821

TOPOGRAPHICAL (a) account of Tattershall, in the county of Lincoln ; collected from the best authorities. [By G. Weir. The second edition.] 8vo. Pp. 23. Horncastle, 1813

TOPOGRAPHICAL (a) and historical account of Hayling Island, Hants. [By Richard Scott.] 4to. [J. P. Anderson's *Brit. Topography.*]
Havant, 1826

TOPOGRAPHICAL (a) and historical account of Linlithgowshire. By the late John Penny. [Really by George Chalmers.] 12mo. Pp. xi. 223.
Edinburgh, 1831
Copied, almost verbatim, from *Chalmers' Caledonia*, and published as the work of Penny by J. Maidment, who added a preface and appendix.

TOPOGRAPHICAL (a) and historical account of the city and county of Norwich, its antiquities and modern improvements. . . . [By John Stacy.] 8vo. [*Brit. Mus.*] Norwich, 1819

TOPOGRAPHICAL (a) and historical description of the County of Suffolk. . . . [By John Kirby.] 8vo. [*Brit. Mus.*] Woodbridge, 1829
Other editions have the author's name and the title " The Suffolk traveller."

TOPOGRAPHICAL (a) description of the State of Ohio, Indiana Territory, and Louisiana. By a late officer in the U.S. Army [Jervase Cutler]. 8vo. [Cushing's *Init. and Pseud.*]
Boston, 1812

TOPOGRAPHICAL (the) dictionary of England and Wales. [By Thomas Dugdale.] 8vo. Nos. 1-4. [Corns and Sparke's *Bibl. of Unf. Books*, p. 74.]
London [1860]
This is really " Dugdale's England and Wales delineated : edited by C. L. Blanchard," but with different title-pages.

TOPOGRAPHICAL (a) history, and description of Bawtry and Thorne, with the villages adjacent. By W. P. [William Peck]. 4to. 2 parts. [*Brit. Mus.*] Doncaster, 1813

TOPOGRAPHICAL (a) history of Stonyhurst and Mytton. . . . By an old Antiquarian [Peter Armstrong Whittle]. 8vo. [Sparke's *Bibl. Bolt.* p. 148.] Preston, 1821-37

TOPOGRAPHICAL memoranda of the ward of Farringdon without. By an antiquary [—— Underhill]. 4to.
London [1850 ?]

TOPOGRAPHICAL (a), statistical, and historical account of the borough of Preston . . . including a correct copy of the charter granted in the reign of Charles II. . . . By Marmaduke Tulket [Peter A. Whittle]. 12mo. 2 vols. [Sparke's *Bibl. Bolt.* p. 148.]
Preston, 1821-37

TOPOGRAPHY (the) of all the known vineyards, containing a description of the kind and quality of their products and a classification. . . . [An abridged translation of " Topographie de tous les vignolles connus," by André Jullien.] 12mo. Pp. xvi. 248. [*Brit. Mus.*]
London, 1824

TOPSAIL-SHEET blocks; or, the naval foundling. By "The old sailor ": author of *Tough yarns*, etc. [Matthew Henry Barker]. 12mo. 3 vols.
London, 1838

TOPSY turvy ; with anecdotes and observations illustrative of leading characters in the present government of France. By the editor of *Salmagundi* [Rev. George Huddesford, M.A.]. 8vo. Pp. 56. London, 1793

TOR (the) hill. By the author of *Brambletye House*, etc. [Horace Smith]. 12mo. 3 vols. [Green's *Bibl. Somers.* iii. 320.] London, 1826

TORIES' (the) "Refuge for the destitute," or political advertiser . . . and The House of reform that Jack built [in verse. By William Hone ?]. Third edition. 8vo. Pp. 24. [*Brit. Mus.*]
London [1832]
For the first edition, see " The house of reform that Jack built . . ."

TORIO-WHIGGO-MACHIA ; or, the battle of the Whigs and Tories : a political satire, in four cantos. [By Benjamin Cole.] 4to. London, 1806

TORMENTOR (the). [A novel.] By Benjamin Swift [William Romaine Paterson]. 8vo. Pp. 296. [*Brit. Mus.*]
London, 1906

TORN (a) leaf from a lost life. [A poem. By J. Smith.] 8vo.
Birmingham, 1864

TORN sails. [A novel.] By Allen Raine [Mrs Beynon Puddicombe, *née* Anne Adaliza Evans]. 8vo.
London, 1900

TORQUATO Tasso, his Jerusalem delivered, Englished in octaves by Hugh Bent [George Atty]. 12mo. 2 vols. London, 1856

TORQUAY. By John Presland [Gladys Skelton]. 8vo. Pp. vii. 190. [*Brit. Mus.*] London, 1920

TORRINGTON Hall; being an account of two days, in the autumn of the year 1844, passed at that magnificent and philosophically conducted establishment for the insane. By Arthur Wallbridge, author of *Jest and earnest*, etc. [A. W. Lunn]. 8vo. Pp. x. 135. [*Bodl.*] London, 1845

TORY (a) plot; a story of the attempt to kill General Washington in 1776. By James Otis [James Otis Kaler]. 8vo. Pp. iv. 227. New York [1898]

TORY (the) Quaker; or, Aminadab's new vision in the fields, after a cup of the creature. [By Edward Ward.] 8vo. Pp. 24. [Smith's *Anti-Quak.* p. 442.] London, 1717

TOTALL (the) and finall demands already made by, and to be expected from, the agitators and army; vpon the concession whereof they will rest fully satisfied. . . . [By William Prynne.] 4to. Pp. 8. London, 1647

TOTALL (the) svmme; or, no danger of damnation vnto Roman Catholiques for any errour in faith : nor any hope of saluation for any sectary vvhatso-euer that doth knovvingly oppose the doctrine of the Roman Church. This is proued by the confessions, and sayings of M. William Chillingvvorth his booke. [By John Floyd, S. J.] 4to. Pp. 104. [Oliver's *Collections*; Sommervogel's *Dictionnaire*.] [St Omer] 1639

T O T 'S tales. By Cue [A. Leonard Summers]. 8vo. Pp. 30. [*Brit. Mus.*] London, 1917

TOTTIE'S trial. By "Kay Spen" [Henry Courtney Selous]. 8vo. London, 1872

TOUCH (the) of sorrow. [A novel.] By Edith Hamlet [Hon. Mrs Alfred Lyttleton]. 8vo. Pp. 323. [*Brit. Mus.*] London, 1896

TOUCHING the subject of supremacy in causes ecclesiastical ; diatriba quædam Oxoniensis cujusdam : tending to peace and setling, by shewing how the powers civil and ecclesiastical may act in their own sphæres without incroachment on one another. [By John Geree, M.A.] 4to. Pp. 8. [*Bodl.*] 1647

TOUCHSTONE (the), exhibiting Universalism and Restorationism as they are, moral contraries. By a consistent Restorationist [Adin Ballou]. 12mo. Pp. 32. Providence, R.I., 1837

TOUCHSTONE (a) for a communicant. . . . By E. F. [Edward Fisher]. 12mo. [*D. N. B.* vol. 19, p. 56.] London, 1647

TOUCH-STONE (a) for physick, directing by evident marks and characters to such medicines, as without purgers, vomiters, bleedings, issues, minerals, or any other disturbers of nature, may be securely trusted for cure in all extreamities. . . . [By William Walwyn.] 12mo. Pp. 110. [*W.*] London, 1667 "To the Reader" signed : W. W.

TOUCHSTONE (the) of peril; a tale of the Indian Mutiny. By D. H. Thomas [R. E. Forest]. 8vo. 2 vols. [*Calc. Imp. Lib.*] London, 1886

TOUCH-STONE (the) of the new religion; or, sixty assertions of Protestants try'd by their own rule of Scripture alone, and condemn'd by clear and express texts of their own Bible. [By Matthew Killison, D.D., re-edited by Richard Challoner, Bishop of Debra.] 12mo. [*D. N. B.* vol. 30, p. 345.] London, 1748

TOUCHSTONE (the) of the Reformed Gospel ; wherein sundry chief heads and tenents of the Protestant doctrine . . . are briefly refuted. . . . [By Matthew Kellison]. 12mo. Pp. 140, 92. [*D. N. B.* vol. 30, p. 345.] St Omers, 1652

TOUCHSTONE (a) ; or, a perfect tryal by the scriptures, of all priests, bishops and ministers who have called themselves the ministers of the gospel, whose time and day hath been in the last ages past, or rather in the night of apostacy ; unto which is annexed, Women's speaking justified. [By Margaret Fell, afterwards Fox.] 4to. [*Brit. Mus.*] London, 1667 Signed : M. F.

TOUCH-STONE (the) ; or, historical, critical, political, philosophical, and theological essays on the reigning diversions of the town : designed for the improvement of all authors, spectators, and actors of operas, plays, and masquerades. . . . By a person of some taste and quality [James Ralph]. With a preface, giving some account of the author and the work. 12mo. London, 1728 The epistle dedicatory is signed : A. Primcock, pseud. of J. Ralph.

TOUCHSTONE [*i.e.* —— Herring] to the people of the United States on the Choice of a President. 8vo.
New York, 1812

TOUCH-STONE (a) to try whether we be Christians in name onely, or Christians in deed ; or, the character of a true believer. By R. Y. [Richard Younge] of Roxwell, in Essex. 4to. [*Brit. Mus.*[London, 1648

TOUCH-STONE (a) ; whereby the Protestant religion, as it stands at this day in England may be tryed : that in the light of Christ, people of all sorts may see the degeneration, and great apostacy, which these last dayes and perillous times have produced. . . . By a friend to all that love pure religion, and follow after righteousness [John Collins]. 4to. Pp. 9, 18. [*Bodl.*]
London, 1660
Signed : J. C.

TOUGH yarns ; a series of naval tales and sketches to please all hands, from the swabs in the shoulders down to the swabs in the head. By the old sailor, author of *Greenwich Hospital*, etc. [Matthew Henry Barker]. Illustrated by George Cruikshank. 8vo. Pp. 351. [*Brit. Mus.*] London, 1835

TOUN'S (the) Great Bible ; or, a brief account of the gift of Gilbert Hervie . . . of Aberdein to the Gild Brethren's Hospital. [By John Philip Edmond.] 8vo. Pp. 10.   Aberdeen, 1885
Signed : J. P. E.

TOUR (a) around New York. By Felix Oldboy [Rev. John Flavel Mines]. 8vo.   Harper, 1893

TOUR (a) in Brazil, and on the River Plate ; with notes on sheep-farming. By T. D. [T. Dillon]. 8vo. [*Birm. Free Lib.*]   1867

TOUR (a) in Connaught ; comprising sketches of Clonmacnoise, Joyce country, and Achill. By the author of *Sketches in Ireland* [Rev. Caesar Otway]. 12mo. [Anderson's *Brit. Topog.*]   Dublin, 1839
Wrongly attributed to Thomas Newte. This work was afterwards expanded, with another title, " Prospects and observations on a tour . . ."

TOUR (a) in England and Scotland, in 1785. By an English gentleman [William Thomson, LL.D.]. 8vo. Pp. x. 367. [*D. N. B.* vol. 56, p. 275.]
London, 1788

TOUR in England, Ireland, and France, in the years 1828 & 1829 ; with remarks on the manners and customs of the inhabitants, and anecdotes of distinguished public characters : in a series of letters. By a German prince [Hermann Ludwig Heinrich, Prinz von Pückler-Muskau]. Translated by Sarah Austin. 8vo. 4 vols. London, 1832
Vols. III. and IV. have the following title : Tour in Germany, Holland and England, in the years 1826, 1827, & 1828, etc. This work is, strictly speaking, not anonymous, as the translator in his preface states that rumour has generally ascribed it to Prince Pückler-Muskau. It is a translation of a part only of the original *Briefe eines Verstorbenen.*

TOUR (a) in France and Italy, made by an English gentleman [J. Clenchy], 1675. 4to. [*Brit. Mus.*]
London, 1676

TOUR (a) in France during 1802. [By Mrs Frances Elizabeth King.] 12mo. Pp. 91. [*Brit. Mus.*] London, 1804

TOUR (a) in Germany, and some of the Southern provinces of the Austrian empire, in the years 1820, 1821, 1822. [By John Russell.] 12mo. 2 vols.
Edinburgh, 1824
A new edition, published at Edinburgh in 1828, has the author's name.

TOUR in Holland in the year 1819 [with some notes of a second tour in 1822-23. By Lady —— Murray ?]. 12mo. [*Brit. Mus.*]   London [1825 ?]

TOUR (a) in Ireland in 1813 and 1814 ; with an appendix, written in 1816, on another visit to that Island. By an Englishman [John Gough]. 8vo. [*Brit. Mus.*]   Dublin [1817]

TOUR (a) in Ireland in 1775 ; with a map, and a view of the salmon-leap at Ballyshannon. [By Richard Twiss.] 8vo. Pp. 204. [*Bodl.*] London, 1776

TOUR (a) in pursuit of ideas ; being a picturesque view of all the Yarmouth Public-houses : a poem. By Dr Sigma [David Service]. 8vo. Pp. 27.
Yarmouth, 1822

TOUR (a) in quest of genealogy, through several parts of Wales, Somersetshire, and Wiltshire, in a series of letters to a friend in Dublin ; interspersed with a description of Stourhead and Stonehenge ; together with various anecdotes, and curious fragments from a manuscript collection ascribed to Shakespeare. By a barrister [Richard Fenton]. 8vo. Pp. iv. 338. [*D. N. B.* vol. 18, p. 327 ; *Gent. Mag.* xci. ii. 644.]
London, 1811

TOUR (a) in 1787, from London, to the Western Highlands of Scotland; including excursions to the lakes of Westmoreland and Cumberland, with minute descriptions of the principal seats, castles, ruins, &c. throughout the tour. [By Rev. Stebbing Shaw, Rector of Hartshorne.] 12mo. Pp. ix. 303. [*Gent. Mag.* lxxiii. i. 10 ; lviii. ii. 805 ; *Mon. Rev.* lxxix. 537.]
London, 1787

TOUR (a) in Tartan-Land. By Cuthbert Bede, author of *Glencreggan ; or, a Highland home in Cantire*, etc. [Edward Bradley]. 8vo. Pp. xv. 430.
London, 1863

TOUR (a) in Teesdale ; including Rokeby and its environs. [By Richard Garland.] Second edition. 12mo. Pp. 96. [Boyne's *Yorkshire Lib.* p. 188-9.] York, 1813

TOUR (a) in the Isle of Wight, in the autumn of 1820. [By the Countess of Blessington.] 12mo. Pp. 84. [Martin's *Cat.*] London, 1822

TOUR (a) in Wales, and through several counties of England, including both the Universities, performed in the summer of 1805. [By William F. Mavor, LL.D.] 8vo. [*D. N. B.* vol. 37, p. 109.] London, 1806

TOUR (a) in Wales, 1773. [By Thomas Pennant.] 8vo. Dublin, 1779
Other editions bear the author's name.

TOUR (a) in Zealand, in 1802 ; with an historical sketch of the Battle of Copenhagen. [By Andreas Anderson.] 8vo. [*Brit. Mus.*]
London, 1805

TOUR (the) of a Cathedral organist. [Signed : J. E. R. *i.e.* John Elliott Richardson, of Salisbury.] 8vo. [*Brit. Mus.*] London, 1870

TOUR of a German artist [Johann David Passavant] in England. [Translated by Lady Elizabeth Eastlake.] 8vo. 2 vols. London, 1836

TOUR (a) of Asia ; the most popular modern voyages and travels. . . . By T. Clark [John Galt]. Second edition. 12mo. Pp. vi. 402. [*D. N. B.* vol. 20, p. 390 ; *Brit. Mus.*] London [1820 ?]

TOUR (the) of Dr Prosody, in search of the antique and picturesque, through Scotland, the Hebrides, the Orkney and Shetland Isles. [By William Combe.] 8vo. [*Brit. Mus.*]
London, 1821

TOUR (the) of Doctor Syntax, in search of the picturesque ; a poem. [By William Combe.] 8vo. Pp. iii. 275.
[London, 1812]

TOUR (the) of His Royal Highness the Prince of Wales through British America and the United States. By a British Canadian [Henry James Morgan]. 8vo. Montreal, 1860

TOUR (the) of Holland, Dutch Brabant, the Austrian Netherlands and part of France ; in which is included a description of Paris. . . . [By Harry Peckham.] 8vo. London, 1772
Later editions have the author's name and the title, "A tour through Holland . . ."

TOUR (the) of the Don ; a series of extempore sketches made during a pedestrian ramble along the bank of that river, and its principal tributaries : originally published in the *Sheffield Mercury*, during the year 1836. [By John Holland, of Sheffield.] 12mo. 2 vols. [Boyne's *Yorkshire Lib.* p. 108.]
London, 1837

TOUR (the) of Valentine. [By Rev. Joseph Holden Pott, M.A.] 8vo. [Nichols' *Lit. Anec.* ix. 73 ; *Mon. Rev.* lxxv. 315.] London, 1786

TOUR (a) on the banks of the Thames, from London to Oxford in 1829, by a pedestrian [A. Walton, or R. Walton]. 12mo. London, 1834

TOUR (a) on the prairies. By the author of *The sketch-book* [Washington Irving]. 8vo. New York, 1835

TOUR (a) round the world. By an ex-Lord Provost of Glasgow [Sir John Ure]. 8vo. [*Brit. Mus.*]
Glasgow, 1885

TOUR (a) through Ireland ; in several entertaining letters. . . . By two English gentlemen [—— Chetwood]. 8vo. Pp. 246. London, 1748

TOUR through Ireland in 1779. [By Philip Luckombe.] 12mo. [*N. and Q.* 10th April 1858, p. 308.] 1780

TOUR through Ireland, particularly the interior & least known parts : containing an accurate view of the parties, politics, and improvements in the different Provinces ; . . . By the Rev. James Hall, A.M. [William Thomson, LL.D.]. 8vo. 2 vols.
London, 1813

TOUR (a) through Normandy, described in a letter to a friend. [By Andrew Coltee Ducarel, D.C.L.] 4to. [*D. N. B.* vol. 16, p. 85.] London, 1754

TOUR (a) through part of Belgium and the Rhenish provinces. [By John Henry Manners, Duke of Rutland.] 4to. Pp. 131. [*Bodl.*] London, 1822

TOUR (a) through part of France, containing a description of Paris, Cherbourg, and Ermenonville; with a rhapsody, composed at the tomb of Rousseau: in a series of letters. [By Right Hon. John Charles Villiers.] 8vo. Pp. viii. 323. [*Biog. Dict.* 1816.]
London, 1789

TOUR (a) through part of Virginia in the summer of 1808; also some account of the Azores. [By J. Caldwell.] 8vo. Pp. 63. [Rich's *Bibl. Amer.* ii. 51.]
Belfast, 1810

TOUR through parts of England, Scotland and Wales in 1778; in a series of letters. [By Richard Joseph Sulivan.] [Watt's *Bibl. Brit.*]
London, 1780
The second edition bears the author's name.

TOUR through parts of the United States and Canada. By a British subject [—— Beaufoy]. 8vo. Pp. viii. 141. [Rich's *Bibl. Amer.*]
London, 1828

TOUR (a) through the Island of Rügen, in the Baltic, 1805. . . . By a temporary inhabitant [Johann Jakob Grümbke]. 8vo. Pp. 64. [Cushing's *Init. and Pseud.*]
London, 1807

TOUR (a) through the Isle of Thanet, and some other parts of East Kent, including a particular description of the churches in that extensive district, and copies of monumental inscriptions, etc. [By Zachariah Cozens.] 4to. Pp. 507. [Smith's *Bibl. Cant.* p. 315; *Upcott*, i. 437.]
London, 1793

TOUR (a) through the Land of the West [United States]. . . . [By N. Smith.] 8vo. [*Birm. Ref. Lib.*] 1894

TOUR (a) through the South of England, Wales, and part of Ireland, made during the summer of 1791. [By Edward Daniel Clarke, LL.D.] 8vo. Pp. xxx. 403. [Mayo's *Bibl. Dors.* p. 9.]
London, 1793

TOUR (a) through the upper provinces of Hindostan; comprising a period between the years 1804 and 1814: with remarks and authentic anecdotes: to which is annexed, a guide up the river Ganges, with a map from the source to the mouth. By A. D. [Mrs A. Deare]. 8vo. [*Brit. Mus.*]
London, 1823

TOUR (a) thro' the whole island of Great Britain, divided into circuits or journies: giving a particular and diverting account of whatever is curious and worth observation. . . . By a gentleman [Daniel Defoe]. 8vo. [Wilson's *Life of Defoe.*] London, 1724
Vol. II. 1724; Vol. III. 1727. Continued by William Richardson.

TOUR (a) through Upper and Lower Canada. By a citizen of the United States [Rev. John Cosens Ogden]. 8vo. [Cushing's *Init. and Pseud.*]
Litchfield, 1799

TOUR (a) to Cheltenham Spa; or, Gloucestershire display'd: containing an account of Cheltenham, its mineral water, public walks, amusements, environs, etc. . . . [By Simeon Moreau.] 12mo. Pp. 173. [*Brit. Mus.*]
Bath, 1783

TOUR to La Vendée in 1835, interspersed with novel and interesting remarks addressed to the judgement, not the prejudices of mankind. [By Alex. Marjoribanks.] 12mo. 1836
An edition of 1837 bears the author's name and the title, "Tour from modern Athens . . ."

TOUR (a) to the caves in the environs of Ingleborough and Settle, in the West Riding of Yorkshire . . . in a letter to a friend. [By Rev. John Hutton, vicar of Burton in Kendal.] The second edition, with large additions. 8vo. Pp. 100. [Boyne's *Yorkshire Lib.* p. 125.]
London, 1781

TOUR (a) to the Rhine, with antiquarian and other notices. [By William George Meredith.] 8vo. Pp. 106. [*Martin's Cat.*]
London, 1825

TOUR (a) to the sepulchres of Etruria. By Prosper E. Biardot [Miss Elizabeth Caroline Gray]. 8vo. [M. L. Solon's *Ceramic literature*, p. 30.]
[1840?]
The second edition, 1841, has the author's name.

TOUR (a) twenty years ago. By "Umbra" [Charles Cavendish Clifford, M.P.]. 8vo. [Cushing's *Init. and Pseud.*]
London, 1863

TOURIST'S (the) assistant; a popular guide to watering places in England and Wales, with a railway key to the Paris exhibition. By Frank Foster, author of *Number one; or, the way of the world*, etc. [Daniel Puseley]. First annual issue. 8vo. Pp. 234.
London, 1867

TOURIST'S (the) companion for Penzance and its neighbourhood. [By John H. Hancock.] 12mo. Pp. 24. [Boase and Courtney's *Bibl. Corn.*]
Penzance, 1869

TOURIST'S (the) guide ; being a concise history and description of Ripon, Studley Royal, Fountains Abbey, Markenfield, Brimham Rocks, Hackfall, and Newby Hall. [By John Richard Walbran.] 12mo. Pp. 106. [Boyne's *Yorkshire Lib.* p. 138.]
Ripon, 1837
A third edition appeared in 1841, under the title of "The Harrogate visitor's pictorial pocket guide to Ripon, Studley, &c." In 1844, a similar pictorial guide was published, with the author's name.

TOURIST'S (a) guide to Lucknow. . . . By one of the beleaguered garrison [Edward H. Hilton]. Fifth edition. 8vo. [*Calc. Imp. Lib.*]
Lucknow, 1905
TOURIST'S guide to Penzance, St Michael's Mount, Land's End. . . . By J. H. H. [John H. Hancock]. 12mo. [*Brit. Mus.*]　　Penzance [1875]
A later edition of the "New guide to Penzance . . ."

TOURMALIN'S time cheques ; a farcical extravaganza. By F. Anstey [Thomas Anstey Guthrie]. 8vo. Pp. ii. 172. [*Brit. Mus.*]　　Bristol [1891]

TOURNAMENT (the) ; a poem. [By Rev. Luke Aylmer Conolly, B.A., T.C.D.] 12mo. [O'Donoghue's *Poets of Ireland.*]　　Belfast, 1832

TOURNAY ; or, Alaster of Kempencairn. By the author of *The fire-eater* [James Wilson]. 12mo. Pp. 471.
London, 1824
TOURNEY (the) of the thirty-six ; an idyll of the King. [A mock-heroic poem on the election of the first Town Council of Cheltenham. By James Batten Winterbotham.] 8vo. Pp. 4. [Hyett and Bazeley's *Gloucest. Lit.*]
[Cheltenham] 1876
TOWARDS a new architecture. By Le Corbusier [Charles Edouard Jeanneret]. Translated . . . by Frederick Etchells. 8vo. Pp. 289. [*Brit. Mus.*]
London, 1927
TOWARDS democracy. [By Edward Carpenter, M.A.] 8vo. [*Brit. Mus.*]
Manchester, 1883
TOWARDS the sunset ; teachings after thirty years. By the author of *Recreations of a country parson* [Andrew K. H. Boyd, D.D.]. 8vo. [*D. N. B.* First *Supp.* vol. 1, p. 245.]
London, 1883
TOWARDS Utopia ; being speculations in social evolution. By a Free Lance [Frank Hill Perry Coste]. 8vo. Pp. vi. 252. [*Brit. Mus.*]　London, 1894

VOL. VI.

TOWER (the). By "Watchman" [Warwick Draper]. 8vo. Pp. 144.
London, 1918
A later edition (1919) has the author's name and a different title, "The new Britain."

TOWER (the) bridge : an imperial question. By "Aquarius" [Lowis d'Aguilar Jackson]. 8vo. [*Brit. Mus.*]
London, 1878
TOWER (the) menagerie ; natural history of animals in that establishment. [By Edward Turner Bennett.] 8vo. [*D. N. B.* vol. 4, p. 241.]
London, 1829
TOWER (the) of Pereemont, and Marianne. By George Sand [Madame A. L. A. Dudevant]. Translated. 8vo.
London, 1881
TOWER (the) of Taddeo. [A novel.] By "Ouida" [Louise de la Ramée]. 8vo. Pp. 288.　　London, 1899
TOWER (the) of the Hawk ; some passages in the history of the House of Hapsburg. By the author of *Chillon* [Miss Jane Louisa Willyams]. 8vo. Pp. xii. 484. [*Brit. Mus.*]
London, 1871
TOWER (the) of the Mirrors ; and other essays on the spirit of places. By Vernon Lee [Violet Paget]. 8vo. Pp. 254.　　London, 1914
TOWN and country. [By Lord Francis Egerton, afterwards Earl of Ellesmere.] 8vo. Pp. 16.
London, private print, 1836
TOWN and country sketches. By Andrew Halliday [Andrew Halliday Duff]. 8vo. [Cushing's *Init. and Pseud.*]
London, 1866
TOWN and forest. By the author of *Mary Powell* [Anne Manning, later Mrs Rathbone]. 12mo. Pp. iv. 286. [*Brit. Mus.*]　　London, 1860
TOWN (a) eclogue. [By Rev. George William Auriol Hay Drummond.] 8vo. Pp. 33. [*Brit. Mus.*]　Edinburgh, 1804
TOWN fashions ; or, modern manners delineated, a satirical dialogue ; with James and Mary, a rural tale. [By Hector Macneill.] 12mo. [Rogers' *Mod. Scot. Minst.* i. 79.]
Edinburgh, 1810
TOWN (a) in its truest glory ; a discourse wherein the state of all our towns is considered. [By Cotton Mather.] 12mo. Pp. 58. [G. Brinley's *Amer. Lib.*]　　Boston, 1712
TOWN (the) lady and the country lass. [A novel.] By Florence Warden [Florence Alice Price, later Mrs George E. James]. 8vo. Pp. 316.
London, 1900

TOWN life. By the author of *Liverpool life* and *Rambles in the Lake district* [Hugh Shimmin, journalist]. 8vo. [*Brit. Mus.*] Liverpool, 1858

TOWN mice in the country; a story of holiday adventure. By M. E. Francis [Mrs Mary E. Blundell, *née* Sweetman]. 8vo. Pp. 160.
London, 1894

TOWN (the) on the hill. [A novel.] By Mrs George Norman [Mrs George Blount]. 8vo. Pp. 288. [*Brit. Mus.*]
London [1927]

TOWN (a) romance. By Carl Swerdna [Catherine March]. [*Brit. Mus.*]
London [1890 ?]

TOWN Talk, the Fish Pool, the Plebeian, the Old Whig, the Spinster, etc. By the author of *The Tatler, Spectator*, and *Guardian* [Joseph Addison]; with notes and illustrations. 12mo. [*T. C. D. Lib.*] Dublin, 1790

TOWNS and types. By Mark Allerton [William Ernest Cameron, LL.B.]. 8vo. London, 1905

TOWNSMAN'S (the) farm. By "Home Counties" [John W. Robertson Scott]. 8vo. Pp. xiv. 304. [*Brit. Mus.*]
London, 1908

TOWNSHIP (the) of Birkenhead. [By P. Sulley.] 8vo. Pp. 352. [*Brit. Mus.*]
[Birkenhead, 1893]

TOXAR; a novel. By the author of *Thoth* [Prof. John Shield Nicholson, LL.D.]. 8vo. [*Brit. Mus.*]
London, 1892

TOXIN; a sketch. By "Ouida" [Louise de la Ramée]. 8vo. Pp. 184. [*Lit. Year Book.*] London, 1895

TOXOPHILUS; the schole of shootinge conteyned in two bookes; to all gentlemen and yomen of Englande, pleasaunte for theyr pastyme to rede and profitable for theyr use to folow, both in war and peace. [By Roger Ascham.] 4to. B. L. Londini, 1545

TRACED and tracked; or, memories of a city detective. By James M'Govan [William C. Honeyman]. 8vo.
Edinburgh, 1884

TRACINGS of men and things. By Trevelyan Turnham, Esq. [James Flamank]. 8vo. Pp. 265. [*Cushing's Init. and Pseud.*] London, 1854

TRACK (the) of a storm. By Owen Hall [James Davis, B.A., dramatist]. 8vo. Pp. 288. London, 1895

TRACKED and taken; detective sketches. By Dick Donovan [Joyce E. P. Muddock]. 8vo. Pp. 205.
London, 1890

TRACKED down; a novel. By Headon Hill [Francis E. Grainger]. 8vo.
London, 1902

TRACKED to doom; the story of a mystery and its unravelling. By Dick Donovan [Joyce E. P. Muddock]. 8vo. Pp. vi. 250. London, 1892

TRACKS we tread. [A novel.] By G. B. Lancaster [Miss Edith Lyttleton]. 8vo. Pp. 310. London, 1907

TRACT (a) against the high rate of usurie; presented to the High Court of Parliament, A.D. 1623. [By Sir Thomas Culpeper, Kt.] 4to. M'Culloch's *Lit. of Pol. Econ.* p. 249.]
London, 1623

TRACT (a) concerning schisme and schismatiques; wherein, is briefly discovered the originall causes of all schisme. Written by a learned and judicious divine. Together, with certain animadversions upon some passages thereof. [By John Hales.] 4to. Pp. 33. [*D. N. B.* vol. 24, p. 32.]
Oxford, 1642

TRACT entitled True and faithful relation of a worthy discourse, between Colonel John Hampden and Colonel Oliver Cromwell; preceded by an explanatory preface. [By George Nugent Temple Grenville, Lord Nugent.] 4to. Pp. viii. 61. London, 1847
A work of fiction purporting to be written by Dr William Spurstowe, but really written by Lord Nugent.

TRACT (a) for all time; the Christian or true constitution of man, versus the pernicious fallacies of Mr Combe and other materialistic writers. By Stephen Seedair [Phineas Deseret]. 8vo. Pp. 24. Edinburgh, 1856

TRACT (a) for soldiers. By the author of *The faithful promiser*, etc. [John Ross Macduff, D.D.]. 12mo.
Edinburgh, 1853

TRACT (a) for the times. [By William Penney, Lord Kinloch.] 8vo. Pp. 31.
Edinburgh, 1866

TRACT for the times. By a Minister of the Gospel [William L. Roy]. 8vo. Pp. 24. [*Brit. Mus.*] Brooklyn, 1875

TRACT (a) for the times; how to keep a horse for less than one shilling a day, and two horses at the expense of one, under the old plan: being hints upon feeding. By F. D. P. [Frederick De Porquet]. 8vo. [*Brit. Mus.*]
London, 1852

TRACT (a) for the times. Is endless punishment true or false? Dialogues between a Calvinist, Arminian, Baxterian and Berean. [By John Oakeshott.] 8vo. [*Brit. Mus.*] Brighton [1848]

TRACT (a) on the novel county-rates. Exeter, &c. [By William Holmes.] 8vo. [Davidson's *Bibl. Devon.* p. 28.]
Exeter, 1800

TRACT (a) upon the dispensing power. [By Daniel Defoe.] 4to. [*Wilson's Life of Defoe.*]   London, 1687

TRACT (a) upon tomb-stones; or, suggestions for the consideration of persons intending to set up that kind of monument to the memory of deceased friends. By a member of the Lichfield Society for the encouragement of ecclesiastical architecture [Rev. Francis Edward Paget]. Third edition. 8vo. Pp. 23. London, 1853

TRACTE (a) containing the artes of curious paintinge, caruinge, & buildinge; written first in Italian by Jo. Paul Lomatius [Lomazzo], painter of Milan, and englished by R. H. [Richard Haydocke], student in Physik. Fol. [*Quaritch's Cat.*] Oxford, 1598
Of the seven books forming the original, only five are contained in this translation.

TRACTS and essays . . . By Mr Slender [Philip Freneau]. 8vo. [*Cushing's Init. and Pseud.*] Philadelphia, 1788

TRACTS by Warburton, and a Warburtonian [Richard Hurd]; not admitted into the collections of their respective works. [Edited by Samuel Parr, LL.D.] 8vo. Pp. ii. 281.
London, 1789

TRACTS [ix] for the Church in 1856. [By Henry Drummond and Nicholas Armstrong.] 8vo. Pp. 121.
London, 1856-58

TRACTS for the last days. [By Henry Drummond, M.P.] Vol. I. 8vo. Pp. 400. London, 1844
No more published. The volume consists of 24 tracts, each having a separate title.

TRACTS for the present crisis; first and second series. [By Sir Arthur Hallam Elton.] 8vo. [*Brit. Mus.*]
Bristol [1855-56]

TRACTS for the times on political subjects. [By Rev. Samuel Nicholson Kingdon, B.D.] 8vo. [*Brit. Mus.*]
London [c. 1865]
Four tracts, each 16 pages.

TRACTS for the use of the poor. By Daniel Merdant [Rev. Robert A. Mayow]. 8vo. [*Boase and Courtney's Bibl. Corn.*] 1800

TRACTS on business . . . By a citizen of the United States [David Fosdick]. 8vo. New York, 1838

TRACTS on Christian Socialism. [Nos. 1, 3, 7 and 8 by John F. Denison Maurice.] 8vo. [*Brit. Mus.*]
London [1850]

TRACTS on Irish agricultural interests. [By William Hanley.] 4to.
Dublin, 1872

TRACTS on practical agriculture and gardening; in which the advantage of imitating the garden culture in the field is fully proved by a seven years course of experiments. . . . To which is added, a complete chronological catalogue of English authors on agriculture, gardening, &c. By a country gentleman [Richard Weston]. 8vo. London, 1769
The second edition (1773), enlarged, gives the author's name.

TRACTS on sundry topics of political economy. [By Oliver Putnam.] 8vo. Pp. viii. 156. [*Sabin's Dictionary.*]
Boston, 1834

TRACTS on the Church of England. No. 1. The Liturgy. [By Rev. Wm. N. Kingdon, B.D.] 8vo.
London [c. 1860]
No more published.

TRACTS on the relative duties of married persons, parents, and servants. By a country clergyman [Edward Berens, Archdeacon of Berks]. 12mo.
Oxford, 1820
Each of the tracts has a separate title and pagination.

TRACTS relative to botany, translated from different languages. [By C. D. E. Koenig.] 8vo. [*Brit. Mus.*]
London, 1805

TRACTS, written in the years 1823 & 1828. By C. L. Esq. [Chandos Leigh, first Lord Leigh]. 8vo. Pp. vi. 247. [*Bodl.*] Warwick, private print, 1832

TRADE (the) and navigation of Great Britain considered; shewing that the surest way for a nation to increase in riches is to prevent the importation of such foreign commodities as may be rais'd at home. . . . [By Joshua Gee.] 12mo. [*Brit. Mus.*]
London, 1730

TRADE (the) of the future; a hint to the merchants and traders of London . . . and merchants and traders of every class. . . . By [Thomas Dick] a citizen of Edinburgh . . . 8vo.
London, 1850

TRADE prefer'd before religion, and Christ made to give place to Mammon; reprehended in a sermon relating to the Plantations. . . By the author of *The Negroes Advocate* [Morgan Godwin]. 4to. [*Brit. Mus.*]
London, 1685

TRADE (the) to India critically and calmly considered and prov'd to be destructive to the general trade of Great Britain . . . [By Daniel Defoe.] 8vo. [*Camb. Hist. of Eng. Lit.*]
London, 1702

TRADE (the) with France, Italy, Spain, and Portugal, considered; with some observations on the treaty of commerce between Great Britain and France. [By Daniel Defoe.] 8vo. Pp. 23. [*Brit. Mus.*] London, 1713

TRADER Carson. By John Barnett [John Reginald Stagg]. 8vo. Pp. 303. [*Brit. Mus.*] London, 1914

TRADER'S (the) pocket record. . . . By an accountant [Samuel W. Flint]. 8vo. [*Brit. Mus.*] London, 1886

TRADES (the) increase. [Signed : J. R. *i.e.* John Roberts.] 4to. Pp. 56. London, 1615

TRADESMAN'S (the) guide to book-keeping. By a practical man [J. Stuart, journalist]. 8vo. Pp. 59. [*Brit. Mus.*] London [1896]

TRADESMAN'S (the) jewel; or, a safe, easie, speedy, and effectual means for the incredible advancement of trade, and multiplication of riches. [By W. Potter.] 4to. [M'Culloch's *Lit. of Pol. Econ.* p. 159.] London, 1659

TRADESMEN *versus* salesmen . . . [Signed : S. A. B. *i.e.* S. A. Bunning.] 8vo. [*Brit. Mus.*] London, 1881

TRADIDI vobis; or, the traditionary conveyance of faith cleer'd, in the rational way, against the exceptions of a learned opponent [T. White]. By J. B. [John Belson], Esq. 12mo. [*W.*] London, 1662
Published without the author's consent by S. W., who states in his Epistle to the Reader, that it is an answer to Rushworth's Dialogues [by T. White].

TRADING; finishing the story of "The house in town," etc. By the author of *The wide wide world*, etc. [Susan Warner]. 8vo. Pp. 203—414. London, 1872

TRADITION. By Joseph Conrad [Joseph Conrad Korzeniowski.] 8vo. Private print, 1919

TRADITION is no rule now to Christians, either of faith or practice; being an answer to Dr Brett's *Treatise of tradition.* By S. W. [Samuel Walker], A.B. 8vo. [*Brit. Mus.*] London, 1721

TRADITIONAL nursery songs of England. By Felix Summerley [Sir Henry Cole]. 12mo. [Cushing's *Init. and Pseud.*] London, 1846

TRADITIONALL memoyres on the raigne of King James. [By Francis Osborne.] 12mo. [*Brit. Mus.*] London, 1658

TRADITIONS etc. respecting Sir William Wallace, collected chiefly from publications of a recent date [by Major-General Yuille]. 8vo. Pp. 32. [*Bibl. Wallasiana*, p. 19.] Edinburgh, 1856

TRADITIONS of London, historical and legendary. By "Waters" [William H. C. Russell]. 8vo. London, 1859

TRADITIONS of Palestine; or, scenes in the Holy Land in the days of Christ. By a Wayfarer [Moses H. Sargent]. 8vo. [*Brit. Mus.*] Boston, 1863

TRADITIONS (the) of the Christian Fathers the standard for interpretation of Holy Scripture; a sermon. . . . By a Presbyter of the diocese [Rev. Charles Jobson Lyon]. 8vo. N.P. 1838

TRADITIONS (the) of the Jews; or, the doctrines and expositions contained in the Talmud and other Rabbinical writings; with a preliminary preface, or an inquiry into the origin, progress, authority, and usefulness of those traditions . . . [by Rev. John Peter Stehelin, F.R.S.]. 8vo. 2 vols. [Horne's *Introduction*, v. 455.] London, 1742
Translated from the High Dutch of Dr John Andrew Eisenmenger, professor of Oriental languages in the University of Heidelberg : the preface by Rev. J. P. Stehelin. [*W.*]

TRAFALGAR; or, the sailors play. [By William Perry, M.D., of Hillingdon.] [*N. and Q.* 20th December 1856, p. 499.] Uxbridge, 1807

TRAGE-COMEDY, acted by the late ministry; or, an answer to a scandalous pamphlet, entitul'd, A defence of the king. [By John Asgill.] 8vo. Pp. 22. [*Bodl.*] London, N.D.

TRAGEDIE (the) of Alceste and Eliza; as it is found in Italian, in La croce racquistata : collected, and translated into English, in the same verse, and number, by Fr. Br. Gent. [Francesco Bracciolini], at the request of the right vertuous lady, the Lady Anne Wingfield. . . . 8vo. No pagination. [*Bodl.*] London, 1638

TRAGEDIE (the) of Antonie. [By Robert Garnier.] Doone into English by the Countess of Pembroke. 8vo. No pagination. London, 1595

TRAGEDIE (the) of Cleopatra, Queen of Egypt [in five acts, and in verse]. By T. M. [Thomas May]. 12mo. [*Brit. Mus.*] London, 1639

TRAGEDIE (the) of King Richard the second, as it hath beene publikely acted by . . . the Lorde Chamberlaine his servants. [By William Shakespeare.] 4to. London, 1597

TRAGEDIE (the) of Mariam, the fair queene of Jewry; written by that learned, vertuous, and truly noble ladie, E. C. [Elizabeth Cary, Viscountess Falkland]. 4to. No pagination. [*Brit. Mus.*] London, 1613
Attributed also to Lady Elizabeth Carew. [Baker's *Biog. Dram.*]

TRAGEDIE (the) of Solimon and Perseda; wherein is laide open, loues constancie, fortunes inconstancie, and deaths triumphs. [By Thomas Kyd.] 4to. No pagination. [Baker's *Biog. Dram.*] London, 1599

TRAGEDIE (the) of Tancred and Gismund. Compiled by the gentlemen of the Inner Temple. . . . Newly revived and polished . . . by R. W. [Robert Wilmot]. 4to. [Greg's *English Plays.*] London, 1591

TRAGEDIES and comedies collected into one volume. . . . [By John Marston.] 8vo. London, 1633
Later issues of the same year bear the author's name.

TRAGEDY (a) in marble. [A tale.] By Adam Lilburn [Lillias Wasserman]. 8vo. Pp. 251. [*Brit. Mus.*] London, 1898
Title-page of her "Road of life."

TRAGEDY (a) in the Imperial Harem at Constantinople. . . . By Leila-Hanoum [Madame Adrienne Piazzi]; translated from the French with notes by R. E. Colston. 8vo. Pp. v. 299. [*Brit. Mus.*] New York, 1883

TRAGEDY (the) of a throne. By Hildegard Ebenthal [Princess Catherine Radziwill]. 8vo. London, 1917

TRAGEDY (the) of Antigone the Theban Princesse [in five acts, and in verse]. Written by T. M. [Thomas May]. 8vo. [*Brit. Mus.*] London, 1631

TRAGEDY (the) of Christopher Loue at Tower-hill. By the ingenious author of *Iter boreale* [Robert Wild, D.D.]. 4to. Pp. 8. [*Bodl.*] London, 1660

TRAGEDY (the) of Chrononhotonthologus; being the most tragical tragedy that ever was tragediz'd by any company of tragedians. Written by Benjamin Bounce, Esq. [Henry Carey]. 12mo. Pp. 22. [*Brit. Mus.*]. Dublin, 1773

TRAGEDY (the) of Count Alarcos. By the author of *Vivian Grey* [Benjamin Disraeli, later Lord Beaconsfield]. 8vo. Pp. vii. 108. [*Brit. Mus.*] London, 1839
Dedication signed : Δ

TRAGEDY (a) of errors. [A dramatic poem. By Mary Lowell Putnam.] 8vo. Pp. 249. [*Brit. Mus.*] Boston, 1862

TRAGEDY (the) of Gray-Beard; or, the brandy botle of Kinkegolaw. . . . [By Alexander Pennecuik.] 8vo. [*Brit. Mus.*] Edinburgh, 1700

TRAGEDY (the) of Hoffman; or, a reuenge for a father, as it hath bin diuers times acted with great applause, at the Phenix in Druery-lane. [By Henry Chettle.] 4to. No pagination. London, 1631
"This tragedy was written by Henry Chettle, a very voluminous dramaticke author, having written at least as many plays as Shakspeare, either solely or with the assistance of other men. See the titles of 38 of his pieces in my Shakspeare, vol. I. P. 11. p. 308 & seq. The tragedy of Hoffman was first acted in Jany 1602-3. Of all his dramas this only, and *Patient Grissel* and *The blind beggar of Bethnal Green* remain. In the former he was assisted by Thos. Dekker and Wm. Haughton, in the latter by John Day. Chettle was a stationer. Since this was written I have observed that he likewise wrote the Second Part of Robert Earl of Huntingdon, in conjunction with Anthony Mundy, and the Valiant Welchman in conjunction with Drayton and Haughton : both which are extant."—MS. note by Malone.

TRAGEDY (the) of Judas Iscariot; a modern drama in a prologue and five acts. By Gregorio d'Arci [F. Tavani]. 8vo. Pp. 72. [*Brit. Mus.*] Amersham [1926]

TRAGEDY (the) of Julia Agrippina, Empresse of Rome. By T. M. Esq. [Thomas May]. 12mo. No pagination. [Baker's *Biog. Dram.*] London, 1639

TRAGEDY (the) of King Lear, as lately published, vindicated. [By Charles Jennins or Jennens.] 8vo. Pp. 42. [Wilson's *Shaksperiana*, 62.] N.P. [1772]
No title-page.

TRAGEDY (the) of King Richard the third; containing his treacherous plots against his brother Clarence. . . . As it hath bene lately acted by the . . . Lord Chamberlaine his servants. [By William Shakespeare.] 4to. [*Brit. Mus.*] London, 1597

TRAGEDY (the) of King Saul; written by a deceas'd person of honour, and now made publick at the request of several men of quality who have highly approv' of it. [By Joseph Trapp.] 4to. Pp. 67. [Arber's *Term Cat.* iii. 336.] London, 1703
The author's name appears in the 12mo. edition published in 1739.

TRAGEDY (the) of Mustapha. [By Fulke Greville, Lord Brooke.] 4to. [*Bodl.*] London, 1609
"This is the first edition. It was printed without the author's knowledge. There is a second in folio, printed in 1633."—M[alone].

TRAGEDY (the) of Nero newly written. 4to. London, 1633
Wrongly attributed to Matthew Gwinne, who wrote a Latin play with that title.

TRAGEDY (the) of pardon. Diane. [Two plays.] By the author of *Borgia* [Michael Field, *i.e.* K. H. Bradley and E. E. Cooper]. 8vo. Pp. 251. [*Brit. Mus.*] London, 1911

TRAGEDY of success. [By Mary Lowell Putnam.] 8vo. Pp. 191. [Sabin's *Dictionary.*] Boston, 1862

TRAGEDY (the) of that famous Roman oratour Marcus Tullius Cicero. [By Fulke Greville, Lord Brooke.] 4to. No pagination. [*Bodl.*] London, 1651

TRAGEDY (the) of the Great Emerald. [A novel.] By Weatherby Chesney [Charles J. Cutcliffe Hyne]. 8vo. Pp. 316. London, 1904

TRAGEDY (the) of Thierry King of France, and his brother Theodoret; as it was diuerse times acted at the Blacke-Friers by the Kings Majesties seruants. [By Francis Beaumont and John Fletcher.] 4to. [Baker's *Biog. Dram.*] London, 1621

TRAGEDY (the) of tragedies; or, the life and death of Tom Thumb the great: as it is acted at the theatre in the Hay-Market, with the annotations of H. Scriblerus Secundus. [By Henry Fielding.] The third edition. 8vo. Pp. 6, 54. London, 1737
The title of an earlier edition (1730) is: "Tom Thumb, a tragedy . . ."

TRAGEDY (the) of Wild River Valley. By Martha Farquharson [Martha Finlay]. 8vo. Pp. 231. New York [1893]

TRAGIC (a) contract. [A novel.] By Mount Houmas [Mrs Gill]. 8vo. London, 1903

TRAGIC dramas from Scottish history. Heselrig. Wallace. (Second edition.) James the First of Scotland. [By Robert Buchanan, M.A., professor of logic in the University of Glasgow.] 8vo. Pp. vi. 233. Edinburgh, 1859
Another edition (with additional dramas) appeared in 1868, in two volumes, with the title, "Tragic dramas from history with legendary and other poems," and with the author's name.

TRAGIC (a) honeymoon. By Alan St Aubyn [Frances Marshall]. 8vo. London, 1902

TRAGIC (the) Mary; a tragedy in five acts [in prose and verse]. By Michael Field [Miss Katherine H. Bradley and Miss Edith Emma Cooper]. 8vo. Pp. viii. 261. [*Brit. Mus.*] London, 1890

TRAGIC (the) Muse; a poem addressed to Mrs Siddons. [Dedication signed: W. R. *i.e.* William Russell, LL.D.] 4to. [*Brit. Mus.*] London, 1783

TRAGIC romances. By Fiona Macleod [William Sharp]. 8vo. London, 1903

TRAGICAL (the) history of two English louers, 1563, written by Ber. Gar. [Bernard Garter]. 8vo. [Lowndes' *Bibl. Man.*] [London] 1565

TRAGICALL (a) historie of the troubles and civile warres of the Lowe Countries, otherwise called Flanders; by —— Théophile: translated out of French into Englishe by T. S. [Thomas Stocker]. 4to. B. L. [*Christie-Miller Cat.*] London, N.D.

TRAGICALL (the) history of D. Faustus; as it hath bene acted by the . . . Earl of Nottingham his seruants. Written by Ch. Marl. [Christopher Marlowe]. 4to. [*D. N. B.* vol. 36, p. 183.] London, 1604
The edition of 1609 has the title: "The tragicall history of the horrible life and death of Doctor Faustus."

TRAGI-COMICALL (a) history of our times under the borrowed names of Lisander and Calista. [Translated by William Duncombe from the French of Vital d'Audiguier.] Fol. London, 1627
Wrongly attributed to G. de Costa.

TRAGIDIE (the) of Ferrex and Porrex, set forth without addition or alteration but altogether as the same was shewed on stage before the Queenes Maiestie, about nine yeares past, viz. the xviij. day of Ianuarie, 1561. By the gentlemen of the Inner Temple. [By Thomas Norton.] 8vo. B. L. No pagination. London, N.D.
The two last acts by Thomas Sackville, Lord Buckhurst.

TRAIL (the) of adventure. By Ben Bolt [Rev. Ottwell Binns]. 8vo. [*Who's Who in Lit.*] London, 1923

TRAIL (the) of fear. By Anthony Armstrong [George Anthony Armstrong Willis]. 8vo. Pp. 310. [*Brit. Mus.*] Philadelphia [1927]
The English edition bears the title "Jimmy Rezaire."

TRAIL (the) of the barbarians ; being "L'outrage des barbares." By Pierre Loti [M. Julien Viaud, Captain in the French Navy]. Translated by Ford Max Hueffer. 8vo. Pp. 30.
London, 1918

TRAIL (the) of the Sandhill stag. By E. Seton-Thompson [Ernest Thompson Seton]. 12mo. Pp. 94.
London, 1899

TRAIL (the) of the serpent. [A novel.] By the author of Lady Audley's secret [Mary E. Braddon, later Mrs John Maxwell]. 8vo. London, 1892

TRAIL (the) of the white mule. [A novel.] By B. M. Bowen [Bertha M. Sinclair]. 8vo. London, 1923

TRAIL-HUNTER (the) ; a tale of the Far West. By Gustave Aimard [Olivier Gloux]. Translated from the French by Sir Frederick C. Lascelles Wraxall. 8vo. London [1879]

TRAINING in tracking. By Gilcraft [F. Gidney and George Moore]. 8vo. Pp. 190. [Brit. Mus.] London, 1927

TRAITOR (the) to him = self, or mans heart his greatest enemy ; a moral interlude in heroic verse, representing, the carless, hardned, returning, despairing, renewed heart ; with inter-maskes of interpretation at the close of each several act : as it was acted by the boys of a publick school at a breaking up, and published as it may be useful, on like occasion. [By William Johns.] 4to. Pp. 43. [Bodl.]
Oxford, 1678

TRAITOR'S (a) escape ; a story of the attempt to seize Benedict Arnold after he had fled to New York. By James Otis [James Otis Kaler]. 8vo. Pp. 234. New York [1898]

TRAITOR'S (a) wooing. [A novel.] By Headon Hill [Francis E. Grainger]. 8vo. Pp. 304. [Amer. Cat.]
London, 1909

TRAITS and anecdotes of animals. [By William White Cooper.] 8vo. [Brit. Mus.] London, 1861
Another edition of "Zoological notes and anecdotes."

TRAITS and scenes of Scottish life, and pictures of scenes and character. [By William Bennet.] Second edition. 8vo. 3 vols. [Mitchell and Cash's Scot. Topog.] London, 1832

TRAITS and stories of the Irish peasantry ; second series. [By William Carleton.] 8vo. 3 vols. [Brit. Mus.]
Dublin, 1833

TRAITS and trials of early life. By L. E. L. author of The improvisatrice, etc. [Letitia Elizabeth Landon, later Mrs Maclean]. 8vo. London, 1836

TRAITS of American humour, by native authors ; edited and adapted by the author of Sam Slick, etc. [Thomas Chandler Haliburton]. 8vo. 3 vols.
London, 1852

TRAITS of character, pursuits, manners, etc., manifested by the inhabitants of the North-eastern States. By Uncle Daniel [Anson Wrifford]. 8vo.
Portland, Maine, 1837

TRAITS of character ; twenty-five years' literary and personal recollections. By a contemporary [Miss Eliza Rennie]. 8vo. 2 vols. [Courtney's Secrets, p. 65.] London, 1860

TRAITS of private life. By L. A. [Louisa Anthony]. 8vo. Pp. vii. 364. [N. and Q. Feb. 1869, p. 169.]
London, 1844

TRAITS of the aborigines of America ; a poem. [By Mrs Lydia Sigourney, née Huntley.] 8vo. [Brit. Mus.]
Cambridge [Mass.] 1822

TRAITS of the Tea Party ; being a memoir of G. R. T. Hewes, one of the last of its survivors : with a history of that transaction, reminiscences of the massacre, and the siege, and other stories of old times. By a Bostonian [Benjamin Bussey Thatcher]. 12mo. Pp. 265. [Cushing's Init. and Pseud. i. 38.] New York, 1835

TRAITS of travel ; or, tales of men and cities. By the author of High-ways and by-ways [Thomas C. Grattan]. 12mo. 3 vols. [Brit. Mus.]
London, 1829

TRAMP (a) abroad. By Mark Twain [Samuel Langhorne Clemens]. 8vo. 2 vols. [Brit. Mus.] London, 1880

TRAMPING with tramps ; studies and sketches of vagabond life. By Josiah Flynt [Josiah Flynt Willard]. 8vo. [Amer. Cat.] New York, 1899

TRANCE (a) ; or, newes from hell, brought fresh to towne. By Mercurius Acheronticus [James Howell]. 4to. Pp. 19. [Bodl.] London, 1649

TRANSACTIONEER (the) ; with some of his philosophical fancies, in two dialogues. [By William King, LL.D.] [Gent. Mag. xlvi. 465.] 1700

TRANSACTIONS in India, from the commencement of the French war in seventeen hundred and fifty-six, to the conclusion of the late peace, in seventeen hundred and eighty-three. . . . [By John Moir?] 8vo. Pp. 505. [Catalogue of Authors, 1788.]
London, 1786

TRANSACTIONS of the Loggerville Literary Society. [By William Sandys, F.S.A.] 8vo. [Nat. Lib. of Scot.]
London, 1867

TRANSALPINE memoirs ; or, anec-
dotes and observations, shewing the
actual state of Italy and the Italians.
By an English Catholic [John Richard
Digby Beste]. 12mo. 2 vols. [Green's
Bibl. Somers. ii. 525.]   Bath, 1826

TRANSATLANTIC rambles ; or,
twelve months' travel in the United
States, Cuba, and the Brazils. By
a Rugbæan [—— Dixon]. 12mo.
                          London, 1851
TRANSATLANTIC sketches. By
Porte-plume [W. M. Harding]. 8vo.
[Cushing's *Init. and Pseud.*]
                        New York, 1870
TRANSCENDENT and multiplied re-
bellion and treason, discovered by the
laws of the land. [By Edward Hyde,
Earl of Clarendon.] 4to. [*D. N. B.*
vol. 28, p. 388.]   London, 1645

TRANSCENDENTAL magic ; its
doctrine and ritual. By Eliphas Levi
[the Abbé Alphonse Louis Constant] ;
translated by A. E. Waite. 8vo.
[F. L. Gardner's *Rosicrucian Books*,
p. 43.]   London, 1896

TRANSCRIPT (the) ; also the memorial,
and other poems. [By William Ball.]
12mo. Pp. viii. 288.
                  Private print [1853]
An edition of 1855 gives the author's
name.

TRANSCRIPT pieces. By Reynard
[Frank Foxcroft]. 8vo. [Cushing's
Init. and Pseud.] 8vo.
              North Adams, Mass., 1856
TRANSFORMATION (a) in book-
keeping. "Cantab's" [W. P. Hollis's]
loose-leaf system of accounts. 8vo.
Pp. 36. [*Brit. Mus.*]
                    Cambridge [1917]
TRANSFORMATIONS. By Max
Adeler [Charles Heber Clark]. . . .
8vo. Pp. vi. 122. [*Brit. Mus.*]
                     London [1883]
TRANSFORMED. By Faye Hunting-
ton [Mrs Isabella H. Foster]. 8vo.
[Cushing's *Init. and Pseud.*]
                       Boston, 1886
TRANSFORMED Hinduism. By the
author of *God the beautiful* [Emil P.
Berg]. 8vo. 2 vols.   London, 1908

TRANSIENT (the) and permanent in
religion. [Ten essays edited by
W. C. B. *i.e.* William Copeland Bowie.]
8vo. Pp. 318. [*Brit. Mus.*]
                       London, 1908
TRANSITION. [A novel.] By the
author of *A superfluous woman* [Emma
Frances Brooke]. 8vo. Pp. 330. [*Lond.
Lib. Cat.*]   London, 1895

TRANSITION (the) between the
Christian and Millennial dispensations.
A.D. 1848 proved to be A.M. 6000 ! [By
Louis Albert du Puget.] 8vo. Pp. 46.
[*Bodl.*]   London, 1852
Signed : L. A. du P.

TRANSITION (the); the Bible and
science : can the veiled or allegoric
portions of our Scriptures be interpreted by modern science ? By " Rejected " [C. Inglis, M.D.]. 8vo.
Pp. 54.   London, 1892

TRANSITION of Masonry. By Kru-
Cha [Charles Henry Kruse]. 8vo.
[*Amer. Cat.*]   Petersburg, Va., 1910

TRANSLATION from the Italian of
Fortiguerri of the first canto of
Ricciardetto ; with an introduction
concerning the principal romantic,
burlesque and mock heroic poets.
[Translated by Sylvester Douglas,
Lord Glenbervie.] 12mo.
          London, private print, 1821
Reprinted with the translator's name in
1822.

TRANSLATION (a) of a charter granted
to the city of Exeter by K. Charles I.
By a citizen of Exeter [William
Holmes]. 4to. Pp. xii. 78. [Lowndes'
Bibl. Man.]   [Exeter] 1785

TRANSLATION of a comparative
vocabulary, of the Chinese, Corean,
and Japanese languages. . . . By
Philo-Sinensis [Walter Henry Med-
hurst]. 8vo. [*Brit. Mus.*]
                       Batavia, 1835
TRANSLATION of a fragment of the
eighteenth book of Polybius, found in
the Monastery of Ste Laure on Mount
Athos, by the Count D'. [D'Antraigues,
—but rather written by him]. 8vo.
                       London, 1806
A satire on the King of Prussia for his
conduct after the Battle of Austerlitz.

TRANSLATION of a passage in a late
pamphlet of Mallet du Pan, intitled
" Correspondance politique." [By
Francis Maseres.] 8vo. [*D. N. B.*
vol. 36, p. 409.]   London, 1796

TRANSLATION (the) of bishops. [By
Samuel Roffey Maitland, D.D.] 8vo.
Pp. 24. [*Camb. Univ. Lib.*]
                       London, 1834
TRANSLATION (a) of chapters 273
and 287 of the Consolato del Mare,
relating to Prize Law. [By Sir
Christopher Robinson, Admiralty
Lawyer.] 8vo. [*D. N. B.* vol. 49, p. 5.]
                       London, 1800

TRANSLATION (a) of Dante ; Arnaldo, Gaddo, and other unacknowledged poems of Lord Byron. By Odoardo Volpi [Edward W. Shannon, Irish journalist]. 8vo. [O'Donoghue's *Poets of Ireland*.]   London, 1836

TRANSLATION of divers parts of the Holy Scriptures, chiefly from Dr Mill's printed Greek copy, with notes and maps. [By —— Mortimer.] 8vo. [Leslie's *Cat.* 1843.]   London, 1761

TRANSLATION (a) of the fifth Canto of Dante's *Inferno*, and of the entire scene and narrative of Hugolino. [Signed : H. C. J. *i.e.* Henry Constantine Jennings.] 8vo. [*Brit. Mus.*]   [Taunton ? 1798]

TRANSLATION of the first seven books of Homer's *Odyssey* [by Charles Lloyd]. 12mo. [*Brit. Mus.*]   Birmingham, 1810

TRANSLATION (a) of the Latin epistle in the Dreamer. [By William King, D.D.] 8vo. Pp. 28. [*Bodl.*]   London, 1754

TRANSLATION of the letters of a Hindoo Rajah. By [Miss] Elizabeth Hamilton [who really wrote them]. Fifth edition. 12mo. 2 vols.   London, 1811

TRANSLATION (a) of the New Testament from the original Greek, humbly attempted by Nathaniel Scarlett, assisted by men of piety and literature, with notes. [Revised by William Vidler.] 12mo. [Whitley's *Bapt. Bibl.*]   London, 1798

TRANSLATION (a) of the passages from Greek, Latin, Italian, and French writers, quoted in the prefaces and notes to the Pursuits of literature ; a poem, in four dialogues. To which is prefixed, a prefatory epistle, intended as a general vindication of the Pursuits of literature, from various remarks which have been made upon that work. By the translator [Thomas James Mathias]. 8vo. Pp. lxxv. 104.   London, 1798

TRANSLATION (a) of the several charters &c. granted by Edward IV., Henry VII, James I and Charles II to the citizens of Canterbury ; also a list of the bailiffs and mayors, from the year 780 to the present period. By a citizen [Alderman Cyprian Rondeau Bunce]. 8vo. [*W.*]   Canterbury, 1791

TRANSLATION (a) of the twenty-fourth book of the *Iliad* of Homer. [By Charles Lloyd, poet.] 8vo. Pp. 35. [*Brit. Mus.*]   Birmingham, 1807

TRANSLATIONS. By C. C. [Charles Chorley, newspaper editor]. 8vo. Pp. 31. [Boase and Courtney's *Bibl. Corn.*]   Truro, 1866

TRANSLATIONS and imitations, and a few other verses. [By John Cam Hobhouse, Lord Broughton.] 8vo.   Private print [1856]

TRANSLATIONS and poems. [By Sir Edward Hall Alderson.] 12mo. Pp. 42. [*W.*]   London, 1846
    Not published.

TRANSLATIONS and sketches of biography. . . . By a lady [Louisa Minshull]. 8vo. [*Brit. Mus.*]   London, 1839

TRANSLATIONS chiefly from the Greek anthology, with tales and miscellaneous poems. [By Robert Bland, and J. H. Merivale.] 8vo. [*Brit. Mus.*]   London, 1806

TRANSLATIONS chiefly from the Italian of Petrarch and Metastasio. By * * * * * * * M.A., Fellow of New College [Thomas Le Mesurier, B.D.]. 8vo. Pp. iv. 127. [*Bodl.*]   Oxford, 1795

TRANSLATIONS (found in a commonplace book). [By Maurice Baring]. Edited by S. C. 8vo. [*Brit. Mus.*]   Oxford, 1916

TRANSLATIONS from Camoens, and other poets, with original poetry. By the author of *Modern Greece* and the *Restoration of the works of art to Italy* [Felicia Hemans]. 8vo. Pp. 95.   Oxford, 1818

TRANSLATIONS from the German, in prose and verse. [By Ellis Cornelia Knight.] 12mo. Pp. 112. [Martin's *Cat.*]   Windsor, 1812

TRANSLATIONS from the Norse [of Henrik Ibsen and Petter Dass]. By a B. S. S. [Andrew Johnston]. 12mo.   Gloucester, private print [*c.* 1877]
    Presentation copy from the author.

TRANSLATIONS, imitations, etc., etc. By the author of *Ireland, a satire* [Rose Lambart Price]. 12mo. Pp. 8, 179. [Boase and Courtney's *Bibl. Corn.* ii. 527.]   London, 1824

TRANSLATIONS in verse. Mr Pope's Messiah, Mr Philips's Splendid shilling in Latin ; the eighth Isthmian of Pindar in English. [By Thomas Tyrwhitt.] 4to. Pp. 21. [*Dyce Cat.* ii. 379.]   Oxford, 1752

TRANSLATIONS into English verse from the [Welsh] poems of Davyth ap Gwilym. By "Maelog" [Arthur James Johnes]. 8vo. [*Brit. Mus.*]   London, 1834

TRANSLATIONS into Latin and Greek verse, from Milton, Shakespeare, Burns, George Eliot, Gray, Tennyson, Wordsworth, Goethe, Shelley, etc. [By Hugh Andrew Johnstone Munro.] 4to.   1884

Reprinted in 1906 with the author's name.

TRANSLATIONS into verse from comedies of Molière and Casimir Delavigne ; preceded by a cursory view of French dramatic literature. To which are added original poems. . . . By E. F. [Edward Fitzgerald]. 12mo. Pp. iv. 103. [*Ashley Library*.]
Paris, 1829

TRANSLATIONS of German poems, extracted from the musical publications of the author of the German Erato [B. Beresford]. 8vo. [*Brit. Mus.*]
Berlin, 1801

TRANSLATIONS of the Oxford and Cambridge Latin prize poems ; second series. [By Nicholas Lee Forre.] 12mo.   Oxford, 1833

TRANSLATIONS of two passages of the *Iliad*, and of a fragment of Kallinos. [By Edward Craven Hawtrey.] 4to. Pp. iv. 15. [Dobell's *Priv. Prints*, p. 181.]   N.P. 1843

TRANSNATURAL philosophy, or metaphysicks ; demonstrating the essences and operations of all beings whatever, which gives the principles to all other sciences. . . . By J. S. [John Sergeant]. 8vo. [*Brit. Mus.*]
London, 1700

TRANSPORT (a) voyage to the Mauritius and back, touching at the Cape of Good Hope and St Helena. By the author of *Paddiana*, etc. [Dr Adam Blenkinsop]. 8vo. Pp. vii. 303. [Mendelssohn's *South African Bibl.* i. 1377.]   London, 1851

TRANSPROSER (the) rehears'd ; or, the fifth act of [Dryden] Mr Bayes's play : being a postscript to the Animadversions on the preface to Bishop Bramhall's Vindication, &c., shewing what grounds there are of fears and jealousies of Popery. [By Richard Leigh, of Queen's College, Oxford.] 8vo. Pp. 149.   Oxford, 1673

TRANSUBSTANTIATION a peculiar article of the Roman Catholick faith, which was never own'd by the ancient Church or any of the reform'd Churches, in answer to a late discourse call'd, Reasons for abrogating the test. [By Thomas Goodwin.] 4to. Pp. 48. [*Queen's Coll. Lib.* p. 241.]
London, 1688

TRANSUBSTANTIATION contrary to Scripture ; or, the Protestant's answer to the Seeker's request. [By Robert Nelson.] 4to. Pp. 24. [Jones' *Peck*, ii. 364.]   London, 1688

TRANSUBSTANTIATION defended and prov'd from Scripture, in answer to the first part of a treatise [by John Tillotson], intitled, A discourse against transubstantiation. [By John Gother.] 4to. Pp. xxii. 64. [Jones' *Peck*, ii. 389.]   London, 1687

TRANSUBSTANTIATION no doctrine of the primitive Fathers ; being a defence of the Dublin letter herein, against the Papist misrepresented and represented, part 2, cap. 3. [By John Patrick, D.D.] 4to. Pp. 72. [Jones' *Peck*, i. 108.]   London, 1687

TRANSVAAL (the) Boers ; a historical sketch. By Africanus [Sir Malcolm Cotter Cariston]. 8vo. Pp. xv. 158. [*Brit. Mus.*]   London, 1899

TRANSVAAL (the) in 1876 ; notes made by a resident in the Republic previous to the annexation ; with extracts from the diary of the Hon. William Napier. . . . By D. M. D. [Sir Drummond Miles Dunbar]. 8vo. Pp. 74. [Mendelssohn's *South African Bibl.* i. 493.]   Grahamstown, 1881

TRAP (the). [A novel.] By Dick Donovan [Joyce Emerson Preston Muddock]. 8vo. Pp. 320.
London, 1911

TRAP (a) to catch a sunbeam. By the author of *Old Jolliffe*, etc. [Mrs Mackarness *née* Matilda Anne Planché]. 12mo.   London, 1859

TRAPPER'S (the) daughter ; a story of the Rocky Mountains. By Gustave Aimard [Olivier Gloux] ; translated from the French by Sir F. C. L. Wraxall]. 8vo.   London [1878]

TRAPPERS (the) of Arkansas ; a narrative. . . . By Gustave Aimard [Olivier Gloux]. 8vo. London, 1876

TRASH, dedicated without respect to James Halse, Esq., M.P. [By Winthrop Mackworth Praed.] 12mo. Pp. iv. 31. [Boase and Courtney's *Bibl. Corn.* i. 204.]   Penzance, 1833

TRAULUS ; the first part : in a dialogue between Tom and Robin. [By Jonathan Swift.] 8vo. Pp. 8. [*Camb. Hist. of Eng. Lit.*]   Dublin, 1730

TRAVAILES (the) of an Englishman ; containing his sundrie calamities indured by the space of twentie and odd yeres in his absence from his native countrie. . . . By I. H. [Job Hortop]. 4to. [*Christie-Miller Cat.*]
London, 1591

TRAVAILES (the) of the three English brothers, Sir Thomas Sir Anthony Mr Robert Shirley ; an historical play : as it is now play'd by her maiesties seruants. [By John Day.] 4to. No pagination.   London, 1607
" The authors, John Day, William Rowley, and George Wilkins, according to Kirkman." —MS. note by Malone in the Bodleian copy.

TRAVAIGLED (the) pylgrime, bringing newes from all partes of the worlde. . . . [By Stephen Bateman.] 4to. B. L. [*Brit. Mus.*]   London, 1569
An allegorical romance, in verse.

TRAVEL pictures.   By Israfel [Miss —— Hudson].   London, 1904

TRAVELLER (a) returns ; a play in one act.   By Clemence Dane [Winifred Ashton]. 8vo. Pp. 22. [*Brit. Mus.*]   London [1927]

TRAVELLERS (the) ; a tale, designed for young people. By the author of *Redwood* [Catherine Maria Sedgwick]. 12mo. Pp. 202. [*Bodl.*]   London, 1825
TRAVELLER'S (the) breviat ; or, an historicall description of the most famous kingdomes in the world [being part of *Le relationi universali* by Giovanni Botero].   Translated into English [by Robert Johnson].   4to. [*Brit. Mus.*]   London, 1601
Later editions, with variant titles : "The world, or an historical description . . .", "An historicall description . . .", "Relations of the most famous kingdoms and commonweales thorough the world . . ." bear the author's name.

TRAVELLER'S (the) classical guide through France. . . . By J. B. Richard [J. M. V. Audin]. 12mo. [*Brit. Mus.*]   Paris, 1844

TRAVELLER'S (a) diary. [By Daniel Puseley.] 8vo.   London, 1854

TRAVELLER'S (the) dream, and other poems. By Henrietta, authoress of *Poetical pieces on religion and nature* [Henrietta Nethercott]. 12mo. Pp. 192.   Dublin, 1858

TRAVELLER'S (the) guide in Switzerland ; being a complete picture of that interesting country, describing every object of curiosity, and containing sketches of the manners, society and customs of its respective cantons. . . . By Henry Coxe, Esq. author of *The picture of Italy* [John Millard]. 12mo. [*W.*]   London, 1816

TRAVELLER'S (the) guide ; or, a topographical description of Scotland and of the islands belonging to it : with maps and illustrations. [By Rev. Joseph Robertson.] 8vo. [*Watt's Bibl. Brit.*]   Edinburgh, 1798
Many editions followed, enlarged and improved, with varying titles.

TRAVELLER'S (the) guide to Madeira and the West Indies ; being a hieroglyphic representation of appearances and incidents during a voyage out and homewards, in a series of engravings. . . . To which are added Occasional notes, etc.   By a young traveller [George Miller, jun., bookseller]. 8vo. Pp. 120. [Couper's *Millers of Haddington*, p. 265.]   Haddington [1800?]

TRAVELLER'S (the) handbook to Copenhagen and its environs. By Anglicanus [Robert Stephenson Ellis]. 8vo. [*Edin. Univ. Lib.*]   London, 1853
TRAVELLERS in search of truth. By the author of *The antidote to the miseries of human life*, etc. [Harriet Corp]. 12mo. [*Watt's Bibl. Brit.*]   London, 1849
TRAVELLERS' tales retold. By Theta [Julia Hyde]. 12mo.   London, 1860

TRAVELLING anecdotes through various parts of Europe. [By James Douglas.] 8vo. [*Gent. Mag.* Dec. 1819, p. 564.]   Rochester, 1782

TRAVELLING (the) companions ; a story in scenes, reprinted from *Punch*. By F. Anstey [Thomas Anstey Guthrie]. 4to.   London, 1892

TRAVELLING (the) menagerie. . . . By Charles Camden [Richard Rowe, journalist]. 8vo.   London, 1873

TRAVELLING notes in France, Italy and Switzerland of an invalid in search of health. [By John Strang, LL.D.] 8vo. Pp. xix. 266.   Glasgow, 1863
Appeared originally in the *Glasgow Herald*.

TRAVELLING sketches in Egypt and Sinai, including a visit to Mount Horeb . . . translated, corrected and abridged from the French of A. Dumas, by a Bible student [William Cooke Taylor]. 12mo. [*Brit. Mus.*]   London, 1839
Signed : W. C. T.

TRAVELS.   By "Umbra" [Charles Cavendish Clifford] ; being a tour in Iceland twenty years ago. . . . 8vo. Pp. vi. 278.   Edinburgh, 1865

TRAVELS (the) and adventures of Edward Brown, formerly a merchant in London ; containing his observations on France and Italy, his voyage to the Levant, his account of the Isle of Malta, etc., etc. [By John Campbell, LL.D.] 8vo. [*Brit. Mus.*]
London, 1739

TRAVELS (the) and adventures of James Massey [Jacques Massé] ; translated from the French [of S. Tyssot de Patot, by S. Whatley]. 8vo. Pp. 318. [*Brit. Mus.*] London, 1733
　　The French original is attributed also to Pierre Bayle.
　　Another edition of the translation appeared in 1823.

TRAVELS and adventures of John Ledyard. [By Jared Sparks.] 8vo. [Sabin's *Dictionary*.] London, 1834

TRAVELS and adventures of little Baron Trump and his wonderful dog Bulger. By Irwin Longman [Ingersoll Lockwood]. 8vo. [*Amer. Cat.*]
Boston, 1890

TRAVELS (the) and adventures of Mademoiselle de Richelieu. . . . Done into English . . . by the translator of the *Memoirs and adventures of the Marques of Bretagne and Duke of Harcourt* [—— Erskine. A novel]. 12mo. 3 vols. [*Brit. Mus.*]
London, 1744

TRAVELS (the) and observations of Hareach, the wandering Jew ; comprehending a view of the most distinguished events in the history of mankind since the destruction of Jerusalem by Titus. . . . Second edition, revised and improved, with many valuable additions. By the Rev. T. Clark, author of *A tour of Europe* [John Galt]. 12mo. Pp. xviii. 424. [*Nat. Lib. of Scot.*] London, N.D.
　　Preface dated Chelsea ; September, 1820.

TRAVELS (the) and surprising adventures of Baron Munchausen. . . . [By Rudolph Eric Raspe.] 8vo.
London, 1859 [1858]
　　For the titles of other editions, see the note in Vol. I. p. 177.

TRAVELS and tales in verse. [By John Charles Bristow.] 8vo. Pp. xix. 474. [*Brit. Mus.*] London, 1841

TRAVELS and trials of a Dominie. By "Amuena" [Alexander Malcolm, teacher in Bower]. 8vo.
London, 1874

TRAVELS at home, and voyages by the fire-side ; for the instruction and entertainment of young persons. [By Charles Lloyd, LL.D.] 12mo. 2 vols. [*Mon. Rev.* lxxiii. 437.] London, 1814

TRAVELS, by sea and land, of Alethitheras [Laughton Osborn]. 8vo. [Cushing's *Init. and Pseud.*]
New York, 1868

TRAVELS for the heart, written in France. By Courtney Melmoth [Samuel Jackson Pratt]. 8vo. 2 vols. [*Brit. Mus.*] London, 1777

TRAVELS from Paris through Switzerland and Italy in 1801-02 ; with sketches of manners and characters. By a native of Pennsylvania [Joseph Sansom]. 8vo. Pp. 280. [Cushing's *Init. and Pseud.*] Philadelphia, 1808
　　This work appeared in 1805 under a different title—"Letters from Europe, during a tour through Switzerland and Italy."

TRAVELS from the Cape of Good Hope into the interior parts of Africa, including many interesting anecdotes. . . . Translated from the French of Monsieur [François Le] Vaillant [by Elizabeth Holme]. Second edition. 8vo. 2 vols. [*Manch. Free Lib.*]
London, 1791

TRAVELS in Algiers, Spain, etc. ; with a faithful . . . account of the Algerines, etc. [By Mrs Sophia Barnard.] 8vo. [*Brit. Mus.*] London [1820]

TRAVELS in America. By the ex-barber to His Majesty the King of Great Britain [Asa Greene]. 8vo. [Cushing's *Init. and Pseud.*]
New York, 1833

TRAVELS in America ; observations on life and manners in the Free and Slave States. By an Englishman [John Benwell]. 8vo. [Cushing's *Init. and Pseud.*] London, 1853

TRAVELS in Australasia. By Wandanian [R. A. Dyott]. 8vo. [*Birm. Cent. Lib.*] London, 1912

TRAVELS in Europe, Asia, and Africa ; describing characters, customs, manners, laws, and productions of nature and art ; containing various remarks on the political and commercial interests of Great Britain. . . . [By William Thomson.] 8vo. [*D. N. B.* vol. 56, p. 275.] London, 1782

TRAVELS in France, during the years 1814-15 ; comprising a residence at Paris during the stay of the allied armies, and at Aix, at the period of the landing of Bonaparte. [By Sir Archibald Alison, Bart., and Patrick Fraser Tytler.] Second edition, corrected and enlarged. 8vo. 2 vols.
Edinburgh, 1816
　　The first edition was published in 1815.

TRAVELS in Great Britain. [By John Henry Manners, fifth Duke of Rutland : with engravings from drawings by the Duchess of Rutland.] 8vo. 3 vols. [*Brit. Mus.*]
London, private print, 1805
See also "Three years travels . . ."

TRAVELS in North America. . . . [By George Philips.] 12mo. [*Brit. Mus.*]
Dublin, 1824
TRAVELS in North America in the years 1780, 1781 and 1782 ; by the Marquis De Chastellux : translated from the French by an English Gentleman [J. Kent]. 8vo. 2 vols. [Sabin's *Dictionary.*]   London, 1787

TRAVELS in Phrenologasto. By Gio. Battista Balscopo ; translated from the Italian. [Written by John Trotter, jun.] 8vo. [*Nat. Lib. of Scot.*]
London, 1829
Attributed also to Alexander Trotter.

TRAVELS in Portugal. By John Latouche [Oswald John Frederick Crawfurd, H.B.M. Consul at Oporto, who wrote also in the *New Quarterly Magazine* under the name of John Dangerfield]. With illustrations by the Right Hon. T. Sotheron Estcourt. 8vo. Pp. xii. 354. [*Lib. Journ.* iii. 76 ; *Athenæum*, May 26, 1877, p. 672.]
London [1875]
TRAVELS in Scotland. By J. G. Kohl ; translated from the German ; with notes by the translator [John Kesson]. 8vo. [*Brit. Mus.*]   London, 1844

TRAVELS in Scotland, by an unusual route ; with a trip to the Hebrides : containing hints for improvements in agriculture and commerce. . . . By the Rev. James Hall, A.M. [William Thomson, LL.D.]. 8vo. 2 vols.
London, 1807
TRAVELS in the Pyrenees, including Andorra and the coast from Barcelona to Carcassonne. By Odysseus [V. C. Scott O'Connor]. 8vo. [*Lond. Lib. Cat.*]   London, 1913

TRAVELS in the Western Hebrides, from 1782 to 1790. By the Rev. George Lane Buchanan, A.M., missionary minister to the Isles from the Church of Scotland. [By William Thomson, LL.D.] 8vo. Pp. 251. [Watt's *Bibl. Brit.* ; *Mon. Rev.* xii. 154.]   London, 1793

TRAVELS in town. By the author of *Random recollections of the Lords and Commons*, etc. [James Grant]. 12mo. 2 vols.   London, 1839

TRAVELS into Norway, Denmark, and Sweden. By Andrew Swinton [Rev. William Thomson, LL.D.] 8vo. [*D. N. B.* vol. 56, p. 275.]
London, 1792
TRAVELS into several remote nations of the world, in four parts. By Lemuel Gulliver, first a surgeon, and then a captain of several ships. [By Jonathan Swift, D.D.] Second edition. To which are prefixed, several copies of verses explanatory and commendatory ; never before printed. 8vo. 3 vols. [*Camb. Hist. of Eng. Lit.*]   London, 1727
TRAVELS of Ali Bey [Domingo Badia y Leblich] in Morocco, Tripoli, Cyprus, Egypt, Arabia, Syria, and Turkey, between the years 1803 and 1807. Written by himself, and illustrated by maps and numerous plates. 4to. 2 vols.   London, 1816
TRAVELS of an Irish gentleman in search of a religion ; with notes and illustrations by the editor of *Captain Rock's memoirs* [Thomas Moore]. 8vo. 2 vols. [*Brit. Mus.*]
London, 1833
See, a "Reply to the travels . . ." [by Bp. John W. Kaye] ; and "Second travels of an Irish gentleman . . ." [by Joseph Blanco White].

TRAVELS (the) of Cyllenius. [A poem. By Charles Dickinson.] 4to. [*Brit. Mus.*]   London, 1796
The title of an edition, also anonymous, issued in 1820, is "Cyllenius : a poem."

TRAVELS (the) of Edward Brown, Esq., formerly a merchant in London : containing his observations on France and Italy ; his voyage to the Levant ; his account of the Island of Malta ; his remarks in his journies through the Lower and Upper Egypt. . . . [By John Campbell, LL.D.] 12mo. 2 vols. [*N. and Q.* 1923, p. 356.]
London, 1753
The first edition appeared in 1739, with the title "Travels and adventures of Edward Brown . . ." *q.v.*

TRAVELS (the) of ex-barber Fribbleton. [By Asa Greene.] 8vo. [Cushing's *Init. and Pseud.*]   New York, 1835

TRAVELS of Lady Hester Stanhope, forming the completion of her Memoirs, narrated by her Physician [Dr Charles Lewis Meryon]. 12mo. 3 vols. [*Brit. Mus.*]   London, 1845

TRAVELS of my night-cap ; or, reveries in rhyme : with scenes at the Congress of Verona. By the author of *My note-book* [Sir Samuel Egerton Brydges]. 12mo.   London, 1825

TRAVELS (the) of Persiles and Sigismunda ; a Northern history : wherein, amongst the variable fortunes of the Prince of Thule, and this Princesse of Frisland, are interlaced many witty discourses, morall, politicall, and delightfull ; the first copie, beeing written in Spanish [by Miguel de Cervantes Saavedra], translated afterward into French ; and now last into English. 4to. Pp. 399. [Quaritch's *Cat.*]   London, 1619

   Epistle dedicatory sign ed: M. L.

TRAVELS (the) of Sylvester Tramper in Africa. [By George Walker, bookseller in London.] 12mo. [*Brit. Mus.*]
                         London, 1813

TRAVELS (the) of the imagination ; a true journey from Newcastle to London, in a stage-coach : with observations upon the metropolis. By J. M. [Rev. James Murray]. 12mo. [*Nat. Lib. of Scot.*]   London, 1783

TRAVELS of the late Duke du Chatelet in Portugal, with notes by J. F. Bourdoing.   [By ―― Cormartin, one of the Vendean chiefs.] 8vo. 2 vols. [Lowndes' *Bibl. Man.*]
                         London, 1809

TRAVELS (the) of Theodore Ducas in various countries in Europe at the revival of letters and art ; edited [or rather written] by Charles Mills. Part the first : Italy. 8vo. 2 vols. [*D. N. B.* vol. 37, p. 444.]   London, 1822

   No more published.

TRAVELS over the most interesting parts of the globe, to discover the source of moral motion ; communicated to lead mankind through the conviction of the senses to intellectual existence, and an enlightened state of nature. [By John Stewart.] 12mo. [*Watt's Bibl. Brit.*]   London [1792 ?]

   The second volume has the title "The apocalypse of nature . . ."

TRAVELS through Denmark and some parts of Germany [by M. De la Combe de Vrigny] by way of Journal in the retinue of the English envoy [J. Vernon] in 1702 ; done into English from the French original. 8vo. [*Brit. Mus.*]
                         London, 1707

TRAVELS through parts of the United States and Canada. By a British subject [―― Beaufoy, brother of Henry]. 8vo. Pp. 141. [Rich's *Bibl. Amer.* p. 203.]   London, 1828

TRAVELS through Sicily and the Lipari Islands, in the month of December, 1824. By a naval officer [Capt. Edward Boid]. Illustrated with views and costumes from drawings made on the spot, and on stone by L. Haghe. 8vo. Pp. xvi. 367. [*Brit. Mus.*]   London, 1827

TRAVELS through Spain and part of Portugal, with commercial, statistical, and geographical details. [By the Rev. ―― Whittington.] 12mo. 2 vols. [*W.*]   London, 1808

TRAVELS through the interior parts of America. By an Officer [Thomas Anburey, Captain in the 29th Infantry Regiment]. 8vo. 2 vols. [*Sunderland Lib.*]   London, 1789

TRAVELS with Dr Leichhardt in Australia. By the author of *Hortus Tasmaniensis* . . . [Daniel Bunce]. 8vo. [*Sydney Lib. Cat.*]
                         Melbourne, 1859

TRAVESTY (a) without a pun ! Hamlet revamped, modernized and set to music. By the author of *Romeo and Juliet* [Charles Carroll Soule ?]. 8vo. Pp. 48. [*Brit. Mus.*]
                         St Louis, 1880

TRAYTOR (the) ; a tragedy, as it is acted at the New Theatre in Little Lincolns - Inn - Fields ; reviv'd, with several alterations. [By Christopher Bullock.] 8vo.   London, 1718

   This tragedy was originally written by Anthony Rivers, a Jesuit, and was published by James Shirley, with alterations and improvements, in 1635.

TRAYTORS (the) perspective-glass; or, sundry examples of Gods just judgments executed upon many eminent regicides, who were either fomentors of the late bloody wars against the King, or had a hand in his death. . . . Faithfully delineated by J. T. [John Taylor], gent. 4to. [*Brit. Mus.*]
                         London, 1662

TRAYTORS (the) unvailed ; or, a brief and true account of that horrrid (*sic*) and bloody designe intended by those rebellious people, known by the names of anabaptists and Fifth monarchy [men] being upon Sunday the 14th of April 1661 in Newgate on purpose to oppose his Majesties person and laws. [By Thomas Ellis.] 4to. Pp. 7. [Whitley's *Bapt. Bibl.* i. 83.]
                         [London] 1661

TRE (the) Giuli ; translated from the Italian of G. B. Casti : with a memoir of the author, and some account of his other works [by Captain Montagu Montagu, R.N.]. 8vo. London, 1826

TREACHEROUS (a) woman. By Arrah Leigh [Mrs H. C. Hoffman]. 8vo. New York, 1885

TREACHERY. [By Mrs Martin Lucas.] 12mo. 3 vols. London, 1848

TREACHERY no crime; or, the system of courts exemplified in the life . . . of General Dumourier, etc. [By Charles Pigott.] 8vo. [Brit. Mus.] London, 1793

TREASON. . . . By T. [William Henry Trenwith]. 8vo. [Cushing's Init. and Pseud.] Philadelphia, 1866

TREASON detected, in an answer to that traiterous and malicious libel entitled English advice to the free-holders of England [by Francis Atterbury, D.D. By Daniel Defoe]. 8vo. [Camb. Hist. of Eng. Lit.] London, 1715

TREASURE. [A novel.] By W. Danc Bank [William Henry Williamson]. 8vo. Pp. 360. [Brit. Mus.] London, 1915

TREASURE (the) of Christopher. [A novel.] By Ben Bolt [Rev. Otwell Binns]. 8vo. [Who's Who in Lit.] London, 1922

TREASURE (the) of Euonymus, con-teyninge the wonderfull hid secretes of nature touching the most apte formes to prepare and destyl medicines, for the conservation of helth. . . . [By Conrad Gesner]: translated . . . out of Latin by Peter Morwyng. . . . 4to. B. L. [Brit. Mus.] London [1559]

TREASURE (the) of heaven; a romance of riches. By Marie Corelli [Caroline Cody]. 8vo. Pp. ix. 564. [Brit. Mus.] London, 1906

TREASURE (the) of pearls; or, romance of adventures in California. By Gustave Aimard [Olivier Gloux]. 12mo. London [1884]

TREASURE of tempest. By Shann Malory [R. J. K. Russell]. 8vo. London, 1919

TREASURE of Thule. By B. D. Steward [Frank Sidgwick]. 8vo. London, 1912

TREASURE (the) of vowed chastity in secular persons; also the Widdowes glasse [by Leonardus Lepsius]; trans-lated [from Latin] into English by I. W. [William Wright, S.J., D.D.]. 12mo. [D. N. B. vol. 63, p. 135.] [St Omer?] 1621

TREASURE trove. . . . Collected by John o' London [Wilfred Whitten]. 8vo. Pp. 187. [Brit. Mus.] London [1925]

TREASURE-BOOK (the) of consolation for all in sorrow and suffering. By Benjamin Orme [Alexander Hay Japp]. 8vo. [Brit. Mus.] London, 1880

TREASURE-BOOK (the) of devotional reading. By Benjamin Orme [Alexander Hay Japp]. 8vo. [Brit. Mus.] London, 1866

TREASURE-FINDERS (the); a boy's adventure in Nicaragua. By James Otis [James Otis Kaler]. 8vo. New York, 1890

TREASURE-TOWN (the); a story of Malta. By Cousin Virginia [Virginia Wales Johnson]. 8vo. [Amer. Cat.] Chicago, 1892

TREASURES of darkness. [A collec-tion of poems.] By E. L. [Emma Lewis]. 8vo. [Brit. Mus.] Philadelphia, 1854

TREASURIE of auncient and moderne times. [By Thomas Milles.] Fol. 2 vols. [W.; Bliss's Cat.] 1613-19

TREASURY (the) of languages; a rudimentary dictionary of universal philology. [By James Bonwick.] 8vo. Pp. iv. 301. London, 1893

TREASURY (a) of pleasure books for young people. [Edited by Joseph Cundall.] 8vo. [W.; Brit. Mus.] London, 1856
Signed: J. C.

TREASURY (a) of theological know-ledge; wherein Christianity and the divine authority of the Scriptures are proved, and the most plausible objections considered. [By Morgan Williams.] 12mo. 2 vols. [Darling's Cyclop. Bibl.] Garm, 1791

TREASURY (the) of wit; being a methodical selection of about twelve hundred, the best, apophthegms and jests from books in several languages. . . . By H. Bennet, M.A. [John Pinkerton]. 12mo. 2 vols. [Gent. Mag. xcvi. i. 471.] London, 1786

TREATISE (a) concerning the broken succession of the Crown of England. [By Robert Parsons.] 8vo. Pp. 167. [Brit. Mus.] 1655

TREATISE (a) concerning the causes of the present corruptions of Christians, and the remedies thereof. In two parts. [Translated from the French of Jean Frédéric Ostervald, by Charles Mutel.] The second edition cor-rected. 8vo. Pp. 10, 468. London, 1702

TREATISE (a) concerning the Church; wherein it is shewed . . . that the Church of Rome . . . is the only true Church of Christ. Written in Latin by . . . J. Gordon Huntley . . . and translated into English by J. L. [William Wright, D.D., S.J.]. 8vo. [Gillow's Bibl. Dict.] [St Omer] 1614

TREATISE (a) concerning the defence of the honour of the right high, mightie and noble princesse Marie Queene of Scotland, and Dowager of France; with a declaration, as wel of her right, title and interest to the succession of the croune of England. . . . Made by Morgan Philippes, bachelar of diuinitie [John Leslie, bishop of Ross]. 8vo. [*Brit. Mus.*]   Leodii, 1571

TREATISE (a) concerning the dignities, titles, offices, pre-eminences, and yearly revenues, which have been granted to the several kings of England, after the Conquest, for the honour and maintenance of the princes, their eldest sons; with sundry particulars relating thereto. [By Duncan Forbes, Lord President of the Court of Session.] 4to. Pp. viii. 58. [*Nat. Lib. of Scot.*]   London, 1737

T R E A T I S E (a) concerning the division . . . See below, "Treatise (a) concernynge . . ."

TREATISE (a) concerning the fulnesse of Christ. [By Henry Jeanes.] 4to. Pp. 396.   Oxford, 1656

TREATISE (a) concerning the manner of fallowing of ground, raising of grass-seeds, and training of lint and hemp, for the increase and improvement of the linnen-manufactories in Scotland. . . . [By William Macintosh, M.A., of Borlum.] 8vo. Pp. 173. [*Aberd. Quatercent. Studies*, No. 19, p. 336.] Edinburgh, 1724
Wrongly attributed to Richard Bradley.

TREATISE (a) concerning the militia, in four sections. 1. Of the militia in general. 2. Of the Roman militia. 3. The proper plan of a militia for this country. 4. Observations upon this plan. By C. S. [Charles Sackville, 2nd Duke of Dorset]. 8vo. [*Park's Walpole*, iv. 281; *Mon. Rev.* vi. 90.] 1752

TREATISE (a) concerning the origin and progress of fees; or, the constitution and transmission of heritable rights: being a supplement to Spotiswood's Introduction to the knowledge of the stile of writs. [By James Mackenzie.] 8vo. Pp. xii. 276. [*D. Laing.*]   Edinburgh, 1734

TREATISE (a) concerning the payment of tythes and oblations in London. By B. W. [Brian Walton] D.D. 8vo. [R. Thomson's *Chronicles of London Bridge*, p. 297.]   1641

TREATISE (a) concerning the peace of the Church. [By Philip Freher.] 4to. Pp. 82. [Watt's *Bibl. Brit.*] London, 1646

TREATISE (a) concerning the regulation of the coyn of England, and how the East India trade may be preserved and encreased. By R. C. [Roger Cook]. 4to. Pp. 44. [Quaritch's *Cat.*]   London, 1696

TREATISE (a) concerning the right use of the Fathers, in decision of the controversies that are at this day in religion. Written in French by John Daillé. [Preface signed: T. S. *i.e.* Thomas Smith, the translator.] 8vo. Pp. 195. [*Brit. Mus.*] London, 1651

TREATISE (a) concerning the sanctifying of the Lord's day; and particularly the right improvement of a Communion Sabbath: wherein the morality of the Sabbath, and its strict observation under the New Testament dispensation, is maintained. . . . By a minister of the Church of Scotland [Rev. John Willison, Dundee]. 8vo. Pp. 520.
          Edinburgh, 1716
Other editions have varying titles.

TREATISE (a) concerning the use and abuse of the marriage bed; shewing I. The nature of matrimony, its sacred original, and the true meaning of its institution. II. The gross abuse of matrimonial chastity. . . . III. The diabolical practice of attempting to prevent childbearing by physical preparations. IV. The fatal consequences of clandestine or forced marriages, thro' the persuasion, interest, or influence of parents and relations. . . . V. Of unequal matches, as to the disproportion of age. . . . VI. How married persons may be guilty of conjugal lewdness. . . . [By Daniel Defoe.] 8vo. Pp. 406. [Wilson's *Life of Defoe*, 200.]   London, 1727

TREATISE (a) concerning trespasses vi & armis; wherein the nature of trespass is clearly explicated, and the gist of the action stated, and by whom such actions may be brought, and against whom and how to be laid. . . . By the author of *Lex customaria* [Samuel Carter]. 8vo. London, 1704

TREATISE (a) concernynge the division betwene the spiritualtie and temporaltie. [By Christopher Saint-Germain.] 8vo. [*Christie-Miller Cat.*]
          London [*c.* 1532]

TREATISE (a) containing the aequity of an humble supplication which is to be exhibited vnto hir gracious Maiestie and this high court of parliament in the behalfe of the countrey of Wales, that some order may be taken for the preaching of the Gospell among those people. . . . [By John Penry.] 8vo. Pp. 63. [*Bodl.*; Dexter's *Cong. Bibl.* 123.]   Oxford, 1587

TREATISE (a) containing the description and use of a new and curious quadrant, made by J. Rowley for taking altitudes and for solving various mathematical problems. By T. W. [T. Woodford]. 4to. [*W.*]
London, 1756

TREATISE (a) how, by the Word of God, Christian mens almose ought to be distributed. [By Martin Bucer, translated by John Poynet, Bishop of Rochester.] 8vo. Pp. 29. [*Pollard and Redgrave.*] N.P. [*c.* 1566]
Herbert (p. 1753) quotes it from Maunsell's Catalogue.

TREATISE (a) in confutation of the Latin service practised, and, by the order of the Trent Council, continued in the Church of Rome. [By Daniel Whitby.] 4to. Pp. 118. [Jones' *Peck*, ii. 329.] London, 1687

TREATISE (a) in defence of the celibacy of priests. By C. E. [Edward Coffin, *alias* Hatton, S.J.]. 12mo. [Gillow's *Bibl. Dict.*] St Omer, 1619

TREATISE (a) of Baptism; wherein that of believers, and that of infants, is examined by the Scriptures; with the history of both out of antiquity: making it appear that Infants-Baptism was not practised for near three hundred years. . . . By H. D. [Henry D'Anvers]. 8vo. London, 1673
The second edition (1674), with large additions, gives the author's name.

TREATISE (a) of blazing starres in generall, as well supernaturall as naturall; to what countries or people soeuer they appeare in the spacious world. [Translated by Abraham Fleming from the Latin of Friedrich Nause, Bishop of Vienna.] 4to. No pagination. B. L. [Ames' *Typogr. Antiq. ed. Herbert*, ii. 1196.]
London, 1618

TREATISE (a) of Christian religion; or, the whole bodie and substance of Diuinitie. By T. C. [Thomas Cartwright]. Second edition, edited by W. B. [William Bradshaw]. 4to. [*Camb. Univ. Lib.*] London, 1616

TREATISE (a) of civil power in ecclesiastical causes; shewing that it is not lawfull for any power on earth to compell in matters of religion. The author, J. M. [John Milton]. 12mo. Pp. 83. [Masson's *Life of Milton.*]
London, 1659

TREATISE (a) of communion under both kinds; faithfully rendered from the French and dedicated to Thomas Lord Petre. [By Jacques Bénigne Bossuet; translated by John Davis.] 4to. Pp. vi. 116. [Jones' *Peck*, p. 350.]
London, 1687

TREATISE (ane) of conscience, quhairin divers secrects concerning that subject are discovered, as may appeare in the table following. By A. H. [Alexander Hume]. 8vo. [*Christie-Miller Cat.*]
Edinbvrgh, 1594

TREATISE (a) of divine worship; tending to prove, that the ceremonies imposed upon the ministers of the Gospel in England, in present controversie, are in their use unlawful. [By William Bradshaw.] With a preface, containing an account of the antiquity, occasion, and grounds of non-conformity . . . and also, a postscript in defence of a book entituled, Thomas against Bennet, being a reply to Mr Bennet's answer thereto. 8vo. Pp. xxii. 40. [*Camb. Univ. Lib.*]
London, 1703
The " Treatise," the only part by Bradshaw, was first printed in 1604. The " Preface " and " Postscript " were written probably by D. M., who signs the latter.

TREATISE (a) of dreams and visions; wherein the causes, nature, and uses of nocturnal representations, both of good and evil angels, are theosophically unfolded. . . . By Philotheos Physiologus [Thomas Tryon, M.D.]. 12mo. [*Brit. Mus.*] [London, 1695?]

TREATISE (a) of ecclesiasticall and politike power; shewing, the Church is a monarchicall gouernment, ordained to a supernaturall and spiritual end, tempered with an aristocraticall order, (which is the best of all and most comfortable to nature) by the great Pastor of soules Iesus Christ. Faithfully translated out of the Latin originall [of Edmundus Richerius]. . . . 4to. No pagination. [London] 1612
Address to the Prince signed : Δ.

TREATISE (a) of election and reprobation; in vindication of the universal grace and love of God to mankind. By B. L. [Benjamin Lindley]. 4to. [Smith's *Cat. of Friends' Books*, ii. 124.]
London, 1700

TREATISE of equity. [By Henry Ballow.] Fol. [*Brit. Mus.*]
London, 1737
Later editions were enlarged, and issued in 2 vols. 8vo.

TREATISE (a) of eternal nature with her seven essential forms. . . . By J. P. [John Pordage], M.D. 8vo. [*Brit. Mus.*] London, 1681
Forms the second part of the author's " Theologia mystica."

TREATISE (a) of faith; wherein is briefly and plainely shewed a direct way by which every man may resolve and settle his mind in all doubts, questions, and controversies concerning matters of faith. [By John Fisher, S.J.] 8vo. [*Camb. Univ. Lib.*] N.P. 1614

TREATISE (a) of fornication; shewing what the sin is, how to flee it, motives and directions to shun it: upon 1 Cor. vi. xviii.; also a penitentiary sermon upon John viii. 11. By W. B. [William Barlow, rector of Chalgrove, Oxford] M.A. 8vo. Pp. 110. [Darling's *Cyclop. Bibl.*] London, 1690

TREATISE (a) of God's government, and of the justice of his present dispensations in this world; by Salvian: translated from the Latin by R. T. [R. Tesdale], Presbyter of the Church of England. . . . 8vo. London, 1700

TREATISE (the) of heavenly philosophie. By T. P. [Thomas Palfreyman]. 4to. [Lowndes' *Bibl. Man.* p. 1765.] London, 1578

TREATISE (a) of human nature; being an attempt to introduce the experimental method of reasoning into moral subjects. [By David Hume.] 8vo. 3 vols. London, 1739-40

TREATISE (a) of humane reason. [By Martin Clifford, Master of the Charter House, London.] 12mo. Pp. 91. [*D. N. B.* vol. ii. p. 69.] London, 1675
The author's name is given in the edition issued in 1691.

TREATISE (a) of humilitie. Published by E. D., parson sequestered. [Adapted from Alonso Rodriguez.] 12mo. Pp. 241. [*Brit. Mus.*] London, 1654

TREATISE (a) of infallibility, shewing that the Church of Rome's claim to that high privilege is without foundation in Scripture, antiquity, or reason; in answer to a paper on that subject sent by a Popish missionary: with some animadversions on a book [by Robert Manning], entituled, *The shortest way to end disputes about religion.* By a presbyter of the suffering [Episcopal] Church of Scotland [William Harper]. 8vo. Edinburgh, 1752
Contemporary attestation of authorship.

TREATISE (a) of jealousie; or, means to preserve peace in marriage: highly necessary to be considered by all persons before they enter into the state of matrimony, as well as such as are already married. [By Antoine de Courtin.] Translated from the French. 12mo. [*Brit. Mus.*] London, 1684

TREATISE (a) of magistracy, shewing the magistrate hath beene, and for ever is to be the cheife officer in the Church, out of the Church, and over the Church. . . . [The Epistle dedicatory is signed: M. P. *i.e.* Mary Pope.] 4to. Pp. 156. [*Bodl.*] N.P. 1647

TREATISE (a) of marriage, with a defence of the 32 Article of religion of the Church of England, viz. Bishops, priests, and deacons are not commanded by God's law, either to vow the state of single life, or to abstain from marriage. . . . [The epistles dedicatory are both signed: T. H. *i.e.* Thomas Hodges.] 8vo. London, 1673

TREATISE (a) of mental prayer, in which is briefly declared the manner how to exercise the inward actes of vertues; by Fr. Ant. de Molina, Carthusian. Whereunto is adioyned a very profitable Treatise of exhortation to spirituall profit, written by Fr. Francis Arias, of the Society of Jesus: togeather with a Dialogue of attrition and contrition. All translated out of Spanish into English by a Father of the Society of Jesus [John Sweetnam, *alias* Nicholson]. 12mo. Pp. 365. [Oliver's *Collections; Sommervogel.*] [St Omer] 1617

TREATISE (a) of monarchie, containing two parts: 1. Concerning monarchy in generall. 2. Concerning this particular monarchy. . . . Done by an earnest desirer of his countries peace [Philip Hunton]. 4to. [Jones' *Peck*, i. 9.] London, 1643
Attributed also to R. Eyre.

TREATISE (a) of nature and grace; to which is added, the author's idea of providence. . . . By the author of *The search after truth* [Nicholas Malebranche]; translated from the last edition [by Richard Sault]. 8vo. [*Brit. Mus.*] London, 1695

TREATISE (a) of oaths, containing several weighty reasons why the people called Quakers refuse to swear. [By William Penn and Richard Richardson.] 4to. [Smith's *Cat. of Friends' Books.*] N.P. 1675

TREATISE (a) of one hundred and thirteene diseases of the eyes, and eye-liddes; the second time published, with some profitable additions by Richard Banister. . . . [By Jacques Guillemeau.] 12mo. [*Surgeon-General's Cat.*] London, 1622

TREATISE of painting. By Leonardo Da Vinci ; translated [by John Senex]. 8vo. London, 1721

TREATISE (a) of paradise and the principal contents thereof. . . . [By John Salkeld.] 8vo. [Watt's *Bibl. Brit.* ; Queen's *Coll. Cat.* p. 433.] London, 1617

TREATISE (a) of patience ; written by Father Francis Arias, of the Society of Jesus, in his second parte of the Imitation of Christ our Lord ; translated into English. [Epistle signed : T. M. *i.e.* Sir Tobias Matthew.] 12mo. Pp. 225. [Gillow's *Bibl. Dict.*] N.P. 1650

TREATISE (a) of perspective ; or, the art of representing all manner of objects as they appear to the eye in all situations. . . . Written originally in French by Bernard Lamy, priest of the Oratory, and faithfully translated into English by an officer of His Majesties Ordnance. [Dedication signed : A. F. *i.e.* A. Forbes.] 8vo. Pp. (161) 174. London, 1702

TREATISE (a) of power, essential and mechanical : wherein the original, and that part of religion which now is natural, is stated. By J. H. [John Hutchinson]. 8vo. [*Brit. Mus.*] London, 1732

TREATISE (a) of prayer and meditation, compiled by the Rev. Fr. Peter of Alcantara ; translated out of Spanish by R. R. [Richard Rowlands, *alias* Verstegan]. 12mo. [Gillow's *Bibl. Dict.*] Antwerp [*c.* 1575]

TREATISE (a) of prayer, and of the fruits and manner of prayer ; by the Rd. Father John Fisher, Bishop of Rochester ; translated into English by R. A. B. [Bartholomew Alban Roe, O.S.B.]. 12mo. [Gillow's *Bibl. Dict.*] Paris, 1640

TREATISE (a) of prayer ; two quæries resolved touching formes of prayer, and six quæries relating specially to the Lords Prayer. . . . [By Hezekiah Woodward.] 4to. London, 1656
See note at end of his *Law-Power*, 1656.

TREATISE (a) of repentance and of fasting, especially of the Lent fast. [By Symon Patrick, D.D., Bishop of Ely.] 12mo. [Darling's *Cyclop. Bibl.*] London, 1686

TREATISE (a) of ruling elders and deacons, in which these things which belong to the understanding of their office and duty are clearly and shortly set down. By a minister of the Church of Scotland [James Guthrie, of Stirling]. 16mo. Pp. 79. [Scott's *Fasti.*] Edinburgh, 1699

TREATISE (a) of sacramentel covenanting with Christ. By M. M. [John Rawlett]. 12mo. London, 1667
The fifth edition, 1692, has the author's name.

TREATISE (the) of St Catherine of Genoa on Purgatory, newly translated by J. M. A. [Rev. John Marks Ashley, B.C.L.]. 8vo. London, 1878

TREATISE (a) of self deniall. [By John Downame, B.D.] 4to. London, 1646

TREATISE (a) of specters or straunge sights, visions, and apparitions appearing sensibly vnto men ; wherein is delivered the nature of spirites, angels, and divels, as also of witches, sorcerers, enchanters, and such like. [By Peter de Loier ; translated by Zachary Jones.] 4to. [*Brit. Mus.*] London, 1605

TREATISE (a) of taxes & contributions ; shewing the nature and measures of crown-lands, assessments, customs, poll-moneys, lotteries, benevolence, penalties, monopolies, offices, tythes, raising of coins, harth-money, excise, &c. . . . [By Sir William Petty.] 4to. Pp. 75. [M'Culloch's *Lit. of Pol. Econ.* p. 318.] London, 1662

TREATISE (a) of the celibacy of the clergy, wherein its rise and progress are historically considered. [By Rev. Henry Wharton.] 4to. Pp. iv. 168. [Jones' *Peck*, ii. 334.] London, 1688

TREATISE (a) of the Church ; in which is proued M. Iohn White his Way to the true Church, to be indeed no way at all to any Church, true or false : by demonstrating, that his visible company of protestants, is but a chymæra of his owne braine. . . . Written by W. G. [William Wright, S.J.], Professour in Diuinity : in manner of dialogue. 4to. [Dodd's *Ch. Hist.* ii. 136.] [St Omer] 1616

TREATISE (a) of the Churche ; conteininge a true discourse to knowe the true Church by, and to discerne it from the Romish Church and all other false assemblies. . . . [By Bertrand De Loque.] Translated out of French into English by T. W. [Thomas Wilcox]. 8vo. Pp. 384. [*Brit. Mus.*] London, 1581
An edition of 1582 has a slightly different title ; see Watt's *Bibl. Brit.*

TREATISE (a) of the civil power of ecclesiasticals, and of suspension from the Lords Supper. [By Thomas Edwards, M.A.] 4to. [*D. N. B.* vol. 17, p. 128.] London, 1642

TREATISE (a) of the cohabitacyon of the faithfull with the unfaithfull; whereunto is added a sermon. . . . [By Heinrich Bullinger.] 8vo. [*Pollard and Redgrave.*]   [Zurich, 1555]

TREATISE (a) of the confession of sinne, and chiefly as it is made unto the priests and ministers of the Gospel; together with the power of the keys, and of absolution. [By Thomas Ailsbury.] 4to. [Dexter's *Congregationalism*, 1753.]
London, 1657

TREATISE (a) of the felicitie of the life to come, vnsavorie to the obstinate, alluring to such as are gone astray, and to the faithfull, full of consolation. By A. H. [Alexander Hume]. 8vo. [*Christie-Miller Cat.*]
Edinburgh, 1594

TREATISE (a) of the first principles of laws in general; of their nature and design, and of the interpretation of them: translated out of French: being a proper introduction to the New institute of the imperial or civil law, with notes, &c. lately published. [By Thomas Wood, D.C.L.] 8vo. Pp. 144. [*Bodl.*]   London, 1705

TREATISE (a) of the future restoration of the Jews and Israelites to their own land; with some account of the goodness of the country, and their happy condition there, till they shall be invaded by the Turks. . . . [By Samuel Collett.] 8vo. Pp. 87. [*Brit. Mus.*]
London, 1747
Other copies differ slightly in the title.

TREATISE (a) of the groundes of the old and newe religion; devided into two parts, whereunto is added an appendix, containing a briefe confutation of William Crashaw his first Tome of Romish forgeries and falsifications. [By Edward Mayhew.] 4to. [Dodd's *Ch. Hist.* ii. 401.]   1608
The address from the printer to the reader is signed: Your poore Catholike countriman, Thom R.

TREATISE (a) of the Holy Communion. [By Dr Henry Compton.] 12mo. [Leslie's *Cat.* 1843.]   1677

TREATISE (a) of the Holy Sacrifice of the altar called the Masse; in which, by the Word of God, and testimonies of the Apostles and primitive Church, it is proved that our Saviour Jesus Christ did institute the Masse, and the Apostles did celebrate the same. Translated out of Latin [of Antonio Possevino] into English [by Thomas Butler, LL.D.]. 8vo. [Gillow's *Bibl. Dict.* i. 366.]   Antwerp, 1570

TREATISE (a) of the imitation of the holy youth of our Lord and Saviour Jesus Christ: translated from the French original of Mr Charles Gobinet . . . by W. A. M. [Bishop William Maire], C.A.D.A. 12mo. Pp. 126. [Gillow's *Bibl. Dict.*]   London, 1758

TREATISE (a) of the Iudge of controversies; written in Latin by the R. Father Martinus Becanus of the Society of Jesus, professour in diuinity, and englished by W. W. Gent [William Wright, S. J.]. 8vo. [Dodd's *Ch. Hist.* iii. 114.]   [St Omer] 1619

TREATISE (a) of the just interest of the kings of England, in their bill disposing power, and the validity of grants made to their subjects; written at the request of a person of honour in the year 1657, by a person learned in the laws [Sir Matthew Hale? Published by Blackerby Fairfax]. 12mo. [*W.*]   London, 1703

TREATISE (a) of the law of debtor and creditor in Scotland; showing the course of diligence against the person and estate of the debtor before and after bankruptcy, and the conditions of his right to personal freedom. . . . By a Member of the Faculty of Advocates [Alexander Macallan]. 8vo. Pp. xii. 214.   Edinburgh, 1837

TREATISE (a) of the Lords Supper, in two sermons. [By Henry Smith.] 8vo. [*Bodl.*]   London, 1591
Each sermon has a separate pagination.

TREATISE (a) of the love of God; written in French by B. Francis de Sales. . . . Translated into English by Miles Car [really Pinkney], priest of the English College of Doway. 18th edition. 8vo. Pp. 790. [Gillow's *Bibl. Dict.*]   Doway, 1630

TREATISE (a) of the ministery of the Church of England; wherein is handled this question, whether it be [better?] to be separated from or joyned vnto; which is discussed in two letters, the one written for it [by Arthur Hildersam], the other against it [by Francis Johnson]. . . . 4to. Pp. 141. B. L. [*Brit. Mus.*]
[London, 1595?]

TREATISE (a) of the nature and vse of things indifferent; tendinge to prove that the ceremonies in present controversie amongst the ministers of the gospell in the realme of England, are neither in nature or vse indifferent. [By William Bradshaw.] 8vo. Pp. 30.   1605

TREATISE (a) of the nature of Catholick faith and heresie, with reflexion upon the nullitie of the English Protestand Church and Clergy. By N. N. [Peter Talbot, Archbishop of Dublin]. 8vo. [*Brit. Mus.*]   Rouen, 1657

TREATISE (a) of the nature of God. [By Thomas Morton.] 8vo. Pp. 239. [*Bodl.*]   London, 1599

TREATISE (a) of the perpetuall visibilitie, and succession of the true Church in all ages. [By George Abbot, Archbishop of Canterbury.] 4to. Pp. 116. [Simms' *Bibl. Staff.* p. 2.]   [London] 1624

TREATISE (a) of the plague ; being an instruction how one ought to act, in relation, I. To apparel and lodging. II. To diet. III. To antidotes or preservatives. IV. To such medicines, as are necessary to be made use of. . . . By Eugenius Philalethes, Jun. [Robert Samber]. 8vo.
London, 1721

TREATISE (a) of the principall grounds and maximes of the lawes of this kingdome ; very usefull and commodious for all students, and such others as desire the knowledge, and understanding of the lawes : written by that most excellent, and learned expositor of the law, W. N. [William Noy] of Lincolns-Inn, Esquire. 4to. Pp. 130.   London, 1641

TREATISE (a) of the Real Presence, in answer to [Charles Leslie] the author of "The case stated," in which 'tis clearly shewed we have both Scripture and Fathers on our side, and consequently something besides "an unintelligible Jargon of Metaphysicks," p. 150 ; the second part. By the author of *The gentleman instructed* [William Darrell, S.J.]. 12mo. Pp. 400. [Oliver's *Collections ; Sommervogel.*]
London, 1721

TREATISE (a) of the revenue and false money of the Romans. [By —— De Chassipol.] To which is annexed a dissertation upon the manner of distinguishing antique medals from counterfeit ones. [By Guillaume Beauvis.] 8vo. Pp. xxxii. 227. [*Brit. Mus.*]
London, 1741

TREATISE (a) of the souls union with Christ. . . . By J. L. [John Lougher, minister at Beaconsthorpe, Norfolk]. 8vo.   London, 1680

TREATISE (a) of the sufferings and victory of Christ, in the work of our redemption ; declaring by the Scriptures these two questions : that Christ suffered for vs the wrath of God, which we may well terme the paynes of hell, or hellish sorrowes. That Christ after his death on the crosse, went not into hell in his soule. Contrarie to certaine errours in these points publiklie preached in London : anon 1597. [Signed : H. I. *i.e.* Henry Jacob.] 8vo. Pp. 174.   N.P. 1598

TREATISE (a) of the three evils of the last times : I. The sword ; II. The pestilence ; III. The famine, and of their natural and moral causes. [By John Hildrop, D.D.] 8vo. [Watt's *Bibl. Brit.*]   London, 1711

TREATISE (a) of the three-fold state of man, wherein is handled : 1. His created holiness. 2. His sinfulness since the fall. 3. His renewed holiness in his regeneration. [By Rev. Thomas Morton.] 8vo. [Darling's *Cyclop. Bibl.*]   London, 1596

TREATISE (a) of the two sacraments of the Gospell ; Baptisme and the Supper of the Lord : divided into two parts. The first treating of the doctrine and nature of the sacraments in generall, and of these two in speciall; together with the circumstances attending them. The second containing the manner of our due preparation to the receiving of the Supper of the Lord . . . The third edition. By D. R. B. of divin. minister of the Gospel [Daniel Rogers]. 4to. Pp. 360. [*D. N. B.* vol. 49, p. 118.]   London, 1636

TREATISE (a) of the vanity of childish-baptisme ; wherein the deficiency of the baptisme of the Church of England is considered in five particulars thereof. . . . By A. R. [Andrew Ritor]. 4to. [Whitley's *Bapt. Bibl.* i. 12.]   London, 1642

TREATISE (a) of three conversions of England from Paganisme to Christian religion ; the first under the Apostles, in the first age after Christ : the second under Pope Eleutherius and K. Lucius, in the second age : the third, under Pope Gregory the Great, and K. Ethelbert in the sixth age. . . . By N. D. author of the *Ward-word* [Robert Parsons]. 8vo. [Jones' *Peck*, 1. 150.]
1603

TREATISE (a) of traditions; part I. Where it is proved, that we have evidence sufficient from tradition; I. That the Scriptures are the Word of God. II. That the Church of England owns the true canon of the books of the Old Testament. III. That the copies of the Scripture have not been corrupted. IV. That the Romanists have no such evidence for their traditions. V. That the testimony of the present Church of Rome can be no sure evidence of Apostolical tradition. VI. What traditions may securely be relyed upon, and what not. [By Daniel Whitby.] 4to.   London, 1688

——. Part II. Shewing the novelty of the pretended traditions of the Church of Rome. . . . [By Daniel Whitby.] 4to. [Jones' *Peck*, ii. 323.]
London, 1689

TREATISE (a) of Transubstantiation. [By Roger Hesketh, D.D.]   4to. [Gillow's *Bibl. Dict.*]   London, 1688

TREATISE (a) of vnion of the two realmes of England and Scotland. By I. H. [Sir John Haywarde, D.C.L.]. 4to. Pp. 58. [*Brit. Mus.*]
London, 1604

TREATISE (a) of vse and custome. [By Meric Casaubon.] 4to. Pp. 186. [*Camb. Univ. Lib.*]   London, 1638

T R E A T I S E (a) of weights and measures; in which the antient and modern weights and measures of several nations are accurately compared, especially those of Scotland and England. [By William Young.] 12mo.
Aberdeen, 1762

TREATISE (a) of wool, and the manufacture of it; in a letter to a friend occasion'd upon a discourse concerning the great abatements of rents, and low value of lands : wherein is shewed how their worth and value may be advanced by the improvement of the manufacture and price of our English wool. . . . [By George Clarke.] 4to. Pp. 31. [*Bodl.*]   London, 1685

An earlier edition (1677) bears the title "A treatise of wool and cattel, in a letter . . . "

TREATISE (a) on agriculture. [By Adam Dickson.] 8vo. [*Camb. Univ. Lib.*]   London, 1762

TREATISE (a) on agriculture. . . . By a practical farmer [John Armstrong]. 8vo.   Albany, New York, 1819

An edition of 1845 bears the author's name.

TREATISE (a) on air; containing new experiments and thoughts on combustion; being a full investigation of M. Lavoisier's system. . . . By Richard Bewley, M.D. [Robert Harrington, M.D.]. 8vo. Pp. 215. [*Mon. Rev.* vi. 435; xiv. 462.]   London, 1791

TREATISE (a) on captures in war. By Richard Lee, Esq. Second edition; corrected : with additional notes [by Thomas Hartwell Horne]. 8vo.
London, 1803

From a list of his works in the handwriting of the editor.

TREATISE (a) on Church government. By a neighbour [Ebenezer Chaplin]. 8vo. [Evans' *Amer. Bibl.* vol. 4, p. 354.]   Boston, 1773

TREATISE (a) on Civil government. . . . By Sevrup Semaj [James Purves]. 12mo. [*D. N. B.* vol. 47, p. 51.]
Edinburgh, 1791

TREATISE (a) on devotion to the sacred heart of our Saviour J. C. [Compiled by Robert Beeston, S.J.] 12mo. Pp. 53. [Oliver's *Collections; Sommervogel.*]   N.P. 1711

TREATISE (a) on equity jurisprudence. By Platt Potter [John Willard]. 8vo. [Kirk's *Supp.*]   New York, 1875

TREATISE (a) on field diversions. By a Gentleman of Suffolk [—— Symonds] a staunch sportsman; showing the nature of dogs, etc. 12mo. [*Brit. Mus.*]   Norwich, private print, 1776

TREATISE on finance, under which the general interests of the British Empire are illustrated, comprising a project for their improvement. . . . [By David Laurie.] 8vo. Pp. 1268.
Glasgow, 1815

T R E A T I S E (a) on happiness. [By James Flamank.] 8vo. 2 vols.
London, 1832

TREATISE (a) on heresy, as cognizable by the spiritual courts; and an examination of the statute 9th and 10th William III. C. 32. entitled, An Act for the more effectual suppressing of blasphemy and profaneness, in denying by writing, printing, teaching, or advised speaking, the divine original of the Scriptures, or the doctrine of the Holy Trinity. By a barrister at law [Sir Benjamin Hobhouse, Bart.]. 8vo. Pp. 146. [*Biog. Dict.* 1816; *Mon. Rev.* xi. 206.]   London, 1792

TREATISE (a) on justification. . . . By the Rev. Mr Thomas Dutton [or rather by Anne Dutton]. 8vo. Pp. 185. [*Brit. Mus.*]   Glasgow, 1778

TREATISE (a) on mercury, shewing the danger of taking it crude for all manner of disorders, after the present fashion, from its nature, its manner of operating in the human body and facts, with some remarks on the Antient physician's legacy [of Thomas Dover]. [By Henry Bradley.] 8vo. Pp. viii. 52. [*W.*] London, 1733

TREATISE (a) on military finance; containing the pay, subsistence, deductions, and arrears of the forces on the British and Irish establishments; and all the allowances in camp, garrison and quarters, &c. With an enquiry into the method of cloathing and recruiting the army; and an extract from the report of the Commissioners of public accounts, relating to the office of the Paymaster General. [By John Williamson.] 12mo. [*Gent. Mag.* lxxi. ii. 957; *Mon. Rev.* lxviii. 362.] London, 1782

TREATISE (a) on naval discipline; with an explanation of the important advantages which naval and military discipline might derive from the science of phrenology: to which are added, phrenological deductions from the cerebral developement of J——h H——e [Joseph Hume] Esq. [By Capt., afterwards Sir John Ross.] 8vo. London, 1825

TREATISE (a) on pasturage, in two parts. [By Anthony Macmillan.] 8vo. Edinburgh, 1790

TREATISE (a) on penance. By George Douley [William Warford, or Warneford]. 12mo. [*Oliver's Collections.*] St Omer, 1633

TREATISE (a) on R. J. Campbell's sermon preached on "Anthropomorphism," or "Man made in the image of God." [Signed: W. D. F. *i.e.* William D. Forsyth.] 8vo. [*Brit. Mus.*] Littleborough [1908]

TREATISE (a) on rents. By a late Lord Chief Baron [Sir Jeffrey Gilbert]. 8vo. [*Brit. Mus.*] [London] 1758

TREATISE (a) on signals. . . . [By Rev. James Ramsay, M.A.] 8vo. [Watt's *Bibl. Brit.*] London [1784]

TREATISE (a) on skating. . . . By a gentleman [Lieut. Robert Jones]. 8vo. Pp. 64. [*Brit. Mus.*] London [*c.* 1775]

A reissue of the edition of 1772, which bears the author's name.

TREATISE (a) on soap-making; containing, an account of the alkaline materials; tests for discovering the presence of an alkali, &c.; with full directions for manufacturing yellow, pure, white, and perfumed hard soap. . . . By a manufacturer [John Carmichael]. 12mo. Pp. xxii. 132. Edinburgh, 1807

TREATISE (a) on swimming, as taught in the Military College of Berlin. By an Officer of the Coldstream Guards [Charles William Short]. 8vo. [Thomas's *Swimming,* p. 239.] London, 1846

TREATISE (a) on tennis. By a member of the Tennis Club [Robert Lukin]. 8vo. Pp. viii. 120. [*Brit. Mus.*] London, 1822

TREATISE (a) on the application of certain terms and epithets to Jesus Christ. [By Paul Cardale.] 8vo. Pp. 74. [*Brit. Mus.*] London, 1774

TREATISE (a) on the arts, manufactures, manners and institutions of the Greek and Romans. [By Thomas Dudley Fosbrooke, M.A., Rev. Dionysius Lardner, LL.D., and Samuel Astley Dunham, LL.D.] 12mo. 2 vols. London, 1833

Lardner's Cab. Cyclopædia.

TREATISE (a) on the authorship of Ecclesiastes. [By Rev. David Johnston, D.D., Professor in Aberdeen University.] 8vo. [*Brit. Mus.*] London, 1880

TREATISE (a) on the beneficial effects of cold and warm bathing; with an appendix, containing a description of the baths erected at Portobello, near Edinburgh. [By John Millar, M.D.] 8vo. Pp. 62. Edinburgh, 1807

TREATISE (a) on the breeding, training, and management of horses, with practical remarks & observations on farriery, etc.; to which is prefixed the natural history of horses in general, and the antiquity of horse-racing in England; together with an appendix containing the whole law relating to horses. By an old sportsman, etc. [William Flint]. 12mo. [*W.; Brit. Mus.*] Hull, 1815

Signed: W. F.

TREATISE (a) on the choice, buying and general management of live stock. . . . By the author of *The complete grazier* [Thomas Hartwell Horne]. 8vo. [*Brit. Mus.*] London, 1807

TREATISE (a) on the choice of religion ; written in Latin by the R. Father L. Lessius, of the Society of Jesus, and translated into English [by William Wright, S.J.]. 8vo. [Oliver's *Collections ; Sommervogel.*]
St Omer, 1619

TREATISE (a) on the coco-nut tree. . . . By a Fellow of the Linnæan and Horticultural Societies [J. W. Bennett]. 8vo. [*N. and Q.* Feb. 1869, p. 168.]
London, 1831

TREATISE (a) on the Court of Exchequer ; in which the revenues of the crown, the manner of receiving and accounting for the several branches of them, the duty of the several officers employed in the collection and receipt, the nature of the processes for the recovery of debts due to the crown, are clearly explained. . . . By a late Lord Chief Baron of that court [Sir Jeffrey Gilbert]. 8vo. Pp. xvi. 343. [*D. N. B.* vol. 21, p. 326.]
In the Savoy, 1758

TREATISE (a) on the culture of wheat, recommending a system of management founded upon the successful experience of the author. By a practical farmer [John Claudius Loudon]. 8vo.   London, 1812

TREATISE (a) on the dental art. By J. C. F. Maury [Auguste Tillet]. 8vo. [Cushing's *Init. and Pseud.*]
Philadelphia, 1842

TREATISE (a) on the different degrees of the Christian priesthood ; translated from the Latin [of H. Saravia by A. W. Street]. 12mo. [*Brit. Mus.*]
Oxford, 1840
Signed : A. W. S.

TREATISE (a) on the faith and hope of the Gospel ; in two parts. [By Benjamin Ingham.] 12mo. Pp. viii. 183.   [Private print] 1770
Later editions bear the author's name.

TREATISE (a) on the game of cribbage ; shewing the laws and rules of the game, as now played at St James's, Bath, and Newmarket. . . . By Anthony Pasquin, Esq. [John Williams]. 8vo. Pp. 96. [*Biog. Dict.* 1816 ; *Mon. Rev.* viii. 468.]   London, 1792

TREATISE (a) on the hair and teeth . . . . By a surgeon [B. Abrahams]. [Cushing's *Init. and Pseud.*]
New Hampton, New Hampshire, 1849

TREATISE (a) on the improvements made in the art of criticism, collected out of the writings of a celebrated hypercritic. By Philocriticus Cantabrigiensis [John Jackson]. 8vo. Pp. 58. [Sutton's *Life of Jackson*, p. 184.]
London, 1748

TREATISE (a) on the indefinite and infinite powers of credit, circulation of money, and industry. [By —— Garbett.] 8vo. [*Brit. Mus.*]
London, 1784

TREATISE (a) on the manner of raising forest trees, &c. In a letter from the Right Honourable, the Earl of —— [Thomas Hamilton, Earl of Haddington] to his grandson ; to which are added, two memoirs : the one on preserving and repairing forests ; the other on the culture of forests, both translated from the French of M. de Buffon of the Royal Academy at Paris. 12mo. Pp. 129. [*Brit. Mus.*]
Edinburgh, 1761

TREATISE (a) on the manufacture . . . of freigus. . . . By a practical chemist [John Stephen]. 8vo.
Philadelphia, 1860

TREATISE (a) on the method of living well ; a translation [by Thomas Everard, or Everett, S.J.]. 12mo. [Gillow's *Bibl. Dict.*]   St Omer, 1620

TREATISE (a) on the modes and subjects of baptism. . . . [By Samuel Hebden.] 8vo. Pp. 60.
London, 1742

TREATISE (a) on the nature and causes of doubt, in religious questions ; (with a particular reference to Christianity) : with an appendix, on some common difficulties : lists of books, etc. [By David Bristow Baker, M.A., of St John's College, Cambridge.] 12mo.   London, 1831

TREATISE (a) on the nature and constitution of the Christian Church ; wherein are set forth the forms of its government, the extent of its powers, and the limits of our obedience. By a layman [William Stevens]. 8vo. [Watt's *Bibl. Brit. ; Mon. Rev.* xlviii. 419.]   London, 1773

TREATISE (a) on the nature and virtues of the Buxton waters ; with a preliminary account of the external and internal use of natural and artificial warm waters among the ancients. By a physician [Alexander Hunter, M.D.]. 8vo. Pp. 68. London, 1761
The third edition, 1773, has the author's name.

TREATISE (a) on the nature, uses, and effects of the Harrogate mineral waters. By a member of the Royal College of Surgeons [John Thomson, formerly Mayor of Ripon]. 12mo. Pp. 93. [Boyne's *Yorkshire Lib.* p. 138.]

[Ripon, 1841]

Appended to the third edition of *The Tourist's guide*, by John Richard Walbran, published at Ripon in 1841, under the title of *The Harrogate visitor's pictorial pocket guide to Ripon, Studley, &c.*

TREATISE (a) on the office, functions, and dignity of Surrogates ; with some remarks on the projected reform of ecclesiastical courts. [By Thomas Marsden of Durham.] 8vo. Pp. viii. 24. [*Brit. Mus.*] London, 1836

TREATISE (a) on the origin, progressive improvement, and present state, of the silk manufacture. [By George Richardson Porter.] 8vo. Pp. xv. 339.

London, 1831

Lardner's Cab. Cyclop.

TREATISE (a) on the parallactic angle, extracted from a letter to the late Earl of Macclesfield on that subject ; to which is added an appendix, containing a compleat set of solar and lunar tables. . . . [The Dedication is signed : S. C. *i.e.* the Hon. Spencer Cowper, Dean of Durham.] 4to. Pp. viii. 31.

London, 1766

The appendix has a separate pagination [viii. 33].

TREATISE (a) on the passions, so far as they regard the stage ; with a critical enquiry into the theatrical merit of Mr G——k, Mr Q——n, and Mr B——y [Garrick, Quin, and Barry]. The first considered in the part of Lear, the two last opposed in Othello. [By Samuel Foote.] 8vo. [*Brit. Mus.*] London [1747]

TREATISE (a) on the patriarchal system of society . . . in America. By an inhabitant of Florida [Z. Kingsley]. 8vo. [Cushing's *Init. and Pseud.*] 1833

TREATISE (a) on the pleadings in suits in the Court of Chancery by English bill ; in two books. [By John Freeman Mitford, 1st Lord Redesdale.] 8vo. Pp. 128. London, 1780

TREATISE (a) on the police and crimes of the Metropolis. . . . By the editor of *The Cabinet lawyer* [John Wade, LL.D.]. 8vo. [*Brit. Mus.*] London, 1829

TREATISE (a) on the police of the metropolis, explaining the various crimes and misdemeanors which at present are felt as a pressure upon the community ; and suggesting remedies for their prevention. By a magistrate [Patrick Colquhoun, LL.D.]. 8vo.

London, 1796

The edition of 1800 has the author's name.

TREATISE (a) on the powers and duties of Juries, and on the Criminal Laws of England. By William Mavor [Sir Richard Phillips]. 12mo. [*Bibliographer*, vol. 4, p. 168.] London, 1811

TREATISE (a) on the principles and practice of the action of ejectment. . . . By Philo Ruggles [John Adams, of the Middle Temple]. 8vo. [Cushing's *Init. and Pseud.*]

New York, 1821

TREATISE (a) on the principles, practice, and history of commerce. [By John R. MacCulloch.] 8vo. [*Brit. Mus.*] London, 1831

Library of Useful Knowledge.

TREATISE on the progress of literature, and its effects on society ; including a sketch of the progress of English and Scottish literature. [By Robert Thomson.] 8vo. Edinburgh, 1834

TREATISE (a) on the progressive improvement and present state of the manufactures in metal. [By John Holland.] 8vo. 3 vols. [*Brit. Mus.*] London, 1831-34

TREATISE (a) on the proper condition for all horses. By Harry Hieover [Charles Bindley]. 8vo. [*Brit. Mus.*] London, 1852

TREATISE (a) on the religious observation of the Lord's-day, according to the express words of the fourth commandment. [By Dr Samuel Wright.] Second edition. . . . 8vo.

London, 1724

TREATISE (a) on the right of Manors, as deduced from the most ancient and best authorities. . . . [Preface signed : J. S. *i.e.* J. Searle.] 8vo.

London, 1817

TREATISE (a) on the safety and maintenance of states by the means of fortresses ; written originally in French, by M. Maigret, Ingineer in Chief, and Knight of the Royal and Military Order of St Louis [and translated by John Heath]. 8vo. London, 1747

TREATISE (a) on the second sight, dreams and apparitions, with several instances sufficiently attested ; and an appendix of others equally authentic ; the whole illustrated with letters to and from the author on the subject of his treatise. . . . By Theophilus Insulanus [Rev. Donald M'Leod, of Hamer, in Skye]. 12mo. Pp. xxvi. 192. [Boswell's *Tour to the Hebrides.*]

Edinburgh, 1763

TREATISE (a) on the seven stages of man's life, the aged, and word union. By Philomath [Joseph Jenkins]. 12mo. Pp. 28. [*Brit. Mus.*] Penzance, 1865

TREATISE (a) on the solar creation and universal deluge of the earth, by which is illustrated many of the most curious points in natural philosophy. By a native of Manchester [John Lowe, jun.]. 8vo. Pp. viii. 361. [*Manch. Free Lib.*] London [*c.* 1790]

TREATISE (a) on the subjection of Princes to God and the Church. [By Michael Walpole, S.J.] 4to. [*Oliver's Collections ; Sommervogel.*] St Omer, 1608

TREATISE (a) on the theory and practice of seamanship ; containing general rules for manœuvring vessels, with a moveable figure of a ship, so planned that the sails, rudder, and hull may be made to perform the manœuvres according to the rule laid down. . . . By an officer in the service of the India Company [Richard Hall Gower]. 8vo. [*Brit. Mus.*] London, 1793

TREATISE (a) on the third commandment, self-denial, and marriage. By Philomath [Joseph Jenkins]. 12mo. Pp. 28. [*Brit. Mus.*] Penzance [1864]

TREATISE (a) on the vanity of Childish-Baptisme, wherein the deficiency of the Baptisme of the Church of England is considered in five particulars thereof; and wherein also is proved that baptizing is dipping and dipping baptizing. By A. R. [Andrew Ritor]. 4to. Pp. iv. 32. [*Whitley's Bapt. Bibl.*] London, 1642

TREATISE (a) on the virtues and efficacy of a crust of bread, eat early in a morning fasting. . . . [By N. Robinson.] The fifth edition. 8vo. [*Brit. Mus.*] London, 1767

TREATISE (a) on theonomy. . . . . Book I. By Robert Blake [Robert Hely Thompson]. 8vo. London [1907]

TREATISE (a) on trade ; or, the antiquity and honour of commerce, shewing how trade was esteemed by the Egyptians, Jews, Greeks, and Romans, and on what footing of worship it stands with us ; addressed to the country-gentlemen of England. [By —— Perry of Penshurst, Kent.] 8vo. Pp. viii. 64. [*W.*] London, 1750

TREATISE (a) on virtue and vice [by —— Ridgway]. 8vo. Private print, 1783

TREATISE on wheel carriages, showing their present defects ; with a plan and description of a new constructed waggon, which will effectually preserve and improve the public roads, and be more useful, cheap, and handy to the proprietor. [By Samuel Bourn.] 8vo. 3 parts. [*Watt's Bibl. Brit.*] London, 1768

TREATISE (a) parænetical, wherein is shewed the way to resist the Castilian King [Philip II.]. By a pilgrim Spaniard [José Teixeira]. 4to. [*Pollard and Redgrave.*] London, 1598

For a later edition, 1625, see "The Spanish pilgrim . . ."

TREATISE (a) partly theological, and partly political, containing some few discourses, to prove that the liberty of philosophizing (that is making use of natural reason) may be allow'd without any prejudice to piety, or to the peace of any common-wealth ; and that the loss of public peace and religion it self must necessarily follow, where such a liberty of reasoning is taken away. Translated out of Latin [of Benedict de Spinoza]. 8vo. Pp. 452. [*N. and Q.* 28th Feb. 1863, p. 168.] London, 1689

TREATISE (a) shewing how useful, safe, reasonable and beneficial the inrolling and registring of all conveyances of lands may be to the inhabitants of this kingdom. By a person of great learning and judgment [Sir Matthew Hale]. 4to. [*Wood's Athen. Oxon.* iii. 1096.] London, 1694

TREATISE (a) tending to mitigation tovvards Catholicke - subiectes in England ; wherein is declared, that it is not impossible for subiects of different religion, (especially Catholickes and Protestantes) to liue togeather in dutifull obedience and subiection, under the gouernment of his Maiesty of Great Britany : against the seditious wrytings of Thomas Morton minister, & some others. . . . By P. R. [Robert Parsons]. 8vo. Pp. 556. [*Oliver's Collections* ; Sommervogel's *Dictionnaire.*] 1607

TREATISE (a) touching the East-Indian trade ; or, a discourse (turned out of French into English) concerning the establishment of a French company for the commerce of the East-Indies. [By François Charpentier.] 4to. Pp. 62. [*Bodl.*] London, 1664

TREATISE (a) upon coal-mines ; or, an attempt to explain their general marks of indication, acknowledg'd and probable : together with particular instances of their public utility : objections to the mode of their discovery, and to their manufacture, obviated, &c. [By William Sharp, vicar of Long Burton.] 8vo. Pp. 105. [*Brit. Mus.*] London, 1769

TREATISE (a) upon gout, in which the primitive cause of that disease and likewise of gravel is clearly ascertained; and an easy method recommended, by which both may be with certainty prevented, or radically cured. [By Murray Forbes.] 8vo. [*Mon. Rev.* lxxvi. 220 ; xiii. 233.] London, 1786

TREATISE (a) upon the culture of peach trees ; translated from the French [of De Combes]. 8vo. London, 1768

TREATISE (a) upon the modes ; or, a farewell to French kicks. [By John Harris, D.D., Bishop of Llandaff.] 8vo. Pp. viii. 64. [*Bodl.*] London, 1715
Attributed also to John Robinson, Bishop of Bristol. [*Brit. Mus.*]

TREATISE (a) wherein is declared the sufficiencie of English medicines for cure of all diseases, cured with medicines ; whereunto is added a collection of medicines growing (for the most part) within our English climat, approoved and experimented against the jaundice, dropsie, stone, falling sicknesse, pestilence. [By Timothy Bright, M.D.?] 12mo. Pp. 127. [*W.*] London, 1615
The dedication to Lord Zouch is subscribed : T. B.

TREATISE (a) wherein is demonstrated, I. That the East-India trade is the most national of all foreign trades. II. That the clamors, aspersions, and objections made against the present East-India Company, are sinister, selfish, or groundless. III. That since the discovery of the East-Indies, the dominion of the sea depends much upon the wane or increase of that trade, and consequently the security of the liberty, property, and protestant religion of this kingdom. IV. That the trade of the East-Indies cannot be carried on to national advantage in any other way than by a general joynt-stock. V. That the East-India trade is more profitable and necessary to the kingdom of England, than to any other kingdom or nation in Europe. By Φιλοπάτρις [Sir Josiah Child]. 4to. Pp. 43. [M'Culloch's *Lit. of Pol. Econ.* p. 99.] London, 1681

TREATISE (a) whirein is manifestlie proved that reformation and those that sincerely favour the same are unjustly charged to be enemies unto his Majestie and the state : written both for the clearing of those that stande in that cause, and the stopping of the sclanderous mouthes of all the enemies thereof. [By John Penry]. 4to. [*D. N. B.* vol. 44, p. 348.] [Edinburgh ?] 1590
This pamphlet was preceded by a similarly anonymous "Humble (an) motion with submission . . ."

TREATISE (a) written by an author of the communion of the Church of Rome touching transubstantiation ; wherein is made appear, that according to the principles of that Church, this doctrine cannot be an article of faith. [From the French of Louis Dufour, abbé de Longuerne. Published by Abp. Thomas Tenison.] 4to. Pp. 73. London, 1687

TREATISES concerning regeneration. 1. Of repentance ; 2. Of the diet of the soule ; shewing, the one, how it ought to be sought after, and may be attained vnto : the other, how it being gotten, is to be preserued and continued. [By Thomas Morton.] 8vo. Pp. 119. [*Bodl.*] London, 1613

TREATISES on poetry, modern romance, and rhetoric, contributed to the *Encyclopædia Britannica*. [By George Moir.] 8vo. Edinburgh, 1839

TREATISES on printing and typefounding. By T. C. H. [Thomas Curson Hansard]; from the seventh edition of the *Encyclopædia Britannica*. 8vo. Pp. vii. 235. Edinburgh, 1841

TREATMENT (the) of our domestic dogs. By "Magenta" [Captain Maurice Hartland Mahon]. 8vo. Edinburgh, 1868

TREATY (a) of pacification; or, conditions of peace between God and man. By H. I. [Henry Isaacson]. 12mo. [*D. N. B.* vol. 29, p. 61.] London, 1645

TREATYSE (a) cōcernynge diuers of the constitucyons prouynciale and legantines. [By Christopher Saint German?] 8vo. B. L. [*Brit. Mus.*] London [1535 ?]

TREATYSE (a) shewing and declaring the pryde and abuse of women now a dayes. By Charles Bansley. [Edited by John Payne Collier.] 8vo. Pp. 15. [*W.*] [London, 1841]
Reprinted from an unique copy.

TRECAN Farm. [A tale, by Rev. Jonathan Lett Stackhouse.] 12mo. Pp. 47. [Cushing's *Anon.*] London [1865]

TREE (the) of knowledge. [A novel.] By G. M. Robins [Mrs Louis Baillie Reynolds]. 8vo. 3 vols.
London, 1889

TREE (a) planted by the rivers of water; or, an essay upon the . . . improvements which baptized Christians are to make of their sacred Baptism. . . . [By Cotton Mather.] 8vo. Pp. ii. 70. [Whitley's *Bapt. Bibl.* i. 139.]
Boston, 1704

TREE stories. By Mary Muller [Lenore E. Mulets]. 8vo.   Chicago, 1904

TREES and their nature ; or, the bud and its attributes : in a series of letters to his sons, by A. H. [Alexander Harvey, M.D.]. 8vo. [*Brit. Mus.*]
London, 1856

TREES and their uses. [By Harriet Bickersteth, later Mrs Cook.] 12mo. [*Brit. Mus.*]   London, 1862

TREFOIL; verses by three [A., E. *i.e.* Miss E. Synge, and F. *i.e.* Frances Mary Synge, later Mrs Owen]. 8vo. [*Brit. Mus.*]   London, 1868

TREMAINE ; or, the man of refinement. [By Robert Plumer Ward.] Second edition. 12mo. 3 vols.
London, 1825

TREMENDA; the dreadful sound with which the wicked are to be thunderstruck ; in a sermon. . . . [By Cotton Mather.] 12mo. Pp. 41. [G. Brinley's *Amer. Lib.*]   Boston, 1721

TREMLETT diamonds. [A novel.] By Alan St Aubyn [Frances Marshall]. 8vo. Pp. 328.   London, 1906

TRENT (the) Sunday School manual; or, questions . . . on the collects. . . . [By Rev. William Henry Turner.] 12mo. [*Brit. Mus.*]   London, 1840

TREPAN (the) ; or, virtue rewarded : an opera. [Probably by John Maxwell, a blind man.] 8vo. [Baker's *Biog. Dram.*]   York, 1739

TREVELYAN. By the author of *A marriage in high life* [Lady Caroline Lucy Scott]. Second edition. 12mo. 3 vols. [*Brit. Mus.*]   London, 1834

TREVLYN Hold ; or, Squire Trevlyn's heir. By the author of *East Lynne*, etc. [Mrs Henry Wood, *née* Ellen Price]. 8vo. 3 vols. [*D. N. B.* vol. 62, p. 356.]   London, 1864

TREW (the) report of the dysputacyon had & begonne in the convocaycyon hows at london among the clargye there assembled the xviii daye of October in the yeare of our lord M.D.LIIII. [By John Philpot, Archdeacon of Winchester.] 12mo. [Maskell's *Selected centuries of books*, p. 98.]
Imprinted at Basil by Alexander Edmonds, 1554. A fictitious imprint.

TREWE (a) and feythfull hystorie of the redoubtable Prynce Radapanthus. [A pretended reprint from a unique copy printed by Wynkin de Worde ; but the reputed author is John Adey Repton.] 12mo. [*Gent. Mag.* Jan. 1861, p. 109.]   London, 1820

TRIAL (the) and life of Eugene Aram ; several of his letters and poems ; and his plan and specimens of an Anglo-Celtic lexicon : with copious notes and illustrations, and an engraved facsimile of the handwriting of this very ingenious but ill-fated scholar. [By Michael Fryer, of Reeth.] 8vo. Pp. 126.
Richmond, 1842

TRIAL and triumph ; a coronation ode. . . . By Robert Blake [Robert Hely Thompson]. 8vo. Pp. 32.
London, 1902

TRIAL and triumph ; a novel. . . . [By —— M'Gauran.] 8vo. 3 vols. [Cushing's *Anon.*]   London, 1854

TRIAL (the) ; Calvin and Hopkins, *versus* the Bible and common sense. By a lover of the truth [Charles Prentiss]. 8vo. [Allibone's *Dict.*]
Boston, 1819

TRIAL (the) ; more links of the Daisy chain. By the author of *The heir of Redclyffe* [Charlotte Mary Yonge]. 8vo.   London and Cambridge, 1864

TRIAL (the) of a student at the college of Clutha ; in the kingdom of Oceana. [By William Thom, minister of Govan.] 8vo. Pp. 76.   Glasgow, 1768
Reprinted among "The works of the Rev. William Thom . . ." Glasgow, 1799. 12mo.

TRIAL (the) of Abraham ; a dramatic poem. [By Rev. E. Farrer.] 8vo. Pp. vii. 68. [*W.; Brit. Mus.*]
Stamford, 1790

TRIAL (the) of Arminian Methodism ; together with a vindication of the good old Church-of-England doctrines. . . . By the author of *Free Grace* [William Howell]. 12mo. Pp. 32. Leeds, 1798

TRIAL (the) of Elizabeth Fenning for murder ; with an investigation of the mysterious case, and full particulars by Dr J. Watkins [William Hone]. [Nattali and Bond's *Cat.*, Feb. 1858.]
1815

TRIAL (the) of Farmer Carter's dog Porter, for murder ; taken down verbatim et literatim in short-hand, and now published by authority, from the corrected manuscript of Counsellor Clear-point, barrister at law. N.B. This is the only true and authentic copy ; and all others are spurious. [By Edward Long.] 8vo. [*Gent. Mag.* May 1813, p. 490.]
London, 1771

TRIAL (the) of Frederick Kendall, for setting fire to Sydney College, Cambridge; published from notes taken in court by a member of the University [Edward Smedley, M.A.]. 8vo. Pp. 18. [Bowes' *Camb. Books.*]
Cambridge, 1813

TRIAL (the) of man; an allegorical romance. [By Charles Edward Lawrence.] 8vo. Pp. viii. 319. [*Brit. Mus.*] London, 1902

TRIAL (the) of Mr Whitefield's spirit ; in some remarks upon his fourth journal, publish'd when he staid in England on account of the embargo. [By Rev. Samuel Weller, minister of Maidstone.] 8vo. Pp. 55. [*Smith's Bibl. Cant. ; Gent. Mag.* Nov. 1740, p. 576.] London, 1740

TRIAL (the) of republicanism ; or, a series of political papers, proving the injurious and debasing consequences of republican government, and written constitutions : with an introductory address to the Hon. Thomas Erskine, Esq. By Peter Porcupine [William Cobbett]. 8vo. Pp. 63.
London, 1801

TRIAL (the) of Selim the Persian [George Lord Lyttelton], for divers high crimes and misdemeanours. [By Edward Moore, the dramatist.] 4to. Pp. 24. [O'Donoghue's *Poets of Ireland.*] London, 1748

TRIAL of the Duchess of Kingston [Elizabeth Hervey]. Edited by Lewis Melville [Lewis S. Benjamin]. 8vo. Pp. x. 328. [*Brit. Mus.*] London, 1928

TRIAL (the) of the ladies, Hide Park, May Day ; or, the Yellow books partner. [Signed : W. B. *i.e.* William Blake, of Highgate.] 4to. Pp. 46. [*Brit. Mus.*] 1656

TRIAL (the) of the most notable lawsuit of ancient or modern times; the Incorporated Scientific Era Protection Society *v.* Paul Christman and others, in the Court of Common Reason. . . . Issue : Did Christ rise from the dead ? . . . [An allegory, by Robert Roberts.] 8vo. Pp. xii. 282. [*Brit. Mus.*]
London, 1882

TRIAL of the Rev. James Kidd. . . . [By John Davidson.] 8vo. [Robertson's *Aberd. Bibl.*] Aberdeen, 1831

TRIAL (the) of the Unitarians, for a libel on the Christian religion. [By George Wilkins.] 8vo. Pp. 313. [*Aberdeen Pub. Lib.*] London, 1830

TRIAL (the) of the witnesses of the resurrection of Jesus. [By Thomas Sherlock, D.D.] 8vo. [*Brit. Mus.*]
London, 1800

An earlier edition has the title " The tryal . . ." See below.

VOL. VI.

TRIAL (the) of tractarianism by the divine rule " Beware of false prophets. . . . Ye shall know them by their fruits." By Cornelius [Charles Henry Corbett]. 12mo. [*W.*]
London, 1851

TRIALL (the) of a black-pudding; or, the unlawfulness of eating blood proved by Scripture, before the Law, under the Law, and after the Law. By a well-wisher to ancient truth [Thomas Barlow, D.D., bishop of Lincoln ?]. 4to. London, 1652

TRIALL (the) of Lieut. Collonell John Lilburne, by an extraordinary or special Commission, of Oyear and Terminer at the Guild-Hall of London, the 24. 25. 26. of Octob. 1649. . . . Published by Theodorus Verax [Clement Walker]. 4to. [*Brit. Mus.*]
Southwark [1649]

TRIALL (a) of subscription, by way of a preface vnto certaine subscribers ; and, reasons for lesse rigour against non-subscribers : both modestly written ; that neither should offend. [By William Bradshaw.] 8vo. Pp. 10, 28. [*D. N. B.* vol. 6, p. 182.]
[Middleburgh] 1599

TRIALL (the) of Tabacco; wherein his worth is most worthily expressed, as in the name, nature, and qualitie of the sayd hearb; his speciall use in all physicke, with the true and right use of taking it. . . . By E. G. [Edmund Gardner], Gent. and Practicioner in Physicke. 4to. [Bragge's *Books about Tobacco*, p. 7.] London, 1610

TRIALL (the) of the Protestant private Spirit; wherein their doctrine, making the sayd Spirit the sole ground and meenes of their beliefe, is confuted. . . . Written by J. S. [John Spencer] of the Society of Jesus. 4to. Pp. 392. [*De Backer.*] [St Omer] 1630

TRIALOGUS ; a conference betwixt Mr Con, Mr Pro, and Mr Indifferent concerning the Union : to be continued weekly. [By George Mackenzie, Earl of Cromarty.] 4to. [*D. N. B.* vol. 35, p. 147]. 1706

TRIALS ; a tale. By the author of *The favourite of nature*, etc. [M. A. Kelty]. 12mo. 3 vols.
London, 1824

TRIALS (the) of a village priest. By Ruth Buck [Mrs Joseph Lamb]. 8vo. [*Nat. Lib. of Scot.*] London [1862]

TRIALS (the) of life. By the author of *De Lisle* [Mrs Elizabeth C. Grey]. Second edition. 12mo. 3 vols.
London, 1829

TRIALS (the) of Margaret Lyndsay. By the author of *Lights and shadows of Scottish life* [Professor John Wilson]. 8vo.
Edinburgh and London, 1823

TRIANA ; or, a threefold romanza of Mariana, Paduana, Sabina. [By Thomas Fuller.] 12mo. [*Brit. Mus.*]
London, 1654

TRIANGLE (the). . . . By Investigator [Samuel Wheeler]. 8vo. [*Cushing's Init. and Pseud.*]   New York, 1832

TRIANGULAR (a) canon logarith- micall ; or, a table of artificiall sines, tangents, and the complements arith- meticall of sines supplying the use of secants, to radius 100,000,000 and to every degree and minute of the quadrant. [By Richard Norwood, teacher of mathematics.] 4to. 2 parts. [*W. ; Brit. Mus.*]   [1665 ?]

TRIANGULAR (the) society; leaves from the life of a Portland family. [By Elizabeth Chase Akers.] 12mo. [*Foley's Amer. Authors.*]
Portland, Maine, 1886

TRIBE (the) of Levi ; a poem. [By John Tutchin.] 4to. [*Bodl.*]
London, 1691

TRIBES on my frontier ; an Indian naturalist's foreign policy. By Eha [Edward Hamilton Aitken]. 8vo. [*Brit. Mus.*]   London, 1881

TRIBULATIONS (the) of a Princess. By the author of *The martyrdom of an Empress* [Margaret Cunliffe Owen]. 8vo.   London, 1901

TRIBUNAL (the) of the Terror ; a study of Paris in 1793-1795 : from the French of G. Lenôtre [Louis L. T. Gosselin] by Frederick Lees. 8vo. [*Amer. Cat.*]
Philadelphia, 1910

TRIBUNE (the). [By Patrick Delany, D.D.] 8vo. Pp. 84.
Printed at Dublin ; London reprinted, 1729
Consists of xii. numbers.

TRIBUTE (the) ; a collection of pieces in prose and verse. [By Joseph O'Leary, journalist.] 8vo. [*O'Donoghue's Poets of Ireland.*]   Cork, 1833

TRIBUTE (the) ; a panegyrical poem dedicated to the Honorable the Lady Ann Coke, of Holkham Hall. By Philo [—— Maitland]. 8vo. Pp. viii. 28. [*Bodl.*]   Norwich, N.D.
Address to the reader dated 1832.

TRIBUTE (the) of a humble muse to an unfortunate captive Queen, the widow of a murdered King. By W. T. F*** G * * * *, Esq. [W. T. Fitzgerald]. 4to. [*Mon. Rev.* x. 457 ; xiii. 238.]
London, 1793

TRIBUTE to Caesar, how paid by the best Christians, and to what purpose ; with some remarks on the late vigorous expedition against Canada. . . . By Philalethes [Thomas Maule]. 4to. Pp. 29. [*Evans' Amer. Bibl.*]
[Philadelphia, 1712 ?]

TRIBUTE to O'Connell. By a Catho- lic priest of the house of Leinster. [By the Hon. Arthur Philip Perceval, B.C.L.] 8vo. Pp. 11. [*Bodl.*]
Dublin, 1844

TRIBUTE (a) to the life and character of Jonas Chickering. By one who knew him well [Richard Green Parker]. 8vo. [*Cushing's Init. and Pseud.*]
Boston, 1854

TRIBUTE (a) to the memory of Dr Chalmers. By a former pupil [James M'Cosh, D.D., Principal of Princeton College]. 8vo. Pp. 8. [*D. Laing.*]
Brechin, 1847
Signed : J. M.

TRIBUTE (a) to the memory of William Cowper, author of the Task and other poems, occasioned by the perusal of his works, and the memoirs of his life, by Hayley. [By John Talwyn She- well.] 4to. [*Smith's Cat. of Friends' Books*, i. 82 ; ii. 567.]
Ipswich, 1808
Another edition in octavo, was published in the same year, with the author's initials, I. T. S.

TRIBUTE (a) to the memory of William Grover, of Stanstead, in Essex, who died the 11th of 10th month, 1825. By A. F. G. [Atkinson F. Gibson]. 8vo. [*Smith's Cat. of Friends' Books*, i. 95.]   Warwick, 1826

TRIBUTE (a) to the principles, virtues, habits, and public usefulness of the Irish and Scotch early settlers of Pennsylvania. By a descendant [George Chambers, LL.D.]. 8vo. [*Cushing's Init. and Pseud.*] Chambersburg, 1856

TRIBUTES of affection ; with the Slave, and other poems. By a lady, and her brother [Elizabeth Sophia Tomlins ; published by her brother, Sir Thomas Edlyne Tomlins]. 12mo. [*Gent. Mag.* xcviii. ii. 471 ; *Mon. Rev.* xxiv. 214.]
London, 1797

TRICK (a) to catch the old-one ; as it hath beene lately acted, by the children of Paules. [By Thomas Middleton.] 4to. No pagination. [*Baker's Biog. Dram.*]   London, 1608
Another issue has the title :—A tricke to catch the old-one : as it hath beene often in action, both at Paules, and the Black- Fryers : presented before his Maiestie on New-yeares night last. Composde by T. M. [Thomas Middleton]. London, 1608

TRICK, trial, and triumph ; a Scottish clerical detective story. By Andrew Cheviot [Rev. James Hiram Watson]. 8vo. Pp. 128. [Scott's *Fasti* (sec. ed.), ii. 15.]   Glasgow, 1891

TRICK upon trick ; or, the vintner in the suds. [A farce] in two acts. [By Joseph Yarrow.] 12mo. [*Brit. Mus.*]
London, 1786

TRI-COLORED sketches in Paris, during the years 1851 to 1853. By Dick Tinto [Frank Bott Goodrich]. 8vo. [Cushing's *Init. and Pseud.*]
New York, 1855

TRICOTRIN, the story of a waif and stray. By Ouida, author of *Strathmore*, etc. [Louise de La Ramée]. 8vo. 3 vols.   London, 1869

TRIDENT (the) and the net. By the author of *The martyrdom of an Empress* [Margaret Cunliffe Owen]. 8vo. [*Brit. Mus.*]   London, 1905

TRIDENT (the) ; or, the national policy of naval celebration : describing a hieronauticon, or naval temple, with its appendages ; proposing a periodical celebration of naval games, and, on occasion of victories of the first magnitude the granting of triumphs. . . . By a private gentleman [Major John Cartwright]. 4to. Pp. xvi. 208. [Watt's *Bibl. Brit.*]   London, 1802

TRIED and true ; a tale. By Alton Clyde [Mrs Arnold Jeffreys]. 12mo. [*Camb. Univ. Lib.*]   London, 1868

TRIFLER (the); a new periodical miscellany by Timothy Touchstone of Saint Peter's College, Westminster. [By R. Oliphant and J. H. Allan, of Trinity College Cambridge ; Hon. W. Aston and Sir W. E. Taunton, students of Christ Church, Oxford, all of whom were under the age of 20.] 8vo. [Lowndes' *Bibl. Man.*]
London, 1788

TRIFLER (the) ; or, a ramble among the wilds of fancy, the works of nature, and the manners of men. [By Henry Man.] 12mo. 4 vols.
London, 1776-77

TRIFLES from my portfolio ; or, recollections of twenty-nine years' military service. By a staff surgeon [Walter Henry]. 8vo. 2 vols. [F. Boase's *Mod. Eng. Biog.* i. 1433.]
Quebec, 1839

Republished with the author's name in two volumes, 8vo, London, 1843, with the title "Events of a military life ; being recollections after service in the Peninsular war, invasion of France, the East Indies, St Helena, Canada and elsewhere."

TRIFLES in poesy. By W. T. M. [Walter Thomas Meyler]. 12mo. [O'Donoghue's *Poets of Ireland.*]
Dublin, 1840

TRIFLES in verse. [By Henry, Lord Lyttelton.] 8vo. Pp. 52. [*W.*; Martin's *Cat.*]   London, 1803

TRIFLING (a) mistake in Lord Erskine's recent preface, corrected in a letter to his Lordship. By the author of the *Defence of the people* [Sir John C. Hobhouse]. 8vo. [*W.*; *Brit. Mus.*]
London, 1819

TRIMESTER (a) in France and Swisserland ; or, a three months' journey in the months of July, August, September, and October, 1820, from Calais to Basle, through Lyons ; and from Basle to Paris, through Strasburg and Reims. By an Oxonian [Rev. Stephen Weston, B.D.]. 8vo. Pp. 88. [Lowndes' *Bibl. Man.* p. 2882.]   London, 1821

TRIMMED (the) lamp ; and other stories of the Four Million. By O. Henry [William Sydney Porter]. 8vo.
Chicago, 1907

TRIMMER (the) ; or, some necessary cautions, concerning the union of the kingdoms of Scotland and England ; with an answer to some of the chief objections against an incorporating union. [By Sir John Spotswood.] 4to.   Edinburgh, 1706

TRIMMING (the) of Thomas Nashe Gentleman, by the high-tituled patron Don Richardo de Medico Campo, Barber Chirurgion to Trinitie Colledge in Cambridge. [By Richard Lichfield, *pseud.* of Gabriel Harvey.] 4to. Pp. 53.   London, 1597

TRIMSHARP'S account of himself. [By Harvey A. Fuller.] 8vo. [Cushing's *Init. and Pseud.*]
Ann Arbor, Michigan, 1873

TRINCULO'S trip to the jubilee. [By Edward Thompson.] 4to. [Newsam's *Poets of Yorkshire.*]   Moran, 1769

TRINITARIAN (the) controversy reviewed ; or, a defence of the Appeal to the common sense of all Christian people, &c. Wherein every particular advanced by the Reverend Dr M'Donnell in his Sincere Christian's answer to the Appeal, is distinctly considered. . . . By the author of the Appeal [William Hopkins]. 8vo. [*Brit. Mus.*]   London, 1760

TRINITARIAN (the) investigator ; or, an examination into the origin, amongst Christians, and Scripture proofs, of the doctrine of the Trinity, &c. A dispassionate inquiry, whether certain opinions held by the Society of Friends, are the peculiar doctrines of Christianity, or whether they are not heathenish, absurd, unscriptural, antichristian, and derogatory of God, addressed to John Wilkinson, Josiah Forster, Joseph John Gurney, & William Allen, acknowledged by that Society to be " true ministers of Christ, and inwardly moved to the work by the Holy Ghost." [By Joseph Shipton.] 8vo. [Smith's *Cat. of Friends' Books*, i. 99 ; ii. 573.]   Birmingham [1830] Signed : An unlearned layman.

TRINITARIAN (the) scheme of religion, concerning Almighty God and mankind, considered both before and after the (pretended) Fall ; with notes. [By Stephen Nye.] 4to. [*D. N. B.* vol. 41, p. 282.]   London, 1692

TRINITY (the) ; a nineteenth century Passion-Play. The Son ; or, victory of love. [By Karl Pearson, Cambridge.] 8vo. [Bartholomew's *Camb. Books.*] 1882

TRINITY Church case. . . . By Presbyter [Rev. John Morgan]. 8vo. [Cushing's *Init. and Pseud.*] New York, 1856

TRINITY [College] Foot Beagles ; a song by H. S. G. [Gladstone]. 8vo. [Bartholomew's *Camb. Books.*] Cambridge, 1898

TRINITY (the) or Christ—Charity and Shilok, showing Jesus and His seed. . . . [Signed : W. D. F. *i.e.* W. D. Forsyth.] 8vo. Pp. 103. [*Brit. Mus.*] Littleborough [1901]

TRINITY (the), the Christ's, and the Antichrists ; thoughts on 1 John. [By Richard Govett.] 12mo. London, 1874

TRIOLETS. By M. B. [Maurice Baring]. Second series. 8vo. Pp. 24. [Chaundy's *Bibl. of M. B.*] [Private print, 1893]

TRIP (a) down the Thames ; from Oxford to Windsor. By a Lockkeeper [J. Sadler]. 8vo. Sonning, 1877

TRIP (the) of the " Porgie " ; or, tacking up the Hudson. By Bricktop [George G. Smith]. 8vo. [Cushing's *Init. and Pseud.*]   New York, 1874

TRIP round the world . . . Europe. By the author of *Home and its duties*, etc. [Mrs J. Werner Laurie]. 12mo. [*Brit. Mus.*]   London [1869]

TRIP (a) through London ; containing observations on men and things ; to which is added, a brief and merry character of Ireland. By a Berkshire gentleman [Erasmus Jones]. . . . 8vo. London, 1728

TRIP (a) to Calais ; a medley maritime sketch : being the poetical, prosaical production of Timothy Timbertoe, Esq. [Samuel Foote], dedicated to a Duchess [of Kingston]. 8vo. Pp. 60. [*Manch. Free Lib.*]   London, 1775

TRIP (a) to Holland, containing sketches of characters ; together with cursory observations on the manners and customs of the Dutch. [By Andrew Becket.] 8vo. 2 vols. [*Biog. Dict.* 1816 ; *Mon. Rev.* lxxiv. 67 ; lxxv. 138.] London, 1786

TRIP (a) to Jamaica ; with a true character of the people and island. By the author of *Sot's Paradise* [Edward Ward]. Fol. Pp. 16. [*Brit. Mus.*] London, 1698

TRIP (a) to London ; or, the humours of a Berwick smack : interspersed with topographical notices. [By R. Jameson, or Jamieson, advocate.] 12mo. Pp. x. 241. [*Brit. Mus.*] Edinburgh, 1815

TRIP (a) to Maoriland. By Pakeha Maori [John Robin]. 8vo. [*Amer. Cat.*]   New York, 1907

TRIP (a) to Margate. By Paul Pry, Esq. [William Heath]. Oblong 4to. [Jaggard's *Index.*]   London [1825]

TRIP (a) to Mexico ; or, recollections of a ten months' ramble in 1849-50. . . . By a barrister [Alex. C. Forbes]. 8vo. London, 1851

TRIP (a) to New-England ; with a character of the country and people, both English and Indians. [By Edward Ward.] Fol. Pp. 16. [*Camb. Hist. of Amer. Lit.* i. 379.] London, 1699

TRIP (a) to Norway in 1873. By Sixtyone [Rev. George Henry Hely Hutchinson]. 8vo.   London, 1874

TRIP (a) to Paris in July and August 1792. [By Richard Twiss.] 8vo. Pp. 131. [*Mon. Rev.* x. 65.] London [1792 or 3]

TRIP (the) to Portsmouth ; a comic sketch of one act, with songs. [By George Alexander Stevens.] 8vo. Pp. 51. [*D. N. B.* vol. 54, p. 230.] London [1773]

TRIP (a) to Rome in 1869. By C. M. [Charles Mackenzie, bookseller]. 12mo. Pp. 87. Edinburgh, private print, 1869

TRIP (a) to Scotland ; as it is acted at the Theatre Royal in Drury-Lane. [By William Whitehead.] 8vo. Pp. 40. [Baker's *Biog. Dram.*]
London, 1770

TRIP (a) to Shetland. By a Scotsman [David Dakers Black]. 8vo. Pp. 49.
Edinburgh, 1872
Signed : T. G.

TRIP (a) to Taymouth, performed during the late Royal Visit, Sept. 1842. [By Dr Thomas Gillespie.] 12mo. [*Brit. Mus.*]
Cupar, 1843

TRIP (a) to the English Lakes in May, 1864. By a Gourmet [Francis Mewburn, Junr.]. 8vo. Pp. 74. [Dobell's *Priv. Prints*, p. 122.]
N.P. [1865]

TRIP (the) to the Great Exhibition of Barnabas Blandydash and family. By Uncle Joseph [Joseph Banks]. 8vo.
London, 1851

TRIPARTITE division of Tithes. [By John Allen, M.D., Dulwich College.] 8vo.
London, 1833

TRIPLE (the) cord ; or, a treatise proving the truth of the Roman religion, by Sacred Scriptures, taken in the literall sense ; expounded by ancient Fathers, interpreted by Protestant writers : with a discouery of sundry subtile sleights vsed by Protestants, for euading the force of strongest arguments, taken from cleerest texts of the foresaid Scriptures. [By Laurence Anderton.] 4to. Pp. 801. [Gillow's *Bibl. Dict.*]
[St Omer] 1634
The Epistle dedicatory is signed : N. N.

TRIPLET (the) ; Church, state, and vassalage. "Tria juncta in uno." [By Judah Lee Bliss.] 8vo. Boston, 1872

TRIPLETS for the truth's sake. By B. B. [Bernard Barton]. 8vo. [*Brit. Mus.*]
London, 1842

TRIPLICI nodo, triplex cuneus ; or, an apologie for the Oath of Allegiance against the two breves of Pope Paulus Quintus, and the late letter of Cardinal Bellarmine to G. Blackwel the Arch-Priest. [By King James I.] 4to. [*Brit. Mus.*]
London, 1607

TRIPLICITY. [An essay. By Thomas Lance, of Birkenhead.] 8vo. 2 vols.
Liverpool, 1840

TRIPPINGS in author-land. By Fanny Forrester [Emily C. Chubbuck, later Mrs Judson]. 12mo. [Cushing's *Init. and Pseud.*]
New York, 1846

TRIPPINGS (the) of Tom Pepper ; an autobiography. By Harry Franco [Charles F. Briggs]. 8vo. [*Brit. Mus.*]
New York, 1844

TRISTIA ; or, the sorrows of Peter : elegies to the King, Lords Grenville, Petty, Erskine, the Bishop of London, Messrs Fox, Sheridan, &c. &c. By P. Pindar, Esq. [John Wolcott, M.D.]. 8vo. Pp. 169.
London, 1806

TRISTRAM and Iseult. [By Rev. Frederick Millard.] 8vo. Pp. 35. [*Brit. Mus.*]
London, private print, 1870

TRISTRAM of Blent ; an episode in the history of an ancient house. By Anthony Hope [Sir Anthony Hope Hawkins]. 8vo. London, 1901

TRITHEISM charged upon Dr Sherlock's new notion of the Trinity, and the charge made good, in an answer to the Defense of the said notion against the Animadversions upon Dr Sherlock's book, entituled, A vindication of the doctrine of the holy and ever blessed Trinity, &c. By a divine of the Church of England [Robert South, D.D.]. 4to. [*D. N. B.* vol. 53, p. 277.]
London, 1695

TRIUMPH (the) of acquaintance over friendship ; an essay for the times. By a lady [Mrs Hayley]. 12mo. Pp. 87. [*European Mag.* xxix. 183 ; xxxii. 359.]
London, 1796

TRIUMPH (the) of benevolence ; a poem, occasioned by the national design of erecting a monument to John Howard, Esq. A new edition, corrected and enlarged ; to which are added, stanzas on the death of Jonas Hanway, Esq. [By Samuel Jackson Pratt.] 4to. Pp. 30. [Nichols' *Lit. Anec.* ix. 7.]
London, 1786

TRIUMPH (the) of Christianity ; or, the life of Cl. Fl. Julian, the apostate : with remarks contain'd in the resolution of several queries : to which is added, reflections upon a pamphlet, call'd, Seasonable remarks on the fall of the Emperor Julian ; and on part of a late pernicious book, entituled, A short account of the life of Julian, &c. [By John Dowell, M.A., of Christ's College, Cambridge.] 8vo. Pp. 237. [Arber's *Term Cat.*]
London, 1683

TRIUMPH (the) of Count Ostermann. [A novel.] By Graham Hope [Miss Jessie Hope]. 8vo. London, 1903

TRIUMPH (the) of fashion ; a vision. [By Henry James Pye.] 4to. [Watt's *Bibl. Brit.*]
London, 1771

TRIUMPH (the) of friendship ; an historical poem. [By William Golden.] 4to. [*Brit. Mus.*] London, 1791

TRIUMPH (the) of Isis ; a poem : occasioned by [William Mason's] Isis, an elegy. [By Thomas Warton.] Third edition. 4to. Pp. 16. [Coleridge's *Worthies of Yorkshire*, p. 403.]
London, 1750

TRIUMPH (the) of love ; and other stories. By Mimosa [Miss M. Chan-Foon]. 8vo.　　London [*c.* 1900]

TRIUMPH (the) of music ; with other poems. By the blind bard of Cicestria [Francis Champion]. 8vo. [*Camb. Univ. Lib.*]　　Chichester, 1841

TRIUMPH (the) of the Orwell ; with a dedicatory sonnet, and prefatory stanzas. [By Bernard Barton.] 8vo. [Smith's *Cat. of Friends' Books*, i. 196.]
Woodbridge [1817]

TRIUMPH (the) of time and truth ; an oratorio . . . set to music by Mr Handel. [By Cardinal B. Pamfili ; translated by T. Morell.] 4to. [*Brit. Mus.*]　　London, 1758

TRIUMPH (the) of truth ; being an account of the trial of Mr E. Elwall [written by himself] for heresy and blasphemy, at Stafford Assizes, before Judge Denton ; to which are added extracts from William Penn's Sandy foundation shaken, and a few additional illustrations. By the author of *An Appeal to the serious and candid professors of Christianity*, etc. [Joseph Priestley]. 12mo. [*Brit. Mus.*]
London, 1776

TRIUMPH (the) of truth ; or, the Protestant truth vindicated and established by arguments fairly drawn from the Word of God. [By Rev. J. Chapman, Vicar of Likley.] 8vo. Pp. 35.　　Leeds, 1784

TRIUMPH (the) over Midian. By A. L. O. E., author of *The Shepherd of Bethlehem*, etc. [Charlotte Maria Tucker]. 8vo. Pp. 280.
London, 1867

TRIUMPHS of ancient architecture ; Greece and Rome. [Signed : W. H. D. A. *i.e.* William H. Davenport Adams.] 12mo. [*Brit. Mus.*]
London, 1866

TRIUMPHS (the) of Europe in the campaigns of 1812, 1813, 1814, commemorated by a series of twelve views from original drawings in the collection of the Emperor of Russia, to which is prefixed a concise history of those important events. [By Thomas Hartwell Horne.] Fol. [*W ; Brit. Mus.*]
London, 1814

TRIUMPHS (the) of Fabian Field, criminologist. By Dick Donovan [Joyce Emerson Preston Muddock]. 8vo. Pp. 308.　　London, 1912

TRIUMPHS (the) of faith. [By John Bonar.] 12mo. Pp. 364. [*N. and Q.* 1913, 2, 350.]　　London, 1766

TRIUMPHS (the) of folly. By the author of *The Diaboliad* [William Combe]. 4to.　　London, 1777

TRIUMPHS (the) of London ; performed on Monday, October 29, 1683, for the entertainment of . . . Sir Henry Tulse, Knight, Lord Mayor of the City of London : containing a description of the whole solemnity. . . . [By Thomas Jordan.] 4to. [*Brit. Mus.*]
London, 1683
An edition of 1678 is not anonymous.

TRIUMPHS of modern architecture ; a description of some of the celebrated edifices of modern Europe. [Preface signed W. D. A. *i.e.* William Davenport Adams.] 12mo. Pp. 128. [*Brit. Mus.*]　　London, 1886

TRIUMPHS (the) of perseverance and enterprise ; recorded as examples for the young. [By Thomas Cooper.] 8vo. Pp. viii. 280.　　London [1856]

TRIUMPHS (the) of religion ; a sacred poem, in four parts. [By Harriett Cope.] 12mo. Pp. 121. [*Mon. Rev.* lxvi. 320 ; *Brit. Crit.* xxxviii. 519.]
London, 1811

TRIUMPHS (the) of Rome over despised, Protestancie : [By George Hall, Bishop of Chester.] 4to. Pp. 2, 148. [*D. N. B.* vol. 24, p. 65.]
London, 1655
The address "to the victorious Roman Catholique knight, that foyld the vicar, and won the lady" is signed : Your truly Catholique wel-willer, faithfull will-bee vicar of Non-such.

TRIUMPHS of superstition ; an elegy. By a student of Harvard University [Thaddeus Mason Harris, D.D.]. 8vo. [Evans' *Amer. Bibl.* vol. 8, p. 38.]
Boston, 1790

TRIUMPHS of the press ; a poem. [By John Smith.] 8vo.
Edinburgh, 1837

TRIUMPHS (the) of the Prince d'Amour ; a masque presented by his Highnesse at his pallace in the Middle Temple, the 24th of Februarie 1635. [By Sir William D'Avenant.] 4to. Pp. 2, 16. [*Bodl.*]　　London, 1635
Address to every reader signed : W. D. "Will. D'Avenant the author."—WOOD.

TRIUMPHS (the) of time ; the previsions of Lady Evelyn ; with the conclusion. By the author of *Two old men's tales*, etc. [Mrs Anne Marsh Caldwell]. 8vo. Pp. 348. [*D. N. B.* vol. 36, p. 219.]　　London, 1849

TRIUMPHS (the) ouer death; or, a consolatorie epistle, for afflicted minds, in the affects of dying friends: first written for the consolation of one; but nowe published for the generall good of all, by R. S., the authour of *S. Peters complaint, and Mœoniæ his other hymnes* [Robert Southwell, S.J.]. 4to. No pagination. London, 1596

TRIUMVIRADE (the); or, broadbottomry; a panegyri-satiri-serio-comi-dramatical poem. By Porcupinus Pelagius [Macnamara Morgan]. 4to. [*D. N. B.* vol. 39, p. 23.] London [1743]

TRIUMVIRATE (the); or, a letter in verse from Palaemon to Celia, from Bath. [By Leonard Welsted.] Fol. [*D. N. B.* vol. 60, p. 241.] London, 1718

TRIUMVIRATE (the); or, the authentic memoirs of A. B. and C. [By Richard Griffith.] 12mo. 2 vols. [*Watt's Bibl. Brit.*] London, 1765

TRIUMVIRI; or, the genius, spirit and deportment of three men, Mr Ric. Resburg, Mr John Pawson, and Mr G. Kendall, in their late writings against the free grace of God in the redemption of the word. [By John Goodwin, D.D.] 4to. [*D.N.B.* vol. 22, p. 147.] London, 1658

TRIUNE (the); or, the new religion. [By Edward Webster.] 8vo. Pp. 60. London, 1867

TRIVIAL poems, and triolets; written in obedience to Mrs Tomkin's commands, by Patrick Carey, 20th Aug. 1651. [Edited by Sir Walter Scott.] 4to. [*W.*] London, 1820

TRIVIAL (the) round; a confirmation story for girls. By Alan St Aubyn [Frances Marshall]. 8vo. London [1902]

TROADES Englished. By S. P. [Samuel Pordage]. 8vo. Pp. 74. [*D. N. B.* vol. 46, p. 151.] London, 1660

TRODDEN down strength by the God of strength; or, Mrs Drake revived: shewing her remarkable . . . case . . . with the manner how the Lord revealed Himself unto her. . . . Related by . . . Hart On-hi [John Hart, D.D.]. 8vo. [*Brit. Mus.*] London, 1647

TRODDLES and us and others. By R. Andom [Alfred Wilson Barrett]. 8vo. London, 1901

TRODDLES' Farm. By R. Andom [Alfred Wilson Barrett]. 8vo. Pp. 316. London, 1911

TRODDLES in the trenches. By R. Andom [Alfred Wilson Barrett]. 8vo. Pp. 160. London, 1919

TRODDLES—not to mention ourselves. By R. Andom [Alfred Wilson Barrett]. 8vo. Pp. 320. London, 1914

TROJAN (the) horse of the Presbyteriall government unbowelled; wherein is contained, I. The power of the Presbyterian government. II. The persons in whom this power is placed. III. The exercise of the Presbyterian power in Scotland, and the lawes there imposed on the peoples necks. [By Henry Parker, of Lincoln's Inn.] 4to. Pp. 22. [*D. N. B.* vol. 43, p. 241.] 1646

TROLLOPE'S dilemma; a story of a Cambridge Quad. By Alan St Aubyn [Mrs Frances Marshall]. 12mo. Bristol, 1889

TROLLOPIAD (the); or, a travelling gentleman in America: a satirical poem by Nil Admirari, Esq. [Rev. Frederick William Shelton, LL.D.]. 12mo. Pp. 28, 151. [Cushing's *Init. and Pseud.*] New York, 1837

TROOPER Peter Halket of Mashonaland. By Ralph Iron [Olive Schreiner, later Mrs Cronwright]. 8vo. Pp. 133. London, 1897

TROPICAL flowers for Charlotte. By F. H. A. [Francis Harcourt Anton]. 8vo. London, 1825

TROTH (the); a play in one act. By Rutherford Mayn [Samuel Waddell]. 8vo. Pp. 14. [S. J. Brown's *Books on Ireland.*] Dublin, 1909

TROTTY'S book; the story of a little boy. By the author of *Gates ajar* [Miss Elizabeth Stuart Phelps]. 16mo. [*Brit. Mus.*] London [1872]

TROUBADOUR (the); catalogue of pictures, and historical sketches. By L. E. L. author of *The improvisatrice* [Letitia Elizabeth Landon, afterwards Mrs M'Lean]. Third edition. 8vo. Pp. 326. London, 1825

TROUBLED (a) heart and how it was comforted at last. [By Charles Warren Stoddard.] 16mo. [Foley's *Amer. Authors.*] 1885

TROUBLED waters. [A novel.] By Headon Hill [Francis Edward Grainger]. 8vo. Pp. 288. London, 1909

TROUBLES (the) in Jamaica; a condensed statement of facts. [By the Rev. Henry Richard.] 8vo. Pp. 12. London, 1866

TROUBLES (the) of a shovel hat; and other stories. By Max Baring [Charles Messent]. 8vo. London, 1901

TROUBLES (the) of an unlucky boy;
a novel. By John Strange Winter
[Mrs Arthur Stannard, *née* Henrietta
E. V. Palmer]. 8vo. Pp. 118.
London, 1897

TROUBLESOME (the) and hard
adventures in love ; lively setting forth
the feavers, the dangers and the
jealousies of lovers, and the labyrinths
and wildernesses of fears and hopes
through which they dayly passe. . . .
Written in Spanish by that excellent
and famous gentleman, Michael
Cervantes, and exactly translated into
English by R. C. [Robert Codrington],
Gent. 4to. 139 leaves, unpaged.
[*W.*]   London, 1652

The Epistle dedicatory is signed : R. C.
Not by Cervantes.

TROUBLESOME (a) girl ; a novel.
By the author of *Molly Bawn* [Mrs
Argles, later Hungerford, *née* Margaret
W. Hamilton]. 8vo. Pp. 189.
London, 1889

TROUBLESOME (the) life and raigne
of King Henry the Third ; wherein
five distempers and maladies are set
forth. Viz. 1. By the Pope and church-
mens extortions. 2. By the places of
best trust bestowed upon unworthy
members. 3. By patents and monopolies for private favourites. 4. By
needlesse expences and pawning of
jewels. 5. By factious Lords and
ambitious peeres. . . . [By Sir Robert
Cotton.] 4to.   London, 1642

A reprint of " A short view of the long life
and raigne," etc.

TROUBLESOME (a) pair. [A novel.]
By Leslie Keith [Miss Grace Leslie
Keith Johnstone]. 8vo. 3 vols.
London, 1894

TROWEL (the) and the cross ; and
other stories. By Conrad de Bolanden
[Joseph E. Bischoff]. Translated from
the German. 8vo. [*Lib. Journ.* iv. 99.]
New York, 1878

TROY town. By Q. [Sir Arthur T.
Quiller-Couch]. 8vo. London, 1895

TRUANT (the) five. [A tale.] By
Raymond Jacberns [Miss M. Selby
Ashe]. 8vo.   London, 1907

TRUCE (the) in the East and its
aftermath ; being the sequel to *The
re-shaping of the Far East.* By
B. L. Putnam Weale [Bertram Lenox
Simpson]. 8vo. Pp. 644.
London, 1907

TRUCKLEBOROUGH Hall ; a novel.
[By William Pitt Scargill.] 3 vols.
[*Brit. Mus.*]   London, 1827

TRUE (a) account and confutation of
the doctrine of the Sabellians. [By
Daniel Whitby, D.D.] 8vo. [*Brit.
Mus.*]   London, 1716

TRUE (a) account and declaration of
the horrid conspiracy against the late
king, his present Majesty, and the
government ; as it was order'd to be
published by his late Majesty. [By
Thomas Sprat, D.D., Bishop of
Rochester.] The second edition.
Fol. Pp. 167. [*Brit. Mus.*]
In the Savoy, 1685

TRUE (a) account of the author of a
book entituled Εἰκὼν Εδς ιλικὴ [*sic*], or
the Pourtraiture of His Sacred Majesty
in His solitudes and sufferings ; with
an answer to all objections made by
Dr Hollingsworth and others, in defence of the said book. [By Anthony
Walker.] 4to. [Watt's *Bibl. Brit.*]
London, 1692

TRUE (a) account of the behaviour and
conduct of Archibald Stewart, Esq. ;
late Lord Provost of Edinburgh ; in
a letter to a friend. [By David Hume.]
8vo. Pp. 51.   London, 1748

TRUE (a) account of the design and
advantages of the South-Sea trade ;
with answers to all the objections
raised against it ; a list of the commodities proper for that trade, and the
progress of the subscription towards
the South-Sea Company. By the author
of the *Review* [Daniel Defoe]. 8vo.
[*Brit. Mus.*]   London, 1711

TRUE (a) account of the life and
writings of Thomas Burnett, Esq. [By
George Sewell, M.D.] 8vo. [*W.*]
London, 1715

A satirical account of Sir Thomas Burnet,
one of the Justices of the Court of Common
Pleas, and youngest son of Bishop Burnet.

TRUE (a) account of the present state of
Trinity College in Cambridge, under
the oppressive government of their
master Richard Bentley, late D.D.
[By Conyers Middleton, D.D.] 8vo.
Pp. 43. [Rawlinson's *English Topographer*, p. 20.]   London, 1719

TRUE (a) account of the proceedings at
Perth ; the debates in the secret council
there : with the reasons and causes of
the suddain finishing and breaking up
of the rebellion. Written by a rebel
[John, Master of Sinclair]. 8vo.
Pp. 76.   London, 1716

See Preface (p. viii.) to *Memoirs of the
insurrection in Scotland in* 1715. By John,
Master of Sinclair. . . . With notes by Sir
Walter Scott, Bart. Edinburgh, 1858.

TRUE (a) account of the regulation and management of the foundation bursaries of the United College, St Andrews. . . . By a bursar of the College [Charles Roger]. 8vo.
St Andrews, 1843

TRUE (a) account of the sensible, thankful and holy state of God's people ; and of his speaking to them both in the Old and New Covenant. By the servant of Christ, G. F. [George Fox]. 4to. [Smith's *Cat. of Friends' Books*, i. 686.] 1686

TRUE (a) account of the tryals, examinations, confessions, condemnations and executions of divers witches at Salem in New-England, for their bewitching of sundry people and cattel to death. . . . [Signed : C. M. *i.e.* Cotton Mather.] 4to. Pp. 8. [Sabin's *Dictionary*.]
London [1693]

TRUE (a) account of this present blasingstar; presenting it self to the view of the world, this August. 1682. with sundry considerable remarks and observations thereupon. [By Christopher Nesse.] Fol. S. sh. [*Bodl.*]
London, 1682

Signed : C. N. See also "A full and true account of the late blazing star. . . ."

TRUE (the) alarm ! An essay shewing the pernicious influence of houses of industry on the political interests of this country. [By R. Alderson.] 8vo.
London, 1787

TRUE (a) and admirable historie of a mayden of Confolens, in the Prouince of Poictiers, that for the space of three yeeres and more hath liued and yet doth, without receiuing either meate or drinke. . . . [Translated from the French of N. Coeffeteau, by Anthony Munday.] 8vo. [*Brit. Mus.*]
London, 1603

Signed : A. M.

TRUE (the) and ancient manner of reading Hebrew without points, and the art of the Hebrew versification. [By John Robertson, M.D.] 8vo.
London, 1747

TRUE (the) and briefe relation of the great victory obtained by Sir Ralph Hopton, neare Bodmin, in the county of Cornwall, Ianuary 19. Ann. Dom. 1642. [By Peter Heylin, D.D.] 4to. Pp. 37-42. [*Bodl.*] 1642

Complete in itself ; but the pagination shows it to be only a part of a larger work.

TRUE (a) and certaine relation of a strange birth borne at Stone-house. [Signed : Th. B. *i.e.* Bedford Thomas.] 4to. [*Pollard and Redgrave*.]
London, 1635

TRUE and correct tables of time, calculated for the old stile for 784 years, viz. from A.D. 1300 to 2083, both inclusive ; and for the new stile, from its commencement, viz. 1582 to 2083, inclusive, being 501 years. By R. T. [Robert Tailfer], half-pay officer. 8vo. [*Camb. Univ. Lib.*] [London, 1736]

TRUE (the) and eternal divinity of the Great Founder of the Christian dispensation. . . . [By Thomas Fawcett.] 12mo. Pp. 68. Manchester, 1813

TRUE (a) and exact account of Sadler's well, or the new mineral water lately found out at Islington ; treating of its nature and virtues. . . . By T. G. [Thomas Guidott], doctor of Physick. 4to. [*Brit. Mus.*] London, 1684

TRUE (a) and exact history of the succession of the Crown of England ; collected out of records, and the best historians : written for the information of such as have been deluded and seduced by the pamphlet [by Lord Somers], called The brief history of the succession, &c. pretended to have been written for the satisfaction of the Earl of H. [By Robert Brady, M.D.] Fol. Pp. 46. London, 1681

TRUE (a) and exact relation of the strange finding out of Moses his tombe, in a valley neere unto Mount Nebo in Palestina ; with divers remarkable occurrences that happened thereupon, and the severall judgements of many learned men concerning the same. . . . [By Thomas Chaloner.] 8vo. Pp. 39. [Wood's *Athen. Oxon.* iii. 531.]
London, 1657

" This book, at its first appearance, made a great noise, and pusled the presbyterian Rabbies for a time : at length the author thereof being known, and his story found to be a meer sham, the book became ridiculous, and was put to posterior uses." —ANT. À WOOD, *Athen. Oxon.*, ed. Bliss, iii. 533.

Ascribed also to Joseph Georgirenes, Archbishop of Samos. [*Douce Cat.*]

TRUE and exact relation of two Catholics who suffered for their religion at the Summer Assizes held at Lancaster in the year 1628. [By Cornelius Murphy, S.J.?] 8vo. Pp. 68. [Sommervogel's *Dictionnaire*.]
London, 1737

TRUE (a) and faithful account of what was observed in ten years travells into the principal places of Europe, Asia, Africa and America ; written in several letters . . . by R. F. [Richard Flecknoe], Esq. 12mo. 92 leaves. [*Brit. Mus.*] London, 1665

TRUE (a) and faithful narrative of the unjust and illegal sufferings and oppressions of many Christians . . . under, and by several of his Majesties Justices of peace, and others, who are no officers, but informers, in the county of Devon, since the 10th of May, 1670, from a pretended zeal, to put the laws against conventicles in execution. . . . [By John Hicks, minister at Kingsbridge.]   4to.   [Davidson's *Bibl. Devon.* p. 96.]   N.P. 1671
      Somers' *Collection of Tracts*, 2d. ed. vol. vii. pp. 586-615.

TRUE (a) and ful relation of the officers and armies forcible seising of divers eminent members of the Commons House, Decemb. 6. & 7. 1648 ; as also, a true copy of a letter lately written by an agent for the army in Paris, dated 28 of Novemb. 1648. to a member of the said House. . . . [By William Prynne.]   4to.   Pp. 15.   London, 1648

TRUE (the) and genuine account of the life and actions of the late Jonathan Wild . . . taken from his own mouth. [By Daniel Defoe.]   8vo.   Pp. viii. 40. [*Brit. Mus.*]   London, 1725

TRUE (a) and genuine history of the last two wars against France and Spain. . . .   See " Military (the) memoirs of Captain George Carleton . . ."

TRUE (a) and impartial account of the life of the Most Reverend Father in God, Dr James Sharp, Arch-bishop of St Andrews, Primate of all Scotland, and Privy-Counsellor to his Most Sacred Majesty King Charles II. . . . [By David Simson.]   8vo.   [*Nat. Lib. of Scot.*]   1723

TRUE (a) and impartial account of the parliamentary conduct of Sir T. D. Acland, Bart.   By a freeholder of the county of Devon [Rev. John Pike Jones, of North Bovey].   8vo.   [Davidson's *Bibl. Devon.* p. 135.]
                    Exeter, 1819

TRUE (a) and impartial account of the present differences between the Master and Fellows of Trinity College [Cambridge.   By John Paris].   8vo. Pp. 36. [Bartholomew's *Camb. Books.*]
                    London, 1711

TRUE (a) and impartial history of the most material occurrences in the kingdom of Ireland during the two last years, with the present state of both armies. . . .   Written by an eyewitness to the most remarkable passages [George Warter Story].   4to. [Arber's *Term Cat.* ii. 624.]
                    London, 1691
      Part II. gives the author's name.

TRUE (a) and impartial narrative of some illegal and arbitrary proceedings by certain Justices of the Peace against Non-conformists in and near the town of Bedford. . . .   [By John Bunyan ?] 4to.   1670

TRUE (a) and impartial narrative of the most material debates and passages in the late Parliament. . . .   By a member of that Parliament [Slingsby Bethel].   4to.   London, 1659
      Reprinted in the *Somers Tracts*, vol. 4.

TRUE (a) and impartiall relation of the battaile betwixt, his Majesties army and that of the rebells, neare Newbury in Berk-shire, Sept. 20. 1643 ; with the severall actions of the kings army since his Majesties removing it from before Gloucester: sent in a letter from the army to a noble Lord. [By Lord George Digby.]   4to.   Pp. 9. [*Bodl.*]   1643
      " This was writt by my Lord George Digby."—MS. note by Bishop Barlow in the Bodleian copy.

TRUE (a) and impartial state of the Province of Pennsylvania ; containing an exact account of the nature of its government, the power of the proprietaries, and their governors. . . . [By Benjamin Franklin.]   8vo.   Pp. 173, 34. [Evans' *Amer. Bibl.* vol. 3, p. 224.]   Philadelphia, 1759

TRUE (a) and lively representation of Popery, shewing that Popery is only new modelled Paganism, and perfectly destructive of the great ends and purposes of God in the Gospel. [By Thankful Owen, M.A.]   4to.   Pp. 82. [Jones' *Peck*, i. 251.]   London, 1679
      Wrongly ascribed to Henry Hallywell, Cf. *D.N.B.* vol. 42, p. 454.

TRUE (a) and particular history of earthquakes. . . .   Translated from the original Spanish [by Henry Johnson]. . . .   By Philolethus [Pedro Lozano].   8vo. [Sabin's *Dictionary.*]
                    London, 1748

TRUE (a) and perfect narrative of the strange and unexpected finding the crucifix & gold-chain of that pious prince, St Edward the King and Confessor, which was found after 620 years interment : and presented to his most sacred Majesty, King James the Second.   By Charles Taylour, Gent. [Henry Keepe].   4to.   Pp. 34. [*Bodl.*]
                    London, 1688

TRUE (the) and real violations of property ; offered to consideration in some expostulatory queries, concerning the criminal and mischievous nature of those unjust practices, whereby just possessions, rights, or dues, are injuriously invaded, detained, or diminished. [By John Graile, A.M.] 8vo. Pp. 28, 160. [*Bodl.*]
London, 1683

TRUE (a) and strange discourse of the travailes of two English Pilgrimes . . . in . . . Ierusalem, Gaza, Grand Cayro, Alexandria, and other places. [By Henry Timberlake.] 4to. B. L. [*Christie-Miller Cat.*]   London, 1608
An earlier edition was issued in 1603 ; a later edition, in 1631, has a different title : "A relation of the travells of two English pilgrimes . . ."

TRUE (the) and the false infallibility of the Popes : a controversial reply to Dr Schulte, by Joseph Fessler, Bishop. Translated from [the German of] the third edition [by A. Saint John]. 8vo. [*Brit. Mus.*]
London, 1875

TRUE (a) answer to Dr Sacheverell's sermon before the Lord Mayor, Nov. 5. 1709 ; in a letter to one of the Aldermen. [By White Kennett, D.D.] 8vo.   London, 1709

TRUE as steel. [A tale.] By Marion Harland [Mrs Mary Virginia Terhune, *née* Hawes]. 8vo.   London, 1891

TRUE (the) Briton. [By Philip, Duke of Wharton.] 8vo. 2 vols. [*W.*]
London, 1723-4
This Paper consists of seventy-four numbers.

TRUE (the) Briton ; a letter addressed to Sir Samuel Fludyer, Bt., Lord Mayor [by James Churchill]. 8vo.
London, 1762

TRUE (the) cause of depreciation traced to the state of our silver currency. [By A. W. Rutherford.] 8vo. [*Brit. Mus.*]   London [1819 ?]

TRUE (the) character of a Church of England man. [By Samuel Grascome.] 4to.   London [*c.* 1700]

TRUE (the) character of a churchman, shewing the false pretences to that name. [By Richard West, D.D.] 4to. Pp. 7. [*Bodl.*]   [1705]
No title-page.

TRUE (the) character of a noble generall ; seen and allowed by the Earl of Essex. [By William Cooke.] 4to. [Thomason's *Coll. of Tracts*, i. 429.]   London, 1644

TRUE (the) character of a rigid Presbyter ; with a narrative of the dangerous designes of the English and Scotch Covenanters, as they have tended to the rouine of our Church and kingdom : also, the articles of their dogmatical faith, and the inconsistency thereof with monarchy. [By Marchamont Nedham.] To which is added, a Short history of the English rebellion : compiled in verse, by Marchamont Nedham and formerly extant, in his Mercurius Pragmaticus. 4to. Pp. 94.   London, 1661
The "Short history" has a separate title ; but the pagination is continuous. The address to the reader is signed : Mercurius Pragmaticus. A MS. note by Wood states that Nedham "published this merely to curry favour at the king's restauration, w^n he had lost his credit so much, y^t he was many times in danger of his life."

TRUE (the) character of an honest man ; particularly with relation to the publick affairs : dedicated to his Grace the Duke of Marlborough. [By Sir Thomas Burnet.] 8vo. Pp. 32. [*Bodl.*]   London, 1712
Dedication signed : Timon.

TRUE (the) character of John the Baptist. . . . By an impartial hand [Rev. William Ashdowne, Unitarian minister]. 8vo. [*Brit. Mus.*]
London, 1757

TRUE (a) character of Mr Pope, and his writings ; in a letter to a friend. [By John Dennis and Charles Gildon.] 8vo. Pp. 18. [Lowndes' *Bibl. Man.* p. 1920 ; *Dyce Cat.* ii. 189.]
London, 1716

TRUE Christian love ; to bee sung with any of the common tunes of the Psalmes. [By David Dickson.] 12mo. [*Brit. Mus.*]   Glasgow, 1634
The earliest work printed in Glasgow.

TRUE (the) Christian religion againe discovered ; after the long and darke night of apostacy ; which hath overshadowed the whole world ; and the profession and practice thereof for many ages ; witnessed unto by the Scriptures, &c. [By Edward Burrough.] 4to. [Smith's *Cat. of Friends' Books*, i. 35.]   London, 1658

TRUE Christian religion; containing the universal theology of the New [Jerusalem] Church, which was foretold by the Lord in Daniel, Chap. vii. 5, 13, 14, and in the Apocalypse, Chap. xxi., 1, 2: by Emanuel Swedenborg, servant of the Lord Jesus Christ. Translated from the original Latin [by Rev. John Clowes]. 8vo. 2 vols. [Evans' *Amer. Bibl.* vol. 8, p. 360.]
                    Philadelphia, 1789-92

TRUE (the) Christians distinguished from such as go under the name of Christians; with a short epistle concerning the Holy Scriptures of truth: as also concerning Christ the offering; and such as are chosen in Christ, and haue their names written in the book of life before the foundation of the world. By G. F. [George Fox]. 4to. [Smith's *Cat. of Friends' Books,* i. 688.]
                    London, 1689

T R U E (the) chronicle historie of Thomas Lord Cromwell. By W. S. [Wentworth Smith?]. 4to. [*Brit. Mus.*]   London, 1602
    The *D. N. B.* does not accept the attribution.

TRUE (the) Church of Christ shewed by concurrent testimonies of Scripture and primitive tradition; in answer to a book [by Charles Leslie] entitled *The case stated between the Church of Rome and the Church of England.* In three parts. . . . [By Edward Hawarden.] 8vo. 2 vols. [*Brit. Mus.*]   London, 1714-15

TRUE (a) Churchman's reasons for repealing the Corporation and Test Acts. . . . [By Benjamin Hoadly, D.D. ?] 8vo.   London, 1732

TRUE (a) collection of the writings of the author of the *True-born Englishman* [Daniel Defoe]. Corrected by himself. 8vo. [Wilson's *Life of Defoe.*]
                    London, 1703

TRUE (a) confession of the faith which wee, falsely called Brownists, doo hold. [By Henry Ainsworth.] 4to. [*Pollard and Redgrave.*]
                    [Amsterdam?] 1596

TRUE (the) consoler. . . . By W. C. W. [William Chalmers Whitcomb]. 8vo.
                    Boston, 1861

TRUE (the) copies of some letters occasioned by the demand for dilapidations in the archiepiscopal see of Canterbury. [By Archdeacon Thomas Tenison.] 4to. [*W.; Upcott.*]   1716

TRUE (a) copy of a letter written by N. Machiavell in defence of himself. . . . Translated [by Henry Neville]. 4to. [Arber's *Term Cat.*]
                    London, 1691

TRUE (a) daughter of Hartenstein; from the German of E. Vely [Emma Simon]. 8vo.   New York, 1892

TRUE (a) declaration of our innocency, who in scorn are called Quakers, and how we are clear (if we have justice) from the penalties of the late Act made against seditious meetings, and conventicles, as exprest in the preamble and reason of the said Act, &c. Also several reasons, and proofs by the Common-Prayer-Book, and the Holy Scriptures directed to in it, that our meetings, and the manner of them, are according to the Scriptures of truth, and therefore allowed by the liturgy of the Church of England, &c. By J. S. [John Stubbs]. 4to. [Smith's *Cat. of Friends' Books,* ii. 641.]   1670

TRUE (the) defēce of peace, wherin is declarēdde the cause of all warres now a dayes, and how they maye be pacified, called before the Pollecye of warre devysed & lately recognised by Theodore Basille [Thomas Becon]. 12mo. B. L. [*W.*]   London, 1543
    Reprinted in his works under the title of "The policy of war."

TRUE (a) description of the pot-companion poet, who is the founder of all the base and libellous pamphlets lately spread abroad; also, a character of the swilbole cook. [Two characters from the Microcosmographie of John Earle.] 4to. [Murphy's *Character Books.*]   London, 1642

TRUE (a) description out of the word of God of the visible church. [By Henry Barrow.] 4to. [*Pollard and Redgrave.*]
                    N.P. [c. 1610]

TRVE (a) discourse historicall, of the succeeding governours in the Netherlands, and the ciuill warres there begun in the yeere 1565; with the memorable seruices of our honourable English generals, captaines and souldiers, especially vnder Sir Iohn Norice knight, there performed from the yeere 1577, vntill the yeere 1589. and afterwards in Portugale, France, Britaine and Ireland vntill the yeere 1598. Translated and collected by T. C. [Thomas Churchyard] Esquire, and Ric. Ro. [Richard Robinson] out of the reuerend E. M. [Emanuel Meteranus] of Antwerp, his fifteene bookes Historiæ Belgicæ. . . . 4to. Pp. 154. B. L.
                    London, 1602
    Epistle dedicatorie signed : T. C.

TRUE (a) discourse of the two infamous upstart prophets, Richard Farn'ham weaver of White-chappell, and John Bull weaver of Saint Butolphs Algate, now prisoners, the one in Newgate, and the other in Bridewell : with their examinations and opinions taken from their owne mouthes April 16. Anno. 1636: as also of Margaret Tennis now prisoner in Old Bridewell, with the hereticall opinions held by her, at the same time examined. Written by T. H. [Thomas Heywood]. 4to. Pp. 19.
London, 1636
Reprinted by J. Caulfield, 1795.

TRUE (the) dissenter ; or, the cause of those that are for gathered Churches ; being a right state thereof, proposed and settled upon its proper foundations : in opposition to all compliance that is sinful, but in order to that obedience which is lawful, and conducive to the healing of the nation : occasion'd by some late writings, and especially by a book entituled, The cause of their mix'd Churches against (or The axe laid to the root of) separation. [By Stephen Lobb.] 8vo. Pp. 142. [Darling's *Cyclop. Bibl.*]   1685

TRUE (the) doctrine of the New Testament concerning Jesus Christ, considered ; wherein the misrepresentations that have been made of it, upon the Arian hypothesis, and upon all Trinitarian and Athanasian principles, are exposed ; and the honour of our Saviour's divine character and mission is maintained. . . . [By Paul Cardale, Unitarian minister at Evesham.] The second edition, corrected and enlarged. 8vo. Pp. iii. 428.   London, 1771

TRUE (the) dyfferēs between ye regall power and the ecclesiasticall power. [By Edward Fox, Bishop of Hereford.] Translated out of latyn by Henry lord Stafforde. 12mo. B. L. [*Brit. Mus.*]
London [1548]

TRUE (the) effigies of the most eminent painters and other famous artists, that have flourished in Europe, curiously engraven on copper plates ; together with an account of the time when they lived, the most remarkable passages of their lives, and most considerable works. [By Sebastiano Resta.] Fol. *W.; Brit. Mus.*]   Antwerp, 1694
The plates of Belgians only.

TRUE (the) English government, and mis-government of the four last kings, with the ill consequences thereof, briefly noted in two little tracts. [By Edward Stephens.] 4to. Pp. 8. [*Bodl.*]   London, 1689

TRUE (the) Englishman's miscellany, in two parts : Part I. The false guardians outwitted ; a ballad opera, containing twenty one airs : with a prologue and preface, giving some account of the author, and his reasons for this publication. Part II. Containing a collection of dismal songs, pleasant satires, bitter encomiums, terrible poems, epigrams, epitaphs, &c. Never before published. By W. G. [William Goodall]. 8vo.
[London] 1740

TRUE (a) estimate of the light of inspiration and the light of human learning, before and since the apostolic age ; submitted to the candidates for Holy Orders, &c. [By C. E. de Coetlogon.] 4to. [Watt's *Bibl. Brit.; Mon. Rev.* lxxix. 560.]   1788

TRUE (a) exemplary and remarkable history of the Earl of Tirone. By an eye witness [Thomas Gainsford]. 4to. [Lowndes' *Bibl. Man.* p. 854.]
London, 1619

TRUE faith. By an Indian Theist [Kesavachandra Sena]. 8vo. [*Brit. Mus.*]   Calcutta, 1879

TRUE (the) faith. By Herman Heinfetter, author of *Rules for ascertaining the sense conveyed in ancient Greek manuscripts*, etc. [Frederick Parker]. 12mo. Pp. 20.   London, 1862

TRUE (the) faith of the Gospel of peace contended for against the secret opposition of John Bunyan ; or, an answer to his book called *Some Gospel truths opened.* By E. B. [Edward Burrough]. 8vo. [Whitley's *Bapt. Bibl.* i. 64.]
London, 1656

TRUE (the) foundations of natural and reveal'd religion asserted ; being a reply to the Supplement to the Treatise [by Waterland] entitul'd, The nature, obligation, &c. of the Christian sacraments. [By Arthur Ashley Sykes.] 8vo. Pp. 96. [Disney's *Memoir of Sykes*, p. xviii.]   London, 1730

TRUE (the), genuine, Tory-address ; to which is added, an explanation of some hard terms now in use : for the information of all such as read, or subscribe, addresses. [By Benjamin Hoadly.] Fol. Pp. 2. [London] 1710

TRUE genuine Tory-address, and the true genuine Whig-address, set one against another : to which is added a farther explanation of some hard terms now in use, for the information of all such as read, or subscribe addresses : being an answer to a late scandalous paper, falsly call'd The true genuine Tory-address, &c. [By Joseph Trapp, D.D.] Fol. Pp. 12. [*D. N. B.* vol. 57, p. 156.] London, 1710

TRUE (the) good old cause rightly stated, and the false uncaved. [By William Prynne.] 4to. [*W.; Brit. Mus.*]   [London, 1659]

TRUE greatness; or, tributary stanzas to the glorious memory of Lord Viscount Nelson. . . . [By T. Sansom.] 4to. [*Brit. Mus.*]
London, 1806

TRUE (the) Grecian bend; a story in verse. By Larrie Leigh [L. T. Warner]. 8vo. [*Brit. Mus.*]   New York, 1868

TRUE (the) grounds and reasons of the Christian religion, in opposition to the false ones. . . . [By Rev. Thomas Jeffery, dissenting minister.] 8vo. [*Brit. Mus.*]   London, 1725

TRUE (the) grounds of ecclesiasticall regiment set forth in a breife dissertation ; maintaining the kings spirituall supremacie against the pretended independencie of the prelates &c. : together ,with some passages touching the ecclesiasticall power of parliaments, the use of synods, and the power of excommunication. [By Henry Parker.] 4to. [Thomason's *Coll. of Tracts,* i. 47.]   London, 1641

TRUE (the) grounds of the expectation of the Messiah, in two letters; the one printed in the *London Journal,* April the 1st, 1727 ; the other in vindication of it : being a reply to the answer published at the end of a late Letter to Dr Rogers. By Philalethes [Arthur Ashley Sykes]. 8vo. Pp. 68. [Disney's *Memoir of Sykes,* p. xvii. ; Green's *Bibl. Somers.* iii. 214.]
London, 1727

TRUE (the) guide; or, a short treatise wherein is shewed how the weakest Christian may be able to discerne the true way of the Spirit of God. By a Lover of the Truth, R. H. [Richard Hollingworth]. 8vo. [Whitley's *Bapt. Bibl.* i. 24.]   London, 1646

TRUE heart's trials. By Reginald Tierney [Thomas O'Neill Russell]. 8vo.   Dublin, 1910

TRUE (the) heir of Ballymore. [A novel.] By an Ulster Scot [Rev. Henry Henderson, Presbyterian minister in Holywood, Co. Down]. 8vo. Pp. 80. [S. J. Brown's *Ireland in Fiction.*]
Belfast, 1859

TRUE heroism. . . . By A. L. O. E. [Miss Charlotte M. Tucker]. 12mo.
Edinburgh, 1854

TRUE (a) historicall discourse of Muley Hamet's rising to the three kingdomes of Moruecos, Fez, and Sus; the disyunion of the three kingdomes, by ciuill warre. . . . By R. C. [R. Cottington]. 4to. Pp. 74.
London, 1609

TRUE (a) history of a late short administration. [By Charles Lloyd.] 8vo. Pp. 22. [Almon's *Biog. Anec.* ii. 110.]
London, 1766

TRUE (the) history of a little ragamuffin. By the author of *A night in a work house* [James Greenwood. Nos. 1-7]. 8vo. [*Nat. Lib. of Scot.*]
London [1866]
No more published.

TRUE (the) history of Joshua Davidson. [By Mrs E. Lynn Linton.] 8vo. Pp. viii. 279. [*Brit. Mus.*]   London, 1872

TRUE (the) history of the Jacobites, of Ægypt, Lybia, Nubia, &c. their origine, religion, ceremonies, laws, and customs ; whereby you may see how they differ from the Jacobites of Great Britain : translated by a person of quality [Sir Edward Sadleir] from the Latin of Josephus Abudernus, a man of integrity, and born in Cairo in Ægypt. 4to. Pp. 10, 32.
London, 1692

TRUE (a) history of the military government of the Citie of Gloucester to the removall of Col. Edward Massey to the command of the Western Forces. [By John Corbet]. . . . 4to. Pp. 140. [Thomason's *Coll. of Tracts,* i. 545.]
London, 1645

TRUE (a) history of the several designs and conspiracies against His Majesties . . . person and government . . . from 1688 till 1697. . . . By R. K. [Rev. Richard Kingston, D.D.]. 8vo. [*Brit. Mus.*]   London, 1698

TRUE (the) idea of Jansenisme, both historick and dogmatick. By T. G. [Theophilus Gale]. 8vo. Pp. 30, 166.
London, 1669

TRUE (the) impartial history and wars of the Kingdom of Ireland. . . . The second edition, with additions. [Dedication signed: J. S. *i.e.* James Shirley.] 12mo. Pp. 192. [*Brit. Mus.*]
London, 1692

TRUE (a) impartiall narration concerning the Armies preservation of the King [Charles I. By George Joyce]. 4to. [Thomason's *Coll. of Tracts,* i. 515.]   London, 1647

TRUE (a) information to the nation from the people called Quakers. . . . By J. C. [John Crook?]. 4to. Pp. 14. [*Brit. Mus.*]   [London] 1664

TRUE (the) institution of sisterhood ; or, a message and its messengers. By L. N. R. [Mrs Ellen Ranyard]. 8vo. Pp. 32.   London [1862]

TRUE (the) interest of America impartially stated, in certain strictures on a pamphlet [by Thomas Paine] intitled "Common Sense." By an American [Rev. Charles Inglis]. 8vo. Pp. 71. [Evans' *Amer. Bibl.* vol. 5, p. 240.] Philadelphia, 1776

TRUE (the) interest of families ; or, directions how parents may be happy in their children, and children in their parents : to which is annexed a discourse about the right way of improving our time. By a divine of the Church of England [Rev. James Kirkwood, rector of Astwick, in Bedfordshire]. With a preface by A. Horneck, D.D. 8vo. Pp. 18, 224. London, 1692

TRUE (the) interest of the United States, and particularly of Pennsylvania, considered, with respect to the advantages resulting from a State paper currency. . . . By an American [William Barton]. 4to. Pp. 43. [Evans' *Amer. Bibl.* vol. 7, p. 6.] Philadelphia, 1786

TRUE (the) interests of the European powers and the Emperor of Brazil, in reference to the existing affairs of Portugal. By a friend of truth and peace [William Walton]. 8vo. [*W. ; Brit. Mus.*]   London, 1829

With autograph letter from the author.

TRUE judgement ; or, the spiritual man judging all things, but he himself judged of no man ; to them who are growing up into discerning and judgement : and to them, who cannot endure sound judgement. [By George Fox.] 4to. [Smith's *Cat. of Friends' Books*, i. 33.]   London, 1654

TRUE (the) lawe of free monarchies ; or, the reciprock and mutuall dutie betwixt a free king, and his naturall subjects. [By James VI. of Scotland.] 12mo. No pagination.
At London, according to the copie printed at Edinburgh, 1603

The advertisement to the reader is signed : Φιλοπατρις. The first edition was published at Edinburgh in 1598.

TRUE liberty. [By William Alexander, bookseller.] 4to. [Smith's *Cat. of Friends' Books*, Supp. p. 4.] York, N.D.

TRUE (the) liberty and dominion of conscience vindicated, from the usurpations & abuses of opinion, and persuasion. [By John Nalson, LL.D. prebendary of Ely.] 8vo. Pp. 142. [Whitley's *Bapt. Bibl.* i. 108.]
In the Savoy, 1677

TRUE (a) light of alchemy ; containing a correct edition of "The marrow of alchymy ; " the errors of a late tract called "A short discourse of the quintessence of Philosophers." . . . [By Sir George Ripley.] 12mo.
London, 1709

TRUE love at last. [By Mrs Mary S. L. Fisher.] 12mo.   London, N.D.

TRUE love versus fashion. . . . By the author of *Nothing to wear* [William Allen Butler]. 8vo. [*Brit. Mus.*]
London [1859]

TRUE Magdalen. By Bertha M. Clay [Charlotte M. Braeme]. 8vo.
New York, 1888

TRUE (the) meaning of Rom. 13. 7, stated, in a sermon preached in the city of Chester. By a now persecuted clergyman [Thomas Parry]. 4to. [Darling's *Cyclop. Bibl.*]   N.P. 1751

TRUE (the) meaning of the System of nature ; translated from the French of [Claude Arien] Helvetius [by Daniel Isaac Eaton], with notes. 12mo. Pp. 145. [Watt's *Bibl. Brit.*]
Edinburgh, 1799

An edition issued at London in 1811 has a slightly different title : "The true sense and meaning . . ."

TRUE (a) method, 1. For raising of souldiers ; 2. For bringing those seamen that are in the land into the navy ; 3. For the increase of seamen, &c. [By Peter Rowe.] 4to. [*Brit. Mus.*]
London, 1703

TRUE (a), modest, and just defence of the Petition for Reformation exhibited to the King's Majestie : containing an answer to the Confutation. . . . [By John Sprint, D.D.] 8vo. [*D. N. B.* vol. 53, p. 430.]   London, 1618

TRUE (the) mother Church ; or, a short practical discourse upon Acts ii. [41 42] concerning the first Church at Jerusalem. [By Rev. Samuel Johnson.] 8vo. Pp. 20. [*Bodl.*]   London, 1688

TRUE (the) narration of the entertainment of His Royall Maiestie, from the time of His departure from Edenbrough, till his receiving in London. . . . By T. M. [Thomas Middleton]. 4to. [*Brit. Mus.*]   London, 1603

TRUE (a) narrative of an unfortunate elopement [viz. that of Mrs R. Simes]; in a series of letters. By * * * S——, Esq. [Thomas Simes]. 8vo. [*Brit. Mus.*]   London, 1780

TRUE (a) narrative of the controversy concerning the doctrine of the Trinity; being a reply to Dr Berriman's Historical account; wherein the partiality and mis-representations of that author are fully shewn. By the author of the *Reply to Dr Waterland's Defenses* [Rev. John Jackson, of Rossington]. 4to. Pp. 112. [*Brit. Mus.*]   London, 1725

TRUE (a) narrative of the late design of the Papists to charge their horrid Plot upon the Protestants. . . . [By Captain John Bury.] 4to. Pp. 12. [Dix and Dugan's *Dubl. Books.*]
                    Dublin, 1679

TRUE (a) narrative of the proceedings of the Presbytery of Kirkcudbright against one of their number; and that to the sentence of deposition; to which is added the grievances. [By Rev. John MacMillan, Balmaghie.] 4to. [Scott's *Fasti*, second edition.]   1704

TRUE (a) narrative of the sufferings and relief of a young girle; strangely molested, by evil spirits and their instruments, in the West: collected from authentic testimonies there-anent. . . . [By Francis Grant, of Cullen, one of the Lords of Session.] 8vo. Pp. xlvi. 21.   Edinburgh, 1698

TRUE (a) narrative of what pass'd at the examination of the Marquis De Guiscard, at the cock-pit, the 8th of March, 17$\frac{10}{11}$; his stabbing Mr Harley, and other precedent and subsequent facts, relating to the life of the said Guiscard. [Revised by Jonathan Swift, D.D.] 8vo. Pp. 43. [*Camb. Hist. of Eng. Lit.*]   London, 1711

TRUE (the) nature and cause of the tail of comets; elucidated. . . . By an enquirer [John Perkins]. 8vo. [Sabin's *Dictionary*.]   Boston, 1772

TRUE news of the good new world shortly to come. . . . [By William Sherwin.] 4to. [*Brit. Mus.*]
                    N.P. [*c.* 1675]

TRUE (the) non-conformist in answere to the Modest and free conference [by Gilbert Burnet] betwixt a conformist and a non-conformist, about the present distempers of Scotland. By a lover of truth [Robert M'Ward] and published by its order. 8vo. [*Wodrow.*]   1671

TRUE (the) notion of imputed righteousness, and our justification thereby; being a supply of what is lacking in the late book of that most learned person Bishop Stillingfleet, which is a discourse for reconciling the dissenting parties in London. . . . By the Reverend M. S. a country minister [Matthew Smith]. 8vo. Pp. 14, 222.
                    London, 1700
    A presentation copy to Ralph Thoresby, who has given the author's name.

TRUE of heart. [A novel.] By Kay Spen [Henry Courtney Selous, artist]. 8vo. Pp. 310.   London [1891]

TRUE (the), pathetic history of poor Match. By Holme Lee, author of *Legends from fairy land*, etc. [Harriet Parr]. With four illustrations. 8vo. Pp. viii. 219.   London, 1863

TRUE patriotism; an apostrophe inspired by the public loss experienced in the death of Sir J. T. Long. [By Robert Sadler.] 4to. [*Brit. Mus.*]
                    London, 1795

TRUE patriotism; or, poverty ennobled by virtue: a drama [in five acts, prose and verse. By George Holford, M.P.]. 8vo. [*Brit. Mus.*]   Louth, 1799
    Attributed to T. Robinson in *Gent. Mag.* Sept. 1799, p. 748.

TRUE (the) patriot's book. By Orme Agnus [John C. Higginbotham]. 8vo. Pp. 168.   London, 1915

TRUE peace. . . . See "A wise and moderate discourse. . . ."

TRUE (the) penitent instructed. [By Jeremy Taylor.] 12mo. [Leslie's *Cat.* 1843 (415).]   1697

TRUE (the) picture of a modern Whig, set forth in a dialogue between Mr Whiglove & Mr Double, two underspur-leathers to the late ministry. [By Charles Davenant, LL.D.] Seventh edition. 8vo. Pp. 96. [*Bodl.*]
                    London, 1705

TRUE (the) picture of an ancient Tory; a dialogue between a vassal, a Tory, and Freeman, a Whig. [By Charles Davenant, LL.D.] 8vo.
                    London, 1702

TRUE (the) picture of Quakerism; in a summary view of the blasphemies, heresies and treasonable practices of the Quakers of old, taken from their most noted and approv'd writers. By a lover of truth [Zachary Grey, LL.D.]. 8vo. [Watt's *Bibl. Brit.; Gent. Mag.* vi. 295.]   1736

TRUE piety; or, the day well spent. . . . By a Roman Catholic clergyman of Baltimore [Rev. J. B. David]. 8vo. [Cushing's *Init. and Pseud.*]
                    Baltimore, 1809

TRUE (the) plan of a living temple ; or, man considered in his proper relation to the ordinary occupations and pursuits of life. By the author of *The morning and evening sacrifice*, etc. [Thomas Wright]. 12mo. 3 vols.
Edinburgh and London, 1830

TRUE (the) portraiture of the kings of England ; drawn from their titles, successions, raigns and ends : or, a short and exact historical description of every king with the right they have had to the crown, and the manner of their wearing of it especially from William the Conqueror. . . . To which is added the Political Catechism. [Address "to the reader" signed : H. P. *i.e.* Henry Parker, of Lincoln's Inn.] 4to. Pp. 63.   London, 1688

TRUE (the) Presbyterian without disguise ; or, a character of a Presbyterians wayes and actions. [By Sir John Denham. In verse.] 4to. Pp. 6. [*Brit. Mus.*]   London, 1661
    An edition of 1680 gives the author's name.

TRUE (the) priesthood of the Holy Jerusalem vindicated, and the false shepherds exposed ; in a letter to a friend. [By Joseph Noel Paton, senior, a Swedenborgian.] 12mo. Pp. 39. [Beveridge's *Dunferm. Bibl.*]
Dunfermline, 1846

TRUE (the) principles of Roman Catholics. [Preface signed : Philalbion *i.e.* Simon Lucas.] 12mo. [Gillow's *Bibl. Dict.*]   Newport, Isle of Wight, 1796

TRUE (the) principles of the English Reformation, being the substance of a lecture (occasioned by a discussion between the Catholick Church and the Church of England) delivered in Canon-Street chapel, Louth. By the author of *Notitiæ ludæ*, etc. [R. S. Bayley]. 8vo. Pp. 46.
London, 1835

TRUE (a) protestant bridle ; or, some cursory remarks upon a sermon [by William Stephens, rector of Sutton in Surrey] preached before the Right Honourable the Lord Mayor and Aldermen of the city of London at S. Mary le Bow, 30 Jan. 1693. in a letter to Sir P. D. [By Thomas Rogers.] 4to. [Wood's *Athen. Oxon.* iv. 401.]
London, 1694

TRUE (the) protestants appeal to the city and countrey. [By Dr John Nalson.] Fol. [*Lincoln's Inn Lib.*]
London, 1681

TRUE (a) reformation and perfect restitution, argued by Sylvanus and Hymenæus, wherein the true Church of Christ is briefly discovered. . . . By J. G. [John Graunt, of Bucklersbury], a friend to the truth and Church of God. 4to. [*Brit. Mus.*]
London, 1643

TRUE (a) reformer. [By Lieut.-Col. Francis Rawdon Chesney, R.A.] 8vo. 3 vols.
Edinburgh and London, 1873
    Originally published in *Blackwood's Magazine.*

TRUE (a) relation and journall of the manner of the arrivall and magnificent entertainment given to Prince Charles at Madrid. [By George Villiers, first Duke of Buckingham.] 4to. [*W.* ; Bliss' *Cat.*]   London, 1623

TRUE (a) relation of disbanding the Supernumerary Forces amounting to twenty thousand Horse and Foot, and taking off free-quarter from the subject. [By John Rushworth, secretary to the Parliamentary Army.] 4to. [Thomason's *Coll. of Tracts*, i. 596.]
London, 1648

TRUE relation of disbanding the supernumerary forces in several counties to the great ease of the Kingdom. . . . [By Gilbert Mabbot.] 4to. Pp. 8.
London, 1647

TRUE (a) relation of England's happinesse, under the raigne of Queene Elizabeth ; and the miserable estate of Papists under the Pope's tyranny. By M. S. [Matthew Sutcliffe]. 8vo. [*Brit. Mus.*]   [London] 1629

TRUE relation of sundry conferences had betweene certaine Protestand Doctours (Francis White, Daniel Featly) and a Iesuite called M. Fisher [whose real name was John Piercy] . . . with defences of the same. . . . By A. C. 4to. Pp. 86. [*Brit. Mus.*]
N.P. 1626

TRUE (a) relation of that memorable parliament, which wrought wonders, begun at Westminster, 1386, in the tenth yeare of the reign of King Richard the Second ; whereunto is added an abstract of those memorablematters, before and since the said king's reign, done by parliaments : together with the character of the said amiable, but unhappy king, and a briefe story of his life and lamentable death. [By Thomas Fannant.] 4to. [*Brit. Mus.* ; Scott's ed. of Somers' *Tracts*, iv. 174-190.]   1641

TRUE (a) relation of the apparition of one Mrs Veal, the next day after her death, to one Mrs Bargrave at Canterbury, the 8th of September. 1705, which apparition recommends the perusal of Drelincourt's Book of consolations against the fear of death. [By Daniel Defoe.] 4to. [Wilson's *Life of Defoe.*]
London, 1705

TRUE (a) relation of the ceremonies of the creating of the Knights of the Hon. Order of the Bath, 18th and 19th April, 1661 ; with a perfect list of their names. [By Philemon Stephens.] 4to.
London, 1661

TRUE (a) relation of the conversion and baptism of Isuf the Turkish chaous, named Richard Christophilus, on Jan. 30, 1658 in Covent Garden. [By Thomas White.] 12mo.
London, 1658

Contemporary attestation.

TRUE (a) relation of the faction begun at Wisbich, by Fa. Edmonds, alias Weston, a Iesuite, 1595. and continued since by Fa. Walley, alias Garnet, the Prouinciall of the Iesuits in England, and by Fa. Parsons in Rome, with their adherents ; against vs the secular priests their brethren and fellow prisoners, that disliked of nouelties, and thought it dishonourable to the auncient ecclesiasticall discipline of the Catholicke Church, that secular priests should be gouerned by Iesuits. [By Christopher Bagshaw.] 4to. Pp. 97. [*Brit. Mus.*]
1601

Reprinted in T. G. Law's *Conflict between Jesuits and Seculars.*

TRUE (a) relation of the last sicknes and death of Cardinal Bellarmine, who died in Rome the seaventeenth day of September, 1621. By C. E. [Edward Coffin] of the Society of Jesus. 12mo. [Oliver's *Collections.*]
1622

TRUE (a) relation of the late battell fought in New England between the English and the salvages : with the present state of things there. [By Philip Vincent.] 8vo. [*Camb. Hist. of Amer. Lit.* i. 379.]   London, 1637

An edition of 1638 has a slightly different title ; see *Christie-Miller Cat.*

TRUE (a) relation of the passages of God's providence in a voyage for Ireland . . . wherein every day's work is set down faithfully. By H. P. [Rev. Hugh Peters, M.A.], an eyewitness thereof. 4to. [*D. N. B.* vol. 45, p. 76.]   London, 1642

TRUE (a) relation of the proceedings against John Ogilvie, a Jesuit, executed at Glasgow, the last of Februarie, anno 1615. [By Archbishop John Spottiswood.] 4to. [*Brit. Mus.*]
Edinburgh, 1615

TRUE (a) relation of the several facts and circumstances of the intended riot and tumult on Queen Elizabeth's birthday ; gathered from authentick accounts : and published for the information of all true lovers of our constitution in Church and State. [By Jonathan Swift.] 8vo. Pp. 16.
London, 1711

Attributed also to Mrs Mary de la Rivière Manley. [*Brit. Mus.*]

TRUE (a) relation of the storming Bristoll and the taking the town, castle, forts . . . by Sir Thomas Fairfax's army . . . 11th September 1645. . . . [By Thomas Rainsborough, Colonel.] 4to. Pp. 24. [Hyett and Bazeley's *Lit. of Gloucest.*]
London, 1645

TRUE (a) relation of the travels and perilous adventures of Matthew Dudgeon, gentleman ; wherein is truly set down the manner of his taking, the long time of his slavery in Algiers, and means of his delivery : written by himself [really invented by Alfred Henry Huth], and now for the first time printed. 8vo.   London, 1894

TRUE relation of what hath been transacted in behalf of those of the reformed religion, during the treaty of peace at Reswick ; with an account of the present persecution in France. By P. G. D. [Peter Gally de Gaujac]. 4to. [*Mendham Coll. Cat.* p. 118.]
London, 1698

TRUE (a) relation of what past betweene the fleet of his Highnes the Prince of Wales [Charles II.] and that under the command of the Earle of Warwick. [By Sir William Batten.] 4to. [*Brit. Mus.*]
1648

TRUE (a) relation or collection of the most remarkable dearths and famines since the coming of William the Conquerour to Michaelmas, 1745. . . . [By William Penkethman ?] 4to.
London, 1748

TRUE religion. By W. E. H. [Rev. William Edward Heygate]. 12mo. [Boase and Courtney's *Bibl. Corn.*] 8vo. Pp. 12.   Truro [1848]

TRUE religion explained and defended against ye archenemies thereof in these times, in six bookes. [By Hugo de Groat.] . . . 12mo. [*Brit. Mus.*]
London, 1632

TRUE (a) report of the late apprehension and imprisonment of John Nicols, minister at Roan [Rouen], and his confession and answers, made in the time of his durance there. . . . [By Robert Parsons or Persons, S.J.] 12mo. Pp. 34. [*De Backer.*]
Rhemes, 1583

TRUE (a) report of the private colloquy between Mr Smith, *alias* Norrice, and M. Walker, held in the presence of two worthy knights, and of a few other gentlemen, some Protestants ; with a briefe confutation of the false and adulterated summe which M. Walker, Pastour of S. John Euangelist, in Watling-Streete, hath divulged of the same. [By Sylvester Norris, S.J.] 4to. Pp. 63. [Sommervogel's *Diction-naire.*]   [London] 1624

TRUE (a) reporte of the death and matyrdome of M. [Edmund] Campion, Jesuite and Prieste, and M. [Rodulph] Sherwin and M. [Alexander] Bryan, Priestes, at Tiborne, the first of December 1581 ; observed and written by a Catholike priest [Robert Parsons] which was present thereat ; whereunto is annexid certayne verses made by sundrie persons. 8vo. [*W.* ; Lowndes' *Bibl. Man.*]   [Douai, 1582]
    This tract was written in answer to one by Ant. Munday, entitled, "A discoverie of Edmund Campion, and his confederates."

TRUE (a) reporte of the late discoveries, and possession, taken in the right of the Crowne of Englande of the New-found Landes, by that valiaunt and worthye gentleman, Sir Humfrey Gilbert, Knight ; wherein is also breefly sette downe her Highnesse lawfull tytle thereunto, &c. [Dedication signed : G. P. *i.e.* Sir George Peckham.] 4to. [*Brit. Mus.*]
London, 1583

TRUE (a) representation of Presbyterian government ; wherein a short and clear account is given of the principles of them that owne it, the common objections against it answered, and some other things opened that concern it in the present circumstances. The second edition, corrected and much enlarged. By a friend to that interest [Gilbert Rule, D.D.]. 4to. Pp. 19. [Dexter's *Congr. Bibl.* 2378.]
Edinburgh, 1690
    The Address to the reader is signed : G. R.

TRUE (a) representation of the absurd and mischievous principles of the sect, commonly known by the name of Muggletonians. [By John Williams, D.D.] 4to. Pp. 30. [Smith's *Anti Quak.* p. 327.]   London, 1694

TRUE (a) representation of the proceedings of the Kingdome of Scotland; since the late pacification : by the Estates of the Kingdome : against mistakings in the late Declaration, 1640. [By William Kerr.] [*D. N. B.* vol. 31, p. 65.]   N.P. 1640

TRUE (a) representation of the rise, progresse, and state of the present divisions of the Church of Scotland [between Resolutioners and Protesters. By James Wood, Professor at St Andrews]. 4to. Pp. 48.
London, 1657

TRUE (the) riches ; a present of glorious and immense riches plainly and freely tendered. . . . [By Cotton Mather.] 8vo. Pp. 31. [G. Brinley's *American Library.*]   Boston, 1724

TRUE riches ; or, wealth without wings. By the author of *Ten nights in a bar room* [Timothy Shay Arthur]. 8vo. Pp. 224. [*Brit. Mus.*]   London [1881]

TRUE (the) Scripture doctrine of the most holy and undivided Trinity, continued and vindicated from the misrepresentations of Dr Clarke ; in answer to his Reply. By the author of the Scripture-Doctrine published and recommended by Robert Nelson, Esq. [By James Knight, D.D.] 8vo. Pp. 308. [*D. N. B.* vol. 51, p. 16.]
London, 1715
    The authorship is by no means certain ; it has also been attributed to Daniel Scott, LL.D.

TRUE (the) Scripture doctrine regarding Baptism, in six letters to a candid Anti-pædo baptist ; being a full answer to Dr Gill's Baptism a divine commandment to be observed. By Candidus [Henry Mayo]. 8vo. Pp. 72. [Whitley's *Bapt. Bibl.* i. 185.]
London, 1766

TRUE (the) secret history of the lives and reigns of all the Kings and Queens of England from William the First . . . to the end of the reign of . . . Queen Anne. By a person of honour [Lord Somers]. 8vo. 2 vols. [*Camb. Univ. Lib.*]   London, 1725

TRUE (the) sentiments of America ; contained in a collection of letters sent from the House of Representatives of the province of Massachusetts Bay, to several persons of high rank in this kingdom ; together with certain papers relating to a supposed libel on the governor of that province, and a dissertation on the canon and feudal law. [By Thomas Hollis.] 8vo. Pp. 158. [Rich's *Bibl. Amer.* i, 164.]
London, 1768

TRUE (the) settlement of a Christians faith, after shaking assaults, by its own evidence ; and by the internal sealing work of the Spirit ; pointed at, in some special enquiries thereon, in a letter to a friend : with some serious reflections on the present times we are in, and these great vicissitudes of Providence, which have been in the publick state of Britain in this last age, in a II. letter. By a minister of the Gospel [Robert Fleming]. 8vo. Pp. 208. [*D. N. B.* vol. 19, p. 285.]
1692

TRUE (a), short, impartial relation, containing the substance of the proceedings at the assize held . . . 12th and 13th . . . August 1664 at Hertford . . . chiefly . . . against nine prisoners called Quakers. . . . By W. S. [William Smith, of Besthorp]. 4to. [*Brit. Mus.*] [London, 1664]

TRUE, sincere, and modest defence of English Catholiques that suffer for their faith both at home and abroad, against a false, seditious and slaunderous libel [by Lord Burghley] intituled, The execution of justice in England. [By William Allen, Cardinal.] 8vo. [*D. N. B.* vol. 1, p. 321.]
[Ingolstadt, 1584]

TRUE (the) Sonship of Christ investigated ; and his person, dignity and offices explained and confirmed from the Sacred Scriptures. By a clergyman [William Dalgleish, D.D., of Peebles]. 12mo. Pp. 198. [*New Coll. Lib.*] London, 1776

TRUE (the) speeches of Thomas Whitebread, Provincial of the Jesuits in England, William Harcourt, pretended Rector of London, John Fenwick, Procurator for the Jesuits in England, John Gavan, and Anthony Turner, all Jesuits and priests ; before their execution at Tyburn, June the 20th MDCLXXIX. . . . [By David Clarkson.] Fol. Pp. 24. London, 1679

TRUE (the) spirit of the Methodists, and their allies, (whether other enthusiasts, Papists, Deists, Quakers, or Atheists) fully laid open ; in an answer to six of the seven pamphlets (Mr Law's being reserv'd to be consider'd by itself) ; lately publish'd against Dr Trapp's sermons upon being righteous over-much. . . . [By Joseph Trapp, D.D.] 8vo. Pp. 98. [*D. N. B.* vol. 57, p. 157.] London, 1740

TRUE (the) state of Gospel truth establish'd upon the free election of God in Christ ; the agreement, yet difference between Law and Gospel, so that the Gospel cannot be stiled Law. The inconditionateness of the Gospel salvation, the procedure of the Day of Judgment, in the way of a conciliatory discourse upon Mr [Daniel] Williams his concessions. By T. B. [Thomas Beverley]. 8vo. [Arber's *Term Cat.* iii. 399.] London, 1704

TRUE (the) state of the case. . . . [By Robert Dick, D.D.] [Scott's *Fasti*, i. 39.] Edinburgh, 1763

TRUE (a) state of the case concerning the election of a Provost of Queen's-College in Oxford. [By Francis Thompson, B.D.] 4to. Pp. 32. [*Bodl.*] Oxford, 1704

Most of the materials for this pamphlet were collected by Dr Thomas Crosthwait.

TRUE state of the proceedings in the Parliament of Great Britain and the Province of Massachusetts Bay relative to the giving and granting the money to that province. [By Arthur Lee, of Virginia, from material supplied by Benjamin Franklin.] Fol. Pp. 24. [Sabin's *Dictionary*.] London, 1774

TRUE (the) state of the process against Mr Ebenezer Erskine minister of the Gospel at Stirling ; setting forth the proceedings of the Synod of Perth and Stirling against him, and the Act of the late Assembly concerning him, and some other ministers adhering to his protest : together with a preface and appendix, . . . [By Ebenezer Erskine.] 8vo. Pp. 80. [M'Kerrow's *History of the Secession Church* (ed. 1841), p. 818.] Edinburgh, 1733

TRUE (the) state of Trinity College [Cambridge], in a letter to a residing Fellow of that Society ; wherein the trifling impertinencies, malicious aspersions, and bold falshoods of Dr Bentley are answer'd. . . . [By John Paris, D.D., and Samuel White, B.D.] 8vo. Pp. 88. [Bartholomew's *Camb. Books.*] London, 1710

TRUE (a) statement of the circumstances which led to the late change of administration. By Scaevola [John Allen]. 8vo. London, 1807

TRUE stories of cottagers ; the drunkard's boy ; the cottage in the lane, etc. [By Edward Monro, M.A.] 12mo. [*Bodl.*] London, 1849

Each story has a separate title and pagination.

TRUE (a) story, and the recent carnival of crime. By Mark Twain [Samuel Langhorne Clemens]. Illustrated. 16mo. [*Brit. Mus.*] Boston, 1877

TRUE (the) story of Lord and Lady Byron, in answer to Mrs Beecher Stowe. By Outis [John Lucas Tupper]. 8vo. London, 1869

TRUE (the) story of Madam Eccles. By a licensed victualler [—— Jennings]. 8vo. Cambridge, 1885

TRUE (the) subject to the rebell; or, the hurt of sedition, how greivous it is to a commonwealth. Written by Sir John Cheeke, Knight (Tutor and Privy-Counceilour to King Edward the Sixt) 1549: whereunto is newly added by way of preface a briefe discourse of those times, as they may relate to the present, with the author's life [by G. Langbaine]. 4to. [*W.*] Oxford, 1641

TRUE (a) subjects wish; for the happy successe of our royall army preparing to resist the factious rebellion of those insolent Covenanters (against the sacred Maiesty, of our gracious and loving King Charles) in Scotland. [By Martin Parker.] Fol. S. sh. 2 parts. B. L. London, N.D.
Signed: M. P.

TRUE (the) testimonie of a faithfull subject; containing severell exhortations to all estates to continue them in their due obedience. . . . [Signed R. V. *i.e.* Richard Venner.] 8vo. [*Brit. Mus.*] London [1605]

TRUE (a) testimony from the people of God; (who by the world are called Quakers) of the doctrines of the prophets, Christ, and the apostles, which is witnessed unto, by them who are now raised up by the same power, and quickened by the same Spirit and blood of the everlasting Covenant, which brought again our Lord Jesus from the dead. . . . By M. F. [Margaret Fell]. 4to. Pp. 28. [*Smith's Cat. of Friends' Books.*] London, 1660

TRUE (the) text of the Holy Scriptures. By Herman Heinfetter, author of *Rules for ascertaining the sense conveyed in ancient Greek manuscripts*, etc. [Frederick Parker]. Second edition. 12mo. Pp. 30. London, 1861

TRUE (the) theory of rent, in opposition to Mr Ricardo and others. . . . By the author of the *Catechism on the Corn Laws* [Thomas Perronet Thompson]. Fourth edition. 8vo. Pp. 32. London, 1829

TRUE (the) theory of the earth, and philosophy of the predicted end; a solution of some of the great problems of science, and sacred prophecy, on the testimony of the two witnesses, the book of nature and the Word of God; . . . By Research [J. Wood Beilby, Frankston, Victoria]. 8vo. Pp. vii. 229. [*Camb. Univ. Lib.*] Edinburgh, 1869

TRUE Tilda. By "Q." [Sir Arthur T. Quiller-Couch]. 8vo. London, 1909

TRUE (the) time of keeping St Matthias's-day in leap years, shewn in a familiar conference between a church-man and a dissenter; wherein is inserted Dr Wallis's letter to Bp. Fell written on that subject. [By Robert Watts, LL.B.] 8vo. [*Bodl.*] Oxford, 1711

TRUE to her trust; or, womanly past question. [By Miss Dora Havers, later Mrs Boulger.] With illustrative initial devices by F. W. Waddy. 8vo. 3 vols. [Title page of *Pretty Miss Bellew.*] London, 1874
An edition appeared in New York under the pseudonym: Theo Gift.

TRUE to him for ever. By F. W. R. [Miss Frannie W. Rankin]. 8vo. [*Cushing's Init. and Pseud.*] New York, 1874

TRUE to his colours. By Harry Castlemon [Charles A. Fosdick]. 8vo. [*Cushing's Init. and Pseud.*] Philadelphia, 1889

TRUE to life; a simple story. By a sketcher from nature [Mary Stanley]. 8vo. London, 1873

TRUE to trust; or, the story of a portrait. [By Rev. John Rutherford Shortland.] 8vo. Pp. 344. London [1874]

TRUE (the) translation of the Holy Scriptures. By Herman Heinfetter, author of *Rules for ascertaining the sense conveyed in ancient Greek manuscripts*, etc. [Frederick Parker]. 12mo. Pp. 55. London, 1861

TRUE (the) vine. By the author of *The Schönberg-Cotta family* [Mrs Elizabeth Charles, *née* Elizabeth Rundle]. 8vo. [*Brit. Mus.*] London, 1885

TRUE (the) way to vertue and happinesse; intreating especially of constancie in publick calamities and priuate afflictions. [Translated by Andrew Court from Guillaume Du Vair's "De la constance . . ."] 4to. Pp. 165. [*Brit. Mus.*] London, 1623, 1622
Books 2 and 3 have separate title-pages, dated 1622.

TRUE-BLEU Presbyterian loyalty; or, the Christian loyalty of Presbyterians, in Britain and Ireland, in all changes of government, since the Reformation, asserted: more particularly, of the Presbyterians in Ulster, since their first plantation there: when King James the First came to possess the crown of England. . . . [By William Tisdal, D.D., vicar of Belfast.] 4to. Pp. 31.   Dublin, 1709

The title is taken from the Reply by John M'Bride, and must be regarded as ironical, since Dr Tisdall was a violent opponent of the Presbyterians. The work has been ascribed (see Wodrow's Correspondence, i. 412) to Mr Campbell, probably Dr William Campbell, minister of Armagh, who wrote a Vindication of the character and principles of the Presbyterians of Ireland. Dr Reid, however, in his History of the Presbyterian Church of Ireland (iii. 127, 128, 166, 167), ascribes it unhesitatingly to Dr Tisdall.

TRUE-BLUE; a musical entertainment [in verse]; altered from the *Press-gang* [of Henry Carey] . . . and the story of J. Gilpin [by Wm. Cowper]. 8vo. [*Brit. Mus.*]   London, 1787

TRUE-BORN (the) Englishman; a satyr. [By Daniel Defoe.] 4to.
                                              1701

TRUMP (the) card. [A novel.] By Derek Vane [Mrs B. Eaton-Back]. 8vo. Pp. 287. [*Brit. Mus.*]
                              London [1925]

TRUMPET (the) of fame; or, Sir F. Drakes and Sir J. Hawkins Farewell. By H. B. [Henry Roberts]. 4to. Pp. 12. [*W.*: Lowndes' *Bibl. Man.*]
                              London, 1595

TRUMPET (the) of the Lord sounded, and his sword drawn, and the separation made between the precious and the vile; and the vineyard of the Lord dressed by his own husbandmen, and the dead trees cut down, and all the mystery of witchcraft discovered in all professions: by them who have come thorow great tribulation, whose garments have been washed in the blood of the Lamb, who are accounted as the off-scowring of all things for Christs sake, scornfully called by the world Quakers. [By George Fox.] 4to. Pp. 17.   London, 1654

One of what may be called the blasts of the trumpet is signed: G. F.

TRUMPINGTON Church. [By A. C. Moule.] 8vo. Pp. 7. [*Brit. Mus.*]
                              Cambridge, 1923

"TRUMP'S" [*i.e.* William Brisbane Dick's] new card games. Hearts, Boodle, Newmarket, Five or Nine, Domino Whist, Cayenne Whist, Solo and Heart Jackpot. 16mo. Pp. 38. [Jessel's *Bibl. of Playing Cards*, p. 71.]
                              New York, 1886

TRUST (the). [A tale.] By E. J. B. [Mrs E. J. Burbury]. 12mo. [*Brit. Mus.*]   London, 1849

TRUST (a) betrayed; a novel. By John Tipton [Henry Godefroi]. 8vo. 3 vols. [*Brit. Mus.*]   London, 1889

TRUST for trust. [A novel.] By A. J. Barrowcliffe [A. J. Albert Mott]. 8vo. 3 vols. [*Brit. Mus.*]   London, 1859

TRUST her not. [A novel.] By Helena Gullifer [Helen F. Hetherington]. 8vo. 3 vols. [*Brit. Mus.*]
                              London, 1881

TRUST in God; or, Jenny's trials. By Cousin Kate [Catherine Douglas Bell]. 12mo.   London, 1871

TRUST me. By N. D'Anvers [Mrs Nancy Bell, *née* Meugens]. 8vo.
                              London, 1882

TRUSTEE (the). By the author of the tragedy of *The Provost of Bruges*, etc. [George William Lovell]. 12mo. 3 vols. [*Brit. Mus.*]   London, 1841

TRUSTWORTHINESS (the) of the Earl Street Committee examined and disproved. . . . [By James M. M'Culloch, D.D., Greenock.] 8vo. Pp. 28.   Edinburgh, 1828

TRUTH. . . . By T. [William Henry Trenwith]. 8vo. [Cushing's *Init. and Pseud.*]   New York, 1873

TRUTH; a gift for scribblers; with additions and amendments. [In verse; signed: W. J. S. *i.e.* William Joseph Snelling.] 8vo. [*Brit. Mus.*]
                              Boston, 1831

TRUTH; a novel. By the author of *Nothing* [William Pitt Scargill]. 12mo. [*Brit. Mus.*]   London, 1827

TRUTH; a path to justice and reconciliation. By Verax [Francis Bonnet]. 8vo. Pp. 293. [*Brit. Mus.*]
                              London [1926]

TRUTH (the) about an author. [By Arnold Bennett.] 8vo. Pp. 269. [*Calc. Imp. Lib.*]   Westminster, 1903

Chapters in autobiography, reprinted from *The Academy*.

TRUTH about China and Japan. By Putnam Weale [Bertram Lenox Simpson]. 8vo. Pp. 156.
                              London, 1921

TRUTH (the) about Clement Ker . . . told by his second cousin Geoffrey Ker . . . edited [or rather written, as a novel] by George Fleming [Julia Constance Fletcher]. 8vo. Pp. 311. [*Brit. Mus.*]   London, 1888

TRUTH (the) about Ireland. By an English Liberal [Allen Upward]. 8vo.
London, 1884

TRUTH (the) about the Bar and about the Solicitors. . . . By Innes Lincoln, Esq. [Louis de Souza]. 8vo. Pp. 16. [*Brit. Mus.*]   London [1884]

TRUTH (the) about the Land League. [By Hugh Oakeley Arnold-Forster.] 8vo. [*D. N. B.* Second Supp. vol. 1, p. 62.]   London, 1881

TRUTH (the) about the stage. By Corin [—— Lind]. 8vo.
London, 1885

TRUTH (the) about the Tsar and the present state of Russia. By Carl Joubert [Adolphus Waldorf Carl Grottey]. Fourth edition. 8vo. Pp. 265.
London, 1905

TRUTH (the) and certainty of the Protestant faith ; with a short and plain account of the doctrine of the Romish Church. . . . [By Robert Fleming, minister at Rotterdam.] 12mo. Pp. 6, 55. [*D. N. B.* vol. 19, p. 285.]   [Rotterdam] 1678

TRUTH and error ; a calm examination of the doctrines of the Church of Rome for all who are sincere in the search after truth. By an octogenarian [Mrs Tyndall, of Oxford]. 8vo. Pp. 211. xxxii.   Oxford, 1870

TRUTH and error in religious belief ; an exposition of the Nicene Creed [with the text]. . . . By George Frederick Newmarch [G. F. Newman]. 8vo. [*Brit. Mus.*]   Cirencester, 1878

TRUTH and falshood ; a tale [in verse. By Rev. Thomas Francklin]. Fol. Pp. 6. [*D. N. B.* vol. 20, p. 183.]
London, 1755
The subject of the verses is the Duchess of Bedford.

TRUTH and fancy ; tales legendary, historic, and descriptive. By Mary Jane Windle [Mary Jane M'Lane]. 8vo. [Cushing's *Init. and Pseud.*]
Philadelphia, 1850

TRUTH and innocence vindicated ; in a survey of a discourse [by Samuel Parker] concerning ecclesiastical polity ; and the authority of the civil magistrate over the consciences of subjects in matters of religion. [By John Owen, D.D.] 8vo. [*Bodl.*]   London, 1669

TRUTH and its triumph ; or, the story of Jewish twins. By Aunt Friendly [Mrs Sarah S. Baker, *née* Tuthill]. 8vo.
London, 1882

TRUTH and trust. [A tale.] By W. C. [William Chambers]. 12mo. [*Brit. Mus.*]   Edinburgh, 1848

TRUTH (the) as it is in Jesus defined in the constitution and order of the Ecclesia of immersed Believers. . . . [By David Brown.] Third edition. 8vo.   London [1870]

TRUTH (the) come out at last ; a true history of the Wild Methodist [Isaac Abrams] . . . written by himself. 8vo. [Cushing's *Init. and Pseud.*]
Philadelphia, 1831

TRUTH (the) ; comprising an inquiry if a man is justified in proving the truth of his religious tenets. By W. M. R. [W. M. Russell]. 8vo. [*Brit. Mus.*]
London [1852]

TRUTH Dexter. [A novel.] By Sidney M'Call [Mrs Mary M'Neil Fenollosa]. 8vo. [*Amer. Cat.*]   Boston, 1906

TRUTH further cleared from mistakes ; being two chapters out of the book entitled "Primitive Christianity revived." . . . [Signed : W. P. *i.e.* William Penn.] 12mo. Pp. 48. [Smith's *Cat. of Friends' Books.*]   Dublin, 1698

TRUTH, if you can find it ; or, a character of the present M[inistr]y and P[arliamen]t : in a letter to a member of the March Club. [By Sir Thomas Burnet.] 8vo. Pp. 37. [*Brit. Mus.*]   London, 1712

TRUTH it's manifest ; or, a short and true relation of divers main passages of things (in some whereof the Scots are particularly concerned) from the very first beginning of these unhappy troubles to this day. [By David Buchanan.] Pp. 142.   London, 1645
"The author of the present vol. was, I believe, David Buchanan, who in 1644, republished Knox's History of the Reformation in Scotland—and was the author of various other works."—MS. note by Dr David Laing.

TRUTH (the) of revelation demonstrated by an appeal to existing monuments, sculptures, gems, coins, and medals. By a Fellow of several learned Societies [John Murray]. 12mo. Pp. xviii. 276.   London, 1831
The author's name appears on the title-page of the second edition, published in 1840.

TRUTH (the) of Spiritualism. By "Rita" [Mrs W. Desmond Humphreys, *née* Eliza M. J. Gollan]. 8vo.
London, 1919

TRUTH (the) of the Christian religion vindicated from the objections of unbelievers ; particularly of John James Rousseau : in a series of dissertations. By the editors of the *Christian's Magazine.* [By William Dodd, LL.D.] 8vo. [*Gent. Mag.* xlvii. 421.]   1766

TRUTH (the) respecting Italy and Piedmont; diplomatic revelations. By a secret agent of Count Cavour [J. A. Curletti]. Translated from the French. 8vo. [*Brit. Mus.*] London, 1862

TRUTH soberly defended. [By Isaac Marlow.] . . . With a postscript in answer . . . to a paper called An Answer to a brief discourse concerning singing. By H. K. [Hanserd Knollys]. 8vo. [*Brit. Mus.*] London, 1692
The first tract is not anonymous.

TRUTH : the mysteries of Christianity radically developed, and discovered to be physically true. . . . From the French [of —— Bebescourt]. 8vo. 2 vols. [*Brit. Mus.*] London, 1772

TRUTH triumphant. By T. B. [Timothy Brown, P.P. of Castle Lyon, Co. Cork]. 4to. Cork, 1745

TRUTH unlocked; in gleanings and illustrations from the Scripture originals. By a pioneer witness [William Bennoch, later Bennet]. 8vo. Pp. 454. [*Corrie's Glencairn*, p. 198.] Edinburgh, 1875

TRUTH (the) unvailed, &c. in behalf of the Church of England, and at the importunity of one that calls loudly on Mr. Standish for particular instances of such (amongst her profess'd sons) as have ventured upon innovations in her doctrine ; taking occasion from his sermon preach'd before his Majesty, and ordered to be published by royal authority. By a person of quality [Arthur Annesley, Earl of Anglesey]. 4to. Pp. 20-39. [*D. N. B.* vol. 2, p. 3.] 1667

TRUTH vindicated ; being an appeal to the light of Christ within, and to the testimony of Holy Scripture : by way of answer to a pamphlet, entitled, "Extracts from periodical works on the controversy amongst the Society of Friends." [By Henry Martin.] 12mo. [Smith's *Cat. of Friends' Books*, i. 221.] London, 1835

TRUTH vindicated ; or, a detection of the aspersions and scandals cast upon Sir Rob. Clayton and Sir Geo. Treby, justices ; and Slingsby Bethel and Henry Cornish sheriffs of the city of London, in a paper published in the name of Dr Francis Hawkins minister of the Tower entit. The confession of Edw. Fitzharris, Esq. ; &c. [By Sir George Treby.] 4to. [Wood's *Athen. Oxon.* iv. 500.] London, 1681

TRUTH will out ; or, a discovery of some untruths smoothly told by Dr Ieremy Taylor in his Disswasive from Popery : with an answer to such arguments as deserve answer. By his friendly adversary E. W. [Edward Worsley]. 4to. Pp. 217, 4. [Jones' *Peck*, ii. 465.] 1665

TRUTH will out ; the foul charges of the Tories against the editor of the "Aurora" repelled. [By Benjamin Franklin Bache.] 8vo. [*Brit. Mus.*] Philadelphia, 1798

TRUTH without prejudice. [By Miss Wyndham, afterwards Mrs Alfred Montgomery.] 8vo. [*Brit. Mus.*] London, 1842

TRUTHS (the) and errors of liberal Christianity, and of the national conference of 1870. By A Delegate [Rev. Henry Clay Badger]. 8vo. [Kirk's *Supp.*] Cambridge, Mass., 1870

TRUTHS and fancies from fairy land ; or, fairy stories with a purpose. [Preface signed: W. H. D. A. *i.e.* W. H. Davenport Adams.] 8vo. Pp. 128. London [1867]

TRUTHS and their reception, considered in their relation to homœopathy ; to which are added various essays on the principles and statistics of homœopathic practice. [By Marmaduke B. Sampson.] Second edition. 8vo. Pp. 251. [*Manch. Free Lib.* p. 620.] London, 1849

TRUTHS and untruths respecting a restored Apostolate. By a clergyman [Rev. Robert Norton, D.D.]. 8vo. Pp. 24. [*Brit. Mus.*] London, 1876

TRUTHS defence ; or, the pretended examination by John Alexander of Leith, of the principles of those (called Quakers) falsly termed by him Jesuitico-Quakerism, re-examined and confuted, together with some animadversions on the dedication of his book to Sir Robert Clayton, then Mayor of London. By G. K. [George Keith]. 8vo. Pp. 254. [Smith's *Cat. of Friends' Books*, ii. 22.] London, 1682

TRUTHS for all people. [By Alexander Jarvie.] 8vo. London, 1882

TRUTHS for the day of life and the hour of death. By the author of *God is love* [James Grant]. 8vo. London, 1864

TRUTHS illustrated by great authors ; a dictionary of nearly four thousand aids to reflection, quotations of maxims, metaphors, counsels, cautions, aphorisms, proverbs, &c. &c., in prose and verse : compiled from Shakespeare, and other great writers, from the earliest ages to the present. [By William White, publisher.] 12mo. London, 1852

TRUTH'S triumphs in the eternal power over the darke inventions of fallen man. G. F. [George Fox]. 4to. [Smith's *Cat. of Friends' Books*, i. 666.] London, 1661

TRUTH'S triumph over Trent; or, the great gulfe betweene Sion and Babylon : that is, the vnreconcileable opposition betweene the apostolicke Church of Christ, and the apostate synagogue of Antichrist, in the maine and fundamentall doctrine of iustification, for which the Church of England Christs spouse, hath justly, through Gods mercie, for these manie yeares, according to Christs voyce, separated her selfe from Babylon, with whom from henceforth she must hold no communion. By H. B. [Henry Burton] rector of S. Mathews, Friday-Street. 4to. Pp. 373.   London, 1629

TRUTHS victory against heresie ; all sorts comprehended under these ten mentioned : Papists, Familists, Arrians, Arminians, Anabaptists, Separatists, Antinomists, Monarchists, Millenarists, Independents. By J. G. [John Grant]. 4to. Pp. 73. [Whitley's *Bapt. Bibl.* i. 19.]   London, 1645

TRUTHS victory over error ; or, an abridgement of the chief controversies in religion, which, since the apostles days to this time, have been, and are in agitation, between those of the orthodox faith, and all adversaries whatsoever ; a list of whose names are set down after the epistle to the reader. . . . [By David Dickson, Professor of Divinity in the University of Edinburgh.] 12mo. Pp. 371.
Edinburgh, 1684

Really an unacknowledged translation, by George Sinclar (who signs his name at the end of the dedication to the municipal authorities in Edinburgh), of Dickson's academical lectures in Latin. The plagiarism was soon discovered and set forth in the couplet—

No error in this book whatever do I see,
Except that G. S. stands where D.D. ought to be.

In 1752, Robert Wodrow published an edition bearing the name of the author, with a memoir. [*D. N. B.*, vol. 15, p. 42.]

TRUTHTELLERS (the). [A novel.] By John Strange Winter [Mrs Arthur Stannard, *née* Henrietta E. V. Palmer]. 8vo. Pp. 282.   London, 1896

TRUTH-TRIUMPHANT ; in a dialogue between a Papist and a Quaker : wherein (I suppose) is made manifest, that Quaking is the off-spring of Popery : at the least, the Papist and the Quaker, are [patres vterini] both of one venter. [By Charles Stanley, Earl of Derby.] 4to. Pp. 45-58.
London, 1671

TRUYTE (the) of redempcyon. [By Richard Whitford.] 4to. [Copinger's *Bibl. on Predestination.*]
London, 1514

TRY ; a book for boys. By "Old Jonathan" [David Alfred Doudney, D.D.]. 12mo. [*Nat. Lib. of Scot.*]
London, 1857

TRY and try again ; being an outline of the lives of two youths who became clergymen of the Church of England. By "Old Jonathan" [David Alfred Doudney, D.D.]. 8vo. London, 1864

TRYAL (the) and examination of a late libel, intituled, A new test of the Church of Englands loyalty ; with some reflections upon the additional libel, intituled, An instance of the Church of Englands loyalty. [By Samuel Johnson.] 4to. [Jones' *Peck*, i. 66.]   [1687 ?]

No title-page.

TRYAL (the) of dramatic genius ; a poem : to which are added, a collection of miscellaneous pieces. By the same author [William Heard]. 8vo. [*J. Maidment.*]   London [1770]

Heard's father kept the Philobiblian Library in Piccadilly, and was prompter of the theatre at China Hall.

TRYAL (the) of the Roman Catholics, on a Special Commission directed to Lord Chief Justice Reason, Lord Chief Baron Interest, and Mr Justice Clemency, Wednesday, August 5th, 1761. . . . [By Henry Brooke.] 8vo. Pp. 310. [Watt's *Bibl. Brit.*]
Dublin, 1762

TRYAL (the) of the time-killers ; a comedy of five acts. [By Phanuel Bacon.] 8vo. [Baker's *Biog. Dram.*]
London, 1757

TRYAL (the) of the witnesses of the resurrection of Jesus. [By Thomas Sherlock.] 8vo. Pp. 110.
London, 1729

See above, "The trial of the witnesses . . ."

TRYAL (the) of William Whiston, clerk ; for defaming and denying the Holy Trinity, before the Lord Chief Justice Reason : to which is subjoined, a new catechism for the fine ladies : also a specimen of a new version of the Psalms. By Mr Pope, etc. [By Thomas Gordon.] The third edition. 8vo. Pp. 67. [Nichols' *Lit. Anec.* i. 710.]   London, 1740

The first edition appeared in 1734.

TRYAL (the) of witchcraft ; or, witch-craft arraign'd and condemned : in some answers to a few questions anent witches and witchcraft : wherein is shewed, how to know if one be a witch, as also when one is bewitched ; with some observations upon the witches mark, their compact with the devil, the white witches &c. [By John Bell.] 12mo. [*Nat. Lib. of Scot.*]   N.P., N.D.

TRYALL (a) of private devotions ; or, a diall for the houres of prayer. By H. B. [Henry Burton], rector of St Mathevves, Friday-Street. 4to. Pp. 100. [*D. N. B.* vol. 8, p. 7.]
London, 1628
A criticism of John Cosin's "Booke of private devotions."

TRYALS per pais ; or, the law concern-ing juries by nisi-prius, &c. methodi-cally composed for the publick good, in the 16th year of the reign of our Soveraigne Lord Charls the Second, King of England, Scotland, France and Ireland, &c. By S. E. [Giles Duncombe] of the Inner - Temple Esquire. 12mo. Pp. 22, 238.
London, 1665
This work has been erroneously ascribed to Sampson Ever. The letters S. E. are the final letters of Duncombe's names.

TRYING to be useful. By Mrs Madeline Leslie [Harriet Newell Baker]. 8vo. [*Brit. Mus.*]   Boston, 1871

TRYPHENA in love. By Tom Cobb-leigh [Walter Raymond]. 8vo. Pp. 172.   New York, 1895

TSAR'S (the) coronation, as seen by "De Monte Alto," resident in Moscow [Aylmer Maude]. 8vo. [*Brit. Mus.*]
London, 1896

TUCK-NET (the) split. By Pindar [Rev. William Woodis Harvey, M.A.]. 12mo.   London, 1824

TUCK-UP songs. By Ellis Walton [Mrs F. Percy Cotton]. 8vo. Pp. 123. [*Brit. Mus.*]   London, 1895

TUDOR queens and princesses. By Sarah Tytler [Henrietta Keddie]. 8vo. Pp. 418.   London, 1896

TUDORS & Stuarts. By a descendant of the Plantagenet [Frances Mary English]. Vol. I.—Tudors. 12mo.
London, 1858

TUFLONGBO'S journey in search of ogres ; with some account of his early life, and how his shoes got worn out. By Holme Lee, author of *Legends from fairy land*, etc. [Harriet Parr]. With six illustrations by H. Sanderson. 8vo. Pp. vii. 240.   London, 1862

TUILERIES (the). [In verse.] By the author of *Miscellaneous poems* [J. M. Richardson]. 12mo. Pp. 61. [*Brit. Mus.*]   Paris, 1824

TUILERIES (the) ; a tale. By the author of *Hungarian tales*, etc. [Mrs Catherine Frances Gore]. 12mo. 3 vols.   London, 1831

TULLIUS de Amicicia, in English ; here after ensueth a goodly treatyse of amyte or frendshyp, composed in latyn by the most eloquente Romayne, Marcus Tullius Cicero, and lately translatyd in to Englyshe [by J. Tipcroft, Earl of Worcester]. Fol. [*W.*]   [London, 1530?]
A reprint from the edition, published with the De Senectute by Caxton in 1481.

TULLY'S three books of Offices in English ; with notes explaining the method and meaning of the author. [Dedicatory epistle signed : T. C. *i.e.* Thomas Cockman.] 8vo. [*Brit. Mus.*]
London, 1699

TUMBLE-DOWN Dick ; or, Phaeton in the suds : a dramatick entertain-ment of walking, in serious and foolish characters, interlarded with burlesque, grotesque, comick interludes . . . in-vented by Monsieur Sans Esprit. . . . [By Henry Fielding.] 8vo. [*Brit. Mus.*]   London, 1744
The dedication is signed : Pasquin.

TUMBLEDOWN farm ; a novel. By Alan Muir [Rev. Hayes Robinson]. 8vo. 2 vols. [*Lond. Lib. Cat.*]
London, 1889

TUNBRIDGE (the) miscellany. [By Sir Charles Hanbury Williams.] 8vo. 2 pts. [Smith's *Bibl. Cant.* p. 320.]
London, 1713

TUNBRIDGE (the) Wells guide ; or, an account of the ancient and present state of that place. . . . [By J. Sprange.] 8vo. [*Brit. Mus.*]
Tunbridge Wells, 1780

TUNBRIDGE-WALKS ; or, the Yeo-man of Kent ; a comedy : as it is acted at the Theatre Royal by her Majesty's servants. By the authour of the *Humour o' the age* [Thomas Baker]. 4to. Pp. 12, 64. [Baker's *Biog. Dram.*]
London, 1703

TUNBRIDGE-WELLS ; or, a days courtship : a comedy, as it is acted at the Dukes-Theatre. Written by a person of quality. [Attributed to Thomas Rawlins, and by Wood, doubtfully, to Sir Charles Sedley.] 4to. Pp. 42.   London, 1678

TUNBRIDGIALE ; a poem : being a description of Tunbridge, in a letter to a friend at London. By the author of *My time, O ye muses* [John Byrom]. 4to. [Smith's *Bibl. Cant.* p. 320.]
London, 1726

TUNER (the). [By Paul Hiffernan.] 8vo. [Watt's *Bibl. Brit.; Mon. Rev.* Feb. 1754.]   London, 1754, 1755
     The work consists of five letters, each with a separate title and pagination. It is supposed that no more was published.

TUNNEL (the) of Trübau; a tale of the trains. By Tilbury Tramp [Charles James Lever]. 12mo. [*Brit. Mus.*]
London, 1845

TURF (the). By Nimrod [Charles James Apperley]. With illustrations. New edition. 8vo. [*Brit. Mus.*]
London, 1851
     First published in the *Quarterly Review.* See also " The Chace, the Turf, and the Road."

TURF (the); a treatise on racing and steeple-chasing. By "Rapier"[Alfred E. T. Watson]. 8vo. [*Brit. Mus.*]
London, 1898

TURF characters; the officials, and the subalterns. By Martingale, author of *Sporting scenes*, etc. [—— White]. 8vo. Pp. xvi. 128. [*Nat. Lib. of Scot.*]
London, 1851

TURF tales. By Nathaniel Gubbins [Edward Spencer Mott]. 8vo. [*Brit. Mus.*]   London [1902]

TURKEY; being sketches from life. By the Roving Englishman [Eustace Clare Grenville Murray]. 8vo. [*Brit. Mus.*]   London, 1877

TURKEY in agony. By Pierre Loti [Captain M. Julian Viaud, of the French Navy]: translated from the French by B. Sands. 8vo. Pp. 202.
London, 1913

TURKEY in Europe. By Odysseus [Sir Charles Norton Edgecumbe Eliot]. 8vo. Pp. 480. [*Amer. Cat.*]
London, 1900

TURKISH (the) and Pan-Turkish ideal. By Tekin Alp [Albert Cohen]. Fol. Pp. 48. [*Brit. Mus.*]   London [1917]

TURKISH (the) atrocities. [Verse. By Joseph Plimsoll.] 8vo. Pp. 14. [*Brit. Mus.*]   Plymouth [1876?]

TURKISH (the) Empire; embracing the religion, manners and customs of the people. [Translated from the German of Alfred de Bessé;] with a memoir of the reigning sultan . . . by E. J. Morris. Second edition. 12mo. Pp. 216. [*Brit. Mus.*]
Philadelphia, 1855

TURKISH (a) tale; in five cantos. [By George Grey, of Southwick, father-in-law of the first Earl Grey.] 12mo.   London, 1770
     Autograph on J. Maidment's copy.

TURKISH (the) tales; or, how the revenge of the perfidious empress of Persia was baffled. [By Shaikh-zādah; translated from the French version of F. Pétis de la Croix.] 8vo. Pp. 149. [*Brit. Mus.*]   Bombay, 1889

TURKO; or, the little dark boy in Dame Europa's school. By the author of *John justified* [Colonel Charles William Grant]. 8vo. [Green's *Bibl. Somers.* i. 535.]   Bath, 1877

TURN (the) of the road; a play. . . . By Rutherford Mayne [Samuel Waddell]. 8vo. Pp. 71. [S. J. Brown's *Books on Ireland.*]   Dublin, 1907

TURNED adrift; an adventurous voyage. By Harry Collingwood [William J. C. Lancaster]. 8vo. Pp. 296.   London, 1913

TURNING out; or, St S——'s in an uproar; containing particulars of the death and resurrection of the heaven-born ministers; or, the pilots that weathered the storm: a poem. By Peter Pindar, Jun. author of the *Royal Bloods*, and *Royal Lover* [John Agg]. 8vo. Pp. 24.   London, 1812

TURNING (the) wheel; a story of the Charn Hall inheritance. By Dick Donovan [Joyce Emerson Preston Muddock]. 8vo. Pp. 318.
London, 1912

TURNUS and Drances; being an attempt to shew, who the two real persons were, that Virgil intended to represent under those two characters. [By William Beare.] 8vo. Pp. 30.
Oxford, 1750
     " Given by the author, William Beare, M.A. of C.C.C."—MS. note in the Bodleian copy.

TURTLE (the) dove; a tale [in verse] from the French of M. De Florian [by Stephen Weston, B.D.]. 8vo. [*D.N.B.* vol. 60, p. 373.]   Caen, 1789

TURTLE (the) dove (an emblem of the new creature), under the absence and presence of her only choise. . . . By a lover of the celestiall muses [John Fullarton, of Careltoun]. 12mo.
Edinburgh [1664]

TURNER'S (the) manual; a translation of the work of [L. E.] Bergeron [Z. G. J. Salivet]. 4to. [*Patent Office Lib.*]
London, 1877

TUSCAN studies and sketches. By Leader Scott [Mrs Lucy E. Baxter, *née* Barnes]. 8vo. Pp. 329.
London, 1888

TUTAMEN evangelicum ; or, a defence of Scripture-Ordination, against the exceptions of T. G. [Thomas Gipps] in a book intituled, Tentamen novum, proving, that ordination by Presbyters is valid ; Timothy and Titus were no diocesan rulers ; the Presbyters of Ephesus were the apostles successors in the government of that Church, and not Timothy ; the First Epistle to Timothy was written before the meeting at Miletus ; the ancient Waldenses had no diocesan Bishops, &c. By the author of the *Plea for Scripture-Ordination* [James Owen]. 8vo. Pp. 30, 190.
London, 1697
Preface signed : J. O.

TUTOR (the) of truth. By the author of the *Pupil of pleasure*, etc. [Samuel Jackson Pratt]. 12mo. 3 vols. [Green's *Bibl. Somers.* i. 417 ; *D. N. B.* vol. 46, p. 296.]   London, 1779

TUTOR (a) to astronomy and geography; or, the use of the Copernican spheres. . . . By Joseph Moxon [or rather by William Blaeu]. 4to. Pp. 184. [*Brit. Mus.*]   London, 1665
A different work from "A Tutor to astronomie and geographie . . ." by J. Moxon. London, 1659.

TUTOR'S (the) assistant ; or, comic figures of arithmetic, slightly altered and elucidated from a Walking-game, by Alfred Crowquill [Alfred Henry Forrester]. 12mo.   London, 1843

TUTOR'S (the) ward ; a novel. By the author of *Wayfaring sketches*, etc. [Felicia M. F. Skene]. 8vo. 3 vols. [*Nat. Lib. of Scot.*]   London, 1851

TWA (the) cuckolds [by A. Steel]; and the Pint quey, or thrawart Maggy [by R. Gall] : two tales in the Scottish dialect. 12mo. [*W. ; Brit. Mus.*]
Edinburgh, 1796

TWA (the) frien's ; or, the ghost o' Coffer Ha' ; a poem : and Francisco, or the man of brass : also Holy Tammie's prayer. [By David Waters.] Second edition. 8vo. [Sinton's *Bibl. of Hawick.*]   Hawick, 1895

TWA (the) Miss Dawsons. [A tale.] By the author of *The bairns* [Miss Margaret Murray Robertson]. 8vo. Pp. 36. [*Brit. Mus.*]   London, 1880

TWAIN'S [Samuel Langhorne Clemens'] pleasure trip on the Continent ; the complete work previously issued under the title of "The Innocents abroad" and "The new Pilgrim's progress." 8vo. [*Brit. Mus.*]   London [1871]

'TWAS in dhroll Donegal. [Tales.] By "Mac" [James MacManus]. 8vo. Pp. 176.   London, 1897

TWEED and Don ; recollections and reflections of an angler for the last fifty years. [By James Locke.] 8vo. [Mitchell and Cash's *Scot. Topog.*]
Edinburgh, 1860

TWEEDS teares of joy, to Charles Great Brittains King. [By George Lauder.] 4to. Pp. 8. [*D.N.B.* vol. 32, p. 195.]
N.P. [1641]
No title-page.

'TWEEN thou and me. By Elfin Hall [Mrs E. C. Perry]. 4to. [Kirk's *Supp.*]
Albany, N.Y., 1879

TWELFTH (the) note of the Church examined, viz. The light of prophecy. [By William Clagett, D.D., Preacher to the Society of Gray's Inn.] 4to. Pp. 23. [Jones' *Peck*, p. 439.]
London, 1687

TWELVE days in the saddle ; a journey on horse-back in New England, during the autumn of 1883. . . . By Medicus [Daniel Denison Slade, M.D.]. 8vo. [*Lib. Journ.* ix. 94.]   Boston, 1884

TWELVE generall arguments, proving that the ceremonies imposed upon the ministers of the gospell in England, by our prelates, are unlawfull; and therefore that the ministers of the gospell, for the bare and sole omission of them in church service, are most unjustlie charged of disloyaltie to his Majestie. [By William Bradshaw.] 12mo. [*Nat. Lib. of Scot.*]   N.P. 1605

TWELVE hundred questions on the history of the Church of England, with some answer hints. [By Canon E. H. Knowles.] 8vo. London, 1888

TWELVE keys to auction bridge play. By Pachabo [A. E. Whitelaw]. 8vo. Pp. 184. [*Brit. Mus.*] London [1921]

TWELVE letters on the evidences of the Christian religion. By an enquirer [W. Cunninghame]. 8vo. [*Brit. Mus.*]
Serampore, 1802
First printed in the *Oriental Star.*

TWELVE maxims on swimming. By the author of *The cigar* [William Clarke]. 12mo. Pp. 30. [Thomas on *Swimming*, p. 242.] London, 1833
Preface signed : C.

TWELVE months in a Curatorship. By one who has tried it [Charles Lutwidge Dodgson]. 8vo. [S. H. Williams' *Bibl. of Dodgson.*]
[Oxford, private print] 1884
See also "Three years . . ."

TWELVE months in the British legion. By an officer of the Ninth regiment [Charles William Thompson, Major-General]. 12mo. Pp. viii. 273, xxx. [*Brit. Mus.*]   London, 1835

TWELVE (a) months' tour in Brazil and the River Plate ; with notes on sheep-farming. By L. D. [L. Dillon]. 8vo. Pp. 100. [*Brit. Mus.*]
Manchester, 1867

TWELVE moral maxims of my Uncle Newbury. [By George Mogridge.] Second edition. 12mo. Pp. 72. [*Brit. Mus.*]   London, 1832

TWELVE (the) nights. [By Baron Karl von Miltie.] 12mo. Pp. xv. 404.
London, 1831

TWELVE (the) obelisks at Rome. [By John H. Parker.] Second edition, revised. 8vo. Pp. 64.   Oxford, 1879

TWELVE o'clock ; a Christmas story. By the author of *Grandmother's money*, etc. [Frederick William Robinson]. 8vo. [*Brit. Mus.*]   London, 1861

TWELVE (the) pagan principles; or, opinions, for which Thomas Hicks hath published the Quaker to be no Christian, seriously considered, and presented to Mr N. L., citizen of London. By W. L., a lover of every man whose conversation is honest [William Loddington]. 8vo. Pp. 40. [Smith's *Cat. of Friends' Books*, ii. 127 ; Wilson's *Hist. of Diss. Ch.* iii. 392.]
N.P. 1764

TWELVE queries of publick concernment, humbly submitted to the serious consideration of the Great Councell of the Kingdom. By a cordiall well-wisher to its proceedings [William Prynne]. 4to. Pp. 4. [*Brit. Mus.*]
London, 1647

TWELVE rambles in London. By Amicus Patriae [William Burt]. 8vo.
London, 1810

XII. Resolves concerning the disposall of the person of the King in a sharpe reproofe to a Rejoynder to three pamphlets, published in defence of Mr Chaloners Speech (called, A speech without doores, and said to be defended without reason) under pretence of the Parliaments honour. [By Thomas Chaloner.] 4to. [*D. N. B.* vol. 9, p. 460.]   London, 1646

TWELVE sermons [in the Catholic Apostolic Church] at Gordon Square [London. By Rev. John G. Francis, M.A.]. 8vo. [*Brit. Mus.*]
London, 1868

TWELVE sermons, preached to a country congregation. [By Alexander Dallas, M.A.] 12mo. Pp. vii. 231.
Oxford, 1827

TWELVE simple addresses to a communicants' class. By E. M. H. [E. M. Halcombe]. 8vo. Pp. 108. [*Brit. Mus.*]   Oxford [1895]

TWELVE tales for the young. [By Mrs Gertrude Parsons, *née* Hext.] 12mo. [Boase and Courtney's *Bibl. Corn.* ii. 426.]   London [1860]

Of these tales, "The old dripping pan" was written by Daniel Parsons ; and "Too late for school," by Miss A. M. Bridges.

TWELVE trifles, cheerful and tearful. By Theophila North [Dorothea Hollins]. 8vo. Pp. 264. [*Brit. Mus.*]
London, 1904

TWELVE years ago ; a tale. By the authoress of *Letters to my unknown friends* [Sydney Warburton]. 12mo.
London, 1851

TWELVE years' military adventure in three quarters of the globe; or, memoirs of an officer who served in the armies of his Majesty and of the East India Company, between the years 1802 and 1814. . . . [By Major John Blakiston, Madras Engineers.] 8vo. 2 vols. [See his *Twenty years in retirement.*]   London, 1829

TWENTIETH (a) century boy. By Gladys Dudley Hamilton [Marguerite L. Glentworth]. 8vo.   Boston, 1901

TWENTIETH (the) century Church and Club. [A story.] By Don De Neroh [Edwin Horen]. 8vo. [*Amer. Cat.*]
Chicago, 1900

TWENTIETH (the) Epistle of Horace to his book, modernized [in parody] by the author of *Female conduct* [Thomas Marriott]. 8vo. [*Brit. Mus.*]
London, 1759

TWENTY cases of conscience propounded to the bishops, or others, who are called fathers in God; for them to answer; that the blind may not be turned out of the way, nor the people perish for lack of knowledge. . . . By J. C. [John Crook]. 4to. Pp. 8.
London [1667]

TWENTY charges against the Methodists answered by the Word of God, for their encouragement, and conviction of their enemies. [By Rev. John Barnes, of Pembroke.] 12mo. Pp. 22.
Carmarthen, 1764

TWENTY minutes late. By "Pansy" [Mrs Isabella (Macdonald) Alden]. 8vo. Pp. 374.   Boston, 1893

TWENTY sermons upon social duties and their opposite vices. By the author of *The life of David* [Patrick Delany, D.D.]. 8vo. [*Brit. Mus.*]
London, 1750

TWENTY (the) styles of architecture, illustrated by plates. . . . By the editor of the *Hundred greatest men* [W. Wood]. 8vo.   London, 1881

TWENTY years ; a ballad : poetry by the late T. H. B. [Thomas Haynes Bayly], adapted by Mrs T. H. B. to the music of L. van Beethoven. Fol. [Green's *Bibl. Somers.*]
London [1860]

TWENTY years ago ; a book of anecdote, illustrating literary life in London. By F. M. Allen [Edmund Downey]. 8vo. [*Brit. Mus.*]
London, 1905

TWENTY years ago. From the journal of a girl in her teens [Beatrice Walford]; edited by the author of *John Halifax, Gentleman* [Dinah Maria Mulock]. 8vo. Pp. v. 277.
London, 1871

TWENTY years in California ; incidents in the life of a stage-driver [James S. M'Cue]. 8vo.　San Francisco, 1875

TWENTY years' reminiscences of the Lews. By Sixty-one [Rev. George Henry Hely Hutchinson, vicar of Westport, Wiltshire]. 8vo.
London, 1871

TWENTY years' residence among the people of Turkey. By a Consul's daughter and wife [Mrs Fanny Blunt, *née* Sanderson]. 8vo. [Cushing's *Init. and Pseud.*]　London, 1878

TWENTY - EIGHT miscellaneous sermons. By a clergyman of the Church of England [Rev. Andrew Macdonald]. 8vo.　London, 1788
The fourth edition, 1793, has the author's name.

XXVIII prayers. By a prisoner of hope [Georgina Elizabeth Russell]. 8vo. [*Brit. Mus.*]
Leamington, private print [1857]

TWENTY - EIGHT propositions, by which the doctrine of the Trinity is endeavoured to be explained. . . . [By Edward Fowler, D.D.] 4to.
London, 1693
Reissued in 1694, with a different title : " Certain propositions by which the doctrine of the H. Trinity is . . . explain'd . . ."

TWENTY-EIGHT years in India. [By Charles James O'Donnell, Indian Civil Service.] 8vo.　London, 1902

TWENTY-FIVE sermons upon several subjects. . . . By Orthodoxus [Thomas Coney, D.D.]. 8vo. London, 1730-50

TWENTY-FIFE years' history of St George's-in-the-West Parish Church, Aberdeen, 1879-1904. [By James Smith.] 8vo.　Aberdeen, 1904

TWENTY-FIVE years' soldiering in South Africa ; a personal narrative. By a Colonial Officer [Captain Harry Vernon Woon]. 8vo. [Mendelssohn's *South African Bibl.*]　London, 1909

XXIV (the) cases concerning things indifferent in religious worship considered ; or, the resolver better resolved by his own principles ; and nonconformists more confirmed : also the grand case touching ministers conformity, with the double supplement thereunto annexed, briefly discussed. [By Edward Bagshaw.] 4to. Pp. 64.
London, 1663
The second part of the " The great question concerning things indifferent in religious worship, briefly stated, &c." The third part has the author's name.

TWENTY-FOUR reasons for dissenting from the Church of England. [By Thomas Binney ?] 8vo. Pp. 8. [*Brit. Mus.*]　N.P. [1835 ?]

TWENTY-NINTH (the) of May ; rare doings at the Restoration. By Ephraim Hardcastle, author of *Wine and walnuts* [William Henry Pyne]. Second edition. 12mo. 2 vols. [*Bodl.*]
London, 1825

TWENTY-ONE discourses upon the Augsburg Confession. [By Count Nicholas Lewis Zinzendorf.] Translated by F. Okeley. 12mo. [*Brit. Mus.*]　London, 1753

TWENTY-ONE golden rules to depress agriculture, etc. By a Pennsylvanian [Matthew Carey]. 8vo. [Sabin's *Dictionary*.]　Philadelphia, 1824

TWENTY-SIX and one ; and other stories. By Maxim Gorky [Aleksyei Maksimovitch Pyeshkov]. From the Russian. 12mo.　New York, 1902

XXVI letters on religious subjects, with hymns. [By Rev. John Newton.] 12mo.　　　　　　　1774

TWENTY - SIX men and a girl. [Four short tales, translated from the Russian.] By Maxim Gorky [Aleksyei Maksimovitch Pyeshkov]. 8vo. Pp. 214.　　　　London, 1902

TWENTY-THREE years in a House of Mercy. By H. N. [Harriet Nokes]. 8vo. [*Brit. Mus.*]　London, 1886

TWICE lost ; a novel. By the author of *Queen Isabel*, etc. [Menella Bute Smedley]. 8vo. Pp. 323. [*Brit. Mus.*]
London, 1863

TWICE rescued ; or, the story of little Tino. By Nellie Cornwall [Nellie Sloggett]. 8vo. Pp. 224. [*Brit. Mus.*]　London [1888]

TWICKENHAM (the) hotch-potch, for the use of the Rev. Dr Swift, Alexander Pope, Esq. ; and company : being a sequel to the Beggar's opera, etc. . . . Written by Caleb D'Anvers [Nicholas Amhurst]. 8vo. Pp. vii. 54.
London, 1728
" This work will be continued. The end of the first part."

TWIDDLEDETWIT ; a fairy tale. By Martha Farquharson [Martha Farquharson Finley]. 8vo.
New York, 1898

TWIGS for nests ; or, notes on nursery nurture. By the author of the *Expositions of the Cartoons of Raphael* [Richard Henry Smith]. 8vo. [*Brit. Mus.*] London, 1866

TWILIGHT ; a novel. By Frank Danby [Mrs Julia Frankau]. 8vo. Pp. 334.
London, 1916

TWILIGHT ; a poem. By a student at law [Frederick Knight]. 8vo. [Cushing's *Init. and Pseud.*]
New York, 1813

TWILIGHT and candle-shade. [Verses.] By Exul [Richard Le Gallienne]. 8vo. Pp. ix. 163. London, 1888
Inscribed copy.

TWILIGHT and dawn. By the author of *Four messengers*, etc. [Emily Marion Harris]. 12mo. [*Brit. Mus.*]
London, 1873

TWILIGHT hours ; a legacy of verse. By Sadie [Miss Sarah Williams]. 8vo.
London, 1869

TWILIGHT people. [Verse.] By Seumas O'Sullivan [James Starkey]. 8vo. [O'Donoghue's *Poets of Ireland.*]
Dublin, 1905

TWILIGHT shadows, and other poems. By R. M. E. A. [Robert M. Ashe, and Emily Ashe]. 8vo. London, 1886

TWILIGHT thoughts ; stories for children and child-lovers. [By Mary S. Claude.] 12mo. London, 1853

TWIN cousins. By Sophie May [Rebecca Sophia Clarke]. 8vo.
Boston, 1884

TWIN (the) Dianas ; or, virtue sad : a novel. By Roof Roofer [Rufus Randell]. 8vo. Pp. 181.
London, 1896

TWIN (the) sisters ; or, the advantages of religion. [By Mrs Elizabeth Sandham.] 12mo. [*Biog. Dict.* 1816]
1809

TWIN (the) soul ; or, the strange experiences of Mr Rameses : a psychological and realistic romance. [By Charles Mackay, LL.D.] 8vo. 2 vols.
London, 1887

TWIN-BROTHERS (the) ; or, a new book of discipline for infidels and old offenders, in prose and verse. [By —— Graham.] 8vo.
Edinburgh, 1787

TWINKLE and wrinkle ; or, more helps over hard places for boys. By Lynde Palmer [Mrs Mary Louise Peebles, *née* Parmlee]. 8vo.
New York, 1891

TWISTY'S album. By Archie Fell [Miss Mary J. Capron]. 8vo.
Boston, 1885

TWISTY'S trials. By Archie Fell [Miss Mary J. Capron]. 8vo.
Boston, 1885

TWISTY'S tumbles. By Archie Fell [Miss Mary J. Capron]. 12mo.
Boston, 1885

'TWIXT land and sea ; tales. By Joseph Conrad [Joseph Conrad Korzeniowski]. 8vo. Pp. 272. London, 1912

'TWIXT love and hate. [A novel.] By Bertha M. Clay [Charlotte M. Braeme]. 8vo. London [1895]

'TWIXT promise and vow ; and other stories. By Ruth Elliott [Lillie Peck]. 8vo. Pp. 141. [*Brit. Mus.*]
London [1886]

'TWIXT shade and shine. [A novel.] By Annabel Gray [Mrs —— Cox]. 8vo. 3 vols. London, 1883

'TWIXT smile and tear. By Bertha M. Clay [Charlotte M. Braeme]. 8vo.
New York, 1887

'TWIXT town and country ; a book of suburban gardening. By Roma White [Blanche Oram, later Mrs Winder]. 8vo. Pp. 284. London, 1900

'TWIXT wife and fatherland ; a novel. [By Miss Lili Kuper.] 8vo. 2 vols. [*Brit. Mus.*] London, 1875

'TWIXT wood and sea ; a novel. By Elizabeth Godfrey [Jessie Bedford]. 8vo. 3 vols. London, 1892

TWO addresses to the Freeholders of Westmorland. [By William Wordsworth.] 8vo. [*Brit. Mus.*]
Kendal, 1819
Signed : A Freeholder.

TWO and a-half. By "Fleeta" [Kate W. Hamilton]. 8vo.
Philadelphia, 1891

TWO and two ; or, French and English. By the author of *Dethroned*, etc. [Mary Seamer, later Mrs Seymour]. 8vo. [*Brit. Mus.*] London, 1887

TWO apological odes, and an elegy. [By —— Courtney.] 8vo. [*W.*]
1808
Not published.

TWO appeals to the leaders of Spiritualism in England and America. By a disciple of Allan Kardec [G. Parisi]. 8vo. [*Brit. Mus.*]
Florence and Trieste, 1871-73

TWO (the) babies ; a sketch of everyday life. By a mother [Mrs Harriet Miller Davidson]. 12mo. Pp. 17.
London, 1859
Signed : H. D.

TWO bad blue eyes. [A novel.] By "Rita" [Mrs W. Desmond Humphreys, *née* Eliza M. J. Gollan]. 8vo. 3 vols.
London, 1884

TWO (the) banners and the old battle ; or, the Established & Free Churches as they are. By a Highlandman [Hugh M'Intosh, M.A.]. Third edition (25th thousand). 8vo. Pp. 72.
Edinburgh, N.D.

TWO (the) bars ; a tale of rescue. [By Mary Kennion]. 8vo. [*Brit. Mus.*]
London [1882]

TWO Biddicut boys, and their adventures with a wonderful trick-dog. By Paul Creyton [John Townsend Trowbridge]. 8vo. New York, 1898

TWO black pearls ; a novel. By Marie Connor [Mrs Robert Leighton]. 8vo.
London, 1886

TWO blizzards ; and other helps over hard places. By Lynde Palmer [Mrs Mary Louise Peebles, *née* Parmlee]. 8vo. New York, 1891

TWO books in defence of the Bishops voting in Capital Cases in Parliament ; the first, The Honours of the Lords Spiritual asserted, etc. ; the other, The Rights of the Bishops to judge in Capital Cases in Parliament cleared : being a full answer [by Thomas Hunt, lawyer] to two books recently published . . . endeavouring to shew the contrary. The second edition. Fol. [Arber's *Term Cat.*] London, 1680

TWO (the) books of Francis Bacon ; Of the proficience and advancement of learning, divine and human. [Edited by Thomas Markby.] 12mo. [*W.*]
London, 1852
Preface signed : T. M., King's College.

TWO (the) brides ; a tale. By Laval [Rev. Bernard O'Reilly]. 8vo.
New York, 1879

TWO (the) brothers. [A poem, by Rev. Edward Henry Bickersteth, bishop of Exeter.] 8vo. Pp. 22. [*Brit. Mus.*]
London, 1845

TWO (the) brothers. By the author of *The discipline of life*, etc. [Lady Emily Ponsonby]. 8vo. 3 vols.
London, 1858

TWO (the) brothers ; or, the family that lived in the first society. [Translated from the German of Mathilde Raven.] 8vo. 2 vols. [*Brit. Mus.*]
London, 1850

TWO (the) carnations. [A novel.] By Marjorie Bowen [Miss Gabrielle Vere Campbell]. 8vo. Pp. 288.
London, 1913

TWO catechisms for the instruction of young persons. [By Bishop John Skinner.] 12mo. Aberdeen, 1832

TWO (the) Catherines ; or, which is the heroine ? [A novel. By Mrs Mary Anne Hardy, *née* MacDowell.] 8vo. 2 vols. London, 1862

TWO centuries of St Pauls Church Yard ; *una cum indice expurgatorio in Bibliotheca Parliamenti, sive qui librorum prostant venales in vico vulgo vocato* Little Brittain : done into English for the benefit of the Assembly of Divines and the two Universities. [By Sir John Berkenhead.] 8vo. [*Cat. of the Lond. Inst.*]
[*c.* 1650]

TWO charges as they were delivered by T. E. [Thomas Edgar] Justice of the peace for the county of Suffolke . . . wherein appears the necessity of government, and of steps and degrees in it, and the duty . . . not to desert the present government. 4to. [*W.*; *Brit. Mus.*] London, 1650

TWO charity sermons at Madron and Penzance for the public dispensary. [By Rev. Henry Tonkin Coulson.] 8vo. [Boase and Courtney's *Bibl. Corn.*] Penzance, 1826

TWO Christmas stories : Sam Franklin's saving-bank ; A miserable Christmas and a happy new year. By Hesba Stretton, author of *Lost Gip*, etc. [Sarah Smith]. 8vo. Pp. 68.
London, 1876

TWO (the) comings of Christ. [By William Ferguson, LL.D., of Kinmundy.] 8vo. London, 1857

TWO Compton boys. By C. Auton [Augustus Hoppin]. 8vo.
Boston, 1885

TWO conferences, one betwixt a papist and a Jew, the other betwixt a protestant and a Jew ; in two letters from a merchant in London to his correspondent in Amsterdam. [By Richard Mayo.] 12mo. [Wilson's *Hist. of Diss. Ch.*; *Mon. Rev.* xi. 314.]
London, 1699
Ascribed also to John Jacob. [*Mendham Collection Cat.* p. 162.] See also "Two disputations concerning the Messiah. . . ."

TWO copies of verses on the meeting of King Charles the First and his Queen Henrietta Maria, in the Valley of Kineton, below Edge-Hill, in Warwickshire, July 13, 1643. [Edited by William Hamper.] 4to. [*W.*; Martin's *Cat.*] Birmingham, 1822

TWO (the) cousins ; a moral story, for the use of young persons. By the author of *The blind child* [Mrs Pinchard]. 8vo. [*W.*; *Brit. Mus.*].
London, 1794

TWO crowns. By Eglanton Thorne [Emily Charlton]. 8vo. Pp. 298.
London, 1885

TWO daughters of the race. [A novel.] By W. Heimburg [Martha Behrens]; translated from the German by Mrs D. M. Lowry. 8vo. Pp. 329.
New York, 1889

TWO days and a night in the wilderness. By Thomas Twayblade [Archibald Gillies] and Dryas Octopetala [Alexander Copland]. 8vo. [Robertson's *Aberd. Bibl.*] Aberdeen, 1878

TWO days in Cadenabbia. [By Constance, Lady Battersea.] 8vo. [*Camb. Univ. Lib.*] London, 1876

TWO delightful novels; or, the unlucky fair one: being the amours of Milistrate and Prazimone. . . . Translated from the French [of —— Le Maire] by a person of quality. 12mo. Pp. 258. [*Brit. Mus.*] [*c.* 1710]

TWO dialogues; containing a comparative view of the lives, characters, and writings, of Philip, the late Earl of Chesterfield, and Dr Samuel Johnson. [By William Hayley.] 8vo. Pp. xxiv. 240. [*Gent. Mag.* lxxxi. ii. 448; *Mon. Rev.* lxxvii. 457.] London, 1787

TWO dialogues in English, between a doctour of divinity, and a student in the laws of England, of the grounds of the said laws and of conscience. [By C. Saint Germain.] Newly revised and reprinted. 8vo. B. L. [*W.; Brit. Mus.*] London, 1668
Originally published in Latin. In 1531 appeared "The fyrste dyalogue . . ." Many editions followed with varying titles.

TWO discourses at Albury on certain errors. [By John Bate Cardale, solicitor.] 8vo. [*D. N. B.* vol. 9, p. 36.] London, 1860

TWO discourses concerning the adoration of our B. Saviour in the H. Eucharist; the first: Animadversions upon the alterations of the rubrick in the communion-service, in the Common-prayer-book of the Church of England: the second: The Catholicks defence for their adoration of our Lord, as believed really and substantially present in the holy sacrament of the Eucharist. [By Abraham Woodhead.] 4to. [Jones' *Peck*, ii. 355.]
Oxford, 1687

TWO discourses concerning the affairs of Scotland; written in the year 1698. [By Andrew Fletcher, of Salton.] 8vo. Pp. 50, 54. [M'Culloch's *Lit. of Pol. Econ.* p. 296.] Edinburgh, 1698

VOL. VI.

TWO discourses delivered at the public meetings of the Royal Academy of Sciences and Belles Lettres at Berlin, in the years 1785 and 1786; I. On the population of states in general, and that of the Prussian dominions in particular. II. On the true riches of states and nations, the balance of commerce and that of power. By the Baron de Hertzberg, minister of State and member of the Academy: translated from the French [by Joseph Towers, LL.D.]. 8vo. [*Gent. Mag.* lxxiii. i. 355; *Mon. Rev.* lxxvi. 42.]
London, 1786

TWO discourses for the furtherance of Christian piety and devotion; the former asserting the necessity and reasonableness of a positive worship, and particularly of the Christian: the later considering the common hinderances of devotion, and the divine worship, with their respective remedies. By the author of the *Method of private devotion* [Edward Wetenhall, D.D.]. 12mo. Pp. 18, 379. [Arber's *Term Cat.* i. 531.] London, 1671
Each discourse has a separate title-page; but the pagination is continuous.

TWO discourses; of purgatory, and prayers for the dead. [By William Wake, D.D.] 4to. Pp. 71. [*Brit. Mus.*] London, 1687

TWO discourses on the creation of all things by Jesus Christ; and on the resurrection of the dead. [By Robert Tyrwhitt, M.A., of Jesus College, Cambridge.] Third edition. 8vo. [Dyer's *Life of Robert Robinson*, p. 112.] Cambridge, 1787

TWO discourses: I. Concerning the different wits of men; II. Of the mysterie of vintners. [By Walter Charleton, M.D.] 8vo. Pp. 230.
London, 1669
Later editions have the author's name.

TWO discourses: the first concerning the spirit of Martin Luther, and the original of the Reformation: the second, concerning the celibacy of the clergy. [By Abraham Woodhead.] 4to. [Jones' *Peck*, i. 196.]
Oxford, 1687
The two discourses are separately paged, and have also separate titles.

TWO discourses wherein it is prov'd that the Church of England blesseth and offereth the Eucharistick elements; with a preface, shewing in what sense she allows praying for the saints departed: and that mixt wine is not contrary to any of her rubricks. [By George Smith.] 8vo. 1732

I

TWO disputations concerning the Messiah, one between a papist and a Jew, the other between a protestant and a Jew ; contained in two letters from a merchant in Amsterdam. [By Richard Mayo.] 8vo. [*Mon. Rev.* xi, 314.] 1754

    Another edition of " Two conferences . . ." *q.v.*

TWO dissertations concerning sense, and the imagination ; with an essay on consciousness. [By Zachary Mayne.] 8vo. Pp. 231. London, 1728

TWO dissertations on the subject of Carausius, Emperour of Britain, together with that of his supposed wife and son A 3d ; also of him and his successor Allectus ; illustrated with three copper plates, of hitherto unpublished coins : to which is added A letter to the Reverend Dr S—k—y [Stukeley] on the first volume of his extraordinary medallick History of Carausius, observing the many mistakes, unwarrantable assertions, and amazing productions therein. [By John Kennedy.] 4to. London, N.D.

    A general title to "A dissertation . . .", "Further observations . . .", and "A letter to the Reverend Dr S—k—y . . ."

TWO dithyrambic odes. [By John Pinkerton.] 4to. [*Brit. Mus.*] London, 1782

TWO elegies, consecrated to the never dying memorie of the most worthily admyred, most hartily loued, and generally bewayled Prince ; Henry Prince of Wales. [By Christopher Brooke and William Browne.] 4to. [*Christie-Miller Cat.*] London, 1613

TWO (the) Elsies. By Martha Farquharson [Martha Finley]. 8vo. New York, 1885

TWO enquiries into the meaning of demoniacks in the New Testament. By T. P. A. P. O. A. B. I. T. C. O. S. [Arthur Ashley Sykes, D.D.]. 8vo. London, 1737

    The initials on the title stand for " *The Precentor and Prebendary of Alton Borealis in the Church of Salisbury.*"

TWO epistles out of Wales, and other poems. [By William Roscoe.] 8vo. Pp. 42. [*Brit. Mus.*] London, 1808

TWO epistles to Mr Pope, concerning the authors of the age. [By Edward Young, LL.D.] 8vo. Pp. 44. [*Watt's Bibl. Brit.*] London, 1730

TWO essays [on suicide, and on the immortality of the soul. By David Hume]. 8vo. [*Brit. Mus.*] London, 1777

TWO essays ; life, law, and literature. By T. E. Court [Wm. George Thomas Barter]. 8vo. [Kirk's *Supp.*] London, 1863

TWO essays on the ballance of Europe : the first by [De la Mothe Fénelon] the late Archbishop of Cambray . . . translated into English ; the second by the translator of the first essay [William Grant, advocate, Edinburgh]. 8vo. [*Brit. Mus.*] London, 1720

TWO essays on the Remnant. By John Eglinton [William Kirkpatrick Magee]. 8vo. [S. J. Brown's *Books on Ireland.*] Dublin, 1894

TWO fair women. By Bertha M. Clay [Charlotte M. Braeme]. 8vo. New York, 1888

TWO (the) families ; an episode in the history of Chapelton. By the author of *Rose Douglas* [Mrs Sarah R. Whitehead]. 8vo. 2 vols. London, 1852

TWO (the) fathers ; an unpublished original Spanish work. By Adadus Calpe [anagram of A[ntonio] D. de Pascual] ; translated into the English language by the author, and Henry Edgar. 12mo. 3 vols. [*W.*] New York, 1852

    The title is headed " He who taketh the sword shall perish by the sword."

TWO first books of Lucretius, De rerum natura, translated into blank verse [by Sir J. S. Trelawny and Sir Robert Porrett Collier]. 8vo. [Boase and Courtney's *Bibl. Corn.* i. 80.] Devonport, 1842

TWO friends. By the author of *The patience of hope* [Dora Greenwell]. 12mo. [*Brit. Mus.*] London, 1862

TWO gallant sons of Devon ; a tale of the days of Queen Bess. By Harry Collingwood [William J. C. Lancaster]. 8vo. Pp. 364. London, 1912

TWO general epistles to the flock of God, where-ever they are dispersed on the face of the earth, who are separated from the world to bear testimony for the Lord God [by Mrs Margaret Fox, *née* Fell] ; also Pure consolation proclaimed from the spirit of life to the faithful followers of the Lamb, etc. [by J. Park]. 4to. [*W. ; Brit. Mus.*] London, 1664

    Signed : M. F.

TWO (the) generals. [Two poems. By Edward Fitzgerald.] 4to. [*Brit. Mus.*] London [1869 ?]

TWO gentlemen in Touraine. By Richard Sudbury [Charles Gibson]. 8vo. [*Amer. Cat.*] New York, 1906

TWO ghost-tales ; poems. By G. W. A. [G. W. Allen]. 8vo. [Kirk's *Supp.*] Nottingham, 1870

TWO girls. [A story.] By Susan Coolidge [Sarah Chauncey Woolsey]. 8vo. Boston, 1900

TWO grammatical essays: first on a barbarism in the English language, in a letter to Dr S——; second on the usefulness and necessity of grammatical knowledge in order to a right interpretation of the Scriptures. [By William Salisbury, B.D.] 8vo. [*Mon. Rev.* xl. 84, and *Index*.] London, 1768

TWO gray tourists. By Philemon Perch [Robert Malcolm Johnston]. 12mo.
Baltimore, 1885

TWO (the) great mysteries of Christian religion, the ineffable Trinity [and] the wonderful Incarnation, explicated to the satisfaction of mans own naturall reason, and according to the grounds of philosophy. By G. G. G. [Godfrey Goodman, Bishop of Gloucester]. 4to. [*Camb. Univ. Lib.*]
London, 1653

TWO great questions considered, I. What is the obligation of parliaments to the addresses or petitions of the people, and what the duty of the addressers? II. Whether the obligation of the covenant or other national engagements, is concern'd in the treaty of union? Being a sixth essay at removing national prejudices against the union. [By Daniel Defoe.] 4to. Pp. 31. [Wilson's *Life of Defoe*.]
[Edinburgh] 1707

TWO (the) great questions consider'd. I. What the French king will do with respect to the Spanish monarchy. II. What measures the English ought to take. [By Daniel Defoe.] 4to. [Wilson's *Life of Defoe*.]
London, 1700

TWO (the) great questions further considered; with some reply to the Remarks. By the author [Daniel Defoe]. 4to. Pp. 20. [Wilson's *Life of Defoe*.] London, 1700

TWO (the) guardians; or, home in this world. By the author of *Henrietta's wish*, etc. [Charlotte M. Yonge]. 8vo. Pp. vii. 430. London, 1852

TWO heroes. [A novel.] By Zandile [Miss Frances Ellen Colenso, daughter of Bishop Colenso]. 8vo.
London, 1873

TWO homes [of the Fox family, Wodehouse Place and Glendurgan]. By a grandson [Elton Fox]. 8vo. Pp. 102. [*Brit. Mus.*]
Plymouth, private print, 1925

TWO homes; a tale. By the author of *Amy Grant* [C. B. Doggett]. 8vo. Pp. 146. [*Brit. Mus.*] Oxford, 1856
Wrongly attributed to Miss Hopton.

TWO (the) homes; or, earning and spending. By Mrs Madeline Leslie [Harriet Newell Baker]. 8vo. [*Brit. Mus.*] Boston, 1863

TWO homilies concerning the meanes how to resolue the controversies of this time. [By Philippe de Mornay, seigneur Du Plessis.] Translated out of French. 12mo. Pp. 142. [Madan's *Oxf. Books*, i. 82.] Oxford, 1612
In the same year, later, another issue appeared, differing only in the title-page, which bears the author's name.

TWO humorous novels, viz. I. A diverting dialogue between Scipio and Berganza, two dogs belonging to the city of . . . Valladolid. . . . II. The comical history of Riconata and Cortadillo. Both written by the celebrated author of *Don Quixote* [Miguel de Cervantes] and now first translated [by Robert Goadby]. . . . Second edition. 12mo. [*Brit. Mus.*] 1741
The first edition has the translator's name.

201 Bowery songster. By Tony Pastor [Harlan Halsey]. New York, 1867

TWO hundred and twenty six "choice" original hymns. . . . [By —— Thomson.] 8vo. 1776

TWO hundred queries moderately propounded concerning the doctrine of the revolution of humane souls. . . . [By Francis M. van Helmont.] 8vo. Pp. 166. London, 1684

TWO husbands; a novel. By John Strange Winter [Mrs Arthur Stannard, *née* Henrietta E. V. Palmer]. 8vo. Pp. 118. London, 1898

TWO introductory lectures on the study of the early Fathers, delivered in the University of Cambridge by the Rev. J. J. Blunt, B.D., Margaret Professor of Divinity; second edition, with a brief memoir of the author, and table of lectures delivered during his professorship [by William Selwyn]. 8vo. [*W.*]
Cambridge, 1856
The Memoir is signed: W. S.

TWO journeys to Jerusalem, containing first, a strange and true account of the travels of two English pilgrims some years since, and what admirable accidents befel them in their journey to Jerusalem, Grand Cairo, Alexandria, &c. By H. T. [Henry Timberlake]. Secondly, the travels of fourteen Englishmen in 1669. from Scanderoon to Tripoly, Joppa, Ramah, Jerusalem, Bethlehem, Jericho, the river Jordan, the lake of Sodom and Gomorrah, and back again to Aleppo. By T. B. . . . To which is added, a relation of the Great Council of the Jews assembled in the plains of Agayday in Hungaria in 1650. to examine the Scriptures concerning Christ. By S. B. [Brett] an Englishman there present. . . . [By Richard or Robert Burton *i.e.* Nathaniel Crouch.] 12mo. Pp. 232. London, 1683

TWO (the) kinds of truth ; a test of all theories. By T. E. S. T. [W. T. B. Martin]. 8vo.   London, 1890

TWO kisses. . . . By Bertha M. Clay [Charlotte M. Braeme]. 8vo.   New York, 1885

TWO knights errant. By Barbara Yechton [Miss Lyda Farrington Krausé]. 8vo.   New York, 1894

TWO lads and a lass, and other stories. By Florence Warden [Florence Alice Price, later Mrs G. E. James]. 8vo. Pp. 122.   London, 1896

TWO (the) Lady Lascelles. [A novel.] By Sarah Tytler [Miss Henrietta Keddie]. 8vo. Pp. 334.   London, 1908

TWO lady tramps abroad ; a year's travel in India, Greece, Turkey, Switzerland, England, Scotland, etc. By two American ladies [Mrs —— Straiton and ——]. 8vo.   Private print, U.S.A., 1881

TWO Lancashire lovers ; or, the excellent history of Philocles and Doriclea. By Musæus Palatinus [Richard Brathwait]. 8vo. Pp. 268. [*W.* ; Lowndes' *Bibl. Man.*]   London, 1640

TWO (the) last dialogues, treating of the Kingdome of God within us and without us, and of his special providence through Christ over his Church from the beginning to the end of all things. . . . [By Henry More.] [*D. N. B.* vol. 38, p. 422.]   London, 1668

TWO (the) laws, and the necessity of their distinction for the sake of freedom and self-government : in three parts. [By J. J. Brown.] 12mo. Pp. 100.   Glasgow, 1871

TWO lectures read before the Essay Society of Exeter College, Oxford. I. On the supernatural beings of the Middle Ages. II. On the origin of the Romance literature of the XII and XIII centuries. . . . [By Richard John King.] 8vo. [Dobell's *Private Prints.*]   Private print, 1840

TWO letters, addressed to a noble Lord, on the manufactures, agriculture, and apparent prosperity of Scotland ; with a few strictures on the speculations, morals, and manners, of the nineteenth century. [By —— M'Neil.] 8vo. Pp. 55.   Edinburgh, 1804
The letters are signed : Anti-speculator.

TWO letters, addressed to the Right Rev. prelates, who a second time rejected the Dissenters' bill. [By Ebenezer Radcliff.] 8vo. Pp. 108. [*Bodl.*]   London, 1773

TWO letters concerning the present Union [between Scotland and England], from a Peer in Scotland [E. C. *i.e.* George Mackenzie, Earl of Cromarty] to E. W. [the Earl of Wemyss]. 4to. Pp. 28. [*Brit. Mus.*]   [Edinburgh] 1706

TWO letters containing a further justification of the Church of England, against dissenters ; the first, by one of the reverend commissioners for the review of the Liturgy, at the Savoy, 1661 [Thomas Pierce, D.D.]: the second by Dr Laurence Womock Archdeacon of Suffolk, author of the *Verdict upon Melius inquirendum.* 8vo. Pp. 89.   London, 1682

TWO letters, describing a method of increasing the quantity of circulating money upon a new and solid principle. [By Ambrose Weston.] 8vo. 2 parts. [*Brit. Mus.*]   Private print, 1799

TWO letters from a deist [Nicholas Stevens, A.M.] to his friend, concerning the truth and propagation of deism, in opposition to Christianity. With remarks [by Samuel Wesley, M.A.]. 4to. Pp. vi. 37. [*Bodl.*]   London, 1730

TWO letters from Satan to Buonaparte. [By Henry Whitfield, M.A.] 8vo. [Upcott and Shoberl's *Biog. Dict.*, p. 383.]   London, 1803

II letters in defence of the British and Foreign Bible Society, addressed to a friend in the country. [By David Brown, bookseller.] 8vo.   Edinburgh, 1826
Each letter has a separate title and pagination, and is signed : Amicus.

TWO letters in verse. [By Rev. John Fisher, M.A.] 8vo. Pp. 47.   London, 1821

TWO letters of advice ; (1) For the susception of holy orders. (2) For studies theological, especially such as are rational. . . . [Epistle dedicatory signed : H. D. *i.e.* Henry Dodwell, M.A.] 8vo. Pp. 356. [Dix and Dugan's *Dublin Books.*]   Dublin, 1672

TWO letters on Scottish affairs, from Edward Bradwardine Waverley Esq. [John Wilson Croker] to Malachi Malagrowther, Esq. [Sir Walter Scott, Bart.]. 8vo. Pp. 63.   London and Edinburgh, 1826

TWO letters on the subject of the Catholics, to my brother Abraham, who lives in the country. By Peter Plymley [Sydney Smith]. 8vo.   London, 1807

T W O letters on the subject of the present vacancy in the Professorship of Oriental languages. [By Thomas Brown.] 8vo. Pp. 31, 7. [*New Coll. Lib.* p. 116.] Edinburgh, 1813
The Letters are signed : E. P.

TWO letters, one from John Audland a Quaker, to William Prynne; the other, William Prynnes answer. By the author of *Hudibras* [Samuel Butler]. Fol. Pp. 22. London, 1672

TWO letters; the first containing some remarks on the meeting held 5th Nov. 1809 to celebrate the acquittal of Mrs Hardy, J. H. Tooke, Thelwall and others, in November 1794. . . . The second containing a short comparative sketch of our practical constitution in ancient times and the present. . . . By a freeholder of Cornwall [Francis Gregor, M.P.]. 8vo. Pp. 57. [Boase and Courtney's *Bibl. Corn.*] London, 1810

TWO letters, to a British merchant, a short time before the expected meeting of the new parliament in 1796; and suggesting the necessity and facility of providing for the public exigencies, without any augmentation of debt, or accumulation of burdens. [By John Bowles.] The second edition. 8vo. Pp. 84. [*Bodl.*] London, 1796

TWO letters to a clergyman in the country, concerning the choice of members, and the execution of the parliament writ, for the ensuing Convocation. [By Francis Atterbury, D.D.] 4to. [*Bodl.*] London, 1701

TWO letters to a clergyman of the Reformed Dutch Church, on the question whether a man may lawfully marry his deceased wife's sister. By Clericus [Rev. Alexander Gunn, D.D.]. 8vo. New York, 1827

TWO letters to a gentleman attempting to subvert the doctrine of the Arians. [By —— Hanley.] 8vo. Pp. 88. [*Brit. Mus.*] London, 1751

TWO letters to the Earl of Dorset concerning the Ecclesiastical Commission of King James II. [By Thomas Spratt, D.D., Bishop of Rochester.] 12mo. Pp. 36. [*D. N. B.* vol. 53, p. 421.] London, 1711

TWO letters to the Rev. Dr Chalmers, on his proposal for increasing the number of churches in Glasgow. By an observer [James A. Haldane]. 8vo. Pp. 38. [*New Coll. Lib.* p. 163.] Glasgow, 1818

T W O letters to the Reverend Dr Kennicott, vindicating the Jews from the charge of corrupting Deut. xxvii. 4; the first of which was published in the Library for July 1761: the second is now first published, being an answer to Dr Kennicott's remarks, in the Library for August, 1761; and a farther illustration of the argument. [By Robert Findlay, D.D.] 8vo. Pp. 34. London, 1762
Letters signed : Philalethes.

TWO letters to the Rev. Dr Thomas M'Crie, and the Rev. Mr Andrew Thomson, on the parody of Scripture, lately published in *Blackwood's Edinburgh Magazine*. By Calvinus [James Grahame, advocate]. 8vo. Pp. 30. Edinburgh, 1817
Of these letters of Calvinus, there were in all, five, besides a postscript. Their titles are "Another letter . . .", "Two more letters . . .", and "Postscript to the letters of Calvinus."

TWO letters to the Rev. Francis Law, occasioned by his late Address to the Protestants of Salmerbury, Preston. [Signed: A Catholic *i.e.* Richard Norris, S.J.] 8vo. [Sommervogel's *Dictionnaire.*] Preston, 1835

TWO letters to the Right Honourable the Lord Viscount Townshend; shewing the seditious tendency of several late pamphlets; more particularly of, A review of the Lutheran principles, by Tho. Brett, LL.D. Rector of Betteshanger in Kent, and of A letter to the author of the Lutheran Church, from a country school-boy. By a presbyter of the Church of England [Robert Watts, LL.B., St John's Coll., Oxford]. 8vo. Pp. 40. London, 1714
Signed : R. W.

TWO letters, written by a minister of the gospel to a gentleman, concerning Professor Campbell's divinity: letter I. Wherein his scheme concerning the origine, or primary source of moral virtue, contained in his answer to the author of the Fable of the bees, is shewed to be irrational, and antiscriptural; letter II. Wherein his discourse, proving that the Apostles were no enthusiasts, is considered: and the poisonous nature of enthusiasm, together with his mistakes of it, are detected. [By James Hog.] 8vo. Pp. 63. Edinburgh, 1731

TWO letters written to [Samuel Hill] the author of a pamphlet entituled, Solomon and Abiathar; or, the case of the deprived bishops and clergy discussed. [By Samuel Grascome.] 4to. Pp. 43. [Green's *Bibl. Somers.* ii. 480.] London, 1692

TWO (the) lights. By the author of *Struggles for life* [William Leask, D.D.]. 12mo. [*Brit. Mus.*]   London, 1856

TWO little B's. [A tale.] By Maud Carew [Miss Florence M. King]. 8vo. Pp. 162.   London, 1906

TWO little cousins. [A tale]. By Alice Hepburn [Mary Elizabeth Chevallier Boutell]. 12mo. Pp. 159.
London, 1876

TWO little crusoes and three little monkeys. [A tale.] By A. B. Romney [Miss A. Beatrice Rambaut]. 8vo. Pp. 126. [*Brit. Mus.*] London [1912]

TWO little travellers . . . By Ray Cunningham [Mrs Frances Browne Arthur]. 8vo.   London, 1902

TWO little wooden shoes; a sketch. By Ouida, author of *Chandos*, etc. [Louise de la Ramée]. 8vo. Pp. 322.
London, 1874

TWO lives. [In verse]. By Reginald Hainault [G. Keyes]. 8vo. [*Brit. Mus.*]   [Clapton, 1890]

TWO love stories; an Anglo-Spanish romance. By "Waters" [William Russell]. 8vo.   London, 1861
Subscribed: Antony Shandy.

TWO loves; a novel. By Curtis Yorke [Mrs W. S. Richmond Lee] and E. M. Davy. 8vo.   London, 1904

TWO lyric epistles; one to my cousin Shandy, on his coming to town; and the other to the grown gentlewomen, the Misses of * * * * [By John Hall-Stevenson.] 4to. [*D. N. B.* vol. 54, p. 239.]   London, 1760

TWO (the) magistracies; or, the first blast of the seventh trumpet: an address to the Old Light Seceders. [By J. G. Clendinning, shepherd in Eskdale.] 8vo. Pp. 57.
Edinburgh, 1847

TWO marriages. By the author of *John Halifax, Gentleman*, etc. [Dinah Maria Mulock]. 8vo. 2 vols.
London, 1867

TWO men and a governess. [A novel.] By Olivia Ramsay [Laetitia Selwyn Oliver]. 8vo.   London, 1911

TWO men o' Mendip. By Tom Cobbleigh [Walter Raymond]. 8vo.
London, 1899

TWO (the) mentors; a modern story. By the author of *The old English baron* [Clara Reeve]. The third edition. 12mo. Pp. 386. [Nichols' *Lit. Anec.* viii. 138.]   London, 1803

TWO (the) misers; a musical farce: as it is performed at the Theatre Royal in Covent-Garden. By the author of *Midas*, and *The Golden Pippin* [Kane O'Hara]. 8vo. Pp. 32. London, 1775
Taken from *Les deux avares* of Fenouillot de Falbaire.

TWO mistakes. [Two stories.] By Sydney Christian [Miss Maria L. Lord]. 8vo. Pp. 187. [*Brit. Mus.*]
London, 1895

TWO modern little princes, and other stories. By Margaret Sidney [Mrs Harriet M. Lothrop]. 8vo.
Boston, 1886

TWO months abroad; or, a trip to England, France, Baden, Prussia, and Belgium in 1843. By a railroad director of Massachusetts [Elias Hasket Derby]. 8vo. [*Brit. Mus.*]
Boston, 1844

TWO months in Italy; or, passages from the diary of a Sexagenarian [Henry C. Beloe]. 8vo. Pp. 124. [Dobell's *Private Prints*, p. 2117.]
Liverpool, 1872

TWO months in Palestine; or, a guide to a rapid journey to the chief places of interest in the Holy Land. By the author of *Two months in Spain* [James Monteith]. 8vo. Pp. 238.
London, 1871

TWO months in Spain. . . . [By James Monteith.] 8vo.   London, 1869

TWO moods of a man; with other papers and short studies. By Violet Fane [Mary Montgomerie, later Lady Currie]. 8vo. Pp. 274.
London, 1901

TWO more letters (being the fourth and the last), to the Rev. Dr Thomas M'Crie, and the Rev. Mr Andrew Thomson, on the parody of Scripture, lately published in *Blackwood's Edinburgh Magazine*; including a brief view of ministerial character and duty. By Calvinus [James Grahame, advocate]. 8vo. Pp. 29.
Edinburgh, 1817

TWO mothers of one. By Roof Roofer [Rufus Randell]. 8vo. London, 1895

TWO (the) Mr Clarks. (From the *Witness* of 12th April 1843.) [By Hugh Miller.] 12mo. Pp. 18.
Edinburgh, 1843
Reprinted in 1870 in a volume entitled *Leading articles on various subjects*. By Hugh Miller.

TWO (the) Napoleons; a lecture delivered at Dawlish [Devonshire] by "Iconoclast" [J. S. Harding]. 8vo.
Exeter, 1861

TWO (the) Nellies. [A story.] By H. N. R. [Elizabeth Lyon Millar]. 8vo. Pp. 30.   Edinburgh [1880]

TWO new sermons, preached in Oxford, fitted for these times; the one of diuine mysteries: the other of church-schismes, by the vnity of orthodox professors. By J. D. [John Doughty]. [*D. N. B.* vol. 15, p. 258.]
London, 1629

TWO north-country maids; an every-day story. By Mabel Wetheral [Mabel Hodgson]. 8vo.
London, 1887

TWO novels; in letters. By the authors of *Henry and Frances* [Richard and Elizabeth Griffith]. 12mo. 4 vols.
London, 1769

TWO odes. [By George Colman, the elder, and Robert Lloyd, in parody of the odes of William Mason and Thomas Gray.] 4to. Pp. 23. [*Brit. Mus.*]   London, 1760

TWO odes, from the Latin of the cele-brated Rapin; imitated in English Pindaricks, by a gentleman of Cam-bridge [Francis Bragge]. 8vo. [*Brit. Mus.*]   London, 1710

TWO odes of Horace, relating to the cival wars of Rome, and against covetous rich men. Translated into English [by Richard Fanshaw]. 8vo. [Lowndes' *Bibl. Man.*]
London, 1664

TWO offenders. By "Ouida" [Louise de la Ramée]. 8vo. Pp. 265.
Philadelphia, 1897

TWO old men's tales; The deformed, and the Admiral's daughter. [By Mrs Anne Marsh.] Second edition. 12mo. 2 vols.   London, 1834

TWO on an island; an episode. By Curtis Yorke [Mrs W. S. Richmond Lee]. 8vo. Pp. 102.   London, 1892

TWO orations of the Emperor Julian; one to the Sovereign sun, and the other to the Mother of the Gods: translated [by Thomas Taylor, the Platonist]. 8vo. Pp. lxviii. 204. [*Brit. Mus.*]   London, 1793

TWO orphans. [A story taken from *Les deux orphelins* of E. Philippe and P. E. Piestre, by Henry Llewellyn Williams.] 4to. [*Brit. Mus.*]
London, 1878

TWO papers; a theatrical critique, and an essay (being No. 999 of the *Pre-tender*) on sonnet writing, and sonnet-writers in general, including a sonnet on myself, attributed to the editor of the *Ex-m-n-r*, preceded by proofs of their authenticity, founded upon the authority of internal evidence. [By John Poole.] 8vo. Pp. xi. 24. [*Athen. Cat.* p. 486.]   London, 1819

TWO papers of proposals concerning the discipline and ceremonies of the Church of England, presented to His Majesty by Rev. ministers of the Presbyterian Perswasion. [Drawn up by Richard Baxter.] 4to. Pp. 46.
London, 1661

TWO papers on some of the popular dis-contents. By T. B. Temple [Thomas Banister]. 8vo.   London, 1849

TWO (the) parties in the Church brought to the test; or, moderatism and evangelism contrasted. [By Rev. David Carment.] 8vo. Pp. 8. [*New Coll. Lib.* p. 152.]   Edinburgh, 1843

TWO penny-worth of truth for a penny; or, a true state of facts; with an apology for Tom Bull [William Jones of Nay-land] in a letter to Brother John. [By Ann Jebb.] Second edition. 8vo. Pp. 16. [*W.*]   London, 1793
Signed: W. Bull.

TWO petitions presented to the supreame authority of the nation, from thousands of the Lords, owners, and commoners of Lincolneshire; against the old court-levellers, or propriety-destroyers, the prerogative undertakers. [By John Lilburne.] 4to. Pp. 10. [*Bodl.*]
London, 1650

TWO plaies: The city match; a comedy; and The amorous warre; a tragy-comedy [each in five acts and in verse]. Both long since written by J. M. [Jasper Mayne] of Christ Church in Oxon. 4to. [*Brit. Mus.*]
Oxford, 1658

TWO plain letters to the people of England, exhorting them to a more . . . earnest use of the excellent prayers of our Church. By a Lay Churchman [John David Hay Hill]. 12mo. Pp. 31. [*Brit. Mus.*]
London, 1834

TWO (the) prisoners of Lyons; or, the duplicate keys: a melodrama. . . . Altered from the French of Benjamin [Benjamin Antier], Saint Amant [Jean Amand Lacoste], and Paulyanthe [Alexandre Chapponier]. 8vo. [*Brit. Mus.*]   London, 1824

TWO (the) prophets. . . . By Zion Ward [John Ward]. 8vo. [*Brit. Mus.*]   Birmingham, 1847

TWO public letters in reply to Brookes' Farmer. [Signed: Rusticus, *i.e.* Charles O'Conor, M.R.I.A.] 8vo.
Dublin, 1749

TWO questions of present importance briefly stated and argued, viz. Whether 'tis reasonable in point of policy; and Whether 'tis consistent with the safety and welfare of the Establish'd Church, to set the Dissenters free from all legal incapacity to serve the present govern-ment. In a letter to a Member of Parliament. [By William Harris, D.D., Presbyterian minister in Lon-don.] 8vo. Pp. 24.   London, 1717

TWO questions, previous to Dr. Middleton's Free enquiry, impartially considered: viz. What are the grounds upon which the credibility of miracles, *in general*, is founded? and Upon what grounds the miracles of the Gospel, *in particular*, are credible? To which is added, A dissertation upon Mark xvi. 17, 18. These signs shall follow them that believe, &c. [By Arthur Ashley Sykes.] 8vo. Pp. 129.
London, 1750

—— Part II. In which the evidence for the miracles of the primitive Church is fully examined into ; and the miracles of the Gospel are shewn to have sure marks of credibility. [By Arthur Ashley Sykes, D.D.] 8vo. Pp. ix. 5, 209. [Disney's *Memoir of Sykes*, p. xxiii.] London, 1752

TWO (the) Rebellions ; or, treason unmasked. By a Virginian [Angus W. Macdonald]. 8vo. [Cushing's *Init. and Pseud.*] Richmond, Va. 1865

TWO (the) rectors. [By George Wilkins, D.D.] 12mo. Pp. xvi. 458.
London, 1824

TWO (the) rubies ; a novel. By the author of *Recommended to mercy* [Mrs Margaret C. Houstoun]. 8vo. 3 vols. [*Brit. Mus.*] London, 1868

TWO (the) runaways. By Claud Heathcote [James Harwood Panting]. 8vo. London, 1907

TWO schemes of a Trinity considered, and the Divine Unity asserted : four discourses on Philippians ii. 5-11. . . . [By Nathaniel Lardner, D.D.] 8vo. [*Brit. Mus.*] London, 1784

TWO (the) schools. From the Table of the unity of religions. [By T. Martin.] 12mo. [*Brit. Mus.*] London, 1848

TWO seasonable discourses concerning the present parliament. [By Anthony Ashley Cooper, 1st Earl of Shaftesbury.] 4to. Pp. 10. [*Bodl.*] Oxford, 1675

TWO secrets ; and, A man of his word. [Tales.] By Hesba Stretton [Miss Sarah Smith]. 8vo. Pp. 127.
London [1897]

TWO sermons, etc. I. On the national jubilee; II. On the thanksgiving and poems on the majesty of the Godhead. [By Rev. S. Barker, A.M.] 4to. Pp. 63. [*W.;* Martin's *Cat.*]
[Yarmouth] 1815

TWO sermons formerly preach'd in the cathedral-church of Worcester. By a late prebendary of the said church [Miles Stapylton, D.D.]. 8vo. Pp. 73.
London, 1736

TWO sermons on the relative and social duties. [By Joseph Morrison.] 8vo. [Robertson's *Aberd. Bibl.*]
Aberdeen, 1845

TWO sermons on the third [chapter] of the Lamentations, preached at Hanwell in the first yeere of His Majesties reigne, 1602 : the one by I. D. [John Dod], the other by R. C. [Robert Cleaver]. 4to. Pp. 71. [*Brit. Mus.*]
London, 1610

TWO sermons preached by the author of a book entitled *The life of God in the soul of man* [Henry Scougal, D.D.]. 8vo. [Robertson's *Aberd. Bibl.*]
[Aberdeen, 1691]

TWO sermons preached on a fast day during the late war with France. [By Francis Blackburne, M.A.] 8vo. Pp. 11, 28. [*Bodl.*] London, 1778

TWO sermons, preached to a congregation of black slaves, at the parish church of S. P. in the province of Maryland. By an American pastor [Thomas Bacon]. 12mo. Pp. 79. [Sabin's *Dict.*] London, 1749

TWO sermons; the first addressed to seamen ; the second to British West-India slaves. [By James Mackittrick Adair, M.D.] : to which are subjoined Remarks on female infidelity, and a plan of Platonic matrimony, by F. G. 8vo. [Watt's *Bibl. Brit.*] 1791

TWO sketches of France, Belgium, and Spa, in two tours, during the summers of 1771 and 1816; with a portrait of Napoleon's guide at Waterloo. By the author of *Letters from Paris, in* 1802-3 [Stephen Weston, F.R.S.]. 8vo. Pp. vii. 176. London, 1817

TWO small Crusoes. [A story.] By A. B. Romney [A. Beatrice Rambaut]. 8vo. London, 1901

TWO (the) Sosias. . . . [A satire on Dr Mead.] By T. Byfield, M.D. [John Woodward, M.D.]. 8vo. [*Brit. Mus.*]
London, 1719

TWO speeches made in the House of Peers, on Monday, 19 Dec. 1642. [By Edward Hyde, Earl of Clarendon.] 4to. [*D. N. B.* vol. 28, p. 388.]
N.P. [1643]

TWO speeches made in the House of Peers; the one, November 20, 1675 : the other in November 1678. By a Protestant peer of the realm of England [Anthony Ashley Cooper, 1st Earl of Shaftesbury]. 4to. Pp. 15.
Hague, 1680

TWO speeches of a late Lord Chancellor [Charles Yorke, Earl of Hardwicke]. Printed from an authentic copy. 8vo. Pp. 64. London, 1770

TWO (the) spheres of truth, with relation to present-day theories. . . . By T. E. S. T. [W. T. B. Martin]. 8vo. Pp. 377. London, 1892

TWO spheres ; or, mind versus instinct. By T. E. S. T. [W. T. B. Martin]. Revised and enlarged. 8vo. Pp. vii. 518.   London, 1894

TWO stories of the seen and the unseen: The open door ; Old Lady Mary. [By Mrs Margaret Oliphant.] 8vo. Pp. 212.   Edinburgh, 1885
   A later edition, 1912, gives the name of the authoress.

TWO summers in Norway. By the author of *The angler in Ireland* [William Bilton]. 12mo. 2 vols.
                    London, 1840

TWO supplementary letters (being the 5th and 6th of a series) on the circulating medium of the British Isles. . . . [By Rev. Francis John Hext, M.A.] 8vo. Pp. 40. [*Brit. Mus.*] Truro, 1840
   Signed : Y. Z.

TWO tales (Geoffrey the Mesmerist ; Dollie, a psychological romance) told by a sensitive. By Brooke Anstruther [Mary Helen Cameron]. 12mo. [*Brit. Mus.*]   Edinburgh, 1888

TWO tales translated out of Ariosto: the one in dispraise of men, the other in disgrace of women ; with certaine other Italian stanzas and proverbs. By R. T. [Robert Tofte] gentleman. 4to. [*Pollard and Redgrave.*]
                    London, 1597

TWO tellings to Pet. [Ecclesiological notes taken in Wales and Yorkshire.] By "Unda" [Rev. Thomas Muir]. 4to. Pp. 33.
          [Edinburgh, private print, 1877]

2010 A.D. [A novel.] By the author of *The adventures of John Johns* [Frederick Carrel]. 8vo. Pp. 254. [*Brit. Mus.*]
                    London, 1914

TWO tracts shewing that Americans, born before the independence, are by the laws of England, not aliens; first, a discussion, &c.; second, a reply, &c. By a barrister [John Reeves, M.A.]. 8vo. Pp. 100. [Rich's *Bibl. Amer.*, ii. 72.]   1814

TWO tramps . . . By the author of *Probable sons* [Amy Le Feuvre]. 8vo.
                    London, 1900

TWO treatises concerning regeneration : 1. Of repentance. 2. Of the diet of the soule. . . . [By Thomas Morton, D.D., Bishop.] 12mo. Pp. 121, 119. [*Watt's Bibl. Brit.*]   London, 1613

TWO treatises of government; in the former, the false principles and foundation of Sir Robert Filmer, and his followers, are detected and overthrown: the latter is an essay concerning the true original, extent, and end of civil-government. [By John Locke.] 8vo. Pp. 358. [*Camb. Hist. of Eng. Lit.*]
                    London, 1694

TWO treatises; the first, proving both by history & record that the bishops are a fundamental & essential part of our English parliament: the second, that they may be judges in capital cases. [By Laurence Womock, D.D.] Fol.   London, 1680

TWO troubadours. [A romance.] By Esmé Stuart [Miss Amélie Claire Le Roy]. 8vo. Pp. 310.   London, 1912

TWO true ; a story of to-day. [By Mrs Metta Victoria Victor.] 12mo. [Kirk's *Supp.*]   New York, 1868

TWO useful cases resolved.   I. Whether a certainty of being in a state of salvation be attainable ? II. What is the rule by which this certainty is to be attained? [By Richard Blechynder, prebendary of Peterborough.]   4to. Pp. 32. [*Bodl.*]   London, 1685

TWO very godly and comfortable letters, written ouer into England ; the one to a godly and zealous lady : wherin the Annabaptists errour is confuted : and the sinne against the Holye Ghoste plainly declared; the other an answer to a godly merchants letter : written for his comfort, being greeued with the heauye burden of sinne : wherin is declared the true confession of sinne. Written by T. C. [Thomas Cartwright]. 8vo. [*D. N. B.* vol. 9, p. 229.]   London, 1589

TWO (the) vocations ; or, the sisters of mercy at home. A tale. By the author of *Tales and sketches of Christian life in different lands and ages* [Mrs A. P. Charles, *née* Elizabeth Rundle]. 8vo. [*Brit. Mus.*]   London, 1853

TWO voyages, and what came of them. [By Rev. Edward N. Hoare, M.A.] 8vo.   London, 1877

TWO ways of becoming a hunter. By Harry Castlemon [Charles Austin Fosdick]. 8vo.   Philadelphia, 1894

TWO ways of looking at it. By Austin Clare [Miss W. M. James]. 8vo.
                    London, 1885

TWO ways of love. [A novel.] By "Iota" [Mrs Katharine Mannington Caffyn]. 8vo.   London, 1913

TWO (the) weddings; or, holy and unholy matrimony. By S. W. [Miss S. Warren]. 12mo. [*Brit. Mus.*]
                    London [1872]

TWO wise men and all the rest fooles; or, a comicall morall, censuring the follies of the age, as it hath beene diverse times acted. [By George Chapman.] 4to. Pp. 104. [*Baker's Biog. Dram.*]   1619

TWO (the) wizards, and other songs. By Richard Honeywood [Claud Lovat Fraser]. 16mo. [Millard's *Bibl. of Fraser.*] 1913

TWO (the) wolves in lambs' skins ; or, Old Ely's sorrowful lamentation over his two sons. . . . The second edition. By poor old Tom of Bedlam [Rev. Luke Milbourne]. 8vo. Pp. 62. [*Brit. Mus.*] London, 1716

TWO women and a man ; a society sketch of to-day. By Ellam Fenwicke Allan [Mrs Edith Charlton Anne]. 8vo. Pp. 231. [*Brit. Mus.*] London [1897]

TWO women, or one? By Sidney Luska [Henry Harland]. 8vo. London, 1890

TWO words of counsel and one of comfort. [By William Combe.] [*Gent. Mag.* May 1852, p. 467.] 1795

TWO (the) worlds, the natural and the spiritual. By Thomas Brevior [Thomas Shorter]. 8vo. [Boase's *Mod. Brit. Biog.* vol. 6, col. 554]. London, 1864

TWO Wyoming girls. By Carl Louis Kingsbury [Mrs Caroline Louise Marshall]. 8vo. Philadelphia, 1899

TWO years after and onwards ; or, the approaching war amongst the powers of Europe and other future events described as foretold in Scripture prophecy. By the author of *The coming struggle* [David Pae]. 8vo. Pp. viii. 192. London, 1864

TWO years before the mast; a personal narrative of life at sea. [By Richard Henry Dana, Junr.] 8vo. Pp. 124. London, 1841
Reprint of the original American edition. Preface signed : R. H. D. Jr.

TWO years' captivity in German East Africa ; being the personal experiences of Surgeon E. C. H. [Ernest Charles Holtom]. 8vo. Pp. 239. [*Brit. Mus.*] London [1919]

TWO years in Ava ; from May 1824, to May 1826. By an officer on the Staff of the Quarter-Master-General's department [Capt. Thomas Abercrombie Trant]. 8vo. [*Gent. Mag.* April 1832, p. 371.] London, 1827

TWO (a) years' journal in New York, and part of its Territories in America. By C. W. [Rev. Charles Wooley]. 8vo. [*Book Prices Current*, 1921.] London, 1701

TWO years of Church [of England] progress. By the author of *The Church cause and the Church party* [Alex. J. Beresford Hope]. 8vo. Pp. 27. [*Brit. Mus.*] London, 1862

TWOFOLD vindication of the Archbishop of Canterbury [Tillotson], and of the author of the *History of religion.* [By Sir Robert Howard.] 8vo. [Leslie's *Cat.* 1843.] 1696

TYBORNE, and "Who went thither in the days of Queen Elizabeth" ; a sketch, by the authoress of *Eastern hospitals* [Miss Frances Magdalen Taylor]. 8vo. [Boase's *Mod. Eng. Biog.* vi. col. 666.] London, 1859

TYNDALL and materialism ; Gladstone and the Vatican Decrees : two epistles in verse. By J. K. C. [Rev. James Casey, Catholic priest in Sligo]. 8vo. [O'Donoghue's *Poets of Ireland.*] Dublin, 1875

TYPES (the), and a selection from the writings in verse and prose of a lady recently and suddenly deceased. [By Lucy Croggan.] 12mo. Pp. viii. 195. London, 1836

TYPES and antitypes of our Lord Jesus Christ. [By Miss A. E. Gimingham, Weston-super-Mare.] Obl. 4to. Pp. 29, with 29 plates. London [1884]

TYPES of the Turf; anecdotes and incidents from the course and the stable. By "Rapier" [Alfred E. T. Watson]. 8vo. Pp. 115. London, 1883

TYPE-WRITER (the) girl. By Olive Pratt Reyner [Charles Blairfindie Grant Allen]. 8vo. Pp. 261. [Courtney's *Secrets*, p. 106.] London, 1897

TYPHON ; or, the Gyants war with the Gods : a mock poem, in five cantos. [Translated from the French of Scarron by John Phillips ?]. 8vo. Pp. 160. [*Brit. Mus.*] London, 1665

TYPHON ; or, the wars between the Gods and the Giants : a burlesque poem in imitation of . . . Mons. Scarron. [The dedication is signed B. M. *i.e.* Bernard Mandeville.] 4to. Pp. 47. [*Brit. Mus.*] London, 1704

TYPHOON (the) ; and other stories. By Joseph Conrad [Joseph Conrad Korzeniowski]. 8vo. Pp. 310. London, 1903

TYRANNICALL - GOVERNMENT anatomized ; or, a discourse concerning evil-councellors : being the life and death of John the Baptist : and presented to the Kings most excellent Majesty by the author. [A translation of George Buchanan's *Baptistes*, probably by John Milton.] 4to. Pp. 34. [Peck's *Memoirs of Milton*, p. 265.] London, 1642

TYRANNICIDE proved lawful, from the practice and writings of Jews, heathens, and Christians; a discourse, delivered in the mines at Symsbury, in the colony of Connecticut, to the loyalists confined there by order of the Congress, on September 19, 1781. By Simeon Baxter, a licentiate in divinity, and voluntary chaplain to those prisoners in the apartment called Orcus [Rev. Samuel Peters]. 8vo. Pp. vi. 31. Printed in America; London; reprinted, 1782

"I believe this squib is by the Rev. Samuel Peters."—MS. note in the Bodleian copy.

TYRANNUS; or, the mode; in a discourse of sumptuary lawes. [By John Evelyn.] 8vo. Pp. 30. London, 1661

The address "To him that reades" signed: I. E.

"This, which is corrected throughout, by the author (Mr Evelyn) with his own hand, for a second edition . . ."—MS. note on the Mason copy in the Bodleian.

TYRANNY and hypocrisy detected; or, a further discovery of the tyrannical-government, popish-principles, and vile practices of the now-leading quakers. [By William Mucklow.] 8vo. [Smith's *Cat. of Friends' Books*, i. 39; ii. 190.] London, 1673

TYRANNY and popery lording it over the conscience, lives, liberties, and estates both of king and people. [By Roger L'Estrange.] 4to. Pp. 94. London, 1678

The second edition, 1681, has the author's name.

TYRANNY (the) of custom; revised and enlarged. The bagman's vision, etc. Addressed to commercial travellers. By "One of us" [John Martin]. Second edition. 12mo. [Green's *Bibl. Somers.* iii. 387.] Wellington, 1866

TYRANNY (the) of faith; a story of Courland. By Carl Joubert [A. W. C. Grottey]. 8vo. [*Brit. Mus.*] London, 1806

TYRANNY (the) of modern Nonconformity compared with Papal supremacy. By a victim of Nonconformist persecution [Rev. Brewin Grant]. 8vo. [*Brit. Mus.*] London, 1874

TYRANNY (the) of Popery, as seen in Italy by an eye-witness [Rev. Charles Cameron, M.A., Oxford]. 8vo. London, 1853

TYROL (the) and its people. By Clive Holland [Charles J. Hankinson]. 8vo. Pp. 342. London, 1909

TYROLESE (the) patriots of 1809. [By Mrs Harriet Diana Thompson, *née* Calvert.] 8vo. London, 1859

TYRRELL; a tragic play in five acts. [By Kenneth Menzies and Edward Tait.] 8vo. [Inglis' *Dramatic writers of Scotland.*] Edinburgh, 1841

TYTLER'S History of Scotland examined; a review. [By Patrick Fraser, LL.D.] 8vo. Pp. 246. Edinburgh, 1848

Appeared first in the *North British Review.*

U

U. E. (the); a tale of Upper Canada. [Verse. By William Kirby, F.R.C.S.] 8vo. Pp. 180. [*Brit. Mus.*] Niagara, 1859

UGANDA. By Philo-Africanus [Robert Needham Cust, LL.D.]. 8vo. [*Lond. Lib. Cat.*]. Woking, 1892

UGBROOKE park; a poem. [By Rev. Joseph Reeve.] 4to. [Davidson's *Bibl. Devon.* p. 128.] London, 1776

A second edition, Exeter, 1794, has the author's name.

UGLINESS and its uses; a lecture . . . By Jak Wonder [Peter K. Ferguson]. 8vo. [Cushing's *Init. and Pseud.*] New York, 1852

UGLY (the) man. [A novel.] By F. M. Allen [Edmund Downey]. 8vo. London [*c.* 1900]

UGO Bassi; a tale of the Italian Revolution. [Verse.] By Speranza [Lady Francesca Speranza Wilde]. 8vo. [*Brit. Mus.*] London, 1857

ULAD of the dreams. By Fiona Macleod [William Sharp]. 8vo. London, 1904

ULGHAM; its story: printed in aid of the funds for rebuilding Ulgham church. [By William Woodman, of Morpeth.] 4to. Pp. 40. Newcastle, 1861

ULLSMERE; a poem. [By John Charles Bristow.] 8vo. Pp. xv. 271.
London, 1835
Included in his " Collected poems."

ULM and Trafalgar. [A poem. By George Canning, Prime Minister.] 4to. Pp. 10. [*Brit. Mus.*]
London, 1806

ULSTER. [By John James Clancy.] 8vo. [*Lond. Lib. Cat.*] Dublin, 1886

ULSTER (the) Synod; a satirical poem. [By Rev. William Heron.] 8vo. [O'Donoghue's *Poets of Ireland.*]
Belfast, 1817

ULTIMATE (the) generalization; an effort in the philosophy of science. [By John Lord Peck.] 8vo. [*Brit. Mus.*] New York, 1876

ULTIMATE (the) remedy for Ireland. [By Rowley Lascelles.] 8vo. [*Gent. Mag.* April 1831, p. 345.]
London, 1831

ULTRAMONTANISM *versus* education in Ireland; the case of Father O'Keeffe, P.P., shortly stated. By Scrutator [W. R. Aucketill]. 8vo. [*Brit. Mus.*]
London, 1875

ULTRA-PROTESTANT developments at Liverpool; an old warning to evangelicals repeated. By a Liverpool layman [Dan. Radford]. 8vo. Pp. 36. [*Bodl.*] Liverpool, 1856

ULTRA-UNIVERSALISM, and its natural affinities. By Paul [Arthur Granger]. 12mo. Pp. 51. [Eddy's *Universalism in America*, ii. 535.]
Hartford [U.S.A.] 1839

ULUG Beg; an epic poem, comic in intention . . . By Autolycus, a snapper-up of unconsidered trifles [Leonard Bacon]. 8vo. Pp. 292. [*Amer. Cat.*]
New York, 1923

ULYSSES Homer; or, a discovery of the true author of the Iliad and Odyssey. By Constantine Koliades, Professor in the Ionian University [Jean Baptiste Le Chevalier; translated by the Rev. P. Fraser]. 8vo. Pp. xxiv. 67. [*W.*]　London, 1829
Abridged from J. B. Le Chevalier's *Voyage dans la Troade*, 3 vols. 8vo., Paris, 1802.

ULYSSES, or De Rougemont of Troy. By A. H. M. [A. H. Milne]. 8vo.
London, 1899

ULYSSES upon Aiax; written by Misodiaboles to his friend Philaretes. [By Sir John Harington.] 12mo. [*W.;* Lowndes' *Bibl. Man.*]
London, 1596

UMBRELLAS to mend. By Margaret Vandergrift [Margaret Thomson Janvier]. 8vo.　　Boston, 1906

UNANIMITY; a poem: most respectfully inscribed to that truly patriotic nobleman the Duke of Leinster. [By John Macaulay.] 4to. [Watt's *Bibl. Brit.; Mon. Rev.* lxii. 319.]
London, 1780

UNANSWERABLE (an) conviction of the impostures of Popery, and deceits of the Papal agents; with a necessary caution to all sincere and conscientious Christians to beware of them: recommended to all the clergy of England, especially of such parishes, as have any of these deceivers or deceived in them. [By Edward Stephens, of Cherington.] 4to. Pp. 4. [*Bodl.*]　London, 1706

UNANSWERED (an) question, and other stories. By " Alien " [Mrs L. A. Baker]. 8vo. Pp. 318. [*Who's Who in Lit.*]　London, 1906

UNA'S revenge; a story of real life in the nineteenth century. By Melville Gray [Miss Ethel Granger]. 8vo. [*Brit. Mus.*]　London, 1887

UNAUTHORISED (an) appeal to Irish Catholics. [By Rev. Robert R. Suffield.]　New York, 1864
Information from the author.

UNAWARES; a story of an old French town. By the author of *One year* [Frances Mary Peard]. 8vo. Pp. 295. [*Brit. Mus.*]　London, 1870

UNBELEEVERS (the) preparing for Christ. By T. H. [Thomas Hooker]. 4to. [*Bodl.*]　London, 1638

UNBISHOPING (the) of Timothy and Titus; or, a briefe elaborate discourse, prooving Timothy to be no bishop (much lesse any sole, or diocæsan bishop) of Ephesus, nor Titus of Crete; and that the power of ordination, or imposition of hands, belongs Iure divino to presbyters, as well as to bishops, . . . By a well-wisher to God's truth and people [William Prynne]. 4to. Pp. 173, 5.
N.P. 1636

UNCANNY tales. By Ennis Graham [Mrs Mary Louise Molesworth]. 8vo. Pp. 228. [*Who's Who in Lit.*]
London, 1896

UNCASING (the) of heresie; or, the anatomie of Protestancie. Written and composed by O. A. [Oliver Almond, Catholic priest]. 8vo. [Gillow's *Bibl. Dict.*]　　[Louvain ?] 1623

UNCENSORED celebrities. By E. T. Raymond [Edward Raymond Thompson]. 8vo. Pp. 244. [*Manchester Guardian*, 4.4.28.]　London, 1918

UNCERTAINTIES (the) of travel; a plain statement by a certain traveller [George Amory Bethune, M.D.]. 8vo. [Cushing's *Init. and Pseud.;* Kirk's *Supp.*]　　Boston, 1880

UNCERTAINTY (the) of the art of physick ; together with an account of the innumerable abuses practised by the professors of that art : clearly manifested by a particular relation of the beginning and progress thereof. . . . Written in Italian by the famous [Lionardo di] Capoa, and made English by J. L. [J. Lancaster], Gent. 8vo. [Arber's *Term Cat.* ii. 49 and 645.] London, 1683

UNCERTAINTY (the) of the signs of death, and the danger of precipitate interments and dissections, demonstrated. I. From the known laws of the animal oeconomy. II. From the structure of the parts of the human body. And III. From a great variety of amusing and well-attested instances of persons who have return'd to life in their coffins, in their graves, under the hands of the surgeons, and after they had remain'd apparently dead for a considerable time in the water. . . . Illustrated with copper plates. [By Jean Jacques Bruhier-D'Ablaincourt.] 8vo. Pp. 6, 219. [*N. and Q.* Oct. 1868, p. 287 ; Douce *Cat.*] London, 1746

UNCHANGING (the) East. By Luke Sharp [Robert Barr]. 8vo. [*Who's Who in Lit.*] London, 1900

UNCHARITABLENESS (the) of modern charity . . . By Phileleutherus Trinitoniensis [Rev. George Legh, LL.D., Vicar of Halifax, Yorkshire]. 12mo. London, 1732

UNCHARTED (the) island. By Skelton Kuppord [J. Adams]. 8vo. Pp. 350. London, 1899

UNCLAIMED (the) daughter ; a mystery of our own day. Edited by C. G. H. [Mrs C. G. Hamilton], author of *The curate of Linwood*, etc. Second edition. 8vo. Pp. xv. 175. Bath [1853]

UNCLE . . . (Mon oncle et mon curé) ; translated from the French of Jean de La Brète [Mlle. A. Cherbonnel] and edited by J. Berwick. 8vo. Pp. 284. [*Brit. Mus.*] London [1892]

UNCLE and aunt. By Susan Coolidge [Sarah C. Woolsey.] 12mo. [*Amer. Cat.*] Boston, 1902

UNCLE Anthony. By Capt. Carnes [M. J. Cummings]. 12mo. [Cushing's *Init. and Pseud.*] Boston, 1873

UNCLE Armstrong ; a narrative. By Lord B******m, author of *Masters and workmen*, etc. [probably Lord Belfast]. 12mo. 3 vols. London, 1866

UNCLE Bob's niece ; a novel. By Leslie Keith [Miss Grace Leslie Keith Johnstone]. 8vo. 3 vols. London, 1888

UNCLE Charles ; a novel. By John Strange Winter [Mrs Henrietta E. V. Stannard, *née* Palmer]. 8vo. Pp. viii. 323. London, 1902

UNCLE Clive ; a tale. By C. A. M. W. [Rev. Charles Wooley]. 8vo. [*Brit. Mus.*] London, 1865

UNCLE Crotty's relations. [A novel.] By Herbert Glyn [Henry Alford Pettitt]. 8vo. 2 vols. London, 1863

UNCLE Downie's home. By Glance Gaylord [Warren Ives Bradley]. 12mo. [Cushing's *Init. and Pseud.*] Boston, 1866

UNCLE Dudley's odd hours ; Western sketches. [By Morris C. Russell.] 8vo. [*Amer. Cat.*] Lake City, Minn. 1904

UNCLE Frank's pleasant pages for the fireside. [By Francis Channing Woodworth.] 8vo. [*Brit. Mus.*] London, 1857

UNCLE George's stories. [By Rev. Increase Niles Tarbox.] 8vo. [Cushing's *Init. and Pseud.*] Boston, 1808

UNCLE Horace ; a novel. By the author of *Sketches of Irish character*, etc. [Anna Maria Hall]. 8vo. 3 vols. [*Camb. Univ. Lib.*] London, 1837

UNCLE Jem's Stella ; a story for girls. By the author of *The two Dorothys* [Mary E. Martin.] 8vo. Pp. 160. [*Brit. Mus.*] London, 1896

UNCLE John ; or, is it too much trouble ? By Mary Orme [Mary Neal Sergeant Gore, later Mrs Nichols, M.D.]. 8vo. [Cushing's *Init. and Pseud.*] New York, 1855

UNCLE John's letters . . . rocks and sands . . . happiness . . . [By James White.] 8vo. Southampton [1889]

UNCLE Josh's trunkful of fun. [By William B. Dick.] 8vo. [*Amer. Cat.*] New York, 1875

UNCLE (the) of an angel ; and other stories. By Ivory Black [Thomas Allibone Janvier]. 8vo. [*Amer. Cat.*] New York, 1891

UNCLE Paul's stories for boys and girls. [By Samuel Burnham, junr.] 8vo. [Cushing's *Init. and Pseud.*] Boston, 1865

UNCLE Peregrine's heiress ; a novel. By Ann of Swansea, author of *Guilty or not guilty*, etc. [Anne Hatton]. 12mo. 5 vols. [*Brit. Mus.*] London, 1828

UNCLE Philip's conversations . . . about the habits and mechanical employments of inferior animals. [By Francis Lister Hawks.] 12mo. [*Brit. Mus.*]
London, 1834

UNCLE Piper of Piper's Hill: an Australian novel. By Tasma [Jessie Huybers, later Mrs Fraser, then Madame Auguste Couvrier]. 8vo. Pp. viii. 348. London, 1889

UNCLE Ralph; a tale. By the author of *Dorothy* [Margaret Agnes Colville, later Mrs Paul]. 8vo. [*Brit. Mus.*]
London, 1858

UNCLE Reg's school-days. By himself [Page Woodcock]. 8vo. Pp. 134.
London, 1912

U N C L E Remus; his songs and his sayings : the folk-lore of the old plantations. [By Joel Chandler Harris.] 8vo. [Cushing's *Init. and Pseud.*]
New York, 1880

UNCLE Steve's locker. [A novel.] By "Brenda" [Mrs Castle Smith]. 8vo. Pp. 352. [*Brit. Mus.*] London, 1888

UNCLE Timothy Faber; or, the new minister: a story for the old and young. By a Sabbath-school superintendent [Alex. S. Arnold]. 12mo. Pp. 228. [Eddy's *Universalism in America*, ii. 573.] Boston, 1868

UNCOLLEGIATE (the) clergyman's lamentation [over the reading of the Act regarding Captain John Porteous. By Rev. John Glen, minister of Haddo's Hole Kirk, Edinburgh]. 8vo.
Edinburgh, 1737

UNCOMFORTABLE (an) term. By Raymond Jacberns [Miss M. Selby Ashe]. 8vo. Pp. 408. London, 1911

UNCONDITIONAL election, and its dependent doctrines disproved; being an abridgement of Whitby on the Five Points. [By Rev. William Jenkins Rees, M.A.] 8vo. [Upcott and Shoberl's *Biog. Dict.* p. 289.]
London, 1810

UNCONFESSED. [A novel.] By Maxwell Gray [Miss Mary Gleed Tuttiett]. 8vo. Pp. 352.
London, 1910

UNCREATED (the) man. By Austin Fryers [William Edward Clery]. 8vo. Pp. 312. London, 1912

UNCROWNED (an) king. By Agnes Marchbank [Mrs —— Marshall]. 8vo. [*Who's Who in Lit.*] Paisley, 1904

UNCROWNED (the) king; a romance of high politics. By Sydney C. Grier [Miss Hilda Gregg]. 8vo. [*Who's Who in Lit.*] Edinburgh, 1896

U N C U T (an) diamond; and other stories. By Raymond Jacberns [Miss M. Selby Ashe]. 8vo. Pp. 168.
London, 1895

UNDECEIVED; Roman or Anglican? A story of English ritualism. By the author of *A voice from the sea* [Lillie Peck]. 8vo. [*Brit. Mus.*]
London, 1877

UNDECEIVING (the) of the people in the point of tithes; wherein is shewed, I. That never any clergy in the Church of God hath been, or is maintained with lesse charge to the subject, then the established clergy of the Church of England. II. That there is no subject, in the realme of England, who giveth any thing of his own, towards the maintenance of his parish-minister, but his Easter-offering. III. That the change of tithes into stipends, will bring greater trouble to the clergy, then is yet considered; and far lesse profit to the country, then is now pretended. By Ph. Treleinie Gent. [Peter Heylin]. 8vo. Pp. 28.
London, 1651

UNDER a charm; a novel: from the German of E. Werner [Elisabeth Buerstenbinder], by Christina Tyrrell. 8vo. 3 vols. London, 1877

UNDER a cloud. By one who knows what shadows are [Mrs Sawers Mitchell]. 8vo. Pp. x. 434.
Edinburgh, private print, 1867

UNDER a cloud. [A novel.] By the author of *The Atelier du Lys*, etc. [Miss Margaret Roberts]. 8vo. Pp. 281. [*Brit. Mus.*] London [1889]

UNDER a kingly mask. By Lewis Ramsden [Dr A. L. Dowding]. 8vo.
London [*c.* 1900]

UNDER a shadow. By Bertha M. Clay [Charlotte Braeme]. 8vo. [*Amer. Cat.*] New York, 1887

UNDER cliff; a tale. By the author of *The Chorister brothers* [Mrs Mary Charlotte Julia Leith]. 8vo. Pp. iv. 235. London, 1890

UNDER cross and crescent; poems. By Violet Fane [Lady Currie, *née* Mary Montgomerie]. 4to. London, 1896

U N D E R false colours. By G. G. Kilburne [Miss Sarah Doudney]. 8vo.
London, 1888

UNDER fate's wheel; a story of mystery, love, and bicycle. By Lawrence L. Lynch [Mrs Emma Murdoch van Deventer]. 8vo. Pp. 336. [*Who's Who in Lit.*] London, 1903

U N D E R fire; or, the cruise of the *Destroyer*. By "M. Quad" [Charles B. Lewis]. 8vo. New York, 1886

UNDER foot; a novel. By Alton Clyde [Mrs Arnold Jeffreys]. 8vo. [*Who's Who in Lit.*] London, 1870

UNDER God's sky; the story of a cleft in Marland. By Deas Cromarty [Elizabeth Sophia Fletcher, later Mrs Robert A. Watson]. 8vo. Pp. vii. 376. [*Who's Who in Lit.*]   London, 1895

UNDER guiding stars. By Dorothy Prescott [Miss Agnes Blake Poor]. 8vo. [*Amer. Cat.*]   New York, 1905

UNDER love's rule. [A novel.] By the author of *Lady Audley's secret* [Mary E. Braddon, later Mrs John Maxwell]. 8vo.   London, 1897

UNDER mother's wing. [Stories for children.] By L. C. [Lucy Clifford]. 4to. Pp. 32. [*Brit. Mus.*]   [1885]

UNDER seal of confession. By Averil Beaumont, author of *Thornicroft's model* [Mrs Margaret A. W. Hunt]. 8vo. 3 vols. [*Nat. Lib. of Scot.*]   London, 1874

UNDER (the) side of things. By Lilian Bell [Mrs A. H. Bogue]. 8vo.   London, 1897

UNDER strange stars. [A story.] By Ray Cunningham [Frances Browne Arthur]. 8vo.   Stirling [1897]

UNDER temptation. By the author of *Ursula's love story*, etc. [Mrs Gertrude Parsons, née Hext]. 8vo. 3 vols.   London, 1878

UNDER the arches; a tale of the Ragged Schools. By S. B. H. [Mrs Sarah B. Hancock]. 8vo. [*Green's Bibl. Somers.* i. 243.]   Bath, 1871

UNDER the ban (Le Maudit); a tale of the nineteenth century, translated from the French of M. l'Abbé * * * [Jean H. Michon]. 8vo. 3 vols. [*Brit. Mus.*]   London, 1864

UNDER the cherry tree. [A novel.] By Peter Traill [Guy Morton]. 8vo. Pp. 219.   London, 1926

UNDER the Chilian flag; a tale of the War between Chili and Peru, 1879-1881. By Harry Collingwood [William J. C. Lancaster]. 8vo. Pp. 288. [*Who's Who in Lit.*]   London, 1908

UNDER the Chilterns; a story of English village life. By Rosemary [Margaret Watson]. 8vo.   London, 1895

UNDER the dog-star. [A story for the young.] By Mary Vandergrift [Mary Thomson Janvier]. 8vo.   New York, 1881

UNDER the dog-star; a tale of the Borders. By Austin Clare [Miss M. W. James]. 8vo. Pp. 377. [*Who's Who in Lit.*]   London [1895]

UNDER the ensign of the Rising Sun; a story of the Russo-Japanese War. By Harry Collingwood [William J. C. Lancaster]. 8vo. Pp. 348. [*Who's Who in Lit.*]   London, 1917

UNDER the greenwood tree; a rural painting of the Dutch school. By the author of *Desperate remedies* [Thomas Hardy]. 8vo. 2 vols.   London, 1872

UNDER the grey olives. [A novel.] By Marian Keith [Mary Esther Miller MacGregor]. 8vo. Pp. 176. [*Publishers' Weekly*, 3. 9. 27].   New York, 1927

UNDER the Hermes, and other stories. By Richard Dehan [Clotilde Inez Mary Graves]. 8vo. Pp. 341. [*Who's Who in Lit.*]   London, 1917

UNDER the Huguenot cross; a tale of Old Sea Point. By Telkin Kerr [W. Angus Kingon]. 8vo. [*Brit. Mus.*]   Cape Town, 1904

UNDER the iron flail. [A novel.] By John Oxenham [William Arthur Dunkerley]. 8vo. Pp. 400. [*Who's Who in Lit.*]   London, 1902

UNDER the liberty tree; a story of the Boston massacre. By James Otis [James Otis Kaler]. 4to. Pp. 115. [*Who's Who in Lit.*]   Boston, 1896

UNDER the limes. [A novel.] By the author of *Christina North*, etc. [E. M. Archer *i.e.* Eleanor Taylor]. 8vo. 2 vols. [*Camb. Univ. Lib.*]   London, 1874

UNDER the Meteor Flag; the log of a Midshipman. By Harry Collingwood [William J. C. Lancaster]. 8vo. [*Who's Who in Lit.*]   London, 1887

UNDER the microscope; or, "Thou shalt call me my father." [A tale. By Miss Emily S. Elliot.] 8vo. Pp. 111. [*Brit. Mus.*]   London, 1861

UNDER the old roof. By Hesba Stretton [Sarah Smith]. 12mo. Pp. 93.   London [1882]

UNDER the olive; poems. [By Mrs Annie Fields.] 12mo.   Boston, 1881

UNDER the Red Star. [A novel.] By Morice Gerard [Rev. John Jessop Teague]. 8vo. Pp. 286. [*Who's Who in Lit.*]   Edinburgh, 1910

UNDER the rose; a novel. By F. Anstey [Thomas Anstey Guthrie]. 8vo. [*Who's Who in Lit.*]   London, 1894

UNDER the rowan tree; and other stories. By Alan Saint Aubyn [Miss Frances Marshall]. 8vo. Pp. 256. [*Who's Who in Lit.*]   London, 1898

UNDER the shield; a tale. By M. E. Winchester [Margaret E. Whatham]. 8vo. [*Who's Who in Lit.*]   London, 1883

UNDER the skylights. By Stanton Page [Henry B. Fuller]. 8vo. [*Amer. Cat.*]   New York, 1901

UNDER the Southern cross; a tale of the New World. By the author of *The Spanish brothers* [Deborah Alcock]. 8vo.   London, 1873

UNDER the spell. By the author of *Grandmother's money*, etc. [Frederick William Robinson]. 8vo. 3 vols.
London, 1861

UNDER the thatch. [A novel.] By Allen Raine [Mrs Anne Adaliza Puddicombe, *née* Evans]. 8vo. Pp. iv. 346.
London, 1910

UNDER the tide. By Barry Lyndon [George Lowell Austin, M.D.]. 8vo. [Kirk's *Supp*.]   Boston, 1870

U N D E R the upas tree ; a romance of Scotland in the sixteenth century. By Cyril Grey [A. Balfour Symington], author of *The lost earldom*, etc. 8vo. Pp. 256.   London, 1915
Presentation copy from the author, with autograph.

UNDER two flags; a story of the household and the desert. By Ouida, author of *Strathmore*, etc. [Louise de La Ramée]. 8vo. 3 vols.
London, 1867
Originally written for a military periodical.

UNDER Western eyes. By Joseph Conrad [Joseph Conrad Korzeniowski]. 8vo.   London, 1911

UNDER Westminster Bridge ; a tale of the London dynamiters and the unemployed. By J. M. Burton [Joseph Barton Mason]. 8vo. Pp. 100. [*Brit. Mus.*]   London [1888]

UNDER-CURRENTS. [A novel.] By the author of *Phyllis*, etc. [Mrs Margaret Argles, later Hungerford]. 8vo. 3 vols. [*Brit. Mus.*]
London, 1888

UNDERCURRENTS of [English] Church life in the eighteenth century. By [Jane Frances Mary Carter] the author of *Nicholas Ferrar*, etc. 8vo. Pp. xvi. 222. [*Brit. Mus.*]
London, 1899

UNDERCURRENTS overlooked. By the author of *Flemish interiors*, etc. [Mrs William Pitt Byrne, *née* Julia Clara Busk]. 12mo. 2 vols. [*Brit. Mus.*]   London, 1860

UNDERGRADUATE (the); a sketch. By Ross George Dering [Frederick Henry Balfour]. 8vo. 2 vols. [*Brit. Mus.*]   London, 1891

UNDERGRADUATE (the); or, College life in five phases ; a satire. By B.A., Cantab [Gavin F. James]. 8vo. [Bartholomew's *Camb. Books*.]
Cambridge [1885]

UNDERGRADUATE subscription ; extracts from a collection of papers published in Oxford in 1772 on the subject of subscription to the xxxix Articles, required from young persons at their matriculation. With a preface by the Editor [Vaughan Thomas, B.D.]. To which is added, the debate in the House of Commons upon Sir William Meredith's motion on the same subject, Feb. 1773. 8vo. Pp. xix. 44. [*Bodl.*]   Oxford, 1835
Editor's name in the handwriting of Dr Bliss.

UNDERGRADUATES' (the) guide to unseen translations from Latin and Greek literature. [By Rev. Thomas Allen Blyth, B.A.] 8vo.
Oxford, 1881

UNDERGROUND Jerusalem ; discoveries on the hill of Ophel, 1909-11. By H. V. [L. Hugues Vincent]. . . . Translated from the French. . . . 8vo. Pp. xvii. 42. [*Brit. Mus.*]
London, 1911

UNDERGROUND Russia ; revolutionary profiles and sketches. By Stepniak [Sergie Michaelovitch Kravchinsky]. 8vo.   London, 1883

UNDERNEATH the bough ; a book of verses. By Michael Field [Katharine Harris Bradley and Edith Emma Cooper]. 8vo. Pp. 135. [*Brit. Mus.*]
London, 1893

UNDERTONES of the nineteenth century ; a prelude and a prophecy. [By Mrs Edward Trotter.] 8vo. Pp. 105.   London, 1905
The second edition, 1916, has the author's name.

UNDETERMIN'D (the) clergyman's journey on the first Sabbath of September to —— Well, which was at that time impregnate with salutary particles. [By Rev. Robert Kinloch, M.A. of New Kirk, Edinburgh.] 8vo.   Edinburgh, 1737

UNDINE ; a romance. [By F. H. C. de La Motte Fouqué.] Translated from the German by G. Soane. 12mo. [*Brit. Mus.*]   London, 1818

U N D I S C O V E R E D crimes. By "Waters" [William Russell]. 8vo.
London, 1862

UNEQUAL (the) match ; a tale [in verse]. By the author of *The curious maid* [Matthew Prior]. Fol. [*Brit. Mus.*]   London, 1737

UNEQUAL (the) match ; or, the life of Mary of Anjou: an historical novel [translated from the French of Jean de la Chapelle, by Ferrand Spence]. 12mo. [*Brit. Mus.*]   London, 1681

UNERRABLE (an) Church or none ; being a rejoynder to The Unerring unerrable Church against Dr Andrew Salls repley entituled The Catholic Apostolic Church of England. Written by J. S. [Ignatius Brown] and dedicated to the most illustrious Prince James Duke of Ormond, &c. 8vo. Pp. 342. [*Brit. Mus.*] [Douai] 1678

UNERRING(the)and unerrablechurch ; or, an answer to a sermon preached by Mr A. Sall. . . . Written by J. S. [Ignatius Brown, S.J.]. 8vo. Pp. 310. [*Sommervogel; Brit. Mus.*] 1675

UNEXPECTED (the). [A novel.] By Rowland Grey [Miss Lilian Rowland Brown]. 8vo. Pp. 250. [*Who's Who in Lit.*] London, 1902

UNFORTUNATE (the) Court favourites of England, exemplified in some remarks upon the lives, actions, and fall of divers who have been favourites. . . . By R. B. [Richard Burton, *i.e.* Nathaniel Crouch]. 12mo. [*Brit. Mus.*] London, 1696

UNFORTUNATE (the) Politique ; first written in French by C. N. [Nicolas Caussin, S.J.], Englished by G. P. 12mo. Pp. 230. [Madan's *Oxford Books*, i. 205.] Oxford, 1638

A translation of the fourth book of the author's *Cour Sainte*.

UNFORTUNATE (the) shepherd ; a pastoral. [By John Tutchin.] 8vo. [*Brit. Mus.*] London, 1685

UNFOULDYNG (the) of sundry vntruths and absurde propositions, latelye propounded by one I. B. a greate fauourer of the horrible heresie of the Libertines. [By Thomas Wilcocks.] 8vo. No pagination. B. L. [*Bodl.*] London, 1581

UNFOUNDED attacks on British officers in "An absent-minded war," by a British Officer ; a refutation. By XXX and LIX [Colonel J. E. Goodwyn]. 8vo. [*Brit. Mus.*] London, 1901

UNFULFILLED prophecy respecting Eastern nations, especially the Turks, the Russians, and the Jews. [By A. Macleod.] 12mo. London, 1841

UNGROWN-UPS (the). [A novel.] By "Rita" [Mrs W. Desmond Humphreys, *née* Eliza M. J. Gollan]. 8vo. Pp. 382. [*Who's Who in Lit.*] London, 1923

UNHAPPY (an) game at Scotch and English ; or, a full answer from England to the papers of Scotland : wherein their Scotch mists and their fogs, their sayings and gain-sayings, their juglings, their windings and turnings. . . . [By John Lilburne.] 4to. Pp. 26. Edinburgh, 1646

UNHAPPY (the) history of Elizabeth Stuart, Queen of Bohemia. By Marie Hay [Madame de Hindenburg]. 8vo. [*Who's Who in Lit.*] London, 1910

UNHAPPY (the) princesses ; containing, first, the secret history of Queen Anne Bullen, mother to Queen Elizabeth of renowned memory : with an impartial account of the first loves of Henry VIII. to that lady. . . . Secondly, the history of the Lady Jane Grey, who was proclaimed Queen of England. . . . Adorn'd with pictures. By R. B. [Richard, or Robert Burton, *i.e.* Nathaniel Crouch]. 12mo. Pp. 159. London, 1710

UNHOLY matrimony. [A novel.] By John Le Breton [Miss M. Harte-Potts, and T. Murray Ford]. 8vo. Pp. 336. [*Brit. Mus.*] London, 1899

UNINTERRUPTED (the) succession of bishops, proved not necessary to the ministerial office. . . . [By Rev. John Platts.] 8vo. London, 1718

UNIO politico - poetico - joco - seria ; written in the latter end of the year 1703 : and afterwards, as occasion offered, very much enlarged, in severall paragraphs. By the author of *Tripatriarchicon* [Andrew Symson]. 4to. Pp. 32. Edinburgh, 1706

The two concluding lines give the author's initials :—"And if you ask the author's name, here 'tis, A. S. Philophilus, Philopatris."

UNIOMACHIA, or the battle at the Union ; an Homeric fragment, lately given to the world by Habbakukius Dunderheadius [Thomas Jackson], and now rendered into the English tongue by Jedediah Puzzlepate [John Douglas Giles]. 8vo. Pp. 8. [F. Madan.] Oxford, 1833

UNION and no union ; being an enquiry into the grievances of the Scots and how far they are right or wrong, who alledge that the Union is dissolved. [By Daniel Defoe.] 8vo. Pp. 24. [Lee's *Defoe*, 150.] London, 1713

UNION (the); cease your funning. [An answer to a pamphlet by Edward Cooke entitled Arguments for and against an Union between Great Britain and Ireland considered. By the Rt. Hon. Charles Kendal Bushe.] Third edition. 8vo. Pp. 45. [*Brit. Mus.*]   Dublin, 1798
   The title of an edition of 1799 begins " Cease your funning . . ."

UNION Liturgy ; containing forms of prayer for the public services of religion, and also for family worship and private devotion. [By James Thomson, M.D., a Baptist.] 8vo. Pp. 280.   London, 1837

UNION necessary to security ; addressed to the loyal inhabitants of Ireland. By an independent observer [Archibald Redfoord]. 8vo. [*Brit. Mus.*]   Dublin, 1800

UNION (the) of Christ and the Church ; in a shadow. By R. C. [Ralph Cudworth]. 4to. Pp. 35. London, 1642

UNION (the) of Church and State . . . with a glance at confiscation. By a layman [C. N. Cumberlege Ware]. 8vo. [*Brit. Mus.*]   London, 1869

UNION (the) of the British North American Provinces considered. By Obiter Dictum [James Anderson, F.R.S.E., Canadian journalist]. 8vo. [Kirk's *Supp.*]   Montreal, 1859

UNION of the Old Light Seceders with the Established Church ; a review of the proceedings of the Synod of Merse and Teviotdale, as reported in the Kelso Chronicle for October, 1834. [By Adam Thomson, D.D., Coldstream.] 8vo.   Edinburgh, 1834

UNION [between Ireland and England] or not ? By an Orangeman [Harding Giffard]. 8vo.   Dublin, 1799

UNION (the) ; or, select Scots and English poems. [Mainly by Thomas Warton.] 8vo. [*D. N. B.* vol. 59, p. 432.]   London, 1753
   Signed : A Gentleman from Aberdeen.

UNION pursued ; in a letter to Mr Baxter, concerning his late book of National churches. . . . That the Presbyterians and Independants, that have united within themselves, may both be united also with the Church of England. By a lover of him, and follower of peace [John Humfrey]. 4to. Pp. 38. [*Bodl.*]   London, 1691

UNION with the Free Church ; observations upon the pamphlet of the Rev. Matthew Murray. . . . [By Thomas M'Crie.] 8vo.   Edinburgh, 1849

UNION-PROVERB (the) ; viz. If Skiddaw has a cap, Scruffell wots full well of that : setting forth, I. The necessity of uniting. II. The good consequences of uniting. III. The happy union of England and Scotland, in case of a foreign invasion. [By Daniel Defoe.] 8vo. [Wilson's *Life of Defoe*, 105.]   London, N.D.

UNIQUE traditions, chiefly connected with the West and the South of Scotland. [By J. G. Barbour ; preface signed J. G. B—b—r.] 8vo. Pp. xiv. 198.   Edinburgh, 1833

UNITARIANISM, old and new, exemplified . . . in three letters [the first and third by "An old Unitarian," *i.e.* Thomas Sanden ; the second by William Johnson Fox, M.P.]. 8vo. [*Brit. Mus.*]   Chichester, 1817

UNITARIANISM the doctrine of the Bible. By a Unitarian layman [H. J. Huidekoper]. 8vo. [*Brit. Mus.*]   Pittsburg, Penn., 1843

UNITARIANISM tried by Scripture and experience ; a compilation of treatises and testimonies in support of Trinitarian doctrine and evangelical principles. . . . By a layman [John Edmonds Stock]. 8vo. [Green's *Bibl. Somers.* i. 310.]   London, 1840

UNITARIANISM unscriptural. [By Henry Morris, of Magdalen Hall, Oxford.] No. 1. 12mo. [*Brit. Mus.*]   London, 1837
   No more published.

UNITARIAN'S (the) appeal. [By Lant Carpenter.] A new edition, with the texts quoted at length. 12mo. [*Brit. Mus.*]   Bristol, 1817

UNITE or fall. [By Frederick Howard, 5th Earl of Carlisle.] Fifth edition. 12mo. Pp. 23. [*Bodl.*]   London, 1798

UNITED (the) States and England. By an American [Duff Green]. 8vo. [Sabin's *Dict.*]   London, 1842

UNITED (the) States and England ; being a reply to the criticism on Inchiquin's Letters contained in the *Quarterly Review* for January 1814. [By James Kirke Paulding]. 8vo. [*Brit. Mus.*]   London, 1815

UNITED (the) States of North America as they are. By Karl Postl [later Charles Seafield]. 8vo. [*Camb. Hist. of Amer. Lit.* i. 484.]   London, 1827

UNITED (the) States Review and Literary Gazette. [Edited by William Cullen Bryant.] 8vo. 2 vols. [Foley's *Amer. Authors.*]   Boston, 1826-27

UNITED (the) States Sanitary Commission; a sketch of its purpose and work. [By Miss Katharine Prescott Wormeley.] 12mo. [Cushing's *Anon.*]
New York, 1863

"UNITED we stand, divided we fall." By Juba [Rev. Benjamin Allen]. 8vo.   New York, 1812

UNITY and its restoration. By a presbyter of the diocese of Illinois [Hugh Miller Thompson, D.D.]. 8vo.
New York, 1860

UNITY and Trinity; a dissertation establishing that doctrine against the Anti-Trinitarians. [By James Anderson, D.D., minister in London.]
London [1720?]

UNITY (the) of God not inconsistent with the divinity of Christ; being remarks on the passages in Dr Waterland's Vindication, &c. relating to the unity of God and to the object of worship. [By Joseph Hallett.] 8vo. [Watt's *Bibl. Brit.*; Darling's *Cyclop. Bibl.*]   London, 1720
    Ascribed also to Hubert Stogdon.

UNITY (the) of men; or, life and death realities; a reply to Luther Leo, by Anthropos [George Storrs]. 12mo. Pp. 122. [Cushing's *Anon.*]
Philadelphia, 1850

UNITY (the) of medicine; its corruptions and divisions as by law established in England and Wales; with their causes, effects, and remedy. By a Fellow of the Royal College of Surgeons [Frederick Davies]. 8vo. Pp. x. 154. [*Brit. Mus.*]
London, 1858

UNITY of priesthood necessary to the unity of communion in a Church: with some reflections on the Oxford manuscript, and the preface annexed: also a collection of canons, part of the said manuscript, faithfully translated into English from the original, but concealed by Mr Hody, and his prefacer. [By Nathaniel Bisbie.] 4to. Pp. 72.   London, 1692
    This work has been assigned to Mr Webster: but it is ascribed to Bisbie by Rawlinson, in his MS. continuation of the Athenæ. See also Lathbury's *Nonjurors*, p. 137.

UNITY our duty; in twelve considerations humbly presented to the godly, reverend, and learned brethren of the Presbyterian judgement . . . about church government. . . . By I. P. [John Price]. 4to. Pp. 9.
London, 1645

UNIVERSAL and saving grace, asserted and demonstrated; or, a Scriptural refutation of the doctrines of absolute and unconditional predestination, in letters to the proprietors of the Gospel Magazine. Letter the first, in which are noticed, chiefly, some of the arguments, inconsistencies, and contradictions, contained in a treatise on the subject, by the late A. Toplady, A.B., vicar of Hembury, Devon. [By Thomas Scantlebury.] 12mo. [Smith's *Cat. of Friends' Books*, i. 84; ii. 541.]
Sheffield, 1813

UNIVERSAL angler; or, that art improved in all its parts, especially in fly-fishing: the whole interspersed with many curious and uncommon observations. 12mo. [Smith's *Bibl. Ang.*]   London, 1766
    "This book is copied from Bowlker's Art of Angling, printed at Worcester, with some few additions taken from Walton, Cotton and Hawkins."—WM. WHITE.

UNIVERSAL beauty; a philosophical poem, in six books. [By Henry Brooke.] Fol. [*Gent. Mag.* v. 55.]
London, 1735

UNIVERSAL (the) chronologist, from the creation to 1825. By Henry Boyle [William Henry Ireland]. 8vo.
London, 1826

UNIVERSAL (the) Church; an essay on nature, as the universal basis of truth, perfection, and salvation, and their universality, etc. [By John Crook.] 8vo. [*Brit. Mus.*]
London, 1807

UNIVERSAL (the) Church; its faith, doctrine, and constitution. [By John Burley Waring, architect.] 8vo. [*Brit. Mus.*]   London, 1866

UNIVERSAL (the) Church of nature; being a synopsis of *The Universal Church.* . . . By the author of the original pamphlet [John Crook]. 8vo. [*Brit. Mus.*]   London, 1836

UNIVERSAL commerce; or, the commerce of all the mercantile cities and towns of the world. . . . By the editor of Mortimer's *Commercial dictionary* [William Dickinson, of London]. 8vo. [*Edin. Univ. Lib.*]
London, 1818

UNIVERSAL damnation and salvation clearly proved by the Scriptures of the Old and New Testament. . . . [By Rev. John Tyler.] 8vo. [Eddy's *Universalism in America*, ii. 492.]
Boston, 1798
    An edition published in 1815, at Norwich [Conn.] has a different title: "The law and the gospel clearly demonstrated in six sermons."

UNIVERSAL (the) doom; or, the state of mortality: humbly presented to the Right Reverend Father in God Thomas Tanner, D.D. Lord Bishop of St Asaph. [By W. Howard.] 4to. Pp. 12. [*Bodl.*]   London, 1733

UNIVERSAL (the) gardener and botanist. . . . By —— Mawe [John Abercrombie]. 4to. [Rivers' *Lit. Memoirs*, i. 1.]   London, 1778

UNIVERSAL geography; or, a description of all the parts of the world on a new plan. . . . By M. Malte-Brun. [Translated and edited by Henry Dewar, M.D.] 8vo. 10 vols.
      Edinburgh, 1822-33

UNIVERSAL (the) historical bibliotheque; or, an account of the most considerable books, printed in all languages in the month[s] of January [February and March] 1686: wherein a short description is given of the design and scope of almost every book: and of the quality of the author, if known. [By G. Wells, and J. D. de la Crose.] 4to. [*W.*] London, 1687

UNIVERSAL history on Scriptural principles. [By Mary Bowley, afterwards Peters.] Second edition. 8vo. 5 vols. [*Brit. Mus.*] London, 1844-50

UNIVERSAL (an) history of Christian martyrdom . . . originally composed by John Fox . . . and now entirely rewritten by the Rev. J. Milner, M.A. [Francis William Blagdon]. 8vo. [*Brit. Mus.*]   London, 1807

UNIVERSAL (the) passion. See "The love of fame . . ."

UNIVERSAL (the) passion; a comedy, as it is acted at the Theatre-Royal in Drury-Lane by His Majesty's servants. [By James Miller.] 8vo. [*Biog. Dram.*]   London, 1737

UNIVERSAL (the) prayer. By the author of the *Essay on man* [Alexander Pope]. Fol. Pp. 7.
      London, 1738

UNIVERSAL restitution, a Scripture doctrine; this proved in several letters wrote on the nature and extent of Christ's kingdom: wherein the scripture passages, falsly alledged in proof of the eternity of hell torments, are truly translated and explained. [By Rev. Sir James Stonhouse, M.D.] 8vo. [*D. N. B.* vol. 54, p. 418.]
      London, 1762

UNIVERSAL restitution farther defended; being a supplement to the book intitled Universal restitution a Scripture doctrine. . . . [By Rev. Sir James Stonhouse, M.D.] 8vo. Pp. 148. [*D. N. B.* vol. 54, p. 418.]
      Bristol, 1768

UNIVERSAL restitution vindicated against the Calvinists; in five dialogues. . . . [By Rev. Sir James Stonhouse, M.D.] 8vo. Pp. 176. [*D. N. B.* vol. 54, p. 418.]
      Bristol, 1773

UNIVERSAL (the) revival of religion; a few words to Christian ministers, and others. By M. Justitia [John Frearson]. 12mo. Pp. 26.
      London [1858]

UNIVERSAL (the) Spectator. [By Daniel Defoe.] No. 1. 4to. [Lee's *Defoe*, 246.]   1728

UNIVERSAL (the) Spectator, by Henry Stonecastle, of Northumberland, Esq. [Probably by John Kelly, the dramatic writer.] 12mo. 4 vols. [*Athen. Cat.*]   London, 1756

UNIVERSALISM as related to the Church and the State. By [Clement Wise] the author of *Darkness and dawn; or, the peaceful birth of a new age*. 8vo. Pp. xi. 478. Bristol, 1892

UNIVERSALISM false and unscriptural; an essay on the duration and intensity of future punishment. [By Archibald Alexander, D.D.] 12mo. Pp. 104. [Eddy's *Universalism in America*.]   Philadelphia [1851]

UNIVERSALIST'S assistant; or, an examination of the principal objections commonly urged against Universalism. By a believer [Darius Forbes]. 12mo. Pp. 234. [Eddy's *Universalism in America*, ii. 548.]   Boston, 1846

UNIVERSALIST'S (the) book of reference; containing all the principal facts and arguments, and Scripture texts pro and con, on the great controversy between Limitarians and Universalists. . . . [By R. E. Guild.] 12mo. Pp. 381. [Eddy's *Universalism in America*.]   Boston, 1844

UNIVERSE (the); a poem. By the Rev. C. R. Maturin [in reality by Rev. James Wills, D.D.]. 8vo. Pp. 112. [*N. and Q.* 5th Ser. iii. pp. 20, 172, 240, 280, 340.]   London, 1821

UNIVERSITIES (the) and the Church of England. By a Cambridge man [Charles Hardwick, B.D.]. 8vo. [*Camb. Univ. Lib.*] Cambridge, 1854

UNIVERSITIES (the) and the Scientific Corps [of the British Army]. By a Staff Officer [Francis Duncan] and an Oxford Tutor [Francis J. Jayne]. 8vo. Pp. 15. [*Brit. Mus.*]   Oxford, 1872

UNIVERSITIES' Mission to Central Africa; the A B C of the U. M. C. A. Compiled by M. E. W. [M. E. Woodward]. 8vo.   London, 1899

UNIVERSITIES of Scotland Bill; remarks on the condition, necessities, and claims of the Universities of Scotland; with an appendix. By a graduate [Sir John Rose Cormack, M.D.]. 8vo. Pp. xvi. 72. [*Brit. Mus.*]   London, 1858

UNIVERSITY (the) commission; or, Lord John Russell's post bag of April 27, 1850; the first instalment. [By William Sewell, D.D.] 8vo. Pp. vii. 35.   Oxford, 1850
Three other "Instalments" followed, in the same year.

UNIVERSITY education for English Catholics; a letter to the Very Rev. Dr Newman. By an English Catholic Layman [Sir Peter le Page Renouf.] 8vo. [*D. N. B. 3rd Supp.* iii. 295.]
                    London, 1864

UNIVERSITY (the) Library, Cambridge. [By Charles Sayle.] 8vo. [*Bartholomew's Camb. Books.*]
                    Cambridge, 1895

UNIVERSITY of Aberdeen; description of the armorial bearings, portraits, and busts in the Mitchell Hall and portrait gallery, Marischal College. By E. A. [Ellinor Arnott]. 8vo.
                    Aberdeen, 1896

UNIVERSITY (the) of Brecknock. By Veritas [Joseph Hughes, D.D., Bishop of St Asaph]. 8vo. [F. Boase's *Mod. Eng. Biog.* i. 1575.]   1856

UNIVERSITY (the) of Cambridge vindicated from the imputation of disloyalty it lies under on the account of not addressing: as also from the malicious and foul aspersions of Dr B - - - - ly, late Master of Trinity College; and of a certain officer, and pretended reformer in the said University. Written by the author [Styan Thirlby, M.A.]. 8vo. Pp. 35. [*Brit. Mus.*]   London, 1710

UNIVERSITY (the) of Dublin in its relation to the several religious communions. [By Humphrey Lloyd.] 8vo. Pp. 31. [*Brit. Mus.*]
                    Dublin, 1868

UNIVERSITY of London: statements of fact as to Charter. [Signed: W. T. *i.e.* William Tooke, junior.] 8vo. [*D. N. B.* vol. 57, p. 51.] London, 1835

UNIVERSITY Olympians; or, sketches of academic dignitaries. By A. P. [Arthur Ponsford Baker]. 8vo. [*Camb. Univ. Lib.*]
                    Cambridge, 1918 [printed in 1914]

UNIVERSITY (the) question considered. By a graduate [Rev. Dr John M'Caul]. 8vo. [*Cushing's Init. and Pseud.*]
                    Montreal, 1845

UNIVERSITY tests and their abolition, considered in a letter to Sir John Duke Coleridge. . . . [By John Place.] 8vo.
                    London [1870]

UNIVERSITY tests; observations upon the Bill of the Solicitor-General, and upon the counter-proposal of Lord Carnarvon. By the Principal of St Mary Hall, Oxford [Drummond Percy Chase]. 8vo. [*Camb. Univ. Lib.*]
                    Oxford, 1869

UNJUST (an) plea confuted, and Melchisedec and Christ's order vindicated against Antichristianism; in answer to a book called "Moses and Aaron, or the ministers right and the magistrates duty," given forth by Daniel Pointell, a false minister in Kent. . . . By a witness of the way of truth, G. W. [George Whitehead]. 4to. Pp. 28. [Smith's *Anti-Quak.* p. 368.]
                    London, 1659

UNKIND (the) word and other stories. By the author of *John Halifax, gentleman*, etc. [Dinah Maria Mulock, later Mrs Craik]. 8vo. Pp. 305.
                    London, N.D.

UNKINDE (the) desertor of loyall men and true frinds. [By E. S. *i.e.* Nicholas French, titular Bishop of Ferns.] 8vo. Pp. 246 [misprinted 446], 8. [*Brit. Mus.*]   1676
Of this work, seven copies only are known to exist. The Bodleian copy has the author's autograph, and memoranda of donation to Sir Christopher French, his brother.

UNKNOWN (the) and unknowable God; or, the critic criticised. By a Bucolic [John Poole Sandlands]. 8vo. Pp. 91. [*Brit. Mus.*]   London [1903]

UNKNOWN (an) country. By the author of *John Halifax, gentleman* [Mrs Craik, *née* Dinah M. Mulock]. 8vo.   London, 1887

UNKNOWN (the) Eros, and other odes. [By Coventry K. D. Patmore.] 8vo. [Boase's *Mod. Eng. Biog.* vi. col. 364.]   London, 1877
Later editions give the author's name.

UNKNOWN (the) God. By B. L. Putnam Weale [Bertram Lenox Simpson]. 8vo. Pp. 492. [*Brit. Mus.*]
                    London, 1911

UNKNOWN Hampshire. By Clive Holland [Charles James Hankinson]. 8vo. Pp. xv. 260. [*Brit. Mus.*]
                    London, 1926

UNKNOWN (the) power behind the Irish Nationalist party. [By F. O. Trench, Baron Ashtown.] 8vo. Pp. 208. [*Brit. Mus.*]   London, 1907

UNKNOWN (an) river; or, an etcher's voyage of discovery. [By Philip Gilbert Hamerton.] 8vo.
London, 1874

UNKNOWN (the) road; an everyday story. By Curtis Yorke [Mrs W. S. Richmond Lee, *née* Jex-Long]. 8vo. Pp. 284. [*Who's Who in Lit.*]
London, 1920

UNLAWFUL (the) and unholy alliance between Church and State. [By the Rev. Archibald A. Currie, minister in Abercorn.] 12mo.   London, 1870

UNLAVVFVLNES (the) and danger of limited Prelacie; or, perpetvall presidensie in the Chvrch briefly discovered. [By Alexander Henderson, Moderator of the General Assembly, A.M.] 4to. Pp. 23. [*Brit. Mus.*]   N.P. 1641

UNLAWFULNESS (the) of bonds of resignation; first written in the year 1684, for the satisfaction of a private gentleman, and now made publick for the good of others. [By John Wills, D.D.] 8vo. Pp. 30. [*Bodl.*]
London, 1696

UNLAWFULNESS (the) of marriage with a deceased wife's sister. [By John Bate Cardale, solicitor.] 8vo. [*Brit. Mus.*]   London, 1859

UNLAWFULNESSE (the) of subjects taking up armes against their soveraigne, in what case soever; together with an answer to all objections scattered in their severall bookes. [By Dudley Digges.] 4to. Pp. 170. [*Bodl.*]   1643

UNLUCKY; a fragment of a girl's life. By Caroline Austin [Mrs —— Whitway]. 8vo. Pp. 160. [*Brit. Mus.*]   London, 1891

UNLUCKY (the) citizen experimentally described in the various misfortunes of an unlucky Londoner, calculated for the meridian of this city but may serve by way of advice to all the cominalty of England. . . . [By Francis Kirkman.] 8vo. Pp. 317.
London, 1673
The work has an engraved title "The unlucky citizen by F. K."

UNMARRIED (the) woman. By Eliza Chester [Miss Harriet Eliza Paine]. [*Amer. Cat.*]   New York, 1892

UNMASKED. [A novel.] By Annabel Gray [Mrs Cox]. 8vo. [*Lond. Lib. Cat.*]   London, 1884

UNMASKED at last. [A novel.] By Headon Hill [Francis E. Grainger]. 8vo. [*Brit. Mus.*]   London, 1906

UNMASKING of the masse priest. By C. A. [John Lewis]. 4to. [*Pollard and Redgrave.*]   London, 1624
A reissue of Melchizedechs anti-type (1624 also) which bore the author's name.

UNMASKING (the) of the politique atheist. By J. H. [John Hull], Batcheler of Divinitie. 8vo. [*Bliss' Cat.*]   London, 1602

UNNATURAL bondage. By Bertha M. Clay [Charlotte M. Law, later Mrs Braeme]. 8vo. [*Amer. Cat.*]
New York, 1887

UNNATURAL natural history notes. By H. M. L. [Hill Mussenden Leathes]. 8vo. Pp. 139. [*Brit. Mus.*]
London, 1884
See also "Rough notes . . ."

UNPARALLEL'D reasons for abollishing Episcopacy. 1. It will assure his Majesties authority royall. 2. Increase his revenue. 3. Settle a good union in his Majesties owne kingdomes, and between them and other reformed Churches. 4. Cause a good understanding betweene his Majesty and his people. By N. F., Esquire [Nathaniel Fiennes]. 4to. Pp. 8. [*Bodl.*]
London, 1642

UNPARALLEL'D varieties; or, the matchless actions and passions of mankind. . . . Imbelished with pictures. By R. B. [Richard Burton]. 12mo. Pp. 231. [*Brit. Mus.*]   London, 1683
"The contents of this volume were pillaged from Wanley's Wonders of the little world." —MS. note by Douce.

UNPOSTED letters concerning life and literature. By John o' London [Wilfred Whitten]. 8vo. [*Nat. Lib. of Scot.*]
London [1924]

UNPREACHED (the) Gospel. By the author of *The study of the Bible* [Henry Dunn]. 8vo.   London [1863]
Reprinted extract from the author's "Destiny of the human race."

UNPRETENTIOUS rhymes. By H. G. L. [Hugh Graham Lang]. 8vo. [*Brit. Mus.*]   Lewes, 1915

UNPROFESSIONAL tales. By Normyx [Norman Douglas]. 8vo.
London, 1901
First edition, withdrawn by the author.

UNPROTECTED females in Norway; or, the pleasantest way of travelling there, passing through Denmark and Sweden: with Scandinavian sketches from nature. [By Miss Emily Lowe.] 8vo. [*Nat. Lib. of Scot.*]
London, 1857

UNPROTECTED females in Sicily, Calabria, and the top of Mount Ætna. [By Miss Emily Lowe.] 8vo. [*Brit. Mus.*]   London, 1859

UNPROTECTED (the); or, facts in dressmaking life. By a dressmaker [Mary Guignard. Edited, with an introduction, by Rev. W. Landels]. 8vo. [*W.; Brit. Mus.*] London, 1857

UNPUBLISHED writings of Eliphas Levi [Louis Alphonse Constant]. The paradoxes of the Highest Science ; translated from the French MSS. by a student of occultism. 8vo. [*Brit. Mus.*]   London, 1883
  Publications of the Theosophical Society.

UNRAVELLED convictions ; or, my road to faith. [By Lady Amabel Cowper, afterwards Kerr.] 8vo. Pp. 128.   Liverpool, private print, 1876
  Published afterwards, still anonymously, by Burns & Oates, London, 1878.

UNREAD (an) letter. [A novel.] By "Alien" [Mrs L. A. Baker]. 8vo. Pp. 318. [*Who's Who in Lit.*]
                            London, 1909

UNREALITY ; a novel. By Bartimeus [Lewis Anselm Da Costa Ricci]. 8vo. Pp. 320.   London, 1920

UNREASONABLENESS (the) and impiety of Popery ; in' a second letter written upon the discovery of the late plot. [By Gilbert Burnet, D.D.] 4to. Pp. 36. [Clarke and Foxcroft's *Life of Burnet*, Appendix.]   London, 1678

UNREASONABLENESS (the) of separation ; the second part : or, a further impartial account of the history, nature, and pleas of the present separation from the communion of the Church of England. Begun by Edw. Stillingfleet D.D. Dean of St Pauls ; continued from 1640 to 1681 : with special remarks on the life and actions of Mr Richard Baxter. [By Thomas Long, B.D.] 8vo. Pp. 167. [*Bodl.*]
                            London, 1682

UNREASONABLENESS (the) of the Romanists, requiring our communion with the present Romish Church ; or, a discourse drawn from the perplexity and uncertainty of the principles, and from the contradictions betwixt the prayers and doctrine of the present Romish Church ; to prove that 'tis unreasonable to require us to joyn in communion with it. [By William Squire.] 8vo. Pp. 205. [*Bodl.*]   London, 1670

UNREASONABLENESSE (the) of atheism made manifest : a discourse written at the command of a person of honour. [By Sir Charles Wolseley.] 12mo. Pp. 197. [*Brit. Mus.*]
                            London, 1669
  A second edition, in the same year, bears the author's name.

UNREASONABLENESSE (the) of the separation ; made apparant by an examination of Mr [Francis] Johnsons pretended Reasons, published an. 1608. Whereby hee laboureth to justifie his schisme. . . . [By William Bradshaw.] 4to. [*D. N. B.* vol. 6, p. 184.]
                            London, 1614

UNREQUITED (an) loyalty. [A novel.] By Marie Hay [Madame de Hindenburg]. 8vo. [*Lit. Who's Who.*]
                            London, 1901

UNRIVALLED (the) adventures of that great aeronaut and glum Peter Wilkins. . . . By T. Trueman [Robert Paltock. Abridged]. 12mo. [*Brit. Mus.*]
                            London [1802]

UNSATISFACTORY (an) lover. By "The Duchess" [Mrs Hungerford, formerly Mrs Argles, *née* Margaret Hamilton]. 8vo. Pp. 210. [*Who's Who in Lit.*]   Philadelphia, 1896

UNSEEN (the) barrier. [A story.] By Mark Allerton [William Ernest Cameron]. 8vo. Pp. 112. [*Brit. Mus.*]   London, 1924

UNSEEN (the) barrier. [A novel.] By Morice Gerard [Rev. John Jessop Teague]. 8vo. Pp. 320. [*Who's Who in Lit.*]   London, 1911

UNSEEN (the) hand. [A novel.] By Laurence L. Lynch [Mrs Emma M. van Deventer]. 8vo. [*Who's Who in Lit.*]   London, 1902

UNSEEN (the) hand. . . . By Ruth Vernon [Stopford J. Ram]. 8vo.
                            Cincinnati, 1863

UNSEEN horizons. [Poems.] By Frederick Arthur [Col. Frederick Arthur H. Lambert]. 8vo. [*Lit. Who's Who.*]   London, 1915

UNSEEN (the) universe ; or, physical speculations on a future state. [By Professors Peter Guthrie Tait, and Balfour Stewart.] 8vo. Pp. xvi. 212.
                            London, 1875
  Published subsequently with the authors' names.

UNSEEN (the) world ; communications with it, real or imaginary, including apparitions, warnings, haunted places, prophecies, aerial visions, astrology, &c. [By John Mason Neale, D.D.] 8vo.   London, 1847

UNSENTIMENTAL (an) journey through Cornwall. By the author of *John Halifax, gentleman* [Mrs Craik, *née* Dinah M. Mulock]. 4to.
                            London, 1884

UNSEX'D (the) females ; a poem, addressed to the author of the Pursuits of literature. [By Richard Polwhele.] 8vo. Pp. 37. [Boase and Courtney's *Bibl. Corn.* ii. 509.]   London, 1798

UNSPEAKABLE (the) gift ; or, the story of Benjamin and Ruth. By E. W. [E. Wheeler]. 8vo. Pp. viii. 124. [*Brit. Mus.*]   London, 1897

UNSPEAKABLE (the) ; or, the life and adventures of a stammerer. [By James Malcolm Rymer.] 8vo. [*Brit. Mus.*]
                            London [1855]

UNSPOKEN (the) word. [A novel.] By Morice Gerard [Rev. John Jessop Teague]. 8vo. Pp. 286. [*Who's Who in Lit.*] London, 1910

UNSTUDIED songs, devoid of art. By Willow [William Porter, timber merchant], Old Meldrum. 8vo. Pp. 122. [Robertson's *Aberd. Bibl.*] [Aberdeen] private print, 1880

UNTAUGHT (the) muse; poems and songs. By a working man [Henry Syme]. 8vo. [Beveridge's *Dunferm. Bibl.*] Dunfermline, 1849

UNTIL my Lord's return; a romance of a river town. By Admiral Bonaventura Hinton [Valentine Durrant]. 8vo. [*Brit. Mus.*] London, 1892

UNTIL the day-break. By Birch Arnold [Alice Elinor Bartlett]. 8vo. Philadelphia, 1877

"UNTIL the shadows flee away"; a tale. [By Jessie M'Laren.] 8vo. [*Nat. Lib. of Scot.*] Edinburgh, 1869

UNTIMELY (an) birth, called Answers to the Queries. . . . [By Patrick Lindsay, M.P., Provost of Edinburgh.] 8vo. Edinburgh, 1737

UNTO death. By "Fleur de Lys" [Edith S. Floyer]. 8vo. Pp. 357. [*Brit. Mus.*] London, 1891

UNTO the desired haven, and other poems. [By Mrs Hobart Seymour.] 8vo. New York, 1880

UNTO the end. [A tale.] By Pansy [Mrs Alden, *née* Isabella Macdonald]. 8vo. Pp. 324. [*Who's Who in Lit.*] London, 1902

UNTO the perfect day; a homely story. By "Eona" [Miss —— Finniswood]. 8vo. Darlington, 1880

UNTO this generation; ten essays with prayers and hymns. [Preface signed : W. C. B. *i.e.* William Copeland Bowie.] 8vo. Pp. 264. [*Brit. Mus.*] London, 1914

UNTOLD (the) half; a novel. By Alien [Mrs L. A. Baker]. 8vo. [*Who's Who in Lit.*] London, 1900

UNTRAVELLED Berkshire. By L. S. [Miss L. Salmon, afterwards Grant]. 8vo. London, 1909

UNVEILING (the) of the everlasting gospel; with the scripture philosophy of happiness, holiness and scriptural power, specially addressed to the ministers and Church of God at the present crisis. [By Ebenezer Cornwall.] 12mo. London, 1848

UNWELCOME (the) guest; a story for girls. By Esmé Stuart [Miss Amélie Claire Leroy]. 8vo. [*Who's Who in Lit.*] London, 1886

UNWORTHY (the) pact. By Dorothea Gerard [Madame Longarde de Longarde]. 8vo. Pp. 312. [*Who's Who in Lit.*] London, 1913

UP against it in Uganda. By Langa Langa [Harry B. H. Hodge]. 8vo. Pp. 244. [*Brit. Mus.*] London, 1922

UP and down the house. By Amy Lothrop [Anna Bartlett Warner]. 8vo. Philadelphia, 1892

UP and down the Nile. By Oliver Optic [William Taylor Adams]. 8vo. [*Amer. Cat.*] Boston, 1894

UP and war them a' Willie; a letter of congratulation to the Burgher-hero William Smith; upon the glory of his late atchievement in routing the whole body of Antiburghers. [By Adam Gib.] 8vo. Pp. 15. [*New Coll. Lib.*] Edinburgh, 1766

UP Broadway, and its sequel; a life story. By Eleanor Kirk [Mrs Eleanor Ames]. 12mo. [Cushing's *Init. and Pseud.*] New York, 1870

"UP for the season," and other songs of society. By C. C. R. [C. C. Rhys]; being a second edition of *Minora Carmina.* 8vo. Pp. viii. 319. [*Brit. Mus.*] London, 1889

UP north; or, lost and found in Russia and the Arctic wastes. . . . By Janet Gordon [Mrs Janet Hardy, *née* Walker]. 8vo. [Scott's *Fasti*, second edition, ii. 20.] London, 1878

UP the ladder; or, striving and thriving. By Mrs Madeline Leslie [Harriet Newhall Baker]. 8vo. Boston, 1870

UP, the Rebels. By George A. Birmingham [Rev. James Owen Hannay], author of *Spanish gold.* 8vo. [*Who's Who in Lit.*] London, 1919

UP the river; or, yachting on the Mississippi. By Oliver Optic [William Taylor Adams]. 8vo. [*Amer. Cat.*] Boston, 1881

UP the Thames; sketches by S. C. P. [S. C. Pennefather]. Obl. 8vo. [*Brit. Mus.*] London [1874]

UP to fifteen; a tale for boys. By the author of *Only me* [Miss Matilda Mary Pollard]. 12mo. Pp. 154. [*Brit. Mus.*] London [1875]

UP-BYE ballads. By Will Carew [Ernest Milligan]. 12mo. Belfast, 1907

UPHILL (the) climb. [A novel.] By B. M. Bower [Bertram M. Sinclair]. 8vo. London, 1923

UPHOLSTERER (the), or what news? A farce, in two acts, as it is performed at the Theatre Royal, in Drury-Lane. By the author of *The apprentice* [Arthur Murphy]. 8vo. [Baker's *Biog. Dram.*] London, 1753

UPLAND (the) tarn; a village idyll. [By John E. H. Thomson, D.D.] 8vo. Pp. 168. [*Nat. Lib. of Scot.*]
Edinburgh, 1881

UPON a cast. By Charlotte Dunning [Charlotte Dunning Wood]. 8vo.
New York, 1885

UPON Mr Bobards yew-men of the guards to the Physick Garden; to the tune of the counter-scuffle. [By Edm. Geyton.] Fol. S. sh. [*Bodl.*]
N.P. [1662]
" By G. E. [*i.e.*] Edm. Geyton Esq ; Bedle of Arts. Oxon."—MS. note by Wood.

UPON nothing ; a poem. By a person of honour [John Wilmot, 2d Earl Rochester]. Fol. S. sh. N.P., N.D.
A different work from "An Essay on nothing." See above.

UPON the death of Mr Anthony Austin, younger son to Sir James Austin, Knight. By W. A. [William Austin]. 4to. [*Hazlitt.*] [London] 1677

UPON the most hopefull and ever-flourishing sprouts of valour, the indefatigable centrys of the Physick-Garden. [By John Drope, M.A.] Fol. S. sh. [*Bodl.*] Printed 1664
"Joh. Drope M. of A. Fellow of Magd. Coll. the author."—MS. note by Wood.

UPON the pleurality of personages in the "Elohim." . . . By an examining advocate [Edmund Baker]. 8vo. Pp. 44. [*Brit. Mus.*] London, 1867

UPON the rise and progress of criticism ; knowledge of the world, or good company : a dialogue, printed from the MSS. of J. H. [James Harris] of S. [Salisbury]. 8vo. Pp. 48. [*Brit. Mus.*] Private print, 1752

UPON the tree tops. By Oliver Thorne Miller [Mrs Harriet Mann Miller]. 8vo. Pp. 245. [*Amer. Cat.*]
Boston, 1897

UPPER (the) ten thousand ; sketches of American society. By a New Yorker [Charles Astor Bristed]. Reprinted from *Fraser's Magazine.* 8vo. [*Brit. Mus.*] London, 1852
Signed : Frank Manhattan.

UPPINGHAM by the sea ; a narrative of the year at Borth. By J. H. S. [John Henry Skrine]. 8vo. [*Brit. Mus.*] London, 1878

UPS and downs ; a story of Australian life. By Rolf Boldrewood [Thomas Alexander Browne]. 12mo. [*Lib. of Col. Inst.* Supp. i. 687.]
London, 1878
Republished in 1890 as " The Squatter's dream."

UPS and downs of a public school. By a Wykehamist [Frederick Gale, solicitor]. 8vo. [*Brit. Mus.*]
London, 1856

UPS and downs of Ally Sloper ; some humiliating confessions. [By Charles Henry Ross.] 4to. [*Brit. Mus.*]
London, 1882

ϒ″ΨΟΣ (το) ἅγιον ; or, an exercise upon the creation : written in the express words of the sacred text, as an attempt to show the beauty and sublimity of Holy Scripture. [By Francis Peck.] 8vo. [*Brit. Mus.*] London, 1717

UP-TO-DATE (an) parson ; and other stories. By Harry Lindsay [Harry Lindsay Hudson]. 8vo. Pp. viii. 234. [*Who's Who in Lit.*] London, 1899

UP-TO-DATE superstitions in common use, in every-day life. By Manas [Emma D. Mills]. 8vo.
New York, 1895

UPTON (the) letters. By T. B. [Arthur C. Benson]. 8vo. [*Brit. Mus.*]
London, 1905

UPWARDS and downwards, and other stories. By A. L. O. E., author of *The silver casket*, etc. [Charlotte Maria Tucker]. 8vo. Pp. 120.
London, 1873

URAICECHT na Gaedhilge ; a grammar of the Gaelic language. [By William Halliday.] 12mo. Pp. xv. 201.
Dublin, 1808
The Introduction is signed : E. O'C. *i.e.* Edmond O'Connell.

URANIA. [A poem. By Samuel MacArthur.] 8vo. [*Brit. Mus.*]
Edinburgh [1758]

URBAN Grandier, and other poems. By Louis Brand [Louisa Bigg]. 8vo. Pp. 88. [*Smith's Cat. of Friends' Books, Supp.* p. 58.] London, 1872

URBANÉ and his friends. By Cousin Susan [Mrs Elizabeth (Payson) Prentiss]. 12mo. New York, 1874

URIEL, and other poems. [By T. J. de Powis.] 8vo. Pp. 169. [*Reform Club Cat.*] London, 1857

URIEL ; or, the chapel of the angels. By the author of *Lady Glastonbury's boudoir*, etc. [Augusta Theodosia Drane]. 8vo. Pp. iv. 268. [*Brit. Mus.*] London, 1884

URIM and Thummim ; or, the apostolical doctrines of light and perfection maintained : against the opposite plea of Samuel Grevill (a pretended minister of the gospel) in his ungospellike discourse against a book, intituled, A testimony of the light within, anciently writ by Alexander Parker. By W. P. [William Penn]. 4to. 1674

URSULA ; a tale of country life. By the author of *Amy Herbert*, etc. [Elizabeth M. Sewell]. 8vo. 2 vols.
London, 1858
URSULA'S beginnings. [A tale.] By Howe Benning [Mary H. Henry]. 8vo. Pp. 256. [*Brit. Mus.*]
London [1884]
URSULA'S fortune. [A story.] By Esmé Stuart [Miss Amélie Claire Leroy]. 8vo. [*Who's Who in Lit.*]
London, 1886
U R S U L A'S love story. [By Mrs Gertrude Parsons.] 8vo. 3 vols.
London, 1869
US three. By E. A. B. D. [E. A. Bland]. 8vo. Pp. 190. [*Brit. Mus.*]
London [1885]
USAGE (the) of holding Parliaments and of preparing and passing bills of supply, in Ireland, stated from record. [By John Lodge.] 8vo.
Dublin, 1770
To which is added, Annotations, together with an address to His Excellency George Lord Viscount Townshend, lord lieutenant general and general governor of Ireland. By C. Lucas, M.D. one of the representatives of the city of Dublin, in Parlement. Dublin : reprinted 1770. 8vo. Pp. 76.

USE and abuse ; a tale. By the author of *Wayfaring sketches amongst the Greeks and Turks . . . By a seven years resident in Greece* [Felicia M. F. Skene]. 12mo. London, 1849
USE (the) and abuse of Parliaments, in two historical discourses. [Published and edited by James Ralph, architect. The first discourse was written by Algernon Sidney, the remaining portion of the work by Lord Polwarth, afterwards Earl of Macclesfield.] 8vo. 2 vols. [*W.*] London, 1744
USE (the) of catechisms further considered ; with a more full account of God's ambassadors, of saving faith, and of the faith of devils : in a letter to a friend. [By Rev. John Glas.] 12mo. Pp. 47. Edinburgh, 1737
See also the earlier print on " The usefulness of catechisms. . . ."

USE (the) of daily publick prayers, in three positions. [By Meric Casaubon.] 4to. Pp. 28. [*Bodl.*] London, 1641
USE (the) of reason recovered, by the data in Christianity : whereby we know the state we are in : that there are Elahim : what they have done for us : the state they offer us : the terms upon which they offer it : so we have evidence to reason upon, and may make a reasonable choice. By J. H. [John Hutchinson]. 8vo. [*Brit. Mus.*]
London, 1736

USE (the) of sunshine ; a Christmas narrative. By S. M. [Menella Bute Smedley], authoress of *The story of a family*, etc. 8vo. [*Nat. Lib. of Scot.*]
London, 1852
USE (the) of the hand camera ; with remarks upon larger apparatus. . . . By Clive Holland [Charles J. Hankinson]. 8vo. Pp. xx. 198. [*Brit. Mus.*]
London, 1898
USE (the) of the Lord's Prayer vindicated and asserted against the objections of innovators and enthusiasts ; from the French of Mons. D'Espagne [by Archibald Campbell, Scottish bishop]. 12mo. Pp. 48.
Edinburgh, 1688
USEFUL and important questions concerning Jesus the Son of God. . . . [By Isaac Watts, D.D.] 8vo. [*Cushing's Anon.*] London, 1746

USEFUL and ornamental planting. [By Mrs Jane C. Loudon, *née* Webb.] 8vo. London, 1832

USEFUL hints to the agricultural faction. . . . [By Rev. William Atkinson.] 8vo. Bradford, 1815

U S E F U L miscellanies ; or, serious reflections, respecting men's duty to God, and one towards another : with advices civil and religious, tending to regulate their conduct in the various occurrences of human life. Published for general service, by a well-wisher to all mankind [William Dover]. 8vo. [*Smith's Cat. of Friends' Books*, i. 59, 542.] London, 1739

USEFUL revelations of science and disinterested persons on promiscuous dancing. [By Rev. L. X. Fernando.] 16mo. Pp. 16. [*Brit. Mus.*]
Madras, 1897
USEFUL suggestions favourable to the comfort of the labouring people. . . . [By George Chalmers.] 8vo. [*Brit. Mus.*] Edinburgh, 1795

USEFUL transactions in philosophy, and other sorts of learning, for the months of January and February 1708$\frac{9}{10}$, to be continu'd monthly, as they sell. [By William King, LL.D.] 8vo. Pp. 63. [Arber's *Term Cat.* iii. 650.]
London [1709]
There were six numbers in all.

USEFULNESS (the) of catechisms considered, in a letter to a friend. [By Rev. John Glas.] 12mo. Pp. 34.
Edinburgh, 1736
See also a later print, " The use of Catechisms. . . ."

USQUE adeo ; or, what may be said for the Ionian people : being letters addressed to Lord John Russell, Earl Grey, Sir J. Pakington, and Sir H. Ward. . . . By an Ionian (G. D. P.) [G. D. Papanicolas]. 8vo. [*Brit. Mus.*] London, 1853

USURER (the) ; or, the departed not defunct : a comedy, in five acts. [By John Radcliffe Robins.] 8vo. London, 1833

USURER'S (the) daughter. By a contributor to *Blackwood's Magazine* [William Pitt Scargill]. 12mo. 3 vols. [*Brit. Mus.*] London, 1832

USURPATIONS (the) of France upon the trade of the woollen manufacture of England briefly hinted at ; being the effects of thirty years observations, by which that king hath been enabled to wage war with so great a part of Europe. By W. C. [William Carter, clothier]. 4to. [*W.; Brit. Mus.*] London, 1695

U S U R Y explain'd ; or, conscience quieted in the case of putting out mony at interest. By Philopenes [Jo. Huddleston, *alias* Dormer, S.J.]. 8vo. Pp. 8, 116. [*Bodl.*] London, 169⅝

UTAH and its people. By a Gentile [Dyer Daniel Lum]. 8vo. [*Brit. Mus.*] New York, 1882

UTI (the) possidetis, and Status quo : a political satire. [By James Sayers.] 8vo. [*Brit. Mus.*] London, 1807

UTILISATION (the) of the Church Establishment ; a letter . . . by the author of *The Pilgrim and the shrine* [Edward Maitland]. 8vo. [*Brit. Mus.*] Ramsgate, 1870

UTILITY (the) of agricultural knowledge to the sons of landed proprietors of Great Britain. . . . By a Scottish farmer and land-agent [John Claudius Loudon]. London, 1809

UTOPIA found ; being an apology for Irish absentees, addressed to a friend in Connaught. By an absentee, residing in Bath [Rev. Edward Mangin]. 8vo. [Green's *Bibl. Somers.* i. 334.] Bath, 1813

UTOPIA ; written in Latin by Sir Thomas More, Chancellor of England : translated in English [by Gilbert Burnet, Bishop of Salisbury]. 8vo. Pp. xxii. 206. [*W.*] London, 1685

UTRUM horum ; Rome or Geneva ; never a barrel better herring. [By John Gadbury.] 1668

UTRUM horum ? The government or the country ? [By Dennis O'Brien.] 8vo. [*Brit. Mus.*] [London, 1796]

V

V.C. (the) for valour ; a novel. By Dick Donovan [Joyce E. P. Muddock]. 8vo. London, 1898

VACATION (a) excursion from Massachusetts Bay to Paget Sound. By O. R. [Olive Rand]. 8vo. [Cushing's *Init. and Pseud.*] Manchester, New Hampshire, 1884

VACATION labors. By C. E. H. G. [Charles E. H. Gestrin]. 8vo. Montpelier, Vermont, 1879

VACATION rambles. [By James Augustus Atkinson.] 12mo. [*Brit. Mus.*] Manchester [1864]

VACATION trifles. By W. G. [William Gregory]. 8vo. Bath, 1880 (?)

VACATION verses. By two undergraduates [T. A. Bagge and G. R. Pardoe]. 8vo. [*Birm. Cent. Lib.*] Birmingham, 1910

VACCINATION and small-pox. By "Abdiel" [William Thomas Wiseman]. 8vo. Pp. 23. [*Brit. Mus.*] London, 1882

VADE mecum ; a manuall of essayes, morrall, theologicall : inter-woven with moderne obseruations, historicall, politicall. [By Daniel Tuvill.] 12mo. Pp. 6, 246. [*Bodl.*] London, 1629
To the reader, signed : Thine Anonym. Musophil.

VADE mecum ; goe with mee, deare pietie and rare charitie. By Otho Casmanne, preacher at Stoade. Translated out of Latine, by H. T. [Henry Tripp, M.A.], minister. 8vo. [*D. N. B.* vol. 57, pp. 2, 34.] London, 1606

VADE-MECUM (the) ; or, A B C guide to Denmark, Sweden, and Norway. By Elohta Ttenrub [Athole Burnett]. 8vo. London, 1875

VADE mecum ; or, the Fresher's A B C. By J. D. M. [John Dunning Macleod], and G. R. D. [Graham Richards Dawbarn]. 8vo. [*Camb. Univ. Lib.*] Cambridge, 1919

VADE-MECUM to Hatton; a poem. [By James Crossley.] 8vo.
Private print, 1867

VAGABOND and victor. By "Fleeta" [Kate W. Hamilton]. 8vo. [*Amer. Cat.*] Philadelphia, 1880

VAGABOND life in Mexico. By Gabriel Feny [Louis de Bellemare]. 8vo. [*Brit. Mus.*] London, 1856

VAGABOND (a) lover; a novel. By "Rita" [Eliza M. J. Gollan, later Mrs Booth, then Mrs W. Desmond Hamphreys]. 8vo. [*Who's Who in Lit.*] London, 1889

VAGABOND'S (a) note-book. By "Kuklos" [W. Fitzwater Wray]. 8vo. Pp. 232. [*Brit. Mus.*] London, 1908

VAGABUNDULI libellus; the Sea calls [and] Stella maris. [By John Addington Symonds.] 12mo. [*Book prices current,* 1922.] N.P., N.D.
Only a few copies privately printed.

VAGAMUNDS; or, the attaché in Spain. [By John Esaias Warren.] 8vo. [Cushing's *Init. and Pseud.*] New York, 1851

VAGARIES. By Puck Munthe [Axel Munthe]. 8vo. Pp. xiii. 308. [*Brit. Mus.*] London, 1893

VAGARIES in verse. By the author of *An essay on light reading* [Rev. Edward Mangin]. 8vo. [Green's *Bibl. Somers.* i. 335.] London, 1835

VAGARIES (the) of a pen, in prose and verse. By Versatilius [Alexander Watt]. 12mo. London, 1874

VAGRANT viator; Erin-go-Bragh. [Verse.] By Verbosoperegrinubiquitos [Thomas Newton]. 8vo. [*Brit. Mus.*] London, 1885

VAGRANT (a) wife. [A novel.] By Florence Warden [Florence Alice Price, later Mrs George E. James]. 8vo. [*Brit. Mus.*] London, 1885

VAGROM verses. By John Paul [Charles Henry Webb]. 8vo. [Cushing's *Init. and Pseud.*] Boston, 1888

VAIL (the) family; or, doing good. By Theodelinda [Mrs Charles E. Kelsey]. 8vo. [Cushing's *Init. and Pseud.*] Philadelphia, 1862

VAIN boastings of Frenchmen, the same in 1386 as in 1798; being an account of the threatened invasion of England by the French the 10th year of King Richard II: extracted from ancient chronicles. [By Craven Ord.] 8vo. Pp. 15. [*Bodl.*] London, 1798

VAIN (a) thing. [A novel.] By Guy Thorne [Cyril A. E. Ranger-Gull]. 8vo. [*Who's Who in Lit.*] London, 1907

VAIN worship and worshipers detected. . . . [Epistle signed J. H. *i.e.* John Humphrey?] 8vo. London, 1675

VALAZY (the) family, and other narratives. By "Waters" [William Russell]. 8vo. [*Brit. Mus.*] London [1870]

VALDARNO; or, the ordeal of art worship. [By Thomas Gordon Hake, M.D.] 8vo. [Courtney's *Secrets,* p. 99.] London, 1842
A later edition of "Vates; or, the philosophy of madness."

VALE (the) of Apperley, and other poems. [By William Greenwood.] 8vo. [*Camb. Univ. Lib.*] Malton, 1822

VALE (the) of Chamouni; a poem. By the author of *Rome* [John Chaloner, Captain in H.M. 36th Regt.]. 8vo. [*N. and Q.* 5th March 1864, p. 204.] 1822

VALE (the) of Glamorgan; scenes and tales among the Welsh. [By Charles Redwood.] 8vo. [*Brit. Mus.*] London, 1839

VALE (the) of Trent; a poem. [By John Moore Stone.] 12mo. Birmingham, 1801

VALENTINE; a story of ideals. By Curtis Yorke [Mrs S. Richmond Lee]. 8vo. Pp. 304. [*Who's Who in Lit.*] London, 1909

VALENTINE Duval; an autobiography of the last century. . . . [By Anne Manning.] 8vo. London, 1860

VALENTINE'S day; a musical drama, in two acts: as it is performed at the Theatre Royal in Drury-Lane. [By William Heard.] 8vo. [Baker's *Biog. Dram.; Mon. Rev.* liv. 341.] London, 1776

VALERIA; a story of Venice. [By Eleanor Lloyd.] 8vo. [*Brit. Mus.*] London, 1879

VALERIE Aylmer. [A novel.] By Christian Reid [Frances Fisher, later Mrs James M. Tiernan]. 8vo. [Cushing's *Init. and Pseud.*] New York, 1877

VALERIE; or, half a truth. By "The Duchess" [Mrs Maggie Argles]. 8vo. Pp. 220. [*Who's Who in Lit.*] New York, 1888

VALERIE'S fate; and other stories. By Mrs Alexander [Mrs Alexander Hector, *née* Annie French]. 12mo. [*Who's Who in Lit.*] London, 1885

VALERIUS; a Roman story. [By John Gibson Lockhart.] 8vo. 3 vols. Edinburgh, 1821

VALETE, Fratres. [Verses]; dedicated to his fellow-students by the author of *Dulce Cor* [Samuel R. Crockett]. 4to. [*D. N. B.* 1912-21.] Private print, 1886

VALETTA; a novel. By the author of *Denton Hall* [—— Cross]. 8vo. 3 vols. London, 1851

VALIANT (the) knight; or, the legend of St Peregrine. [By Charles Cotton.] 8vo. [*D. N. B.* vol. 12, p. 301.]
London, 1663

VALIANT (the) Welshman; or, the true chronicle history of the life and valiant deedes of Caradoc the Great, King of Cambria, now called Wales: as it hath beene sundry times acted by the Prince of Wales his seruants. Written by R. A. Gent. [Robert Armin]. 4to. No pagination. [*Brit. Mus.*]
London, 1615

VALIDITY (the) of baptism administred by dissenting ministers, and the unreasonableness of refusing burial to children so baptiz'd; first offer'd to the consideration of a dissenting congregation, at two publick baptisms, on the occasion of that new notion, denying all such to be Christians, who have been baptiz'd by persons not episcopally ordain'd. . . . By a Presbyter of the Church of Christ [Ferdinand Shaw]. 8vo. Pp. 22. [*Cresswell's Printing in Nottinghamshire.*]
Nottingham, 1713
Ascribed also to James Peirce.

VALIDITY (the) of the orders of the Church of England made out against the objections of the Papists, in several letters to a gentleman of Norwich, that desired satisfaction therein. [By Dr Humphry Prideaux.] 4to. [*Queen's Coll. Lib.*] London, 1688

VALLEY (the) of a hundred fires. By the author of *Margaret and her bridesmaids*, etc. [Mrs Julia C. Stretton]. 8vo. 3 vols. [*D. N. B.* vol. 36, p. 219.]
London, 1860
Mistakenly attributed to Mrs Anne Marsh-Caldwell and to Henrietta Keddie.

VALLEY (a) of diamonds. By Crona Temple [Miss Corfield]. 8vo.
London, 1883

VALLEY (the) of the Rea. By V. author of *IX. poems*, etc. [Mrs Archer Clive]. 12mo. London, 1851

VALLEY (the) of Sapphires. [A novel.] By Mayne Lindsay [Mrs Clarke]. 8vo. Pp. 312. [*Who's Who in Lit.*]
London, 1899

VALLEY (a) of shadows. [A novel.] By George Colmore [Gertrude Dunn, afterwards Baillie-Weaver]. 8vo. 2 vols. [*Brit. Mus.*] London, 1892

VALLEY (the) of the squinting windows. By Brinsley Macnamara [A. E. Weldon]. 8vo. Pp. 296. [*Brit. Mus.*]
London [1928]

VALLIS Vale; and other poems. By the author of *The Juvenile poetical moralist* [Elizabeth Tuck]. 8vo. [*Brit. Mus.*] London, 1823

VALOUROUS (a) and perillous seafight; fought with three Turkish ships, pirats or men of warre on the coast of Cornwall (or westerne part of England) by the good ship named the Elizabeth of Plimmouth, she being of the burthen of 200 tuns, which fight was bravely fought, on Wednesday the 17 of June last past, 1640. [By John Taylor.] 4to. [Davidson's *Bibl. Devon.* p. 61.]
London, 1640

VALPERGA; or, the life and adventures of Castruccio, prince of Lucca. By the author of *Frankenstein* [Mrs Mary W. Shelley]. 12mo. 3 vols. [Courtney's *Secrets*, p. 60.]
London, 1823

VALUE (the) of a child; or, motives to the good education of children: in a letter to a daughter. [By John Taylor, Dissenting teacher.] 12mo. [Chalmers' *Biog. Dict.; Mon. Rev.* v. 461.] 1751

VAMPIRE (the); a tragedy [in five acts]. By St John Dorset [Rev. Hugo John Balfour]. 8vo. [*Brit. Mus.*]
London, 1821
Attributed also to Geo. Stephens.

VAMPIRES; Mademoiselle Réséda. [Two stories.] By Julien Gordon [Mrs Julia Grinnell Cruger]. 8vo. Pp. 299. [*Camb. Univ. Lib.*]
London, 1891

VAMPYRE (the): a tale. By the Right Honourable Lord Byron. [Really by John William Polidori.] 8vo. [*Dyce Cat.* ii. 385.] London, 1819

VAN Diemen's Land; comprehending a variety of statistical and other information likely to be interesting to the emigrant. [By Henry Melville.] 12mo. [*Sydney Lib. Cat.*]
Hobart Town, 1833

VAN Patten. [A novel.] By B. M. Bower [Bertha Muzzy Sinclair]. 8vo. Pp. vi. 289. [*Brit. Mus.*]
Boston, 1926

VAN Suyden sapphires. By Charles Carey [Charles Carey Waddell]. 8vo. [*Amer. Cat.*] New York, 1905

VANDA. [A tale.] By Esmé Stuart [Miss Amélie Claire Leroy]. 8vo. [*Who's Who in Lit.*] London, 1881

VANDELEUR; or, animal magnetism: a novel. [By Madame Pisani.] 12mo. 3 vols. London, 1836

VANESSA. [By Mrs Margaret Agnes Paul, *née* Colville.] The second edition. 8vo. 2 vols. [*Brit. Mus.*]
London, 1878

VANISHED (the) Empire. By B. L. Putnam Weale [Bertram Lenox Simpson]. 8vo. Pp. ix. 379. [*Brit. Mus.*]   London, 1926

VANISHED (a) lady. [A novel.] By Sarah Tytler [Henrietta Keddie]. 8vo. [*Who's Who in Lit.*]   London, 1908

VANISHED (the) moor. By John Trevena [Ernest George Henham]. 8vo. Pp. 256.   London, 1923

VANISHED (the) pomps of yesterday ; being some random reminiscences of a British diplomat [Lord Frederick Spencer Hamilton]. 8vo. [*Camb. Univ. Lib.*]   London, 1919

VANISHING Aberdeen. [By Dr Alexander Cruickshank.] 4to. [Mitchell and Cash's *Scot. Top.* i. 24.]
                          Aberdeen, 1894

VANITAS ; polite stories. By Vernon Lee [Violet Paget]. Pp. vi. 276. [*Brit. Mus.*]   London, 1892

VANITIE (the) of self-boasters ; or, the prodigious madnesse of tyrannizing Sauls, mis-leading Doegs (or any others whatsoever) which peremptorily goe on, and atheistically glory in their shame and mischiefe. In a sermon preached at the funerall of John Hamnet, Gent. late of the parish of Maldon in Surrey. By E. H. minister of the same, and late Fellow of Merton Colledge in Oxford [Edward Hinton]. 4to. Pp. 52. [*Bodl.*]   London, 1643

VANITY (the) box. [A novel.] By Alice Stuyvesant [Mrs C. N. Williamson]. 8vo. [*Amer. Cat.*]
                          New York, 1911

VANITY Church. [By J. M. Whitelaw?] 8vo. 2 vols.   London, 1861

VANITY Fair album ; a show of sovereigns, statesmen, etc. : with biographical and critical notices. By " Jehu Junior" [Thomas Gibson Bowles]. Fol.   1862-89

VANITY Fair cartoons ; a series of fifty-one coloured portrait cartoons of princes, statesmen, and leading men of the day. . . .   By "Spy" [—— Leslie], with biographical and critical notices by "Jehu Junior" [Thomas Gibson Bowles]. Fol. London, 1894

VANITY (the) of honour, wealth, and pleasure ; with the indispensable duty of amendment of life. By J. H. [Joseph Halsey, M.A.]. 12mo. [Arber's *Term. Cat.*]   London, 1678

VANITY (the) of humane inventions ; in an exercitation on the ceremonies. [By John Willson, minister of Backford, Cheshire.] 12mo. [Cooke's *Bibl. Centr.*]   1666

VANITY (the) of scoffing ; or, a letter to a witty gentleman, evidently shewing the great weakness and unreasonableness of scoffing at the Christian's faith, on account of its supposed uncertainty : together with the madness of the scoffers unchristian choice. [By Clement Ellis, M.A., rector of Kirkby, Nottinghamshire.] 4to. Pp. 38. [*Bodl.* ; Wood's *Athen. Oxon.* iv. 517.]
                          London, 1674
   Ascribed to John Fell, Bishop of Oxford. [*W. ; Brit. Mus.*]

VANITY (the) of the creature. By the author of *The whole duty of man* [Richard Altestree, D.D.]. 8vo. [*Brit. Mus.*]   London, 1684

VANITY (the) of the life of man ; represented in the seven several stages thereof, from his birth to his death : with pictures and poems exposing the follies of every age : to which is added, several other poems upon divers subjects and occasions. By R. B. [Richard or Robert Burton, *i.e.* Nathaniel Crouch]. 12mo. Pp. 30.
                          London, 1688

VANITY ! the confessions of a Court modiste. By "Rita" [Eliza M. J. Gollan, later Mrs Booth, then Mrs W. Desmond Humphreys]. 8vo. [*Who's Who in Lit.*]   London, 1901

VANITY verses. [By Nathaniel Morton Safford.] 8vo. [Cushing's *Anon.*]
                          New York, 1877

VANQUISHED ; a novel. By Mollie Myrtle [Agnes Leonard, later Mrs Hill]. 8vo.   New York, 1866

VARIETIE (the) ; a comedy, lately presented by his Majesties servants at the Black-Friers. [By William Cavendish, Duke of Newcastle.] 12mo. Pp. 87. [*Bodl.*]   London, 1649

VARIETIES. By a wanderer [Arthur Moberley, formerly of St Petersburg]. [*Brit. Mus.*]   London, 1849

VARIETIES in verse. By Sigma [John Begg Shaw, M.A., barrister]. 12mo.
                          London, 1879

VARIETIES of literature, from foreign literary journals and original MSS. now first published. [By William Tooke.] 8vo. 2 vols. [Nichols' *Lit. Anec.* ix. 159.]   London, 1795

VARIETIES of Whist. By Aquarius [Lowis d'Aguilar Jackson]. 8vo. [*Brit. Mus.*]   London, 1888

VARIETY ; a collection of essays : written in the year 1787. [By Humphrey Repton]. 8vo. Pp. viii. 297. [Watt's *Bibl. Brit.*]   London, 1788
   Attributed also to Ann Seward.

VARIETY; a comedy, in five acts: as it is performed at the Theatre-Royal in Drury Lane. [By Richard Griffith]. 8vo. Pp. 71. [Baker's *Biog. Dram.*]
London, 1782

VARIETY: a tale, for married people. [By William Whitehead.] 4to. Pp. 24. [Watt's *Bibl. Brit.*]
London, 1776

VARIOUS accounts of the great convulsion at Axmouth in Devonshire, etc. [Edited by J. H. Hallett.] 8vo. [Davidson's *Bibl. Devon.* p. 118.]
Exeter, 1840

VARIOUS ironic and serious discourses on the subject of physick. . . . [By Dennis De Coetlogon.] 8vo. 7 parts. [*Brit. Mus.*] London, 1749
Various tracts published separately, with a comprehensive title prefixed.

VARIOUS (the) lives of Marcus Igoe. By Brinsley Macnamara [A. E. Weldon]. 8vo. Pp. 282. [*Brit. Mus.*] London, 1929

VARIOUS prospects of mankind, nature and providence. [By Robert Wallace, D.D.] 8vo. [M'Culloch's *Lit. of Pol. Econ.* p. 257.] London, 1761

VARNISHANDO; a serio-comic poem: addressed to collectors of paintings. By an admirer of the arts [Francis Duckinfield Astley]. 8vo. [*Biog. Dict.* 1816; *Brit. Crit.* xxxiii. 632.]
Manchester, 1809
Attributed also to George Charles Vernon, 4th Baron Vernon. [*Brit. Mus.*]

'VARSITY Bloods. By " Growler " [B. B. Watson]. 8vo. [Bartholomew's *Camb. Books.*] Cambridge, 1900

'VARSITY verses, light blue and dark. By H. D. C. [Harry Debron Catling]. 8vo. [*Camb. Univ. Lib.*]
Cambridge, 1901

'VARSITY versicles. By W. H. [William Charles Hennessy]. 8vo. [O'Donoghue's *Poets of Ireland.*]
Dublin, 1879

VASCONSELOS; a romance of the New World. By Frank Cooper [William Gilmore Simms, LL.D.]. 8vo. [Foley's *Amer. Authors.*]
New York, 1885

VASHTI Savage. [A novel.] By Sarah Tytler [Miss Henrietta Keddie]. 8vo. Pp. 320. [*Who's Who in Lit.*]
London, 1897

VAST (the) expense of ignorance to the Queen's subjects. By the oldest School Inspector [Joseph Bentley]. 8vo. [*Brit. Mus.*] London [1870]

VASTY (the) deep; a strange story of to-day. By Stuart C. Cumberland [Charles Garner, of Oxford]. 8vo. 2 vols. [*Brit. Mus.*] London, 1889

VATES : or, the philosophy of madness; being an account of the life, actions, passions, and principles of a tragic writer. [By Thomas Gordon Hake, M.D.] 4to. [Courtney's *Secrets*, p. 99.]
London, 1840
Title afterwards changed to "Valdarno ; or the ordeal of art worship."

VATICAN (the) Council; eight months at Rome during the Vatican Council: impressions of a contemporary. By Pomponio Leto [Cardinal Vitelleschi]. Translated from the original. 8vo. Pp. xx. 340. London, 1876
Although the above work was prepared for the press, and edited by the Marchese Vitelleschi, there is no doubt that the real author was the Cardinal who was present at the Council, and kept a journal of the proceedings. See *The Church Quarterly Review*, July, 1876.

VATICANISM ; or, papal floundering and blundering. [By A. Polhausen.] 8vo. Pp. 16. [*Brit. Mus.*]
Manchester [1875?]

VATICANISM unmasked ; or, Romanism in the United States. By a puritan of the nineteenth century [Rev. Joseph Warren Alden]. 8vo. [Kirk's *Supp.*] Cambridgeport, Mass., 1877

VATICINIUM votivum ; or, Palaemon's prophetick prayer : lately presented privately to His now Majestie in a Latin poem, and here published in English. . . . [By George Wither.] 8vo. [*D. N. B.* vol. 62, p. 264.]
Trajecti [1649]

VAUCENZA ; or, the dangers of credulity. [A novel. By Mrs Mary Robinson, *née* Darby.] 8vo. [*D. N. B.* vol. 49, p. 32.] London, 1792

VAUDEVILLES and other things. By Bunny [Carl Emil Schultze]. 8vo.
New York, 1900

VAURIEN; or, sketches of the times ; exhibiting views of the philosophies, religions, politics, literature, and manners of the age. [By I. Disraeli.] 12mo. 2 vols. London, 1797

VAUXHALL (the) affray ; or, the Macaronies defeated ; being a compilation of all the letters, squibs, etc., on both sides of that dispute. [By Rev. H. Bate Dudley.] 8vo. [Dobell's *Cat.*] London, 1773

VAYENNE. [A novel.] By Christian Lys [Percy John Brebner]. 8vo. [*Amer. Cat.*] New York, 1908

VEGETABLE life; an illustrated natural history reader. By N. D'Anvers [Nancy R. E. Bell, *née* Meugens]. 8vo.
London [1883]

VEGETABLE physiology. Part I. [By John Lindley.] Second edition. 8vo. [*Brit. Mus.*]   London, 1827
Library of Useful Knowledge. No more published.

VEGETABLE substances used for the food of man. [By Dr Edwin Lankester.] 12mo. 2 vols. [*W.*]
London, 1846

VEIL (the) of glamour. [A novel.] By Clive Arden [Lily Clive Nutt]. 8vo. Pp. 356. [*Publishers' Weekly*, 28th Aug. 1926.]   London, 1926

VEIL (a) of gossamer; being some reflections. By Roland Saint-Clair [Roland Sinclair Watson]. 8vo. Pp. 15. [*Brit. Mus.*]   London, 1916

VEIL (the) withdrawn; or, apostacy the result of hypocrisy. . . . [By John Williams, of Bury.] 12mo. [*Brit. Mus.*]   London, 1831

VEILED (the) figure, and other poems. [By Dorothy Hollins.] 8vo.
London, 1895

VEILED (the) lady. [A novel.] By Hatherly Sealis [Charles Freeman Foster]. 8vo. [*Amer. Cat.*]
New York, 1905

VEILED (the) lady. [A novel.] By Florence Warden [Florence Alice Price, later Mrs James]. 8vo. Pp. 318. [*Who's Who in Lit.*]
London, 1909

VEILED (the) lady; a romance. By May Wynne [Mabel Wynne Knowles and Draycott M. Dell]. 8vo. Pp. viii. 286. [*Brit. Mus.*] London [1918]

VEILED (the) man. [A historical romance.] By Owen Rhoscomyl [Owen Vaughan]. 8vo. [*Brit. Mus.*]
London, 1898

VELASQUEZ; his life and work. [By P. G. Konody.] Fol. [*Birm. Ref. Lib.*]   London, 1903

VELINA; a poetical fragment. [By Andrew Macdonald.] 8vo. [Chalmers' *Notes; Mon. Rev.* lxvii. 470.]
London, 1782

VELITATIONES polemicæ; or, polemicall short discussions of certain particular and select questions. By I. D. Phil-Iren-Alethius [John Doughtie, Fellow of Merton]. 8vo. Pp. 335. [Wood's *Athen. Oxon.* iii. 977.]
London, 1651

VELLA Vernell; or, an amazing marriage. By Hattie Hateful [Mrs Sumner Hayden]. 8vo.
New York, 1887

VELOCIPEDE (the); its past, its present, and its future. By J. F. B. [Joseph Firth Bottomley]. 8vo. Pp. 108. [Smith's *Cat. of Friends' Books*, *Supp.* p. 64.]   London, 1896

VELVET (the) cushion. [By Rev. John W. Cunningham, Vicar of Harrow.] 8vo. Pp. 68. [*D.N.B.* vol. 13, p. 314.]
London, 1814
Frequently reprinted. A counter publication is "A new covering to the Velvet cushion" [by John Styles].

VELVET (the) glove. [A novel.] By Henry Seton Merriman [Hugh Stowell Scott]. 8vo. Pp. 125. [*Who's Who in Lit.*]   London, 1901

VENDALO (the) lost property office. By the author of *Copsley annals*, etc. [Emily S. Elliott]. 8vo. [*Bodl.*]
London, 1870

VENERABLE (the) Bede expurgated, expounded, and exposed. By the Prig [Thomas Longueville]. 12mo. [*Brit. Mus.*]   London, 1886

VENETIA. By the author of *Vivian Grey* and *Henrietta Temple* [Benjamin Disraeli, Lord Beaconsfield]. 12mo. 3 vols.   London, 1837
Dedication to Lord Lyndhurst signed: Δ.

VENETIAN (the) bracelet, The lost Pleiad, A history of the lyre, and other poems. By L. E. L., author of the *Improvisatrice, The Troubadour*, and *The golden violet* [Letitia Elizabeth Landon]. 8vo.   London, 1829

VENETIANS (the); a novel. By the author of *Lady Audley's secret*, etc., [Mary Elizabeth Braddon, later Mrs John Maxwell]. 8vo. 3 vols. [*Brit. Mus.*]   London, 1892

VENETIA'S lovers; an uneventful story. By Leslie Keith, author of *Surrender*, etc. [Grace Leslie Keith Johnston]. 8vo. 3 vols.   London, 1884

VENGEANCE (the) of Fionn; poems. By Austin Clare [Miss W. M. James]. 8vo. [*Who's Who in Lit.*]
Dublin, 1917

VENGEANCE (the) of Friedrich Bahl. [A novel.] By Prudens Futuri [Nelly Davidson]. 8vo. Pp. 319. [*Brit. Mus.*]   Antwerp, 1925

VENI, vidi, vici; the triumphs of Oliver Cromwell: written originally in Latine [by Payne Fisher], and faithfully done into English heroicall verse by T. M. [Thomas Manly or Manley]. 4to. Pp. 93. [Thomason's *Coll. of Tracts*, i. 860.]   London, 1652

VENICE; a poem written for the Chancellor's medal. By T. E. H. [Thomas Edwards Hankinson, M.A.]. 8vo. Pp. 19.   Cambridge, 1826

VENICE under the yoke of France and of Austria; with memoirs of the courts, governments, & people of Italy; presenting a faithful picture of her present condition, and including original anecdotes of the Buonaparte family. By a lady of rank [Catherine Hyde, Marchioness Broglio Solari]. . . . 8vo. 2 vols. [*Nat. Lib. of Scot.*]
London, 1824

VENTA, and other poems. By the author of *Pericula urbis* [Rev. William Moore, rector of Appleton]. 8vo. Pp. 3, 133. [Crockford's *Clerical Directory.*]   London, 1882

VENUS and Cupid; or, a trip from Mount Olympus to London. . . . By the author of *The fight at Dame Europa's school* [Henry William Pullen]. 8vo. Pp. 314. [*Brit. Mus.*]
London, 1896

VENUS in the cloister; or, the nun in her smock. [Translated by Robert Samber from the French of l'Abbé Barrin, *i.e.* l'Abbé Duprat.] 8vo. [Straus' *The Unspeakable Curll; Barbier.*]   London, 1724

VENUS of Cadiz. By Richard Fisguill [Richard H. Wilson]. 8vo. [*Amer. Cat.*]   New York, 1905

VERA. By the author of *Elizabeth and her German garden* [Mary Beauchamp, later Countess Russell]. 8vo. Pp. 365. [*Brit. Mus.*]   London, 1921

VÉRA. By the author of *The hôtel du Petit St Jean* [Charlotte Louisa Hawkins Dempster]. 8vo. Pp. viii. 289.   London, 1871

VERA in poppyland. By Vera [Mrs A. Berlyn]. 8vo.   London, 1892

VERBA Verbi Dei; the words of our Lord and Saviour Jesus Christ, harmonized by the author of *Charles Lowder* [Miss Maria French]. 8vo. Pp. 200.   London, 1894

VERBALIST (the); a manual devoted to brief discussions of the right and the wrong use of words. . . . By Alfred Ayres [Thomas Embley Osmun]. 8vo. Pp. 220. [*Brit. Mus.*]
New York, 1882

VERBEIA; or, Wharfdale: a poem, descriptive and didactic: with historical remarks. [By Thomas Maude.] 4to. [*Mon. Rev.* lxix. 167.]   1783
The edition of 1782 mentioned in Upcott, p. 1410, is not anonymous.

VERDICT (the) of you all. By Henry Wade [Henry Lancelot Aubrey-Fletcher]. 8vo. Pp. 254. [*Amer. Cat.*]   London, 1926

VERDICT (the) upon the dissenters plea, occasioned by their Melius inquirendum [by Vincent Alsop]; to which is added, a letter from Geneva to the Assembly of Divines. . . . [By Lawrence Womock, D.D., Bishop of St David's.] 8vo. Pp. 281, 45. [*Bodl.*]
London, 1681

VERDICTS [on the poets of the times—Moore, Lamb, Scott, Rogers, Hood, Shelley, &c. By James Thomas Fields]. 8vo.   London, 1852

VERITAS evangelica; or, the Gospel-truth asserted in sixteen useful questions, which, being seriously searched into, will open the way to find out assuredly the true and saving faith of Christ. . . . Written by T. K. [Thomas Kemeys, Romish priest]. 4to. Pp. 110. [*Gillow's Bibl. Dict.*]
London, 1687

VERITAS in semente; being a moderate discourse concerning the principles and practices of the Quakers: written long since (as they then appeared to the author) in a Middle Way between them and the followers of orthodox truth, that the well-meaning among them might come over to it. . . . [By John Humphrey.] 8vo. Pp. 284. [Smith's *Anti-Quak.* p. 241.]   London, 1705

VERITIES in verses; combining Mottoes and motives, Brotherhood, fellowship and acting together, New Covenant ordinances and order. [By Robert A. Macfie, of Dreghorn.] Second edition, to which are added Jubilee and other rhymings. 8vo. 4 parts.   London, 1888
Presentation copy.

VERMONTERS unmasked. . . . By a citizen of the United States [Charles Phelps]. 8vo. [Evans' *Amer. Bibl.* vol. 6, p. 182.]   New York, 1782

VERNAL (the) walk; a poem. [By Ebenezer Elliott.] 8vo. [Watkins' *Life of Elliott; Mon. Rev.* xxxv. 109.]
London, 1801

VERNER Galbraith's wife. [A novel.] By Derek Vane [Mrs Eaton Back]. 8vo. [*Lit. Year Book.*]
London, 1894

VERNON-IAD (the); done into English from the original Greek of Homer, lately found at Constantinople. [By Henry Fielding. A satire on Edward Admiral Vernon.] 4to. [*Brit. Mus.*]
London, 1741

VERONICA; a novel. By the author of *Aunt Margaret's trouble* [Frances Eleanor Trollope]. 8vo. 3 vols. [*Brit. Mus.*]   London, 1870

VERS de société, and parody. By H. A. Page [Alexander Hay Japp]. 8vo. [*Brit. Mus.*]   London, 1883

VERS de societè; historical fragments, sonnets, etc. [By M. Joseph Denison, M.P.] 8vo. 2 vols. [Martin's *Cat.*]
London, 1849

VERSAILLES; and other poems. [By Colonel William Read.] 8vo. [O'Donoghue's *Poets of Ireland.*]
Belfast, 1821

VERSATILE verses on the 'Varsity, etc. By two Bachelors [H. D. Catling and A. W. Burke Peel]. 8vo. [Bartholomew's *Camb. Books*, p. 256.]
Cambridge, 1896

VERSE. By C. C. [Charles Chorley, journalist]. 8vo. [F. Boase's *Mod. Eng. Biog.* i. 614.]   Truro, 1867

VERSE. By H. W. P. [Henry Webster Parker]. 8vo. [*Brit. Mus.*]
Boston, 1862

VERSE translations from the German, including Bürger's Lenore, Schiller's Song of the Bell, and other poems. [By William Whewell, D.D.] 8vo. Pp. vi. 87. [*D. N. B.* vol. 60, p. 462.]
London, 1847

VERSES. [By J. R. Finlay.] 8vo. Pp. 41.   Private print, 1874
"Nearly all the following pieces were written more than twenty years ago.— J. R. F."

VERSES. [By Sir Ambrose Hardinge Giffard, LL.D., Chief Justice of Ceylon.] 8vo. [O'Donoghue's *Poets of Ireland.*]   Colombo, 1822

VERSES. [By Sir William Cusack Smith, Bart.] 8vo. [*D. N. B.* vol. 53, p. 156.]   Dublin, private print, 1830

VERSES. By A. C. Q. W. [Mrs Ann C. (Quincey) Waterston]. 12mo. [Cushing's *Init. and Pseud.*]
Boston, 1863

VERSES [chiefly hymns]. By a country curate [Rev. John William Hewett, M.A.]. 12mo. Pp. 172. [Julian's *Dict. of Hymnology.*]   London, 1859

VERSES. By A. G. [Alfred Gurney]. 8vo.   Private print, 1868

VERSES. By A. J. G. D. [Anna Julia Grant Duff]. 8vo. Pp. 47. [*Brit. Mus.*] [Edinburgh, private print] 1882

VERSES. By a Maynooth student [Eugene Higgins]. 8vo. [O'Donoghue's *Poets of Ireland.*]
Dublin [1885?]

VERSES. By E. D. W. [Elizabeth DickinsonWest [later Mrs E. Dowden]. 12mo. [O'Donoghue's *Poets of Ireland.*]   Dublin, 1876
A second series appeared in 1883.

VERSES. By "Euoe" [Trevor Mansell]. 8vo. Pp. 20.   Abergavenny [1896]

VERSES. By H. H. [Mrs Helen Maria Jackson, *née* Hunt]. 12mo.
Boston, 1874

VERSES. By J. G. [Mrs Jane Gurney, *née* Birkbeck]. 8vo.
Private print, 1890

VERSES. By L. M. L. [Lady —— Lushington].   Maidstone, 1880

VERSES. By M. T. [M. Tennant]. 8vo. Pp. 192.
Glasgow, private print, 1866

VERSES. By Susan Coolidge [Sarah Chauncey Woolsey]. 12mo.
Boston, 1880

VERSES. By two children [Elaine and Dora Goodale]. 12mo. [Cushing's *Init. and Pseud.*]   New York, 1878

VERSES addressed to Lady Brydges, in memory of her son Edward William George Brydges. [By Sir Samuel Egerton Brydges.] 4to. Pp. 8. [*W.*]
Lee Priory, private print, 1816

VERSES addressed to Sir G. O. Paul on the improvement of County prisons. [By James Dallaway.] 4to. [*Gloucester Pub. Lib.*]   Gloucester, 1785

VERSES addressed to [Alexander Pope] the imitator of the first satire of the second book of Horace. By a lady [Lady Mary Wortley Montagu]. Fol. [*Brit. Mus.*]   London [1733]

VERSES addressed to the ladies of Stockton. [By Joseph Ritson.] 12mo. [*Brit. Mus.*]   [Newcastle? 1780?]

VERSES and opinions. By Matthew Browne [William Brighty Rands]. 8vo. [F. Boase's *Mod. Eng. Biog.* iii. 34.]   London, 1866

VERSES and re-verses. By II [Wilfrid Meynell]. 8vo. Pp. 48.
Cambridge, 1912

VERSES and translations. By C. S. C. [Charles Stuart Calverley]. 8vo. Pp. vi. 203.   Cambridge, 1862

VERSES at random. By "Thistle" [M. C. Anderson]. 8vo.
Paisley [*c.* 1900]

VERSES, chiefly devotional. By Martha W[hewell, later Mrs Statter]. Now collected and arranged by a sorrowing sister [Ann Whewell, later Mrs Newton]. 8vo. Pp. xi. 138. [Bowes' *Cat. of Camb. Books.*]
Cambridge, 1863
A short note is added, signed "W. W." [William Whewell, D.D.].

VERSES, edited by M[ilitia] M[ea] M[ultiplex] [William Tooke, solicitor]. 8vo. Pp. 31. [*D. N. B.* vol. 57, p. 51.]
London, private print, 1860
Verses relating to Tooke's family, etc., by various persons, chiefly himself.

VERSES for children. [By Jane Bragg.] 12mo. Pp. 31. [Smith's *Cat. of Friends' books*, i. 312.]
Carlisle, 1862

VERSES for holy seasons; with questions for examination. By C. F. H. [C. F. Alexander]. Edited by Walter Farquhar Hook, D.D., vicar of Leeds. 8vo. Pp. xi. 232.   London, 1846

VERSES for penitents. [By John Henry Newman, D.D.] 12mo. [*D. N. B.* vol. 40, p. 349.]   Private print, 1860

VERSES for the people. By a rhymer [Thomas Bell, of Fifeshire]. 12mo.
Glasgow, 1844

VERSES for the Sundays and holidays of the Christian year. [By Esther Wigglesworth.] 12mo. London, 1863

VERSES from a mother's corner. By Mrs George Archibald [Anna Campbell, later Mrs George Archibald Palmer]. 8vo.   Boston, 1889

VERSES from Japan. [By George William Thomson. Reprinted from the *Japan Weekly Mail*.] 8vo. Pp. 59. [*Brit. Mus.*]   London, 1878

VERSES humbly addressed to Sir Thomas Hanmer on his edition of Shakspeares works. By a gentleman of Oxford [William Collins]. Fol. [Lowndes' *Bibl. Man.* p. 2314.]
London, 1743

VERSES in memory of Dunbar Collegiate Church. [By George Miller, bookseller.] 8vo. Pp. iv. 40. [Couper's *Millers of Haddington*.]
Edinburgh, 1819
Afterwards included in "St Baldred of the Bars" (1824).

VERSES, miscellaneous and grave. By Fred. H. [Frederick Holland]. 8vo.
Edinburgh, 1881

VERSES, mostly written in India. By G. H. T. [George Herbert Trevor]. 8vo.   London, 1878

VERSES occasioned by reading some strictures on Barclay's Apology. [By Joseph Beck.] 8vo. [Smith's *Cat. of Friends' Books*, i. 73.]   1785

VERSES occasioned by seeing the Palace and Park of Dalkeith anno MDCCXXXII. [By S. Boyse.] Humbly inscribed to his Grace the Duke of Buccleugh. 8vo. Pp. 14.
Edinburgh, 1732

VERSES of a collegian. [By Edwin J. Gerstle.] 8vo. [*Lib. Journ.* xiv. 59.]
New York, 1885

VERSES of other days; printed for friends. [By Abraham Hayward, barrister.] 12mo.   N.P., 1847
Presentation copy from the author. Later issue in 1878.

VERSES of six generations [mostly by Rev. John Mason Neale, D.D.]; edited by M. S. L. 8vo.   Bristol, 1907

VERSES on Dr Mayhew's book of Observations on the character and conduct of the Society for the propagation of the Gospel in foreign parts; with notes. . . . By a gentleman of Rhode-Island Colony [John Aplin, lawyer]. 8vo. Pp. 19. [*Evans' Amer. Bibl.*]
Providence, New England, 1763

VERSES on Her Majesty's birthday, May 19, 1784. [By Anthony Freston (formerly Brettingham), M.A.] 4to. Pp. 18. [*Bowes' Cat. of Camb. Books*, p. 491.]   London, 1784

VERSES on religious subjects [including translations of Latin Hymns. By John Henry Newman, D.D.]. 12mo. Pp. 141. [*Brit. Mus.*]   Dublin, 1853

VERSES on Sir Joshua Reynolds's painted window at New College, Oxford. [By Thomas Warton.] 4to. [*Gent. Mag.* lii. 342.]   1782

VERSES on the celestial sphere. By O. H. [Holt Okes]. 4to. Pp. 14. [*Brit. Mus.*]   London [1910]

VERSES on the death of Dr Samuel Johnson. [By Thomas Percy, LL.D., Fellow of St John's College, Oxford, nephew of the Bishop of Dromore.] 4to. Pp. 16. [*Gent. Mag.* May 1808, p. 470.]   London, 1785

VERSES on the sonship of Christ. . . . [By Rev. John Stevens.] 8vo. [*Brit. Mus.*]   London, 1812
Another edition, with fuller title ("Verses on the sonship and pre-existence of Jesus Christ. . . .") and otherwise enlarged, appeared in 1846.

VERSES on various occasions. [By John Henry Newman, D.D., Cardinal.] 8vo. [*D. N. B.* vol. 40, p. 349.]
London, 1868

VERSES, sacred and miscellaneous. By Harriet [Harriet White, of Cashel]. [*Olphar Hamst*, p. 5.]   1853

VERSES, sacred and profane. By Seumas O'Sullivan [James Starkey]. 12mo. [O'Donoghue's *Poets of Ireland*.]   Dublin, 1908

VERSES spoken at the Encæna. By Mr Smith, Demy of Magdalen College, Oxford [Rev. Walter Birch, B.D.]. 8vo.   Oxford, 1810

VERSES spoken to the King, Queen, and Dutchesse of Yorke in St John's library in Oxford. [By Thomas Laurence.] 4to. Pp. 2. [*Bodl.*]
N.P., N.D.
"These verses were spoken by Thom. Laurence a gent. com. of St John Coll— Afterwards Fellow of Univ. coll."—MS. note by Wood.

VERSES to a lady of quality. . . . [By John Lockman.] 4to. [*Brit. Mus.*]
London, 1741

VERSES to order. By A. G. [Alfred Denis Godley]. 8vo. Pp. 69.
London, 1892

A new and enlarged edition, 1904, gives the author's name.

VERSES to the memory of a brother. [By William Laurence Brown, D.D. Principal of Marischal College, Aberdeen.] 8vo. Pp. 15. [*D. Laing.*]
N.P. [1784]

VERSES to the memory of Garrick; spoken as a monody at the Theatre Royal in Drury Lane [by Richard Brinsley Sheridan]. Second edition. 4to. [*Quaritch's Cat.*] London, 1779

VERSES to the memory of Lord Nelson, and in commemoration of the glorious victory obtained . . . 21st Oct. 1805. [By Thomas Crichton.] 12mo. [*Brit. Mus.*] Paisley, 1805

VERSES to the Right Rev. Father in God, Edward, Lord Bishop of Durham; with an essay towards restoring the original texts of Scripture and reconciling the Hebrew and Septuagint, by the Oriental languages, Fathers, &c. [By John Mawer, M.A.] 8vo. Pp. 27. [*Davies' Mem. of the York Press*, p. 182.]
London, 1731

VERSES; with imitations and translations. By A. M. W. [Mrs Ann M. Wood]. London, 1842

VERSES written in the portico of the Temple of Liberty at Woburn Abbey. . . . [Introduction signed : J. H. W. *i.e.* Jeremiah H. Wiffen.] 4to. Pp. 39. [*Brit. Mus.*]
London, private print, 1836

VERSES written in Westminster Abbey, after the funeral of the Right Hon. Charles James Fox, October 10, 1806. [By Samuel Rogers.] 4to. [*Brit. Mus.*] London [1806]

VERSES written on several occasions, between the years 1712 and 1721. [By Sir Thomas Burnet.] 4to.
London, 1777

VERSICLES from the portfolio of [Robert Rockliff] a Sexagenarian. . . . 16mo. [*Brit. Mus.*] Liverpool, 1862

VERSIFICATION (a) of President Washington's excellent farewell address to the citizens of the United States. By a gentleman of Portsmouth, N.H. [Jonathan Mitchell Sewall]. 8vo. [*Cushing's Init. and Pseud.*]
Portsmouth, N.H., 1798

VERSION (a) of the Psalms of David, attempted to be closely accommodated to the text of Scripture ; and adapted, by variety of measure, to all the music used in the versions of Sternhold and Hopkins, and of Brady and Tate. By a lay-member of the Church of England [John Stow, of Greenwich]. 12mo. Pp. xix. 7, 704. [*Brit. Mus.*]
London, 1809

VERSION (a) of the Psalms; with a comprehensive selection of hymns, chosen from the best authors. [By C. Bassano.] 12mo. [*Brit. Mus.*]
Leamington, 1826

VERSUS inopes rerum, nugæque canoræ; commonly call'd Poems on several occasions. [By Soame Jenyns.] 8vo. Pp. xii. 106. [*Brit. Mus.*]
London [1730?]

VERTUES due; or, a true modell of the life of . . . Katharine Howard, late Countess of Nottingham, deceased. By T. P. [Thomas Powell, attorney]. 8vo. London, 1603

Reprinted by the Roxburghe Club, 1881.

VERTUES encomium ; or, the image of honour. [By Richard Niccolls.] 4to.
London, 1614

Reprinted in the Harleian Miscellany, vol. 10.

VERTUMNUS ; an epistle [in verse] to Mr Jacob Bobart. By the author of *The apparition* [Abel Evans]. 8vo. [*Watt's Bibl. Brit.*] Oxford, 1713

VERTUOUS (the), holy, christian life and death of the late Lady Lettice, Vicountess Falkland, with some additionals. [By John Duncon.] 12mo. [*W.; Brit. Mus.*] London, 1653

VERTUOUS (the) wife is the glory of her husband; or, a good woman in her proper colours. . . . By L. P. [Lawrence Price?] a well-wisher to all good women. 8vo. Pp. 21. [*Brit. Mus.*] London, 1667

VERULAMIANA ; or, opinions on men, manners, literature, politics, and theology, by Francis Bacon, Baron of Verulam, &c. &c. To which is prefixed a life of the author, by the editor [P. L. Courtier]. 12mo. [*Lowndes' Bibl. Man.* p. 97.] London, 1803

VERY (a) brief memoir of dear H.ᵉB. By her brother [Edward W. Barlow, M.A.]. 12mo. Woburn [1840]

VERY genteel. [A novel.] By the author of *Mrs Jerningham's journal*, etc. [Mrs Hart, *née* Fanny Wheeler]. 8vo. Pp. 318. [*Brit. Mus.*] London, 1880

VERY (a) godly and learned exposition, vpon the whole Booke of Psalmes ; wherein is contained the diuision and sense of euery Psalme : as also manifold, necessary and sound doctrines, gathered out of the same, all seruing for the great furtherance and instruction of euery Christian reader. . . . [By Thomas Wilcocks.] 4to. Pp. 600. [*Bodl.*] London, 1591

Epistle dedicatory signed : T. W.

VERY (a) plain state of the case ; or, the Royalty Theatre versus the Theatres Royal. . . . [By George Colman.] 8vo. London, 1787

VERY (a) rough diamond. [A novel.] By Florence Warden [Florence Alice Price, later Mrs George E. James]. 8vo. [*Who's Who in Lit.*] London, 1905

VERY (the) short memory of Mr Joseph Scorer, and other seaside experiences. By John Oxenham [William Arthur Dunkerley]. 12mo. Pp. 184. [*Who's Who in Lit.*] London, 1903

VERY (a) simple story. . . . [By Florence Montgomery.] 4to. [*Nat. Lib. of Scot.*] Sleaford, 1867

VERY (a) woman. [By Menella Bute Smedley.] 8vo. [*Brit. Mus.*] London, 1846

VERY (a) young couple. By the author of *Mrs Jerningham's journal* [Mrs Hart, *née* Fanny Wheeler]. 8vo. [*Camb. Univ. Lib.*] London [1874]

VESPERS (the) of Palermo ; a tragedy. By F. B. [Felicia Browne, later Mrs Hemans]. 8vo. [*Brit. Mus.*] London, 1823

VESPERTILIA, and other verses. By Graham R. Tomson [Mrs Rosamund M. Watson]. 8vo. Chicago, 1895

VESPERTINA. By A. H. B., commoner of St John's College, Oxford [A. H. Baldwin]. 8vo. Pp. viii. 118. [*F. Madan.*] Oxford, 1853

VESTA. By Mrs Hester Benedict [Mrs T. P. Dickinson]. 8vo. [*Cushing's Init. and Pseud.*] Philadelphia, 1872

VESTIGES of civilization ; or, the ætiology of history, religious, æsthetical, political, and philosophical. [By Robert Henry Shannon, *or* James O'Connell.] 8vo. New York, 1851

VESTIGES of the natural history of creation. [By Robert Chambers, LL.D.] Eleventh edition ; illustrated by numerous engravings on wood. 8vo. Pp. iv. 286, lxiv. London, 1840

In reply to numerous criticisms, the author published, anonymously also, " Explanations, a sequel . . ." (1845.)
See also "An expository outline . . ."

VESTIGIA. [A novel depicting Italian life at Leghorn.] By George Fleming [Julia Constance Fletcher]. 12mo. 2 vols. [*Who's Who in Lit.*] London, 1884

VETERAN (the) ; or, matrimonial felicities. [A novel. By Edward Harley.] 8vo. 3 vols. [*Camb. Univ. Lib.*] London, 1819

VETERANS (the) of Chelsea Hospital. By the author of *The subaltern* [George Robert Gleig]. 12mo. 3 vols. London, 1842

VETERES vindicati, in an expostulatory letter to Mr Sclater of Putney, upon his Consensus Veterum &c.; wherein the absurdity of his method, the weakness of his reasons are shewn, his false aspersions upon the Church of England are wiped off, and her faith concerning the Eucharist proved to be that of the primitive Church : together with animadversions on Dean Boileau's French translation of, and remarks upon Bertram. [By Edward Gee.] 4to. [*D. N. B.* vol. 21, p. 107.] London, 1687

VETERINARY (the) surgeon ; or, farriery taught on a new and easy plan. By John Hinds [John Badcock, *or* John Bell]. London, 1827

VETO (the) church ; or, what is nonintrusion. [By Robert Lee, D.D.] 8vo. Edinburgh, 1844

VIA dolorosa ; being the Catholic devotion of the stations ; prepared as a special office for the use of English people, with reference to the sins, the responsibilities, and the portents of these times ; translated and arranged by the author of *From Oxford to Rome*, etc. [E. F. S. Harris]. 8vo. London, 1848

Preface signed : E. F. S. H.

VIA Hudson's Bay. By Stuart Cumberland [Charles Garner, of Oxford]. 8vo. [London, 1905]

VIA lucis ; a novel. . . . By Kassandra Vivaria [Miss Magda Sindici, later Mrs Heinemann]. 8vo. Pp. 480. [*Brit. Mus.*] London, 1898

VIA (the) media ; or, Anglican orthodoxy. By a member of the Oxford Convocation [John Hippisley]. 8vo. Pp. 53. London, 1838

VIA, veritas, vita ; discursive notes on preaching and on some types of the Christian life. By a Presbyter [Rev. Peter Barclay, M.A.]. 8vo. Pp. 94. London, 1881

Published in 1882, with the author's name, with the title—"The Way, the Truth, and the Life."

VIAGGIANA ; or, detached remarks on the buildings, pictures, statues, inscriptions, &c. of ancient and modern Rome. [By Stephen Weston.] 12mo. Pp. iv. 181. [*Dyce Cat.* ii. 417.]
London [1776]

VIATOR, a poem ; or, a journey from London to Scarborough, by the way of York : with notes historical and topographical. [By Thomas Maude.] 4to. Pp. 40, xix. [Boyne's *Yorkshire Lib.* p. 128.]   London, 1782

VIATOR Christianus ; or, the Christian traveller ; by Thomas of Kempis. Translated from the original Latin . . . [by Miles Pinkney, *alias* Thomas Carre]. 8vo. [Gillow's *Bibl. Dict.*]
Paris, 1653

VIC ; the autobiography of a Pomeranian dog ; a true story. [By A. C. Fryer.] 8vo. Pp. 92. [*Brit. Mus.*]
Manchester, 1880

VICAR (the) of Charles ; a poem in commemoration of Plymouth's great preacher [Robert Hawker] in a preceding age. . . . [By Joseph Plimsoll.] 8vo. Pp. 38. [*Brit. Mus.*]
Plymouth, 1868

VICAR (the) of Wakefield ; a tale, supposed to be written by himself. [By Oliver Goldsmith.] 12mo. 2 vols. [*Book prices current*, 1922.]
Salisbury, 1766
First edition ; many later editions bear the author's name.

VICAR'S (the) atonement. By Claud Heathcote [James Harwood Panting]. 8vo. [*Who's Who in Lit.*]
London, 1900

VICAR'S (the) trio ; a story. . . . By Esmé Stuart [Miss Amélie Claire Leroy]. 8vo. Pp. 274. [*Who's Who in Lit.*]   London [1890]

VICAR'S (the) will and codicil. [By William Cooper, of Kirby Wisk.] 8vo.   Newcastle, private print, 1824
A reprint of "The will of a certain northern vicar" (London, 1765). Ascribed also to Rev. John Ellison.

VICE triumphant ; or, the world run mad : a satyre. [By Robert Cockburn.] 8vo. Pp. 15.   Edinburgh, 1719

VICE versâ ; or, a lesson to fathers. By F. Anstey [F. Anstey Guthrie]. New and revised edition. 8vo. Pp. vi. 371.   London, 1883

VICEROY (the) ; a poem addressed to the Earl of Halifax. [By John Langhorne, D.D.] 4to. Pp. xi. 11. [*Watt's Bibl. Brit.*]   London, 1762

VICEROY (the) of Catalonia ; or, the double cuckhold. [By Gabarel de Bremond.] Made English by James Morgan, Gent. 12mo. Pp. 155.
London, 1678

VICES in virtues ; and other vagaries. By the author of *The life of a prig* [Thomas Longueville]. 8vo. Pp. 104. [*Brit. Mus.*]   London, 1913

VICISSITUDES (the) of Bessie Fairfax. By Holme Lee, author of *Basil Godfrey's caprice*, etc. [Harriet Parr]. 8vo. 3 vols.   London, 1874

VICISSITUDES (the) of commerce ; a tale of the cotton trade. [By Thomas Greenhalgh.] 12mo. 2 vols.
London, 1852
Mistakenly attributed to Thomas Hall. This work was revised and reissued, with the author's name (Liverpool, 1854), as "Lancashire life ; or, the vicissitudes of commerce . . ."

VICISSITUDES (the) of Darley. Part I. Philip Colborne's love matters. By Hans Kiste [John Box]. 8vo. Pp. 88. [*Brit. Mus.*]   London [1890 ?]

VICISSITUDES of life ; exemplified in the interesting memoirs of a young lady, in a series of letters. [By Jane West.] 12mo. 2 vols. London, 1815

VICISSITUDES (the) of life ; or, the balloon : a Canterbury tale for young persons. [By Mrs Cumming.] 8vo. [*Brit. Mus.*]   Canterbury, 1845

VICTIM (the) ; a tragedy [in five acts and in verse]. Written by Mr [Charles] Johnson [on the basis of Jean Racine's *Iphigénie*]. 12mo. [*Brit. Mus.*]
London, 1714

VICTIM (the) of fancy. By a lady, author of *The conquests of the heart* [Elizabeth Sophia Tomlins]. 12mo. 2 vols. [*Mon. Rev.* xxvii. 331 ; lxxvi. 446.]   London, 1787

VICTIM (a) of the Falk Laws ; the adventures of a German priest in prison and in exile, told by the victim [Frederick Mills Raymond Barker, of Oriel College]. 8vo.   London, 1879

VICTIMS. [A novel.] By Theo Gift [Dorothea Hamilton Havers, later Mrs Boulger]. 8vo. [*Who's Who in Lit.*]   London, 1887

VICTOR Pelham's love-story. By Bertha M. Clay [Charlotte M. Braeme]. 8vo. [*Brit. Mus.*]   London, 1911

VICTORIA. By "Grapho" [James Alonzo Adams]. 8vo. [*Amer. Cat.*]
Chicago, 1901

VICTORIA ; or, the heiress of Castle Cliffe. By May Carleton [May Agnes Fleming]. 8vo. [*Brit. Mus.*]
New York [1864 ?]

VICTORIA Bess ; or, the ups and downs of a doll's life. By Brenda [Mrs Castle Smith]. 8vo. [*Brit. Mus.*]
London [1880 ?]

VICTORIA Britannia ; plan for cele-
brating the reign of Queen Victoria by
the inauguration of political changes
in the British constitution. By Hollis
True [T. C. Chegwidden]. 12mo.
                          New York, 1879
VICTORIA (the) Cross ; how it was
won, how it was lost, and how it came
back again. By Morice Gerard [Rev.
John Jessop Teague]. 8vo. Pp. 156.
[*Who's Who in Lit.*]   London, 1892

VICTORIA, Queen of England ; her
girlhood and womanhood. By Grace
Greenwood [Mrs Sara Jane Lippincott].
8vo. [*Who's Who in Lit.*]
                          London, 1884
VICTORIA, the British Eldorado ; or,
Melbourne in 1869 : showing the
advantages of that Colony as a field
for emigration. By a Colonist of
twenty years' standing [C. R. Carter].
12mo. [*Lib. of Col. Inst.* i. 127.]
                          London, 1870
VICTORIAD (the) ; or, the New World :
an epic and illustrative lay . . . of the
Victorian era. By an old looker-on of
change [Edmund Carrington]. 8vo.
[Kirk's *Supp.* i. 297.]   London, 1861

VICTORIAISM ; or, a re-organization
of the people : moral, social, economical, and political : suggested as a
remedy for the present distress :
respectfully addressed to the Right
Hon. Sir Robert Peel, Bart. [By
William C. Coward.] 8vo. [*Camb.
Univ. Lib.*]   London, 1843
Signed : W. C. C.

VICTORIAN novelists. By Lewis Melville [Lewis Samuel Benjamin]. 8vo.
Pp. 334. [*Brit. Mus.*] London, 1906

VICTORIES (the) of the British armies;
with anecdotes illustrative of modern
warfare. By the author of *Stories of
Waterloo*, etc. [William Hamilton
Maxwell, rector of Ballagh, Connaught].
8vo. 2 vols.   London, 1839

VICTORIES (the) of Wellington and
the British armies. By the author of
Stories of Waterloo, etc. [William
Hamilton Maxwell]. 8vo. [*Brit. Mus.*]
                          London, 1852
VICTORIOUS (the) stroke for old
England ; all preachers make all
hearers one man against her enemies
and down Jericho, etc. [By John
Henley.] Third edition. 8vo. Pp. 54.
[*Brit. Mus.*]   London, 1748

VICTORIOUS (a) union. By Oliver
Optic [William T. Adams]. 8vo.
Pp. 361. [*Amer. Cat.*] Boston, 1893

VICTORS (the). By Luke Sharp
[Robert Barr]. 8vo. [*Who's Who
in Lit.*]   London, 1902

VICTORY ; an island tale. By Joseph
Conrad [Joseph Conrad Korzeniowski].
8vo. Pp. 424.   London, 1915

VICTORY (the) ; and other stories. By
A. L. O. E., author of *Fairy Frisket*,
etc. [Charlotte Maria Tucker]. 8vo.
Pp. 64.   London, 1875

VICTORY (the) murders. By Foster
Johns [Gilbert Seldes]. 12mo. Pp. 304.
[*New York Evening Post, Lit. Rev.*
9th April 1927.]   New York, 1927

VICTORY (the) of suffering ; a prize
poem, recited in Rugby School, June 10,
1842. [By John Conington.] 8vo.
Pp. 11. [*Brit. Mus.*]   Rugby, 1842

VICTORY (the) of the vanquished ; a
tale of the first century. By the author
of *Chronicles of the Schönberg-Cotta
family*, etc. [Mrs Elizabeth Charles,
née Rundle]. 8vo. Pp. 458.
                          London, 1871
VICTORY (the) that overcometh. By
H. A. D. [Helen A. Dallas]. 8vo.
                          London, 1901
VICTORY ! Victory ! [By Amelia M.
Hull.] 8vo. [*Brit. Mus.*]
                          London, 1864
" VICTORY (the) won"; a brief memorial
of the last days of G. R. [By Miss
Catherine Marsh.] Second edition.
8vo. Pp. 84. [*Brit. Mus.*]
                          London, 1855
Preface signed : W. M. *i.e.* William
Marsh.

VIDA ; study of a girl. By Amy Duns-
muir [Amy M. Oliphant, later Smith].
8vo. 2 vols.   London, 1880

VIENNA. Noe art can cure this hart ;
wherein is storied yᵉ valorous atchieve-
ments . . . of St Paris of Vienna, and
the . . . Faire Vienna. By M. M.
[Mathew Mainwaringe]. 4to. [*Brit.
Mus.*]   London [1650]
Wrongly attributed to Richard Mynshull.

VIERA ; a romance 'twixt the real and
the ideal. By Rob. Appleton [Roman
I. Zubof]. 8vo.   New York, 1890

VIEW (a) of a printed book [by Henry
Parker] intituled Observations upon
His Majesties late answers and ex-
presses. [By Sir John Spelman.] 4to.
Pp. 45. [*Bodl.*]   Oxford, 1642
Author's name in the handwriting of
Barlow.

VIEW (a) of an ecclesiastick in his socks and buskins ; or, a just reprimand given to Mr [Vincent] Alsop for his foppish, pedantick, detractive and petulant way of writing. [By Robert Ferguson]. 4to. [*Brit. Mus.*]
London, 1698

VIEW (a) of antient history ; including the progress of literature and the fine arts. By William Rutherford, D.D. master of the academy at Uxbridge. [In reality by John Logan, minister of Leith.] 8vo. 2 vols.
London, 1788-93

VIEW (a) of antiquity. See "ΑΡΧΑΙΟΣ-ΚΟΠΙΑ."

VIEW (a) of certain wonderful effects of late dayes come to passe, and now newly conferred with the presignifica-tions of the comete . . . which appered . . . the x day of Novem . . . 1577. Written by T. T. [Thomas Twyne?]. 4to. B. L. [*Brit. Mus.*]
London, 1578

VIEW (a) of Christianity, containing a short account of religion from the creation to the end of the 4th cent. ; with the complete duty of a Christian : laid down in two catechisms. [By Thomas Deacon.] 8vo. [*Lathbury's Nonjurors.*]   1747

  The second edition, 1748, has the title : "A view of Christianity, succinctly and fully laid down in two catechisms."

VIEW (a) of Fraunce. [By Sir Robert Dallington.]   4to.   No pagination. [*Brit. Mus.*]   London, 1604

VIEW (a) of French literature during the eighteenth century. [By Baron Brugière de Barante.] Translated. .8vo. [*Brit. Mus.*]   London, 1814

VIEW (a) of life in its several passions. [By James Fortescue, D.D.] 8vo. [*Brit. Mus.*]   Oxford, 1749

VIEW (a) of Lord Bolingbroke's philo-sophy, compleat, in four letters to a friend ; in which his whole system of infidelity and naturalism is exposed and confuted : with the apology pre-fixed. [By William Warburton, D.D.] The third edition. 12mo. Pp. xlviii. 335. [*Bodl.*]   London, 1756

VIEW (a) of many errors and some gross absurdities in the old translation of the Psalms in English metre ; as also in som other translations lately published : shewing how the Psalms ought to be translated, to be accept-able and edifying. . . . By W. B. [William Barton], M.A. and minister of the Gospel. 4to. Pp. 6, 18.
London, 1654

VIEW (a) of real grievances, with remedies proposed for redressing them; humbly submitted to the consideration of the legislature. [By —— Powell.] 8vo. [*Queen's Coll. Lib.; Mon. Rev.* xlviii. 19.]   London, 1772

VIEW (a) of society and manners in France, Switzerland, and Germany ; with anecdotes relating to some emi-nent characters. By a gentleman who resided several years in those countries [John Moore, M.D.]. 8vo. 2 vols.
London, 1779

VIEW (a) of some exceptions which have beene made by a Romanist to the Lord Viscount Falkland's Discourse of the infallibilitie of the Church of Rome. Submitted to the censure of all sober Christians ; together with the Dis-course it selfe of infallibilitie prefixt to it. [By Henry Hammond, D.D.] 4to. Pp. 4, 204.   Oxford, 1646

VIEW (a) of Stourton Gardens with strictures on a late abusive Ode upon the same subject ; somewhat, it is said, in imitation of Horace, Book II, Ode 13. [By Rev. John Chapman.] 8vo. Pp. 11. [*W.; Upcott.*] [*c.* 1810]

VIEW (a) of the advantages of inland navigations ; with a plan of a navigable canal intended for a communication between the ports of Liverpool and Hull. . . . [By R. Whitworth.] 8vo. Pp. 40. [*Manch. Free Lib.*]
London, 1765

VIEW of the agriculture of Oxfordshire, drawn up for the Board of Agriculture and internal improvement. By the secretary to the Board [Rev. Arthur Young]. 8vo. [*W.*]   London, 1809

VIEW (a) of the art of colonization. . . . [By Edward Gibbon Wakefield.] 8vo. [*D. N. B.* vol. 58, p. 450.] London, 1849

VIEW (a) of the British Empire, more especially Scotland ; with some pro-posals for the improvement of that country, the extension of its fisheries, and the relief of the people. [By John Knox, bookseller.] 8vo.
London, 1784
  The author's name appears in the third edition, 1785.

VIEW (a) of the Christian religion. By one of the people [William Godson]. 8vo. Pp. 37. [*Brit. Mus.*]
Liverpool [1864 ?]
  Preface signed : W. G.

VIEW of the conduct of the English clergy, as relates to civil affairs. [By Sir Edmund Thomas.] 8vo. [*Leslie's Cat.* 1843 (414).]   1737

VIEW (a) of the controversy between Great-Britain and her colonies; including a mode of determining their present disputes, finally and effectually; and of preventing all future contentions: in a letter to the author of A full vindication of the measures of the Congress, from the calumnies of their enemies. By *A. W.* Farmer, author of *Free thoughts*, etc. [Dr Samuel Seabury, Bishop of Connecticut]. 8vo. Pp. 90. [*Bodl.*]
New-York, printed: London reprinted, 1775

VIEW (a) of the Court of St Germain, 1690 to 1695; with an account of the entertainment Protestants meet with there. [By John Macky.] 4to. Pp. 32. [*Times Lit. Supp.* 28th June 1928.]
London, 1696

VIEW (a) of the Dissertation upon the Epistles of Phalaris, Themistocles, &c. lately publish'd by the Reverend Dr Bentley; also of the examination of that Dissertation by the Honourable Mr Boyle: in order to the manifesting of the incertitude of heathen chronology. [By Rev. John Milner, B.D.] 8vo. Pp. 87. [Bartholomew's *Bibl. of Bentley*, p. 31.]   London, 1698

VIEW (a) of the *Edinburgh Review*; pointing out the spirit and tendency of that paper. [By Edward Johnston, minister at Moffat.] 8vo.
Edinburgh, 1756

VIEW (a) of the elections of bishops in the primitive Church; wherein is shewed, what were the several shares of the bishops, inferior clergy and people in these elections: as also, of the Emperors, after they became Christians: and the nature of the Church, its unity and government are likewise explained. By a presbyter of the [Episcopal] Church of Scotland [James Dundass]. 8vo. Pp. 242.
Edinburgh, 1728

VIEW (a) of the English acquisitions in Guinea and the East Indies; with an account of the religion, government, wars, strange customs, etc. . . . By R. B. [Richard Burton, *alias* Nathaniel Crouch]. 12mo. [*Brit. Mus.*]   London, 1686

VIEW (a) of the English Constitution; a translation of Montesquieu's sixth chapter of the eleventh book of *L'Esprit des loix*. [By Baron Francis Maseres.] 8vo. [*D. N. B.* vol. 36, p. 409.]   London, 1781

VIEW of the evidence for proving that the present Earl of Galloway is the lineal heir male and lawful representative of Sir William Stuart of Jedworth, so frequently mentioned in history from the year 1385 to the year 1429. [Drawn up by Rev. E. Williams, his lordship's chaplain.] 4to. [*W.*] 1796

VIEW (a) of the gold coin and coinage of England from Henry the Third to the present time, with copper plates. [By Thomas Snelling.] Fol. Pp. iv. 36. [*W.*]   London, 1763

VIEW (a) of the heresy of Aerius; consisting of the following articles. . . . [By Rev. John Glas.] 8vo. Pp. 59. [Glas' *Works*, 1782.] Edinburgh, 1745

VIEW (a) of the internal evidence of the Christian religion. [By Soame Jenyns.] 8vo. [*D. N. B.* vol. 29, p. 333.]   London, 1776

VIEW (a) of the internal policy of Great Britain. [By Robert Wallace, D.D.] 8vo. Pp. xxiii. 288. [*Brit. Mus.*]
London, 1764

VIEW (a) of the Iewish religion; containing the manner of life, rites, ceremonies and customs of the Iewish nation throughout the world at this present time: together with the articles of their faith, as now received. Faithfully collected by A. R. [Alexander Ross]. 8vo. Pp. 427. [Lowndes' *Brit. Lib.* p. 1253.]   London, 1656

VIEW (a) of the Lancashire dialect, by way of dialogue; to which is added, a glossary of all the Lancashire words and phrases therein used. By T. Bobbin, Opp'n Speyker o' th' Dialect [John Collier, of Milnrow]. 12mo. [*W.*]   Manchester [1746]

VIEW (a) of the life of King David; wherein are observations on divers historical passages therein recited. [By W. Skilton, horologist, *i.e.* Peter Annett?] 8vo. Pp. 38. [*Brit. Mus.*]
London [1768]

VIEW (a) of the naval force of Great Britain; in which its present state, growth, and conversion of timber: construction of ships, docks and harbours; regulations of officers and men in each department, are considered and compared with other European powers. . . . By an officer of rank [Sir John Borlase Warren]. 8vo. Pp. 203, 74. [Watt's *Bibl. Brit.*; *Mon. Rev.* vi. 221.]   London, 1791

VIEW (a) of the necessitarian or best scheme; freed from the objections of M. Crousaz, in his examination of Mr Pope's Essay on Man. [By William Dudgeon.] 8vo. Pp. 25.
London, 1739

VIEW (a) of the new directorie, and a vindication of the ancient liturgie of the Church of England; in answer to the reasons pretended in the ordinance and preface, for the abolishing the one, and establishing the other. [By Henry Hammond, D.D.] The third edition. 4to. Pp. 120. Oxford, 1646

> Wrongly assigned to Henry Jeanes. First edition, 1645.
>
> An edition, said to be the third, with some variations was printed at Oxford, by the same printer [Henry Hall], in the same year, with a different pagination.

VIEW (a) of the political state of Scotland at Michaelmas 1811; comprehending the rolls of the freeholders, an abstract of the setts or constitutions of the royal burghs, and a state of the votes at the last elections throughout Scotland: to which is prefixed an account of the forms of procedure at elections to parliament from the counties and burghs of Scotland. [By James Bridges, W.S.] 8vo. [Watt's *Bibl. Brit.*] Edinburgh, 1812

VIEW (a) of the political state of Scotland at the late general election; containing, an introductory treatise on the election laws, lists of the peers, and the procedure at their late election, with the effect of their protests, the rolls of the freeholders of Scotland, an abstract of the sets of the Royal boroughs, and the names of their delegates, &c. &c. . . . [By Alexander Mackenzie.] 8vo. Edinburgh, 1790

VIEW (a) of the present state and future prospects of the free trade and colonization of India. [By John Crawfurd.] 8vo. [M'Culloch's *Lit. of Pol. Econ.* p. 110.] London, 1829

VIEW of the present state of affairs in the kingdom of Ireland; in three discourses, viz. I. A list of the absentees of Ireland. [By Thomas Prior.] . . . 8vo. [*Brit. Mus.*] London, 1730

VIEW (a) of the present state of Ireland; with an account of the origin . . . of the disturbances in that country. . . . By an Observer [Denis O'Bryen]. 8vo. London, 1797

VIEW (a) of the present state of the Dutch settlements in the East Indies. By a person long resident in India [Philippe Firmin, M.D.]. 8vo. [*Christie-Miller Cat.*] 1780

VIEW (a) of the principal courts of the Isle of Man. [By James Clarke.] 8vo. Liverpool, 1817

VIEW (a) of the real danger of the Protestant succession. [By Daniel Defoe.] 8vo. Pp. 46. London, 1714

VIEW of the real power of the Pope, and of the power of the priesthood over the laity; with an account how they use it. [By Thomas Hawkins.] 8vo. Pp. 520. [Leslie's *Cat.* 1841.] London, 1733

> Ascribed also to T. Hart, T. Haddon and T. Hutchinson.

VIEW (a) of the reign of Henry the III.; shewing the danger of the subjects' arrogancy, the methods of great men's rise and fallings, the wrong the King and his subjects suffer from evil counsellors. . . . [By Sir Robert Cotton.] 4to. [Arber's *Term Cat.* i. 543.] London, 1682

> See also "A short view of the reign of King Henry III. . . ."

VIEW (a) of the relative situation of Great Britain and the United States of America. By a merchant [Henry M. Bird]. 8vo. [Sabin's *Dict.*] London, 1794

VIEW (a) of the relative situations of Mr Pitt and Mr Addington, previous to, and on the night of, Mr Patten's motion. By a member of parliament [Robert Plumer Ward]. Second edition. 8vo. [Pellew's *Life of Sidmouth*, ii. 146; *Mon. Rev.* xliii. 328.] London, 1804

VIEW (a) of the rise, progress, and present state of the tea-trade in Europe. [By Robert Wissett.] 8vo. [*Brit. Mus.*] [London, 1801]

VIEW of the Romish hydra and monster, traison against the Lord's Anointed; condemned by David, 1 Sam. 26, and nowe confuted in seven sermons, to perswade obedience to princes, concord among ourselves, and a general reformation and repentance in all states. [By Laurence Humphrey.] 12mo. B.L. [Wood's *Athen. Oxon.*] Oxford, 1588

VIEW (a) of the Scots rebellion; with some inquiry into what we have to fear, from the rebels? and what is the properest method to take with them? [By Daniel Defoe.] 8vo. Pp. 40. [Lee's *Defoe*, 171.] London, 1715

VIEW (a) of the Scripture revelations concerning a future state; laid before his parishioners by a country pastor [Richard Whately]. 12mo. Pp. 322. [Darling's *Cyclop. Bibl.*] London, 1829

VIEW (a) of the several schemes with respect to America, and their comparative merit in promoting the interest and dignity of Great Britain. [By Capel Lofft.] 8vo. Pp. 55. [Rich's *Bibl. Amer.* i. 468.] 1776

VIEW (a) of the silver coin and coinage of England, from the Norman Conquest to the present time ; considered with regard to type, legend, sorts, rarity, weight, fineness and value. [By Thomas Snelling.] 4to. [*W.* ; *Brit. Mus.*]
London, 1762

VIEW (a) of the soul, in several tracts. The first, being a discourse of the nature and faculties, the effects and operations, the immortality and happiness of the soul of man. The second, a cordial against sorrow, or a treatise against immoderate care for a man's own posterity, and grief for the loss of children. The third consists of several epistles to the Reverend John Tillotson, D.D. and Dean of Canterbury, tending to the further illustration of the former arguments concerning the soul of man, and the proof of a particular providence over it. By a person of quality [R. Saunders]. Fol. [Lowndes' *Brit. Lib.* p. 804.]
London, 1682

VIEW (a) of the stage. By —— Wilkes [Samuel Derrick]. 8vo. [*D.N.B.* vol. 14, p. 399.]
London, 1759

VIEW (a) of the state of religion in the diocese of St David's about the beginning of the eighteenth century; with some account of the causes of its decay, together with considerations of the reasonableness of augmenting the revenues of impropriate Churches. By E. S. [Erasmus Saunders] D.D. 8vo. Pp. 128. [Darling's *Cyclop. Bibl.*]
London, 1721

VIEW (a) of the times, their principles and practices, in the Rehearsals. By Philalethes [Charles Leslie]. Fol. [Darling's *Cyclop. Bibl.*] 1708-9
Second edition in 6 vols. 12mo. London, 1750.

VIEW (a) of the Treaty of Commerce with France, signed at Versailles, Sept. 20 [rather, 26] 1786, by Mr Eden. [By Dennis O'Bryen]. 8vo. Pp. viii. 127. [*Brit. Mus.*]
London, 1787

VIEW of the Valley of the Mississippi. By R. B. [Robert Baird]. 12mo. [*Brit. Mus.*]
Philadelphia, 1834

VIEW (a) of the whole controversy between the Representer and the Answerer, with an answer to the Representer's last reply ; in which are laid open some of the methods by which Protestants are misrepresented by Papists. [By William Clagett, D.D., preacher to Gray's Inn.] 4to. Pp. 123. [*Bodl.*]
London, 1687

VIEWS and interviews on journalism. By Carlfried [Charles F. Wingate]. 8vo.
New York, 1875

VIEWS and opinions. By Matthew Browne [William Brighty Rands]. 8vo. Pp. xviii. 294. [*Brit. Mus.*]
New York, 1866

VIEWS and reviews in American literature, history, and fiction. By the author of *The Yemassee*, etc. [William Gilmore Simms]. 8vo. [*Brit. Mus.*]
New York, 1845

VIEWS in London. By an amateur [Hon. Elizabeth Susan Abbot, afterwards Baroness Colchester]. Sketched from a window in the Palais de la Vérité : and extracts from an album. 8vo. [*Brit. Mus.*] Chiswick, 1833

VIEWS in Orkney, and on the North-Eastern Coast of Scotland, taken in 1805 and etched in 1807. [By Elizabeth Leveson Gower, Duchess of Sutherland.] Fol. Pp. 27. [*Martin's Cat.*] [1807 ?]

VIEWS of Canada and the colonists, embracing the experience of a residence ; views of the present state, progress and prospects of the colony ; with detailed and practical information for intending emigrants. By a four years' resident [James Bryce Brown]. 8vo. [*Camb. Univ. Lib.*]
Edinburgh, 1844

VIEWS (the) of Christopher. [By Elkin Mathews.] 8vo. London, 1904

VIEWS of Inverness and district. [By Alexander I. M'Connochie.] 8vo.
Aberdeen, 1906

VIEWS of ports and harbours, watering places, fishing villages, and other picturesque objects on the English coast. Engraved by W. and E. Finden. [With a descriptive letterpress by W. A. C. *i.e.* William Andrew Chatto.] 4to. [*Universal Cat. of Books on art*, i. 275.]
London, 1838

VIEWS of society and manners in America ; in a series of letters from that country to a friend in England, during the years 1818, 1819, and 1820. By an Englishwoman [Frances Wright]. 8vo. Pp. x. 523. [Rich's *Bibl. Amer.* ii. 130.]
London, 1821

VIEWS of the American press on the Philippines ; edited by T. Bruce [Thomas Bruce Esty]. 8vo. [*Amer. Cat.*]
New York, 1899

VIEWS of the Holy Trinity, doctrinal and experimental. [By Mrs —— Fludd, of Charleston, South Carolina.] 12mo. Pp. 197. Charleston, 1853

VIEWS of the seats of noblemen and gentlemen in England, Wales, Scotland and Ireland; from drawings by J. P. Neale. [With letterpress descriptions by Thomas Moule.] 6 vols. [*W.*]
London, 1818-23
Second Series. 5 vols. London, 1824-9.

VIEWS on slavery. By an American [Edward Habich]. 12mo. [*Brit. Mus.*]
Boston, 1855

VIGIL (the) of Venus, and other poems. By "Q" [Sir Arthur Quiller-Couch]. 8vo. Pp. viii. 137. [*Brit. Mus.*]
London, 1912

VIGILEMUS et oremus. By E. W. B. [Rev. Edward Waller Barker]. 8vo. [*Brit. Mus.*]
London, 1876

VIGILIUS, or the awakener, making a brief essay to rebuke first the natural sleep . . . and then the moral sleep. . . . [By Cotton Mather, D.D.] 8vo. [Evans' *Amer. Bibl.* vol. 1, p. 276.]
Boston, 1719

VIGNETTE stories. By "Rita" [Eliza M. J. Gollan, later Mrs Von Booth, then Mrs W. Desmond Humphreys]. 8vo. [*Who's Who in Lit.*]
London, 1896

VIGOR; a novel. By Walter Barrett, clerk [Joseph A. Scoville]. 12mo. [Sabin's *Dict.*]
New York, 1864

VIKING (the). By M. R. [Margaret Richmond Cartmell]. 8vo.
London, 1879

VILLA (the) of the peacock, and other stories. By Richard Dehan [Clotilde Graves]. 8vo. [*Who's Who in Lit.*]
London, 1921

VILLA Rubein; a novel. By John Sinjohn [John Galsworthy]. 8vo. Pp. 262. [*Brit. Mus.*]
London, 1900

VILLAGE belles; a tale of English country life. By the author of *Mary Powell* [Anne Manning, later Mrs Rathbone]. New edition, revised. 8vo. Pp. iv. 348.
London, 1860

VILLAGE (the) blacksmith. [A novel.] By Darley Dale [Francesca M. Steele]. 8vo. 3 vols. [*Who's Who in Lit.*]
London, 1892

VILLAGE (the) carol singers; a musical juvenile drama, in two acts. . . . [Signed H. F. *i.e.* Henry Formby.] 8vo. [*Brit. Mus.*]
London, 1852

VILLAGE (the) Church. [A poem.] By the author of *The phylactery* [Rev. Arthur Bononi Evans, D.D.]. 8vo.
London, 1843

VILLAGE (a) commune. By "Ouida" [Louise De La Ramée]. 8vo. 2 vols. [*Lit. Year Book.*]
London, 1881

VILLAGE (a) contest. By Marian Thorne [Miss Ida T. Thurston]. 8vo. [*Amer. Cat.*]
Boston, 1899

VILLAGE conversations; or, the vicar's fire-side. [By Sarah Renou.] Dedicated to Mrs Hannah More. 12mo. Pp. xvii. 227.
London, 1815

Dedication is signed: S. R.

VILLAGE (the) convict. By C. H. White [Heman W. Chaplin]. 8vo. [*Amer. Cat.*]
New York, 1884

VILLAGE (the) curate; a poem. [By James Hurdis, D.D.] 8vo. [Courtney's *Secrets*, p. 119.]
Bishopstone, 1797

Printed at the author's private press.

VILLAGE (a) drama. By V. Schallenberger [Mrs Vesta S. Simmons]. 8vo. Pp. 199. [*Amer. Cat.*]
New York, 1896

VILLAGE (the) lesson book; for the use of schools. By Martin Doyle, author of *Hints to small farmers*, etc. [Rev. William Hickey]. 12mo. Pp. 116.
London, 1855

VILLAGE (the) life; a poem. [By J. H. Stoddart, LL.D.] 8vo. [F. Boase's *Mod. Eng. Biog.* vi. col. 627.]
Glasgow, 1879

VILLAGE memoirs; in a series of letters between a clergyman and his family in the country, and his son in town. [By Joseph Cradock.] 12mo. [Cradock's *Mem.* i. xix.; *Mon. Rev.* lii. 139.]
London, 1775

VILLAGE missionaries; or, every one to his work. [By Miss Emily Steele Elliot.] 8vo.
London, 1866-72

VILLAGE (the) nurse. By the author of *Margaret Whyte* [Mrs Lucy L. Cameron]. 12mo. [*Brit. Mus.*]
London, 1824

VILLAGE (the) on the cliff. By the author of *The story of Elizabeth* [Anne Isabella Thackeray, later Mrs R. Ritchie]. 8vo. Pp. 318. [*Brit. Mus.*]
London, 1867

VILLAGE (the) pastor. By one of the authors of *Body and soul* [George Wilkins, D.D.]. 12mo. [*Brit. Mus.*]
London, 1825

VILLAGE (the) pastor. By the author of *The retrospect, Ocean*, etc., formerly a Lieutenant in the Royal Navy, and now a minister in the Established Church [Richard Marks]. 12mo. 2 vols. [*Brit. Mus.*]
London, 1827

VILLAGE (the) patriarch; a poem [with notes and an appendix. By Ebenezer Elliott]. 12mo. [*Brit. Mus.*]
London, 1829

VILLAGE politics, addressed to all mechanics, journeymen, and day-labourers in Great Britain. By Will Chip, a country carpenter [Hannah More]. Fifth edition. 12mo. [Green's *Bibl. Somers.* ii. 235.]
Bath, 1793

VILLAGE (the) poorhouse. By a country curate [Rev. James White]. 12mo. [*D. N. B.* vol. 61, p. 51.]
London, 1832

VILLAGE reminiscences. By an old maid [Mrs Monkland]. 12mo. 3 vols.
London, 1834

VILLAGE scenes; a poem: in two parts. [By James Cargill Guthrie.] 12mo.
                Edinburgh and London, 1850
VILLAGE (the) school; a collection of entertaining histories for . . . children. [Preface signed: M. P. *i.e.* Dorothy Kilner.] New edition. 12mo. Pp. 88. [*Brit. Mus.*]   1828

VILLAGE (the) school; a poem. By Moralisto, poet "lariat" of Carthage [J. M. Dill]. 8vo. [*Lib. Journ.* vi. 16.]
                    Cincinnati, 1885
VILLAGE sermons. By a country clergyman [Edward Berens, Archdeacon of Berks]. 12mo. Pp. viii. 202.
                    Oxford, 1820
VILLAGE sermons. By a Northamptonshire rector [Granville Hamilton Forbes]. With a preface on the inspiration of Holy Scripture. 8vo. Pp. xliv. 321.
                London and Cambridge, 1863

VILLAGE sketches; or, hints to pedestrians: reprinted from the *Doncaster Gazette*, 1849-50. [By C. W. Hatfield.] 12mo. Pp. 350. [Boyne's *Yorkshire Lib.* p. 108.]
                    Doncaster, N.D.
VILLAGE society; a sketch. [By John Coakley Lettsom, M.D.] 8vo. [*Brit. Mus.*]   London, 1800

VILLAGE tales. By Oliver Oakwood [Stacy Gardner Potts]. 8vo.
                    Trenton, 1827
VILLAGE verses. By **Guy Roslyn** [Joseph Hatton]. 12mo. [*Brit. Mus.*] 12mo.   London, 1876

VILLAGE virtues; a dramatic satire: in two parts. [By Matthew Gregory Lewis.] 4to. Pp. 45. [*N. and Q.* 8th June 1861, p. 458.]   London, 1796

VILLAGE (the) watch-tower. [A tale.] By Kate Douglas Wiggin [Mrs George C. Riggs]. 8vo. [*Who's Who in Lit.*]
                    London, 1895
VILLAGE (the) wedding; or, the faithful country maid: a pastoral entertainment of music, as it is performed at the Theatre-Royal at Richmond. [By James Dance.] 8vo. [Baker's *Biog. Dram.; Mon. Rev.* xxxvii. 152.]   1767

VILLAGERS (the). By Billy Burgundy [Oliver V. Limerick]. 12mo. [*Amer. Cat.*]   New York, 1904

VILLAINY (the) of stock-jobbers detected, and the causes of the late run upon the bank and bankers discovered and considered. [By Daniel Defoe.] 4to. [Wilson's *Life of Defoe,* 19.]   London, 1701

VILLANIES discouered by lanthorne and candle-light, and the helpe of a new cryer called O per se O; being an addition to the belman's second nightwalke, and a laying open to the world of those abuses, which the bel-man (because he went i' the darke) could not see, with canting songs neuer before printed. [By Thomas Dekker.] 4to. No pagination. B. L.
                    London, 1616
VILLETTE. By Currer Bell, author of *Jane Eyre,* etc. [Charlotte Brontë]. 8vo. 3 vols.   London, 1853
VINCENT Trill, of the detective service. By Dick Donovan [Joyce E. P. Muddock]. 8vo. [*Who's Who in Lit.*]
                    London, 1899
VINCIGLIATA and Maiano. By Leader Scott [Mrs Lucy E. Baxter, *née* Barnes]. 4to. [*Lond. Lib. Cat.*]
                    Florence, 1891
VINDICATION (a) and defence of Mr George Meldrum's Sermon, preached May 16, 1703, against the reflections and censure of [John Sage] the author of the Examination of some things in the sermon, and [George Brown] the author of Toleration defended. [By George Meldrum, minister at Edinburgh.] 4to. Pp. 30. Edinburgh, 1703
VINDICATION (a) of a book, intituled, A brief account of many of the prosecutions of the people call'd Quakers, &c.; lately presented to the members of both Houses of Parliament: shewing the fallacy and injustice of the calculations and remarks in a late book call'd An examination, &c. . . . To which are added, remarks on the poor vicar's Plea. With Bishop Burnet's description of the ecclesiastical courts. [By Joseph Besse.] 8vo. Pp. 138. [Smith's *Cat. of Friends' Books,* i. 254.]
                    London, 1737
    Six other parts followed, dated 1739-1742. See Smith's *Cat. of Friends' Books.*

VINDICATION (a) of a discourse concerning the unreasonableness of a new separation, on account of the oaths [by Edward Stillingfleet], from the exceptions made against it in a tract called, A brief answer to a late discourse, &c. [By John Williams, D.D.] 4to. Pp. 40.
                    London, 1691
    Ascribed by some to Stillingfleet.

VINDICATION (a) of a discourse entituled the Principles of the Cyprianic age, with regard to episcopal power and jurisdiction; being a reply to Gilbert Rule's Cyprianic bishop examin'd and found not to be diocesan. . . . [By Bishop John Sage.] 4to. [*D. N. B.* vol. 50, p. 115.]
                    London, 1701

VINDICATION (the) of a late pamphlet (entituled, Obedience and submission to the present government, demonstrated from Bp. Overal's Convocation-book) from the false glosses, and illusive interpretations of a pretended answer [by Thomas Wagstaffe]. By the author of the first pamphlet [Zachary Taylor, M.A.]. 4to. Pp. 36. [*Cat. Lond. Inst.* ii. 34.] London, 1691

VINDICATION (a) of a late pamphlet, intituled, The case of the Hanover troops considered; with some further observations upon those troops: being a sequel to the said pamphlet. [By Philip Dormer Stanhope, Earl of Chesterfield, and Edmund Waller.] 8vo. Pp. 60. [*D. N. B.* vol. 54, p. 28.] London, 1743

VINDICATION (a) of a printed letter addressed to the Calvinistic Baptists of the Western Association on the subject of doxologies. . . . [By Job David.] 8vo. [Whitley's *Bapt. Bibl.* vol. ii.] Trowbridge, 1789

VINDICATION (a) of an Essay concerning critical and curious learning ; in which are contained some short reflections on the controversie betwixt Sir William Temple and Mr Wotton, and that betwixt Dr Bentley and Mr Boyl. In answer to an Oxford pamphlet. By the author of that essay [Thomas Rymer]. 8vo. Pp. 49. [Bartholomew's *Bibl. of Dr Bentley*, p. 30.] London, 1698

VINDICATION (a) of an undertaking of certain gentlemen, in order to the suppressing of debauchery, and profaneness. [By Edward Fowler, D.D., Bishop of Gloucester.] 4to. Pp. 16. [*Bodl.*] London, 1692

VINDICATION (a) of Bishop Colenso. By the author of *The eclipse of faith* [Henry Rogers]. 8vo. Pp. 105. [*Brit. Mus.*] Edinburgh, 1863
Signed : Vindex.

VINDICATION (a) of Bishop Taylor, from the injurious misrepresentation of him by the author of the Letter to the clergy of the Church of England in the county of Northumberland; with a few remarks upon some other passages in that letter. [By Thomas Sharp, D.D., Archdeacon of Northumberland.] 8vo. Pp. 16. [Smith's *Bibl. Anti-Quak.* pp. 39, 392.] 1733

VINDICATION (a) of commerce and the arts ; proving that they are the source of the greatness . . . of a state: being an examination of Mr [——] Bell's Dissertation upon populousness. . . . [By William Temple of Trowbridge.] 8vo. [*Lond. Lib. Cat.*] London, 1758

VINDICATION (a) of Demosthenes from the charge of corruption : in a letter to a friend. [By William Melmoth, junr.] 8vo. [Green's *Bibl. Somers.* i. 348.] London [1770]

VINDICATION (a) of Dr [Henry] Hammonds Addresse . . . from the exceptions of Eutactus Philodemius, in two particulars ; concerning the power supposed in the Jew over his owne freedome, [and] the no-power over a mans own life. . . . [By Henry Hammond himself.] 4to. [*Brit. Mus.*] London, 1649
This evoked "An answer to the Vindication of Dr Hamond against the exceptions of Eutactus Philodemius. . . ."

VINDICATION (a) of Dr Sherlock Dean of St Paul's, in answer to Mr Nathaniel Taylor's late treatise, entituled, Dr Sherlock's Case of Church communion, and his letter to Anonymous, consider'd, &c. ; together with a reply to his vindication of the dissenters from the charge of schism. [By Benjamin Hoadley, D.D.] 4to. Pp. 72. London, 1702

VINDICATION (a) of Doctor Tail [Traill], from the charge of heresy ; being a defence of a sermon entitled, The happiness of dead clergymen, &c. By the Reverend Doctor Tail [William Thom, minister at Govan]. 8vo. Glasgow, 1770

VINDICATION (the) of Dr Troy refuted. By S. N. [Thomas Elrington, D.D., Bishop of Ferns]. 8vo. [*D. N. B.* vol. 17, p. 333.] Dublin, 1804

VINDICATION of Edmund Burke's Reflections on the Revolution in France, in answer to all his opponents. [By Edmund Burke.] 8vo. Pp. 147. London, 1791

VINDICATION (a) of Exeter School, by its master, J. L. [John Lemprière, D.D.]. 8vo. [Davidson's *Bibl. Devon.* p. 29.] Exeter, 1818

VINDICATION (a) of free grace, in opposition to an Arminian position of Mr J. Goodwin. . . . By S. L. [Samuel Lane]. 4to. Pp. 72. [Copinger's *Bibl. on Predestination.*] London, 1645

VINDICATION (a) of Freemasonry from charges in the *Edinburgh News.* By several Freemasons [chiefly William Hunter]. 12mo. Edinburgh [1858]

VINDICATION (a) of Friends. . . . By an Irish lady [Mrs J. R. Greer]. 8vo. [Cushing's *Init. and Pseud.*] Philadelphia, 1852

VINDICATION (a) of General Richard Smith, Chairman of the select Committee of the House of Commons, as to his competency to preside over . . . an investigation into the best mode of providing the investment for the East India Company's . . . ships. . . . [By Captain Joseph Price.] 8vo. [*Brit. Mus.*] London, 1783

VINDICATION (a) of God's sovereignty, the doctrines of election, reprobation, and original sin ; from a late pamphlet intituled, Free and impartial thoughts on the sovereignty of God, &c. By W. B. [Richard Finch]. 8vo. [*Smith's Cat. of Friends' Books*, i. 610.] London, 1745
     Afterwards formed part of a volume entitled " Tracts,—By Richard Finch."

VINDICATION (a) of his Excellency the Lord C——t from the charge of favouring none but Tories, high-church-men and Jacobites. By the Reverend Dr S——t [Jonathan Swift, D.D.]. 8vo. Pp. 27. London, 1730

VINDICATION (a) of His Majesties government and judicatures, in Scotland ; from some aspersions thrown on them by scandalous pamphlets, and news-books : and especially, with relation to the late Earl of Argyle's process. [By Sir George Mackenzie.] 4to. Pp. 29.
     Printed at Edinburgh : re-printed at London, 1683

VINDICATION (a) of His Majesty [King Charles I.] and the Army from a paper by M. Reymes, as also the grounds of the Armies guarding His Majesties person. [By George Joyce.] 4to. [Thomason's *Coll. of Tracts*, ii. 526.] London, 1647

VINDICATION of informers of the breaches of the laws against prophaneness and immorality ; asserting and proving the lawfulness and necessity of informing : shewing that all sober Christians, and good neighbours, are called in duty to joyn therein. . . . [By Francis Grant, Lord Cullen.] 4to. Edinburgh, 1701

VINDICATION (a) of Isaac Bickerstaff Esq. ; against what is objected to him by Mr Partridge, in his Almanack for the present year 1709. By the said Isaac Bickerstaff Esq. [Jonathan Swift, D.D.]. 8vo. Pp. 8. London, 1709

VINDICATION (a) of King Charles the Martyr, proving that His Majesty was the author of ΕΙΚΩΝ ΒΑΣΙΛΙΚΗ ; against a memorandum, said to be written by the Earl of Anglesey : and against the exceptions of Dr Walker, and others. [By Thomas Wagstaffe, A.M.] 8vo. Pp. 46. [*Wood.*] London, 1693
     A second edition appeared in 1697, with a preface containing a refutation of a passage in Bayle's Dictionary relating to the controversy ; and a third, in 1711, with large additions, and some original letters of Charles I.

VINDICATION (a) of lawful authority ; against some principles lately advanc'd to undermine the same ; or, a confutation of Hobbism in politicks, as it is reviv'd by some modern doctors ; wherein Dr Broughton's Grand apostacy is consider'd ; and his notion concerning the divine right of power is set in its true light ; according to the Holy Scriptures, and the testimony of the primitive Church. [By George Smith.] 8vo. Pp. 80. [*W.; Brit. Mus.*] [London] 1718

VINDICATION (the) of liturgies, lately published by Dr Falkner, proved no vindication of the lawfulness, usefulness and antiquity of set-forms of publick ministerial prayer, to be generally used by, or imposed on all ministers ; and consequently an answer to a book, intituled, A reasonable account why some pious nonconformists judge it sinful, for them to perform their ministered acts in by [*sic*] the prescribed forms of others. . . . By the author of the *Reasonable account, and supplement to it* [John Collinges, D.D.]. 8vo. Pp. 30, iv. 258, 3. [*Brit. Mus.*] London, 1681

VINDICATION (a) of mankind, or freewill asserted in answer to a philosophical inquiry concerning human liberty [by Anthony Collins] ; to which is added an Examination of Mr Lock's scheme of freedom. [By S. Lowe?] 8vo. [*W.; Brit. Mus.*] London, 1717

VINDICATION (a) of marriage, as solemnized by Presbyterians, in the North of Ireland. . . . By a minister of the Gospel [John Macbride]. 4to. Pp. 71. [*D. N. B.* vol. 34, p. 427.] 1702

VINDICATION (a) of Mr Foster's Account of the late Earl of Kilmarnock. [By Richard Finch.] 8vo. [*Brit. Mus.*] London, 1746

VINDICATION (a) of Mr George Buchanan, in two parts. Part I. Vindicating him from the vile aspersion cast on him by Camden, that he repented, when dying, of what he wrote against Mary Queen of Scots. . . . Part II. Vindicating him from the horrible ingratitude he is charged with to Q. Mary, in extolling her so high in his dedication of his paraphrase of the Psalms, and there after writing so bitterly against her in the Detection and History. . . . [By John Love.] 8vo. [Chalmers' *Life of Ruddiman*, p. 224.]
Edinburgh, 1749

VINDICATION (a) of Mr James Colmar, Bachelor of physick and Fellow of Exeter College in Oxford; from the calumnies of three late pamphlets. 1. A paper publish'd by Dr Bury, 1659. 2. The account examin'd. 3. The case of Exeter College related and vindicated. . . . [By James Harrington.] 4to. Pp. 4, 43. [*D. N. B.* vol. 24, p. 436.]   London, 1691

VINDICATION (a) of Mr [William] Nation's sermon; in a letter to Mr P. C. [By Micaiah Towgood.] To which is annex'd a letter from Mr Nation to the author, in vindication of himself with respect to his orthodoxy. . . . 8vo. [*Brit. Mus.*] London, 1732

VINDICATION (a) of Mr Pope's Essay on man, from the misrepresentations of Mr de Crousaz, professor of philosophy and mathematicks in the university of Lausanne. By the author of *The divine legation of Moses demonstrated;* in six letters. [By William Warburton, D.D.] 12mo. Pp. 118. London, 1740
    There is added A seventh letter, which finishes the Vindication, with a separate title-page, and having the author's name.

VINDICATION (a) of Mr Robert Keith, and of his young grand nephew Alexander Keith, from the unfriendly representations of Mr Alexander Keith junior of Ravelstone, one of the underclerks in the Court of Session. [By William Douglas.] 8vo. Pp. 22.
                               N.P. [1750]
    "A few copies of this tract were printed for private circulation, in the year 1750, by Bishop Keith, author of the History of the affairs of Church and State in Scotland." —MS. note by Dr David Laing.

VINDICATION (a) of my Lord Bishop of Worcester's [George Morley's] letter touching Mr Baxter from the animadversions of D. E. [Edward Bagshaw]. [By Sir Henry Yelverton.] 4to. Pp. 14. [*Bodl.*]   London, 1662

VINDICATION (a) of my Lord Shaftesbury on the subject of ridicule, being remarks upon [John Brown's] "Essays on the characteristics." [By Charles Bulkley.]   8vo.   [*Brit. Mus.; Mon. Rev.* v. 285; vii. 41.]   London, 1751

VINDICATION (a) of natural society; or, a view of the miseries and evils arising to mankind from every species of artificial society; in a letter to Lord * * * *. By a late noble writer [Edmund Burke, imitating the style of Lord Bolingbroke]. 8vo. Pp. 106. [*Bodl.*]   London, 1756

VINDICATION (a) of oaths and swearing in weighty cases, as lawful and useful under the Gospel. By J. C. [John Cheyney], and approved by Mr Richard Baxter. The second edition. 4to. Pp. 38. [*D. N. B.* vol. 10, p. 224.]   London, 1680

VINDICATION (a) of Plain-dealing, from the base and malicious aspersions of two country curates, contained in a little scurrilous pamphlet, entitled, Plain-dealing proved to be plain-lying. [By Rev. Charles Owen, D.D.] 8vo. [*W.;* Lowndes' *Bibl. Man.*]
                              London, 1716

VINDICATION (a) of Presbyterian ordination; from Scripture and antiquity, the judgment of the Reformed Churches, and particularly of the Church of England: with a brief reflection upon the arguments offered by Mr Cautrell of Derby against it. [By Rev. John Hartley, of Ashby-de-la-Zouch.] 8vo. Pp. 72. [Darling's *Cyclop. Bibl.*]   Nottingham, 1714
    This was followed by "A defence of the Vindication": see above.

VINDICATION (a) of Protestant charity, in answer to some passages in Mr E[dward] M[eredith]'s Remarks on a late conference. [By James Harrington.] 4to. [Jones' *Peck,* i. 140.]   Oxford, 1688
    The above is printed with "Some reflexions upon a treatise called Pietas Romana et Parisiensis, &c.," *q.v.*

VINDICATION (a) of Protestant principles. By Phileleutherus Anglicanus [John William Donaldson, D.D., headmaster of King Edward's School, Bury St Edmunds]. 8vo. [*Brit. Mus.*]
                              London, 1847

VINDICATION (a) of Psalme 105, 15 (Touch not mine Anointed, and doe my Prophets no harme) from some false glosses lately obtruded on it by Royalists, proving that this divine inhibition was given to Kings, not Subjects; to restraine them from injuring . . . Gods servants. . . . [By William Prynne.] 4to. Pp. 8. [*Brit. Mus.*]   [London] 1642

VINDICATION (a) of Robert Barclay's Apology for the principles of the people call'd Quakers, against the attempts of William Notcutt in a late pamphlet, entituled, "An impartial review of Robert Barclay's pretended 'Apology.'" In a letter to a friend at Ipswich, by H. B. [Henton Brown]. 8vo. Pp. 120. [Smith's *Anti-Quak.* p. 342.]
London, 1732

VINDICATION (a) of St Gregorie his dialogues; in which the great St Gregory is proved the author of that work. [By James Mumford, S.J.] 4to. Pp. 20. [De Backer.]   London, 1660

VINDICATION of St Ignatius of Loyola from fanaticism. [By William Darrell, or Darell, S.J.] 4to. [Oliver's *Collections;* Sommervogel's *Diction-naire.*]   London, 1688

VINDICATION (a) of scriptural Unitarianism, and some other primitive Christian doctrines, in reply to Vindex's Examination of an appeal to the Society of Friends. By Verax [Thomas Foster]. 8vo. Pp. 324. [*Mon. Rev.* lxiii. 442.]   London, 1810

VINDICATION (a) of Sir Robert King's designs and actions in relation to the late and present Lord Kingston. [By Tobias Pullen, D.D., bishop of Dromore.] 8vo. [*D. N. B.* vol. 47, p. 22.]
[Dublin] 1699

VINDICATION (a) of Sir William Lewis [Governor of Portsmouth] from one part of his particular charge by an undeniable evidence of ancient date. [By Wm. Prynne.] 4to. [*Brit. Mus.*]   1647

VINDICATION (a) of some among our selves against the false principles of Dr Sherlock; in a letter to the Doctor, occasioned by the sermon which he preached at the Temple-Church, on the 29th of May, 1692: in which letter are also contained reflexions on some other of the Doctor's sermons, published since he took the oath. [By George Hickes, D.D.] 4to. Pp. 51. [*D. N. B.* vol. 26, p. 354.]   London, 1692

VINDICATION (a) of some passages in a Discourse concerning communion with God, from the exceptions of William Sherlock, rector of St George Buttolph-Lane. By the author of the said Discourse [John Owen, D.D.]. 8vo. Pp. 237. [*Bodl.*] London, 1674

VOL. VI.

VINDICATION (a) of some truths contained in the Scriptures, by the exercise of reason only. [By Joseph Lancaster.] 12mo. [Smith's *Cat. of Friends' Books,* i. 78.]   London, 1801

VINDICATION (a) of Strictures on the origin of moral evil. . . . [By William Parry.] 8vo. [*Brit. Mus.*]
London, 1808

VINDICATION (a) of that prudent . . . Knight Sir Henry Vane from the lies and calumnies of Mr Richard Baxter. By a true friend and servant of the Commonwealth of England [Henry Stubbe]. 4to. [*D. N. B.* vol. 58, p. 129.]
London, 1659

VINDICATION (a) of the account of the double doctrine of the ancients; in answer to a Critical enquiry into the practices of the antient philosophers. [By Arthur Ashley Sykes, D.D.] 8vo. Pp. 38. [Disney's *Memoir of Sykes,* p. xxii.]   London, 1747

VINDICATION of the Address made by the Episcopal clergy to the General Assembly of the Presbyterians anno M.DC.XC.II., from the sinistruous and false constructions put upon it by the enemies of that order; but more especially of that particular address, given in by Mr Robert Irving minister of Towie, and Mr John Forbes minister of Kincardine; in name of, and by commission from, their brethren, the ministers of the synod of Aberdeen: they being expressly reflected upon, and named by [James Hadow] the author of the Remarks upon the case of the Episcopal clergy. [By Robert Irving.] 4to. Pp. 40. [*Nat. Lib. of Scot.*]   1704

VINDICATION (a) of the Address to the inhabitants of the British Settlements, on the slavery of the negroes in America. By a Pennsylvanian [Benjamin Rush]. 8vo. [Evans' *Amer. Bibl.* vol. 4, p. 391.]
Philadelphia, 1773

VINDICATION (a) of the Answer to some late papers concerning the unity and authority of the Catholick Church, and the reformation of the Church of England. [By Edward Stillingfleet, D.D.] 4to. [Jones' *Peck,* i. 16.]
London, 1687

VINDICATION (a) of the Answer to the Humble remonstrance, from the unjust imputations of frivolousnesse and falsehood; wherein the cause of liturgy and episcopacy is further debated, by the same Smectymnuus [Stephen Marshall, Edmund Calamy, Thomas Young, Matthew Newcomen and William Spurstowe]. 4to.   1641

M

VINDICATION (a) of the Answer to the Popish address presented to the ministers of the Church of England ; in reply to a pamphlet abusively intituled, A clear proof of the certainty and usefulness of the Protestant rule of faith, etc. [By John Williams, D.D.] 4to. Pp. 41. [Jones' *Peck*, ii. 316.]
London, 1688

VINDICATION (a) of the Apamean medal ; and of the inscription NΩE : together with an illustration of another coin struck at the same place, in honour of the Emperor Severus. By the author of the *Analysis of ancient mythology* [Jacob Bryant]. 4to. [*W.*]
London, 1775

VINDICATION (a) of the Apostles from a very false imputation laid on them in several English pamphlets, viz., that they refused constant, and held only occasional communion with one another, and with one another's Churches. [By Rev. William Wall, vicar of Shoreham, in Kent.] 4to.
London, 1705

VINDICATION (a) of the authenticity of the narratives contained in the first two chapters of the Gospels of St Matthew & St Luke ; being an investigation of objections urged by the Unitarian editors of the improved version of the New Testament : with an appendix, containing strictures on the variations between the first and fourth editions of that work. By a layman [John Bevan]. 8vo. [Smith's *Cat. of Friends' Books*, i. 91.]
London, 1822

VINDICATION (a) of the authority of Christian princes over ecclesiastical synods from the exceptions made against it by Mr [Samuel] Hill. [By Dr John Turner.] 8vo.
London, 1701
Attributed also to Archbishop Wake. [Watt's *Bibl. Brit.*]

VINDICATION (a) of the Bishop of Condom's Exposition of the doctrine of the Catholic Church ; in answer to a book [by W. Wake] entituled, An exposition of the doctrine of the Church of England, etc. : with a letter from the said Bishop. [By Henry Joseph Johnston, O.S.B.] 4to. Pp. 122. [Jones' *Peck*, i. 113.]   London, 1686

VINDICATION (a) of the Bishop of Durham [Thomas Morton, D.D.] from the vile and scandalous calumnies of a libell intituled the Downfall of hierarchie. . . . [By Thomas Morton himself.] 4to.   London, 1641

VINDICATION (a) of the Bishop of Landaff's sermon. By a son of truth and decency [Rev. Charles Inglis]. 8vo. [Evans' *Amer. Bibl.* vol. 4, p. 136.]   New York, 1768

VINDICATION (a) of [Gilbert Burnet] the Bishop of Salisbury and Passive Obedience ; with some remarks upon a speech which goes under his Lordship's name ; and a Postscript, in answer to a book, just publish'd, entitul'd, Some considerations humbly offer'd to the Right Reverend the Lord Bishop of Salisbury [by Edmund Curll]. . . . [By Gilbert Burnet, D.D.] 8vo. Pp. 16.   N.P. 1710

VINDICATION (a) of the Brief discourse concerning the Notes of the Church ; in answer to a late pamphlet, entituled, The use and great moment of the Notes of the Church, as delivered by Cardinal Bellarmin, De Notis Ecclesiæ, justified. [By William Sherlock.] 4to. [Jones' *Peck*.]
London, 1687

VINDICATION (a) of the British colonies, against the aspersions of the Halifax gentleman, in his letter to a Rhode-Island friend. [By James Otis.] 8vo. Pp. 32.   Boston, 1765
Reprinted with author's name, 1769.

VINDICATION of the calendar tables and rules annexed to the Act for regulating the commencement of the year, and correcting the calendar, against the objections made to it, with respect to the time appointed for the celebration of Easter-day ; to which is added a more full account of that Act : written whilst it was depending in the House of Commons. [By Peter Daval.] 4to. [Nichol's *Lit. Anec.* ii. 372 ; *Mon. Rev.* xxiv. 468.]   1761

VINDICATION of the captors of Major André. [Signed "Curator," *i.e.* Egbert Benson.] 8vo. [*Brit. Mus.*]
New York, 1817

VINDICATION (a) of the Case of indifferent things, used in the worship of God ; in answer to a book, intituled, The case of indifferent things used in the worship of God, examined, stated on the behalf of the dissenters, and calmly argued. [By John Williams, D.D.] 4to. Pp. 57. [*Brit. Mus.*]
London, 1684

VINDICATION of the Case of the Hanover forces in the pay of Great Britain . . . with some further observations. [By Philip Dormer Stanhope, Earl of Chesterfield, and E. Waller.] 8vo. [*Brit. Mus.*]   London, 1743

VINDICATION (a) of the Character of a Popish successor; in a reply to two pretended answers to it. By the author of the Character [John Phillips]. Fol. Pp. 15. [*Bodl.*] London, 1681
Attributed also to Elkanah Settle.

VINDICATION of the character of the late Right Hon. William Pitt, from the calumnies against him contained in the fifth article of the *Edinburgh Review* for April, 1810. [By James Walker.] 8vo. [*N. and Q.* 28th June 1862.] Edinburgh, 1810

VINDICATION (a) of the Christian religion and Reformation, against the attempts of a late letter pretending to show that all religions have a like plea. . . . [By William King, archbishop of Dublin.] 4to. [*Brit. Mus.*] N.P. 1688

VINDICATION (a) of the Church and clergy of England, from some late reproaches rudely and unjustly cast upon them. [By White Kennett, D.D.] 8vo. Pp. vi. 120. [*Bodl.*]. London, 1709

VINDICATION (a) of the Church and clergy of England from the misrepresentations of the *Edinburgh Review.* By a beneficed clergyman [Henry Soames, M.A., Dean of St Paul's]. 8vo. [*Crockford's Clerical Directory.*] London, 1823

VINDICATION (a) of the Church of England from the aspersions of a late libel, intituled, Priestcraft in perfection, &c.; wherein the controverted clause of the Church's power in the xxth Article is shewn to be of equal authority with all the rest of the Articles. . . . By a priest of the church of England [Hilkiah Bedford]. 8vo. London, 1710

VINDICATION (a) of the Church of England from the foul aspersions of schism and heresie unjustly cast upon her by the Church of Rome. [By Michael Altham.] 4to. 2 parts. [*Jones' Peck*, i. 168.] London, 1687

VINDICATION (a) of the Church of England, in answer to Mr Pierce's Vindication of the dissenters; wherein abundance of historical mistakes are rectified; several groundless calumnies thrown upon the most worthy and deserving prelates of our Church, refuted: and many Fathers of the most primitive ages of Christianity clear'd from misrepresentations. In two parts. By a presbyter of the Church of England [Zachary Grey, LL.D., vicar of St Peter's and Giles', Cambridge]. 8vo. [*Bodl.*] London, 1720

VINDICATION (a) of the Church of Scotland; being an answer to a paper, intituled, Some questions concerning episcopal and presbyterial government in Scotland: wherein the latter is vindicated from the arguments and calumnies of that author; and the former is made appear to be a stranger in that nation. By a minister of the Church of Scotland, as it is now established by law [Gilbert Rule]. 4to. [*Nat. Lib. of Scot.*] London, 1691

VINDICATION (a) of the " Clanronald of Glengary " against the attacks made upon them in the *Inverness Journal* and some recent printed performances; with remarks as to the descent of the family who style themselves " of Clanronald." [By John Riddell.] 8vo. Pp. 97, xxx. Edinburgh, 1821

VINDICATION (a) of the clergy, from the contempt imposed upon them by [John Eachard] the author of The grounds and occasions of the contempt of the clergy and religion. 8vo. Pp. 135. London, 1686

The attribution to John Bramhall, Bishop of Derry, by Wood seems to be a mistake, as Bramhall died in 1663.

VINDICATION (a) of the commands and doctrine of Christ Jesus and of his people in their faithful obedience to him against all swearers and swearing whatsoever. . . . By a lover of righteousness and truth . . . W. B. [William Bayly]. 4to. [*Brit. Mus.*] [London, 1663]

VINDICATION (a) of the conforming clergy from the unjust aspersions of heresie, &c.; in answer to some part of M. Jenkyn's funeral sermon upon Dr Seaman: with short reflexions on some passages in a sermon preached by Mr J. s. upon 2 Cor. 5, 20: in a letter to a friend. [By Robert Grove, D.D.] 4to. Pp. 74. [*Bodl.*] London, 1676

VINDICATION (a) of the convention lately concluded between Great Britain and Russia, in six letters; addressed to —— —— [By Charles Jenkinson, Earl of Liverpool.] 8vo. Pp. 124. London, 1801

VINDICATION (a) of the Convocation and the Lord Chancellor of Ireland, in answer to the Englishman's Defence of the C——s [Commons]: in a letter . . . By the editor of Aristides [Dr Patrick Delany]. 8vo. [*Brit. Mus.*] Dublin, 1714
Signed: Philalethes.

VINDICATION (a) of the deprived Bishops, asserting their spiritual rights against a lay-deprivation, against the charge of schism, as managed by the late editors of an anonymous Baroccian MS. In two parts. . . . [By Henry Dodwell, Senior.] 4to. [Green's *Bibl. Somers.* ii. 487.]　　　London, 1692

This was followed, in 1695, by a "Defence of the Vindication . . . " See above.

VINDICATION (a) of the divine attributes ; in some remarks on his Grace [W. King] the Archbishop of Dublin's sermon, intituled, Divine predestination and foreknowledg consistent with the freedom of man's will. [By John Edwards, D.D.] 8vo. Pp. 38.
London, 1710

VINDICATION (a) of the divine authority and inspiration of the Old and New Testament ; in answer to a Treatise [by Jean Le Clerc] lately translated [by John Locke] out of French, entituled, "Five letters concerning the inspiration of the Holy Scriptures." [By William Lowth, B.D.] The second edition. 8vo. [Arber's *Term Cat.* iii. 148.]　　London, 1699

VINDICATION (a) of the divine perfections, illustrating the glory of God in them, by reason and revelation; methodically digested into several heads. By a person of honour [James Dalrymple, 1st Viscount of Stair]. 8vo. [*D. N. B.* vol. 13, p. 415.]
London, 1695

The preface is signed : W. Bates, J. Howe, the editors.

VINDICATION (a) of the doctrine contained in Pope Benedict XII. his Bull, and in the General Councill of Florence, under Eugenius the III. concerning the state of departed souls. In answer to a certain Letter. . . . By S. W. [John Sergeant], a Roman Catholick. 12mo. Pp. 202. [Gillow's *Bibl. Dict.*]　　　　　Paris, 1659

VINDICATION (a) of the doctrine of grace, from the charge of antinomianism ; contained in a letter to a minister of the gospel [Ralph Erskine]. [Signed : I. H. *i.e.* James Hog.] 8vo. Pp. 24.　　　　　Edinburgh, 1718

VINDICATION (a) of the doctrine of the Catholic Church concerning the Eucharist. [By —— Gilbert.] 12mo.
London, 1800

VINDICATION (a) of the doctrine of the Divine person and eternal Sonship of Christ. [By James Waters.] 8vo.　　　　　London, 1733

VINDICATION (a) of the doctrine of the Trinity from the exceptions of a late pamphlet entituled An essay on spirit &c. By a divine of the Church of England [Thomas Randolph, D.D.]. Part I. 8vo. [Darling's *Cyclop. Bibl.*]
Oxford, 1753

Part II. was also published in 1753, and part III. in 1754. The name of the author is given in the Appendix, which also appeared in 1754.

VINDICATION of the drama, the stage, and public morals. [By Joseph Parkes.] 8vo.　　　　　Birmingham, 1826

VINDICATION (a) of the ecclesiastical part of Sir James Dalrymple's Historical collections ; in answer to a late pamphlet [by John Gillane], intituled, The life of the Reverend Mr John Sage, &c. : wherein some things are added towards the clearing the ancient government of the Church of Scotland from the mistakes of a late author : together with a defence of what Sir James hath advanced concerning the opinion of the Scottish historians in relation to King Robert the Second's marriage with Elizabeth Muir, in answer to Mr John Sage his criticism on that subject in his introduction to Hawthornden's works. [By Sir James Dalrymple, Bart., of Borthwick.] 8vo. Pp. 73. [D. Laing.] Edinburgh, 1714

VINDICATION (a) of "The end of religious controversy" from the exceptions of the RR. Dr Burgess, bishop of St Davids, and the Rev. Richard Grier, A.M. By the Rev. J. M. [John Milner], D.D., F.S.A. 8vo. Pp. 359. [*Brit. Mus.*]　London, 1822

VINDICATION (a) of the Enquiry into charitable abuses, with an exposure of the misrepresentations . . . in the *Quarterly Review* . . . [By Henry Bellenden Kerr.] 8vo. Pp. 129. [*Manch. Free Lib.*]　　London, 1819

VINDICATION (a) of the facts in the Free Enquirer's [Mr M——y's] Letter, and the misrepresentations in the Reply thereto [by A. Nimmo] considered. . . . By A. M. [Rev. Alexander Murray]. 8vo.
Newcastle, 1767

VINDICATION (a) of the Faithful rebuke to a false report against the rude cavils of the pretended Defence. [By Vincent Alsop.] 8vo. Pp. 152.
London, 1698

The Report and Defence were written by Stephen Lobb.

VINDICATION (a) of the Faults on both sides, from the reflections of the Medley, the Specimen-maker, and a pamphlet [by Joseph Trapp] entituled, Most faults on one side; with a dissertation on the nature and use of money and paper-credit in trade. . . . By the author of the *Faults on both sides* [Richard Harley]. 8vo. Pp. 43. London, 1710

"Faults on both sides" has been ascribed to Defoe, and to Clements, secretary to the Earl of Peterborough, as well as to Harley. —Note in *Nat. Lib. of Scot. Cat.*

VINDICATION (a) of the freedom & lawfulness of the late General Assembly begun at St Andrews, and continued at Dundee; in answer to the reasons alledged against the same in the Protestation and Declinatore given in at St Andrews, and in another paper contrived since. . . . [By James Wood, Professor at St Andrews.] 4to. Pp. 49. [D. Laing.] London, 1652

VINDICATION (a) of the friendly conference between a minister and a parishioner of his, inclining unto Quakerism, from the exceptions of Thomas Ellwood, in his pretended Answer to the said conference. By the same author [Edward Fowler, D.D.]. 8vo. [Smith's *Bibl. Anti-Quak.* p. 21.] London, 1678

The authorship is doubtful.

VINDICATION (a) of the Fundamental charter of presbytery [by John Sage] from the exceptions of [John Anderson] the contry-man in his letter to [R. Calder] a curate. . . . By a true son of the afflicted Church of Scotland [John Gillan]. 8vo. Edinburgh, 1713

VINDICATION (a) of the government, doctrine, and worship, of the Church of England, established in the reign of Queen Elizabeth; against the injurious reflections of Mr Neale, in his late History of the Puritans: together with a detection of many false quotations and mistakes in that performance. [By Zachary Grey, D.D.] 8vo. Pp. 362. [*Brit. Mus.*] London, 1733

Wrongly ascribed to Isaac Madox.

VINDICATION of the Hindoos from the aspersions of the Rev. Claudius Buchanan, M.A.; with a refutation of the arguments exhibited in his Memoir on the expediency of an ecclesiastical establishment for British India, and the ultimate civilization of the natives by their conversion to Christianity. . . . By a Bengal officer [Major John Scott-Waring]. 8vo. Pp. 171. [*Brit. Mus.*] London, 1808

Wrongly ascribed to Charles Stewart.

VINDICATION (a) of the Historiographer of the University of Oxford, and his works, from the reproaches of the Lord Bishop of Salisbury [Gilbert Burnet] in his Letter to [Lloyd] the Lord Bishop of Coventry and Litchfield, concerning a book lately published, called, A specimen of some errors and defects in the History of the reformation of the Church of England, by Anthony Harmer [*i.e.* Henry Wharton]. Written by, E. D. To which is added the Historiographer's Answer to certain animadversions made in the before-mentioned History of the reformation, to that part of Historia & antiquitates universitatis Oxon, which treats of the divorce of Queen Catherine from King Henry the Eighth. [By Dr Thomas Wood, of New College, Oxford.] 4to. Pp. 30. [Wood's *Athen. Oxon.* i. cxiv. note.] London, 1693

Wrongly ascribed to James Harington. [*Upcott*, p. 1089.]

VINDICATION (a) of the history of the Gunpowder-treason, and of the proceedings and matters relating thereunto, from the exceptions which have been made against it, and more especially of late years by the author of the Catholic apology, and others. To which is added, a parallel betwixt that, and the present Popish plot. [By John Williams, D.D.] 4to. Pp. 95. [*Bodl.*] London, 1681

Ascribed also to Gilbert Burnet, D.D. [*Mendham Collection Cat.* p. 51.]

VINDICATION of the history of the Septuagint from the misrepresentations of the learned Scaliger, Dupin, Dr Hody, Dr Prideaux, and other modern criticks. [By Charles Hayes.] 8vo. Pp. v. 176. [*D. N. B.* vol. 25, p. 289.] London, 1736

Wrongly attributed to Sir Richard Ellis, Bart.

VINDICATION (a) of the honour and justice of Parliament against a most scandalous libel entitled the Speech of John A—— Esq. [By Daniel Defoe.] Pp. 36. [Lee's *Defoe*, p. 209.] London [1721]

VINDICATION of the honour of God; in a Scriptural refutation of the doctrines of eternal misery, and universal salvation. . . . [By George Clarke.] 8vo. Pp. 284. London, 1782

VINDICATION (a) of the honour of King Charles I. against the prodigious calumnies of the regicide, Ludlow, publisht in what he calls A letter from Major-General Ludlow, to Sir E. S. [By Edmund Elys.] 8vo. Pp. 14. [*Bodl.*] 1691

Author's name in the handwriting of Wood.

VINDICATION (a) of the imprisoned and secluded members of the House of Commons, from the aspersions cast upon them, and the maiority of the House, in a paper lately printed and published: entituled, An humble answer to the generall councel of the officers of the army under his Excellency Thomas Lord Fairfax, to the demands of the Honourable Commons of England in parliament assembled; concerning the late securing or secluding some members thereof. [By William Prynne.] 4to. Pp. 34. London, 1649

VINDICATION of the Irish nation, and particularly its Catholic inhabitants, from the calumnies of libellers. By Julius Vindex [Dennis Taafe]. 8vo. [*Brit. Mus.*] Dublin, 1802

VINDICATION (a) of the Kings Letter concerning the regulation of preachers. [By Robert Seppius.] 4to. London, 1664

VINDICATION (a) of the King's sovereign rights; together with a justification of his royal exercise thereof, in all causes, and over all persons ecclesiastical (as well as by consequence) over all ecclesiastical bodies corporate, and cathedrals: more particularly applyed to the King's Free Chappel and Church of Sarum, upon occasion of the Dean of Sarum's Narrative and Collections. . . . [By Thomas Pierce, Dean of Salisbury]. Fol. Pp. 44. [*Bodl.*] London, 1683

VINDICATION (a) of the late Archbishop Sancroft, and of his brethren the rest of the depriv'd bishops, from the reflections of Mr Marshal in his Defence of our constitution in Church and State; particularly with regard to their refusing to publish an abhorrence of the Prince of Orange's invasion, their meeting at Guild-Hall, and their endeavours for a regency. In a letter to a friend. [By Hilkiah Bedford.] 8vo. London, 1717

VINDICATION (a) of the late House of Commons, in rejecting the Bill for confirming the eighth and ninth articles of the treaty of navigation and commerce between England and France. By a citizen [John Egleton]. 8vo. [*W.; Brit. Mus.*] London, 1714

VINDICATION (a) of [Lord King] the learned and honourable author of The history of the Apostles Creed, from the false sentiment, which Mr Simson has injuriously imputed to him. [By James Hadow, D.D.] 8vo. [*Nat. Lib. of Scot.*] Edinburgh, 1731

VINDICATION (a) of the Letter out of the North concerning Bp. Lake's declaration of his dying in the belief of passive obedience, &c. [By W. Eyre.] 4to. London, 1690

VINDICATION (a) of the licensed chapels in Scotland; being an answer to the objections exhibited against them, in a Letter addressed to the Reverend Mr Grant at Edinburgh. By Philanthropos [G. Blaikie]. 8vo. Pp. 46. Edinburgh, 1749
Wrongly ascribed to James Grant.

VINDICATION (a) of the literal sense of three miracles of Christ: I. His turning water into wine; II. His whipping the buyers and sellers out of the Temple; III. His exorcising the devils out of two men; against the objections of Thos. Woolston. [By Benjamin Andrews Atkinson.] 8vo. [*Trin. Coll. Dub. Lib.* p. 145.] London, 1729

VINDICATION (a) of the literary character of the late Professor Porson, from the animadversions of the Right Reverend Thomas Burgess, D.D. F.R.S. F.A.S. P.R.S.L. Lord Bishop of Salisbury, in various publications on 1 John v. 7. By Crito Cantabrigiensis [Thomas Turton, D.D.]. 8vo. [*N. and Q.* 28th April 1860, p. 332.] Cambridge, 1827

VINDICATION (a) of the Lord Bishop of Ely's visitatorial jurisdiction over Trinity-College in general, and over the Master thereof [Bentley] in particular. [By John Colbatch, D.D.] 4to. Pp. 44. [*Bodl.*] London, 1732

VINDICATION (a) of the ministers and ruling elders of the Church of Scotland who have taken the Abjuration [Oath]; wherein it is made evident, that they are not thereby engaged in their stations to oblige the successor when he comes to the crown, to join in communion with the Church of England. . . . [By Alexander Lauder, minister at Mordentoun.] 4to. [Scott's *Fasti*, new edition, vol. 2, p. 57.] Edinburgh, 1712

VINDICATION of the ministers of the Church of Scotland, who have prayed for the Queen by name, notwithstanding the order in Council on that subject. By a presbyterian [Thomas M'Crie, D.D.]. The second edition. 8vo. Edinburgh, 1820
Ascribed also to Andrew Thomson, D.D.

VINDICATION (a) of the ministers of the Gospel, in and about London, from the unjust aspersions cast upon their former actings for the Parliament, as if they had promoted the bringing of the King to capital punishment. [Drawn up by Cornelius Burgess, D.D., though signed by other ministers.]   4to. [Reid's *Hist. of Western Divines*, i. 80.]
London, 1648

VINDICATION (a) of the Miscellanea Analytica; in answer to a late pamphlet entitled Observations, &c.   [By John Wilson, M.A., St Peter's College, Cambridge.]   8vo.   Pp. 22.
Cambridge, 1709

VINDICATION (a) of the Modern history of Hindostan, from the gross misrepresentations, and illiberal strictures of the Edinburgh reviewers, by the author [Thomas Maurice].   8vo. Pp. 88.   London, 1805

VINDICATION (a) of the New theory of the earth from the exceptions of Mr Keill and others; with an historical preface of the occasions of the discoveries therein contained : and some corrections and additions. [By William Whiston.]   8vo.   Pp. 10, 52.
London, 1698

VINDICATION (a) of the Nine Reasons of the House of Commons against the votes of Bishops in Parliament; or, a reply to the Answers made to the said Reasons in defence of such votes. [By Cornelius Burgess, D.D.]   4to. [Madan's *Oxford Books*, ii. 157; *D.N.B.* vol. 7, p. 303.]   London, 1641
Another edition of " An humble examination of a printed abstract of the answers &c.," *q.v.*

VINDICATION (a) of the Oath of Allegiance, in answer to a paper disperst by Samuel Eaton, pretending to prove the Oath of Allegiance voyd and non-obliging. By the author of the *Exercitation concerning usurped powers* [Edward Gee].   4to.   [*D.N.B.* vol. 21, p. 104.]   N.P. 1650
Attributed also to Richard Hollinworth. [*Cat. London Institution*, ii. 30.]

VINDICATION (a) of the Observations on the rapid decline of the clerical credit and character. By the author [Rev. Thomas Hunter, vicar of Wavorham, in Cheshire]. 8vo. London, 1782

VINDICATION (a) of the opposition to the late intended bill for the relief of Roman Catholics in Scotland; in which an address to the people on that subject, by the Reverend Dr Campbell, Principal of Marischal College, Aberdeen, is particularly considered. [By John Erskine, D.D.] 8vo. Pp. 53.
Edinburgh, 1780

VINDICATION (a) of the ordinations of the Church of England; in which it is demonstrated that all the essentials of ordination, according to the practice of the primitive and Greek Churches, are still retained in our Church : in answer to a paper written by one of the Church of Rome to prove the nullity of our Orders; and given to a person of quality.   [By Gilbert Burnet, D.D.]   The second edition. 4to. Pp. xxviii. 94.   London, 1688
The first edition, 1677, has the author's name on the title-page.

VINDICATION (a) of the orthodox clergy, in answer to two scurrilous libels, pretending to be vindications of the Lord Archbishop of Canterbury, but scandalously reflecting upon his grace, and our most orthodox clergy. [By Wm. Taswell, D.D.]   8vo.
London, 1720

VINDICATION (a) of the orthodoxe Protestant doctrine against the innovations of Dr Drayton and Mr Parker. [By John Tendring.]   4to.   Pp. 77. [Thomason's *Coll. of Tracts*, ii. 194.]
London, 1657

VINDICATION of the outbreak at Eton.   [By Jeremiah Milles, M.A., barrister.]   8vo.   Pp. 18.   1795

VINDICATION (a) of the Oxford Reply to two discourses [by Abraham Woodhead] there printed 1687; concerning the adoration of our blessed Saviour in the Eucharist, from the exceptions made to it in the second appendix [by Obadiah Walker] to a compendious discourse on the Eucharist [by Abraham Woodhead], published from the same press.   [By Henry Aldrich, D.D.]   4to.   Pp. 91. [Jones' *Peck*, p. 359.]   N.P., N.D.

VINDICATION (a) of the penalty of death for the crime of murder. [By Edmund Holmes.]   8vo.   [*Brit. Mus.*]
London [1850 ?]

VINDICATION (a) of the people of God, called Quakers ; directed unto Roger Boyle, called Earl of Orrery, Charles Coote, called Earl of Mountrath, Theophilus Jones, called Sir Theophilus Jones ; being an answer to a book, dedicated to them, by one George Pressick of Dublin. . . . By E. B. [Edward Burrough].   4to. Pp. 24.   London, N.D.

VINDICATION (a) of the practice of England in putting out money to use. [By John Dormer, *alias* Huddleston, S.J.]. 8vo. [Gillow's *Bibl. Dict.*]
London, 1699

VINDICATION (a) of the Presbyterian ministers in the North of Ireland; subscribers and non-subscribers: from many gross and groundless aspersions cast upon them, in a late scandalous libel, entituled, An account of the mind of the Synod at Belfast 1721, in a short reply to Mr Dugud's remarks upon their declaration. By a sincere lover of truth and peace [James Kirkpatrick]. Published and recommended by Victor Ferguson, M.D. 8vo. Pp. 82. [Witherow's *Presb. in Ireland*, i. 227.]   Belfast, 1721

VINDICATION (a) of the primitive Church, and diocesan episcopacy; in answer to Mr Baxter's Church history of bishops, and the councils abridged: as also to some part of his Treatise of episcopacy. [By Henry Maurice, D.D.] 8vo. Pp. 64, 567. [Watt's *Bibl. Brit.*; Orme's *Life of Baxter*, ii. 383.]
London, 1682

VINDICATION (a) of the principles of the author of the answer to the compiler of the Nubes Testium from the charge of popery; in answer to a late pretended letter from a dissenter to the divines of the Church of England. [By Rev. Edward Gee, rector of St Benedict, Paul's Wharf, London.] 4to. [Darling's *Cyclop. Bibl.*]
London, 1688

VINDICATION (a) of the privilege of the people, in respect of the right of free discussion; with a retrospect to various proceedings relative to the violation of that right. [By George Chalmers.] 8vo. Pp. 80. [*Brit. Mus.*]
London, 1796

VINDICATION (a) of the proceedings against the six members of E[dmund] Hall, Oxford. By a gentleman of the University [William Browne]. 8vo. Pp. 20. [*Bodl.*]   London, 1768

VINDICATION (a) of the proceedings of his Majesties ecclesiastical commissioners against [Hen. Compton] the Bishop of London, and the Fellows of Magdalen College. [By Henry Care.] 4to. [*Brit. Mus.*]   London, 1688

VINDICATION (a) of the proceedings of some members of the Lower House of the last Convocation, with relation to the archbishop's prorogation of it upon the eighth of May; in a letter to the publisher of the Late narrative of the proceedings of that House about adjournments. [By Charles Trimnell, D.D.] 4to. Pp. 8. [*Bodl.*]
[London] 1702

VINDICATION (a) of the proceedings of the Edinburgh Bible Society, relative to the Apocrypha, against the aspersions of the "Eclectic Review"; in a letter to the members of the comitee of the parent institution. [By Alexander Haldane.] 8vo. Pp. 35. [*Brit. Mus.*]   London, 1825

VINDICATION (a) of the proceedings of the late Parliament of England, An. Dom. 1689; being the first in the reign of their present Majesties King William and Queen Mary. [By John, Lord Somers.] 4to. Pp. 25. [*D.N.B.* vol. 53, p. 222.]   London, 1690

VINDICATION (a) of the proceedings of the University of Oxford, against the allegations of an act of the council of the city of Oxford, dated Sept. 6. 1703. By a private hand [Thomas Wood, D.C.L.]. 4to. Pp. 7. [*Bodl.*]
No title-page.

VINDICATION (a) of the Protestant doctrine concerning Justification, and of its preachers and professors, from the unjust charge of Antinomianism; in a letter from a minister in the city, to a minister in the countrey. [By Robert Traill, M.A.] 4to. Pp. 42. [*Aberdeen Lib.*]   London, 1692

VINDICATION (a) of the Protestant Reformation; containing I. A brief account of the origin of Popery. II. Presumptions against. III. A refutation of its main doctrinal errors. IV. A display of the unscriptural idolatrous worship of the Romish Church. . . . [By Samuel Bourne, minister in Birmingham.] 12mo. Pp. 10, 202.
London, 1746

VINDICATION (a) of the real Reformation-principles of the Church of Scotland concerning separation, &c.; in which the Essay on separation is vindicated, and the arguments of the Reverend Mr Wilson, for separation from this Established Church, in his Defence, are considered. . . . By the author of the Essay on separation [John Currie]. 8vo. Pp. xiv. 8, 360. [*New Coll. Lib.*]   Edinburgh, 1740
Address to the reader signed: J. C.

VINDICATION (a) of the realm, and Church of England, from the charge of perjury, rebellion, & schism, unjustly laid upon them by the non-jurors: and the rebellion and schism shewn to lie at their own doors. [By William Wake.] 8vo. Pp. 68. [Darling's *Cyclop. Bibl.*]   London, 1716

VINDICATION (a) of the Reasonable-
ness of Christianity, &c. from Mr
Edwards's Reflections. [By John
Locke.] 8vo. Pp. 40. [*Brit. Mus.*]
London, 1695

VINDICATION (a) of the Reasons and
Defence, &c. Part I. Being a reply
to the first part of No sufficient reason
[by Nathaniel Spinckes] for restoring
some prayers and directions of King
Edward VI.'s first liturgy. By the
author of *Reasons and Defence* [Jeremy
Collier]. 8vo. London, 1718

——. Part II. Being a reply to the
second part of No sufficient reason for
restoring some prayers and directions
of King Edward VI's first liturgy. By
the author of the *Reasons and Defence*
[Jeremy Collier]. 8vo. London, 1719

VINDICATION (a) of the religious and
civil principles of the Irish Catholics ;
in a letter to . . . the Marquis
Wellesley. By J. K. L. [James
Warren Doyle, Romish Bishop of
Kildare and Leighlin]. Third edition.
8vo. [*Camb. Univ. Lib.*]
Dublin, 1823

This was followed by a Defence of his
Vindication, after it had drawn forth "Observations" [from Dr Samuel O'Sullivan]
and a statement of the "Case of the Church
of Ireland" [by Dr William Phelan].

VINDICATION (a) of the Remarks on
the Bishop of Derry's [William King's]
Discourse about human inventions,
from what is objected against them in
the admonition annext to the second
edition of that Discourse. By the
author of the Remarks [Joseph Boyse].
12mo. [*Brit. Mus.*] London, 1695

VINDICATION (a) of the Remarks
upon Mr Cha. Leslie's First Dialogue
on the Socinian controversy. [By
Thomas Emlyn.] 4to. Pp. 8.
[1708 ?]
No title-page.

VINDICATION (a) of the reverend
Dr Henry Sacheverell from the false,
scandalous and malicious aspersions
cast upon him in a late infamous
pamphlet entitled The modern
fanatick [by Rev. William Bisset]. . . .
In a dialogue between a Tory and a
Wh—g. [By William King, LL.D.,
with the co-operation of Charles Lambe,
M.A., and Dr Sacheverell.] 8vo. Pp.
viii. 99. [F. Madan, in the *Bibliographer*, vol. 4, p. 108.]
London [1710]

VINDICATION (a) of the Rev. Mr
Wesley's last minutes ; occasioned by
a circular, printed letter, inviting
principal persons, both clergy and
laity, as well of the dissenters as of
the established Church, who disap-
prove of those minutes, to oppose
them in a body, as a dreadful heresy.
. . . In five letters, to the Hon. and
Rev. author [Walter Shirley] of the
Circular letter. By a lover of quiet-
ness and liberty of conscience [John
William Fletcher]. 12mo. Pp. 98.
[*Gent. Mag.* lvi. 29.] Bristol, 1771
Letters signed : J. F.

VINDICATION (a) of the Review; or,
the exceptions formerly made against
Mr Horn's Catechisme, set free from
his late allegations, and maintained
not to be mistakes. By J. H. [Joseph
Hacon], parson of Massingham, p.
Norf. 8vo. [*Camb. Univ. Lib.*]
Cambridge, 1662

VINDICATION (a) of the Right Rev.
Dr Stillingfleet, Mr [Richard] Baxter,
Mr Humfrey, and Mr Clark, against
Dr Chauncey's late book. . . . [By
John Humfrey.] 4to. London, 1700

VINDICATION (a) of the Right Reverend the Lord Bishop of Exeter [Dr
Blackall], occasioned by Mr Benjamin
Hoadly's reflections on his Lordship's
two sermons Of government, preached
in St Dunstan's church, March 8, 1704,
and before her Majesty, March 8, 1708.
[By William Oldisworth.] 8vo. Pp.
87. [*Bodl.*] London, 1709

VINDICATION (a) of the Right Reverend the Ld. Bishop of Norwich, from
the undeserved reflections of the Reverend Mr John Johnson, in his book
entituled The unbloody sacrifice and
altar unvailed and supported . . . in
a letter to the Reverend Mr Johnson.
By a Christian [John Lewis, D.D.,
Vicar of Margate]. 8vo. Pp. 23.
[*Bodl.*] London, N.D.

VINDICATION (a) of the Right Reverend the Lord Bishop of Winchester,
against the malicious aspersions of
those who uncharitably ascribe the
book, intituled, A plain account of the
nature and end of the Sacrament of
the Lord's Supper, to his Lordship.
By the author of the *Proposal for the
revival of Christianity* [Philip Skelton,
B.A., rector of Fintona, Ireland]. 8vo.
Pp. 71. [*D. N. B.* vol. 52, p. 332.]
Dublin printed : London,
reprinted, 1736
An ironical production.

VINDICATION (a) of the rights of
brutes. [By Thomas Taylor, the
Platonist.] 12mo. [*Brit. Mus.*]
London, 1792

VINDICATION (a) of the rights of men, in a letter to the Right Honourable Edmund Burke; occasioned by his Reflections on the Revolution in France. [By Mary Wollstonecraft.] 8vo. [*W.*]   London, 1790

VINDICATION (a) of the Roman Catholicks of the English nation, from some aspersions lately cast upon them; in a letter from a Protestant gentleman in the country, to a citizen of London. [By R. Caron.] 4to. [*Bibliotheca Grenvilliana*, i. 117.]
London, 1660

VINDICATION (a) of the royal martyr King Charles I. from the Irish massacre in the year 1641, cast upon him in the " Life of Richard Baxter," wrote by himself, and since in the "Abridgement" by Edmund Calamy; being a case of present concern : in a letter to a member of the House of Commons. [By Rev. Thomas Carte.]   Second edition.   [*Cat. of the Lond. Inst.*]
1704

VINDICATION (a) of the Scottish Covenanters; consisting of a review of the first series of the "Tales of my landlord," extracted from the Christian Instructor for 1817. [By Thomas M'Crie, D.D.] With an appendix, containing various extracts, illustrative of the principles and character of the Reformers. 12mo.   Glasgow, 1824

VINDICATION (a) of the Scottish Presbyterians & Covenanters, against the aspersions of the author of "Tales of my landlord." By a member of the Scottish bar [James Grahame]. 8vo. Pp. 32.   Glasgow, 1817

VINDICATION (a) of the scripture doctrine of original sin from Mr Taylor's Free and candid examination of it. [By Rev. David Jennings, D.D.] 8vo. Pp. vi. 130. [Darling's *Cyclop. Bibl.*]   London, 1740

VINDICATION (a) of the sentence of the Synod of Relief in the case of the organ; and an answer to the misrepresentations of the Rev. William Anderson in his "Chapter of organ history." By a member of Synod [Rev. Alexander Harvey]. 8vo. Pp. 44.
Glasgow, 1829

VINDICATION (a) of the Short history of the Corporation and Test Acts. [By Capel Lofft.] 8vo. Pp. 35. [*Bodl.*]   London, 1790

VINDICATION of the speeches of Thomas Dromgole, M.D. [By John Lanigan, D.D.] 8vo.   Dublin, 1814

VINDICATION of the subject's right to deliberate and vote at County meetings. [By W. Peters.] 8vo.   1817

VINDICATION (a) of the Surey demoniack as no impostor : or, a reply to a certain pamphlet publish'd by Mr Zach. Taylor, called The Surey impostor : with a further clearing and confirming of the truth as to Richard Dugdale's case and cure. By T. J. [Thomas Jolly] one of the ministers who attended upon that affair from first to last. . . . 4to. Pp. 32. [*Bodl.*]
London, 1698

VINDICATION (a) of the Test-Act; or, the right of Protestant Dissenters to be admitted into all civil offices, fully and impartially consider'd. By a member of the House of Commons [Thomas Sherlock, D.D.]. 8vo. London, 1736

VINDICATION (a) of the Theory of Mahometanism unveiled, against the strictures of a writer in No. XIII. of the British Critic, and Quarterly Theological Review; in a letter to the Rev. Hugh James Rose, B.D., Christian Advocate in the University of Cambridge. [By the Rev. Charles Forster, author of the work.] 8vo. [*W.*; Martin's *Cat.*]   [London] 1830

VINDICATION (a) of Thomas Jefferson. . . . By Grotius [De Witt Clinton]. 8vo. [Sabin's *Dictionary.*]
New York, 1800

VINDICATION (a) of the Treatise of monarchy, containing an answer to Dr Fernes reply; also a more full discovery of three maine points : 1. The ordinance of God in supremacie. 2. The nature and kinds of limitation. 3. The causes and meanes of limitation in governments.   Done by the authour of the former treatise [Philip Hunton]. 4to.   London, 1644

VINDICATION (a) of the truth of Christian religion, against the objections of all modern opposers : written in French by the Reverend and learned Dr Jacques Abbadie; rendered into English by H. L. [Henry Lussan], of New Colledg, Oxford. 8vo. [Arber's *Term Cat.* ii. 491.]   London, 1698

This translation was denounced by the author as incorrect, and thus misrepresenting his views.

VINDICATION (a) of the twenty third Article of the Church of England, from a late exposition, ascribed to my Lord [Gilbert Burnet], Bishop of Sarum. [By William Thornton, Principal of Hart-Hall.] 4to. Pp. 26. [*Bodl.*]
London, 1702

Ascribed also to Bernard de Mandeville, and to Robert Burscough.

VINDICATION (a) of the worship of the Lord Jesus Christ, on the Unitarian principles ; in answer to what is said on that head by Mr Jos. Boyse, in his Vindication of the Deity of Jesus Christ. [By Thomas Emlyn.] 4to. [*D. N. B.* vol. 17, p. 359.]   N.P. 1705

VINDICATION (a) of their Majesties authority to fill the sees of the deprived bishops ; in a letter out of the country, occasioned by Dr B—— [Beveridge]'s refusal of the bishoprick of Bath and Wells. [By Edward Stillingfleet, D.D.] 4to. Pp. 27.   London, 1691

VINDICATION (a) of those who take the oath of allegiance to his present Majestie from perjurie, injustice, and disloyaltie, charged upon them but such as are against it ; wherein is evidently shewed that the common good of a nation is what is primarily and principally respected in an oath, and therefore when the oath is inconsistent with that, the persons who have taken it, are absolved from it ; in proving of which the case of Maud and King Stephen is particularly consider'd ; in a letter to a non-juror. [By Thomas Hearne.] 8vo. [*W.*]   1731

Preface to the Reader by —— Bilstone, M.A., of All Souls.

VINDICIÆ Academiarum ; containing, some briefe animadversions upon Mr Webster's book, stiled, The examination of academies ; together with an appendix concerning what M. Hobbs, and M. Dell have published on this argument. [By Seth Ward, D.D., Bishop of Salisbury.] 4to. Pp. 65. [Wood's *Athen. Oxon.* iv. 249.]
Oxford, 1654

The tract is signed : H. D., the final letters of the author's names. The prefatory epistle is signed : N. S., John Wilkins [finals] of Wadham College, afterwards Bishop of Chester ; this addition has also been wrongly assigned to Nathaniel Stephens.

VINDICIAE Anti-Baxterianae ; or, some animadversions on a book, entituled Reliquiae Baxterianae, or the life of Mr Richard Baxter. [By Samuel Young.] 12mo. [Arber's *Term Cat.* iii. 74.]
London, 1698

VINDICIÆ Biblicæ ; a series of notices and elucidations of passages in the Old and New Testament, which have been the subject of attack and misrepresentation by deistical writers. [By David Walther.] 8vo. [Lowndes' *Brit. Lib.* p. 314.]   London, 1832

VINDICIÆ Britannicæ ; being strictures on a late pamphlet by Gilbert Wakefield, A.B. late Fellow of Jesus College, Cambridge, intitled, The spirit of Christianity compared with the spirit of the times in Great Britain. By an undergraduate [William Penn, descendant of the Quaker]. 8vo. Pp. 66. [*Gent. Mag.* June 1863, p. 800 ; *Mon. Rev.* xv. 225.]   1794

VINDICIÆ Calvinisticæ ; or, some impartial reflections on the Dean of Londonderry's Considerations, and Mr Chancellor King's Answer thereto, in which he no less unjustly than impertinently reflects on the Protestant dissenters : in a letter to a friend. By W. B., D.D. [Joseph Boyse].   4to. [Jones' *Peck*, i. 155.]   Dublin, 1688

Published among Boyse's Works, ii. 45.

VINDICIÆ Carolinæ; or, a defence of ʼΕικων Βασιλική, the portraicture of his sacred Majesty in his solitudes and sufferings: in reply to a book intituled ʼΕικονοκλαστής, written by Mr Milton, and lately re-printed at Amsterdam. [By Richard Hollingworth, D.D.] 8vo. Pp. 12, 144. [Lowndes' *Bibl. Man.* p. 723.]   London, 1692

Ascribed also to John Wilson, author of a Treatise on necromancy. [*W.; Brit. Mus.*]

VINDICIÆ contra tyrannos; a defence of liberty against tyrants ; or of the awfull power of the prince over the people, and of the people over the prince ; being a treatise written in Latin and French by Junius Brutus [Hubert Languet] and translated out of both into English [by William Walker]. 4to.   London, 1648, 1689

" The original of this work has been attributed to Theodore Beza. M'Crie in his Life of Andrew Melville, vol. i. p. 424, says that this work resembles Hotman's Franco Gallia, and that Languet's work is properly only an enlargement of Beza's suppresst work, De Jure Magistruum, and although more guarded yet is still far from evasive in the expression of liberal opinions. In the British Museum copy of the edition of 1689, is the following Manuscript note— " This translation of the Vindicæ contra tyrannos was the work of Mr William Walker of Darnal near Sheffield, Yorkshire, the person who cut off King Charles's head. It was first printed in 1649 [1648] and reprinted at the Revolution as above."

VINDICIAE Flavianae; or, a vindication of the testimony given by Josephus concerning our Saviour Jesus Christ. [By Jacob Bryant.] 8vo. Pp. 83. [*Dyce Cat.*]   London, 1777

VINDICIAE juris regii ; or, remarques upon a paper [by Gilbert Burnet, D.D.], entituled, An enquiry into the measures of submission to the supream authority. [By Jeremy Collier.] 4to. Pp. 48. [*D. N. B.* vol. 11, p. 345.]
London, 1689

VINDICIÆ laicæ; or, the right of the laity to the unrestricted reading of the Sacred Scriptures, vindicated. By a clergyman of the Established Church [Rev. W. B. Mathias]. 8vo. Pp. 66.
Dublin, 1825

VINDICIÆ Landavensis ; or, strictures on the Bishop of Landaff's late charge, in a letter to his Lordship. [By William Mavor, LL.D.] 4to. Pp. 19.
Oxford, 1792

VINDICIÆ pietatis ; or, a vindication of godlinesse, in the greatest strictness and spirituality of it, from the imputations of folly and fansy ; together with several directions for the attaining and maintaining of a godly life. By R. A. [Richard Alleine]. 8vo. Pp. 12, 331. [*Brit. Mus.* ; Green's *Bibl. Somers.* ii. 107.]   London, 1664

VINDICIAE Priestleyanae; addressed to the students of Oxford and Cambridge. By a late member of the University of Cambridge [Theophilus Lindsay, B.A.]. 8vo. [*D. N. B.* vol. 33, p. 318.]
London, 1784
A second part appeared in 1790.

VINDICIAE regiae ; or, a defence of the kingly office: in two letters, to [Charles, the third] Earl Stanhope. [By John Ireland, D.D.] 8vo. [*Brit. Mus.; D. N. B.* vol. 29, p. 30.]   London, 1797
Two editions were issued.

VINDICIAE spei. . . . By D. C. [Daniel Cawdrey]. 4to.   London, 1641

VINDICIAE veritatis; or, an answer [by Nathaniel Fiennes] to a discourse [by David Buchanan], intituled, Truth it's manifest. . . . 4to. Pp. 246. [*Brit. Mus.*]   London, 1654

VINDICIAE veritatis ; or, an impartial account of two late disputations between Mr Dawson, late minister of Sandwich in Kent, and Mr Ives of London upon this question (viz.), whether the doctrine of some true believers final apostasy be true or no? Published to prevent false reports; together with an appendix. . . . By a lover of truth and peace [Jeremiah Ives]. 8vo. [Whitley's *Bapt. Bibl.* i. 98.]
London, 1672

VINDITIAE Paedo-Baptismii ; or, a confirmation of an Argument lately emitted for infant baptism : in a letter to a Reverend Divine of the Church of England. By R. B. [Richard Burthogge], M.D.   8vo.   [Arber's *Term Cat.* ii. 112 and 611]
London, 1685
The "Argument for Infant's Baptism " is not anonymous.

VINE and olive; or, Young America in Spain and Portugal. By Oliver Optic [William T. Adams]. 12mo. Pp. 309.
Boston, 1877

VINE culture for amateurs; being plain directions for the successful growing of grapes. . . . By "Practical Hand" [W. J. May]. 8vo. [*Brit. Mus.*]
London [1875]

VINE (the) Hunt. By "Sexagenarian" [Rev. Edward Austen-Leigh]. 8vo. [*N. and Q.* 1922, p. 437.]
Private print [*c.* 1870]

VINEGAR and mustard; or, wormwood lectures. By J. W. [John Wade, ballad writer]. 8vo. [*Brit. Mus.*]
London, 1673

VINETA. [A novel treating of love and patriotism.] By E. Werner [Elizabeth Bürstenbinder]; translated from the German. 8vo. Boston, 1877

VINETUM Britannicum ; or, a treatise of cider, and such other wines and drinks that are extracted from all manner of fruits growing in this kingdom. . . . With copper-plates. By J. W. Gent. [John Worlidge]. 8vo. Pp. 19, 186. [*Bodl.*]   London, 1676

VINEYARD (the). By John Oliver Hobbes [Mrs Pearl Mary Teresa Craigie, *née* Richards]. 8vo.
London, 1904

VINEYARD (the) of Naboth ; a dramatic fragment : translated from the original Hebrew [by Dr Edward Andrews, minister of Beresford Church, Walworth]. 8vo. Pp. 36.
London, private print, 1825

VINOVO and its porcelain ; a page of the history of art in Piedmont. By L. De Mauri [Ernesto Sarasino]. 8vo. Pp. 38. [*Brit. Mus.*]   London, 1925

VINTAGE (the) of vice. By Guy Thorne [Cyril A. E. Ranger-Gull]. 8vo. Pp. 490.   London, 1913

VINTNERS (the) answer to some scandalous pamphlets, published, as is supposed by Richard Kilvert. [By Henry Parker.] 4to. [Thomason's *Coll. of Tracts*, i. 97.]   London, 1642

VINUM Britannicum; or, an essay on the properties and effects of malt liquors: wherein is considered in what cases, and to what constitutions, they are either beneficial or injurious; with a plain mechanical account how they are serviceable or disserviceable to human bodies. [By James Sedgwick.] 8vo.   London, 1727

VIOLA. By the author of *Caste*, etc. [Emily Jolly]. 8vo.   London, 1869

VIOLA; or, 'tis an old tale. [By Isabel Goldsmid.] 8vo.   London, 1852
    Another edition of "'Tis an old tale," *q.v.*

VIOLENTA; or, the rewards of virtue: turn'd from Bocacce into verse [by Mrs Mary Pix]. 8vo. [*Brit. Mus.*]
                    London, 1704
VIOLENZIA; a tragedy. [By William Caldwell Roscoe.] Pp. xiii. 140. [*Bodl.*]
                    London, 1851
VIOLET and daisy; or, the picture with two sides. By M. H. [Matilda Horsburgh]. 8vo. [*Brit. Mus.*]
                    Edinburgh, 1868
VIOLET Bank and its inmates. [By Mrs Henrietta Camilla Jenkin.] 8vo. 3 vols.   London, 1858

VIOLET; or, the danseuse: a portraiture of human passions and character. [By —— Beasley.] 8vo. 2 vols. [*N. and Q.* 4th Ser. pp. 176, 324, 397, 492, 543.]   London, 1836

VIOLET Stuart; a tale of Gibraltar. By H. E. P. [Harriet Eleanor Phillimore]. 8vo. [*Lib. Journ.* iii. 310.]
                    London, 1879
VIOLET, the American Sappho; a realistic novel of bohemia. By Rob. Appleton [Roman L. Zubof]. 8vo.
                    New York, 1894
VIOLETS and jonquils. [A tale. By Thomas Henry Wilkins.] 12mo. 2 vols. [*Brit. Mus.*]   London, 1857

VIOLET'S victory. By A. K. C. [Antoinette K. Crichton]. 12mo.
                    London, 1877
VIOLIN (the); how to master it. By a professional player [William C. Honeyman]. 8vo. [*Brit. Mus.*]
                    Edinburgh [1894]
VIPER (the) of Milan. By Marjorie Bowen [Gabrielle Vere Campbell]. 8vo. Pp. 356. [*Who's Who in Lit.*]
                    London, 1906
VIRGIDEMIARUM; six bookes: first three bookes, of toothlesse satyrs. 1. Poeticall. 2. Academicall. 3. Morall. [By Joseph Hall, Bishop of Norwich.] 8vo. Pp. 85. [Hart's *Index Expurg. Angl.* p. 33.]
                    London, 1597

VIRGIDEMIARUM; the three last bookes; of byting satyres. [By Joseph Hall, Bishop of Norwich.] 8vo. Pp. 111. [Hart's *Index Expurg. Angl.* p. 33.]   London, 1598
VIRGIL in London; or, town eclogues: to which are added, imitations of Horace. [By George Daniel.] 8vo. [*D. N. B.* vol. 14, p. 22.]
                    London, 1814
VIRGILIUS; this boke treateth of the lyfe of Virgilius, and of his deth, and many marvayles that he did, in hys lyfe-tyme, by whychcrafte and nygromancye thorough the helpe of the devyls of hell. [Reprinted and edited by E. Vernon Utterson.] 4to. Pp. 22. [*W.*; Martin's *Cat.*]   London [1812]

VIRGILS Eclogues translated into English. By W. L. Gent. [William Lisle]. 8vo. Pp. 14, 193.
                    London, 1628
VIRGIL'S husbandry; or, an essay on the Georgics: being the first book, translated into English verse: to which are added the Latin text, and Mr Dryden's version: with notes critical, and rustick. [By William Benson.] 8vo. Pp. xv. 50. [Lowndes' *Bibl. Man.* p. 2784.]   London, 1725
    The second book, with title-page as above, was published in the previous year, 1724.

VIRGIL'S first pastoral [a poem based on his first eclogue]. By Eta [William Cunningham, of Edinburgh]. 4to.
        Private print [Edinburgh, 1883]
    Presentation copy from the author.

VIRGIL'S two seasons of honey. . . . With a method of investigating the rising and setting of the fixed stars. [By Bishop Samuel Horsley.] 4to. [*Birm. Cent. Lib.*]   London, 1805

VIRGIN (the) and the fool. By Ellenor G. Linne [F. Britten Austin and Lambert F. Williams]. 8vo. Pp. vii. 64. [*Ashley Lib.*]   London, 1904

VIRGIN (the) birth, one of the principal foundations of the Christian faith; an account of some of the various ways it was explained: collected and presented to the twentieth century by a Bibliophile [Rev. Walter Begley]. 8vo.
                    Private print, 1905
VIRGIN (the) Mary misrepresented by the Roman Church, in the traditions of that Church, concerning her life and glory; and in the devotions paid to her, as the mother of God. . . . Part I. Wherein two of her feasts, her conception and nativity are considered. [By John Patrick.] 4to. Pp. 153. [Jones' *Peck*, p. 417.]   London, 1688

VIRGIN (the) unmask'd ; or, female dialogues betwixt an elderly maiden lady and her neice. . . . [Signed: B. M. *i.e.* Bernard Mandeville.] 8vo. [*Brit. Mus.*]   London, 1709

VIRGIN (the) widow. [A novel.] By A. Matthey [Arthur Arnould]. Translated from the latest French edition. 8vo. Pp. 259. [*Brit. Mus.*]
London, 1887

VIRGIN (a) widow ; a novel. By Oliver Grey [Henry Rowland Brown, junior]. 8vo. 3 vols.   London, 1886

VIRGIN (the) widow ; a tragedy. [By the Rev. Thomas Comber, LL.D., rector of Buckworth, Huntingdonshire.] 8vo.   Huntingdon, 1777

VIRGIN (the) wife. By John Carruthers [John Young Thomson Greig]. 8vo. Pp. 336. [*Brit. Mus.*]
London, 1925

VIRGINALIA ; or, spiritual sonnets in prayse of the most glorious Virgin Marie, upon everie severall title of her litanies of Lareto. . . . By I. B. [John Brereley, *i.e.* Lawrence Anderton, S.J.]. Pp. 48. [Sparke's *Bibl. Bolt.* p. 6.]   1632

VIRGINIA ; a pastoral drama, on the birth-day of an illustrious person. [By John Parke.] 4to. [*Mag. of Hist.* extra no. 91.]   Philadelphia, 1776

VIRGINIA ; a Roman sketch. By H. A. D. [Miss Henrietta A. Duff]. 8vo. [*Brit. Mus.*]   London, 1877

VIRGINIA ; a tragedy, as it is acted at the Theatre-Royal in Drury-Lane, by his Majesty's servants. [By Samuel Crisp, of Chesington.] 8vo. Pp. 74. [*D. N. B.* vol. 13, p. 98.]   London, 1754
    Wrongly ascribed to Henry Crisp, and to Frances Moore, afterwards Mrs Brooke.

VIRGINIA (the) comedians ; or, old days in the Old Dominion ; edited from the MSS. of Champ Effingham [John Esten Cooke]. 12mo. 2 vols. [Wegelin's *Bibl. of J. E. Cooke.*]
New York, 1854

VIRGINIA land grants ; a study of conveyancing in relation to colonial politics. [Introduction signed : F. H. *i.e.* Fairfax Harrison.] 8vo. Pp. 184. [*Brit. Mus.*]   Richmond, Va., 1925

VIRGINIA of the Rhodesians. [A novel.] By the author of *Poppy* [Cynthia Stockley]. 8vo. Pp. 278. [*Who's Who in Lit.*]   London, 1910

VIRGINIA ; or, the Roman father : a tragedy [in verse. By H. Mackenzie]. 8vo. Pp. 62. [*Brit. Mus.*]
Private print, N.P. [1820 ?]

VIRGINIA Tennant. By the author of *Christina North* [Miss E. M. Archer]. 8vo. [*Brit. Mus.*]   London, 1888

VIRGINIAN (a) holiday. By Hope Daring [Anna Johnson]. 8vo. [*Amer. Cat.*]   New York, 1910

VIRGINIANS in Texas ; a story for young old folks, and old young folks. [By William M. Baker.] 8vo.
New York, 1878

VIRGINIE'S husband ; a novel. By Esmé Stuart [Miss Amélie Claire Leroy]. 8vo. Pp. 370. [*Who's Who in Lit.*]   London [1892]

VIRGIN'S (the) vengeance ; or, how the Irish got Home Rule. By Ross George Dering [Frederic Henry Balfour]. 8vo. Pp. 78. [*Brit. Mus.*]
Oxford, 1889

VIRTUE the source of pleasure. [By E. Barnard.] 8vo. [Baker's *Biog. Dram.* i. 21 ; *Mon. Rev.* xvii. 603.]
1757

VIRTUES (the) of honey in preventing many of the worst disorders. . . . [By John Hill, M.D.] 8vo. [*Brit. Mus.*]
London, 1759

VIRTUE'S tragedy ; a novel. By Eff Kaye [Miss E. Konstam, later Mrs Price]. 8vo. [*Brit. Mus.*]
London, 1899

VIRTUOSO'S (the) companion and coin collector's guide. [By Thomas Prattent and M. Denton.] 8vo. 8 vols. [*Brit. Mus.*]   London, 1795-7

VIRTUOUS (the) wife ; a sentimental tale. By G. C. L. [Gervase C. Leverland]. 8vo. [*Brit. Mus.*]
Sudbury, private print, 1812

VIRTUS post funera vivit ; or, honour tryumphing over death, being true epitomes of honourable, noble, learned and hospitable personages. By W. P. [William Sampson]. 4to. 36 leaves. [*W ;* Lowndes' *Bibl. Man.*]
London, 1636

VIRTUS rediviva ; a panegyrick on our late King Charles the First, of ever blessed memory ; attended with severall other ingenious pieces from the same pen. . . . By T. F. [Thomas Forde]. 8vo. [Wood's *Athen. Oxon.* iii. 1097 ; iv. 245.]   London, 1660

VISIBLE (the) God, and our relation to Him in creation and redemption. [By William Marshall.] 8vo. Pp. viii. 365. [*Brit. Mus.*]   London, 1890

VISION (the) ; a poem. [By Daniel Defoe.] 4to. Pp. 4.
[Edinburgh, 1706]
    Wrongly ascribed to Thos. Hamilton, Earl of Haddington.

VISION (the) ; a poem containing reflections on fashionable attachments, fashionable marriages, and fashionable education. By an enemy to them all [Thomas Grady]. 8vo. [O'Donoghue's *Poets of Ireland.*]   Dublin, 1798

VISION (the) ; compylit in Latin be a most lernit clerk, in time of our hairship and oppression, anno 1300, and translatit in 1524. [Verse : subscribed "Quod Ar. Scot." *i.e.* Allan Ramsay.] 8vo. Pp. 15. [*D. N. B.* vol. 47, p. 232]. [Edinburgh] 1748

VISION (the) ; from Dante ; translated by H. F. C. [Rev. Henry Francis Cary]. 12mo. [O'Donoghue's *Poets of Ireland*, p. 36.]   London, 1814

VISION (the) and discourse of Henry the Seventh, concerning the unitie of Great Brittaine. . . . Related by T. G. [Thomas Gainsford, in verse]. 4to. [*Brit. Mus.*]   London, 1610

VISION (the) of a Highlander. [By D. Dewar.] 8vo. [*Brit. Mus.*]
                    London [1886]

VISION (the) of angels. By Kythe Wylwynne [Miss M. F. Hyland]. 8vo. [*Who's Who in Lit.*]   Edinburgh, 1896

VISION (the) of Barabbas and other poems. [By C. E. Bourne.] 8vo. Pp. 103. [*Brit. Mus.*]   London, 1891

VISION (the) of Constantine, and other poems. [Signed : R. G. M. *i.e.* Robert Gerald Mooney, B.A.] 12mo. [O'Donoghue's *Poets of Ireland.*]
                    Dublin, 1828

VISION (the) of Esther ; a sequel to the *Vision of Nimrod.* By Louis Barnaval [Charles De Kay]. 8vo.
                    New York, 1882

VISION (a) of Hell ; a poem. [By John Abraham Heraud.] 12mo. Pp. 165.   Glasgow, 1831

VISION (a) of Hell, and a discovery of some of the consultations and devices there in the year 1767. By Theodorus Van Shermain [Jacob Green]. 12mo. Pp. 35. [Evans' *Amer. Bibl.* vol. 4, p. 230.]   New-London, 1770

VISION (the) of J. L. [John Lacy], Esq., and prophet, on Thursday the 9th of June, 1715 (Bloody Thursday). . . . 8vo. Pp. 24. [*Brit. Mus.*]
                    London, 1715
    The "Vision" was occasioned by the Rebellion in favour of the Pretender.

VISION (the) of judgment. By Quevedo Redivivus [George Gordon Byron, Lord Byron], suggested by the composition so entitled by the author [Robert Southey] of "Wat Tyler." 8vo. Pp. 24.   London, 1824

VISION (the) of judgment ; or, the return of Joanna [Southcott] from her trance. [Introduction signed : C. W. T. *i.e.* Charles William Twort.] 8vo. 2 parts. [*Brit. Mus.*]   London, 1829

VISION (the) of judgment ; or, the South Church : ecclesiastical councils viewed from celestial and Satanic stand-points. By Quevedo Redivivus, Jr. [Robert William Wright]. 8vo. [*Sabin's Dict.*]   New York, 1867

VISION (the) of judgment revived. By Bloc [Clarence F. Cobb]. 8vo. [Cushing's *Init. and Pseud.*]
                    Washington, D.C., 1870

VISION (the) of Mary ; or, a dream of joy : a poem in honour of the immaculate conception. By R. B. J., barrister-at-law : Temple [Robert Baker Jones]. 8vo. [Olphar Hamst, p. 108.]
                    London, 1856

VISION (a) of memory, and other poems. By a young gentleman [Fortescue Hitchins]. 8vo. [Cushing's *Init. and Pseud.*]
                    Plymouth, New England, 1803

VISION (the) of Mons. Chamillard concerning the Battle of Ramilies and the miraculous Revolution in Flanders begun May the 12th, 1706 : a poem, . . . By a nephew of the late Mr John Milton [John Phillips]. [*D. N. B.* vol. 45, p. 206.]   London, 1706

VISION (the) of Nimrod ; an oriental romance. By Louis Barnaval [Charles De Kay]. 8vo.   New York, 1882

VISION (the) of Pierce Plowman. . . . [By Robert Langland.] 4to. Pp. cxvii. B. L.   London, 1550

VISION (the) of Purgatory, anno 1680 ; in which the errors and practices of the Church and Court of Rome are discover'd. By Heraclito Democritus [Edward Pettit, M.A.]. 12mo. Pp. 10, 156.   London, 1680

VISION (the) of Rubeta ; an epic story of the Island of Manhattan. [By Laughton Osborn.] 8vo. [*Brit. Mus.*]
                    Boston, 1838

VISION (a) of splendid hope. By Conrad Hawthorne Carroder [Walter John Tripp]. 12mo.   London, 1903

VISION (a) of Sumeru, and other poems. By Choshee Chunder Dutt [J. A. G. Barton]. 8vo.   London [1878]

VISION (the) of the Lord of Hosts, faithfully declared in his own time. By a handmaid of the Lord, M. H. [Mary Howgill]. 4to. [*Brit. Mus.*]
                    [London] 1662

VISION (the) of the three T.'s ; a threnody by the author of *The new belfry*, etc. [Rev. Charles L. Dodgson, M.A.]. 12mo. [*Brit. Mus.*]
                    London, 1873

VISION (the) of the years. [A novel.] By Curtis Yorke [Mrs W. S. Richmond Lee, *née* —— Jex-Long]. 8vo. Pp. 316. [*Who's Who in Lit.*]   London, 1913

VISION (the); or, a dialog between the soul and the bodie, fancied in a morning dream. [By James Howell.] 8vo. Pp. 176. [Bliss' *Cat.* 154.]   1651

VISION (the) splendid; some verse for the time and the time to come. By John Oxenham [William Arthur Dunkerley]. 12mo. Pp. 96. [*Who's Who in Lit.*]   London, 1917

VISION (a) written by F. P. . . . [Fr. Plumer] in two letters to a friend. 8vo. [*Brit. Mus.*]
        London, private print, 1781

VISIONARY (the): Nos. I., II., III. [By Sir Walter Scott. Political satires, signed: Somnambulist.] 8vo. [*Brit. Mus.*]   Edinburgh, 1819

VISIONS and jewels; an autobiography. By Moysheh Oyved [Edward Good]. 8vo. Pp. 174. [*The Observer*, 1, 5, 27.]   London, 1925

VISIONS in verse, for the entertainment and instruction of younger minds. [By Nathaniel Cotton, M.D.] Eighth edition, revis'd and enlarg'd. 8vo. Pp. 141. [*Bodl.*]   London, 1771

VISIONS (the) of Dom Francisco de Quevedo Villegas, Knight of the Order of St James; made English by R. L. [Roger L'Estrange]. 8vo. [*Brit. Mus.*]   London, 1667

VISIONS (the) of John Bunyan; being his last remains; recommended by him as necessary to be had in all families. [*Not* by John Bunyan, but by George Larkin, junior.] 8vo. [Brown's *Life of Bunyan*, pp. 447-8.]
        London, 1725
    The original title of this work was "The world to come; the glories of heaven and the terrors of hell lively displayed under the similitude of a vision: by G. L." London, 1711.

VISIONS (the) of sapience; or, a report of the speeches delivered at an extraordinary congress, convened by his Satanic Majesty, for the purpose of . . . presenting James Douglas [of Newcastle] with a vote of thanks for his late attempts, in two pamphlets [entitled "Methodism condemned" and "The system of Methodism exposed"] to render Methodism contemptible and Devilism respectable: with notes. By Criticos [James Everett] and Castigator [William Naylor]. 8vo. Pp. 60. [*Brit. Mus.*]
        Leeds, 1815

VISIONS (the) of Sir Heister Ryley, with other enterteinments, consisting of 200 discourses and letters, representing by way of image and description, the characters of Virtue, Beauty, Affection, Love, and Passion, etc. etc. [By Charles Povey.] 4to. Vol. I. [*N. and Q.* 24th March 1855, p. 234.]
        [1711]

VISIONS of the night . . . . [By William Naismith.] 8vo.   Paisley, 188—

VISIONS (the) of the soul, before it comes into the body; in several dialogues. Written by a member of the Athenian Society [John Dunton]. 8vo. Pp. 151.   London, 1692

VISIONS of the Western railways; to which are added, Thoughts on the British Association at Liverpool in 1837, and miscellaneous poems. [By Richard E. A. Townsend.] 8vo.
        London, private print, 1838

VISIT (the) for a week; or, hints on the improvement of time: containing original tales, anecdotes from natural and moral history, &c.; designed for the amusement of youth. By the author of *The six princesses of Babylon*, etc. [Lucy Peacock]. Second edition, revised. 12mo. Pp. 330. [*Brit. Mus.*]
        London, 1794

VISIT (the) to Clarina; or, the effects of revenge: an Irish story. By M. F. D. [Maria Frances Dickson, later Mrs Smith]. 12mo. Pp. iv. 176. [*Brit. Mus.*]   London, 1842

VISIT (a) to Coventry fair; with the story of Lady Godiva . . . a legendary rhyme. [By Charles Dyall.] 8vo. Pp. 16.   Manchester [1863]

VISIT (the) to Dolby Hall, and what came of it; and the Mystery of a five-pound note. By the author of *Maud Hamilton*, etc. [Anna Kent]. 8vo. Pp. 125. [*Brit. Mus.*] London, 1906

VISIT (a) to Dublin. [By William Knox.] 8vo. [*N. and Q.* 26th December 1863, p. 529.]   Edinburgh, 1824

VISIT (a) to grandpa; or, a week at Newport. [By Sarah S. Cahoone.] 12mo. Pp. 213. [Sabin's *Dictionary*.]
        New York, 1840
    Reprinted, 1842, also anonymous, as "Sketches of Newport . . .", *q.v.*

VISIT (a) to Iona [in 1846] by an American clergyman [James C. Richmond]. 8vo.   Glasgow, 1849
    Presentation copy.

VISIT (a) to my birthplace. [By Mrs Selina Bunbury.] 12mo. [*Brit. Mus.*[
        Dublin [1828?]

VISIT (a) to my discontented cousin. [By James Moncreiff Baron, of Tullie-bole.] 8vo. [F. Boase's *Mod. Eng. Biog.* Supp. vol. 6, col. 229.]
London, 1871

VISIT (a) to Saint Saviour's, South-wark ; with advice to Dr Sacheverell's preachers there. By a divine of the Church of England [White Kennett, D.D.]. 8vo. London, 1710

VISIT (a) to the Antipodes ; with remi-niscences of a sojourn in [South] Australia. By a squatter [E. Lloyd]. 12mo. [*Sydney Public Lib.*]
London, 1846

VISIT (a) to the Celestial City ; revised by the Committee of the American Sunday School Union. [By Nathaniel Hawthorne.] 16mo. [Foley's *Amer. Authors.*] Philadelphia [1843]

VISIT (a) to the Eastern necropolis of Dundee, on 30th August 1865, in seven chapters. By Norval [James Scrymgeour]. 12mo. Pp. 33. [*And. Jervise.*] Dundee [1865]
Reprinted from the *Dundee Advertiser* for private circulation.

VISIT (a) to the Falls of Niagara in 1800. [By John Maude.] 8vo. [*Quaritch's Cat.*] London, 1826

VISIT (a) to the headquarters of Sloyd. [Signed : J. S. T. *i.e.* Joseph Smith Thornton.] 8vo. [*Brit. Mus.*]
London [1892 ?]

VISIT (a) to the New Forest ; a tale. By Harriet Myrtle, author of *The water-lily*, etc. [Mrs Lydia Falconer Miller]. Illustrated with twenty-five engravings, from drawings by William Harvey, George Thomas, Birket Foster, and Harrison Weir. 8vo. Pp. 158.
London, 1859

VISIT (a) to the rectory of Passy ; with sketches of character and scenery. [By J. W. Peers.] 8vo. Pp. 228.
London, 1826

VISIT (a) to the United Service Institu-tion in 1849. By Bosquecillo [Lieuten-ant D. B. Shaw]. 12mo. London, 1849

VISIT (a) to the Waldenses. By a Kentish vicar [Rev. Edward Vesey Bligh, M.A.]. 8vo. [*Brit. Mus.*]
London [1873]

VISIT (a) to the Wild West ; or, a sketch of the Emerald Isle. By an English traveller [Ralph D'Israeli]. 8vo. London, 1843

VISIT (a) to Vaucluse, Nismes, Orange, Pont-du-Gard, Avignon, Marseilles, &c. &c. in May, MDCCCXXI. By the author of the *Trimester*, in MDCCCXX. [Rev. Stephen Weston, B.D.]. 8vo. Pp. 111. London, 1822
Author's name in the hand-writing of Dyce.

VOL. VI.

VISITATION (the) of dens ; an appeal to the women of England. By the author of *Work among the lost* [Ellice Hopkins]. 12mo. Pp. 29.
London [1874]

VISITATION (a) of heavenly love unto the seed of Jacob yet in captivity ; to whom the love of the Lord is, who is gathering, and will gather it, for it belongs unto him. By one who feeleth the springs of life opened from which this is given forth, D. W. [Dorothy White, of Weymouth]. 4to. Pp. 9. [Smith's *Cat. of Friends' Books.*]
London, 1660

VISITATION (a) of love unto the King [Charles II.], and those called Royal-lists ; consisting of an Answer to several Queries proposed to the people called Quakers, from a supposed Royallist. . . . [Signed : E. B. *i.e.* Edward Burrough.] 4to. Pp. 39. [Smith's *Cat. of Friends' Books.*]
London, 1660

VISITATION (the) of the County of Lincoln in 1562-64. [By Robert Cooke.] Edited by Walter C. Metcalfe. 8vo. [Anderson's *Brit. Top.*]
London, 1881

VISITATION (the) ; or, long look'd-for comes at last, in the submission of Mr Baxter, Mr Jenkins and others to . . . the Act of Uniformity. [Preface signed : R. L. *i.e.* Sir Roger L'Estrange.] 8vo. Pp. 28. [*Brit. Mus.*] London, 1662

VISITATION (a) speech at Colchester in Essex, 1692. [By John Hansley, Archdeacon of Colchester.] 4to. Pp. 14. London, 1662

VISITATION (a) to the Jewes from them whom the Lord hath visited from on high, among whom he hath per-formed his promise made with Abra-ham, Isaac, and Jacob, and to his seed, which Moses saw, &c. Given forth by G. F. [George Fox]. 4to. [Smith's *Cat. of Friends' Books*, i. 651.]
London, 1656

VISITATIONS for Cornwall. [By Sir Nicholas Harris Nicolas.] Fol. Pp. 28. N.P., N.D.
The above is a made-up title. The work was never published.

VISITED on the children ; a novel. By Theo. Gift [Dora Havers]. 8vo. 3 vols. London, 1881

VISITING my relations, and its results ; a series of small episodes in the life of a recluse. [By Mary Ann Kelty.] 8vo. [*D.N.B.* vol. 30, p. 360.]
London, 1851

N

VISITING societies and lay readers ; a letter to the Lord Bishop of London. By Presbyter Catholicus [Rev. William Harness, incumbent of All-Saints, Knightsbridge]. 8vo. [Darling's *Cyclop. Bibl.*] London, 1844

VISITOR'S hand-book for Cheltenham ; containing brief notices of the spas, pump rooms, and places of fashionable resort and amusement ; also of its churches, chapels, and public institutions ; with chronological notices of events connected with its history, &c. &c. [By Henry Davies.] 8vo. Pp. viii. 78. [*Bodl.*] London, 1840
    Advertisement signed : H. D.

VISITOR'S (the) hand-book to Corfe Castle and its neighbourhood, including notices of Swanage, Tilly-whim, Encome, Lulworth Castle, Bindon Abbey . . . and other objects of interest. . . . [By David Sydenham.] 12mo. Pp. iv. 56. [Mayo's *Bibl. Dors.* p. 138.] London, 1853

VISITOR'S handbook to Weston-super-Mare and its vicinity. [By Miss L. E. H. Jackson.] 12mo. [*Brit. Mus.*] Weston-super-Mare [1877]

VISTA (a). [Poems.] By John Crichton [Norman Gregor Guthrie]. 8vo. Pp. 85. [*Brit. Mus.*] Montreal, 1921

VISTAS Mexicanas ; the land of the Sun. By Christian Reid [Frances Fisher, later Mrs James N. Tiernan]. 8vo. New York, 1895

VITA (la) mia ; a sonnet chain of life and thought. By W. H. [William Hastie, D.D., Professor in Glasgow University]. 8vo. Pp. 70. Edinburgh, private print, 1896

VITAL lies ; studies of some varieties of recent obscurantism. By Vernon Lee [Violet Paget]. 8vo. 2 vols. [*Who's Who in Lit.*] London, 1912

VITAL (the) Spark and her queer crew. By Hugh Foulis [Neil Munro]. 8vo. Pp. 184. [*Brit. Mus.*] Edinburgh, 1906

VITAL truth and deadly error. [By T. A. Tyng.] 8vo. [*Brit. Mus.*] Cincinnati, 1853

VITALITY ; an appeal to the Fellows of the Royal Society of London for improving natural knowledge. By a Fellow [Lionel Smith Beale, M.D.]. 8vo. [*Camb. Univ. Lib.*] London, 1899

VITIS degeneris ; or, the degenerate-plant : being a treatise of ancient ceremonies, containing an historical account of their rise and growth, their first entrance into the Church, and their gradual advancement to superstition therein. Written originally in French, but now, for general information and benefit, faithfully translated into English [by Thomas Douglas]. [By John Wilson.] 8vo. Pp. 45, 173. [*Bodl.*] London, 1668

VITTORIA Colonna ; a tale of Rome in the nineteenth century. [By Charlotte A. Eaton.] 12mo. 3 vols. Edinburgh, 1827
    Published in 1820, with the title "Rome in the nineteenth century."

VIVA. [A novel.] By Mrs Forrester [Mrs —— Bridges]. 8vo. 3 vols. London, 1878

VIVE Jesus ; the Rule of St Austin with the Constitutions and Directory for the religious sisters of the Visitation. Translated out of French [by Charles Townely]. Pp. 312. Paris, 1678

VIVIAN Grey. [By Benjamin Disraeli.] 12mo. 5 vols. [*Brit. Mus.*] London, 1826-27

VIVIENNE ; a novel. By "Rita" [Mrs W. Desmond Humphreys, *née* Eliza M. J. Gollan]. 8vo. [*Who's Who in Lit.*] London, 1884

VIVIER of Vivier, Longman and Company, bankers ; a novel. By Barclay North [W. C. Hudson]. 8vo. London, 1890

VIVISECTION ; a farce in one act [and in prose]. By W. J. M. [William John Massey]. 8vo. [*Brit. Mus.*] [London, 1877]

VIXEN ; a novel. By the author of *Lady Audley's secret*, etc. [M. E. Braddon]. 8vo. 3 vols. London, 1879

VIZIER Ali Khan ; or, the massacre of Benares ; a chapter in British Indian history. By J. F. D. [Sir John Francis Davis]. Second edition. 8vo. London, private print, 1871
    The first edition appeared in 1844.

VIZIER'S (the) son ; or, the adventures of a Mogul. By the author of *Pandurang Hari* [William Brown Hockley]. 8vo. 3 vols. London, 1831

VOCABULARY (a) containing Chinese words and phrases peculiar to Canton and Macao. By J. F. D. [Sir John Francis Davis]. 8vo. [*Brit. Mus.*] Macao, 1824

VOCABULARY of English-Chinyanja and Chinyanja-English as spoken at Likoma, Lake Nyasa. Compiled by M. E. W. [Miss M. E. Woodward]. Second edition. 8vo. Pp. 88. [*Brit. Mus.*]   London, 1895

VOCABULARY (a) of the English and Malay languages. By B. P. K. [Benjamin Peach Keasberry]. 8vo. [*Brit. Mus.*]   London, 1863

VOCABULARY (a) of the English, Bugis, and Malay languages, containing about 2000 words. [By Th. Thomsen.] 8vo. Pp. vi. 66.
                    Singapore, 1833

V O C A B U L A R Y (a); or, pocket dictionary; to which is prefixed a compendious grammar of the English language. [By John Baskerville.] 12mo. [*Brit. Mus.*]
                    Birmingham, 1765

VOCABULARY (a) to Bland's Latin Hexameters and Pentameters. By a Harrow tutor [Cecil Frederick Holmes]. 12mo. Pp. vii. 45.
                    London, 1863
Introduction signed : C. F. H.

VOCAL (the) organ ; or, a new art of teaching the English orthographie, by observing the instruments of pronunciation. By O. P. [Owen Price], Master of Arts and Professor of the Art of Paedagogie. 8vo. [*Brit. Mus.*]
                    Oxford, 1665

VOCAL parts of an entertainment [by Mr Rich], called Apollo and Daphne : or, the Burgo-master trick'd ; as perform'd in the Theatre Royal in Lincoln's-Inn-Fields. [By Lewis Theobald.] The fourth edition, with alterations and additions. 8vo. Pp. 15.   London, 1726

VOCAL sounds. By Edward Search [Abraham Tucker]. 8vo. [*D. N. B.* vol. 57, p. 278.]   Private print, 1773

VOCATION (the) of the soul : being meditations given in the Confraternity of the Divine Love. [By Mother Elizabeth.] 8vo. Pp. 125. [*Brit. Mus.*]   London, 1916

VOCES populi. By F. Anstey [Thomas Anstey Guthrie]. Two series. 4to. [*Who's Who in Lit.*] London, 1890-92

VOICE (a) from America to England. By an American gentleman [Calvin Colton]. 8vo. [Allibone's *Dict.*]
                    London, 1839

VOICE (a) from heaven. [By Thomas Lake Harris.] 8vo.
                    Fountain-Grove, 1879

VOICE (a) from heaven, to the Commonwealth of England. [By Arise Evans.] 8vo. Pp. 75. [Thomason's *Coll. of Tracts* i. 883.]   London, 1652

VOICE (a) from Palace Yard! addressed to Sir Robert Peel and members of both houses of parliament by George Canning. [By Francis Stack Murphy.] 8vo. Pp. 24. [*Athen. Cat.*]
                    London [1844]

VOICE (a) from Rome, A.D. 1842. [By Frederick Meyrick, M.A.] 12mo. Pp. 50. [*Brit. Mus.*]   London, 1843

VOICE (a) from St Peter's and St Paul's; being a few plain words . . . on some late accusations against the [English] Church establishment. . . . By a member of the University of Oxford [William Lisle Bowles]. 8vo. [*Brit. Mus.*]   London, 1825

VOICE (a) from the back pews to the pulpit and front seats ; an answer to "What think ye of Christ?" By a back-pewman [Elihu Burritt]. 8vo.
                    London, 1872

VOICE (a) from the factories; in serious verse: dedicated to the Right Honourable Lord Ashley. [By the Hon. Caroline Elizabeth Sarah Norton.] 8vo.   London, 1836

V O I C E (a) from the far Interior of Australia. By John Sidney. [Really written by his brother, Samuel Sidney.] 8vo. [*D. N. B.* vol. 52, p. 240.]
                    London, 1847

VOICE (a) from the font. [By George Wilkins, D.D.] 12mo. London, 1838

VOICE (a) from the North ; an appeal to the people of England on behalf of their Church. By an English priest [Samuel Brown Harper]. 8vo. 3 parts.   London, 1850

VOICE (a) from the ocean grave. . . . By a philanthropist [Josiah Harris]. 8vo. [Boase and Courtney's *Bibl. Corn.*]   Truro, 1859

VOICE (a) from the pew to the pulpit, against the practice of reading sermons. [By Rev. Thomas Kay, of Ladyburn Church, Greenock.] 8vo.
                    Edinburgh [c. 1850[

VOICE (a) from the pews ; or, a Tabernacle supplement. By A men der [Benjamin F. Burnham]. 8vo. [*Lib. Journ.* iv. 171.]   Boston, 1877

VOICE (a) from the place of S. Morwenna, in the rocky land, uttered to the sisters of mercy, at the Tamar Mouth ; and to Lydia, their lady in the faith, "whose heart the Lord opened." By the vicar of Morwenstow, a priest in the diocese of Exeter [Robert Stephen Hawker]. 12mo. Pp. 13.   London, 1849
Signed : R. S. H.

VOICE (a) from the police-court ; or, the danger of too much punch. By Saint Meva [Josiah Harris]. 8vo. [Boase and Courtney's *Bibl. Corn.*]
                    Plymouth, [1856?]

VOICE (a) from the sea ; or, the wreck of the Eglantine. By Ruth Elliott [Lillie Peck]. 8vo. [*Lib. Journ.* iii. 379.] London, 1876

VOICE (a) from the South ; or, an address from some Protestant dissenters in England to the Kirk of Scotland. [By Daniel Defoe.] 4to. Pp. 8. [Wilson's *Life of Defoe*, 99.] [1707]
No title-page.

VOICE (a) from the vintage, on the force of example, addressed to those who think and feel. By the author of *The women of England* [Mrs William Ellis, *née* Sarah Stickney]. . . . [The second edition.] 12mo. Pp. 80. London, 1843

VOICE (the) in singing ; translated from the German of Emma Seiler, by a Member of the American Philosophical Society [Rev. William H. Furness]. 8vo. [*Brit. Mus.*] Philadelphia, 1868

VOICE (the) of a flower. By E. G. Gerard [Mrs Emily Gerard Laszowska]. 8vo. [*Amer. Cat.*] New York, 1893

VOICE (the) of a tree from the Middlesex Fells. By Pinus Strobus [Elizur Wright]. 8vo. [*Lib. Journ.* xiii. 390.] Boston, 1883

VOICE (the) of beauty ; or, woman's life : sketches. . . . By the author of *The language of the eye* [Joseph Turnley]. 8vo. [*Brit. Mus.*] London, 1857

VOICE (the) of Christian life in song ; or, hymns and hymn-writers of many lands and ages. By the author of *Tales and sketches of Christian life* [Mrs Elizabeth Charles]. 8vo. Pp. v. 303. London, 1858

VOICE (the) of Dashin ; a romance of wild mountains. By "Ganpat" [Martin Louis Alan Gompertz]. 8vo. Pp. 320. [*Brit. Mus.*] London, 1926

VOICE (the) of God in a tempest. . . . [By Cotton Mather, D.D.] 8vo. [Evans' *Amer. Bibl.* i. 323.] Boston, 1723

VOICE (the) of Okharon from the golden book of life. By Azelda. . . . Transmitted through Paul Black [G. M. Nash] & Oliver Fox [H. G. Callaway]. 8vo. Pp. 48. [*Brit. Mus.*] London [1926]

VOICE (the) of one crying in a wilderness ; or, the business of a Christian, both antecedaneous to, concomitant of, and consequent upon, a sore and heavy visitation ; represented in several sermons. . . . By S. S. a servant of God in the Gospel of his Son [Samuel Shaw]. 12mo. Pp. 21, 248. [*Brit. Mus.*] London, 1667

VOICE (the) of praise ; a selection of hymns and tunes, by Karl Reden [Charles Crozat Converse]. 8vo. Richmond, Va., 1872

VOICE (the) of prayer ; being a new edition . . . of a Plain manual of religious exercises. . . . [By J. J. Douglas.] 16mo. Pp. 47. [*Brit. Mus.*] Aberdeen, 1873
Signed : J. J. D., B.D.

VOICE (the) of the addressers ; or, a short comment upon the chief things maintain'd, or condemn'd in our late modest addresses. [By Benjamin Hoadly, D.D.] 8vo. Pp. 31. [*Bodl.*] London, 1710

VOICE (the) of the bird. . . . [By Mrs Jane E. Saxby, *née* Browne.] 8vo. [Boase's *Mod. Eng. Biog.* vol. 6, col. 531.] London, 1875

VOICE (the) of the city. By O. Henry [William Sydney Porter]. 8vo. [*Amer. Cat.*] New York, 1908

VOICE (the) of the just uttered. . . . [Signed : T. S. *i.e.* Thomas Symonds.] 4to. Pp. 8. [*Brit. Mus.*] London, 1657

VOICE (the) of the people, in a memorial to the Prince Regent of Great Britain and Ireland. By an elector of Westminster, author of *The universal Church*, etc. [John Crook]. 8vo. Pp. 62. [*Brit. Mus.*] Westminster, 1819

VOICE (the) of the people, no voice of God ; or, the mistaken arguments of a fiery zealot [Daniel Defoe], in a late pamphlet entitl'd Vox populi, vox Dei, since published under the title of the Judgment of whole kingdoms and nations, &c. fully confuted, and his designs prov'd to be pernicious and destructive to the publick peace. . . . By F. A. [Francis Atterbury, D.D.]. 8vo. 1710

VOICE (the) of the [English] Prayer-Book on the Holy Communion [in reply to M. F. Sadler on "The one offering"]. By the author of *The physician's daughters* [Mrs Lucy Nelson]. 12mo. [*Brit. Mus.*] London, 1877

VOICE (the) of the silence ; being chosen fragments from the "Book of the Golden Precepts," for the daily use of Lanoos. . . . Translated and annotated by H. P. P. [Helena P. Blavatsky]. 8vo. Pp. xi. 97. [*Brit. Mus.*] London, 1889

VOICE (the) of warning to Christians on the ensuing election of a President of the United States. [By Rev. John Mitchell Mason, D.D.] 8vo. [Cushing's *Anon.*] New York, 1800

VOICE (a) to America; or, the model republic, its glory, or its fall : with a review of the causes of the . . . failure of the republics of South America, Mexico, and of the Old World: applied to the present crisis in the United States. [By F. Saunders and T. B. Thorpe.] 12mo. Pp. 404. [*Brit. Mus.*] New York, 1855

VOICELESS (the) victims. [A novel.] By Guy Thorne [Cyril A. E. Ranger-Gull]. 8vo. [*Lit. Year Book.*] London, 1922

VOICES. [A novel.] By J. E. Buckrose [Mrs Falconer Jameson]. 8vo. Pp. 354. [*Who's Who in Lit.*] London, 1908

VOICES from dead nations. [By Kenneth Robert Henderson Mackenzie.] 8vo. [*Brit. Mus.*] London [1860 ?]

VOICES from the garden ; or, the Christian language of flowers. By S. W. P. [Samuel William Partridge]. 8vo. London, 1851

VOICES (the) from the heart. [Hymns.] By Mary Alphonsus [Miss —— Leaby]. 12mo. Dublin, 1868

VOICES from the hearth ; a collection of verses. By Isidore [Isidore G. Ascher]. 12mo. [*Lib. of Col. Inst.* Supp. I. p. 678.] Montreal, 1863

VOICES from the rocks ; or, proofs of the existence of man during the palæozoic or most ancient period of the earth : a reply to the late Hugh Miller's *Testimony of the rocks.* [By William Elfe Tayler.] 8vo. [*Brit. Mus.*] London, 1857

VOICES in solitude. [Verses.] By R. G. H. [Roland G. Hill]. 8vo. London [*c.* 1900]

VOICES of nature to her foster-child the soul of man ; a series of analogies between the natural and spiritual world. By the author of *A reel in a bottle* [George B. Cheever]. Edited by Rev. Henry T. Cheever. 12mo. [*Brit. Mus.*] New York, 1852

VOICES of the dead. By Abel Reid and A. N. Broome [William James Linton]. 8vo. Boston, 1869

VOICES of the past, recalled by R. N. C. [Robert Needham Cust] and E. S. K. [E. Seton-Karr]. 8vo. Pp. 134. Hertford, private print, 1895

VOICES of the stones. [Poems.] By A. E. [George William Russell]. 8vo. pp. 61. [*Brit. Mus.*] London, 1925

VOICES of to-day ; studies of representative modern preachers. By Hugh Sinclair [Mrs Emma Herman]. 8vo. London, 1912
Information from the husband of the authoress.

VOLCANO (the) diggings ; a tale of California law, by a member of the Bar [Leonard Kip]. 8vo. [Cushing's *Init. and Pseud.*] New York, 1851

VOLCANO (the) under the city. By a volunteer special [Wm. Osborn Stoddard]. 8vo. New York, 1887

VOLO ; or the will : what is it ? how to strengthen it ; how to use it. By Arthur Lovell [David Arthur Lovell Williams]. 8vo. Pp. 150. [*Who's Who in Lit.*] London, 1897

VOLPONE ; or, the fox : by way of fable, very applicable to the present times. [By Joseph Browne, D.D.] 4to. Pp. 19. [*Bodl.*] London, 1706

VOLTAIRE in his letters. By S. G. Tallentyre [Miss E. Beatrice Hall]. 8vo. [*Who's Who in Lit.*] London, 1919

VOLTAIRE in the shades ; or, dialogues on the deistical controversy. [By William Julius Mickle.] 8vo. Pp. xvi. 214. [*Watt's Bibl. Brit.*] London, 1770

VOLUNTARY Church Association, and their manifesto against Establishments considered. . . . [By Rev. John Cormack, D.D., of Stow.] 12mo. Edinburgh, 1832

VOLUNTARY (the) principle tried by the Scriptures of the New Testament. [By the Hon. Arthur Philip Perceval.] 12mo. Pp. 24. London, 1836

VOLUNTARY (the) system. By a Churchman [Samuel Roffey Maitland]. 8vo. 7 parts. London, 1834-5

VOLUNTARYISM unscriptural, unsuccessful, and unsafe ; being a reply to the recent manifesto of the United Presbyterian Church on Disestablishment. [By Dr —— Graham.] 8vo. Pp. 23. Glasgow, 1873

VOLUNTAS Dei. By the author of *Pro Christo et ecclesia* [Lily Dougall]. 8vo. [*Brit. Mus.*] London, 1912

VOLUNTEER (the) force ; its rise and progress. By an Ex-Volunteer [William Reid]. 8vo. Pp. 56. [Mowat's *Bibl. of Caithness*, p. 537.] Wick, 1891

VOLUNTEER (the) levee ; or, the remarkable experiences of Ensign Sopht : written and illustrated by himself. Edited by the author of *How not to do it* [Robert Michael Ballantyne]. 8vo. Pp. 56. [*Brit. Mus.*] Edinburgh, 1860

VOLUNTEER (the), the militiaman, and the regular soldier; a conservative view of the armies of England. . . . By a Public School boy [Richard Harrison, Major-General.] 8vo. Pp. xii. 116. [*Brit. Mus.*] London, 1874

VOLUNTEERS (the); or, taylors to arms! A comedy in one act, as performed at the Theatre Royal, Covent Garden. [By George Downing.] The music by Mr Hook. 8vo. [Baker's *Biog. Dram.; Mon. Rev.* lxii. 411.]
London, 1780

VOLUNTEER'S (a) scrap-book. By the author of *A Cambridge scrap-book* [John Lewis Roget]. 8vo. [*Brit. Mus.*] London, 1860

VORTIGERN ; an historical tragedy, in five acts, represented at the Theatre Royal, Drury Lane ; and Henry the Second, an historical drama; supposed to be written by the author of *Vortigern.* [By William Henry Ireland.] 8vo. 2 parts. London [1799]

VORTIGERN under consideration; with general remarks on Mr James Boaden's Letter to George Steevens, Esq. relative to the manuscripts, drawings, seals, &c. ascribed to Shakespeare, and in the possession of Samuel Ireland, Esq. [By W. C. Oulton.] 8vo. Pp. 67.
London, 1796
Author's name is in the handwriting of Samuel Ireland, to whom the pamphlet belonged.

VOTE by ballot ; a comedy. By one of the great unplayed [Alfred Farthing Robbins]. 8vo. [*Lond. Lib. Cat.*]
London [1880]

VOTIVAE Angliae ; or, the desires and wishes of England : contained in a patheticall discourse, presented to the king on new-yeares day last : wherein are vnfolded and represented, many strong reasons, and true and solide motiues, to perswade his Majestie to drawe his royall sword, for the restoring of the Pallatynat, and Electorat, to his sonne in law Prince Fredericke, to his onely daughter the Lady Elizabeth. . . . Written by S. R. N. I. [John Reynolds]. 4to. No pagination. [Hart's *Index Expurg. Angl.* p. 63.] Vtrecht, 1624
Wrongly attributed to Thomas Scot.

VOW (the). [A novel.] By Paul Trent [Edward Platt]. 8vo. Pp. 308. [*Brit. Mus.*] London, 1911

VOW (the) of the peacock, and other poems. By L. E. L., author of *The improvisatrice*, etc. [L. E. Landon]. 8vo. London, 1835

VOX clamantis. [By Ralph Sadler]. 8vo. London, 1891

VOX clamantis. [On socialism.] By Numa Minimus [Frederick Scott Oliver]. 8vo. [*Lond. Lib. Cat.*]
London, 1911
Attributed also to Sir Stanley M. Leathes. [*Brit. Mus.*]

VOX cleri ; or, the sense of the clergy, concerning the making of alterations in the established liturgy : with remarks on the discourse concerning the Ecclesiastical Commission, and several letters for alterations : to which is added, an historical account of the whole proceedings of the present Convocation. [By Thomas Long, B.D., Exeter.] The second edition. 4to. [*D. N. B.* vol. 32, p. 111.]
London, 1690

VOX coeli ; or, newes from heaven : of a consultation there held by the high and mighty princes, King Hen. 8. King Edw. 6. Prince Henry, Queene Mary, Queene Elizabeth, and Queene Anne ; wherein Spaines ambition and treacheries to most kingdomes and free estates of Europe, are vnmaskd and truly represented, but more particularly towards England, and now more especially under the pretended match of Prince Charles, with the Infanta Dona Maria. . . . Written by S. R. N. I. [John Reynolds]. 4to. [Hart's *Index Expurg. Angl.* p. 63.]
Elisium, 1624
Wrongly attributed to Thomas Scott, B.D.

VOX Dei. [By Thomas Scott, B.D.] 4to. Pp. 9, 86. [*Pollard and Redgrave.*] N.P. [1624]

VOX militis ; foreshewing what perils are procured where the people of this, or any other kingdome liue without regard of marshall discipline, especially when they stand and behold their friends in apparent danger, and almost suberted by there enemies vniust persecution, and yet with hold their helping hand and assistance. . . . 4to. Pp. 8, 38. London, 1625
Epistle dedicatorie signed : G. M.
"This is Barnaby Rich's Allarum to England originally printed 4° 1578. the matter abridged, the language modernized, and the whole newly adapted to the age in which it appeared."—MS. note by Dr Bliss, who wrongly attributes this edition to Gervase Markham.

"VOX oculis subjecta;" a dissertation on the most curious and important art of imparting speech and the knowledge of language, to the naturally deaf, and (consequently) dumb. . . . By a parent [Francis Green]. 8vo. [Nichol's *Lit. Anec.* viii. 125.] London, 1783

VOX piscis; or, the book fish, containing three treatises, which were found in the belly of a cod-fish in Cambridge Market, on Midsummer Eve last, Ao. 1626. [By Richard Tracey, or Tracy.] 8vo. [Lowndes' *Bibl. Man.* p. 2704; Wood's *Athen. Oxon.* i. 245.]   1627
  "Vox piscis" is a reprint of "Of the preparation to the cross and to death, and of the comfort under the cross and death." 8vo. London, 1540.

VOX populi, expressed in xxxv. motions to this present Parliament; being the generall voyce and the humble and earnest request of the people of God in England to that most honorable and religious assembly, for reforming the present corrupt state of the Church. Published by Irenæus Philadelphus [Louis Du Moulin]. 4to. Pp. 12.   1641

VOX populi, fax populi; or, a discovery of an impudent cheat and forgery put upon the people of England by Elephant Smith and his author of Vox Populi: thereby endeavouring to instil the poysonous principles of rebellion into the minds of His Majesties subjects. [By John Nelson.] 4to. [Whitley's *Bapt. Bibl.* i. 112.]
                            London, 1681

VOX populi; or, newes from Spayne, translated according to the Spanish coppie. . . . [By Rev. Thomas Scott, B.D., Utrecht.] 4to. No pagination.
                                  1620
  Reprinted as the work of Sir Robert Cotton, with a different title ("A choice narrative of Count Gondamor's trans-actions. . . ." 1659).

VOX populi; or, the people's complaint . . . [By Nicholas Grimald, M.A.] 4to. [*D. N. B.* vol. 23, p. 250.] London, 1549

VOX populi, vox Dei; being true maxims of government; proving, I. That all kings, governors and forms of government proceed from the people. II. The nature of our constitution is fairly stated, with the original contract between king and people, and a journal of the late revolution. . . . [By Daniel Defoe.] 8vo. [Wilson's *Life of Defoe*, 113.]   London, 1709
  Reprinted under the title of "The judgment of whole kingdoms and nations," etc.

VOX populi vox Dei. Lord Weymouth's appeal to a General Court of India proprietors considered. [By Alexander Dalrymple.] 4to. [*Brit. Mus.*]
                            London, 1769

VOX populi, vox Dei; or, the voice of the people the voice of God. [By —— Brewster, barrister.] 8vo. [Gillow's *Bibl. Dict.* iv. 209.]   N.P. [1716]

VOX regis. [By Thomas Scott, B.D.] 4to. Pp. 5, 74. [*Pollard and Red-grave.*]   N.P. [1623]
  Address to the reader signed: T. S.

VOX turturis; vel, columba alba Albionis; the voice of the turtle, or England's white dove in the deluge of division, the second time sent forth from Gods arke. . . . By E. M. [Edward Marbury]. 4to.   London, 1647

VOX veritatis; or, the voice of truth: earnestly recommended to the perusal of the members of the Church of Rome in particular. By a minister of the Gospel, formerly educated . . . for the Catholic priesthood [J. E. Cullen]. 8vo. [*Brit. Mus.*]   Devonport, 1833
  A second edition, enlarged, was issued in 1840.

VOYAGE en zigzag. [By Miss Elizabeth Tuckett.] 8vo. [*Brit. Mus.*]
                            London, 1866

VOYAGE (a) in the S.S. *Oceanic.* By H. J. [H. Jardine], of Alderley. 4to. [*Brit. Mus.*]   1882

VOYAGE (a) into the Levant; a brief relation of a journey lately performed by Master H. B. gentleman, from England by the way of Venice, into Dalmatia, Sclavonia, Bosnia, Hungary, Macedonia, Thessaly, Thrace, Rhodes and Egypt, unto Gran Cairo: with particular observations concerning the moderne condition of the Turks, and other people under that empire. [By Sir Henry Blunt.] 12mo. Pp. 228.
                            London, 1636

VOYAGE (the) of a Vice-Chancellor. By A. E. S. [Arthur Everett Shipley]. 8vo. [*Camb. Univ. Lib.*]
                            Cambridge, 1919

VOYAGE (the) of Captain Popanilla. By the author of *Vivian Grey* [Benjamin Disraeli]. 12mo. Pp. viii. 243.   London, 1828

VOYAGE (the) of Columbus; a poem. [By Samuel Rogers.] 4to. Pp. viii. 48. [*Brit. Mus.*]   London, 1810

VOYAGE (the) of France; or, a compleat journey through France with the character of the people, and the description of the chief towns, fortresses, churches, monasteries, universities, pallaces and antiquities, as also of the interest, government, riches, etc. By P. H. [Peter Heylin], D.D. 8vo. Pp. 362.   London, 1673
  "This is the spurious edition alluded to in Wood's Athenæ ii. 283: but there must have been a previous edition."—Douce.
  "Reprint of the first of Heylin's Two journeys, published in 1656."—Note in *Bodl. New Cat.*

VOYAGE (the) of the ark ; as related by Dan Banim. By F. M. Allen [Edmund Downey]. Second edition. 8vo. Pp. viii. 128. [*Brit. Mus.*] London, 1888

VOYAGE (the) of the *Aurora.* By Harry Collingwood [William J. C. Lancaster]. 8vo. [*Who's Who in Lit.*] London, 1887

VOYAGE (the) of the lady. By the author of *The three paths* [Herbert Grey]. 8vo. [*Brit. Mus.*] London, 1860

VOYAGE (the) of the wandring knight. By Jean de Cartigny : translated out of French into English by W. G. [W. Goodyeare] of Southampton, merchant. [Edited by R. N.] 4to. B. L. [*Brit. Mus.*] London, 1661
   See another edition, "The wandering knight."

VOYAGE (a) round the world, but more particularly to the north-west coast of America, performed in 1785-88. . . . By Captain George Dixon. [Really written by William Beresford.] 4to. [*Brit. Mus.*] London, 1789

VOYAGE (a) round the world, in the years MDCCXL, I, II, III, IV. By George Anson, Esq. ; commander in chief of a squadron of his Majesty's ships, sent upon an expedition to the South-Seas : compiled from papers and other materials of the Right Honourable George Anson, and published under his direction, by Richard Walter, M.A., chaplain of his Majesty's ship the Centurion, in that expedition : illustrated with forty-two copper-plates. [Completely revised and rewritten by Benjamin Robins, F.R.S.] 4to. Pp. 30, 417. [*D.N.B.* vol. 48, p. 435.] London, 1748
   The copper-plates occupy a separate volume.

VOYAGE (a) round the world ; or, a pocket-library, divided into several volumes : the first of which contains the rare adventures of Don Kainophilus, from his cradle to his 15th year. . . . Done into English by a lover of travels. . . . [By John Dunton.] 8vo. Pp. 24, 158. London, 1691

VOYAGE (a) to Abyssinia. By Father Jerome Lobo : from the French [by Samuel Johnson, LL.D.]. [Simms' *Bibl. Staff.* p. 251.] London, 1735
   Johnson's first prose work.

VOYAGE (a) to Barbary for the redemption of captives ; translated from the French [of Francis C. de la Motte Philemon, and Joseph Bernard] ; with notes historical, critical, and explanatory. 8vo. [*Watt's Bibl. Brit.*] London, 1735

VOYAGE (a) to Boston ; a poem. By the author of *American liberty : a poem* [Philip Freneau]. . . . [*Evans' Amer. Bibl.* vol. 5, p. 131.] 12mo. Pp. 24. New York [1775]

VOYAGE (a) to India ; and other poems, on various subjects. By an Officer, late of the Indian Army, author of *Occasional poems* [Captain Thomas Hall]. 8vo. Pp. viii. 214. [*Brit. Mus.*] London, 1853

VOYAGE (a) to Locuta. By Lemuel Gulliver, jun. [Mrs Elizabeth Susanna Graham]. 8vo. [Cushing's *Secrets,* p. 53.] London, 1818

VOYAGE (a) to Mexico and Havanna. By an Italian [Carlo Barinetti]. 8vo. [Cushing's *Anon.*] New York, 1841

VOYAGE (a) to New South Wales. . . . By George Barrington [George Waldron]. 8vo. [*Brit. Mus.*] London [1796 ?]

VOYAGE (a) to Peru, performed by the [ship] Condé of St Malo, in the years 1745-1749 ; written by the chaplain [Courte de la Blanchardière, Abbé] ; with an appendix. . . . 12mo. [Sabin's *Dictionary.*] London, 1753

VOYAGE (a) to Quebec, in an Irish emigrant vessel. By a cabin passenger [Robert Whyte]. 8vo. Boston, 1848

VOYAGE (a) to South America, with an account of a shipwreck in the river La Plata, in the year 1817. By the sole survivor [George Fracker]. 8vo. [Cushing's *Init. and Pseud.*] Boston, 1826

VOYAGE (a) to the East-Indies ; giving an account of the Isles of Madagascar and Mascareigne, of Suratte, the coast of Malabar, of Goa, Gameron, Ormus, and the coast of Brasil . . . of the inhabitants, as also a treatise of the distempers peculiar to the Eastern countries. . . . By Gabriel Dellon. [Translated from the French by Jodocus Crull.] 8vo. 2 parts. [*Brit. Mus.*] London, 1698
   Signed : J. C., Med. D.

VOYAGE (a) to the East Indies in 1747 and 1748 ; containing an account of the islands of St Helena and Java, of the city of Batavia, of the government and political conduct of the Dutch ; of the empire of China, with a particular description of Canton, interspersed with many useful and curious observations and anecdotes, and illustrated with copper-plates. [By C. F. Noble ?] 8vo. [*W. ; Brit. Mus.*] London, 1762

VOYAGE (a) o the Eastern part of Terra Firma; or, the Spanish Main in South America during the years 1801 . . . 1804. By F. Depons. . . . Translated by an American gentleman [Washington Irving]. 8vo. 3 vols. [Sabin's *Dictionary*.] New York, 1806

VOYAGE (a) to the Island of Mauritius (or Isle of France), the Isle of Bourbon, the Cape of Good Hope, etc.; with observations and reflections upon nature and mankind. By a French Officer [Jacques Henri Bernardin de Saint Pierre]. Translated by J. Parish. 8vo. Pp. 291. [*Brit. Mus.*]
London, 1775
A different translation was issued in 1800 ("A voyage to the Isle of France . . .").

VOYAGE (a) to the island of the Articoles. By André Maurois [Emile Herzog]. Translated . . . by David Garnett. . . . 8vo. Pp. 63. [*Observer*, 1st Feb. 1931.] London, 1928

VOYAGE (a) to the South-Seas, and to many other parts of the world, performed from the month of September in the year 1740, to June 1744, by Commodore Anson, in his Majesty's ship the Centurion, having under his command the Gloucester, Pearl, Severn, Wager, Trial, and two store-ships. . . . By [Richard Walter] an Officer of the fleet. [Completely revised and rewritten by Benjamin Robins.] 8vo. Pp. 408. [*D.N.B.* vol. 48, p. 435.] London, 1744

VOYAGE (a) to the South Seas, by His Majesty's Ship *Wager*. [By John Bulkeley and J. Cummins.] 8vo.
London, 1743
Another edition of the same year has the authors' names.

VOYAGE (a) to the world of Cartesius. Written originally in French [by Gabriel Daniel], and now translated into English. 8vo. Pp. 12, 298, 6.
London, 1692
The translator was T. Taylor, who signs the dedication.
This has been attributed to Defoe, but in Wilson's list of Defoe's works, it is set down as doubtful.

VOYAGE (a) up the Thames. [By Thomas Bryan Richards, F.S.A.] 8vo.
London, 1738
Wrongly ascribed to —— Weddell.

VOYAGES and adventures. By Jacques Massé [Simon Tyasot de Patot]; translated by S. Whatley. 8vo. [*Brit. Mus.*] London, 1733

VOYAGES (the) and adventures of Captain Robert Boyle, in several parts of the world; intermixed with the story of Mrs Villars, an English lady, with whom he made his surprising escape from Barbary; likewise including the history of an Italian captive, and the life of Don Pedro Aquilo, &c. Full of various and amazing turns of fortune. [By William Rufus Chetwood.] 12mo. Pp. 266. [*N. and Q.* February 1920, p. 45.] Edinburgh, 1726
Ascribed also to Benjamin Victor. [*Brit. Mus.*]

VOYAGES and travels of a Sea-Officer [Francis V. Vernon]. 8vo.
Dublin, 1792
Presentation copy from the author.

VOYAGES (the), dangerous adventures and imminent escapes of Captain Richard Falconer; containing the laws, customs and manners of the Indians of America, and intermixed with voyages and adventures of Thomas Randal, Cork pilot. [By William Rufus Chetwood.] 12mo. 2 parts. [*N. and Q.* 28th January 1860, p. 66.] London, 1720

VOYAGES to the Madeira, and Leeward Caribbean Isles; with sketches of the natural history of these islands. By Maria R ****** [Maria Riddell]. 12mo. Pp. ix. 105. Edinburgh, 1792

VOYCE (the) of him that is escaped from Babylon; reasons given forth to all sober minded people, why I departed from the ministery of those called ministers of parishes: and why I departed from the ministery of those called Anabaptists: and why I have, and what I have contended for, some years past. [By Robert West, of Devizes.] 4to. Pp. 40. [Smith's *Cat. of Friends' Books*, i. 36.] London, 1658

VRONINA. [A novel.] By Owen Rhoscomyl [Owen Vaughan]. 8vo. [*Who's Who in Lit.*] London, 1907

VULGAR (the) tongue; comprising two glossaries of slang, cant, and flash words and phrases. By Ducange Anglicus [Bernard Quaritch]. 12mo.
London, 1857

VULGAR verses, in dialect and out of it. By Jones Brown [Arthur Joseph Munby]. 8vo. Pp. x. 208. [*Brit. Mus.*]
London, 1891

VULGARISMS and other errors of speech; including a chapter on taste and one containing examples of bad taste. [By Richard Meade Bache.] 8vo. [*Brit. Mus.*] Philadelphia, 1868

VULGUS Britannicus; or, the British Hudibrass. [By Edward Ward.] 8vo. [*Brit. Mus.*] London, 1710

VULTURES (the); a novel. By Henry Seton Merriman [Hugh Stowell Scott]. 8vo. [*Who's Who in Lit.*]
London, 1902

VULTURE'S (the) nest, and other stories. By Ascott R. Hope [Robert Hope Moncrieff]. 8vo. [*Who's Who in Lit.*]   London, 1886

VYNER; a family history. [With pedigree. By Charles James Vyner.] 8vo.   London, 1885

VYVYANS (the); or, the murder in the Rue Bellechasse. By Andrée Hope [Mrs A. J. Harvey]. 8vo. Pp. 211. [*Brit. Mus.*]   London, 1893

W

W. F. Clarke . . . his life and letters, hospital sketches and addresses. By E. A. W. [Mrs E. A. Walker]. 8vo. Pp. viii. 297. [*Brit. Mus.*]
London, 1885

WACOUSTA; or, the prophecy: a tale of the Canadas. By the author of *Ecarté* [Major John Richardson]. 12mo. 3 vols. [*Nat. Lib. of Scot.*]
London, 1832

WAES (the) o' war; or, the upshot o' the History o' Will and Jean. [By Hector Macneill.] 8vo. 4 parts. Pp. 32. [*Watt's Bibl. Brit.*]   Edinburgh, 1796

WAGE (the) of character; a social study. By Julien Gordon [Mrs Julie Van Rennselaer, *née* Julie Grinnell Cruger]. 8vo. Pp. 272. [*Amer. Cat.*]
New York, 1901

WAGES (the) of sin; a novel. By Lucas Malet [Mrs St Leger Harrison, *née* Mary Kingsley]. 8vo. [*Brit. Mus.*]   London, 1892

WAIFS. By Herbert Martyne [Wm. Tait Ross]. [*Brit. Mus.*]
London [1880?]

WAIFS and strays. [A collection of poems. By Richard Hill Sandys, M.A., barrister.] 8vo. [*Brit. Mus.*]
London, 1847

WAIFS and strays; twelve stories . . . together with a representative selection of critical and biographical comment. By O. Henry [William Sydney Porter]. 8vo. Pp. 305. [*Brit. Mus.*]
New York, 1919

WAIKNA; or, adventures on the Mosquito shore. By Samuel A. Bard [Ephraim George Squier, M.D.]. 8vo. [*Brit. Mus.*]   London, 1855

WAIL (the) of Scotia; a poem, in which the former and present states of Scotland are contrasted. By Philopatris [Rev. Paul Hamilton, Minister of Broughton]. 12mo. Pp. 12.   Glasgow, 1794

WAITING for the verdict: an autobiography. Edited by Berkeley Aikin [Fanny Aikin Kortright]. 8vo. [*Brit. Mus.*]   London, 1863

WAKEFIELD and its adjacent scenery. By an amateur [Rev. Thomas Kilby]. 8vo.   1843

WALBURY (the) case. [A novel.] By Ashton Hilliers [Henry M. Wallis]. 8vo. [*Brit. Mus.*]   London, 1923

WALDEMAR, surnamed Seir, or the Victorious; translated from the Danish of Bernhard S. Ingemann, by a lady [Miss Jane Frances Chapman]. 12mo. 3 vols. [*Camb. Univ. Lib.*]
London, 1841

WALDENBERG; a poem, in six cantos. By M. E. M. J. [Margaret Elizabeth Mary Jones]. 12mo. Pp. viii. ix. 108. [*N. and Q.* 25th July 1857, p. 71.]
London, 1837

WALFORD. [A tale.] By Henry Hayes [Mrs Ellen Olney Kirk]. 12mo. [*Kirk's Supp.*]   Boston, 1892

WALK (the), and other poems. By Mercator [John A. Chapman]. 8vo.
Newberry, S.C., 1875

WALK (a) from Keith to Rothiemay. [By Robert Sim.] 8vo. [Mitchell and Cash's *Scot. Topog.* i. 98.]   Elgin, 1862

WALK (a) from the town of Lanark to the Falls of Clyde, on a summer afternoon. [By C. Buchanan.] 8vo. Pp. 88.   Glasgow, 1816
Presentation copy signed by the author.

WALK knaves, walk; a discourse intended to have been spoken at court, and now published for the satisfaction of all those that have participated of the sweetnesse of publique employments. By Hodg Turbervill, chaplain to the late Lord Hewson [Edmund Gayton]. 4to. Pp. 14. [Wood's *Athen. Oxon.* iii. 756.]   London, 1659

WALK (a) round Dorchester; containing an account of everything worthy the observation of the traveller and antiquary within that ancient town. . . . [By James Criswick.] 8vo. Pp. xxvi. 125. [Mayo's *Bibl. Dors.* p. 146.]
Dorchester, 1820

WALK (a) round the boundaries of Morayshire ; with map specially prepared from Ordnance survey, by a pedestrian [James Pirie]. 8vo. Pp. viii. 91.   Banff, 1877

WALK (a) through Leeds ; or stranger's guide to everything worth notice in that ancient and populous town ; with an account of the woollen manufacture of the West Riding of Yorkshire : with plates. [By Francis T. Billam.] 12mo. Pp. 55. [Boyne's *Yorkshire Lib.* pp. 84, 85.]   Leeds, 1806

WALK (a) through Leicester ; being a guide to strangers, containing a description of the town and its environs ; with remarks upon its history and antiquities. [By Susanna Watts.] 12mo. [*Upcott*, i. 548.]   Leicester, 1804

WALK (a) through Rochester Cathedral. [By Charles Spence.] 12mo. [*Brit. Mus.*]   London, 1840

WALK (a) to Islington. . . . By the author of *The poet's ramble after riches* [Edward Ward]. Folio. Pp. 12. [*Brit. Mus.*]   London, 1701

WALKER (the) family; a true story. By Uncle Silas [James W. Poland]. 12mo.   Boston, 1847

WALKER'S manly exercises. By Craven [J. W. Carleton]. 12mo. [Olphar Hamst's *Swimming*, p. 243.]   London, 1839

WALKING amusements for chearful Christians, or trades spiritualized. [By George Wright, author of *The Rural Christian.*] 12mo.   London, 1775

WALKING (a) gentleman ; a novel. By James Prior [James Prior Kirk]. 8vo. Pp. 386. [*Brit. Mus.*]   London, 1907

WALKING in the light. . . . By R. P. S. [Robert Pearsall Smith]. 8vo. [Cushing's *Init. and Pseud.* i. 258.]   Boston, 1872

WALKING (a) tour in Normandy. By the author of *All round Ireland on Foot* [William Whittaker Barry]. 8vo. [*Brit. Mus.*]   London, 1868

WALKING (a) tour round Ireland in 1865. By an Englishman [William Whittaker Barry]. 8vo. [*Brit. Mus.*]   London, 1867

WALKS about New York ; facts and figures gathered by the Secretary of the City Mission [I. Orchard]. 8vo. Pp. 120.   New York, 1865

WALKS abroad and evenings at home. [By Robert Kemp Philp.] With numerous illustrations. 8vo. Pp. viii. 328. [Boase and Courtney's *Bibl. Corn.* ii. 494.]   London, 1861

WALKS and talks. By Uncle Walter [Walter T. Sleeper]. 8vo. [Cushing's *Init. and Pseud.* i. 303.]   Boston, 1875

WALKS and talks of an American farmer in England. [By Frederick Law Olmsted.] 8vo. [Cushing's *Init. and Pseud.* i. 14.]   New York, 1852

WALKS and wanderings in the world of literature. By the author of *Random recollections*, etc. [James Grant, journalist]. 12mo. 2 vols. [*Nat. Lib. of Scot.*]   London, 1839

WALKS in a forest; or poems descriptive of scenery and incidents characteristic of a forest at different seasons of the year. [By Thomas Gisborne, sen.] 4to. [*Brit. Mus.*]   London, 1794

WALKS in our Churchyards, old New York, Trinity parish. By Felix Oldboy [John Flavel Mines]. 12mo. Pp. 181. [*Amer. Cat.*]   New York [1895]

WALKS in the neighbourhood of Sheffield. [By John Thomas.] Two series. 12mo.   Sheffield, 1843-44

WALKS round Alston. . . . By Jonathan Dale [Isaac E. Page]. 8vo. [*Bodl.*]   Newcastle, 1896

WALKS round Auchterarder. [By Mrs Haldane, *née* Edith Nelson.] 12mo. Pp. 64.   Edinburgh, 1896

WALKS through Leeds ; or the stranger's companion to the public buildings, churches, chapels, charitable institutions, &c., in that ancient and populous town : and various historical occurrences connected therewith. [By John Robert Blesard.] 12mo. Pp. viii. 132. [Boyne's *Yorkshire Lib.* p. 85.]   Leeds, 1835

WALKS through London, including Westminster and the borough of Southwark, with the surrounding suburbs ; describing every thing worthy of observation in the public buildings, places of entertainment, exhibitions, commercial and literary institutions, &c. down to the present period : forming a complete guide to the British metropolis. By David Hughson, LL.D. [Dr Edward Pugh]. 8vo. 2 vols. [*Upcott*, iii. 1478.]   London, 1817
    Ascribed also to William Hamilton Reid, and to Mrs Reid.

WALL (a) Street bear in Europe. . . . By T. Q. [Samuel Young]. 8vo. [Cushing's *Init. and Pseud.* i. 243.]   New York, 1855

WALLACE ; a fragment. [Verse. By Robert Pierce Gillies.] 8vo. [*Brit. Mus.*]   Edinburgh, 1813

WALLACE ; a tragedy. [By James Grahame.] 8vo. Pp. 94. [*D. N. B.* vol. 22, p. 366.]   Edinburgh, 1799
    Six copies only were printed.

WALLACE ; a tragedy, in five acts. [By Robert Buchanan, professor of rhetoric in the University of Glasgow.] 8vo. Pp. 96.   Glasgow, 1856

   Afterwards included in " Tragic dramas from Scottish History " (1859), also anonymous, q.v.,and " Tragic dramas from History" (1868), which bears the author's name.

WALLACE ; or, the fight of Falkirk ; a metrical romance. [By Miss Margaret Holford, later Mrs Hodson.] 4to. [Gent. Mag. March 1810, p. 251.] London, 1809

   The second edition (1810) bears the name of the author.

WALLACE ; or, the vale of Ellerslie : with other poems. [By John Finlay.] 8vo. [Watt's Bibl. Brit.]
                            Glasgow, 1802

WALLADMOR ; "freely translated into German from the English of Sir Walter Scott " [but really composed by William Haering] ; and now freely translated from the German into English [by Thomas De Quincey]. 8vo. 2 vols. [Brit. Mus.; T. A. Green's Bibl. of De Quincey.]   London, 1825

WALLAMANNUMPS; or, the triumph of religious principles. By a minister [Rev. Henry M. Bridge]. 8vo.
                            Boston, 1856

WALLENSTEIN ; a dramatic poem: from the German of Johan C. F. von Schiller. [By G. Moir.] 8vo. 2 vols. [Brit. Mus.]   Edinburgh, 1827

WALLENSTEIN'S camp ; from the German : and original poems. [By Lord Francis Leveson-Gower.] 8vo. Pp. 167. [D.N.B. vol. 17, p. 154.]
                            London, 1830

WALLIS'S pocket itinerary ; being a new and accurate guide to all the principal direct and cross-roads, throughout England, Wales, and Scotland. [By Thomas Hartwell Horne.] 18mo.   London, 1803

   " The publisher inscribed his own name on the title-page."—From a list of his works in the handwriting of the author.

WALLOGRAPHY ; or the Britton describ'd : being a pleasant relation of a journey into Wales, wherein are set down several remarkable passages that occur'd in the way thither. . . . By W. R. a mighty lover of Welch travels [William Richards, M.A.]. 8vo. [Wood's Athen. Oxon.] London, 1682

WALPOLIANA. [Collected by John Pinkerton.] 12mo. 2 vols. [N. and Q. 26th December 1863, p. 516.]
                            London, N.D.

WALPOLIANA ; or, a few anecdotes of Sir Robert Walpole. [By Philip Yorke, second Earl of Hardwicke.] 4to. [D.N.B. vol. 63, p. 352.]
                            London, 1783

WALSH Colville ; or, a young man's first entrance into life : a novel. [By Anna Maria Taylor.] 8vo.   London, 1797

WALSINGHAM; or the pupil of nature. [By Mrs Mary Robinson.] Second edition. 12mo. 4 vols. [D.N.B. vol. 49, p. 32.]   London, 1805

WALTER Ashwood ; a love story. By Paul Siegvolk [Albert Mathews]. 8vo. [Brit. Mus.]   New York, 1860

WALTER Clayton ; a tale of the Gordon riots. [By —— M'Gauran.] 12mo. 3 vols.   London, 1844

WALTER Colyton ; a tale of 1688. By the author of Brambletye House, etc. [Horace Smith]. 12mo. 3 vols. [D.N.B. vol. 53, p. 54.] London, 1830

WALTER Stanhope. [A novel.] By John Copland [Walter Copland Perry]. 8vo. Pp. 439. [Brit. Mus.]
                            London, 1888

WALTER, the schoolmaster. [By Edward Monro, M.A.] 8vo. Pp. 2, 252. [D.N.B. vol. 38, p. 183.]
                            London, 1854

WALTZ (the) ; an apostrophic hymn. By Horace Hornem, Esq. [George Gordon, Lord Byron]. 8vo. [D.N.B. vol. 8, p. 139.]   [London, 1813]

   This work proved a failure, and was disowned by the author, but appears in his works (1824).

WALTZING. By Philagathus [John Haven Dexter]. 8vo. [Cushing's Init. and Pseud. i. 229.] 8vo. Boston, 1868

WANDA. By Ouida [Louise de la Ramée]. 8vo. 3 vols. London, 1883

WANDA, a dramatic poem. By Colonel J. Przyiemski, author of Sketches of the Polish mind : translated by A. M. M. [Miss Anna Maria May]. 8vo. [Dobell's Priv. Prints, p. 187.]
                            N.P. 1863

WANDERER (a).   By H. Ogram Matuce [Charles Francis Keary]. 8vo. Pp. vii. 211. [Brit. Mus.]
                            London, 1888

WANDERER (the).   By Owen Meredith, author of Clytemnestra [Edward Robert Bulwer-Lytton, Lord Lytton]. Second edition. 8vo. Pp. xvi. 436. [Brit. Mus.]   London, 1859

WANDERER (the) and traveller. [A dramatic poem. By Rev. John Wallace, minister in Ayr.] 8vo.
                            Glasgow, 1733

WANDERER (the).   Fantasia and Vision. . . . By The Smith of Smitheden [Daniel M'Ivor]. 8vo. Pp. vii. 381.   Edinburgh, 1857

WANDERER (the) in Africa ; a tale illustrating the thirty-second Psalm. By A. L. O. E., authoress of *Clermont tales*, etc. [Charlotte M. Tucker]. 8vo. Pp. 96. [*Brit. Mus.*] Edinburgh, N.D.

WANDERER (the) in Syria. [By George William Curtis.] 8vo.
London, 1852
Published later (1857) under the title " The Howadji in Syria," with the author's name. See also " Nile notes of a Howadji."

WANDERER (the) in Washington. [By George Watterston.] 8vo.
Washington, 1867

WANDERER (the) of the West, and other poems. By a Scottish Borderer [John Rutherford, of Thickside, Jedburgh]. 8vo. Pp. 118.
Jedburgh, 1890

WANDERER (the) ; or, Edward to Eleonora : a poem. [By John Bell.] 4to. [*Nat. Lib. of Scot.*]
[London] 1785

WANDERER (the) ; or female difficulties. By the author of *Evelina, Cecilia,* and *Camilla* [Frances Burney, later Madame D'Arblay]. 8vo. 5 vols. [*Brit. Mus.*] London, 1814

WANDERERS (the) by sea and land. By Peter Parley [Samuel Griswold Goodrich]. 12mo. London [1855]

WANDERING (the) bard ; and other poems. [By John Walker Ord.] 8vo. Pp. 135. [Tweddel's *Bards and Authors of Cleveland and South Durham,* p. 251.] Edinburgh, 1833

WANDERING Heath ; stories, studies, and sketches. By Q. [Arthur Thomas Quiller-Couch]. 8vo. [*Brit. Mus.*]
London, 1895

W A N D E R I N G homes, and their influences. By the author of *The Physician's daughters* [Mrs Lucy Nelson]. 8vo. Pp. 357. [*Brit. Mus.*]
London, 1864

WANDERING (the) islander ; or, the history of Mr Charles North. [By Charles Henry Wilson, of the Middle Temple.] 12mo. 3 vols. [*Gent. Mag.* May 1808, p. 469.] London, 1792

WANDERING (the) Jew ; or, the travels and observations of Hareach the Prolonged : comprehending a view of the most distinguished events in the history of mankind since the destruction of Jerusalem by Titus. . . . Compiled from a MS. supposed to have been written by that mysterious character. By the Rev. T. Clark [John Galt]. 12mo. [*W.*] London, 1820
At p. 437, the letters of the author's name are found commencing the sentences in the last paragraph of the book. These words are : — *It, Over, History, Nevertheless, Greatness, All, Literally, To.*

WANDERING (the) Jews chronicle ; or, The old historian His brief declaration Made in a mad fashion Of each coronation That past in this nation Since William's invasion For no great occasion But meer recreation To put off vexation. [By Martin Parker.] S. sh. Folio. B. L. [*Bodl.*]
N.P., N.D.
Signed : M. P.

WANDERING (the) knight. [By J. de Cartigny.] Newly translated into English from the edition of 1572 [by A. J. Hanmer]. 8vo. Pp. xvi. 346. [*Brit. Mus.*] London, 1889
The translator's preface is signed : A. J. H. For an earlier translation, see " The voyage of the Wandring Knight."

WANDERING (the) minstrel ; a collection of original poems. [By Samuel Howell.] 8vo. London, 1820
The second edition (1827) bears the author's name.

WANDERING (the) spy ; or, the merry observator. . . . [By Edward Ward.] 8vo. 6 parts. [*Brit. Mus.*]
London, 1724

WANDERING thoughts ; or memoranda of past phases of life. [Poems.] By a man of business [Thomas A. Welton]. 8vo. Pp. 93. [*Brit. Mus.*]
London, 1913

WANDERING Willie. The sponsor. [By Edward Monro, M.A., perpetual curate of Harrow Weald.] 8vo. Pp. 29. [*Bodl.*] London, 1845
Signed : E. M.

WANDERINGS in the Isle of Wight. By the author of *The Old Sea Captain* [George Mogridge]. 12mo. [*Brit. Mus.*] London [1846]

WANDERINGS in West Africa (1860-61), from Liverpool to Fernando Po. By a F.R.G.S. [Captain Sir Richard F. Burton]. 12mo. 2 vols. [*Brit. Mus.*]
London, 1862

WANDERINGS of a beauty. [By Mrs Edwin James.] 8vo. New York, 1873

WANDERINGS of a journeyman tailor through Europe and the East, 1824-40. [By P. D. Holthaus.] 8vo. [Cushing's *Init. and Pseud.* i. 143.]
New York, 1842

WANDERINGS of a pilgrim. [By David Addison Harsha.] [Cushing's *Init. and Pseud.* i. 235.] 8vo.
New York, 1854

WANDERINGS of a pilgrim in search of the picturesque during four-and-twenty years in the East ; with revelations of life in the Zenana. [By Fanny Parks, later Mrs Parlby.] 8vo. 2 vols.
London, 1850
The author's name is given in Arabic character on the title-page.

WANDERINGS of a vagabond; an autobiography, edited by John Morris [John O'Connor]. 8vo. [Cushing's *Init. and Pseud.* i. 198.]
New York, 1873

WANDERINGS of an antiquary. . . . [By Thomas Wright.] 8vo. [Cushing's *Init. and Pseud.* i. 17.]   London, 1861

WANDERINGS of an artist among the Indians of North America. . . . [By Paul Kane.] 8vo. [Cushing's *Init. and Pseud.* i. 20.]   London, 1859

WANDERINGS (the) of Lucan and Dinah; a romance. By M. P. K. [Morgan Peter Kavanagh]. 8vo. [Boase's *Mod. Eng. Biog.* ii. 161.]
London, 1824

WANDERINGS (the) of a pen and pencil. By F. P. Palmer and A. Crowquill [Alfred H. Forrester]. 8vo. [*Brit. Mus.*]   London, 1846

WANDERINGS (the) of Persiles and Sigismunda; a northern story. By Miguel de Cervantes Saavedra. Translated from the Spanish by L. D. S. [Louisa Dorothea Stanley]. 12mo. [*Camb. Univ. Lib.*]
London, 1854

WANDERINGS over Bible lands and seas. By the author of *Chronicles of the Schönberg-Cotta family*, etc. [Mrs Elizabeth Charles, *née* Rundle]. 8vo. Pp. 301. [*Brit. Mus.*]   London, 1868

WANDERINGS through the conservatories at Kew. [By Philip Henry Gosse.] 12mo. [*Brit. Mus.*]
London [1860]

WANDRING (the) lover; a tragycomedie: being acted severall times privately at sundry places by the author and his friends with great applause. Written by T. M. gent. [Thomas Meriton]. 4to. Pp. 6, 31. [Baker's *Biog. Dram.*]   London, 1658

WANG Keaou-Lwan Pïh Nëen Han; or, the lasting resentment of Miss Keaou Lwan Wang: a Chinese tale . . . translated by Sloth [Robert Thom]. 8vo. [Cushing's *Init. and Pseud.* i. 268.]   Canton, 1839

WANG the ninth; the story of a Chinese boy. By Putnam Weale [Bertram Lenox Simpson]. 8vo. Pp. 252. [*Brit. Mus.*]   London, 1920

WANLEY Penson; or the melancholy man: a miscellaneous history. [By—— Sadler, of Chippenham.] 8vo. 3 vols. [Britton's *Top. of North Wiltshire*.]
London, 1792

"WANTED." [A tale.] By "Pansy" [Mrs Isabella Alden, *née* Macdonald]. 8vo. [*Lit. Year Book.*]   London, 1894

WANTED, a cook; domestic dialogues. By Alan Dale [Alfred J. Cohen]. 8vo. [*Brit. Mus.*]   Indianapolis, 1904

WANTED! A detective's strange adventure. By Dick Donovan [Joyce E. Preston Muddock]. 8vo. Pp. 316. [*Lit. Year Book.*]   London, 1904

WANTED—a home. [A novel.] By the author of *Morning clouds* [Mrs A. J. Penny]. 8vo. 3 vols. [*Brit. Mus.*]   London, 1864

WANTED, a husband. By the author of *A Bad boy's diary* [Mrs Metta Victoria Victor, *née* Fuller]. 8vo. Pp. 33. [*Brit. Mus.*]   London [1883]

WANTED—a king; or, how Merle set the nursery rhymes to rights. . . . By Maggie Browne [Margaret Hamer, later Mrs Andrewes]. 8vo. Pp. 183. [*Brit. Mus.*]   London, 1890

WANTED—a pedigree. By Martha Farquharson [Mrs Martha Farquharson Finley]. 8vo. [Cushing's *Init. and Pseud.* i. 99.]   New York, 1870

WANTED, a wife; a story of the Sixtieth Dragoons; and other tales. By John Strange Winter [Mrs Arthur Stannard, *née* Henrietta E. V. Palmer]. 8vo. [*Lit. Year Book.*]   London, 1887

WANTED; and other stories. By James Otis [James Otis Kaler]. 8vo. [Cushing's *Init. and Pseud.* i. 220.]
London, 1912

WAR. By Pierre Loti [Julien M. J. Viaud]. Translated from the French by M. Laurie. 8vo. Pp. 228. [*Brit. Mus.*]   London [1917]

WAR, a system of madness and irreligion; to which is subjoined, by way of conclusion, The Dawn of universal peace. . . . By Humanitas [George Miller, bookseller]. 8vo. Pp. 64. [Couper's *Millers of Haddington*, p. 265.]
[Edinburgh] 1796

WAR aims; the need for a Parliament of the Allies. By Norman Angell [Ralph Norman Angell Lane]. 8vo. Pp. 127. [*Brit. Mus.*]   London, 1917

WAR; an epic satire. [By Stephen Barrett.] [*Gent. Mag.* xvii. 156.]
1747

WAR and peace; a tale of the retreat from Caubul. By A. L. O. E., authoress of *The young pilgrim*, etc. [Charlotte M. Tucker]. 8vo. Pp. 256. [*Brit. Mus.*]   London, 1862

WAR and sport in India, 1802-06; an Officer's diary. [By Lieut. John Pester.] 8vo. [*Lond. Lib. Cat., Supp.*]
London, 1913

WAR and the essential realities. By Norman Angell [Ralph Norman Angell Lane]. 8vo. Pp. 78. [*Brit. Mus.*]
London, 1913

WAR and the workers. By Norman Angell [Ralph Norman Angell Lane]. 8vo. Pp. 63. [*Brit. Mus.*]
London, 1913

WAR at sea ; modern theory and ancient practice. By " Barfleur " [Sir Reginald Neville Constance]. 8vo. [*Lond. Lib. Cat.*] London, 1919

WAR betwixt the two British Kingdoms consider'd, and the dangerous circumstances of each, with regard thereto, layd open ; by a full view of the consequences of it on both sides. . . . By the author of *The rights and interests of the two British Monarchies* [James Hodges]. 8vo. [Arber's *Term Cat.* iii. 694.] London, 1705

WAR (the) correspondence of the " Daily News," from the capture of Orleans by the Germans to the Peace. [By Archibald Forbes.] 8vo. [*D. N. B. First Supp.* ii. 223.] London, 1871

WAR flying ; the letters of " Theta " to his home people, written in training and in War. By a Pilot [Captain —— Hutcheon]. 8vo. Pp. 117. London, 1917

WAR in disguise ; or, the frauds of the neutral flags. [By James Stephen.] The second edition. 8vo. Pp. 216. [Rich's *Bibl. Amer.* p. 21.] London, 1805

Also attributed to John Brown, of Yarmouth.

WAR (the) in Florida ; being an exposition of its causes and an accurate history of the campaigns of Generals Clinch, Gaines, and Scott. By a late Staff-officer [Woodbourne Potter]. [Cushing's *Init. and Pseud.* i. 165.] Baltimore, 1836

WAR (the) in Texas. . . . By a citizen of the United States [Benjamin Lundy]. 8vo. [Cushing's *Init. and Pseud.* i. 59.] Philadelphia, 1837

WAR (the) in the Far East, 1904-5. By the military correspondent of " The Times " [Charles A'Court Repington]. 8vo. [*Brit. Mus.*] London, 1905

WAR (the): is it just, or necessary ? [By R. W. Smiles.] 4to. Pp. 4. [*N. and Q.* February 1869, p. 169.] N.P., N.D.

Signed : R. W. S.

WAR letters of a disbanded volunteer. [By Joseph Barber.] 8vo. [Cushing's *Init. and Pseud.* i. 81.] New York, 1864

WAR lyrics ; dedicated to the friends of the dead. By A. and L. [Arabella and Louisa Shore]. 8vo. Pp. 48. [*Brit. Mus.*] London, 1855

A second edition, containing additional poems, was published in the same year.

WAR memories ; a book of verse. . . . [By J. Lynch.] 12mo. [*Brit. Mus.*] Plymouth [1919]

Preface signed : Serowe.

WAR (the) of the bachelors ; a story of the Crescent city at the period of the Franco-German War. By Orleanian [George Frederick Wharton]. 8vo. [*Lib. Journ.* vii. 280.] New Orleans, 1882

WAR (the) of the surplice ; a poem, in three cantos. By Anti-Empiricus [John Wesley Thomas]. London, 1845

The second edition (1871) bears the author's name.

WAR (the) Office and the Volunteer Force. [By James F. Macpherson.] 8vo. N.P. 1873

WAR Office rhymes. By Aegocerus [Edgar Roger Brown]. 8vo. [*Who's Who in Lit.*] London, private print, 1921

WAR poems. By " X " [T. W. H. Crosland]. 8vo. Pp. 96. London, 1916

WAR sketches, from Cedar Mountain to Bull Run. By a staff officer [James T. Lyon]. 8vo. [Cushing's *Init. and Pseud.* i. 273.] Buffalo, 1872

WAR times ; or, the lads of Craigross. [A tale.] By Sarah Tytler [Henrietta Keddie]. 8vo. Pp. 263. [*Brit. Mus.*] London, 1893

WAR to the knife ; or Tangata Maori. By Rolf Boldrewood [Thomas A. Browne]. 8vo. Pp. 420. [*Brit. Mus.*] London, 1899

WAR with France, the only security of Britain, at the present momentous crisis, set forth in an earnest address to his fellow subjects. By an old Englishman [James Rennell]. 8vo. [Watt's *Bibl. Brit.*] London, 1794

WAR with the devil ; or the young mans conflict with the powers of darkness : in a dialogue, discovering the corruption and vanity of youth, the horrible nature of sin, and deplorable condition of fallen man. . . . The fourth impression. By B. K. [Benjamin Keach]. 8vo. Pp. 208. [*Brit. Mus.*] London, 1676

WAR with the saints. By Charlotte Elizabeth [Charlotte Elizabeth Tonna, *née* Browne]. 12mo. [*Brit. Mus.*] [London] 1848

WAR with the senses ; or, free thoughts on snuff-taking. By a friend to female beauty [Richard Russell, woolstapler]. 8vo. [*Gent. Mag.* liv. 821.] London, 1782

WARBLINGS and waitings of leisure hours. By Scotus [Captain John Robertson.] 12mo. Three Rivers, 1859

WARD and Lock's pictorial guide to London. [By George Rose Emerson.] 12mo. London [1879]

WARD (a) in Chancery. By Mrs Alexander [Mrs Alexander Hector, *née* Annie French]. 8vo. 2 vols. [*Brit. Mus.*]   London, 1894

WARD (the) of Navarre. [A historical romance.] By Morice Gerard [Rev. John Jessop Teague]. 8vo. [*Who's Who in Lit.*]   London, 1920

WARD (the) of the crown; a historical novel. By the author of *Seymour of Sudley* [Hannah D. Wolfensberger]. 12mo. 3 vols.   London, 1845

WARDEN (the) of Galway; a tragedy, in verse. [By Rev. Edward Groves, B.A.] 8vo. [O'Donoghue's *Poets of Ireland*.]   Dublin, 1832

WARDEN (the) of the marches; a novel. By Sydney C. Grier [Hilda C. Gregg]. 8vo. [*Amer. Cat.*]   London, 1901

WARDS (the) of London; comprising a historical and topographical description of every object of importance within the boundaries of the city: with an account of all the companies, institutions, buildings, ancient remains, &c. &c. and biographical sketches of all eminent persons connected therewith. By Henry Thomas [Henry Ride]. 8vo. 2 vols. London, 1828
"This book is said to have been written by Henry Ride, formerly of S. John's Coll. Oxford. Vide 'Memoirs of Shakspeare's tavern the late Boar's Head, Eastcheap'—note at bottom of page 3."—MS. note on the Douce copy in the Bodleian.

WARFARE and victory; a record of Bible-class work. [By M. J. Fox.] 8vo.   London, 1878

WARFARE and work, or life's progress. [By Helen Clacy.] 12mo. [*Brit. Mus.*]   London, 1859
Signed: Cycla.

WARLEY; a satire [in verse] addressed to the first artist in Europe [Sir Joshua Reynolds.] ("The swashing blades of Warley; a ballad"). [By George Huddesford.] 4to. 2 parts. [*Brit. Mus.*]   London, 1778
Wrongly attributed to Thomas Maurice.

WARLICK (a) captain attack'd by a single soldier; or, a letter from A . . . . w S . . . . n [Andrew Stevenson] writer in Edinburgh, to the Reverend Mr T . . . . s N . . . n [Thomas Nairn] minister of the Gospel at Abbotshall: wherein the said Mr N . . . n's reasons of secession from the A . . . . e P . . . . y [Associate Presbytery], and the bad effects it hath already produced, are briefly consider'd. . . . 12mo. Pp. 55.   Edinburgh, 1743
Letter signed : A . . . . w S . . . . n.
Inscribed copy in the British Museum.

WARLOCK (the). By the old sailor, author of *Land and sea tales*, etc. [Matthew Henry Barker]. A new edition. 8vo. Pp. 272. London, 1860

WARM corners in Egypt. By one who was in them [Walter Ralph Goodall]. 8vo.   London, 1886

WARNING (a) agaynst the dangerous practices of Papistes, and specially the parteners of the late rebellion. [By Thomas Norton.] 8vo. B. L. [Strype's *Annals*, p. 554, 562.]
[London, 1569]

WARNING (a) for the Church of England. . . . See "A Warning to the Church . . ."

WARNING (a) from the Lord to the Pope and to all his train of idolatries; with a discovery of his false imitations, and likenesses, and traditional inventions, which is not the power of God. . . . By a lover of souls, G. F. [George Fox]. 4to. Pp. 19. [Smith's *Cat. of Friends' Books*, i. 651.]
London, 1656

WARNING; or the beginning of the end; an address . . . by C. Jones [Charles Inglis, M.D.]. 8vo. [*Gladstone Lib. Cat.*]   London, 1866

WARNING (the); recommended to the serious attention of all Christians, and lovers of their country. [By Eliza Coltman.] 12mo. [Smith's *Cat. of Friends' Books*, i. 80.] London, N.D.

WARNING (a) to all teachers of children, which are called schoolmasters and school-mistresses, and to parents, which doth send their children to be taught by them, that all schoolmasters and school-mistresses may train up children in the fear of God, etc. By G. F. [George Fox]. 4to. [*Brit. Mus.*]   [London, 1657]

WARNING (a) to all the merchants in London, and such as buy and sell; with an advisement to them to lay aside their superfluity, and with it to nourish the poor. By G. F. [George Fox]. 4to. Pp. 8. [Smith's *Cat. of Friends' Books*, i. 656.] London, 1658

WARNING (a) to England to repente and to turne to God from idolatrie and Poperie by the terrible example of Calece given the 7 of March. Anno D. 1558. By Benthalmai Outis [Bartholomew Traheron]. 8vo. [*Brit. Mus.*]   [Wesel?] 1558
Sixteen leaves without pagination.

WARNING (a) to the Church of England. [By John Bramhall, Archbishop of Armagh.] 4to. [*Brit. Mus.*]
London [1706]
A reprint of the "Fair warning against the deception of the Scotch discipline . . ."
Another copy issued in the same year begins, "A warning for the Church . . ."

WARNING (a) to the dragon and all his angels. [By Eleanor Audeley.] 4to. [*Trin. Coll. Dubl. Lib.*] N.P. 1625

WARNING to the eldership. [By John Longmuir, LL.D.] 12mo. Pp. 4. [*And. Jervise.*]   N. P. [1869]
Reprinted from the *Aberdeen Free Press* of 19th March 1869.

WARNING (a) to the inhabitants of England and London in particular. By M. A. [Mary Adams]. 8vo. [*Brit. Mus.*]   London, 1676

WARNING (a) to wives ; or, the Platonic lover : a novel. By the author of *Cousin Geoffrey*, etc. [Mrs Yorick Smythies, *née* Gordon]. 12mo. 3 vols. [*Brit. Mus.*]   London, 1847

WARNING (the) voice. [By P. L. Courtier.] 4to. [*Watt's Bibl. Brit.*]
N.P. 1798

WARNINGS and exhortations to those who are waiting for the coming again of the Lord Jesus Christ. [By Wm. F. Pitcairn.] 8vo. Pp. 72. [*Brit. Mus.*]
Edinburgh, 1858

"WARNINGS (the) of the war"; a letter to the Right Hon. Lord Palmerston, Prime Minister. By "A British Commoner" [Edward Rupert Humphreys, LL.D., Head Master of the Cheltenham Grammar School]. 8vo. Pp. 53. [*Brit. Mus.*]   London, 1855

WARN-WORD (the) to Sir Francis Hastinges Wast-word ; conteyning the issue of three former treateses, the Watch-word, the Ward-word and the Wast-word (intituled by Sir Francis, an apologie or defence of his Watchword) ; togeather with certaine admonitions & warnings to the said Knight and his followers : whereunto is adioyned a brief reiection of an insolent and vaunting minister [Matthew Sutcliffe] masked with the letters O. E. who hath taken vpon him to wryte of the same argument in supply of the Knight. . . . By N. D. author of the Ward-word [Nicholas Doleman, *i.e.* Robert Parsons]. 8vo. Pp. 15. ff. 131, 138 ; pp. 21. [Jones' *Peck*, i. 54.]
[Antwerp] 1602

WARP (the) and woof of Cornish life and character. By Open Eyes [Mrs C. P. Penberthy]. 8vo.
London [1898]

WARP and woof ; or, the reminiscences of Doris Fletcher. By Holme Lee, author of *Sylvan Holt's daughter*, etc. [Harriet Parr]. 8vo. 3 vols. [*Lond. Lib. Cat.*]   London, 1861

WARRANTABLENESS (the) of the Associate Synod's sentence, concerning the religious clause of some Burgess-Oaths, proved; and some notes of two sermons vindicated : upon occasion of a late pamphlet [by Ralph Erskine], intitled, The lawfulness of the religious clause of some Burgess Oaths asserted ; . . . [Part I. by Rev. Thomas Mair, of Orwell ; Part II. by Rev. Alexander Moncrieff, of Abernethy.] 8vo. 2 parts. Pp. 55.   Edinburgh, 1747

WARRENIANA ; with notes, critical and explanatory, by the Editor of a Quarterly Review [William Frederick Deacon]. 12mo. [*D. N. B.* vol. 14, p. 249.]   London, 1824
A burlesque imitation of popular authors.

WARRES (the) of Pompey and Cæsar. By G. C. [George Chapman]. 4to. [*W.*]   London, 1631

WARRIOR and Pacificus; or, dialogues on war. By the author of *Remarks on the theatre*, etc. [Ann Alexander, *née* Tuke]. 12mo. [Smith's *Cat. of Friends' Books*, i. 8.]   York, 1819

WARRIOR (a) king; the story of a boy's adventures in Africa. . . . By J. Evelyn [E. J. Bowen]. 8vo. Pp. 120. [*Brit. Mus.*]   London, 1890

WARRIOR'S (the) soul. By Joseph Conrad [Joseph Conrad Korzeniowski]. 4to. Pp. 40. [*Brit. Mus.*]
London, private print, 1920
Only twenty-five copies printed.

WARS (the) and causes of them, between England and France, from William I. to William III.; with a treatise on the Salique Law. By D. J. [David Jones], and revised by R. C. 4to.
London, 1698

WARS (the) in England, Scotland, and Ireland . . . during the reign of King Charles the First . . . and till the Restoration. By R. B. [Richard (or Robert) Burton, *i.e.* Nathaniel Crouch]. Sixth edition, revised. 12mo. Pp. 184. [*D. N. B.* vol. 8, p. 15.] London, 1697
See the note appended to "Admirable curiosities."

WARS (the) of Wapsburgh. By the author of *The heir of Redclyffe*, etc. [Charlotte Mary Yonge]. 8vo.
London, 1864

WARS (the) of the Cross; or the history of the Crusades. By the author of *The Mediterranean illustrated*, etc. [William Henry Davenport Adams]. 8vo. Pp. 163. [*Brit. Mus.*]
London, 1883

WARSTOCK (the); a tale of to-morrow. By Wirt Gerrare [William Greener]. 8vo. Pp. 234. [*Brit. Mus.*]
London, 1898

WAR-TIME in our street; the story of some companies behind the firing-line. By J. E. Buckrose [Mrs Falconer Jameson]. 8vo. Pp. 158. [*Lit. Year Book.*]   London, 1917

WARWICK (the) woodlands. By Frank Forester [Henry William Herbert]. 8vo. [Cushing's *Init. and Pseud.* i. 104.]   London, 1849

WARWICKSHIRE (the) hunt, from 1795 to 1836; describing many of the most splendid runs. . . . By Venator [John Cooper]. 8vo. [*Brit. Mus.*]
London, 1837

WARWICKSHIRE (the) medley, or convivial songster. By John Free [John Freeth]. 8vo. [*Birm. Cent. Lib.*]   Birmingham [1780?]

WARWICKSHIRE (Shakespeare country); painted by Frederick Whitehead, R.B.A.; described by Clive Holland [Charles J. Hankinson]. 8vo. [*Brit. Mus.*]   London, 1906

WAS Hamlet mad? or, the lucubrations of Messrs Smith, Brown, Jones and Robinson [James Smith, Dr Neild, Charles Bright, David Blair, and Archibald Michie]. 8vo.
Melbourne, 1868

WAS it a dream? and, The new church-yard. By the author of *Stories on the Lord's Prayer*, etc. [Elizabeth Missing Sewell]. 12mo. [*Brit. Mus.*]
London, 1849

WAS it a ghost? By J. B. [Henry Johnson Brent]. 8vo. [Cushing's *Anon.*]   Boston, 1868

WAS it wise? A novel. By "Volo non valeo" [Miss M. S. Gibbons]. 8vo.
Exeter, 1872

WAS Shakespeare a lawyer? A selection of passages from "Measure for Measure." . . . By H. T. [Hull Terrell]. 8vo.   London, 1871

WAS she engaged? . . . By "Jonquil" [J. L. Collins]. 8vo. [Cushing's *Init. and Pseud.* i. 143.] Philadelphia, 1875

WAS she tamed? A novel. By the author of *Only three weeks* [Geraldine Penrose Fitzgerald]. 8vo. London, 1875

WAS she to blame? A novel. By Mrs Alexander [Mrs Alexander Hector, *née* Annie French]. 8vo. Pp. 235. [*Brit. Mus.*]   Chicago, 1893

WASH Bolton, M.D.; or, the life of an orator. By Ducdame [Henry Hooper]. 8vo. [Cushing's *Init. and Pseud.* i. 84.]   London, 1872

WASHER (the) of the ford. By Fiona Macleod [William Sharp]. 8vo. [*Brit. Mus.*]   London, 1898

WASHINGTON and Napoleon: a fragment. [By Franz Lieber.] 8vo. [*Brit. Mus.*]   New York, 1864

WASHINGTON; historical sketches of the capital city of our country. [By John P. Coffin.] 8vo. Pp. 343.
Washington, 1887

WASHINGTON, outside and inside. By Laertes [George Alfred Townsend]. 8vo. [Cushing's *Init. and Pseud.* i. 164.]   Hartford, 1874

WASHINGTON (the) sketch-book. By Viator [Joseph B. Varnum, jun.]. 8vo. [Cushing's *Init. and Pseud.* i. 294.]
New York, 1864

WASHINGTON'S birthday; an historical poem, with notes and appendix. By a Washingtonian [John Lovett]. 8vo. [Cushing's *Init. and Pseud.* i. 304.]   Albany, N.Y., 1812

WASTED moments; poems. [By G. B. Rose, of Little Rock, Arkansas.] 12mo.   Buffalo, private print, 1891

WAT Tyler; a dramatic poem. [By Robert Southey, LL.D.] 12mo. Pp. xi. 70. [*D. N. B.* vol. 53, p. 287.]
London, 1817

WATCH (the) below; naval sketches and stories. By "Taffrail," author of *Carry on* [Henry Taprell Dorling]. 8vo. Pp. 125. [*Brit. Mus.*]
London, 1919

WATCH (the) house: a farce, in two acts. [By John Galt.] 8vo. [*Brit. Mus.*]   London, 1814

WATCHED by wolves . . . and other anecdotes of animals from personal experience. By Lindon Meadows [Charles Buller Greatrex]. 8vo. Pp. 141. [*Brit. Mus.*]   London [1896]

WATCHER (the); a true story. By the author of *Where can I find it?* [I. Hingston Wakeham]. 8vo. [*Brit. Mus.*]   London, 1873

WATCHMAN (the). [By Charles Edward Stuart Gleig.] 8vo. [*Brit. Mus.*]   London [1876]

WATCH-TOWER (the); or, man in death, and the hope for a future life. . . . By Homo [George Storrs]. 8vo.
New York, 1858

VVATCH-VVOORD (a) to Englande to beware of traytours and tretcherous practises, which haue beene the ouer-throwe of many famous kingdomes and common weales; written by a faithfull affected freend to his country: who desireth God long to blesse it from traytours, and their secret conspiracyes. . . . [By Anthony Munday.] 4to. [*Pollard and Redgrave.*] B. L.
London, 1584

Epistle dedicatory signed: A. M.

WATCHWORDS for the warfare of life; from Doctor Martin Luther: translated and arranged by the author of *Chronicles of the Schönberg-Cotta Family* [Mrs Elizabeth Charles, *née* Rundle]. 8vo. Pp. xix. 354. [*Brit. Mus.*]   London, 1869

WATER (the) lily. By Harriet Myrtle [Mrs Lydia Falconer Miller]. With illustrations by Hablot K. Browne; engraved by Thomas Bolton. 8vo. Pp. 84.   London, 1854

WATER (the) witch; or, the skimmer of the seas: a tale. By the author of *The borderers*, etc. [James Fenimore Cooper]. 12mo. 3 vols. [*Brit. Mus.*]   London, 1830

WATER-BAPTISTS (the) reproach repel'd; being a further Reply offering a defence of R. Hobbs to his pretended Impartial Narrative of one C. Bayly, hereto a pretended Quaker; a story of eleven years standing: in defence of an Answer to the said Narrative, clearing the people called Quakers. By T. R. [Thomas Rudyard, Quaker attorney]. 4to. Pp. 24. [*Smith's Anti-Quak.* p. 232.]   London, 1673

WATER-COLOUR painting. By Penumbra [Mary L. Breakell]. 8vo. [*Amer. Cat.*]   London, 1904

WATERDALE (the) neighbours. By the author of *Paul Massie* [Justin M'Carthy]. 8vo. 3 vols. [*Brit. Mus.*]   London, 1867

WATER-FINDER (the). [A novel.] By Lucas Cleeve [Mrs Howard Kingscote, *née* Adelina G. I. Wolff]. 8vo. Pp. 222. [*Brit. Mus.*] London, 1897

WATER-LILY (the) on the Danube; being a brief account of the perils of a pair-oar during a voyage from Lambeth to Pesth. By the author of the *Log of the Water Lily* [Robert Blackford Mansfield] and illustrated by one of the crew. 8vo. [*Bodl.*]   London, 1853

WATERLOO; a poem, in two parts: inscribed by permission, to his Grace the Duke of Wellington, &c. by his respectful and obliged humble servant, the author of *Triumphs of religion*, etc. [Harriett Cope]. 8vo. [*Edin. Univ. Lib.*]   London [1822]

WATERLOO; a poetical epistle to Mr Sergeant Frere, master of Downing College, and Vice Chancellor of Cambridge in 1820. [By Rev. John Wing, of Pembroke College, Cambridge.] 8vo. Pp. viii. 28. [*Bodl.*; Bartholomew's *Camb. Books*, p. 262.]
                    London, 1820

WATERLOO; a tale of the Hundred Days. By Emile Erckmann and Pierre A. Chatrian: a new translation by Theodore Taylor [John Camden Hotten]. 8vo. [*Brit. Mus.*]
                    London [1871]

WATERMAN (the); or, the first of August: a ballad opera, in two acts, as it is performed at the Theatre-Royal, Hay-Market. [By Charles Dibdin.] 8vo. [Baker's *Biog. Dram.*]
                    London, 1774

WATER-QUEEN (the); or the mermaid of Loch Lene (translated from the Gaedhic) and other tales. [By H. Coates.] 12mo. 3 vols. [*Nat. Lib. of Scot.*]   London, 1832

WATERS of comfort; a small volume of devotional poetry of a practical character, addressed to the thoughtful and the suffering. By the author of *Visiting my relations* [Mary Ann Kelty]. 8vo. [*D. N. B.* vol. 30, p. 360.]   Cambridge, 1856

WATERS (the) of Edina; a novel. By Ouida [Louise de la Ramée]. 8vo. [*Lit. Year Book.*]   London, 1903

WATERS (the) of Hercules; a novel. By E. D. Gérard [Mrs Von Laszouski]. 8vo.   New York, 1885

WATERS (the) of Marah sweetned; a thanks-giving sermon [on Exod. xv. 23, 24, 25], preached at Taunton, in the county of Somerset, May 11. 1647. for the gracious deliverance of that poore towne from the strait and bloody siege. By T. B. Master of Arts, and a minister of the Gospel in that county [Timothy Batt]. 4to. Pp. 23. [Green's *Bibl. Somers.* ii. 124.]
                    London, 1648

WATERSIDE sketches; a book for wanderers and anglers. By Red Spinner [William Senior]. 8vo. Pp. viii. 253. [*Brit. Mus.*] London, 1875

WATERY (the) war; a poetical description of the existing controversy between the Pedo-baptists and Baptists on the subjects and mode of baptism. By John of Enon [David Benedict, D.D.]. 12mo. Pp. 34. [Cushing's *Init. and Pseud.* i. 143.]   Boston, 1808

WATTLE blossoms; some of the grave and gay reminiscences of an old Colonist. [By George Wright.] 8vo. [Cushing's *Init. and Pseud.* i. 210.]
                    Melbourne, 1857

WATTY and Meg; or, the wife reform'd: a tale. [By Alexander Wilson.] [*D. N. B.* vol. 62, p. 75.] 12mo. Pp. 8.   Paisley, 1820
Misattributed for a time to Robert Burns.

WAVE (the) of bliss (Anandalaharî); translated [from the Sanskrit] with commentary by Arthur Avalon [Sir John George Woodroffe]. 8vo. [*Brit. Mus.*]   London, 1917

WAVERLEY; or 'tis sixty years since. [By Sir Walter Scott.] 12mo. 3 vols. Edinburgh, 1814

WAY (the) about Surrey. . . . [By Herbert Stanley Vaughan.] 8vo. [*Brit. Mus.*] London, 1891
  Introduction signed: H. S. V.

WAY (the) and the fare of a wayfaring man; in two letters to a friend. [By William Huntington.] 8vo. [*Brit. Mus.*] [London? 1830]
  Signed: W. H.

WAY (the) home. [By Mrs Margaret F. Barbour.] 12mo. Edinburgh, 1856

WAY (the) home. By the author of *The inner shrine* [Basil King]. 8vo. [*Brit. Mus.*] London, 1914

WAY (the) of deception. By "Pan" [Leslie Beresford]. 8vo. [*Lit. Year Book.*] London, 1922

WAY (a) of escape; a novel. By Graham Travers [Miss Margaret G. Todd, M.D.]. 8vo. Pp. 390. [*Who's Who in Lit.*] Edinburgh, 1902

WAY (the) of good men for wise men to walk in. [By Rev. Charles Morton, of Charlestown, N.E.] 8vo. Pp. 95. London, 1681
  Advertisement at the end of his "Spirit of Man" (1693).

WAY (the) of life; book of prayers and instruction for the young. [By Rev. E. Hoskins.] 32mo. London, 1871

WAY (the) of peace. By Henry Fielding [Henry Fielding-Hall]. 8vo. [*Lond. Lib. Cat.*] London, 1917

WAY (the) of the [Episcopal] Church with children. . . . [By Rev. George W. Doane.] 8vo. Burlington, N.J., 1848

WAY (the) of the wilderness, and other poems. By E. C. C. B. author of *The protoplast* [Mrs E. C. C. Baillie]. 8vo. [*Camb. Univ. Lib.*] London [1862]

WAY (the) of the world. [A novel.] By the author of *De Lisle*, etc. [Elizabeth C. Grey]. 12mo. [*Brit. Mus.*] London, 1831

WAY (a), propounded to make the poor in these and other nations happy, by bringing together a fit, suitable, and well qualified people unto one household government or little-commonwealth. Whereunto is also annexed An Invitation to this society or little commonwealth. By Peter Cornelius, Van-Zurik-Zee [Hugh Peters]. 8vo. [*Brit. Mus.*] London [1659]
  The "Invitation" has a separate title-page, but the pagination is continuous.
  "I believe this pamphlet was made by Mr Hugh Peeters, who hath a man named *Cornelius* Glover."—MS. note by George Thomason in the British Museum copy.

WAY (the) out; a Northumbrian pitman's story. By Austin Clare [Miss W. M. James]. 8vo. [*Who's Who in Lit.*] London, 1890

WAY (the) the Lord hath led me. [By Harriet Perfect.] 8vo. London, 1870

WAY (the) things happen; a drama. By Clemence Dane [Winifred Ashton]. 8vo. [*Who's Who in Lit.*] London, 1923

WAY (the) thither. [By Mrs L. F. Field, *née* Story.] 8vo. 2 vols. London, 1882

WAY (the) to be happy; or, the story of Willie the gardener's boy. By Cousin Kate [Catherine Douglas Bell]. 12mo. [*Brit. Mus.*] London, 1871

WAY (the) to be rich and respectable; addressed to men of small fortune. . . . [By John Trusler, LL.D.] Fifth edition: to this edition is added a variety of estimates or plans of living. . . . 8vo. Pp. 59. [*D. N. B.* vol. 57, p. 269.] London [1780?]
  The seventh edition (1796) bears the author's name.

WAY (the) to be wise and wealthy; or, the excellency of industry and frugality. By Mr J. S. [John Sowter]. 8vo. Pp. 95. [*Manch. Free Lib.*] Exon, 1716

WAY (the) to fortune; a series of short essays, with illustrative proverbs and anecdotes. [By Alexander Hay Japp.] 8vo. London, 1881

WAY (the) to God. . . . [By Henry James Prince.] 8vo. [*Brit. Mus.*] London, 1877
  Signed: B.

WAY (the) to happiness. [By J. Ecclestone.] 8vo. N.P. [abroad] 1726

WAY (the) to health, long life and happiness; or, a discourse of temperance and the particular nature of all things requisit for the life of man, as all sorts of meats, drinks, air, exercise, &c. with special directions how to use each of them to the best advantage of the body and mind. . . . Communicated to the world for a general good, by Philotheos Physiologus [Thomas Tryon]. 8vo. Pp. 12, 669. [*Bodl.*] London, 1683

WAY (the) to keep him ; a comedy in three acts. [By Arthur Murphy.] 8vo. [Baker's *Biog. Dram.*]
London, 1760

WAY (the) to make all people rich ; or, wisdoms call to temperance and frugality, in a dialogue between Sophronio and Guloso, one a lover of sobriety, the other addicted to gluttony, and excess. By Philotheos Physiologus, the author of *The way to health, The countrymans companion* [Thomas Tryon]. 8vo. Pp. 6, 130. [*Douce Cat.* 279.]   [London] 1685

WAY (the) to peace amongst all Protestants ; being a letter of reconciliation sent by Bp. Ridley to Bp. Hooper : with some observations upon it. [By Samuel Johnson, chaplain to William, Lord Russell.] 4to. Pp. 8. [*Bodl.*]
London, 1688

WAY (the) to salvation ; or, the doctrine of life eternal ; laid down in several texts of Scripture, opened and applyed. . . . By J. H. [John Hieron]. 8vo. [*Brit. Mus.*]   London, 1668

WAY (the) to things by words, and to words by things ; being a sketch of an attempt at the retrieval of the antient Celtic, or, primitive language of Europe: to which is added, a succinct account of the Sanscort, or learned language of the Bramins. . . . [By John Cleland.] 8vo. [Lowndes' *Bibl. Man.*]
London, 1766

WAY (the) to win. By Cannibal Jack [Charles Beach]. 8vo. [*Cushing's Init. and Pseud.* i. 49.]   London, 1869

VVAY (the) tovvards the finding of a decision of the chiefe controversie now debated concerning Church government. [By John Hales, of Eaton.] 4to. Pp. 42. [Wood's *Athen. Oxon.* iii. 413.]   London, 1641
    "Authore John Hales è Coll. Eatonensi, ut creditur."—MS. note by Barlow in the Bodleian copy.
    By some ascribed to John Dury.

WAY (the) women love ; a novel. By E. Owens Blackburne, author of *A woman scorned*, etc. [Elizabeth Owens Casey]. 8vo. 3 vols.   London, 1877

WAYFARER (the). By Fiona MacLeod [William Sharp]. 12mo. Pp. xi. 47. [*Lit. Year Book.*]
Portland, Maine, 1906

WAYFARER (a) in Hungary. By George A. Birmingham [James Owen Hannay, D.D.]. 8vo. [*Who's Who in Lit.*]   London, 1925

WAYFARERS all ; a home story. By Leslie Keith [Grace Leslie Keith Johnston]. 8vo. Pp. 320. [*Who's Who in Lit.*]   London, 1902

WAYFARER'S (a) notes on the shores of the Levant, and the valley of the Nile. [By Cuthbert G. Young.] 8vo. [*Cushing's Init. and Pseud.* i. 304.]
London, 1848

WAYFARER'S (a) treasurers. [Verses.] By C. O. G. [C. Oscar Gridley]. 8vo. Pp. 188. [*Brit. Mus.*]   London, 1911

WAYFARING men ; a story of theatrical life. By Edna Lyall [Ada Ellen Bayly]. 8vo. [*Who's Who in Lit.*]
London, 1904

WAYFARING notes ; Sydney to Southampton, by way of Egypt and Palestine. [By Dr John Smith, Professor of Chemistry in Sydney.] 8vo. [*Brit. Mus.*]   Sydney, private print, 1865
    Preface signed : J. S.

WAYFARING notes ; second series. A holiday tour round the world. . . . [By John Smith, M.D., Professor of Chemistry in Sydney.] 8vo. Pp. ix. 405.   Aberdeen, 1876
    Preface signed : J. S.

WAYFARING sketches among the Greeks and Turks, and on the shores of the Danube. By a seven years' resident in Greece [Felicia M. F. Skene]. 8vo. Pp. 343. [*D. N. B.* First Suppl. iii. 348.]   London, 1847

WAYLAND Well. By C. A. M. W. [Charles Wooley]. 8vo.
London [1871]

WAYMARKS in the life of a wanderer. [By Caroline E. Rush.] 8vo.
Philadelphia, 1855

WAYMARKS ; or, Sola in Europe. [By Joseph Tyler]. 8vo. New York, 1885

WAYS and means. By Margaret Vandergrift [Margaret Thomson Janvier]. 8vo. [*Cushing's Init. and Pseud.* i. 292.]   Philadelphia, 1879

WAYS and means whereby his Majesty may man his navy with ten thousand able sailors, etc. [By Thomas Robe.] 8vo. [*Brit. Mus.*]   London, 1726

WAYS (the) of the line : a monograph on excavators. [By Anna R. Tregelles.] 8vo. [Smith's *Cat. of Friends' Books*, ii. 821.]   N.P. 1858

WAYS (the) of the world. [A novel.] By Esca Gray [Mrs Frances A. Adamson.] 8vo. Pp. 296.
London, 1901

WAYS (the) of women ; their virtues, vices, charms. . . . By Stephen Yorke [Mary Linskill]. 8vo. [*Who's Who in Lit.*]   London, 1885

WAYS to kill care ; a collection of original songs, chiefly comic. Written by Young D'Urfey [Frederick Forrest]. 8vo. Pp. xii. 112. [Lowndes' *Bibl. Man.*]   London, 1761

WAYSIDE flowers. By Carrie Carlton [Mrs Mary Booth Chamberlain]. 8vo. [*Lib. Journ.* i. 193.]   Milwaukee, 1862

WAYSIDE flowers, gathered by a wayfarer along the highway of life [Alex. Laing]. 8vo.   Edinburgh, 1871

WAYSIDE notes and fireside thoughts. By Eudora [Mrs E. L. South]. 12mo. St Louis, 1885

WAYSIDE pillars. By the author of *The Feast of Sacrifice* [Miss Emily Steele Elliott]. 12mo. Pp. viii. 207. [*Brit. Mus.*]   London, 1866

WAYSIDE (a) snowdrop. . . . By M. E. Winchester [M. E. Whatham]. 8vo. Pp. 265. [*Brit. Mus.*] London, 1884

WAYSIDE talks with boys and girls on Sunday afternoons. By E. W. W. [E. W. Winterbotham]. 8vo. Pp. 122. [*Brit. Mus.*]   London [1891]

WAYSIDE thoughts. By a Christian pilgrim [Rev. James Grantham Faithfull, M.A.]; The recreation of weary days: the solace of suffering nights, 1860-62. 8vo.   London, 1863

WAYSIDE verses. By Thomas Brevior [Thomas Shorter]. 12mo. [*Brit. Mus.*]   London, N.D.

WAYSIDE wisdom for wayfarers; or voices from silent teachers. By the author of *Hymns for the household of faith* [Mrs J. Williamson, of Bath]. 8vo. [*Brit. Mus.*]   London, 1873 Signed: J. W.

WAYWARD Anne. [A novel.] By Curtis Yorke [Mrs W. S. Richmond Lee, *née* Jex-Long]. 8vo. Pp. 316. [*Who's Who in Lit.*]   London, 1910

WAYWARD Dosia, and the generous diplomatist. By Henry Gréville [Madame Alice Durand]. Translated from the French. 8vo. Pp. 212. [*Brit. Mus.*]   London, 1880

WAYWARD (the) son. By Maria [Maria D. Weston]. 8vo. Boston, 1849

WE all. [A story of negro life in the United States]. By Octave Thanet [Alice French]. 8vo. [Cushing's *Init. and Pseud.* i. 281.] New York, 1891

WE are worldlings. [A novel.] By the author of *Rosa Noel* [Bertha de Jongh]. 8vo. 3 vols. [*Brit. Mus.*] London, 1876

"WE can't afford it!" Being thoughts upon the aristocracy of England. Part the second. By Isaac Tomkins, Gent. [Lord Henry Brougham]. 8vo. Pp. 30. [Thomas's *Bibl. List of Lord Brougham's publications.*] London, 1835

"WE donkeys" in Devon. By "Volo non valeo" [Miss M. S. Gibbons]. 8vo. [*Brit. Mus.*]   Exeter, 1885 *We donkeys on Dartmoor*, published in the following year, bears the author's name.

WE know what we worship. [By Rev. John Henry Blunt.] 8vo. Pp. 16. London, 1858

WE mothers and our children. By Frank Danby [Mrs Julia Frankau]. 8vo. [*Who's Who in Lit.*]   London, 1918

"WE pity the plumage, but forget the dying bird"; an address to the people on the death of the Princess Charlotte. By the Hermit of Marlow [Percy Bysshe Shelley]. 8vo. Pp. 16. [*D. N. B.* vol. 32, p. 35.] [London, 1843]
    A reprint of the lost edition of 1817.

WE ten; or, a story of the Roses. By Barbara Yechton [Miss Lyda Farrington Krausé]. 8vo. [*Amer. Cat.*] New York, 1896

WE three. By "Fleeta" [Kate W. Hamilton]. 12mo. [*Amer. Cat.*] Philadelphia, 1877

WE three and troddles. By R. Andom [Alfred W. Barrett]. 8vo. [*Brit. Mus.*] London, 1897

WE two; a novel. By Edna Lyall [Ada Ellen Bayly]. 8vo. [*Lit. Year Book.*]   London, 1884

WE Von Ardens. By Edith Douglas [Mrs Clara Louise Burnham, *née* Root]. 8vo. [Cushing's *Init. and Pseud.* i. 83.] Chicago, 1881

WE win; the life and adventures of a young railroader. By F. Benton Williams [Herbert Elliott Hamblen]. 8vo.   New York, 1899

WEAKER than a woman. By Bertha M. Clay [Charlotte M. Braeme]. 8vo. [*Amer. Cat.*]   New York, 1890

WEAKNESS (the) and inefficiency of the government of the United States. By a late American Statesman [Charles Fenton Mercer]. 8vo. [Cushing's *Init. and Pseud.* i. 165.] Philadelphia, 1863
    Attributed also to Charles Astor Bristed.

WEAKNESSES (the) of Brutus exposed; or some remarks in vindication of the constitution proposed by the late Federal Convention. . . . By a citizen of Philadelphia [Pelatiah Webster]. 12mo. Pp. 23. [Evans' *Amer. Bibl.* vii. 184.]   Philadelphia, 1787
    Reprinted in his Political Works.

WEALTH (the) and biography of the wealthy citizens of New York. [By Moses Yale Beach.] . . . Eleventh edition. 8vo. [*Brit. Mus.*] New York, 1846

WEALTH and labour; a novel. By Lord B******* author of *Masters and Workmen, Farce of Life*, etc. [Frederick R. Chichester]. 12mo. 3 vols. London, 1853
    This series of novels have been variously attributed to Lord Belfast and Lord Brougham, but both are unlikely.

WEALTH; definitions by Ruskin and Mill compared. By W. C. [William Cassels]. 8vo.   Glasgow [1882]

WEALTH discovered; or, an essay upon a late expedient for taking away all impositions and raising a revenue without taxes: published and presented to his most excellent Majesty King Charles the II., by F. C., a lover of his country [Francis Cradock]. Whereunto is added His Majesty's gracious answer. 4to. Pp. viii. 44. [Green's *Bibl. Somers.* ii. 336.]   London, 1661

WEALTH the name and number of the beast, 666, in the Book of Revelation. [By John Taylor.] 8vo. [*Nat. Lib. of Scot.*]   London, 1844

WEARIN' (the) o' the green; a novel. By Basil [Rev. Richard Ashe King]. 8vo. [*Brit. Mus.*]   London, 1884

WEARING the Willow; or, Bride Fielding: a tale of Ireland and of Scotland sixty years ago. By the author of *The nut-brown maids* [Henrietta Keddie]. 8vo. Pp. 343.   London, 1860

WEARITHORNE; or, in the light of to-day. By Fadette [Mrs Minnie Reeves Rodney; *or* Marian C. Legare Reeves]. 8vo. [Cushing's *Init. and Pseud.* i. 98.]   Boston, 1872

WEARY (the) traveller his eternal rest; being a discourse of that blessed rest here which leads to endless rest hereafter. By H. H. [H. Harrison], D.D., rector of Snaylwell, and Canon of Ely. 8vo. [Arber's *Term Cat.* i. 550.]   London, 1681

WEATHERCOCK (the); a musical entertainment of two acts; as performed at the Theatre-Royal, Covent-Garden. [By Theodosius Forrest.] 8vo. Pp. 3, 37. [Baker's *Biog. Dram.*]   London, 1775

WEATHERCOCK (the); or the difference between faith and sight. By Cesar Malan, D.D.; with a preface on personal assurance by the translator [Rev. Samuel Carr, M.A., of Colchester]. Second edition. 12mo. Pp. 70.   London, 1831
Note by a friend of the translator.

WEATHER-COCKE (the) of Romes religion; with her severall changes: or, the world turn'd topsie-turvie by Papists. [By Alexander Cooke.] 4to. Pp. 16. [*Bodl.*]   London, 1625

WEAVER (a) of webs. By John Oxenham [William Arthur Dunkerley]. 8vo. Pp. 320. [*Brit. Mus.*] London, 1904

WEAVERS and weft; a novel. By the author of *Lady Audley's Secret* [Mary E. Braddon, later Mrs John Macwill]. 8vo. 3 vols. [*Brit. Mus.*]
London, 1877

WEAVER'S (the) family. By the author of *Dives and Lazarus*, etc. [William Gilbert]. 8vo. Pp. 347. [*Camb. Univ. Lib.*]   London, 1860

WEAVERS (the) pocket-book; or, weaving spiritualized: in a discourse, wherein men employed in that occupation are instructed how to raise heavenly meditations, from the several parts of their work. . . . By J. C. [John Collinges, or Collings] D.D. 8vo. Pp. 8, 145, 4.   Edinburgh, 1723

WEAVING the web. [A novel.] By Huan Mee [—— and —— Mansfield, two brothers]. 8vo. Pp. 336.
London, 1902

WEB (the). [A novel.] By Rolf Bennett [W. Marten]. 8vo. Pp. viii. 276. [*Brit. Mus.*]   London, 1917

WEB (the) of life. By Morgan Douglas [Madame Winterhalter]. 8vo. [*Who's Who in Lit.*]   Edinburgh, 1913

WEDDED and parted. By Bertha M. Clay [Charlotte M. Braeme]. 8vo. [*Amer. Cat.*]   New York, 1885

WEDDED, but not a wife. [A novel.] By Florence Warden [Florence Alice Price, later Mrs George E. James]. 8vo. Pp. 320. [*Who's Who in Lit.*]
London, 1911

WEDDED hands. [A novel.] By the author of *Madam's ward* [C. Andrews]. 8vo. [*Amer. Cat.*]   London, 1887

WEDDING (the) among the flowers. [Verse.] By one of the authors of *Original poems* [Ann Taylor]. 4to. [*Brit. Mus.*]   London, 1808
Signed: A.

WEDDING! and bedding! The R——l nuptials!! or, epithalamium extraordinary!! A poem, by Peter Pindar, Esq. author of the R——l courtship, etc. [John Wolcot, M.D.]. Third edition. 8vo. Pp. 27.   London, N.D.

WEDDING (a) and other stories. By Julien Gordon [Mrs Julia Van Rensselaer Cruger]. 8vo. Pp. 229. [*Amer. Cat.*]   Philadelphia [1896]

WEDDING (the) feast. By Faith Latimer [Mrs John A. Miller]. 8vo. [Cushing's *Init. and Pseud.* i. 166.]
New York, 1884

WEDDING (the) guest; Jesus in Yessa, first and second visit. [By Thomas Lake Harris.] 8vo.
Fountain-Grove, 1878

WEDDING (the) ring; an opera. [By Charles Dibdin.] 8vo. [Baker's *Biog. Dram.*]   London, 1773

WEDLOCK; or, yesterday and to-day. By the author of *The maid's husband* [Henrietta Camilla Campbell, later Mrs Jenkin]. 12mo. 3 vols.
London, 184

WEDNESDAY Club Law; or the injustice, dishonour, and ill policy of breaking into parliamentary contracts for public debts. [By —— Broome.] 8vo. Pp. 38. [*N. and Q.* June 1853, p. 576.]   London, 1717

WEE MacGreegor. By J. J. B. [John Joy Bell]. 12mo. [*Brit. Mus.*]
       Glasgow, 1903
WEE MacGreegor again; a sequel. By J. J. B. [John Joy Bell]. 8vo. [*Eng. Cat.*]   Glasgow, 1904

WEE wee songs. By Leila Lee [Miss R. Coe]. 8vo. [Cushing's *Init. and Pseud.* i. 170.]   Boston, 1859

WEE wee stories. By Aunt Louisa [Mrs Richard Valentine]. 8vo.
      New York, 1874
WEE wifie; a tale. By the author of *Nellie's memories* [Rosa Nouchette Carey]. 8vo. 2 vols. [*Brit. Mus.*]
      London, 1869
Nellie's memories is not anonymous.

WEEDS and wild flowers. By E. G. L. B. [Sir Edward George Bulwer-Lytton, Lord Lytton]. [Martin's *Cat.*]
    Paris, private print, 1826
WEEDS from the Isis; a miscellany of prose and verse. By a few Oxonians; edited by Vaughan Dayrell [Wiltshire Stanton Austin, B.A., barrister]. 8vo. [*Brit. Mus.*]   London, 1856

WEEK (a) at a cottage; a pastoral tale. [By William Hutchinson.] 12mo. Pp. 222. [Nichol's *Lit. Illust.* i. 421.]
      London, 1776
WEEK (the) of darkness; a short manual for the use and comfort of mourners in a house wherein one lies dead. By the author of *Ye maiden and married life of Mary Powell, afterwards Mistress Milton* [Anne Manning]. 12mo. Pp. viii. 195. [*Brit. Mus.*]
      London, 1856
WEEKLY (the) journal; or Saturday's Post (Mist's). [Daniel Defoe first found in it at No. 37, and continued to No. 101, 15 Nov. 1718. Defoe again connected with Mist's Journal, 31. January, 1719, and continued its management, writing letters introductory until the beginning of July, 1720; after which he only watched the paper, and translated the articles on foreign affairs and occasionally contributed articles.] Each number 1½ sheets. Small folio. 24 August, 1717, to 15 Nov. 1718. 3 Jan. 1719 to July, 1720; and occasionally afterward, until Oct. 24, 1724. [Lee's *Defoe*, 183.]

WEEKLY memorials for the ingenious; or, an account of books lately set forth in several languages: with other accounts relating to arts and sciences. [By —— Beaumont.] 4to. Pp. 6, 390, 8. [*Bodl.*]   London, 1683
   The work consists of 50 numbers.

WEEKLY (the) miscellany; giving an account of the religion, morality and learning of the present times. By Richard Hooker, of the Temple, Esq. [William Webster, D.D.]. 8vo. 2 vols. [*W.*]   London, 1736
   The first number of this paper was published on Dec. 16, 1732, and was continued until June 27, 1741. It met with but little success, and from the number of religious essays that it contained, it acquired the appellation of "Old Mother Hooker's Journal." See Nichol's *Lit. Anec.* ii. 36; v. 161, 169, 175, etc.

WEEKLY (the) pacquet of advice from Rome; or the history of Popery: a deduction of the usurpations of the Bishops of Rome, and the errors and superstitions by them from time to time, brought into the Church. . . . [By Henry Care.] 4to. 5 vols. [*D. N. B.* vol. 9, p. 45.]
      London, 1679-83
   The first number was published on the 3 of Dec. 1678 and the last of vol. 5 on July 13, 1683.

WEEK'S (a) delight; or, games and stories for the parlor and fireside. By E. M. [Emily Mayer, later Mrs Higgins]. 8vo. [*Brit. Mus.*]
      New York, 1854
WEEK'S (a) morning and evening prayers for families. . . . By Vita [Lady Victoria A. M. Louisa Welby-Gregory]. 4to. [*Brit. Mus.*]
      London, 1892
WEESILS (the); a satyrical fable (on Dr Wm. Sherlock) giving an account of some argumental passages happening in the Lion's Court about Weesilion's taking the oaths. [By Thomas Browne, B.D.] 4to. [Lathbury's *History of the Convocation*, 2nd ed., pp. 338-9.]   London, 1691

WEIGHED in the balance; a novel. By Christian Reid [Frances Fisher, later Mrs James N. Tiernan]. 8vo. [Cushing's *Init. and Pseud.* i. 249.]
      Boston, 1900
WEIGHT (the) of a crown; a tragedy. By Feragus [C. H. Williams]. [*N. and Q.*, 26th March 1870, p. 332.]
      1852
WEIRD (a) gift. [A novel.] By Georges Ohnet [Georges Hénot]: translated from the French, by A. D. Vandam. 8vo. [*Brit. Mus.*]   London, 1890

WELCH (the) freeholder's farewell epistles to the Right Rev. Samuel [Horsley], Lord Bishop (lately of St David's), now of Rochester; in which the Unitarian dissenters, and the dissenters in general, are vindicated from the charges advanced against them in his Lordship's circular letter on the case of the emigrant French clergy; with a copy of that letter. [By David Jones, of Llandovery.] 8vo. Pp. 68. [Murch's *Dissenters*, p. 518.]   London, 1794

WELCH (the) freeholder's vindication of his letter to the Right Rev. Samuel [Horsley] Lord Bishop of St David's; in reply to a letter from a clergyman of that diocese; together with strictures on the said letter. [By David Jones, of Llandovery.] 8vo. Pp. 61. [Murch's *Dissenters*, p. 518.]   London, 1791

WELCOME and farewell; a tragedy. [By Rev. William Harness.] 8vo. Pp. 122. [Martin's *Cat.*]
London [1837]

WELCOME (the) of Isis; a poem, occasioned by an unexpected visit of the Duke of Wellington to the University of Oxford. By the author of *The Oxford Spy* [James Shergold Boone, M.A.]. 8vo. Pp. 31. [*N. and Q.* Aug. 1863, p. 153.]
Oxford, 1834

WELL met gossip; or, tis merrie when gossips meete; newly enlarged with diuers merrie songs. [By Samuel Rowlands.] 4to. No pagination. [*Pollard and Redgrave.*]
London, 1619

For other editions, see "A crew of kind London gossips, . . ." " 'Tis merry when gossips meet . . ." and "A whole crew of kind gossips . . ."

WELL (the) of Sainte Claire. By Anatole France [Jacques Anatole Thibault]; a translation by Alfred Allinson. 8vo. Pp. 310. [*Brit. Mus.*]
London, 1908

WELL won. By Mrs Alexander [Mrs Alexander Hector, *née* Annie French]. 8vo. [*Amer. Cat.*]   New York, 1891

WELLS in Baca's Vale. [By Gray Campbell Fraser.] 8vo.
Aberdeen, 1866

WELLS of Baca; or, solaces of the Christian mourner, and other thoughts on bereavement. By the author of *The faithful promiser*, etc. [John Ross MacDuff]. Fourth edition. 12mo. Pp. 70. [*Brit. Mus.*] London, 1845

WELLS (the) of Scripture, illustrated in verse. By the author of *The pastor's legacy* [Henrietta Joan Fry]. 8vo. [Smith's *Cat. of Friends' Books*, i. 816.]
London, 1847

WELSH (the) cottage. [By Mary Martha Butt, later Mrs Sherwood]. 12mo. [*Brit. Mus.*]   London, 1820

WELSH legends, in humorous English verse. By Edward Johns [R. J. Edwards]. 8vo. Pp. 51. [*Brit. Mus.*]   Aberystwyth, 1899

WELSH (the) looking-glass; or, thoughts on the state of religion in North Wales. By a person who travelled through that country at the close of the year 1811 [Rev. Thomas Jones, rector of Great Creaton]. 8vo. [*Brit. Mus.*]
London, 1812

WELSH (the) magistracy. By "Adfyfr" [T. J. Hughes]. 8vo. [*Brit. Mus.*]
Cardiff [1888]

WELSH (the) peasant boy; a novel. . . . By the author of *The Maid of Avon* [Mrs Peck]. 12mo. 3 vols. [*Brit. Mus.*]   London, 1808

WELSH (a) singer. [A novel]. By Allen Raine [Mrs Beynon Puddicombe, *née* Anne Adaliza Evans]. 8vo. [*Who's Who in Lit.*]
London, 1897

WELSH sketches, chiefly ecclesiastical, to the close of the twelfth century. By the author of *Proposals for Christian union* [Ernest Silvanus Appleyard]. Second edition. 12mo. Pp. viii. 160. [*Brit. Mus.*]   London, 1852

Advertisement signed: E. S. A. The first edition appeared in 1851.

—— Second series, 1852. Pp. viii. 153.

—— Third series, 1853. Pp. viii. 192.

WELSH (the) witch; a tale of rough places. By Allen Raine [Mrs Beynon Puddicombe, *née* Anne Adaliza Evans]. Fifth edition. 8vo. Pp. 440. [*Who's Who in Lit.*]   London, 1904

WENHAM water-works; statements by W. P. P. [Willard P. Phillips]. 8vo. [Cushing's *Init. and Pseud.* i. 223.]   Salem, Mass., 1867

WENSLEYDALE; or rural contemplation: a poem. [By Thomas Maude.] The third edition. 4to. Pp. xii. 13-54. [*Gent. Mag.* lxix. 163.]   London, 1780

The fourth edition (1816) has the author's name.

WEPT (the) of Wish-Ton-Wish; a tale. By the author of *The Pioneers*, etc. [James Fenimore Cooper]. New edition. 8vo. 2 vols. [Allibone's *Dict.*]   Philadelphia, 1836

WE'RE all low people then; and other tales. By the author of *Caleb Stukely* [Samuel Phillips, LL.D.]. 8vo. Pp. 255. [*Brit. Mus.*]   London, 1854

Reprinted from *Blackwood's Magazine.*

WERNERIA; or short characters of earths : with notes according to the improvements of Klaproth, Vauquelin and Hauy. By Terræ Filius [Rev. Stephen Weston, B.D.]. 12mo. 2 parts. [*Manch. Free Lib.*]
London, 1805-06
WERTER to Charlotte ; a poem. [By Edward Taylor, of Tipperary.] 4to. [O'Donoghue's *Poets of Ireland*.]
London, 1784
Founded on Goethe's novel, *The sorrows of Werther*.
WESLEYAN local preachers. [By William D. Lawson.] 8vo.
Newcastle, 1874
WESLEYAN Methodism as it respects the temperance question, agreeably to the writings of the Rev. John Wesley, A.M. . . . Compiled by a leader of the Methodist Society [Francis Carne]. 12mo. Pp. 12.
Falmouth [1839]
WESLEYAN Methodism in Scotland. [By H. W. Holland.] Pp. 12. [*Bodl.*]
Leeds, 1864
WESLEYAN (the) Methodist Sunday hymn-book ; edited by W. H. R. [William Harris Rule]. 8vo. [Cushing's *Init. and Pseud.* i. 246.] London, 1851
WESLEYAN takings ; or, centenary sketches of ministerial character. By Rev. Joseph Beaumont [Rev. James Everett]. 8vo. 2 vols. [Cushing's *Init. and Pseud.* i. 715.]
London, 1841-51
WESLEYANS (the) vindicated from the calumnies contained in "The Church of England compared with Wesleyan Methodism," in a dialogue between a Churchman and a Methodist. [By Rev. Thomas Jackson.] 8vo. London, 1837
WESSEX ; painted by Walter Tyndale, described by Clive Holland [Charles J. Hankinson]. 8vo. [*Lond. Lib. Cat.*]
London, 1906
WEST (the) Briton ; a collection of poems on various subjects. [By Thomas O'Grady.] 4to. Dublin, 1800
WEST coast ballads and other pieces. By J. C. A. [J. Carfine Alston]. 8vo.
Glasgow, 1889
WEST (the) country farmer (Number 2), consisting of three parts : I. The landlord's answer to his tenant's complaint. . . . II. The farmer's reply, in which the errors of his brethren are excused. . . . III. A postscript to the farmers themselves, exhorting them to put a due value on their persons and professions. . . . [By Francis Squire.] 8vo. [*Bodl.*; Green's *Bibl. Somers.* ii. 399.] Taunton, N.D.
The Farmer signs himself : Ofellus ; the Landlord : X. Y. Z. For No. 1, *see below* "The West-Country farmer . . ."

WEST India eclogues. [By Edward Rushton.] 4to. [*Mon. Rev.* lxxvii. 283.] London, 1787
WEST (the) India question practically considered. [By Sir Robert J. W. Horton, M.A., M.P.] 8vo. [*Brit. Mus.*] London, 1826
WEST (the) India sketch-book. [By Trelawney Wentworth.] 8vo. 2 vols.
London, 1834
WEST (the) Indian; a comedy, as it is performed at the Theatre Royal in Drury-Lane. By the author of *The Brothers* [Richard Cumberland]. 8vo. Pp. 102. [Baker's *Biog. Dram.*]
London, 1771
WEST Indian yarns. By "X. Beke" [G. H. Hawtayne]. 8vo. Pp. 137. [*Brit. Mus.*] Demerara, 1884
WEST (the) Indians defended. By a gentleman [Edward Samuel Byam]. 8vo. Bath, 1811
Signed at end : Edward White.

WEST of Indian life. By Nivedita [Margaret Elizabeth Noble]. 8vo. [*Brit. Mus.*] London, 1904
WEST Point colors. By Amy Lothrop [Anna Bartlett Warner]. 8vo. [*Amer. Cat.*] Chicago, 1904
WEST Somerset ballads. [By John Barwick Hodge.] 4to. Pp. 32. [*Lond. Lib. Cat.*] London [1895]
WEST Ward rhymes ; and other verses. By "The Member for the West Ward" [W. J. Townsend Collins]. 8vo. Pp. ii. 80. [*Brit. Mus.*] Newport, 1898
WEST-COUNTRY (the) farmer ; or, a fair representation of the decay of trade, and badness of the times : in a letter of complaint from a tenant in the country, to his landlord in London. [By Francis Squire.] 12mo. Pp. 50. [*Bodl.*] Taunton, N.D.
The preface is signed : Ofellus. For a continuation, *see above* "The West country farmer . . ."

WESTERN Australia. By "The Vagabond" [Julian Thomas]. 8vo. [*Lib. of Col. Inst.*, Supp. i. 35.]
Melbourne, 1896
WESTERN Australia ; with some account of the settlement of Australind. [By Alfred Gill.] 12mo.
London, 1842
WESTERN (the) mail ; being a selection of letters made from the bag taken from the Western Mail when it was robbed by George —— in 17—. [By Annabella Plumptre.] 12mo. [Watt's *Bibl. Brit.*] N.P. 1801

WESTERN (the) martyrology; or, bloody assizes: containing the lives, trials, and dying speeches of all those eminent Protestants that suffer'd in the West of England, and elsewhere, from the year 1678, to this time: together with the life and death of George L. Jeffreys: the fifth edition: to which is now added, to make it compleat, an account of the barbarous whippings of several persons in the West: also the trial and case of Mr John Tutchin (the author of the Observator). . . . [By Thomas Pitts.] 8vo. Pp. 14, 279. [*Mendham Collection Cat.*]
London, 1705

WESTERN (the) wanderings of a Typo. [By John S. Robb.] 8vo. [Cushing's *Init. and Pseud.* i. 289.]
Philadelphia, 1846

WESTERN (a) wildflower. [A novel.] By Katharine Lee [Katharine Lee Jenner]. 8vo. 3 vols. [*Brit. Mus.*]
London, 1882

WESTMINSTER Abbey; a poem. [By John Dart.] 8vo. Pp. 3, 64. [*Dyce Cat.*]
London, 1721

WESTMINSTER Abbey; or, the days of the Reformation. By the author of *Whitefriars*, etc. [Miss Emma Robinson]. 12mo. 3 vols. [*Brit. Mus.*]
London, 1854

WESTMINSTER Abbey; with other occasional poems, and a free translation of the Oedipus Tyrannus of Sophocles. By the author of *Indian antiquities* [Thomas Maurice]. 8vo.
London, 1813

A previous edition (1784) of Westminster Abbey bears the author's name.

WESTMINSTER chimes, and other poems. By Maxwell Gray [Mary Gleed Tuttiett]. 8vo. [*Brit. Mus.*]
London, 1890

WESTMINSTER Fayre, newly proclaimed. A satire on the Westminster Assembly of divines. [By John Taylor, the water poet.] 4to. Pp. 8.
[London] 1647

WESTMINSTER Hall; or, anecdotes and reminiscences of the bar, the bench, and the woolsack. [Compiled by Henry and Thomas Roscoe.] 8vo. 3 vols. [Lowndes' *Bibl. Man.* p. 2880.]
London, 1825

WESTMORLAND (the) dialect, in three familiar dialogues; in which an attempt is made to illustrate the provincial idiom. By A. W. [Ann Walker]. 12mo. Pp. 95, 12. [*Bodl.*]
Kendal, 1790

Ascribed also to H. Wheeler.

WESTWARD Ho! . . . By the author of *The Dutchman's fireside* [James Kirke Paulding]. 8vo. 2 vols. [Kirk's *Supp.*]
New York, 1833

WET (the) blanket; or Edith's bright autumn. By the author of *The Dalrymples* [Sibella Jones]. 8vo. [*Brit. Mus.*]
London [1872]

WET days. [Poems.] By a farmer [John Affleck Bridges]. 8vo. Pp. xii. 218. [*Brit. Mus.*]
London, 1879

WET days at Edgewood. By Ik Marvel [Donald Grant Mitchell, LL.D.]. 8vo. [Cushing's *Init. and Pseud.* i. 184.]
New York, 1888

WEYMOUTH (the) guide; exhibiting the ancient and present state of Weymouth and Melcombe Regis, with a description of Lulworth Castle, the Island of Portland and other places worthy the attention of Strangers. . . . [By Peter Delamotte.] 8vo. Pp. 96. [Mayo's *Bibl. Dors.* p. 253.]
London, 1785

WHALE (the) and its captors. By Major Marble [Rev. Henry T. Cheever]. 8vo. [Cushing's *Init. and Pseud.* i. 183.]
New York, 1849

WHARNCLIFFE; a play, in three acts: time occupied, one day. [By James Hobson Aveling, M.D.] 12mo. Pp. 36.
London, 1854

WHAT a boy! Problems concerning him. By Julia A. Willis [Julia A. Kempshall]. 8vo. [Cushing's *Init. and Pseud.* i. 308.]
Philadelphia, 1874

WHAT a life! An autobiography. By E. V. L. and G. M. [Edward Verrall Lucas and George Morrow]. 8vo. Pp. 126. [*Brit. Mus.*]
London, 1911

WHAT a woman will do; a society drama. By Lucas Cleeve [Mrs Howard Kingscote, *née* Adelina G. I. Wolff]. 8vo. Pp. 316. [*Who's Who in Lit.*]
London, 1899

WHAT aileth thee? By the author of *The melody of the Twenty-third Psalm* [Anna Bartlett Warner]. 8vo. [Kirk's *Supp.*]
London, 1881

WHAT am I? Where am I? What ought I to do? How am I to become qualified and disposed to do what I ought? By the author of *Outlines of social economy*, etc. [William Ellis]. 8vo. Pp. 66. [*Bodl.*]
London, 1852

WHAT an old myth may teach. By Leslie Keith [Grace Leslie Keith Johnston], author of *A simple maiden*. 8vo. Pp. 139. [*Nat. Lib. of Scot.*]
London, 1878

WHAT, and how of the eternal worker: the work and the plan? [By Emanuel Swedenborg.] 8vo.
Private print, 1862

WHAT? and who says it? An exposition of the statement that the Established Church "destroys more souls than it saves," by T. Chalmers . . . in a letter. . . . Edited by John Search [Rev. Thomas Binney]. Second edition. [*Brit. Mus.*]
Worcester [1838?]

WHAT are the causes of prolonged depression in trade? By a Scotch banker [George Drummond Charles]. 8vo.   London, 1879

WHAT are the English Roman Catholics to do? The question considered in a letter to Lord Edward Howard. By Anglo-Catholicus [Lord John Manners]. 8vo. [*Bodl.*]
London, 1841

WHAT came to me in the silence. By A. E. S. [Annie E. Stapley]. 8vo. Pp. 100. [*Brit. Mus.*] London, 1899

WHAT can't be cured must be endured ; or Christian patience and forbearance in practice. [By Anna Letitia Waring.] 8vo. [*Brit. Mus.*]   London, 1854
Signed : A. L. W.

WHAT do you go to Church for? A question to Christian men and women. By S. W. [Miss S. Warren]. 8vo. [*Brit. Mus.*]   London [1869]

WHAT does it profit a man? University education and the memorialists. By the son of a Catholic country squire [Roger William Bede Vaughan, R. C. archbishop of Sydney]. 8vo. [*D. N. B.* vol. 58, p. 178.]
London, 1865

WHAT Dolly and Robbie did. By "Fleeta" [Kate W. Hamilton]. 8vo. [*Amer. Cat.*]   Philadelphia, 1891

WHAT dreams may come. By Frank Lin [Mrs Gertrude Franklin Atherton]. 8vo.   Chicago, 1888
A later edition (1889) bears the author's name.

WHAT election and reprobation is, clearly discovered, and the ignorance of such who hold election and reprobation of persons, manifested. By G. F. [George Fox]. 4to. [Smith's *Cat. of Friends' Books*, i. 679.]   1679

WHAT Emmet means in 1915. By A. Newman [Herbert Moore Pim]. 8vo. [*Lond. Lib. Cat.*]   Dublin, 1915
Tracts for the times, published by the Irish Publicity League, No. 1.

WHAT Fide remembers. By Faye Huntington [Mrs Isabella H. Foster]. 8vo. [Cushing's *Init. and Pseud.* i. 134.]   New York, 1884

WHAT gold cannot buy ; a novel. By Mrs Alexander [Mrs Alexander Hector, *née* Annie French]. 8vo. Pp. 304. [*Lit. Year Book.*]   London, 1896

WHAT happened after the battle of Dorking ; or the victory of Tunbridge Wells. [By Charles John Stone, barrister.] 8vo.   London [1871]

WHAT have the Whigs done? . . . By Caleb Wilkins [George Sheppard]. [Cushing's *Init. and Pseud.* i. 307.]
Newark, 1838

WHAT have thirty years of Church revival done? [By Rev. John Henry Blunt.] 8vo. Pp. 24. [*Brit. Mus.*]
London, 1861
Reprinted from *The Ecclesiastic.*

WHAT I know about Ben Eccles. By Abraham Page, Esq. [John Saunders Holt]. [Cushing's *Init. and Pseud.* i. 223.]   Philadelphia, 1869

WHAT I think of South Africa, its people and its politics. By Stuart Cumberland [Charles Garner, of Oxford]. 8vo. Pp. 224. [*Brit. Mus.*]
London, 1896

WHAT if the Swedes should come? With some thoughts about keeping the army on foot, whether they come or not. [By Daniel Defoe.] 8vo. Pp. 38. [Wilson's *Life of Defoe*, 160.]   London, 1717

WHAT is a Christian? By A. L. O. E., authoress of *The Claremont tales*, etc. [Charlotte M. Tucker]. 8vo. Pp. 208.   Edinburgh, N.D.

WHAT is a pound? A letter on the new currency measures. [By John Taylor, publisher.] 8vo.
London, 1844

WHAT is baptism? By a clergyman of the diocese of Exeter [Rev. George Ferris Whidborne]. 8vo.
London, 1835

WHAT is baptism? Is it a fiction? Considered by a no-party man [Henry Hayes]. 8vo. [*Brit. Mus.*]
Holloway, 1859

WHAT is free trade? By Émile Walter, a worker [Alexander Delmar]. 8vo. [*Lib. Journ.* vi. 322.] New York, 1867

WHAT is good English? and other essays. By Rafford Pyke [Harry Thurston Peck]. 8vo. [*Amer. Cat.*]
New York, 1899

WHAT is good iron ; and how is it to be got? [By R. H. Cheney.] 8vo. [*Brit. Mus.*]   London, 1862
The second edition (1862) bears the author's name.

"WHAT is he?" By the author of *Vivian Grey* [The Rt. Hon. Benjamin Disraeli]. 8vo. Pp. 16. [*D. N. B.* vol. 15, p. 101.]   London, 1833

WHAT is law? What are personal rights under law? and what are personal obligations? By "Legalis" [J. P. Philpott]. 8vo. [*Amer. Cat.*]
Nashville, Tenn., 1887

WHAT is man? And other essays. By Mark Twain [Samuel Langhorne Clemens]. 8vo. [*Lit. Year Book.*]
London, 1919

WHAT is meant by Apostolical Succession? A question answered by a clergyman of the Scottish Episcopal Church [Rev. John Gabriel Ryde, M.A., of Aberdeen]. 8vo. Pp. 67.
Aberdeen, 1856

WHAT is mesmerism? And what its concomitants, clairvoyance and necromancy? [By Francis Sitwell.] Second edition enlarged. 12mo. Pp. 32. [*Brit. Mus.*]   London, 1862

WHAT is occultism? A philosophical and critical study. By Papus [Gérard Encausse]. Translated [from the French] by Fred Rothwell. 8vo. Pp. 101. [*Brit. Mus.*]   London, 1913

WHAT is our situation, and what are our prospects? By an American [Joseph Hopkinson]. 8vo. [*Cushing's Init. and Pseud.* i. 13.]
Philadelphia, 1799

WHAT is she? A comedy, in five acts [and in prose. By Charlotte Smith]. 12mo. [*Brit. Mus.*]   Dublin, 1799

WHAT is the Church of Christ? [By George Hill.] 12mo.   N.P. 1843

WHAT is the duty of Seceders in reference to Union with the Free Church? By a working man [Thomas Robertson, elder in Clola]. 8vo. Pp. 16.   Edinburgh, 1851

WHAT is the Municipal Mortgages Act? The question answered in a letter to the ratepayers of Birmingham. [By George James Johnson.] 8vo.
Birmingham, 1867

WHAT is the truth? [By A. Fellowes.] 8vo. Pp. xvi. 160.
Tunbridge Wells, 1892
Signed : A. F.

WHAT is the War about? [By William Edward Armitage Axon.] 8vo. [*Brit. Mus.*]   Manchester, 1877

WHAT is truth? By "Africanus" [H. G. Soames]. 8vo. Pp. 28. [Mendelssohn's *South Afr. Bibl.* i. 335.]
Johannesburg [1902]

WHAT is truth? A consideration of the doubts as to the efficacy of prayer, raised by evolutionists, materialists, and others. By "Nemo" [Leonard William Thrupp]. 8vo. Pp. xiii. 265.
London, 1890

WHAT is wine? An interesting dialogue on wines. . . . By F. and I. [—— Forster and —— Ingle]. 8vo. 2 parts. [*Brit. Mus.*]   London [1856]

WHAT is worship? A second question on Churchgoing. By S. W. [Miss S. Warren]. 8vo. [*Brit. Mus.*]
London [1870]

WHAT it feels like. By A. Newman [Herbert Moore Pim]. 8vo. [*Lond. Lib. Cat.*]   Dublin, 1915
Tracts for the times, published by the Irish Publicity League, No. 8.

WHAT Katy did; a story. By Susan Coolidge [Sarah Chauncey Woolsey]. 12mo. Pp. viii. 238. [*Lit. Year Book.*]   London, [1873]

WHAT Katy did next. [A story for the young.] By Susan Coolidge [Sarah Chauncey Woolsey]. 8vo. Pp. 288. [*Lit. Year Book.*]   Boston, 1886

WHAT killed Mr Drummond, the lead or lancet? By an old army surgeon [Samuel Dickson]. 8vo. [*Brit. Mus.*]
London, 1843

WHAT lay beneath; a story of the Queensland Bush. By "Coo—ee" [William Sylvester Walker]. 8vo. Pp. 301. [*Brit. Mus.*]   London, 1909

WHAT lies beneath. [A novel.] By Benjamin Swift [William Romaine Paterson]. 8vo. [*Brit. Mus.*]
London, 1917

WHAT made you join the English Church? [By Rev. William Macdonald Meredith, M.A.] 8vo. Pp. 20.   Edinburgh, 1885

WHAT may be effected by union; a fragment of mission history. [By Rev. G. Pearce.] 8vo.   Calcutta, 1870
Signed : G. P.

WHAT may I learn? or, sketches of school-girls. By Cousin Kate [Catherine Douglas Bell]. 8vo. [*Cushing's Init. and Pseud.* i. 157.]
Edinburgh, 1849

WHAT men call love; a story of South Africa in the days of Cetewayo. By Lucas Cleeve [Mrs Howard Kingscote, *née* Adelina G. I. Wolff]. 8vo. [*Lit. Year Book.*]   London, 1901

WHAT men like in women. By the author of *How to be happy though married* [Rev. Edward John Hardy, M.A.]. 8vo. [*Lond. Lib. Cat.*]
London, 1906

WHAT might have been; a true story. By the author of *English hearts and English hands*, etc. [Catherine M. Marsh]. 8vo. Pp. vii. 127. [*Brit. Mus.*]   London, 1881

WHAT might have been: the story of a social war. Anonymous. [By Ernest Brahmah.] 8vo. Pp. 380. [*Bookman*, Jan. 1923, p. 184.]
London, 1907
Published afterwards under the title "The Secret of the League," with the author's name.

WHAT next? or the peers and the third time of asking. [By Sir Henry Rich.] 8vo. [*Brit. Mus.*]
London, 1837

WHAT one can do with a chafing-dish; a guide for amateur cooks. By H. L. S. [H. L. Sawtelle]. New edition. 8vo. Pp. 150. [*Brit. Mus.*]
New York [1899]

WHAT one work of mercy can I do this Lent? A letter to a friend. [By Henry Edward Manning.] 12mo. [*Brit. Mus.*] London, 1847

WHAT ought she to do? [A novel.] By Florence Warden [Florence Alice Price, later Mrs George E. James]. 8vo. Pp. 306. [*Lit. Year Book.*] London, 1904

WHAT ought the Church and people of Scotland to do now? By a Seceder [Rev. William White, minister of Knox's Free Church, Haddington]. Second edition. 8vo. Pp. 28. [*New Coll. Lib.*] Edinburgh, 1840

WHAT ought the diocese to do? Considerations addressed to [episcopal] Churchmen of the diocese of New York. By a layman [Orlando Meads]. 8vo. [*Brit. Mus.*] [New York] 1845

WHAT ought the General Assembly to do at the present crisis? [By Thomas M'Crie, D.D.] 8vo. Pp. 58.
Edinburgh, 1833

WHAT peace to the wicked? or, an expostulatorie answer to a derisorie question, lately made concerning peace. By a free-man, though a prisoner [George Wither]. The author spares his name; not, that he dares not to let you know it; but, that he cares not. 4to. Pp. 6. [*D. N. B.* vol. 62, p. 264.] N.P. 1646

WHAT saith the Scriptures about witchcraft? [By Caroline Pearse.] 12mo. Pp. 8. [*Brit. Mus.*] Launceston [1865]
Signed: C. P.

WHAT Scotch fowk think. Brethren in the Keel-howes; or, questionings as to Christian doctrine and Plymouthism. [By James Moir Porteous, D.D.] Fourth edition. 8vo. Pp. 204. London, 1874
The sixth edition, entitled "Brethren in the Keel-howes . . ." bears the author's name.

WHAT set him right; with other chapters to help. . . . [By Andrew K. H. Boyd, D.D.] 8vo. [*D. N. B.* First Supp. vol. i. p. 245.]
London, 1885

WHAT shall be done with Cardinal Wiseman? An inquiry. By an English journalist [William Charles Mark Kent]. 8vo. [*Brit. Mus.*]
London, 1850

WHAT shall be the end of these things? An inquiry regarding the probable issues of the Scottish Free Church controversy. By the author of *Considerations for the conscientious* [Rev. James W. Taylor, of Flisk]. 12mo. Pp. 117. [*New Coll. Lib.*] Perth, 1844

WHAT shall I do with my money? By Old Chatty Cheerful [William Martin]. 12mo. [Cushing's *Init. and Pseud.* i. 210.] London [1863]

WHAT shall we do at Delphi? An Englishman's [Edmund Wheeler's] letter to the humanitarians. 8vo. [Cushing's *Init. and Pseud.* i. 92.]
London 1857

WHAT shall we do to-night? or, social amusements. By Leger D. Mayne [W. B. Dick, S. A. Frost, and W. Taylor]. [Cushing's *Init. and Pseud.* i. 186.] New York, 1873

WHAT she came through. By Sarah Tytler, author of *Citoyenne Jacqueline*, etc. [Henrietta Keddie]. 8vo. 3 vols. [*Brit. Mus.*] London, 1877

"WHAT she could." By the author of *The wide wide world* [Susan Warner]. 8vo. Pp. 259. [Allibone's *Dict.*]
London, 1870

WHAT the bird said to Bertha. By Laura Caxton [Lizzie B. Comins]. 8vo. [Cushing's *Init. and Pseud.* i. 53.] Boston, 1888

WHAT the Book of Job teaches; compiled largely from Prof. S. R. Driver and A. B. Davidson . . . by K. S. M. [Rev. Kenneth S. Macdonald, D.D.]. 8vo. Pp. 4. [*Brit. Mus.*]
Calcutta, 1898

WHAT the boy thought. Thoughts wise and otherwise; a social satire. By Little Jim [James S. Little]. Second edition. 12mo. Pp. 58. [*Brit. Mus.*] London, 1884

WHAT the Gospels teach on the Divinity and humanity of Jesus Christ. By a layman [Thomas Crowther Brown, of Further Barton, Cirencester]. 8vo. Pp. xv. 91. London, 1877

WHAT the old tell me! A reverie. [By Rev. Frederick W. B. Bouverie.] 8vo. Aberdeen [1865?]

WHAT the people ought to do, in choosing their representatives at the general election, after the passing of the Reform Bill. By Junius Redivivus [William Bridges Adams]. 8vo. [*D. N. B.* vol. i, p. 109.]
London, 1832

WHAT the seven did; or the doings of the Wordsworth Club. By Margaret Sidney [Mrs Harriet Mulford Lathrop]. 8vo. Pp. 405. [*Brit. Mus.*]
Boston, 1882

WHAT they couldn't ; a home story. By "Pansy" [Mrs Isabella Alden, *née* Macdonald]. 8vo. Pp. 424. [*Lit. Year Book.*]   Boston, 1895

WHAT think ye of Christ? By a Farmer [William Mill]. 8vo. Pp. 52.
                                    Wick, 1878

WHAT think ye of the Congress now? or an enquiry how far the Americans are bound to abide by and execute the decisions of the late Congress. [By Thomas Bradbury Chandler.] 8vo. Pp. 52. [*Evans' Amer. Bibl.* v. 109.]
                              New York, 1775
  There is added, "A Plan of a proposed union between Great Britain and the Colonies of New-Hampshire, Massachusetts-Bay, etc."

WHAT to do, and how to do it, when an election comes. By the oldest School Inspector [Joseph Bentley]. 8vo. [*Cushing's Init. and Pseud.* i. 214.]
                                  London, 1868

WHAT was the Fall? Or a brief statement of the doctrine of divines on the First and the Second Death ; with observations. . . . [By Edward White, Congregational minister.] 8vo.
                                  London, 1845

WHAT we must all come to ; a comedy in two acts, as it was intended to be acted at the Theatre-Royal in Covent-Garden. [By Arthur Murphy.] 8vo. Pp. 52. [*Baker's Biog. Dram.*]
                                  London, 1764
  Afterwards produced as "Three weeks after marriage."

WHAT will be the practical effects of the Reform Bill? [By Montague Gore.] 8vo.   London, 1831

WHAT will come of it? By E. W. B. [Miss E. W. Barnes]. 8vo.
                              Philadelphia, 1877

WHAT will he do with it? By Pisistratus Caxton, author of *My novel*, etc. [Sir Edward Bulwer-Lytton]. 8vo. 4 vols. [*W.*]   Edinburgh, 1859

WHAT will he say? By Ojos Morenos [Mrs Josephine Russell Clay]. 8vo. [*Lib. Journ.* iii. 168.]
                              Philadelphia, 1873

WHAT will the Lords do? [By Sir Henry Rich.] 8vo. [*Brit. Mus.*]
                                  London, 1831

WHAT woman wills. [A novel.] By Lucas Cleeve [Mrs Howard Kingscote, *née* Adelina G. I. Wolff]. 8vo. Pp. 314. [*Lit. Year Book.*] London, 1908

WHEAT and tares ; a tale. [By Sir Henry Stewart Cunningham, K.S.I.E.] 12mo. Pp. 411. [*Camb. Univ. Lib.*]
                                  London, 1861

WHEAT in the ear. [A tale.] By "Alien" [Mrs L. A. Baker]. 8vo. [*Lit. Year Book.*]   London, 1898

WHEEL (the) of fortune ; or, the dignity of labour. By Madeline Leslie [Harriett N. Baker]. 8vo. [*Brit. Mus.*]
                                  Boston [1866]

WHEEL (the) of God. [A novel.] By George Egerton [Mrs Egerton Clairmonte, *née* Dunn]. 8vo. Pp. 322. [*Brit. Mus.*]   London, 1898

WHEELS within wheels. [A novel.] By Huan Mee [—— and —— Mansfield, two brothers]. 8vo.
                                  London, 1901

WHEN Auntie Lil took charge. By May Wynne [May Wynne Knowles]. 8vo. Pp. 223. [*Brit. Mus.*]
                              Glasgow [1915]

WHEN Grandmamma was fourteen. By Marion Harland [Mrs Mary Virginia Terhune, *née* Hawes]. 8vo. [*Lit. Year Book.*]   Boston, 1905

WHEN hearts are young ; an idyll. By Deas Cromarty [Mrs Robert L. Watson, *née* Elizabeth Sophia Fletcher]. 8vo. [*Who's Who in Lit.*]
                                  London, 1896

WHEN I was a little girl ; stories for children by the author of *St Olave's* [Miss Eliza Tabor]. Illustrated by L. Frolich. 8vo. Pp. vi. 2, 249. [*Nat. Lib. of Scot.*] London, 1871

WHEN I was young. . . . By Charles Camden [Richard Rowe]. 8vo. [*F. Boase's Mod. Eng. Biog.* iii. 326.]
                                  London, 1872

WHEN Israel Putnam served the King. . . . By James Otis [James Otis Kaler]. 8vo. [*Cushing's Init. and Pseud.* i. 220.]   Boston, 1888

WHEN it was dark ; the story of a great conspiracy. By Guy Thorne [Cyril A. E. Ranger-Gull]. 8vo. Pp. 436. [*Who's Who in Lit.*]
                                  London, 1903

WHEN it was light ; a reply to When it was dark. By a well-known author [Andrew Lang]. 8vo. Pp. 208.
                                  London, 1906

WHEN knighthood was in flower ; or, the love-story of Charles Brandon and Mary Tudor. By Edwin Caskoden [Charles Major]. 8vo. [*Amer. Cat.*]
                              New York, 1898

WHEN Santiago fell ; or, the war adventures of two chums. By Captain Ralph Bonehill [Edward Stratemeyer]. 8vo. [*Amer. Cat.*]   New York, 1899

WHEN terror ruled. [A novel.] By May Wynne [May Wynne Knowles]. 8vo. Pp. 252. [*Brit. Mus.*]
                                  London, 1907

WHEN the bour-tree blooms. [A tale.] By Leslie Keith [Grace Leslie Keith Johnston]. 8vo. Pp. 256. [*Brit. Mus.*]
                                  London [1894]

WHEN the devil drives. [A novel.] By Florence Warden [Florence Alice Price, later Mrs George E. James]. 8vo. Pp. 304. [*Who's Who in Lit.*]
London, 1910

WHEN the eagle flies seawards. [By Patrick Vaux and Lionel Gaxley.] 8vo. [*Who's Who in Lit.*] London, 1907

WHEN the Great War came. By "Navarcus" [Patrick Vaux and another]. 8vo. [*Who's Who in Lit.*]
London, 1908

The above is a slightly different edition of "The World's awakening."

"WHEN the King comes to his own." A pastoral play. . . . [By Frances J. Armour.] 8vo. Pp. 19.
Waterloo [1903]

WHEN the snow comes down. [A tale of the winter sports.] By W. L. S. [Rev. William L. Stephen, M.A., of Dumbarton]. 8vo. Pp. 243.
London [1915]

WHEN the swallows come again. [A story.] By M. F. W. [M. F. Wilson]. 8vo. [*Brit. Mus.*] London [1891]

WHEN the trumpet is calling; and other poems. By Clarice Laurence [Miss C. L. Hancock]. 8vo. [*Who's Who in Lit.*] London, 1919

WHEN the wicked man. [A novel.] By Guy Thorne [Cyril A. E. Ranger-Gull]. 8vo. Pp. 317. [*Who's Who in Lit.*] London, 1916

WHEN the world reeled. [A novel.] By Guy Thorne [Cyril A. E. Ranger-Gull]. 8vo. [*Who's Who in Lit.*]
London, 1924

WHEN Washington served the King. . . . By James Otis [James Otis Kaler]. 8vo. [*Cushing's Init. and Pseud.* i. 220.] New York, 1905

WHEN wheat is green. By Joseph Wilton [Beatrice Chambers]. 8vo.
London, 1895

WHENCE comest thou? The Devil and Satan; a critical examination of all the texts in which the words Diabolos and Satan are found in Holy Scripture. By Omega [Thomas Walter Good]. 8vo. Pp. 103. [*Brit. Mus.*] London, 1877

WHERE are the dead? And will any suffer eternal torment? A debate between Antipas, F[idei] D[efensor] . . . and the Rev. Eli Clarke . . . and the Rev. F. D. Thomson. [By James Martin, publisher.] 8vo. Pp. 63.
London, 1885

WHERE are the dead? or, spiritualism explained. . . . By Fritz [Frederic A. Binney, solicitor]. Third edition. Pp. viii. 228. London, 1875

WHERE billows roll; a tale of the Welsh Coast. By Allen Raine [Mrs Beynon Puddicombe, *née* Anne A. Evans]. 8vo. Pp. 360. [*Who's Who in Lit.*] London, 1909

WHERE did King Oswald die? A summary (by A[skew] R[oberts]) of the arguments in favour of Oswestry [by Howel William Lloyd,† M.A.] and Winwick [by O. Cockayne]. 8vo. [*Brit. Mus.*] Shrewsbury, 1879

WHERE ghosts walk; the haunts of familiar characters in history and literature. By Marion Harland [Mary Virginia Hawes, later Mrs Terhune]. 8vo. Pp. x. 292. [*Who's Who in Lit.*] London, 1913

WHERE highways cross. By a son of the soil [Joseph Smith Fletcher]. 8vo. New York, 1895

WHERE honor leads. By Lynde Palmer [Mrs Mary Louise Peebles, *née* Parmlee]. 8vo. [*Cushing's Init. and Pseud.* i. 224.] New York, 1894

WHERE honour sits. By Reginald Wray [W. B. Home-Gall]. 8vo. [*Who's Who in Lit.*] London, 1906

WHERE is your husband? [A novel.] By George Frost [Mrs Octavius Eddison]. 8vo. Pp. 188. [*Brit. Mus.*]
London, 1901

WHERE men only dare to go; or, the story of a boy Company, C.S.A. By an Ex-boy [R. W. Figg]. 8vo.
Richmond, Va., 1885

WHERE ought the new cemetery to be placed? In the Meadows? or in the King's Park? [By Patrick Neill, printer.] 8vo. Pp. 7.
Edinburgh, 1832

Signed: A Citizen.

From a MS. note in the Brit. Mus. copy in Lord Henry Cockburn's handwriting.

WHERE Pharaoh dreams. By Irene Osgood [Irene Harvey, later Mrs Robert Harborough Sherard]. 8vo.
London, 1908

WHERE science and religion meet. By William Scott Palmer [M. E. Dowson]. 8vo. Pp. 287. [*Brit. Mus.*]
London [1919]

WHERE shall I worship when I am saved? In verse. By F. W. [Frances Wilson]. 12mo. [*Brit. Mus.*]
London, 1879

WHERE shall we go? A guide to watering-places in Great Britain. By Ascott R. Hope [Robert Hope Moncrieff]. 8vo. [*Who's Who in Lit.*]
London, 1892

WHERE Socialism failed. An actual experiment. . . . With illustrations and a map. [On William Lane's experiment at New Australia and Cosine in Paraguay.] By Stewart Grahame [Graeme Douglas Williams]. 8vo. Pp. xii. 266. [*Brit. Mus.*]
London, 1912

WHERE the battle was fought. [A novel.] By Charles Egbert Cradock [Mary Noailles Murfree]. 8vo. Pp. 423. [*Brit. Mus.*]   Boston [1885]

WHERE the forest murmurs. By Fiona Macleod [William Sharp]. 8vo. [*Who's Who in Lit.*]   London, 1907

WHERE the wind sits. By the author of *Honoria's patchwork* [Mercedes Macandrew]. 8vo. Pp. 308. [*Brit. Mus.*]   London, 1907

WHERE there's a will there's a way. [By Rosina Anne Doyle Wheeler, later Lady Lytton Bulwer]. 8vo. [F. Boase's *Mod. Eng. Biog.* ii. 554.]
N.P. 1871

WHERE to go abroad. By Ascott R. Hope [Robert Hope Moncrieff]. 8vo. [*Who's Who in Lit.*]   London, 1893

WHERE to spend a half-holiday; one hundred and eighty walks around Bradford. By Johnnie Gray [Harry Speight]. 8vo. Pp. 188. [*Brit. Mus.*]   Bradford, 1890

WHERE to spend a holiday. [By Louisa M. Hubbard.] 8vo. Pp. 64. [*Brit. Mus.*]   London, 1887
Signed: L. M. H.

WHERE truth lies. By Jane Wardle [Oliver Madox Hueffer]. 8vo. Pp. 320. [*Who's Who in Lit.*]
London, 1909

WHERE was Protestantism before Luther? With an appendix. By a layman [James Creighton M'Clellan]. 12mo. Pp. 52.   York, 1852

WHERE will it end? A view of slavery in the United States, in its aggressions and results. . . . [By Edmund Quincy.] 8vo.   Providence, 1863

VVHETHER Christian faith maye be kepte secret in the heart, without confession therof openly to the worlde as occasion shal serue; also what hurt cōmeth by the that hath receiued the gospell, to be presēt at masse vnto the simple and vnlearned. [By Robert Horne.] 8vo. No pagination. [*D.N.B.* vol. 27, p. 361.]
From Roane [M. Wood, London] 1553
Wrongly ascribed to John Hooper.

WHETHER the parliament be not in law dissolved by the death of the Princess of Orange? And how the subjects ought, and are to behave themselves in relation to those papers emitted since by the stile and title of Acts? With a brief account of the government of England; in a letter to a country gentleman, as an answer to his second question. [By Robert Ferguson.] 4to. Pp. 59.
No title-page. Letter dated April 24, 1695.

WHETHER the preserving the Protestant Religion was the motive unto or the end that was designed in the late Revolution? In a letter [by Robert Ferguson, "the Plotter"] to a country gentleman. 4to. [*D.N.B.* vol. 18, p. 353.]   N.P. 1695

WHETSTONE (the) of witte, whiche is the second parte of arithmetike; containyng the extraction of rootes. . . . [By Robert Record.] 4to.
London, 1557
Record's name is given in the text of the dedication.

WHICH? [A novel.] By Edith Nowell [Mrs Hubert Barclay]. 8vo. [*Who's Who in Lit.*]   London, 1908

WHICH is? or, the unknown God. By an unknown man [A. H. Pilkington]. 8vo.   London, 1909

WHICH is the lunatic? A farce in one Act. By Henry Francis [William Henry Francis Basevi]. 8vo. Pp. 21.
Allahabad, 1904

WHICH loved him best? A novel. By Bertha M. Clay [Charlotte M. Braeme]. 8vo. Pp. 342. [*Amer. Cat.*]
New York [1897]

WHICH party breaks the law and resists God's ordinance? [By Alexander Murray Dunlop.] 8vo. Pp. 4. [*New Coll. Lib.*]   Edinburgh, N.D.

WHICH party still breaks the law? [By Alexander Murray Dunlop.] 8vo. Pp 8. [*New Coll. Lib.*]
Edinburgh, N.D.

WHICH shall it be? [A novel.] By Mrs Alexander [Mrs Alexander Hector, *née* Annie French]. 8vo. [*Brit. Mus.*]   London, 1876

WHICH sister? A story. By Sydney Mostyn [William Clark Russell]. 8vo. 2 vols. [*Brit. Mus.*]   London, 1873

WHICH temple ye are. By A. H. W. (Canada) [A. H. Wigmore]. 8vo.
London, 1913

WHICH wins, love or money? By the author of *Whitefriars*, etc. [Emma Robinson]. 8vo. Pp. 262. [*Brit. Mus.*]   London, 1862

WHIFFS from a short briar. By Max Baring [Charles Messent]. 8vo. Pp. 124. [*Brit. Mus.*]   London [1896]

"WHIG claims on national confidence" examined. . . . [By John Ramsay.] 8vo.   Aberdeen, 1835

WHIG (the) Club ; or a sketch of the manners of the age. . . . By the author of *The Jockey Clubs* [Charles Pigott]. 8vo. [*Brit. Mus.*]   London, 1794

WHIG (the) Featheration ; or fireside legislation in Council : an original melodrama, in two acts, with songs. By Demos [James Woods]. 8vo. [O'Donoghue's *Poets of Ireland*.]
                              Mullingar, 1893

WHIG government ; or two years' retrospect. [By Sir Henry Rich.] 8vo. Pp. 24. [*Brit. Mus.*] London, 1832

WHIGS (the) and the Dissenters ; a letter to Edward Baines, Esq., M.P. [By John Middleton Hare.] 8vo. Pp. 23.   London [1839]
  Signed : J. M. H.

WHIG'S (a) apology for his consistency ; in a letter from a member of parliament to his friend in the borough of ****. [By Robert Adair.] 8vo. Pp. 198. [*Watt's Bibl. Brit.*]
                              London, 1795

WHIGS turn'd Tories, and Hanoverian-Tories, from their avow'd principles, prov'd Whigs ; or, each side in the other mistaken. Being a plain proof, that each party deny that charge which the other bring against them : and that neither side will disown those principles, which the other profess. [By Daniel Defoe.] 8vo. Pp. 4, 40. [Wilson's *Life of Defoe*, 145.]
                              London, 1713

WHIGS (the) unmask'd ; being the secret history of the Calf's-Head-Club : shewing the rise and progress of that infamous society since the grand rebellion : containing all the treasonable songs and ballads, sung as anthems by those saints, at their king-killing anniversaries : much enlarg'd and improv'd . . . Adorn'd with cuts suitable to every particular design : to which are added, Several characters by Sir John Denham and other valuable authors. . . . By Mr Butler, author of *Hudibras*. [By Edward Ward.] The eighth edition, with large additions. 8vo. Pp. 14, vi. 224.
                              London, 1713

WHIGS (the) unmask'd ; or, the history of the Calf's-Head-Club farther expos'd ; in a full account of the rise and progress of that impious society, since their horrid rebellion in forty-one : with all the treasonable ballads, sung by the villanous Whigs, as anthems, on the xxxth of January : much enlarg'd, . . . [By Edward Ward.] The ninth edition. 8vo. Pp. 14, vi. 224.
                              London, 1714

WHIM (a) and its consequences. [By George Payne Rainsford James.] 12mo. [*Brit. Mus.*]   London, 1847

WHIMS. [Tales.] By "Wanderer," author of *Fair Dianas*, etc. [Elim H. D'Avigdor]. 8vo. Pp. 305. [*Brit. Mus.*]   London, 1889

WHIMSICAL (the) bachelor ; or, married at last. A comedy in two acts. Written by a novice who has never beheld the interior of the greenroom [Henry Victor]. 8vo. Pp. 43. [*Brit. Mus.*]   Penzance [1865]

WHIMSICAL rhymes. By Edmund Evans [Charles Henry Ross]. 8vo. [F. Boase's *Mod. Eng. Biog.* vi. 498.]
                              London, 1881

WHIP (the) hand ; a comedy for husbands. By Keble Howard [John Keble Bell]. 8vo. Pp. 307. [*Who's Who in Lit.*]   London, 1906

WHIPPER (the) whipt ; being a reply upon a scandalous pamphlet, called the Whip : abusing that excellent work of Cornelius Burges, Dr in divinity, one of the Assembly of divines, entituled, The fire of the sanctuary newly discovered. [By Francis Quarles.] 4to. Pp. 2, 44. [*D. N. B.* vol. 47, p. 94.]
                              N.P. 1644

WHIRL (a) asunder. By Frank Lin [Mrs Gertrude Franklin Atherton]. 8vo. Pp. 192. [*Amer. Cat.*]
                              New York [1896]

WHIRLIGIG (the). [A novel.] By Mayne Lindsay [Mrs Clarke]. 8vo. Pp. 312. [*Who's Who in Lit.*]
                              London, 1901

WHIRLIGIG (the) of time. [A political satire, by Sir R. K. Douglas ; reprinted from *Blackwood's Magazine*.] 8vo. Pp. 32.   Edinburgh, 1885

WHIRLIGIG (the) papers. By Herman Grimbosh [Charles Mackay, LL.D.]. 8vo. [Cushing's *Init. and Pseud.* i. 121.]
                              London, 1855

WHIRLIGIGS. [A novel.] By O. Henry [William Sydney Porter]. 8vo. [*Amer. Cat.*]   New York, 1910

WHIRL-WIND (the) of the Lord gone forth as a fiery flying roule, with an alarm sounded against the inhabitants of the North-countrey; being a forewarning to all the rulers in England, of the mighty and terrible day of the Lord which shall overtake the wicked : but especially and in particular, to the persecuting rulers, priests, and people, in the county of Westmorland. . . . C. T. [Christopher Taylor]. 4to. Pp. 17. [*Bodl.*]   London, 1656
　　First printed in 1655.

WHIRLWIND (the) sown and reaped. [A story.] By Saladin [William Stewart Ross]. 8vo. [*Who's Who in Lit.*]   London [1884]

WHISKERS (the) whisk'd ; or, a farewel sermon prepared to be preach'd in Turners-Hall in Phillpot-Lane, by the Irreverend J—— J—— [Joseph Jacob], doctor of enthusiasm. [By John Tutchin, author of the Observator.] 4to. Pp. 26. [*Bodl.*]   London, 1703

WHISPER (a) to a newly-married pair ; from a widowed wife [Margaret Graves Derenzy]. 8vo. [*Brit. Mus.*]
　　　　　　Wellington, Salop, 1824
WHISPERER (the) ; or tales and speculations. By Gabriel Silvertongue [James Montgomery]. 12mo. [*D.N.B.* vol. 38, p. 318.]   London, 1798
　　Containing 24 Nos., the first dated May 28, 1795 ; the last, Nov. 5, 1795.
　　The copy in the British Museum contains the following note by Archdeacon Wrangham : " There is only one other copy, it is believed, of this work in existence, and that is in the author's hands. He has sedulously destroyed the remaining few which ever got into circulation."

WHISPERING (the) unseen ; or be ye doers of the Word. By A. L. O. E. [Miss Charlotte M. Tucker]. 8vo. [*Brit. Mus.*]   London, 1881

WHISPERINGS from life's shore ; a bright shell for children. By S. W. L. [Mrs S. W. Landor]. 8vo.
　　　　　　　　Boston, 1849
WHISPERS ; a novel. By George Colmore [Mrs Baillie Weaver]. 8vo. Pp. 312. [*Who's Who in Lit.*]
　　　　　　　　London, 1914
WHISPERS from dreamland. By Nellie Graham [Mrs Annie Dunning, *née* Ketchum]. 12mo. [Cushing's *Init. and Pseud.* i. 119.]
　　　　　　　　New York, 1861
WHIST ; a poem, in twelve cantos. [By Alexander Thomson.] 8vo. Pp. 194.   London, 1791
　　From the title-page of his *Paradise of taste.*

WHIST developments ; American leads, and the unblocking game. By " Cavendish " [Henry Jones]. 8vo. [*Brit. Mus.*]   London, 1894
WHIST for all players. . . . By Captain Rawdon Crawley [George Frederick Pardon]. A new edition, revised by his son, Rawdon Crawley, Bart., of Queen's Crawley, Hants [Charles Frederick Pardon]. 32mo. Pp. 37. [F. Jessel's *Bibl. of Playing Cards.*]
　　　　　　　　London, 1889
WHIST in diagrams ; a supplement to American Whist Illustrated. . . . By G. W. P. [George William Pettes]. 8vo. Pp. 290. [*Brit. Mus.*]
　　　　　　　　Boston, 1891
WHIST, or bumblepuppy? Thirteen lectures addressed to children. By Pembridge [John Petch Hewby]. 12mo. [*Reform Club Cat.* p. 601.]
　　　　　　　　London, 1880
WHIST (the) player ; the laws and practice of short whist explained and illustrated. By B . . . [Lieut.-Col.
—— Blyth]. Second edition. 4to.
　　　　　　　　London, 1858
WHIST (the) table ; a treasury of notes on the royal game. By " Cavendish " [Henry Jones], C. Mossop, A. E. Ewald, Charles Hervey, and other distinguished players. The whole edited by " Portland " [James Hogg]. 8vo. Pp. 472. [F. Jessel's *Bibl. of Playing Cards*, p. 129.] London, 1894
WHIST universal ; an analysis of the game as improved by the introduction of American leads, and adapted to all methods of play. By G. W. P. [George William Pettes]. 8vo. Pp. xiii. 258. [*Brit. Mus.*]   Boston, 1887
WHIST ; which card to lead. By Cam [Waller Lewis, M.D.]. 32mo. Pp. 11. [F. Jessel's *Bibl. of Playing Cards.*]
　　　　　　　　London, 1865
　　The second edition (1865) reads : "Whist; what to lead."

WHIST, with and without perception ; illustrated by means of Endhands from actual play. By B. W. D. and " Cavendish " [Henry Jones]. 12mo. Pp. xv. 71. [*Brit. Mus.*]   London, 1889

WHISTLE-BINKIE ; or the piper of the party. [By William Miller.] Second edition. 12mo. 2 vols.
　　　　　　　　Glasgow, 1839
　　The first edition (1832) runs : "Whistle-Binkie, or a collection of comic and sentimental songs. . . ."

WHISTLER ; or, the manly boy. By Walter Aimwell [William Simonds]. 8vo. [Cushing's *Init. and Pseud.* i. 8.]
　　　　　　　　New York, 1885

WHIST-SCORES, and card-table talk. By Rudolph H. Rheinhardt [George Hempl]. 8vo.   Baltimore, 1887

WHIST-WHITTLINGS, and forty fully annotated games. By Five of Clubs [Richard Anthony Proctor]. 8vo. [*Brit. Mus.*]   London, 1885

WHITBY (the) spy. [A series of thirty periodical essays. By William Watkins.] 12mo. Pp. vi. 246. [Smales' *Whitby Authors.*]   Whitby, 1784

WHITE (the) Africans. [In verse.] By Pardio [John Nott Pyke-Nott, B.A.]. 8vo. Pp. vii. 86.   London, 1879

WHITE and black; a story of the Southern [United] States. [By Caroline Ashurst Biggs.] 8vo. 3 vols. [*Brit. Mus.*]   London, 1862

WHITE and black lies; or, truth better than falsehood. By Mrs Madeline Leslie [Harriet Newells Baker]. 8vo. [Cushing's *Init. and Pseud.* i. 181.]
                            Boston [1864]

WHITE and black magic; or, practical instructions for students of occultism. By F. H. [Franz Hartmann]. 8vo. Pp. iv. 149.   Boston, 1885

WHITE and blue; sketches of military life. [By Mrs Julia Clara Byrne, *née* Busk.] 8vo. 3 vols. [*Brit. Mus.*]
                            London, 1862

WHITE (the) bear's den; a tale. . . . By A. L. O. E. [Charlotte M. Tucker]. 8vo. [*Brit. Mus.*]   Edinburgh, 1884

WHITE (the) beaver. By Harry Castlemon [Charles Austin Fosdick]. 8vo. [*Amer. Cat.*]   New York, 1899

WHITE (the) Chapel; a story. By Esmé Stuart [Amélie Claire Leroy]. 8vo. Pp. 211. [*Brit. Mus.*]
                            London [1881]

WHITE (the) charger that cost me two hundred pounds; lost me seventy thousand pounds; drove me from society; eventually deprived me of my friends: and finally compelled me to quit the service. By the author of *The horse guards*, etc. [Lieut.-Col. Richard Hort]. 8vo. [*Brit. Mus.*]
                            London, 1850

WHITE (the) chateau: a tragedy. [By Thomas M'Nicoll, editor of the *British Quarterly Review.*] 8vo. Pp. 68. [*R. Inglis.*]   London, 1852

WHITE (the) comrade. By Katherine Hale [Amelia Warnock Garvin]. 8vo. [*Who's Who in Lit.*]   London, 1915

WHITE (the) cottage. [A novel.] By "Zack" [Miss Gwendoline Keats]. 8vo. Pp. 270. [*Who's Who in Lit.*]
                            London, 1901

WHITE (the) cottage; a tale. [By Arthur Mower.] 12mo. Pp. 344. [*Noctes Ambrosianæ,* iv. 306.]
                            Edinburgh, 1817

WHITE (the) countess. [A novel.] By Florence Warden [Florence Alice Price, later Mrs George E. James]. 8vo. [*Brit. Mus.*]   London, 1907

WHITE (the) feather. By Tasma [Madame Couvreux, *née* Jessie Huybers]. 8vo. [*Brit. Mus.*]
                            London, 1892

WHITE fire. By John Oxenham [William Arthur Dunkerley]. 8vo. Pp. 350. [*Brit. Mus.*]   London, 1908

WHITE (the) hand (Baylaya Kuka); a narrative. By Carl Joubert [Adolphus Waldorf Carl Grottey]. 8vo. [*Brit. Mus.*]   London, 1906

WHITE (the) hands of justice. [A novel.] By Ben Bolt [Rev. Ottwell Binns]. 8vo. [*Who's Who in Lit.*]
                            London, 1922

WHITE heat. [A novel.] By Pan [Leslie Beresford]. 8vo. [*Who's Who in Lit.*]   London, 1915

WHITE heather. [Three Irish tales.] By "Aroon" [Mrs K. E. O'Connell]. 8vo. [S. J. Brown's *Ireland in Fiction.*]
                            Dublin, 1903

WHITE knights. [A tract on purity.] By Beatrice Chase [Olive Katharine Parr], and [two poems by] John Oxenham [William Arthur Dunkerley]. 12mo. [*Brit. Mus.*]   London [1917]

WHITE (the) lady; a legend of Artagh; in verse. By T. W. B. [Thomas Wentworth Beaumont]. 8vo. [O'Donoghue's *Poets of Ireland.*]   London, 1827

WHITE magic. [By Henry Fothergill Chorley]. [Cushing's *Anon.*]
                            London [*c.* 1850]

WHITE (the) month. By the author of *The Rose garden* [Frances Mary Peard]. 8vo. [*Camb. Univ. Lib.*]
                            London, 1880

WHITE (the) nun; or, the Black Bog of Dromore: a novel, by a young gentleman of note [Charles Richard Sumner, scholar at Eton, later bishop of Winchester]. 8vo. [Harcourt's *Eton Bibl.* p. 23.]   London, 1809

WHITE poppies; a novel. By May Kendall [Leonora Blanche, Mrs Andrew Lang]. 8vo. Pp. iv. 232.
                            London, 1893

WHITE rose and red; a love-story. [In verse.] By the author of *St Abe* [Robert Williams Buchanan]. 8vo. Pp. 243. [*Brit. Mus.*] London, 1873

WHITE (the) scalper; a story of the Texan war. By Gustave Aimard [Ollivier Gloux]. 8vo. [*Brit. Mus.*]
                            London [1861]

WHITE (the) slave; and the Russian prince. By the author of *Revelations of Russia* [Charles Frederick Henningsen]. Second edition. 12mo. 3 vols. [*Brit. Mus.*]   London, 1846

WHITE (the) slave ; or memoirs of a fugitive. [By Richard Hildreth.] 8vo. Pp. 408. [*Brit. Mus.*]   Boston, 1852

WHITE (the) stone. By Anatole France [Jacques Anatole Thibault] ; translated by Charles E. Roche. 8vo. Pp. 240. [*Brit. Mus.*]   London, 1910

WHITE (a) umbrella ; and other stories. By the author of *Soul Shapes* [Alice Dew-Smith]. 8vo.   London, 1895

WHITE webs ; a romance of Sussex. By Theo Douglas [Mrs H. D. Everett]. 8vo. Pp. 308. [*Lit. Year Book.*]
London, 1912

WHITE (the) wife ; with other stories, supernatural, romantic and legendary. Collected and illustrated by Cuthbert Bede [Edward Bradley], author of *Verdant Green*, etc. 8vo. Pp. vii. 252. [*Brit. Mus.*]   London, 1865

WHITE (a) witch. [A novel.] By Theo Douglas [Mrs H. D. Everett]. 8vo. Pp. 340. [*Lit. Year Book.*]
London, 1908

WHITE (the) wolf, and other fireside tales. By "Q" [Sir Arthur T. Quiller-Couch]. 8vo. Pp. v. 368. [*Lit. Year Book.*]   London, 1902

WHITEFRIARS ; or, the days of Charles the Second : an historical romance. [By Emma Robinson.] 8vo. 3 vols. [*Brit. Mus.*]   London, 1844

WHITEHALL (the) Evening Post. [Commenced and edited by Daniel Defoe ; published every Tuesday, Thursday, and Saturday : he continued to write in it occasionally until June, 1720.] 2 leaves. Sm. 4to. [Lee's *Defoe*, 189.]
18 Sep. 1718 to June, 1720

WHITEHALL ; or, the days of Charles I. : an historical romance. By the author of *Whitefriars* [Emma Robinson]. 12mo. 3 vols. [*Brit. Mus.*]
London, 1845
Wrongly ascribed to Joseph Robinson.

WHITEHALL ; or, the days of George IV. [By William Maginn, LL.D.] 8vo. [*Dub. Univ. Mag.* xxiii. 86.]
London [1827]
A parody on a work by Horace Smith.

WHITHER? A novel. By M. E. Francis [Mary E. Sweetman, later Mrs Francis Blundell]. 8vo. 3 vols. [*Who's Who in Lit.*]   London, 1902

WHITHER drifting? By the author of *The light of thy truth* [Edward John Adams]. 8vo. Pp. 96. [*Brit. Mus.*]
London [1914]

WHITTIER with the children. By Margaret Sidney [Mrs Lothrop, *née* Harriet Mulford Stone]. 8vo. Pp. 59. [Cushing's *Init. and Pseud.* i. 267.]
Boston, 1893

WHITTINGTON and his cat ; the "Royal" grand Christmas pantomime for 1881-82. Written by R. L. Westland [Robert W. Lowe]. . . . 8vo. Pp. 38. [*Nat. Lib. of Scot.*]
Edinburgh, 1881

WHITTLINGS from the West ; with some account of Butternut Castle. By Abel Log [Charles Butler Greatrex, rector of Stanton-upon-Hine]. 8vo. Pp. vi. 442. [*Nat. Lib. of Scot.*]
Edinburgh, 1854

WHO are the happy ? A poem on the Christian beatitudes ; with other poems on sacred subjects. [By Rev. William Hamilton Drummond, D.D.] 8vo. [O'Donoghue's *Poets of Ireland.*]
Dublin, 1818

"WHO breaks—pays." (Italian proverb.) By the author of *Cousin Stella* [Henrietta Camilla Campbell, later Mrs Jenkin]. 8vo. [*Brit. Mus.*]
London, 1861

WHO did it ? [A novel.] By Headon Hill [Frank E. Grainger]. 8vo. [*Who's Who in Lit.*]   London, 1912

WHO fares best, the Christian, or the man of the world ? Or, the advantage of a life of real piety to a life of fashionable dissipation. By a marine officer [Major-General Andrew Burn]. 8vo. [Watt's *Bibl. Brit.*]
London, 1789

WHO goes there ? By the author of *Aunt Sarah and the War* [Wilfrid Meynell]. 8vo. Pp. 94. [*Brit. Mus.*]
London, 1916
Third impression of "Halt ! who goes there ? "

WHO goes there ? or, men and events. By Sentinel [William Henry Bogart]. [Cushing's *Init. and Pseud.* i. 265.]
New York, 1866

WHO is responsible for the War ? By Scrutator [Rev. Malcolm MacColl, M.A., D.D.]. 8vo. Pp. viii. 154. [*Brit. Mus.*]   London, 1871

WHO is she ? A mystery of Mayfair. By the author of *The Honeymoon* [the Duke de Medina Pomar]. Second edition. 8vo. 3 vols. [*Brit. Mus.*]
London, 1878

WHO is the author ? or, a letter to the Rev. R. Frost, A.M., containing an examination into the authenticity of a letter bearing his name, addressed to the Warden and Fellows of the Collegiate Church, Manchester. By Verax [T. Hutchinson]. 8vo. Pp. 16.
Manchester, 1836

WHO is the legitimate King of Portugal?
A Portuguese question, submitted to
impartial men by a Portuguese residing
in London [Paolo Midosi]. Translated
from the Portuguese. 8vo. [Brit.
Mus.]   [London, 1828]
WHO is the real enemy of Germany?
[Translated from the German of Onno
Klopp]. 8vo.   London, 1868
WHO is to be Speaker [in the House of
Commons]. [By Sir Henry Rich.]
8vo. [Brit. Mus.]   London, 1835
WHO is to have it? A novel. By the
author of The Netherwoods of Otter-
pool [Mrs J. C. Bateman]. 8vo. Pp.
434. [Brit. Mus.]   London, 1859
WHO lived there? By the author of
My Neighbour Nellie, etc. [George
Dalziel]. 8vo. Pp. 144. [Brit. Mus.]
                         London [1887]
WHO ought to win? Oom Paul or Queen
Victoria? By S. Randolph [Thomas
B. O'Connor]. 8vo. [Amer. Cat.]
                         Chicago, 1900
WHO poisoned Hetty Duncan? and
other detective stories. By Dick
Donovan [Joyce E. P. Muddock].
8vo. Pp. 313. [Who's Who in Lit.]
                         London, 1890
WHO saved the ship? By "Jak"
[Annie Bowles Williams]. 8vo. [Kirk's
Supp.]   New York, 1887
WHO sent thee to baptize? or, "A
Clergyman's Christian baptism" not
the baptism of Christ. [By John
Bellows, printer.] 8vo. Pp. 24.
[Brit. Mus.]   London, 1872
    A reply to a pamphlet entitled "Christian
Baptism, a reply to a pamphlet issued by
the Society of Friends. By a Clergyman."
WHO shall rule: Briton or Norman?
By Cynicus [Martin Anderson]. 8vo.
Pp. 48. [Brit. Mus.]   Tayport, 1911
WHO told it to me? By Margaret
Sidney [Mrs Harriet M. Lothrop].
8vo. [Cushing's Init. and Pseud.
i. 267.]   Boston, 1884
WHO was Caxton? William Caxton,
merchant, ambassador, historian,
author, translator, and printer. A
monograph by R. H. B. [Rowland
Hill Blades]. 8vo.   London, 1877
    Presentation copy from the author.
WHO was Lady Thurne? [A novel.]
By Florence Warden [Florence Alice
Price, later Mrs George E. James].
8vo. Pp. 320. [Brit. Mus.]
                         London, 1905
WHO wrote Cavendish's Life of Wolsey?
[By Joseph Hunter, of Bath.] 4to.
Pp. 56. [Bodl.]   London, 1814
WHO wrote Shakespeare? [By M. L.
Horr.] 8vo. [Brit. Mus.]
                         [Denver, 1885]
    Signed: Multum in parvo.

WHO wrote the Waverley novels? Being
an investigation into certain mysterious
circumstances attending their production, and an inquiry into the literary
aid which Sir Walter Scott may have
received from other persons. [By
William John Fitzpatrick.] 8vo. Pp.
88. [Brit. Mus.; Boase's Mod. Eng.
Biog. v. 307.]   London, 1856
    The Introduction is signed: W. J. F.
    A second edition, revised, was issued later
in the same year.
WHO'D be an author? With the answer.
By Frank Foster [Daniel Puseley].
8vo. Pp. vi. 264. [D.N.B. vol. 47,
p. 53.]   London, N.D.
WHOLE (the) art of husbandry; or the
way of managing and improving of
land . . . to which is added the
Country-man's Kalendar. By J. M.
[John Mortimer] Esq., F.R.S. 8vo.
[Brit. Mus.]   London, 1707
WHOLE Book of Psalms, as they are
now sung in churches, with the singing
notes of time and tune set to every
syllable, made plain and easie to the
understanding of all that can read, etc.
"Never before done in England." By
T. M. [Thomas May]. 8vo. [W.]
                         N.P. 1688
WHOLE (a) crew of kind gossips, all
met to be merry. [By Samuel Rowlands.] 4to. No pagination.
                         London, 1609
    Address "To the maids of London,"
signed: S. R.
    For other editions see "A crew of kind
London gossips, . . ." "'Tis merry when
gossips meet . . ." and "Well met,
gossip. . . ."
WHOLE (the) doctrine of the Sabbath
as set forth in the Holy Scriptures, in
the writings of the Fathers, and by the
most eminent Reformers and orthodox
modern divines. . . . By J. W. [John
Wauchope]. 8vo. Pp. 60.
                         Edinburgh, 1851
WHOLE (the) duty of a Christian, and a
guide to perfection; with directions to
parents in the Christian education of
their children. By M. P. [Michael
Benedict Pembridge, O.S.B.]. 8vo.
[Gillow's Bibl. Dict. v. 254.] N.P. 1775
WHOLE (the) duty of a Christian . . .
being a faithful abstract of the Trent
Catechism. [By Sylvester Jenks, D.D.]
12mo. [D.N.B. vol. 29, p. 316.]
                         London, 1707
WHOLE (the) duty of a Christian; by
way of question and answer; exactly
pursuant to the method of the Whole
duty of man, and designed for the use
of the charity schools, lately erected
in and about London. [By Robert
Nelson.] 12mo. Pp. 93, 3. [D.N.B.
vol. 40, p. 212.]   London, 1705

WHOLE (the) duty of a Christian ; or, the character of a true believer. . . . Second impression . . . inlarged. By R. Y. [Richard Young, or Younge] of Rexwell in Essex. 8vo. [*Brit. Mus.*]
London, 1653

WHOLE (the) duty of man consider'd, under its three principal and general divisions, namely, the duties we owe to God, ourselves, and neighbours ; faithfully extracted from that excellent book so entitled, and published for the benefit of the poorer sort. By a gentleman [Browne Willis, LL.D.]. 12mo. Pp. x. 52. [*D. N. B.* vol. 62, p. 17.]   London, 1717
Regarding the authorship, see the note appended to " The Art of contentment."
Though this work proved so welcome to many readers that more than thirty editions were issued, it was perceived by the more thoughtful to deal to such an extent with externalities that the inner life of man received too little regard. The first attempt to remedy this defect was not made till 1693, when another anonymous writer issued " The Whole Duty of man, Part II., teaching a Christian . . . how to prepare himself for an happy death. . . ." Even this, however, failed to supply what was lacking, and thus made little impression on the public mind : and a longer interval elapsed before better light and leading were supplied. In 1704, however, there appeared a shorter and more acceptable treatise, entitled " The Whole Duty of man, by way of question and answer, exactly pursuant to the Whole Duty of man . . ." [by Robert Nelson] ; many editions were issued, including some with the author's name. A summary of the original " Whole Duty" was prepared [by Dr Browne Willis] and sent forth in 1717 as " The Whole Duty of man consider'd " : see above. Next followed. in 1729, a similarly unambitious work, " The Whole Duty of man, laid down in a familiar way, for the use of all, but especially the meanest reader . . ." In 1744, still another anonymous writer published " The New Whole Duty of man, containing the faith as well as practice of a Christian . . . with devotions proper for several occasions ; also an help to reading the Scriptures." Public appreciation of this work was proved by the constant demand for reprints, which have numbered more than forty.
As the original " Whole Duty of man," however, continued its hold on the mind of many well-disposed persons, even after the revival of religion during the eighteenth century, another work was required, presenting a full outline of Evangelical theology to supply the long-felt want : this was provided in 1763 by Henry Venn of Huddersfield in a volume bearing the significant title, " The Complete Duty of man." Later editions, revised and improved, have numbered nearly twenty. [See the *Bibliographer*, vol. ii. pp. 24, 73, and 124.]

The very first form of " The Whole Duty of man " had a fuller title : see " The Practice of Christian graces . . ."

WHOLE (the) Duty of man, laid down in a plain and familiar way. . . . [By Richard Allestree, D.D.] 12mo.
London, 1669
The title of the first edition of this popular work (issued in 1658) begins thus : " The Practice of Christian graces ; or the whole duty of man. . . ." Regarding the authorship, see the note to " The Art of Contentment. . . ." See also *N. and Q.* March 1920.

WHOLE (the) duty of mourning, and the great concern of preparing ourselves for death, practically considered : written, some years since, by the author of The Whole Duty of man [Dr Richard Allestree], and now published. . . . 12mo. [*Brit. Mus.*]   [London, 1695]

WHOLE (the) duty of receiving worthily the blessed Sacrament, laid down in six days of preparation ; consisting of prayers, meditations, and soliloquies before it, and after the Lord's Supper. By the author of *The Whole Duty of Man* [Richard Allestree, D.D.]. 12mo.
London, 1696
Regarding the authorship, see the note appended to " The Art of Contentment."

WHOLE (the) duty of woman. By a lady [rather by William Kenrick, LL.D.]. Written at the desire of a noble lord. 8vo. [*D. N. B.* vol. 31, p. 17.]   London, 1753
Another edition, " with considerable improvements," was published at Boston, Mass., in 1807.

WHOLE (the) Psalter, translated into English metre [by Matthew Parker, Archbishop of Canterbury], which contayneth an hundreth and fifty Psalmes. The first Quinquagene. 4to. [Lowndes' *Bibl. Man.*]
London [1557]

WHOLE (the) question of ecclesiastical establishments stated and considered. [By Rev. William Lowrie, of Lander.] 12mo. [Cushing's *Anon.*]
Edinburgh, 1833

WHOLE (the) truth. Address to the freemen of New England, Nov. 1, 1808. By Hancock [Jonathan Russell]. 8vo. [Cushing's *Init. and Pseud.*, ii. 72.]   Boston, 1808
See also " Essex Junta exposed . . ."

WHOLE (the) truth and nothing but the truth about the social evil in Edinburgh, showing fuller and deeper investigations. [By James Glass Bertram, journalist.] 8vo. Pp. 56.
Edinburgh, 1868

WHOLE (the) truth, and nothing but the truth ; or a dialogue [regarding the Irish elections] between Irish Tom, and Jack, and English Will. [By Jonas Hanway.] 8vo. [*Camb. Univ. Lib.*] Dublin, 1761

Signed : Thomas Trueman.

WHOLSOME advices from the Blessed Virgin, to her indiscreet worshippers. Written by one of the Roman communion [Adam Widenfelt] and done out of the French into English, by a gentleman of the Church of England [James Taylor] ; with a preface shewing the motives to the translation. 4to. Pp. xvi. 20. [Jones' *Peck*, i. 102 ; ii. 421.] London, 1687

WHOLSOME severity reconciled with Christian liberty ; or, the true resolution of a present controversie concerning liberty of conscience : here you have the question stated, the middle way betwixt popish tyrannie and schismatizing liberty approved, and also confirmed from Scripture, and the testimonies of divines, yea of whole Churches : the chiefe arguments and exceptions used in The bloudy tenent, The compassionate Samaritane, M. S. to A. S. &c. examined. . . . [By George Gillespie.] 4to. [*D. N. B.* vol. 21, p. 360.] London, 1645

WHOM shall we hang ? The Sebastopol enquiry. [By Sir Peter Benson Maxwell.] 8vo. [*Scotsman*, Jan. 14, 1856.] London, 1855

WHOM to follow—Gladstone or Beaconsfield : in two parts. [Part I. by George Smith, C.I.E., LL.D. ; Part II. by Sir George Adam Smith, D.D., LL.D.] 8vo. Pp. 132. Edinburgh, 1879

WHO'S afraid ? A farce of one act : with songs. [By Sir Richard Paul Jodrell, M.D.] 8vo. [Baker's *Biog. Dram.*] London, 1787

WHOSE poems ? [By E. D. Girdlestone.] 8vo. [*Brit. Mus.*] London, 1850

WHOSO breaketh an hedge. [A novel.] By "Iota" [Mrs Mannington Caffyn]. [*Lit. Year Book.*] 8vo. London, 1909

WHY am I a Presbyterian ? By a mother [Mrs N. W. Campbell]. 8vo. Philadelphia, 1852

WHY are not hydropathic establishments more successful ? By A. M. [Alexander Munro, M.D., of Cluny-Hill Hydropathic, Forres]. 8vo. Pp. 48. Dunfermline [1881]

WHY are you a churchman ? A plain question answered in a dialogue between Mr Fitz Adam and John Oakley. [By Thomas Drewitt, of Chedder.] 12mo. [*Mon. Rev.* xxxii. 314.] London, 1800

WHY Church is better than chapel or meeting. By M. E. S. [Mary E. Simpson]. 8vo. London, 1863

WHY Dissenters are not . . . guilty of Schism . . . [By Charles Owen, D.D.] 8vo. [*D. N. B.* vol. 42, p. 401.] London, 1717

WHY do men starve ? By Iconoclast [Charles Bradlaugh]. 8vo. No title-page. [*Brit. Mus.*] London [1867]

WHY do not women swim ? A voice from many waters. [By Susan Rugeley Powers.] 8vo. Pp. 16. [Olphar Hamst's *Swimming.*] London [1859]

WHY do you object to vaccination ? [By Caroline Pearse.] 8vo. Pp. 8. Launceston [*c.* 1865]

WHY do you take strong drink ? . . . By the author of *Bound by fetters*, etc. [Emily Foster]. 8vo. [*Brit. Mus.*] Manchester, 1887

WHY don't you say your prayers ? A few words addressed to those who never pray. [By Julia Elizabeth Marshall.] 8vo. London [1895]

WHY emigrate ? The cultivation of our own lands is the sure source of general employment for our population. . . . [By H. B. Gaskin.] 8vo. London, 1819

WHY freedom matters. By Norman Angell [Ralph Norman Angell Lane]. 8vo. Pp. 60. [*Who's Who in Lit.*] London, 1916

WHY [General Charles G.] Gordon perished [at Khartoum] ; or the political and military causes which led to the Sudan disasters. By a War correspondent . . . [Alexander Macdonald]. 8vo. Pp. viii. 318. London, 1896

WHY have you become a Pædobaptist ? A dialogue between Hezekiah Hastie, a Baptist, and Simon Searche, a Pædobaptist . . . By John Bull [Rev. Benjamin Parsons, Congregationalist]. 8vo. [*Brit. Mus.*] Stroud, 1835

WHY how now, Gossip [Alexander] Pope ? Or the sweet-singing bird of Parnassus taken out of its pretty cage to be roasted. . . . [By John Henley.] 8vo. Pp. 16. [*Brit. Mus.*] London, 1743

WHY I am a conservative. By an elector [Henry Llewellyn Williams]. 8vo. [*Brit. Mus.*] London [1885]

WHY I'm single. [A novel.] By Albert Ross [Linn Boyd Porter]. 8vo. Pp. 360. [*Brit. Mus.*] New York, 1892

WHY is history read so little ? By a student of history [Edward Denham]. 8vo. [Kirk's *Supp.*] New Bedford, 1876

"WHY Johnny didn't interfere." An answer to "The fight at Dame Europa's school." [By Frank Chancellor.] 12mo. Pp. 11. [*F. Madan.*]
London, 1871
Signed: Johnny.

WHY not? Eight queries made to the Parliament from the people of England in 1649. [By James Frese?] Folio. S. sh. [*Brit. Mus.*]   London, 1649

WHY one should join the Theosophical Society. [By Bertram Keightley.] 8vo.   London [1890?]
Signed: B. K.

WHY Paul Ferroll killed his wife. By the author of *Paul Ferroll* [Mrs Caroline Clive, *née* Wigley]. 12mo. [*Brit. Mus.*]   London, 1860

WHY Pennsylvania should become one of the Confederate States of America. By a native of Pennsylvania [George MacHenry]. 8vo. [Cushing's *Init. and Pseud.* i. 201.]   London, 1862

WHY she left him. [A novel.] By Florence Warden [Florence Alice Price, later Mrs George E. James]. 8vo. Pp. 320. [*Who's Who in Lit.*]
London, 1914
WHY should the Chinese go? By Kwang Ching Ling [Alexander Delmar]. 8vo. [*Lib. Journ.* iv. 457.]
San Francisco, 1878
WHY should we oppose the licensing clauses? [By A. S. Cook.] [Robertson's *Aberd. Bibl.*] [Aberdeen, 1890?]

WHY should you secede? Containing observations on spiritual independence and non-intrusion in reference to secession. [By George Munro, advocate.] 8vo. Pp. 31.   Edinburgh, 1843

WHY, sir, it's better and better . . . By E. C. [Edward Crowley]. 8vo.
Southampton [1865]
WHY the Liberals are leaving the League; a letter to Sir B. Heywood. By a Manchester Liberal [John Heugh]. 8vo. [*Brit. Mus.*]   Manchester [1857]

WHY the martyrs of Manchester died. By A. Newman [Herbert Moore Pim]. 8vo. [*Lond. Lib. Cat.*]   Dublin, 1915
Tracts for the times, published by the Irish Publicity League, No. 9.

WHY we live. By Summerdale [Alexander Young]. 8vo. [Cushing's *Init. and Pseud.* ii. 141.]   Chicago, 1880

WHYCHCOTTE of St John's; or, the court, the camp, the quarter-deck, and the cloister. [By Erskine Neale.] 12mo. 2 vols. [*N. and Q.* 3rd Feb. 1855, p. 91.]   London, 1833

WHY'S? (the) and the How's? or, a good enquiry: a sermon [on Matt. ii. 3] preach'd before their Majesties in their chappel at St James's the 2d. Sunday of Advent, December 6th. 1685. By J. D. of the Society of Jesus [John Dormer]. Published by his Majesties command. 4to. Pp. 34. [*Brit. Mus.*]
London, 1687
WHYTE dyed black; or a discouery of many most foule blemishes, impostures, and deceiptes, which D. Whyte haith practysed in his book entituled The way to the true Church. Writen by T. W. P. [Thomas Worthington, Priest]; and dedicated to the Vniuersity of Cambridge. 4to. Pp. 18, 183. [*Bodl.*]   N.P. 1615

WICKED (the) plots, and perfidious practises of the Spaniards, against the 17. provinces of the Netherlands, before they took up armes; being gathered out of severall Dutch writers, by a lover of truth, and an unfained hater of oppression and tyrannie, the bane of commonwealths. [By Thomas Scot, B.D.] No pagination. 4to. [*Pollard and Redgrave.*]   N.P., N.D.
Printed at the end of Scot's Second part of Spanish practises, under the title of "An adioynder of sundry other particular wicked plots and cruell, inhumane, perfidious; yea, unnatural practises of the Spaniards." Signed: S. O.

WICKEDEST (the) woman in New York. By John Paul [Charles Henry Webb]. 8vo. [*Amer. Cat.*]
New York [*c.* 1900]
WICKER (the) work woman; a chronicle of our own times. By Anatole France [Jacques Anatole Thibault]; translated from the French. 8vo. Pp. 274. [*Brit. Mus.*]   London, 1910

WICKHAM wakened; or, the Quaker's madrigall in rime dogrell. [By Martin Llewellyn.] 4to. Pp. 8. [Smith's *Bibl. Anti-Quak.* p. 275.]   N.P. 1672

WICLIF; an historical drama. [By Charles E. Sayle.] 8vo. [Bartholomew's *Camb. Books*, p. 269.]
Oxford, 1887
WIDDOWES (the) teares; a comedie. Written by Geor. Chap. [George Chapman]. 4to. [*Brit. Mus.*]
London, 1612
WIDE awake. By Martha James [Martha Claire MacGowan Doyle]. 8vo. [*Amer. Cat.*]   Boston, 1902

WIDE of the mark. By the author of *Recommended to mercy* [Mrs Matilda Charlotte Houstoun]. 8vo. 3 vols.
London, 1871

WIDE (the), wide world. By Elizabeth Wetherell [Susan Warner]. Complete edition. 8vo. Pp. 446. [Allibone's *Dict.*] London [1877]

WIDER (a) world. By Crona Temple [Miss —— Corfield]. 8vo.
London, 1885

WIDOW (the) and her daughter. By the authors of *The wide, wide world* [Susan and Anna Bartlett Warner]. 12mo. [Allibone's *Dict.*]
London, 1864

WIDOW (the) Bedott papers. [By Mrs Frances M. Whitcher.] 8vo. Pp. 228.
New York, 1893

WIDOW (the) bewitch'd ; a comedy, as it is acted at the Theatre in Goodmans-Fields. [By John Mottley.] 8vo. Pp. 64. [Baker's *Biog. Dram.*]
London, 1730

WIDOW Guthrie ; a novel. By Philemon Perch [Robert Malcolm Johnston]. 8vo. [Cushing's *Init. and Pseud.* i. 228.]
New York, 1890

WIDOW Magoogin. [A novel.] By John J. J. [John J. Jennings]. 8vo.
New York, 1900

WIDOW O'Callaghan's boys. By Gulielma Zollinger [William Zachary Gladwin]. 8vo. [*Amer. Cat.*]
Chicago, 1905

WIDOW (the) of Malabar ; a tragedy, in three acts. [By Miss Mariana Starke]. Third edition. 8vo. Pp. 47. [Baker's *Biog. Dram.*]   London, 1791

WIDOW (the) of the city of Naïn ; and other poems. By an under-graduate of the University of Cambridge [Thomas Dale]. 8vo. [*Brit. Mus.*]
London, 1819
Inscribed copy in the British Museum.

WIDOW (the) of the wood. [By Benjamin Victor.] 12mo. [*D. N. B.* vol. 58, p. 302.]   London, 1755
A reprint was issued at Glasgow in 1769. The work was so offensive to the family of Sir William Wolseley, that they destroyed every copy they could secure.

WIDOW Wakefull's mission ; or gleaning's in mil-dewed and blighted fields. [By Catherine Grant.] 8vo. [P. J. Anderson's *Inverness Bibl.* p. 126.]
London, N.D.

WIDOW Wiley. [A novel.] By Brown Linnet [Miss Ella Tomlinson]. 8vo.
London, 1911

WIDOW (the) Wyse. [By Mrs Helen Mar Bean.] 8vo. [Cushing's *Anon.*]
Boston, 1884

WIDOWHOOD (the) of Gabrielle Grant. By Eglanton Thorne [Emily Charlton]. 8vo. [*Who's Who in Lit.*]
London, 1903

WIDOW'S (the) cottage ; a poem . . . By the author of *The beauties of Walden* [Mrs Hannah Carnes]. 12mo. [*Brit. Mus.*]   Cambridge, 1840

WIDOW'S (the) jewels ; in two stories. By a lady [Hannah Maynard Pickard].
London, 1831

WIDOW'S (the) lodgings ; a novel. [By John Ballantyne.] 12mo. 2 vols. [*Cat. of the Philos. Inst. Edin.*, p. 336.]
Edinburgh, 1813

WIDOW'S (the) mite ; or, questions of the greatest moment, humbly offered for reviving true piety and religion in the life and power thereof. [By John Warden.] 12mo. [*Nat. Lib. of Scot.*]
Edinburgh, 1721

WIDOW'S (a) reminiscences of the siege of Lucknow. [By Mrs Katherine Mary Bartrum.] 12mo.
London, 1858

WIDOW'S (the) tale : and other poems. By the author of *Ellen Fitzarthur* [Caroline Bowles, later Mrs Southey]. 12mo. Pp. 222. [*D. N. B.* vol. 53, p. 282.]   London, 1822

WIDOW'S (the) vow ; a farce, in two acts, as it is acted at the Theatre Royal, Hay-Market. [By Elizabeth Inchbald, *née* Simpson.] 8vo. Pp. 35. [Baker's *Biog. Dram.*]   London, 1786

WIELAND ; or, the transformation. By C. B. B. [Charles Brockden Brown]. 8vo. [Cushing's *Init. and Pseud.* i. 23.]
New York, 1798

WIFE (the). By Mira, one of the authors of *The female spectator*, and *Epistles for ladies* [Eliza Haywood]. 12mo. Pp. 282. [*Brit. Mus.*]
London, 1756

WIFE and woman ; from the German of L. Haidheim [Mrs Luise Ahlborn, *née* Jäger]. 8vo. [Holzmann and Bohatta's *Deuts. Pseud-Lexikon.*]
New York, 1891

WIFE (the) and woman's reward. [By Hon. Mrs Caroline E. S. Norton.] 12mo. 3 vols.   London, 1835

WIFE (the) hunter, and Flora Hunter ; tales by the Moriarty family : edited by Denis Ignatius Moriarty, Esq. [By John O'Brien Grant.] 12mo. 3 vols. [*Bodl.*]   London, 1838

WIFE (a) in name only. By Bertha M. Clay [Charlotte M. Braeme]. 8vo. [*Amer. Cat.*]   New York, 1886

WIFE (a) not ready made, but bespoken by Dicus the batchelor, and made up for him by his fellow shepheard Tityrus : in four pastorall eclogues. [By Robert Aylett.] The second edition ; wherein are some things added but nothing amended. 8vo. [*Brit. Mus.*]
London, 1653
Signed : R. A.

WIFE (a), now a widdowe. [By Sir
Thomas Overbury.] 8vo. No pagi-
nation. [*Bodl.*]   London, 1614
WIFE (the) of Leon, and other poems.
By two sisters of the West [Mrs
Catharine Ann Warfield, *née* Ware,
and Mrs Eleanor Percy Lee, *née* Ware].
8vo. [Cushing's *Init. and Pseud.*
i. 288.]   New York, 1844
WIFE (a) well manag'd; a farce [in one
act, and in prose. By Susanna
Carrol, later Mrs Centlivre]. 12mo.
[Baker's *Biog. Dram.*]   London, 1715
WIFE-CHASE (the) ; a monitory poem.
[By Joshua Jenour.] 8vo.
                    London [1780 ?]
WIFE-LENDING ; how to preserve the
poor. . . . By Walter James [James
Dennis Hird]. 8vo. Pp. 110. [*Brit.
Mus.*]   London, 1894
WIFE'S (the) domain. [A domestic
manual.] By Philomalos [James
Whitehead, M.D.] Second edition.
8vo. Pp. vii. 162. [*Manch. Free Lib.*]
                    Manchester, 1874
    Presentation copy from the author.
WIFE'S (a) secret. By Bertha M.
Clay [Charlotte M. Braeme]. 12mo.
[*Amer. Cat.*]   New York, 1885
WIFE'S (a) story, and other tales. By
the author of *Caste*, etc. [Emily Jolly].
8vo. 3 vols. [*Brit. Mus.*]
                    London, 1875
WIFE'S (the) temptation, a tale of Bel-
gravia. By the authoress of *The sister
of charity*, etc. [Mrs Annie E. Challice].
12mo. 2 vols. [*Camb. Univ. Lib.*]
                    London, 1859
WIFE'S (the) trials ; a novel. [By
Emma Jane Worboise.] 8vo. 3 vols.
[*Brit. Mus.*]   London, 1855
WIG (the) and the Jimmy ; or, a leaf in
the political history of New York.
[By John J. Davenport.] 8vo.
[Cushing's *Anon.*]   New York, 1869
WIGWAM (the) and the cabin. By the
author of *The Yemassee*, etc. [William
Gilmore Simms]. 8vo. [*Brit. Mus.*]
                    New York, 1845
WIGWAM (the) and the war-path. . . .
By Ascott R. Hope [Robert Hope
Moncrieff]. 8vo. Pp. 392. [*Brit.
Mus.*]   London, 1892
WILBERFORCE'S doctrine of the
Eucharist refuted. By Theophilus
Secundus [Rev. Stephen Jenner, M.A.].
12mo. [*Brit. Mus.*]   London, 1854
WILD animal play for children. . . .
By Ernest Seton-Thompson [Ernest
Thompson Seton]. 8vo. Pp. 80.
[*Lond. Lib. Cat.*]   London, 1900
WILD animal ways. By Ernest Seton-
Thompson [Ernest Thompson Seton].
8vo. [*Lond. Lib. Cat.*]
                    New York, 1916

WILD animals at home. By Ernest
Seton-Thompson [Ernest Thompson
Seton]. 8vo, [*Lond. Lib. Cat.*]
                    London, 1913
WILD animals I have known. . . . By
E. Seton-Thompson [Ernest Thomp-
son Seton]. 8vo. Pp. 360. [*Lond.
Lib. Cat.*]   London, 1898
WILD (the) beast fighter. [By Henry
Llewellyn Williams.] 8vo.
                    London, 1890
WILD (a) beauty. [A novel.] By Dick
Donovan [Joyce E. Preston Muddock].
8vo. Pp. 320. [*Who's Who in Lit.*]
                    London, 1909
WILD (a) bouquet. By Leon Claire
[Edwin C. Barnes].
                    Syracuse, N.Y., 1874
WILD (the) brier ; or, lays by an un-
taught minstrel. By E. N. L. [Elizabeth
N. Lockerby]. 8vo. [Cushing's *Init.
and Pseud.* i. 159.]
                    Charlottetown, 1866
WILD (the) flora of Lampeter and
neighbourhood. By a lover of flowers
[Rev. J. Eli Evans]. 8vo. 2 parts.
[*Brit. Mus.*]   N.P. 1910
WILD (the) flower of Ravensworth. By
the author of *John and I*, etc. [Matilda
Betham Edwards]. 8vo. 3 vols. [*Brit.
Mus.*]   London, 1866
WILD flowers from the wayside.
[Poems.] By Thomasine [Olivia
Knight]. 8vo. [O'Donoghue's *Poets
of Ireland.*]   Dublin, 1883
WILD (the) flowers of Dover and its
neighbourhood. . . . [By Frederick
Apthorp Paley.] 12mo. Pp. xii. 76.
[*Brit. Mus.*]   London [1850 ?]
WILD flowers of South Australia. By
F. E. D. [Miss F. E. De Mole]. 4to.
                    Adelaide, 1861
WILD flowers of the West. By an old
prairie hen [Catherine Nichols]. 8vo.
                    Chicago, 1874
WILD flowers of Wisconsin. [Poems.]
By Porte Crayon [Bernard Isaac
Durward]. 8vo. [*Lib. Journ.* vi. 16.]
                    New York, 1872
WILD (the) garland ; or, prose and
poetry connected with English wild
flowers : intended as an embellishment
to the study of botany. By the author
of *The life of Linnæus, in a series of
letters* [Miss S. Waring]. 12mo.
[Smith's *Cat. of Friends' Books*, ii. 859.]
                    London, 1827
WILD (the) heart. [A novel.] By M. E.
Francis [Mrs Francis Blundell, *née*
Mary Evans Sweetman]. 8vo. Pp.
330. [*Who's Who in Lit.*]
                    London, 1910

WILD honey from various thyme. [Poems.] By Michael Field [Mrs Katherine H. Bradley, and Edith Emma Cooper]. 8vo. Pp. 208. [*Brit. Mus.*]   London, 1908

WILD (the) Irish boy. . . . By the author of *Montorio* [Rev. Charles Robert Maturin]. 12mo. 3 vols. [*Brit. Mus.*]   London, 1808

WILD life in a southern County. By the author of *The gamekeeper at home* [Richard Jefferies]. 8vo. [*Brit. Mus.*]   London, 1879

WILD Mike and his victim. By the author of *Misunderstood* [Florence Montgomery]. 8vo. Pp. 146.
                London, 1875

WILD notes from the backwoods. . . . By R. A. P. [Rhoda Ann Paige, later Mrs Falkner]. 8vo. [Sabin's *Dictionary*.]   Cobourg, 1850

WILD oats ; from the French of H. Gréville [Madame Alice Durand]. 8vo. [*Brit. Mus.*]   New York, 1889

WILD olive ; by the author of *The inner shrine* [Basil King]. 8vo. [*Lond. Lib. Cat.*]   London [1910]

WILD roses. . . . By Cousin Sue [Susan A. Wright]. 8vo. [Cushing's *Init. and Pseud.* i. 276.]
                Philadelphia, 1868

WILD roses. [Poems.] By Ellis Walton [Mrs F. Percy Cotton]. 12mo. [*Brit. Mus.*]   London, 1894

WILD (the) Ruthvens ; a home story. By Curtis Yorke [Mrs W. S. Richmond Lee, *née* Jex-Long]. 8vo. [*Who's Who in Lit.*]   London, 1900

WILD shrubs of Alabama ; or, rhapsodies of restless hours. By the minstrel maiden of Mobile [Julia Mildred Harriss]. 8vo. [Cushing's *Init. and Pseud.* i. 195.]
                New York, 1852

WILD sports in Ireland, with rod, gun, and camera. By John Bickerdyke [Charles Henry Cooke]. 8vo.
                London, 1897

WILD sports of the West ; with legendary tales, and local sketches. By the author of *Stories of Waterloo* [Capt. William Hamilton Maxwell]. 8vo. 2 vols. [*D. N. B.* vol. 37, p. 138.]
                London, 1832

WILD thyme gathered on the mountains of Israel. [Poems.] By C. S. [Charles Sabine]. Third edition. 12mo. Pp. 191. [*Brit. Mus.*]   London, 1857

WILD Western scenes ; a narrative of adventures. . . . By a squatter [John B. Jones]. 8vo. [Cushing's *Init. and Pseud.* i. 273.]   Philadelphia, 1869

WILD wheat ; a Dorset romance. By M. E. Francis [Mrs Francis Blundell, *née* Mary Evans Sweetman]. 8vo. Pp. 300. [*Amer. Cat.*] London, 1905

WILD wooing ; a novel. By Florence Warden [Florence Alice Price, later Mrs George E. James]. 8vo. [*Brit. Mus.*]   London, 1893

WILDERNESS (the). [A novel.] By Lucas Cleeve [Mrs Howard Kingscote, *née* Adeline G. I. Wolff]. 8vo. Pp. 306. [*Who's Who in Lit.*]
                London, 1906

WILDERNESS (the) and its lessons. . . . By F. E. R. [F. E. Raven]. 8vo. Pp. 137.   London, 1898

WILDERNESS (the) cure. By Vandyke Brown [Marc Cook]. 8vo.
                New York, 1881

WILDERNESS (the) ; or, Braddock's times : a tale of the West. By Solomon Secondsight [James M'Henry, M.D.]. 8vo. [*D. N. B.* vol. 35, p. 108.]
                New York, 1823
    Wrongly assigned to Thomas Berkeley Greaves.

WILDFLOWER. By the author of *The house of Elmore* [Frederick William Robinson]. 8vo. 3 vols. [*Brit. Mus.*]   London, 1857

WILD-FOWL and sea-fowl of Great Britain. By "A son of the marshes" [Denham Jordan]. Edited by J. A. Owen. [*Brit. Mus.*] 8vo. Pp. 326.
                London, 1895

WILDMOOR. By Edith Lee [Florence Burckett]. 8vo. [Cushing's *Init. and Pseud.* i. 170.]   Philadelphia, 1875

WILDS (the) of London. By the Amateur Lambeth Casual [James Greenwood]. 8vo.   London, 1866

WILDWOOD'S magazine. [By Fred. E. Pond.] Vol. I., May-Oct. 1888. 8vo.   Chicago, 1888
    No more published.

WILES (the) of Wilhelmina. [A novel.] By Florence Warden [Florence Alice Price, later Mrs George E. James]. 8vo. Pp. 312. [*Brit. Mus.*]
                London, 1913

WILFRED and his record. By a pioneer [F. Harris]. 8vo.
                Adelaide, 1887

WILFRED'S widow ; a novel. By the author of *Mrs Jerningham's Journal* [Mrs Hart, *née* Fanny Wheeler]. 8vo. [*Brit. Mus.*]   London, 1883

WILFUL (a) maid. By Bertha M. Clay [Charlotte M. Braeme]. 8vo. [*Amer. Cat.*]   New York, 1887

WILFUL Ward ; a novel. By Florence Warden [Florence Alice Price, later Mrs George E. James]. 8vo. [*Brit. Mus.*]   London, 1891

WILFUL (the) ward ; a novel. By the author of the *Young doctor*, etc. [Jane Vaughan Pinkney]. 12mo. 3 vols. [*Nat. Lib. of Scot.*] London, 1853

WILHELM Meister's apprenticeship ; a novel. From the German of Goethe [by Thomas Carlyle]. 8vo. 3 vols. [*D. N. B.* vol. 9, p. 113.] Edinburgh, 1824

WILHELM'S wanderings ; an autobiography. [By William Swift.] 8vo. [*Brit. Mus.*] London, 1878

WILL. [A novel.] From the French of G. Ohnet [Georges Hénot]. 8vo. Pp. 408. [*Brit. Mus.*] London, 1896

WILL Denbigh, nobleman. [By Dinah Maria Mulock, later Mrs Craik.] 12mo. [Cushing's *Anon.*] Boston, 1877
Also ascribed to Mrs Emily Fox.

WILL it come? a story. By Leland Searcher [William Wallace Hebbard, M.D.]. [Cushing's *Init. and Pseud.* i. 263.] Hyde Park, Mass., 1870

WILL (the) o' the Wisps ; or, St John's Eve in the Forest. [A tale.] By the authoress of *The Princess Ilse* [Marie Petersen]. Translated from the German. 8vo. [*Brit. Mus.*] Edinburgh, 1865

WILL (the) of a certain Northern vicar. [By Rev. W. Cooper, rector of Kirkby Wiske.] Second edition, to which is annex'd a codicil. 4to. [*N. and Q.* 18th March 1882, p. 209.] London, 1765
The above was reprinted as " The vicar's will and codicil " (Newcastle, 1824).
Also ascribed to Rev. John Ellison.

WILL (the) ; or, the half-brothers : a romance. [By —— M'Gauran.] 8vo. 3 vols. London, 1846

WILL religious equality do good or harm throughout the counties in which Gaelic is more or less spoken ? By a Free Church Elder [Thos. M'Micking]. 8vo. Pp. 8. Glasgow [1880?]

WILL Romanism prevail in the Church of England ? By an English Churchman [Rev. George Thomas Horn, M.A.]. 4to. Oxford, 1877

WILL Rood's friendship. [A novel.] By Glance Gaylord [Warren Ives Bradley]. 12mo. [Cushing's *Init. and Pseud.* i. 111.] Boston, 1868

WILL Shakespeare ; an invention in four acts. By Clemence Dane [Winifred Ashton]. 8vo. [*Camb. Univ. Lib.*] London, 1921

WILL you be confirmed? A word to the young. By a London curate [William Dalrymple Maclagan, afterwards Archbishop of York]. 8vo. [*D.N.B.*, Second Supp., vol. 2, p. 532.] London [1859]

WILL you have your Church repaired ? [By Sir Henry Rich, Bart.] 8vo. London, 1837

WILL-FORGERS (the). By the Rev. Allan Temple [Rev. Charles Benjamin Tayler, M.A.]. 8vo. London, 1847

WILLIAM and Ellen ; a tale. [By Eaglesfield Smith.] 12mo. Pp. 22. [*Mon. Rev.* xxi. 467 ; xxiii. 108.] London, 1796

WILLIAM and Lucy : an opera of two acts : an attempt to suit the style of the Scotch music. [By —— Paton.] 8vo. [Baker's *Biog. Dram.*] Edinburgh, 1780

WILLIAM and Marion ; a story for children. [By Lady Sarah Savile.] 12mo. London, 1842

WILLIAM and Nanny ; a ballad farce, in two acts, as performed at the theatre in Covent Garden. [By Richard Josceline Goodenough.] 8vo. [Baker's *Biog. Dram.*] London, 1779

WILLIAM Barnes, poet and philologist. By Leader Scott [Mrs Lucy E. Baxter]. [*Who's Who in Lit.*] 8vo. London, 1887

WILLIAM by the Grace of God. [A novel.] By Marjorie Bowen [Gabrielle Vere Campbell]. 8vo. Pp. vi. 312. [*Brit. Mus.*] London, 1916

WILLIAM Douglas ; or, The Scottish exiles : a historical novel. [By Henry Duncan, D.D., of Ruthwell.] 12mo. 3 vols. [Scott's *Fasti.*] Edinburgh, 1826

WILLIAM Holman Hunt and his works. [By Frederic George Stephens, art critic.] 8vo. [*Brit. Mus.*] London, 1860

WILLIAM Makepeace Thackeray ; a biography. By Lewis Melville [Lewis Samuel Benjamin]. 8vo. 2 vols. [*Who's Who in Lit.*] London, 1899

WILLIAM Orleigh. [A novel.] By Esme Hope [Rev. R. M'Kerron, M.A., of Clatt, Aberdeenshire]. 8vo. London, 1890
Also ascribed to George Alexander Selbie.

WILLIAM Penn and the Quaker in unity, the Anabaptist mistaken and in enmity ; or a brief reply to a sheet sent abroad by Jeremiah Ives, entituled William Penn's Confutation of a Quaker ; or an answer to a late libel. [By William Shewen.] 4to. Pp. 12. [Smith's *Anti-Quak.* p. 245.] N.P. 1674

WILLIAM Penn and the Quakers either impostors, or apostates, which they please ; proved from their avowed principles, and contrary practices. By Trepidantium Malleus [Samuel Young]. 12mo. Pp. 4, 134. [Smith's *Bibl. Anti-Quak.* p. 459.]
London, 1696

WILLIAM Robinson Pirie [Principal of Aberdeen University]. In memoriam. [By Penelope E. Pirie.] 8vo. Pp. 165. Private print, Aberdeen, 1888

WILLIAM Shakespeare not an impostor. By an English critic [George Henry Townsend]. 8vo. Pp. vi. 122. [*Olphar Hamst*, p. 180.] London, 1857

WILLIAM Tell ; a tragedy : translated from the German of Schiller by "Tarkari" [Peter Reid, of Aberdeen]. [*R. Inglis.*] Aberdeen, 1879

WILLIAM the Silent, and the Netherland War. By Mary Barrett [Mary O. Nutting]. 8vo. [*Lib. Journ.* iv. 23.]
Boston, 1869

WILLIAM Wyrcestre redivivus ; notices of ancient church architecture, in the fifteenth century, particularly in Bristol: with hints for practicable restorations. [By Rev. James Dallaway.] 4to. Pp. 32. [*Brit. Mus.*] Bristol [1823]

WILLIE ; a story of a children's hospital. By M. Calderford [William Ford Robertson, M.D., Edinburgh]. 8vo. Pp. 49. London, 1899

WILLIE Armstrong ; a Scottish drama, in three acts. By a man wise enough to know that amusement, even though somewhat coarse, is at times as salutary as any article in the pharmacopæia [Dr Richard Poole]. 8vo. Pp. 60. Edinburgh, 1843

WILLIE Wabster's wooing and wedding on the braes of Angus. [By Dorothea Ogilvy, of Clova.] 8vo. Pp. 62. [*A. Jervise.*] Montrose, 1868

WILLIE'S first English book : written for young Maoris who can read their own Maori tongue, and who wish to learn the English language. [By William Colenso, F.L.S.] 12mo. [*Brit. Mus.*] Wellington, N.Z., 1872

WILLING (the) horse ; a novel. By Ian Hay [John Hay Beith]. 8vo. Pp. 300. [*Lit. Year Book.*] London, 1921

WILLING (the) run. By Captain Ralph Bonehill [Edward Stratemeyer]. 8vo. [*Amer. Cat.*] New York, 1905

WILLOUGHBY ; or reformation : the influence of religious principles. By the author of *The Decision*, etc. [Grace Kennedy]. 12mo. 2 vols. [*Brit. Mus.*] London, 1823

WILLOW brook ; a sequel to "The little camp on Eagle hill." By the author of *The wide, wide world*, etc. [Susan Warner]. 8vo. [*Allibone's Dict.*] London, 1874

WILLOWS (the) of Amwell [in Hertfordshire]. By a lady [Elizabeth Barrand]. 8vo. Pp. 74. [*Brit. Mus.*]
Hertford, 1853

WILMINGTONS (the) ; a novel. By the author of *Two old men's tales*, etc. [Mrs Anne Marsh - Caldwell]. 8vo. 3 vols. [*D. N. B.* vol. 36, p. 219.]
London, 1850

WILMOT'S child ; a domestic incident. By Atey Nyne [=89], student and bachelor [Joseph Parker, D.D.]. 8vo. [*Brit. Mus.*] London, 1895

WILTON Castle ; its present condition and past history, and some notes on the adjoining bridge. By the vicar of the parish [Henry Wilson Tweed]. 8vo. Pp. 44. [*Brit. Mus.*]
London, 1884

WIN her and take her, or, old fools will be meddling ; a comedy, as it is acted at the Theatre-Royall, by their Majesties servants. [By John Smyth, M.A.] 4to. [Baker's *Biog. Dram.*] London, 1691
Ascribed also to C. Underhill [*Arber*, ii. 625.]

WINCHESTER, and a few other compositions, in prose and verse. [By Rev. Charles Townsend, rector of Kingston-on-the-sea, near Brighton.] 4to. Pp. 82. [*Martin's Cat.*]
Winchester, 1835

WINCHESTER (the) converts ; or, a full and true discovery of the real usefulness and design of a late right seasonable and religious treatise, entitled, A plain account of the nature and end of the sacrament of the Lords Supper : in three dialogues. [By Thomas Tovey, D.D., Principal of New Inn Hall, Oxford.] 8vo. Pp. 78. [*Bodl.*] Oxford, 1735

WINCHESTER (the) guide ; or, a description of the antiquities and curiosities of that ancient city. [By Thomas Warton, B.D.] A new edition. 12mo. Pp. 115. [*D. N. B.* vol. 59, p. 436.]
Winton, 1780
For an earlier edition see "A description of the City, College and Cathedral of Winchester . . ."

WIND and whirlwind. By Mr Thom White [Charles Wyllys Elliott]. 12mo. [Cushing's *Init. and Pseud.* i. 307.]
New York, 1868

WIND, rain and soil. Poems. By Charman Edwards [Frederick Anthony Edwards]. 8vo. Pp. 51. [*Who's Who in Lit.*] Enfield, 1924

WINDFALL (the). By Charles Egbert Craddock [Mary Noailles Murfree]. 8vo. Pp. 452. [*Who's Who in Lit.*] London, 1912

WINDFALLS. [Essays.] By Alpha of the plough [Alfred George Gardiner]. 8vo. Pp. xvi. 270. [*Nat. Lib. of Scot.*] London, 1920

WINDFALLS. By the author of *Aspects of humanity* [Richard Randolph]. 8vo. [*Brit. Mus.*] Philadelphia, 1871

WINDFALLS; some stray leaves gathered by a rolling stone. [A novel.] By Robert Aitken [Robert Aitken Swan]. 8vo. Pp. 310. [*Who's Who in Lit.*] London, 1903

WINDFALLS; two hundred and odd [scraps of blank verse. By W. J. Linton]. 12mo. Pp. 96. [*Dobell's Private Prints*, p. 110.] Appledore Private Press, N.D.

WINDING (the) road. [A novel.] By Elizabeth Godfrey [Jessie Bedford]. 8vo. Pp. 360. [*Amer. Cat.*] London, 1902

WINDING (the) way; a novel. By "A Son of the Soil" [Joseph Smith Fletcher]. 8vo. Pp. 309. London, 1890

WINDING-SHEET (a) for England's ministry, which hath a name to live, but is dead; sent to John Owen, called Dr. in that ministry, and late Vice-Chancellor of Oxford: and is in answer to his printed paper concerning tythes. . . . [By T. Foster, of Norfolk?] 4to. [Smith's *Cat. of Friends' Books*, i. 626.] N.P., N.D.
Signed: "By a member of the true Church and of that Society, which the world calls Quakers."

WINDOW (a) in Paris. [A novel.] By Marianne Farningham [Marianne Hearne, of Farningham]. 8vo. Pp. vi. 358. [*Brit. Mus.*] London, 1898

WINDS of the dawn. (Some common-sense occasional papers—for the times.) By John Oxenham [William Arthur Dunkerley]. 8vo. [*Brit. Mus.*] London, 1919

WINDSOR Castle; or, the fair maid of Kent: an opera, as performed at the Theatre-Royal, Covent-Garden, in honour of the marriage of their Royal Highnesses the Prince and Princess of Wales. By the author of *Hartford-Bridge*, etc. [William Pearce]. 8vo. Pp. 40. [Watt's *Bibl. Brit.*] London, 1795

WINDSOR walks; or pedestrian time guide for business or recreation. By "Windsor Bee" [B. R. Bambridge]. 12mo. Pp. 103. [*Brit. Mus.*] Windsor, 1895

WIND-SWEPT (the) wheat; poems. By Madeline Bridges [Madeline A. De Vere]. 8vo. Boston, 1904

WINDY Haugh. . . . By Graham Travers [Margaret Todd, M.D.]. 8vo. [*Who's Who in Lit.*] London, 1898

WINDYGAP. [A novel.] By Theo Douglas [Mrs H. D. Everett]. 8vo. Pp. 216. [*Lit. Year Book.*] Bristol, 1898

WINE; a poem: to which is added, Old England's New Triumph; or, the Battle of Oudenard: a song. [By John Gray.] 8vo. [*Brit. Mus.*] London, 1709

WINE and walnuts; or, after dinner chit-chat. By Ephraim Hardcastle, citizen and dry-salter [William Henry Pyne]. 8vo. 2 vols. [*Lowndes' Bibl. Man.* p. 2015.] London, 1823

WINE (the) merchant; a familiar treatise on the art of making wine. [By William Robert Loftus.] 12mo. [*Brit. Mus.*] London, 1865

WINE the mocker. By Guy Thorne [Cyril A. E. Ranger-Gull]. 8vo. Pp. 320. [*Who's Who in Lit.*] London, 1919

WINEFRIDE Jones; a very ignorant girl. [By Mrs Harriet Diana Thompson, *née* Calvert.] 8vo. London, 1854

WINFIELD the lawyer's son, and how he became a Major-General [Hancock]. By Major Penniman [Charles Wheeler Denison]. 8vo. [Cushing's *Init. and Pseud.* i. 227.] Philadelphia, 1865

WINGED Arrow's medicine. By Harry Castlemon [Charles Austin Fosdick]. 8vo. [*Brit. Mus.*] Philadelphia, 1901

WINGED destiny; studies in the spiritual history of the Gael. By Fiona Macleod [William Sharp]. 8vo. Pp. 378. [*Who's Who in Lit.*] London, 1904

WINGED (the) victory. [A novel.] By Sarah Grand [Mrs Haldane M'Fall, *née* Frances Elizabeth Clarke]. 8vo. [*Brit. Mus.*] London, 1916

WINGS and stings; a tale for the young. By A. L. O. E., authoress of the *Claremont tales*, etc. [Charlotte M. Tucker]. 8vo. Pp. 160. London, 1863

WINGS of courage; and, the cloud-spinner. By George Sand [Madame Amandine L. A. Dudevant]; translated. 8vo. [*Brit. Mus.*] London, 1883

WINIFRED and the stockbroker. By Charles Eddy [Charles E. Rose]. 8vo. [*Who's Who in Lit.*] London, 1902

WINIFRED Bertram, and the world she lived in. By the author of *Chronicles of the Schönberg-Cotta family*, etc. [Mrs Elizabeth Charles, *née* Rundle]. 8vo. Pp. 476. London, 1866

WINIFRED Power ; a novel. [By Bella Duffy.] 8vo. 3 vols. London, 1883

WINIFRID, afterwards called Boniface, A.D. 680-755. [A poem. By William Selwyn.] 4to. Pp. 41.
Cambridge, 1864
Private information from a friend.

WINKEY'S whims. [By Wells Egelshem.] London, 1769

WINKLES ; a winner. By G. G. [Henry George Harper]. 8vo. Pp. 250. [*Brit. Mus.*] London, 1899

WINNING hazard. [A novel.] By Mrs Alexander [Mrs Alexander Hector, *née* Annie French]. 8vo. [*Who's Who in Lit.*] New York, 1905

WINNING his shoulder straps ; or Bob Anderson at Chetham military school. By Norman Brainerd [Samuel Richard Fuller]. 8vo. [*Amer. Cat.*]
Boston, 1909

WINNING (the) of May. By the author of *Dr Edith Romney* [Anne Elliot]. 8vo. [*Brit. Mus.*] London [1893]

WINNING the eagle prize ; or, the pluck of Billy Hazen. By Norman Brainerd [Samuel Richard Fuller]. 8vo. [*Amer. Cat.*] Boston, 1910

WINNIPEG (the) country ; or, roughing it with the eclipse party. By a Rochester fellow [Samuel Habbard Scudder]. 8vo. Boston, 1886

WINTER amusements ; an ode read at Lady Miller's assembly, Dec. 3, 1778. [By Christopher Anstey.] 4to.
[Bath], 1778
See the note to " Poetical amusements at a villa near Bath."

WINTER comforts, and how to knit them. [By Miss H. P. Ryder.] 8vo. [*Brit. Mus.*] Richmond, Yorks [1866]

WINTER displayed ; a poem. By an American [Samuel Low]. 8vo. Pp. 40. [Sabin's *Dictionary*.]
New York, 1784

WINTER (a) dreame. [By James Howell.] 4to. Pp. 20. [*Bodl.*]
N.P. 1649
Sometimes attributed to George Wither.

WINTER evening conversations between a father and his children on the works of God. [By Rev. Alex. Arthur of Dalkeith.] Edinburgh, 1810

WINTER evening entertainments, containing—I. Ten pleasant and delightful relations. II. Fifty ingenious riddles. [By Nathaniel Crouch.] Sixth edition. 12mo. [*D. N. B.* vol. 8, p. 15.]
London, 1737

WINTER (the) evening fireside. . . . [By William Giles Dix.] 12mo. [*Brit. Mus.*] Boston, 1847
Signed : W. G. D.

WINTER evenings at College ; a familiar description of the manners, customs, sports, and religious observances of the Ancient Greeks ; with a short account of the state of Modern Greece ; and reflections on the revolutions of empires. By a clergyman [Benjamin Thomas Holcott Cole]. 8vo. 2 vols. [*Camb. Univ. Lib.*] London, 1829

WINTER (a) evening's conversation upon the doctrine of original sin, between a minister and three of his neighbours. . . . [By Rev. Samuel Webster.] 8vo. [Evans' *Amer. Bibl.* iii. 185.] Boston, 1757

WINTER evenings ; or, lucubrations on life and letters. [By Vicesimus Knox, D.D.] 12mo. 3 vols. [*Brit. Mus.*]
London, 1788

WINTER (a) in Bath ; or love as it may be, and friendship as it ought to be : a novel. [By Mrs E. G. Bayfield.] 12mo. 4 vols. [Green's *Bibl. Somers.* i. 55.] Bath, 1807
The second edition (1808) gives the author's name.

WINTER (a) in Edinburgh ; or, the Russian brothers : a novel. By Honoria Scott [Mrs —— Frazer]. 12mo. 3 vols. London, 1822
" Mrs Frazer, who some years ago published several popular works under the name of Honoria Scott, . . ."—Newspaper cutting (July 1824) in Mr Maidment's copy.

WINTER (a) in the West. By a New Yorker [Charles Fenno Hoffman]. 8vo. 2 vols. [Cushing's *Init. and Pseud.* i. 203.] New York, 1835

WINTER (a) journey from Gloucester to Norway. [By John Bellows.] 8vo. [*Brit. Mus.*] London, 1867

WINTER leaves. [Poems by Rev. John Fairbairn and Professor Charles M'Dowall.] 8vo. [R. Inglis' *Dram. Writers of Scotland*, p. 149.]
Edinburgh, 1835

WINTER sketches from the saddle. By a Septuagenarian [John Codman]. 12mo. New York, 1888

WINTER (a) story. By the author of *The rose garden*, etc. [Frances Mary Peard]. 8vo. Pp. 292. [*Camb. Univ. Lib.*] London, 1875

WINTER (a) with Robert Burns ; being annals of his patrons and associates in Edinburgh, 1786-7, and details of his inauguration as poet-laureate of the Can. Kil. [Canongate Kilwinning. By James Marshall, S.S.C.]. 8vo.
Edinburgh, 1846

WINTER-EVENING (a) conference between neighbours. [By John Goodman, D.D.] Third edition. 8vo. 3 parts. [*Camb. Univ. Lib.*]
London, 1686
Several editions were issued later, with the author's name.

WINTERING hay. [A novel.] By John Trevena [Ernest George Henham]. 8vo. Pp. 518. [*Brit. Mus.*]
London, 1912

WINTER-PIECE (the); a poem written in 1740. [By Joseph Phipps.] Folio. [Smith's *Cat. of Friends' Books*, i. 66.]
London, 1763

WINTER'S (a) tale; a romance. [By James Norris Brewer]. 8vo. [*D. N. B.* vol. 6, p. 293.] London, 1799

WISDOM; a poem. [By Edward Wilkinson, M.D.] Fourth edition. 8vo. Pp. 21. [Smith's *Cat. of Friends' Books*, ii. 933.] London, 1798

WISDOM and policy of the French in the construction of their great offices; so as best to answer the purposes of extending their trade and commerce and enlarging their foreign settlements. With some observations in relation to the dispute now subsisting between the English and French colonies in America. [By Henry McCulloh.] 8vo. [*Brit. Mus.*] London, 1755
See also, " A miscellaneous essay . . ."

WISDOM for the foolish. By Lambkin Sprinx [Celia Louise Crittenton]. 8vo. [*Amer. Cat.*] Boston, 1908

WISDOM from above; or, considerations tending to explain, establish, and promote the Christian life, or that holiness, without which no man shall see the Lord. By a lover of truth, and of the souls of men [Rev. John Mapletoft, M.D.]. 12mo. 2 parts. Pp. 155. [*D. N. B.* vol. 36, p. 115.]
London, 1714-17

WISDOM, intelligence, and science, the true characteristics of Emmanuel Swedenborg. . . . By Medicus Cantabrigiensis [John Spurgin]. 8vo. [*Brit. Mus.*] London, 1862

WISDOM (the) of Damaris. [A novel.] By Lucas Malet [Mrs St Leger Harrison, *née* Mary Kingsley]. 8vo. [*Who's Who in Lit.*] London, 1914

WISDOM (the) of looking backward, to judge the better of one side and t'other by the speeches, writings, actions, and other matters of fact on both sides, for the four years last past. [By White Kennett, D.D.] 8vo. [*D. N. B.* vol. 31, p. 5.] London, 1715

WISDOM (the) of passion; or the motives of human nature. By Salvarona [Harry G. Waters]. 8vo. [*Amer. Cat.*] Boston, 1901

WISDOM (the) of the son of David; an exposition of Proverbs i.-ix. [By Rev. Richard Meux Benson.] 12mo. [*D. N. B.* Third Supp.] London, 1860

WISDOM (the) of the wise; a comedy, in three acts. By John Oliver Hobbes [Mrs Reginald Walpole Craigie, *née* Pearl Teresa Richards]. 8vo. [*Who's Who in Lit.*] London [1901]

WISDOM on the hire system; containing full details of the "Insidecompleteuar Britannia-ware" prize competition. By E. V. L. [Edward V. Lucas] and C. L. G. [Charles L. Graves]. 4to. Pp. 56. [*Brit. Mus.*] London, 1903
A skit on the tenth edition of the *Encyclopædia Britannica*. See also "Wisdom while you wait."

WISDOM the first spring of action in the Deity; a discourse, in which, among other things, the absurdity of God's being actuated by natural inclinations, and of an unbounded liberty, is shewn. . . . [By Rev. Henry Grove, of Taunton.] 8vo. Pp. iv. 110. [Watt's *Bibl. Brit.*] London, 1734
The second edition (1742) bears the author's name.

WISDOM triumphant over vain philosophy; or, What is truth? By Zion Ward [John Ward]. 8vo. Pp. viii. 73. [*Brit. Mus.*] Birmingham [1810]

WISDOM *versus* Satan on the stage of time. By "Elijah the prophet" (not Elijah the Tishbite) [James A. Moncrieff, C.E.]. See Malachi iv. 5-6. 8vo. Pp. viii. 664. [*Manch. Free. Lib.*] Belfast, 1871

WISDOM while you wait; being a foretaste of the glories of the "Insidecompleteuar Britanniaware." [By Edward V. Lucas and Charles L. Graves.] 8vo. Pp. 95. London, 1903
Preface signed: E. V. L., C. L. G.

WISDOM'S conquest; being an explanation and grammatical translation of the 13th Book of Ovid's Metamorphoses [by Thomas Hall]. 8vo. [Lowndes' *Bibl. Man.*]
London, 1651

WISDOM'S way; notes of lectures. By F. F. R. [F. E. Raven]. 8vo. Pp. 99. [*Brit. Mus.*] London, 1900

Q

WISE (a) and moderate discourse, concerning Church-affaires; as it was written, long since, by the famous authour [Francis, Lord Bacon] of those Considerations, which seem to have some reference to this: now published for the common good. 4to. N.P. 1641

   Reprinted in 1663 with the title, "True peace: or, a moderate discourse to compose the unsettled consciences and greatest differences in ecclesiastical affaires."

WISE and otherwise. [A tale.] By "Pansy" [Mrs Isabella Alden, *née* Macdonald]. 8vo. Pp. 320. [*Brit. Mus.*]   London [1888]

WISE (the) Christian's study; or, the true way of serving God in a most perfect manner. From the Spanish of Alphonse, by F. M. [John Gregory Mallet, O.S.B.]. 12mo. [Gillow's *Bibl. Dict.* iv. 399.]   Douay, 1680

WISE (the) judgment; being a chapter on the competing models for the Manchester Wellington testimonial. By Gabriel Tinto, Esq. [G. W. Anthony]. 8vo. Pp. 11. [*Manch. Free Lib. Cat.*]
Manchester, 1853

WISE (the) or foolish choice; or the wisdom of choosing Christ, and the folly of choosing the world for our portion: discovered and asserted by Solomon the Wise, in a paraphrase on the Song of Solomon, and an abstract of the book of Solomon called Ecclesiastes. . . . Both done in metre by one of the ministers of the Gospel in Glasgow, I. C. [Rev. James Clark, minister at Innerwick, afterwards at Glasgow]. 8vo. Pp. 62. [R. Inglis' *Dramatic Writers of Scotland*, p. 141.]
Edinburgh, 1703

WISE sayings; and stories to explain them. By M. H. [Matilda Horsburgh], author of *Rose Lindesay*, etc. 12mo. Pp. 192. [*Brit. Mus.*]
Edinburgh [1860]

WISE to win. [A tale.] By "Pansy" [Mrs Isabella Alden, *née* Macdonald]. 4to. [*Brit. Mus.*]   London [1894]

WISE words and loving deeds: a book of biographies for girls. By E. Conder Gray [Alexander Hay Japp, LL.D.]. 8vo. Pp. 394. [*D. N. B.*, Second Supp., ii. 363.]   London, 1880

WISEMAN versus Pascal the younger; the Church of Rome's defence against "Cases of conscience," with a reply. By Pascal the younger [Pierce Connelly]. 8vo. [*New Coll. Lib.*]
London, 1851

WISHES (the) of a free people; a dramatic poem. [By Paul Hiffernan, M.D.] 8vo. [O'Donoghue's *Poets of Ireland*.]   London, 1761

WISTONS; a story in three parts. By Miles Amber [Mrs Ellen Melicent Sickert, *née* Cobden]. 8vo. Pp. 282. [*Brit. Mus.*]   London, 1902

WIT a sporting in a pleasant grove of new fancies. By H. B. [Henry Bold]. 8vo. [Lowndes' *Bibl. Man.*]
London, 1657

WIT against reason; or the Protestant champion, the great, the incomparable Chillingworth, not invulnerable. . . . By H. E. [Edward Hawarden,† D.D.] 8vo. [*D. N. B.* vol. 25, p. 186.]
Brussels, 1735

WIT and drollery; jovial poems, never before printed; by Sir J. M. [Sir John Mennis], Ja. S. [James Smith], Sir W. D. [Sir William Davenant], J. D. [John Donne], and other admirable wits. [Preface signed: J. P. *i.e.* John Phillips.] 8vo. Pp. 160. [*D. N. B.* vol. 45, p. 205.]   London, 1656

   J. D. has been wrongly interpreted as John Dryden and J. P. as John Playford. An edition was issued in 1661 with the preface signed: E. M. (unidentified).

WIT (the) and honesty of James Hoskins, etc. consider'd in remarks on their late pamphlet call'd "The Pennsylvania Bubble." By the translator of *The Pattern of Modesty* [Elias Bockett]. 8vo.   London, 1726

   Also tentatively attributed to Thomas Story against whom "The Pennsylvania Bubble" was directed.

WIT and wisdom from Edgar Saltus. By G. F. Monkshood [W. J. Clarke]. 8vo. [*Brit. Mus.*]   [London?] 1903

WIT bought; or the life and adventures of Robert Merry [Samuel G. Goodrich]. 12mo.   London, N.D.

WIT, humor, and pathos. By Eli Perkins [Melville D. Landon]. 8vo. [Cushing's *Init. and Pseud.* i. 228.]
Chicago, 1887

WIT (the) of a woman; as it now acted at the New Theatre in Little Lincoln's-Inn-Fields, by Her Majesty's sworn servants. [By Thomas Walker.] 4to. Pp. 8, 34. [Baker's *Biog. Dram.*]
London, 1705

WIT revived; or, a new excellent way of divertisement, digested into most ingenious questions and answers. Published under the name of Asdryasdust Tossoffacan [Edmund Gayton]. 12mo. Pp. 72. [Wood's *Athen. Oxon.* iii. 756.]   London, 1660

WITCH Demonia; a child's fairy tale. By Raymond Jacberns [Miss Georgina M. Selby Ash]. 8vo. [*Who's Who in Lit.*]   London, 1895

WITCH (the) of Malton Hill. [By Mrs Harriet Diana Thompson, *née* Calvert.] 8vo.   London, 1849

WITCH (a) of the hills ; a novel. By Florence Warden [Florence Alice Price, later Mrs George E. James]. 8vo. Pp. 203. [*Brit. Mus.*]
London, 1889

WITCH (the) of the rocks. By M. E. Winchester [M. E. Whatham]. 8vo. [*Who's Who in Lit.*]   London, 1886

WITCH (the) of the woodlands ; or, the cobler's new translation. Written by L. P. [Lawrence Price]. 8vo. Pp. 22. B. L. [*Bodl.*]   London, 1655

WITCHCRAFT cast out from the religious seed and Israel of God ; and the black art, or, necromancy, inchantments, and witchcraft discovered, with the ground, fruits and effects thereof. . . . Also some things to clear the truth from reproaches, and false accusations, occasioned by D. Bott, and his slander-carriers. [By Richard Farnworth.] 4to. [*Brit. Mus.*]   London, 1655
Signed : R. F.

WITCHCRAFT farther display'd. Containing I. An account of the witchcraft practis'd by Jane Wenham of Walkerne, in Hertfordshire, since her condemnation, upon the bodies of Anne Thorn and Anne Street. . . . II. An answer to the most general objections against the being and power of witches. . . . To which are added, the tryals of Florence Newton, a famous Irish witch, at the assizes held at Cork, anno 1661 ; as also of two witches at the assizes held at Bury St Edmonds in Suffolk, anno 1664. [By Francis Bragge, A.B., late of Peterhouse in Cambridge.] 8vo. Pp. 39.   London, 1712
Introduction signed : F. B.

WITCH-CRAFT proven, arreign'd, and condemn'd in its professors, professions and marks, by diverse pungent and convincing arguments, excerpted forth of the most authentic authors, divine and humane, ancient and modern. . . . By a lover of the truth [Rev. John Bell, minister of Gladsmuir]. 12mo. Pp. 16. [J. Ferguson's *Witchcraft Lit. of Scot.* p. 25.]
Glasgow, 1697

WITCH-FINDER (the). By May Wynne [Mabel Wynne Knowles]. 8vo. Pp. 256. [*Brit. Mus.*]
London, 1922

WITCH-FINDER (the); or, the wisdom of our ancestors : a romance. By the author of *The Lollards*, etc. [Thomas Gaspey]. 12mo. 3 vols. [*Brit. Mus.*]
London, 1824

WITCH-WIFE (the). By Sarah Tytler [Henrietta Keddie]. 8vo. Pp. 280. [*Who's Who in Lit.*]   London, 1897

WITENHAM-HILL ; a descriptive poem. By T. P—— A.M. [Thomas Pye, A.M.]. 4to. Pp. 26. [*Bodl.*]
London, 1777
Ascribed also to Thomas Pentycross. [Watt's *Bibl. Brit.*]

WITH aimless feet. By M. C. Ramsay [Mary Ramsay Calder]. 8vo. Pp. 272. [*Who's Who in Lit.*]
London, 1906

WITH airship and submarine ; a tale of adventure. By Harry Collingwood [William Joseph Cosens Lancaster]. 8vo. Pp. 384. [*Who's Who in Lit.*]
Glasgow, 1907

WITH brains, Sir. [By John Brown, M.D.] 8vo. Pp. 12.   N.P., N.D.
From the *Monthly Journal of Medical Science*, for February 1851. Signed : J. B.

WITH cords of love ; a tale. By E. Livingston Prescott [Edith Katherine Spicer-Jay]. 8vo. Pp. 256. [*Who's Who in Lit.*]   London, 1904

WITH edged tools. [A novel.] By Henry Seton Merriman [Hugh Stowell Scott]. 8vo. Pp. 386. [*Who's Who in Lit.*]   London, 1903

WITH General Sheridan in his last campaign. By a staff officer [Lieut.-Colonel Frederick C. Newhall]. 8vo. Pp. 235.   Philadelphia, 1866

WITH harp and crown ; a novel. By the authors of *Ready-money Mortiboy*, etc. [Sir Walter Besant and James Rice]. 8vo. 3 vols. [*Brit. Mus.*]
London, 1875

WITH hooks of steel. By Crona Temple [Miss —— Corfield.] 8vo. Pp. 224.
London [1887]

WITH King James' Bible as exclusive authority, can the Protestant Christian question the Eucharist? By Consistency [John Thaddeus Foley]. [*Amer. Cat.*]   Marquette, Mich., 1909

WITH Lafayette at Yorktown ; a story of how two boys joined the Continental Army. By James Otis [James Otis Kaler]. 8vo. Pp. 303. [*Cushing's Init. and Pseud.* i. 220.]
New York, 1896

WITH my regiment from the Aisne to La Bassée. By "Platoon Commander" [Arthur Frederick Hobart Mills]. 8vo. [*Lond. Lib. Cat.*]   London [1915]

WITH Porter in the "Essex" ; a story of his famous cruise in Southern waters during the war of 1812. By James Otis [James Otis Kaler]. 8vo. [Cushing's *Init. and Pseud.* i. 220.]
Boston, 1901

WITH rank and file ; or, side-lights on soldier life. By Arthur Amyand [Major Andrew C. P. Haggard]. 8vo. Pp. vi. 261. [*Brit. Mus.*]   London, 1895

WITH rod and line in Colorado waters. By "Bourgeois" [L. B. France]. 8vo.
Denver, 1884

WITH Rogers' Rangers. By Victor St Clair [George Waldo Browne]. 8vo. [*Amer. Cat.*]   Boston, 1906

WITH signals clear. [A collection of railway stories.] By Ramsay Guthrie [Rev. J. G. Bowran]. 8vo. [*Who's Who in Lit.*]   London, 1915

WITH swallow's wings. By Crona Temple [Miss —— Corfield]. 8vo.
London, 1883

WITH the best intentions. By Marian Harland [Mrs Mary Virginia Terhune, *née* Hawes]. 8vo. [*Amer. Cat.*]
New York, 1890

WITH the best intentions ; a story of undergraduate life. By John Bicker-dyke [Charles Henry Cook]. 8vo. [*Who's Who in Lit.*] London, 1884

WITH the guns. By F. O. O. [Forward Observation Officer, *i.e.* C. J. C. Street]. Second edition. 8vo. [*Lond. Lib. Cat.*]
London, 1916

WITH the Harrises seventy years ago. By the author of *The Subaltern*, etc. [Rev. George R. Gleig, D.D.]. 8vo. Pp. xii. 499. [*Brit. Mus.*]
London, 1889

WITH the procession ; a novel. By Stanton Page [Henry B. Fuller]. 8vo. Pp. 336.   New York, 1895

WITH the R.N.R. By "Windlass" [John B. Hicks]. 8vo. Pp. 251. [*Brit. Mus.*]   London, 1918

WITH the Russians in Manchuria. By Max Baring [Charles Messent]. 8vo. Pp. 222. [*Brit. Mus.*] London, 1905

WITH the tide ; or, a life's voyage : a story for young people. By Sidney Daryl [Douglas Straight]. 8vo. [*Brit. Mus.*]   London, 1868

WITH the treasure-hunters ; a story of the Florida Cays. . . . By James Otis [James Otis Kaler]. 8vo. Pp. 340. [Cushing's *Init. and Pseud.* i. 220.]   Philadelphia, 1903

WITH the trees. By E. M. Hardinge [Maud Going]. 8vo. [*Amer. Cat.*]
New York, 1903

WITH the wild flowers, from pussy-willow to thistle-down. By E. M. Hardinge [Maud Going]. 8vo. [*Amer. Cat.*]   New York, 1901

WITH the woodlanders, and by the tide. By "A son of the marshes" [Denham Jordan]. Edited by J. A. Owen. 8vo. Pp. 305. [*Brit. Mus.*]
London, 1893

WITH wind and tide ; a story of the East Coast. By the author of *The Dean's little daughter* [Frances Marshall]. 8vo. [*Lit. Year Book.*]
London, 1892

WITHIN an hour of London town ; among wild birds and their haunts. By "A son of the marshes" [Denham Jordan]. Edited by J. A. Owen. 8vo. Pp. 314. [*Brit. Mus.*]
London, 1892

WITHIN Fort Sumter ; or, a view of Major Anderson's garrison family for one hundred and ten days. By one of the company [Miss A. Fletcher]. 8vo. [Cushing's *Init. and Pseud.* i. 216.]   New York, 1861

WITHIN the enemy's lines. By Oliver Optic [William Taylor Adams]. 8vo. Pp. 349.   Boston, 1890

WITHIN the sound of the sea. [A novel.] By the author of *Vera*, etc. [Charlotte L. H. Dempster.] 8vo. 2 vols. Pp. ix. 395. [*Brit. Mus.*]
London, 1879

WITHIN the tides. [Four stories.] By Joseph Conrad [Josef Konrad Korzeniowski]. 8vo. Pp. 288. [*Brit. Mus.*]   London, 1915

WITHIN the vail ; and other poems. By C. L. S. [Charitie Lees Smith, later Mrs Julian Bancroft]. 12mo.
London, 1867

WITHIN the veil ; studies in the Epistle to the Hebrews. By the author of *Chronicles of the Schönberg-Cotta family* [Mrs Elizabeth Charles *née* Rundle]. 8vo. Pp. 104. [*Brit. Mus.*]   London [1891]

WITHIN, without and over ; or memorials of the earnest life of Henry C. Hall. [By Amanda H. Hall.] [*Lib. Journ.* iv. 24.]
Northampton, Mass., 1878

WITHOUT a friend in the world. By the author of *Worth her weight in gold* [H. Colson]. 8vo. [*Brit. Mus.*]
London, 1866

WITHOUT a reference ; a Christmas story. By Brenda [Mrs —— Castle Smith, *née* —— Meyrick]. 8vo. Pp. 266. [*Brit. Mus.*] London, 1882

WITHOUT faith, without God. . . . [By Robert Barclay, the Berean.] 8vo.
N.P. 1769

WITHOUT sin ; a novel. By Martin J. Pritchard [Mrs Augustus Moore]. 8vo. Pp. 310.   New York, 1896

WITNESS (the) of Assyria ; or, the Bible contrasted with the monuments. By Chilperic Edwards [Edward John Pilcher]. 8vo. Pp. v. 183. [*Brit. Mus.*]   London, 1893

WITNESSES (the) in sackcloth; or a descriptive account of the attack made upon the Reformed Churches of France in the seventeenth century; with a bibliographical and literary appendix, including notices of the subsequent history of the French Protestants. By a descendant of a refugee [Henry Samuel Baynes.] 8vo. Pp. viii. 304. [*Brit. Mus.*] London, 1852

WITS (the) and beaux of society. By Grace and Philip Wharton, authors of *The Queens of society* [Mrs Katherine B. and John Cockburn Thomson]. 8vo. 2 vols. [*Olphar Hamst.*]
London [1860]

WIT'S bedlam, where is had, whipping cheer to cure the mad. [By John Davies, of Hereford.] 8vo. [Lowndes' *Bibl. Man.*] London, 1617

WITS common-wealth; or, a treasury of divine, moral, historical, and poetical admonitions, similies and sentences for the use of schools. [Compiled by John Bodenham.] Newly corrected and enlarged. 8vo. Pp. 270. [*Brit. Mus.*] London, 1722
A reprint. For the original editions (1597 *et seq.*) see " Politeuphuia . . ."

WITS extraction, conveyed to the ingenious in riddles, observations and morals. By W. B. [William Bagwell], Truth's servant. 12mo. [Lowndes' *Bibl. Man.*] London, 1664

WITS, fits, and fancies; or a generall and serious collection of the sententious speeches, answers, jests, and behaviours of all sortes of estates, from the throane to the cottage. . . . Newly corrected and augmented. [By Anthony Copley.] 4to. B. L. [*Brit. Mus.*]
London, 1614

WITS interpreter; the English Parnassus; or, a sure guide to those admirable accomplishments that compleat our English gentry, in the most acceptable qualifications of discourse or writing. . . . The 3d edition with many new additions. By J. C. [John Cotgrave]. 8vo. Pp. 11, 520. [Arber's *Term Cat.* i. 532.] London, 1671

WITS labyrinth. By J. S. [James Shirley?]. 4to. London, 1648

WITS led by the nose; or a poets revenge; a tragi-comedy [from William Chamberlaine's "Love's Victory"]; acted at the Theatre-Royal. 4to. [Baker's *Biog. Dram.*] London, 1677

WITS (the); or, sport upon sport: in select pieces of drollery, digested into scenes by way of dialogue. . . . [By Francis Kirkman.] Part I. 8vo. Pp. 186. London, 1662

WITS (the) paraphras'd; or paraphrase on paraphrase; in a burlesque on the several late translations of Ovid's epistles. [By M. Stevenson.] [Arber's *Term Cat.* i. 532.] London, 1680

WITS private wealth, stored with choyse commodities to content the minde. [By Nicholas Breton.] 4to. [*Pollard and Redgrave.*] London, 1625
Many editions (1612, 1613, 1615, 1629, 1634) bear the author's name.

WITS theater of the little world. 8vo. Ff. 3, 269, 6. [London] 1599
This used to be ascribed to John Bodenham but is now considered to be by Robert Allott whose name it bears at the dedication.

WITT against wisdom; or a panegyrick upon folly: penned in Latin by Desiderius Erasmus; rendered into English [by White Kennett, D.D.]. 12mo. [*D. N. B.* vol. 31, p. 2.]
Oxford, 1683

WITTY (the) and humorous side of the English poets. By Arthur H. Elliott [William Henry Davenport Adams]; with a variety of specimens. . . . 8vo. [*Brit. Mus.*] London, 1880

WITTY apophthegms delivered at several times, and upon several occasions, by King James, King Charles, the Marquess of Worcester, Francis, Lord Bacon, and Sir Thomas Moor. Collected and revised [by Thomas Baily, D.D., Subdean of Wells]. 8vo. Pp. 2, 186. [*Brit. Mus.*]
[London] 1671

WITTY (a) combat; or, the female victor: a tragi-comedy, as it was acted by persons of quality in Whitsun-week with great applause. Written by T. P. Gent. [Thomas Porter]. 4to. No pagination. [*Bodl.*]
London, 1663

WITTY sayings. By John Brighte [J. Duncan]. 8vo. [Cushing's *Init. and Pseud.* i. 39.] London, 1875

WIVES and mistresses. [By Mrs Anne Stevenson, *née* Reddie.] 8vo.
Edinburgh [1880?]

WIZARD (the) Peter; a song of the Solway. [By Charles Kirkpatrick Sharpe.] 8vo. Pp. 32.
Edinburgh, 1834

WIZARD'S (the) cave. By Eglanton Thorne [Emily Charlton]. 8vo. Pp. 78. [*Brit. Mus.*] London [1910]

WOBURN Park; a fragment in rural rhyme. [By George Castleden.] 12mo.
Woburn, 1839

WOFULL cry of unjust persecutions, and grievous oppressions of the people of God in England . . . and this may serve for an answer in full to all such who have presented . . . the innocent people in scorn called Quakers. . . . By E. B. [Edward Burrough]. 4to. [Smith's *Cat. of Friends' Books.*]
London [1657]

WOLF (the) ; a novel. By J. E. Buckrose [Mrs Falconer Jameson]. 8vo. Pp. 324. [*Who's Who in Lit.*]
London, 1908

WOLF (the) at the door. [A novel.] By Florence Warden [Florence Alice Price, later Mrs George E. James]. 8vo. [*Brit. Mus.*] London, 1909

WOLF hunting and wild sport in Brittany. By the author of *Paul Pendril, Dartmoor Days*, etc. [Rev. Edward W. L. Davies]. 8vo. [Shum's *Bath books*, p. 62.] London, 1875

WOLF (the) in the fold ; or a new phase of the perils of Ritualism, and a plain statement of facts in the case of All Saints, Newington. By a parishioner [John Waddington, D.D.]. 8vo. [*Brit. Mus.*] London [1867]

WOLF (the) stript of his shepherd's cloathing ; in answer to a late celebrated book [by James Owen] intituled Moderation a vertue : wherein the designs of the dissenters against the Church, and their behaviour towards her Majesty both in England and Scotland are laid open. By one call'd an Highchurchman [Charles Leslie]. With my service to Dr D'Avenant. 4to. [Smith's *Anti-Quak.* p. 272.]
London, 1704

WOLFE (the) of Badenoch ; a historical romance of the fourteenth century. [By Sir Thomas Dick Lauder, of Fountainhall, East Lothian.] 12mo. 3 vols. [*D. N. B.* vol. 32, p. 598.]
Edinburgh, 1827

WOLFE of the Knoll ; and other poems. By Virginia Gabriel [Constance Crane, later Mrs Marsh]. [Cushing's *Init. and Pseud.* i. 111.] New York, 1860

WOLFVILLE. [Stories of the South West.] By Dan Quin [Alfred H. Lewis]. 8vo. Pp. 337. New York [1897]

WOLSEY, the Cardinal, and his times ; courtly, political, and ecclesiastical. By George Howard, Esq. author of *Lady Jane Grey, and her times* [Lieut. Francis C. Laird, R.N.]. 8vo.
London, 1824

WOLSEY'S bell in Sherborne Abbey Church ; some account of it, together with a tabular comparison of the bells at Exeter and Sherborne. . . . [By Edward Harston.] 8vo.
Sherborne, 1866

WOMAN ; a poem. [By Eaton Stannard Barrett.] 8vo. [O'Donoghue's *Poets of Ireland.*] London, 1810
Another edition, with additions, in 1818.

WOMAN and artist. [A story of London life.] By Max O'Rell [Paul Blouet]. 8vo. [*Brit. Mus.*] London, 1900

WOMAN and her Saviour in Persia. By a returned missionary [Thomas Laurie, D.D.]. 8vo. [Cushing's *Init. and Pseud.* i. 250.] Boston, 1863

WOMAN and her social position. [By Margaret Milne, or Mylne.] 8vo.
London [private print], 1872

WOMAN and Moses. By Lucas Cleeve [Mrs Howard Kingscote, *née* Adelina Georgina Isabella Wolff]. 8vo. [*Lit. Year Book.*] London, 1901

WOMAN and the wits ; epigrams on woman, love, and beauty ; collected by G. F. Monkshood [William James Clarke]. 8vo. Pp. viii. 174. [*Brit. Mus.*] London, 1899

WOMAN (a) at the helm. [A novel.] By the author of *Dr Edith Romney* [Anne Elliot]. 8vo. 3 vols. [*Lond. Lib. Cat.*] London, 1892

WOMAN beautiful. By "Mme Qui Vive" [Helen Follett Stevans]. 12mo.
Chicago, 1899

WOMAN (the) decides. [A romance.] By "Nomad" [Adèle Crafton-Smith]. 8vo. Pp. 339. [*Who's Who in Lit.*]
London, 1910

WOMAN (the) errant ; chapters from the Wonder Book of Barbara, the Commuter's Wife [Mrs Mabel Osgood Wright]. 8vo. Pp. 388. [*Brit. Mus.*] London, 1904

WOMAN (the) hater ; as it hath beene lately acted by the children of Paules. [By Francis Beaumont and John Fletcher.] 4to. No pagination. [*Pollard and Redgrave.*] London, 1607
This is the first edition. The edition published in 1648 has the name of John Fletcher only.

WOMAN ; her glory, her shame, and her God. By Saladin [William Stewart Ross, M.A.]. 8vo. 2 vols. [*Brit. Mus.*] London, 1894

WOMAN ; her true place and standing. An address by An American clergyman [John S. Davenport]. Third edition. 8vo. Pp. 16. Edinburgh, 1877

WOMAN (the) I loved, and the woman who loved me. By the author of *Agnes Tremorne*, etc. [Isabella Blagden]. 8vo. Pp. 292. [*Camb. Univ. Lib.*] London, 1865
Agnes Tremorne is not anonymous.

WOMAN (a) in armor. By H. M. Lewtral [Mary Hartwell, later Mrs Catherwood]. 8vo. [Cushing's *Init. and Pseud.* i. 171.]   New York, 1875

WOMAN (a) in it; a sketch of feminine misadventure. By "Rita" [Eliza M. J. Gollan, later Mrs W. Desmond Humphreys]. 8vo. Pp. x. 247. [*Lit. Year Book.*]   London, 1895

WOMAN (the) in the firelight. [A novel.] By Oliver Sandys [Mrs Marguerite Barclay.] 8vo. Pp. 284.   London, 1911

WOMAN (a) intervenes; or, the mistress of the mine. By Luke Sharp [Robert Barr]. 8vo. Pp. 375. [*Bril. Mus.*]   New York [1896]

WOMAN (a) of emotions, and other poems. By Rowland Thirlmere [John Walker]. 8vo. Pp. 198. [*Who's Who in Lit.*]   London, 1901

WOMAN (the) of feeling. [By William Henry Ireland.] 12mo. 4 vols. [*Brit. Mus.*]   London, 1804
Signed "Paul Persius" at the end of Vol. IV.

WOMAN (a) of fortune; a novel. By Christian Reid [Mrs Frances C. Tiernan, *née* Fisher]. 8vo. Pp. 285. [Cushing's *Init. and Pseud.* i. 249.]   New York, 1896

WOMAN (a) of forty; a monograph. By Esmé Stuart [Amélie Claire Leroy]. 8vo. 3 vols. [*Brit. Mus.*]   London, 1894

WOMAN (a) of impulse; a sentimental episode. By Joseph Prague [Andrew Lang Nisbet]. 8vo. Pp. 317. [*Brit. Mus.*]   London, 1912

WOMAN (the) of mystery. By Georges Ohnet [Georges Hénot]. Translated from the French by F. Rothwell. 8vo. Pp. 374. [*Lond. Lib. Cat.*]   London, 1911

WOMAN (the) of Samaria. [By Ann Alexander, *née* Tuke.] 12mo. [Smith's *Cat. of Friends' Books*, i. 8.]   London, 1846

WOMAN (a) of Samaria. [A novel.] By Rita [Eliza M. J. Gollan, later Mrs W. Desmond Humphreys]. 8vo. Pp. 338. [*Brit. Mus.*]   London, 1900

WOMAN (the) of the world; a novel. By the authoress of the *Diary of a désennuyée* [Mrs Catherine Grace Frances Gore]. 12mo. 3 vols. [*Brit. Mus.*]   London, 1838

WOMAN (the) Ruth. [A novel.] By Curtis Yorke [Mrs W. S. Richmond Lee, *née* —— Jex-Long]. 8vo. Pp. 316. [*Lit. Year Book.*]   London, 1914

WOMAN (a) scorned; a novel. By E. Owens Blackburne, author of *The quest of the heir*, etc. [Elizabeth Owens Blackburne Casey]. 8vo. 3 vols.   London, 1876

WOMAN; sketches of the history, genius, disposition, accomplishments, employments, customs, and importance of the fair sex, in all parts of the world. . . . By a friend to the sex [Rev. John Adams, M.A.]. 12mo. Pp. 400. [Watt's *Bibl. Brit.*]   London, 1790

WOMAN (a) snared. By Bertha M. Clay [Charlotte M. Braeme]. 8vo. Pp. 252. [*Amer. Cat.*] London [1912]

WOMAN suffrage; a refutation and an appeal. By a citizen [Mrs M. S. Wolstenholme]. 8vo.   Sydney, N.S.W., 1896

WOMAN (a) ventures. By John Graham [David Graham Phillips]. 8vo.   New York, 1902

WOMAN (the) who came between. [A novel.] By Effie Adelaide Rowlands [E. Maria Albanesi]. 8vo. Pp. 251. [*Brit. Mus.*]   London, 1920

WOMAN (the) who dared. [A novel.] By Lawrence L. Lynch [Emma M. Murdoch, later Mrs Van Deventer]. 8vo. Pp. 472. [*Who's Who in Lit.*]   London [1902]

WOMAN (the) who didn't. [A novel.] By Victoria Cross [Miss Vivian Cory]. 8vo. [*Who's Who in Lit.*]   London, 1898

WOMAN (the) who looked back. By M. Hamilton [Mrs Churchill Luck, *née* —— Spottiswoode-Ashe]. 8vo. Pp. 296. [*Who's Who in Lit.*]   London, 1914

WOMAN (the) who vowed. By Ellison Harding [Edmund Kelly]. 8vo.   London, 1908
Originally published in New York (1907) with the title "The Demetrian."

WOMAN (the) who wouldn't. [A novel.] By Lucas Cleeve [Mrs Howard Kingscote, *née* Adelina G. I. Wolff]. 8vo. Pp viii. 225. [*Brit. Mus.*]   London, 1895

WOMAN (a) with a secret. [A novel.] By Paul Cushing [Roland Alexander Wood-Seys]. 8vo. [*Brit. Mus.*]   London, 1885

WOMAN (the) with the diamonds; a novel. . . . By Florence Warden [Florence Alice Price, later Mrs George E. James]. 8vo. Pp. 102. [*Who's Who in Lit.*]   London, 1895

WOMAN (the) with two words. [A tale.] By Sarah Tytler [Henrietta Keddie]. 8vo. Pp. vi. 208. [*Brit. Mus.*]   London, 1885

WOMAN'S a riddle ; a romantic tale. By Anne of Swansea, author of *Conviction, Cesario Rosalba*, etc. [Anne Hatton]. 12mo. 4 vols.
London, 1824
Also ascribed to Julia Ann Kemble.

WOMAN'S (the) advocate. [Edited by T. J. H. *i.e.* Thomas J. Haslam.] Nos. 1-3. 8vo. [*Brit. Mus.*] Dublin, 1874

WOMAN'S (a) aye and nay. [A novel.] By Lucas Cleeve [Mrs Howard Kingscote, *née* Adelina G. I. Wolff]. 8vo. Pp. 318. [*Who's Who in Lit.*]
London, 1908

WOMAN'S (the) conquest ; a tragicomedy, as it was acted by the Duke of York's servants. Written by the Honourable E. H. [Edward Howard]. 4to. [Arber's *Term Cat.* i. 532.]
London, 1671

WOMAN'S devotion ; a novel. [By Mrs Julia C. Stretton.] 8vo. 3 vols.
London, 1855
Wrongly ascribed to Mrs Anne Marsh-Caldwell, and to Henrietta Keddie.

WOMAN'S dower ; a sketch in black and white. . . . By Austin Clare [Miss W. M. James]. 8vo. [*Who's Who in Lit.*] London, 1887

WOMAN'S (a) error. By Bertha M. Clay [Charlotte M. Braeme]. 8vo. [*Amer. Cat.*] New York, 1886

WOMAN'S (a) example, and a nation's work ; a tribute to Florence Nightingale. [By Fred. Milnes Edge.] 12mo. London, 1864

WOMAN'S (a) face ; a romance. By Florence Warden [Florence Alice Price, later Mrs George E. James]. 8vo. [*Brit. Mus.*] London, 1890

WOMAN'S heart. [A novel.] By Mrs Alexander [Mrs Alexander Hector, *née* Annie French]. 8vo. 3 vols. [*Brit. Mus.*] London, 1894

WOMAN'S (a) heart. By Mrs Mark Peabody [Mrs Metta Victoria Victor, *née* Fuller]. 8vo. [*Cushing's Init. and Pseud.* i. 226.] New York, 1865

WOMAN'S (the) kingdom ; a love story. By the author of *John Halifax, Gentleman*, etc. [Dinah Maria Mulock, later Mrs Craik]. 8vo. 3 vols.
London, 1869

WOMAN'S love ; or the triumph of patience : a drama, in five acts. [By Thomas Wade.] 12mo. [*Brit. Mus.*]
London, 1829

WOMAN'S (a) love-story. By Bertha M. Clay [Charlotte M. Braeme]. 12mo. [*Amer. Cat.*] New York, 1887

WOMAN'S (a) poems. [By Mrs Sarah Morgan Piatt, *née* Bryan.] 8vo. [*Cushing's Init. and Pseud.* i. 309.]
Boston, 1871

WOMAN'S service on the Lord's Day. [By Emily Bickersteth.] 8vo.
London, 1861

WOMAN'S sphere in the world. [By Alexander Ledingham.] 8vo.
[1886]

WOMAN'S (a) temptation. By Bertha M. Clay [Charlotte M. Braeme]. 12mo. [*Amer. Cat.*] New York, 1885

WOMAN'S (a) thoughts about women. By the author of *John Halifax, Gentleman*, etc. [Dinah Maria Mulock, later Mrs Craik]. 8vo. Pp. v. 348.
London, 1858

WOMAN'S (a) tragedy ; or, the detective's task. [A novel.] By Lawrence L. Lynch [Mrs Emma van Deventer, *née* Murdoch]. 8vo. Pp. 324. [*Who's Who in Lit.*] London, 1904

WOMAN'S (a) trials. By Grace Ramsay [Kathleen O'Meara]. 8vo. 3 vols. [*Brit. Mus.*] London, 1867

WOMAN'S (a) vengeance ; a novel. By the author of *Cecil's tryst, Lost Sir Massingberd*, etc. [James Payn]. 8vo. 3 vols. [*Brit. Mus.*] London, 1872

WOMAN'S (a) victory ; a novel. By the author of *Elsie ; a lowland sketch* [Agnes C. Maitland]. 8vo. 3 vols. [*Brit. Mus.*] London, 1876

WOMAN'S (the) victory ; and other stories. By Maarten Maartens [Josef M. W. van der Poorten-Schwartz]. 8vo. Pp. 364. [*Brit. Mus.*]
London, 1906

WOMAN'S (a) war. By Bertha M. Clay [Charlotte M. Braeme]. 12mo. [*Amer. Cat.*] New York, 1887

WOMAN'S witchcraft ; or, the curse of coquetry. By Corinne L'Estrange [Henry Hartshorne, M.D.]. 8vo.
Philadelphia, 1854

WOMEN and their work ; wives and daughters of the Old Testament. By Marianne Farningham [Marianne Hearne, of Farningham]. 8vo. Pp. 124. [*Brit. Mus.*] London, 1906

WOMEN as they are ; or, the manners of the day. [By Mrs Catherine Grace Frances Gore.] Second edition. 12mo. 3 vols. [*D. N. B.* vol. 22, p. 237.]
London, 1830

WOMEN composers. By C. Herman [Otto Ebel]. 12mo. New York, 1902

WOMEN in the East. Les femmes en Orient. Par Mme. la Comtesse Dora d'Istria [The Princess Koltzoff-Massalsky, *née* Helena Ghika, daughter of the Prince Alexander Ghika, Exhospodar of Wallachia]. 2 vols. [*Athenæum*, 3rd August 1861, p. 148.] Zurich and London, 1861

WOMEN must weep. By F. Harold Williams [Rev. F. W. Orde Warde]. 8vo. [*Who's Who in Lit.*] London, 1890

WOMEN must weep. By Sarah Tytler, author of *Jean Keir of Craigneil*, etc. [Henrietta Keddie]. 8vo. [*Brit. Mus.*] London, 1901

WOMEN (the) of India, and what can be done for them. [By Rev. John Murdoch.] 8vo. Madras, 1888

WOMEN (the) of Paris. By the author of *Women of London*, etc. [Bracebridge Hemyng]. 8vo. [*Brit. Mus.*] London [1884]

WOMEN (the) of the Gospels, The three wakings, and other verses. By the author of *Chronicles of the Schönberg-Cotta family* [Mrs Elizabeth Charles, *née* Rundle]. New edition, with additions. 8vo. Pp. 276. London, 1868

WOMEN of the last days of old France. By the author of *On the edge of the storm*, etc. [Margaret Roberts]. 8vo. Pp. vi. 403. [Courtney's *Secrets*, p. 68.] London, 1872

WOMEN of the Salons, and other French portraits. By S. G. Tallentyre [Beatrice Hall]. 8vo. Pp. 244. [*Who's Who in Lit.*] London, 1901

WOMEN (the) of the South. By Mary Forrest [Julia Deane Freeman]. 8vo. [Cushing's *Init. and Pseud.* i. 104.] New York, 1860

WOMEN ; or, pour et contre : a tale. By the author of *Bertram*, etc. [Charles Robert Maturin]. 12mo. 3 vols. [Watt's *Bibl. Brit.*] Edinburgh, 1818

WOMEN types of to-day ; the Venus, the Juno, the Minerva ; or modern casts from ancient moulds. By "Da Libra" [Colonel —— Brain]. 8vo. Pp. x. 366. London, 1907

WOMEN who work. By Theo. Gift [Dora Havers, later Mrs Boulger]. 8vo. London, 1874

WOMEN'S conquest of New York. By Ivory Black [Thomas Allibone Janvier]. 8vo. New York, 1893

WOMEN'S degrees. By D. C. H. [Harry D. Catling]. Verses. 8vo. [Bartholomew's *Camb. Books*, p. 274.] Cambridge, 1897

WOMENS speaking justified, proved and allowed by the Scriptures, all such as speak by the spirit and power of the Lord Jesus, and how women were the first that preached the tidings of the resurrection of Jesus, etc. [By Margaret Fox, *née* Fell.] 4to. [*Brit. Mus.*] London, 1667
Signed : M. F.

WON ! By the author of *Jennie of "The Prince's"* [Mrs Bertha H. Buxton]. 8vo. 3 vols. [*D. N. B.* vol. 8, p. 105.] London, 1877

WON by waiting. [A novel.] By Edna Lyall [Ada Ellen Bayly]. 8vo. London, 1888

WONDER (the) of a kingdome ; dedicated to the Junto at Westminster. . . . [By John Taylor, the water poet.] 4to. [*D. N. B.* vol. 55, p. 437.] London, 1648

WONDER (the) of Lourdes ; what it is and what it means. By John Oxenham [William Arthur Dunkerley]. 8vo. Pp. 62. [*Brit. Mus.*] London, 1924

WONDER (the) of the Bishop of Meaux [Bossuet], upon perusal of Dr Bull's books, consider'd and answer'd. [By Edward Stephens.] 4to. Pp. 12. [*D. N. B.* vol. 54, p. 171.] London, 1704

WONDER (a) ; or, an honest Yorkshire-man : a ballad opera, as it is perform'd at the theatres with universal applause. [By Henry Carey.] 8vo. [*N. and Q.* 18th February 1860, p. 126.] London, 1736

WONDER (the) ; or propositions for a safe and well-grounded peace : proposed by a Parliament-man [Henry Anderson]. 4to. [*Brit. Mus.*] London, 1648

WONDERFUL (the) adventure. [A novel.] By Mrs George Norman [Mrs George Blount]. 8vo. Pp. 318. [*Catholic Who's Who.*] London, 1914

WONDERFUL (the) adventures of Captain Priest . . . with other legends. By the author of *A stray Yankee in Texas* [Samuel A. Hammett]. 12mo. [*Brit. Mus.*] New York, 1855

WONDERFUL (the) adventures of Tuflongbo and his elfin company, in their journey with Little Content through the enchanted forest. By Holme Lee, author of *Legends from fairy land*, etc. [Harriet Parr]. 8vo. Pp. vi. 245. [*Brit. Mus.*] London, 1861

WONDERFUL (a) book ; or, my experience in three trances. [By William Wilson.] 8vo. Pp. 15. [*Brit. Mus.*]
Toronto, 1895

WONDERFUL cities of the world. By Hazel Shepard [Helen Ainslie Smith]. 4to.   London, 1887

WONDERFUL (the) confirmation of the succession of the Kingdom of Christ at 1697, derived from the 42 moons then ending ; given by prophecy, etc. [By T. Beverley.] 4to. [*Brit. Mus.*]   [London, 1690 ?]

WONDERFUL (a) cure. *See* "Home plays for ladies."

WONDERFUL curiosities, rarities, and wonders in England, Scotland, and Ireland. By R. B. [Richard or Robert Burton, *i.e.* Nathaniel Crouch]. 12mo. [*D. N. B.* vol. 8, p. 15.] London, 1682

WONDERFUL (the) deeds and doings of the little giant Boab, and his talking raven, Tabib. By Irwin Longman [Ingersoll Lockwood]. 8vo. [*Amer. Cat.*]   Boston, 1891

WONDERFUL (the) drama of Punch and Judy, and their little dog Toby. By Papernose Woodensconce, Esq. [Robert Barnabas Brough] ; with illustrations by "The Owl" [Charles Henry Bennett]. [Cushing's *Init. and Pseud.* i. 309.]   London, 1854

WONDERFUL (the) life. By Hesba Stretton, author of *Lost Gip*, etc. [Sarah Smith]. 8vo. Pp. viii. 251.
London, 1875
See the note to "Alone in London."

WONDERFUL love ; being the romantic adventures of Glory West, actress. By "Pan" [Leslie Beresford]. 8vo. Pp. viii. 342. [*Who's Who in Lit.*]
London, 1916

WONDERFUL (the) love of God to men ; or, heaven opened in earth. [By William Peckitt.] 8vo. [*Brit. Mus.*]   York, 1794
Peckitt's name is given only in the text on the last page.

WONDERFUL mates. [A tale.] By Brenda [Mrs —— Castle Smith, *née* —— Meyrick]. 8vo. Pp. 320. [*Who's Who in Lit.*]   London, 1900

WONDERFUL (the) narrative ; or, a faithful account of the French profits, their agitations, extasies, and inspirations. . . . In a letter to a friend. [By Charles Chauncy, D.D., of Boston.] 12mo. Pp. 130.   Glasgow, 1742
Signed : Anti-Enthusiasticus.

WONDERFUL prodigies of judgment and mercy ; discovered in above three hundred memorable histories. . . . Faithfully collected from antient and modern authors, of undoubted authority and credit, and imbellished with divers curious pictures, of several remarkable passages therein. By R. B. author of the *History of the wars of England*, etc. [Richard or Robert Burton, *i.e.* Nathaniel Crouch]. 12mo. Pp. 2, 235. [*Bodl.*]   London, 1682

WONDERFUL (the) travellers . . . containing "A journey into the interior of the earth," and "Five weeks in a balloon." By Jules Verne. [Translated from the French by Fred Amadeus Malleson.] 8vo.   London [1877]

WONDERFUL (the) wapentake. By a "Son of the Soil" [James S. Fletcher]. 8vo.   Chicago, 1895

WONDERFUL works ; or, the miracles of Christ. By a clergyman's daughter [Mrs Ellen Clacy]. 12mo. [Cushing's *Init. and Pseud.* i. 63.] London, 1864

WONDERFULL (a), strange and miraculous, astrologicall prognostication for this yeer of our Lord God, 1591 ; discouering such wonders to happen this yeere, as neuer chaunced since Noes floud : wherein if there be found one lye, the author will loose his credit for euer. By Adam Fouleweather, student in asse-tronomy [Thomas Nash]. 4to. B. L. No pagination. [*D. N. B.* vol. 40, p. 104.]
London [1591]
A counter attack on Richard Harvey, astrologer and divine, who had attacked Nash, Greene and Lyly, in his "Theological Discourse of the Lamb of God," and in his "Plaine Percevall." This strife was a re-echo of the Martin Mar-Prelate controversy.

WONDERFULL (the) yeare, 1603 ; wherein is shewed the picture of London, lying sicke of the plague : at the ende of all (like a mery epilogue to a dull play) certain tales are cut out in sundry fashions, of purpose to shorten the liues of long winter nights, that lye watching in the darke for us. [By Thomas Dekker.] 4to. Pp. 48. B. L. [Corser's *Collectanea Anglo-Poetica*, v. 129.]   London, N.D.

WONDERS in flowers and plants, as seen in Kew Gardens. [By Philip Henry Gosse.] 8vo. [*Brit. Mus.*]
[London, 1859]

WONDERS no miracles; or, Mr Valentine Greatrates gift of healing examined, upon occasion of a sad effect of his stroaking, March the 7, 1665 at one Mr Cressets house in Charter-House-Yard: in a letter to a reverend divine living near that place. [By David Lloyd, M.A., Canon of St Asaph.] 4to. [*Bodl.; D. N. B.* vol. 33, p. 417.]   London, 1666

WONDERS of electricity. . . . By Ascott R. Hope [Robert Hope Moncrieff]. 8vo. Pp. 128. [*Brit. Mus.*]   London [1881]

WONDERS (the) of God in the wilderness; or, the lives of the most celebrated saints of the oriental desarts. Collected out of the genuine works of the holy fathers and other ancient ecclesiastical writers. . . . [By Bishop Richard Challoner.] 8vo. [*D. N. B.* vol. 9, p. 443.]   London, 1755

WONDERS of sculpture. . . . Translated from the French of L. Viardot by N. D'Anvers [Mrs Nancy Bell, *née* Meugens]. 8vo. [*Brit. Mus.*]   London, 1872

WONDERS (the) of the heavens displayed, in twenty lectures. By the author of *The hundred wonders of the world* [ostensibly the Rev. C. C. Clarke, but really Sir Richard Phillips]. 8vo. Pp. xxxv. 315.   London, 1821

WONDERS of the ice world. . . . By Ascott R. Hope [Robert Hope Moncrieff]. 8vo. Pp. 128. [*Brit. Mus.*]   London [1884]

WONDERS (the) of the vegetable kingdom display'd; in a series of letters. By the author of *Select female biography* [Mary Roberts]. 8vo. Pp. 5, 243. [Smith's *Cat. of Friends' Books*, ii. 500.]   London, 1822

WONDERS of the vegetable world. [By William Henry Davenport Adams.] 12mo. Pp. 127.   London, 1867
Preface signed: W. H. D. A.

WONDERS of the volcano. By Ascott R. Hope [Robert Hope Moncrieff]. 8vo. Pp. 128. [*Brit. Mus.*]   London [1880]

WONDERS of the West. By a Canadian [James Lynne Alexander]. 8vo. [Cushing's *Init. and Pseud.* i. 49.]   Toronto, 1825

WONDERS (the) of to-morrow; and the crown of life: two addresses. [By James Munro Sandham.] 8vo. [*Brit. Mus.*]   Frome Selwood, 1853

WONDROUS strange; a novel. By the author of *Mabel*, etc. [Mrs Emma Newby, *née* Barry]. Second edition. 12mo. 3 vols. [Boase's *Mod. Eng. Biog.*]   London, 1864

WONDROUS (the) tale of Alroy. The rise of Iskander. By the author of *Vivian Grey*, etc. [Benjamin Disraeli]. 12mo. 3 vols. [*D. N. B.* vol. 15, p. 116.]   London, 1833

WONSTON confirmation tracts. [By Alexander Robert Charles Dallas, rector of Wonston, Hants.] 12mo.   London, 1840
These tracts are twelve in number, having all the general title as given above. Each tract has, however, an addition, explanatory of the particular aspect in which Confirmation is viewed by the author.

WOO-CREEL (the); or, the Bill o' Bashan: a tale. [By Sir Alexander Boswell.] 4to. Pp. 11. [*Brit. Mus.*]   Auchinleck, 1816
Dedication signed: A. B.

WOOD (the) end; a novel. By J. E. Buckrose [Mrs Falconer Jameson]. 8vo. [*Who's Who in Lit.*]   London, 1907

WOOD, hay, and stubble. By Fleeta [Kate W. Hamilton]. 8vo. [*Amer. Cat.*]   Philadelphia, 1886

WOOD Island light; or, Ned Sanford's refuge. By James Otis [James Otis Kaler]. 8vo. Pp. 246. [Cushing's *Init. and Pseud.* i. 220.]   Boston [1895]

WOOD notes; or, Carolina carols: a collection of North Carolina poetry, compiled by La Tenella [Mrs Mary Clarke, *née* Bayard]. 8vo. [Kirk's *Supp.*]   Raleigh, N.C., 1854

WOOD (the) nymph; a novel. By the author of *Ariel*, etc. [Thomas Dutton, M.A.]. 8vo.   London, 1806
Ariel (1796) bears the author's name.

WOOD-CART (the); and other tales from the South of France. By F. M. P. [Frances Mary Peard]. 8vo. [*Brit. Mus.*]   London, 1867

WOODCRAFT. By Nessmuk [George W. Sears]. 8vo. [Cushing's *Init. and Pseud.* i. 203.]   New York, 1884

WOODCRAFT; a story of the South at the close of the Revolution. By Frank Cooper [William Gilmore Simms]. 8vo. [Cushing's *Init. and Pseud.* i. 67.]   New York, 1885

WOODEN (the) horse for the rounder, and the horse without a head. . . . By Robin Baragwaneth [John Jeffery]. 12mo. [Cushing's *Init. and Pseud.* i. 30.]   Penzance, 1824

WOODEN (the) works of Thomas Anonymous [Thomas Childs]. 8vo. [*Amer. Cat.*]   Sumter, So. Carolina, 1904

WOODEN (the) world dissected; in the character of a ship of war: as also, the characters of all the officers, from the captain to the common sailor. . . . By a lover of mathematics [Edward Ward]. The second edition. 12mo. Pp. 86. [*Lond. Lib. Cat. Supp.*]
London, 1707

WOODLAND (the) companion; or a brief description of British trees, with some account of their uses. By the author of *Evenings at home* [John Aikin, M.D.]. 12mo. [*Brit. Mus.*]
London, 1815
Signed: J. A.

WOODLAND, moor, and stream; being the notes of a naturalist [Denham Jordan]; edited by J. A. Owen. 8vo. Pp. 224. [*Brit. Mus.*] London, 1889

WOODLEIGH. By the author of *One and twenty*, etc. [Frederick William Robinson]. 8vo. 3 vols. [*Brit. Mus.*]
London, 1859

WOODMAN (the). [A novel.] By Jules de Glouvet [Guernay de Beaure-paire]: translated from the French. 8vo. [*Baker's Guide to Fiction.*]
New York, 1892

WOOD-NUTS from a fairy hazel bush, cracked for little people. By Jean D'Ensinge [John Marten]. 8vo. Pp. viii. 201. [*Brit. Mus.*] London, 1869

WOODRANGERS' tales. By Victor St Clair [George Waldo Browne]. 8vo. [*Amer. Cat.*]
Brooklyn, N.Y., 1907

WOODS and wild flowers. By E. G. L. B. [Edward George Lytton Bulwer, first Lord Lytton]. 8vo. London, 1875

WOOD'S plot discovered by a member of his society; with his apology to his countrymen. [By Jonathan Swift.] 12mo. [*Brit. Mus.*] Dublin, 1724

WOOD-SPIRIT (the); a novel. [By Ernest Charles Jones.] 12mo. 2 vols.
London, 1841

WOODSTOCK; an elegy. [By Hugh Dalrymple.] 4to. [*N. and Q.* 1 Ser. ix. 589.] 1761

WOODSTOCK; or, The cavalier: a tale of the year Sixteen hundred and fifty-one. By the author of *Waverley*, etc. [Sir Walter Scott]. 8vo. 3 vols.
Edinburgh, 1826

WOOING!! and cooing!! or, C——tte and Co——gh; a poem. By Peter Pindar, Esq. [John Wolcot, M.D.]. Second edition. 8vo. Pp. 27.
London [1816]
On the contemplated marriage between Princess Charlotte and Prince Leopold.

WOOING and warring in the wilderness. By Se De Kay [Charles D. Kirke]. [*Cushing's Init. and Pseud.* i. 79.]
New York, 1860

WOOING (the) o't; a novel. By Mrs Alexander [Annie Hector, *née* French]. 8vo. 3 vols. London, 1873

WOOING (the) of May. [A novel.] By Alan St Aubyn [Frances Marshall]. 8vo. Pp. vi. 292. [*Brit. Mus.*]
London, 1897

WOOING (the) of Webster, and other stories. By A. M. [A. Murdoch]. 8vo. Pp. 290. [*Brit. Mus.*] London [1899]

WOOL encouraged without exportation; or, practical observations on wool and the woollen manufacture. . . . By a Wiltshire clothier, F. A. S. [Henry Wansey]. 8vo. [*Brit. Mus.*]
London, 1791

WOOLLEN draper's (a) letter on the French treaty to his friends and fellow tradesmen all over England. [By Lieut. J. Mackenzie.] 8vo. Pp. 48.
London, 1786
Signed: R. J. Woollen Draper. Dedication in MS. signed by the author.

WOOLLEN (a) shroud; or learn to dye: to be given at burials. By C. B. [Clement Barksdale]. 12mo. [*Camb. Univ. Lib.*] London, 1679

WOORE (the) country. [Verses. By Rowland E. Egerton Warburton.] 8vo. Chester, 1834
See the title-pages of subsequent works.

WORCESTER dumb-bells; a ballad: to the tune of All in the land of Essex. [By Thomas Warton.] S. sh. [*Bodl.*]
N.P., N.D.

WORCESTER gaudy, 1858. By a late fellow [James Thomas Bainbridge Landon, M.A.]. 4to. Pp. 3.
N.P., N.D.

WORCESTERS apophthegmes; or, witty sayings of Henry, late Marquess of Worcester. By T. B. [Thomas Bayly, D.D.]. 4to. Pp. 114. [*Thomason's Coll. of Tracts*, i. 801.] London, 1650

WORCESTERS elegie, and evlogie. By J. T. [John Toy] Mr. of Arts. 4to. No pagination. [*Lowndes' Bibl. Man.*]
London, 1638

WORCESTER-SHIRE (the) petition to the parliament for the ministry of England defended, by a minister of Christ in that county; in answer to xvi. queries, printed in a book, called, A brief discovery of the threefold estate of Antichrist: whereunto is added, xvii. counter-queries, and an humble monition to parliament, people and ministers. [By Richard Baxter.] 4to. Pp. 4, 40. [*Smith's Bibl. Anti-Quak.* p. 59.] London, 1653

WORD (a) about a new election, that the people of England may see the happy difference between English liberty and French slavery; and may consider well, before they make the exchange. [By Daniel Defoe.] 8vo. [Wilson's *Life of Defoe*, 122.]   1710

WORD (the) and the life. [Poems. By R. H. Cooke, F.R.C.S.] 12mo. [*Brit. Mus.*]   Private print, 1883

WORD (a) at parting; in a letter to the Rev. Edward Manley; being a sequel to the "Brief account of the Unitarians"; with a commentary on that writer's "Creed of Contradictions," and an answer to his "Questions proposed to the illuminati." By the author of *An Appeal to Scripture and tradition* [Sir Charles A. Elton]. 12mo. [Green's *Bibl. Somers.* ii. 386.]
London, 1825

WORD (a) for inquiry previous to decision in the matter of the present manifestations of, or pretentions to, the gifts of speaking with unknown tongues and prophesying. By one of the congregation of the National Scotch Church [William Harding]. 8vo. Pp. 56.   London, 1832

WORD (a) for that section in the Church, who, in the recent struggle, took up what may be called a medium position. [By David Logan, minister of Stenton.] 8vo. Pp. 4. [*D. Laing.*]
Edinburgh [1844]

WORD (a) for the Empire. By Rowland Thirlmere [John Walker]. 8vo. [*Who's Who in Lit.*]   London, 1907

WORD (a) from the Bible . . . on behalf of enslaved British subjects. By H. P. [Henry Pownall]. 8vo. London, 1829

WORD (a) in behalf of the king, that he may see who they are that honour all men, and love the brother-hood, that fear God, and honour the king, according as it is written in the Scriptures of truth, see 1 Pet. 2. 17. [By George Fox.] 4to. Pp. 15. [Smith's *Cat. of Friends' Books*, i. 659.]   London, 1660
Signed: G. F.

WORD (a) in season; being a parallel between the intended bloody massacre of the people of the Jews, in the reign of King Ahasuerus; and the hellish powder-plot against the Protestants, in the reign of King James. . . . By H. C., a lover of true Protestants [Henry Care]. 4to. Pp. 2, 47. London, 1679

WORD (a) in season; or, how the corn-grower may yet grow rich, and his labourer happy; addressed to the Stout British Farmer. [By Rev. Samuel Smith, M.A., vicar of Lois-Weedon-by-Weston, Towcester.] 8vo. [*Nat. Lib. of Scot.*]   London, 1849

WORD (a) in season to all in authority; with weighty considerations what persons, practices and things, doth chiefly cause division and contention, rending of kingdoms, and distresse of nations. . . . Published by a lover of truth and the kingdom of peace, J. C. [John Collens]. 4to. Pp. 26. [*Brit. Mus.*]   London, 1660
The Postscript was written by John Anderdon.

WORD (a) in season to all sorts of well-minded people in this miserably distracted and distempered nation, plainly manifesting, that the safety and well-being of the commonwealth under God dependeth on the fidelity and steadfast adherence of the people to those whom they have chosen, and on their ready compliance with them. . . . [By John Sadler, M.D.] 4to. [*Brit. Mus.*]
London, 1646

WORD (a) in season to the traders and manufacturers of Great Britain. [By William Combe.] Sixth edition. 8vo. Pp. 22. [*D. N. B.* vol. 11, p. 433.]
London, printed: Edinburgh, reprinted, 1792
Signed: A true-born Englishman.

WORD (a) in season to working women. By Austin Clare [Miss W. M. James]. 8vo. Pp. vi. 119. [*Who's Who in Lit.*]   London, 1889

WORD (the) made flesh; or the true humanity of God in Christ demonstrated from the Scriptures. [By Thomas Carlyle, advocate.] 8vo. Pp. 234. [*G. C. Boase.*]   Edinburgh, 1829

WORD (a) more on the Moderatorship; in a letter to the Rev. William Cunningham, of Trinity College Church, Edinburgh. By a bystander [James Moncrieff]. 8vo. Pp. 54.
Edinburgh, 1837

WORD (a) of caution and of comfort to the middle and lower classes of society; being a pastor's advice to his flock in time of trouble. [By Rev. Thomas Frognall Dibdin.] [*Olphar Hamst*, p. 182.]   London, 1831

WORD (a) of comfort; or, a discourse concerning the late lamentable accident of a fall of a roome, at a catholike sermon in the Black-friars at London. By I. R.-P. [John Floyd, priest]. 4to. [*Brit. Mus.*]   St Omer, 1623

WORD (a) of comfort to a melancholy country. By Amicus Patriæ [Rev. John Wise]. 8vo.   Boston, 1721

WORD (a) of friendly admonition to a Jew. [By Joel Abraham Knight.] The second edition. 12mo. [*Brit. Mus.*]   London, 1796

WORD (the) of God and Anglo-Israelism; an argument founded on Scripture. By C. M. G. [Colonel C. M. Gumm]. 8vo. Bath, 1885

WORD (the) of God the best guide to all persons, at all times, and in all places ; or, a collection of Scripture-texts, plainly shewing such things as are necessary for every Christians knowledg and practice. By the author of *The Best companion* [William Howell]. 8vo. Pp. 10, 213, 3. [*Bodl.*] Oxford, 1689

WORD (a) of information to them that need it ; briefly opening some most weighty passages of God's dispensations among the sons of men, from the beginning ; and insisting a little upon the state and condition of the nations, wherein they now stand, and particularly of England : . . . By W. T. [William Tomlinson]. 4to. Pp. 47. [*Bodl.*] London, 1660

WORD (a) of reproof, and advice to my late fellow-souldiers and officers of the English, Irish and Scotish army ; with some inrhoad made upon the hireling and his mass-house, university, orders, degrees, vestments, poperies, heathenism, etc. With a short catalogue of some of the fighting priests, and for just cause given, have given them a blow in one of their eyes (pickt out of the whores head) which they call, a fountain of religion, but is a sink of iniquity . . . . By a lover of good men, good laws, good governments and governours, good judges and ministers, as at the beginning : who hates nor fears no man, and is a lover and honourer of all men in the Lord, but cannot give flattering title, or respect the person of any man. E. B. [Edward Billing]. 4to. Pp. 96. [*Bodl.*] London, 1659

WORD (a) of testimony ; or, a corrected account of the evidence adduced by the Trustees of the National Scotch Church in support of their charges against the Rev. Edward Irving, and his defence. [By William Harding.] 8vo. Pp. 86. London, 1832

WORD (the) of the Lord, To his beloved Citty New-Ierusalem, come from God, cloathed with the excellency of the glory of his love ; and is the bride the Lambs wife, with the flowings of the tender compassionate bowels of the Lord Jesus, to all the mourners in Sion. . . . [By William Dewsbury.] (Given forth in York Castle, the 19. of the first moneth, 1663.) 4to. Pp. 7. N.P. [1663]

WORD (the) of the Lord to Sion the new Jerusalem, the bride the Lambs wife, the excellency of all the glory that is amongst the people ; though she be now in deep sufferings, in fulness of time God will· clear the innocency of her children. . . . [By William Dewsbury.] 4to. Pp. 8. London, 1664 Signed : W. D.

WORD (a) of warning to his countrymen, regarding the relation existing between the nation and the Church. By an aged Scotsman [David Ker]. 8vo. Pp. 8. Edinburgh, 1882

WORD (a) of wisdom for the witty, addressed to Isaac Tomkins, author of " Thoughts upon the aristocracy of England." [By John Richards, M.P.] 8vo. Pp. 24. [*Manch. Free Lib. Cat.*] London, 1835

WORD (a) or two about the new Poor Law, addressed to his parishioners by a beneficed clergyman in Buckinghamshire. [By Lord Sidney Godolphin Osborne.] 8vo. [*Brit. Mus.*] London, 1835 Signed : S. G. O.

WORD (a) or two in vindication of the University of Oxford and of Magdalen College in particular from the posthumous aspersions of Mr Gibbon. [By James Hurdis, D.D.] 4to. Pp. 44. [Bishopstone, 1797]

WORD (a) or two of advice to William Warburton ; a dealer in many words. By a friend [Zachary Grey, LL.D.] ; with an appendix containing a taste of William's spirit of railing. 8vo. Pp. 26. [*Bodl.*] London, 1746 The Advice is signed : Thy friend in the truth, A. E. See above " A free and familiar letter." The letters A. E. are the vowels in Zachery Grey.

WORD (a) or two on the Liturgy, offered to the younger members of the English Church. . . . By A. M. [Alfred Miles]. 12mo. Pp. 72. [*Brit. Mus.*] London, 1837

WORD (a) or two ; or, architectural hints, in lines, in two parts, addressed to those Royal Academicians who are painters : written prior, as well as subsequent to the day of annual election for their president, 10th December 1805. . . . By Fabricia Nunnez, Spinster [Peter Coxe]. 4to. Pp. 49. [*Gent. Mag.* Dec. 1844, p. 653 ; Feb. 1808, p. 143.] London, 1806 See above, " Another word or two . . ."

WORD (a) or two to the 228 Members [of Parliament] who voted against the second reading of the Jews' Relief Bill, May 17. [By P. Anchini.] 8vo. London, 1830

WORD (the); the Star out of Jacob. By the author of *The golden ladder* [Anna Bartlett Warner and Susan Warner]. 8vo. Pp. vii. 271.
London, 1872
Preface signed : A. W.

WORD (a) to a drunkard. [By John Wesley, M.A.] 12mo. Pp. 4.
[London, 1780?]

WORD (a) to a young governess. By an old one [Katharine Naish]. 12mo. [Green's *Bibl. Somers.* i. 370.]
Bath, 1860

WORD (a) to Christ's ministers at the beginning of the year. [By Rev. Josiah Viney.] 12mo.
London [1864]

WORD (a) to his parishioners on their duty to the church at the present [Tractarian] crisis. By W. S. B. [William Simcox Bricknell]. 8vo. [*Brit. Mus.*]   London, 1837

WORD (a) to Mr Madan; or, free thoughts on his late celebrated defence of polygamy; in a letter to a friend. [By Rev. Henry Moore, Unitarian.] 8vo. [Murch's *Dissenters*, p. 512.]   N.P. 1781

WORD (a) to Mr [Hugh] Peters, and two words for the Parliament and Kingdom. By a friend to the Parliament, City, and Ministery of it [Rev. Nathaniel Ward]. 4to. Pp. 38. [*N. and Q.* March 1837, p. 237.]   London, 1647

WORD (a) to Mr Wil. Prynn, Esq. ; and two for the parliament and army : reproving the one, and justifying the other in their late proceedings : presented to the consideration of the readers of Mr William Prynn's last books. [By Henry Marten.] 4to. Pp. 16. [*Bodl.*]   London, 1649

WORD (a) to Parmenas, on his "Address to the members of the Baptist Church at Shrewsbury." By R. D. [Rev. Richard De Courcy, vicar of Shrewsbury]. 8vo. [Whitley's *Bapt. Bibl.* i. 202.]
Shrewsbury, 1776

WORD (a) to the Hutchinsonians; or, remarks on three extraordinary sermons lately preached before the University of Oxford, by the Rev. Dr Patten, the Rev. Mr Wetherall, and the Rev. Mr Horne. By a member of the University [Benjamin Kennicott, D.D.]. 8vo. Pp. 44. [*Darling's Cyclop. Bibl.*]   London, 1756

WORD (a) to the officers of the Army. [By Thomas Zachary.] 4to.
London, 1657
Signed : T. Z.

WORD (a) to the public. By the author of *Lucretia, Rienzi*, etc. [Edward G. E. Lytton Bulwer-Lytton, Lord Lytton]. 12mo. [*Brit. Mus.*]   London, 1847

WORD (a) to the quiet of the land, on the present dissensions in the Church. [By Andrew Coventry Dick, advocate.] 8vo. Pp. 46.   Edinburgh, 1838

WORD (a) to the sons of Africa. [By Luke Howard.] 8vo. [Smith's *Cat. of Friends' Books*, i. 92.]
London, 1822

WORD (a) to the wavering ; or an answer to the Enquiry into the present state of affairs : whether we owe allegiance to the King in these circumstances? &c. [By George Hicks.] With a postscript of subjection to the higher powers by Dr G. B—— [Gilbert Burnet]. 4to. Pp. 10. [*D. N. B.* vol. 26, p. 354 ; Clarke and Foxcroft's *Life of Burnet*, Appendix.]
London, 1689

WORD (a) to the wise ; in a letter to a city clergyman, recommended to the consideration of his brethren of the clergy especially those of the younger sort. [By Joseph Rawson, D.D.] 8vo. [Kennett's *Wisdom*, p. 110.]   London, 1711

WORD (a) to the wise ; or, an exhortation to the Roman Catholic clergy of Ireland. By a member of the Established Church [George Berkeley, Bishop of Cloyne]. 8vo. [*Trin. Coll. Dubl. Cat.*]   Dublin, 1749

WORD (a) to the world answering the darkness thereof concerning the perfect word of God to salvation. [By John Perrot.] 4to. Pp. 8. [*Brit. Mus.*]
London, 1658
Signed : J. P.

WORD (a) upon Deuteronomy. [By Rev. Daniel Edward.] 8vo. Pp. 58. [*New Coll. Lib.*]   Edinburgh, 1878

WORD (the) ; walks from Eden. By the author of *The wide, wide world* [Susan Warner]. 8vo. Pp. vi. 284. [Allibone's *Dict.*]   London, 1866

WORD-BOOK of the English tongue. By C. L. D. [Charles Louis Dessoulavy]. 8vo. Pp. vii. 216. [*Brit. Mus.*]   London, 1917

WORDS and their uses, past and present ; a study of the English language. By a Yankee [Richard Grant White]. [Cushing's *Init. and Pseud.* i. 311.]
New York, 1870

WORDS (the) and works of our Blessed Lord and their lessons for daily life. By the author of *Brampton rectory* [Mary M. Howard]. 8vo. 2 vols. [*Brit. Mus.*]   London, 1860

WORDS by an eye-witness ; the struggle in Natal. By "Linesman" [Captain Maurice Harold Grant]. 8vo. [*Brit. Mus.*]   Edinburgh, 1901

WORDS for peace. By a layman [Alfred Robert Cooke, journalist]. 8vo.
London, 1879

WORDS for the hour. [By Mrs Julia Ward Howe.] 12mo. [*Cushing's Anon.*] Boston, 1857

WORDS from a layman's ministry at Barnard Castle. [By George Brown.] 8vo. London, 1871

WORDS heard in quiet ; searchings out of the Book of the Lord. By E. A. W. [Miss Emily A. Wanton]. 12mo.
London, 1870

WORDS made visible ; or grammar and rhetorick accommodated to the lives and manners of men : represented in a country school for the entertainment and edification of the spectators. [By Samuel Shaw.] 8vo. Pp. 6, 187. [*Dyce Cat.* ii. 295.] London, 1679

WORDS of comfort to persecuted Catholics, written in exile, anno 1607. Letters from a cell in Dublin Castle, and diary of the Bohemian war of 1620. By H. F. [Henry Fitzsimon, S.J.]. 8vo. Pp. 284. [*Gillow's Bibl. Dict.*] Dublin, 1881

WORDS of counsel ; a mother's monitory to the daughter. [By Henriette Gislesen]. Translated from the fifth Norwegian edition by John Hazeland. 8vo. Christiania, 1869

WORDS of hope and comfort for those in sorrow. [By Mrs Julias C. Hare.] 8vo. London, 1874

WORDS (the) of Jesus. By the author of *The morning and night watches,* etc. [John Ross MacDuff, D.D.]. Fourth edition. 8vo. Pp. 127. [*Brit. Mus.*] London, 1854

WORDS of life's last years ; containing Christian emblems ; metrical prayers and sacred poems, translated from foreign writers. By the author of *Thoughts on devotion,* etc. [John Sheppard, of Frome.] 8vo. [*Olphar Hamst;* Green's *Bibl. Somers.* iii. 244.]
London, 1862

WORDS (the) of the hymnal noted complete ; with scriptural references. [By Thomas Helmore, M.A.] 12mo. Pp. 132, 8. [*D. N. B.* vol. 25, p. 372.]
London [*c.* 1870]

WORDS (the) of the songs, duets, glees, and other compositions in the operatic farce of " Arrived at Portsmouth. . . ." By the author of *Hartford Bridge* [William Pearce]. 8vo. [*Baker's Biog. Dram.*] London, 1794

WORDS (the) of the songs . . . in " The Nunnery," a comic opera. [By William Pearce.] 8vo. [*Baker's Biog. Dram.*]
London, 1785

WORDS (the) of the wise, designed for the entertainment and instruction of younger minds. [By John Potter.] 12mo. [*European Mag.* v. 283.]
London, 1768

WORK about the Five Dials. [By the Hon. Alethea Maude Stanley.] [*Lib. Journ.* iii. 348 ; iv. 25.] London, 1878
Mistakenly ascribed to George Barnett Smith.

WORK among the lost. By the author of *Home thoughts for mothers and mothers' meetings* [Jane Ellice Hopkins]. 12mo. Pp. 95. London, 1870

WORK and conflict ; or divine life in progress. By the author of *The divine life* [John Kennedy, D.D., Stepney]. 8vo. London [1858]
Another issue gives the author's name.

WORK and warfare. By " Cycla " [Mrs Helen Clacy]. 8vo. [*Cushing's Init. and Pseud.* i. 72.] London, 1858

WORK for a cooper ; being an answer to a libel, written by Thomas Wynne the cooper, the aleman, the quack, and the speaking-Quaker : with a brief account how that dissembling people differ at this day from what at first they were. By one who abundantly pities their ignorance and folly [William Jones, of North Wales]. 4to. [*Smith's Bibl. Anti-Quak.* p. 257.]
London, 1679

WORK (a) for none but angels & men ; that is, to be able to look into, and to know our selves : or a book shewing what the soule is, subsisting and having its operations without the body ; its more then a perfection or reflection of the sense, or temperature of humours. . . . [Verse. By Sir John Davies.] 4to. Pp. 54. [*Bodl.*] London, 1653
The second elegy of the " Nosce te ipsum."

WORK of the future for the Society of Friends. [By William Henry Richardson.] 8vo. Pp. 56. [*Smith's Cat. of Friends' Books,* Supp. p. 22.]
London, 1874

WORK (the) of God's power in man, with something that the spirit of truth leads to practice, and what it leads to deny. . . . By W. S. [William Smith, of Besthorpe]. 4to. [*Smith's Cat. of Friends' Books.*] London, 1663

WORK (the) of the sixth day illustrated. [By Frances Walter.] 8vo. [*Brit. Mus.*] London, 1851

WORKE (a) entytled of yᵉ olde god & the newe, of the olde faythe & the newe, of the olde doctryne and yᵉ newe, an orygynall begynnynge of Idolatrye. [Written originally in German by Judas Nazarei, *pseud.* of Joachim von Watt, under the title of, "Vom alten und neuen Gott, Glauben und Lere." Translated from the Latin version of Hartmannus Dulichius, by Wm. Turner, Dean of Wells.] 8vo. B. L. [*Brit. Mus.*]   N.P. 1534

WORKE for a masse-priest. [By Alexander Cooke]. 4to. Pp. 14. [*Bodl.*]
London, 1617

WORKE, more worke, and a little more worke for a masse-priest. [By Alexander Cooke.] 4to. [*Mendham Collection Cat.* p. 83.]   London, 1630

WORKERS together; or, an endless chain. By "Pansy" [Mrs Isabella Alden, *née* Macdonald]. 8vo. Pp. 280. [*Brit. Mus.*]   London, 1887

WORKES (the) of a young wyt, trust up with a fardell of pretie fancies, profitable to young poetes. . . . Done by N. B., gentleman [Nicholas Breton]. 4to. [*D. N. B.* vol. 6, p. 277.]
London [1577]

WORKHOUSE (the) boy; containing his letters, with a short account of him. By the author of *Friendly advice to parents on the management and education of their children* [Mrs Louisa Hoare]. 12mo. [Smith's *Cat. of Friends' Books*, Supp. p. 192.]
London [*c.* 1830]

WORKING designs for ten Catholic Churches, containing all dimensions, details, and specifications. . . . By an ecclesiastical architect [Charles Sholl]. Folio. Pp. 72.   New York, 1869

WORKING (a) man's refutation of [John] Stuart Mill. [By Johann Georg Eccarius.] 8vo.   London, 1869

WORKING of the Tithe Commutation Act. [By the Hon. Arthur Philip Perceval.] 8vo. [*Bodl.*] London, 1838

WORKING (a) woman's life; an autobiography. By Marianne Farningham [Marianne Hearne, of Farningham]. 8vo. Pp. 282. [*Lit. Year Book.*]
London, 1907

WORKING-MAN'S (the) way in the world: being the autobiography of a journeyman printer. [By Charles Manby Smith.] 12mo. [*N. and Q.* Feb. 1869, p. 168.]   London, N.D.

WORKMAN! What of your house? Specially addressed to the working men in small towns and villages. By one who knows [Charles James Wahab]. 8vo. [*Brit. Mus.*]
Edinburgh, 1867

WORKS for the times; an appeal for the heathen. . . . By a Christian witnesser [J. F. Paysley]. 8vo. [*Brit. Mus.*]   Dublin, 1867
Signed: J. F. P.

WORKS (the) of Anacreon and Sappho, with pieces from ancient authors [Bion, Moschus, Virgil, and Horace], and occasional essays; illustrated by observations on their lives and writings, explanatory notes from established commentators, and additional remarks by the editor: with the classic and introductory poem. [By Edward Burnaby Greene.] 12mo. [*D.N.B.* vol. 23, p. 63.]   London, 1768
Signed: E. B. G.

WORKS (the) of Anacreon, Sappho, Bion, Moschus, and Musæus, translated into English. By a gentleman of Cambridge [Rev. Francis Fawkes, M.A.]. 12mo. [*D. N. B.* vol. 18, p. 275.]   London, 1760

WORKS (the) of Ben Jonson; with a memoir of his life and writings. By Barry Cornwall [Bryan Waller Procter]. 8vo. Pp. lvi. 819. [Allibone's *Dict.*]
London, 1838

WORKS (the) of Cheviot Tichburn. [By William Harrison Ainsworth.] 8vo. [*D. N. B.* vol. 1, p. 197.] London, 1825

WORKS (the) of darknesse brought to light and reproved; in answer to divers false doctrines . . . of J. Wells concerning the word and the gospel. . . . By him that loves the truth as it is in Jesus. . . . F. H. [Francis Howgill]. 4to. Pp. 23. [*Brit. Mus.*]
London, 1659

WORKS (the) of Geoffrey Chaucer, compared with the former editions and many valuable MSS., out of which, three Tales are added which were never before printed; by John Urry, Student of Christ Church, Oxon, deceased: together with a glossary, by a Student of the same College [Timothy Thomas]. To the whole is prefixed the author's life, newly written [by —— Dart, corrected and enlarged by William Thomas], and a preface, giving an account of this edition [by Timothy Thomas]. Folio. [*W.*]   London, 1721

WORKS (the) of Jacob Boehme. (Translated out of the German—the Epistles.) [By J. E. *i.e.* John Ellistone. A reprint.] With introduction by a graduate of Glasgow University (F. F.). 4to.   Glasgow, 1886

WORKS (the) of Mr John Cleveland, containing his poems, orations, epistles, collected into one volume, with the life of the author. [Edited by J. Lake and S. Drake.] 8vo. [*W.*] London, 1687
Epistle Dedicatory signed: J. L., S. D.

WORKS (the) of Nobody [William Stevens, F.S.A.]. 8vo. [Watt's *Bibl. Brit.*]   London [1780?]

WORKS (the) of Peter Pindar, Esq. [John Wolcot, M.D.]. 8vo. 4 vols. [*W.*]   London, 1794-6

WORKS (the) of Plato [translated and] abridg'd [by Joseph Stennett]; illustrated by notes by M. Dacier. 8vo. 2 vols. [Whitley's *Bapt. Bibl.* i. 137.]   London, 1701

WORKS (the) of Salomon Gessner; translated . . . with some account of his life and writings. [By Mrs Rose Lawrence.] 8vo. 3 vols. [*Brit. Mus.*]   London, 1802

WORKS (the) of Tacitus; to which are prefixed political discourses upon that author. [By Thomas Gordon, of Kirkcudbright.] Folio. 2 vols. [*Brit. Mus.*]   London, 1728-31

WORKS (the) of the author of *Night-Thoughts* [Rev. Edward Young, LL.D.], revised and corrected by himself. A new edition. 8vo.   London, 1762
> Many copies have an engraved frontispiece, containing a miniature and the name of the author.

WORKS (the) of the Caledonian bards; translated from the Galic [by John Clark]. Volume I. 8vo. Pp. 200. [Lowndes' *Bibl. Man.* p. 347.]   Edinburgh, 1778

WORKS (the) of the ever-memorable John Hales of Eton, collected [by Sir David Dalrymple, Lord Hailes]. 8vo. 3 vols. [Lowndes' *Brit. Lib.*]   Glasgow, 1765

WORKS (the) of the very learned and Reverend Father in God, John Jewell, not long since Bishop of Salisburie, newly set forth with some amendments of divers quotations; and a brief discourse of his life [by Daniel Featley. The whole edited by Nicholas Fuller]. Folio. 4 parts. [*D. N. B.* vol. 29, p. 382.]   London, 1609
> The Dedication was written by John Overal, and the appendix by Bishop Morton. The book was published under the direction of Archbishop Bancroft.

WORKS (the) of William Browne; containing Britannia's Pastorals: with notes and observations by the Rev. W. Thompson, late of Queen's-College, Oxford. The Shepherd's Pipe: consisting of Pastorals, the Inner Temple Masque, never published before; and other poems; with the life of the author [by Thomas Davies, the bookseller]. 12mo. [*D. N. B.* vol. 7, p. 75.]   London, 1772

WORKS (the) of William Hogarth (including the Analysis of beauty), elucidated by descriptions, critical, moral, and historical: to which is prefixed some account of his life. By Thomas Clerk. [The engravings by Thomas Clerk. The text by Thomas Hartwell Horne.] 8vo. 2 vols. London, 1821
> From a list of Horne's works in the handwriting of the author.

WORKS on alchemy and chemistry. [By H. C. Bolton.] 8vo. [*Birm. Cent. Lib.*] 8vo.   London, 1891

WORLD (the). By a deserter [Rev. Alexander Robert Charles Dallas]. Nos. 1 and 2. 8vo.   London, 1838-9

WORLD (the). By Ascott R. Hope [Robert Hope Moncrieff]. 8vo. Pp. 192. [*Brit. Mus.*]   London, 1908

WORLD (the) alarm'd: a surprizing relation of a new burning island lately raised out of the sea near Tercera; with . . . a brief history of the other ignovomous mountains at this day . . . in the world: in a letter. . . . [By Thomas Forster, F.R.S.] 12mo. [*Brit. Mus.*]   Boston, N.E., 1721

WORLD (the) and a man. [A novel.] By Z. Z. [Louis Zangwill]. 8vo. Pp. 357. [*Brit. Mus.*]   London, 1896

WORLD (the) and Delia. [A novel.] By Curtis Yorke [Mrs W. S. Richmond Lee, *née* —— Jex-Long]. 8vo. Pp. 318. [*Who's Who in Lit.*]   London, 1907

WORLD (the) as it goes; a poem. By the author of *The Diaboliad* [William Combe]; dedicated to one of the best men in his Majesty's dominions. . . . The second edition. 4to. Pp. 37. [*D. N. B.* vol. 11, p. 433.]   London, 1779

WORLD (the) at auction; a play. By Michael Field [Katherine Harris Bradley and Edith Emma Cooper]. 4to. Pp. 116.   Edinburgh, 1898

WORLD (the) at Westminster; a periodical publication. By Thomas Brown, the younger [Thomas Moore]. 12mo. [*D. N. B.* vol. 38, p. 382.]   London, 1816
> The work consists of thirty numbers.

WORLD (a) between them. By Bertha M. Clay [Charlotte M. Braeme]. 8vo. [*Amer. Cat.*]   New York, 1886

WORLD (the) bewitch'd; a dialogue between two astrologers and the author. . . . [By Edward Ward.] 4to. [*D. N. B.* vol. 59, p. 313.]   London, 1699

WORLD (the) conquered, or a believer's victory over the world; laid open in several sermons on 1 John 5, 4. By R. A. [Richard Alleine]. 8vo. Pp. 320. [Green's *Bibl. Somers.* ii. 108].   London, 1668

WORLD (the); how to square it. By Harry Hieover [Charles Bindley]. 8vo. [*Brit. Mus.*]　　　London, 1854

WORLD (the) in the Church. By F. G. Trafford, author of *The moors and the fens*, etc. [Mrs Charlotte E. L. Riddell]. Second edition. 8vo. 3 vols. [*D. N. B.* Second Supp., vol. 3, p. 193.]
London, 1863

WORLD (the) in which I live, and my place in it. By E. S. A. [Miss Letitia Willgoss Stone]. 8vo. London, 1856
　　Wrongly ascribed to Ernest Silvanus Appleyard.

WORLD (a) in white ; and other poems. By Lindon Meadows [Rev. Charles Butler Greatrex]. 8vo. [*Brit. Mus.*]
London [1889]

WORLD (the) of bewilderment. By John Travers [Mrs G. H. Bell]. 8vo. [*Who's Who in Lit.*]　　London, 1913

WORLD (the) of graft. By Josiah Flynt [Josiah Flynt Willard]. 8vo.
Chicago, 1898

WORLD (the) of phantoms ; a poem. [By Cornelius Black, M.D.] 8vo.
London, 1862

WORLD (the) soul. By Henry Fielding [Henry Fielding-Hall]. 8vo. Pp. xx. 311. [*Lond. Lib. Cat.*] London, 1913

WORLD (the) to come, as presented in the Epistle of James ; notes of lectures, by F. E. R. [F. E. Raven]. 8vo. Pp. 52. [*Brit. Mus.*]　　London [1902]

WORLD (the) to come ; the glories of heaven and the terrors of hell lively described under the similitude of a vision. By G. L. [George Larkin]. 8vo. [Brown's *Life of Bunyan*, p. 447.]
London, 1711

WORLD (the) unmask'd ; or, the philosopher the greatest cheat ; in twenty-four dialogues between Crito a philosopher, Philo a lawyer, and Erastus a merchant ; in which true virtue is distinguished from what usually bears the name or resemblance of it. . . . Translated from the French [of Marie Huber]. 8vo. [*N. and Q.* 13th Dec. 1856, p. 476 ; 28th March 1857, p. 256 ; 25th April 1857, p. 334.]
London, 1736
　　Wrongly ascribed to Bernard de Mandeville.

WORLD (a) view of Free Trade, tariff reforms, and the Empire's duty to mankind. By N. D. H. [Colonel North Dalrymple Hamilton]. 8vo.
London, 1905

WORLD (a) without souls. [By the Rev. J. W. Cunningham, A.M., vicar of Harrow.] 12mo. [Darling's *Cyclop. Bibl.*]　　London, 1805

WORLDLING'S (the) progress ; a biographical fragment. By F. R. B. [F. R. Beecheno]. 8vo. Pp. 72. [*Brit. Mus.*]　　London [1885]

WORLDLY (the) hope. By F. O. O. [Forward Observation Officer, *i.e.* C. J. C. Street]. 8vo. Pp. 315. [*Brit. Mus.*]　　London, 1917

WORLD-MENDER (the). [A novel.] By Maxwell Gray [Mary Gleed Tuttiett]. 8vo. Pp. 400. [*Who's Who in Lit.*]　　London, 1916

WORLD'S (the) awakening. By "Navarcus" [Patrick Vaux and another]. 8vo. [*Who's Who in Lit.*]
London, 1908
　　A later edition of the same work bears a different title : "When the Great War Came."

WORLD'S (the) blackmail ; a novel. By Lucas Cleeve [Mrs Howard Kingscote, *née* Adelina G. I. Wolff]. 8vo. Pp. vi. 312. [*Who's Who in Lit.*]
London, 1900

WORLD'S (the) epitaph ; a poem. [By Thomas Gordon Hake.] 8vo. Pp. vii. 128. [*Brit. Mus.*]
London, private print, 1866

WORLD'S (the) great restavration ; or, the calling of the Ievves, and (with them) of all the nations and kingdomes of the earth, to the faith of Christ. Published by William Gouge, B. of D., and preacher of God's Word in Blackfryers, London. [Written by Henry Finch.] 4to. Pp. 234. [*Bodl.*]
London, 1621

WORLD'S (the) honour detected, and, for the unprofitableness thereof, rejected ; and the honour which comes from God alone, asserted, and reduced to practice ; or, some reasons why the people of God called Quakers do deny the accustomary honour and salutations of the world, consisting in putting off the hat, bowing, titling, bidding goodmorrow, good-night, &c. . . . By a friend to truth, who is no respecter or regarder of persons, called a Quaker, B. F. [Benjamin Furly]. 4to. [Smith's *Cat. of Friends' Books*, i. 827.]
London, 1663

WORLD'S (the) idol. Plutus ; a comedy written in Greek by Aristophanes. Translated by H. H. B. [Henry Burnell]. 4to. [*W.*] London, 1659

WORLD'S (the) laconics ; or the best thoughts of the best authors. By Everard Berkeley [Tryon Edwards]. 12mo. Pp. 432. [*Brit. Mus.*]
London, 1853

WORLD'S (the) mercy ; and other tales. By Maxwell Gray [Mary Gleed Tuttiett]. 8vo. [*Who's Who in Lit.*]
London, 1900

WORLD'S (the) mistake in Oliver Cromwell; or, a short political discourse, shewing that Cromwell's maladministration, (during his four years and nine moneths pretended Protectorship), layed the foundation of our present condition in the decay of trade. [By Slingsby Bethel.] 4to. [*Lowndes' Bibl. Man.*] London, 1668

WORLD'S (the) people. [Short stories.] By Julien Gordon [Mrs Julia Grinnell Cruger]. 8vo. Pp. 358. [*Who's Who in Lit.*] London, 1905

WORLD'S (the) verdict. By the author of *The morals of May Fair*, etc. [Mrs Annie Edwardes]. 8vo. 3 vols. [*Camb. Univ. Lib.*] London, 1861

WORLD-WIDE (the) want. [By the Rev. George Hunt Jackson.] 8vo. [*Brit. Mus.*] London [1866]

WORM (the) that ceased to turn. By Gorham Silva [Elizabeth Lawrence]. 12mo. New York, 1895

WORM (the) that God prepared; a novel. By John Oliver Hobbes [Mrs Walpole Craigie, *née* Pearl Maria Teresa Richards]. 8vo. [*Brit. Mus.*] London, 1901

WORME (the) of Lambton. [Edited by Sir Cuthbert Sharp.] 4to. Pp. 15. [*Martin's Cat.*] Durham, 1830

WORN-OUT neology; or, brief strictures upon the Oxford Essays and Reviews; by the author of the Hartley Wintney Tracts [Francis Osbern Giffard]. 8vo. [*Brit. Mus.*] London [1861]

WORSHIP (the), rites, and ceremonies of the Church of Scotland. . . . [By George W. Sprott, D.D.] 8vo. Edinburgh, 1863

WORSHIPFUL (the) Company of Needlemakers of the city of London; with a list of the court of assistants and livery. [By John Edward Price.] 4to. London, 1874

WORTH and wealth; or, Jessie Dorr. By Madeline Leslie [Harriet Newells Baker]. 8vo. [*Brit. Mus.*] Boston, 1870

WORTH having. By "Pansy" [Mrs Isabella Alden, *née* Macdonald]. 8vo. Pp. 250. [*Brit. Mus.*] Boston, 1893

WORTH her weight in gold. . . . [By H. Colson]. 8vo. [*Brit. Mus.*] London, 1863

WORTH (the) of a baby and How Apple-Tree Court was won. By Hesba Stretton, author of *Jessica's first prayer*, etc. [Sarah Smith]. 8vo. Pp. 58. London, 1876
See note to "Alone in London."

WORTH while. By Archie Fell [Mary J. Capron]. 12mo. [*Cushing's Init. and Pseud.* i. 100.] Boston, 1870

WORTHLESSNESS (the) of Christianity. By a Japanese [Oertse Yvempo]. 8vo. London, 1904

WORTHY of His name. By Eglanton Thorne [Emily Charlton]. 8vo. Pp. 192. [*Who's Who in Lit.*] London, 1892

WORTLEBANK (the) diary, and some old stories from Kathie Brande's portfolio. By Holme Lee, author of *Sylvan Holt's daughter*, etc. [Harriet Parr]. 8vo. 3 vols. [*Lond. Lib. Cat.*] London, 1860

WOUNDED and a prisoner of War. By an exchanged officer [Captain M. V. Hay]. 8vo. [*Lond. Lib. Cat., Supp.*] Edinburgh, 1916

WRAITH (the) of Olverstone. [A novel.] By Florence Warden [Florence Alice Price, later Mrs George E. James]. 8vo. Pp. 123. [*Who's Who in Lit.*] London, 1916

WRANGLING (the) lovers; or, the invisible mistress; a comedy [in five acts, and in prose. By Edward Ravenscroft]. 4to. [*Brit. Mus.*] London, 1677

WRATH (the) of echo, and other pieces in verse. By G. M. [G. Middleton]. 12mo. London, 1876

WREATH (the); an old glee: with numerous songs. [By Richard Scrafton Sharpe.] 8vo. London, N.D.

WREATH (a) from the wilderness; being a selection from the metrical arrangements of Accola Montis-Amœni. [By Robert Barnard.] 8vo. [*Smith's Cat. of Friends' Books*, i. 87, 193.] Ironbridge, 1816
Reprinted in 1817, with the author's name, and with a change in the latter part of the title.

WREATH (a) of carols from the Fatherland. [By Alice Mannington.] 12mo. Pp. 48. London, 1864

WREATH (the) of fashion; or, the art of sentimental poetry. [By Richard Tickell.] 4to. Pp. iv. 14. [*Brit. Mus.*] London, 1778

WREATH (a) of Indian stories. By A.L.O.E., honorary missionary at Amritsar, author of *The young pilgrim*, etc. [Charlotte M. Tucker]. 8vo. Pp. 211. London, N.D.

WREATH (a) of ivy, and Christmas wild flowers: gathered and twined by "Amicitiæ." [By Charles Augustus Hulbert.] 8vo. Pp. 34. [*Bodl.*] Shrewsbury, 1823
A few copies only, printed for presentation.

WREATH (the) of lilies; a tale for the young. By the writer of *Infant hymnings* [Jane E. Leeson]. 12mo. Pp. 240. [*Brit. Mus.*] London, 1847

WREATH (a) of smoke. By A. L. O. E., authoress of *The wanderer in Africa*, etc. [Charlotte M. Tucker]. 8vo. Pp. 191.   London [1871]

WREATHS of song from a course of divinity. By the author of *Wreaths of song from courses of Philosophy* [Rev. Timothy J. O'Mahony, D.D.]. 8vo. Pp. viii. 96. [O'Donoghue's *Poets of Ireland.*]   London, 1903

WREATHS of song from fields of philosophy. [By Rev. Timothy J. O'Mahony, D.D.] 8vo. [O'Donoghue's *Poets of Ireland.*]   Dublin, 1890

WRECK (the) of the circus. . . . By James Otis [James Otis Kaler]. 8vo. [Cushing's *Init. and Pseud.* i. 220.]   Boston, 1900

WRECK (the) of the Golden Galleon. [A novel.] By Lucas Malet [Mrs St Leger Harrison, *née* Mary Kingsley]. 8vo. Pp. 214. [*Who's Who in Lit.*]   London, 1910

WRECK (the) of the "Grosvenor." [By W. Clark Russell.] 8vo. [*Lib. Journ.* iii. 271.]   London, 1878

WRECK (the) of the "Grosvenor," and other South African poems. [By William Charles Scully.] 8vo.   London, 1886

WRECK (the) of the "Ocean Queen." By James Otis [James Otis Kaler]. 8vo. [Cushing's *Init. and Pseud.* i. 220.]   Boston, 1907

WRECKED at the outset; a novel. By Theo Gift [Dora Boulger, *née* Havers]. 8vo. [*Brit. Mus.*]   London, 1894

WRECKED, but not lost. By Faith Templeton [Harriet Boomer Barber]. 8vo. [Cushing's *Init. and Pseud.* i. 281.]   Philadelphia, 1880

WRECKED on a reef; or, twenty months in the Auckland Isles: a true story of shipwreck, adventure, and suffering. [By F. E. Raynal: translated from the French.] 8vo. Pp. xiv. 350. [Collier's *New Zeal. Lit.* p. 155.]   London, 1885

WRECKED on Spider Island; or, how Ned Rogers found the treasure. By James Otis [James Otis Kaler]. 8vo. Pp. 276. [Cushing's *Init. and Pseud.* i. 220.]   New York [1896]

WRECKERS (the). By the author of *Smugglers and foresters* [Mary Rosa Stuart Kettle]. 8vo. 3 vols. [*Brit. Mus.*]   London, 1857

WREN (the) and eagle in contest; or, a short method with the Unitarian nobility. By Aquae Homo, A.B. [Jotham Waterman]. 8vo.   Boston, 1819

WREN (a) in the burning bush, waving the wings of contraction to the congregated clean fowls of the heavens, in the ark of God, Holy Host of the Eternal Power, Salutation. [By John Perrot.] 4to. [*Brit. Mus.*]   London, 1660
Signed: J. P.

WRINKLES; or, hints to sportsmen and travellers on dress, equipment, and camp life. By the Old Shekarry, author of *The forest and the field*, etc. [Major Henry Astbury Leverson]. A new edition, fully illustrated. 8vo. Pp. 2, 294. [*Brit. Mus.*]   London, 1874

WRIT in water. [A novel.] By Sydney C. Grier [Hilda C. Gregg]. 8vo. Pp. 358. [*Who's Who in Lit.*]   Edinburgh, 1913

WRITER (the); a series of original essays, moral and amusing. By a gentleman of Massachusetts [Gamaliel Bradford]. 8vo. [*Brit. Mus.*]   Boston, 1822

WRITER (a) of books. By George Paston [Emily Morse Symonds]. 8vo. Pp. 344. [*Brit. Mus.*]   London, 1898

WRITER (a) of fiction. By Clive Holland [Charles J. Hankinson]. 8vo. Pp. 153. [*Brit. Mus.*]   London, 1898

WRITER'S (the) and student's assistant: or, a compendious dictionary, rendering the more common words and phrases in the English language into the more elegant or scholastic. . . . [By John Henry Brady.] 12mo. 2 vols. [*Brit. Mus.*]   London, 1827

WRITER'S (the) and student's grammar of the English language. [By John Henry Brady.] 12mo. [*Brit. Mus.*]   London, 1838

WRITERS (the) of hymns, ancient and modern, with notes and index, giving the Greek, Latin, and German first lines. [By Rev. Robert M. Moorsom, M.A.] 8vo. Pp. 48.   Alton, N.D.

WRITINGS (the) and character of Lord Byron. [By A. Norton.] 8vo.   Boston, 1825

WRITINGS (the) of a person in obscurity, and a native of the Isle of Wight [T. Nutt]. 12mo. [Gilbert and Godwin's *Bibl. Hanton.* p. 50.]   London, 1808

WRITINGS (the) of Solomon; comprising the Book of Proverbs, Ecclesiastes, Song of Songs, and Psalms lxxii., cxxvii.: translated by F. B. [Francis Barham]. 4to. [F. Shum's *Cat. of Bath Books.*]   Bath, 1870

WRITTEN in the rain. [A novel.] By John Trevena [Ernest George Henham]. 8vo. Pp. 352. [*Who's Who in Lit.*]   London, 1910

WRITTEN to order; being some account of the journeyings of an irresponsible egotist. . . . By the author of *A day of my life at Eton*, etc. [George Nugent Banks]. 8vo. Pp. ii. 366. [*Brit. Mus.*]   London, 1885

WRONG (the) end of religion. By "Rita" [Mrs W. Desmond Humphreys, *née* Eliza M. J. Gollan]. 8vo. Pp. 154. [*Brit. Mus.*]   London, 1918

WRONG (the) prescription. [A novel.] By Lanoe Falconer [Miss Mary Elizabeth Hawker]. 8vo. [*Brit. Mus.*]
London, 1893

WRONGS (the) of Africa. [A poem. By William Roscoe.] 4to. 2 parts. [*D. N. B.* vol. 49, p. 223.]
London, 1787-8

WRONGS (the) of Poland; a poem in three cantos: comprising the siege of Vienna, with historical notes. By the author of *Parental wisdom* [John Antrobus]. 8vo. [*Camb. Univ. Lib.*]
London, 1849

WRONGS (the) of the Caffre nation; a narrative. By "Justus" [Beverley Mackenzie]. With an appendix containing Lord Glenelg's despatches. [Mendelssohn's *South African Bibl.* i. 121.] 8vo. Pp. 20, 333.
London, 1837
Ascribed also to the Rev. John Philip, D.D.

WRONGS (the) of woman. By Charlotte Elizabeth [Mrs Charlotte Elizabeth Tonna, previously Mrs Phelan]. 12mo. 4 parts. [*D. N. B.* vol. 57, p. 34.]   London, 1843-4

WUTHERING Heights and Agnes Grey. By Ellis and Acton Bell [Emily Jane, and Anne Brontë]. A new edition, revised, with a biographical notice of the authors, a selection from their literary remains, and a preface, by Currer Bell [Charlotte Brontë]. 12mo. [*D. N. B.* vol. 6, p. 412.]
London, 1850

WYCH Hazel. By the author of *The wide, wide world*, etc. [Susan Warner]. 8vo. Pp. iv. 422. [Allibone's *Dict.*]
London, 1876

WYCLIFFE; his biographers and critics; republished from the *British Quarterly*. [By Robert Vaughan, D.D.] 8vo.   London, 1858

WYCLIFFE to Wesley; heroes and martyrs of the Church in Britain. [By Gregory J. Robinson.] 8vo. Pp. 8, 248.   London, 1879

WYLLARD'S weird; a novel. By the author of *Lady Audley's secret*, etc. [Miss M. E. Braddon]. 8vo. 3 vols.
London [1885]

WYNDHAM (the) family; a story of modern life. By the author of *Mount St Clair* [Mrs Harriet Diana Thomson, *née* Calvert]. 8vo. 2 vols.
London, 1876

WYNDHAM'S loan. [A tale.] By Mignon [Mrs —— Baseley]. 8vo. [*Brit. Mus.*]   Manchester, 1902

WYNVILLE; or clubs and coteries. A novel. By the author of *The age of Pitt and Fox* [Daniel Owen Madden]. 12mo. 3 vols. [*Brit. Mus.*]
London, 1852

X

X. Y. Z.; a comedy, in two acts. [By George Colman, the younger.] 12mo. [Bakers' *Biog. Dram.*]   Dublin, 1820

    A later (undated, London) edition, bearing Colman's name, was "Printed from the acting copy, with remarks, biographical and critical, by D— G. [George Daniel]."

XANTIPPE; or the scolding wife, done from the Conjugium of Erasmus. By W. F. of D. [W. Forbes of Disblair]. 4to. Pp. 27.   Edinburgh, 1724

XARIFFA'S poems. [By Mrs Mary Ashby Townsend, *née* Van Voorhis.] 12mo.   Philadelphia, 1870

XÉNIE'S inheritance; a tale of Russian life. From the French of Henri Gréville [Madame Alice Durand]. 12mo. [*Amer. Cat.*]   New York, 1891

XENOPHON'S defence of the Athenian democracy; translated from the Greek: with notes, and an appendix, containing observations on the democratic part of the British government, and the existing constitution of the House of Commons. [By Henry James Pye.] 8vo. Pp. iv. 106. [Watt's *Bibl. Brit.*]
London, 1794

XENOPHON'S History of the affairs of Greece. By the translator of Thucydides [Rev. William Smith, D.D.]. 4to. [*Brit. Mus.*]   London, 1770

Y

YACHT (the) sailor; a treatise on practical yachtmanship cruising and racing. By Vanderdecken [William Cooper]. 12mo. [*Brit. Mus.*]
London, 1862

YACHT (a) voyage to Iceland in 1853. [By Rev. J. E. Cross.] 12mo.
London, 1854

YACHTING and rowing. By the Hon. Secretary of the Royal Eastern Yacht Club [Archibald Young]. 8vo.
London, 1866

YACHTING (a) cruise in Norway. By the parson and the lawyer [Edward Trustram]. 8vo.   London, 1895

YACHTING in Australia. By "The Vagabond" [Julian Thomas]. 8vo. [*Lib. of Royal Col. Inst.*, Suppl. i. 61.]
Melbourne, 1895

YACHTMAN'S (a) holidays or cruising in the West Highlands. By the "Governor" [John Inglis]. 8vo. Pp. viii. 151.   London, 1879

YACHTS and yachting. . . . By Vanderdecken [William Cooper]. 8vo. [*Brit. Mus.*]   London, 1873

YANKEE (a) among the nullifiers; an autobiography. By Elnathan Elmwood, Esq. [Asa Greene]. 8vo. [Cushing's *Init. and Pseud.* i. 89.]
New York, 1833

YANKEE (a) at the court of King Arthur. By Mark Twain [Samuel Langhorne Clemens]. 8vo. [*Amer. Cat.*]   London, 1890

YANKEE (the) conscript; or, eighteen months in Dixie, 1861-62. [By George Adams Fisher.] 8vo. [Cushing's *Init. and Pseud.* i. 311.]
Philadelphia, 1864

YANKEE (a) Crusoe. By Allan Eric [Charles W. Willis]. 8vo. [*Amer. Cat.*]   Boston, 1900

YANKEE (a) in Canada. [By Henry David Thoreau.] 8vo. [Cushing's *Init. and Pseud.* i. 311.] Boston, 1866

YANKEE notions; a medley. By Timothy Titterwell, Esq. [Samuel Kettell]. 8vo. [Cushing's *Init. and Pseud.* i. 284.]   Boston, 1838

YANKEE (a) steamer on the Atlantic—New York; its hotels, waterworks, and things in general. . . . By J. W. Hengiston [Cyrus Redding]. 8vo. [*Brit. Mus.*]   London, 1852-3

YANKO-SEQUOR (the); disquisitions upon several things in America. . . . [By Martin Regul Pilon.] 8vo. [Cushing's *Init. and Pseud.* i. 311.]
New York, 1874

YARICO to Inkle, an epistle. By the author of an *Elegy written among the ruins of an abbey* [Edward Jerningham]. 4to. Pp. 19. [*Brit. Mus.*]
London, 1766

YARN (the) of a bucko mate; his adventures in two oceans. By F. Benton Williams [Herbert Elliott Hamblen.] 8vo. [*Amer. Cat.*]
New York, 1899

YARNS. [In verse.] By a Manchester spinner [John Cameron]. 8vo. [*N. and Q.* Feb. 1869, p. 168.]
Manchester, N.D.

YARNS. By an old Tar [James Thomson, senior]. Pp. 76.   Cupar-Fife, 1877

YARNS from the Never-Never. By "Sundowner" [Herbert Tichborne]. 8vo.   London, 1898

YAXLEY and its neighbourhood; a novel. By the author of *Myself and my relatives* [Anne J. Robertson]. 8vo. 3 vols. [*Brit. Mus.*]   London, 1865

YE shall be as gods. [A novel.] By Derek Vane [Mrs B. Eaton Back]. 8vo. [*Brit. Mus.*]   London, 1902

YEA (the) and nay stock-jobbers; or, the 'Change-Alley Quakers anatomized. In a burlesque epistle to a friend at sea. [By Elias Brockett.] 8vo. Pp. 32.   London, 1720
Signed: Damon.

YEA or nay? or, the union question tried and tested. By "a country minister" of the Free Church [—— Philip]. 8vo. Pp. 16.
Edinburgh, 1870

YEAR (a) abroad; stories and sights in France and Italy. By Grace Greenwood [Sarah Jane Clarke]. 8vo. Pp. 221. [*Brit. Mus.*] Edinburgh [1869]

YEAR after year; a tale. By the author of *Paul Ferroll* and *IX poems by V.* [Mrs Caroline Clive]. Third edition. 12mo. Pp. vii. 365. [*Brit. Mus.*]
London, 1858

YEAR (a) and a day. By Guy Thorne [Cyril A. E. Ranger-Gull]. 8vo. Pp. 303. [*Brit. Mus.*]   London, 1922

YEAR (a) and a day; a novel in two volumes by Madame Panache, author of *Manners* [really Miss Frances Moore, later Mrs Brooke]. 8vo. [Boase's *Mod. Eng. Biog.* ii. 947.]
London, 1818

YEAR (a) and a day; a story of Canadian life. By the author of *Christie Redfern's troubles*, etc. [Margaret Murray Robertson]. 8vo. [*Nat. Lib. of Scot.*]
London [1886]

YEAR (a) at Poplar Row. By March Ellinwood [Mrs N. Proudfit Burch]. 8vo.   New York, 1879

YEAR (the) book of the Holy Souls. By the author of *Vera*, etc., C. L. H. D. [Charlotte Louisa Hawkins Dempster]. 8vo. [*Brit. Mus.*]   London, 1901

YEAR (the) 1851. [A poem. By William Steere.] 8vo. [*Brit. Mus.*]
                                    London, 1852

YEAR (a) in Spain. By a young American [Captain Alexander Slidell Mackenzie]. 8vo. 2 vols. [*Brit. Mus.*]   London, 1831

YEAR (a) in Sunday-school; from the journal of an old teacher. [By Mrs Margaret Hosmer.] 8vo. [Cushing's *Init. and Pseud.* i. 213.]
                           Philadelphia, 1869

YEAR (a) in Tasmania; including some months' residence in the capital; with a descriptive tour through the Island. By the author of *Five Years in the Levant* [Captain Henry Butler Stoney]. 8vo.   Hobart, 1854

YEAR (the) nine; a tale of the Tyrol. By the author of *Mary Powell* [Anne Manning, later Mrs Rathbone]. 8vo. [*Brit. Mus.*]   London, 1858

YEAR (the) of liberation; a journal of the defence of Hamburgh against the French army under Marshal Davoust, in 1813, with sketches of the battles of Lutzen, Bautzen, etc., etc. [By George Croly, LL.D., rector of St Stephen's, Walbrook.] 12mo. 2 vols. [*Camb. Univ. Lib.*]   London, 1832

YEAR (the) of preparation for the Vatican Council; including the original and English of the Encyclical and Syllabus, and of the Papal documents connected with its convocation. [By Herbert Alfred Vaughan, D.D., Cardinal.] 8vo. 2 parts. [*Brit. Mus.*]
                            London, 1869-70

YEAR (a) of wreck; a true story. By a victim [George Chittenden Benham]. 8vo. [Cushing's *Init. and Pseud.* i. 294.]   New York, 1880

YEAR (the); with other poems. By the author of *The fall of the Indian*, etc. [Isaac M'Lellan]. 8vo. Pp. 60. [Cushing's *Anon.*]   Boston, 1832

YEAR (a) with the birds. By an Oxford tutor [William Warde Fowler]. 8vo. [*Brit. Mus.*]   Oxford, 1886

YEAR (a) with the Everards. A tale. By the author of *Little Elsie's Summer at Malvern* [Marion Clifford Butler, Baroness Dunboyne]. 8vo. [*Brit. Mus.*]   London, 1874

YEAR (a) worth living. By George F. Harrington [Rev. William Mumford Baker]. 12mo. [Cushing's *Init. and Pseud.* i. 126.]   Boston, 1887

YEAR'S (the) mind; Hamworth happenings. By the author of *Leaves from a life* [Mrs Jane Ellen Panton]. 8vo. Pp. 348. [*Brit. Mus.*]   London, 1913

YEARS of hate. By Guy Thorne [Cyril A. E. Ranger-Gull]. 8vo. Pp. 304. [*Who's Who in Lit.*]   London, 1921

YEAST; a problem. [By Charles Kingsley.] Reprinted, with corrections and additions, from *Fraser's Magazine*. 12mo. Pp. vi. 379. [*D. N. B.* vol. 31, p. 177.]
                                    London, 1851

YELLOW (a) aster. [A novel.] By "Iota" [Mrs Kathleen Mannington Caffyn]. Sixth edition. 8vo. 3 vols. [*Brit. Mus.*]   London, 1894

YELLOW (the) claw. By Sax Rohmer [Arthur Sarsfield Ward]. 8vo. Pp. 320. [*Lond. Lib. Cat.*]   London [1915]

The *Brit. Mus.* now gives this author's surname as Wade.

YELLOW (the) fiend. [A novel.] By Mrs Alexander [Mrs Alexander Hector, *née* Annie French]. 8vo. Pp. 332. [*Who's Who in Lit.*]   London, 1902

YELLOW (the) shoe-strings. . . . By J. P. [James Pedder, journalist]. 8vo. [Cushing's *Init. and Pseud.* i. 222.]
                                    Boston [1850]

YELLOW (the) van. [A novel.] By the author of *No. 5 John Street* [Richard Whiteing]. 8vo.   London, 1903

YELLOW (the) war. By "O," author of *On the heels of De Wet* [Capt. Lionel James]. 8vo. Pp. 312. [*Brit. Mus.*]
                                  Edinburgh, 1905

YELLOWLEAF. By Sacha Gregory [Baroness von Hutten]. 8vo. [*Lond. Lib. Cat.*]   London, 1919

YELLOWSTONE letters. By Rube Shuffle, valet [Augustus George Heaton]. 8vo.
                          Washington, D.C., 1906

YEMASSEE (the); a romance of Carolina. . . . By the author of *Guy Rivers*, etc. [William Gilmore Simms]. 12mo. 3 vols. [*Brit. Mus.*]
                                  New York, 1835

YEOMAN Fleetwood. [A novel.] By M. E. Francis [Mrs Francis Blundell, *née* Mary Evans Sweetman]. 8vo. Pp. 412. [*Who's Who in Lit.*]
                                    London, 1900

YEOMAN'S (the) [Sir William Cusack Smith's] second letter to the Right Honourable William Wickham, one of his Majesty's most honourable privy council, etc., etc., etc. Occasioned by the second edition of an Irish Catholic [Mr Scully]'s advice to his brethren. Second edition. 8vo. Pp. 98.
                                    Dublin, 1804

YES and no ; a tale of the day. By the author of *Matilda* [Constantine Henry Phipps, Marquis of Normanby]. 12mo. 2 vols. [Smales' *Whitby Authors*, p. 158.] London, 1828

YES and no ; or glimpses of the great conflict. [By Rev. Dr Henry Robert Reynolds and his brother Sir John Russell Reynolds.] 8vo. 4 vols. [*D. N. B.* First Supp. iii. 295.] Cambridge, 1860

YESTERDAY and to-day in Kruger's Land ; the personal knowledge and experiences of a lady from South Africa. [By M. E. Vaughan-Williams.] 8vo. Pp. 88. London, 1900

YESTERDAY framed in to-day ; the story of the Christ, and how to-day received Him. By "Pansy" [Mrs Isabella Alden, *née* Macdonald]. 8vo. [*Amer. Cat.*] Boston, 1899

YESTERDAY in Ireland. By the author of *To-day in Ireland* [Eyre Evans Crowe]. 12mo. 3 vols. [*D. N. B.* vol. 13, p. 238.] London, 1829

YET a course at the Romyshe foxe ; a disclosynge or openynge on the Manne of Sinne, cōtayned in the late declaratyon of the Popes olde faythe, made by Edmunde Boner, Bysshopp of London ; wherby Wyllyam Tolwyn was then newelye professed at Paules Crosse openlye into Antichristes Romyshe relygyon agayne, by a new solempne othe of obedyence, notwythstādinge the othe made to hys prynce afore to the contrarye, etc. Compyled by Johan Harrison [John Bale, Bishop of Ossory]. 16mo. [Watt's *Bibl. Brit.*] Zurich, 1543

YET another plan for the resumption of specie payments, easy and early. By A. P. [A. Penfield]. 8vo. [Cushing's *Init. and Pseud.* i. 221.] Washington, 1869

YETTS (the) o' Muckart ; or the famous picnic and the brilliant barn ball ; in hairst, auchteen hunder an' seventy one. [By Miss Edith Stevenson.] 12mo. Pp. 54. Edinburgh, private print, 1872

YEWS (the). [A Westmoreland tale.] By the author of *How to see the English Lakes* [Mrs Bitha Lloyd, *née* Fox]. 8vo. Pp. 108. [*Brit. Mus.*] London [1859]

Y N S O E R. By Allen Raine [Mrs Beynon Puddicombe, *née* Anne Adaliza Evans]. 8vo. [*Who's Who in Lit.*] London, 1894

YOKE (the) of the Thorah. [A novel.] By Sidney Luska [Henry Harland]. 8vo. Pp. 320. [*Lond. Lib. Cat.*] London [1888]

YOLANDA, the maid of Burgundy. By Edwin Caskoden [Charles Major]. 8vo. [*Amer. Cat.*] New York, 1905

YOLANDE the Parisienne. By Lucas Cleeve [Mrs Howard Kingscote, *née* Adelina Georgina Isabella Wolff]. 8vo. [*Who's Who in Lit.*] London, 1900

YORICK, and other poems. [By James Warren Ward.] 12mo. Cleveland, Ohio, 1838

YORICK'S Sentimental Journey [by Laurence Sterne] continued. By Eugenius [John Hall - Stevenson]. 12mo. London, 1784
See above, "A Sentimental Journey. . . ." Hall-Stevenson was a friend of Sterne, and was introduced by Sterne into both "Tristram Shandy," and the "Sentimental Journey" under the name of Eugenius. This disgraceful continuation of the "Sentimental Journey" was first published in 1769 within a year of Sterne's death.

YORK (the) Congress and Church rites. By the author of *The Church cause and the Church party* [Alexander James Beresford Hope]. 8vo. [*Brit. Mus.*] London, 1867

YORK (the) musical festival ; a dialogue. [By Rev. William Hett, M.A.] 4to. Pp. 60. London, 1825

YORK-SHIRE (a) dialogue in its pure natural dialect, as it is now commonly spoken in the north parts of Yorkshire ; being a miscellaneous discourse or hotchpotch of several country affaires. [By George Meriton.] 4to. Pp. 18. [*W.*] York, 1683
Reprinted with "The Praise of York-shire ale," York, 1697, 12mo.

YORKSHIREMAN (the) ; a religious and literary journal. By a Friend [Luke Howard, F.R.S.]. 8vo. 5 vols. [*Bodl.*] Pontefract, 1833-7

YOU and me ; or sketches for both of us. By Hans Patrick Le Connor [Jacob L. Bowman]. 8vo. St Louis, 1867

YOU have heard of them. [By Charles G. Rosenberg.] 8vo. London, 1845

YOUNG America in Germany. By Oliver Optic [William Taylor Adams]. 8vo. [Cushing's *Init. and Pseud.* i. 219.] New York, 1872

YOUNG (the) angler's guide ; comprising instructions in the arts of fly-fishing, bottom-fishing, trolling, etc. [By John Cheek, who published it.] 8vo. [Westwood and Satchell's *Bibl. Pisc.*] London, 1839

YOUNG (the) apprentice's monitor ; or, the seasonable advice of a friend with respect to his conduct, as well as at his first entrance into . . . his apprenticeship. . . . By a person unknown [Henry Dixon, schoolmaster at Bath]. 12mo.   Bath, 1747

YOUNG (a) artist's [Leonard Holme's] life. [By Alexander D. R. W. Baillie Cochrane, Baron Lamington, M.P.] 8vo. [*Nat. Lib. of Scot.*]
London, 1864

YOUNG (the) bandmaster. By Captain Ralph Bonehill [Edward Stratemeyer]. 8vo. [*Amer. Cat.*]   New York, 1900

YOUNG barbarians. By Ian Maclaren [Rev. John Watson, D.D.]. 8vo. Pp. iv. 318. [*Who's Who in Lit.*]
London, 1901

YOUNG (the) baronet ; a novel. By the author of *The Scottish heiress*, etc. [Robert Mackenzie Daniel]. 12mo. 3 vols. [*Camb. Univ. Lib.*]
London, 1846

YOUNG blood. By Ian Hay [John Hay Beith, M.A.]. 8vo. [Bartholomew's *Camb. Books*, p. 21.]
London, 1905

YOUNG Brown or the law of inheritance. By the author of *The member for Paris*, etc. [Eustace Clare Grenville Murray]. 8vo. 3 vols. [*Brit. Mus.*]
London, 1874

YOUNG (the) chaplain. By his mother [Mrs Marianne C. Johnston, *née* Howe]. 8vo.   New York, 1876

YOUNG (the) Chevalier ; or, a genuine narrative of all that befell that unfortunate adventurer, from his fatal defeat to his final escape. . . . By a gentleman who was personally acquainted . . . with many of the actors [Henry Goring ?]. Pp. iv. 108.
London [1746 ?]

YOUNG (the) churchman's manual ; containing reasons for, and explanations of, the services of morning and evening prayer. By a member of the Church of England [J. A. Thornthwaite]. 12mo. [*Brit. Mus.*]
London, 1837

YOUNG (the) clergyman's companion, in visiting the sick. [By Rev. Richard Batty.] [Watt's *Bibl. Brit.*]   1756

YOUNG (the) commander ; a novel. By the author of *The two midshipmen*, etc. [F. Claudius Armstrong]. 12mo. 3 vols. [*Camb. Univ. Lib.*]
London, 1856

YOUNG (the) communicants ; written for the use of the poor school, Bermondsey, and respectfully dedicated to the Reverend Peter Butler, by the author of *Geraldine, a tale of Conscience* [Miss E. C. Agnew]. With the approbation of the Right Reverend Dr Griffiths, V.A.L. 12mo. Pp. 116. [*Bodl.*]   London, 1840

YOUNG (the) cottager ; a true story. By the author of *The dairyman's daughter* [Legh Richmond, M.A., rector of Turvey, Bedfordshire]. 32mo. Pp. 40. [*Brit. Mus.*]   London [1826]

YOUNG (the) curate ; or the quicksands of life. [By John Harvey Ashworth, M.A.] 8vo. [F. Boase's *Mod. Eng. Biog.* i. 98.]   London, 1859

YOUNG (the) days of Admiral Quilliam. [A historical novel of Lord Nelson's time.] By F. Norreys Connell [Conal O'Connell O'Riordan]. 8vo. [O'Donoghue's *Poets of Ireland*.]   London, 1906

YOUNG days of authors. By Ascott R. Hope [Robert Hope Moncrieff]. 8vo. Pp. 380. [*Brit. Mus.*]
London, 1885

YOUNG (the) doctor ; a novel. By the author of *Lady Granard's nieces* [Jane Vaughan Pinkney]. 8vo. 3 vols. [*Brit. Mus.*]   London, 1851

YOUNG (a) dragon. [A tale of moorland life near the English border.] By Sarah Tytler [Henrietta Keddie]. 8vo. Pp. 276. [*Who's Who in Lit.*]
London, 1900

YOUNG (the) dragoon ; or, everyday life of a soldier. By one who has served [Major-General Alfred Wilkes Drayson, R.A.]. 12mo. [*Brit. Mus.*]
London [1870]

YOUNG (the) duke. By the author of *Vivian Grey* [Benjamin Disraeli]. 12mo. 3 vols. [*D.N.B.* vol. 15, p. 116.]   London, 1831

YOUNG Emily. By Ann Jane [Mrs Ann Jane Morgan]. 48mo. Pp. 16. [*W.*]   London

YOUNG Fawcett's Mabel. By Albert Ross [Linn Boyd Porter]. 8vo. Pp. 312. [*Brit. Mus.*]   New York, 1896

YOUNG folks' travels in Asia and Africa. By Rupert Van West [Daniel Clarke Eddy]. 4to. [Cushing's *Init. and Pseud.* i. 292.]   Chicago, 1887

YOUNG folks' travels in Europe. By Rupert Van West [Daniel Clarke Eddy]. 4to. [Cushing's *Init. and Pseud.* i. 292.]   Chicago, 1887

YOUNG (the) game-warden. By Harry Castlemon [Charles Austin Fosdick]. 8vo. Pp. 411. [*Amer. Cat.*]
New York, 1896

YOUNG heads on old shoulders. By Ascott R. Hope, author of *A peck of troubles*, etc. [Robert Hope Moncrieff]. 8vo. Pp. 3, 179. [*Brit. Mus.*]
London [1879]

YOUNG hearts. By J. E. Buckrose [Mrs Falconer Jameson]. 8vo. Pp. 315. [*Brit. Mus.*]   London, 1920

YOUNG (the) housekeeper as daughter, wife, and mother; forming a perfect "young woman's companion" in all her social relations. . . . Compiled by the editor of *The family friend* [Robert Kemp Philp]. 8vo. Pp. viii. 376. [*D. N. B.* vol. 45, p. 226.]
London, N.D.

YOUNG (the) Huguenots; or the soldiers of the Cross; a story of the seventeenth century. By "Fleur de Lys" [Edith S. Floyer]. 12mo.
New York, 1884
Later editions bear the author's name.

YOUNG husbands. [A comedy.] By John Daly [John Besemeres, merchant in Calcutta]. 8vo. [Cushing's *Init. and Pseud.* i. 77.]   London, 1852

YOUNG (the) idea; a sketch for "old boys," by one of them. By the author of *Culmshire folk* [James Franklin Fuller]. 8vo. Pp. 171. [*Brit. Mus.*]
London, 1884

YOUNG (the) knight-errant. By Oliver Optic [William Taylor Adams]. 12mo. [Cushing's *Init. and Pseud.* i. 219.]
Boston, 1892

YOUNG (the) lady's friend; practical advice and instruction to young females. By a lady [Mrs Eliza R. Farrar]. 8vo.   London, 1837

YOUNG (the) lady's geography; containing an accurate description of the several parts of the known world. . . . [By —— Demarville.] 12mo. [*Brit. Mus.*]   London, 1765

YOUNG (the) lady's introduction to natural history. . . . By the editor of the *Young Lady's Geography* [—— Demarville]. 12mo. [*Brit. Mus.*]
London, 1766

YOUNG (the) Lord. By the author of *The discipline of life*, etc. [Lady Emily Ponsonby]. 8vo. 2 vols. [*Nat. Lib. of Scot.*]   London, 1856

YOUNG Lord Stranleigh. By Luke Sharp [Robert Barr]. 8vo. [*Amer. Cat.*]   New York, 1908

YOUNG (a) man married. [A novel.] By Sydney C. Grier [Hilda C. Gregg]. 8vo. Pp. 348. [*Who's Who in Lit.*]
London, 1909

YOUNG (a) man's account of his conversion from Calvinism. [By Sylvester Judd.] 12mo.   Boston, 1838

YOUNG (a) man's difficulties with his Bible. By the author of *The Christian in the World* [Daniel Worcester Faunce]. 12mo. [Kirk's *Supp.*]
London, 1877
The first edition (New York, 1876) bears the author's name.

YOUNG (the) man's fancy; and other tales. By Mrs Forrester [Mrs —— Bridges]. 12mo. 3 vols. [*Amer. Cat.*]
New York, 1887

YOUNG (the) man's guide. [By William A. Alcott.] 12mo. [*Brit. Mus.*]
Boston, 1833

YOUNG (the) man's guide in the choice of a benefit society; or, the danger of choosing a bad club, and the advantage of entering a well-regulated friendly society, illustrated: in three dialogues. By a Suffolk clergyman [Samuel Hobson]. 12mo. [*Brit. Mus.*]
London, 1846

YOUNG (the) man's guide through the wilderness of this world to the Heavenly Canaan. [By Thomas Gouge.] 8vo. [*Brit. Mus.*]
London, 1672

YOUNG (a) man's year. By Anthony Hope [Sir Anthony Hope Hawkins]. 8vo. Pp. 351. [*Brit. Mus.*]
London, 1915

YOUNG Master Kirke. By Penn Shirley [Sarah J. Clarke]. 12mo. Pp. 156. [*Amer. Cat.*]   Boston [1895]

YOUNG (the) mechanic; a book for boys: containing directions for the use of all kinds of tools, and for the construction of steam engines and mechanical models, including the art of turning in wood and metal. By the author of *The lathe and its uses*, etc. [Rev. James Lukin]. 8vo. Pp. iv. 346. [*Brit. Mus.*]   London, 1871

YOUNG Miss Giddy. [A novel.] By Albert Ross [Linn Boyd Porter]. 8vo. [*Brit. Mus.*]   New York, 1893

YOUNG Mistley. [A novel.] By Henry Seton Merriman [Hugh Stowell Scott]. 8vo. [*Brit. Mus.*]   London, 1888

YOUNG (the) mountaineer; or Frank Miller's lot in life: the story of a Swiss boy. [From the French of Mlle. Julie Gouraud, *pseud.* for Louise d'Aulnan.] By Daryl Holme [David Herbert]. 8vo. [*Nat. Lib. of Scot.*]
Edinburgh, 1870

YOUNG (the) mountaineers; short stories. By Charles Egbert Craddock [Mary Noailles Murfree]. 8vo. Pp. 262. [*Brit. Mus.*]   Boston, 1897

YOUNG Mrs Jardine. By the author of *John Halifax, gentleman*, etc. [Dinah Maria Mulock, later Mrs Craik]. 8vo. 3 vols. [*Brit. Mus.*]   London, 1879

YOUNG Mrs Teddy. By Barbara Yechton [Lyda Farrington Krausé]. 8vo. [*Amer. Cat.*]   New York, 1901

YOUNG (the) navigators. By Oliver Optic [William Taylor Adams]. 8vo. [Cushing's *Init. and Pseud.* i. 219.]
Boston, 1894

YOUNG (the) O'Briens; being an account of their sojourn in London. By the author of *Elizabeth's children* and *Helen Blackiston* [Margaret Westrup, later Mrs Sydney Stacey]. 8vo.   London, 1906

YOUNG Ofeg's ditties. By Ola Hansson, translated from the Swedish by George Egerton [Mrs Mary C. Clairmonte]. 8vo. Pp. 191. [*Brit. Mus.*]   London, 1895

YOUNG (a) Oxford maid, in the days of the King and the Parliament. By Sarah Tytler [Henrietta Keddie]. 8vo. Pp. 320. [*Who's Who in Lit.*]
London [1890]

YOUNG (the) patriot, and other poems. By J. B., a friend of the Aborigines Protection Society [John Burtt]. 8vo. [Sabin's *Dictionary.*]
Manchester [1846]

YOUNG (the) patroon; or Christmas in 1690 : a tale of New York. By the author of *The First of the Knickerbockers* [P. Hamilton Myers]. 12mo. [*Brit. Mus.*]   New York, 1849

YOUNG (the) people. By one of the old people [Stephen Paget, M.D.]. 8vo. [*Brit. Mus.*]   London, 1906

YOUNG (the) pilgrim; a tale illustrative of "The Pilgrim's progress." By A. L. O. E., author of *The Shepherd of Bethlehem*, etc. [Charlotte M. Tucker]. 8vo. Pp. 286. [*Brit. Mus.*]
London, 1889

YOUNG (the) Quaker; a comedy : as it is performed at the Theatre Royal in Smock-Alley, with great applause. [By John O'Keefe.] 12mo. Pp. 36. [Smith's *Bibl. Anti-Quak.*, pp. 45, 345.]
Dublin, 1784

YOUNG (the) rebels; a story of the Battle of Lexington. By Ascott R. Hope [Robert Hope Moncrieff]. 8vo. [*Brit. Mus.*]   London, 1878

YOUNG (the) Roscius. By Bisset [W. H. W. Betty]. [*Birm. Ref. Lib.*]
N.P. 1804

YOUNG Sam and Sabina. [A novel.] By the author of *Gentleman Upcott's daughter* [Walter Raymond]. 8vo. Pp. 188. [*Brit. Mus.*] London, 1894

YOUNG Sam; or, the native American's own book. By a native American [E. Hutchinson]. 8vo. [Cushing's *Init. and Pseud.* i. 201.]
New York, 1855

YOUNG (a) savage. By Barbara Yechton [Lyda Farrington Krausé]. [*Amer. Cat.*]   Boston, 1899

YOUNG Scarron. [By Thomas Mozeen.] 12mo. [Lowndes' *Bibl. Man., s. v. Scarron.*]   London, 1751

YOUNG (the) seigneur; or, nation-making. By Wilfrid Châteauclair [William D. Lighthall]. Pp. vi. 200. [*Brit. Mus.*]   Montreal, 1888

YOUNG Singleton. [A novel.] By Talbot Gwynne [Josepha Heath Gulston]. 2 vols. 12mo.
London, 1856
The author's name is given as Galston in the *Brit. Mus. Catalogue.*

YOUNG (the) sportsman's complete manual of fowling, fishing, and field sports in general. By Frank Forester [Henry William Herbert]. 8vo. [Cushing's *Init. and Pseud.* i. 104.]
London, 1852

YOUNG (the) sportsman's instructor in angling, fowling, hawking, hunting, ordering singing birds, hawks, poultry, coneys, hares and dogs, and how to cure them. By G. M. [Gervase Markham]. 8vo. Pp. 140. [Arber's *Term Cat.* iii. 528.]   [London, 1706]

YOUNG (the) sportsman's manual; with some account of the game of the British Islands. By "Craven" [Captain John William Carleton]. 8vo. [*Brit. Mus.*]   London, 1849

YOUNG (the) spy. By "Bruin" [J. F. C. Adams]. 8vo. [Cushing's *Init. and Pseud.* ii. 20.]   New York, 1877

YOUNG (the) squire's resolve. By Waldo Gray [Luther Winther Caws]. 8vo.   London, 1901

YOUNG (the) step-mother; or, a chronicle of mistakes. By the author of *The heir of Redclyffe*, etc. [Charlotte Mary Yonge]. 8vo. Pp. 482. [*Brit. Mus.*]   London, 1861

YOUNG (the) student's library, containing extracts and abridgements of the most valuable books printed in England. . . . [By John Dunton.] Folio.   London, 1682

YOUNG travellers' tales. . . . By Ascott R. Hope [Robert Hope Moncrieff]. 8vo. Pp. 288. [*Brit. Mus.*]   London [1895]

YOUNG (the) violinist. By Emma von Rhoden [Emmy von Friedrich-Friedrich]; translated from the twelfth edition of the German. . . . 8vo. [*Amer. Cat.*]   Akron, O., 1906

YOUNG (the) widow; a novel. By the author of the *Scotish heiress*, etc. [Robert Mackenzie Daniel]. 12mo. 3 vols. [*Brit. Mus.*]   London, 1844

YOUNG (the) widow ; or, the history of Cornelia Sedley, in a series of letters. [By William Hayley.] 12mo. 4 vols. [Nichols' *Lit. Anec.* ix. 50.]
London, 1789

YOUNG (a) wife's trial ; or, Ralph Ryder of Brent. [A novel.] By Florence Warden [Florence Alice Price, later Mrs George E. James]. 8vo. Pp. 312. [*Who's Who in Lit.*]
London, 1893

YOUNG (the) wild-fowlers. By Harry Castlemon [Charles Austin Fosdick]. 12mo. [*Amer. Cat.*]
Philadelphia, 1885

YOVNGER (the) brother his apologie, or a fathers free power disputed, for the disposition of his lands, or other his fortunes to his sonne, sonnes, or any one of them ; as right reason, the lawes of God and nature, the civil, canon, and municipall laws of this kingdome doe command. [By J. Ap-Robert.] 4to. Pp. 56. [*Madan's Oxf. Books.*] Oxford, 1624 [for 1634]
Epistle to the reader signed : J. A. Erroneously assigned to J. Allen.

YOUNGER (the) sister. [By Anne Dawe.] 12mo. 2 vols. [*Gent. Mag.* xciv. 1. 136.]   London, 1770

YOUNGER (a) sister. [A novel.] By the author of *The Atelier du Lys*, etc. [Margaret Roberts]. 8vo. Pp. 314. [*Brit. Mus.*]   London, 1892

YOUNGEST (the) Miss Brown. [A novel.] By Florence Warden [Florence Alice Price, later Mrs George E. James]. 8vo. Pp. 320. [*Who's Who in Lit.*]
London, 1905

YOUNG-LADYISM ; a handbook on the education, accomplishments, duties, dress, and deportment of the upper ten thousand. By Democritus Machiavel Brown, Esq. [James Macgrigor Allan]. 12mo.   London [1859]
Title-page of his " The Intellectual Severance of Men and Women."

YOUNGSTERS' Yarns. By Ascott R. Hope [Robert Hope Moncrieff]. 8vo. Pp. x. 372. [*Brit. Mus.*]
London, 1888

YOUR fortune in your name ; or Kabalistic astrology. By "Sepharial" [Walter Gorn Old]. 8vo. Pp. 96. [*Brit. Mus.*]   London, 1910

YOUR life. By the author of *My life, by an Ex-Dissenter* [George Rawston]. 8vo.   London, 1841

YOURS and mine. By Amy Lothrop [Anna Bartlett Warner]. [*Kirk's Suppl.*] 8vo.   New York, 1889

YOUTH ; a narrative ; and two other stories. By Joseph Conrad [Joseph Conrad Korzeniowski]. 8vo. Pp. 384. [*Brit. Mus.*]   Edinburgh, 1902

YOUTH ; and Gaspar Ruiz. By Joseph Conrad [Joseph Conrad Korzeniowski]. 8vo. Pp. 192. [*Brit. Mus.*]
London, 1920

YOUTH (the) and manhood of Cyril Thornton. [By Capt. Thomas Hamilton.] 8vo. 3 vols. [*Nat. Lib. of Scot.*]
Edinburgh, 1827

YOUTH (the) and womanhood of Helen Tyrrel. By the author of *Brampton Rectory, Compton Merivale*, etc. [Mary Matilda Howard]. 12mo. [*Gent. Mag.* Oct. 1851, p. 406.]
London, 1854

YOUTH in twelve centuries ; poems by M. E. B. [Mrs Mary Elizabeth Blake, née M'Grath]. 8vo.   Boston, 1886

YOUTH, know thy selfe. [A poem. By Richard Turner.] 4to. [*Brit. Mus.*]   London, 1624

YOUTH (the) of Shakspeare. By the author of *Shakspeare and his friends* [R. Folkestone Williams]. 12mo. 3 vols. [Jaggard's *Shakespeare Bibl.*]
London, 1839

YOUTHFUL pilgrims ; or, memorials of young persons of the Society of Friends. [By Esther Seebohm.] 8vo. [*Brit. Mus.*]   London, 1854

YOUTHFUL (the) prophet, and Israel's first king. By the author of *Mothers in council* [Harriet Bickersteth, later Mrs Cook]. 8vo. [*Brit. Mus.*]
London [1866]

YOUTHFUL sprouts of poesy. [By R. Gibson.] 12mo. Pp. 100.
Edinburgh [private print], 1897

YOUTH'S (the) business guide ; a practical manual for those entering life. By " Experientia " [John Southward, printer]. 12mo. Pp. 145.
London, 1883

YOUTH'S comedy ; or the soul's tryals and triumph : a dramatick poem, with divers meditations intermixt. . . . By the author of *Youth's tragedy* [Thomas Sherman]. 8vo. [*Arber's Term Cat.* i. 381.]   London, 1680

YOUTH'S friendly monitor ; being a set of directions, prudential, moral, religious, and scientific . . . together with Theophilus, a character worthy of imitation. By the author of *Britain's Remembrancer* [James Burgh]. 12mo. 2 parts. [*Brit. Mus.*]   London, 1724

YOUTH'S history of California. By
Lucia Norman [Mrs S. M. Heaven].
12mo. [Cushing's *Init. and Pseud.*
i. 205.]				San Francisco, 1867
YOUTH'S (the) miscellany; or, a
father's gift to his children. . . . By
the author of the *Juvenile Olio*, etc.
[William Fordyce Mavor, LL.D.].
12mo. Pp. xi. 286. [*D. N. B.* vol. 37,
p. 108.]				London, 1798
   A later edition (1814) with the title "A
Father's gift to his children" bears the
author's name.

YOUTH'S (the) spelling, pronouncing,
and explanatory theological dictionary.
. . . By E. D. [Emerson Dowson].
8vo.				London, 1818

YOUTH'S tragedy; a poem, drawn up by
way of dialogue between youth, the
devil, wisdom, time, death, the soul and
the Nuncius. By T. S. [Thomas
Sherman]. 4to. [Arber's *Term Cat.*
i. 532.]				London, 1671
YULE (the) log, for everybody's Christmas
hearth; showing where it grew, where
it was cut out and brought home, and
how it was burnt. By the author of
The Chronicles of the Bastile [Louis
Alexis Chamerovzow]. 12mo. [*Bodl.*]
				London, 1847
YULE-TIDE; faces in the fire. By a
clergyman's wife [Mrs Fanny Hart,
née Wheeler]. 12mo. Pp. 15.
				Manchester, N.D.

Z

ZADKIEL'S almanac for 1851, etc. [By
Lieut. Richard James Morrison.] 8vo.
[*Brit. Mus.*]				London, 1851

ZADOC, the outcast of Israel; a tale.
By Charlotte Elizabeth [Mrs Charlotte
Elizabeth Tonna, *née* Browne]. 12mo.
[*D. N. B.*, vol. 57, p. 34.] London, 1825

ZADOK the Israelite. [A poem. By
Mrs Ann Wilson.] 12mo. [*Brit.
Mus.*]				London, 1837

ZAIDA'S nursery note-book; for the
use of mothers. By A. L. O. E.,
author of *Shepherd of Bethlehem*, etc.
[Charlotte M. Tucker.] 8vo. Pp. 135.
[*Brit. Mus.*]				London, 1867

ZAMBRA the detective. [A novel.]
By Headon Hill [Frank E. Grainger].
8vo. [*Who's Who in Lit.*]
				London, 1894
ZANA; or the heiress of Clair Hall.
By the author of *Fashion and famine*
[Mrs Ann S. Stephens]. 12mo.
				London, 1854
Fashion and famine is not anonymous.

ZANONI. [A novel.] By the author of
Night and Morning [Edward George
Earle Lytton Bulwer - Lytton, Lord
Lytton]. 8vo. 3 vols. [*D. N. B.* vol.
34, p. 386.]				London, 1842

ZARA, and other stories. By the author
of *Molly Bawn* [Mrs Margaret W.
Hungerford, *née* Hamilton]. 12mo.
[*Brit. Mus.*]				London, 1890

ZARA, at the Court of Annamaboe, to
the African Prince now in England.
[By William Dodd, LL.D.] 4to.
Pp. 15. [Watt's *Bibl. Brit.*]
				London, 1749
   See also "The African Prince now in
England, to Zara . . ."

ZARA; or, the black death: a poem of
the sea. By the author of *Naufragus*
[M. J. Horne]. 8vo. Pp. xii. 220.
[*Brit. Mus.*]				London, 1833
ZARAILLA; a novel. By "Beulah"
[Fanny D. Bates]. 8vo. Pp. 323.
[Cushing's *Init. and Pseud.* i. 35.]
				New York, 1889
ZAREEFA; a tale, and other poems.
By the author of *Cephalus and Procris*,
etc. [Helen Lowe]. 8vo. Pp. vii. 171.
[*Eng. Cat.*]				London, 1844
ZASTROZZI; a romance. By P. B. S.
[Percy Bysshe Shelley]. 8vo. Pp. 252.
[*D. N. B.* vol. 52, p. 32.] London, 1810
   Shelley's first publication. He was aged
sixteen and still at Eton.

ZAYDA; a Spanish tale, in three cantos;
and other poems, stanzas, and canzonets.
By Oscar [Mrs Leman Grimstone].
12mo. Pp. ix. 163. [*Nat. Lib. of Scot.*]
				London, 1820
ZEAL without innovation; or the present
state of religion and morals considered;
with a view to the dispositions and
measures required for its improvement.
. . . [By James Bean, vicar of Olney.]
8vo. Pp. 392. [*Camb. Univ. Lib.*]
				London, 1808

ZEALOUS (the) and impartial Protestant; shewing some great but less heeded dangers of Popery. . . . [By Joseph Glanvill, M.A.] 4to. Pp. 64. [*D. N. B.* vol. 21, p. 409.] London, 1681

ZEALOUS beleevers are the best subjects to Cæsar; or, an exhortation to all good Christians to pray for their princes. . . . Published by J. F. [John Ferret]. 8vo. [*Brit. Mus.*]
[Amsterdam] 1643

ZEBULON advised. . . . By a minister of the Gospel [Rev. Nathanael Clap]. 8vo.   Newport [U.S.A.], 1738

ZELIA in the desert; from the French [of Mad. Marguérite Daubenton] by a lady. 12mo. 3 vols. [Barbier's *Dictionnaire*.]   London, 1789

ZELIDA; a tragedy. By the author [Thomas Horde]. 8vo. Pp. 55. [*Brit. Mus.*]   Oxford, 1772

ZELINDA. [A poem. By Mrs Eardly Hall.] 8vo. [*Brit. Mus.*]
Brighton [1850?]

ZELMANE; or, the Corinthian Queen; a tragedy. [By William Mountfort.] As it is acted at the New-Theatre in Lincoln's-Inn-Fields by Her Majesties servants. 4to. [Baker's *Biog. Dram.*]
London, 1705

ZELOTES and Honestus reconciled; or, an equal check to Pharasaism and Antinomianism continued: being the first part of the Scripture-scales to weigh the gold of Gospel-truth:—to balance a multitude of opposite Scriptures;—to prove the Gospel-marriage of free-grace and free-will: and restore primitive harmony to the Gospel of the day. . . . By a lover of the whole truth as it is in Jesus [John Fletcher]. 12mo. Pp. xxvi. 204.   London, 1705
There is a second part, with a half title, occupying from p. 205 to p. 443.

ZELUCO; various views of human nature, taken from life and manners, foreign and domestic. [By John Moore, M.D.] 8vo. 2 vols. [*D. N. B.* vol. 38, p. 364.]   London, 1789

ZEMINDARY (the) settlement of Bengal. [By R. H. Hollingbery.] 8vo. 2 vols.   Calcutta, 1879

ZENANA (the); or a Nuwab's leisure hours. By the author of *Pandurang Hari* [William Browne Hockley]. 12mo. 3 vols. [*Brit. Mus.*]
London, 1827

ZENITH distances, observed with the mural circle at the Royal Observatory, Cape of Good Hope, and the calculation of the geocentric south polar distances for 1836-7. [By Thomas Maclear, F.R.A.S., Her Majesty's astronomer at the Cape of Good Hope.] 4to. [*W.*]   N.P. 1837

ZENOBIA; a tragedy, as it is performed at the Theatre Royal in Drury-Lane. By the author of *The Orphan of China* [Arthur Murphy]. 8vo. Pp. 82. [Baker's *Biog. Dram.*]
London, 1768

ZENOBIA; or the fall of Palmyra: a historical romance: in letters of Lucius M. Piso from Palmyra, to his friend Marcus Curtius at Rome. [By Rev. William Ware.] 8vo. 2 vols. [*Brit. Mus.*]   London, 1844

ZETETIC astronomy; a description of several experiments which prove that the surface of the sea is a perfect plane, and that the earth is not a globe! Being the substance of a paper read before the Royal Astronomical Society on the evening of Dec. 8, 1848. By Parallax [Dr Samuel Birley Rowbotham]. 12mo. Pp. 16. [*Bookseller*, Jan. 7. 1885.]
Birmingham, 1849

ZETETIC astronomy; an experimental enquiry proving the earth to be a plane, and the only world in the universe. By Parallax [Dr Samuel Birley Rowbotham]. 12mo. [*Brit. Mus.*]   London, 1865

ZIEKE Reiziger; or, rambles in Java and the Straits in 1852. By a Bengal Civilian [Charles Walker Kinloch]. 8vo.   Teignmouth, 1853

ZIGZAG to Paris, and straight home. [By Francis H. Jessop.] 8vo. [*Brit. Mus.*]   London, 1850

ZIG-ZAGGING amongst Dolomites. [By Miss Elizabeth Tuckett.] Folio. [*Brit. Mus.*]   London, 1871
Also ascribed to M. and R. W. Dunlop.

ZIKE Mouldom; a novel. By Orme Agnus [John C. Higginbotham]. 8vo. [*Who's Who in Lit.*]   London, 1902

ZILLAH; a tale of the Holy City. By the author of *Brambletye House*, etc. [Horace Smith]. Second edition. 3 vols. 12mo.   London, 1828

ZION'S warrior; or the Christian soldier's manual in which the duties and occupations of the military life are spiritualised and improved. [By Robert Hawker, D.D.] 8vo. [*Brit. Mus.*]   London, 1802

ZION'S works; new light on the Bible from the coming of Shiloh, the Spirit of truth, 1828-37 [edited by C. B. Holinsworth, of Birmingham]. [By John Ward.] [*Birm. Cent. Lib.*]
Birmingham, 1899-1904

ZIT and Zoe; their early experiences. [A novel. By Henry Curwen, journalist.] Originally published in *Blackwood's Magazine*. 8vo. Pp. 131. [*Brit. Mus.*]   Edinburgh, 1886

ZOBEIR ; or, Turkish misrule. By
William St Clair [William Ford,
C.I.E.]. 8vo. Pp. 248. [*Who's Who
in Lit.*]   London, 1899
ZODIACAL (the) chess-board. By J.
H. S. [Joseph Houghton Spencer].
Folio. [*Brit. Mus.*]   Taunton, 1899
ZODIAKE (the) of life ; written by the
godly and zealous poet Marcellus
Palingenius Stellatus [Pietro Angelo
Manzolli] : newly translated into
Englishe verse by Barnabie Googe.
B. L. 8vo. [*Brit. Mus.*]
                             London, 1565
    For previous editions, *see* " The firste thre
    bokes . . ." and " The firste syxe bokes . . ."

ZOE ; a Sicilian Sayda. [By Lloyd
Wharton Bickley.] 8vo. [*Cushing's
Anon.*]   Philadelphia [1830 ?]
ZOË ; an Athenian tale. [By John
Campbell Colquhoun, of Killermont.]
12mo. Pp. ix. 115. Edinburgh, 1824
    Printed for private circulation.

ZOË the dancer. [A novel.] By Ida
Wild [Mrs Meynell Pearson]. 8vo.
Pp. 302.   London, 1911
ZOE'S 'brand'. . . [By Mrs M. C.
Houstoun.] 8vo. 3 vols.
                             London, 1864
ZOFLOYA ; or, the Moor : a romance
of the fifteenth century. By Charlotte
Dacre [Mrs Byrne, better known as
Rosa Matilda, author of the Nun of
St Omers, Hours of solitude, etc.].
12mo. 3 vols.   London, 1806
ZOHRAB the hostage. By the author
of *Hajji Baba* [James Justinian Morier].
12mo. 3 vols. [*Brit. Mus.*]
                             London, 1832
ZONE (the) of fire. [A novel.] By
Headon Hill [Frank E. Grainger].
8vo. Pp. 432. [*Who's Who in Lit.*]
                             London, 1897

ΖΩΟΛΟΓΙ'Α ; or, the history of animals,
as they are useful in physick and
chirurgery. . . . By John Schroder.
[Translated by T. B. *i.e.* T. Bateson.]
8vo. Pp. 159. [*Brit. Mus.*]
                             London, 1659
ZOÖLOGICAL notes and anecdotes.
By Sestertius Holt [William White
Cooper, surgeon-oculist]. 8vo. [*Brit.
Mus.*]   London, 1852
ZOOLOGY (the) of Beloochistan and
Southern Afghanistan. [By James A.
Murray.] 8vo. [*Calc. Imp. Lib.*]
                             Bombay [1887]
ZOPHIËL ; or, the bride of seven. By
Maria del Occidente [Maria Brooks].
8vo.   London, 1833
ZORAH ; a love-tale of modern Egypt.
By D. T. S. [Elizabeth Batch]. 8vo.
                             Edinburgh, 1886
ZORAIDA ; a tragedy ; as it is acted
at the Theatre-Royal in Drury-Lane :
to which is added a postscript, con-
taining observations on tragedy. [By
William Hodson.] 8vo. Pp. 104.
[Baker's *Biog. Dram.*]   London, 1780
ZULEKA ; being the history of an
adventure in the life of an American
gentleman. By " R." [Clinton Ross].
8vo. Pp. 222. [*Amer. Cat.*]
                             Boston, 1897
ZULNEIDA ; a tale of Sicily. By the
author of *The White cottage* [A.
Mower]. 8vo. 3 vols. [*Nat. Lib. of
Scot.*]   London, 1837
ZULU (the) war ; giving a descriptive
account of Isandula, Rorke's Drift,
Saving the colours, Cetywayo and his
chiefs in Council, Flogging the troops,
the Prince Imperial, Lord Chelmsford's
victories, etc. [In verse.] By a Cape
Correspondent [George Walter Boyce].
12mo. Pp. 30. [Mendelssohn's *South
Afr. Bibl.* i. 177.]   Wells, 1879

SUPPLEMENT

An asterisk (*) signifies an addition or correction to an entry which has already appeared in the main part of the Dictionary.

A

A bon chat bon rat, tit for tat ; a new and idiomatic course of instruction in the French language. By Chrysostôme Dagobert [Jean Baptiste Alphonse Led'huy]. 8vo. [*Brit. Mus.*]
London [1855]

A. E. Housman ; a list of adversaria, etc. . . . Compiled by A. S. F. G. [Andrew S. F. Gow]. 8vo. Pp. 11. [*Brit. Mus.*] Cambridge, 1926

À vous, and others. By Veritas [Miss D. Allbeury]. 8vo. Pp. 16. [*Brit. Mus.*] London [1914]

A B C (the) of fair trade ; addressed especially to the British workman. By "S. N." [Stuart James Nicholson]. 8vo. Pp. 36. [*Brit. Mus.*]
London [1905]

A B C (the) of the U.M.C.A. [Universities' Mission to Central Africa]. Prose and pictures for young and old. Compiled by M. E. W. [M. E. Woodward]. Obl. 8vo. Pp. 30. [*Brit. Mus.*]
London [1899]

*A B C (an) or holy alphabet . . .
Author's advertisement signed : E. C.
The author's name is also spelt Cancellar. There were previous editions of this work, under the title "The Alphabet of prayers" in 1565, 1570, 1573, 1576 and 1591. The last was issued under the Initials J. C. ; the others were not anonymous.

A B C (the) ; or, the institution of a Christian, etc. [containing the Creed, Lord's Prayer, Scripture texts, etc., published by William Bedell, Bishop of Kilmore and Ardagh. In English and Irish]. 8vo. Pp. 13. [*Brit. Mus.*] Dublin, 1631
The Irish text is printed with the Irish types presented by Queen Elizabeth to J. O'Kearney, with which he printed his Catechism, 1571.

A, B, C, or, thoughts on the principles of Biblical interpretation. . . . [By James Wapshare.] 8vo. 3 parts. [*Brit. Mus.*] [London, 1867]
Signed : J. W., Octogenarius.

VOL. VI.

ABIMELECH ; an oratorio. The music by Mr Arnold. [The words by Christopher Smart.] 4to. Pp. 23. [*Brit. Mus.*] [London, *c.* 1768]

ABOLITION (the) of the slave trade, peace, and . . . reform, essential to the salvation of England. [By William Ward.] 8vo. Pp. 24. [Whitley's *Bapt. Bibl.*] N.P. 1796

ABOUT mending the coyn. [By Thomas Neale, Groom-Porter to their Majesties.] Fol. S. sh. [*Brit. Mus.*]
London, 1695

ABRACADABRA ; or, freemasonry secrets revealed. [By Reginald Stuart.] 8vo. Pp. 7. [*Brit. Mus.*] London [1928]
Authorship disclosed in the preface to his "Freemasonry."

ABRAHAM Christian lawmaker. [A tale.] By Prudens Futuri [Nelly Davidson]. 8vo. Pp. 340. [*Brit. Mus.*] Printed in Holland, 1925

ABRIDGEMENT (an) of a discourse on self-dedication, by John Howe. . . . [Edited by J. A. *i.e.* John Audley.] 8vo. Pp.xv. 73. [*Brit.Mus.*] Cambridge,1785

ABRIDGEMENT (an) of the evidence before the select committee appointed . . . to consider the . . . means of preventing bribery, corruption, and intimidation in the election of members to serve in Parliament. With remarks. [By Thomas Martin.] 8vo. [*Brit. Mus.*] London, 1837
Signed : M.

*ABRIDGEMENT (the) or svmmarie of the Scots chronicles . . .
The first edition (1612) was not anonymous.

[ABRIDGMENT of cases to the end of Henry VI. By Nicholas Statham.] 4to. [*D. N. B.* vol. 54, p. 112 ; *Pollard and Redgrave.*] [Rouen, 1490]

ABRIDGMENT (an) of ecclesiastical history (by J. L. von Mosheim) . . . translated . . . by A. Maclaine . . . and now abridged by a layman [J. Parkinson]. 8vo. [*Brit. Mus.*] 1787

S

ABRIDGMENT of modern voyages and travels. By T. Clark [John Galt]. 12mo. [*Eng. Cat.*, 1801-1836, p. 118.] London, 1819

ABRIDGMENT (a) of Swedenborg's work entitled The true Christian religion. . . . [By Rev. John Hyde]. 8vo. Pp. xviii. 318. [*Swedenborg Bibl.* p. 577.] London, 1868

Reprinted at Boston in 1869.

ABSENTEEISM injurious to Ireland; a brief argument in answer to an essay or dialogue entitled Absenteeism. [By Thomas Falconer of Lincoln's Inn.] 8vo. [Falconer's *Letters and Notes on the Texas Santa Fé Expedition* (ed. F. W. Hodge), p. 145.] Bath, 1829

ABSTRACT of a Bill for the reformation of the High Court of Chancery. [By Edgar Taylor.] 8vo. [*Lincoln's Inn Lib.*] London, 1831

ABSTRACT (an) of a treatise concerning the payment of tythes and oblations in London. [By Bryan Walton.] 4to. [*Lincoln's Inn Lib.*] London, 1662

ABSTRACT of Colenso on the Pentateuch. . . . To which is appended an essay on the nation and country of the Jews. [By William Henry Burr.] 8vo. Pp. 48. [*Brit. Mus.*] New York, 1871

ABSURDITY (the) of that new devised state-principle (viz.) that in a monarchy the legislative power is communicable to the subject, and is not radically in sovereignty in one, but in more; in a letter, to a friend. [By John Brydall.] 4to. [*Lincoln's Inn Lib.*] London, 1681

A B U S E S discovered whereby the creditors are meerly cheated; the officers of law and gaolers are unjustly inriched; and the poor debter and their families destroyed. [By William Gery?] Fol. S. sh. [*Brit. Mus.*] [London, 1649]

Signed: W. G.

ABUSES of the laws. By Guy Mitford [George Moore, of Warrington]. 8vo. [Sutton's *Lancashire Authors.*] 1832

ACADEMICAL (the) sportsman; or, seven wise men of Gotham: burletta in three acts. [By Rev. Robert Burrowes?] [O'Donoghue's *Poets of Ireland*, p. 16.] Dublin [1795?]

A skit on "The academic sportsman, or a winter's day: a poem. By Rev. Gerald Fitzgerald" (1773).

ACCOMPLISH'D (the) maid; a comic opera. . . . [Translated from Goldoni's *La Buona Figlia* by Edward Toms.] 8vo. Pp. ii. 59. [*Library of Congress, Cat. of Opera Librettos.*] London, 1767

*ACCOMPLISHT (the) physitian. . . .

The *Brit. Mus.* attributes this to Gideon Harvey.

ACCORDING to Jill. By Nora K. Strange [Mrs E. Gower Stanley]. 8vo. Pp. 252. [*Brit. Mus.*] London, 1926

ACCOUCHEUR (the): a letter to the Rev. Mr Tattershall . . . on the evils of man-midwifery. By a student [John Browne]. 8vo. [*Brit. Mus.*] London [1859]

ACCOUNT (an) from the children of light . . . why we have been kept from joyning to, or worshipping in, those formes at Law, and formes of worships, that have been imposed upon us against our consciences. . . . [By J. N. *i.e.* James Nayler and R. H. *i.e.* Richard Hubblethorn.] 8vo. Pp. 55. [*Brit. Mus.*] London, 1660

ACCOUNT (an) of a rich illuminated manuscript, executed for John, Duke of Bedford . . . by R. G. [Richard Gough]. 4to. [*Brit. Mus.*] London, 1794

ACCOUNT (an) of Barbarossa, the usurper of Algiers; being the story on which the tragedy [by John Brown, D.D., vicar of Newcastle] is founded, now in rehearsal at Drury Lane. 8vo. [*Brit. Mus.*] London, 1755

ACCOUNT (an) of Russia, 1767. [By George, Lord Macartney.] 8vo. [*Brit. Mus.*] London, 1768

*ACCOUNT (an) of some remarkable passages . . .

This is not accepted as Defoe's work by Trent (*Camb. Hist. of Eng. Lit.*, vol. 9) or by Dottin. There is a copy in St Deiniol's Library, Hawarden, Chester, which has written on it "by Thomas Woodcock" in a nearly contemporary handwriting, and this may be taken as more probable.

*ACCOUNT (an) of Switzerland . . .

Not by Temple Stanyan but by his brother Abraham. See *D. N. B.* vol. 54, p. 88.

ACCOUNT (an) of the abolishing of duels in France, being extracts out of the edicts of the Kings, the regulations of the Marshals, and the records of the Parliaments in France. [By John Evelyn?] 8vo. Pp. 67. London, 1713

See the note to "The Laws of honor . . ."

ACCOUNT (an) of the Bill lately depending in Parliament, for the better regulating the proceedings of ecclesiastical courts. [By Edmund Gibson, D.D.] Folio. [*Camb. Univ. Lib.*] London [1733?]

ACCOUNT (an) of the cedar of Libanus, now growing in the garden of Queen Elizabeth's Palace at Enfield. [By R. Gough.] Fol. [*Brit. Mus.*] [London?] 1788

ACCOUNT (an) of the glacieres, or ice alps in Savoy, in two letters ; one from an English gentleman [Col. William Windham, assisted by R. Price and B. Stillingfleet] . . . the other from P. Martel. . . . 4to. [*Brit. Mus.*] London, 1744

*ACCOUNT (an) of the growth of knavery . . .
For another edition (1679) see " The Parallel ; or, an account of the growth of knavery . . ."

ACCOUNT (an) of the late attempt at mutiny on board the U.S. brig *Somers* . . . and an original letter to President Tyler on the subject, by a Bostonian [James Lloyd Homer?]. 12mo. Pp. 24. [*Brit. Mus.*] Boston, 1842
Signed : J. L. H.

ACCOUNT (an) of the latter days of R. V. Pryor ; to which is prefix'd a brief sketch of his life and character. [By John Scandrett Harford.] 12mo. [*Brit. Mus.*] Bristol, 1808
Signed : J. S. H.

ACCOUNT (an) of the life and writings of Herman Boerhaave. . . . [By John Burton, M.D.] 8vo. Pp. ix. 226. [*Manch. Free. Lib.*] London, 1743

ACCOUNT (an) of the life, ministry, and writings of the late Rev. John Fawcett, D.D. . . . [By his son, John Fawcett, of Ewood Hall.] 8vo. [*Edin. Univ. Lib.*] London, 1818

ACCOUNT (an) of the new north wing and recent additions to University College, London. [By Prof. Henry Morley.] 4to. [*Brit. Mus.*] London [1881]

*ACCOUNT of the remains of a Roman villa . . .
Attributed also to G. Tupper. [*Leeds Univ. annotated copy of Halkett and Laing.*]

ACCOUNT (an) of the rescue of five of the family of G. Jackson. [By Major John Leathart.] 8vo. [*Brit. Mus.*] [*c.* 1820]

ACCOUNT (an) of the seminary that will be opened on Monday the fourth day of August at Epsom in Surrey. [By William Godwin.] 8vo. [*F. K. Brown's Godwin.*] London, 1783

*ACCOUNT (an) of the Societies for Reformation of manners, in England and Ireland . . .
By —— Yates, barrister of the Temple. See Nicholson's *Letters*, i. 191.

ACCOUNT (an) of the Spanish settlements in America. . . . To which is annexed a succinct account of the climate . . . manufactures, etc., of Old Spain. With a map. [By John Campbell, LL.D.]. 8vo. [*Sabin's Dictionary.*] Edinburgh, 1762

ACCOUNT (an) shewing the progress of the Colony of Georgia in America, from its first establishment. [By Benjamin Martyn.] Folio. [*Book Prices Current*, 1921.] London, 1741

ACCURATE (an) tho' compendious history of the ancient Parliaments of France. By Count Henri de Boulainvilliers, in fourteen letters [translated from the French by C. Forman]. 8vo. 2 vols. [*Brit. Mus.*] London, 1754

ACHILLES in petticoats ; an opera. By Gay ; with alterations [by George Colman the younger]. 8vo. [*Brit. Mus.*] London, 1774

ACHILLES ; or, Iphigenia in Aulis ; a tragedy [translated from the French of Jean Racine] by Mr [Abel] Boyer. 4to. [*Brit. Mus.*] London, 1700

ACQUITAL (the) or purgation of the moost catholyke Christen Prince, Edwarde the VI. . . . against al suche as blasphemously and traitorously infame hym . . . of heresie or sedicion. [By John Old.] 8vo. [*Camb. Univ. Lib.*] Waterford, 1555

ACTOR'S (an) notebooks ; being some memories, friendships, criticisms, and experiences of Frank Archer [Frank Bishop Arnold]. 8vo. [*Camb. Univ. Lib.*] London [1912]

ACTS (the) and miracles of the holy, true, Apostolic Catholic Church ; wherein her infallibility is asserted and proved. [Signed : Arthur O'Leary's Ghost, *i.e.* S. Sapsford]. 12mo. Pp. iv. 83. [*Brit. Mus.*] London, 1807

ACTUAL state of the question between our Colonial slave proprietors, and the Parliament and abolitionists of this country : illustrated in a series of articles originally published in the *Glasgow Free Press* newspaper. [By William Bennet]. 8vo. Glasgow, 1836
Private information.

ADAM and Eve stript of their furbelows ; or, the fashionable virtues and vices of both sexes expos'd. . . . [By Edward Ward?] The second edition. 8vo. Pp. 224. [*Brit. Mus.*] London [*c.* 1710]
The first edition appeared under the title " The modern world disrob'd," *q.v.*

ADAM'S Daughters. By John Carruthers [John Young Thomson Greig]. 8vo. Pp. 320. London, 1926

ADDINGTONIAN extinguisher. By an impartial observer [J. Corry]. 12mo. [*Eng. Cat.*, 1801-1836, p. 5.] Macclesfield, 1811

ADDITION (an) to the book [by Elias Hookes], entitled, The spirit of the martyrs revived, it being a short account of some remarkable persecutions in New-England, especially of four faithful martyrs of Our Lord and Saviour Jesus Christ, who suffered death at Boston. [By Joseph Bolles.] 4to. Pp. 20. [*Book Prices Current*, 1921.]
[New York] 1758

*ADDITIONAL (an) dialogue of the dead . . .

Internal evidence shows that this was not by the author of the Dialogue between Pericles and Cosmo [*i.e.* George, Lord Lyttleton]. It was probably by John Brown, D.D., Vicar of Newcastle-upon-Tyne. [*D. N. B.* vol. 7, p. 11.]

ADDITIONAL hymns, compiled for use with " Hymns for the Christian Church and Home" at Rosslyn Hill Chapel, Hampstead. [By Thomas Sadler.] 12mo. [*Brit. Mus.*]   London, 1876

*ADDITIONS to Common Sense . . .
Only partly by Thomas Paine. *See* the note in the Supplement to "Large Additions to Common Sense."

ADDRESS (an) delivered in St George's Hall, Philadelphia, January 21, 1894. By an Evangelist of the Catholic Apostolic Church [John Sidney Davenport]. 8vo. [*Brit. Mus.*]   [1894]

ADDRESS (the) of the minority in the Virginia Legislature to the people of that State ; containing a vindication of the constitutionality of the alien and sedition Laws. [By Henry Lee.] 8vo. Pp. 16. [E. G. Swem's *Bibl. of Virginia*, pt. ii., p. 84.]   [Richmond] 1799

ADDRESS to a medical student. [By William A. Greenhill.] 16mo. Pp. xii. 172. [*Brit. Mus.*]   London, 1843

ADDRESS (an) to a young student, on his entrance into College. By Eumenes [John Walker]. 8vo. Pp. 13. [*Brit. Mus.*]   Dublin, 1798

*ADDRESS (an) to Baptists of all denominations . . .
For Frazer, *read* Fraser. The author's full name is Peter Lovett Fraser.

ADDRESS (an) to Major-general Tryon, written in consequence of his late expedition into Connecticut. [Signed : Juvenis, *i.e.* Samuel Bostwick.] 4to. [*Magazine of History*, Extra No. 95.]
[Hartford ?] 1779

ADDRESS to prophetical students in the Church of Rome ; on the revelation of the man of sin and the coming of the Lord. [By William Tarbet.] 8vo. Pp. 36. [*Brit. Mus.*] London, 1856

ADDRESS (an) to the clergy concerning the first article of the Church of England. By a person of a truly scrupulous conscience [Francis Hoffman ?] 8vo. [*Brit. Mus.*] London, 1724

ADDRESS (an) to the Congress of the United States, on the utility and justice of restrictions upon foreign commerce. [Signed : C. B. B. *i.e.* Charles Brockden Brown.] 8vo. [*Brit. Mus.*]
Philadelphia, 1809

ADDRESS (an) to the females of Great Britain [on the Reform Bill]. By an Englishwoman [Jane Alice Sargant ?] 8vo. Pp. 15. [*Brit. Mus.*]
London, 1832

ADDRESS (an) to the government of the United States on the cession of Louisiana to the French, and on the late breach of treaty by the Spaniards. [By Charles Brockden Brown.] 8vo. Pp. 56. [*Brit. Mus.*]
[Philadelphia] 1803

ADDRESS (an) to the House of Commons of Ireland [on the Accommodation Bill]. By a Freeholder [Sir James Caldwell]. Third edition. 8vo. [*Camb. Univ. Lib.*]   [Dublin ?] 1771

ADDRESS (an) to the inhabitants of Fakenham [on the subject of baptism. By Charles Norris]. 8vo. [*Brit. Mus.*]   Fakenham, 1825
Signed : C. N.

ADDRESS (an) to the inhabitants of Ireland. By C. L—as, M.D. [C. Lucas]. 8vo. [*Brit. Mus.*]   Dublin, 1753

*ADDRESS to the inhabitants of Loughborough . . .
For Frazer, *read* Fraser. The author's full name is Peter Lovett Fraser.

ADDRESS (an) [in verse] to the inhabitants of Manchester, on theatricals. By a townsman [James Watson]. 8vo. [*Brit. Mus.*]   Manchester [1803]

ADDRESS (an) to the inhabitants of Scarborough on the profanation of the Lord's Day. [By Thomas Hinderwell.] 8vo. [*Brit. Mus.*]   1799
Signed : T. H.

ADDRESS (an) to the peers of England. [In reference to the proceedings in the House of Lords against Queen Caroline.] By an Englishwoman [Jane Alice Sargant]. 8vo. Pp. 20. [*Brit. Mus.*]   London, 1820

ADDRESS (an) to the people of the United States on the policy of maintaining a permanent navy. By an American citizen [Enos Bronson ?]. 4to. [*Magazine of History*, Extra No. 71.]   Philadelphia, 1802

ADDRESS to the working classes of England. By a poor man [R. Detrosier]. 24mo. [*Eng. Cat.*, 1801-1836, p. 5.]
London, 1836

ADMINISTRATION (the) of Ireland. By "I. O." [Major C. J. C. Street]. 8vo. [*Bookman*, October 1922, p. 8.] London, 1922

ADMIRAL'S (the) daughter. . . . By Margaret Stuart Lane [Margaret Ashworth]. 8vo. Pp. 287. [*Brit. Mus.*] London, 1921

ADMIRALTY (the). By a flag officer [Sir William Fanshawe Martin]. . . . (Second edition.) 8vo. Pp. 27. [*Brit. Mus.*] Portsmouth, 1870
From an inscribed copy.

*ADMONITION (an) to the Parliament holden . . .
First edition [1572].

ADMONITION (an) upon the nature, propriety and advantages of confirmation. [By Edward Owen, Rector of Warrington?] 12mo. Pp. 24. [Hawkes' *Lancashire Books*, p. 131.] Warrington, 1788

ADMONITIOUN (the) to the Lordis. [A ballad. By Robert Sempill, Baron Sempill.] [*Pollard and Redgrave.*] Edinburgh, 1570

ADOPTED ; a farce in one act. By Richard Henry [Richard Butler and Henry Chance Newton]. 12mo. Pp. 22. [*Brit. Mus.*] London [1893]

ADVANCED building construction. . . . By the author of *Notes on building construction* [Percy Gaillemard Llewellyn Smith, Major-General, R.E.]. 8vo. Pp. xv. 239. [*Brit. Mus.*] London, 1892

ADVANTAGES (the) and disadvantages of the married state. New edition. [By Archibald Courage.] 8vo. [*Aberd. Publ. Lib.*] Aberdeen, 1852

ADVANTAGES of Russia in the present contest with France ; with a short description of the Cozacks. [By William H. C. C. Bentinck-Scott, 4th Duke of Portland?] 8vo. Pp. 65. [*Brit. Mus.*] London, 1807

*ADVENT addresses . . .
For Willington, *read* Wellington.

ADVENTURE (an). By Elizabeth Morison and Frances Lamont [Anne Moberly and Eleanor Jourdain]. 8vo. Pp. vi. 162. [*T. L. S.*, 19th February 1931.] London, 1911
A later edition (1930) bears the authors' names.

ADVENTURE (an) among the Rosicrucians. By a student of occultism [Franz Hartmann]. 8vo. Pp. 181. [*Brit. Mus.*] Boston, 1887

ADVENTURE (the) of the Lady Ursula: a comedy in four acts. By Anthony Hope [Sir Anthony Hope Hawkins]. 8vo. Pp. 125. [*Brit. Mus.*] New York, 1898

ADVENTURES among the Red Indians. By H. W. G. Hyrst [Sidney Harry Wright]. 8vo. [*Amer. Cat.*] Philadelphia, 1910

ADVENTURES among wild beasts. By H. W. G. Hyrst [Sidney Harry Wright]. 8vo. [*Amer. Cat.*] Philadelphia, 1907

ADVENTURES in contentment. By David Grayson [Ray Stannard Baker]. 8vo. Pp. ix. 203. [*Amer. Cat.*] New York, 1907

ADVENTURES in friendship. By David Grayson [Ray Stannard Baker]. 8vo. Pp. 232. [*Amer. Cat.*] New York, 1910

ADVENTURES in the Arctic regions ; romantic incidents and perils of travel. . . . By H. W. G. Hyrst [Sidney Harry Wright]. 8vo. [*Amer. Cat.*] Philadelphia, 1909

ADVENTURES of a book agent. By Audrey Allison [Jennie Margerie Bly]. 8vo. Pp. 212. [*Publishers' Weekly*, 30th January 1926.] Boston, 1925

ADVENTURES (the) of a hackney coach. [By Dorothy Kilner.] Seventh edition. 8vo. [*Courtney's Secrets*, p. 21.] Dublin, 1781

ADVENTURES (the) of Abdalla, son of Hanif, sent by the Sultan of the Indies to make a discovery of the Island of Borico . . . translated into French [but rather wholly written in French] by M. de Sandisson [Jean Paul Bignon] . . . also an account of Rauschen . . . done into English by W. Hatchett. 8vo. [*Brit. Mus.*] London, 1729

*ADVENTURES of Bilberry Thurland.
For Hooton, *read* Horton.

ADVENTURES (the) of Dick Distich. [By George Daniel.] 12mo. [*Brit. Mus.*] London, 1912

*ADVENTURES of half-an-hour . . .
For Stephen Bullock, *read* Christopher Bullock. [*D. N. B.* vol. 7, p. 253.]

ADVENTURES (the) of Harry Rochester ; a tale of the days of Marlborough and Eugene. By Herbert Strang [George Herbert Ely and C. J. L'Estrange]. 8vo. Pp. ix. 418. [*Brit. Mus.*] London, 1906

ADVENTURES (the) of James Webb, at Claverton, Bath, Cheltenham, etc. By W. M. [Miles Watkin], gent. 8vo. [Shum's *Bath Books*, p. 223.] Bath, 1827

ADVENTURES (the) of Louis de Rougement [Henri Louis Grin] as told by himself. 8vo. Pp. xx. 396. [*Brit. Mus.*] London, 1899

ADVENTURES (the) of Philip Quarll, the English Hermit. . . . [A chapbook, abridged from "The Hermit," by Peter Longueville.] 8vo. Pp. 24. [*Brit. Mus.*]   [1823]

   See also "The English Hermit," "The Hermit," "Philip Quarll," and "The surprising adventures of Philip Quarll."

ADVENTURES (the) of Pomponius, a Roman Knight ; or, the history of our times. [By —— Labadie.] Made English from the Rome edition of the French original by Mr Macky. 12mo. 2 parts. [*Brit. Mus.;* Barbier's *Dictionnaire.*]   London, 1726

ADVENTURES (the) of Sir Lyon Bouse, Bart., in America during the Civil War, being extracts from his diary. [By Richard Grant White.] 12mo. [Foley's *Amer. authors.*]
                    New York, 1867

ADVENTURES (the) of Telemachus, in blank verse ; from the French of Fenelon . . . by J. Y. [J. Youde]. 12mo. [*Brit. Mus.*]   [1793?]

ADVENTURES (the) of Theagenes and Clariclea. Translated from the Greek (of Heliodorus) [by Charles Gildon]. 12mo. 2 vols. [R. Straus' *The Unspeakable Curll*, p. 248.]   London, 1717

   Dedication signed : C. G.

ADVENTUROUS (the) voyage ; telling of the deeds of some famous heroes. [By Maurice Kerr.] 8vo. Pp. 93. [*Brit. Mus.*]   London [1930]

ADVERTISEMENT (an) for a runaway wife. Family fracas. [By William Smith, stationer, of Edinburgh.] 8vo. [*Brit. Mus.*]   [Edinburgh, 1825?]

ADVERTISEMENT to the Parliament of England, from many grave, learned and pious divines beyond seas, in the year 1572 ; declaring the many and great errours at that present in the discipline and government of the English Church. . . . [By John Field or Feilde and Thomas Wilcox.]
                    London, 1644

   A reprint of "An Admonition to the Parliament, 1572," *q.v.*

A D V I C E to a friend. [By Symon Patrick.] [*D. N. B.* vol. 44, p. 47.]
                    London, 1673

   Signed : S. P.

*ADVICE to a painter . . .

   More probably by Henry Savile. See H. M. Margoliouth's *Marvell's poems and letters*, vol. 1, pp. 197, 321, 322.

*ADVICE to editors of newspapers. [With a letter signed : Emendator, *i.e.* Caleb Whitefoord.]

   The main work is not by Emendator.

ADVISE of a sonne, now professing the Religion established in the present Church of England, to his deare mother, yet a Roman Catholike. [By Anthony Hungerford.] [*D. N. B.* vol. 28, p. 253.]   Oxford, 1616

   A later (1639) edition bears the author's name.

ADVOCACY (the) of Christ. [By William Kelly of Guernsey.] 8vo. Pp. 28. [*Brit. Mus.*] London [1875]

ÆSOP at court ; or, state fables. [Verse. By Thomas Yalden.] 8vo. Pp. 43. [*Brit. Mus.*]   London, 1702

ÆTHIOPIAN (an) historie, written in Greeke by Heliodorus, translated into English by T. V. [Thomas Underdowne]. 4to. [*Christie - Miller Cat.*]
                    London, 1606

   Earlier editions give the author's name in full.

AFFECTIONATE (an) address to Church people and dissenters. By a lay churchman [John David Hay Hill]. 8vo. Pp. 18. [*Brit. Mus.*]
                    London, 1834

   Signed : J. D. H. H.

AFFECTIONATE (the) shepheard. [By Richard Banfield.] 4to. [*Pollard and Redgrave.*]   London, 1594

AFFECTIONS gift to a beloved godchild. By M. H. [Mary Ann Hedge]. 12mo. [*Brit. Mus.*] Colchester, 1819

AFLOAT in freedom's cause ; the story of two boys in the War of 1812. By James Otis [James Otis Kaler]. 8vo. [*Amer. Cat.*]   New York, 1908

AFRICA pilot. . . . Part I. Third edition. [Advertisement signed : F. J. E. *i.e.* Sir Frederick J. O. Evans.] 8vo. [*Brit. Mus.*]   London, 1880

AFRICAN lessons. Wolof and English. [By Mrs Hannah Kilham.] 12mo. 3 parts. [*Brit. Mus.*] London, 1823

AFTER confirmation ; a sketch of modern life in Norway. By Margrethe [Bolette Gjør]. Translated from the Norwegian by Th. Eggen. [Pettersen's *Norsk-Lexikon*, p. 11.]
                    Minneapolis, 1900

AFTER-RECKONING (an) with Mr Saltmarsh ; or, an appeal to the impartial and consciencious reader . . . against his last paper, called, An end of one controversy, or an answer or letter to M. Leys large last book. Written by L. M. a student in divinity. [By John Ley.] [*D. N. B.* vol. 33, p. 208.]   London, 1646

*AGE (the) [a poem, in eight books].

   Not by Philip James Bailey. The work referred to in the *D. N. B.* is a different one.

AGIATIS, queen of Sparta, or, the civil wars of the Lacedemonians, in the reigns of the Kings Agis and Leonidas. Translated out of French [of Pierre d'Ortigue de Vaumorière]. 8vo. [Barbier's *Dictionnaire*.]   London, 1686

AGNES Willoughby. . . . [A novel. By William Stephens Hayward.] 8vo. Pp. iv. 336. [*Brit. Mus.*]
London [1884]

AGNUS dei ; the lamb of God. [By Rev. Robert Norton, of Holbeck.] 12mo. [*Brit. Mus.*]   London, 1867

AGREEMENT (an) of the Associated Ministers and Churches of the counties of Cumberland and Westmerland : with something for explication and exhortation annexed. [By Richard Gilpin.] [Calamy's *Nonconf. Mem., Palmer's ed.* i. 302.]   London, 1656

AGRICULTURAL and administrative reform in Bengal. By a Bengal civilian [A. P. MacDonnell, afterwards Lord MacDonnell]. 8vo.
London, 1883
Certification by a friend of the author.

AIDS to development ; or mental and moral instructions exemplified in conversations between a mother and her children. [By Mary Atkinson Maurice.] 12mo. 2 vols. [*Brit. Mus.*]
London, 1829

AIDS to the divine life in a series of practical Christian contemplations. . . . (Originally published by "T. S." [Thomas Sherman]). 16mo. [*Brit. Mus.*]   1865

AILEY Moore. By Father Baptist [Rev. Richard Baptist O'Brien]. 8vo. Pp. 311. [S. J. Brown's *Ireland in fiction*.]   Dublin [1856]

*AIMS and ends . . .
The footnote is incorrect. The work there referred to is not the same.

AIR (the) patrol ; a story of the northwest frontier. By Herbert Strang [George Herbert Ely and C. J. L'Estrange] . . . 8vo. Pp. 442. [*Brit. Mus.*]   London, 1913

AIR-BUILT castles ; stories from the Spanish of Fernan Caballero [Cecilia Francisca Josefa Arrom de Ayala]. Translated by Mrs Pauli. 8vo. Pp. 240. [*Brit. Mus.*]   London [1887]

AIRS, duets, choruses, etc., in the new comedy called A day in Turkey, or the Russian slaves. [By Hannah Cowley.] 8vo. [*Brit. Mus.*]   London, 1791

AIRS, duets, glees, chorusses, etc., in the opera of The lad of the Hills, or Wicklow Gold Mine. [By John O'Keefe.] 8vo. Pp. 40. [*Brit. Mus.*]
London, 1796

AIRS, duets, trios, etc., in the new comic opera, called False Alarms ; or, My cousin. [By James Kenney.] 8vo. Pp. 23. [*Brit. Mus.*]   London, 1807

ALARM (an) to the hous-holders and heritors of the City of Edinburgh, in copies of proposals sent off by some in the city for procuring an Act of Parliament to impose a poor-rate thereon. . . . [By John Home.] 8vo. Pp. 28. [*Bibl. Lind.*]   Edinburgh, 1749

ALARUM (an) to England to prevent its destruction by the loss of trade and navigation. . . . By W. C. [William Carter, clothier]. Pp. v. 40. [*Brit. Mus.*]   London, 1700
The author refers on p. 3 to his work, "England's Interest, by the benefit of the woollen manufacture." This is known to be by William Carter.

ALARUM (an) to London ; or, the famous London's blowing up by Londoners. Sounded not to fire their buildings but to quench their burnings. In a letter to Major Generall Browne. [By William Beech.] 4to. Pp. 18. [*Brit. Mus.*]   London, 1650
Subscribed : Benjamin. A reissue in the same year bears the author's name.

ALARUM (an) to the House of Lords, against their insolent usurpation of the common liberties and rights of this nation. . . . [By Richard Overton.] [*D. N. B.* vol. 42, p. 386-7.]   1646

ALCINA ; an opera, as it is performed at the Theatre Royal in Covent Garden. [Translated from the *Alcina delusa da Ruggiero* of Antonio Marchi. The music by Haendel.] 8vo. Pp. 48. [*Library of Congress, Cat. of Opera Librettos*.]   London, 1736

ʾΑΛΕΚΤΟΡ. The Cock. (By Bartélemy Aneau.) [Translated by J. Hammon ?] 4to. [*Pollard and Redgrave.*]
London, 1590

ALEXANDER Pope ; notes towards a bibliography of early editions of his writings. [By C. S. Livingston.] 8vo. Pp. 50. [O'Leary's *Eng. Lit. Hist.* p. 157.]   Iowa, Cedar Rapids, 1910

ALEXANDER the Great ; or, the conquest of Persia : a grand heroic pantomime composed by M. J. D'Egville. [A scenario, by John Philip Kemble.] 8vo. Pp. 8. [*Brit. Mus.*] London [1795]

ALGIERS voyage in a journall, or briefe reportary of all occurrents hapning in the fleet of ships sent out by the King . . . as well against the pirates of Algiers, as others : . . . under the command of Sir R. Mansell . . . expressed by one that went along in the voyage (J. B. [*i.e.* J. Button]). 4to. [*Pollard and Redgrave.*]
[London ?], 1621

ALL and sundry. [Sketches of contemporary characters.] By E. T. Raymond [Edward Raymond Thompson]. 8vo. Pp. 283. [*Brit. Mus.*]
London, 1919

ALL the famous Battels that have bene fought in our age throughout the worlde, as well by sea as lande, set foorth at large liuely described. . . . Collected out of sundry good authors [by John Polman]. [Cockle's *Bibl. of military books*, p. 19.] London [1586]

ALLAHAHBARRIES C. C. [By Sir James M. Barrie.] 8vo. Pp. 12. [Garland's *Bibl. of Barrie*.]
Private print, 1893

ALL'S well that ends well; a story of Brittany. By S. G. [Selina Gaye], author of *Dickie Winters*. 8vo. Pp. 240. [*Brit. Mus.*] London, 1891

ALMIGHTY gold. By J. J. Connington [Alfred Walter Stewart]. 8vo. Pp. 334. [*Amer. Cat.*] London, 1924

ALMOST faultless; a story of the present day. By the author of *A book for governesses* [Emily Peart]. 8vo.
Edinburgh, 1870

ALPHABET (the) of prayers. [By James Canceller, or Cancellar.] 16mo. [*Pollard and Redgrave.*] London, 1591
Signed: J. C. There were previous editions, in 1565, 1570, 1573 and 1576, none of them anonymous. For a later edition [signed: E. C.] with a different title, see "An A B C or holy alphabet . . . "

ALPHABET (an) of the holy Proverbs of King Salomon. [By Robert Allen.] 8vo. [*Pollard and Redgrave.*]
London, 1596
Signed : R. A., a minister of God's word.

*ALPINE sketches . . .
For George Wyndham Bridges *read* George Wilson Bridges. [*Edin. Univ. Lib.*]

ALTAR book of the Norwegian evangelical lutheran church with scripture lessons and collects : a translation [by E. G. Lund]. [Pettersen's *Norsk Lexikon*, p. 16.] Minneapolis, 1915

ALTERNATE (the) sex; the female intellect in man, and the masculine in woman. By Hans Breitmann [Charles Godfrey Leland]. 8vo. [*Amer. Cat.*]
New York, 1904

*ALTHORP (the) picture-gallery . . .
The *Brit. Mus.* gives the author's name as Jordan.

ALVAREDA (the) family; a novelette. Translated from the Spanish of Fernan Caballero [Cecilia Francisca Josefa Arrom de Ayala] by Viscount Pollington. 8vo. [*Brit. Mus.*] London, 1872

ALZIRA; or, Spanish insult repented; a tragedy [in verse] written by Aaron Hill [or rather adapted by him from the French of Voltaire]. 8vo. [*Brit. Mus.*] [London, 1760]

AMATEUR art; oil and water colour painting, painting on china, etc. By Henri Clarise [Mrs Henrietta Clarissa Jackson Cosgrove]. 8vo. [*Amer. Cat.*] Chicago, 1909

AMATEUR'S (the) workshop. By the author of *Pattern Making*, etc. [Joseph Gregory Horner]. 8vo. [*Brit. Mus.*]
London, 1889

AMATONDA; a tale from the German of Anton Wall [Christian Lebrecht Heyne. Translated by Henry Crabb Robinson]. 12mo. Pp. xxiii. 288. [*Brit. Mus.*] London, 1811

AMBROSE McEvoy. [By R. M. Y. G. *i.e.* Reginald M. Y. Gleadowe.] 4to. Pp. 29. [*Brit. Mus.*] London, 1924
"Contemporary British Artists."

AMBROTOX and Limping Dick. [A novel.] By Oliver Fleming [Ronald and Philip Macdonald]. 8vo. Pp. 315. [*Brit. Mus.*] London, 1920

AMELIA Mansfield : translated from the French of Madame C * * * * [Sophie R. Cottin]. 12mo. 4 vols. [*Brit. Mus.*] London, 1803

AMERICA; being the latest and most accurate description of the New World, containing the original of the inhabitants and the remarkable voyages thither; the conquest of the vast empires of Mexico and Peru, and other large provinces and territories. . . . [Largely based on " De niewe en onbekende weereld . . . " by Arnoldus Montanus] ; with maps and plates by John Ogilvie.] Folio. [*Book prices current*, 1921.] London, 1771

AMERICAN adventure by land and sea ; being remarkable instances of enterprise and fortitude among Americans. [By Epes Sargent.] 8vo. [Foley's *Amer. authors*.] New York, 1841

AMERICAN insects. By Max Vernon [Vernon Lyman Kellogg]. Second edition, revised. 4to. [*Amer. Cat.*]
New York, 1908

*AMERICAN memoranda.
Preface signed : J. L.

AMERICAN (an) poilu. [Letters from the front. By Elmer Stetson Harden.] 8vo. Pp. xii. 244. [*Amer. Cat.*]
Boston, 1919
The letters are signed : E.

AMERICAN (the) register, or general repository of history. [Edited by C. B. B. *i.e.* Charles Brockden Brown.] 8vo. 7 vols. [*Brit. Mus.*]
Philadelphia, 1807-11

AMERICA'S insular possessions. By Charles Harcourt [Charles Harcourt Ainslie Forbes Lindsay]. 8vo. 2 vols. [*Amer. Cat.*]   Philadelphia, 1907

AMONG French inns. By Richard Sudbury [Charles Gibson]. 8vo. [*Amer. Cat.*]   Boston, 1905

AMONG privileged people ; a novel from the Afrikaans. By Marie Linde [Elise Bosman]. 8vo. Pp. 352. [*T. P.'s Weekly*, 2nd April 1927.]
London, 1927

AMONG the heather. . . . By A. C. Hertford [Adelaide M. Cameron]. New edition. 8vo. Pp. 320. [*Brit. Mus.*]   London, 1891

AMONG the ruins of Pompei. By F. and A. M. [F. and A. Mavrogordato]. 16mo. Pp. 44. [*Brit. Mus.*]
[Naples] 1925

AMONG the Shoshones. By Uncle Nick [Elijah Nicholas Wilson]. 8vo. [*Amer. Cat.*]   Salt Lake City, 1910

AMONG the tombs of Colchester. [By Mrs Mary Benham.] 8vo. Pp. 76. [*Brit. Mus.*]   Colchester, 1880

AMOROUS Fiametta ; wherein is sette downe a catalogue of all and singular passions of loue and iealousie. . . . First written in Italian by Master John Boccace . . . and now done into English by B. Giouano del M. Temp. [Bartholomew Young, of the Middle Temple]. . . . 4to. Ff. 123. B. L. [*Pollard and Redgrave.*] London, 1587

*AMOROUS (the) warre . . .
    The 1659 edition was "By J. M. St. of Ch. Ch. in Oxon."

AMOURS (the) of Bonne Sforza, Queen of Polonia. [Translated from the French by P. B. *i.e.* Peter Bellon]. 12mo. Pp. 155. [*Brit. Mus.*]
London, 1684
    Bentley's "Modern Novels," vol. 8.

AMPHORA. [Poems. By Aleister Crowley.] 8vo. Pp. 80. [*Brit. Mus.*]
London, 1908

*ANABAPTISTS (the) groundwork for reformation . . .
    For I. H., read I. E.

ANALECTA. By Roland Saint-Clair [Roland Sinclair Watson]. 8vo. Pp. 22. [*Brit. Mus.*]   London [1925]

ANALECTIC (the) magazine, containing selections from foreign reviews and magazines. . . . [Edited by Washington Irving.] 8vo. 6 vols. [*Foley's Amer. authors.*]   Philadelphia, 1813-15

ANALYSIS by a student of prophecy [Robert Mackenzie Beverley] of "Thoughts on the Apocalypse" by B. W. Newton, of Plymouth. 8vo. Pp. 51. [*Brit. Mus.*]   London, 1845
    In a bound volume of tracts by Beverley in the British Museum, many bearing his name. The binding bears the title *Castoreana*, this being a pun on Beverley's name from *castor* = a beaver.

ANALYSIS of pnematics and moral philosophy ; for the use of students in the College of Edinburgh. [By Adam Ferguson, LL.D., Professor.] 8vo. Pp. 55.   Edinburgh, 1766

ANALYSIS of the late correspondence between our Administration and Great Britain and France. . . . [By John Lowell.] 8vo. [*Brit. Mus.*]
New York, 1814

ANATOMIE (the) of the Common Prayer-Book, wherein is remonstrated the unlawfulness of it, and that by five several arguments. . . . By Dwalphintramis [John Bernard]. [*Brit. Mus.*]   1661

ANATOMIE (the) of abuses. By Philip Stubbes. [The introduction signed : J. P. C. *i.e.* John Payne Collier.] 4to. [*Brit. Mus.*]   London [1870]

ANATOMIE (the) of basenesse ; or the foure quarters of a knave. [By John Andrewes.] 4to. [*Pollard and Redgrave.*]   London, 1615

ANATOMIE (an) of the world. . . . See "An anatomy of the world. . . ."

ANATOMIST (the) ; or, the sham doctor : a farce. [Adapted from Edward Ravenscroft's comedy.] 8vo. Pp. 43. [*Brit. Mus.*] London [1762 ?]

*ANATOMY (the) of baseness . . .
    The correct title is "The Anatomie of baseness," and the author is John Andrewes. [*Pollard and Redgrave.*]

ANATOMY (the) of the body of God ; being the supreme revelation of cosmic consciousness. By Frater Achad [C. Stansfeld Jones]. 4to. Pp. xv. 111. [*Brit. Mus.*]   Chicago, 1925

*ANATOMY (the) of the heretical Synod . . .
    Signed : T. L.

ANATOMY (an) of the world ; wherein by occasion of the untimely death of Mistris Eliz. Drury the frailty and decay of this whole world is represented. [By John Donne.] 8vo. [*Pollard and Redgrave.*] London, 1611
    There was an edition in 1625 entitled "An anatomie of the world . . ." Editions in 1612 and 1621 were entitled "The First anniversarie. An anatomy of the world . . ." *q.v.*

ANCHOR (the) of hope ; or, some of God's words of hope in the Old Testament. . . . [By John Ross Macduff.] 8vo. 2 parts. [*Brit. Mus.*]
London [1881]

ANCHOR (the) of the soul. By the author of *The lamplighter* [Francis Bourdillon]. 12mo. [*Brit. Mus.*]
London [1863]
Signed : F. B.

ANCIENT and modern Malta : a full account of the islands of Malta and Goza, by L. Du Boisgelin. [Translated by Mrs —— Lutwyche.] 4to. 2 vols. [Shum's *Bath Books*, p. 133.] 1805

ANCIENT (the) and present state of the County of Down : a chorographical description, with natural and civil history. ./. . [By Walter Harris ?] 8vo. [*Brit. Mus.*] Dublin, 1744

ANCIENT (the) bounds, or liberty of conscience, tenderly stated, modestly asserted, and mildly vindicated. [By Francis Rous.] [*M'Alpin Coll. Cat.*]
London, 1645
Attribution by Dr Charles A. Briggs.

ANCIENT (the) of dayes is come ; the judgment is set. . . . Written by a lover of peace and truth, J. G. [John Gibson, Quaker]. 4to. [*Brit. Mus.*]
London, 1657

ANCIENT tales of Hindustan. By A. C. A. [A. C. Albers]. 8vo. Pp. 105. [*Brit. Mus.*] Calcutta [1923]

ANCIENT (the) vessel found in the parish of Tune, Norway. [By Oluf Rygh. Translated by Gerhard Gade ?] 8vo. [Pettersen's *Norsk Lexikon*, p. 18.]
Christiania, 1872

ANCILLA'S share ; an indictment of sex antagonism. Anonymous. [By Elizabeth Robins.] 8vo. Pp. 313. [*Brit. Mus.*] London, 1924

ANECDOTAL reminiscences of distinguished characters. By Leigh Cliffe [George Jones]. 12mo. [*Eng. Cat.*, 1801-1836, p. 121.] London, 1830

ANGELA and I. By L. Du G. [L. Du Garde Peach]. 8vo. Pp. 240. [*Brit. Mus.*] London, 1925

ANGELA goes to school. [A novel.] By May Wynne [Mabel Wynne Knowles]. 8vo. Pp. 253. [*Who's Who in Lit.*] London, 1922

ANGLIÆ ruina ; or, England's ruine, represented in the barbarous and sacrilegious outrages of the sectaries of this kingdom, committed upon the lives, consciences and estates of all His Maj. loyal subjects. . . . [Containing the Mercurius Rusticus of Bruno Ryves and The Querela Cantabrigiensis of John Barwick.] [*D. N. B.* vol. 50, p. 71.] 1647

*ANGLIÆ speculum morale . . .
For Sir Richard Grahame *read* Richard Grahame, Viscount Preston. [*Brit. Mus.*] For a later edition, see " The Moral State of England . . ."

ANGLO-INDIAN literature. [A collection of specimens. By Sir Edward Buck, Secretary to the Government of India]. 8vo. Pp. 103.
Calcutta, private print, 1883
Authorship certified by a friend of the collector.

ANGLO-IRISH essays. By John Eglinton [W. K. Magee]. 8vo. Pp. 130. [Boyd's *Ireland's Lit. Renaissance.*]
Dublin, 1917

ANGLO-ISRAELISM true, not false ; being an answer to the Rev. Canon C. D. Bell. By Philo-Israel [—— Bird, Indian Civil Service]. 8vo. Pp. 16. London, 1882

*ANGLO-MANIACS (the).
The author's name is given in Foley's *Amer. Authors* as Mrs Burton Harrison.

ANGLO-SCOTUS again ; or the lucubrations of a Rev. correspondent of the United Secession and Voluntary Magazines exposed. . . . By Anglo-Scotus [John Lockhart ?]. 8vo. Pp. 16. [*Brit. Mus.*]
Newcastle-upon-Tyne, 1834

ANIMADVERSIONS, upon a paper, entituled, The speech of the late Lord Russell. . . . [By Dr John Nalson.] Folio. [*Lincoln's Inn Lib.*]
London, 1683

ANIMADVERSIONS upon [the Rev.] Dr [John] Brown's three essays on the Characteristics [written by the Earl of Shaftesbury]. [By Rev. Robert Andrews, minister in Bridgnorth.] 8vo. [Sparke's *Bibl. Bolt.*]
Wrongly ascribed to Rev. Robert Colvill, or Colville.

ANIMAL magnetism. . . . By . . . William Gregory. [Preface signed : M.A. Oxon. *i.e.* William S. Moses.] 8vo. Pp. viii. 252. [*Brit. Mus.*]
London, 1884

ANIMAL magnetism ; a farce. . . . By Mrs Inchbald . . . with remarks . . . by D— G. [George Daniel]. 12mo. Pp. 33. [*Brit. Mus.*] London [1827]

ANN and her mother; a story of Scottish manse life. By Olivia Douglas [Ann Buchan]. 8vo. [*Brit. Mus.*]
London, 1922

*ANNALS of a fishing village.
Delete with Mrs Jane Owen Visger. The title-page continues, "edited by J. A. Owen."

ANNALS (the) of an Indian family (Cherry). [By Charles Minchin.] 8vo. Pp. 48. [*Brit. Mus.*]
Harrogate, private print, 1898, 1908

ANNALS (the) of Europe for the year 1739. [By George Gordon, historian.] 8vo. [*Brit. Mus.*]   London, 1740
The work was continued to include 1743.

ANNALS of the parish of Halton. Collected and edited by E. M. [E. Mackreth]. 8vo. Pp. 24. [*Brit. Mus.*]   London [1888]

ANNALS of Waverley Abbey Hospital. By Nurse W. [Edith M. Ware]. 8vo. Pp. 16. [*Brit. Mus.*] Farnham [1916]

ANNAN (the) jewel. By Patricia Wentworth [Mrs —— Dillon, *née* D. O. Ellis]. 8vo. Pp. 311.   London, 1924

ANNE Grey, a novel, edited by the author of *Granby* [Thomas Henry Lister]. 12mo. [*Brit. Mus.*]   London, 1834

ANNIE and Pierre, or, "Our Father's letter :" a book for the holidays. By K. M. [Kate Maclellan]. 12mo. [*Brit. Mus.*]   New York [1874]

ANNIE ; or, the life of a lady's maid. . . . [By William Stephens Hayward.] 8vo. Pp. 316. [*Brit. Mus.*]   London [1884]

ANNIVERSARIES upon his Panarete. [By Richard Brathwait.] 8vo. [*Pollard and Redgrave.*]   London, 1634

ANNOTATIONS on a sermon preached before the University of Oxford on . . . June 7, 1761, by George Horne, D.D. [By Martin Madan.] 8vo. Pp. 60. [*Bibl. Lind.*]   London, 1762

ANN'S an idiot. A novel. By Pamela Wynne [Winifred Mary Scott]. 8vo. Pp. viii. 408. [*Brit. Mus.*]   London, 1923

ANNUAL (the) Register for 1758. [By Edmund Burke. Also for the years 1759-63.] 8vo. [R. Straus' *Robert Dodsley.*]   London, 1759-64

ANONYMA. . . . [A novel. By William Stephens Hayward.] 8vo. Pp. vi. 327. [*Brit. Mus.*]   London [1884]

ANONYMOUS criticism ; an essay. By Robert Blake [Robert Hely Thompson]. 8vo. [O'Donoghue's *Poets of Ireland.*]   London, 1877

ANOTHER ballad, called The libertines lampoone, or the curvets of conscience. . . . By the authour of *The Geneva ballad* [Samuel Butler]. Fol. S. sh. [*Brit. Mus.*]   [*c.* 1675]

ANOTHER home ; or, hope for the old and poor. By the author of *The lamplighter* [Francis Bourdillon]. 12mo. [*Brit. Mus.*]   London [1862]
Signed : F. B.

*ANOTHER word or two . . .
For Nunnery, *read* Nunnez.

ANSWER (an) or necessary animadversions upon some late impostumate observations invective against his sacred Majesty, bearing the face of the publick, but boldly pen'd and publish't by a Privado [Richard Burney]. 4to. [Wood's *Athen. Oxon.* ii. 885.]   London, 1642

ANSWER (an) to a late pamphlet [by Daniel Defoe], entitled, The Experiment, or the shortest way with the Dissenters exemplified. . . . [By Hugh James.] 4to. Pp. 52. [*Bibl. Lind.*]   London, 1707

ANSWER (an) to a Letter of enquiry [signed : T. B. *i.e.* John Eachard] into the grounds and occasions of the contempt of the clergy. [By John Bramhall, Archbishop of Armagh.] 8vo. Pp. 91. [*Brit. Mus.*]   London, 1671

ANSWER (an) to a letter to Edward Long Fox, M.D. [Signed : C. T. S. *i.e.* Samuel Taylor Coleridge.] 8vo. Pp. 8. [*Ashley Library.*]   Bristol [1795]

ANSWER (an) to a pamphlet entit'led A declaration of the Commons of England . . . expressing their reasons and grounds of passing the late resolutions touching no further addresse . . . to be made to the King. [By Edward Hyde, afterwards Earl of Clarendon.] 4to. Pp. 13. [*Brit. Mus.*]   1648

ANSWER (an) to a pamphlet entituled considerations on the propriety of requiring a subscription to the articles of faith [by Edmund Law. By Thomas Randolph, Archdeacon of Oxford]. 8vo. Pp. 52. [*Brit. Mus.*]   Oxford, 1774

ANSWER (an) to a Papisticall Byll, cast in the streetes of Northampton, and brought before the Iudges at the last Syses, 1570. [By Thomas Knell.] B. L. [*Christie-Miller Cat.*]   1570
A ballad.

ANSWER (an) to an infamous and trayterous pamphlet, entituled, A Declaration of the Commons of England in Parliament, expressing their reasons and grounds of passing the late resolutions, touching no further addresse or application to be made to the King. [By Edward Hyde, Earl of Clarendon.] Pp. 166 [for 186]. [*Bibl. Lind.*]   [London, 1648]

ANSWER (an) to Dr D . . . ., y's [Patrick Delany's] Fable of the pheasant and the lark. [By Benjamin Swift.] 8vo. Pp. 8. [*Bibl. Lind.*]   [Dublin ?] 1730

ANSWER (an) to Dr Rotheram's apology for the Athanasian creed ; in a letter to a friend. [By William Adams, Master of Pembroke College, Oxford.] 8vo. Pp. 70. [*Brit. Mus.*] London, 1773

ANSWER (an) to M. I. Forbes of Corse, his peaceable warning [*i.e.* to John Forbes' "A peaceable warning to the subjects in Scotland." This answer is ascribed to David Calderwood.] 4to. [*Pollard and Redgrave.*]
[Holland?] 1638

ANSWER (an) to Mr J. G. [John Goodwin] his xl. queries . . . in which answer the undueness of mixt communion is declared. . . . By W. A. [William Allen]. 4to. [*Brit. Mus.*]
London, 1653

ANSWER (an) to several new laws and orders made by the rulers of Boston in New-England. . . . By G. F. [George Fox]. 4to. Pp. 7. [*Brit. Mus.*] 1678

ANSWER (an) to the pamphlet call'd The Conduct of the Ministry impartially examined. . . . By the author of the *Four Letters to the people of England* [John Shebbeare, M.D.]. 8vo. Pp. 100. [*Brit. Mus.*] London, 1756

ANSWER (an) to the question, Is any church worth preserving? By Scrutator [Edward Bennett]. 8vo. Pp. 24. [*Brit. Mus.*] Chester [1878?]

ANSWERE (an) in defence of the truth ; againste the apologie of private masse. [By Thomas Cooper.] [*Camb. Univ. Lib.*] Londini, 1562

ANSWERE (an) to a papystycall exhortacyon pretendynge to auoyde false doctryne. [By John Bale, Bishop of Ossory.] 8vo. [*Pollard and Redgrave.*]
N.P. [1548?]

ANSWERE (an) to the Proclamation of the Rebels in the North. . . . See "An Aunswere . . ."

ANSWERS to inquiries in regard to the Catholic Apostolic Church. [By John Sidney Davenport.] 12mo. Pp. 8. [*Brit. Mus.*] [*c.* 1860]

ANTHOLOGY (an) of invective and abuse. Compiled . . . by Hugh Kingsmill [Hugh Kingsmill Lunn]. 8vo. Pp. xii. 221. [*Brit. Mus.*]
London, 1929

ANTHOLOGY (an) of modern verse. Chosen by A. M. [Sir Algernon Methuen]. With an introduction by Robert Lynd. 8vo. Pp. xlv. 240. [*Brit. Mus.*] London, 1921

ANTHONY Fairfax. A novel. [By Margery Hollis.] 8vo. 3 vols. [*Brit. Mus.*] London, 1885

*ANTICIPATION, 1778 . . .
The *D.N.B.* queries the ascription to Tickell very strongly.

ANTI-CORSICAN (the) ; a poem inscribed to the volunteers of Great Britain. [By Matthew Rolleston.] 4to. [*Eng. Cat.*, 1801-1836, p. 21.]
Exeter, 1805

*ANTIDOTE (an) against lay-preaching . . .
Not anonymous. It bears Bewick's name.

ANTIDOTE (an) against melancholy, made up in pills compounded of witty ballads, jovial songs, and merry catches. [By Thomas Ourfey.] 4to. [*Christie-Miller Cat.*]
London, 1661
An edition was published in 1870 by J. P. C. *i.e.* John Payne Collier. [*Brit. Mus.*]

ANTIDOTE (the): strictures upon two anonymous pamphlets. [By J. Mills.] 8vo. [*Birm. Ref. Lib.*] 1820

ANTIQUARY (the) ; a national drama, founded on the celebrated novel of the same name, by the author of Waverley . . . as performed at the Theatre-Royal, Edinburgh. [By Isaac Pocock.] 12mo. Pp. 66. [*D.N.B.* vol. 46, p. 4.]
[Edinburgh, 1822]

ANTIQUITY (the) and excellency of globes. . . . [By William Grent?] 4to. [*Brit. Mus.*] London, 1652

*ANTONIOS rewenge. . .
For the first part, see "The History of Antonio and Mellida. . . ."

ANY man ; or, it means me. "Peace, false and true." By W. T. P. W. [W. T. P. Wolston]. 16mo. Pp. 16. [*Brit. Mus.*] Edinburgh [1884]

APHORISMS(the)of the Mimausa philosophy by Jaimini. . . . [Edited by J.R.B. *i.e.* James Robert Ballantyne.] 8vo. [*Brit. Mus.*] Allahabad, 1851

APHORISMS (the) of the Nyáya philosophy by Gautama. . . . [Edited by J. R. B. *i.e.* James Robert Ballantyne.] 8vo. [*Brit. Mus.*] 1851

APHORISMS (the) of the Sánkhya philosophy of Kapíla. . . . [Edited by J. R. B. *i.e.* James Robert Ballantyne.] 8vo. [*Brit. Mus.*] Allahabad, 1852

APHORISMS of whist. By "Nestor" [Thomas D. Lowther]. 8vo. Pp. 40. [Jessel's *Bibl. of playing cards.*]
Chicago, 1901

APOCALYPSE (the) of S. John the Divine, represented by figures. . . . [Described by H. O. C. *i.e.* Henry Octavius Coxe.] 4to. [*Brit. Mus.*]
London, 1876
Roxburghe Club.

APOCRYPHAL (the) gospel of St Peter ; the Greek text of the newly discovered fragment. [Preface signed: H. B. S. *i.e.* Henry Barclay Swete.] 8vo. Pp. 14. [*Brit. Mus.*] London, 1892

APOLLO'S cabinet; or the Muse's delight: an accurate collection of English and Italian songs, cantatas, and duetts, set to music for the harpsichord, violin, german-flute, etc. . . . [Edited by John Sadler, bookseller, of Liverpool.] 8vo. 2 vols. [Hawkes' *Lancashire Printed Books*, p. 37.]
Liverpool, 1757
Originally issued (1754) under the title "The Muses delight."

APOLLO'S feast; or, wit's entertainment: consisting of pleasant intrigues, delightful stories . . . writ by Jo. Haynes and Mr Pinkeman. . . . Now published by the author of the *Pills to purge melancholy* (Dr Merryman) [Henry Playford]. 12mo. Pp. 170. [*Brit. Mus.*] London, 1703

APOLOGIE diffidentis. By W. Compton Leith [Ormonde Maddock Dalton]. 8vo. Pp. 211. London, 1908

APOLOGIA pro vita Ecclesiae Anglicanae; in reply to John Henry Newman, D.D. [By William Josiah Irons?] 8vo. Pp. 24. [*Brit. Mus.*]
London [1864]

APOLOGIE (an) of priuate Masse sediciously spredde abroade in wrtynge without name of the author. . . ." See "A Levvde Apologie of pryuate Masse . . ."

APOLOGIE (the) of the Romane Church, devided into three severall tractes . . . all which are undertaken and proved by testimonies of the learned Protestantes themselves. [By Lawrence Anderton, *alias* John Brerely.] 4to. Pp. 191. [*Brit. Mus.*] N.P. 1604
Secretly printed. The advertisement is signed: I. Br.
See A. J. Hawkes in *The Library*, Sept. 1926, and C. A. Newdigate in *The Library*, Dec. 1926.

*APOLOGIE (an) or defence of such true Christians . . .
By Henry Ainsworth and Francis Johnson. [*D.N.B.* 1/192 and *Pollard and Redgrave*.]

APOLOGY for the conduct of Mrs Teresia Constantia Phillips. [Edited by Paul Whitehead.] 3 vols. [*D. N. B.* vol. 61, p. 105.] 1748

APOLOGY (an) for the life of Mrs Shamela Andrews, in which the many notorious falsehoods and misrepresentations of a book called Pamela [by Samuel Richardson] are exposed. . . . By Conny Keyber [Henry Fielding]. 8vo. Pp. xv. 59. [*Times Lit. Supp.* 4 Dec. 1930.] London, 1741

APOLOGY (an) of T. F. [Thomas Fitzherbert] in defence of himselfe . . . falsely charged with a fayned conspiracy against her Maiesties person. . . . 4to. [*Camb. Univ. Lib.*]
[St Omer] 1602

APOLOGY (the); or, the genuine memories of Madam Maria Manchini, Constabless of Colonna. . . . Written in Spanish by her own hand. [By Gabriel de Brémond.] . . . 8vo. Pp. 160. [Arber's *Term Cat.*]
London, 1679

APOLOGY to the travellers' club; or anecdotes of monkeys. [By W. S. Rose.] 8vo. [*Eng. Cat.*, 1801-1836, p. 22.] London, 1825

APOSTACY (the). [By William Tarbet.] 12mo. Pp. 12. [*Brit. Mus.*] [1866?]

APOSTLE (the) of the Alps; a tale. By the author of *Moravian life in the Black Forest*, etc. [Mrs Beatrice Batty, *née* Stebbing]. 12mo. [*Brit. Mus.*]
London, 1863

APOSTOLICAL (the) and true opinion concerning the Holy Trinity, revived and asserted; partly by twelve arguments levyed against the traditional and false opinion about the Godhead of the Holy Spirit. [By John Bidle.]
London, 1653
Reprinted in "The Faith of One God," 1691.

APPEAL (the) of five fellows of Saint John's College to the visitor. . . . [By C. E. C. B. Appleton.] 8vo. Pp. 24. [*Brit. Mus.*] Oxford, 1869
Preface signed: C. E. A.

*APPEAL to reason.
By H. Halkerstoun, of Rathillet.

APPEAL (the) to Rome; a letter from an English clergyman [Rev. —— Hatherway] to a Roman Catholic friend. . . . 8vo. Pp. 16.
London, 1850

*APPEAL (an) to the conscience of a fanatick. [By John Brydall.] [*Lincoln's Inn Lib.; D. N. B.* vol. 7, p. 159.]

APPEAL (an) to the impartial public by the Society of Christian Independents congregating in Gloucester. [By Epes Sargent.] 8vo. Pp. 39. [Eddy's *Universalism in America*, ii. 488.]
Boston, 1785

APPEAL (an) to the public on the subject of the framework knitters' Fund. [By Rev. Robert Hall.] 8vo. [*Brit. Mus.*] Leicester, 1819
As opposition was raised against his proposal, the author next published (again anonymously), "A Reply to the principal objections . . ." *q.v.*

APPEAL (an) to the Scriptures on the ordinance of Baptism ; interpreted with the concessions of learned and judicious writers who espoused infant sprinkling. By the author of the *Spiritual Cabinet* [Jabez Burns, D.D.]. 12mo. Pp. 24. [Whitley's *Bapt. Bibl.*]
London, 1830
An enlarged edition, with the author's name, was published in 1831.

APPEAL (an) to the Society of Friends on the primitive simplicity of their Christian principles and Church discipline. . . . [By Thomas Foster.] 8vo. Pp. 233. [*Brit. Mus.*]
London, 1801

APPEALS in criminal cases and amendment of law. [By Charles Nash.] 8vo. [*Brit. Mus.*]   [1860 ?]
Two leaves.

APPENDIX to an address to the inhabitants of Loughborough . . . on the erection of a Roman Catholic Chapel in that town. By Aristogeiton [Rev. Peter Lovett Fraser]. 12mo. Pp. 12. [*Brit. Mus.*]   London, 1824
See "An address to the inhabitants . . ."

*APPLES of Eden ; a realism. By the author of *Estelle.*
The entry is incorrect. The title reads : By Estelle ; and the author is not known.

APPLESEED Johnny ; a poetic drama of pioneer days. By Donald Thistle [H. Clark Brown]. 8vo. Pp. 54. [*Publishers' Weekly*, 28th Jan. 1928.]
[Charles City, Iowa] 1927

APPRENTICE'S (the) monitor ; or, indentures in verse, shewing what they are bound to do. [Together with] The Golden Rule in verse. [By Hannah More.] Fol. S. sh. [*Brit. Mus.*]
Bath [1795 ?]
Signed : Z.

APPRENTICESHIP *v.* Conscription. [By R. C. T. Evans ?] Fol. Pp. 13. [*Brit. Mus.*]   Herne Bay, 1912

APPROACH to the holy altar ; by Bishop Ken. . . . [Edited by J. L. A. *i.e.* John L. Anderdon.] 8vo. Pp. vii. 148. [*Brit. Mus.*]   London, 1852

APRON (the) farmer. By a bird at Bromsgrove [John Crane]. 12mo. [*Brit. Mus.*]   London [1802]

AQUARIAN (the) Gospel of Jesus the Christ ; the philosophic and practical basis of the religion of the aquarian age of the world and of the church universal. Transcribed from the book of God's remembrances, known as the Akashic records by Levi [Levi H. Dowling]. . . . 8vo. Pp. 260. [*Brit. Mus.*]
London, 1911

ARABIAN (the) trudgman, that is, certaine Arabicke termes, as names of places, titles of honour &c. . . . expounded according to their . . . etymologie. . . . By W. B. [William Bedwell]. 4to. 2 parts. [*Brit. Mus.*]
[London] 1615

ARABINIANA. [By Blencowe Churchill.] 8vo. [*Lincoln's Inn Lib.*]
London, 1843

ARBOR (the) of amorous deuises. By N. B. Gent. [Nicholas Breton]. 4to. [*Christie-Miller Cat.*]   1597

ARCANA aulica ; or Walsingham's manual of prudential maxims for the states-man and the courtier. [Translated by Edward Walsingham from the Traicté de la cour of Eustache du Refuge.] 12mo. Pp. 153. [*Brit. Mus.*]   London, 1652
See also " Walsingham's manual. . ."

ARCANE teaching ; or, secret doctrine of the ancient Atlantis, Egypt, Chaldea, and Greece. By Yogi Ramacharaka [William Walker Atkinson]. Second edition. 8vo. Pp. 336. [*Amer. Cat.*]
Boston, 1909

ARCH (the) of Titus. [Verse signed : D. C. W. *i.e.* D. C. Wrangham ?] 8vo. [*Brit. Mus.*]   N.P. 1824

ARCHÆOLOGIÆ philosophicæ ; or, the ancient doctrine concerning the originals of things. . . . By Thomas Burnet. . . . [With a " Letter to Mr E. Curll " signed : C. B. *i.e.* Charles Blount ?] 8vo. [*Brit. Mus.*]
London, 1729

ARCHER (the) and the Steppe ; or, the Empires of Scythia : a history of Russia and Tartary. . . . By F. R. Grahame [Catherine Laura Johnstone]. 12mo. Pp. 479. [*Brit. Mus.*]   London [1860]

ARCTIC (the) world ; its plants, animals, and natural phenomena : with a historical sketch of arctic discovery. [By William Henry Davenport Adams.] 4to. [*Brit. Mus.*]   London, 1876

ARE the late wars of Prussia a fulfilment of prophesy ? By H. H. [Henry Hewetson]. 8vo. [*Brit. Mus.*]
London, 1871

ARGAL ; or the silver devil, being the adventures of an evil spirit . . . related by himself. [By George Hadley.] 12mo. 2 vols. [*Brit. Mus.*]
London [1793]

ARGUMENT (an) for the authority of Holy Scripture ; from the Latin of Socinus . . . to which is prefixed a short account of his life. [By Edward Combe.] 8vo. [*Brit. Mus.*]
London, 1731

ARGUMENT (the) of Mr Peter de la Marteliere . . . made in Parliament . . . for the Rector and University of Paris . . . against the Jesuits. . . . Translated [by George Browne]. . . . 4to. Pp. 71. [*Brit. Mus.*]
London, 1689
The dedication signed : G. B. An edition of 1612 contains the translator's name.

ARGUMENT (an) to prove that the abolishing of Christianity in England may, as things now stand, be attended with some inconveniences. . . . [By Jonathan Swift, D.D.] 8vo. Pp. 38. [*Brit. Mus.*]
London, 1717

ARGUMENTS against some of the popular errors of whist, with an analysis of some of the leading features of the game. By W. H. C. [W. H. Collins]. 16mo. Pp. 32. [F. Jessel's *Bibl. of playing cards.*] Whitehaven, 1880

ARGUMENTS and reasons to prove the inconvenience and unlawfulness of taking the New Engagement. [By John Aucher, D.D. ?] 4to. [*D. N. B.* vol. 2, p. 246.]
London, 1650

ARGUMENTS from Scripture for pure diet and living. By I. O. and M. A. [Gideon J. R. Ouseley]. Being a reply to alleged objections to vegetarianism. . . . 8vo. Pp. 12. [*Brit. Mus.*]
[Paris ? 1890]

*ARIDÆ frondes . . .
For Siddon, *read* Siddons.

ARIEL, or the life of Shelley. By André Maurois [Émile Herzog]. Translated by Ella D'Arcy. 8vo. Pp. viii. 310. [*Observer*, 1st Feb. 1931.] London, 1924

ARIOSTO'S satyres, in seven famous discourses. By G. Markham [or, rather Robert Tofte]. 4to. [*Pollard and Redgrave.*] London, 1608
For a later edition, see the following entry.

ARIOSTOS seven planets governing Italie, or his satyrs in seven famous discourses. . . . Newly corrected and augmented. [Translated by Robert Tofte.] 4to. Pp. 100, 24. [*Pollard and Redgrave.*] London, 1611

ARISTOPHANES at Oxford. O(scar) W(ilde). [A satire on Oscar Wilde.] By Y. T. O. [L. C. M. S. Amery, F. W. Hirst and H. A. A. Cruso]. 8vo. Pp. vi. 85. [Stuart Mason's *Bibl. of Oscar Wilde.*] Oxford [1894]

'ΑΡΚΑΙΟΣΚΟΠΙΑ ; or, a view of antiquity: presented in a short . . . account of some of the fathers . . . who lived within or near the first three hundred years after Christ. . . . By J. H. [John Howe], M.A. 8vo. [*Brit. Mus.*]
London, 1677

ARMADA days ; a dramatic sketch. By N. S. S. [N. S. Shaler ?]. 8vo. Pp. 92. [*Brit. Mus.*] London, 1898

ARMOUR, or the never failing engine. [A poem. By Basil Kennet ?] [R. Straus' *The Unspeakable Curll*, p. 275.]
London, 1724

ARMY (the) harmlesse ; or, a dispassionat and sober discussion of the late and present proceedings of the Army under the command of his Excellencie, Sir Thomas Fairfax. [By John Goodwin ?] [Thomason's *Coll. of Tracts*, i. 533.] London, 1647

ARNALDO ; Gaddo ; and other unacknowledged poems by Lord Byron, and some of his contemporaries ; collected by Odoardo Volpi. 8vo. [*Brit. Mus.*] Dublin, 1836
Spurious. Not by Lord Byron.

ARNE ; or, peasant life in Norway : a Norwegian tale by Bjørnstjerne Bjørnson. Translated from the second edition by a Norwegian [Thomas Krag]. [Pettersen's *Norsk Lexikon*, p. 28.] Bergen [1861]

ARRAIGNMENT (the), conviction and condemnation of the Westminsterian Juncto's engagement, with a cautionarie exhortation to all honest English spirits, to avoid the danger of perjurie by taking of it. [By William Prynne.] 4to. [*Lincoln's Inn Lib.*] N.P. 1649

ARRIAN'S (the) vindication of himself against Dr Wallis's Fourth letter on the Trinity. [By William Freke.] [M'Lachlan's *Nonconformist Lib.* p. 64.]
1691
No title-page.

ARROL'S engagement. By Charlotte May Kingsley [Thomas W. Hanshew]. 8vo. Pp. 383. [*Brit. Mus.*]
London, 1903

ARS moriendi ex variis sententiis collecta. . . . [Translated from the Latin by William Caxton ? Edited by W. B. *i.e.* W. Blades.] 4to. B.L. [*Brit. Mus.*] [London, 1868]
Only 54 copies printed.

ARS punica sive flos linguarum ; the art of punning. By the labour and industry of Tom Pun-sibi [Jonathan Swift]. 8vo. [*Camb. Hist. of Eng. Lit.*] London, 1719

*ARSINOE, Queen of Cyprus. . . . [Translated from Tommaso Stanzani.] [*Library of Congress, Cat. of Opera Librettos.*]

ART (the) and science of change ringing. By William Banister. [Edited by S. B. G. *i.e.* Samuel B. Goslin.] 8vo. Pp. vii. 179. [*Brit. Mus.*] London, 1879

*AR'T asleepe, husband?
For Paledonius, *read* Panedonius.

ART crafting in metal for amateurs. By
F. Alexander [F. Alexander Chandler].
8vo. [*Amer. Cat.*]   Boston, 1909

ART (the) of chymistry : as it is now
practised. From the French of P.
Thibaut. Translated into English by
a fellow of the Royal Society [William
Aglionby]. 8vo. [Arber's *Term Cat.*
i. 187.]   London, 1668
   A later edition (1674) is " Englished by
W. A., Fellow of the Royal Society."

*ART (the) of getting into practice in
physic . . .
   A satire on Dr Richard Mead. For a
counter satire, see " The life and adventures of Don Bilioso de l'Estomac. . . .''

*ART (the) of heraldry . . .
   The 1685 edition is not anonymous. The
Brit. Mus. however possesses a 1693 edition
in which Blome's name does not occur,
unless indeed this is an imperfect copy,
wanting the epistle dedicatory.

ART (the) of knowing women ; or, the
female sex dissected, in a faithful
representation of their virtues and
vices. . . . Written in French by the
Chevalier Plante - Amour [François
Bruet] and by him published at the
Hague 1729. Now faithfully made
English with improvements. 8vo.
Pp. iv. 237. [*Brit. Mus.*; Barbier's
Dictionnaire.]   London, 1730

ART (the) of Latin poetry ; founded on
the work of C. D. Jani. By [Edward
Baines] a Fellow of a College [Christ's
College] in Cambridge. 8vo. [*Camb.
Univ. Lib.*]   Cambridge, 1828

ART (the) of numbring by speaking-rods,
vulgarly termed Nepeir's [*i.e.* J. Napier,
of Merchistoun] bones. . . . Published
by W. L. [William Leybourn]. 12mo.
[*Brit. Mus.*]   1667

*ART (the) of punning . . .
   For Tom Pun-Sibe, *read* Tom Pun-Sibi.
The correct title, however, is " Ars punica,
sive flos linguarum . . ." *q.v.*

*ART (the) of ringing improved . . .
   For Stedman, *read* Steadman.

ARTAXERXES, an English opera, as
it is performed at the Theatre Royal
in Covent Garden. [Translated from
Metastasio by T. A. Arne.] 8vo.
Pp. 31. [*Library of Congress, Cat. of
Opera Librettos.*]   London, 1792

ARTEMUS Ward (C. F. Browne) in
London. . . . [Edited by E. P. H.
i.e. Edward P. Hingston.] 8vo. Pp.
195. [*Brit. Mus.*]   London [1870]

ARTICLES originally published in the
Biblical Repertory for April, 1834.
[By William Stockton Martien.] 8vo.
Pp. 35. [*Brit. Mus.*]
          Princeton, N.J. [1834]

ARTIS logicæ rudimenta. [By Henry
Aldrich.] With illustrative observa-
tions on each section [by John Hill,
B.D.]. Sixth edition. 12mo. [*Brit.
Mus.*]   Oxford, 1850

AS common mortals. [By Mrs Annie
Coombs, *née* Sheldon.] 12mo. [Kirk's
Supp.]   New York, 1886

AS good as a comedy ; or, the Tennes-
seean's story. By an editor [William
Gilmore Simms]. 12mo. [Foley's
Amer. Authors.]   Philadelphia, 1852

AS it was. By H. T. [Mrs Helen
Thomas]. 8vo. Pp. 116. [*Times
Lit. Supp.* 29th Jan. 1931.]
          London, 1926
   A portrait under a concealed name of her
husband, the poet Edward Thomas.

AS it was in the beginning : a poem.
By Joaquin Miller [Cincinnatus H.
Miller]. 4to. [*Amer. Cat.*]
          San Francisco, 1903

*ASAPH.
   For Schimmelpeninck, *read* Schimmel-
penninck.

*ASCENTS of the soul . . .
   For Henry Hare, *read* Hugh Hare. The
date of publication was 1665.

ASPECTS of biography. By André
Maurois [Emile Herzog]. Translated
. . . by S. C. Roberts. 8vo. Pp. 187.
[*Observer*, 1st Feb. 1931.]
          Cambridge, 1929

ASPECTS of Jewish life and thought.
The letters of Benammi [Mordecai
Epstein]. 8vo. Pp. 223.
          London, 1922
   Information from a friend of the author.

ASPIRATIONS (the) of Bulgaria.
Translated from the Serbian of Bal-
kanicus [Stojan M. Protić]. 8vo. Pp.
xxvii. 249. [*Brit. Mus.*] London, 1915

ASSEMBLY (the) of God. . . . [By
C. H. Mackintosh.] New edition,
revised. 8vo. [*Brit. Mus.*]
          London [1874]

ASSES (the) complaint against Balaam ;
or, the cry of the country against
ignorant and scandalous ministers.
[By Lewis Griffin.] Fol. S. sh. [*Brit.
Mus.*]   London, 1661

ASSIMILATIVE memory ; or, how to
attend, and never forget. By Alphonse
Loisette [Marcus Dwight Larrowe].
8vo. Pp. 170. [*Brit. Mus.*]
          New York, 1896

ASSUMPTIONS (the) of the [episcopal] clergy as the only ministers of Christ, calmly refuted in a letter to a friend. By Philagathon [Thomas Finch, of Harlow]. 8vo. Pp. 50. [Whitley's *Bapt. Bibl.*]   London, 1837

ASTRÆA, a romance written in French by . . . H. d'Urfé. . . . [With a preface signed : J. D. *i.e.* John Dryden ?] Fol. 3 vols. [*Brit. Mus.*]
London, 1657-58

ASTRÆA'S return ; or, the halcyon days of France in the year 2440 : a dream. Translated from the French [of Louis Sebastien Mercier] by Harriot Augusta Freeman. 8vo. Pp. xii. 308. [*Brit. Mus.*]   1797

ASTRONOMICAL essays. By "Catholicus" [George Vincent Leahy]. 8vo. Pp. 283. [*Amer. Cat.*]
Brighton, Mass., 1910

ASTRONOMY. [By Sir Benjamin Heath Malkin.] 8vo. Pp. 256. [*Brit. Mus.*]   London, 1829

Society for diffusing useful knowledge.

ASTRONOMY and geology as taught in the Holy Scriptures. [By William Tarbet.] 8vo. Pp. 23. [*Brit. Mus.*]
1855

AT century's ebb. [A novel.] By Cyprian Cope [James C. Biddle-Cope, afterwards Baron Cope]. 8vo. 2 vols. [*Brit. Mus.*]   London, 1893

AT Mrs Beam's ; a comedy. By C. K. Munro [Charles W. K. Macmillan]. 8vo. Pp. 72. [*Brit. Mus.*]
London [1925]

AT the sign of the palm-tree ; a record of some idle hours in sunset land, by Madge Mortimer. Edited [but rather written] by R. L. N. J. [R. L. N. Johnston]. Pp. viii. 152. [*Brit. Mus.*]   London, 1899

ATALANTIS ; a story of the sea, in three parts. [By William Gilmore Simms.] 8vo. [Foley's *Amer. Authors.*]
New York, 1832

ATHANASIAN (the) Creed ; suggestions submitted for consideration, by a Lay member of the General Synod [Sir John Napier]. 8vo. [*Lincoln's Inn Lib.*]   Dublin, 1876

ATHANASIAN (the) Creed weighed in the balance, and found wanting. [By —— Hale ?] 8vo. [*Birm. Cent. Lib.*]
London, 1858

ATHEISM and anarchy. [By M. Hale.] 8vo. Pp. 10. [*Brit. Mus.*]
St Albans [1924]

ATHEISM or theism ? Debate between Iconoclast [Charles Bradlaugh], the accredited champion of Atheism, and others, and William Honeyman Gillespie. . . . 8vo. [*Brit. Mus.*]
London, 1869

ATHUALPA, the last of the Incas. By Hugh M'Nab [Hugh M'Nab Humphry, barrister]. 8vo. Pp. 87.
London, 1923
From an inscribed copy.

ATONEMENT (the) made by Christ as the vicarious sacrifice for sin. . . . [By W. F. Pitcairn.] 8vo. Pp. 35. [*Brit. Mus.*]   Edinburgh, 1873

ATTEMPT (an) at an English translation, in terra rima, of the first canto of Dante's Inferno. (A translation of Claudian's Epigram on the old man who lived in the territory of Verona. . . .) By a late scholar of Trinity College, Cambridge [Jonathan Hatfield]. 8vo. Pp. 16. [*Brit. Mus.*]
London, 1832

AUCTION bridge ; lessons for the unskilled. By " Major Terrace " [George Washington Bailey ?]. 8vo. Pp. 125. [*Amer. Cat.*]   London, 1928

AUCTION (the) bridge manual. By John Doe [F. R. Roe]. 8vo. Pp. 144. [Jessel's *Bibl. of playing cards.*]
London, 1910

AUDI et alteram partem ; or, a few cursory remarks on . . . A Vindication of the Hindoos from the aspersions of the Rev. Claudius Buchanan . . . by [Charles Stuart] a Bengal officer. [By Adam Clark, LL.D.] 8vo. 3 parts. [Whitley's *Bapt. Bibl.*]
Dunstable, 1814

AUDI (the) filia ; or, a rich cabinett full of spirituall jewells. By Juan De Avila. Translated out of Spanish [by L. T. *i.e.* Sir Tobias Matthew]. 4to. [*Pollard and Redgrave.*]   [St Omer] 1620

AULD Grannie's advice to witless mithers and their belle daughters, who bring them up to deceive themselves and their lads wi' their braw dresses. . . . [By William Smith, stationer, of Edinburgh.] 8vo. [*Brit. Mus.*]
Edinburgh, 1825

AULD (ane) Prophecie, bot doubte be Merlyne or Thomas of Erceldoune, fundin under yᵉ altar-stane of yᵉ Quenyis College of yᵉ Haly Trinitie besyde Edenburgh, And diligentlie comparit with yᵉ Cronyclis and auld Wrytingis quhilk yairto effeir, be Maister D. Doubleyowe, ane Brither of yᵉ Auncient Fraternitie of yᵉ Antiquaries [Sir Daniel Wilson, LL.D.]. 4to.   1849

AUNSWERE (an) to the Proclamation of the rebels in the North [T. Percy, Earl of Northumberland and C. Nevill, Earl of Westmoreland. By William Seres? In verse.] 12mo. B. L. [*Brit. Mus.*] London, 1569

Signed : W. S.

Another edition in the same year runs "An answere . . ."

AUSTRALASIA and prison discipline. [By Henry Melville, of Tasmania.] 8vo. [*Camb. Univ. Lib.*] London, 1851

AUSTRALASIAN Board of Missions ; report of . . . proceedings. . . . [Edited by E. H. *i.e.* Ernest Hawkins.] 16mo. [*Brit. Mus.*] London, 1851

AUSTRALIA directory; volume II. . . . Third edition. [Advertisement signed : F. J. E. *i.e.* Sir Frederick J. O. Evans.] 8vo. [*Brit. Mus.*] London, 1879

AUSTRALIAN (the) babes in the wood ; a true story told in rhyme for the young. By the author of *Little Jessie,* etc. [Sarah Maria Fry]. 12mo. Pp. 47. London, 1866

AUTARCHY ; or, the art of self-government, in a moral essay. . . . [By George Burghope.] 8vo. Pp. 158. [*Brit. Mus.*] London, 1691

The Epistle Dedicatory signed : G. B. The second edition, corrected (1713), runs "'Αυταρχία, or the art of self-government . . ."

AUTHENTIC copy of a letter from Mr Pitt to His Royal Highness the Prince of Wales, containing the restrictions on the intended regency, with His Royal Highness's answer. [The answer was written by R. B. Sheridan.] 8vo. Pp. 24. [*Times Lit. Supp.* 28th June 1928.] London, 1799

AUTHENTICK (an) narrative of the late proceedings and cruel execution at Thorn. [By Jean Bion]. . . . 8vo. Pp. xvi. 44. [*Brit. Mus.*] London, 1725

AUTHOR (an) to be lett ; being a proposal . . . address'd to the . . . Society of the Bathos. By . . . Iscariot Hackney [Alexander Pope ?]. No. I. 4to. Pp. 12. [*Brit. Mus.*] London, 1729

AUTOBIOGRAPHICAL (an) chapter in the life of Jane, Duchess of Gordon. [Edited by J. W. G. *i.e.* J. Wyllie Guild.] 4to. Pp. viii. 19. [*Brit. Mus.*] Glasgow, private print, 1864

*AUTOBIOGRAPHY of Jack Ketch.

Also attributed to Charles Whitehead. [*Eng. Cat.,* 1801-1836, p. 33.]

A'ΤΤΟΜΑΧΙΑ ; or, the selfe contradiction of some that contend about Church Government ; dialogue-wise digested into a scholasticall discourse between religion, reason, prejudice and partiality. . . . By Irenæus Philalethes [Louis Du Moulin ?]. 4to. [*Brit. Mus.*] London, 1643

A'ΤΤΟΦΟΝΙΑ ; or, self-murther arraign'd and condemn'd as utterly unlawful by the judgment of learned heathens, Jews and Christians. [By John Brydall.] 4to. [*Lincoln's Inn Lib.*] London, 1705

AUTUMN Crocus ; a play in three acts. By C. L. Anthony [Dodie Smith]. 8vo. Pp. 127. [*Brit. Mus.*] London, 1931

AVENGING (the) ray. [A novel.] By Seamark [Austin J. Small]. 8vo. Pp. 314. [*Brit. Mus.*] London [1930]

AVERAGE (an) woman. By W. Dane Bank [William Henry Williamson]. 8vo. Pp. 437. [*Brit. Mus.*] London, 1916

AVERAGES ; a story of New York. By Eleanor Stuart [Eleanor Stuart Childs]. 8vo. Pp. viii. 4to. [*Brit. Mus.*] New York, 1899

AWFUL (an) memorial of the state of Francis Spina after he turn'd apostate from the Protestant Church to Popery. [Abridged from Nathaniel Bacon.] 12mo. [*D.N.B.,* vol. 2, p. 365.] Falkirk, 1815

AXEL ; a poem. [By Bishop E. Tegner]. Translated from the Swedish by Rowland Muckleston. 8vo. [*Brit. Mus.*] London, 1864

AXEL Ebersen, the graduate of Upsala. [A tale.] By André Laurie [Paschal Grousset]. . . . 8vo. Pp. vi. 286. [*Brit. Mus.*] London, 1892

'ΑΞΙΩΜΑ βασιλικὸν ; the unanimous, or consentient opinion of the learned : namely Digges, Heath, Croke, Glanvill, Lord Digby, Elliot . . . and others, in the explication . . . of that celebrated maxim . . . The King can do no wrong. [By John Brydall.] 4to. [*Lincoln's Inn Lib.*] London, 1703

*AZARIA and Hushai.

Not by Elkanah Settle. The author was Samuel Pordage. See the *D.N.B.* and *Bibliography of Settle* (1910).

B

BAB comes into her own. [A novel.]
By Clementia [Sister Mary Edward
Feehan]. 8vo. Pp. 298. [*Publishers'
Weekly*, 20th Feb. 1926.]
Chicago, 1925

BABES (the) in the wood. . . . A panto-
mime . . . written by the author of
. . . *The three bears* [John Baldwin
Buckstone?]. 8vo. [*Brit. Mus.*]
London, 1856

BABOONS, banks and branches. By a
descendant man [Henry F. Morriss].
12mo. Pp. 89. [*Brit. Mus.*]
London [1927]

BABY John. By the author of *Miss
Toosie's Mission* [Evelyn Whitaker].
8vo. [*Amer. Cat.*]   London, 1892

BABYLON and Jerusalem; a letter [on
Popery] addressed to Ida, Countess of
Hahn-Hahn; from the German [of
Dr Hermann Abeken]; with a preface
by the translator [signed : W.]. 12mo.
Pp. xii. 116. [*Brit. Mus.*]
London, 1851

Ascribed also to Dr Nitsch, of Berlin.

BABYLON and the beast. [By William
Kelly, of Guernsey.] 8vo. Pp. 47.
[*Brit. Mus.*]   London [1875 ?]

BABYLON destroyed; or, the history
of the Empire of Assyria. . . . By
the author of *Lily Douglas*, etc. [Miss
Grierson]. 12mo. [*Camb. Univ. Lib.*]
Edinburgh, 1827

BABYLONISH (the) Baptist; or, H. G.
[Henry Grigg] contradicting H. G. in
his book stiled, Light from the Son of
righteousness; which is proved meer
confusion and darkness. [By George
Whitehead.] 4to. Pp. 7. [*Brit. Mus.*]
[London, 1672]

Signed : G. W.

BABYLON'S babes. [An exposure of
the Romish conventual system.] By
the editor of the *Indian Watchman*
[Wallace J. Gladwin]. 8vo. Pp. 32.
[*Brit. Mus.*]   Bombay, 1893

BABYON (the); a family chronicle.
By Clemence Dane [Winifred Ashton].
8vo. Pp. v. 380. [*Brit. Mus.*]
London, 1928

*BACHELARS (the) banquet . . .
See the note in this supplement appended
to "The Batchelar's banquet . . ."

BACK numbers. [Literary essays, reprinted from the *Saturday Review*.]
By "Stet" [Thomas Earle Welby].
8vo. Pp. xi. 226. [*Brit. Mus.*]
London, 1929

BACK stage; a story of the theatre. By
Roland Oliver [Henry White]. 8vo.
Pp. 284. [B. Mantle's *American Play-
wrights of Today*, p. 302.]
London [1926]

BACKSLIDER (the) bewailed, the care-
less warned, and the faithful en-
couraged. . . . By P. Hendrick. . . .
Translated . . . by W. C. [William
Caton?]. 4to. Pp. 12. [*Brit. Mus.*]
N.P. 1665

BACKWARD (the) swing, and other
stories. By A. L. O. E. [A Lady of
England, Charlotte M. Tucker]. 16mo.
[*Brit. Mus.*]   London, 1875

BAKER'S (the) dream; or, death no
bad change to the poor and good.
[By Mrs Hannah More.] 8vo. [*Brit.
Mus.*]   London [1797 ?]

Signed : M.

BALLAD (a) of the Queen's Majesty,
June 22, 1897; an Aldine leaf. [By
Austin Dobson.] 8vo. Pp. 4. [F.
Shay's *Bibl. of Dobson*.]   1897

BALLAD (a) supposed to have been
written about the year eighteen hundred
and fifty two. By I. H. A. Etonensis
[John Hungerford Arkwright]. 12mo.
[*Camb. Univ. Lib.*]   Windsor, 1852

BALLOON (the) travels of Robert
Merry, and his young friends, over
various countries in Europe. By Peter
Parley [Samuel Griswold Goodrich].
12mo. [*Camb. Univ. Lib.*]
London, 1856

BANCHORY Ternan sixty years ago;
reminiscences of bygone days. By an
old residenter [Charles Ogg]. 8vo.
[*Aberd. Free Lib.*]   Aberdeen, 1870

BANE and antidote together; the un-
exampled philology of the Newer
Testament and the unsuspected geology
of genuine scripture. . . . A letter
. . . from an octogenarian advocate
of inspiration [Andrew Thom?]. 8vo.
Pp. 31. [*Brit. Mus.*]   London, 1884

Signed : A. T.

BANGKOK calendar. . . . Compiled
by D. B. B. [D. B. Bradley]. 8vo.
[*Brit. Mus.*]   Bangkok, 1859-69

BANK (the) torpedo. . . . [By Benjamin
Davies.] [H. E. Miller's *Banking
theories in the U.S.*, p. 229.]
New York, 1810

BANNER (the) unfurled; choice selections from Christian writers. Edited
by E. A. H. [Mrs Elizabeth Anna
Gordon]. 8vo. [*Brit. Mus.*]
London, 1874

BANQUET (a) of jests, or change of cheare. . . . [By Archibald Armstrong.] 12mo. [*Huntington Lib. Checklist.*]
London, 1630
Second part, 1633.

BAPTISM. [By C. W. Boase.] 8vo. Pp. 24. [*Brit. Mus.*]   Dundee [1866]

BAPTISMAL regeneration contrary to the New Testament. . . . Being a reply to three sermons preached by the Rev. W. R. Cosens. . . . By a layman [J. P. Shorthouse.] 8vo. Pp. 8. [*Brit. Mus.*]   Birmingham [1874]

BAPTIST-CATECHISM (the) ; agreeable to the Confession of faith. . . . [By Benjamin Keach.] Fifteenth edition. 12mo. [*Brit. Mus.*]   London, 1747

BARBARA goes to Oxford. By Barbara Burke [Oona Howard Ball]. 8vo. [*Who's Who in Lit.*]   London, 1907

BARDS (the) of Bon Accord, 1375-1860. [By William Walker, Dean of Aberdeen and Orkney.] 8vo. [Mitchell and Cash's *Scot. Top.* ii. 40.]
Aberdeen, 1887

BARRICADE. [A novel.] By John Presland [Gladys Skelton]. 8vo. Pp. 316. [*Brit. Mus.*]   London, 1926

BART'LEMY Fair, or an enquiry after wit ; in which due respect is had to a Letter [by A. A. Cooper, Earl of Shaftesbury] concerning enthusiasm. . . . By Mr [William] Wotton [or rather, Mary Astell]. 8vo. [*Brit. Mus.*]
London, 1709

BASIS (the) of Scripture prophecy. By Sepharial [Walter Gorn Old]. 8vo. Pp. 98. [*Brit. Mus.*]   London [1927]

BASKET (the) of first-fruits ; or, worship and service. By the compiler of *The golden grain almanack*, J. E. H. [James E. Hawkins]. 16mo. [*Brit. Mus.*]
London [1873]

BASKET (a) of fragments ; being fundamental truths, precepts, devotions of the One Holy Catholic Divine-Human Apostolic Church of Israel, with a brief introductory comment by I. O. and M. A. [*i.e.* by G. J. R. Ouseley]. 8vo. Pp. 190. [*Brit. Mus.*]   Paris [1888 ?]

*BATCHELER'S (the) banquet . . .
This is not an original work but a translation of *Les quinze joies de mariage*.
Dekker's authorship is now impugned. It is suggested that the author may have been Robert Tofte. See *The Year's Work in English Studies*, 1928, p. 194.

BATHSHEBAES instructions to her Sonne Lemvel ; containing a fruitfull and plaine exposition of the last chapter of the proverbs. . . . [By Robert Cleaver.] [*M'Alpin Coll. Cat.*]
London, 1614

BATTLE (the). By Claude Farrère [Charles Bargone]. Translated by E. de Claremont Tonnere. 8vo. Pp. 293. [*Brit. Mus.*]   London, 1912

BATTLE (the) for native industry ; the debate upon the Corn Laws. . . . Reprinted . . . from Hansard. [Edited by A. S. O'B. *i.e.* Augustus Stafford O'Brien.] 8vo. 2 vols. [*Brit. Mus.*]
London [1846]

BATTLE (the) of Bothwell Bridge, viewed by spirits in Paradise : reported by Strathclutha [William Jolly, Inspector of Schools]. 8vo.
Hamilton [1902]
Presentation copy from the author.

BATTLE (the) of London. By Hugh Addison [Collinson Owen]. 8vo. Pp. 312. [*Brit. Mus.*]   London, 1923

BATTLE (a) of wits. By Scott Campbell [Frederick William Davis]. 8vo. [*Amer. Cat.*]   New York, 1906

BATTLEFIELD fragments ; and other poems. By an old trooper [C. H. Capern]. 8vo. [*Birm. Ref. Lib.*]
Birmingham, 1913

BATTLERIDGE ; a historical tale founded on facts. By a lady of quality [Mrs Cooke]. 12mo. 3 vols. [*Letters of Jane Austen*, i. 159.] London, 1799

BAXTER'S second innings ; specially reported for the —— School Eleven. [By H. Drummond.] 8vo. Pp. 58. [*Brit. Mus.*]   London, 1892

BAY (the) of Hartlepool ; a series of sketches in pen and ink. [By William Hutton.] 8vo. Pp. 24. [*Bibl. Lind.*]
Sunderland, 1856
Presentation copy from the author, with his autograph.

BEAU Brummell ; his life and letters. By Lewis Melville [Lewis S. Benjamin]. . . . 8vo. Pp. 313. [*Brit. Mus.*]
London, 1924

BEAUFORD ; or a picture of high life : a novel. [By Henry Card, D.D.] 8vo. 2 vols. [*D.N.B.* vol. 9, p. 36.]
London, 1811

BEAUTIES of the monopoly system in New Jersey. By a Citizen of Burlington [Henry C. Carey]. 8vo. [Sabin's *Dictionary*, iii. 329.] Philadelphia, 1848

BEAUTIFUL (a) young nymph going to bed. Written for the honour of the fair sex. To which are added Strephon and Cloe, and Cassinus and Peter. [By Jonathan Swift.] 4to. [*Brit. Mus.*]
Dublin printed ; London reprinted, 1734

BEAUTY ; an ode. . . . By Taliessen de Monmouth [Thomas Powell]. 4to. [*Brit. Mus.*]   London, 1794

BEAUTY (the) of daily duties, and others. By Gilbert Guest [Sister Mary Angela]. 12mo. Pp. 196. [*Publishers' Weekly*, 16th Jan. 1926].   Omaha, 1925

BEAUTY (a) spot ; a novel. By Huan Mee [—— and —— Mansfield, two brothers]. 8vo.   London [1894]

BEAUX (the) stratagem ; a comedy as it is acted at the Theatre-Royal in Drury Lane and Covent Garden. [By George Farquhar]. 12mo. Pp. 72. [*Bibl. Lind.*]   London, 1763

*BECKET, an historical tragedy . . .
    Ascribed also to George Darley.

BECKY Compton, ex-dux. [A tale.] By Raymond Jacberns [Georgina M. Selby Ash]. 8vo. [*Lit. Year Book.*]
                    London, 1910

BEDESMAN (the) on Nidside. (Legendary fragments.) [Verse. Generally ascribed to Robert Riddell.] [F. Miller's *Poets of Dumfriesshire*, p. 178.]   London, 1790
    The first "fytte" of the Bedesman appeared in *The Edinburgh Magazine* or *Literary Miscellany* for January 1788.

BEE (the) preserver ; or practical directions for the management and preservation of hives : by Jonas de Gelieu. Translated from the French [by Clementina Stirling Graham]. 8vo. [*Camb. Univ. Lib.*]
                    Edinburgh, 1829
    The translator's name is given in the second edition (1876).

BEFORE and after. [Verse. By W. E. Gladstone.] 8vo. Pp. 6. [*Brit. Mus.*]
                    N.P. [1885]

BEGINNER'S (a) star-book ; an easy guide to the stars and to the astronomical uses of the opera-glass, the field-glass and the telescope. By Kelvin MacKready [Edgar Gardner Murphy]. 4to. Pp. vii. 148. [*Amer. Cat.*]   New York, 1912

BEGINNING (the) and the end ; a domestic drama. . . . By Maria Lovell . . . with remarks . . . by D. G. [George Daniel]. 12mo. Pp. 44. [*Brit. Mus.*]   London [1855]

BEGINNING (the) of the reign of Queen Elizabeth. By Sr. J. H. [Sir John Hayward]. 12mo. [*Brit. Mus.*]
                    London, 1636

BEHIND a throne. [A novel.] By Nick Carter [John Russell Coryell]. 8vo. [*Amer. Cat.*]   New York, 1906

BELLE. [A tale.] By the author of *Laddie*, etc. [Evelyn Whitaker]. 8vo. [*Amer. Cat.*]   Edinburgh, 1898

BELLE (the) of Loveland river. By Olivia Dawn [Mrs Carrie Olivia Chesley Davis]. 12mo. Pp. 192. [*Publishers' Weekly*, 19th Jan. 1929.] New York, 1928

BELLE (the) of New York ; a musical comedy in two acts. Words by Hugh Morton [C. M. S. McLellan]. . . . 8vo. Pp. 32. [*Brit. Mus.*]
                    London [1901]

BELL'S edition of Shakespeare's plays. . . . With notes critical and illustrative. By the author of *The Dramatic Censor* [Francis Gentleman]. 12mo. [*Brit. Mus.*]   1774, etc.

BELOVED (the) Persis ; a memoir of Mrs Tarbett. By her pastor [J. Burrell ?]. 12mo. [*Brit. Mus.*]
                    London, 1855

BELPHEGOR, or the wishes ; a comic opera. . . . [By Miles Peter Andrews.] 8vo. Pp. 29. [*Library of Congress, Cat. of Opera Librettos.*] Dublin, 1788

BEMMO ; or, an exposition of error : being a treatise directed against Christianity. . . . By Jasui Shiuhei. [Translated from the Japanese by J. H. Gubbins.] 8vo. Pp. 30. [*Brit. Mus.*]   Yokohama, 1875

BENEFIT (the) of sanctified afflictions. [By Samuel Maddock.] 16mo. [*Brit. Mus.*]   London [1871]
    Signed : S. M.

* BENJAMIN Renton.
    For Renton, *read* Kenton.

BEPPO ; a Venetian story. [By George Gordon Noel Byron, Lord Byron]. 8vo. Pp. 49. [*Brit. Mus.*]
                    London, 1818

BERASHITH ; an essay in ontology, with some remarks on ceremonial magic. By Abhavananda [Aleister Crowley]. 4to. [*Crowley's Works*, 1903.]   Private print [1903]

BERMUDA verses. By Larry Chittenden [William Lawrence Chittenden]. 8vo. [*Amer. Cat.*]   New York, 1909

BERNARD Quesnay. Translated from the French of André Maurois [Emile Herzog] by Brian W. Downs. 8vo. Pp. 256. [*Observer*, 1st Feb. 1931.]
                    London, 1927

BERTIE, Bobbie, and Belle ; a tale of three young lads in Brittany. By May Wynne [Mabel Wynne Knowles]. 8vo. [S. J. Brown's *Ireland in fiction.*]
                    London, 1924

BESSIE Binney. By Ramsay Guthrie [John George Bowran]. 8vo. Pp. 221. [*Brit. Mus.*]   London [1921]

BESSY Bell and Mary Gray. [By Allan Ramsay.] 8vo. [A. Gibson's *Allan Ramsay*, p. 128.]   [Edinburgh, 1720]

BEST (the) friend ; a little book of thoughts and prayers for women. By A. M. N. [A. M. Newton]. 16mo. Pp. 15. [*Brit. Mus.*]   London [1916]

BEST (the) improvement of the . . . death of . . . G. Whitefield . . . addressed to the people of the Tabernacle and the Chapel, in Tottenham-Court-Road. By W. M. [William Mason, of Rotherhithe]. 12mo. [*Brit. Mus.*]
London, 1770

BEST (the) man ; eights' week 1906. [By James Elroy Flecker.] 4to. Pp. 16. [Danielson's *Bibl. of Modern Authors.*] Oxford, 1906

BEST (the) of chums. [A novel.] By May Wynne [Mabel Wynne Knowles]. 8vo. Pp. 256. London, 1922

BEST seller ; the story of a young man who came to New York to write a novel. By N. O. Youmans [Allen Clark Marple]. 8vo. Pp. 314. [*Amer. Cat.*] Indianapolis [1930]

BEST (the) way of disposing of hammer'd money and plate, as well for the advantage of the owners thereof, as for raising one million of money, in, and for the service of, the year 1697 by way of a lottery. [By Thomas Neale.] Fol. S. sh. [*Brit. Mus.*] London, 1696/7
Signed : T. N.
See also " A proposal concerning the coin," " A way to make plenty of money . . ." and " A profitable adventure . . ."

BETHIAH, the glory which adorns the daughter of God . . . [A sermon. By Cotton Mather.] 8vo. [*Brit. Mus.*]
Boston, 1722

BETRAYAL (the) of Wales. By the Member for Treorky [Ernest B. B. Rowlands]. 8vo. Pp. 120. [*Brit. Mus.*] London, 1908

BETTESWORTH (the) book ; talks with a Surrey peasant. By George Bourne [George Sturt]. 8vo. Pp. 332. [*Brit. Mus.*] London, 1901

BETWEEN the flags. By "Sabretache" of "The Tatler" [A. S. Barrow]. 8vo. Pp. 255. [*Brit. Mus.*] London [1921]

BÉZIQUE and cribbage. By "Berkeley" [W. H. Peel]. 8vo. Pp. 63. [Jessel's *Bibl. of playing cards.*] London, 1890
One of " The Club Series."

BIBLE (the) and the Church. [By William Tarbet.] 8vo. Pp. 4. [*Brit. Mus.*] [c. 1860]

" BIBLE (the)" ; by the Rev. Walter Wood . . . examined. By Mnason [David Walther]. 12mo. [*Brit. Mus.*]
Aberdeen, 1880
Scottish Tracts for the times.

BIBLE readings ; the life of Abraham. By A. H. L. [A. H. Lowndes]. Revised by R. Lowndes. 8vo. [*Brit. Mus.*]
London [1861]

BIBLE (the) series [of religious tracts. Signed : L. *i.e.* L. Laurenson]. 16mo. 4 parts. [*Brit. Mus.*]
Edinburgh [c. 1900]

BIBLE (the) Translation Society of the Baptist shown to be uncalled for and injurious. . . . By a Baptist [Henry Burgess]. 8vo. [*Brit. Mus.*]
London, 1840

BIBLE (the) true. By an unknown Christian [Albert E. Richardson]. 8vo. Pp. 144. [*Brit. Mus.*]
London [1928]

BIBLIOGRAPHY (a) of [John Bunyan's] *Grace abounding.* [By W. Perkins.] 8vo. [*Manch. Ref. Lib.*]
London, 1906

BIBLIOGRAPHY (a) of the writings . . . forming the history of philately. [By Edward Denny Bacon.] Fol. [*Bibl. Lind.* vol. 7.] London, 1911

*BIBLIOTHECA arcana. . . . By "Speculator Morum."
The author is given in Maggs' *Cat.* No. 267, 1911, as W. L. Clowes.

BIG (the) book of animal stories. By Margaret Stuart Lane [Margaret Ashworth]. 4to. Pp. 192. [*Brit. Mus.*] London, 1928

" BIG, strong man !" [A novel.] By Charman Edwards [Frederick Anthony Edwards]. 8vo. Pp. 318. [*Who's Who in Lit.*] London [1923]

BIJOUX (les) indiscrets ; or, the indiscreet toys. Translated from the Congese language, printed at Monomatapa. [By Denis Diderot.] 8vo. 2 vols. [Barbier's *Dictionnaire.*]
Tobago, 1749

BILL Bruce of Harvard. By Burt L. Standish [Gilbert Patten]. 8vo. [*Amer. Cat.*] New York, 1910

BILL (a) of divorcement ; a play in three acts. By Clemence Dane [Winifred Ashton]. 8vo. Pp. 92. London, 1921

BILL (a) of fare for a Saturday night's supper, a Sunday morning breakfast, and a Munday dinner, described in a pleasant new merry ditie. [By Martin Parker ?] Fol. S. sh. B. L. [*Brit. Mus.*] London [1635 ?]
Signed : M. P.

BILLA vera ; or, the arraignment of Ignoramus ; put forth out of charity for the use of grand inquests and other jury's ; the sworn assertors of truth and justice : in a letter to a friend. [By Laurence Womock.] [*D. N. B.* vol. 62, p. 347.] London, 1682

BILLESDON Coplow, Monday, February 24th, 1800. [Verses by Robert Lowth, M.A., of Christ College, Oxford, describing a fox-hunt.] 8vo. [*Brit. Mus.*] Melton Mowbray [1800]

BIOGRAPHICAL (a) encyclopædia of Massachusetts of the nineteenth century. [By Henry Clay Williams.] 8vo. [Kirk's *Supp.*]   Boston, 1876

BIOGRAPHICAL (a) sketch of Henry [Dundas, first] Lord Viscount Melville ; originally published in the Edinburgh Correspondent. [By William Douglas, advocate.] 8vo. [*Edin. Univ. Lib.*]
Edinburgh, 1811

BIOGRAPHICAL sketch of Mother Margaret Mary Hallahan . . . abridged from her life [by Augusta Theodosia Drane]. 8vo. Pp. 248. [*Brit. Mus.*]
London, 1871

BIOGRAPHY of James G. Blaine. By Gail Hamilton [Abigail Dodge]. 8vo. 2 vols. [*Camb. Mod. Hist.* vol. 7, p. 822.]   Norwich, 1895

BIRD (the) in the cage. [By R. Sempill ?] S. sh. [*Pollard and Redgrave.*]
Edinburgh, 1570

BIRD (the) of truth, and other fairy tales. By Fernan Caballero [Cecilia Francisca Josefa Arrom de Ayala]. (Translated by J. H. Ingram.) 8vo. Pp. xi. 241. [*Brit. Mus.*]   [1881]
Illustrated Library of Fairy Tales.

BIRDS (the) of Aristophanes. Translated by J. H. Frere. [Edited by J. W. C. *i.e.* John Willis Clark.] 8vo. Pp. 84. [*Brit. Mus.*]
Cambridge, 1883

BIRINTHEA, a romance. Written by J. B. Gent [John Bulteel]. 8vo. [*Brit. Mus.*]   1664

BIRTH (the) and early days of our ambulance trains in France, August 1914, to April 1915. By "Wagon-Lit" [George Abraham Moore]. 8vo. Pp. 19.   London, 1921

BISHOPS (the) downfall ; or, the Prelates snare ! By E. E. [Edmund Ellis ? Verse]. 4to. [*Christie-Miller Cat.*]   N.P. 1642

BLACK (a) candle. By Janey Canuck [Emily F. Murphy]. 8vo. [*Who's Who in Lit.*]   London, 1922

BLACK folk tales ; retold from the Haussa of Northern Nigeria. By Erick Berry [Mrs Allena Best, *née* Champlin]. 8vo. Pp. x. 80. [*Amer. Cat.*]   New York, 1928

BLACK Humphrey ; a story of the old Cornish coaching and kidnapping days. By James Cassidy [Mrs E. M. Story]. 8vo. Pp. 295. [*Brit. Mus.*]
London [1911]

BLACK Munday ; or, a full and exact description of that great . . . Eclipse of the Sun which will happen on the 29 day of March 1652. . . . [By John Booker.] 4to. Pp. 6. [*Brit. Mus.*]
1651

BLACK Partridge ; or, the fall of Fort Dearborn. [A story.] By H. R. Gordon [Edwin Sylvester Ellis]. 8vo. Pp. 302. [*Brit. Mus.*]   London, 1908

BLACK Valley. By Hugo Wast [G. Martínez Zuviria]. Translated by Herman and Miriam Hespelt. 8vo. Pp. 302. [*Brit. Mus.*]   London, 1928

*BLACKE (the) booke.
Signed : T. M.

BLACK'S guide to Norway. [By Robert Bowden.] Second edition. [Pettersen's *Norsk Lexikon*, p. 51.]
Edinburgh, 1877

BLAKES (the) of Culveredge. [A tale.] By C. E. M. [Constance E. Miller]. 8vo. Pp. 253.   London [1893]

BLANCHE and Beryl ; or, the two sides of life. By Madame de Stolz [Countess de Bégon]. Translated from the French. 8vo. [*Brit. Mus.*]
London, 1874

BLANCHE Heriot ; or, the Chertsey Curfew (from the drama by Albert Richard Smith). By the author of *The Hebrew maiden*, etc. [Clara Reeve]. 8vo. Pp. 141. [*Brit. Mus.*]
London, 1851

BLESSED (the) hope ; some thoughts on the second coming of our Lord. By J. A. C. [James A. Campbell, of Stracathro, M.P.]. 12mo.
Edinburgh, 1889
Private information.

BLESSINGS (the) of universal peace. By Evah Rawon [reversed spelling of " Have no war," *i.e.* Hugo Weissenborn]. 8vo. [*Amer. Cat.*]
Jersey City, N.J., 1905

BLIND Alice and her benefactress. By A. L. O. E. [A Lady of England, Charlotte M. Tucker]. 8vo. [*Brit. Mus.*]   London [1877]

BLIND (the) lady ; a comedy. [By Sir R. Howard.] 8vo. [*Brit. Mus.*]
[London, 1660 ?]
A fragment of a collection. The pagination begins on p. 29.

BLIND Maggie. [By C. B. Doggett.] 16mo. [*Brit. Mus.*]   London [1871]

BLIND (the) musician. [A Russian story.] By Vladimir Korolenko. Translated from the Russian by "Stepniak" [Sergius Kravtchinsky] and W. Westall. 8vo. [Baker's *Guide to Fiction*, p. 409.]
New York, 1890

BLIND (the) passenger. By Friedrich Laun [Friedrich August Schulze]. 16mo. [*Brit. Mus.*]   1826
Specimens of German Romance, vol. 3.

BLIND (the) pieman's fancies. By Sydney Longdale [Sydney Temple]. 16mo. [*Brit. Mus.*]
Chippenham [1926]

BLONDEL. [A novel.] By Hugh Kingsmill [Hugh Kingsmill Lunn]. 8vo. Pp. 250. [*Brit. Mus.*]
London, 1927

BLONDELLE; a story of the day. [By Sir Henry Drummond Wolff.] 8vo. Pp. viii. 314. [*Brit. Mus.*]
London, 1852

BLOODY (the) Assizes; or, a compleat history of the life of George Lord Jefferies . . . wherein is given an account of his . . . cruelties in his whole Western Circuit. . . . By James Bent [John Dunton]. 4to. Pp. 70. [*Nichols' Lit. Anec.*]   London, 1689

BLOODY (the) proiect; or, a discovery of the new designe, in the present war: being a perfect narrative of the present proceedings of the severall grandee factions for the prevention of a just peace, and promoting of a causeless warre. . . . By W. P. Gent [William Walwyn]. [*D. N. B.* vol. 59, p. 328.]
1648

BLUE flames. [A novel.] By Hubert Wales [William Piggott]. 8vo. Pp. 320. [*Brit. Mus.*]   London, 1918

BLUE Jack; and other temperance tales. . . . By the author of *Clary's confirmation*, etc. [F. E. Reade]. 8vo. Pp. 160. [*Kirk's Supp.*] London [1884]

BLUE magic. [A novel.] By Roy Devereux [Mrs Devereux Pember]. 8vo. Pp. 319. [*Brit.Mus.*] London, 1927

"BLUE Peter"; a romance of the Navy in the Great War. By Paul Trent [Edward Platt]. 8vo. Pp. 224. [*Brit. Mus.*]   London [1919]

BLUE (the) pool. [A novel.] By Valentine [Arthur Valentine Peachey]. 8vo. Pp. 256. [*Brit. Mus.*]
London, 1930

BLUESKIN; a romance. [By Edward Viles]. 8vo. [*N. and Q.* 29th April 1922, p. 332.]   London [1867]

BLYTHE House. [A story.] By R. F. H. [Rosa F. Hill]. 8vo. [*Brit. Mus.*]   London, 1864

BOA Constrictor, alias Helluo Curiarum; observations on the "resolved-on" absorption of the Vice-Chancellor's Court, and the Master of the Rolls Court, with the Lord High Chancellor's Court. [By Jeremy Bentham]. 8vo. Pp. 24. [*Brit. Mus.*] [London, 1831]

BOKE (the) for to lerne a man to be wyse, in buylding of his howse for the helth of body to holde quyetnes for the helth of his soule and body: the boke for a good husbande to lerne. [By Andrew Birde.] 8vo. B. L. [*Brit. Mus.*]   [London, 1540?]
The first eight chapters of the author's "Compendious regiment or dietary of helth."

BOKE (the) of the fayre gentylwoman, that no man shulde put his truste, or confydence in: that is to say, Lady Fortune, etc. [In verse. By Sir Thomas More.] 4to. [*Brit. Mus.*] 1875
Fugitive Tracts, series 1. Reprinted from an edition published in 1540.

BOKE (the) of wysdome. [Translated from the "Fiore di vertu" by John Larke.] 8vo. [*Pollard and Redgrave.*]
London, 1532
A later edition [1565] bears Larke's name.

BOKE (the); reade me frynde and be not wrothe. [By William Roy; with preface by L. R.] 12mo. [*Pollard and Redgrave.*]
Henry Nicholson, Wesel, 1546
For the first edition (1528) see "Rede me and be nott wrothe . . ."

BOLDNESS of them that have been with Jesus. [A sermon on Acts iv. 13. By J. E. B. Mayor.] 12mo. Pp. 28. [*Brit. Mus.*]   Cambridge [1890]

BOLSTER (the) book; a book for the bedside (compiled from the occasional writings of Reginald Drake Biffin). By Col. D. Streamer [Coldstreamer, *i.e.* Capt. Harry J. C. Graham, of the Coldstream Guards]. 8vo. [*Amer. Cat.*]   New York, 1910

"BOMBA" shrieks for help. [Verse.] By Rettop Elliverg Samoht [Thomas Greville Potter]. Fol. S. sh. [*Brit. Mus.*]   [London] 1860
The name reversed.

BONAPARTE; a poem. [By Rev. Edward Hincks?] 8vo. Pp. 64. [*O'Donoghue's Poets of Ireland,* p. 1.]
Cork, 1816

BONNIE Scotland; tales of her history, heroes, and poets. By Grace Greenwood [Mrs Sarah Jane Lippincott]. 8vo.   New York, 1903

BOOK (the) intytulyd The art of good lywyng and good deyng. [Translated by Alexander Barclay.] Fol. [Johnstone and Robertson's *Bibl. Aberd.* i. 6.]
Parys [1503]
A free translation with additions of *Le Livre intitulé L'Art de bien vivre: et de bien mourir.* This was the first book printed in Scots idiom.

BOOK (the) of Benjamin; appointed to be read by the electors of England. [By A. Capel Shaw.] Part I. 12mo. [*Birm. Ref. Lib.*]   [London, 1879?]
A burlesque directed against Benjamin Disraeli, later Earl of Beaconsfield.

BOOK (the) of blunders. . . . Selected and edited by the compiler of *Gleanings for the curious* [Charles C. Bombaugh]. 12mo. Pp. 212. [*Brit. Mus.*]
Philadelphia, 1871
Preface signed: C. C. B.

BOOK (the) of Cardiff; edited by a University graduate [John Austin Jenkins]. 8vo. Pp. viii. 132. [*Brit. Mus.*] Cardiff, 1912

BOOK (the) of hymns or praises. . . . [Metrical translations of Psalms 90 to 107]. By F. R. [Francis Roberts, D.D.]. 8vo. [W. L. Taylor's *Coll. of Psalm Versions*, p. 111.] London, 1674

BOOK (the) of James [Annesley]; with an hymn of thanksgiving on his deliverance from the hands of Richeth [Richard, Earl of Anglesey]. Translated from the original Arabick of Belshazzar Kapha, the Jew. [By Robert Dodsley.] 8vo. 2 parts. [*Brit. Mus.*] N.P. 1743-4

Another edition has the title " The book of the chronicle of James the nephew . . ."

BOOK (a) of new epigrams. By the same hand that translated Martial [Henry Killigrew, D.D.]. 8vo. 2 parts. [*Brit. Mus.*] London, 1695

BOOK (the) of Rabelais. By Jake Falstaff [Herman Fetzer]. Illustrated by Guy Arnoux. 8vo. Pp. ix. 246. [*Amer. Cat.*] Garden City, 1928

BOOK (the) of religion, ceremonies and prayers of the Jews. . . . Translated . . . from the Hebrew by Gamaliel ben Pedhazur, Gent. [Abraham Mears]. 8vo. 2 parts. [*Brit. Mus.*] London, 1738

BOOK (the) of rubies; a collection of the most notable love poems in the English language. [Edited by Thomas Dunn English.] 8vo. [*Foley's Amer. authors.*] New York, 1866

BOOK (the) of the choir. [By W. A. C. Macfarlane.] 16mo. [*Brit. Mus.*] London, 1874

Signed: W. A. C. M.

BOOK (the) of the Fathers; containing the lives of the celebrated Fathers of the Christian Church, and the spirit of their writings. [By Elizabeth Frost, later Mrs Byron, later Mrs Strutt.] 8vo. Pp. viii. 446. [*Brit. Mus.*] London, 1837

BOOK (the) of the Psychic Society; a study of the fourteen unseen powers that control human life. By Edmund Shaftsbury [Webster Edgerly]. 8vo. [*Amer. Cat.*] Washington, D.C., 1909

BOOK (the) of the visions and instructions of Blessed Angela of Foligno. . . . Translated . . . by a secular priest [Alexander P. J. Cruikshank]. . . . 8vo. Pp. xxiv. 349. [*Brit. Mus.*] London, 1871

BOOK (a) of thoughts. [Selections.] By H. A. [Henry Attwell]. 16mo. Pp. 166. [*Brit. Mus.*] London, 1865

BOOK sales of 1895, 1896 etc. . . . with introduction, notes, and index. By Temple Scott [J. H. Isaacs]. 8vo. [*Brit. Mus.*] London, 1896, etc.

BOOK (the) to keep the spirits up in dull and gloomy hours. By John Brighte [J. Duncan]. 8vo. Pp. 238. [Cushing's *Init. and Pseud.* i. 39.] Wakefield [1850?]

BOOK (a) without a title. [By G. A. D. *i.e.* George Arthur Dunn.] 8vo. Pp. 215. [*Brit. Mus.*] London [1923]

BOOKE (a) called the lyfe and deathe of the Merry Devill of Edmonton. . . . By T. B. [Thomas Brewer]. 4to. [*D.N.B.* vol. 6, p. 296.] London, 1608

A later edition (1631) gives the author's name: a reprint was issued in 1819.

BOOKE (a) containing the true portraiture of the countenances and attires of the kings of England, from William the conqueror unto our soveraigne lady Queene Elizabeth. . . . Collected by T. T. [T. Timms? or Thomas Twyne?]. 4to. [*Brit. Mus.*] London, 1597

BOOKE (the) of nurture for men servauntes; with Stans puer ad mensam. . . . [By Hugh Rhodes.] 4to. B. L. [*Pollard and Redgrave.*] London, 1568

Most other editions, both earlier and later, are not anonymous.

BOOKE (a) of secrets: shewing divers waies to make and prepare all sorts of inke and colours. . . . Translated out of Dutch . . . by W. P. [William Phillip?]. . . . 4to. B. L. [*Pollard and Redgrave.*] London, 1596

BOOKE (the) of thrift. [By Jacques Bellot.] 8vo. [*Pollard and Redgrave.*] London, 1589

Signed: J. B.

BOOKS in general. By Solomon Eagle [Jack Collings Squire]. 8vo. Pp. 256. [*Bookman*, Feb. 1923.] London, 1918

BORDERER (the). [A novel.] By Adam Lilburn [Lillias Wasserman]. 8vo. Pp. viii. 385. [*Brit. Mus.*] London, 1896

Title-page of her *Road of Life*.

BORDERERS (the); a romance of the 14th century. [By Mrs Byron.] 12mo. 3 vols. [*Eng. Cat.*, 1801-1836, p. 66.] London, 1812

BOSS (the) of Camp Four. . . . By Emart Kinsburn [Arthur Preston Hankins]. 8vo. Pp. 284. [*Brit. Mus.*] London [1927]

BOSTON (the) book; being specimens of Metropolitan literature. [Edited by James Thomas Fields.] 12mo. [*Foley's Amer. authors.*] Boston, 1850

BOSTON Common. [By Nehemiah Adams.] 8vo. Pp. 63. [*Brit. Mus.*]
Boston, 1842

BOSWELL again. By Philalethes [Thomas Davis]. 12mo. [*Lincoln's Inn Lib.*]   London, 1878

BOY artists; or sketches of the childhood of Michael Angelo, Mozart, Haydn. . . . Translated from the French of Eugénie Foa [Eugénie Rebecca Gradis, *née* Rodrigues]. 16mo. [*Bibl. Nat. de Paris.*]
Boston, 1868

BOYHOOD (the) of the king. By Herbert Strang [George Herbert Ely and C. J. L'Estrange]. 8vo. [*Brit. Mus.*]   London [1911]

BOY'S (the) friend; or, the maxims of a cheerful old man. By Carlton Bruce [George Mogridge]. 18mo. [*Eng. Cat.*, 1801-1836, p. 70.] London, 1834

BOYS of the Fort. By Captain Ralph Bonehill [Edward Stratemeyer]. 8vo. [*Amer. Cat.*]   New York, 1901

BOY'S (the) own annual; a holiday companion for all seasons: consisting of original tales. By Old Chatty Cheerful [William Martin]. 8vo. [*Brit. Mus.*]   London, 1861
Signed: W. M.

BRACKIE the fool. [A novel.] By Klabund [Alfred Henschke]. Translated by H. G. Scheffauer. 8vo. Pp. 261. [*Amer. Cat.*]
New York, 1927

BRADFORD'S history of the Plymouth Settlement, 1608-1650. Rendered into modern English by Valerian Paget [Harold and Zoe Paget]. 8vo. Pp. xxvi. 349. [*Brit. Mus.*] London, 1909

BRADSHAW'S ultimum vale; being the last words that are ever intended to be spoke of him. . . . By J. O., D.D. [John Owen] Time Server general of England. 4to. [*Brit. Mus.*]
Oxon, 1660

BRAINS (the) of the family. . . . By E. J. Rath [J. Chauncey Covey Brainerd and Edith Rathbone Brainerd]. 8vo. Pp. 284. [*Brit. Mus.*] London [1926]

BRAMBLE (the); or, the old fable of Jotham applied to the present times [in defence of George II.]. By R*** B*** [Richard Barton], B.D. 8vo. [*Camb. Univ. Lib.*]   Dublin, 1746

*BRAY of Buckholt.
This was produced under the author's real name: Edmund White.

BREACHES in the family fireside. By the late Rev. Hugh Stowell. [Edited by C. B. *i.e.* Charles Bullock.] 16mo. Pp. 12. [*Brit. Mus.*] London [1865]

BREAD cast upon the waters. [Religious tracts signed: C. S. *i.e.* Charles Stanley, Sheffield.] 32mo. 16 nos. [*Brit. Mus.*]   London [1893]

BREAKING point [of twentieth-century civilization]. . . . By Jeffery E. Jeffery [Jeffery Eardley Marston]. 8vo. Pp. 159. [*Amer. Cat.*]
London, 1921
New Era Series, vol. 11.

BREFE (a) and compendious register or table of the pryncyple histories and mooste commune artycles in the Old and Newe Testament. The thyrde boke of the Machabees not founde in the Hebrew Canons, but translated out of the Greke into Latyn. [By John Marbecke.] 12mo. [*Book prices current*, 1922.]   London, 1550

BRIDE (the) of Ludgate; a comic drama. . . . By Douglas Jerrold. . . . With memoir of Mr Cooper and remarks by D. G. [George Daniel]. 12mo. Pp. 47. [*Brit. Mus.*]
London [1872]
Lacy's Acting Edition of Plays, vol. 93.

BRIDE (the) of Triermain; or, the Vale of S. John: a poem. [By Sir Walter Scott.] 12mo. [*Eng. Cat.*, 1801-1836, p. 73.]   Edinburgh, 1813

BRIDGE conventions. By John Doe [F. R. Roe]. 8vo. Pp. ii. 204. [Jessel's *Bibl. of playing cards.*]
Allahabad, 1899

BRIDGE in brief; do's and don'ts. By Eiram Ecyrb [Marie Bryce]. 12mo. Pp. 40. [Jessel's *Bibl. of playing cards.*]   New York, 1904

BRIDGE (the) manual; an illustrated practical course of instruction and complete guide to the conventions of the game. By John Doe [F. R. Roe]. 8vo. Pp. v. 122. [Jessel's *Bibl. of playing cards.*]   London, 1900

BRIDGE (a) of fancies; tales and episodes. By James Cassidy [Mrs E. M. Story]. 8vo. Pp. 317. [*Brit. Mus.*]
London [1909]

BRIEF (a) account of some expressions in Saint Athanasius his Creed, for the satisfaction of those who think themselves thereby oblig'd to believe all things therein contain'd to be absolutely necessary to salvation. [By Gabriel Towerson.] 4to. [*Camb. Univ. Lib.*]   Oxford, 1663

*BRIEF (a) account of the Hospital . . .
Signed: C. L.

BRIEF (a) account of the life of Howell Harris extracted from papers written by himself. To which is added a . . . collection of his letters, etc. [Edited by B—— * * T—— *i.e.* Benjamin La Trobe.] 8vo. Pp. 224. [*Brit. Mus.*]
Trevecka, 1791

BRIEF (a) and necessary instruction, verye needeful to bee knowen of all housholders. [By Edward Dering.] 8vo. [*Pollard and Redgrave.*]
London, 1572
Signed : E. D.   See also, "A bryefe and necessary . . ."

BRIEF (a) and plain declaration, containing the desires of those faithful ministers who seek discipline and reformation of the Church of England. . . . By Dudley Fenner [but really by Dr William Fulke, as affirmed by Brook]. 8vo. [*D. N. B.* vol 18, p. 318, and vol. 20, p. 307.]   London, 1584

BRIEF (a) bibliography of Scottish history for the use of teachers. [By II. W. Meikle.] 8vo. Pp. 8. [*Brit. Mus.*]   London, 1910
Signed : H. W. M.

BRIEF (a) chronicle of the late intestine wars in the three Kingdoms of England, Scotland, and Ireland . . . from 1637 to 1663. By H—, J. olim St. Eccl. Ch. Oxon. [James Heath]. 8vo. [*Brit. Mus.*]   London, 1663

BRIEF conclusions of dancers and dancing, condemning the prophane use thereof. . . . As also true physicall observations for the preservation of the body in health, by the use of the same exercise.   By an Out-landish doctor (J. L. Roscio) [John Lowin]. 4to. [*Brit. Mus.*]   London, 1609
A reissue of a work published in 1607 with a different title : "Conclusions upon dances . . ."

*BRIEF description of the ancient vessel found near Sandefjord in Norway.
In Petterson's *Norsk Lexikon*, p. 58, this is attributed to Oluf Rygh.

BRIEF (a) description of the battles, victories and triumphs of the Duke of Parma.   Translated by E. A. [Edward Aggas]. 4to. [*Pollard and Redgrave.*]
London [1591]

BRIEF (a) discovery of the corruption of the ministry of the Church of England : or, three clear and evident grounds from which it will appear that they are no ministers of Christ. . . . Published for the information of all by T. C. [Thomas Collier ?]. 8vo. [*Brit. Mus.*]   London, 1647

BRIEF (a) examination of some passages in the chronological part of a letter written to Dr Sherlock in his vindication ; in a letter to a friend. [By John Milner.] [*D. N. B.* vol. 38, p. 13.]
London [1700 ?]
Also ascribed to Samuel Grascome.

BRIEF exposition of the Epistle of James.   By J. N. D. [John Nelson Darby.] Translated from the Italian. 8vo. [*Brit. Mus.*]   London [1879]

BRIEF (a) guide to Westminster Abbey. [Signed : L. E. T. *i.e.* Lawrence Edward Tanner.] 8vo. Pp. 16. [*Brit. Mus.*]   London [1930]

BRIEF (a) history of Cheshunt Great House and the manors of Andrewes and Le Mote in the county of Hertford. [By C. E. Mayo.] 8vo. Pp. 12. [*Brit. Mus.*]   Sherborne [1899]
Signed : C. E. M.

BRIEF (a) history of the Tabernacle Congregational Church, Narberth, Pembrokeshire. [By Elsie F. Francis.] 8vo. Pp. 31. [*Brit. Mus.*]
Narberth, 1928
Private information.

BRIEF (a) inquiry concerning human knowledge and belief . . . being a sequel to A general view of the materialistic philosophy edited [but rather written] by James Hibbert. 8vo. Pp. 47. [*Brit. Mus.*]
Preston, 1882

BRIEF (a) memoir of an Eton boy (Henry C—— [*i.e.* Henry Slingsby Cookesley]).   Second edition.   16mo. Pp. 62. [*Brit. Mus.*]   London, 1851

BRIEF (a) memoir of the late Joseph Hunter, F.S.A., with a descriptive catalogue of his principal separate publications. . . . [By Sylvester J. Hunter.] 8vo. [*Lincoln's Inn Lib.*]
London, private print, 1861

BRIEF (a) relation of the irreligion of the northern Quakers ; wherein their horrid principles and practises, doctrine and manners . . . are plainly exposed to the view of every intelligent reader. [By Francis Higginson.]   [*D. N. B.* vol. 26, p. 373.]   London, 1653
Signed : F. H.

BRIEF remarks on the defence of the Halifax libel on the British American colonies. [By James Otis.] [Evans' *Amer. Bibl.*]   Boston, 1765

BRIEF remarks on the work of David Brown, entitled "Christ's Second Coming, is it pre-millenial"?   By J. N. D. [John Nelson Darby]. 12mo. [*Brit. Mus.*]   London [1865]

*BRIEF (a) reply to the History of standing armies in England [by J. Trenchard].
The reply was written by Daniel Defoe. [*Brit. Mus.*]

BRIEF (a) summary of the four books of the Imitation of Christ [written in Latin by Thomas à Kempis] shewing the general scope of the works and the connexion between the different chapters.   From the Italian. [Edited by Michael Gibson.] 12mo. [*Camb. Univ. Lib.*]   London, 1853
Signed : M. G.

BRIEF (a) treatise conteinyng many proper tables and easie rules, verie necessary and needful for the use and commoditie of all people. Collected [by Richard Grafton] . . . 8vo. B. L. [*Brit. Mus.*]   London [1573]

BRIEF view of the Baptist missions and translations. . . . Compiled from the printed Accounts of the Baptist Missionary Society [by Andrew Fuller]. 8vo. [*Brit. Mus.*]   London, 1815

BRIEFE (a) and faythfull declaration of the true fayth of Christ, made by certeyne men suspected of heresye. Per me J. B. [John Bradford? or John Bale?]. 8vo. B. L. [*Brit. Mus.*]
     [London] 1547
   No pagination.

BRIEFE (a) and necessaie catechisme for househoulders ; with prayers to the same adjoyning. [By Edward Dering.] 4to. [*Brit. Mus.*]   London, 1597
   A later edition of " A Shorte catechisme for househoulders. . . ." 1582.

BRIEFE (a) and necessary instruction, verye needeful to bee knowen of all householders, whereby they maye the better teach and instruct their families in such points of Christian religion as is most meete. . . . [By Edward Dering.] 8vo. B. L. [*Brit. Mus.*]
     [London] 1572
   The "Epistle to the Christian Reader," which is prefixed, is to be found again in "A briefe and necessarie catechisme or instruction" included in "Maister Dering's Works," 1590.

BRIEFE (a) and plaine declaration concerning the desires of all those faithful ministers, that have and do seeke for the discipline and reformation of the Church of Englande. .. . [By Walter Travers.] [*D. N. B.* vol. 18, p. 318.]
     London, 1584
   Attributed by Brook to William Fulke.

BRIEFE (a) description of the portes, creekes, bays and havens of the West India ; translated out of the Castlin tongue by J. F. [John Frampton] : the originall whereof was directed to the mightie Prince Don Charles, King of Castile. 4to. B. L. [*Christie-Miller Cat.*]   London, 1578
   The Spanish author was Martin Fernandes Denciso.

BRIEFE (a) discourse of the troubles begun at Frankeford in Germany, An. Dom. 1554 ; about the Booke of Common Prayer and Ceremonies. . . . First published in the yeare 1575 and now reprinted. . . . [By William Whittingham.] [*D. N. B.* vol. 61, p. 151.]   London, 1642

BRIEFE (a) historie of the martyrdom of 12 reuerend priests, executed within these twelue monthes for confession and defence of Catholicke faith, but under false pretence of treason : a note of sundrie things that befel them in their life and imprisonment, and a preface declaring their innocence. [By William Allen, Cardinal.] 8vo. [*D.N.B.* vol. 1, p. 321.]   N.P. 1582

BRIEFE (a) introduction to syntax ; collected out of Nebrissa his Spanish copie concordance by J. H. [John Hawkins]. 8vo. [*Pollard and Redgrave.*]   London, 1631

BRIEFE (a) of the art of rhetorique (of Aristotle). By T. H. [Thomas Hobbes]. 12mo. [*Pollard and Redgrave.*]
     London [1637 ?]

BRIEFE (a) refutation of John Traskes iudaical and novel fancyes. . . . By B. D. Catholike Deuine [John Falconer]. 4to. Pp. 102. [*Brit. Mus.*]
     [St Omer] 1618

BRIEFE (a) relation of the gleanings of the idiotismes and absurdities of Miles Corbet. . . . By Antho. Roily [John Taylor, the water-poet]. 4to. [*D.N.B.* vol. 55, p. 437.]   London, 1646
   The pen-name is an anagram.

BRIEFE (a) report of the militarie services done in the Low Countries by the Erle of Leicester ; written by one that served in good place there, in a letter to a friend of his. [By Thomas Digges, M.A.] 4to. [*Walker's Pet. Bibl.* p. 39.]   London, 1587
   Of two copies in the *Brit. Mus.*, one has " T. D." at the end.

BRIEFE (a) treatise conteynynge a . . . declaration of the Pope's usurped primacye. Written in Greke . . . by Nilces. . . . [The address "to the reder," in verse, is signed B. G. *i.e.* Barnaby Googe ?] 8vo. B. L. [*Brit. Mus.*]   London, 1560
   No pagination.

BRIER-PATCH philosophy. By Peter Rabbit [William Josiah Long]. 8vo. [*Amer. Cat.*]   Philadelphia, 1906

BRIGHT tales and funny pictures. By Maggie Browne [Margaret Hamer, later Mrs Andrewes]. 4to. Pp. 80. [*Brit. Mus.*]   London, 1894

BRISTOL and its famous associations. By Stanley Hutton [Albert Edward Tilling]. 8vo. Pp. viii. 406.   1905-7

BRITANNIA ; a poem. [By James Thomson.] Fol. Pp. 16. [*Brit. Mus.*]   London, 1729

BRITANNUS and Africus. . . . By the author of *Sacred History in familiar dialogues* [Hannah Neale]. 12mo. [Whitley's *Bapt. Bibl.*]   London, 1798

BRITISH battles of destiny. By Boyd Cable [Ernest Andrew Ewart]. 8vo. Pp. 341. [*Brit. Mus.*]   London, 1926

BRITISH (the) heroine ; or, an abridgment of the life and adventures of Mrs Christian Davies. . . . By J. Wilson . . . surgeon in the army. [Ascribed to Daniel Defoe and to Nathaniel Crouch.] 8vo. [*Brit. Mus.*] London, 1742

BRITISH maritime supremacy ; a brief analysis of its past, present and possible future condition. . . . By a retired Naval Officer [John Richards]. 8vo. Pp. 16. [*Brit. Mus.*]   London, 1876

BRITISH (the) prison ship ; a poem in four cantoes. . . . To which is added a poem on the death of Captain N. Biddle. . . . [By Philip Freneau.] 8vo. Pp. 23. [Evans' *Amer. Bibl.* vi. 122.]   Philadelphia, 1781

BRITISH-AMERICAN Association and Nova-Scotia Baronets. Report of the Action of Damages for alleged libel, Broun (soi-disant) Sir Richard against the " Globe " Newspaper, with introductory remarks. [Edited by William Barclay David Donald Turnbull.]
Edinburgh, 1846
From a signed presented copy from the editor.

BROB-DINGNAGIANS (the) ; being a key to Gulliver's voyage to Brobdingnag. . . . [Subscribed C. D. M. *i.e.* Corolino di Marco *pseud.* for Jonathan Swift.] 12mo. Pp. 22. [*Brit. Mus.*]   Dublin, 1727

BROKER'S (the) correspondent ; being a letterwriter for the Stock Exchange business. By James Martin [Edward Latham]. 12mo. Pp. 67. [*Brit. Mus.*]   [1892]
Wilson's Legal Handy Books.

BROTHERHOOD, fellowship, and acting together. . . . A sequel to *New Covenant ordinances and order.* [By Robert A. Macfie, of Dreghorn.] 8vo. Pp. viii. 30.   London [1887]
Presentation copy.

BROTHERHOOD (the) of rest. By Mrs Arthur W. [Mrs Arthur Waterhouse]. 12mo. [Holling's *Cat.* 15th Jan. 1927.]   Reading, 1886

BRYEFE (a) and necessary catechisme or instruction. [By Edward Dering.] 8vo. [*Pollard and Redgrave.*]
London, 1583
Signed : Ed. De. See also " A brief and necessary . . ."

BRYEFE (a) and plaine declaracion of certayne senteces in this litle boke folowing, to satisfie the consciences of them that have judged me therby to be a favourer of the Anabaptistes. . . . A brife and faythfull declaration of the true fayth of Christ. . . . Per me J. B. [John Bradford ? or John Bale ?] 8vo. B. L. [*Brit. Mus.*]
[London, 1547]
Twenty leaves without pagination. Whitley (*Bapt. Bibl.* i. 1) gives by John Bale ?

BUCHANAN, the sacred bard of the Scottish Highlands ; his confessions and his Spiritual Songs, with his Letters and a sketch of his life. [By Lachlan Macbean.] 8vo. [Scott's *Fasti*, new edition, iv. 187.]
London, 1919

BUCKSTONE'S adventure with a Polish princess : an original farce in one act. By Slingsby Lawrence [George Henry Lewes]. 12mo. [*Brit. Mus.*]
London [1855]
Lacy's Acting Edition of Plays, vol. 22.

BUCKWHEAT (the) cake ; a poem. [By Henry Pickering.] 8vo. [*Magazine of History*, extra no. 94.] Boston, 1831

BUCOLICA Virgilii. . . . With short English notes. . . . [Edited by H. H. *i.e.* Henry Hayman ?] 16mo. Pp. iv. 34. [*Brit. Mus.*]   Oxford, 1854

BUDGE and Toddie ; their haps and mishaps : an illustrated edition of *Other people's children.* . . . [By John Habberton.] 8vo. [*Brit. Mus.*]
New York, 1878

BUDGET (the) of the people. Collected by Old Hubert [—— Parkinson]. 8vo. 2 parts. [*Brit. Mus.*] London [1793 ?]

BUNDLE (a) of sticks ; being some account of the Peckett family, collected by a twig from various sources. [By William Mortimer Charles Peckett.] 8vo.   Winchester, private print, 1914
Private information.

BUNDLE (a) of soul convincing . . . truths. By Roger Brierley. [Edited by J. C. *i.e.* John Cheney ?] 8vo. [*Brit. Mus.*]   Edinburgh, 1670

BURDEN (the). By Jeffery E. Jeffery [Jeffery Eardley Marston]. 8vo. Pp. 361. [*Amer. Cat.*]   London, 1924

BURKE'S address to the " Swinish Multitude " [Verse. By Thomas Spence, bookseller ?] 12mo. [*Brit. Mus.*]   [1793 ?]

BURMESE (the) almanack for 1879. . . .
By A. W. L. [A. W. Lonsdale]. 8vo.
[*Brit. Mus.*]   1878

*BURNING (the) bush not consumed.
. . . Perused by I. D. [Jeremiah
Dykes?] and divers other divines.
12mo. [*Brit. Mus.*] Edinburgh, 1679
Preface signed : I. H. *i.e.* John Hart.

BURNING (the) light; a sermon
preached at a visitation in Christs
Church, London. [By John Stoughton.]
[*M'Alpin Coll. Cat.*]   London, 1640
See his " XV. Choice Sermons," 1640.

BURNING (the) spear ; being the
experience of Mr John Lavender in
time of war. By A. R. P.-M. [John
Galsworthy]. 8vo. Pp. 255.
                                    London, 1919
Reprinted in 1923 with the author's
name.

BURTHEN (the) of a loaden conscience ;
or the miserie of sinne : set forth by
the confession of a miserable sinner.
[By Richard Kilby.] 8vo. Pp. 98.
[*Camb. Univ. Lib.*]   Cambridge, 1608

BURY and its environs ; a poem. . . .
[By John Winter, M.D.] Fol. [*Brit.
Mus.*]   London, 1747

BUSINESS trifles that tell. By the
managing-director of a well-known
business organization [John M.
Ouseley]. 8vo. Pp. 123. [*Brit. Mus.*]
                                London [1928]
An earlier edition under the title " 100
trifles that tell in business" bears the
author's name.

BUT in ourselves. [A novel.] By
Michael Maurice [Conrad Arthur
Skinner]. 8vo. Pp. 287. [*Brit. Mus.*]
                                London [1928]

BY J. C. of Lincoln's Inn, Esq. [Jamineau
Chevely] ; appendix to his pamphlet
containing thoughts on the easy reduction of the National Debt. 8vo.
[*Brit. Mus.*]   [London, 1783?]

BY the waters of Babylon. [Autobio-
graphical reminiscences. By Laurance
Lyon.] 8vo. Pp. 287. [*Brit. Mus.*]
                                London [1930]
The authorship is disclosed internally by
the author's references (pp. 254 *et seq.*) to
his work *The Pomp of Power.*

BYRON. By André Maurois [Emile
Herzog]. Translated . . . by Hamish
Miles. 8vo. Pp. 464. [*Observer,*
1st Feb. 1931.]   London, 1930

*BYWAYS of Empire . . .
Not by Harry Lindsay, but by Mayne
Lindsay [Mrs —— Clarke].

C

C. R. W. Nevinson. [By Osbert Sitwell.]
4to. Pp. 30, pl. 35. [*Brit. Mus.*]
                                London, 1925
Signed : O. S.

CADET'S (the) guide to India ; containing information and advice to a young
man about to enter the army of the
Hon. East India Company. By a
Lieutenant of the Bengal establishment [Henry Vigo Cary?]. 12mo.
[*Brit. Mus.*]   London, 1820

*CÆSAR'S column. . . . By Ignatius
Donnelly [Edmund Boisgilbert].
Transpose to read : By Edmund Boisgilbert
[Ignatius Donnelly].

CÆSAR'S dogs; or, a familiar communication containing the first institution of a subject in allegiance to his
soveraigne. [By E. Nisbet.] 16mo.
[*Brit. Mus.*]   London, 1601

CAIRN (the) o' Mount and Clochnaben.
By Dryas Octopetala [Alexander
Copland]. 8vo. [*Aberd. Free Lib.*]
                                Aberdeen, 1892

CALCULUS made easy ; being a very
simplest introduction to those beautiful
methods of reckoning which are generally called by the terrifying names of
the Differential Calculus and the
Integral Calculus. By F.R.S. [Silvanus
Phillips Thompson]. 8vo. Pp. 178.
                                London, 1910

CALCULUS (the) of form. [By Oliver
Byrne.] 4to. [*Brit. Mus.*]
                                N.P. [*c.* 1860]
Only two copies printed ; no title-page.

CALCUTTA in days of yore ; the
memoirs of Asiaticus [John Scott
Waring?] : or, ecclesiastical . . . and
historical sketches respecting Bengal.
. . . 8vo. [*Brit. Mus.*]
                                Calcutta, 1869

CALEB D'Anvers's [Nicholas Amhurst's]
petition to the squire of Alsatia for a
pension, setting forth some of his
merits both in writing and painting.
Fol. S. sh. [*Brit. Mus.*]
                                London [1740?]

CALEDONIAN (the) comet [*i.e.* Sir Walter Scott. A satirical poem. By John Taylor, the author of *Monsieur Tonson*]. 8vo. [*Brit. Mus.*]
London, 1810

*CALEDONIAN (the) comet elucidated.
The J. Taylor (John Taylor, author of *Monsieur Tonson*) to whom this has been wrongly ascribed, was in fact the author of the original *Caledonian comet*, q.v.

*CALENDARS of the ancient charters . . .
The introduction is said to have been written by Thomas Astle. [Gross' *Sources of Engl. Hist.* p. 57.]

CALIFORNIA and its gold mines; being a series of recent communications . . . upon the present condition and future prospects of quartz mining. [By Thomas Allsop]. 8vo. Pp. 149. [*Brit. Mus.*]   London, 1853
Signed : A. T.

CALIFORNIA; its characteristics and prospects. (From the New Englander for Feb. 1858). [By Horace Bushnell.] 8vo. Pp. 42. [*Sabin's Dictionary*.]
N.P. 1858

CALIFORNIAN (the) crusoe; or, the lost treasure found : a tale of Mormonism. [By Robert Richards.] Second edition. 8vo. Pp. iv. 162.
London, 1858
The first edition, 1854, is not anonymous.

CALL (a) to prayer, in two sermons. . . . With an account of the principles and practice of the Quakers. . . . By the author of *The skirmish upon Quakerism* [John Cheney]. 8vo. [*Brit. Mus.*]
London, 1677
Preface signed : J. C.

CALL (a) upon H.R.H. the Duke of Kent, with the means, by his return to save and serve his country. . . . [Subscribed : The author of *The discovery*, *i.e.* George Edwards, M.D.] 8vo. [*Brit. Mus.*]   London [1817]

CALL-BOX (the) mystery. By John Ironside [E. M. Tait]. 8vo. Pp. vi. 226. [*Brit. Mus.*]   London, 1923

CALM (a) answer to a bitter invective, called, A letter to the late author of *The Preparation for martyrdom*. By that author [Zachary Cawdrey]. [*M'Alpin Coll. Cat.*]   London, 1643
See "The Preparation for martyrdom . . ."

*CALUMNY display'd. . . .
The author's name appears in a petition at the end of Part I.

CAMDEN and other poems. By Cave Winscom [John Cave]. 8vo. [*Brit. Mus.*]   London, 1876

CAMILLA; a drama, adapted from the French of A. Dumas [by Matilda Heron]. 8vo. [F. Boase's *Mod. Eng. Biog.* i. 1445.]   N.P. 1856

*CAMILLUS . . .
For Moncrief, *read* Moncrieff.

CAMP (the) Fire Boys at Log Cabin Bend. By Oliver Lee Clifton [St George Rathborne]. 8vo. Pp. 248. [*Amer. Cat.*]   New York, 1923
Part of a series called "The Camp Fire Boys Series," all by the same author.

*CAMPANALOGIA; or, the art of ringing improved . . .
Ascribed also to Rev. Francis Scatesgood. [*Leeds Univ. annotated copy of Halkett and Laing.*]

CAN a Jew sit in Parliament? Why not? A letter . . . to a brother clergyman. By Clericus Cambrensis [J. C. Edwards]. 8vo. [*Brit. Mus.*]
London, 1855

CAN we enter into treaty with the new slave trading confederacy? [By W. Alexander.] 8vo. Pp. 8. [*Sabin's Dictionary*.]   Leeds [1861]

CANADAS (the) as they now are; comprehending a view of their climate, rivers, lakes . . . etc. By a late resident [Andrew Picken]. 12mo. Pp. xv. 116. [*D. N. B.* vol. 45, p. 239.]
London, 1833
The information in the book was supplied by John Galt.

CANDID (a) examination of Dr [Jonathan] Mayhew's Observations on the charter and conduct of the Society for the propagation of the Gospel in foreign parts. . . . By one of its members [Samuel Johnson, D.D., of Stratford, Connecticut]. 8vo. . . . [*Brit. Mus.*]
Boston, New England, 1763
See also, above, a later "Answer to Dr Mayhew's Observations . . ." [By Archbishop Thomas Secker]; and "The Claims of the Church of England seriously examined. . . ." [by Caleb Fleming].

CANDIDATES (the) guide; or, the electors right decided : shewing the determination of the rights of elections by . . . the Commons. . . . By J. C. Gent. [J. Cowley]. 8vo. [*Brit. Mus.*]
London, 1735

CANST thou bind the sweet influences of the Pleiades? Job 38 : 31. [By] S. R. D. [Samuel Rolles Driver]. 8vo. [*Camb. Univ. Lib.*]   N.P. [1882]

CANTICLES (the) and anthems used at morning and evening prayer, divided and marked for chanting. [By W. L. Dickinson.] 16mo. Pp. 19. [*Brit. Mus.*]   Manchester, 1857

CANTICLES (the) . . . with the Gregorian tones adapted to them. . . . [Edited by W. B. H. *i.e.* William Beadon Heathcote.] 12mo. [*Brit. Mus.*] Oxford, 1844

*CAPE (the) of Good Hope . . . By a traveller.
   For —— Gilchrist, *read* John Mac-Gilchrist. [*Boase's Mod. Eng. Biog.*]

CAPE Town Dicky; or, Colonel Jack's boy. . . . By Theo Gift [Dora Havers, later Mrs Boulger]. 4to. Pp. 64. [*Brit. Mus.*] London, 1888

CAPRICE; a comedy in three acts. By Sil-Vara [Geza Silberer]. (Adapted by Philip Moeller.) 8vo. Pp. 119. [*Amer. Cat.*] London, 1929

CAPRICES (the) of a royal incognita. Told by herself. [By William R. H. Trowbridge.] 8vo. Pp. vii. 327. [*Brit. Mus.*] London, 1903

CAPTAIN Calamity. By Rolf Bennett [W. Marten]. 8vo. Pp. 254. [*Brit. Mus.*] London, 1916

CAPTAIN Java. By Louis Moresby [Mrs Lily Adams Beck]. 8vo. Pp. 285. [*Amer. Cat.*] London, 1928

CAPTAIN Kid's millions. [A tale.] By Alan Oscar [W. B. Whall]. 8vo. Pp. 390. [*Brit. Mus.*] London, 1897

CAPTAIN Lucifer. [A novel.] By Ben Bolt [Otwell Binns]. 8vo. Pp. 317. [*Brit. Mus.*] London, 1928

CAPTAIN (the) of the watch; a farce in one act. (Freely rendered from a . . . comedy by M. Lockroy [Joseph Philippe Simon] entitled "Le Chevalier du Guet.") By J. R. Planché. 12mo. [*Brit. Mus.*] London [185—]
   Lacy's Acting Edition, vol. 18.

CAPTAIN Smith and Princess Pocahontas; an Indian tale. [By John Davis, of Salisbury.] 12mo. [*Brit. Mus.*], 1817 Richmond [Va.], 1817

CAPTAIN Tom's ballad; or Captain Tom's lamentation for his mob's tribulation. [By Daniel Defoe.] Fol. S. sh. [*Brit. Mus.*] N.P. 1710

*CAPTAIN Trafalgar. . . . By Annie Laurie [Winifred Black].
   Read By André Laurie [Paschal Grousset]. [*Brit. Mus.*]

CAPTAINS and Kings; three dialogues on leadership. By André Maurois [Emile Herzog]. Translated by J. Lewis May. 8vo. Pp. 157. [*Observer*, 1st Feb. 1931.] London, 1925

CAPTAIN'S (the) wife. By John Lloyd [Jacque Lloyd Morgan]. 8vo. [*Amer. Cat.*] New York, 1908

CAPTIVATING Mary Carstairs. [A novel.] By Henry Second [Henry Sydnor Harrison]. 8vo. 1911
   The London (1914) edition has the author's real name.

CARD tricks and puzzles. By "Berkeley" [W. H. Peel] and J. B. Rowland. 8vo. Pp. viii. 120. [Jessel's *Bibl. of playing cards.*] London, 1892
   One of "The Club Series."

CARDANNA; that is to say, a Poeme in honour of our King Charles Iames, Queene Anne and Prince Charles. By James Anne-son [James Maxwell]. 4to. [*Christie-Miller Cat.*] [London, 1619]

CARDILLAC. By Luke Sharp [Robert Barr]. 8vo. [*Amer. Cat.*] New York, 1909

CARDINAL Newman; reminiscences of fifty years since. By one of his oldest living disciples [Rev. William Lockhart, B.A.]. 8vo. [*D.N.B.* vol. 34, p. 53.] London, 1891

*CARDINALISMO (il) di Santa Chiesa.
   The name of the translator (G. H.) is George Havers.

CAREW Quarterings. — Pedigree of Carewe, of Carewe Castle, Co. Pembroke, and Mohun's Ottery, Co. Devon, and the branches of Maccombe, Antony, Bury, and Crowcombe. [By Sir Thomas Phillipps.] Fol. [*Brit. Mus.*] [Middle-Hill, 1830]

CARNAL reason; or, the wisdom of the flesh, how foolish, deceitful, dangerous, reprobate, and divilish; together with rectified reason, how divine, transcendent, safe, profitable, and delightful. . . . By Junius Florilegus [Richard Younge]. 8vo. [*Brit. Mus.*] London, 1669
   Signed: R. Junius.

CARNARVON Castle. [Verse.] By M. L. D. [M. L. Dawson]. 8vo. Pp. 12. [*Brit. Mus.*] Hay, 1911

CARNARVON Castle; or, the birthplace of the Prince of Wales; an opera in two acts, and in prose. [By Rev. John Rose.] 8vo. [*Brit. Mus.*] London, 1793

CAROLI του μακαριτου παλιγγενεσια. [In English verse. By Thomas Pierce, Dean of Salisbury.] 8vo. Pp. 11. [*Brit. Mus.*] 1649

CAROLINE [Queen Consort of George IV.]; a poem, in blank verse. [By William Hone.] 8vo. [*Camb. Univ. Lib.*] London, 1820

CARPENTER (the); or, the danger of evil company. [A ballad. By Hannah More.] Fol. S. sh. [*Brit. Mus.*] Bath [1795 ?]
   Signed: Z.

CARPENTER'S (the) daughter. By the authors of *The wide, wide world* [Susan and Anna Bartlett Warner]. 16mo. [*Brit. Mus.*] London, 1864

CARRIAGE and cab driving on the Lord's Day; reprinted from *The Christian*. [By Frederick Edward Gretton?] 16mo. [*Brit. Mus.*]
London [1873]
Signed: F. E. G.

CARROUSE (a) to the Emperour, the Royal Pole [John III. Sobieski], and the much-wrong'd Duke of Lorraine [Charles V.]. [A ballad, on the occasion of the victory over the Turks at Vienna, Sept. 11, 1683. By Thomas D'Urfey.] Fol. S. sh. B. L. [*Brit. Mus.*] [London, 1683]

CASE (the) is altered; how? Ask Dalio and Millo. [Signed F. T. *i.e.* Francis Thynne?] 4to. B. L. [*Brit. Mus.*] London, 1604

CASE (the) of Dunkirk faithfully stated and impartially considered. By a Member of the House of Commons [Henry St John, Viscount Bolingbroke]. 8vo. [*Camb. Hist. of Eng. Lit.*] London, 1730

CASE (the) of our fellow creatures, the oppressed Africans, respectfully recommended to the serious consideration of the Legislature of Great Britain. By the people called Quakers. [By Anthony Benezet.] 8vo. Pp. 13. [Sabin's *Dictionary*.] London, 1784

CASE (the) of the Church of Ireland stated, in a letter (a second letter) . . . in reply to the charges of J. K. L. [*i.e.* J. Doyle, R.C. Bishop of Kildare and Leighlin in his "Vindication of the Principles of the Irish Catholics"]. By Declan [William Phelan, D.D.]. 8vo. 2 parts. [Jebb's *Life of Phelan*, p. 49.] Dublin, 1823-4

CASE (the) of the Roman Catholics of Ireland; in a course of letters from a member of the Protestant Church in that kingdom [Henry Brooke] to his friend in England. 8vo. [*Camb. Univ. Lib.*] Dublin, 1760

CASE (the) with nine solutions. By J. J. Connington [Alfred Walter Stewart]. 8vo. Pp. 287. [*Amer. Cat.*] London, 1928

CASE (a) without a clue. By Nick Carter [John Russell Coryell]. 8vo. [*Amer. Cat.*] New York, 1907

CATALOGUE (a) of divers visible professors of the Catholike Faith . . . in all ages since Christ. Taken out of the Appendix to the Reply of A. D. [*i.e.* John Fisher, S.J.]. 12mo. [*Pollard and Redgrave.*]
[St Omers] 1614

CATALOGUE (a) of engraved British portraits, from Egbert the Great to the present time; with an appendix containing the portraits of such foreigners as may claim a place in the British series. By Henry Bromley [Anthony Wilson]. 4to. [*D. N. B.* vol. 62, p. 78.] London, 1793

CATALOGUE (a) of engravings by William Miller, H.R.S.A. 1818 to 1871. By W. F. M. [W. F. Miller]. 4to. Pp. xxxv. [*Brit. Mus.*]
London, 1886
Fifty copies only were printed.

CATALOGUE of manuscripts relating to genealogy and heraldry, preserved in the Library of the Faculty of Advocates, at Edinburgh. [By W. B. D. D. Turnbull.] 8vo. [*Bibl. Lind.*]
London, 1852
Only ten copies printed.

CATALOGUE (a) of modern law-books; being a supplement to *Bibliotheca legum Angliae* [of John Worrall]. . . . [By Edward Brooke.] 12mo. [*Brit. Mus.*] London, 1794
Advertisement signed: E. B. Continued London, 1800, by E. B. and J. R. [E. Brooke and J. Rider].

CATALOGUE (a) of new books by way of supplement to the former: being such as have been printed from that time till Easter-term, 1660. [By William London, bookseller?] 4to. [*Brit. Mus.*] London, 1660
Signed: W. L.

CATALOGUE (a) of portraits in the possession of Pembroke College, Oxon. [By Arthur R. Bailey.] 8vo. Pp. 73. [*Brit. Mus.*] Oxford, 1895

CATALOGUE (a) of Scots poets, from the earliest period. [By W. Gowans.] 8vo. Pp. 24. [O'Leary's *Eng. Lit. Hist.* p. 139.] New York, 1852

CATALOGUE (a) of such testimonies in all ages as plainly evidence Bishops and Presbyters to be both one, equall and the same in iurisdiction, office, dignity, order, and degree. . . . [By William Prynne.] [*M'Alpin Coll. Cat.*]
1637
Attribution by Dr Charles A. Briggs.

CATALOGUE (a) of such testimonies in all ages as plainly evidence bishops and presbyters to be both one, equal, and the same in jurisdiction. . . . [By William Prynne.] 4to. N.P. 1641
A marginal note on A 4 recto refers to the author's "The Unbishoping of Timothy and Titus."

CATALOGUE (a) of the Bradshaw collection of Irish books in the University Library, Cambridge. [By Charles Edward Sayle.] 8vo. 3 vols. [*Brit. Mus.*]   Cambridge, 1916

CATALOGUE of the Burrell collection of Wagner documents, letters and other biographical material. [Compiled by Peter E. Wright.] 8vo. Pp. xi. 99. [*Brit. Mus.*]   London, 1929

*CATALOGUE of the Chancellors of England . . .
    For Philipot, *read* Philpot.

CATALOGUE of the pictures at Dalkeith House. [By Lord Henry Francis Scott and Hon. Hew Hamilton Dalrymple.] 4to. Pp. xi. 165. [*Brit. Mus.*]   Private print, 1911
    Preface signed : " H. S. " " H. H. D."
    Only fifty copies printed.

CATALOGUE of the special exhibition of ancient musical instruments, 1872. [At the South Kensington Museum. Edited by C. E. *i.e.* Carl Engel.] 4to. [*Brit. Mus.*]   London [1873]

*CATALOGUE (a) of the subscription library at Kingston upon Hull. [Compiled by J. C. *i.e.* Joseph Clarke.] 8vo. [*Brit. Mus.*]   Liverpool, 1822

CATALOGUE (a) of works of art and curiosities at Normanhurst Court, Battle. [By Alfred Maskell.] 8vo. Pp. 164. [*Brit. Mus.*]   [London] 1878
    Preface signed : A. M.

CATALOGUS librorum A. C. D. A. [Archibald Campbell Duke of Argyle]. 4to. 2 tom. [*Brit. Mus.*]
                    Glasgow, 1748

CATALOGUS Protestantium ; or the Protestants Kalender. . . . [By George Webbe, Bishop of Limerick.] 4to. [*Camb. Univ. Lib.*]   London, 1624
    Epistle to the reader signed by John Gee.

CATAPLUS ; or, Æneas his descent to Hell : a mock poem in imitation of the sixth book of Virgil's Aeneid. . . . [Dedication signed : M. A. *i.e.* M. Atkins ?] 8vo. Pp. 88. [*Brit. Mus.*]
                    London, 1672

CATECHISME for children in yeeres and children in understanding ; chiefly intended for their instruction in the family. [By John Stalham.] 8vo. Pp. 19. [*Brit. Mus.*]   London, 1644
    For the second impression issued "by I. S. of Terling," see "Catechism for children . . ."

*CATECHISME (a) or institution of Christian Religion . . .
    The first edition (1570) was entitled " A Catechisme or first instruction and learning of Christian Religion."

CATHEDRAL (the) Church of Canterbury. . . . . [By Hartley Withers.] 8vo. Pp. 127. [*Brit. Mus.*]
                    London, 1896
    Preface signed : H. W.

CATHEDRAL (the) Church of the Blessed Virgin Mary of Salisbury. By J. M. J. F. [James M. J. Fletcher]. 8vo. Pp. 16. [*Brit. Mus.*]
                    Salisbury, 1926

CATHEDRAL (the) of Trondhjem ; a statement of the resolutions relative to the restoration of the Trondhjem cathedral by the government and storting. [By P. A. Wessel-Berg.] [Pettersen's *Norsk Lexikon*, col. 68.]
                    Kristiania, 1921

CATHERINE Douglas ; a tragedy. [By Sir Arthur Helps.] 8vo. [Keynes' *William Pickering.*]   London, 1843

CATHOLIC (the) Epistles and Revelation. [A translation and commentary by W. H. *i.e.* William Hebenden, the younger.] 8vo. [*Brit. Mus.*]
            London, private print [1836]

CATHOLIC (the) florist ; a guide to the cultivation of flowers for the altar. [By W. H. J. Weale.] . . . 12mo. Pp. xxii. 327, xxix. [*Brit. Mus.*]
                    London, 1851

CATHOLICK (the) poet ; or, Protestant Barnaby's sorrowful lamentation ; an excellent new ballad. [By John Oldmixon.] Fol. [R. Straus' *The Unspeakable Curll.*]   London, 1716

*CATHOLICKE (a) apologie . . . By E. D. L. I. C.
    For Pierre du Belloy, *read* Pierre de Belloy. The attribution to Belloy is by Barbier. Lelong's explanation of E. D. L. I. C. as E[dmond] D[e] L['Allouette,] J[uris] C[onsulte], is accepted by the British Museum, and Pollard and Redgrave.

CATO ; a tragedy. . . . By Joseph Addison ; with . . . notes . . . by D. G. [George Daniel]. 12mo. Pp. 50. [*Brit. Mus.*]   London [1874]
    Lacy's Acting Edition of plays, vol. 99.

CATO'S principles of self-preservation and publick liberty, truly stated and fairly examined. . . . The second edition. By a subject of Cæsars [John Gaynam, chaplain of the Fleet]. 8vo. [*Lincoln's Inn Lib.*]   London, 1722

CAULDRON (the) bubbles. By N. A. Temple Ellis [Neville Aldridge Holdaway]. 8vo. Pp. vii. 275. [*Brit. Mus.*]
                    London, 1930

CAUSE (the) of a crisis ; Flurscheim's theory. By A. J. O. [A. J. Ogilvy]. 8vo. Pp. 19. [*Brit. Mus.*]
                    Hobart, 1894

CAUSE (the) of the greatnesse of cities. Translated [from the Italian of Giovanni Botero] by Sir T. H[awkins]. 12mo. [*Pollard and Redgrave.*]
London, 1635

CAUSIDICADE (the); a panegyri-serio-comic dramatical poem, on the strange resignation and stranger pro-motion. By Porcupine Pelagius [Macnamara Morgan]. 4to. [*D.N.B.* vol. 39, p. 23.]   London, 1743
A satire on the appointment of William Murray (later Earl of Mansfield) as Solicitor-General.

CAUTION (a) against sacriledge; or sundry queries concerning tithes; where-in is held forth the propriety and title that ministers have in them . . . Collected and composed by one that hath no propriety in tithes [Samuel Clarke]. . . . [*M'Alpin Coll. Cat.*]
London, 1659
See also, "An item against sacriledge . . ."

*CAUTION (a) to the readers of . . .
This is by J. J. Penstone and is not anonymous. [*Brit. Mus.*]

CAVALRY taught by experience; a forecast of cavalry under modern war conditions. By " Notrofe " [Ernest Frederick Orton]. 8vo.   Pp. 64. [*Brit. Mus.*]   1910

CEASE your funning; or, the rebel detected. Seventh edition, with a pre-face and notes by the author. [By Charles Kendal Bushe.] 8vo. Pp. 48. [*D.N.B.* vol. 8, p. 34.]   Dublin, 1799
The third edition (? also 1st and 2nd) reads "The Union; cease your funning. . . ." See the note thereto.

CECI Morel; a tale [in verse, professing to be written by Leofwine, of Seniston; edited [but really written] by Robert William Essington. 8vo. [*Brit. Mus.*]
London, 1853

CEDRIC'S diaries and letters from America. [Preface signed: C. C. B. *i.e.* Cedric Clifton Brown.] 8vo. Pp. xv. 143. [*Brit. Mus.*]
London, private print, 1928

CEDRIC'S [Cedric Clifton Brown's] letters during the Great War, 1914-1919. 8vo. Pp. ix. 162. [*Brit. Mus.*]
London, private print, 1926

CELEBRATED (the) jumping frog of Calaveras County, and other sketches. By Mark Twain [Samuel Langhorne Clemens]. 8vo.   Pp. 198.   [*Brit. Mus.*]   New York, 1867

CELEBRATED trials of all countries, and remarkable cases of criminal juris-prudence; selected by a member of the Philadelphia Bar [J. J. Smith]. 8vo. [*Brit. Mus.*]   Philadelphia, 1835

CELEBRITY (the) Zoo. Rhymes and caricatures. By Mac [Herbert W. MacKinney]. 4to. [*Brit. Mus.*]
[Dublin] 1925

CELESTIAL filiation; being a vindica-tion of the pre-existence of the Lord Jesus Christ, in which the erroneous assertions . . . of Mr [Frederick] Silver . . . are exposed and refuted. By a lover of his creed [Rev. John Stevens]. 12mo. 2 parts. [*Brit. Mus.*]   [London] 1833

CELTIC (the) romance.   By Brynjulf Asalris [Card Johan Sel]. [Pettersen's *Norsk Lexikon*, col. 69.]
Stavanger, 1907

CENSURE (a) upon Lilly's grammar. By R. G. [Richard Garthwaite] formerly of the Free School in Newcastle. 12mo. [*Brit. Mus.*]   London, 1684

CENSURES (the) of the Church revived, in the defence of a short paper, published by the first Classis within the province of Lancaster . . . in three full answers. . . .   [Edited by J. Harrison?] 4to. [*Brit. Mus.*]
London, 1657

CENSUS (the). [A tract, by Francis Bourdillon.] 8vo. [*Brit. Mus.*]
London [1861]
Signed : F. B.

CENTENNIAL gleanings. . . .   Short poems by K. M. [Kate M'Carthy]. 12mo.   [O'Donoghue's *Poets of Ireland.*]   New York, 1876

*CENTRUM naturæ concentratum . . .
Not anonymous.   Brice's name is at the end of the preface.

*CERTAIN briefe observations and antiquæries . . .
Also attributed to John Goodwin. [Pease's *Leveller movement*, 73, and *M'Alpin Coll. Cat.*]

CERTAIN misstatements and errors exposed in a conversation between a village schoolmaster and an Ana-baptist. [By Samuel Hobson.] 12mo. Pp. 24. [*Brit. Mus.*]
Birmingham, 1846

CERTAINE articles, collected and taken (as it is thought) by the Byshops out of a litle boke entituled an Admonition to the Parliament, wyth an answere to the same. . . . [By Thomas Cart-wright?] [*Camb. Univ. Lib.*]
London, 1572

*CERTAINE considerations touching the better pacification . . .
The note is incorrect.   There were two editions in 1604, and both bearing that date.

CERTAINE devout and godly petition, commonly called Iesus psalter. [Ascribed to Richard Whitford.] 16mo. B. L. [*D. N. B.* vol. 61, p. 128 ; *Pollard and Redgrave.*]

[London ? 1545 ?]

For other editions see "An invocacyon glorious . . . " (1529) and "The psalter of Jesus . . ." (1618).

CERTAINE Englishe Verses [entitled : "The triumph of trophes"] presented unto the Queenes most excellent Maiestie, by a courtier : in joy of the most happie disclosing, of the most dangerous conspiracies pretended by the late executed traitours, against her royall person, and the whole estate. [By] L. L. [Lodowick Lloyd ?]. 4to. [*Brit. Mus.*] London, 1586

CERTAINE irrefragable propositions worthy of serious consideration. [By Joseph Hall, Bishop of Exeter, later of Norwich.] 4to. [Madan's *Oxford Books*, i. 290.] London, 1639

The same sheets, treating of oaths and covenants, were issued under a different title, ostensibly printed at Oxford, but probably printed elsewhere ("The lawfulnes and unlawfulnes of an oath or covenant, set downe in short propositions . . . 1643).

CERTAINE precepts or directions for the well ordering and carriage of a mans life. . . . [By William Cecil, Lord Burghley.] 4to. [*Brit. Mus.*] London, 1617

The titles of later editions begin " Precepts or directions . . . " and give the author's name.

CERTAINE psalmes reduced into English meter by H. D. [H. Dod]. 8vo. [*Pollard and Redgrave.*]

Edinburgh, 1603

CERTAINE queries touching the ordination of ministers ; soberly propounded to the serious consideration of all the parochiall ministers of England. . . . By W. A. [William Aspinwall]. [*M'Alpin Coll. Cat.*]

London, 1647

Attribution by Dr Charles A. Briggs.

*CERTAYNE matters . . . 1603.

The first edition [1594 ?] begins " Certaine matters . . ." Another edition (1603) begins " Certeine matters . . ."

CERTAYNE sermons of the ryghte famous and excellente clerk Master B. Ochine . . . now . . . an exyle in this lyfe, for the faithful testimony of Jesus Christe. Faythfully translated into Englyshe. [No. 1-6 by Richard Argentine ; No. 7-18 by Lady Anne Cooke, afterwards Bacon]. 8vo. B. L. [*Pollard and Redgrave.*]

London [1550]

CESARIO Rosalba : a romance. By Anne of Swansea [Anne Hatton]. 12mo. 5 vols. [*Eng. Cat.*, 1801-1836, p. 20.] London, 1819

Also attributed to Julia Anne Kemble.

CHAIN (a) of events : a dramatic story in eight acts. By Slingsby Lawrence [George Henry Lewes] and Charles James Mathews. 8vo. [*Brit. Mus.*] London, 1852

CHAINS of lightning. By Jonathan Brooks [John Calvin Mellett]. 8vo. Pp. 313. [*Amer. Cat.*] Indianapolis, 1929

CHANCERY and Exchequer ; hints on the pending schemes for receiving the suitors in Courts of Equity. [By Edgar Taylor.] 8vo. [*Lincoln's Inn Lib.*] London, 1830

CHANCERY (the) compensation to the six clerks, sworn clerks, agents and record keeper, under 5 & 6 Vict. chap. 103 ; statement in support of renewed motion by Mr Watson, Q.C. [By William Richard Ripley.] 8vo. 2 parts. [*Lincoln's Inn Lib.*] London, 1845-6

CHANCES and changes ; a story of love and friendship. By the author of *My first grief* [Charles Beckett]. 8vo. Pp. iv. 274. [*Brit. Mus.*] 1859

*CHANGEABLE (the) covenant . . .

The *D. N. B.* considers the attribution to Thomas May doubtful.

CHAPERON to Cupid. By John Oxenham [William Arthur Dunkerley]. 8vo. Pp. 288. London, 1924

CHAPTER (a) from the book called The ingenious gentleman Don Quijote de la Mancha, which by some mischance has not till now been printed. [By Arthur Machen.] 8vo. Pp. 16. [Danielson's *Bibl. of Machen.*] London [1887]

CHAPTER (a) on bishops ; occasioned by Dr Hampden's elevation to the See of Hereford. [By Robert Mackenzie Beverley.] 8vo. Pp. 39. [*Brit. Mus.*] London, 1848

In a bound volume of tracts by Beverley in the British Museum. See the note to "Analysis by a student of prophecy . . ." in the supplement.

*CHARACTER (the) of a primitive bishop . . .

By Joseph Pitts. [*Leeds Univ.* ; author's own copy.]

*CHARACTER (the) of a right Malignant. . . .

The *D. N. B.* considers the attribution to Thomas May doubtful.

CHARACTER (the) of Dr Johnson, with illustrations from Mrs Piozzi, Sir John Hawkins and Mr Boswell. [By Rev. William Johnston Temple.] 8vo. Pp. 23. [*Times Lit. Supp.* 22nd May 1930.] London, 1792

CHARACTER (the) of Holland. [A poem. By Andrew Marvell.] 4to. [*D. N. B.* vol. 36, p. 324.]
London, 1665

CHARACTER sketches, containing a series of dramatic, comical, humorous and descriptive account [*sic*] of the official and home-life of the revenue officials in the Mofussil. C. P. S. N. [C. P. Srihari Nāyudu]. . . . 8vo. Pp. 76. [*Brit. Mus.*] Madras, 1898

CHARACTERISTICKS of a believing Christian. . . . By Francis Bacon. . . . With a preface by a clergyman [John Green]. 8vo. Pp. 8. [*Brit. Mus.*]
London, 1749
Preface signed : J. G.

CHARGE (the) of schism renewed against the separatists, in answer to the renewer of that pretended peaceable design, which is falsly called an Answer to Dr Stillingfleet's late sermon. [By Samuel Thomas.] [*D. N. B.* vol. 56, p. 190.] London, 1680

CHARGE (the) to the jury ; or, the sum of the evidence on the trial of A. B., C. D. and E. F. All, M.D. for the death of one Robert at Orped, at a Special Commission of Oyer and Terminer . . . before Sir Asculapius Dosem, Dr Timberhead and others. . . . [By Henry Fielding ?] 8vo. Pp. 46. [*Brit. Mus.*] London, 1745

CHARIOTEER (the). [A novel.] By John Presland [Gladys Skelton]. 8vo. Pp. 288. [*Brit. Mus.*] London, 1930

CHARITABLE (the) surgeon ; or the best remedies for the worst maladies revealed : being a new and true way of curing (without mercury) the several degrees of the venereal distemper in both sexes. . . . [By John Marten ?] [R. Straus' *The Unspeakable Curll*, p. 206.] London, 1708
See the note to "A new method of curing without internal medicines. . . ."

CHARITY commended ; or, a Catholick Christian soberly instructed. By J. C., M.D. [John Collop]. 8vo. [*Brit. Mus.*] London, 1667
Other copies have the title : "Medici catholicon. . . ."

CHARITY (the) of Jesus Christ. By Francis Arias. [With a preface signed : H. J. C. *i.e.* Henry James Coleridge.] 8vo. Pp. xii. 222. [*Brit. Mus.*]
London, 1880

CHARLES Shannon. [By E. B. G. *i.e.* Eric B. George.] 4to. Pp. 29. [*Brit. Mus.*] London, 1924
"Contemporary British Artists."

CHARLIE Burton : a tale. [By Jane Alice Sargant.] 8vo. Pp. 127. [*Brit. Mus.*] London [1880]

CHARM, enthusiasm and originality : their acquisition and use. By William Sime [William Henry Schoenan]. 8vo. Pp. 128. [*Brit. Mus.*]
Los Angeles [1929]

CHARMERS (the) ; a poem : humbly inscribed to the Hon. Lady Gore. [By John Marshall.] 4to. [O'Donoghue's *Poets of Ireland.*] Dublin, 1743

CHASING the sun ; or, rambles in Norway. [By Robert Michael Ballantyne.] [Pettersen's *Norsk Lexikon*, col. 69.] London, 1864

CHASTE (the) Diana. [A novel.] By E. Barrington [L. Adams Beck]. 8vo. Pp. 332. [*Brit. Mus.*] London, 1923

CHEAP repository. [A collection of 37 tracts, those signed "Z" being written by Hannah More. With woodcuts attributed to T. Bewick.] [*Brit. Mus.*] London [1795-6]

*CHEAPE and good husbandry . . .
The first edition was in 1614. There was a sequel in the same year entitled, "The second booke of the English Husbandman. . . . By G. M."

*ΧΕΙΡΟΘΕΣΙΑ τῶν πρεσβυτέρων . . .
For τῶν πρεσβυτέρων read τοῦ πρεσβυτερίου. The *D.N.B.* ascribes to Henry Hickman (signed with penultimates). [*D. N. B.* vol. 26, p. 358.]

CHELSEA way. By André Maurois [Emile Herzog]. Translated by Hamish Miles. 8vo. Pp. 58. [*Observer*, 1st Feb. 1931.] London, 1930

CHEMIN (le) abregé ; or, a compendious method for the attaining of sciences in a short time. . . . Englished by R. G. [Richard Gentilis]. 12mo. Pp. 120. [*Brit. Mus.*] London, 1654

CHEMISTRY. [By John Frederick Daniell.] 8vo. [*Lib. of Useful Knowledge.*] London, 1838

CHESHUNT collection of psalms and hymns, from various authors, chiefly designed for public worship. [Compiled by M. M. P. *i.e.* M. M. Preston.] 24mo. [*Brit. Mus.*] London [1850 ?]

CHESS made easy ; new and comprehensive rules for playing the game of chess, with examples from Philidor [François André Danican], Cunningham, etc. ; to which is prefixed a pleasing account of its origin [by —— Faret]. 12mo. [*Brit. Mus.*]
London, 1797
See "Analysis of the game of chess."

CHESTER'S triumph in honor of her prince. [By Robert Amerie.] 4to. [*Huntington Lib. Checklist.*]
London, 1610

CHEVALIER'S (the) hopes. [By Philip Skelton.] 8vo. [*Camb. Univ. Lib.*] 8vo. Dublin, 1745
An account of Prince Charles Edward Stuart.

CHEWTON-ABBOT; and other tales. By Hugh Conway [Frederick John Fargus.] 8vo. Pp. 144. [*Brit. Mus.*]
Edinburgh [1884]

CHICHESTER (the) guide. [By T. Valentine.] 8vo. [*Eng. Cat.*, 1801-1836, p. 110.] Chichester, 1811

CHICKS A'! [Verses.] By Chanticleer [G. F. Joy]. 8vo. Pp. 96. [*Brit. Mus.*] London [1910]

CHILBURY folk. [A tale.] By C. E. M. [Constance E. Miller]. 8vo. Pp. 92. [*Brit. Mus.*] London [1896]

CHILD (a) of the Orient. By Demetra Vaka [Mrs Kenneth Brown]. 8vo. [*Bodl.*] London, 1914

CHILDE Harold's monitor; or, lines occasioned by the last canto of Childe Harold, including hints to other contemporaries. [By Francis Hodgson.] [*Brit. Mus.*] London, 1818

CHILDE Rocliff's pilgrimage. [By J. K. Paulding.] 12mo. 3 vols. [*Eng. Cat.*, 1801-1836, p. 110.]
London, 1833

CHILDREN at Calvary; being the stations of the Cross in metre for singing. [By Richard Frederick Littledale.] 32mo. [*Brit. Mus.*]
London, 1872
Preface signed: R. F. L.

CHILDREN at the altar. [By G. D. N. *i.e.* George Davenport Nicholas and R. J. I. *i.e.* Robert James Ives.] 32mo. Pp. 48. [*Brit. Mus.*] London [1873]

CHILDREN busy, children glad, children naughty, children sad. . . . Stories by L. C. [Lucy Clifford]. 4to. Pp. 40. [*Brit. Mus.*] London [1881]

CHILDREN in Norway; or, holiday on the Ekeberg: a book for boys and girls. By Pater [John Benjamin Stone]. [Pettersen's *Norsk Lexikon*, col. 70.] London, 1884

CHILDREN (the) of chance. By Anthony Carlyle [Mrs Patrick Milton]. 8vo. [*Who's Who in Lit.*] 1922

*CHILDREN (the) of the Chapel; a tale. By the author of *Mark Dennis*. [The prose portion was written by —— Gordon, later Mrs Disney Leith, the verse interludes by her cousin, Algernon Charles Swinburne]. 8vo. Pp. 124. [Shepherd's *Bibl. of Swinburne*.] London, 1864

CHILDREN of the hills; tales and sketches of Western Ireland in the old time and the present day. By Dermot O'Byrne [Arnold Bax]. 8vo. Pp. 156. [Boyd's *Ireland's Lit. Renaissance.*] Dublin, 1913

CHILDREN'S (the) bread; a communion office for the young. [By Richard Frederick Littledale.] 32mo. [*Brit. Mus.*] London, 1872
Preface signed: R. F. L.

CHILDREN'S (the) garland; a picture story book. By A. L. O. E. [A Lady of England, Charlotte M. Tucker]. 4to. [*Brit. Mus.*] London, 1875

CHILDREN'S (the) hour. By E. W. S. and S. W. M. [Silas Weir Mitchell]. [*Publishers' Weekly*, 9th June 1923.]
Philadelphia, 1846

CHIMNEY-SWEEPER'S (the) friend and climbing boy's album. [By J. Montgomery.] 12mo. [*Eng. Cat.*, 1801-1836, p. 111.] London, 1824

CHINAMAN'S (a) opinion of us and of his own country. . . . By Hwuy-Ung . . . Translated by J. A. Makepeace . . . [With an introduction—or rather, written?—by Theodore J. Tourrier.] 8vo. Pp. x. 296. [*Brit. Mus.*]
London, 1927

CHIT-CHAT; or, natural characters and the manners of real life. [By John Collet.] 8vo. 2 vols. [Straus' *Robert Dodsley*.] London, 1754

*CHOICE (a) banquet of witty jests . . .
In the first edition the epistle dedicatory is signed: J. G. T. J. was the printer.

CHOICE (a) collection of 120 loyal songs, all of them written since the two late plots. [Edited by N. T. *i.e.* Nathaniel Thompson.] 12mo. [*Brit. Mus.*] London, 1684
In 1685 the same edition published "A choice collection of 180 loyal songs. . . ."

CHOICE (the) humorous works of Mark Twain . . . with . . . a life of the author [by J. C. H. *i.e.* John Camden Hotten]. 8vo. [*Brit. Mus.*]
London [1873]

*CHOICE thoughts from Shakespeare. By the author of *The book of familiar quotations* [L. C. Gent.] [*Brit. Mus.*]
Not by John Bartlett.

CHORUSES from the Iphigeneia in Aulis and the Hippolytus of Euripides. Translated by H. D. [Hilda Doolittle]. 8vo. [*Brit. Mus.*] London, 1919

CHRIS; a love story. By John Ironside [E. M. Tait]. 8vo. Pp. 288. [*Brit. Mus.*] London [1926]

CHRIST above all. [By Countess A. C. E. di Tergolina.] 12mo. [*Brit. Mus.*] London [1868]

CHRIST and Nicodemus; or, an evening conference in which the nature, necessity and marks of the new birth is . . . described and explained both from Scripture and experience. . . . The second edition, much improved. [By J. Wakelin?] 12mo. [*Brit. Mus.*]
London, 1760
Signed: J. W.

CHRIST and the Church. [By J. G. Francis.] 8vo. [*Brit. Mus.*]
London, 1852
Another edition in the same year was "By a minister of the Catholic Apostolic Church."

CHRIST exalted and Dr Crisp vindicated in several points called Antinomian, being cleared from Neonomian suggestions alledged, by some remarks on Mr A - - - his rebuke to Mr Lob . . . Done by a happy, tho' unworthy branch of the said doctor [Samuel Crisp]. [*M'Alpin Coll. Cat.*] London, 1698
Epistle dedicatory signed: Hananiel, Philalethes.

CHRIST (the) of the red planet. By Eleanor Kirk [Mrs Eleanor M. E. Ames]. 8vo. [*Amer. Cat.*]
New York, 1909

CHRIST our law. By the author of *Christ our example* [Caroline Fry, later Mrs Wilson]. 8vo. [*Brit. Mus.*]
London, 1842

CHRIST tempted and sympathising. [By William Kelly, of Guernsey.] 12mo. Pp. 64. [*Brit. Mus.*]
Manchester, 1871

*CHRISTEN (a) exhortacion unto customable swearers . . .
Pollard and Redgrave, *S. T. C.*, attribute this definitely to John Bale, Bishop of Ossory.

CHRISTEVANGEL. [A series of tracts. By J. S. *i.e.* James Silvester.] 8vo. [*Brit. Mus.*]
Clacton-on-Sea, 1911, *et seq.*

CHRISTIAN (a) almanacke, needefull and true for all countreys, persons and times: faithfully calculated . . . not onely for this present yeare 1612, but also for many yeeres to come. Written by J. M. [John Monipennie]. 16mo. B. L. [*Brit. Mus.*] London, 1612

CHRISTIAN blessings; being notes of lectures. . . . By J. B. S. [J. B. Stoney]. 8vo. Pp. 117. [*Brit. Mus.*]
London [1893]

CHRISTIAN liberty, as it was soberly desired in a letter to certain forreign states upon occasion of their late severity to several of their inhabitants. [By William Penn.] . . . 4to. Pp. 8. [*Brit. Mus.*] N.P. 1674

CHRISTIAN ministry. [By William Kelly, of Guernsey.] 8vo. [*Brit. Mus.*]
[*c.* 1875]

CHRISTIAN (the) physician and anthropological magazine. [Edited, and mainly written, by John Epps, M.D.] 8vo. 4 vols. [*D. N. B.* vol. 17, p. 382.]
London, 1835-8
Of a new series, begun as "The phrenological (anthropological) magazine and Christian physician," in 1839, only Part 1. appeared.

CHRISTIAN (the) pilgrim; or, the travels of the children of Israel spiritualized. [By John Allen, pastor of a Baptist church, in Petticoat Lane.] [*Brit. Mus.*] London, 1857
Earlier editions, 1803, 1809, 1818 were not anonymous.

*CHRISTIAN (the) pilgrime in his spirituall conflict and conquest. [In two parts, *i.e.* i.] The spiritual conflict . . . first published in Spanish by . . . J. Castañiza [translated by Thomas Vincent Faustus Sadler]. . . . The second edition [and ii.] The spiritual conquest in five treatises [written by Arthur Anselm Crowther and T. V. F. Sadler]. 12mo. 2 parts. [*Brit. Mus.*]
Paris, 1652, 51

*CHRISTIAN policie . . .
The translator was James Mabbe. [*Brit. Mus.*] See also "Policie unveiled . . ."

CHRISTIAN (the) religion not founded on allegory; or a vindication of our faith from falshood objected against it [by Anthony Collins] in a late Discourse of grounds and reasons of the Christian religion. [By H. Crofts, of King's College.] 8vo. Pp. 152. [*Bibl. Lind.*] London, 1724

CHRISTIAN religion: substantially, methodicallie, plainlie, and profitablie treatised. [By Thomas Cartwright.] [*M'Alpin Coll. Cat.*] London, 1611

CHRISTIANITY and war; letters of a Serbian [Nicholai Velimirovic] to his English friend. 8vo. [*Camb. Univ. Lib.*] London, 1917

CHRISTIANITY; being notes on lectures delivered in 1895. By J. B. S. [J. B. Stoney]. 8vo. Pp. 102. [*Brit. Mus.*] London [1896]

CHRISTIANITY in Egypt; letters and papers concerning the Coptic Church in relation to the Church of England, during the primacy of Archbishop Howley, 1836-1848. [Edited by B. H. *i.e.* Benjamin Harrison.] 8vo. Pp. 97. [*Brit. Mus.*] London, 1883

CHRISTIANITY; its truth and blessedness: a ministry delivered in the Catholic Apostolic Church, Canning St., Liverpool, on the first Sunday in Advent. [By William Tarbet.] 12mo. Pp. 11. [*Brit. Mus.*] [1874]

CHRISTIANS (the) combat ; or, his true spiritual welfare. [A sermon on Ephes. v. 13-17.] By C. L., later preacher of God's. word in the City of London [Christopher Love]. 16mo. B. L. [*Brit. Mus.*]   London, 1664
With a portrait of the author prefixed.

CHRISTIAN'S (the) daily guide ; or, parochial manual of instruction and devotion.   By the editor of *The Churchman's guide to faith and piety* [Robert Brett].   12mo.   3 parts. [*Brit. Mus.*]   London, 1863

CHRISTIAN'S (the) defence against the fears of death.   By Charles Drelincourt. [Translated by M. d'Assigny.] . . . To which is now added A true relation of the apparition of Mrs Veal [by Daniel Defoe]. . . .   8vo.   Pp. 410.   [*Brit. Mus.*]   London [*c.* 1800]

CHRISTIANS liberty to the Lords Table, discovered by eight arguments, thereby proving, that the Sacrament of the body and blood of our Lord does as well teach to grace, as strengthen and confirm grace . . . occasioned by the contrary doctrine, taught by a strange minister in Woolchurch, on the 29th of June last.   By I. G. a parishioner there [John Graunt]. [*Brit. Mus.*]   London, 1645

CHRISTIANS (the) rule of love, as it respects their conduct to one another, exhibited in a clear and distinct light : in a discourse on the duty of love. . . . By the author of a *Paraphrase on Chaps. v., vi. and vii. of Matthew* [Samuel Collet].   8vo.   [*Camb. Univ. Lib.*]   London, 1742

CHRISTINA, Queen of Sweden : a brief notice of her life, conversion and death. . . .   By M. T. [Margaret T. Taunton]. 16mo.   [*Brit. Mus.*]   London, 1862

CHRISTMAS ; a vigil. By C. J. C. [C. J. Cruttwell].   16mo.   [Madan's *Daniel Press.*]   [Frome] 1851

CHRISTMAS (a) and a New Year dinner, garnished with the compliments of the season, 1927-1928. [By Eric H. Partridge.]   8vo.   Pp. 16.   [*Brit. Mus.*]   [London, 1927]
From an inscribed copy in the British Museum.

CHRISTMAS Bells.   By Truda [Mrs George Robbins].   8vo.   Pp. 136. [*Brit. Mus.*]   1887

CHRISTMAS (a) box for true reformers ; wherein is shown the true birth of Christ, and the origin of Christmas day, never before understood. . . . By Zion Ward [John Ward].   8vo. [*Birm. Lib. Cat.*]   [Birmingham] 1864

*CHRISTMAS (a) carol . . .
The *Brit. Mus.* now supplies the author's Christian name : Rev. Theodore Edwards.

*CHRISTMAS day ; taking to heart . . .
The title should read : "Christmas day, the old heathens feasting day, in honour of Saturn their idol-god . . . taking to heart . . . "

CHRISTMAS Eve, and other stories. By K. M. [Kate Maclellan].   18mo. [*Brit. Mus.*]   New York [1864 ?]

CHRISTMAS (a) gathering of leaves for the little ones. [By Y. S. N. *i.e.* Mary Dutton.]   16mo.   [*Brit. Mus.*] London, 1861

CHRISTMAS leaves, 1877.   Our villas. Furnished by the authors of *Ready-money Mortiboy* [Sir Walter Besant and J. Rice], F. Marryat, and others. 8vo.   [*Brit. Mus.*]   London [1877]

CHRISTMAS (a) legend.   [A poem. By Frank Sidgwick.]   8vo.   [*Brit. Mus.*] London [1921]
Signed : F. S.

CHRIST'S crown-jewels.   [By Rev. Duncan Macgregor.]   16mo.   [*Brit. Mus.*]   Glasgow [1874]

CHRIST'S transfiguration ; or, Tabor's teachings : a glimpse of Christ's glory and intercourse with his people for ever.   By the author of *Heaven our Home* [William Branks]. . . . Seventh thousand.   [*Brit. Mus.*] Edinburgh, 1868

CHRIST'S yoke an easy yoke, and yet the gate to heaven a strait gate : in two excellent sermons. . . . By a learned and reverend divine [Jeremy Taylor].   8vo.   [*Camb. Univ. Lib.*] London, 1675

*CHRISTUS Dei . . .
The ascription to Thomas Morton, Bishop of Durham, is supported by *D. N. B.* vol. 39, p. 165, and Madan's *Oxford Books*, ii. 1099.

CHRONICLE (the) and institution of the Order of the Seraphicall Father S. Francis. . . .   Set foorth first in the Portugall [by Marcos da Silva, Bishop of Oporto] . . . and now in the English tongue [by William Cape].   4to.   Pp. 748.   [*Brit. Mus.*]   S. Omers, 1618

CHRONICLE (a) of certain events which have taken place in the Church of Christ, principally in England, between the years 1826 and 1852. [By T. Douglas, or Douglass.]   8vo. Pp. vi. 47.   [*Brit. Mus.*] London, 1852
Signed : T. D.

CHRONICLE of London.   See "In this booke is conteyned . . ."

CHRONICLE (a) of the conquest of Granada.   From the MSS. of Fray Antonio Agapida by Washington Irving [or rather written by Irving]. 12mo.   2 vols.   [*Brit. Mus.*] Philadelphia, 1829

CHRONICLE of the family of Percy. By Willam Peeris. [Edited by J. B. *i.e.* John Besly.] 8vo. [*Brit. Mus.*]
1845

CHRONICLE (the) of William the son of George ; with all that passed at the Battle of Tournay, the mighty acts of W . . . . . k [Waldeck] the Prince, and I . . . . dsby [Ingoldsby] the Brigadier. . . . By Dathan the Jew [Christoph Gottlieb Richter]. 12mo. [*Bodl.*] London, 1745

CHRONICLES (the) of a virgin fortress [*i.e.* Widden]. . . . By William V. Herbert [William V. Harlessem]. 8vo. Pp. xvi. 346. [*Brit. Mus.*]
London, 1896

*CHRONICLES of an illustrious house. Usually ascribed to Anne Hatton. See " Cambrian pictures."

CHRONICLES of Bagdad ; an oriental fantasy. By Abd'ul Hassan [George Steele Seymour]. 12mo. Pp. 114. [*Amer. Cat.*] Chicago, 1923

CHRONICLES (the) of Cooperstown. [By James Fenimore Cooper.] 12mo. [Sabin's *Dictionary.*]
Cooperstown, 1838

CHRONOLOGICAL (a) abridgement of the history of England, its constitution and laws, from the Norman Conquest to the Revolution in 1688. [By William Cruise.] 8vo. [*Camb. Univ. Lib.*] London, 1815

CHRONOLOGICAL (a) list of the books printed at the Kelmscott Press. . . . [Preface signed : G. P. W. *i.e.* George Parker Winship.] 8vo. Pp. 42. [*Brit. Mus.*] Boston, 1928

CHRONOMETER accuracy : verification of the longitude of Paris. [By Edward John Dent, chronometer maker.] Extract from the *Nautical Magazine.* 8vo. [*D. N. B.* vol. 14, p. 378.] London, 1838

CHUDLEIGH memorials : Devonshire. [By W. P. A. Hardwick.] 8vo. [*Camb. Univ. Lib.*] Private print [1916]

CHURCH (the) and the education question ; remarks on the Church's opposition to the Government plan of national education. By a Churchman [John Hinde Palmer]. 8vo. [*Lincoln's Inn. Lib.*] London, 1840

CHURCH (the) and Thisbe Grey. By John Le Breton [Miss M. Harte-Potts and T. Murray Ford]. 8vo. Pp. 350. [*Brit. Mus.*] London, 1908

CHURCH Army series. By E. H. H. [Evan Henry Hopkins.] 16mo. No. 1. [*Brit. Mus.*] London [1883]

CHURCH (the) as a denomination. [By David Melville.] 8vo. Pp. 15. [*Brit. Mus.*] London [1869]

CHURCH (a) child's life of S. Paul. By D. O. [Dorothy Owen]. With map and illustrations. 8vo. Pp. 80. [*Brit. Mus.*] London, 1906

CHURCH (a) history of the first seven centuries. By Milo Mahan. [Edited by J. H. H. *i.e.* John Henry Hopkins, Jr.] 8vo. Pp. xxxiv. 595. [*Brit. Mus.*] New York, 1872

*CHURCH life . . . Not by William John Blew, but by George Smith Drew. [*D. N. B.* vol. 16, p. 16.]

CHURCH (the) of England, the British Empire, and the Chinese. By Kuklos [John Harris, LL.D.]. 8vo. [*Camb. Univ. Lib.*] 8vo. Montreal, 1876

CHURCH principles and Church measures ; a letter to Lord John Manners : with remarks on [Charles Cavendish Fulke Greville's] Past and present policy of England towards Ireland. By the author of *Maynooth, the Crown, and the Country* [Christopher Wordsworth, Bishop of Lincoln]. 8vo. [*Camb. Univ. Lib.*] London, 1845

CHURCH (the) ; the case of non-graduate clergymen . . . considered in a letter . . . to . . . William, Lord Archbishop of Canterbury. By a Yorkshire Incumbent [William Snowden]. 8vo. Pp. 44. [*Brit. Mus.*]
London, 1830

CIRCE'S daughter. [A novel.] By Priscilla Craven [Mrs William Teignmouth Shore]. 8vo. Pp. 384. [*Amer. Cat.*] 8vo. Pp. 384.
London, 1913

CIRCLE (the) of the seasons ; and perpetual key to the calendar. [By T. Forster.] 12mo. [*Eng. Cat.*, 1801-1836, p. 117.] London, 1827

CIRCULAR (the) of the National Club. [A criticism. Signed D. C. L. *i.e.* Alexander James Beresford Hope.] Reprinted from the *Morning Chronicle.* 8vo. [*Brit. Mus.*] London [1850]

CIRCUMSTANTIAL evidence. [A novel.] By Arthur Ward Basset [Albert E. Bull]. 8vo. [*Who's Who in Lit.*] London, 1905

CITIZENS (the) sacred entertainment ; being an essay to ingratiate the practice of vertue, to consummate the happiness of humane nature, and to gratifie ingenuous and religious spirits. By T. F. [Thomas Fydge]. 8vo. [*Brit. Mus.*] London, 1666

CITY (the) and County Readers. Edited by a University Graduate [J. A. Jenkins]. 8vo. 2 parts. [*Brit. Mus.*] Cardiff [1912]

CITY (the) of lilies. [A novel.] By the author of *Jenny Essenden* [Agnes Russell Weekes] and R. K. Weekes. 8vo. Pp. 334. [*Who's Who in Lit.*]
1923

CITY (the) of to-morrow and its planning. By Le Corbusier [Charles Edouard Jeanneret]. Translated from the 8th French edition of Urbanisme. . . . 8vo. Pp. xxvii. 301. [*Brit. Mus.*]
London, 1929

*CIVIL comprehension recommended . . . Signed: N. N.

CLAIM (the) of the American Loyalists reviewed and maintained upon incontrovertible principles of law and justice. [By Joseph Galloway.] 8vo. Pp. viii. 138. [*Brit. Mus.*]
London, 1788

CLAIR de lune. [A novel.] By the author of *Jenny Essenden* [Agnes Russell Weekes]. 8vo. Pp. 320. [*Who's Who in Lit.*] London, 1922
Published in New York as by John Anthony.

CLANCY of the Mounted Police. [A novel.] By Ben Bolt [Rev. Ottwell Binns]. 8vo. [*Who's Who in Lit.*]
London, 1923

CLANKING (the) of chains. By Brinsley Macnamara [A. E. Weldon]. 8vo. Pp. 241. [*Brit. Mus.*]
Dublin, 1920

CLANSHIP and the Clans; containing a popular sketch of the constitution and traditions of the Clans of Scotland, with notices of the Highland garb and arms. . . . By M. H. Towry [Mary Helen White]. 12mo. Pp. 123.
Edinburgh [1870]
Private information.

CLARA Gazul; or, honi soit qui mal y pense: a novel. [By Harriette Wilson.] 3 vols. [*Eng. Cat.*, 1801-1836, p. 117.] 1830

CLARIOR e tenebris; or, a justification of two books; the one . . . The grand inquest;—the other . . . The royal favourite cleared. . . . By J. G. of the Inner Temple, Esq. [John Garbrand]. 4to. [*Lincoln's Inn Lib.*]
London, 1683

CLASS (the) book; or, three hundred and sixty-five reading lessons adapted to the use of schools. . . . By the Rev. D. Blair [Sir Richard Phillips]. 8vo. Pp. 496. [*Brit. Mus.*] London, 1806
But Eliza Fenwick claims that she compiled this manual for Sir R. Phillips. [E. Fenwick's *The Fate of the Fenwicks*, p. 83.]

CLASSES (the) and orders of the Linnæan system of botany. [By Richard Duppa]. . . . 8vo. 3 vols. [*Brit. Mus.*] London, 1816

CLASSICAL enigmas, adapted to every month in the year. . . . By a lady [A. Ritson]. 16mo. [*Brit. Mus.*]
London, 1811

CLAUDIUS; or, the messenger of Wandsbeck. [Edited with a sketch of his life by H. J. C. *i.e.* Henry James Coleridge.] 8vo. [*Brit. Mus.*]
London, 1859

CLEARE (a) and evident way for enriching the nations of England and Ireland. . . . [A reprint of Sir Walter Raleigh's "Observations upon trade."] 4to. [*Brit. Mus.*] London, 1650

CLEM. By Erica Maxwell [Lillian M. Pyke]. 8vo. Pp. 314. [*Brit. Mus.*]
London [1925]

CLEOPATRA. By Claude Ferval [Baronne Marguerite Thomas-Galline Aimery de Pierrebourg]. Translated by M. E. Poindexter. 8vo. Pp. 328. [*Publishers' Weekly*, 24th April 1926.]
New York, 1926

CLERGY (the) and the present ministry defended; being a letter to the Bishop of Salisbury, occasioned by his Lordship's new preface to his *Pastoral Care*. [By George Sewell.] 8vo. [*Brit. Mus.*] London, 1713
The fourth edition (in the same year) bears the author's name.

CLERGY (the) vindicated; or, the rights and privileges that belong to them asserted. . . . [By John Brydall.] Fol. [*Lincoln's Inn Lib.*]
London, 1679

CLERGYMAN'S (the) companion in the celebration of divine service for 1847. [Edited by William Atkinson Warwick?] 8vo. [*Brit. Mus.*]
London [1846]
Signed: A. W.

CLEVER girls of our time; and how they became famous women. . . . By the author of *Heroines of our time* [Joseph Johnson]. Third edition. 8vo. Pp. iv. 276. [*Brit. Mus.*]
London, 1863

CLIFTON College twenty-five years ago; the diary of a fag. [By Sir Francis George Newbolt.] 8vo. Pp. 191. [*Brit. Mus.*] London, 1904
A later edition (1927), "Clifton College Forty years ago: the diary of a praepostor," bears the author's name.

CLOATHING for the naked woman; or, the second part of The dissembling Scot set forth in his colours: being a corection of Mr David Brown his errors in his pamphlet called The naked woman. . . . Written by the minister of Christ-Church, London [Samuel Chidley]. 4to. Pp. 11. [*Brit. Mus.*] London, 1652

*COACH and sedan . . .
   The dedication is signed : Mis-Amaxius.
COBLER (the) of Preston ; an opera.
[By Christopher Bullock.] [*Brit.
Mus.*]   London, 1732
   A previous (1716) and a subsequent
(1767) edition bear the author's full name.
CODRUS ; or, the Dunciad dissected :
being the finishing stroke. [By
Edmund Curll and Elizabeth Thomas.]
To which is added Farmer Pope and
his son. A tale by Mr [Ambrose]
Philips. 8vo. [R. Straus' *The Un-
speakable Curll*, p. 287.] London, 1728
   The title-page is arranged to make it look
as if Philips wrote the whole.
COLDE (the) Tearm ; or, the frozen
age, or the metamorphosis of the river
of Thames. [A ballad. By John
Taylor, the water poet?] Fol. S. sh.
[*Brit. Mus.*]   N.P. [1621]
COLE'S escheats ; index of persons.
[By Sir Thomas Phillipps.] Fol. Pp. 4.
[*Brit. Mus.*]   [Middle Hill, 1852?]
COLIN'S kisses ; being twelve new songs
designed for music. [By Robert
Dodsley.] 4to. Pp. 16. [Straus'
Dodsley].   London, 1742
COLIN'S mistakes ; written in imitation
of Spencer's style. [By Matthew
Prior.] Fol. Pp. 6. [*Brit. Mus.*]
                      London, 1721
COLLAPSE (the) of Germany ; the
facts about reparations. [By Joseph
King, M.P.] 8vo. Pp. 31. [*Brit.
Mus.*]   London, private print, 1923
*COLLECTION (a) of all the wills . . .
   Signed : J. N.
COLLECTION (a) of hymns from various
authors, intended as a supplement to
Dr Watt's hymns. [Collected by
George Burder.] 12mo. [*Brit. Mus.*]
                      Coventry, 1784
COLLECTION (a) of interesting letters
[by John Almon] upon the govern-
ment, liberty, and constitution of
England from the public papers.
12mo. [Watt's *Bibl. Brit.*]
                      London, 1760
COLLECTION (the) of miniatures in
Montagu House. [By Andrew
MacKay.] 4to. Ff. 183. [*Brit.
Mus.*]   London [1896]
   Preface signed : A. M.
COLLECTION (a) of original papers
relative to the history of the colony of
Massachusetts-Bay. [Edited by H.
i.e. Thomas Hutchinson.] 4to. Pp.
576. [*Brit. Mus.*]   Boston, 1769
COLLECTION (a) of original poems, by
Scotch gentlemen. [Vol. ii. contains
much material by James Boswell, of
Auchinleck, and Captain Erskine, its
editors.] 8vo. 2 vols.   1760-2

COLLECTION (a) of psalms and hymns
for public worship. [Compiled by
W. D. *i.e.* W. Day.] 12mo. [*Brit.
Mus.*]   Evesham, 1795
COLLECTION (a) of sundry matters,
tending to prove it necessary for all
persons, actually to walke in the use
and practise of the substancial
ordinances in the Gospell appointed
by God for his visible church spiritually
politicall. [By Henry Jacob?] 12mo.
[*Camb. Univ. Lib.*]
        [R. Schilders, Middelburg] 1616
COLLECTIONS [of names of patrons
of livings] for Gloucestershire. By
T. P. [Sir Thomas Phillipps]. 8vo.
Pp. 12. [*Brit. Mus.*]
        Typis Medio-Montanis, 1861
COLLECTOR'S (the) whatnot. By
Cornelius Obenchain van Loot [Booth
Tarkington], Milton Kilgallen [Kenneth
Roberts] and Murgatroyd Elphinstone
[Hugh Kahler]. [*New York Times*,
10th August 1924.] New York, 1924
COLLEEN (the) Bawn ; or, the Col-
legian's wife : a tale of Garryowen
originally entitled, *The Collegians*.
[By Gerald Griffin.] 8vo. [*Brit.
Mus.*]   London, 1861
COLLEGE recollections. [By Rev.
Samuel O'Sullivan.] 12mo. [*D.N.B.*
vol. 62, p. 296.]   London, 1825
COLONEL Gore's cases ; No. 5 : the
Mendip mystery. By Lynn Brock
[Alister M'Allister]. 8vo. Pp. 250.
[*Brit. Mus.*]   London [1929]
COLONEL Gore's second case. By
Lynn Brock [Alister M'Allister]. 8vo.
Pp. 389. [*Brit. Mus.*] London, 1925
COLONEL Gore's third case ; the kink.
By Lynn Brock [Alister M'Allister].
8vo. Pp. 289. [*Brit. Mus.*]
                      London [1927]
COLONIAL (the) history of the city of
San Francisco. [By R. C. Hopkins.]
Third edition. 8vo. [*Brit. Mus.*]
                   San Francisco, 1866
COLONIST'S (a) plea for land national-
isation. By A. J. O. of Tasmania
[A. J. Ogilvy]. . . . 8vo. Pp. 51.
[*Brit. Mus.*]   London [1888]
   Land Nationalisation Society Tracts,
No. 23.
COLORS (the) of the United States first
raised over the Capitol of the Con-
federate States, April 3, 1865. [By
Henry Barton Dawson.] 8vo. [*Brit.
Mus.*] Morrisania, private print, 1866
   Signed : H. B. D. Only 26 copies printed.
COLUMBIA encyclopædia of useful
knowledge ; showing the newest and
most wonderful inventions. Edited by
Marshall Everett [Henry Neil]. 8vo.
[*Amer. Cat.*]   Chicago, 1908

COLVILE'S case ; a statement of facts. [By Henry Charles Shelley.] 8vo. Pp. 85. [*Brit. Mus.*]   London [1901]
Bound with the British Museum copy are seventeen letters from Sir H. E. Colvile to the author.

COMBERMERE   (the)   pamphlet ; dietetic and digestible hints on keeping animals economically and in blooming health. [By G. H. Bonnor.] 12mo. Pp. 78. [*Brit. Mus.*]
London [1888]

COME and welcome to Jesus Christ, or a plain and profitable discourse on John vi. 37. [By John Bunyan.] 12mo. [*Brit. Mus.*]   London, 1774

COME in ! An old soldier's invitation. [Verse.]   By J. C. R. [James C. Richardson].   8vo.   Pp. 11.   [*Brit. Mus.*]   [London, 1927]

"COME thou with us" ; a call by the way to the House of God. [By Francis Bourdillon.]   12mo.   [*Brit. Mus.*]
London [1865]
Signed : F. B.

COMFORT (the) of love ; addressed to any anxious or dejected soul. [By William Tarbet.]   8vo.   S. sh.   [*Brit. Mus.*]   [1870 ?]

COMIC (the) almanack. . . .   By Thackeray. . . . [The introduction signed : J. C. H. *i.e.* John Camden Hotten.]   8vo.   2 vols.   [*Brit. Mus.*]
London, 1870-8

COMIC keepsake.   By Alf Crowquill [A. H. Forrester].   1835. [*Eng. Cat.*, 1801-1836, p. 128.]   London, 1834

COMICALL (the) history of Alphonsus, King of Aragon ; as it hath been sundrie times acted. Made by R. G. [Robert Greene].   4to.   [*Pollard and Redgrave.*]   London, 1599

COMICALL (a) satyre of Every man out of his humor. As it was first composed by the author B. J. [Ben Jonson].   4to. [*Brit. Mus.*]   London, 1600

COMING (the) Christ.   Christ in humanity.   By Jōhannā [Mrs Jane Fisher].   8vo.   [*Bodl.*]
Letchworth, 1914

COMING (the) Christ. Christ in you. By Jōhannā [Mrs Jane Fisher].   8vo. [*Bodl.*]   Letchworth, 1914

COMMANDER Lawless, V.C. By Rolf Bennett [W. Marten].   8vo.   Pp. 254. [*Brit. Mus.*]   London, 1916

COMMENTARIES of that divine John Calvine vpon the prophet Daniell, translated [by A. G. *i.e.* Arthur Golding]. . . .   4to.   Pp. 120.   B. L. [*Brit. Mus.*]   London, 1570

COMMERCIAL nationalism *v.* Anti-Nationalism ; or the relative desirableness and values of imports and exports. . . . By the author of *Mongredien answered* [Francis John Bodfield Hooper]. New edition, revised. 4to. Pp. 10. [*Brit. Mus.*]   Leeds [1881]

COMMON   (the)   chord. . . .   By Wynoth Dale [M. G. B. Ryves].   8vo. [*Bodl.*]   London, 1902

COMMON (the) life. By J. B. [J. Brierley].   8vo.   [*Amer. Cat.*]
New York, 1904

COMPANION (a) in a tour round Southampton . . . and a tour of the Isle of Wight. . . . [By John Bullar.] 12mo. [J. P. Anderson's *Brit. Top.*]
Southampton, 1799
Later editions, enlarged, give the author's name.

COMPANY (the) of Cain. By Al Carthill [Sir John Perronet Thompson]. 8vo. Pp. 316. [*Brit. Mus.*]
Edinburgh, 1929

COMPARISON (a) of the life of man, concerning how fickle his estate doth stand. . . . [By Richard Climsell ?] Fol. S. sh. B. L.   London [*c.* 1635] Signed : R. C.

COMPENDIOUS (a) view of the grounds of the Teutonic philosophy ; with considerations by way of enquiry into the . . . writings of J. Behmen [Jacob Boehme] : also several extracts from his writings. Published by a gentleman retired from business. [A treatise of eternal nature.] By J. P. [John Pordage], M.D. 12mo. 3 parts. [*Brit. Mus.*]   London, 1770

COMPENDIUM (a) of colours, and other materials used in the arts dependant on design ; with remarks on their nature and uses, including the method of drawing in chalk, crayons, etc. [By Charles   Taylor.]   8vo.   [*Quaritch's Cat.*]   London, 1797

COMPENDIUM (a) of the theological writings of Swedenborg. By S. M. W. [Samuel M. Warren].   8vo.   [*Kirk's Supp.*]   Philadelphia, 1875

COMPLAINT (the) of liberty and property against arbitrary government. . . . [By Dr John Nalson.]   Fol. [*Lincoln's Inn Lib.*]   London, 1681

COMPLAINT (the) of the Shepheard Harpalus. [A song. By D. M. *i.e.* Sir D. Murray.] Fol. S. sh. B. L. [*Brit. Mus.*]   [London, *c.* 1645]

COMPLAYNT (a) of them that be to soone maryed. [By Robert Copland.] B. L. [*Christie-Miller Cat.*]
London, 1535
See also " Here begynneth the complaynte of them that ben to late maryed."

COMPLEAT (a) and authentick history of the rise, progress, and extinction of the late Rebellion and of the proceedings against the principal persons concerned therein. [By Henry Fielding?] 8vo. Pp. 155. [*Brit. Mus.*]
London, 1747

COMPLEAT (a) key to the Non-juror . . .
The *Brit. Mus.* now follows the *D. N. B.* (vol. vi. p. 289) in ascribing this to John Durant de Breval who frequently used the pseudonym Joseph Gay. The *Nonjuror* was by Colley Cibber, and in this work he is accused of stealing his characters from various sources, chiefly from Molière's *Tartuffe*.

COMPLEAT (a) vindication of the Licensers of the Stage. . . . [By Samuel Johnson.] London, 1739
Wrongly entered as " A complete vindication . . ."

COMPLEMENTUM Fortunarum Insularum, Part II. ; sive, Galathea vaticinans : being part of an epithalamium upon the auspicious match of . . . Charles II. and . . . Catharina, Infanta of Portugal. . . . Written originally in French by P. D. C. [P. D. Cardonnel] Gent. and since translated by him in Latin and English. . . . 8vo. 4 parts. [*Brit. Mus.*] London, 1662

*COMPLETE (the) captain . . .
For John Cruss, *read* John Cruso.

COMPLETE (a) concordance to the comedies . . . of Aristophanes. By H. Dunbar. [The preface signed : W. D. G. *i.e.* William Duguid Geddes.] 4to. Pp. iv. 342. [*Brit. Mus.*] 1883

COMPLETE (a) course in life electricity, with vital laws for living longer. By Edmund Shaftesbury [Webster Edgerly]. 8vo. Pp. 414. [*Publishers' Weekly*, 14th August 1926.]
Meriden, Conn., 1926

COMPLETE (a) key to a Tale of a tub ; with some account of its authors. [By Edmund Curll.] 8vo. [R. Straus' *The Unspeakable Curll*.] London, 1710

COMPLETE (the) letter-writer for ladies and gentlemen. . . . [By Henry Frith.] 8vo. [*Brit. Mus.*] London, 1906

COMPLETE (the) works of William Shakespeare. . . . [Edited by Dr D. *i.e.* Nicolaus Delius.] 8vo. Pp. xx. 1060. [*Brit. Mus.*] Leipzig, 1854

COMPOSITION in portraiture. By Sidney Allan [Sadakichi Hartmann]. 8vo. [*Amer. Cat.*] New York, 1909

COMRADES courageous. By Russ Ruscom [Russell Whitcomb]. 8vo. [*Amer. Cat.*] Boston, 1907

*COMRADES in arms. By A. Amyand.
The *Brit. Mus.* gives the author's name as Edward Arthur Haggard.

CONCEALED turnings. By Pamela Wynne [Winifred Mary Scott]. 12mo. Pp. 378. [*Publisher's Weekly*, 14th Jan. 1928.] New York, 1927

CONCERNING dragons ; a rhyme. By H. D. C. P. [Hilary Douglas C. Pepler]. 16mo. [*Brit. Mus.*]
Ditchling, 1928

CONCERNING prayer, its nature, its difficulties and its value. By the author of *Pro Christo et ecclesia* [Lily Dougall, and others]. 8vo. Pp. xiii. 504. [*Brit. Mus.*] London, 1916

CONCERNING the priviledge of the vnder clarks in the court of chancery as now in clayme and practise. [By John Duke, of Worlingham.] 4to. Pp. 8. [*Bodl.*] London, 1649

*CONCERNING this present Cain . . .
The author is more usually known as Ludwig Friedrich Gifftheyl.

CONCERNINGS. [Prose sketches.] By Y. [Y. Battiscombe]. 8vo. Pp. 94. [*Brit. Mus.*] Frome, 1928

CONCESSIONS. [A novel.] By Sydney Schiff [Stephen Hudson]. 8vo. Pp. 351. London, 1913

CONCEYTED letters, newly layde open : or, a . . . bundle of new wit, wherin is knit up together all the perfections or arte of episteling. . . . [By Gervase Markham.] 4to. [*Brit. Mus.*]
London, 1618
Preface signed : I. M.

CONCISE (a) account of the material events and atrocities which occurred in the late Rebellion . . . and an answer to Veritas's Vindication of the Roman Catholic Clergy of the town of Wexford. By Veridicus [Sir Richard Musgrave]. 8vo. [*Lincoln's Inn Lib.*]
Dublin, 1799

CONCISE (a) sketch of the history of St Botolph's Church, Boston, in the County of Lincoln. Reprinted from the original edition . . . with a few alterations and additions. [Edited by T. N. M. *i.e.* T. N. Morton.] 8vo. Pp. xv. 92. [*Brit. Mus.*] London, 1895

CONCISE whist ; the principles of modern whist as modified by American leads presented in a simple and practical form. By C. S. S. [Charles Stuart Street]. 16mo. Pp. 71. [F. Jessel's *Bibl. of playing cards*, p. 273.]
Salem, 1890

CONFERENCE (a) betwixt a modern atheist and his friend. By the methodizer of the second Spira [J. Sault]. [*M'Alpin Coll. Cat.*] London, 1693

CONFERENCE (a) betwixt a Protestant and a Jew ; or a second letter from a Merchant in London, to his correspondent in Amsterdam. [By Richard Mayo.] [*Brit. Mus.*]   London, 1678
  This is the second of two conferences which were published separately in this year and also together with a common title-page. For the first conference see "A Conference betwixt a Papist and a Jew . . ." and for the joint issue, see "Two Conferences, one betwixt a Papist and a Jew, the other . . ."

CONFESSION (the) and conversion of . . . my lady C. of L. [Helen Livingston, Countess of Linlithgow]. . . . 16mo. [*G. P. Johnston's edition*, 1924.]
                              Edinburgh, 1629
CONFESSION (a) and protestation of the faith of certaine Christians in England, holding it necessary to observe and keepe all Christes true substantiall ordinances . . . though the same doe differ from the common order of the land. [By Henry Jacob.] 12mo. [*Camb. Univ. Lib.*]
          [R. Schilders, Middelburg] 1616
  See a similar book entitled "A Collection of sundry matters . . ."

CONFESSION (a) of faith.   By an unorthodox believer [Edmond Gore Alexander Holmes]. 8vo. Pp. 194. [*Brit. Mus.*]   1895
CONFESSION (a) of my faith, and a reason of my practice : or, with who, and who not, I can hold Church-fellowship or the communion of Saints. . . . [By John Bunyan.] [Groshart's *Bunyan*, No. 10.]   London, 1672
  To the reader, signed : J. B.

CONFESSIONS (the) of a Catholic priest. [Translated from the Hungarian of Baron Caesar Mednyánsky.] 8vo. Pp. v. 320. [*Brit. Mus.*]
                              London, 1858
CONFESSIONS of a medium. [By —— Chapman.] 8vo. Pp. xvi. 282. [*Soc. for Psychical Research Cat.*, p. 83.]
                              London, 1882
CONFESSIONS of an Oxonian. [By Thomas Little.] 8vo. 3 vols. [*Camb. Univ. Lib.*]   London, 1826
CONFESSIONS of Mrs May.   By Thomas Le Breton [T. Murray Ford]. 8vo. Pp. 250. [*Brit. Mus.*]
                              London, 1923
CONFESSIONS (the) of the Nun of St Omer ; a tale. By Rosa Matilda [Charlotte Dacre, later Mrs Byrne]. 12mo. 3 vols. [*Brit. Mus.*]
                              London, 1805
CONFESSIONS of Zeno. Translated by Beryl De Zoete [from the Italian of Italo Svevo, *i.e.* Ettore Schmitz]. 8vo. Pp. 412. [*Brit. Mus.*]   London, 1930

*CONFLAGRATION of London . . .
  The title really begins "Conflagratio Londinensis poetice depicta. . . ." Ascribed also to James Langham [*Leeds Univ. annotated copy of Halkett & Laing*].
CONFLICT (the) of Job, by way of dialogue ; compiled for illustration or opening of that great encounter. . . . By R. H. [Richard Humfrey]. 4to. [*Camb. Univ. Lib.*]   London, 1607
CONFUTATION (the) of Tortura Torti. (By Martinus Becanus.) Translated by W. J. P. [J. Wilson, Priest]. 4to. [*Pollard and Redgrave.*]
                              St Omer, 1610
CONFUTATION (a) of the Popish transubstantiation ; together with a narration how that the masse was at sundrie times patched and peeced by sundrie Popes. Translated out of French [of Jean de l'Espine] by Peter Allibond. 16mo. [*Pollard and Redgrave.*]   London, 1592
*CONGRATULATORY (a) address to the Rev. John Cross . . .
  Signed : Trim.
CONGRATULATORY (a) poem ; presented to . . . Sr. J. Sheldon . . . Lord Maior of London. Composed by the author of the *Geneva Ballad* [Samuel Butler]. Fol. S. sh. [*Brit. Mus.*]
                         [London] 1675
CONGREGATIONAL independency ; declaration of the faith . . . of the Congregational . . . churches. . . . [Edited by W. H. *i.e.* William Hopkins.] 8vo. [*Brit. Mus.*]
                         Melbourne [1869]
CONJUGAL right ; and other stories. By "Rita" [Mrs W. Desmond Humphreys, *née* M. J. Gollan]. 8vo. [*Lit. Year Book.*]   London, 1922
*CONNECTED (a) view of the whole internal navigation . . .
  Attributed in Sabin's *Dictionary* to Matthew Carey.
CONQUERED (a) self. By S. Moore Carew [Salome Hocking, later Mrs Fifield]. 8vo. Pp. 181. [*Brit. Mus.*]
                              London, 1894
  Tavistock Library, No. 3.
CONQUEST (the) of Taranto ; or, St Clara's Eve : a play. By the author of *The peasant boy* [William Dimond]. 8vo. [*Brit. Mus.*]   London, 1817
*CONQUEST of the moon . . . By Annie Laurie [Winifred Black].
  Read By André Laurie [Paschal Grousset]. [*Brit. Mus.*]
CONSEQUENCES. [A novel.] By E. M. Delafield [Elizabeth Monica De La Pasture, afterwards Dashwood]. 8vo. Pp. 344. [*Brit. Mus.*]
                              London, 1919

CONSERVATION of the natural tree-cover; water systems of the earth; arid lands. By Felix St Xavier [Mrs Rose M. Harrington]. 8vo. [*Amer. Cat.*]   New York, 1902

CONSERVATIVE (the) mind. By a Gentleman with a duster [Harold Begbie]. 8vo. Pp. 157. [*Amer. Cat.*]   London, 1924

CONSERVATIVES and Liberals judged by their conduct to the Catholics of England and Ireland. By a Catholic [Myles W. P. O'Reilly]. 8vo. Pp. 18. [*Brit. Mus.*]   Dublin, 1867

CONSIDERATIONS. By Zachary Waynflete [Sir Ian Malcolm]. 8vo. Pp. 166.   London, 1913

CONSIDERATIONS on behalf of the colonists; in a letter to a noble lord. [By James Otis.] 8vo. Pp. 52. [*Sabin's Dictionary*.]   London, 1765
  Signed: F. A. A reply to "The objections to the taxation of our American Colonies . . ."

CONSIDERATIONS on Macknight's hypothesis that St Luke's was the first Gospel written. [By C. Dunster.] 8vo. [*Eng. Cat.*, 1801-1836, p. 131.]   London, 1808

CONSIDERATIONS on patronage. [By John Maclaurin, Lord Dreghorn.] [*D. N. B.* vol. 35, p. 199.]   1766

CONSIDERATIONS on taxes, as they are supposed to affect the price of labour in our manufactures. . . . In a letter to a friend [by J. Cunningham?] 8vo.   London, 1765

CONSIDERATIONS on the accumulation of capital, and its effects on profits and on exchangeable value. [By John Cazenove.] 8vo. Pp. 64. [*Brit. Mus.*]   London, 1822

CONSIDERATIONS on the date of S. Matthew's Gospel. By a country clergyman [C. Dunster]. 8vo. [*Eng. Cat.*, 1801-1836, p. 131.] London, 1807

*CONSIDERATIONS on the law of libel . . . By John Search.
  The *Eng. Cat.*, 1801-1836, p. 131, attributes this to Richard Whately.

CONSIDERATIONS on the laws of honour, occasioned chiefly by a late melancholy event. [By W. B. Orme.] 8vo.   London, 1804

CONSIDERATIONS touching that question, whether the prelates have right to sit among the Lords and vote . . . in capital cases. [By Henry Briggs.] 8vo. [*Lincoln's Inn Lib.*]   London, 1682

*CONSIDERATIONS upon the American Enquiry . . .
  Internal evidence shows that this could scarcely have been by Joseph Galloway. Neither does Sir Robert Dallas, although given by Sabin, seem much more likely.

CONSIDERATIONS upon two Bills sent down from the R— H— [Right Honourable] the H— of L— [House of Lords] to the H—ble [Honourable] H— of C— [House of Commons] relating to the clergy of I . . . . . d [Ireland. By Jonathan Swift]. 8vo. [*Camb. Univ. Lib.*]   London, 1732

*CONSTANCE. [By Mrs Katherine Thomson.]
  The *Eng. Cat.*, 1801-1836, p. 131, giving the title as "Constance; or life as it is" ascribes this to "Mrs Thompson."

CONSTANT, faire, and fine Betty; being the young man's praise of a curious creature. . . . [A ballad, by Richard Climsell?] Fol. S, sh. B. L.   London [*c.* 1635]
  Signed: R. C.

CONSTANT (the) lover, who his affection will not move, though he live not where he love. [A ballad. By Peter Lowberry?] Fol. S. sh. 2 parts. [*Brit. Mus.*]   London [1630?]
  Signed: P. L.

CONSTANTINE; a tragedy. [By Philip Francis, D.D.] 12mo. [*Camb. Univ. Lib.*]   Dublin, 1754
  Other editions give the author's name.

*CONSTANTINE and Eugene . . .
  A presentation copy has lately passed through the stock of Mr John Grant, of Edinburgh, inscribed: "From the author, C. Kelsall."

CONSTITUTIONAL (the) crisis in Norway. [By H. L. Brækstad.] [Pettersen's *Norsk Lexikon*, col. 76.]   London, 1883

CONSTITUTIONAL (the) criterion. By a member of the University of Cambridge [William Jones]. 8vo.   London, 1768

CONSTRUCTIVE rationalism. [By Annie Besant.] 8vo. [*Brit. Mus.*]   London, 1876

CONSUMPTION (the) of opium in India; a critique of the memorandum presented by Sir William Roberts, M.D. . . . [By James Robert Wallace.] 8vo. Pp. 51. [*Brit. Mus.*]   Calcutta, 1895

CONTADINI (i) bizzarri; a new comic opera, to be performed at the King's Theatre. . . . Translated by John Mazzinghi. (The words by Signor N—— [*i.e.* Tommaso Grandi], with additions and alterations by the Poet of this theatre [Lorenzo da Ponte].) 8vo. Pp. 56. [*Brit.Mus.*] London [1794]

CONTENTED (the) home ; or, the wreath of hop blossom. By the author of *The basket of flowers* [Christoph von Schmid]. 8vo. Pp. 174. London [1879]

CONTES du temps passé, ou les contes de ma mère l'Oye ; avec des morales. . . . Sixième edition. . . . Tales of passed times by Mother Goose. . . . Englished by R. S. Gent. [Robert Samber]. *Fr.* and *Eng.* 8vo. [*Brit. Mus.*] London, 1764

*CONTEST (the) of the twelve nations . . .
The *Nat. Lib. of Scot.* and the *Brit. Mus.* give the author as William Howison, philosophical writer of Edinburgh, and the author of two other works about the same time. The *Edin. Univ. Lib.* and the *Eng. Cat.*, 1801-36, p. 132, give the author as W. Hewison, apparently otherwise unknown.

CONTINENTAL travelling. By Arthur Ward Basset [Albert E. Bull]. 8vo. [*Who's Who in Lit.*] London, 1913

CONTINUATION (a) of the Acts and monuments of our late Parliament ; or a collection of the acts, orders, votes, and resolves that hath passed in the House, from June 9 to July 7, 1659. . . . By John Canne [Samuel Butler?] Intelligencer Generall. [A satire.] 4to. Pp. ix. 723. [*Bibl. Lind.*] London, 1659

CONTINUATION (a) of the comical history of the most ingenious knight Don Quixote de la Mancha, by the licentiate (Alonzo) Fernandez de Avellaneda [Alain René Le Sage]; being a third volume, never before printed in English : translated by Captain John Stevens. 8vo. [*Arber's Term Cat.* iii. 480.] London, 1705

CONTINUATION (a) of The grand conspiracy by the Insolent Usurper and the Regall Intruder ; described in the two following sermons. By J. A. [John Allington] a suffering son of the Church of England. 12mo. Pp. 80. [*Brit. Mus.*] London, 1660

CONTROVERSIES of the day. Seven questions with answers. [By Professor Freidrich Max Mueller.] 8vo. Pp. 4. [*Brit. Mus.*] N.P. [1860 ?]
Signed : Philindus.

CONTROVERSY between the four elements. [Verse. By Aaron Niles.] 12mo. Pp. 23. [*Brit. Mus.*] Wrentham, 1812

CONTROVERSY in Ireland ; an appeal to Irish journalists. By A. E. [George William Russell]. 8vo. Dublin, N.D.

CONVENTICLE (the) ; or, a narrative of the Dissenters new plot against the present constitution in Church and State. . . . To which is added the reasons for disabling all Dissenters for ever voting more for Parliament-men, and for wholly repealing the Act of Toleration. . . . By Philaret [John Dunton]. 8vo. Pp. 100. [*Brit. Mus.*] London, 1714

CONVERSATIONS between two old friends. [By Mrs Harriet Rodd.] 12mo. [*Brit. Mus.*] London, 1845
Signed : H. R.

*CONVERSATIONS on Church polity.
The title continues "By a lady."

CONVERSION (the) of England. By Count Charles F. R. de Montalembert. Authorised translation from the French [by Mrs Margaret O. Oliphant]. 8vo. 3 vols. [*D. N. B.*, First Suppl., vol. 3, p. 233.] London, 1867
Vols. 3, 4, 5 in "The Monks of the West."

COOK book. [Verse.] By Joe Beamish [John F. Cook]. 8vo. Pp. 80. [*Amer. Cat.*] Syracuse, 1928

COOKERY rational, practical and economical, treated in connection with the chemistry of food. By Hartlelaw Reid [Robert Hardie]. 8vo. Edinburgh, 1853

COOPER Mitchell's discourse on Sister Susie. Written by Valentine [Arthur Valentine Peachey.] 4to. [*Brit. Mus.*] London, 1916

COPIE (the) of a letter writen out of Scotland by an English Gentlemā of credit and worship serving ther, vnto a frind and kinsman of his, that desired to be informed of the truth and circumstance of the slaunderous and infamous reportes made of the Quene of Scotland, at that time restreined in maner as prisoner in England, vpon pretense to be culpable of the same. [By John Leslie, Bishop of Ross?] 12mo. Pp. 65. [*D. N. B.* vol. 33, p. 99.] N.P. [1570 ?]

COPY (the) of a letter addressed to the Father Rector at Brussels, found amongst some Iesuites taken at London, about the third yeere of His Majesties raigne. . . . [By John Maynard.] [*D. N. B.*, vol. 37, p. 156.] London, 1643
Signed : J. M.

COPY of a letter from a member of the Association of Science, to a friend. [By George Fleming Richardson.] 4to. [*Brit. Mus.*] [1846]
No separate title-page.

COPY (a) of a letter written to an officer of the army by a true Commonwealths-man, and no courtier, concerning the right and settlement of our present Government and Governors. [By Richard Goodgroom.] [*M'Alpin Coll. Cat.*]   London, 1656

COPY (the) of a letter written to Mr Alexander Hinderson. [By John Dury.] [*M'Alpin Coll. Cat.*]
                    London, 1643
    Attribution by Dr Charles A. Briggs.

COPY (a) of an excellent letter wrote by the Rev. Mr J. E. [Joseph Eliot] of Guildford, deceased, to his brother Mr B. E. [Benjamin Eliot] of Roxbury. . . . 12mo. [*Brit. Mus.*] Boston, 1738

COPYRIGHT condensed and explained. By Lewis C. Russell [Lewis Charles Rudd]. 8vo. Pp. 64. [*Brit. Mus.*]
                    London [1922]

COR Jesu. (By J. M., S.J. [J. M. Martins]. Fourth edition.) 16mo. Pp. xii. 124. [*Brit. Mus.*]   Belgaum, 1923

CORD and creese. By the author of *The Dodge Club* [James De Mille]. 8vo. Pp. 199. [*Brit. Mus.*]
                    New York, 1869

CORINTHIAN'S (a) bride. [A novel.] By Ben Bolt [Ottwell Binns]. 8vo. Pp. 256. [*Brit. Mus.*]   London, 1926

CORK (the) surgeon's antidote against the Dublin apothecary's poyson for the citizens of Dublin. By Anthony Litten [Sir Richard Cox, Bart.]. 8vo. 7 nos. [*Brit. Mus.*]   Dublin, 1749

CORNISH (the) pilchard fishery. By J. C. O. [John Cardell Oliver]. 12mo. Pp. 8. [*Brit. Mus.*]   Truro, 1872

CORONER'S (the) understudy. By Captain Coe [E. C. Mitchell; but probably by Lincoln Springfield.] 8vo. [*Nat. Lib. of Scot.*]   Bristol [1891]

CORREGGIO; a tragedy, by Oehlenschlager. Sappho; a tragedy, by Grillparzer . . . . Translated . . . [by E. L. *i.e.* E. B. Lee]. 16mo. [*Brit. Mus.*]   1846

CORRESPONDENCE between the Commissioners for investigating the affairs of the joint companies and a Citizen of Burlington [Henry C. Carey]. 8vo. Pp. 15. [Sabin's *Dictionary*, iii. 329.]   Philadelphia, 1850

CORRESPONDENCE (the) of Theodosius and Constantia, from their first acquaintance to the departure of Theodosius, with the letters which passed between them after Constantia had taken the veil. A new edition. [By J. L. *i.e.* John Langhorne.] 8vo. Pp. 290. [*Brit. Mus.*]   London, 1799
    Several other editions, earlier and later, with varying titles, bear the author's full name.

CORRESPONDENCE [of Philindus, *i.e.* Professor Friedrich Max Mueller, Indophilus, *i.e.* Sir Charles Trevelyan, and others], relating to the establishment of an Oriental College in London. Reprinted from the "Times." . . . 8vo. Pp. 40. [*Brit. Mus.*]   London, 1858

CORRESPONDENTS (the); an original novel, in a series of letters. 12mo.
                    London, 1775
    "Said to be the real correspondence of George, Lord Lyttleton, and Mrs Peach, who afterwards married his son."—A pencil note in a copy.

CORSAIR (the); or, the foundling of the sea; a romance. By Harry Hazel [Justin Jones]. 8vo. [*Cushing's Init. and Pseud.* i. 127.]   London, 1847

CORSICA; a poetical address. [By William Richardson, Professor.] Second edition. 8vo. Pp. 15. [*Brit. Mus.*]
                    Glasgow, 1769

*COSI fan tutte . . .
    For Senolo, *read* Scuolo.

*COSMIC symbolism . . .
    For Gorm, *read* Gorn.

COSMO de' Medici; the False one; Agramont and Beaumont: three tragedies; and the Deformed—a dramatic sketch. By the author of *Ginevra* [Francis H. H. Terrell]. 8vo.
                    London, 1884

COSMOS and diacosmos; processes of nature physiologically treated. By Theophilus Middling [Denton Jaques Snider]. 8vo. [*Amer. Cat.*]
                    St Louis, 1909

*COSTLY stones . . .
    The preface is signed E. L. (not W. E. L. as in text), and as the preface shows that the writer is a lady, the *Brit. Mus.* interpretation as Emily Lumb is probably correct.

COTTAGE bread for cottage children. [Poems.] By C. S. [Charles Sabine]. 8vo. Pp. xii. 148. [*Brit. Mus.*]
                    London, 1857

*COTTAGE farming . . .
    For Ross Hickey, *read* William Ross Hickey.

COTTAGER'S (a) remarks [by Charles O'Conor] on the Farmer's Spirit of party [by Henry Brooke]. 8vo. [*Camb. Univ. Lib.*]   Dublin, 1754

COUGHS and colds. (Cure for colds and indigestion, *etc.*) [By Charles Babington Sharpe.] 8vo. 7 parts. [*Brit. Mus.*]   [Bath] 1901-5
    Signed: C. B. S.

COUNSEL from the heavenly spheres and thoughts thereon. By H. B. [Heather Bellairs]. 8vo. Pp. 131. [*Brit. Mus.*]   London, 1914

X

*COUNSELLOR Manners . . .

We have not been able to trace this "third edition" said to have been written by J. D. There were at least four previous editions, 1673, 1676, 1693, and 1694 (see Arber). A later edition (1710) was alleged on its title-page to be by Sir R. L. S., probably an attempt to secure a sale by giving the impression that it was by Sir Roger L'Estrange. The edition of 1694 runs "Councellor Manners . . . "

COUNTERPOISE (the); being thoughts on a militia and a standing army. By W— T—, Esq. [W. Thornton?]. 8vo. [*Brit. Mus.*] London, 1752

COUNTESS (the) of Dellwyn. By the author of "David Simple" [Sarah Fielding]. 12mo. [*Brit. Mus.*]
London, 1759
Issued also as "The history of the Countess . . . "

COUNTREY-MAN'S (the) rudiments; or, an advice to the farmers in East Lothian how to labour and improve their ground. [Dedication signed: A. B. C. *i.e.* John Hamilton, second Lord Belhaven.] 8vo. Pp. 48. [*Brit. Mus.*] 1699

COUNTRY (the) housewife's garden. . . . Together with the husbandry of bees. [By Gervase Markham.] 4to. 3 parts. [*Brit. Mus.*] London, 1623

COUNTRY (the) of thirty-six thousand wishes. By Andre Maurois [Emile Herzog]. (Translated by Katharine I. Monro.) 4to. Pp. 59. [*Observer*, 1st Feb. 1931.] London, 1930

COUNTRY (the) week; how it was started and what it is doing for the poor children in Boston. (Written for The Dayspring by W. F. W. [W. F. Whitcomb].) 8vo. Pp. 7. [*Brit. Mus.*] Boston, 1883

COURSE (a) in popular song-writing. [By Henry Rogers.] 8vo. 2 vols. [*Brit. Mus.*] London [1925]

COURT (the) and camp of Buonaparte. [By S. D. Whitehead.] 8vo. Pp. viii. 326. [*Brit. Mus.*] London, 1829

*COURT (the) convert . . .

This book is by Henry Waring. It was issued under two pseudonyms, occurring at the end of the dedicatory epistles, *viz.* (respectively) Henry Anderson and Henry Audley. In each case the words By H. A. Gent. alone occur on the title-page.

COURT (the) of honour: or, the Laws, Rules, and Ordinances established for the suppression of duels in France. . . . [By John Evelyn?] 4to. Pp. 100. London, 1720
See the note to "The Laws of honor . . . "

*COURT poems . . .

" . . . a small volume of satirical pieces which most critics now assign severally to Gay, Pope, and . . . Lady Mary Wortley Montagu, though the Lady maintained that she was their sole author."—R. STRAUS' *The Unspeakable Curll*, p. 50.

*COURT tales; a history of the amours . . .

The edition which bears John Oldmixon's name is the second edition, 1732. Watt's note is quite wrong. Oldmixon is the author (see *Lowndes*, *Brit. Mus.*), and while it may be an infamous production, it would be still more surprising from the pen of the respectable Crull. Was Watt confusing Crull with Curll?

COURTSHIP (the) of Captain Silas Porter. By Rolf Bennett [W. Marten]. 8vo. Pp. 252. [*Brit. Mus.*]
London [1916]

COUSIN Christopher. [A novel.] By M. E. Francis [Mary E. Blundell]. 8vo. Pp. 271. [*Brit. Mus.*]
London [1925]

COUSIN Geoffrey and I. . . . By Caroline Austin [Mrs —— Whitway]. 8vo. Pp. 288. [*Brit. Mus.*]
London, 1890

COUSIN Ivo. [A novel.] By Mrs Andrew Dean [Mrs Alfred Sidgwick]. 8vo. Pp. 346. [*Publishers' Circular*, 8th October 1927.] London, 1899

COVENANT (the) with a narrative of the proceedings and solemn manner of taking it by the Honourable House of Commons, and Reverend Assembly of Divines the 25th day of September, at Saint Margarets in Westminster. [By John White, of Dorchester, the Elder.] . . . 8vo. Pp. 34. [F. Rose Troup's *John White*, p. 446.]
London, 1643

COVENANTS (the) and prophecies concerning Jehovah's ancient people of Israel, Jerusalem and the land and the church of God. [By William Marrable, D.D.] 8vo. Pp. 44. [*Brit. Mus.*] Edinburgh [1886?]

*COVENT Garden drollery . . .

The *D. N. B.* says this is not by Brome, and the *Brit. Mus.* now follows suit. It may be by Mrs Aphra Behn. [*Brit. Mus.*]

COZY (a) couple: a farce, in one act. By Slingsby Lawrence [George Henry Lewes]. 12mo. [*Brit. Mus.*]
London [1856]
Lacy's Acting Edition of Plays, vol. 24.

CRADLE (the). By the author of *Margaret Whyte*, etc. [Lucy L. Cameron]. 12mo. Pp. 16. [*Brit. Mus.*] London, 1823
Signed: L.

CRAFT (the) to liue well and to die well. [Translated by Andrew Chertsey.] Fol. [*Pollard and Redgrave.*]
London, 1505

CRAFTIE Cromwell ; or, Oliver ordering our new state : a tragi-comedie . . . written by Mercurius Melancholicus [Marchamont Nedham?]. (The second part of Crafty Crumwell : or Oliver in his glory as King) : a trage commedie . . . written by Marcurius Pragmaticus [M. Nedham]. 4to. 2 parts. [*Brit. Mus.*]
London, 1648

The two parts would seem to be written by the same author, the dedicatory poem at the beginning of the second part being headed "To the readers of my former peece."

CRAFTY (the) whore ; or, the mistery and iniquity of bawdy houses laid open in a dialogue between two subtle bawds. [Translated in part from Pietro Aretino's Capricciosi ragionamenti.] . . . 8vo. Pp. 112. [*Brit. Mus.*]
London, 1658

CRANSTONS (the) ; a tale of two brothers. By Ramsay Guthrie [John George Bowran.] 8vo. Pp. 240. [*Brit. Mus.*]
London [1909]

CRAVEN (the) dialect exemplified in a dialogue between farmer Giles and his neighbour Bridget. By a native of Craven [William Carr. Abridged edition]. 12mo. Pp. 62. [*Brit. Mus.*]
Skipton, 1834

*CRAZY tales . . .
The dedication which is signed A. S. is by the author to himself. A. S. are the initials of Antony Shandy, the pseudonym which Hall - Stevenson employed in his "Two lyric epistles . . ." issued two years previously, *q.v.*

CREATION (the) ; a lecture on Genesis i. and ii. [By William Kelly, of Guernsey.] 8vo. [*Brit. Mus.*]
[1879?]

CREATURES tame. By Maggie Browne [Margaret Hamer, later Mrs Andrewes]. 4to. [*Brit. Mus.*]
London [1884]

CREDENDA, agenda, postulanda ; or, the faith, duty and prayers of a Christian missionary. [By Henry Bailey.] 8vo. [*Brit. Mus.*]
Canterbury, 1855
Signed : H. B.

CREEDS (the) of the Church. [By William Gresley.] 12mo. [*Brit. Mus.*]
London, 1841
Signed : G.

*CREEL (a) of peat . . .
For Chapman-Houston, *read* Chapman-Huston.

*CREW (a) of kind London gossips , . .
The first (1602) edition begins " 'Tis merrie when gossips meete . . ." ; the 1609 edition, "A whole crew of kind gossips . . ." The 1613 edition begins "A crew of kind gossips . . . " ; and there is a 1619 edition called "Well met gossip . . ."

CRIBBAGE. By Rawdon Crawley, Bart., of Queen's Crawley, Hants. [Charles Frederick Pardon]. 32mo. Pp. 28. [Jessel's *Bibl. of playing cards.*]
London, 1889

CRIME and Christening : a farce. By Richard Henry [Richard Buller and Henry Chance Newton]. 8vo.
London, 1891

CRIME (the) in the office. [A novel.] By Arthur Ward Basset [Albert E. Bull]. 8vo. [*Who's Who in Lit.*]
London, 1905

CRIME (the) of the camera. By Nick Carter [John Russell Coryell]. 8vo. [*Amer. Cat.*]
New York, 1907

CRIMINAL courts, criminal procedure and recent changes in the criminal law of France. [By Abraham Hayward.] 8vo. [*Brit. Mus.*]   [London, 1833]
Signed : H. An extract from the *Law Magazine*, vol. 8.

CRIMINAL trials. [By David Jardine.] 12mo. 2 vols. [*Brit. Mus.*]
London, 1832-5
Library of Useful Knowledge.

CRISIS (the) and the remedy. By Publius [James de Peyster Ogden ?]. [H. E. Miller's *Banking Theories in the U.S.*, p. 233.]   New York, 1842

CRISIS (the) in farming ; its radical causes and their only remedies. . . . By the author of *Hints to landlords and tenants* [S. G. Finney]. 8vo. Pp. 40. [*Brit. Mus.*]
London, 1880

CRISIS (the) of 1859. [By William Tarbet.] 8vo. 2 parts. [*Brit. Mus.*]
[1859]

CRISIS (the) ; or, a defence of Administration against the imaginary victory and ill-grounded triumph of Opposition. [By Joseph Cawthorne.] 8vo. [*Camb. Univ. Lib.*]   London, 1875
Signed : Veridicus.
The reference is to the Union of Great Britain and Ireland.

*CRITIC (the) ; or a tragedy rehearsed . . .
Probably not by Sheridan, and possibly by the same hand as "The General fast ; a lyric ode . . ." *q.v.* (and in the supplement). The *D. N. B.* ascribes on doubtful evidence to Israel Pottinger. See Mr R. Crompton Rhodes in the *T. L. S.* 26th Aug. 1926.

CRITICA juris ingeniosa ; or, choice cases in the common-law. Digested [and translated from Les quaeres de Mounsieur [Edmund] Plowden]. By H. B., Esq. 8vo. Pp. 304. [*Brit. Mus.*]   London, 1661

CRITICAL observations on Mr Kemble's performances at the Theatre Royal, Liverpool. [By Augustus Bozzi Granville.] 8vo. [*Brit. Mus.*]
                              Liverpool, 1811
     Signed : A. B. G* * * * * * * *

CRITICAL researches in philology and geography. [By James or John Bell.] 8vo. [*Brit. Mus.*]   Glasgow, 1824

*CRITICAL review of the public buildings . . . 1734.
     Not by James Ralph, miscellaneous writer. The 1734 edition was entirely anonymous, but there was an edition in 1783, as By —— Ralph, architect. For a century it has been currently ascribed to James Ralph, but it is not by him (see *D. N. B.* 47/223 and *N. and Q.* iii. vi. 9 and iii. vi. 72). The second edition, 1736, was called "A new critical review . . ." and the fourth edition, 1783, was edited and added to [by William Nicholson, Chemist].

C R I T I Q U E (the) of the vision of Rubeta ; a dramatic sketch in one act. By Autodicus [Laughton Osborn]. 8vo. [Foley's *Amer. authors.*]
                              Philadelphia, 1838

CROQUET. By Straw Hat [J. Jeffery]. 8vo. Pp. 63. [*Brit. Mus.*]   [1899]
     Dean's Champion Handbooks.

CROSS (the) and the crown; a tale of the revocation of the Edict of Nantes. . . . By the author of *The Spanish Brothers* [Deborah Alcock]. 8vo. Pp. 127. [*Brit. Mus.*]   London [1886]

CROSS (the) in baptism; a sermon principally entreating of the crosse in baptisme. By R. H. [Roger Hacket]. 8vo. [*Camb. Univ. Lib.*]
                              London, 1606

*CROSSING of proverbs. . . . By N. B. Gent. . . .
     Pollard and Redgrave, *S. T. C.*, quoting from the unique fragmentary copy in the H. E. Huntington Library, state that the title reads "By B. N. Gent."

CROTCHETS and Quavers; or the making of the Brixwell young people's band. By Noel Hope [Sarah L. Morewood]. . . . Edited by . . . Mildred Duff. 8vo. Pp. 174. [*Brit. Mus.*]
                              London, 1921

CROWN (the) or the Tiara ? Considerations on the present condition of the Waldenses, addressed to the statesmen of civilised Europe. [By William Stephen Gilly.] 8vo. [*Camb. Univ. Lib.*]   London, 1842

CROWS (the) of Shakespeare. By J. B. [Mrs J. Blackburn]. 8vo. [*Camb. Univ. Lib.*]   Edinburgh, 1899

CRUELL (a) murther committed lately, upon the body of A. Geatsy, who liv'd in the parish of Westmill in the County of Harford. . . . [A ballad by Richard Climsell ?] Fol. S. sh. B. L. [*Brit. Mus.*]   London [1635]
     Signed : R. C.

CRUISE (the) of the Blue Jacket and other sea stories. By Lieut. Warneford [William Howard Russell ?]. [Allibone's *Dict.*]   London, 1862

CRUISING in "The Kid," and Fowey River memories. [Verse.] By Nautic [George Llewellyn Ridley]. 8vo. Pp. 24. [*Brit. Mus.*]   Fowey [1927]

CRUMBS of bread for the dove in the clefts of the rock, and the secret places of the stairs, Cant. ii. 14 ; or, helps to meditation, on conversion, mortification, sanctification. . . . For a friend, by J. T. [John Tickell, minister in Abingdon]. 12mo. [*Brit. Mus.*]
                              [Oxford, 1682]

CRUMS (the) of comfort; with godly prayers. (Thankfull remembrances of Gods wonderfull deliverances of this land.) [Compiled by M. S. *i.e.* Michael Spark.] Corrected and amended. . . . Seventh edition. 12mo.   2 parts. [*Brit. Mus.*]   London, 1628

CRY (a) for more money ; the depression of trade ; the cause and the remedy. By a London merchant [Hermann Lorenz Feuerheerd]. 8vo. [*Camb. Univ. Lib.*]   London, 1886

CRY (the) of innocent blood ; sounding to the ear of each member in Parliament ; being a short relation of the barbarous cruelties inflicted lately upon the peaceable people of God called Quakers. . . . By C. H. [Charles Harriss]. 4to. Pp. 8. [Smith's *Cat. of Friends' Books,* i. 914.]   1670

CRY (the) of the pendulum ; and other poems. By an Undergraduate of Gonville and Caius Colleges [Robert Bruce Bousfield]. 8vo. [*Camb. Univ. Lib.*]   [Cambridge, 1907]

CRYSTAL (the) age. [By William Henry Hudson.] 8vo. Pp. iv. 288.
                              London, 1887
     The second edition, 1906, bears the author's name.

CRYSTALINA ; a fairy tale. By an American [John Milton Harney]. 8vo. Pp. 112. [Appleton's *Dict. of Amer. Biog.*]   New York, 1816

CUCKOO'S-NEST (the) at Westminster, or the Parlement between the two lady-birds, Queen Fairfax and Lady Cromwell, concerning negotiations of estate and their severall interests in the kingdom, sadly bemoaning the fate of their deer and ab-hored husbands. By Mercurius Melancholicus [Marchamont Nedham?] 4to. [*Brit. Mus.*]
London, 1648

CUDWORTH defended; and Unitarianism delineated. By a lover of Cudworth and truth [Rev. George B. Cheever]. ... From the *Salem Gazette.* 8vo. Pp. 27. [Sabin's *Dictionary*, p. 563.] Salem, 1833

CUMBERLAND'S minor theatre, with remarks, biographical and critical [by D. G. *i.e.* George Daniel]. 12mo. 16 vols. [*Brit. Mus.*]
London, 1828-40

CUMBRIANA; or, fragments of Cumbrian life. By the compiler of the *Glossary of Cumberland words and phrases* [William Dickinson]. Second edition. 8vo. [*Camb. Univ. Lib.*]
London, 1876

CUP (the). [A poem. By Alfred, Lord Tennyson.] 8vo. Pp. 48. [*Brit. Mus.*] London, private print, 1881

CUPID'S understudy. By Childe Harold [Edward Salisbury Field]. 8vo. [*Amer. Cat.*] New York, 1909

CURATE (the) of Wildmere; a novel. [By Julia Addison.] 8vo. 3 vols. [*Bibliotheca Jacksoniana.*] 1847
MS. attribution.

CURE (a) for the tongue-evill; or a receipt against vain oaths: being a plain and profitable poem. [By Thomas Jordan.] 4to. [*Christie-Miller Cat.*] London, 1662

CURIOSITIES for the ingenious. [By Joseph Taylor.] 18mo. Pp. 192. [Jessel's *Bibl. of playing cards.*]
London, 1821

CURIOUS (a) collection of ancient paintings . . . engraved from . . . drawings lately done after the originals. [Signed G. T. *i.e.* George Turnbull.] . . . Fol. [*Brit. Mus.*]
London, 1741

*CURIOUS (the) maid . . .
It is now generally agreed that this was not by Matthew Prior, but by Hildebrand Jacob. [*D. N. B.* vol. 29, p. 118.]

CURIOUS revelations concerning the working of the Irish Church Temporalites Commission, by X. Y. Z. [Horatio Nelson Creeny]. Fol. Pp. 7. [*Brit. Mus.*] Belfast [1872?]

CURIOUS (a) uncommon account of the great eclipse of the moon, October the 10th, 1725. [By Francis Hoffman.] . . . 8vo. 5 parts. [*Brit. Mus.*]
London, 1725

CURIOUSLY planned. By Camilla Hope [Grace E. Thompson]. 8vo. Pp. 288. [*Amer. Cat.*] London, 1928

CURLIAD (the); a hypercritic upon the Dunciad variorum, with a farther key to the new characters. [By Edmund Curll.] 12mo. [Straus' *Curll.*]
London, 1729

CURLICISM display'd; or, an appeal to the Church: being just observations upon some books publish'd by Mr Curll. [By Edmund Curll.] 12mo. [Straus' *Curll.*] London, 1718

CURRENCY and coinage; a guide to the solution of the exchange, and allied problems, based on a reduction to ultimate factors. By Vrill [F. A. Perroux]. 8vo. Pp. 36. [*Brit. Mus.*] Calcutta, 1892

CURSORY remarks on An Enquiry into the expediency and propriety of public or social worship; inscribed to G. Wakefield, the author of this work. . . . By Eusebeia [Mary Hays]. Second edition, with a postscript. 8vo. Pp. 28. [*Brit. Mus.*] London, 1792

CUT flowers. [A novel.] By Oliver Onions [George Oliver]. 8vo. Pp. 287. [*Brit. Mus.*] London, 1927

*CUT with his own diamond . . .
For Wood, *read* Wood-Seys.

CYMBERINA; an unnatural history in woodcuts and verse. By L. H. [Loyd Haberly]. 4to. Pp. 45. [*Brit. Mus.*]
Long Crendon, 1926

"CYMRU Fydd." Landlordism in Wales. By Adfyfr [T. J. Hughes]. . . . English edition. 8vo. Pp. 52. [*Brit. Mus.*]
Cardiff, 1887

CYNTHIA abroad. By Norah K. Strange [Mrs E. Gower Stanley]. 8vo. Pp. 250. [*Brit. Mus.*] London, 1927

CYNTHIA in the wilderness. By Hubert Wales [William Piggott]. 8vo. Pp. 312. [*Brit. Mus.*] London, 1907

D

DAFFODIL (the) murderer ; being the Chantrey Prize poem. By Saul Kain [Siegfried Sassoon]. 8vo. Pp. 32. [*Who's Who.*] London, 1913

DAGOBERT'S [J. B. A. Led'huy's] pocket library in French and English. . . . 16mo. [*Brit. Mus.*] London [1863]

DAGWORT (the) Coombe murder. By Lynn Brock [Alister M'Allister]. 8vo. Pp. 243. [*Brit. Mus.*] London, 1929

DAILY meditations ; one for each day in the week. [By R. F. M. and H. T. H. *i.e.* Henry Thomas Hamblin.] 16mo. [*Brit. Mus.*] Bosham [1929]

DAILY (a) message in the words of Jesus. [Compiled by A. A. Saunders.] 16mo. Pp. 85. [*Brit. Mus.*] Lincoln [1890]

DAILY (the) round ; meditation, prayer, and praise adapted to the course of the Christian year. [By T. B. Pollock.] 8vo. Pp. 415. [*Brit. Mus.*] London, 1880

DAILY strength for daily needs. . . . Selected by the editor of *Quiet hours* [Mrs Mary W. Tileston]. 8vo. Pp. 378. [*Brit. Mus.*] Cambridge, U.S.A., 1890

DAISY and Marguerite. [Two tales. By Mr and Mrs Cyril Andrews.] 8vo. Pp. 22. [*Brit. Mus.*] Ditchling, 1923

DALILAH ; or, the little house in Piccadilly. . . . [By William Stephens Hayward.] 8vo. Pp. iv. 327. [*Brit. Mus.*] London [1884]

DAMON and Pythias ; a tragedy. [By R. L. Sheil and John Banim. In verse.] 8vo. [*Brit. Mus.*] London, 1821

DAMOZEL Blanche, and other faery tales. By M. B. [Maurice Baring]. 8vo. Pp. 16. [Chaundy's *Bibl. of Baring.*] Eton, 1891

DANCE (the) ; historic illustrations of dancing from 3300 B.C. to 1911 A.D. By an Antiquary [Nathaniel H. J. Westlake]. 8vo. Pp. viii. 68. [*Brit. Mus.*] London, 1911

*DANCE (the) of death . . .
By Ambrose Bierce and T. A. Harcourt [Starrett's *Bibl. of Bierce*].

*DANCING-MASTER (the) . . .
The eighth and subsequent editions are by Henry Playford, signing himself : H. P.

*DANGER (the) of enthusiasm . . .
Signed : W. A.

DANGERFIELD (the) talisman. By J. J. Connington [Alfred Walter Stewart]. 8vo. Pp. 272. [*Publishers' Weekly,* 29th Sept. 1928.] London, 1926

DANGEROUS connections ; or, letters collected in a society, and published for the instruction of other societies. By M. C**** de L*** [Choderlos de Laclos. Translated from the French.] 12mo. 4 vols. [*Brit. Mus.*] London, 1784

DANIEL Evelyn, heretic. [A novel.] By Cadvar Rhys [David Delta Evans]. 8vo. Pp. x. 449. [*Brit. Mus.*] London, 1913

DANISH fairy legends and tales. . . . Second edition enlarged ; with a memoir of the author [Hans Andersen, by the translator, signed C. P. *i.e.* Caroline Peachey]. 8vo. Pp. xl. 535. [*Brit. Mus.*] London, 1852
First edition, 1846.

DANISH (the) pilot. By Vice-admiral Zahrtmann. [Edited by F. B. *i.e.* Sir Francis Beaufort.] 8vo. Pp. xii. 552. [*Brit. Mus.*] London, 1853

DANTE'S mystic love ; a study of the Vita Nuova, Odes, etc., from the allegorical standpoint. By Marianne Kavanagh [Marion J. Spain]. 8vo. Pp. 122. [*Innisfail, a quarterly magazine*, No. 1.] Edinburgh, 1921

DAPHNIS and Chloe ; excellently describing the weight of affection, the simplicitie of love, the purport of honest meaning, the resolution of men, and disposition of fate, finished in a pastorall . . . termed by the name of The shepheard's holidaie. [Translated from the French version by Jacques Amyot of the Greek of Longus and "The shepheard's holidaie" written] by Angell Daye. 4to. B. L. [*Brit. Mus.*] London, 1587

DARK (the) chapter. [A novel.] By E. J. Rath [J. Chauncey Corey Brainerd and Edith Rathbone Brainerd]. 8vo. Pp. 316. [*Brit. Mus.*] London [1925]

DARKNESS : an ode, written 6th Jan. 1832. [By Sir Samuel Egerton Brydges.] Fol. S. sh. [*Brit. Mus.*] [Geneva, 1832]
Signed : S. E. B.

DARKNESSE and ignorance expelled by the light shining forth. . . . In answer to a book called Innocents no saints. Published by one Edward Dodd. . . . His . . . arguments confounded . . . By one of the Lamb's followers . . . F. H. [Francis Howgill]. 4to. Pp. 29. [*Brit. Mus.*] London, 1659

DAUGHTER (the) of Madame Angot :
a comic opera in three acts. [Music]
by C. Lecocq [words by Clairville,
Paul Sirandin, and Victor Koning.]
Translated from the French by W. D.
Davison. 8vo. [*Brit. Mus.*]
London [1874]
The words only.
Clairville is a *pseud.* for Louis François
Nicolau, the younger.

DAUGHTERS (the) of Pola ; family
letters relating to the persecution of
Diocletian, now first translated from
an Istrian MS. [By John Mason
Neale.] 8vo. Pp. 104. [*Brit. Mus.*]
London [1861]

DAVID the shepherd who became king.
By Mildred Duff and Noel Hope
[Sarah L. Morewood]. 8vo. Pp. 144.
[*Brit. Mus.*]   London [1926]

*DAVID'S musick . . .
Pollard and Redgrave query the attribution to Alleine.

DAWN (the) of science in Glasgow ; a
poem occasioned by the appearance of
the Glasgow Repository of Literature.
[By Robert Buchanan, M.A.] 8vo.
Glasgow, 1805
From a copy bearing this ascription in the
handwriting of Principal Lee.

DAWNLAND (the) experiment ; the
story of the M'Ardle peerage : second
edition. By Evelyn Tempest [Edward
W. D. Cuming]. 8vo. Pp. xi. 305.
[*Brit. Mus.*]   London, 1911

DAWN'S (the) delay. [Three stories.]
By Hugh Kingsmill [Hugh Kingsmill
Lunn]. 8vo. Pp. 203. [*Brit. Mus.*]
London, 1924

DAWSONS (the) of Glenara ; a story
of Scottish life. [By Henry Johnston,
lawyer in Glasgow.] 8vo. 3 vols.
[*Brit. Mus.*]   London, 1877

DAY (a) by the fire, and other papers.
. . . By Leigh Hunt. [Edited by
J. E. B. *i.e.* J. E. Babron.] 8vo. Pp.
368. [*Brit. Mus.*]   London, 1870

DAY-DAWN (the). By the author of
Memorials of Captain Hedley Vicars
[Catherine M. Marsh]. 16mo. [*Brit.
Mus.*]   London, 1866

DAYS at Leighscombe ; a tale for
children. [By Mrs J. F. Foster.]
16mo. [*Brit. Mus.*]   London [1870]

DE bello Germanico ; a fragment of
trench history. . . . By the author of
Undertones of War [Edmund Blunden].
8vo. Pp. 83. [*Brit. Mus.*]
Hawstead, 1930

DE Municipium juramento. A serious
enquiry into the burgess oaths of
Edinburgh, Perth and Glasgow.
Wherein the matter and form of the
said oaths (and the other burgess
oaths used thro' Scotland, in so far as
coinciding therewith) are examined.
. . . By a lover of the publick welfare
[Andrew Stevenson]. 8vo. Pp. 102.
Edinburgh, 1746

DEACONESSES, and early sisterhoods ;
two sermons. . . . By J. M. Neale.
[With an introduction signed : J. H.
i.e. Joseph Haskoll.] 8vo. [*Brit.
Mus.*]   London, 1869

DEAD men's tales. By Bennet Copple-
stone [Frederick Harcourt Kitchin].
8vo. Pp. 330. [*Publishers' Weekly*,
16th Oct. 1926.]   Boston, 1926

DEARLY (the) beloved of Benjamin
Cobb. By Clemence Dane [Winifred
Ashton]. 8vo. Pp. 43. [*Brit. Mus.*]
London, 1927

DEATH at Swaytling Court. By J(ohn)
J(ervis) Connington [Alfred Walter
Stewart]. 8vo. Pp. 292. [*Publishers'
Weekly*, 29th Sept. 1928.] London, 1926

DEATH (the) of a diplomat. By Peter
Oldfield [Vernon Oldfield Bartlett].
8vo. Pp. 254. [*Brit. Mus.*]
London, 1928

*DEATH (the) of Bonaparte . . .
For Samuel William Henry Ireland, *read*
Samuel Ireland ?

DEATH (the) of Napoleon ; a prize
poem recited in Rugby School, June 22,
MDCCCXLVII. [By Alexander Miller.]
8vo. Pp. 6. [*Brit. Mus.*] Rugby, 1847

DEATH (the) of Napoleon ; a prize
poem, recited in Rugby School, June
xxii, MDCCCXLVII. [By C. G. Blom-
field.] 8vo. Pp. 6. [*Brit. Mus.*]
Rugby, 1847

DEATH wake of Maga of the East, or
the editor's lamentation for the down-
fall of his journal [*i.e.* the East-Lothian
Literary and Statistical Journal. By
G. Tait]. 8vo. Pp. 8. [*Brit. Mus.*]
G. Tait, Edinburgh, 1831

DEATH'S test. . . .   [By George
William Foote.] 8vo. [*Brit. Mus.*]
London [1882]

DEBATE (the) in the House of
Commons April 25, 1814, upon cor-
ruption of blood. Published by B. M.
[Basil Montagu]. 8vo. [*Brit. Mus.*]
London, 1814

DEBATE (the) in the House of Lords
April 2, 1813, upon a bill for abolishing
the punishment of death. [Edited by
B. M. *i.e.* Basil Montagu.] 8vo.
[*Brit. Mus.*]   London, 1816

DEBIT the account. [A novel.] By
Oliver Onions [George Oliver]. 8vo.
Pp. 312.   London, 1913

*DECADENT (the). . . .

 For R. A. Crane, *read* R. A. Cram.

DECLARATION (a) and plainer opening of certain points, with a sound
confirmation of some other, contained
in a treatise intituled, The Divine
beginning and institution of Christes
true visible and ministeriall Church.
. . . [By Henry Jacob.] [*Dexter's
Cong. Bibl.* 391.]   N.P., 1612

DECLARATION of rights. [By Percy
Bysshe Shelley.] Fol. S. sh. [*Brit.
Mus.*]   Dublin, 1812

*DECLARATION (a) of the Kings
Majesties intentioun and meaning.
See "A Declaratioun of the King's
Majesties intentioun . . ."

DECLENSION. By a Gentleman with
a duster [Harold Begbie]. 8vo. Pp.
157. [*Amer. Cat.*]   London, 1925

DECLINE (the) and fall of whist. An
old-fashioned view of new fangled play.
By the author of *Whist or Bumblepuppy* [John Petch Hewby]. 16mo.
Pp. 75. [F. Jessel's *Bibl. of playing
cards,* p. 228.]   London, 1884

DECREE (a) made at Rome, the second
of March 1679, condemning some
opinions of the Jesuits and other
casuists. [Translated by Gilbert
Burnet.] [*Brit. Mus.*] London, 1679
 Included in his "Collection of Several
Tracts," 1685.

DEDUCTIONS (the) of Colonel Gore.
By Lynn Brock [Alister M'Allister].
8vo. Pp. 310. [*Brit. Mus.*]
                          London [1924]

*DEEDS of the olden time.
 Usually ascribed to Anne Hatton. *See*
 "Cambrian pictures."

DEEPS (the) of Hell ; a plea for English
convict prison reform. By Jeffrey
Swithin [Alastair Jeffreys Davis].
12mo. [*Brit. Mus.*] [London] 1930

DEFENCE (a) and vindication of the
right of tithes, against sundry late
scandalous pamphlets . . . Penned by
a friend of the Church of England,
and a lover of truth and peace [John
Downame]. [*M'Alpin Coll. Cat.*]
                          London, 1646

DEFENCE (a) of Bridge. By Bads-
worth [Allan Lindsay Lister]. 8vo.
Pp. iii. 16. [F. Jessel's *Bibl. of playing
cards.*]   London [1904]

DEFENCE (a) of Dr Sherlock's notion
of a Trinity in Unity, in answer to the
animadversions upon his vindication
of the doctrine of the Holy and ever
blessed Trinity. [By William Sherlock.]
[*D. N. B.* vol. 52, p. 97.] London, 1694

DEFENCE of our national character.
By Guy Mitford [George Moore of
Warrington]. [*Sutton's Lanc. authors.*]
                                 1816

DEFENCE (a) of Sir Fopling Flutter,
a comedy written by Sir G. Etheridge.
[By John Dennis.] 8vo. Pp. 24.
[*Brit. Mus.*]   1722

DEFENCE (the) of Stonington against
a British Squadron, August 9th to 12th,
1814. [Contemporary accounts, edited
by T. *i.e.* James H. Trumbull.] 4to.
[*Brit. Mus.*]
 Hartford [Conn.], private print, 1864

*DEFENCE (a) of the conduct of the
Warden of Winchester College . . .
 In Straus' *Dodsley* this is attributed to
 Robert Lowth.

DEFENCE (a) of the ministers of the
nation, in answer to an epistle
["Christ's innocency pleaded"] lately
published by Thomas Speed. [Signed :
W. T. *i.e.* William Thomas.] 4to.
Pp. 56. [*Brit. Mus.*]   N.P. [1656 ?]

*DEFENCE (a) of the Missionaries
Arts . . .
 See the note to "The Missionaries Arts
 discovered . . ." in this supplement.

DEFIANCE (the) of death ; being some
thoughts on the death of a brave
soldier, preached . . . by F. W. M.
[F. W. Merryweather]. In memoriam :
Capt. Ball. 8vo. Pp. 16. [*Brit. Mus.*]
                          London [1918]

*DEIRDRE . . .
 For Æ, *read* AE.

DEIRDRE of the sorrows ; an opera.
[Preface signed : W. M. C. *i.e.* William
Mervyn Crofton.] 4to. Pp. 35. [*Brit.
Mus.*]   Dublin, 1926

DELECTABLE (the) story of Princess
Pirlipatine and the Nutcracker. [A
translation of Alexandre Dumas' version
of E. T. W. Hoffmann's story, by
P. B. M. Allan.] . . . 8vo. Pp. 146.
[*Brit. Mus.*]   London [1924]
 Signed : P. B. M. A.
 For an earlier edition of this translation
 see "Princess Pirlipatine . . ."

*DELENDA Carthago.
 This was not by Shaftesbury who died in
 1683 ; there is a reference to the year 1694
 on page 8. The confusion has arisen from
 Shaftesbury's famous speech in 1671 :
 Delenda est Carthago [*i.e.* Holland]. It
 was probably by Charles Leslie who in 1696
 wrote a tract on similar lines : "Now or
 never." There is a copy in the *Brit. Mus.*
 with Leslie's name inscribed.

*DELICIOUS (the) answer . . .
 For answer, *read* amour.

DELIGHTS for the ingenious ; or, a
monthly entertainment for the curious
of both sexes. . . . [By John Tipper,
teacher.] 8vo. [*Brit. Mus.*]
                          London, 1711

DELMOUR ; or, a tale of a sylphid, and other poems. [By Edward George Earle Bulwer, later Lord Lytton.] 8vo. [*Brit. Mus.*]　　　　　London, 1823

DEMETRIAN (the). By Ellison Harding [Edmond Kelly]. 8vo. Pp. 315.　　　　　New York, 1907
　　Republished in London (1908) under the title " The Woman who vowed."

DEMETRIUS ; an opera. . . . [Translated from Metastasio by Angelo Cori.] 8vo. Pp. 61. [*Library of Congress, Cat. of Opera Librettos.*]
　　　　　　　　　　London, 1731

DEMOCRACY ; an American novel. [By Henry Brooks Adams.] 8vo. Pp. 374. [*Publishers' Weekly*, 7th Aug. 1926.]　　　　　New York, 1880

DEMONSTRATION (a) of the truth of the Christian religion, from the Latin of Socinus. [By Edward Combe.] Second edition. 8vo. [*Brit. Mus.*]
　　　　　　　　　　London, 1732
　　This is really the same as " An argument for the authority of Scripture" (published in 1731), with a new title-page.

DEPLORABLE (the) state of New-England by reason of a covetous and treacherous governour [Joseph Dudley] and pusillanimous counsellors. . . . [By Sir Henry Ashhurst.] 4to. [*Brit. Mus.*]　　　　　London, 1708
　　The " Epistle dedicatory " signed : A. H.

DEPOSITION (the) ; a dramatic piece. [By John Maclaurin, Lord Dreghorn.] 8vo. [R. Inglis' *Dramatic Writers of Scotland*, p. 143.]　Edinburgh, 1757
　　A satire on the Rev. J. Home, the author of *Douglas*.

DERWENT'S Horse. [A novel, on the early stages of the South African War.] By Victor Rousseau [Victor Rousseau Emanuel]. 8vo. Pp. viii. 275. [Mendelssohn's *South Afr. Bibl.* i. 522.]
　　　　　　　　　　London, 1901

DESCRIPTION (the) of a plain instrument, that . . . will discover the situation of any vertical plane . . . and how to draw a dyal upon any such plane. . . . By A. M. [Adam Martindale]. 12mo. [*Brit. Mus.*]
　　　　　　　　　　London, 1668

DESCRIPTION (a) of Mr West's picture of Death on the pale horse. . . . [By John Galt.] 4to. [*Brit. Mus.*]
　　　　　　　　　　London, 1818

DESCRIPTION (a) of Pitcairn's Island and its inhabitants ; with an authentic account of the mutiny of the ship Bounty, and of the subsequent fortunes of the mutineers. [By John Barrow, F.R.S.] 8vo. [*Brit. Mus.*]
　　　　　　　　　　New York, 1845

DESCRIPTION (a) of South Carolina ; containing many curious and interesting particulars relating to the civil, natural, and commercial history of that colony. . . . [By Dr —— Glen.] 8vo. Pp. viii. 110. [Sabin's *Dictionary.*]
　　　　　　　　　　London, 1761
　　It has been attributed to James Glenn, Governor of South Carolina.

DESCRIPTION (a) of the grand signour's seraglio or Turkish Emperor's court. By Robert Withers. [Really a translation from the Italian of Ottaviano Bon.] [*Year's Work in English Studies*, 1928, p. 192.]
　　　　　　　　　　London, 1650

*DESCRIPTION (a) of three hundred animals. . . .
　　Attributed also to a Mr Maquin. [*N. and Q.* June 1926, p. 446.]

DESCRIPTIVE (a) and historical account of the Isle of Man, with a view of its society, manners and customs. [By Nathaniel Jefferys.] . . . 8vo. Pp. 200. [*Brit. Mus.*]
　　　　　Newcastle-upon-Tyne, 1809
　　Another issue bears the author's name.

DESCRIPTIVE catalogue of the pictures and other works of art at Oulton Park, Cheshire. [Signed : P. de M. G. E. *i.e.* Sir Philip de Malpas Grey Egerton.] 4to. [*Brit. Mus.*]
　　　　　London, private print, 1864

DESERT dreams ; a romance of friendship. By Patrick Weston [—— Souter]. 4to.　　　　　London, 1914

DESERTER (the), a new musical drama. [Adapted by C. Dibdin from *Le Déserteur* of M. J. Sedaine.] . . . 8vo. Pp. 36. [*Brit. Mus.*]
　　　　　　　　London [1810 ?]

DESIGNED (a) end to the Socinian controversy. . . . By John Smith. [Edited by J. D. *i.e.* John Disney.] 12mo. Pp. xi. 61. [*Brit. Mus.*]
　　　　　　　　　　London, 1793

DESIRES ; poems of main things. By John Doe [Victor Sampson, Judge of the Supreme Court of South Africa]. [*Bookman's Journal*, i, 1925, p. 172.]
　　　　　　　　　　London, 1924

DESPISED and rejected. By A. T. Fitzroy [Rosa Annatelli]. 8vo. Pp. 350.　　　　　London, 1918

DESTINY (the) of America ; with an appendix, Who are the Japanese ? By the Roadbuilder [William Gordon Mackendrick]. 8vo. Pp. xvi. 269. [*Amer. Cat.*]　　　Toronto [1921]
　　Many subsequent editions bear the author's name.

DESTINY (the) of Rome, or the probability of the speedy . . . destruction of
the Pope. . . . In a letter to a divine
of the Church of England from a divine
of the Church of the First-born [John
Toland]. 8vo. [*Brit. Mus.*]
London, 1718
Signed: X. Z.

DESULTORY (a) conversation between
two young aristocratic Ceylonese [on
British rule. Signed Henry Candidus
i.e. Henry White?] 8vo. [*Brit. Mus.*]
[Colombo] 1853

DESULTORY (a) examination of the
reply of the Rev. W. V. Harold to a
Catholic Layman's Rejoinder. By a
Catholic Layman [Matthew Carey].
To which is annexed . . . the above
reply verbatim. 8vo. Pp. 72. [Sabin's
Dictionary, iii. 339.] Philadelphia, 1822

DESULTORY (the) man. By the author
of *The Gypsy* [George P. R. James].
8vo. 3 vols. [*Eng. Cat.*, 1801-1836,
p. 160.] London, 1836

DETAIL (a) of the facts respecting the
late attempt to tune the organ of
St Paul's Chapel. [By Alexander
Anderson.] [Robertson's *Aberd. Bibl.*]
Aberdeen, 1800

DEVIL (the) of a duke; or, Trapolin's
vagaries; a farcial ballad opera.
[Altered from The duke and no duke
of N. Tate, by R. Drury.] 8vo. [*Brit.
Mus.*] London, 1732

DEVIL (the) turn'd hermit; or, the
Adventures of Astaroth banished from
Hell: a satirical romance. . . . Trans-
lated from the original French of Mr
de M * * * [P. L. Saumery]. . . .
Second edition. 12mo. 2 vols. [*Brit.
Mus.*] London, 1751

DEVIL'S (the) tower. [A novel.] By
Oliver Ainsworth [Sir Henry Sharp].
8vo. Pp. 306. [*Brit.Mus.*] London, 1927

DEVOTIONAL aids for the private use
of the clergy. [By James Frederick
Secretan Gabb.] 16mo. [*Brit. Mus.*]
London, 1653
Signed: J. F. S. G.

*DEVOTIONS. First part . . .
The place and date of the first edition are
now known to be Paris, 1668. There is a
copy in Marsh's Library, Dublin.

DEVOUT (the) Christian's companion;
or, a compleat manual of devotions,
fitted for most of the concerns of
human life. . . . Collected from the
works of Abp. Tillotson, Bp. Patrick,
Bp. Kenn, Bp. Beveridge, Bp. Taylor,
Dr Scott, Dr Horneck, Dr Stanhope.
. . . [By Rev. Robert Warren.] 12mo.
3 parts. [R. Straus' *The Unspeakable
Curll*, p. 204.] London, 1707
The second part, second edition (1733),
bears Warren's name.

*DEVOUT (the) companion . . .
This is not given in the *D. N. B.* as stated.
Arber, however, *Term Cat.*, has it.

*DEVOUT entertainments . . . trans-
lated by J. M. Q. . . .
For J. M. Q., *read* J. M. W.

*DEVOUT (the) soul . . .
For J. H., B. N. *read* Jos. H. B. N.

DEUOUTE (a) man's purposes; being
zealous and comfortable meditations, to
weane a man from this world, and the
vanities thereof. [With a dedication
signed: E. M. *i.e.* Edmund Mats, the
bookseller for whom the work was
printed and possibly the author.]
12mo. Pp. 153. [*Brit. Mus.*]
London, 1597

DEWDROP (the) . . . Poems. By
E. G. V. [E. G. Varnham]. 8vo. Pp.
vi. 218. [*Brit. Mus.*] London, 1834

DIABOLUS amans; a dramatic poem.
[By John Davidson.] 8vo. Pp. 143.
[*T. L. S.* 31st Dec. 1930.]
Glasgow, 1885

DIALOGUE (a) between a blind man
and death. [In verse. By Richard
Standfast.] 8vo. Pp. 8. [*Brit. Mus.*]
[1700?]

DIALOGUE (a) between a Japanese and
a Formosan about some points of the
religion of the time. By G. P—m—r
[George Psalmanazar—a pseudonym
assumed by an adventurer, perhaps a
native of Formosa who lived latterly
in England]. 8vo. [*Brit. Mus.*]
London, 1707

DIALOGUE (a) between the Devil and
Prince Rupert [in verse] written at the
Leaguer before Chester upon Prince
Rupert's coming to relieve the said
city. . . . Written by E. B. [Ellis
Bradshaw]. 4to. [*Brit. Mus.*]
London [1649]
The author's name, however, appears on
page 8.

DIALOGUE (a) between the ghost of
General [Richard] Montgomery just
arrived from the Elysian Fields and an
American delegate in a wood near
Philadelphia. [By Thomas Paine.]
8vo. Pp. 14. [Sabin's *Dictionary*.]
Philadelphia, 1776
There was a private reprint, eighty copies,
New York, 1865.

DIALOGUE (the) in English betweene
a Doctor of Divinitie and a student of
the Laws of England: newly corrected
and imprinted, with new additions.
[By Christopher Saint - Germain.]
[*Camb. Univ. Lib.*] London, 1598

DIALOGUE (a) on the Christian's hope, the future destiny of man, and the visible creation. By a working man [J. Manders]. . . . Second edition. 8vo. Pp. 48. [*Brit. Mus.*]
London, 1874
Signed : J. M.

DIALOGUE (a) on the unity of Christ's One Holy Catholic Church. By a working man [J. Manders]. 8vo. Pp. 48. [*Brit. Mus.*] London, 1874
Signed : J. M.

*DIAMOND (the) buckled shoe . . .
The author is not Quiller-Couch, but the Rev. Otwell Binns. [*Brit. Mus. ; Lit. Year Book.*]

DIAMOND cut diamond ; a comedy in two acts. Translated from the French of Guerre ouverte, ou ruse contre ruse [of A. J. Dumaniant, *pseud.* of Joseph André Bourlain by Lady W. [Lady Eglantine Wallace]. 8vo. [*Brit. Mus.*] London, 1787

DIAMOND (the) new pointed ; being a supplement to Diamond cut diamond : containing three letters which Mr Jefferys sent to the Earl of Moira . . . with observations thereon. . . . By Philo-veritas [Thomas Gilliland]. 8vo. Pp. 30. [*Brit. Mus.*] London, 1806

*DIANA of Rosenburgh . . .
For Diana of Rosenburgh, *read* Diana Rosenburgh. The attribution to Miss Corfield is not given in the *Brit. Mus.* as stated.

*DIANNE de Poytiers.
Marie Hay is not a *pseud.*, but the maiden name of Madame de Hindenburg.

DIARY (the) of a communist schoolboy. Translated from the Russian [of N. Ognyov, *i.e.* Mikhail Grigor'evich Rozanov] by Alexander Werth. 8vo. Pp. 288. [*Brit. Mus.*] London, 1928

DIARY (the) of a U-boat Commander. With an introduction and explanatory notes by Etienne [Stephen King-Hall]. . . . 8vo. Pp. 288. [*Brit. Mus.*] London, 1920

DIARY (the) of a young lady of fashion in the year 1764-1765. By Cleone Knox. Edited by her kinsman Alexander Blacker Kerr. [Written by Magdalen King-Hall.] 8vo. Pp. vii. 245. [*Brit. Mus.*] London, 1925

DIARY (a) of the Great Warr (A Second Diary—A last Diary). By Samuel Pepys, Junior [R. M. Freeman and Robert Augustus Bennett]. With effigies. . . . 8vo. 3 vols. [*Brit. Mus.*] London, 1917-9

*DICK and his cousin. . . .
For " Flccta," *read* " Fleeta."

DICTIONARY (a) of quotations from the British poets. . . . By the author of the Peerage and Baronetage charts [William Kingdom]. 12mo. 3 parts. [*Brit. Mus.*] London, 1824

DIELLA, certaine sonnets, adioyned to the amorous poeme of Dom Diego and Gineura : by R. L. Gentleman [Richard Linch ?]. 16mo. [*Brit. Mus.*] London, 1596

DIES Iræ. [With a verse translation by R. C. Winthrop.] 8vo. Pp. 15. [*Brit. Mus.*]
Cambridge [Mass.] 1892
Signed : W.

DIET (a) of Worms ; a metrical fragment from D'Aubigné's *History of the Reformation.* [The preface signed : C. S. *i.e.* Charles Sabine.] 12mo. Pp. 48. [*Brit. Mus.*] London, 1845

DIGITUS Dei ; or, good newes from Holland : sent to the worll Iohn Treffry and Iohn Trefusis, Esquires ; as also to all that have shot arrows agaynst Babels Brats, and wish well to Sion wheresouer. [By Hugh Peters.] 4to. [*Brit. Mus.*] Rotterdam, 1631
Signed : H. P.
There seems little doubt that H. P. is Hugh Peters. He signs himself "your lo. kinsman, H. P." John Treffry was Peters' uncle or grandfather, and Peters is known to have been in Holland in 1631.

DILEMMAS ; or questions on important subjects. By T. P. [Sir Thomas Phillipps]. 8vo. Pp. 3. [*Brit. Mus.*]
[Middle Hill, 1840 ?]

DING Dong ; or, Sir Pitifull Parliament on his deathbed . . . his last will and testament, with his death, buriall and epitaph. By Mercurius Melancholicus [Marchamont Nedham ?]. 4to. [*Brit. Mus.*] [London], 1648

DIOTREPHES his dialogues : wherein it appears beyond all possible evasion, that the doctrine of Gods decrees, and the Articles annexed . . . [Three points] . . . [By Laurence Womock.] [*D. N. B.* vol. 62, p. 346.]
London, 1661

DIPLOMATIC (a) woman. By Huan Mee [—— and —— Mansfield, two brothers]. 8vo. Pp. 181.
London, 1900

DIRECTION (a) for the weaker sort of Christians, shewing in what manner they ought to fit and prepare themselves to the worthy receiving of the Sacrament. . . . By W. B. [William Bradshaw]. To hereunto is adioned a verie profitable treatise of the same argument . . . written by another [Arthur Hildersam]. 12mo. 2 parts. [*Brit. Mus.*] London, 1609

DIRECTIONS for preparing manure from peat ; instructions for foresters. [By Allan Maconochie, Lord Meadowbank.] 8vo. Pp. 98. [*Brit. Mus.*]
       Edinburgh, 1815

DISCIPLINE in the School of God ; its nature and effect. By J. B. S. [J. B. Stoney]. 8vo. 3 vols. [*Brit. Mus.*]
       London [1903]

DISCONTENTED (the) lady ; a new song. . . . [By T. D'Urfey. With the musical notes.] Fol. S. sh. [*Brit. Mus.*]
     [London, 1685 ?]

DISCOURSE (a) against profane swearing . . . Second edition. [By Samuel Wright, D.D.] 8vo. Pp. 32. [*Watt's Bibl. Brit.*]   London, 1732

DISCOURSE (a) concerning the currencies of the British Plantations in America. . . . [By William Douglass.] 8vo. [*Brit. Mus.*] Boston, 1740
  Reprinted, London, 1751.

*DISCOVRSE (a) concerning the svccesse of former Parliaments.
  The author's name appears on the second (1644) edition.

DISCOURSE (a) of an unconverted man's enmity against God. . . . By J. H. [John Howe]. 12mo. [*Brit. Mus.*]   London, 1700

*DISCOURSE (a) of duels . . .
  For T. C. [Thomas Comber, D.D.], *read* T. C. [Thomas Comber] D.D.

DISCOURSE (a) of natural and reveal'd religion ; in several essays : or, the light of nature a guide to divine truth. [By Timothy Nourse.] 8vo. Pp. 363. [Arber's *Term Cat.* ii. 367, 377.]
       London, 1691
  An edition later in the same year bears the author's name.

DISCOURSE (a) of the judgements of God ; composed for the present times against atheism and prophaneness. [By Thomas Beverly.] [*M'Alpin Coll. Cat.*]   London, 1668
  Dedication signed : T. B.

*DISCOURSE (a) of the nature, ends, and difference of the two covenants. . . .
  Not by William Allen, Vicar of Bridgewater, Somersetshire, but by William Allen, tradesman, of London, writer on baptism, justification and similar subjects, called in the British Museum catalogue, *Controversial Writer*. It is included in his collected works.

*DISCOURSE (a) of the true and visible markes . . .
  Translated by Thomas Wilcox. The original edition [1582], which bears Beza's full name, also bears Wilcox's initials : T. W.

*DISCOURSE [on II Cor. 13/14] . . .
  Signed : R. N.

DISCOVERIES. [Poems. By Siegfried Sassoon.] Private print, 1915

DISCOVERIES of the Day-dawning to the Jewes ; whereby they may know in what state they shall inherit the riches and glory of promise. [By] J. P. [John Perrot]. 4to. Pp. 15. [*Brit. Mus.*]   London, 1661
  Signed "Johan" in Hebrew characters.

*DISCOVERIES of the French . . .
  The title continues "By M* * *, formerly a captain in the French navy." *For* Captain, *read* Count.

*DISCOVERY (the) of a new world : or, a description of the South Indies . . .
  By Joseph Hall, Bishop of Exeter, translated by J. H. *i.e.* John Healey. [*Brit. Mus.*]

DISCOVERY (a) of the unnaturall and traiterous conspiracie of Scottish Papists against God, his Kirk, their native countrie, the Kinges Majesties persone and estate, set downe, as it was confessed and subscrivit be M. George Ker and D. Grahame. . . . [By John Davidson.] 4to. Pp. 32. B. L. [Johnstone and Robertson's *Bibl. Aberd.* i. 91.] Edinburgh [1592]

DISEASES (the) of pigeons. By Squills [Alfred Henry Osman]. 8vo. Pp. 33. [*Brit. Mus.*]   London, 1924

*DISH (a) of first-fruits. . . . By Zi. S. S. S. . . .
  For Zi. S. S. S., *read* Z. : S. S. S.

*DISILLUSION . . .
  For Johnson, *read* Jonson.

DISINGAG'D (a) survey of the Engagement, in relation to publike obligations. 1. Precedent. 2. Present, in the Oaths of allegiance and supremacy, the Protestation, and Covenant, and under the present juncture of affaires. [By John Durie, or Dury.] 4to. [*D. N. B.* vol. 16, p. 263.] London, 1650

DISPUTATION between the body and the soul. [Founded upon an old poem in the Auchinleck MS., by T. M. *i.e.* Sir Theodore Martin. With several cuttings inserted containing other poems by the same author signed E. N., Martinus Scriblerus and I. G.] 12mo. Pp. 15. [*Brit. Mus.*]
   Edinburgh [private print], 1838

DISRAELI ; a picture of the Victorian age. By Andre Maurois [Emile Herzog]. Translated by Hamish Miles. 8vo. Pp. x. 334. [*Observer*, 1st Feb. 1931.]   London, 1927

DISRAELI ; the alien patriot. By E. T. Raymond [Edward Raymond Thompson]. 8vo. Pp. 361. [*Brit. Mus.*]   London [1925]

DISSENTERS recalled to their duties and their interests. . . . By a clergyman of the Church of England [Thomas Chamberlain]. 12mo. Pp. 17. [*Brit. Mus.*]   London, 1837

DISSERTATION (a) concerning private judgment and authority. By the author of the *Short method with the deists* [Charles Leslie]. 8vo. Third edition, corrected. [*Brit. Mus.*]
London, 1726

DISSERTATION (a) upon English typographical founders and founderies. By Edward R. Mores. [With an appendix by J. N. *i.e.* John Nichols.] 8vo. Pp. 100. [*Brit. Mus.*]
[London] private print, 1778
Only eighty copies printed.

DISSERTATION (a) upon the sugar of milk. . . . Wrote in French by J. L. Dyvernois. . . . [Translated by D. D'E. *i.e.* D. d'Escherny.] 8vo. Pp. viii. 32. [*Brit. Mus.*]   London, 1753

DISSOLUTION, 1536-7. Suffered by Brother Ambrose, of Beeleigh Abbey. Compiled by A. E. G. [Alexandra E. E. M. S. von Herder, *later* Grantham, *then* Munthe]. . . . 8vo. Pp. 47. [*Brit. Mus.*]   London, 1917

DISSOLUTION (the) of the Union. A sober address to all those who have any interest in the welfare, the power, the glory, or the happiness of the United States. . . . By a Citizen of Pennsylvania [Matthew Carey]. Second edition. 8vo. Pp. 36. [Sabin's *Dictionary*, iii. 340.]
Philadelphia, 1832
Signed : Hamilton.

DISTRESSED (the) virgin; or, the false young man and the constant maid. . . . [A ballad. By Martin Parker?] Fol. S. sh. B. L. [*Brit. Mus.*]   [London, 1670?]

DITTIES of Dublin, and other things. Penned and pictured by Pater Padus [J. W. Poe]. 8vo. Pp. 32. [*Brit. Mus.*]   Dublin [1904]

DIVAN (a) of the dates. Micah, and other poems. By Swithin Saint Swithaine [Thomas Meadows]. 8vo. Pp. xii. 178. [*Bibl. Lind.*]   London, 1900

DIVERTING (the) history of John Gilpin! Shewing how he went farther than he intended and came safe home again. [By William Cowper.] Fol. S. sh. [*Brit. Mus.*]
Birmingham [1790?]
For other editions, see "Gilpin's rig . . .", "The journey of John Gilpin . . . ", "The history of John Gilpin . . . ", and "John Gilpin's journey . . . "

*DIVERTING (the) works of the famous Miguel de Cervantes . . .
Not the work of Cervantes. It is a translation by Edward Ward of the "Para todos" of Juan Perez de Montalban. For a reissue (1710) see "A Week's entertainment at a wedding . . .''

DIVINE meditations written by an honourable person. Whereto is adjoyned a determination of the question, whether men ought to kneele at the receipt of the Holy Communion, and an essay on friendship. [By Sir Isaac Wake.] 8vo. Pp. 162. [*Oxf. Bibl. Soc. Proc.* II. ii. 105.]   London, 1641

DIVINE observations upon the London-Ministers letter against toleration : By his synodicall, priestbyter - all, nationall, provinciall, classicall . . . Reverend Yongue Martin Mar-Priest, sonne and heir to Old Martin the Metropolitane. . . . [Richard Overton]. [*D. N. B.* vol. 42, p. 386.]   Europe, 1646

DIVINE (the) promises considered, and the duty of Christians to be followers of those who thro' faith and patience, inherit them ; a funeral discourse [on Heb. vi. 12] occasion'd by the death of Mrs Hannah Williams. [By Thomas Prince.] 8vo. [*Brit. Mus.*]
Boston, 1746

*DIVINE (the) sacrament . . .
Signed : W. M.

DIVORCE (the) ; a musical entertainment. . . . [By Lady Dorothea Dubois.] 8vo. Pp. 18. [*Library of Congress, Cat. of Opera Librettos.*]
London, 1771

DIVYSION (the) of the places of the lawe and of the Gospell, gathered owt of the Hooly Scripture by Petrum Artopocum [John Bradford, Prebendary of St Paul's]. 8vo. B. L. [*D. N. B.* vol. 6, p. 157.]   London, 1584

DOCTOR Cæsar Crowl ; mind-curer : a novel. By Paul Cushing [Roland Alexander Wood-Seys]. 8vo. 3 vols. [*Brit. Mus.*]   London [1888]

DR Esperanto's [*i.e.* L. Samenhof's] International tongue. Preface and complete method. Edited for Englishmen by J. St. 8vo. Pp. 39. [*Brit. Mus.*]   Warsaw, 1888

DOCTOR Knock ; a comedy in three acts. By Jules Romain [Louis Farigoule]. In an English version by H. Granville-Barker. 8vo. Pp. 95. [*Brit. Mus.*]   London, 1925

DR Syntax in search of the picturesque. [By William Combe.] 16mo. Pp. 282. [*Brit. Mus.*]   London [*c.* 1845]

DOCTRINE (the) of Christ's glorious kingdom, or the New Jerusalem State, now shortly approaching, is exceeding comfortable and very advantageous to all faithful Christians. . . . [By William Sherwin.] 4to. Pp. 4. [*Brit. Mus.*]   [London?] 1672
No title-page.

DOCTRINE (the) of life, with some of its theological applications. [By William B. Greene.] 12mo. [*Brit. Mus.*]   Boston, 1843
Signed : W. B. G.

DOCTRINE (the) of our Lord and his Apostles cleared from the false glosses and misrepresentations of . . . W. Law in his late dialogue between a Methodist and a Churchman. . . . By a hearer of the Apostles [William Cudworth]. 8vo. [*Brit. Mus.*]   London, 1761

DOCTRINE (the) of the Church of England, established by Parliament against disobedience and wilfull rebellion. Published by O. I. for satisfaction of his parishioners of Watton in the County of Hartford. [By William Ingoldsby ?] [Thomason's *Coll. of Tracts*, i. 207.]   London, 1642

DOCTRINE (the) of the Holy Trinity placed in its due light, by an answer to a late book, entituled, Animadversions upon Dr Sherlock's Book, &c. Also the doctrine of the incarnation of our Lord asserted and explain'd. [By William Sherlock.] [*Brit. Mus.*]   London, 1694

DOCUMENTS and proceedings connected with the donation of a free public Library . . . by William Brown, Esq., M.P., to . . . Liverpool. [Edited by A. H. *i.e.* Abraham Hume.] 8vo. Pp. 87. [*Brit. Mus.*]   Liverpool, 1858

DOCUMENTS connected with the foundation of the Anglican Bishopric in Jerusalem ; and with the protest against Bishop Gobat's proselytism. [Collected and edited by J. M. Neale.] 8vo. [*Brit. Mus.*]   London, 1853
Signed : J. M. N.

DOINGS in London ; or day and night scenes of the frauds, frolics, manners and depravities of the Metropolis. [By George Smeeton.] . . . Seventh edition. 8vo. Pp. iv. 423. [*Brit. Mus.*]   [1840?]
Preface signed : G. S.

DOLLAR Share values ; Malayan Rubber Company prospects critically analysed by the Straits Times. [By A. W. Still.] 8vo. Pp. 119. [*Brit. Mus.*]
                    Singapore [1911]
Preface signed : A. W. S.

DOLPHIN (the) ; or, Grand Junction nuisance : proving that seven thousand families in Westminster and its suburbs are supplied with water, in a state, offensive to the sight . . . and destructive to health. [By John Wright.] 8vo. Pp. viii. 104. [*Brit. Mus.*]   1827

DOMESTIC portraiture ; or the successful application of religious principle in the education of a family, exemplified in the memoirs of three of the deceased children of the Rev. Legh Richmond. [By Thomas Fry, M.A., Rector of Emberton.] 8vo. [*Brit. Mus.*]   1833

DOMINOES and solitaire. By "Berkeley" [W. H. Peel]. 8vo. Pp. 56. [Jessel's *Bibl. of playing cards.*]
                    London, 1890
One of "The Club Series."

DOMUS doloris. By W. Compton Leith [Ormonde Maddock Dalton]. 8vo. Pp. 222.   London, 1919

DON Cæsar de Bazan ; a drama. . . . Translated from the French of Dumanoir and Dennery. . . . With remarks . . . by D. G. [George Daniel]. 12mo. Pp. 45. [*Brit. Mus.*]
                    London [1848]

DON Juan. [A novel.] By Azorin [José Martinez Ruiz]. Translated from the Spanish by Catherine A. Phillips. 8vo. Pp. 144. [*Brit. Mus.*]
                    London, 1923

*DON Juan Lamberto . . .
The *D. N. B.* says this is undoubtedly by Thomas Flatman.

*DON Tarquinio . . . By Fr. Rolfe [Fred. Baron Corvo].
Reverse. Corvo is the *pseud.* and Rolfe the author's name.

*DON Zara del Fogo . . .
For another edition in the same year (1656) see "Wit and Fancy in a maze . . . "

DONNA Julia. Original opera. [By Harald Schmidt.] [Pettersen's *Norsk Lexikon*, col. 91.]   Christiania [1876]

DON'T-KNOW (the) family : a story for everybody. By Noel Hope [Sarah L. Morewood]. With illustrations by the author. 8vo. Pp. 151. [*Brit. Mus.*]   London [1904]

DONZELLA desterrada ; or, the banished virgin. By Gio. Fran. Biondi. Englished by I. H. of Graies Inne, Gent. [James Hayward]. 4to. [*Pollard and Redgrave.*]
                    London, 1635

DOOM (the) dealer. [A novel.] By R. O. Chipperfield [Isabel Egenton Ostrander]. 8vo. Pp. 288. [*Brit. Mus.*]   London [1925]

DOOR (the). [A poem.] By E. H. W. M. [E. H. W. Meyerstein]. 8vo. Pp. 23. [*Brit. Mus.*]   Oxford, 1911

DORES de Gualdim ; a tale of the Portuguese Revolution of 1640. [By John Mason Neale]. 8vo. Pp. 94. [*Brit. Mus.*]   London [1866]

DORMIE one, and other golf stories. By Holworthy Hall [Harold Everett Porter]. 8vo. Pp. xiii. 349. [*Brit. Mus.*]   New York, 1917

DOROTHY Dix, her book ; an everyday book for everyday people. [By Mrs Elizabeth Meriwether Gilmer.] 8vo. Pp. 370. [*Publishers' Weekly*, 11th Sept. 1926].   New York, 1926

DOROTHY'S dilemma ; a tale of the time of Charles I. . . . By Caroline Austin [Mrs —— Whitway]. 8vo. Pp. 192. [*Brit. Mus.*]   London [1886]

DOUBLE (the) scoop. [A novel.] By Boyd Cable [Ernest Andrew Ewart]. 8vo. Pp. 288. [*Brit. Mus.*]   London, 1924

DOUBTS (the) of Diana. [A novel.] By Evelyn Tempest [Edward W. D. Cuming]. 8vo. Pp. xi. 312. [*Brit. Mus.*]   London [1911]

DOWN river. [A novel.] By Seamark [Austin J. Small]. 8vo. Pp. 320. [*Brit. Mus.*]   London [1929]

*DOWN the corridors of time. . . .
For Grafton-Smith, *read* Crafton-Smith.

*DOWNAM'S Bulletin. . . .
For Downam's, *read* Downman's.

DOZEN (a) ballads for the times about Church abuses. [By T. *i.e.* Martin F. Tupper.] Reprinted . . . from *The Daily News*. 12mo. [*Brit. Mus.*]   London, 1854

DRAUGHTS and backgammon. By "Berkeley" [W. H. Peel]. 8vo. Pp. 128. [Jessel's *Bibl. of playing cards*.]   London, 1890
One of "The Club Series."

DRAUGHTSMEN. Edna Clarke Hall, Henry Rushbury, Randolph Schwabe, Leon Underwood. [By Reginald H. Wilenski.] 4to. Pp. 27, pl. 36. [*Brit. Mus.*]   London, 1924
Signed : R. H. W.

DRAWNLINE (the). [A novel.] By E. Shaw Cowley [Elsie Mary Boulton]. 8vo. Pp. 319. [*Brit. Mus.*]   London, 1923

*DREADFULL (the) character of a drunkard . . .
The tenth edition (1681) was issued under the name of Andrew Jones, a name Hart makes use of elsewhere. See " The Dying man's last sermon . . . "

DREAM (the) man. [A novel.] By Pamela Wynne [Winifred Mary Scott]. 8vo. Pp. 336. [*Brit. Mus.*]   London, 1924

DREAM (the) of Ravan ; a mystery. [Preface signed : G. R. S. M. *i.e.* G. R. S. Mead.] 8vo. [*Brit. Mus.*]   London, 1895

DREAM, trance or vision ? . . . By Ram's Horn : C. W. B. [Charles Wesley Brabner]. 8vo. Pp. 23. [*Brit. Mus.*]   London, 1915

DREAMER (the) and other poems. By Helen Cash [Helen Stocker]. 8vo. Pp. 62. [*Who's Who in Lit.*]   London, 1918

DREAMING spires ; a novel. By Diana Patrick [Mrs Desemea Newman Wilson]. 8vo. Pp. 288. [*Who's Who in Lit.*]   London, 1924

DRONE (the) ; a play in three acts. By Rutherford Mayne [Samuel Waddell]. 8vo. Pp. 68.   Dublin, 1909

DRUM-WAVE (the) island and other verses of the China coast. By B. N. [Bernard Nunn]. 4to. Pp. 58. [*Brit. Mus.*]   Hong Kong, 1904

DRY fish and wet ; tales from a Norwegian seaport by Elias Kræmmer [Anthon Bernhard Nilsen]. [Pettersen's *Norsk Lexikon*, col. 95.]   London, 1922

DUBLIN (a) ballad. By Dermot O'Byrne [Arnold Bax].   1918

DUBLIN (the) strike. By A. E. [George William Russell]. 8vo.   Dublin [1913]

DURHAM Sanctuary. Sanctuarium Dunelmense. . . . [Preface signed : T. C. *i.e.* Temple Chevallier.] 8vo. [*Brit. Mus.*]   Durham, 1837
Surtees Society publication.

DUSTBIN doggerels. By Gulielmus Vulpes [W. H. Fox]. 8vo. Pp. 55. [*Brit. Mus.*]   London, 1926

DUTY (the) and support of believers in life and death ; a funeral sermon [on Gen. xlix. 18] on the death of Mrs M. Smith. . . . [By Timothy Cruso.] 4to. Pp. 27. [*Brit. Mus.*]   London, 1688
Signed : T. C.

DYBBUK (the) ; a play in four acts. By S. Ansky [Solomon Rappoport]. Translated from the original Yiddish by H. G. Alsberg and Winifred Katzin. . . . 8vo. Pp. 145. [*Brit. Mus.*]   London, 1927

DYING (the) speech of Old Tenor, on the 31st of March 1750. [Verse. By Joseph Green.] Fol. S. sh. [*Magazine of History*, extra No. 94.]   Boston, 1750

D'YOU know this one ? A collection of . . . humorous stories . . . retold by Artemas [Arthur Telford Mason]. Third edition. 8vo. Pp. 128. [*Brit. Mus.*]   London [1924]

E

E. W. Montagu. An autobiography. [Edited, or rather written, by Y. *i.e.* E. V. Kenealy.] 8vo. [*Brit. Mus.*]
1869

EAGLE (the) and the robin; an apologue, translated from the original of Æsop. . . . By H. G. L. Mag [Horatio Gram, Master of Laws]. 8vo. [*Brit. Mus.*]
London, 1709

EAGLES black and white. The fight for the sea. By Augur [Vladimir Polyakov]. 8vo. Pp. 205. [*Amer. Cat.*]
London, 1929

*EARLE (the) of Pembroke's speech in the House of Peeres. . . .   1648
By Samuel Butler? [*Brit. Mus.*]

EARLY English printed books in the University Library, Cambridge. [A catalogue. By C. E. Sayle.] 8vo. 4 vols. [*Brit. Mus.*]
Cambridge, 1900-7
Signed: C. E. S.

EARLY (an) news-sheet; the Russian invasion of Poland in 1563. . . . With an introduction and historical notes, and a full translation into English [by J. C. H. *i.e.* John Camden Hotten]. 8vo. [*Brit. Mus.*]   London, 1874

EARLY (the) Paris editions of Columbus's First "Epistola." Extract from the *Centralblatt für Bibliothekswesen.* [By Henri Harrisse.] 8vo. Pp. 6. [*Brit. Mus.*]   Leipzig, 1893
Signed: B. A. V.

EARTHOLOGY; humanity characterized by the earth, sun and zodiac: with prognostications from the moon. By Albert Raphael [Albert Raphael Borrill]. 8vo. Pp. 222. [*Amer. Cat.*]
London, 1901

EAST (the) Indian chronologist, where the historical events respecting the East India Company are briefly arranged in succession, from the date of their charter in 1600 to the 4th of June 1801. [By John Hawkesworth.] 4to. Pp. vi. 90. [*Brit. Mus.; Bengal Past and Present,* xxxii. 155.]
Calcutta, 1801 [-02]

EASTER Day, and other stories, on the Book of Common Prayer. By K. M. [Kate Maclellan]. 12mo. [*Brit. Mus.*]
New York [1864?]

EASTER holidays; or domestic conversations designed for the instruction . . . of young people. [By Althea Fanshawe.] 8vo. Pp. iv. 336. [*Brit. Mus.*]   Bath, 1797

EBB and flow; the curiosities and marvels of the sea shore. . . . Edited by the editor of *Elements of physical science* [Robert William Fraser]. New edition. 8vo. [*Brit. Mus.*]
London, 1865
The edition of 1860 bears the author's name.

ECARTE and euchre. By "Berkeley" [W. H. Peel]. Illustrated. 8vo. Pp. 79. [Jessel's *Bibl. of playing cards.*]   London, 1890
One of "The Club Series."

ECCENTRICS in Paradise, and other essays. [By William Inglis Morse.] 8vo. Pp. 94. [*Publishers' Weekly,* 1st Jan. 1927.]   Boston, 1926

*ECCLESIA Dei . . .
For Frew, *read* Drew. It has been wrongly attributed to William John Blew.

ECHOES. By two writers [Rudyard Kipling and his sister Beatrice]. 12mo. Pp. vi. 72. [Martindell's *Bibl. of Kipling.*]   Lahore [1884]

ECHOES from "The Tin Trumpet," or heads and tales for the wise and waggish. By Paul Chatfield, M.D. [Horace and James Smith]: compiled by J. Ingram. 12mo. Pp. 128. [*Brit. Mus.*]   Glasgow, 1891
See "The Tin Trumpet."

ECLECTISISM; an historical dissertation. [By H. F. Corbyn?] Fol. [*Brit. Mus.*]   Calcutta [1884]

*EDINBURGH'S address to the country.
This is now ascribed tentatively to Allan Ramsay. See A. Gibson's *Allan Ramsay,* p. 105.

EDUCATION in Turkey. [Signed: T. C. T. *i.e.* Tillman C. Trowbridge.] 8vo. [*Brit. Mus.*]   London [1872]

*EDWARD Irving and the Catholic Apostolic Church. . . .
The *Brit. Mus.* attributes this to William Tarbet.

EFFIGIES Amoris, in English; or the picture of love unveil'd. [Translated from the Latin of Robert Waring by Phil-icon-erus, *pseud.* for John Norris.] 8vo. Pp. 126. [*D.N.B.* vol. 59, p. 386.]   London, 1682
The Latin original entitled "Amoris effigies" [1649?] was also anonymous. For another translation, see "The effigies of love."

EGREGIOUS (the) English. By Angus MacNeill [Thomas William Hodgson Crosland]. 8vo. Pp. 200. [*Brit. Mus.*]   London, 1903

EGYPT, Ethiopia, and the Peninsula of Sinai. [A review of "Letters from Egypt, Ethiopia, and the Peninsula of Sinai," by R. Lepsius.] Reprinted from the *Journal of Sacred Literature*. [By Reginald Stuart Poole.] 8vo. Pp. 18. [*Brit. Mus.*]   London, 1854
    Signed: R. S. P.

EIGHT centuries of reports ; or, eight hundred cases solemnly adjudged in the Exchequer Chamber, or upon writs of error. Publish'd originally in French and Latin by Judge Jenkins. Now carefully translated. . . . Second edition. . . . By a Gentleman of the Middle-Temple [Theodore Barlow]. Fol. Pp. x. 341. [*Brit. Mus.*]
                    [London] 1734

EIGHTEEN of them ; singular stories. By Warwick Simpson [William Pett Ridge]. 8vo. Pp. 250. [*Brit. Mus.*]
                    London [1894]

EIGHTH (the) day. [A poem. By Richard Beling.] The second edition. 4to. Pp. 78. [*Brit. Mus.*]
                    London, 1661

*EIKΩN τοῦ Θηρίου . . .
    Ascribed also to Thomas Delaune. [Whitley's *Bapt. Bibl.*]

ELEANOR. [A tale.] By the author of *A visit to my birthplace* [—— Bunbury]. 12mo. [*Brit. Mus.*]
                    Dublin, 1830

ELECTION (the); an interlude: written some years since. [By D. H. Urquhart?] 8vo. Pp. 21. [*Brit. Mus.*]   N.P. 1784

*ELECTION (the) of aliens . . .
    This is a republication of three pamphlets, issued in the same year. "An extract from the case of the electors . . .", "A letter to the Rev. Dr M.," and "A second letter to Dr M." *See above.*

ELECTRIC (the) eel. [A poem. By James Perry.] 4to. [*Bibl. Arcana,* 1885.]   London, 1777

ELECTRICAL Gold Extraction. By W. M. [Walter Mills]. 8vo. Pp. 12. [*Brit. Mus.*]   London, 1888

ELEGANT epistles. [By Vicesimus Knox.] 8vo. [*Camb. Univ. Lib.*]
                    London, 1790
    An improved and enlarged edition appeared in 1807. See also "Models of letters . . ."

ELEGIAC lines on C. V. de Bonstetten. [By Sir Samuel Egerton Brydges.] Fol. S. sh. [*Brit. Mus.*]
                    [Geneva, 1832]
    Signed : S. E. B.

ELEGY (an) in memory of that valiant champion, Sir Robert Grierson of Lag . . . who died Decem. 23rd, 1733. (The sixth edition, corrected and enlarged.) [Probably by William Irving, Schoolmaster of Hoddam.] [F. Miller's *Poets of Dumfriesshire*, p. 98.]
                    Glasgow, 1757
    Other editions are entitled "Lag's elegy," "The Laird of Lag's elegy," and "An elegy on Sir Robert Grierson of Lag." It has been ascribed to two other schoolmasters—John Orr, and William Wilson, schoolmaster at Douglas.

ELEGY on Maggy Johnston (John Cowper. — Lucky Wood. — Lucky Spence's last advice.). [By Allan Ramsay.] Pp. 16. [A. Gibson's *Allan Ramsay*, p. 123.]   [Edinburgh, 1719]
    No title-page. The first three appeared in 1718 with a title-page "Elegies on Maggy Johnston, etc." and with Ramsay's name.

*ELEGY (an) on the death of an amiable young lady . . . To which are prefixed three . . . letters [signed, G. D., A. E. *i.e.* Hon. Andrew Erskine, and J. B. *i.e.* James Boswell]. 4to. [*Brit. Mus.*]
                    Edinburgh, 1761

ELEGY (an) on the deplorable and never enough to be lamented death of the illustrious and serene Charles II. [With an epitaph signed P. K. *i.e.* Patrick Ker.] Fol. S. sh. [*Brit. Mus.*]
                    London, 1685

ELEGY (an) on the late Honorable Titus Hosmer, Esq., one of the Counsellors of the State of Connecticut. [By Joel Barlow.] 16mo. [Evans' *Amer. Bibl.*]
                    Hartford [1780]

ELEGY (an) to a young lady, in the manner of Ovid. By - - - - [James Hammond]. With an answer by a lady, author of the *Verses to the imitator of Horace* [Lady Mary Wortley Montagu]. Fol. Pp. 8. [*Brit. Mus.*]   London, 1733

ELEGY (an) written at Amwell, in Hertforshire, MDCCLXVIII. [By John Scott.] 4to. Pp. 8. [*Brit. Mus.*]
                    London, 1769

ELEGY (an) written in an empty Bath Assembly room. [By Richard Owen Cambridge.] 4to. [Straus' *Robert Dodsley.*]   1753

ELEMENTA opticæ ; nova . . . et compendiosa methodo explicata. [By Thomas Powell, Canon of St David's.] 8vo. [Wood's *Athen. Oxon.* iii. 507.]
                    Londini, 1651
    Dedication signed : T. P.
    In two congratulatory Latin poems prefixed, the author is addressed by the brothers Vaughan as "Docte Poelle !"

ELEMENTARY (the) principles of tactics, with new observations on the military art. Written in French by Sieur B—— [Le Roy de Bosroger] and translated by an officer of the British army. 8vo. [*Brit. Mus.*]
London, 1771

ELEMENTS of conveyancing. . . . [By Charles Barton.] 8vo. [*Brit. Mus.*]
London, 1802

ELEMENTS of criticism. [By Henry Home, Lord Kames.] With the author's last corrections and additions. First American from the seventh London edition. 8vo. 2 vols. [*Brit. Mus.*]
Boston, 1796

ELEMENTS (the) of fortification . . . Translated . . . from the works of the most celebrated authors. . . . [Edited by Stephen Riou?] 4to. [*Brit. Mus.*]
London, 1746

ELEMENTS (the) of French grammar. By Lhomond. Revised and enlarged by A. M. D. G * * * [J. N. Loriquet]. 12mo. Pp. 158. [*Brit. Mus.*]
London, 1826

ELEMENTS (the) of geography. . . . [By Alfred Mills.] 8vo. Pp. 31. [*Brit. Mus.*]   London [*c.* 1840]

ELEMENTS (the) of geography, astronomy and chronology. [By William Plume?] 12mo. [*Brit. Mus.*]
London [1839]

ELEMENTS of Latin Grammar. [By Richard Valpy.] Eighth edition. 12mo. [*Brit. Mus.*]   London, 1809

ELEMENTS of modern gardening ; or, the art of laying out of pleasure grounds. . . . [By John Trusler?] 8vo. [*Brit. Mus.*]   London [*c.* 1800]

ELEMENTS of mythology ; or, an easy and concise history of the pagan deities. . . . [By Richard Valpy.] 12mo. [*Brit. Mus.*]   London, 1815

ELEUSINIA. By a former member of H. C. S. [Hereford Cathedral School, Arthur Machen]. 8vo. Pp. 16. [Danielson's *Bibl. of Machen.*]
Hereford, 1881

11,506 knots in the Sunbeam in 1883. [By Thomas, Earl Brassey.] . . . 8vo. Pp. 56. [*Brit. Mus.*]
London, private print, 1884

ELIA ; or Spain fifty years ago. Translated from the Spanish of Fernan Caballero [Cecilia Francisca Josefa Arrom de Ayala]. 12mo. [*Brit. Mus.*]   New York, 1868

ELIANA ; being the hitherto uncollected writings of Charles Lamb. [Edited by J. E. B. *i.e.* J. E. Babron.] 8vo. Pp. 437. [*Brit. Mus.*]
New York, 1866

ELIDUKE, Count of Yoeloc ; a tragedy. [By William Caldwell Roscoe, barrister]. 8vo. [F. Boase's *Mod. Eng. Biog.* iii. 282.]   London, 1846

*ELIM and Maria ; a pastoral tragedy in two acts. By a friend to the oppressed [Thomas Muir, of Huntershill, advocate]. 8vo. Pp. 26. [R. Inglis' *Dram. Writers*, p. 144.]
Glasgow, 1792

ELISE, or Innocencie guilty ; a new romance, translated into English [from the French of Jean Pierre Camus] by Jo. Jennings, Gent. Fol. Pp. 150. [*Brit. Mus.*]   1655

ELIUS ; a romance. [Verse. By W. Bilderdijk]. 8vo. [*Brit. Mus.*]
Amsterdam, 1788

*ELIZABETH'S children . . .
  For Westrop, *read* Westrup.

ELIZAES memoriall. King James his arrival. And Romes Downefall. [In verse. Signed A. N. *i.e.* Anthony Nixon?] 4to. [*Brit. Mus.*]
London, 1603

ELLAN Vannin. [Poems.] By J. K. [Josephine Kermode]. 8vo. Pp. 80. [*Bibl. celtica*, 1910]
Douglas, Isle of Man, 1911

ELLEN Gray ; or unselfishness. [A tract. By Martha Landels.] 24mo. [*Brit. Mus.*]
[London ?] private print, 1861
  Signed : M. L.

ELOHIM ; I am that I am. The Lord God Jehovah. . . . By L. T. J. [L. T. James]. 16mo. Pp. 47. [*Brit. Mus.*]
Bristol, 1930

ELOPE if you must. By E. J. Rath [J. Chauncey Corey Brainerd and Edith Rathbone Jacobs Brainerd]. 8vo. Pp. 288. [*Publishers' Weekly*, 31st July 1926].   New York, 1926

ELOPEMENT (the) ; or, the deadly struggle. [A novel. By Lionel Bouverie.] 8vo. 3 vols. [F. Boase's *Mod. Eng. Biog.* iii. 328.] London, 1838

*ELSIE. Translated . . .
  For Wilhelm Heimburg [Martha Behrens], *read* W. Heimburg [Bertha Behrens].

EMANUEL Swedenborg : a lecture revised and extended. By a Bible Student [Rev. John Hyde]. Seventh edition. 8vo. Pp. viii. 120. [*Swedenborg Bibl.* p. 670.]   London, 1901
  The first edition appeared as " Swedenborg, the man of the age."

EMERITUS - PROFESSOR (the) ; a sketch of the last years of William Swan, LL.D., Professor of Natural Philosophy in the University of St Andrews. By J. L. G. [James L. Galbraith, Librarian in Glasgow University]. 8vo. Pp. iv. 68.   Private print, Selkirk [1895 ?]
  Presentation copy from the author.

EMPEROR (the) Napoleon III., and
England. [By Viscount L. É. A. de la
Guerronnière.] Translated from the
French. 8vo. [*Brit. Mus.*]
London, 1858
EMPIRE anthem. [By Mary Jane
Sloan.] 8vo. S. sh. [*Brit. Mus.*]
N.P. [1905]
Signed : Naols.
EMPORIUM (the) ; a novel of modern
society. By Alec Holmes [Lady ——
Scott]. 8vo. Pp. vi. 363. [*Brit.
Mus.*] London, 1912
ENCHANTED (the) lake of the Fairy
Morgana ; from the Orlando Inamorato
of Francesco Berni. [Translated by
R. A. *i.e.* Richard Alsop.] 8vo. Pp.
vii. 67. [*Brit. Mus.*] New York, 1806
END (the) of a world. By Claude Anet
[Jean Schopfer]. Translated by
Jeffery E. Jeffery. 8vo. Pp. 268.
[*Publishers' Weekly*, 20th Aug. 1927.]
New York, 1927
*END (the) of oppression . . .
For F. Spence, *read* Thomas Spence,
bookseller.
ENDIMION and Phœbe. . . . [By
Michael Drayton. Edited by J. P. C.
i.e. John Payne Collier.] 4to. [*Brit.
Mus.*] London [*c.* 1870]
ENGLAND and Ireland ; a counter-
proposal. By C. B. [Rt. Hon. Charles
Booth]. 8vo. Pp. 7. [*Brit. Mus.*]
London, 1886
ENGLAND bought and sold ; or, a
discovery of a horrid design to destroy
the antient liberty of all the free-holders
in England. . . . By a late libel en-
tituled *The certain way to save England.*
[By Dr John Nalson.] Fol. [*Lincoln's
Inn Lib.*] London, 1681
ENGLAND'S duty to Israel's Sons. . . .
By a clergyman of the Church of
England [Alexander MacCaul]. 8vo.
[*Brit. Mus.*] London, 1849
*ENGLAND'S faithful reprover . . .
For Adlington, *read* Allington.
ENGLAND'S joy. [Verses on the defeat
of Irish rebels under the Earl of
Tyrone. By Richard Verstegan.] 4to.
[*Brit. Mus.*] [1601 ?]
Signed : R. V.
*ENGLISH (the) and India . . .
Signed : H. L.
ENGLISH (the) ayre. By Peter
Warlock [Philip Heseltine]. 8vo. Pp.
142. [*Brit. Mus.*] London, 1926
ENGLISH (the) bijou almanack for 1836
[etc.] . . . Poetically illustrated by
L. E. L. [Letitia Elizabeth Landon]. . . .
4to. [*Brit. Mus.*] London, 1835, *et seq.*

ENGLISH (an) Carmelite ; the life of
Catharine Burton. . . . Collected . . .
by Father Thomas Hunter. [Edited by
H. J. C. *i.e.* Henry James Coleridge.]
8vo. Pp. xxxii. 282. [*Brit. Mus.*]
London, 1876
" Quarterly Series," vol. 18.
ENGLISH (the) dancing master ; or,
plaine and easie rules for the dancing
of country dances, with the tune to
each dance. [With an introduction
by J. P. *i.e.* John Playford.] 4to.
[*Brit. Mus.*] London, 1651
The first edition. The second and sub-
sequent editions were published under the
title " The dancing master," *q.v.*
ENGLISH handwriting. [By Robert
Bridges.] With thirty-four facsimile
plates, etc. 8vo. [*Brit. Mus.*]
Oxford, 1926
Signed : R. B. S. P. E. Tract No. 23.
*ENGLISH hexameter translations from
Schiller, Göthe, Homer, Callinus and
Meleager. Signed : J. F. W. H. *i.e.*
Sir John F. W. Herschel, W. W. *i.e.*
William Whewell, J. C. H. *i.e.* Julius
Charles Hare, and E. C. H. *i.e.* Edward
Craven Hawtrey.] 8vo. Pp. vii. 275.
[*Brit. Mus.*] London, 1847
*ENGLISH (the) Iarre . . .
The initials I. W. P. of the translator are
now given (*Pollard and Redgrave ; Brit.
Mus.*) as John Wilson, Priest.
ENGLISH Iliads ; or, a sea-fight re-
viewed in a poem, occasioned by the
death of a person of honour (Lord
Maidstone) slain in the late war
between the English and the Dutch.
By J. W. [John Warly ?]. 4to. Pp.
22. [*Brit. Mus.*] London, 1674
*ENGLISH (the) in India . . .
Not by T. H. Ottley, but by W. B.
Hockley. Ottley was at one time considered
as a possible author of *Pandurang Hari* but
this is now given up.
ENGLISH miscellanies ; consisting of
various pieces of divinity, morals,
politicks, philosophy and history.
[Dedication signed : J. T. *i.e.* John
Tompson.] 8vo. Pp. 608. [*Brit.
Mus.*] Gottingen, 1737
ENGLISH (an) padlock. [A poem. By
Matthew Prior.] Fol. S. sh. [*Brit.
Mus.*] London, 1705
ENGLISH (the) pilot. Describing the
sea-coasts, capes, head-lands, sound-
ings, sands . . . in the whole northern
navigation. [By John Seller.] Fol.
Pp. 78. [*Brit. Mus.*] London, 1770
*ENGLISH Presbyterian eloquence . . .
For T. L—, *read* T. L - - -
*ENGLISH Puritanisme . . .
Editions in 1640 and 1641 were published
as Written by William Ames, D.D.

ENGLISH-IRISH (an) dictionary, containing upwards of eight thousand English words, with their corresponding explanation in Irish. [By T. Connellan.] 12mo. Pp. vii. 144. [*Brit. Mus.*] Dublin, 1814

ENGLISHMAN'S (the) choice and true interest in a vigorous prosecution of the war against France, and serving King William and Queen Mary, and acknowledging their right. [By Daniel Defoe.] 4to. [*Brit. Mus.*]
London, 1694

ENGLISHMAN'S (an) love letters. [By Thomas W. H. Crosland.] 8vo. Pp. 74. [W. S. Brown's *Life of Crosland.*] London, 1901
A parody of "An Englishman's love-letters" by Laurence Housman.

*ENQUIRY (an) after happiness . . .
Signed : R. L.

ENQUIRY (an) into the conduct of Capt. M—n [Savage Mostyn]; being remarks on the minutes of the Court Martial, and other incidental matters. . . . By a Sea-officer [Admiral Edward Vernon]. 8vo. [*D. N. B.* vol. 58, p. 271.] London, 1745

ENQUIRY (an) into the danger and consequences of a war with the Dutch. [By Daniel Defoe?] 8vo. Pp. 40. [*Brit. Mus.*] London, 1712

*ENQUIRY (an) into the late supposed manifestations.
For Percival, *read* Perceval.

ENQUIRY (an) into the state of the manufacturing population, and the causes and cures of the evils therein existing. [By William Rathbone Greg.] 8vo. Pp. 40. [*Brit. Mus.*]
London, 1831

ENQUIRY (an) whether the guilt of the present civil war in America ought to be imputed to Great Britain or America. [By John Roebuck.] [*Brit. Mus.*]
Dublin, 1776

ENTERPRISING (the) burglar. By Hearnden Balfour [Beryl Hearnden and Eva Balfour]. 8vo. Pp. 305. [*Amer. Cat.*] London [1928]

ENTERTAINING (an) dialogue called The toy-shop, exhibiting a true picture of the follies and foibles of men and women. [By Robert Dodsley.] 8vo. [*Brit. Mus.*] Belfast, 1827
Earlier editions, 1735, etc. bear the author's name.

ENTERTAINING (the) history of Betsy Bloomer ; or, little stories, made still less. [By Eleanor Congleton.] 12mo. [*Sotheby's Cat.* 30th April 1928.]
Bastia [*c.* 1795]

ENTERTAINMENT (the) of the high and mighty monarch King Charles I. into his auncient and royall city of Edinburgh, June 15, 1633. [By William Drummond, of Hawthornden?] 4to. [*Pollard and Redgrave.*]
Edinburgh, 1633
In a copy of Crawford's History of the University of Edinburgh, which is in the library of Alexander Gardyne, Esq., of Hackney, there is the following MS. note by George Chalmers, the celebrated Scotch antiquary—"1633, June.—Mr John Adamson, Principal of the Ministry ; Mr William Drummond, of Hawthornden ; and Mr Thomas Crawford, Master of the High School devised the pageants and composed the speeches for the reception of Charles I. in Edinburgh." [R. Inglis, *Dramatic Writers of Scotland*, p. 141.]

*ENTHRALLED and released . . .
For Burstenlinden, *read* Burstenbinder.

ENTHUSIASM. By the author of *Natural History of Enthusiasm* [Isaac Taylor, of Stanford Rivers]. 8vo. [*Eng. Cat.*, 1801-1836, p. 188.]
London, 1836

ENTHUSIASM explained ; or a discourse on the nature, kind and cause of enthusiasm. . . . Extracted from a learned piece of a late eminent writer [*i.e.* from the enthusiasmus triumphatus of Henry More, written under the pseudonym Philophilus Parresiastes]. 8vo. Pp. 32. [*Brit. Mus.*]
London, 1739

EOLOPOESIS ; American Rejected Addresses now first published from the original manuscripts. [By Jacob Bigelow.] 8vo. Pp. 240. [*Sabin's Dict.*] New York [1855]

EONEGUSKI, or, the Cherokee chief: a tale of past wars. By an American [Robert Strange]. 8vo. 2 vols. [*Appleton's Dict. of Amer. Biog.*]
Washington, 1839

EPIGRAMS and humorous verses. By Rambling Richard [Rowland Eyles Egerton-Warburton]. 8vo. Pp. vii. 74. [J. E. Bailey's *The Warburtons of Arley*, p. 23.] London, 1867

EPIGRAMS of Martial Englished [by Henry Killigrew, D.D.] . . . 8vo. Pp. 316. [*Brit. Mus.*] London, 1693

EPILOGUE (the) to Tamerlane, on the suppression of the rebellion. [By Horace Walpole, Lord Orford]. Fol. [Straus' *Robert Dodsley*.] 1746

EPILOGUE (an) to the praise of Angus. By Seumas O'Sullivan [James Starkey]. 8vo. Pp. 38. [Boyd's *Ireland's Lit. Renais.*] Dublin, 1914

EPISCOPACY; what ground is there in Scripture or in history for accounting it an institution of God? By J. N. D. [John Nelson Darby]. 12mo. [*Brit. Mus.*]   London [1874]

EPISODES. [Short stories.] By E. Jayne Gilbert [Eliza Margaret J. Humphreys]. 8vo. Pp. 284. [*Brit. Mus.*]   London [1924]

A later edition was issued under the author's better known pseudonym " Rita."

*EPISTLE (the) exhortatorye . . .
For [London], *read* [Antwerp?].

EPISTLE (an) to His Royal Highness the Prince of Wales; occasioned by the state of the nation. By H. Stanhope [William Bond?] 8vo. Pp. 15. [R. Straus' *The Unspeakable Curll*, pp. 133, 263.]   London, 1720

EPISTLE (an) to the Chevalier ; and a congratulatory poem to Mr Secretary Addison. [By Nicholas Amherst.] [R. Straus' *The Unspeakable Curll*, p. 246.]   London, 1717

EPISTLE (an) to W— H— [William Hamilton, of Gilbertfield] on the receiving the compliment of a barrel of Loch-Fyne herrings from him, 19th December 1719. [By Allan Ramsay.] 8vo. [A. Gibson's *Allan Ramsay*, p. 128.]   [Edinburgh, 1719]
Signed : A. R.

EPITAPH on the late deceased, that truely-noble and renowned lady, Elizabeth Cromwel, mother to his Highness the Lo. Protector, etc. [By J. L. *i.e.* J. Long.] Fol. S. sh. [*Brit. Mus.*]   London, 1655

EPITHALAMIUM on occasion of the nuptials of the Marquis de Villeneuve-Esclapon-Vence and of the Princesse Jeanne Bonaparte. By W. C. B. W. [W. C. B. Wyse]. 4to. Pp. 15. *Eng. and Fr.* [*Brit. Mus.*] Plymouth, 1882

EPITHALAMIUM (an) on the marriage of William Faversham and Julie Opp. [By Richard Le Gallienne.] 8vo. [Lingel's *Bibl. of Le Gallienne*.]   Private print, N.D.

EPITHALAMIUM (an) upon the marriage of Capt. William Bedloe.

I, he, who sung of humble Oates before Now sing a Captain and a man of war.

[By Richard Duke.] Fol. S. sh. [*D. N. B.* vol. 4, p. 117.]   [London, 1679]
A satire. See also " Funeral tears upon the death of Captain William Bedloe." For the reference to Oates, see " Panegyrick upon Oates."

EPITOME of Latin prosody, for the use of schools. [By S. Connor.] 12mo. [*Brit. Mus.*]   Derby, 1823

EPITOME (an) of the history of faire Argenis and Polyarchus put in French [from the Latin of John Barclay] by N. Coeffetean ; translated into English [by Judith Man]. 8vo. [*Pollard and Redgrave.*]   London, 1640
The Latin originals (1622-34) are not anonymous.

ERA Victoriæ Humanæ. The era of " Victoria the humane." . . . By a German Metaphysician [Johann Lhotsky]. 8vo. [*Brit. Mus.*]
London, private print, 1847

ERLE Robert's mice ; a tale in imitation of Chaucer, etc. By M. P. [Matthew Prior] Esq., corrected from the errors of a spurious edition. Fol. Pp. 4. [*Brit. Mus.*]   London, 1712

ERNEST Struggles ; or the comic incidents and anxious moments in connection with the life of a station master. By one who endured it [Hubert Simmons]. 8vo. [*Brit. Mus.*]
London, 1880

ERRORS (the) of the Church of Rome ; or, a demonstration that the Church and her Councils have erred. . . . [By Daniel Whitby.] 4to. [*Brit. Mus.*]   London, 1687
Other copies bear the title " The fallibility of the Roman Church demonstrated," *q.v.*

ESCAPE. By Jeffery E. Jeffery [Jeffery Eardley Marston]. 8vo. Pp. 319. [*Amer. Cat.*]   London, 1922

ESSAY (an) concerning the true original extent and end of civil government. [By John Locke.] 8vo. [*Brit. Mus.*]
London, 1694

*ESSAY (an) on happiness . . .
Wrongly ascribed to T. Newcomb. The second edition (1772) bears the author's name (John Duncan).

ESSAY on legacies for the Scots Law class (John S. More, Esq., Professor), 19th March 1860. [By Francis Deas, LL.B., advocate.]   1860
Presentation copy from the author.

ESSAY on liberalism ; being an examination of the nature and tendency of the liberal opinions. . . . By the author of *Italy and the Italians in the nineteenth century* [André Vieusseux]. 8vo. Pp. xii. 238. [*Brit. Mus.*]
London, 1823

*ESSAY (an) on ridicule.
Not by William Whitehead. This is a confusion with a poem by Whitehead with the same title and bearing his name. [*Brit. Mus.*]

ˣESSAY (an) on tactics.
The title continues " By an adjutant."

ESSAY (an) on the character and doctrines of Socrates. [By Robert Eyres Landor.] 4to. [*London Mercury*, April 1927.]   Oxford, 1802

ESSAY (an) on the constitutional power of Great Britain over the Colonies in America ; with the resolves of the Committee of the Province of Pennsylvania, and their instructions to their representatives in Assembly. [By John Dickinson.] 8vo. Pp. viii. 126. [*Brit. Mus.*]   London, 1774

This was followed by " A New Essay . . ."

ESSAY on the dissolution of the Union threatened by the Nullifiers of South Carolina. . . . Second part. Third edition, improved. [By Matthew Carey.] 8vo. Pp. 23-26. [Sabin's *Dictionary*, iii. 340.]
Philadelphia, 1832

Signed : Hamilton.
For the first part, see " The Dissolution of the Union . . ."

*ESSAY (an) on the original genius and writings of Homer . . . 1775.

This edition was not anonymous. An earlier edition (1769) with the title " An Essay on the original genius of Homer" was anonymous. The work is an enlarged edition of the first part of "A comparative view of the antient and present state of the Troade," which was not anonymous (1767).

ESSAY (an) on the pre-existence and divinity of Christ. [By Rev. Samuel Barnard.] 12mo. [Cushing's *Anon.*]
Boston [1790 ?]

ESSAY (an) on the war and its duration. By A. J. S. [A. J. Smyth]. 8vo. [*Brit. Mus.*]   N.P. 1916

ESSAY (an) to the pious memory of . . . G. Trosse of . . . Exon . . . By J. M. [J. Mortimer ?]. 4to. [*Brit. Mus.*]
Exon, 1713

ESSAY (an) towards an impartial account of the Holy Trinity and the deity of our Saviour as contained in the Old Testament. [By Edward Wells, D.D.] . . . 8vo. Pp. 46. [*Brit. Mus.*]   London 1712

ESSAY (an) towards real moderation. [By Daniel Defoe.] The second edition. 8vo. Pp. 15. [P. Dottin's *Daniel De Foe.*]   London, 1716

ESSAY towards the probable solution of this question, whence comes the stork, the turtle, the crane, and the swallows. . . . By a person of learning and piety [Rev. Charles Morton, of Charlestown, N.E.]. 8vo. Pp. 50. [*Brit. Mus.*]   London, 1703

ESSAY (an) upon improving and adding to the strength of Great Britain and Ireland by fornication. [By Daniel Maclauchlan, minister in Ardnamurchan.] 8vo. [Scott's *Fasti*, second edition, vol. 4, p. 106.]   [1734 ?]

The writer was deposed for neglect of duty, immoral conduct, and publishing this pamphlet.

ESSAY (an) upon the civil wars of France. . . . By Mr de Voltaire. To which is prefixed a short account of the author, by J. S. D. D. D. S. P. D. [Jonathan Swift, D.D., Dean of St Patrick's, Dublin]. 8vo. Dublin, 1760

*ESSAYES, or morall discourses . . .

Not by Thomas Culpeper [*Brit. Mus.*] The author is unknown.

ESSAYS in the intervals of business. [By Sir Arthur Helps.] 8vo. [*Brit. Mus.*]   London, 1841

ESSAYS on Jewish life and thought. (The letters of Benammi [Mordecai Epstein] : second series.) 8vo. Pp. 237.   London, 1924

Information from a friend of the author.

ESSAYS on the subjects of Church establishment, toleration, and the carelessness of the clergy, as productive of grievances and complaints. [By a licentiate of the Church of Scotland [W. S. Charlestown, of Aberlour]. 8vo. Pp. vii. 58. [*Bibl. Lind.*]
London, 1831

ESSAYS social and political. By the Rev. Sydney Smith. [With a memoir of the author signed : S. O. B. *i.e.* Samuel Orchart Beeton.] 8vo. Pp. 548. [*Brit. Mus.*]   London [1877]

*ESSENCE (the) of Algernon Sydney's work . . .

Not by William Scott, Baron Stowell, but by William Scott, of the Middle Temple.

ESSEX (the) champion ; or, the famous history of Sir Billy of Billerecay and his squire Ricardo. [By William Winstanley.] 4to. Pp. 72. [*Brit. Mus.*]
London [*c.* 1690]

E S S E X Junta Exposed. The whole truth. By Hancock [Jonathan Russell]. 8vo. [Cushing's *Init. and Pseud.* ii. 72 ; Sabin's *Dictionary.*]
New York, 1809

ESTHER ; a novel. By Francis Snow Compton [Henry Brooks Adams]. [*Publishers' Weekly*, 7th August 1926.]
New York, 1884

ESULE (L') di Roma ; the exile of Rome, a heroic melodrama, in two acts . . . as represented at the King's Theatre. . . . [By Domenico Gilardoni.] 8vo. Pp. 53. [*Brit. Mus.*]
London, 1832

In Italian and English.

ETHEL Norman's secret. By Paul Trent [Edward Platt]. 8vo. [*Brit. Mus.*]   London, 1915

ETHICA Lincolniensia. [Quotations, mostly Latin. Collected by Christopher Wordsworth, Bishop of Lincoln.] 16mo. Pp. 40. [*Brit. Mus.*]
Lincolniæ, 1875
Dedication signed : C. L.

ETHNOGRAPHICAL and folklore catechism. [By W. Crooke.] 4to. Pp. 28. [*Brit. Mus.*]
Mirzapur [1892]
In English, Hindi and Hindustani.

ETON letters, 1915-18. By a House Master[H. M. *i.e.* Hugh Macnaughten]. 8vo. Pp. vii. 184. [*Brit. Mus.*]
Eton, 1921

ETON records. [Edited by R. A. Austen Leigh.] 8vo. Pp. viii. 96. [*Brit. Mus.*]   1903
Signed : R. A. A. L.

ETONA. [A poem. By C. L. *i.e.* Capel Lofft.] 4to. S. sh. [*Brit. Mus.*]
Bury [1806]

EUCHARISTIC meditations for choristers. . . . [The preface signed : D. G. *i.e.* David Greig.] 12mo. [*Brit. Mus.*]
Oxford, 1872

EUCHRE ; how to play it : with rules, problems, cases, etc., and a chapter on progressive euchre. By the author of *Poker: how to play it* [Charles Welsh]. 8vo. Pp. 125. [F. Jessel's *Bibl. of playing cards*, p. 291.]
London, 1886

EUCHRE ; its methods and maxims. By Lieut. Bougher [Charles Frederick Pardon]. Edited by Rawdon Crawley, Bart., of Queen's Crawley, Hants. 32mo. Pp. 16. [Jessel's *Bibl. of playing cards*.]   London, 1889

Rawdon Crawley, Bart., of Queen's Crawley, Hants, is also a *pseud.* for C. F. Pardon. See "Cribbage."

EURHYTHMY ; the art of movement, as inaugurated by Rudolf Steiner. . . . [By D. S. O. *i.e.* D. S. Osmond, and M. K.] 8vo. Pp. 28. [*Brit. Mus.*]
London, 1924

EUROPE as it ought to be at the end of 1861. [By Hans Ross.] [Pettersen's *Norsk Lexikon*, col. 110.] London, 1860

EUROPEAN Years ; the letters of an idle man [Hermann Jackson Warner]. Edited by G. E. Woodberry. 8vo. Pp. xii. 373. [*Brit. Mus.*]
Boston, 1911

EUTHANASIA. [By Annie Besant.] 8vo. [*Brit. Mus.*]   Edinburgh [1875]

EVANGELICAL (the) Alliance the embodiment of the Spirit of Christendom ; addressed to Dr . . . Sievewright, the Moderator of the Free Church. By [Rev. James Wright, Original Seceder] the author of a *Letter to Dr Chalmers on the present position of the Free Church, etc.* 8vo. Pp. v. 130.   Edinburgh, 1847
Signed : "A Free Church Presbyterian." Information from a friend of the author.

EVANGELICAL sermons. By Thomas Adam, Rector of Wintringham. [Edited by J. S. *i.e.* James Stillingfleet.] 8vo. Pp. xliv. 377. [*Brit. Mus.*]
London, 1781

EVANGELIUM regni . . .
For C— Vitall, *read* Christopher Vitell.

EVENING rest ; or, closing thoughts for every day in the Christian year. . . . [The preface signed : T. T. C. *i.e.* Thomas Thellusson Carter.] 16mo. [*Brit. Mus.*]   London, 1868

EVENING (the) visit. By the author of *Margaret Whyte*, etc. [Lucy L. Cameron]. 12mo. Pp. 16. [*Brit. Mus.*]   London, 1824
Signed : L.

EVERYBODY'S guide to Parliament, giving the growth, development, and life of the Mother of Parliaments. By "P. W. W." [Philip Whitwell Wilson]. 16mo. Pp. 136. [*Brit. Mus.*]
London [1917]

*EVESHAMS (the) ; a novel. By Edmund White [James Blythe Patton].
Incorrect. Edmund White is the author's real name, and Patton is a *pseud.* used by him.

EVIDENCE (the) that would have been given by Mr —— [John Cazenove], late a Continental merchant, before the Committee of secrecy appointed to inquire into the expediency of renewing the Bank [*i.e.* Bank of England] charter. 8vo. Pp. 22. [*Brit. Mus.*]
London, 1832

EVIDENT (the) advantages to Great Britain and its allies from the approaching war : especially in matters of trade. . . . [By Daniel Defoe.] 8vo. Pp. 44. [*Brit. Mus.*]   London, 1727

EVIL (the) that men do ; a military story of the period of the Indian Mutiny. By "Artax" [John Lancelot Eden]. 8vo. Pp. 338. [*Brit. Mus.*]
London, 1926

EVOLUTION (the) of the modern organ, and its control. . . . By J. M. B. [John Melvill Boustead]. 8vo. Pp. 47. [*Brit. Mus.*]   London, 1919

EXACT (an) account of Romish doctrine in the case of conspiracy and rebellion. . . . See "An exact discoverie of Romish doctrine . . . "

*EXACT (an) discoverie of Romish doctrine . . .
A later edition (1679) runs "An exact account of Romish doctrine . . . "

EXAMINATION of a tract on the alteration of the tariff written by Thomas Cooper, M.D. By a Pennsylvanian [Matthew Carey]. To which is annexed the tract of Judge Cooper, verbatim. 8vo. Pp. vii. 36, 27. [Sabin's *Dictionary*, iii. 335.]
                              Philadelphia, 1824

EXAMINATION of the Charleston (S. C.) Memorial. [By Matthew Carey.] 8vo. Pp. 29. [Sabin's *Dictionary*, iii. 340.] [Philadelphia] N.D.
Signed : Jefferson.

EXAMINATION (an) of the Connecticut claims to lands in Pennsylvania. With an appendix containing extracts and copies taken from original papers. 8vo. Pp. 94, 32. [By William Smith, of Philadelphia.] [Evans' *Amer. Bibl.*]
                              Philadelphia, 1774

*EXAMINATION (an) of the new tariff.
For C. Churchill, Cambreleng, *read* Churchill C. Cambreleng.

EXAMINATION of the pretensions of New England to commercial pre-eminence. [By Matthew Carey.] 8vo. [Sabin's *Dictionary*, iii. 340.]
                              Philadelphia, 1814

EXAMINATION (an) of the Treaty of Paris, 30th March 1856; with some remarks on the proceedings of the Russian government. . . . By Marcus [John Cochrane]. 8vo. [*Lincoln's Inn Lib.*]   London, 1878

*EXAMINATION (the) of Tilenus . . .
Signed : N. N.

*EXAMPLES of the ornamental heraldry. . . .
The Editor's preface is signed in a monogram : W. S. M.

EXCELLENCIE (the) of the mysterie of Christ Jesus. Declared in an exposition or meditation upon the 16. verse of the first epistle of Saint Paul unto Timothie. [By P. M. *i.e.* P. Muffet ?] 8vo. [*Brit. Mus.*]   London, 1590

EXCELLENT (an) and right learned meditacion in two prayers, bewailing the deserued plages of England. [By John Bale, Bishop of Ossory.] 8vo. [*Pollard and Redgrave.*] London, 1554

EXCELLENT memorables for all mourners. . . . Gathered out of Mr B.'s [Richard Baxter's] prepared (though not preached) farewel sermon at Kederminster, Aug. 24, 1662, upon . . . John 16, 22. Fol. S. sh. [*Brit. Mus.*]   London, 1691

EXCEPTIONS against Will. Rogers's Cavills at J. P.'s Complaint, etc., taken out of his sixth part of his Christian-Quaker. [By John Pennington.] 4to. Pp. 14. [*Brit. Mus.*]   London, 1682
Signed : J. P.

*EXCURSION (an) from Paris to Fontainebleau. . . .
The author's name is Sir *Edward* Harrington. John is an error.

EXCURSION (an) through Denmark and Sweden to Norway and North Germany. By L. I. G. P. [Louise I. G. Pyne]. Illustrated by photographs. [Pettersen's *Norsk Lexikon*, col. 113.]
                              Dublin, 1878

EXEMPLA minora; or new English etiquette to be rendered into Latin ; adapted to the rules of the Latin Grammar lately printed at Eton. . . . A new edition revised [by T. M. *i.e.* Thomas Morell]. 12mo. [*Brit. Mus.*]
                              Eton, 1765

EXEMPLA moralia ; or, a second book of new English examples, to be rendered into Latin. . . . [By T. M. *i.e.* Thomas Morell.] 12mo. Pp. 273. [*Brit. Mus.*]   Eton, 1762
A third book was published in 1765.

EXERCISE (the) of a Christian life. Written in Italian by . . . Jaspar Loarte. . . . Corected by the translator (J. Saucer) [Stephen Brinkley]. 8vo. [*Brit. Mus.*]   [N.P. 1679 ?]

EXHORTACION (an) to the carienge of Chrystes crosse, wyth a true and brefe confutacion of false and papisticall doctryne. [By Miles Coverdale.] 16mo. B. L. [*Pollard and Redgrave.*]
                              [London ? 1550 ?]

EXHORTATION (an) to the taking of the Solemne League and Covenant for reformation and defence of religion, and honour and happinesse of the King, and the peace and safety of the three kingdomes of England, Scotland and Ireland. [By Philip Nye.] [*D. N. B.* vol. 41, p. 281.] London, 1643
There was another edition in the following year.

EXPATRIATED (the); a tale of modern Poland. By Leigh Cliffe [George Jones]. 12mo. [*Eng. Cat.*, 1801-1836, p. 121.]   1836

EXPEDIENT (an) to preserve peace and amity among Dissenting brethren. By a Brother in Christ [Stephen Marshall]. [*D. N. B.* vol. 36, p. 247.]
London, 1647

*EXPERIENCED (the) butcher . . .
For J. Plumptree, *read* James Plumptre.

EXPERIENCES (the) of a lady detective. . . . [A novel. By William Stephens Hayward.] 8vo. Pp. 308. [*Brit. Mus.*] London [1884]

*EXPERIMENTALL (an) discouerie of Spanish practises . . .
This book declares itself to be translated by T. S. of V. *i.e.* Thomas Scott of Utrecht, but was really written by him.

EXPIATION. By the author of *Elizabeth and her German garden* [Mary Beauchamp, later Countess von Arnim, then Countess Russell]. 8vo. Pp. 381. [*Brit. Mus.*] London, 1929

EXPLANATION (an) of the fashion and vse of three and fifty instruments of chirurgery, gathered out of Ambrosius Pareus . . . and done into English by H. C. [Helkiah Crooke]. 4to. Pp. 117. [*Brit. Mus.*] London, 1634

EXPLANATION (an) of the state of the case of the Edinburgh representation in Parliament. [By Henry Cockburn, Lord Cockburn.] 8vo. [*Brit. Mus.*]
Edinburgh, 1826

EXPOSITION of the Apostles' Creed. By Bishop [Thomas] Ken; from his Practice of divine love. [The introduction signed I. L. A. *i.e.* John Lavicourt Anderdon.] 8vo. [*Brit. Mus.*]
London, 1852

EXPOSITION (an) of the whole fifth chapter of S. John's Gospel; also notes on other choice places of Scripture, taken by a reverend divine now with God, and found in his study after his death written with his own hand. . . . [By William Gouge.] [*Camb. Univ. Lib.*] London, 1630

EXPOSITION (an) uppon the Booke of the Canticles, otherwise called Schelomons Song. Published . . . by T. W. [Thomas Wilcox]. 8vo. Pp. 285. [*Brit. Mus.*] London, 1585

EXPOSURE (an) of the spy-system pursued in Glasgow during the years 1816-20. . . . The whole edited . . . by a Ten-pounder [Peter Mackenzie]. 8vo. 15 Nos. [*Brit. Mus.*]
Glasgow, 1833

EXQUISITE (the) Perdita. [A novel.] By E. Barrington [L. Adams Beck]. 8vo. Pp. v. 372. [*Who's Who.*]
London, 1926

EXTEMPORE to Walter Scott, Esq., of the publication of the new edition of the Bridal of Triermain. . . . [Signed: S. K. C., *i.e.* Robert Pierce Gillies?] 4to. [*Brit. Mus.*] [Edinburgh, 1829]

EXTRA Turns; or footlight flashes from a music hall matinee as heard in the stalls. By "Cue" [A. Leonard Summers]. 8vo. Pp. 51. [*Brit. Mus.*]
London [1911]

EXTRACT (an) for every day in the year. By B. B. [Sarah Anne Matson]. 16mo. [*Brit. Mus.*] London, 1850
The second edition, 1860, has the author's name.

*EXTRACT from a late ingenious author.
For By J. Law, *read* By William Law, author of *A Serious Call*.

EXTRACT (an) from a treatise on the spirit of prayer; or, the soul rising out of the vanity of time into the riches of eternity. [By Anthony Benezet.] . . . 12mo. [*Brit. Mus.*]
Philadelphia, 1780

*EXTRACT (an) from the case of the electors . . .
Followed by "A letter to the Rev. Dr M." and "A second letter to Dr M." All three were republished in the same year, also anonymously under the title "The election of aliens . . ." *q.v.*

EXTRACT (an) from the Spirit of Prayer [by William Law, author of *A Serious Call*]. 12mo. [*Brit. Mus.*]
Dublin, 1757

*EXTRACT (an) of letters, by Mrs L***
[Mrs Lefevre. Edited by J. W. *i.e.* John Wesley]. Bristol, 1769
Subsequent editions (1773, 1792, 1796 and 1808) were not anonymous.

EXTRACT (an) of the life of M. de Renty. . . . [Abridged from the French of J. B. de Saint Jure] by the Rev. J. Wesley. . . . Ninth edition. 24mo. Pp. 71. [*Brit. Mus.*]
London, 1830

EXTRACTS from a journal of travels in North America. By Ali Bey [S. L. Knapp]. 8vo. Pp. 124. [*Brit. Mus.*]
Boston, 1818

EXTRACTS from Juvenilia, or poems by G. Withers. [Edited with notes by Aretephilos, *i.e.* Alexander Dalrymple.] 12mo. [*Brit. Mus.*] London, 1785

EXTRACTS from the pilgrimage of St Caroline; with notes by an Englishwoman [Jane Alice Sargant. A satire, in verse]. 8vo. Pp. 87. [*Brit. Mus.*]
1821

EXTRACTS from the Register Bill, with notes explanatory. . . . [By Lewis Duval.] 8vo. [*Lincoln's Inn Lib.*]
London, 1831

EXTRACTS on various subjects, religious and secular, selected and original. [By John Bragg.] 8vo. [*Brit. Mus.*]
London, 1862
Preface signed : J. B.

EXTRAVAGANT (the) sheepherd ; a pastoral comedie, written in French by T. Corneille. Englished by T. R. [Thomas Rawlins ?] 1654. 4to. Pp. 62. [*Brit. Mus.*]
London, 1654 [for 1655]

EXTRAVAGANT (the) shepherd. The anti-romance. Or, the history of the shepherd Lysis. Translated [from the French of C. Sorel by J. Davies]. Folio. Pp. 264-96. [*Brit. Mus.*]
London, 1653

EX-WIFE. [A novel. By Katherine Ursula Parrott.] 8vo. Pp. 287. [*Brit. Mus.*]
London, 1929

EYE (the) in the Museum. By J. J. Connington [Alfred Walter Stewart]. 8vo. Pp. 287. [*Amer. Cat.*] London, 1929

F

FABLE (a) for critics. [By James Russell Lowell.] 12mo. [*Brit. Mus.*]
New York, 1848

FABLE (the) of Jotham to the Borough Hunters. [By Richard Owen Cambridge.] [Straus' *Robert Dodsley*.]
1754

FABLES. By G. Washington Æsop [George Thomas Lanigan]. Taken anywhere, anywhere out of the world. 4to. [Foley's *Amer. authors*.]
New York, 1878

FABLES. By Mrs Teachwell [Eleanor, Lady Fenn] ; in which the morals are drawn incidentally in various ways. 12mo. [*Brit. Mus.*]   London [1783]
The author issued also, in the same year, "Fables in monosyllables."

FABLES and morals. By Job Crithannan [Nathan Birch]. 8vo. [*Eng. Cat.*, 1801-1836, p. 144.] London, 1834

*FABLIAUX or tales. . . . By M. Le Grand. . . . With a preface and notes [by G. E. *i.e.* George Ellis]. 4to. Pp. xxxvii. 280. [*Brit. Mus.*] London, 1796

*FACTS and arguments against the election of General Caro . . .
For Caro, *read* Cass.

FACTS and arguments respecting the great utility of an extensive plan of inland navigation in America. By a Friend to National Industry [Turner Carnac]. [*Brit. Mus.*]
Philadelphia, 1805

FACTS and fancies. [By Douglas William Jerrold.] 8vo. Pp. 335. [*Brit. Mus.*]   London, 1826

FADED leaves. T. G. A. [Thomas Gold Appleton]. 4to. [Foley's *Amer. authors*.]   Boston, 1872

FAIR (the) parricide ; a tragedy founded on a late melancholy event. [By Edward Crane of Manchester.] 8vo.
London, 1752
Founded on the murder committed by Mary Blandy at Henley on Thames.

FAIR (the) Quakers ; a poem. [By John Bingley.] Fol. Pp. 12. [*Brit. Mus.*]
London, 1713

*FAIRIES (the). . . .
This was repudiated by Garrick. [*Library of Congress, Cat. of Opera Librettos.*]

FAITH and conduct ; an essay on verifiable religion. [By Percy Gardiner.] 8vo. Pp. xiv. 387. [*Brit. Mus.*]
London, 1887

FAITH and practice ; or, the necessity of a frequent and worthy reception of the blessed sacrament of the Lord's supper : a sacred poem. [By William Howard.] 4to.   London, 1718
Presentation copy, signed by the author.

FAITH triumphant, exemplified in the death of Mrs T. [*i.e.* Trotter. Signed : J. T. *i.e.* J. Trotter]. 12mo. [*Brit. Mus.*]
London, 1771

FAITHFUL Bessie. By the author of *Dick and his donkey* [Mrs C. E. Bowen]. 8vo. Pp. 32. [*Brit. Mus.*]   [1867]

FAITHFUL memoirs of the life, amours and performances of that justly celebrated . . . actress . . . Mrs Anne Oldfield, interspersed with several other dramatic memoirs. By William Egerton, Esq. [Edmund Curll]. 8vo. Pp. 212. [R. Straus' *The Unspeakable Curll*, p. 291.]   London, 1731

FAITHFUL (the) servant ; or, the history of Elizabeth Allen. [By Mrs Amelia Bristow.] . . . Second edition. 12mo. Pp. xii. 216. [*Brit. Mus.*]
London, 1824

FAITHFUL (a) servant ; the journal of what took place in the . . . Temple during the captivity of Louis XVI. . . . By J. B. Cléry. . . . Translated from the French [by James F. Cobb]. 16mo. Pp. 127. [*Brit. Mus.*] London [1874]

FALCONHURST [in Kent. Signed : G. J. T. *i.e.* George John Talbot]. 8vo. Pp. 51. [*Brit. Mus.*]
London, private print, 1922

*FALL (the) and redemption of man . . .
By E. S. A.
    The *Brit. Mus.* now attributes this to
Miss Letitia Willgoss Stone.

FALL (the) of the clay-pit; a true
narrative.   By the author of *The
Lamplighter* [Francis Bourdillon].
12mo. [*Brit. Mus.*]   London [1861]
    Signed: F. B.

FALSE dawn. By Al Carthill [Sir John
Perronet Thompson]. 8vo. Pp. vi.
224. [*Brit. Mus.*]   Edinburgh, 1926

FALSEHOOD (the) of Mr William
Pryn's Truth triumphing, in the antiquity of Popish Princes and Parliaments; to which he attributes a sole
sovereigne legislative, coercive power
in all matters of religion. . . . [By
Henry Robinson.] [*D. N. B.* vol. 49,
p. 15.]   London, 1645

FAMILIAR epistles between W— H—
[William Hamilton, of Gilbertfield]
and A— R— [Allan Ramsay]. 8vo.
Pp. 24. [A. Gibson's *Allan Ramsay*,
p. 126.]   Edinburgh [1719]

FAMILY (the) compact. [By Rev. John
Rose, rector of St Martin's Outwich,
London.] 8vo. [*N. and Q.* 9th Aug.
1824, p. 107.]   London, 1792

*FAMILY (a) tour through South
Holland . . .
    Ascribed in the *Brit. Mus.* to Robert Batty.

FAMOSUS defamator; the infamous
libeller . . . arraign'd and condemned.
. . . By Octavius Terminalis [John
Brydall] in a letter to Marcus Aemilius.
4to. [*Lincoln's Inn Lib.*]
                        London, 1706

FAMOUS (the) and delightful history
of the renowned and valiant Prince
Amadis of Gaul. . . . The whole now
abridged by J. S. Gent. [John Shirley,
author of *The triumph of wit*]. . . .
12mo. Pp. 187. [*Brit. Mus.*]
                        London, 1702

FANNY. [A poem. By Fitz-Greene
Halleck.] 8vo.   New York, 1821
    The first edition (1819) is not anonymous.

FAREWELL to Virianne [John Williams,
missionary; verses by J. C. *i.e.* John
Campbell, D.D., and others]. 12mo.
Pp. 8. [*Brit. Mus.*]   N.P. 1838

FARMER Ellicot; or, begin and end
with God. By the author of *Dick and
his donkey* [Mrs C. E. Bowen]. 8vo.
Pp. 32. [*Brit. Mus.*]   [1867]

FARMER (the) of Chappaqua. By a
Greeleyite [Thaddeus Hyatt. Verses].
4to. [*Brit. Mus.*]   London [1872]

FARMER'S (a) life. With a memoir of
the farmer's sister. By George Bourne
. . . [George Sturt]. 8vo. Pp. 208.
[*Brit. Mus.*]   London, 1922

*FARRAGO : containing essays . . .
    The author is not known. Lowndes' note
is incorrect. The work which has Richard
Barton's name in an acrostic to the reader
is the next entry, "Farrago . . . 1739."

FARTHER (a) defence, etc., being an
answer to a reply [by N. Spinckes]
to the Vindication of the Reasons and
defence for restoring some prayers and
directions in King Edward VI.'s first
Liturgy. By the author of the *Reasons*
[Jeremy Collier]. 8vo. [Darling's
Cyclop. Bibl.]   London, 1720

FASCICULUS florum; or a nosegay of
flowers, translated out of the gardens
of severall poets, and other authors.
. . . By Lerimos Uthalmus [Thomas
Willmer ?]. 12mo. [*Pollard and Redgrave.*]   London, 1636

FASCICULUS myrrhæ; or, a briefe
treatise of Our Lord and Saviour's
passion. Written by the R. Fa. I. F.
of the Society of Jesus [John Falconer].
12mo. Pp. 130. [*Brit. Mus.*]
                        [St Omer] 1633

FASHION in language. By I. S. L.
[I. S. Lidbury]. 8vo. Pp. 64. [*Brit.
Mus.*]   London, private print, 1906

FAST workers; a comedy farce in three
acts. By Roland Oliver [Henry White].
8vo. Pp. 85. [B. Mantle's *American
Playwrights of To-day*, p. 302.]
                        London [1927]

FASTI Ecclesiæ Scotianæ. New edition.
Volume III. A critical examination.
[A review of the work by Hew Scott.
By John Warwick]. Reprinted from
the *Kilmarnock Standard.* 8vo. Pp. 7.
[*Brit. Mus.*]   1921
    Signed : A.

FATAL (the) vesper; or, a true . . .
relation of that accident, hapning on
Sunday . . . the 26 of October last,
by the fall of a roome in the Black
Friars. . . . [By William Crashaw ?]
4to. [*Brit. Mus.*]   London, 1623
    Signed : W. C.

FATALITY ; a drama. . . . By Caroline
Boaden . . . with remarks . . . by
D— G. [George Daniel]. 12mo. Pp.
28. [*Brit. Mus.*]   London [1830]

FATHER Christmas; our little ones'
budget. Edited by N. D'Anvers [Nancy
Bell, *née* Meugens]. 4to. [*Brit. Mus.*]
                        London, 1877

FATHER Jones of Cardiff; a memoir of
the Rev. Griffith Arthur Jones, for over
thirty years Vicar of S. Mary's, Cardiff.
By two former curates J. W. W. and
H. A. C. [John Woollaston Ward and
Hector Albert Coe]. . . . 8vo. Pp.
xi. 122. [*Brit. Mus.*] London [1908]

FATHER (the) ; or, American Shandy-
ism. Written by a citizen of New
York [William Dunlap] ; a comedy in
five acts. 8vo. [Foley's *Amer.
authors*.]   New York, 1789

FATHER Paul. [A tale.] By James
Cassidy [Mrs E. M. Story]. 8vo.
Pp. viii. 326. [*Brit. Mus.*]
London, 1908

FATHER Tyrrell's modernism : an
expository criticism of " Through Scylla
and Charybdis " in an open letter to
Mr Athelstan Riley. By Hakluyt
Egerton [Arthur Boutwood]. 8vo.
Pp. viii. 216. [*Brit. Mus.*]
London, 1909

FATHERS (the) counsell ; or . . . useful
directions for all young persons . . .
left in a fatherlesse . . . condition. By
W. T. [William Typing ?]. 12mo.
[*Brit. Mus.*]   London, 1644

FATHER'S (the) hope ; or, the wanderer
returned. By the author of *Going
Abroad* [Nona Bellairs]. 12mo. Pp.
35. [*Brit. Mus.*]   London, 1857

FATHER'S (a) legacie ; with precepts
and prayers. [By John Norden.]
8vo. [*Pollard and Redgrave.*]
London, 1625

FAUST ; a poem. [By Arthur M.
Forrester.] [Hodgson's *Cat.* 28th Jan.
1927.]   1834

FAYTHFULL (a) admonycion of a
certen trewe pastor and prophete, sent
vnto the germanes. . . . Translated
in to Inglyssh [from Luther's " Warn-
ung an seine liebe Deutschen "]. 8vo.
B. L. [*Brit. Mus.*]
Grenewych [printed abroad], 1554

FEAST (the) of sacrifice, and the feast
of remembrance. . . .   [By Emily
Steele Elliott.] 16mo. Pp. viii. 240.
[*Brit. Mus.*]   London, 1864

FEED my lambs . . . a selection of the
simplest texts . . . explained . . . by
a mother [Mrs Charles Jones]. 16mo.
[*Brit. Mus.*]   1852
Signed : C. J.

FELICIA to Charlotte ; being letters
from a young lady in the country to
her friend in town, containing a series
of the most interesting events, interspersed with moral reflections, chiefly
tending to prove that the seeds of
virtue are implanted in the mind of
every reasonable being. [By Mary
Collyer.] 12mo. Pp. 312. [*Bibl.
Lind.*]   London, 1749

FELICITY ; a novel. By Katherine
Harrington [Mrs Rolf Bennett]. 8vo.
Pp. 284. [*Brit. Mus.*]   London, 1919

FEMALE (the) husband ; or, the surpris-
ing history of Mrs Mary *alias* Mrs
George Hamilton, who was convicted
of having married a young woman of
Wells and lived with her as her husband.
. . . [By Henry Fielding ?]   8vo.
Pp. 23. [*Brit. Mus.*]   1746

FEMALE (the) phaeton. [By Matthew
Prior or the Hon. Simon Harcourt.]
Fol. [R. Straus' *The Unspeakable
Curll*, p. 255.]   London, 1719

FEMALE (the) ; or, modern fine lady :
a ballad opera. . . . [By Joseph
Dorman ?] 8vo. Pp. 51. [*Library of
Congress, Cat. of Opera Librettos.*]
London, 1736

FERDINAND ; or, the triumphs of filial
love. By Father Charles [John Andrew
Houban]. 12mo. Pp. v. 208. [*Brit.
Mus.*]   Dublin, 1860

FESTIVAL (the) of St Iago ; a Spanish
romance. [By Mrs S. Green.] 8vo.
[*Brit. Mus.*]   London, 1810

FEW (a) fragments of fairyology, shewing
its connection with natural history.
[By Michael Aislabie Denham.] 8vo.
[*Brit. Mus.*]
Civ. Dunelm. [Durham] 1859
Signed : M. A. D.

FEW (a) ideas ; being hints to all
would-be Meltonians. [Six humorous
coloured plates. By Henry Aiken.]
London, 1825
See Schwerdt's edition of Alken's " Pano-
rama of the progress of Human Life "
(1930), p. 5.

FEW (a) odds and ends for cheerful
friends ; a Christmas gift [in verse.
By J. P. C. *i.e.* John Payne Collier].
4to.   [London] private print, 1870

FEW (a) original ideas of a Manchester
man [Richard Burn ?] respecting our
bad trade and government interference.
8vo. Pp. 32. [*Brit. Mus.*]
Manchester [1876]

*FEW (a) plain reasons why a Protes-
tant . . .
Author's postscript signed : N. N.

FEW (a) popular rhymes, proverbs, and
sayings, relating to fairies, witches
and gypsies. [By Michael Aislabie
Denham.] [*Brit. Mus.*]
Civ. Dunelm. [Durham] 1852
Signed : M. A. D.

FEW (a) self-contradictions of the Bible.
[By William Henry Burr.] . . . 8vo.
Pp. xxi. 43. [*Brit. Mus.*]
London [1866]
The title of an edition of 1860 reads " Self
contradictions of the Bible."

FEW (a) thoughts. By a member of
the bar [Phineas Bacon Wilcox]. 8vo.
[Allibone's *Dict.*]   Columbus, O., 1836

FEW (a) words in answer to two plausible scruples as to receiving the Sacrament of the Lord's Supper. [By Richard Pearson.] 12mo. Pp. 4. [*Brit. Mus.*]   Lowestoft [1835]
    Signed : R. P.

FEW (a) words in reply to the remarks of a Welsh clergyman on What says the Church? By a Welsh Rector [Evan Lloyd of Llangelynin]. 8vo. Pp. 16. [*Brit. Mus.*]   Bangor, 1842

FEW (a) words of advice and consolation to the worshippers of St Lawrence's, who . . . lament the removal of their . . . pastor [W. B. Cadogan]. In three letters [signed J. N. *i.e.* John Newton?] to Christiana. 8vo. [*Brit. Mus.*]
               Reading, 1812

FEW (a) words of counsel and advice to all the sons and daughters of men. [Signed : A. T. *i.e.* Anthony Tompkins]. A short testimony . . . unto all young men. [Signed : R. N. *i.e.* Richard Needham.] 4to. Pp. 6. [*Brit. Mus.*]
               London, 1687

FEW (a) words on reform addressed to John Handy-workman, by J. Brainworkman [Joshua Williams]. 8vo. [*Lincoln's Inn Lib.*]   London, 1867

FEW (a) words to the mothers of little children. By the author of *A few words to Schoolmistresses* [Louisa M. Hubbard]. 16mo. Pp. 32. [*Brit. Mus.*]   London, 1880
    Signed : L. M. H.

FIDDLER Matt. By Adam Lilburn [Lillias Wasserman]. With illustrations by A. March. 8vo. Pp. viii. 192. [*Brit. Mus.*]   London, 1908
    Title-page of her " Road of Life."

FIERY (a) flying roll ; being the last warning piece at the dreadfull Day of Judgement. [By Abiezer Coppe.] 4to. [Thomason's *Coll. of Tracts*, i. 782.]
               London, 1650
    This was followed by "A second fiery flying roule." Parliament ordered that all copies should be seized and burned.

FIFTY New Testament Scripture reasons why one should hesitate to believe in a co-equal and co-eternal Trinity. . . . By a Unitarian [John William Brown]. 8vo. Pp. 14. [*Brit. Mus.*]
               London, 1888

FIFTY-ONE substantial reasons against any modification whatever of the existing tariff : whereby the consistency and propriety of the opposition of the cotton planters, the tobacco planters, and the merchants to the "Infernal Bill" are fully justified. By a Pennsylvanian [Matthew Carey]. 8vo. Pp. 12. [Sabin's *Dictionary*, iii. 340.]
               Philadelphia, 1824

FIGHT (a) at sea famously fought by the Dolphin of London, against five of the Turkes men of warre and a satty the 12 of January last 1616. [By John Taylor, the water poet.] 4to.
               London, 1617
    This is included in an edition of Taylor's collected works, supervised by himself.

FIJI ; records of private and public life, 1875-1880. [Introduction signed : S. *i.e.* Arthur, Baron Stanmore.] 8vo. 4 vols. [*Brit. Mus.*]
    Edinburgh, private print, 1897-1912

FILLI di Sciro ; or, Phillis of Scyros : an excellent pastorall. Written in Italian by C. Guidubaldo de' Bonarelli. Translated into English by J. S. [Jonathan Sidnam]. 4to. Pp. 114. [*Brit. Mus.*]   London, 1655

FINAL (the) count. [A novel.] By Sapper [Herman Cyril MacNeill]. 8vo. Pp. 319. [*Brit. Mus.*]
               London, 1926

FINAL message preparatory to Christ's coming. By Recorder [J. Warren Owen]. 8vo. [*Brit. Mus.*]
               Birmingham [1925]

FINAL (the) sentence. [A novel.] By Michael Maurice [Conrad Arthur Skinner]. 8vo. Pp. 280. [*Brit. Mus.*]
               London, 1926

FINGER (the) of fate. [A novel.] By Sapper [Herman Cyril MacNeile]. 8vo. Pp. 320. [*Brit. Mus.*]
               London [1930]

FIRE from Heaven. Burning the body of one Iohn Hittchell. . . . Written by Iohn Hilliard. . . . With the fearefull burning of the towne of Dorchester vpon friday the 6. of August last 1613 [by John White of Dorchester, the Elder]. 8vo. [F. Rose-Troup's *John White*, p. 446.]   London, 1613

FIRE of the altar. [Verse. By R. M. Marchant ?] 8vo. Pp. 24. [*Brit. Mus.*]   London [1894]
    Signed : W.

FIREFLY ; a novel. By Diana Patrick [Mrs Desemea Newman Wilson]. 8vo. Pp. 322. [*Publishers' Weekly*, 9th Jan. 1926.]   New York, 1926

*FIRESIDE and camp stories.
    For Allcott, read Alcott.

FIRESIDE magic. 100 fascinating conjuring tricks. . . . By Carol Luck [Charles Platt]. 8vo. Pp. 120. [*Brit. Mus.*]   London [1930]

FIRESIDE poems. By "Pansy" [Ida M. Loder Donisthorpe]. 8vo. Pp. 31. [*Brit. Mus.*]   N.P. [1929]
    From a copy inscribed by the author.

FIRST (the) anniversarie ; an anatomie of the world. (The second anniversarie ; of the progres of the soule.) [By John Donne.] 8vo. [*Pollard and Redgrave.*] London, 1612

For an earlier edition, see "An anatomy of the world . . ."

FIRST (the) book of Amadis of Gaule ; discoursing the adventures and love of many knightes and ladies, as well of the realme of Great Brittayne, as sundry other countries, etc. [Translated from the French by Anthony Munday.] 4to. B. L. Ff. 201. [*Pollard and Redgrave.*]

[London, 1590 ?]

The second book was also translated by Munday under the *pseud.* of Lazarus Pyott. See above, "The second book . . ."

FIRST (the) book of Euclid's Elements with alterations and familiar notes. . . . [By Thomas Perronet Thompson.] 8vo. [*Brit. Mus.*] London, 1830

The first edition of "Geometry without axioms . . ."

FIRST (the) of April : a farce. . . . By Caroline Boaden . . . with remarks . . . by D— G. [George Daniel]. 12mo. Pp. 36. [*Brit. Mus.*] London [1829]

FIRST (the) parte of [Thomas] Churchyardes chippes. . . . [Edited by J. P. C. *i.e.* John Payne Collier.] 4to. [*Brit. Mus.*] London [*c.* 1870]

FIRST (the) rung ; an attempt to deal with the poverty problem. [By Alfred Richard Millbourn.] 8vo. [*Lincoln's Inn Lib.*] London, 1906

FIRST the blade ; a comedy of growth. By Clemence Dane [Winifred Ashton]. 8vo. Pp. 288. [*Brit. Mus.*]

London, 1919

FIRST thoughts on the soul ; for the poor. [By John Fitzgerald, the younger.] 12mo. 2 parts. [*Brit. Mus.*] London, 1830-1

FIRST (the) years of Christianity, and What is the Church? By C. S. [Charles Stanley, Sheffield]. 8vo. Pp. 143. [*Brit. Mus.*] London [1893]

FIRSTE (the) thre bokes of the most christiã Poet Marcellus Palingenius [Pietro Angelo Manzolli] called the Zodyake of lyfe ; newly translated out of latin into English by Barnabe Googe. 8vo. B. L. [*Brit. Mus.*]

London, 1560

In the next year "The firste syxe bokes . . ." were issued. For the complete translation (1565) see "The Zodiake of life . . ."

FISHING ; a translation from the Latin of Naniere. . . . With a brief introduction and . . . notes [by J. H. *i.e.* Joseph Haslewood]. 8vo. [*Brit. Mus.*] London, 1809

FISHKE the lame. By Mendele Mocher Seforim [Shalom Yakov Abramovich]. Freely translated from the Yiddish . . . by Dr Angelo S. Rappoport. 8vo. Pp.224. [*Brit.Mus.*] London [1929]

FIT to govern ! [Short biographies of members of the first labour government in Great Britain. With portraits.] By "Iconoclast" [Mary Agnes Hamilton]. 8vo. Pp. 80. [*Brit. Mus.*] London, 1924

FIVE (the) books of Marcus Manilius . . . done into English verse, with notes [by T. C. *i.e.* Thomas Creech]. 8vo. [*Brit. Mus.*] London, 1697

FIVE counter-theories to the Ridsdale judgment. . . . [By John Tomlinson.] 8vo. Pp. 47. [*Brit. Mus.*] 1877

FIVE godlie sermons. Preached by R. T. [Ralph Tryer ?] Bachiler of diuinitie. 8vo. Pp. 309. [*Brit. Mus.*] London, 1602

FIVE hundred French and English everyday idioms and idiomatical sentences. Compiled . . . by M. W. W. [*i.e.* M. W. Wedderburn]. 8vo. Pp. 16. [*Brit. Mus.*] London, 1892

FIVE minutes' advice on drinking the waters of Leamington. [By J. Beck ?] 12mo. Pp. 16. [*Brit. Mus.*]

Leamington [1850 ?]

*FIVE (the) orders of the Church . . .

For Bromby, *read* Bromley.

FIVE years of Irish freedom. By Pat [Patrick D. Kenny]. 8vo. Pp. 61.

London [1927]

FIVE years' penal servitude. By one who has endured it [William Hamilton Thomson, Sheriff-substitute of Inverness-shire.] 8vo. 1877

From a copy with a note in MS. by Lord Rutherford—"Lord Fraser assured me that this book was written by . . . William Hamilton Thomson, Sheriff-Substitute of Inverness-shire, who was in 1871 convicted in the High Court of Justiciary."

FIVE-AND-THREEPENNY-PIECE (a) ; or, a dialogue between a Methodist preacher and one of his hearers. [Verse. By John Cooke, Dissenting minister in Rochdale.] 8vo. [*Brit. Mus.*]

Southwold, 1812

FLEET (the) Annual and Naval Year Book. . . . Compiled by Lionel Yexley [James Woode]. 8vo. [*Brit. Mus.*] London, 1905

FLEUR de lys ; the story of a crime. By J. G. Sarasin [Geraldine Gordon Salmon]. 8vo. Pp. 288. [*Amer. Cat.*] London [1929]

FLIGHT (the) in vain ; showing where true safety lies. By the author of *The lamplighter* [Francis Bourdillon]. 12mo. [*Brit. Mus.*] London [1864]

Signed : F. B.

FLIGHT (the) of religious piety from Scotland upon the account of [Allan] Ramsay's lewd books. [By Alexander Pennecuik?] ... 12mo. [*Brit. Mus.*] [Edinburgh? 1736?]

FLIGHT (a) to a finish. By Valentine [Arthur Valentine Peachey]. 8vo. Pp. 256. [*Brit. Mus.*] London, 1929

FLOCK (the) at the fountain. [By Sarah Flower Adams.] 12mo. Pp. 36. [*Brit. Mus.*] London, 1845

FLORILEGIUM poeticum. [By George Whittaker.] 18mo. [*Eng. Cat.*, 1801-1836, p. 209.] London, 1814

FLOWER-GARDEN (the); shewing how all flowers are to be ordered, the time of flowering. ... By W. H. [William Hughes]. 12mo. [*Brit. Mus.*] London, 1671

FLOWERS from foreign fields. By Father Charles [John Andrew Houban]. 16mo. 6 parts. [*Brit.Mus.*] Dublin, 1857

FLYING (the) courtship; a novel. By E. J. Rath [J. Chauncey Corey Brainerd and Edith Rathbone Brainerd]. 8vo. Pp. 311. [*Brit. Mus.*] London, 1929

FŒROÆ et Fœroa Reserata, that is a description of the Islands and inhabitants of Fœroe ... written in Danish by Lucas Debes: Englished by J. S. [John Sterpin]. 8vo. Pp. 406. [*Brit. Mus.*] London, 1676

FOLIA caduca; verses to three grandchildren (1880-1893). By J. P. M. [James P. Muirhead]. 8vo. Pp. 44. [*Brit. Mus.*] [1895?]

*FOLIOUS appearances ...
The author's name is given in the *Brit. Mus.* as John Tapling.

FOLK song and dance. [By A. H. Fox-Strangways.] ... 8vo. Pp. 20. [*Brit. Mus.*] London [1925]

FOLLOWING (the) speech being spoke off hand upon the debates in the House of Commons, you cannot expect in it the exactness of Roman eloquence. ... [By Sir John Knight.] [*McAlpin Coll. Cat.*] 1694
No title-page.

FOOD for the desert; being choice selections from J. N. D. [John Nelson Darby] ... and others. 8vo. Pp. 112. [*Brit. Mus.*] London, 1877

FOOL'S (the) paradise, and other poems. By Ethna Kavanagh [Sara Spain]. 8vo. Pp. 16. [*Innisfail, a quarterly magazine,* No. 1.]

FOOTMAN'S (the) friendly advice to his brethren of the livery. ... Also a postscript in answer to Squire Moreton's pamphlet, intituled, Every body's business is no body's. [By Robert Dodsley.] 8vo. [*Brit. Mus.*] London [*c.* 1725]
Signed: R. D.

*FOOTPRINTS (the) of Abbé. ...
For Abbé, *read* Albe.
For Brennar, *read* Brennan.

FOR a blank page. "Never a palinode." Q. [Austin Dobson]. 8vo. Pp. 4. [Shay's *Bibl. of Dobson.*] Private print, 1913

*FOR another's fault ...
For Wilhelm Heimburg [Martha Behrens], *read* W. Heimburg [Bertha Behrens].

FOR asmoche as late ... I translated aboke out of frensshe into Englissh named Recuyel of the histories of Troye ... therefor I intend to translate the ... boke of thistories of Jason, etc. [Translated from the French of Raoul Le Fèvre by William Caxton.] Fol. B. L. [*Brit. Mus.*] [Westminster, 1477?]

FOR Christ and the world; a new missionary song service. [By J. J. Kilpin Fletcher.] 8vo. Pp. 9. [*Brit. Mus.*] Jamaica, 1913

FOR her namesake; an anthology. ... Edited by Stephen Langton [Daniel S. O'Connor]. 8vo. Pp. viii. 346. [*Brit. Mus.*] London, 1911
An enlarged edition, 1926, has the title "By what sweet name?"

*FOR His name's sake ...
For R. Anderson, *read* Sir Robert Anderson.

FOR Maurice; five unlikely stories. By Vernon Lee [Violet Paget]. 8vo. Pp. li. 223. [*Brit. Mus.*] London, 1927

FOR me alone. By André Corthis [Mme. Andrée Lécuyes, née Husson]. Translated by Frederick Taber Cooper. 8vo. Pp. 267. [*Amer. Cat.*] London, 1921

FOR prevention of the unpardonable sin against the Holy-Ghost; a demonstration that the spirit and works of Christ were the finger of God. [By Richard Baxter.] [Grosart's *Baxter*, No. 12, p. 16.] London, 1655

FOR sons of gentlemen. By Kerr Shaw [Ronald Gurner]. 8vo. Pp. vii. 245. [*New Statesman*, 23rd Jan. 1932.] London, 1926

FOR the King and Parliament and his Council and Teachers, and to every individual person ... that have a hand against the innocent people called Quakers; one visitation and warning more from the Lord to you. [By William Bayly.] [Smith's *Cat. of Friends' Books*, i. 218.] 1664
Signed at end: W. B.

FORBIDDEN fruit. Edited by Vrill [F. A. Perroux]. 8vo. [*Brit. Mus.*] Calcutta, 1896, etc.

FORECAST (a) of the Sun's eclipse, on 22nd April 1715. By a gentleman in Kelso—On this great eclipse. A poem. By A. R. [Allan Ramsay]. [A. Gibson's *Allan Ramsay*, p. 101.]
Edinburgh, 1715

FOREFRONT (the). [A novel.] By Andrew Loring [Lorin Andrew Lothrop]. 8vo. Pp. 329. [*Brit. Mus.*]
London, 1908

*FOREIGNER (the): a tale . . .
For Charles W. Connor, *read* Charles W. Gordon.

FOREST of Montalbano. A novel. By the author of *Santo Sebastiano* [Catherine Cuthbertson]. 12mo. 4 vols. [*N. and Q.*, June 1911, p. 475.]
London, 1810

FOREST (the) runner. [A novel.] By S. Carleton [Susan Carleton Jones]. 8vo. Pp. 268. [*Brit. Mus.*]
London, 1925

FORETOLD and fulfilled: the Church of Rome a sign of the end. An examination of the Bible prophecy concerning Rome, and the approaching end of this age. [By] "Discipulus" [Basil Stewart]. 8vo. Pp. 94. [*Brit. Mus.*]
London, 1926

FORGED in strong fires. [A novel.] By John Ironside [E. M. Tait]. 8vo. Pp. 318. [*Brit. Mus.*]   London, 1912

FORGOTTEN Seigneurs of the Alençonnais, by . . . F. Le Grix W[hite]. 8vo. Pp. ix. 146. [*Brit. Mus.*]   Penrith, private print [1880?]

FORLORNE (the) traveller, whose first beginning was pleasure and joy. . . . [A ballad, by Richard Climsell?] Fol. S. sh. B. L. [*Brit. Mus.*]
London [*c.* 1635]
Signed: R. C.

FORMOSA; the life of a beautiful woman. . . . [A novel. By William Stephens Hayward.] 8vo. Pp. viii. 310. [*Brit. Mus.*]   London [1884]

FORSAKEN (the); a tale. By the author of *Caius Marius*, etc. [Richard Penn Smith]. 12mo. 2 vols. [Foley's *Amer. authors.*]   Philadelphia, 1831

FORTRESS (the), an historical tale of the Fifteenth Century, from Records of the Channel Islands, etc. [By Amelia W——.] 12mo. 3 vols.
London, 1840
At the end of vol. ii. there is a poem reprinted from the Belle Assemblée, in which it was signed: Amelia W——.

FORT-ROYAL (the) of Holy Scriptures; or, a new concordance . . . The second edition. Revised and enlarged by J. H. [John Hart]. . . . 12mo. Pp. 415. [*Brit. Mus.*]   London, 1652

FORTUNATE (the) lovers; an opera. [By J. Howell, of Edinburgh, known as the Polyphonist.] 8vo. [R. Inglis' *Dramatic Writers of Scotland*, p. 145.]
Edinburgh, 1809

FORTUNE'S football. [An autobiography for children. By Isaac Jenner.] 12mo. Pp. 120. [*Brit. Mus.*]
London, 1806

FORTUNES (the) of Nigel; or, George Heriot: a historical drama, founded on the celebrated novel of the former title, by the author of *Waverley* . . . performed at the Theatre-Royal, Edinburgh. [By Daniel Terry.] 12mo. Pp. 70. [*Brit. Mus.*]
[Edinburgh, 1823]

FORTUNIO. [A fairy tale. Translated and abridged from the French of Marie Catherine La Mothe, Comtesse d'Aulnoy.] Illustrated by J. W. 4to. [*Brit. Mus.*]   Edinburgh, 1847

FORTY select poems on several occasions. By the Right Honourable the Earl of . . . [Thomas Hamilton, 7th Earl of Haddington]. 12mo. Pp. 210. [*D. N. B.* vol. 24, p. 212.]
N.P. 1767

*FORTY years ago . . .
Signed: F. B. The author is Francis Bourdillon. [*Brit. Mus.*]

FOUNDLING (the). By the author of *Hymns and scenes of childhood* [Jane Euphemia Leeson]. 32mo. [Julian's *Dict.*]   1850
Signed: J. E. L.

*FOUR (the) ages of life . . .
For Wetherelt, *read* Wetherell.

FOUR fantastic little stories, a tiny fairy play and some odds and ends. By O. M. S. [Olga M. Somech]. . . . 8vo. Pp. 18. [*Brit. Mus.*]
Southport [1914]

FOUR grande enquiries. I. Whether this whole nation be a Church. . . . II. Whether by priviledge of infant baptism, all are to be admitted to all Church-Communions. . . . III. Whether there can be any suspension from or excommunication out of their Church. . . . IV. Whether infants borne of parents notorious for their ignorance and prophaneness . . . may be admitted to baptism. . . . [By Hezekiah Woodward.] [*M'Alpin Coll. Cat.*]
London, 1656
See the note at the end of his "Law-Power," 1656.

FOUR small copies of verses upon sundry occasions. [By Richard Peers?] 4to. Pp. 18. [*Brit. Mus.*]
Oxford, 1667

FOURE letters and certaine sonnets. . . . [By Gabriel Harvey. The introduction signed : J. P. C. *i.e.* John Payne Collier.] 4to. Pp. 81. [*Brit. Mus.*] [London, 1870]

FOURE sermons of Iohn Calvin, upon the Song that King Ezechias made after hee had been sicke . . . . Translated out of Frenche into English [by A. L. *i.e.* A. Lock ?]. 8vo. [*Brit. Mus.*] London, 1574

FOURFOLD (the) sacrament. [Poems.] By the author of *A book of prayers written for use in an Indian college* [John Somervell Hoyland]. 8vo. Pp. 124. [*Brit. Mus.*] Cambridge, 1924
Preface signed : J. S. H.

FOURTH (the) book of Artemas [Arthur Telford Mason]. 8vo. [*Brit. Mus.*] London [1926]

FOURTH (the) centenary of Martin Luther. Luther, an auto-biographical sketch. . . . [By Samuel Lloyd.] 16mo. Pp. 47. [*Brit. Mus.*] Birmingham [1883]
Preface signed : S. L.

FOURTH essay on free trade and finance humbly offered to the consideration of the public. By a citizen of Philadelphia [Pelatiah Webster]. 8vo. Philadelphia, 1780
There were seven in all, 1779-85.

FOURTH (a) letter from a friend to the Right Honourable. See "A second (-fourth) letter . . . "

FOURTH (the) paper, presented by Maior Butler, to the Honourable Committee of Parliament, for the propagation of the Gospel. . . . By R. W. [Roger Williams]. [Whitley's *Bapt. Bibl.* ii. 652.] London, 1652

*FOXES and firebrands . . .
There were two distinct editions of this in 1681, both called second edition. In 1682 there was an edition called "The second edition : in two parts." Part 2 was by Robert Ware and the whole was re-edited by him : his preface to part 1 was signed W. R. and to part 2 R. W. For this second part, see "The second part of Foxes and firebrands . . ." In 1689 Robert Ware published a third part "Foxes and firebrands . . . (The third part)," and in this he adopted the *pseud.* Philirenes used in part 1 by John Nalson who had died in 1686.

FRAGMENT of a poem occasioned by a visit to the old mansion of Denton. [By Sir Samuel Egerton Brydges.] 8vo. [*Brit. Mus.*] Lee Priory, 1814
Signed : S. E. B.

*FRAGMENT (a) of an ancient prophecy . . .
For F. Spence, *read* Thomas Spence, bookseller.

FRAGMENTS from the Mediterranean Budget. [Verse. By James Kennedy.] 12mo. [*Brit. Mus.*] N.P. [1800?]

FRAGMENTS on ethical subjects, by the late George Grote. [Edited by A. B. *i.e.* Alexander Bain.] 8vo. [*Brit. Mus.*] London, 1876

FRANC (le) discours. A discourse presented of late to the French King. [From the French of Antoine Arnauld.] 8vo. [*Pollard and Redgrave.*] [London ?] 1602

FRANCE, after the revolution of Bonaparte, on the eighth of November 1799. Hastily translated from a French pamphlet [by J. F. Michaud] intituled "Les adieux à Bonaparte." 8vo. [*Brit. Mus.*] London, 1800

FRANCE the Empire of civilization. [By Edward Peacock.] 8vo. Pp. 48. [*Brit. Mus.*] London, 1873

*FREE (a) and impartial inquiry into the causes of that very great esteem . . .
The *D.N.B.* queries the attribution to John Eachard.

*FREE (a) enquiry into the authenticity . . .
Signed : C. B. M.

FREE Grace exalted, and thence deduced ; evangelical rules for evangelical sufferings : in two discourses made 29. March and 10. May, 1670. [By Henry Stubbe.] [*M'Alpin Coll. Cat.*] Oxford, 1670
Contemporary MS. attribution, and "taken from his mouth by the ready pen of Mr Sam. Crispe."

*FREE (a) translation of the preface . . .
For Beloc, *read* Beloe.

FREEDOM (the) of the seas. [By Darrell Figgis.] 12mo. [Holling's *Cat.*, June 1927.] [1918]

FREE-HOLDERS (the) grand inquest touching our soveraigne Lord the King and his Parliament. 4to. Pp. 64. [By Sir Robert Filmer.] [*D.N.B.* vol. 18, p. 441 ; *Brit. Mus.*] [1647 ?]
Also attributed to Sir Robert Holborne. It was republished in 1679 under Filmer's name.

FRENCH exercises, selected chiefly from Wanostrocht. . . . By the Instructer [Henry Wadsworth Longfellow]. 12mo. [Livingston's *Bibl. of Longfellow.*] Brunswick, 1830

*FRENCH (the) gardiner . . .
Translator's dedication signed : J. E.

FRENCH (the) kinges declaration and confirmation of the proclamation of Nantes. . . . Faythfully translated . . . by J. B. [John Barnes ?]. 12mo. [*Brit. Mus.*] 1613

FRENCH verbs. [By S. H. Wall.] Third edition. 4to. Pp. 12. [*Brit. Mus.*]
Buckhurst Hill, 1925
Signed : S. H. W.

FRIEND (the) that loveth at all times. By the author of *The brother born for adversity* [Robert Hawker]. 12mo. [*Brit. Mus.*] London, 1804
Signed : R. H.

*FRIENDLY (a) debate between a Conformist and a Nonconformist . . . 1669
An earlier edition [1668] reads "A Friendly debate betwixt two neighbours, the one a Conformist . . ." Symon Patrick's authorship is upheld by the *D. N. B.* vol. 44, p. 46, but it is also elsewhere ascribed to Robert Wild [*D. N. B.* vol. 61, p. 225].

FRIENDLY (the) road ; new adventures in contentment. By David Grayson [Ray Stannard Baker]. [Manly and Rickert's *Contemp. Amer. Lit.*] 1913

FRIENDS and adventures. By "T" of Punch [Joseph Thorp]. 8vo. Pp. 283. [*Brit. Mus.*] London, 1931

FROM Charles Bonaparte to Napoleon II. By the Berkeley men [Edwin Williams and Charles Edwards Lester]. 8vo. [Cushing's *Init. and Pseud.* i. 34.] New York, 1853
Previously published (1852) as "The Napoleon dynasty."

FROM Dartmouth to the Dardanelles ; a midshipman's log. [By Wolston B. C. W. Forester.] Edited by his mother [Elsbeth Lascelles Forester]. 8vo. Pp. xi. 174. [*Brit. Mus.*]
London, 1916

FROM different standpoints. By Pansy [Mrs Isabella Alden, *née* Macdonald] and Faye Huntington [Mrs Isabella H. Foster]. 8vo. [*Brit. Mus.*] [1895]

FROM Snotty to Sub. By the authors of *From Dartmouth to the Dardanelles* [Wolston B. C. W. Forester, edited by his mother Elsbeth Lascelles Forester]. 8vo. Pp. xi. 142. [*Brit. Mus.*]
London, 1918

FROM the beginning ; or, the story of Mary Jones and her Bible. Collected . . . and re-told by M. E. R. [Mary Emily Ropes]. . . . 8vo. Pp. ix. 156. [*Brit. Mus.*] London [1883]

*FROM the Mither Kirk and the Laigh Tollbooth o' Abirdene these stanes were taen. [A description of the Summer House, Aberdeen. By Alexander Walker.] 8vo. Pp. 7. [*Brit. Mus.*] Aberdeen, 1885
Signed : A. W.

FROM two points of view. By Moira O'Neill [Mrs Skrine, *née* Nesta Higginson]. 8vo. Pp. vi. 304. [S. J. Brown's *Ireland in Fiction.*]
Edinburgh, 1924

FRUITLESS (the) enquiry ; being a collection of several entertaining histories and occurrences, which fell under the observations of a lady in her search after happiness. By the author of the *Female-Spectator* [Mrs Eliza Haywood]. 12mo. [*D. N. B.* vol. 25, p. 315.] London, 1747

FRUITS (the) of folly. [A survey of European politics.] By the author of *The Pomp of Power* [Laurance Lyon]. 8vo. Pp. 320. [*Brit. Mus.*]
London, 1929

FUGITIVE poems. By W. B. N. [W. B. Noel ?]. 8vo. Pp. 60. [*Brit. Mus.*] London, 1849

*FULL (a) and true account of a horrid and barbarous revenge by poison . . .
The date of publication was 1716. The reference is to the dispute between Edmund Curll and Pope after the publication of a satire on the court called "Court poems" (*q.v.*) in which Curll had implicated Pope. Pope arranged a meeting between himself and Curll, at which he actually contrived to add an emetic to the latter's glass of sack. Pope made two further attacks on Curll in the same year, "A further account of the most deplorable condition of Mr Edmund Curl . . ." and "A strange but true relation how Mr Edmund Curll . . . went into Change Alley," *q.v.* And see R. Straus' *The Unspeakable Curll*, p. 50, *et seq.*

FULL (a) and true account of the late blazing star, with some probable prognosticks upon what may be its effects. [By Christopher Nesse.] 4to. [*Brit. Mus.*] London, 1680
Signed : C. N. See also "A True account of this present blasing-star . . . 1682 . . ."

*FULNESS (the) of time . . .
For Samuel, *read* Samuels.

FUNDAMENTAL (the) principles and rules of modern American whist explained and compiled by a Milwaukee Lady [Kate Whelock]. 8vo. Pp. 22. [Jessel's *Bibl. of playing cards*, p. 292.]
Chicago, 1887

FUNDAMENTAL (the) truths of Christianity . . . By George Keith. [With a preface signed : R. B. *i.e.* Robert Barclay.] 8vo. 2 parts. [*Brit. Mus.*] London, 1688

FUNERAL (the) orations of [J. B.] Bossuet . . . at the interment of Henrietta, Duchess of Orleans, and Louis of Bourbon, Prince of Condé. Translated [by Edward Jerningham]. 8vo. Pp. 59. [*Brit. Mus.*] London, 1800

FUNERAL tears upon the death of Captain William Bedloe. [In verse. By Richard Duke.] Fol. S. sh. [*D. N. B.* vol. 4, p. 118.]
London, 1680]

A satire. See also "An Epithalamium upon the marriage of Capt. William Bedloe."

FUNERALL elegies. [By Robert Allyne.] 4to. [*Pollard and Redgrave.*]
London, 1613

FUNERALL (a) sermon, preached at the buriall of the Lady Jane Maitland, daughter to the Right Noble Earl, John Earle of Lauderdail, at Hadington, the 19 of December 1631. By Mr I. M. [John Maitland]. Together with diverse epitaphs . . . 8vo. Pp. 48. [Johnstone and Robertson's *Bibl. Aberd.* i. 261.]
Edinburgh, 1633

*FURMETARY (the) . . .
The preface is signed : And per se And

FURTHER (a) account of the most deplorable condition of Mr Edmund Curl, Bookseller, since his being poison'd on the 28th of March. To be publish'd weekly. [By Alexander Pope.]   London, 1716
See the note to "A full and true account of a horrid . . . revenge by poison . . ."

FURTHER (a) exposure of . . . Dr R. Wardlaw, his Meeting-House and his Voluntary Associates, in a letter addressed to him by Anglo-Scotus [John Lockhart ?] 8vo. [*Brit. Mus.*]
Newcastle-upon-Tyne, 1834

FURTHER proposals for the entire reconstruction of the whole law. By an Outsider [Sir John Nodes Dickinson]. 8vo. [*Lincoln's Inn Lib.*]
London, 1871

FURTHER remarks on the currency of the United States. By Publius [James de Peyster Ogden ?]. [H. E. Miller's *Banking Theories in the U.S.*, p. 233.]
New York, 1841

G

G. H. Q., Montreuil-sur-mer. By G. S. O. [Frank Fox]. 8vo. Pp. 306. [*Brit. Mus.*]   London, 1920

GAGG (a) to love's advocate ; or, an assertion of the justice of the Parliament in the execution of Mr Love. By J. H. [John Hinde ?] Esq. 4to. [*Brit. Mus.*]   London, 1651

GAIN (the) of godliness ; a sermon. [By William Mandell.] 8vo. Pp. 15. [*Brit. Mus.*]   Thames Ditton [1835]

GALANT (the) seamans return from the Indies ; or, the happy meeting of two faithful lovers. [A ballad.] By T. L. [Thomas Lanfiere ?]. Fol. S. sh. [*Brit. Mus.*]   [London, 1670 ?]
Another edition in the same (?) year in Black Letter runs : "The Gallant Seaman's return . . . "

GALIGNANI'S traveller's guide through France (Italy, Switzerland), compiled from the works of Coxe [*i.e.* Henry Coxe, *pseud.* of John Millard]. 12mo. 3 vols. [*Brit. Mus.*]   1819-23

GALLANT (the) ladies ; or, the mutual confidence ; a novel. [By —— Poisson.] Translated out of French. 12mo. [*Brit. Mus.*]   1685

GALLANTS. [A novel.] By E. Barrington [Mrs L. Adams Beck]. 8vo. Pp. 308. [*Brit. Mus.*] London, 1927

GALLERY of notable men and women. Compiled and selected by the editor of *The treasury of modern biography* [Robert Cochrane]. 8vo. [*Brit. Mus.*]
Edinburgh, 1879

GAMBLE (a) with hearts. By Anthony Carlyle [Mrs Patrick Milton]. 8vo. [*Who's Who in Lit.*]   London, 1922

*GAMBLING (the) world . . . By "Rouge et Noir."
F. Jessel (*Bibl. of playing cards*, p. 214) attributes this to Charles William Heckethorn.

GAME of Cinch and Draw Pedro. By "Trumps" [William Brisbane Dick]. 8vo. Pp. 8. [Jessel's *Bibl. of playing cards*, p. 73.]   New York, 1891

GAME (the) of solo-sixty. Edited from traditional sources by Junius [Frank A. Hilliard]. 24mo. Pp. 40. [Jessel's *Bibl. of playing cards.*] Cleveland, 1888

GAME (the) of speculation ; a comedy in three acts and in prose [an adaptation of Balzac's comedy "Mercadet"] by Slingsby Lawrence [George Henry Lewes]. 12mo. [*Brit. Mus.*]
London [1851]
Lacy's Acting Edition of Plays, vol. 5.

GAME (the) of whist. By "Q. P. Index" [William McCrillis Griswold]. 8vo. [Jessel's *Bibl. of playing cards.*]
Bangor, Me., 1881
An extra number of *The Monograph.*

GAME (the) of whist. By "Trumps" [William Brisbane Dick]. 8vo. Pp. 31. [Jessel's *Bibl. of playing cards*, p. 72.]   London [1870?]

GAMEKEEPER'S (the) and game-preserver's account book and diary. By I. E. B. C. [Irvine E. B. Cox]. 4to. Pp. 134. [*Brit. Mus.*]
London, 1881

*GAMING-HUMOR (the) . . .
Not by Charles Morton, of Charlestown, N.E., but by Charles Morton, rector of Blisland, Cornwall.

GARDEN (the) manual; or, practical instruction for the cultivation of all kinds of vegetables, fruits and flowers. . . . By the editors . . . of *The cottage gardener* [George William Johnson and others]. 8vo. [*Brit. Mus.*]
London [1857]

GARDEN (the) of Adonis. By Al Carthill [Sir John Perronet Thompson]. 8vo. Pp. 360. [*Brit. Mus.*]
Edinburgh, 1927

*GARDENERS (the) labyrinth . . . By Didymus Mountain.
In a later edition (1652) only the initials "D. M." appear.

GARDENER'S (the) new kalendar, divided according to the twelve months of the year. . . . [By Sir John Hill, M.D.] 8vo. [*Brit. Mus.*]
London, 1758

GARDENING for the many; being practical monthly directions. . . . By contributors to *The cottage gardener* [George William Johnson and others]. Third edition. 8vo. [*Brit. Mus.*]
London [1856]

GASPARDS (the) of Pine Croft. [A novel.] By Ralph Connor [Charles William Gordon]. 8vo. Pp. 350. [*Brit. Mus.*]   London [1923]

GATHERING (the) storm; studies in economical and social tendencies. By a Rifleman [Victor Wallace Germains]. 8vo. Pp. vi. 297. [*Brit. Mus.*]
London, 1913

GAY cottage. [A tale.] By Glance Gaylord [Warren Ives Bradley]. 16mo. [*Brit. Mus.*]   Boston [1866]

GEBEL Tevi [*i.e.* the mountain of birds. Essays. By William Tudor]. 12mo. [Foley's *Amer. authors.*]
Boston, 1829

GEM of the Peak; or, Matlock Bath and its vicinity. By the author of *Excursions to Chatsworth*, etc. [William Adam]. 12mo. Pp. 86. [*Brit. Mus.*]   Derby [*c.* 1850]
Other editions have the author's name. A second part has the title "Gem of the Peak; containing excursions to Buxton . . ."

GEMIXTE pickles. By K. M. S. [Kurt M. Stein]. 8vo. Pp. 94. [*Publishers' Weekly*, 20th Aug. 1927.]
Chicago, 1927

GEMS of Lancashire, No. 1 Kelup's Kersmas Goose. By M. R. L. [M. R. Lahee]. . . . 8vo. Pp. 16. [*Brit. Mus.*]   Manchester [1871]

GEMS of promise. . . . By Emart Kinsburn [Arthur Preston Hankins]. 8vo. Pp. 280. [*Brit. Mus.*]
London [1926]

GENEALOGICAL (a), chronological, historical and geographical atlas; exhibiting all the Royal Families in Europe, their origin. . . . By A. Le Sage [Marin Joseph Emmanuel Auguste Dieudonné de las Casas, Marquis de la Caussade]. Fol. [*Brit. Mus.*]   London, 1801

GENEALOGICAL memoirs of the Browne family of Caverswall and Shredicote, co. Stafford; Bentley Hall, co. Derby; Greenford, co. Middlesex; Withington and Caughley, co. Salop; also of the Peploe family of Garnstone, co. Hereford. Compiled by G. B. M. [George Blacker Morgan]. 4to. [*Brit. Mus.*]   London, 1888, *et seq.*

GENEALOGY (a) of the ancestors and descendants of George Augustus and Louisa Trumbull of Trumbull Square, Worcester, Mass. [By J. H. Lea.] 8vo. Pp. 46. [*Brit. Mus.*]
Private print, 1886
Signed: J. H. L.

GENEALOGY (the) of the family of Gylle or Gill, of Hertfordshire, Essex and Kent. . . . [Edited by G. G. *i.e.* Gordon W. J. Gyll.] 8vo. 2 parts. [*Brit. Mus.*]   London, 1842-52
Reprinted from *Collectanea Topographica.*

GENERAL accommodations by addresse. [Proposals for an office of general agency, by Adolphus Speed.] 4to. Pp. 15. [*Brit. Mus.*]
[London, 1650]

GENERAL (a) and rational grammar, containing the fundamental principles of the art of speaking . . . translated from the French of Messrs de Port-Royal [Antoine Arnauld and C. Lancelot]. 8vo. [*Brit. Mus.*]
London, 1753

GENERAL Bramble. By André Maurois [Emile Herzog]. Translated . . . by Jules Castier and Ronald Boswell. 8vo. Pp. vi. 188. [*Observer*, 1st Feb. 1931.]   London, 1921

GENERAL Crack. By George R. Preedy [Gabrielle Margaret Vere Long]. 8vo. Pp. xiii. 497. [*Daily Mail*, 3rd Feb. 1931.]   London, 1928

GENERAL (a) description of Nova Scotia. [Attributed variously to T. C. Haliburton and to Walter Bromley.] 8vo. [*Brit. Mus.*]   1823

GENERAL (the) election in the great centres of population. By R. S. S. [Robert Scarr Sowler]. 8vo. Pp. 29. [*Brit. Mus.*]   London, 1869

*GENERAL (the) fast ; a lyric ode . . .

This is accepted as Sheridan's by Mr Walter Sichel in his *Sheridan*, but it appears to be doubtful. It may be by the same hand as " The Critic, or a tragedy rehearsed . . ." which according to the *D. N. B.* on doubtful evidence was by Israel Pottinger. See Mr R. Crompton Rhodes in the *T. L. S.* 26th August 1926.

*GENERAL (the) post-bag. . . . By Humphrey Hedgehog.

The *Eng. Cat.*, 1801-1836, p. 225, attributes this to John Gifford.

GENERAL regulations for inspection and control of all the prisons. . . . [By Sir George Onesiphorus Paul, Bart.]   Gloucester [1790]

GENERAL thoughts on the construction, use and abuse of the great offices. . . . [By Henry M'Culloh]. 8vo. [*Brit. Mus.*]   1754

GENERALL (a) charge, or impeachment of high-treason, in the name of justice, equity, against the communality of England : as was presented by experienced reason. Anno 1647 . . . Likewise the communalities objections to the said articles. With the answer of experienced reason . . . This penned by L. C., a friend of the inslaved communality [Laurence Clarkson, or Claxton]. 4to. Pp. 28. [*D. N. B.* vol. 11, p. 6.]   London, 1647

A tract against the parliament.

GENEROUS (the) surgeon. [By John Marten ?]   London, 1710

See the note to " A new method of curing without internal medicines . . ."

GENESIS : an interpretation. [In verse.] By S. H. S. [Samuel Henry Summerscales]. 8vo. Pp. 15. [*Brit. Mus.*]   Winnipeg [1918]

GENEVA (the) ballad, to the tune of 48. [A satire against the Puritans. By Samuel Butler.] Fol. S. sh. [*Brit. Mus.*]   [London] 1674

GENTLE Jesus. By the author of *The Little Lamb* [Mrs Charles Jones]. 8vo. Pp. 32. [*Brit. Mus.*] London [1907]

GENTLEMAN (the) farmer; or certain observations made by an English gentleman upon the husbandry of Flanders, and the same compared with that of England. . . . By a person of honour in the county of Norfolk [Hon. Roger North]. 12mo. [R. Straus' *The Unspeakable Curll*, p. 277.]   London, 1726

GENTLEMAN (the) from Texas. By Hearnden Balfour [Beryl Hearnden and Eva Balfour]. [*New York Times, Book Review*, 26th Aug. 1928.]   1927

*GENTLEMAN (a) of Virginia.

For Percy John Brebner, *read* Percy James Brebner.

GENTLEMAN'S (the) accomptant : or, an essay to unfold the mystery of accomptes by way of debtor and creditor. . . . Done by a person of honour [Hon. Roger North]. 12mo. [R. Straus' *The Unspeakable Curll*, p. 225.]   London, 1714

*GENTLEMAN'S (the) guide in his tour through France . . .

A later edition (1867) was issued under the *pseud. :* Hy. Coxe.

GENTLEMEN of the Sea. By Paul Trent [Edward Platt]. 8vo. Pp. 318. [*Brit. Mus.*]   London, 1915

*GENUINE (a) account of the Ship S[usse]x . . .

For J. D—n *read* J—n D—n.

GENUINE (the) copy of a letter written from Constantinople by an English lady who was lately in Turkey. . . . [By Lady Mary Wortley Montagu.] 4to. [*Lincoln's Inn Lib.*]   London, 1719

GEOGRAPHY of the British colonies and dependencies. . . . [By James Hewitt.] 8vo. 6 Nos. [*Brit. Mus.*]   London, 1860

Signed : J. H.

GEORGE (the) Meredith birthday book. Selected and arranged by D. M. [Mrs Daisy Meredith]. 8vo. [*Brit. Mus.*]   London [1898]

GEORGE the fourth ; a poem. . . . By the author of *Hours of solitude* [Charlotte Dacre]. 16mo. [*Brit. Mus.*]   London, 1822

GEORGIAN poetry, 1911-1912. [Compiled by E. M. *i.e.* E. H. Marsh.] Third edition. 8vo. Pp. 197. [*Brit. Mus.*]   London, 1913

GEORGICA Virgilii . . . With short English notes. . . . [Edited by H. H. *i.e.* Henry Hayman ?] 16mo. Pp. 71. [*Brit. Mus.*]   Oxford, 1854

*GEORGICS (the) of Bacchicles.

Not by F. D. Morice. The translator was William Jackson Brodribb. [*Information from Mr C. W. Brodribb, the translator's son.*]

*GERALDINE : a tale . . .

For Eleanor C. Agnew, *read* Miss E. C. Agnew. Her Christian name is unknown.

GERMAN accidence for the use of Rugby School. [By J. W. J. Vecqueray.] 12mo. Pp. 34. [*Brit. Mus.*]   Rugby, 1856

GERMAN (the) army from within. By a British Officer [Thomas Burke, of Eltham] who has served in it. 8vo. Pp. 192. [*Brit. Mus.*] London, 1914

GERMANY in Europe. By Augur [Vladimir Polyakov]. 8vo. Pp. 91. [*Amer. Cat.*] London [1927]

GESÙ Bambino, and other records. [By M. D. Stenson.] 8vo. Pp. 224. [*Brit. Mus.*] London, 1922
Signed : M. D. S.

GHOSTLY visitors . . . By "Spectre Stricken." With an introduction by M.A., Oxon. [William S. Moses]. 8vo. Pp. vi. 128. [*Brit. Mus.*]
London, 1882

GIFT (a) for mothers. By the author of *Aids to developement* [Mary Atkinson Maurice]. 8vo. [*Brit. Mus.*]
London, 1833
Introduction signed : M.

GIFT (the) of life ; a romance. By James Cassidy [Mrs E. M. Story]. 8vo. Pp. 414. [*Brit. Mus.*] London, 1897

GILBERT White of Selborne . . . (Private reprint of a proof as revised by the author for the *Dictionary of National Biography*.) [By Alfred Newton.] 8vo. Pp. 34. [*Brit. Mus.*]
Cambridge [1899?]

GILBERT'S last summer at Rainford, and what it taught. By Glance Gayford [Warren Ives Bradley]. 8vo. [*Brit. Mus.*] Boston, 1868

GILPIN'S rig ; or the wedding-day kept : a droll story . . . containing an account of John Gilpin, the bold linen draper of Cheapside, how he went farther and faster than he intended, and came home safe at last. [By William Cowper.] 8vo. Pp. 15. [*Brit. Mus.*] London [1784]
Other anonymous editions with varied titles are " The diverting history of John Gilpin . . .", " The history of John Gilpin . . .", "John Gilpin's journey . . .", and " The journey of John Gilpin . . ."

GIN and Bitters. By A. Riposte [Evelyn May Clowes, later Mrs Wiche]. 8vo. Pp. 306. [*Brit. Mus.*]
New York, 1931

*GINEVRA . . .
For Francis H. H. Terrell, *read* Francis A. H. Terrell.

GIN-SHOP (the) ; or, a peep into a prison. [By Hannah More.] Fol. S. sh. [*Brit. Mus.*] Bath [1795]
Signed : Z.

GIRALDA . . . A comic drama . . . Adapted from . . . M. Scribe . . . with remarks . . . by D. G. [George Daniel]. 12mo. Pp. 45. [*Brit. Mus.*]
London [1850]

GIRL (a) among the anarchists. By Isabel Meredith [Olive and Helen Rossetti]. 8vo. Pp. x. 302. [*Ashley Library.*] London, 1903

GIRL (the) from up there ; musical comedy in three acts. Words by Hugh Morton [C. M. S. M'Lellan]. 8vo. Pp. 32. [*Brit. Mus.*]
London [1901]

GIVE me the willow-garland ; or, the maiden's former fear. . . . [A ballad. By Lawrence Price ?] Fol. S. sh. B. L. [*Brit. Mus.*] [London, 1670?]
Signed : L. P.

GLADSTONE (the) A.B.C. [By George Stronach.] 4to. [*Brit. Mus.*]
Edinburgh [1883]

GLANCE (a) at the glories of sacred friendship. By E. B., Esq. [Edward Benlowes ?]. [*D. N. B.* vol. 4, p. 227.]
London, 1657

GLASSE (the) of vaine-glorie (of Saint Augustine). [Translated by W. Prid.] 12mo. [*Pollard and Redgrave*].
London, 1585
Signed : W. P.

GLEANINGS in Europe. By an American [James Fenimore Cooper]. 12mo. 2 vols. [*Brit. Mus.*]
Philadelphia, 1837-38

GLEN (the) is mine, and The lifting ; two plays of the Hebrides. By John Brandane [Dr John MacIntyre]. 8vo. Pp. 250. [Smith's *Cat.*, Glasgow, 1926]
London, 1925

*GLIMPSE (a) of Sion's Glory . . .
Whitley's *Bapt. Bibl.* i. 11, and *M'Alpin Coll.* attribute the whole work to William Kiffin.

GLIMPSES of eternity ; a vision. By T. J. C. H. [Thomas J. C. Hutt]. 8vo. Pp. xii. 181. [*Brit. Mus.*]
London, 1886

GLOBE notes. By R. H. [Richard Holland]. 8vo. N.P. 1666
The second edition, 1678, bears the author's name.

GLORIES (the) of Jesus ; readings for a month. By the author of *The Year of Our Lord* [Frederick Harper]. 8vo. Pp. x. 66. [*Brit. Mus.*] London, 1907

GLORIOUS Apollo. [A novel.] By E. Barrington [Mrs L. Adams Beck]. 8vo. Pp. viii. 371. [*Who's Who in Lit.*] London, 1926

GLORIOUS glimmerings of the life of love, unity, and pure joy. Written in Rome . . . but conserved . . . until my arrival at Barbados in the year 1662. . . . By J(ohn) P[erret]. 4to. Pp. 15. [*Brit. Mus.*] London, 1663

GLORY (the) of Egypt ; a romance. By Louis Moresby [Lily Adams Beck]. 8vo. Pp. 281. [*Amer. Cat.*]
London, 1926

*GLORY (the) of women . . . by H. C.
Gent.
　Certainly not by Henry Care who was
only six years old in 1652. Possibly by
Hugh Crompton. The book is addressed
to Mrs Elizabeth Crompton from "your
faithful friend and kinsman."

GLORY-CHRISTIAN (the). By an
unknown Christian [Albert Ernest
Richardson]. 8vo. Pp. 133. [*Brit.
Mus.*]   London [1925]

GLOWEROWER : Scottish idylls. By
Innes Adair [Euphemia A. M. Inglis].
8vo. Pp. 92. [*Brit. Mus.*]
                           Haddington, 1924

*GLYGLUMGLEAGH . . .
　For Thomas Hingston Harvey, *read*
Thomas Kingston Harvey.

GO to Joseph ; or, "Bow the Knee."
By W. T. P. W. [W. T. P. Wolston].
12mo. Pp. 16. [*Brit. Mus.*]
                           Edinburgh [1884]

*GOD and man : conferences . . .
　Signed : H. D. L.

GOD (the) in the garden ; an August
comedy. By Keble Howard [John
Keble Bell]. 8vo. Pp. 338. [*Brit.
Mus.*]   London, 1904

GOD, no impostor, nor deluder. [By
William Prynne.] Pp. 27. [*M'Alpin
Coll. Cat.*]   [1629 ?]
　No title-page. The second edition in the
same year bears the author's name.

G O D L Y (a) and learned sermon,
preached before an honourable audi-
torie the 26. day of Februarie. 1580.
[By William Fulke.] [*Camb. Univ.
Lib.*]   [1580 ?]

GODLY (a) sermon [on Mark xiv. 68, 70]
of Peter's repentance, after he had
denyed his Lord and Master. . . .
By a godly pastor [John Hart, D.D.].
12mo. [*Brit. Mus.*]   London, 1663
　In the thirteenth edition (1680) the
author's name occurs in the publisher's
advertisement at the end. It was reprinted
(1776) under the title "Peter's repentance . . . ", *q.v.*

GODLY (a) sermon preached in the
Court at Greenwich . . . 1552 . . .
By B. G. [Bernard Gilpin]. 8vo. Pp.
76. [*Brit. Mus.*]   London, 1581

GOD'S call to unconverted sinners to
turn to the Lord . . . The fifth edition
with additions . . . by T. P. [By
Richard Baxter.] 8vo. Pp. 22. [*Brit.
Mus.*]   London, 1663

GOD'S commonwealths, British and
American. . . . By the Roadbuilder
[William Gordon Mackendrick]. 8vo.
Pp. xv. 287. [*Brit. Mus.*]
                           London [1928]

GOD'S dark, and other bedtime verses
and songs. By John Martin [Morgan
Shepard]. 12mo. No pagination.
[*Publishers' Weekly*, 24th Sept. 1927.]
                           New York, 1927

GODS (the) of war. By A. E. [George
William Russell]. 4to.
　　　Dublin, private print, 1913

GODS trumpet sounding the alarme,
summoning all persons speedily to
repent and turne to God. . . . [By
William Attersoll.] [*D. N. B.* vol. 2,
p. 240.]   London, 1632
　Bound up and issued next year as one of
"Three treatises " bearing the author's
name.

GOLDEN (the) boke of Marcus Aurelius
Emperour and eloquente oratour. [By
Antonio de Guevara.] (Translated
oute of Frenche by John Bourchier.)
8vo. B. L. [*Brit. Mus.*]
                           London, 1546

GOLDEN (a) chaine or the description
of theologie, containing the order of
the causes of salvation and damnation
. . . Written in Latine and translated
by R. H. . . . [By William Perkins.]
[*Camb. Univ. Lib.*]   Cambridge, 1597
　To the Christian Reader signed : W. P.

GOLDEN (the) hills : a story of the
Irish famine. By the author of *Cedar
Creek* [Miss E. H. Walshe]. 8vo.
Pp. viii. 272. [*Brit. Mus.*]
                           London, 1858

GOLDEN (the) oportunity, and how to
improve it ; being prize essays. . . .
[Edited by J. G. *i.e.* James Gabb.]
8vo. [*Brit. Mus.*]   London, 1861

GOLDEN thoughts ; a memento of the
jumble of the church buildings in South
Grove, Highgate, of the Highgate
Congregational Church. [Edited by
G. C. P. *i.e.* G. C. Postans]. . . . 8vo.
Pp. 79. [*Brit. Mus.*]
                           Guildford, 1909

GOLDEN Web. By Wilhelmina Stitch
[Ruth Collie]. 8vo. Pp. 63. [*Brit.
Mus.*]   London, 1928

GONE native ; a tale of the South Seas.
By "Asterisk".[R. J. Fletcher]. 8vo.
Pp. xi. 303. [*Brit. Mus.*]
                           London, 1924

GOOD ! (A proposition on the National
Debt.) [By Luke James Hansard.]
8vo. [*Brit. Mus.*]   London [1845]
　Signed : L. J. H.

GOOD counsell to the petitioners for
Presbyterian government. . . . [By
Katherine Chidley.] Fol. S. sh.
[*Brit. Mus.*]   [London, 1645]
　Signed : K. C.

*GOOD (the) fight of faith . . .
　For Mrs —— Freeland, *read* Mrs Carrie J.
Freeland.

GOOD Friday. [A sermon on Luke xxiii. 35. By William Tarbet.] 12mo. Pp. 13. [*Brit. Mus.*] [1870]
GOOD Friday ; a few words to those who neglect it. . . . By the author of *The Lamplighter* [Francis Bourdillon]. 8vo. [*Brit. Mus.*] London [1859]
Signed : F. B.
GOOD (the) girl. [A novel.] By Seumas O'Sullivan [James Starkey]. 8vo. Pp. 318. [Boyd's *Ireland's Lit. Renais.*] London, 1912
GOOD (a) man? [By M. K. Malcolmson.] 8vo. Pp. xi. 81. [*Brit. Mus.*] London, 1918
Originally published (1907) under the title "What think ye of Christ . . ."
GOOD references. [A novel.] By E. J. Rath [J. Chauncey C. Brainerd and Edith Rathbone Brainerd]. 8vo. Pp. vi. 282. [*Brit. Mus.*] London [1925]
GOOD-NATURED (the) lady. [A novel.] By J. E. Buckrose [Mrs Annie Edith Jameson]. 8vo. Pp. 315. [*Brit. Mus.*] London [1927]
GORDON ; a life of faith and duty. By W. J. G. [William John Gordon]. Illustrated by R. André. 4to. Pp. 36. [*Brit. Mus.*] [1885]
GORDON ; a woman's memories of him . . . [By Elizabeth Surtees-Alnett.] 8vo. Pp. iii. 74. [*Brit. Mus.*] 1885
Signed : E. S. A.
GORGEOUS poetry, 1911-1920. First series. [By J. B. M. *i.e.* J. B. Morton.] 8vo. Pp. 63. [*Brit. Mus.*] London, 1920
Parodies. The title would seem to be based on E. H. Marsh's "Georgian poetry, 1911-1912," *q.v.*
GOSPEL (the) drama ; its symbolism and interpretation. By John Mysticus [George Arthur Gaskell]. 8vo. Pp. ix. 160. [*Brit. Mus.*] London, 1916
GOSPEL (the) of Philip the Evangelist. Reprinted from Spiritual Truth. [An automatic script. Edited by F. B. B. *i.e.* Frederick Bligh Bond.] 4to. Pp. 47. [*Brit. Mus.*] London [1925]
GOSSIPS (the) greeting ; or a new discouery of such females meeting, wherein is plainely set forth the sundry sorts of those kinds of women, with their seueral humors and conditions. [Verse. By Henry Parrot.] 4to. [*Christie-Miller Cat.*] London, 1620
GOUERNAYLE (the) of helthe ; with the medecyne of ye stomache. [Verse. By John Lydgate?] 4to. [*Brit. Mus.*] [Westminster, 1489]
GOVERNOR (the) of Kattowitz. By Graham Seton [Lieut.-Col. Graham Seton Hutchison]. [*Times Lit. Supp.* 27th Nov. 1930.] London, 1930

GRACE, the power of unity and of gathering. By J. N. D. [John Nelson Darby]. 8vo. [*Brit. Mus.*] London [1867]
GRACES (the) ; an intermezzo . . . [By Charles Dibdin.] 8vo. Pp. 24. [*Library of Congress, Cat. of Opera Librettos.*] London, 1782
GRAMMAR (a) of the Tahitian dialect of the Polynesian language. [By John Davies, missionary.] 12mo. Pp. 43. [*Brit. Mus.*] Tahiti, 1823
GRAND (the) Duke's finances. [A novel.] By Frank Heller [Gunnar Serner]. 8vo. Pp. viii. 351. [*Brit. Mus.*] London [1925]
GRANDMOTHER Martin is murdered. By John Courtney [John Cournos]. 8vo. Pp. 255. [*Brit. Mus.*] London [1930]
GRANITE ; a tragedy. By Clemence Dane [Winifred Ashton]. 8vo. Pp. 75. [*Brit. Mus.*] London, 1926
GRAVE (the) facts of the housing situation. [Articles reprinted from the *Westminster Gazette*, signed : M. J. L. *i.e.* M. J. Landa.] 8vo. Pp. 51. [*Brit. Mus.*] London [1927]
GRAY'S "Elegy written in a Country Churchyard." Put into French verse by R. L. S. [Robert Louis Sanderson]. 8vo. [*Brit. Mus.*] [New Haven, Conn., 1912]
GREAT (the) analysis ; a plea for a rational world-order. [By William Archer.] With an introduction by Gilbert Murray. 8vo. Pp. xii. 122. London, 1912
A later edition (1931) bears the author's name.
GREAT (the) and wonderful works of God humbly represented, and the just and equal distributions of providence demonstrated : with an appendix concerning St Paul. By an ancient Doctor of Physick [Walter Harris, M.D.]. 8vo. [*Brit. Mus.*] London, 1727
GREAT (the) day to come. By the author of *The Lamplighter* [Francis Bourdillon]. 12mo. [*Brit. Mus.*] London, 1862
Signed : F. B.
GREAT (the) delusion ; a study of aircraft in peace and war. By Neon [Mrs Marion W. Acworth]. . . . 8vo. Pp. xxxix. 288. [*Times*, 18th Feb. 1931.] London, 1927
GREAT English painters. By Francis Downman [Ernest James Oldmeadow]. With thirty-two illustrations. 8vo. Pp. 294. [*Brit. Mus.*] London, 1908
GREAT (the) gulf. By the author of *The Lamplighter* [Francis Bourdillon]. 8vo. [*Brit. Mus.*] London [1859]
Signed: F. B.

GREAT (the) literary salons, XVII and XVIII centuries ; lectures of the Musée Carnavalet. By . . . Nozière [Fernand Weyl, and others]. . . . 8vo. Pp. 223. [*Brit. Mus.*] London, 1930

GREAT possessions. [A novel.] By David Grayson [Ray Stannard Baker]. [Manly and Rickert's *Contemp. Amer. Lit.*] 1917

GREAT (the) pyramid ; its construction, symbolism and chronology. By Discipulus [Basil Stewart]. 8vo. Pp. 79. London, 1925
The second edition (1927) bears the author's name.

G R E A T (the) Russian bear . . . a comedietta. . . . By Thomas Morton . . . with . . . remarks by D— G. [George Daniel]. 12mo. Pp. 32. [*Brit. Mus.*] London [1862]

GREAT (the) treaty of peace . . . part whereof was preached at the funeral of Mrs Anne Kyrl. . . . By H. S., Minister of the Gospel [Henry Stubbe?]. 8vo. [*Brit. Mus.*] London, 1677

GREAT (the) world. [A novel.] By a Gentleman with a duster [Harold Begbie]. 8vo. Pp. 320. [*Amer. Cat.*] London, 1925

G R E A T E S T (the) scandals of the present century. . . . By a worker (Herbert Ainley [Herbert Ainley Reader].) 4to. [*Brit. Mus.*] London [1923]

GREECE in 1824. By the author of *War in Greece* [Col. Napier]. 8vo. London, 1824
From an inscribed copy.

GREEK vocabulary ; or, exercises on the declinable parts of speech. [By J. R. M. *i.e.* John Richardson Major.] 12mo. London, 1833

GREEKS (the) and Trojans warres—
Caused by that wanton Trojan Knight Sir Paris,
Who ravishes Hellen and her to Troy carries. . . .
With a fit allusion, before the conclusion [to Ireland—
"Ireland is our Hellen fair
Ravished from us through want of care."
A ballad.] By H. C. [Humfrey Crouch ?] Fol. 2 parts. B. L. [*Brit. Mus.*] London [1640?]

GREENES groatsworth of witte. [Edited by J. H. *i.e.* John Hind?] 4to. B. L. [*Brit. Mus.*] London, 1617

GREENES [*i.e.* Robert Green's] Newes both from heaven and hell, commended to the presse [or rather written] by B. R. [Barnaby Rich]. [*Pollard and Redgrave*, p. 270.] London, 1593

GRETNA (the) blacksmith's story. By the author of *Romances of Gretna Green* [R. P. Macdougall]. 8vo. Pp. 132. [*Brit. Mus.*] London [1929]

GRETNA Green; a comic opera. . . . [By Charles Stuart.] 8vo. Pp. 22. [*Library of Congress, Cat. of Opera Librettos.*] Dublin, N.D.

*GRETNA-GREEN and its traditions. By Claverhouse.
The Bibliotheca Jacksoniana Catalogue gives the author's name as Miss Fowle Smith.

GREVILLE Landon ; a novel. By Pier Lisle [John Percy Gordon]. 8vo. 3 vols. [*Brit. Mus.*] London, 1863

*GRILLION'S Club from its origin . . .
The preface, signed : H., is by Richard Monckton Milnes, Lord Houghton.

*GROANS of the quartern loaf.
For Walcot, *read* Wolcot.

GROG time yarns, spun by the merry men of 17 Mess. By Lionel Yexley [James Woode]. 8vo. Pp. iv. 157. [*Brit. Mus.*] London, 1904

GRUB-STREET (the) opera ; as it is acted at the theatre in the Hay-Market. By Scriblerus Secundus [Henry Fielding]. 8vo. Pp. 56. [*Brit. Mus.*] London, 1731

GUIDE (a) for passing Advent holily. By J. B. E. Avrillon. Translated . . . and adapted to the use of the English Church [by E. B. P. *i.e.* Edward Bouverie Pusey]. 8vo. Pp. lxiv. 285. London, 1844

GUIDE (a) for the penitent. [By Brian Duppa. Edited by C. I. B. *i.e.* Charles Ingham Black ?] 8vo. Pp. 32. [*Brit. Mus.*] London, 1852

GUIDE to Bergen with a map of the town. [By Viljam Olsvig.] [*Pettersen's Norsk Lexikon*, col. 181.] Bergen [1888]

GUIDE (a) to Madeira ; containing a short account of Funchall : with instructions to such as repair to that island for health. [By Dr J. Adams ?] 8vo. [*Brit. Mus.*] London, 1801

GUIDE (a) to Mahomedan Law. By A., B.A., LL.B. [Trikamlāl Ranchhoḍlāl Desāi]. 8vo. Pp. 104. [*Brit. Mus.*] Bombay, 1902

GUIDE (a) to the city of Perth and its environs, and to the principal tours through the County ; with notes. [By David Morison, the publisher.] 8vo. [D. C. Smith's *Historians of Perth*, p. 108.] Perth, 1812

GUIDE (a) to the Indian Penal Code, Act XLV. of 1860 . . . in the form of questions and answers. . . . New edition. [Compiled by P. N. V. *i.e.* Vijayaranga Pillai, P.V.] 8vo. Pp. lxvii. 314. [*Brit. Mus.*] Madras, 1895

GUIDE (a) to the vikingship from Gokstad in the Christiana-museum. . . . [By Ingvald Undset.] [Pettersen's *Norsk Lexikon*, col. 182.] Kristiania, 1886

GUIDE (a) unto Sion; or certaine positions concerning a true visible Church; wherein the nature of a true Church is so plainely described, as all men may easily discerne the same from false assemblies. Written by a learned and judicious divine [Henry Ainsworth]. The third edition. 12mo. [*D. N. B.* vol. 1, p. 193.]
Amstelredam, 1640

GUILD (a) of cripples. By K. P. [Kineton Parkes.] An article reprinted from the *Manchester Evening Chronicle*. . . . 8vo. Pp. 16. [*Brit. Mus.*]
Hanley, 1903

GULLIVER'S Travels. . . . Edited by a clergyman [J. Lupton]. 16mo. [*Brit. Mus.*] 1867
Signed: J. L.

GUY Mannering; or, the gypsey's prophecy: a musical drama founded on the celebrated novel of the same name . . . as performed at the Theatre - Royal, Edinburgh. [By Daniel Terry.] 12mo. Pp. 60. [*D. N. B.* vol. 56, p. 84.] [Edinburgh], N.D.

GUY'S porridge pot; a poem in twenty-four books. The first part (Books I-VI.) [A satire on Dr Samuel Parr. By Robert Eyres Landor?] 8vo. [*London Mercury*, April 1927.]
London, 1808
No more published.

GWELYGORDD; or, the child of sin; a tale of Welsh origin. . . . By the author of *The Infernal Quixote*, etc. [Charles Lucas]. 12mo. 3 vols. [*Eng. Cat.*] London, 1820

GWILLIANS (the) of Bryn Gwilliam. [A novel. By Susanna C. Venn.] 8vo. 2 vols. [*Brit. Mus.*] London, 1875

H

HAILSOME (the) admonitioun. . . . [By Robert Sempill, Baron Sempill.] [*Pollard and Redgrave.*] 1570

HALF-CENTURY (a) history of the Farmington Avenue Congregational Church organized as the Pearl Street Congregational Church in Hartford, Connecticut, 1851-1901. [By William De Loss Love.] 8vo. Pp. 84. [*Brit. Mus.*] [Hartford, Conn.], 1901
Introduction signed: W. D. L.

HALLVARD Halvorsen; or, the avalanche: a story. . . . By Nellie Cornwall [Nellie Sloggett]. 8vo. Pp. 316. [*Brit. Mus.*] London [1887]

HAND (the) of horror. [A tale.] By Owen Fox Jerome [Oscar Jerome Friend]. 8vo. [*Publishers' Weekly*, 13th Aug. 1927.] New York, 1927

HANDBOOK (a) for travellers in Algeria. . . . [By Sir R. L. Playfair.] 8vo. Pp. viii. 239. [*Brit. Mus.*]
London, 1874
"Murray's Handbooks."

HAND-BOOK for travellers in France. [By John Murray, publisher.] 12mo. [*Brit. Mus.*] London, 1843

HANDBOOK of bézique. By J. R. W. [James Redding Ware]. 48mo. Pp. 96. [Jessel's *Bibl. of playing cards*, p. 289]. London, 1869

HAND-BOOK (a) of French conversation. By F. Ahn, with . . . additions . . . by . . . Chrysostôme Dagobert [Jean Baptiste Alphonse Led'huy]. 12mo. Pp. 122. [*Brit. Mus.*] London, 1857

HAND-BOOK (a) of German conversation. By F. Ahn with additions . . . by . . . Chrysostôme Dagobert [Jean B. A. Led'huy]. 12mo. Pp. 142. [*Brit. Mus.*] London, 1857

HANDBOOK (a) of the Boer War. With general map of South Africa and 18 sketch maps and plans. [By Wyndham Tufnell.] 8vo.
London and Aldershot, 1910
From a copy containing a signed letter from the author.

HANDBOOK of the Dyce and Forster Collections in the South Kensington Museum, with engravings and facsimiles. [By William Maskell.] 8vo. Pp. viii. 105. [*Brit. Mus.*]
London [1880]

HANDBOOK of whist. By J. R. W. [James Redding Ware]. 48mo. Pp. 92. [Jessel's *Bibl. of playing cards*, p. 288.] London, 1866

HANDBOOK (a) of whist and ready reference manual of the modern scientific game. By Major Tenace [George Washington Bailey]. 8vo. Pp. iv. 110. [Jessel's *Bibl. of playing cards*.] London, 1885

HAND-BOOK (the) of women's work. Edited by L. M. H. [Louisa M. Hubbard]. 8vo. [*Brit. Mus.*]
London, 1876

HANDEL'S Oratorio of Solomon. [The words by Thomas Morell.] 4to. Pp. 8. [*Brit. Mus.*] London [1840?]

HANG pinching ; or, the good fellowes observation. [A ballad. By William Blunden?]. Fol. S. sh. B. L. [*Pollard and Redgrave.*]
London [1636]

HANS Breitmann's barty, and other ballads. By C. G. Leland ; with . . . notes by J. C. H. [John Camden Hotten] and H. L. W. 8vo. 2 parts. [*Brit. Mus.*]   London, 1869

HAPPY (the) ending ; a play in three acts. By Ian Hay [John Hay Beith]. 8vo. Pp. 83. [*Brit. Mus.*]
London [1927]

HAPPY (a) exchange. By Herbert B. Thorneley [Osmund Bartle Words-worth]. 8vo. Pp. 311. [*Brit. Mus.*]
[1915]

HAPPY (a) husband. . . . By Patrick Hannay, Gent. . . . To which is adjoyned The good wife . . . with an exquisite discourse of epitaphs . . . by R. B., Gent. [Richard Brathwait]. 8vo. [*Brit. Mus.*]   London, 1628

HAPPY (the) lovers ; or, the beau meta-morphos'd : a ballad farce. . . . [By Henry Ward.] 8vo. Pp. 28. [*Library of Congress, Cat. of Opera Librettos.*]
1736

HAPPY (the) pair ; a new song. [By John Glanvill.] Fol. [*D. N. B.* vol. 21, p. 407.]   London [1706?]

HAPPY (the) readers. Edited by Herbert Strang [George Herbert Ely and C. J. L'Estrange]. 8vo. [*Brit. Mus.*]   London [1929, etc.]

HAPPY (the) state of believers immedi-ately after death. . . . To which is added Divine Grace Displayed. A poem (by S. A.). By J. W., author of *The Evening Conference of Christ and Nicodemus* [J. Wakelin?]. 12mo. 2 parts. [*Brit. Mus.*] London [1787?]

HARD-US'D (the) poet's complaint : inscribed to the theatric-managers and bibliopolians, of the great, little world. By Scriblerus Tertius [Paul Whitehead]. Fol. [*Brit. Mus.*]   London [1760?]

HARDYKNUTE, a fragment. [Verse. By Elizabeth Lady Wardlaw.] Fol. [*Brit. Mus.*]   Edinburgh, 1719

HARMONIZED Gregorian tones, for the Psalter. . . . [Edited by W. B. H. *i.e.* William Beadon Heathcote.] 8vo. [*Brit. Mus.*]   Oxford, 1849

HAROLD'S cross ; a romance of common freedom. [A play, in verse. Signed : J. C. N. *i.e.* John Cheesman Norwood]. 8vo. Pp. 31. [*Brit. Mus.*]
[Glasgow, 1927]

HARRY [Hapgood ; a biographical sketch.] By Neith Boyce [Mrs Hutchins Hapgood]. 8vo. Pp. 144. [*Brit. Mus.*]   New York, 1923

HARVEST thoughts. By the author of *The Lamplighter* [Francis Bourdillon]. 12mo. [*Brit. Mus.*]
London [1862]
Signed : F. B.

HATE. By Allen Grant [Arthur Douglas Howden Smith]. 8vo. Pp. 319. [*Amer. Cat.*]   New York, 1928

HATE (the) of treason ; with a touch of the late treason. By N. B. [Nicholas Breton]. 4to. [*Christie-Miller Cat.*] 1816

HATTIGE ; or, the amours of the King of Tamaran : a novel. [Translated from the French of Gabriel de Bremond by B. B.] 12mo. [*Brit. Mus.*]   1692

HAVE with you to Saffron-Walden ; or, Gabriell Harvey's hunt is up. . . . [By Thomas Nash. The introduction signed : J. P. C. *i.e.* John Payne Collier.] 4to. Pp. 155. [*Brit. Mus.*]
London, 1870

*HAWKSTONE ; a tale of and for England . . .
Not by Elizabeth Missing Sewell but by William Sewell. See *Brit. Mus. ; D. N. B. ;* Boase's *Mod. Eng. Biog.*

HAWKSTONE (the) handbook ; an illustrated guide to Hawkstone Park, with a notice of the Hill family. . . . Third edition. [By H. R. H. Southam and R. E. Davies.] 8vo. Pp. 48. [*Brit. Mus.*]   Shrewsbury, 1905
Preface signed : H. R. H. S. and R. E. D.

HAYDN. By Michel Brenet [Marie Bobillier]. Translated by C. Leonard Leese. . . . 8vo. Pp. xii. 143. [*Brit. Mus.*]   London, 1926

HEADS of chemistry. [By John Aiken, M.D.] 8vo. Pp. 76. [Hawkes' *Lanca-shire Books*, p. 133.] Warrington, 1781

HEART (the) of a slave girl. By Anthony Armstrong [George Anthony Armstrong Willis]. 8vo. Pp. 256. [*Brit. Mus.*]   London, 1922

*HEART (the) of Hindustan. By Ed-mund White [James Blythe Patton].
Incorrect. Edmund White is the author's real name, and Patton is a *pseud.* used by him.

HEART'S (the) journey. [Poems. By Siegfried Sassoon.] 8vo. Ff. 28. [*Brit. Mus.*]   New York, 1927

HEART'S - EASE (the) ; poems on sacred subjects. [By S. M. Grainger?] 16mo. [*Brit. Mus.*]   London, 1845
Signed : S. M. G.

HEATHER — Hay—Houses — Health ; being a description of land reclamation near the New Forest, and leaves from the life of a land lover. By the author of *Garden first in Land Development* [William Webb]. 8vo. Pp. 168. [*Brit. Mus.*]   Boscombe, 1929
Garden first in Land Development (1919) is not anonymous.

HEIRE (the); a comedy . . . Written by T. M. [Thomas May]. 4to. [*D.N.B.* vol. 37, p. 144.] 1620

Reprinted in Dodsley's *Old Plays.*

HELICON Hill; being a pleasant posy of rather wild flowers gathered at the foothills of Parnassus. . . . By Felix Folio, Gent. of London [William Maas]. 16mo. Pp. 46. [Millard's *Bibl. of Lovat Fraser.*] London, 1921

HELL destroyed! Now first translated from the French of d'Alembert [or rather from *L'Enfer détruit* of Baron d'Holbach], etc. (Part II. A critical dissertation on the torments of Hell . . . Now first translated from the French [*i.e.* from a french version of the work *Of the torments of Hell* by Samuel Richardson, Baptist Minister]. 12mo. 2 parts. Pp. 83. [*Brit. Mus.*] London, 1823

HELL in an uproar, occasioned by a scuffle that happened between the lawyers and the physicians, for superiority. [Verse. By Richard Burridge.] Fol. Pp. 16. London, 1700

Authorship revealed in the advt. at the end of his "The Apostate Prince."

HELPS to worship; a manual for Holy Communion . . . Compiled by two priests [Charles Boyd and H. G. J. Meara]. 16mo. Pp. vi. 74. [*Brit. Mus.*] Oxford [1877]

HENRIE Cornelius Agrippa, of the Vanitie and Uncertaintie of artes and sciences. Englished by Ia. San. Gent. [James Sanford]. 4to. B. L. [*Brit. Mus.*] London, 1569

HENRY Lamb. [By G. L. K. *i.e.* George L. Kennedy.] 4to. Pp. 29. [*Brit. Mus.*] London, 1924

"Contemporary British Artists."

HENRY of Navarre, Ohio. By Holworthy Hall [Harold Everett Porter]. 8vo. Pp. 191. [*Brit. Mus.*] New York, 1914

HENRY'S first scripture lessons . . . By the author of *Home and its duties* [Mrs J. Werner Laurie]. 16mo. [*Brit. Mus.*] London [1869]

HEPTAMERON (the) . . . new translation from the French [by William M. Thomson]. 8vo. [*Brit. Mus.*] [1896]

Signed : W.

HER privates we. By Private 19022 [Frederic Manning]. 8vo. Pp. 453. [*Brit. Mus.*] London, 1930

Previously published under the title, "The middle parts of fortune," *q.v.*

HERALD (the) of literature; or, a review of the most considerable publications that will be made in the course of the ensuing winter; with extracts. [By William Godwin.] 8vo. [F. K. Brown's *Godwin.*] London, 1784

HERBERT Tresham; a tale. . . . By J. M. Neale. [With an introduction signed : J. H. *i.e.* Joseph Haskoll.] 8vo. [*Brit. Mus.*] London, 1870

HERCULES, king of clubs! A farce . . . By F. F. Cooper . . . with . . . remarks by D. G. [George Daniel]. 12mo. Pp. 22. [*Brit. Mus.*] London [1871]

Lacy's Acting Edition of Plays, vol. 89.

HERE beginneth a song of the Lordes Supper. [By Emery Tilney.] [*Pollard and Redgrave.*] London [1550?]

Signed : E. T.

Wrongly attributed to Edmund Tilney.

HERE begynneth a newe treatyse deuyded in thre parties.

The fyrst is to know, ꝛ have ĩ mynde The wretchednes of all mankynde . . .

[By Miles Hogarde?] 4to. B. L. [*Brit. Mus.*] [London, 1550?]

But Pollard and Redgrave, *S. T. C.,* give no attribution at all.

HERE begynneth a lytell Cronycle, translated (out of Frenche) [by Alexander Barclay] and im-printed at the cost and charge of Rycharde Pyn-son . . . [Johnstone and Robertson's *Bibl. Aberd.* i. 22.] London [1517?]

HERE begynneth the castell of laboure. [Translated by Alexander Barclay from Pierre Gringoire's *Le Chateau de labour.*] [*D. N. B.* vol. 3, p. 161.] London [1505]

For a later edition see "The castell of labour."

HERE begynneth the Kalendar of Shepherdes. [Translated by Alexander Barclay?] Fol. [Johnstone and Robertson's *Bibl. Aberd.* i. 9.] London, 1506

The copy in the Grenville collection (*Brit. Mus.*) is the only one known. For an earlier edition see "The Kalendayr of the shyppars."

HERE ensueth a lytell treatyse named the Tauerne of goostly helthe. [By Alexander Barclay.] 12mo. Pp. 16. [Johnstone and Robertson's *Bibl. Aberd.* i. 26.] London, 1522

HERE is a merry jest of the mylner of Abington. [Sometimes ascribed to Andrew Borde.] 4to. [*Pollard and Redgrave.*] London, N.D.

Another edition begins, "A right pleasant historie . . ." *q.v.*

*HEREDITARY right exemplified : . . .

The full title continues " . . . to his son H—y, upon his late discipline at Westminster."

It was certainly not by Curll himself but is merely put into his mouth. R. Straus (*The Unspeakable Curll,* p. 289) conjectures that the author may have been Samuel Wesley.

*HERMIT (the) in Van Dieman's Land.
The *Brit. Mus.* now attributes this to Henry Savary.

HERO (a) from the forge; a biographical sketch of Elihu Burritt. [By A. S. Dyer.] 8vo. [*Brit. Mus.*]
London [1877]

HEROINE (the) musqueteer; or, the female warriour: a true history . . . of pleasant adventures in the campaignes of 1676 and 1677. Translated out of French [of the Sieur de Préchac]. 8vo. Pp. 270. [*Brit. Mus.*]
London, 1700

HEROINES of the faith. [By Frank Mundell.] 8vo. Pp. 160. [*Brit. Mus.*]
[1928]
The first edition bears the author's name.

*HEZEKIAH'S return of praise . . .
For Litleton, *read* Littleton.

HIDDEN joy; points of meditation on the life of our Blessed Lord. . . . Compiled by a priest of the Diocese of Birmingham (C. J. B.) [Charles J. Bowen]. 16mo. [*Brit. Mus.*]
London, 1869

HIDDEN (the) Kingdom. By Francis Beeding [John Leslie Palmer and Hilary Aidan St George Saunders]. 8vo. Pp. 320. [*Amer. Cat.*]
London [1927]

HIDDEN out; a detective story. By Howard Fielding [Charles Witheril Hooke]. 12mo. Pp. 256. [*Publishers' Weekly*, 18th Feb. 1928.]
New York, 1927

HIGH ground; a novel. By Jonathan Brooks [John Calvin Mellett]. 8vo. Pp. 317. [*Amer. Cat.*]
Indianapolis [1928]

HILARY Thornton. [A novel.] By Hubert Wales [William Piggott]. 8vo. Pp. 318. [*Brit. Mus.*] London [1909]

*HILLS (the) of Hell . . .
For W. M. Chapman Houston, *read* Wellesley Desmond Mountjoy Chapman-Huston.

HIMATIA-POLEOS; the triumphs of olde draperie: or, the rich cloathing of England. Performed . . . at the enstalment of Sr Thomas Hayes Knight in the high office of Lord Maior of London . . . the 29 day of October, 1614. Devised and written by A. M., Citizen and draper of London [Anthony Munday]. 4to. [*Brit. Mus.*] London, 1614
See also "Metropolis coronata . . ." and "Sidero-Thriambos . . ."

HINDU law in Bombay; a plea for its codification. [By Framji Rustamji Bhikaji.] 8vo. Pp. 49. [*Brit. Mus.*]
Bombay, 1892
Signed: F. R. V.

HINDU music. [By Sir Sourindro Mohun Tagore.] Reprinted from the "Hindoo Patriot." 8vo. Pp. x. 43. [*Brit. Mus.*] Calcutta, 1874

HINTS concerning the means of promoting religion in ourselves and others. [By Thomas Richards, curate of St Sepulchre's, London.] Fol. S. sh. [*Brit. Mus.*] [London, 1750?]

HINTS for the times; or, modern popery illustrated: being a few deductions drawn from the principles advocated in the Oxford Tracts for the times. By a Clergyman [Rev. —— Attwood, of Mytholm Bridge, Holmfirth.] 12mo. Pp. 40. [*Brit. Mus.*] Oxford, 1837

HINTS on popular song writing. [By D. M. Winkler.] 8vo. Pp. 23. [*Amer. Cat.*] New York [1928]

HINTS on the culture of character by . . . G. Croly . . . H. M. Villiers. . . . [Edited by J. H. *i.e.* James Hogg.] 8vo. [*Brit. Mus.*] Edinburgh, 1855-6

HIS Imperial Highness the Grand Duke Alexis in the United States of America during the winter of 1871-72. [By William W. Tucker.] 8vo. Pp. 221. [*Brit. Mus.*] Cambridge [Mass.] 1872

*HISTORICAL (an) account of the antient rights . . .
The attribution to Andrew Fletcher, of Saltoun, is repudiated in Macfie's *Bibl. of A. Fletcher*, p. 22.

*HISTORICAL (an) outline of the Greek Revolution.
An edition in the following year (1826) bears the author's name.

HISTORICAL sketch of and remarks upon Congressional Caucuses for President and Vice-President. [By Matthew Carey.] From *The Olive Branch*. 8vo. Pp. 36. [Sabin's *Dictionary*, iii. 340.]
Philadelphia, 1816
The Olive Branch is not anonymous.

HISTORICAL sketches of civil liberty; from the reign of Henry VIIth to the accession of the House of Stuart. [By James Brewster.] 8vo. London, 1788

HISTORICAL (an) treatise written by an author of the Communion of the Church of Rome [L. Du Four de Longuerue] touching transubstantiation. Wherein is made appear that according to the principles of that Church, this doctrine cannot be an article of Faith. [Translated from the French and edited by W. Wake.] 4to. [*Brit. Mus.*] London, 1687

HISTORIE (the) of the Council of Trent. . . . Written in Italian by Pietro Goave [Pietro Sarpi] and faithfully translated into English by Nathaniel Brent. Fol. Pp. 825. [*Brit. Mus.*] London, 1620

HISTORIE (the) of the reformation of the Church of Scotland. [Edited by D. B. *i.e.* David Buchanan.] Fol. [*Brit. Mus.*] 1644
The title of an edition of 1790 begins: "The history of the reformation . . ."

HISTORIES or tales of past times told by Mother Goose; with morals. Written in French by M. Perrault and Englished by G. M. Gent. [Guy Miège?] [*Brit. Mus.*] London, 1719
This is the eleventh edition of "The tales of Mother Goose."

HISTORY (the) and antiquities of Colchester. [By P. Morant.] 8vo. Pp. 226. [*Brit. Mus.*]
Colchester, 1789
*HISTORY (the) and the mystery of Good Friday.
Published under the pseudonym: Lewis Carbonell.

HISTORY (the) and philosophy of earthquakes, from the remotest to the present times. . . . By a member of the Royal Academy of Berlin [John Bevis]. 8vo. Pp. 351. [*Brit. Mus.*] London, 1757

HISTORY (the) of Agathon. Translated from the German [of Wieland, by John Richardson, of Eworth, Yorkshire]. 12mo. 4 vols. [W. Taylor's *Historic Survey of German Poetry.*] London, 1773
*HISTORY (the) of America . . .
For Jendidiah *read* Jedidiah.

*HISTORY of England and France . . .
A later edition (1861) bears the author's name.

HISTORY (the) of female favourites. . . . Translated from "Histoire des Favorites," par Mademoiselle D * * * [—— de la Roche-Guilhem]. 8vo. [*Brit. Mus.*] 1772

HISTORY (a) of Hadleigh, Suffolk. [By Hugh Pigot.] 8vo.
Hadleigh, 1859
From an inscribed copy.

*HISTORY (the) of Miss Clarinda Cathcart. . . . [By Mrs Jane Marshall.]
The *Brit. Mus.* now corrects this name to Jean Marishall.

HISTORY (the) of Mr Fantom. [By Hannah More.] 12mo. [*Brit. Mus.*]
London, 1831
Signed: Z.

HISTORY (the) of New Holland. . . . With a particular account of its produce and inhabitants, and a description of Botany Bay. [By George Barrington.] . . . 8vo. Pp. xxiv. 254. [*Brit. Mus.*]
London, 1787

HISTORY (the) of Nourjahad. By the editor of *Sidney Bidulph* (Frances Sheridan). [Edited by H. V. M. *i.e.* H. V. Marrot.] 8vo. Pp. ix. 120. [*Brit. Mus.*] London, 1927
*HISTORY of Prince Titi . . .
The title-page really begins: "Histoire du Prince Titi, A.R. The History of Prince Titi. . . ." The original, published in the same year (1736) as this translation, was also anonymous. For another translation see "Memoirs and history of Prince Titi."

HISTORY (the) of Rome from the earliest times to the fall of the Empire; for schools and families. [By Thomas Milner, M.A., F.R.G.S.] 12mo. [*Brit. Mus.*] London [1848]
*HISTORY (the) of S. Elizabeth . . .
For History, *read* Historie.

*HISTORY of the Athenian Society . . . By L. R.
"By L. R." is a mistake. No indication of authorship appears on the title-page. The Epistle dedicatory is signed: R. L.

HISTORY (the) of the Cathedral Church of Hereford. [By Richard Rawlinson.] [*Gross' Sources of Engl. Hist.* p. 126.]
London, 1717
*HISTORY of the discovery of America . . .
The author was not the Rev. James Steward, but Henry Trumbull (not *Turnbull* as given in the footnote). The first edition, 1810, was issued as "By a Citizen of Connecticut," but editions of 1822 and 1836 bear Trumbull's name. The Rev. James Steward, D.D., has caused much trouble. There was an issue in 1810 which bears this name on the title-page as the author. This was probably the second issue of the first edition, the typography with the exception of the imprint, being identical. But the imprint "Brooklyn (L.I.), Printed by Grant & Wells for J. W. Carew" is fictitious, and as the Rev. James Steward has been found in no work of American Biography, he too may be considered equally fictitious. The whole matter is a bibliographical mystery. See the *Bulletin of the Bibliographical Society of America*, vol. 4, no. 3, 4, p. 46.

HISTORY of the families of Skeet, Somerscales, Widdrington, Wilby, Murray, Blake, Grimshaw, and others. By a connection of the same [Francis John Angus Skeet]. 4to. Pp. 179. [*Brit. Mus.*] London, 1906

HISTORY of the First International. By Yu. M. Steklov [Ovshy Moiseevich Nakhamkis]. 8vo. Pp. xi. 463. [*Brit. Mus.*] London, 1928

HISTORY (the) of the French Academy. . . . Written in French by M. Paul Pellison. [Translated by H. S. *i.e.* Henry Some.] 8vo. [*Brit. Mus.*]
London, 1657

HISTORY (the) of the intrigues and gallantries of Christina, Queen of Sweden and of her court, whilst she was at Rome. [By Christian Gottfried Franckenstein.] Faithfully render'd into English [by Philip Hollingworth]. . . . 12mo. Pp. 328. [Barbier's *Dictionnaire; Brit. Mus.*]
London, 1697

HISTORY of the late war; including sketches of Buonaparte, Nelson and Wellington. For children. [By John Gibson Lockhart.] 12mo. [*Brit. Mus.*]
London, 1832

Preface signed: I. G. L.

HISTORY (the) of the life and death of David, with moral reflections; a translation from the French [of F. T. de Choisy]. . . . 8vo. Pp. 163, 39. [*Brit. Mus.*]
London, 1741

HISTORY of the reign of George the Third. . . . With a review of the late war. [By Robert Macfarlane.] 8vo. [*D. N. B.* vol. 35, p. 76.] London, 1770

HISTORY (the) of the royal genealogy of Spain . . . [Abridged from Mariana and others] by the translator of Mariana's History of Spain [Mlle. de la Roche-Guilhem?]. 8vo. [*Brit. Mus.*]
1724

HISTORY (the) of the serail and of the court of the Grand Seigneur. [By Michel Baudier.] Translated by E. G(rimestone). 4to. 2 parts. [*Pollard and Redgrave.*] London, 1635

*HISTORY of the war in America. . . . [By Patrick Gordon.]

Sabin merely states "Lowndes attributes the work to P. Gordon." There does not seem to be any authority for "Patrick."

*HISTORY (the) of the workhouse. . . . By A. W. . . .

Signed: A. W. The initials are not on the title-page.

*HISTORY (the) of Wales . . .

For By a lady of the Principality of Wales, *read* By a lady of the Principality.

HOB'S wedding; a new farce of two acts. [By John Leigh.] Being the sequel of *The Country Wake.* 12mo. [*Brit. Mus.*] London, 1720

HOGS caracter of a projector; wherein is disciphered the manner and shape of that vermine. [From *Machiavel* by Thomas Heywood.] . . . 4to. Pp. 6. [*Brit. Mus.*] London, 1642

HOLIDAY (a) in Scandinavia. [By —— Kinross.] 8vo. [Pettersen's *Norsk Lexikon,* col. 207.] Glasgow, 1871

HOLIDAY notes of some days in the land of the Tsar, July 1st to 24th, 1901. [By William H. Macleod.] 4to.
N.P., N.D.

Presentation copy signed by the author.

HOLY Baptism. [By John Sidney Davenport.] 8vo. [*Brit. Mus.*]
[1881]

HOLY (the) Catholic Church; an Anglican essay. By Hakluyt Egerton [Arthur Boutwood]. 8vo. Pp. 93. [*Brit. Mus.*] London, 1921

HOLY (the) desires of death: or, a collection of some thoughts of the Fathers of the Church to shew how Christians ought to despise life and to desire death. By the R. F. Lalemant. Englished by T. V. [Thomas Vincent F. Sadler]. . . . 12mo. Pp. 336. [*Brit. Mus.*] N.P. 1678

HOLY (a) oyl and a sweet perfume: taken out of the Sanctuary of the most sacred scriptures. . . . By J. H. [James Harrington]. . . . Fol. [*Brit. Mus.*] [London] 1669

The eighth treatise is entitled "Noah's Dove," and bears the date 1645. Prefixed are the portraits of Sir James and of Lady Katherine Harrington, dated 1654.

HOLY (an) priesthood and spiritual sacrifices. [By William Tarbet.] 8vo. Pp. 8. [*Brit. Mus.*] [1870?]

*HOME life in Russia . . .

For Krystn, *read* Krystyn.

HOME (the) Secretary. [A novel.] By Wilmot Kaye [Edward Platt]. 8vo. Pp. 319. [*Brit. Mus.*]
London, 1910

HOMERIC ballads; with translations and notes by the late William Maginn. [Edited by J. C. *i.e.* John Conington?] 8vo. Pp. xii. 299. [*Brit. Mus.*]
London, 1850

HOMESPUN. By Wilhelmina Stitch [Ruth Collie]. 8vo. Pp. 63. [*Brit. Mus.*] London, 1930

HOMILY; Christmas Eve, 1871. (Homily; Christmas 1879.) [By William Tarbet.] 8vo. 2 parts. [*Brit. Mus.*] 1871-79

HONEST (the) jury; or, Caleb triumphant. [A ballad, by William Pulteney, afterwards Earl of Bath, upon the acquittal of Nicholas Amhurst.] Fol. S. sh. [*Brit. Mus.*]
[London, 1729]

HONEY-COMB (the), containing the life of Taulerus, Young's Poem on resignation, a hymn by Addison. [Edited by W. A. *i.e.* William Alexander, of York?] 24mo. 3 parts. [*Brit. Mus.*] York, 1831

HONEYMOON dialogues. By James James [Arthur Henry Adams]. 8vo. Pp. 159. [*Brit. Mus.*] London, 1916

HONORARY (the) whip; a sporting novel. By Raymond Carew [Frank Victor Hughes-Hallett]. 8vo. Pp. vi. 309. [*Brit. Mus.*] London, 1909

*HONOUR (the) of the seals . . .
   According to Ralph Straus (*The Unspeak-
   able Curll*, p. 305), this was written by
   Edmund Curll.

*HOOP-PETTICOAT (the) . . .
   Not by J. Durand de Breval, but by
   Francis Chute. See the note to "The
   Petticoat . . ." in the supplement.

H O R O M E T R I A ; or, the compleat
   diallist ; wherein the whole mystery
   of the art of dialling is plainly taught.
   . . . By Thomas Stirrup, Philomath.
   Whereunto is added an appendix . . .
   by W. L. [William Leybourn]. 4to.
   Pp. 203. [*Brit. Mus.*]   London, 1652

HOROSCOPE (the) ; a quarterly review
   of astrology and occult science. Edited
   by Rollo Ireton [Ralph Stirling]. 8vo.
   [*Brit. Mus.*]   London, 1902-4

*HORSE (the) Guards . . .
   For John Josiah Hort, *read* Richard
   Hort.

HOUNSLOW-HEATH ; a poem. . . .
   [By Wetenhall Wilkes.] 4to. Pp. 21.
   [*Brit. Mus.*]   London, 1747

HOUSE (a) divided. By E. M. Jameson
   [Elaine Anthony Jones]. . . . 8vo.
   Pp. viii. 312. [*Brit. Mus.*]
                     London, 1905

H O U S E (the) of Dr Edwardes. By
   Francis Beeding [John Leslie Palmer
   and Hilary Aidan St George Saunders].
   8vo. Pp. 308. [*Amer. Cat.*]
                     London [1927]

HOUSE (the) of the secret—La Maison
   des hommes vivants. By Claude
   Farrère [Charles Bargone]. Authorised
   translation by Arthur Livingston. 8vo.
   Pp. 234. [*Brit. Mus.*]   London, 1923

HOUSEHOLDERS (the); another story
   of the Orkneys, by H. C., author of
   Island notes in wartime [H. Camp-
   bell]. 8vo. Pp. 72. [*Brit. Mus.*]
                     Edinburgh, 1921

HOUSES, haunts and works of Rubens.
   . . . By F. W. Fairholt. [Edited by
   J. D. *i.e.* James Dafforne.] 8vo. [*Brit.
   Mus.*]   London, 1871

HOW and whither a Chrysten man
   ought to flye the horryble plague of
   the pestilence ; a sermon . . . translated out of hie Almaine into Englishe
   [by Miles Coverdale]. 8vo. [*Brit.
   Mus.*]   London [*c.* 1560]

HOW sin is strengthened and how it is
   overcome. [By James Nayler.] 8vo.
   Pp. 15. [*Brit. Mus.*]   London, 1660
   Signed : J. N.

HOW to come to Christ. By the author
   of *Our new life in Christ.* Edited
   by a parish priest [Hon. Charles Leslie
   Courtenay]. 8vo. [*Brit. Mus.*]
                     London, 1873
   Signed : C. L. C.

HOW to get married. By E. Montale
   [P. Poliakoff]. 8vo. Pp. 41.
                     London, 1921
   Acknowledgment by the author.

HOW to go racing with pleasure and
   comfort in England and France. By
   a member of Tattersalls [W. Shake-
   shaft]. 8vo. [*Brit. Mus.*]   1901

HOW to grow and cure your own
   tobacco. [By W. A. S. Hellyar.] 8vo.
   Pp. 15. [*Brit. Mus.*]   London [1923]

HOW to play draughts well. By
   Chequerist [Rowland Addams Wil-
   liams]. 8vo. Pp. 32. [*Brit. Mus.*]
                     London [1894?]

HOW to sail a dinghy. . . . By Centre-
   board [C. A. Grant]. 8vo. Pp. 30.
   [*Brit. Mus.*]   London [1930]

HOW to spell correctly. [By Charles
   Platt.] 8vo. Pp. 92. [*Brit. Mus.*]
                     London [1925]

HOW to study the Bible. . . . [By
   John Clifford and others. Edited by
   F. A. A. *i.e.* F. A. Atkins.] Third
   edition. 8vo. Pp. v. 69. [*Brit. Mus.*]
                     London [1890]

HOWLING (the) mob ; an indictment
   of democracy. By a Gentleman with
   a duster [Harold Begbie]. 8vo.
   Pp. 126. [*Brit. Mus.*]   London, 1927

HOYLE abridged ; a treatise on back-
   gammon : or, short rules for short
   memories, with the laws of the game.
   Adapted either for the head or pocket.
   By Bob Short, Jun. [Robert Withy].
   Printed for the benefit of families to
   prevent wrangling. 24mo. Pp. 24.
   [Jessel's *Bibl. of playing cards*, p. 303.]
                     London, 1819

HOYLE abridged ; a treatise on the
   game of chess. . . . Selected principally from the stratagem of chess. By
   Bob Short [Robert Withy]. 16mo.
   Pp. 24. [Jessel's *Bibl. of playing
   cards*, p. 303.]   London, 1824

HOYLE abridged ; short rules for short
   memories at the game of whist, with
   the laws of the game. Adapted either
   for the head or pocket. By Bob Short
   [Robert Withy]. Printed for the benefit
   of families to prevent scolding.
   [Jessel's *Bibl. of playing cards*, p. 302.]
                     London, 1793
   Part II. appeared in the same year.

HUDIBRAS [*i.e.* George Sacheverell]
   on Calamy's imprisonment and Wild's
   poetry. To the Bishops. Fol. S. sh.
   [*D. N. B.* vol. 61, p. 224.]
                     [London, 1663]
   An answer to Robert Wild's ironical verses
   of sympathy on Calamy's imprisonment,
   and was in turn answered in " Your servant,
   Sir, by Ralpho to Hudibras " and " Hudibras
   answered by True de Case."

HUGH Herbert's inheritance. . . . By Caroline Austin [Mrs —— Whitway]. 8vo. Pp. 287. [*Brit. Mus.*] London, 1889

HUMAN sacrifice. [By Sir J. E. D. D. Acton?] 8vo. Pp. 47. [*Brit. Mus.*] London, private print [1864?]

HUMBLE (an) supplicacion unto God, for the restoringe of hys holye woorde, into the Churche of Englande. [By Thomas Becon.] 8vo. [*Pollard and Redgrave.*] Strasburgh in Elsas [London] 1544

HUMOROUS and dramatic sketches, monologues, recitations, rhymes and songs. By "Cue," author of *Extra Turns* [A. Leonard Summers]. 8vo. Pp. 55. [*Brit. Mus.*] London [1912]

HUMOR'S looking glasse. [By Samuel Rowlands. The introduction signed: J. P. C. *i.e.* John Payne Collier.] 4to. Pp. 24. [*Brit. Mus.*] [London, 1870]

HUNDRED (a) points on how to make money. By Pensive [Walter E. Sleight]. 8vo. Pp. 63. [*Brit. Mus.*] Cleethorpes [1929]

HUNTED down. By Charles Dickens; with some account of T. C. Wainewright . . . [by J. C. H. *i.e.* John Camden Hotten]. 8vo. [*Brit. Mus.*] London [1871]

HUNTING the fox. By Sabretache [A. S. Barrow]. 8vo. Pp. 23. [*Brit. Mus.*] London [1926]

HUNTSMAN'S (the) delight, or the forrester's pleasure. [A song.] By J. M. [Joseph Martin?]. Fol. S. sh. [*Brit. Mus.*] [London, 1670?]

HYDRO-SIDEREON; or, a treatise of ferruginous waters, especially the Ipswich Spaw. . . . [By William Coward?] 8vo. [*Brit. Mus.*] [London, 1717] Signed: W. C.

*HYMN (an) to the Redeemer. . . . For William Godwin, *read* William Goldwin.

HYMNS and poems for very little children. By the Hon. M. E. L. [Hon. Mary Emma Lawrence?]. 8vo. 2 series. [*Brit. Mus.*] London [1871-75]

HYMNS for the use of St Paul's, Oxford. [By Alfred Hackman?] 24mo. Pp. 250. [*Brit. Mus.*] Oxford, 1859

HYSTORIE (the) of Hamblet. [Translated from Les histoires tragiques of François de Belleforest.] 4to. B. L. [Gollancz's *Sources of Hamlet.*] London, 1608

I

I HOPE they won't mind. [Reminiscences. By Percy Colson.] 8vo. Pp. 270. [*Who's Who.*] London, 1930

I REMEMBER; or, photographs from a home album. . . . By the author of *Copsley annals* [Emily Steele Elliott]. 8vo. Pp. 164. [*Brit. Mus.*] London, 1870

*IADES. . . . For Iades, *read* Iadis. The date of publication was [1888].

IDEA; the shepheard's garland. . . . [By Michael Drayton. Edited by J. P. C. *i.e.* John Payne Collier.] 4to. [*Brit. Mus.*] London [*c.* 1870]

IDYLL (an) on the peace [of Ryswick. By John Oldmixon]. Fol. Pp. 10. [*Brit. Mus.*] London, 1697

IF four walls told; a village tale in three acts. By Edward Percy [Edward Percy Smith]. 8vo. Pp. 92. [*Brit. Mus.*] London, 1922

"I'LL Neville you." . . . [A letter to the Editor of the *Gateshead Observer*. By Michael Aislabie Denham.] 8vo. [*Brit. Mus.*] [Durham, 1851] Signed: M. A. D.

ILLS (the) of industry; or, Britain's industrial muddle. . . . By "Hospitaller" [Henry H. Spittall]. 8vo. Pp. 15. [*Brit. Mus.*] Glasgow, 1927

ILLUSTRATED guide to Abergele and Pensarn. . . . [By E. L. *i.e.* Egerton Leigh.] (New edition.) 8vo. Pp. vii. 31. [*Brit. Mus.*] Abergele, 1900

ILLUSTRATED narrative of the dreadful murders on the Maungatapan Mountain, and track between the Wakamarina River and Nelson . . . New Zealand. [By D. M. Luckie.] 8vo. [*Brit. Mus.*] Nelson, N.Z., 1866 Signed: D. M. L.

*ILLUSTRATIONS of baptismal fonts . . . Signed: T. C.

ILLUSTRATIONS of manners and expences of antient times in England, in the fifteenth, sixteenth, and seventeenth centuries. . . . [By John Nichols.] 4to. [Gross's *Bibl. of municipal history.*] London, 1797

ILLUSTRIOUS (the) French lovers; being the true histories of the amours of several French persons of quality. . . . Written originally in French [by Robert Challes] and translated into English by Mrs P. Aubin. 12mo. 2 vols. [Barbier's *Dictionnaire*.] London, 1739
Second edition; the first was issued in 1727.

ILLUSTRIOUS (the) Hugo Grotius of the law of warre and peace, with annotations. [Translated by C. B. *i.e.* Clement Barksdale.] 8vo. [*Brit. Mus.*] 1654

ILLUSTRIOUS (the) shepherdess. [Translated from the "Sucessos y Prodigios de Amor" of J. Perez de Montalban by E. P. *i.e.* Edward Phillips.] 8vo. [*Brit. Mus.*] London, 1656

IMAGO regia; the churchman's religious remembrance of the two hundred and fiftieth anniversary of the decollation of King Charles the First . . . [Compiled] by D. M. [Douglas Macleane]. 8vo. Pp. 35. [*Brit. Mus.*] London [1899]

IMITATIONS and translations from Classics; with original poems [some signed L. B. *i.e.* Lord Byron] never before published: collected by John Cam Hobhouse. 8vo. [*Brit. Mus.*] London, 1809

IMMANUEL the salvation of Israel. The word of the Lord came unto me the twelfth day of the sixth month, in the year accompted, 1657. Concerning the Iewes and scattered tribes of Israel. . . . Written by . . . J. P. [John Perrot]. 4to. Pp. 10. [*Brit. Mus.*] London, 1658

IMMORTALITY; an essay in discovery. . . . [By] B. H. Streeter . . . the author of *Pro Christo et ecclesia* [Lily Dougall]. 8vo. Pp. xiv. 380. [*Brit. Mus.*] London, 1917

IMPARTIAL history of the life, character, amours, travels and transactions of Mr John Barber, City-printer and Lord Mayor of London. Written by several hands. [Edited by Edmund Curll.] 8vo. [Straus' *Curll.*] London, 1741

IMPARTIAL (an) representation of the poor cotton spinners in Lancashire. . . . [Signed: W. C. and R. M. *i.e.* Ralph Mather]. 8vo. [*Brit. Mus.*] London, 1780

*IMPERFECT (an) pourtraicture . . .
The sheets of this edition were published later in the same year with a new title-page, "Charles the Second, King of Great Britain, France and Ireland . . . ", bearing the author's name.

*IMPERIAL (an) manifesto. . . . By Mahaba.
For Mahaba, *read* Maharba.

IMPERIOUS (the) brother. [Translated from the "Sucessos y Prodigios de Amor, novel 3, of J. Pérez de Montalban, by E. P. *i.e.* Edward Phillips.] 8vo. Pp. 84. [*Brit. Mus.*] London, 1656

*IMPORTANCE (the) and advantage of Cape Breton . . .
This is now ascribed to William Bollan by all authorities.

IMPORTANCE (the) of the British plantations in America to this kingdom; with the state of their trade, and methods for improving it. [By F. Hall.] 8vo. Pp. 114. [*Brit. Mus.*] London, 1731
Another issue in the same year has the author's name at the dedication.

IMPORTANT questions and other useful information for Protestants of all denominations. [Signed: D. O'C. *i.e.* Daniel O'Connor, of Cork.] 8vo. Pp. 53. [*Brit. Mus.*] [Cork, 1877]

IMPOSSIBLE (the) island; Corsica: its people and its sport. By "Snaffle" [Robert Dunkin]. . . . 8vo. Pp. 224. London, 1923

IMPOSSIBLE (an) thing; a tale. [Translated from La Fontaine by William Congreve. Verse.] 4to. Pp. 16. [*Brit. Mus.*] London, 1720

IMPRESSIONS of Jesus; being an account of how he impressed the friends among whom he grew up. By one of his followers [Buchanan Blake]. 8vo. Pp. 255. [*Brit. Mus.*] London [1925]

IMPUDENT (the) babbler baffled, or the falsety of that assertion utter'd by Bradshaw in Cromwell's new erected slaughter-house, namely that Charles I. was no hereditary but an elective king . . . detected and confuted. . . . [By John Brydall.] 4to. [*Lincoln's Inn Lib.*] London, 1703

IMPRISONMENT (the) and death of King Charles I., related by one of his judges: being extracts from the memoirs of E. Ludlow. [Edited by J. T. H. *i.e.* J. T. Hornby.] 8vo. [*Brit. Mus.*] Edinburgh, 1882
Aungervyle Society, publication No. 10.

IMPROPRIETY (the) of open-communion between Baptists and Pædobaptists in the Lord's Supper. . . . By N. S. [Joseph Jenkins, of Wrexham]. 12mo. Pp. 16. [Whitley's *Bapt. Bibl.* vol. ii. p. 14.] 1786

IN clay and bronze; a study in personality. By Brinsley Macnamara [A. E. Weldon]. 8vo. Pp. 262. New York, 1921
Previously published as "The Irishman. By Oliver Blyth."

IN commemoration of the royal marriage, March 10th, 1863; lines to the Prince of Wales. . . . [By Albert Hiscock.] 12mo. S. sh. [*Brit. Mus.*]
[London, 1863]
Signed: A. H.

IN exile. [Verse.] By R. R. [Sir Ronald Ross]. 8vo. Pp. 84. [*Brit. Mus.*] Liverpool, 1906
A later edition (1931) bears the author's name.

IN Lawrence's Bodyguard. By Gurney Slade [Stephen Bartlett]. 8vo. Pp. xi. 267. [*Brit. Mus.*] London, 1930

IN memoriam; Dr Gee. [By Norman Moore.] 8vo. [*Brit. Mus.*]
[London, 1912]
Signed: N. M.

IN memoriam: Isaac Todhunter. Cambridge Review, March 5, 12 and 19 [1884]. [By J. E. B. Mayor.] 8vo. Pp. 60. [*Brit. Mus.*] Cambridge, 1884
Signed: J. E. B. M.

IN memoriam of the Prince Imperial of France; four sonnets by a grand nephew of Napoleon the Great [W. C. Bonaparte Wyse]. 4to. Pp. 8. [*Brit. Mus.*] Plymouth, 1879

IN memoriam Sir Thomas Lauder Brunton, F.R.S., 1844-1916. [By D'Arcy Power.] 8vo. Pp. 9. [*Brit. Mus.*] [London, 1917]
Signed: D'A.

IN memorie of that lively patterne of true pietie and unstain'd loyaltie, Mrs S. Harris. [An elegy, by Sir George Wharton?] Fol. S. sh. [*Brit. Mus.*] [London, 1649]
Signed: W. G.

IN pursuit of Dulcinea; a quixotic journey. By Henry Bernard [Henry Baerlein]. With fifteen illustrations by H. C. Brewer. 8vo. Pp. xiv. 250. [*Brit. Mus.*] London, 1904

IN the foreign legion. By Erwin Rosen [Erwin Carlé]. 8vo. Pp. xiv. 285. [*Brit. Mus.*] London, 1910

IN the honor of yᵉ passion of our lorde; and the compassyon of our blyssed lady moder of Chryste. [By Alexander Barclay.] 12mo. Pp. 39. [Johnstone and Robertson's *Bibl. Aberd.* i. 26].
London, 1522

*IN the land of the Brora . . .
For Brora, *read* Bora.

IN this booke is conteyned the names of yᵉ baylifs custos mairs a. sherefs of lōdon. [By Richard Arnold.] Fol. [*Pollard and Redgrave.*]
[Antwerp, 1503?]
Known as Arnold's Chronicle. There was another edition, also anonymous, in 1521.

IN time of war. [Hymns written and translated by R. M. M. *i.e.* R. M. Moorsom.] 8vo. Pp. 12. [*Brit. Mus.*] Winchester [1900?]

INCOGNITA; a tale of love and passion. [By William Stephens Hayward.] 8vo. Pp. viii. 312. [*Brit. Mus.*] London [1884]

INCONSISTENT (the) villains. By N. A. Temple Ellis [Neville Aldridge Holdaway]. 8vo. Pp. viii. 284. [*Brit. Mus.*] London, 1929

INCORPORATE your borough! A letter to the inhabitants of Manchester. By a radical reformer [Richard Cobden]. 8vo. Pp. 16. [*Brit. Mus.*] Manchester [1838]
No title-page.

"INCORRIGIBLE (the)"; or, naughty tricks of a merry school-girl. By O. M. S. [Olga M. Somech]. 8vo. Pp. 48. [*Brit. Mus.*] Southport, 1915

INCREDIBLE (the) truth. By Roy Devereux [Mrs Devereux Pember]. 8vo. Pp. 288. [*Brit. Mus.*]
London [1930]

*INDECORVM . . .
Signed: S. E.

INDEX (an) list of all printed editions of the English Scriptures down to 1640, in the library of the British and Foreign Bible Society. [By H. F. Moule.] 4to. [*Brit. Mus.*] 1901
Signed: H. F. M.

INDEX of places to Dugdale's Warwickshire. Second edition, by Dr Thomas. [Compiled by Sir Thomas Phillipps?] Fol. [*Brit. Mus.*] [1844?]
Dugdale's *Warwickshire*, vol. 2.

INDEX to Cartularies now or formerly existing since the dissolution of Monasteries. By T. P. [Sir Thomas Phillipps]. 12mo. [*Brit. Mus.*]
[Middle Hill] private print, 1839

INDEX to the Baker manuscripts by four members of the Cambridge Antiquarian Society (J. J. S. [John James Smith?], C. C. B. [Charles Cardale Babington], C. W. G. [Charles Wycliffe Goodwin], J. P. [John Power]). 8vo. Pp. viii. 176. [*Brit. Mus.*]
Cambridge, 1848

INDEX to the genealogies of the Tenants in capite in Domesday Book. By T. P. [Sir Thomas Phillipps]. Fol. 4 parts. [*Brit. Mus.*]
[Middle Hill, private print, 1838-42]

INDEXES to the County Visitations in the Library at Middle Hill, 1840, and to a few others in the Harl. MSS. British Museum, the Bodleian Library, and Queen's College, Oxford. [By Sir Thomas Phillipps.] Fol. Pp. 56. [*Brit. Mus.*]   [Middle Hill] 1841
Signed : T. P.
The second edition (1842) bears the author's full name.

INDIAN card reading ; the art of fortune telling by means of ordinary playing cards, explained. . . . By an adept [Caxton Hall]. Third edition. 8vo. Pp. 31. [*Brit. Mus.*]
Blackpool [1907]
A later edition (1924) bears the author's name.

INDIAN (the) prophet ; or, a review of Babu Keshub Chunder Sen's lecture "Am I an inspired prophet ?" . . . A lecture delivered at . . . Dacca [by Sitalākānta Chaṭṭopādyāya]. 8vo. Pp. 44. [*Brit. Mus.*]   Dacca, 1879
Signed : S. C.

*INDUSTRIAL (the) arts . . .
Signed : W. M.

INGENIOUS (an) and scientific discourse of witchcraft. [By John Bell, minister at Gladsmuir.] 12mo. [J. Ferguson's *Witchcraft Lit. of Scot.* p. 28.]   1705

INGOMAR the barbarian ; a play. . . . By Maria Lovell . . . with remarks . . . by D. G. [George Daniel]. . . . 12mo. Pp. 61. [*Brit. Mus.*]   London [1855]

*INNER (the) life ; hymns . . .
Not by Miss Phillipps (this is the proper spelling), but by Lucy Fletcher, afterwards Massey. *Thoughts from a girl's life* (1864) bears the latter's name.

INNER (the) life of the Navy: being an account of the inner social life led by our naval seamen. . . . By Lionel Yexley [James Woode]. 8vo. Pp. xiv. 392. [*Brit. Mus.*]   London, 1918

INNKEEPER (the) of Abbeville . . . A drama. . . . By E. Fitzball. . . . With . . . remarks by D. G. [George Daniel]. 12mo. Pp. 32. [*Brit. Mus.*]
London [1871]
Lacy's Acting Edition of Plays, vol. 90.

INNOCENCY against envy ; in a brief examination of Francis Bugg's two invective pamphlets . . . the one styled, The Quakers detected ; the other, Battering Rams against New-Rome. . . . By G. W. [George Whitehead], and S. C. [Samuel Cater ?]. 4to. Pp. 18. [*Brit. Mus.*]   London, 1691

INQUIRY into the causes of the present disarrangement of public credit in Great Britain. [By Joseph Smith, Barrister.] 8vo.   1793
MS. note on Messrs Harding's copy.

INQUIRY (an) into the genuineness of a letter dated 3rd February 1613, and signed "Mary Magdaline Davers." [Edited by J. B. *i.e.* John Bruce, F. S. A.?] 4to. Pp. 30.   London, 1864
Camden Miscellany, vol. 5.

INSTITUTIONAL religion. By Hakluyt Egerton [Arthur Boutwood]. 8vo. Pp. 24. [*Brit. Mus.*]   1914
Modern Oxford Tracts.

INSTITUTIONS, essays and maxims, political, moral and divine ; divided into four centuries. [By Francis Quarles.] 12mo. Pp. 286. [*Brit. Mus.*]
London, 1695
The first edition (1640) and many others have the title *Euchiridion* and are not anonymous. A later edition, 1698, with this same title "Institutions . . ." bears on the title-page "By the Right Honoura[ble] L. Marquis of H[alifax]." Another anonymous edition was issued in 1698, with the title "Wisdom's better than money . . ." *q.v.* [*The Library*, September 1928.]

INSTRUCTION (an) how to pray and meditate well . . . composed . . . by Father I. Balsamo . . . and translated out of French into English by Iohn Heigham [or rather, J. Everard]. 24mo. Pp. 331. [*Pollard and Redgrave.*]   St Omers, 1622

INSTRUCTION made easy ; polyglot copy and exercise books for teaching languages. By Chrysostôme Dagobert [J. B. A. Led'huy]. 4to. [*Brit. Mus.*]
London [1858]

INTEREST (the) of England, as it stands with relation to the trade of Ireland, considered ; the arguments against the Bill for prohibiting the exportation of woollen manufactures from Ireland to forreign parts fairly discusst. . . . [By —— Clements.] 4to. Pp. 23. [*Book prices current*, 1921.]   London, 1698

INTERESTING (an) historical holiday ramble to Mid Calder. . . . By the author of *A History of West Calder* [W. C. Learmonth]. 12mo. Pp. 23. [*Brit. Mus.*]   Hamilton [1887]

INTRODUCTION (an) to Royal Arch Masonry. By "Essex Master" [George Edward Roebuck]. 8vo. Pp. 111. [*Brit. Mus.*]   London, 1931
Signed : G. E. R.
Acknowledgment by the author.

INTRODUCTION (an) to the history of the revolt of the [American] Colonies. [By George Chalmers.] 8vo. [*Book prices current*, 1922.] London, 1782

    This work was suppressed by the author, who afterwards published a *History of the rise and progress of the American Colonies.*

INTRODUCTION (an) to the love of God (by Saint Augustine). [Translated by R. Fletcher.] 8vo. [*Pollard and Redgrave.*] London, 1574

INTRODUCTION (an) to the study of English rhythms, with an essay on the metre of Coleridge's " Christabel." [By H. D. Bateson.] 8vo. Pp. 24. [*Brit. Mus.*] [Manchester, 1896]

    Reprint from the *Manchester Quarterly.*

INTRODUCTORIE (a) for to lerne to rede, to pronounce and to speake French trewly; compyled for the ryghte hyh, excellent and moste vertuous lady, the lady Mary of England, doughter to our mooste gracious souerayne lorde Kynge Henry the eight. [By Giles Dewes.] B. L. 4to. [*Quaritch's Cat.*] London [*c.* 1540]

INUECTIVE (an) agaynst treason. [A ballad on the accession of Queen Mary. By Thomas Waterstoune.] Fol. S. sh. B. L. [*Pollard and Redgrave.*] London, 1553

    Signed: T. W.
    Misprinted "A ninuective . . ."

INVESTIGATION (an) into the affairs of the Delaware and Raritan Canal and Camden and Amboy Railroad Companies in reference to certain charges. By a citizen of Burlington [Henry C. Carey]. 8vo. [*Sabin's Dictionary*, iii. 329.] Newark, 1849

*INVESTIGATOR (the) . . . 1762.

    For William Whitehead, *read* Allan Ramsay, the younger. Now accepted in the *Brit. Mus.*

INVOCACYON (an) gloryous named ye psalter of Iesus. [Ascribed to Richard Whitford.] 16mo. [*D. N. B.* vol. 61, p. 128; *Pollard and Redgrave.*] London, 1529

    For other editions, see " Certaine devout and godly petition . . . " (1545) and " The psalter of Jesus . . ." (1618).

*INWARD (the) light. Reprinted from *The Inquirer* for December 1838.

    Also attributed to Robert Mackenzie Beverley. In a bound volume with other pamphlets by Beverley in the British Museum.

IPHIGENIA in Tauris. Translated from the German of W. von Goethe . . . by P. M. E. [Phillos Marion Ellis]. 8vo. [*Brit. Mus.*] London, private print, 1883

IRELAND and Norway. [By H. L. Brækstad.] 8vo. [Pettersen's *Norsk Lexikon*, col. 234.] London, 1884

IRELAND before its connection with England: and Irish land tenures under English rule. [By J. Bellows.] 4to. [*Birm. Cent. Lib.*] Birmingham [1886]

IRELAND in tears; or, a letter to St Andrew's eldest daughter's youngest son. By Major Sawney M'Cleaver [Lionel Cranfield Sackville, Duke of Dorset]. 8vo. [*Lincoln's Inn Lib.*] London, 1755

IRISH (the) Massacre; or, a true narrative of the unparallel'd cruelties exercised in Ireland upon the British Protestants . . . [By Henry Parker.] 4to. [Thomason's *Coll. of Tracts.*] [London, 1646]

*IRISHMAN (the) . . . By Oliver Blyth.

    For John Weldon, *read* A. E. Weldon. It was published in the U.S.A. as by " Brinsley Macnamara."

IRON (the) ore deposits of Dunderland. [By Hjalmar Sjögren.] [Pettersen's *Norsk Lexikon*, col. 234.] Upsala, 1894

IROQUOIS (the); or, the bright side of Indian character. By Minnie Myrtle [Mrs Anna C. Miller, *née* Johnson]. 8vo. [*Allibone's Dict.*] New York, 1855

IRREGULAR verses, suggested by the baptismal oath of the Church of England, and by her utter inability to convert heathen nations to Christianity. By J. F. L. [J. F. Laing?]. 12mo. [*Brit. Mus.*] London, 1867

IS it good English? By John O'London [Wilfred Whitten]. 16mo. Pp. 175. [*Brit. Mus.*] London [1924]

IS King Oscar II. a constitutional king? [By H. L. Brækstad.] 8vo. [Pettersen's *Norsk Lexikon*, col. 234.] London, 1895

IS Kitchener dead? By Frank Power [Arthur Vectis Freeman]. 8vo. [*Brit. Mus.*] London, 1926

IS the Comforter come? and is he gone? . . . By J. N. D. [John Nelson Darby]. 12mo. [*Brit. Mus.*] London [1865]

IS the New Theology Christian? By Hakluyt Egerton [Arthur Boutwood]. 8vo. Pp. v. 174. [*Brit. Mus.*] London, 1907

*ISAGOGE ad Dei providentiam . . . By T. C.

    This is Thomas Crane. See *D. N. B.*; *Arber*; *Brit. Mus.* Case never used any anonymity.

ISIS (the) . . . [A magazine.] Edited by a lady [E. S. Carlisle]. 4to. [*Brit. Mus.*] London, 1832

ISLAND (the) Empire ; or, the scenes of the first exile of the Emperor Napoleon . . . together with a narrative of his residence on the island of Elba . . . By the author of *Blondelle* [Sir Henry Drummond Wolff]. 8vo. Pp. xv. 324. [*Brit. Mus.*]   London, 1855

ISLAND folk songs. By H. C., author of *Island notes in war time* [H. Campbell]. 8vo. Pp. 38. [*Brit. Mus.*]
                                      Kirkwall, 1920
ISLAND notes in war time. By H. C. [H. Campbell. On the Orkneys]. 8vo. Pp. 69. [*Brit. Mus.*]
                                      Edinburgh, 1918
ISLES of Illusion ; letters from the South Seas. Edited by Bohun Lynch. [By R. J. Fletcher.] 8vo. Pp. xvi. 334. [*Brit. Mus.*]   London, 1923
Signed : Asterisk.

*ISMENIA and the Prince . . .
     For Hon. Mrs Stanley, *read* Hon. Mrs Eliza Stanley.

ISOE, and other poems. By Cave Winscom [John Cave]. 8vo. [*Brit. Mus.*]   London, 1871

ISRAEL ; with an appendix on the future restoration of God's ancient people. By Charisos [Robert Grace]. 8vo. [Whitley's *Bapt. Bibl.*]
                                      London, 1835

"IT is time to seek the Lord." [A tract, by Francis Bourdillon.] 12mo. [*Brit. Mus.*]   London [1859]
Signed : F. B.

*ITALIAN (the) convert . . .
     There was an earlier edition (4to) with this title in 1635. For other editions with different titles, see "Newes from Italy of a second Moses . . ." (1608) and "A president to the nobilitie . . ." (1612).

ITALIAN (the) sketch book. By an American [Henry Theodore Tuckerman]. 8vo. Pp. 216. [Appleton's *Dict. of Amer. Biog.*]   Philadelphia, 1835
     The second edition (1837) bears the author's name.

ITER boreale ; or, Tyburn in mourning for the loss of a saint [the Earl of Shaftesbury?] ; a new song . . . written by J. D. [J. Dean ?]. Fol. S. sh. [*Brit. Mus.*]   London, 1682

ITINERARY of Buonaparte, from the period of his residence at Fontaine-bleau to his establishment on the Island of Elba ; to which is prefixed an account of the Regency at Blois. [Translated from the French of J. B. G. Fabry.] 8vo. Pp. 291-420. [*Brit. Mus.*]   London, 1815
     A separate issue, with a special title-page of the addition to the second edition of the "Secret Memoirs|of Napoleon Buonaparte" published anonymously by C. Doris.

J

JABBEK'S [Jacob Kopelowitz'] new methodic primer . . . for the use of foreign Jews, adults, to enable them to learn the English language. 8vo. Pp. 33. [*Brit. Mus.*]   London [1902]

*JACK and I in Lotus Land. . . .
     Frances Little is a *pseud.* and the author's real name is Mrs Fannie Macaulay, *née* Caldwell.

JACK of Clubs ; a novel. By John Ironside [E. M. Tait]. 8vo. Pp. 319. [*Brit. Mus.*]   London, 1931

JAMES. [A novel.] By W. Dane Bank [William Henry Williamson]. 8vo. Pp. 315. [*Brit. Mus.*]   London, 1914

JAMES Vraille : the story of a life. By Jeffery C. Jeffery [Jeffery Charles Marston]. 8vo. 2 vols. [*Brit. Mus.*]
                                      London, 1890
JANET Syme Mackie ; reminiscences for the grand-children. By J. B. M. [John Beveridge Mackie]. 16mo. Pp. viii. 109. [*Brit. Mus.*]
                                      Edinburgh, 1888

JAPANESE (a) Don Juan and other poems. By John Paris [Frank Trelawny Arthur Ashton-Gwatkin]. 4to. Pp. 126. [*Brit. Mus.*]   London [1926]

JENNY ; a novel. By Sigrid Undset. [Translated by W. Emmé.] 8vo. [Pettersen's *Norsk Lexikon*, col. 239.]
                                      London [1920]
JESS of the Abbey School. By Elsie Jeanette Oxenham [Elsie Jeanette Dunkerley]. 8vo. Pp. 311. [*Brit. Mus.*]   London [1927]

JESUS Christ : conferences delivered at Notre Dame in Paris, by Père Lacordaire, of the Order of St Dominic. Translated from the French . . . by a Tertiary of the same order [Henry D. Langdon]. 8vo. [*Brit. Mus.*]
                                      London, 1872
Signed : H. D. L.

JESUS Christ the model of the priest. [By G. Frassinetti.] Translated from the Italian by the Rev. J. L. Patterson. 16mo. Pp. 108. [*Brit. Mus.*]
                                      London, 1855

JESUS, Maria, Joseph, or, the Devout Pilgrim of the Ever Blessed Virgin Mary, in his holy exercises, affections, and elevations. . . . Published for the benefit of the pious Rosarists by A. C. and T. V., religious monks of the Holy Order of S. Bennet [Arthur Anselm Crowther and Thomas Vincent Faustus Sadler]. 12mo. Pp. 648. [Gillow's *Bibl. Dict.* i. 604.]
Amsterdam, 1657

JEWEL (the) of death. . . . By Huan Mee [—— and —— Mansfield, two brothers]. 8vo. Pp. 330.
London, 1902

JEWISH fairy tales and fables. By Aunt Naomi [Gertrude Landa]. . . . 8vo. Pp. 169. [*Brit. Mus.*]
London, 1908

JEWISH (the) peril; protocols of the learned Elders of Zion. By S. A. Nilus. [A translation of the Russian adaptation of Maurice Joly's *Dialogue aux enfers.*] 8vo. Pp. vi. 95. [*Brit. Mus.*] London, 1920

JIM Brent. [A novel.] By Sapper [Herman Cyril MacNeile]. 8vo. Pp. 316. [*Brit. Mus.*] London [1926]

JIMMY makes the 'varsity. . . . By Jonathan Brooks [John Calvin Mellett]. 8vo. Pp. 283. [*Amer. Cat.*]
Indianapolis [1928]

JIMMY Rezaire. By Anthony Armstrong [George Anthony Armstrong Willis]. 8vo. Pp. 255. [*Brit. Mus.*]
London, 1927
Published in the same year in America with the title "The Trail of Fear."

JOE Smith and his waxworks. Written by Bill Smith, with the help of Mrs Smith and Mr Saunders ; with pictures by Mr Pitcher. [By W. F. Stanley.] 8vo. Pp. viii. 294. [*Brit. Mus.*]
London, 1896
Signed : W. F. S.

JOHN Bull and his three partners ; "which things are an allegory." [By R. S. *i.e.* R. Swiney.] 8vo. Pp. 8. [*Brit. Mus.*]   Cheltenham [1894]

JOHN Gilpin. Iter Johannis Gilpini ; carmen Latinum, auctore Roberto Scott. . . . Edited by J. P. M. [James P. Muirhead]. 8vo. Pp. 35. [*Brit. Mus.*]   N.P., private print, 1897
Includes the English text of Cowper.

JOHN Hadland's advice ; or, a warning for all young men that have means. . . . [A ballad, by Richard Climsell]. Fol. S. sh. B. L. [*Brit. Mus.*]
London [*c.* 1640]
Signed : R. C.

JOHN Walters ; from The Lieutenant and others, etc. By Sapper [Herman Cyril MacNeile]. 8vo. Pp. 316. [*Brit. Mus.*]   London [1927]

JOHN'S looking-glass ; or, true and false zeal delineated. . . . By R. D. [Richard de Courcy]. 12mo. [*Brit. Mus.*]   Edinburgh, 1772

JOHNSON of Lansing. By Hawley Williams [William Heyliger]. 8vo. Pp. 332. [*Amer. Cat.*] New York, 1914

*JOLLY-BOAT (the) or, perils . . .
For William Russell, *read* William Howard Russell ? [Allibone's *Dict.*]

JOSEPH of Arimathæa ; a romantic morality in four scenes. By Edward Percy [Edward Percy Smith]. 8vo. Pp. ix. 37. [*Brit. Mus.*] London, 1920

*JOURNAL (a) kept on a journey. . . .
The British Museum ascribes this tentatively to Samuel Evers.

JOURNAL of a second expedition into the interior of Africa . . . by the late Commander Clapperton. . . . [With an introduction signed : J. B. *i.e.* Sir John Barrow.] 4to. Pp. xxiii. 355. [*Brit. Mus.*]   London, 1829

JOURNAL (a) of a tour in Italy in the year 1821, with a description of Gibraltar. . . . By an American [Theodore Dwight]. 8vo. Pp. 468. [Appleton's *Dict. of Amer. Biog.*] New York, 1824

JOURNAL of a tour through part of the Western Highlands of Scotland in the summer of 1839, by T. H. C. [Chauncy Hare Townsend ?]. 8vo. [*Brit. Mus.*]
Newcastle, 1839

*JOURNAL of a voyage up the Nile . . .
Not by F. L. Hawks. See the preface to the work itself. The author is unknown.

JOURNAL of a wanderer ; being a residence in India, and six weeks in North America. [By John G. Reilly ?] 8vo. Pp. xviii. 250. [*Brit. Mus.*]
London, 1844

JOURNAL (a) of visitation to a part of the diocese of Quebec by the Lord Bishop of Montreal. [Edited by E. H. *i.e.* Ernest Hawkins.] 16mo. Pp. 80. [*Brit. Mus.*]   London, 1844
"Church in the Colonies," No. 2.

JOURNALS of the House of Commons, etc. (A general index to . . . vols. 18 to 34. [By Edward Moore of Stockwell.]) Fol. [*Brit. Mus.*] 1742, etc.

JOURNEY (a) in candour ; being the . . . chronicle of a springtime pilgrimage into the wilds of Worcester. . . . By Gordon Lee [Gordon Lee Wheeler]. 8vo. Pp. 159. [*Brit. Mus.*]
London [1929]

*JOURNEY (a) through England . . .
Not by John Macky. [*Times Lit. Supp.* 28th June 1928.]

*JOURNEY through the Austrian Netherlands . . .

Not by John Macky. [*Times Lit. Supp.* 28th June 1928.]

JOURNEY (a) to Jerusalem ; or, a relation of the travels of fourteen Englishmen in . . . 1669 from Scanderoon to Tripoly, Joppa, Ramah, Jerusalem. . . . In a letter from T. B. [R. Burton, *pseud. i.e.* Nathaniel Crouch]. . . . 12mo. [*Brit. Mus.*]   London, 1672

Augmented and republished (1683) as, "Two Journeys to Jerusalem," *q.v.*

JOVIALL (the) broome man ; or, a Kent Street souldiers exact relation of all his travels in every nation. [A ballad, by Richard Climsell ?] Fol. S. sh. B. L. [*Brit. Mus.*]
London [*c.* 1640]

Signed : R. C.

JOY is my name. By Nicholas Fay [Wilkinson Sherren]. 8vo. Pp. 94. [*Who's Who in Lit.*]   London, 1922

JOY (the) of tears. . . . [In verse. By Sir William Mure.] 8vo. [*Brit. Mus.*]
1635

JOYCE'S little maid. By Nellie Cornwall [Nellie Sloggett]. 8vo. Pp. 127. [*Brit. Mus.*]   London, 1886

JOYFUL (a) new ballad, declaring the happie obtaining of the great Galleazzo. . . . [By Thomas Deloney ?] Fol. S. sh. [*Brit. Mus.*]   London, 1588

Signed : T. D.

JUBILEE and other rhymings, patriotic and domestic in English and Scotch. By a Lothian Justice, quondam M.P. [Robert A. Macfie, of Dreghorn]. 8vo. Pp. 20.   London [1888]

From an inscribed presentation copy.

JUBILEE (a) jaunt to Norway. By three girls [Violet Crompton-Roberts, Mildred Crompton Roberts, and another girl]. 8vo. [Pettersen's *Norsk Lexikon*, col. 247.]   London, 1888

JUDGE (the) ; wherein is shewed how Christ our Lord is to judge the world at the last day. . . . Translated [from Francesco Aria's "De la Imitacion," lib. vii., by G. M. *i.e.* Sir Toby Matthew]. 8vo. Pp. 253. [*Pollard and Redgrave.*]
[St Omer] 1621

JUDGEMENT (the) of dreames (of Artemidorus Daldianus). [Translated by Robert Wood, of Norfolk.] 8vo. [*Pollard and Redgrave.*]   London, 1606

For a later edition (1644) with initials R. W., see "The Interpretation of dreames."

*JUDGMENT on Alexander and Cæsar . . .

Translated from St Evremond. "The comparison of Plato and Aristotle" is not the same work.

JUDICIUM, a pageant. . . . [Edited by F. D. *i.e.* Francis Douce.] 4to. B. L. [*Brit. Mus.*]   London, 1822

Roxburghe Club publication.

JULIUS Levine ; a novel. By a Gentleman with a duster [Harold Begbie]. 8vo. Pp. 314. [*Brit. Mus.*]
London, 1927

JURY (a) of the virtuous. [A novel.] By Patrick Hood [Mary Louisa Gordon]. 8vo. Pp. 368. [*Brit. Mus.*]
London, 1907

JUS primogeniti ; or, the dignity, right and priviledge of the first-born . . . in a letter to a friend in the country. By B. J. Esq. [John Brydall]. 4to. [*Lincoln's Inn Lib.*]   London, 1699

JUST (a) and seasonable reprehension of naked breasts and shoulders. Written by a grave and learned papist [Jacques Boileau]. Translated by Edward Cooke, Esquire . . . 8vo. Pp. 150. [Barbier's *Dictionnaire ; Brit. Mus.*]
London, 1678

The original "De l'abus des nuditez de gorge" (1675) was also anonymous.

Also attributed to De Neuilly, curé of Beauvais.

JUST (a) character of the Revd. Mr Boyce. Written by Mr R— C— [Richard Choppin]. Fol. S. sh. [*Brit. Mus.*]   N.P. [1728 ?]

JUST Peggy. . . . By Margaret Stuart Lane [Margaret Ashworth]. 8vo. Pp. 159. [*Brit. Mus.*] London, 1925

JUST thoughts. [Verse.] By A. M. [Anthony Mildmay]. 8vo. Pp. 24. [*Brit. Mus.*]
London, private print [1915]

JUSTICE (the) and necessity of a war with Holland, in case the Dutch do not come into her Majesty's measures, stated and examined. [By Daniel Defoe.] 4to. Pp. 36. [Dottin's *De Foe ; Cambridge Hist. of Eng. Lit.* ix. 423.]   London, 1712

JUSTIFICATION by faith vindicated in a letter to a friend : with remarks on 1 Timothy v. 17, 18. [By J. Lethem ?] 8vo. [*Brit. Mus.*]   Leith, 1834

MS. attribution in *Brit. Mus.* copy.

JUVENILE (the) gleaner ; or, anecdotes and miscellaneous pieces designed for amusement and instruction. By the author of a *Brief historical catechism of the Holy Scriptures* (W. A.) [William Alexander, of York]. 12mo. Pp. 220. [*Brit. Mus.*]   York, 1825

JUVENILIA. By A. C. Swinburne [or rather Sir Anthony Coningham Sterling]. 8vo. Pp. 37. [*Brit. Mus.*]
London, private print, 1912

K

K. Blake's way. By Margaret Warde [Edith Kellogg Dunton]. 8vo. Pp. 271. [*Brit. Mus.*] London, 1929

KALENDAYR (the) of the shyppars. [Translated by Alexander Barclay?] Fol. [Johnstone and Robertson's *Bibl. Aberd.* i. 7.] Parys, 1503
A free translation with additions of *Le Compost et Kalendrier des bergiers* (1497 edition). Only 3 copies of this translation are known to survive. For another edition, see "Here begynneth the Kalendar of Shepherdes."

*KANSAS and its constitution. . . .
For Sidney George Fisher, *read* Charles Edward Fisher. [Cushing's *Init. and Pseud.;* Sabin's *Dict.*]

*KASIDAH (the) of Haji Abdu 'l-Yazdi.
F. B. stands for Frank Baker, one of the pseudonyms which Sir R. F. Burton used.

KATE Hamilton. . . . [A novel. By William Stephens Hayward.] 8vo. Pp. 332. [*Brit. Mus.*] London [1884]

*KEEKIAD (the); a poem. . . .
For Keekiad, *read* Keekeiad.

KENYA calling. By Nora K. Strange [Mrs E. Gower Stanley]. 8vo. Pp. 256. [*Brit. Mus.*] London, 1928

KEY notes. [Verse.] By Arbor Leigh [Louisa Sarah Bevington, later Mrs Guggenberger]. 8vo. Pp. 23. [*Brit. Mus.*] London, 1876
Afterwards republished under her own name.

KEY (a) to Hamel's exercises. . . . Translated by Chrysostôme Dagobert [J. B. A. Led'huy]. 12mo. [*Brit. Mus.*] London, 1856

KEY to the juvenile historian's genealogical table of the royal families of England. [By Mary Poole Hastings.] 8vo. Pp. 32. [*Brit. Mus.*] Chester, 1834
Signed : M. P. H.

KEY to two hundred miscellaneous questions in *Questions and answers on . . . the four Georges.* By M. P. H. [Mary Poole Hastings]. 8vo. Pp. 41. [*Brit. Mus.*] Chester, 1835

KEZIAH in search of a friend : a story for schoolgirls. By Noel Hope [Sarah L. Morewood]. . . . 8vo. Pp. 174. [*Brit. Mus.*] London, 1908

KIMONO. By John Paris [Frank Trelawny Arthur Ashton-Gwatkin]. 8vo. Pp. viii. 345. [*Brit. Mus.*] London [1921]

KIND (the) hearted creature ; or, the prettiest jest that e'er you know. . . . [A song, by Richard Climsell?] Fol. S. sh. B. L. [*Brit. Mus.*] London [*c.* 1640]
Signed : R. C.

*KING Robert Bruce . . .
In A. W. Robertson's *Aberd. Bibl.*, quoting an edition (Aberdeen, 1833) he attributes this to David Anderson, author of "The Scottish Village : a poem " (Aberdeen, 1808).

KINGDOM (the) of darkness ; or, the history of dæmons, spectres, witches, etc. By R. B. [Richard Burton, *i.e.* Nathaniel Crouch]. 8vo. [*Book prices current,* 1921.] London, 1695

KINGDOM (the) of Heaven is at hand. By the author of *The Gospel of Hope* [W. N. Roundy]. . . . 8vo. Pp. 64. [*Brit. Mus.*] Davenport, Ia., 1927

KINGDOME (the) of God in the soule . . . Composed by . . . Fa. Iohn Evangelist. [Translated by B. P. S. *i.e.* Peter Salvin, O.S.B.] 12mo. Pp. 436. [*Brit. Mus.*] Paris, 1657

KINGFISHER (the) and other poems. By John Doe [Victor Sampson]. 8vo. Pp. 28. [*Brit. Mus.*] London, 1923

KING'S (the) ode, in answer to Peter Pindar, on the subject of his pension. . . . [By John Wolcot.] 4to. [*Brit. Mus.*] London [1788]

KIRKBY-STEPHEN Railway. By "Veritas" [John Close]. Dedicated to Mr Chambers. Fol. S. sh. [*Brit. Mus.*] [Kirkby-Stephen, 1858]

KITCHENER (the) mystery. By Frank Power [Arthur Vectis Freeman]. 8vo. Pp. 98. [*Brit. Mus.*] London, 1926

KNAVES'-ACRE Association. Resolutions adopted at a meeting of placemen . . . Copied by Old Hubert [—— Parkinson]. 8vo. [*Brit. Mus.*] 1793

KNOWING God. By an unknown Christian [Albert Ernest Richardson]. 8vo. Pp. 128. [*Brit. Mus.*] London [1929]

*KOREA, and the ten lost tribes . . .
Signed : N. M.

L

LA Vellma's [David J. Lustig's] vaude-
ville budget for magicians, mind-
readers and ventriloquists. 8vo. Pp.
96. [*Amer. Cat.*]
Somerville, Mass., 1921

LABOUR defended against the claims
of capital. By a Labourer [Thomas
Hodgskin]. 12mo.   London, 1825
From an inscribed copy.

LABYRINTH.   (An improved species
of cribbage.)   [Rules.   By J. F.
Knight?] 4to. Pp. 3. [*Brit. Mus.*]
[Lowcester, 1882]

LAD (the) with the loaves ; or, not lost
in a crowd. . . .   By the editor of
Kind Words [Benjamin Clarke]. 16mo.
[*Brit. Mus.*]   London, 1869

LADENSIUM ἀυτοκατακρισις, the Canter-
burians self-conviction. [By Robert
Baillie.] 4to. [*Huntington Lib.
Checklist.*]   [Amsterdam] 1640

LADIES (the) dressing-room unlock'd.
[A later edition of *Mundus muliebris*
by John Evelyn.] 4to. Pp. 23. [*Brit.
Mus.*]   London, 1700

LADIES (the) parliament. [A satire.
By Henry Neville.] 8vo. [*Brit. Mus.*]
[London, 1647]
See also "The ladies a second time
assembled in Parliament . . ."

LADS afoot. By Gordon Lee [Gordon
Lee Wheeler]. 8vo. Pp. 128. [*Brit.
Mus.*]   Guildford [1929]

LADS (the) of the Don, Donside Gordon
Highlanders, "D" Company, Alford,
24th August 1904. [By Peter Adam.]
4to. [*Edinb. Univ. Lib.*]
Aberdeen, 1904
Preface signed : P. A.

LADY (the) and her Ayah, an Indian
story. By the author of *Little Henry
and his bearer* [Mrs M. M. Sherwood.]
12mo. [*Brit. Mus.*]   Dublin, 1816

*LADY (the) of the decoration. . . .
Frances Little is a *pseud.* and the author's
real name is Mrs Fannie Macaulay, *née*
Caldwell.

LADY Pamela's pearls. By John Ironside [E. M. Tait]. 8vo. Pp. 311.
[*Brit. Mus.*]   London [1927]

LADY'S (the) Museum. By the author
of *The female Quixote* [Charlotte
Lennox, *née* Ramsay]. 8vo. 2 vols.
[*Brit. Mus.*]   London [1760-61]

LADY'S (a) visit to the Vöring-Fos.
By M. F. D. [M. F. Dickson].
8vo. [Pettersen's *Norsk Lexikon*, col.
288.]   Dublin, 1870

LAGHU   (the)   Kaumudi . . . by
Varadarāja ; with an English version.
. . . [The preface signed : R. T. H. G.
i.e. Ralph T. H. Griffith.] 8vo.
[*Brit. Mus.*]   Benares, 1867

LAG'S elegy . . . See "Elegy (an) in
memory of that valiant champion . . ."

*LAIRD (the) of Coul's Ghost . . .
This entry from Martin's *Cat.* is very
incorrect.   Mrs Elizabeth Steuart (not
Stuart) was only the editor of this 1808
(not 1810) edition. The author was the
Rev. William Ogilvie, minister of Innerwick, whose name in fact appears on the
title-page of every edition, as in fact does
Mrs Steuart's on the title-page of the 1808
edition. The work is therefore not anonymous at all. The earlier editions (1751,
onwards) were entitled "A copy of several
conferences and meetings. . . ." Most subsequent editions were called "The Laird
of Coul's (or Cool's) Ghost," but this
1808 edition by Mrs Steuart was entitled
"Narrative of four conferences between the
Ghost of Mr Maxwell of Coul and the
Rev. Mr Ogilvie. . . ." For further information regarding this interesting chapbook,
see "The Laird of Coul's Ghost," by Mr
Frank Miller, of Annan, to whom we are
indebted for calling our attention to this
erroneous entry.

LAIRD (the) of Lag's elegy . . . See
"Elegy (an) in memory of that valiant
champion . . ."

LAITY in Church Councils ; a speech
delivered in the Diocesan Synod of
Aberdeen, 1867. [By John Comper.]
Revised. 8vo. Pp. 18. [*Brit. Mus.*]
Aberdeen, 1867

LAMENTABLE (the) and true tragedie
of M. Arden of Feuersham in Kent,
who was most wickedly murdered by
the meanes of his disloyall and wanton
wife, who for the loue she bare to one
Mosbie, hyred two desperate ruffins,
Blackwill and Shakbag, to kill him.
[By William Shakespeare.] Second
edition. 4to. [Jaggard's *Shakespeare
Bibl.*]   London, 1599

LAMENTABLE (the) tragedy of Locrine,
the eldest sonne of King Brutus.
By W. S.   London, 1595
To Wentworth Smith have been un-
warrantably ascribed the three plays
"Locrine," "The Puritan," and "Cromwell."
. . . There is no clue to the authorship.
[*D. N. B.* vol. 53, p. 138.]

LAMENTATION (a) in whiche is shewed what ruyne and destruction cometh of seditious rebellyon. [By Sir J. Cheke?] 4to. B. L. [*Brit. Mus.*]   Londini, 1536

LAMENTATIONS (the) of Jeremiah paraphras'd. By W. B. [William Brown]. 4to. [*Brit. Mus.*]
                              Edinburgh, 1708

LAND (the) of the midnight sun; a cruise in Norwegian waters. [By Sir William Christopher Leng.] 8vo. Pp. 29. [Pettersen's *Norsk Lexikon*, col. 289.]   Sheffield, 1886
    A later edition (1887) bears the author's name.

LANDLORDS (the) to the tradesmen. [A handbill in favour of the corn laws. By Sir Thomas Phillipp?] 4to. S. sh. [*Brit. Mus.*]   Broadway, 1839

LARACHE; a tale of the Portuguese church in the sixteenth century. [By John Mason Neale.] 8vo. Pp. 94. [*Brit. Mus.*]   London [1861]

*LARGE additions to Common Sense . . .
    Evans' *Amer. Bibl.* says this was a compilation by the publisher and only partly by Thomas Paine. "Additions to Common Sense" (*q.v.*) is a revised edition of "Large Additions. . . ." Neither is included in later editions of "Common Sense" and neither is included in "The Writings of Thomas Paine, collected by M. D. Conway, 1894-96."

LARKS Creek. [A story.] By Virgil B. Fairman [Andrew F. Klarmann]. 12mo. Pp. 200. [*Publishers' Weekly*, 14th January 1928.]   New York, 1927

LASLETT (the) affair. By a gentleman with a duster [Harold Begbie]. 8vo. Pp. 317. [*Brit. Mus.*]   London, 1928

LASS (the) of the hill. [A song. By Mary Jones.] Fol. S. sh. [*Brit. Mus.*]
                              [London? 1740?]

LAST (the) and great Antichrist. [By John Sidney Davenport.] Pp. 14. 8vo. [*Brit. Mus.*]   1895

LAST (a) appeal to the stockholders of the Chesapeake and Delaware Canal on the injustice exercised towards Mr Randall, the contractor for the eastern section. [By Matthew Carey.] 8vo. Pp. 8. [Sabin's *Dictionary*, iii. 340.]   N.P. [1825]

LAST (the) check to Antinomianism; a polemical essay on the twin doctrines of Christian imperfection and a death purgatory. By the author of *The Checks* [John William Fletcher]. 12mo. Pp. 327.   London, 1775
    A reply to Sir Richard Hill's *Creed for Arminians and Perfectionists*.

LAST (the) evening of the year. By the author of *The lamplighter* [Francis Bourdillon]. 12mo. [*Brit. Mus.*]
                              London [1863]
    Signed: F. B.

LAST (the) great naval war; an historical retrospect. By A. Nelson Seaforth [George Sydenham Clarke, Baron Sydenham]. 8vo. Pp. 20. [*Brit. Mus.*]   London, 1891

LAST (the) hour & other plays. By George Graveley [George Graveley Edwards]. 8vo. Pp. 143. [*The Carthusian*, July 1928.]   London, 1928

LAST (the) moments of . . . Geo. IV. . . . his submission to the divine will . . . [Verse. By E— Elliot?] 8vo. [*Brit. Mus.*]   London [1830]

LAST (the) speech, confession, and dying words of Dominus Defunctus, sometime Inquisitor in the city of Juxtamare: faithfully translated from the original. [Written by James Playfair, D.D.] 8vo. Edinburgh, 1809
    "Juxtamare" [juxta mare] is St Andrews. By the Principal of the United College in St Andrews against Principal Hill, of St Mary's College, who had taken a chief part in initiating a charge of immorality against the writer.

LAST (the) visitation, conflicts and death of Mr Thomas Peacock. . . . Published by E. B. [Edward Bagshaw]. 12mo. Pp. 66. [*Brit. Mus.*]
                              London, 1660

LATE (the) Col. T. G. Montgomerie, R.E. [A biographical sketch. By Sir Henry Yule.] 8vo. Pp. 8. [*Brit. Mus.*]   1878
    Signed: H. Y.

*LATE (the) Rev. Thomas Streatfield . . . .
    For L. E. L., *read* L. B. L.

LATE (the) W. B. D. D. Turnbull, Esq. From *The Herald and Genealogist*, January 1864, with some corrections. [By J. Walter K. Eyton.] 8vo. Pp. 12. [*Brit. Mus.*]   [London, 1864]
    Only 25 copies printed.

LATIN (the) prayers used at St Paul's School in 1644. . . . [With an advertisement signed J. H. L. *i.e.* J. H. Lupton.] 12mo. [*Brit. Mus.*]   1890

LATINÆ grammaticæ rudimenta; or, an introduction to the Latin tongue. [A reprint of W. Lilly's *Grammar*, with additions.] 12mo. [*Brit. Mus.*]
                              Londini, 1841

LATTICED windows. By Norah K. Strange [Mrs E. Gower Stanley]. 8vo. Pp. 284. [*Brit. Mus.*]
                              London, 1924

LAUREL (the) ; fugitive poetry of the XIXth century. [Collected by Miss S. Lawrence.] 12mo. [*Brit. Mus.*]
London, 1830

*LAW (the) of Obligations and conditions . . . By T. A. of Gray's Inn, Esq.
The attribution to Thomas Ashe has never had the authority of the *Brit. Mus. Catalogue* and is impossible.
The author is not known.

LAWS and regulations of Short Whist as adopted by the Washington Club of Paris, with maxims and advice for beginners by A. Trump, Junior [William Pembroke Fetridge]. 8vo. Pp. 112. [Jessel's *Bibl. of playing cards*, p. 87.]   Paris, 1880

LAWS (the) of fourhanded bézique adopted by the Portland Club, with a guide to the game. By "Persicus" [Baron George de Reuter]. 8vo. Pp. v. 96. [F. Jessel's *Bibl. of playing cards*, p. 247.]   London, 1903

LAWS (the) of honor ; or, an account of the suppression of duels in France extracted out of the King's Edicts, Regulation of the Marshals, Records of Parliament. [By John Evelyn?] 8vo. Pp. 198. [Levi and Gelli's *Bibl. del Duello*, p. 23.]   1685
The attribution is exceedingly doubtful.
For other editions, see "An account of the abolishing of duels . . .", and "The court of honour . . ."

LAWS (the) of race as connected with slavery. [By Sidney George Fisher.] 8vo. [A. J. Beveridge's *Abraham Lincoln*, p. xx.]   Philadelphia, 1860

LAWYERS (the) : a comedy in three acts. By Slingsby Lawrence [George Henry Lewes]. 12mo. [*Brit. Mus.*]
London [1855]
Lacy's Acting Edition of Plays, vol. ii.

*LAY baptism invalid . . .
The fourth edition (1723) bears the author's name.

LAY (a) churchman's letter to his neighbours upon dissent from the Established Church. [By John David Hay Hill.] 12mo. Pp. 22, 5. [*Brit. Mus.*]   Dereham, 1834
Signed : J. D. H. H.

LAY (the) of the Lincoln's Inn Legion. Monday, 10th April 1848. [By Martin Archer Shee]. 4to. [*Brit. Mus.*]
[London, 1848]
Signed : M. A. S.

LAY (the) of the purple falcon ; a metrical romance, now first printed from the original manuscript, in the possession of the Hon. R. Curzon. *End* Ci finit li lai du Bon et digne Roi Syr Claudius Pantagruelle. [By R. Curzon, Baron de la Zouche?] 4to. B. L. [*Brit. Mus.*]   London, 1847
Only 30 copies printed.

LAY (a) of the Queen's Torpid, 1880. [Signed : R. W. B. *i.e.* Richard Warwick Bond?] 8vo. Pp. 12. [*Brit. Mus.*]   N.P. 1926

LAY sermons on the theory of Christianity, by a Company of Brethren. No. 1 (and No. 2). The Fidianism of Saint Paul, by Victorius Analysis [Dr Samuel Brown].   London, 1841
From an inscribed copy that belonged to the Dr John Brown family.

LAYS (the) of the pious minstrel ; selections by J. B. H. [John Bawtree Harvey]. 12mo. Pp. xii. 343. [*Brit. Mus.*]   London [1862]

*LAYS on land . . .
For Macken, *read* Macker.

LAYTON (the) Court Mystery. By "?" [Anthony Berkeley Cox]. 8vo. Pp. 316. [*Brit. Mus.*]   London, 1925

LAZY Laurie ; or, the mote and the beam. [Signed : M. E. R. *i.e.* Mary Emily Ropes.] 16mo. Pp. 16. [*Brit. Mus.*]   London [1872]

LE Sage's [Marin Joseph Emmanuel Auguste Dieudonné de las Casas, Marquis de la Caussade] historical, genealogical, chronological and geographical atlas . . . Fol. [*Brit. Mus.*]
London, 1813

LEADS (the) at whist ; comprising the altered leads suggested by "Cavendish." Compiled by R. T. [Rosella Trist]. Revised by N. B. T. [Nicholas Browse Trist]. 16mo. Pp. 15. [Jessel's *Bibl. of playing cards*, p. 283.]   New Orleans, 1889

LEAFLETS for letters. By the author of *Copsley Annals* [Mrs Emily Steele Elliott]. 32mo. [*Brit. Mus.*]
Brighton [1873]

LEAGUE (the) of discontent. By Francis Beeding [John Leslie Palmer and Hilary A. St G. Saunders]. 8vo. Pp. 312. [*Brit. Mus.*]   Boston, 1930

LEAGUES of nations, ancient, mediæval and modern. By Elizabeth York [Mrs S. V. Bracker]. 8vo. Pp. vi. 337. [*Brit. Mus.*]   London, 1919

LEARN to live ; firstlings by a working man [Robert Kerr, of Kilmarnock]. 12mo.   1860
Attestation by a friend of the author.

LEARNING to converse. [By George Mogridge.] 18mo. [*Brit. Mus.*]
London [1854]

LEARNING to feel. [By George Mogridge.] 12mo. [*Brit. Mus.*]
London [1845]

LEAVES from the journal of a subaltern during the Campaign in the Punjaub, Sept. 1848 to March 1849. [By Daniel Augustus Sandford.] 8vo. Pp. ii. 227. [*Brit. Mus.; Annual Register*, 1849.]
Edinburgh, 1849

LEAVES in the wind. [By] Alpha of the plough [Alfred George Gardiner]. . . . 8vo. Pp. xvi. 270. [*Brit. Mus.*]
London, 1918

LEAVES of grass. [By Walt Whitman.] 8vo. Pp. 382. [*Brit. Mus.*]
London [1881]
Many other editions, both previous and subsequent, were not anonymous.

LECTURE (a) on the Vedánta, embracing the text of the Vedánta Sára (by Sadánanda Yogíndra. Delivered by J. R. B. [James Robert Ballantyne]). 8vo. [*Brit. Mus.*]   Allahabad, 1850

LECTURES on the revival of religion, by ministers of the Church of Scotland. [Edited by W. H. M. *i.e.* William Maxwell Hetherington?] 12mo. [*Brit. Mus.*]
Glasgow, 1840

LECTURES on the subdivision of knowledge and their mutual relations. . . . [By James Robert Ballantyne.] 8vo. 3 parts. [*Brit. Mus.*]
Calcutta, 1848-49
Preface signed : J. R. B.

LECTURES upon the first and second Epistles of Paul to the Thessalonians. . . . By . . . R. Rollock. [Edited by H. C. *i.e.* Henry Charteris, and W. A.] 8vo. [*Brit. Mus.*]   Edinburgh, 1606

LEFT her home. . . . [A novel. By William Stephens Hayward.] 8vo. Pp. iv. 315. [*Brit. Mus.*]
London [1884]

LEGACY (the) of Liberalism. By Al Carthill [Sir John Perronet Thompson]. 8vo. Pp. v. 168. [*Brit. Mus.*]
London, 1924

LEGEND (the) of the House of Yonne. [By Richard Grenville, Duke of Buckingham.] 4to. Pp. 83. [*Brit. Mus.*] [Stowe, private print, 1830]
Twenty-five copies only printed.

LEITH-HILL ; a poem. [By Rev. Peter Cunningham?] 4to. [*Brit. Mus.*]   London, 1779

LENT lectures for 1859, illustrating the soundness . . . of the Church of England. . . . [By various writers ; preface signed : B. A. *i.e.* Berkeley Addison?] 8vo. Pp. iv. 146. [*Brit. Mus.*]   London [1859]

LENTEN (a) prologue refus'd by the players. [By Thomas Shadwell.] Fol. S. sh. [*Brit. Mus.*]
[London? 1683?]

LEONARD & Gertrude ; a popular story, written originally in German [by J. H. Pestalozzi], translated into French and now attempted in English [by Sir T. Ledgard]. . . . 8vo. Pp. 367. [*Brit. Mus.*]   Bath, 1800

LESS eminent Victorians. [Limericks, with woodcuts reproduced from Victorian periodicals.] By R. D. [Randall Davies]. 8vo. [*Brit. Mus.*]
London, 1927

LESSONS for children . . . from two to four years old. [By A. L. Aikin, later Barbauld.] 12mo. 4 parts. [*Brit. Mus.*]   London, 1808

LESSONS for middle age ; with some account of various cities and men. By the author of *The recreations of a country parson* [A. K. H. Boyd]. 8vo. [*Brit. Mus.*]   London, 1868

LESSONS on number, as given in a Pestalozzian school, Cheam, Surrey. [By C. Reiner.] 12mo. [*Brit. Mus.*]
London, 1831

LET us be divorced. [A translation of V. Sardou's comedy " Divorçons."] 8vo. Pp. 67. [*Brit. Mus.*]
London [1881]

LET us be happy together. [By C. Jefferys.] The factory girl. [Songs.] 4to. S. sh. [*Brit. Mus.*]
[London, 1860?]

LET youth but know ; a plea for reason in education. By Kappa [William Archer]. 8vo. Pp. 256. [*Brit. Mus.*]
London, 1905

LETTER (a) addressed to J. C., Esq. [John Cobbold], containing some observations on his late conduct . . . as Lord of the Manor. [By Robert Small?] 8vo. [*Brit. Mus.*]
London, 1816

*LETTER (a) from a city minister . . .
The letter is signed : N. or M.

LETTER (a) from a distinguished English Commoner [Edmund Burke] to a Peer of Ireland [Lord Kenmare] on the repeal of a part of the penal laws against the Irish Catholics. 8vo. Pp. viii. 29. [*Brit. Mus.*]
London, 1785
Reprinted in 1824.

*LETTER (a) from a Dublin apothecary . . .
Letter signed : C. L.

LETTER (a) from a friend at J—— [Jamaica] to a friend in London, giving an impartial account of the violent proceedings of the Faction in that Island. [By Dr James Smith, of Kingston.] 8vo. [*Brit. Mus.*] [1747?]

LETTER (a) from a gentleman in Ireland to his brother in England, relating to the concerns of Ireland in matters of trade. [By Andrew Marvell.] 4to. Pp. 24. [*Brit. Mus.*] London, 1677

" This was written by Mr Marvyl, under the notion of a younger brother in Ireland to an elder brother in England ; the reason was that it might not be thought his writing because he was not willing to disoblige the North Country members, being his friends, they being for that Act." [An alarum to England.... By W[illiam] C[arter], p. 19.]

LETTER (a) from a gentleman to the minister of his parish, occasioned by this minister never bowing at the name of Jesus. . . . [Signed: A. B. *i.e.* Caleb Parfect?] 8vo. [*Brit. Mus.*] London, 1749

LETTER (a) from a minister, to a person of quality, showing some reasons for his nonconformity. [By Richard Baxter.] Fol. [London? 1679]

Signed: A. B. It is clear from internal evidence that this was written by the author of the Nonconformist's Advocate.

LETTER (a) from a P—me S—j—t [Prime Serjeant] to a H—gh P—t [High Priest, *i.e.* George Stone, primate of Ireland] concerning the present posture of affairs. [Signed : A - - - - - - M - - - - - - *i.e.* Anthony Malone]. . . . 8vo. Pp. 151. [*Brit. Mus.*]
Printed in Scratchland [Dublin] by Thomas Roastum, 1745

*LETTER (a) from a Protestant gentleman . . .
Signed : N. N.

*LETTER (a) from H. G—g, Esq. . . .
For H. G—g, *read* H - - - - G - - - - G.

*LETTER (a) from Irenopolis . . .
Attributed in Whitley's *Bapt. Bibl.* to Morgan Edwards.

LETTER (a) from the author of *Siris* [George Berkeley, Bishop of Cloyne] to Thomas Prior, Esq., concerning the usefulness of tar-water in the plague. 8vo. Pp. 20. [*Brit. Mus.*]
Dublin, 1747
See also ",A letter to T— P— . . ."

LETTER (a) from the D. of D. [Duke of Dorset] to the L—d C—ll—r [Lord Chancellor] of Ireland [on the memorial by the Earl of Kildare as to the misappropriation of money voted for barracks]. 8vo. [*Brit. Mus.*]
London, 1753

LETTER (a) from the Reverend Mr * * * * * * [Erasmus Middleton] to A * * * * D * * * *, Esq., [on walking with God]. 8vo. [*Brit. Mus.*]
[Edinburgh] 1772

*LETTER (a) of a Catholicke man . . .
Cancel this entry. It is incorrect and duplicates the previous entry.

LETTER (a) of advice to a young poet ; together with a proposal for the encouragement of poetry in this kingdom. [By Jonathan Swift.] 8vo. Pp. 32. [*Brit. Mus.*] Dublin, 1721
Signed : E. F.

LETTER of an Italian refugee [Baron Borso di Carminati] on his exile ; addressed to the Countess Dowager of Belmore. 8vo. [*Brit. Mus.*]
London, 1827

LETTER of Christopher Columbus describing his first voyage to the Western Hemisphere. [Edited by S. L. M. B. *i.e.* Samuel L. M. Barlow.] 8vo. [*Brit. Mus.*]   New York, 1875
Only 50 copies printed.

LETTER (a) of [to] Sir R. H. Inglis . . . on the relative numbers, influence and benevolence [of] Churchmen and Dissenters. Second edition, enlarged. [Signed : Presbyter, *i.e.* E. Edwards, Curate of Marsden, Yorkshire.] 12mo. Pp. 12. [*Brit. Mus.*]   London [1837]

LETTER (a) on restrictions and fetters in trade. [By H. H. B. Sawbridge.] 8vo. [*Brit. Mus.*]   1828

LETTER I., to Lord Viscount Althorp, on the ruinous consequences of an oligarchical system of government. By J. V. [J. Veitch]. 8vo. Pp. 33. [*Brit. Mus.*]   London, 1831

LETTER (a) out of Scotland from Mr R. L. S. [Roger L'Estrange] to his friend H. B. in London. Fol. [*Brit. Mus.*]   [London] 1681
Signed : R. L. [*i.e.* Roger L'Estrange].

LETTER (a) sent from a worthy divine [Adoniram Byfield?] to the . . . Lord Maior of . . . London [Sir Richard Gurney]. Being a true relation of the battaile fought betweene his Majesties forces, and . . . the Earle of Essex. . . . Fol. S. sh. [*Brit. Mus.*]
London, 1642
MS. note by Thomason.

LETTER (a) to a friend [giving some account of the life and works of C. Hayes. By E. Y. *i.e.* Edward Yardley?]. 4to. [*Brit. Mus.*]
London [1761 ?]

LETTER (a) to a friend in the country, on the late expedition to Canada, with an account of former enterprises, a defence of that design, and the share the late M - - - - - rs had in it. [By Jeremiah Dummer.] 8vo. Pp. 22. [Sabin's *Dictionary;* Evans' *Amer. Bibl.*]   London, 1712

LETTER (a) to a friend shewing from Scripture, fathers, and reason how false that State maxim is. Royal authority is originally and radically in the people. [By John Brydall of Lincoln's Inn.] Fol. [*Lincoln's Inn Lib.*]   London, 1679

LETTER (a) to a friende, touching Mardochai his age, which helpeth much to holde the trueth. . . . [By Hugh Broughton.] 4to. No pagination, B. L. [*Brit. Mus.*]
[London] 1590

LETTER (a) to a gentleman in Edinburgh upon the apology for the Presbyterians in Scotland. [By John Bisset, the Elder.] 8vo. [Robertson's *Aberd. Bibl.*]   [Aberdeen] 1742
The third edition, 1743, bears the author's name.

LETTER (a) to a gentleman in the country, giving an account of the two Insurance offices, the Fire office & Friendly Society. [Signed : N. B. *i.e.* Nicholas Barbon.] Fol. Pp. 4. [*Brit. Mus.*]   London, 1684

*LETTER (a) to a lady : wherein the canonical authority of St Matthew's Gospel is defended . . .
The *Brit. Mus.* and *D. N. B.* both now attribute this definitely to Brandon Gurdon.

*LETTER (a) to a member of the Convention of States in Scotland. By a lover of his religion and country.
This is the complete title. R. A. Scott Macfie considers this may be by Andrew Fletcher of Saltoun. [*Bibl. of A. Fletcher*, p. 24.]

LETTER (a) to Aaron Robertson, Esq., late Chairman of the Commission for investigating the affairs of the Joint Companies. By a Citizen of Burlington [Henry C. Carey]. 8vo. [Sabin's *Dictionary*, iii. 329.]
Philadelphia, 1852

LETTER (a) to all the saints on the general duty of love. [By Mrs Anne Dutton.] 8vo. Pp. 52. [*Brit. Mus.*]
1742

LETTER (a) to Colonel Chesney. . . . By an old brother officer [Colonel William Martin Leake ?]. 8vo. [*Brit. Mus.*]   1824

*LETTER (a) to General Monck . . .
Ascribed also to Roger Matthews. [*Brit. Mus.*]

LETTER (a) to Her Majesty the Queen from a widowed wife [Jane Alice Sargant ?]. 8vo. Pp. 7. [*Brit. Mus.*]
[1821]

LETTER to his R. H. the Duke of Kent upon the revulsion of trade. . . . [By John Ashton Yates.] 8vo. Pp. 168.
Liverpool [1816]

LETTER to [the ?] Hon. Howell Cobb on currency. [By Peter Scriber.] 8vo. [H. E. Miller's *Banking Theories in the U. S.* p. 234.]   New York, 1857

LETTER (a) to James S. Hulme, Esq., late Commissioner. By a Citizen of Burlington [Henry C. Carey]. 8vo. [Sabin's *Dictionary*, iii. 329.]
Philadelphia, 1851

LETTER (a) to Mr C. Goulding upon the Epistles to the seven churches in Asia, Popery, and Catholic emancipation ; in answer to his preface to Mr Huntington's last sermon. [By Matthew Hutchinson.] 8vo. [*Brit. Mus.*]   London, 1814
Signed : Y. Z.

LETTER to Mr Gallatin. . . . By " Publicola " [Ferris Pell ?]. 8vo. [H. E. Miller's *Banking Theories in the U. S.* p. 233.]   New York, 1815

LETTER (a) to Sir R. H. Inglis . . . on the relative numbers, influence and benevolence of Churchmen and Dissenters. [By Edward Edwards, Perpetual Curate of Marsden, Yorks.] 12mo. Pp. 12. [*Brit. Mus.*]
Leeds, 1834

LETTER (a) to Sir Robert Ladbroke, first senior Alderman, and one of the representatives of the City of London ; with an attempt to show the good effects which may reasonably be expected from the confinement of criminals in separate apartments. [By Rev. Samuel Denne.] 8vo. [*Lincoln's Inn Lib.*]   London, 1771

LETTER (a) to Sir William Stirling Maxwell, Bart. . . . tendering a respectful remonstrance against the royal commissioners reporting to Her Majesty, and publishing abbreviates of royal letters, and other manuscripts, as if new historical materials discovered under the auspices of the Royal Commission. . . . [By Mark Napier.]
N.P. 1872
No author's name given on title or in the book. There is however a portrait with the subscription, Mark Napier, 1872. A copy has been seen with a note on the fly-leaf, by the author : " Privately printed—only a very few copies with the photo of the author."

LETTER (a) to the Bishop of Sarum [Gilbert Burnet], being an answer to his Lordship's pastoral letter. From a minister in the countrey [Mr Louthrope]. 4to. [*Lincoln's Inn Lib.*]
London, 1690

LETTER to the Emperor of the French on the Eastern question, and the re-establishment of the independence of Poland. [By the Duke de Persigny.] 8vo. [*Brit. Mus.*]   London, 1854

LETTER (a) to the members of the Hon. House of Commons on the Catholic question. [By General Sir James Affleck.] 8vo. 1823

LETTER (a) to the people of Ireland, on the expediency and necessity of the present associations in Ireland in favour of our own manufactures ; with some cursory observations on the effects of a Union. [By Right Hon. Henry Flood.] 8vo. [*D. N. B.* vol. 19, p. 334.] Dublin, 1779

LETTER (a) to the rector of Fryerning [R. Doyly ?] upon his refusing to pay his rates to the Parish assessments. [Signed : C. H. *i.e.* Charles Hornby.] 8vo. [*Brit. Mus.*] London, 1732

*LETTER (a) to the Rev. Dr M. [Thomas Morell] . . .

Preceded by " An extract from the case of the electors . . ." and followed by " A second letter to Dr M." All three were republished in the same year under the title : " The election of aliens . . .", *q.v.*

*LETTER (a) to the Rev. Dr John Martin. . . .

By William Allen, F.R.S. [*Brit. Mus.*]

LETTER (a) to the reviewer of the Memoirs of Don Manuel de Godoy, prince of the peace, etc. [By Henry Richard, Lord Holland.] 8vo. [*Lincoln's Inn Lib.*] London, 1836

LETTER (a) to the Right Hon. the Lord Viscount Molesworth. By M. B. Drapier [Jonathan Swift]. 16mo. [*Brit. Mus.*] Dublin [1724]

LETTER (a) to the Senate and House of Assembly of the State of New Jersey. By a Citizen of Burlington [Henry C. Carey]. 8vo. [Sabin's *Dictionary*, iii. 329.] Burlington, 1851

LETTER (a) to the shop-keepers, tradesmen, farmers and common people of Ireland, concerning the brass halfpence coined by Mr Woods, with a design to have them pass in this kingdom. . . . By M. B., Drapier [Jonathan Swift]. 16mo. [*Brit. Mus.*] Dublin [1724]

LETTERS addressed to the electors of the County of Antrim. By a freeholder [Hugh Boyd]. Published previous to the General Election. 12mo. [*D. N. B.* vol. 6, p. 92.] Dublin, 1776

LETTERS addressed to the Rev. W. F. Hook . . . on the Eucharist, the Mass, and Communion under one species. . . . By Verax, a Catholic layman [M. D. Talbot]. 12mo. Pp. 151. [*Brit. Mus.*] London, 1840

LETTERS between Emilia and Harriet. [By Maria Susanna Cooper.] 8vo. Pp. 175. [*Brit. Mus.*] London, 1762

LETTERS by J. N. D. [John Nelson Darby], 1849-1875 ; extracts translated from the French. 8vo. Pp. 120. [*Brit. Mus.*] London [1881]

LETTERS from a sister. [Edited by G. C. *i.e.* George Cooke.] 12mo. Pp. iv. 51. [*Brit. Mus.*] Doncaster [1841]

LETTERS from a veiled politician [Mrs S. K. Bevan, of Birmingham]. 8vo. [*Birm. Cent. Lib.*] London, 1910

LETTERS from India. Written by J. S. H. [John Somervell Hoyland]. 8vo. Pp. 88. [*Brit. Mus.*] London [1919]

LETTERS from literary characters to E. Barton ; edited by F. Danier : with a prefatory notice by E. Barton [Sir William Cusack Smith] of Captain Rock. 8vo. Pp. xxiv. 150. [*Brit. Mus.*] Dublin, 1824

LETTERS from the Bishop of New Zealand (G. A. Selwyn). [Preface signed G. W. D. *i.e.* George Washington Doane, Bishop in New Jersey.] 8vo. [*Brit. Mus.*] [Burlington, N.J.] 1844

LETTERS from the Bishop [of New Zealand] to the Society for the propagation of the Gospel. . . . [Edited by C. B. D. *i.e.* Charles Browne Dalton.] 8vo. Pp. iv. 111. London, 1844

*LETTERS from the Irish Highlands . . . 1825.

This could not have been by Mrs Henry Wood who was not born until 1814. According to Maria Edgeworth the author was Mrs Blake.

*LETTERS illustrative of Italian scenery . . .

The *Brit. Mus.* ascribes this tentatively to Robert Cotton Money, who wrote the " Journal of a tour in Persia . . ."

LETTERS of Celia Thaxter. Edited by A. Fields and R. L. [Rose Lamb]. 8vo. [*Brit. Mus.*] 1895

LETTERS of Ninon de Lenclos to the Marquiss de Sévigné. Translated from the French [of Louis Damours]. 12mo. Pp. xii. 276. [Barbier's *Dictionnaire*.] London, 1751

LETTERS of Pontius Pilate written during his governorship of Judæa to his friend Seneca in Rome. Edited [or rather written] by W. P. Crozier. 8vo. Pp. 160. [*Brit. Mus.*] London, 1928

LETTERS on currency and banking in Scotland. [By William Smitton.] 8vo. [1879]

*LETTERS on spiritual subjects . . .

For tested, *read* tasted.

LETTERS on the manners of the French, and on the follies and extravagancies of the times : written by an Indian at Paris [rather by the Marquis de L. A. Caraccioli, in French, and translated, with an introduction, by Charles Shillito]. 12mo. 2 vols. [*Brit. Mus.*] London, 1790

*LETTERS on the present state of Newfoundland. . . .

The *Brit. Mus.* now supplies the author's Christian name, Richard Howley.

LETTERS originally addressed to the inhabitants of Cork, in defence of revealed religion, occasioned by the circulation of Mr [Thomas] Paine's "Age of reason" in that city. [By Thomas Dix Hincks.] Second edition, with . . . additions. 4to. [*Brit. Mus.*] Cork, 1796

LETTERS to an honourable gentleman, for the encouragement of faith under various trials. [By Mrs Anne Dutton.] 12mo. [Whitley's *Bapt. Bibl.* ii. 212.] London, 1743

Two more volumes were issued later.

LETTERS to and from the Countess du Barry, the last mistress of Lewis XV. of France . . . including the history of that favourite. . . . Translated from the French [of M. F. Pidansat de Mairobert]. 8vo. [*Brit. Mus.*] London, 1779

LETTERS to Monsieur H*** [Hérinch] concerning the most antient gods or kings of Egypt, and the antiquity of the first monarchs of Babylon and China. . . . Translated from the French [of Dominique Révérend]. 8vo. [*Brit. Mus.*] London, 1734

LETTERS to the Hon. Levi Woodbury, Secretary of the Treasury of the United States. By "Franklin" [Isaac H. Bronson ?]. 8vo. [H. E. Miller's *Banking Theories in the U.S.* p. 228.] New York, 1837

*LETTERS to the inhabitants of Wigan . . .

Besides Holland and Toulmin, H. Kirkpatrick, Rev. George Wicke and Rev. Lewis Loyd took part in the composition of these letters. See Hawkes' *Lancashire Printed Books*, p. 153.

LETTERS to the people of New Jersey, on the frauds, extortions and oppressions of the Railroad Monopoly. By a Citizen of Burlington [Henry C. Carey]. 8vo. [Sabin's *Dictionary*, iii. 329.] Philadelphia, 1848

LETTERS which passed between Bishop Atterbury and Mr Dean Stanhope on . . . baptism in private. . . . [Edited by R. C. *i.e.* Caleb Parfect, Rector of Cuxton.] 8vo. [*Brit. Mus.*] [London] 1758

LETTERS written from Lausanne. Translated from the French [*i.e.* from the "Caliste" of Madame Saint Hyacinthe de Charrières]. 12mo. 2 vols. [*Brit. Mus.*] London, 1799

LETTER-WRITER for ladies. . . . (Letter-writer for gentlemen.) [By Henry Frith.] 8vo. 2 parts. [*Brit. Mus.*] London, 1924

An issue of "The complete letter-writer" (*q.v.*) in two parts.

LEVIATHAN. [Essays.] By William Bolitho [William B. Ryall]. 8vo. Pp. 157. [*Publishers' Weekly*, 1st Sept. 1928.] London [1923]

LEX mercatoria ; or, the merchant's companion. [By Giles Jacob.] 8vo. [Straus' *The Unspeakable Curll.*] London, 1718

LEX terræ ; a discussion of the law of England regarding claims of inheritable rights of peerage. By Sir S. E. B. [Samuel Egerton Brydges]. 8vo. [*Brit. Mus.*] Geneva, 1831

LIBERAL theology and the ground of faith : essays towards a conservative restatement of apologetic. By Hakluyt Egerton [Arthur Boutwood]. 8vo. Pp. 248. [*Brit. Mus.*] London, 1908

LIBRARY (the) ; a poem. [By Thomas Crichton ?] 12mo. [*Brit. Mus.*] Paisley, 1804

LIBRARY (the) of entertaining knowledge ; The New Zealanders. [By George Lillie Craik.] 8vo. Pp. iv. 424. [Collier's *Lit. of New Zealand*, p. 15.] London, 1830

Afterwards published as "The New Zealanders," *q.v.*

LIBRARY (the) of fiction, or family story-teller ; consisting of original tales, essays, and sketches of character. [By Charles Dickens.] 8vo. 2 vols. [*Book prices current*, 1922.] London, 1836-37

LIFE (the) and adventures of Don Bilioso de L'Estomac ; translated from the original Spanish into French, done from the French into English : with a letter to the College of Physicians. [A satire on Dr John Woodward. By Dr Richard Mead.] 8vo. [*Brit. Mus.*] London, 1719

For a counter-satire, see "The art of getting into practice in physic . . ."

LIFE (the) and adventures of Don Pablos the Sharper, an example for vagabonds and a mirror for scamps. By Don Francisco de Quevedo y Villegas. Translated by Francisco Villamiquel y Hardin [Frank Mugglestone]. 8vo. Pp. 220. [*Brit. Mus.*] Leicester, 1928

LIFE and adventures of Timothy Murphy, the benefactor of Schoharie. [By —— Sigsby.] 8vo. Pp. 32. [*Brit. Mus.*]   Schoharie, N.Y., 1839

LIFE (the) and death of John Smith. [By Thomas Piggott.] 16mo. Pp. 50. [Whitley's *Bapt. Bibl.* i. 7.]   1613
No title-page. Signed : T. P. Only one copy known.

LIFE (the) and death of Mr James Sharp, archbishop of St Andrews ; with a short digression touching the rise and progress of Mr Andrew Honeyman, Bishop of Orkney. [By Alexander Hamilton, Laird of Kinkell?] 12mo. Pp. 174.   1719
See also " The life of Mr James Sharp ..."

*LIFE and death of Silas Barnstarke ...
For Gulston, *read* Galston.

*LIFE (the) and death of Sir Thomas Moore ...
The initials to the epistle dedicatory, M. C. M. E., stand for Magister Cresacre More Eboracensis.

LIFE (the) and doctrine of our Lord Jesus Christ ; being a continuous narrative compiled from the four Gospels, all in the words of the Authorised Version, with references thereto. [By C. C. Bartholomew.] 8vo. Pp. 153. [*Brit. Mus.*]   Rotherham [1854]

LIFE (the) and letters of John Martin ; with sketches of Thomas Devin Reilly, Father John Kenyon, and other " young Irelanders." By the author of *Life of John Mitchel*, etc. (P. A. S. [*i.e.* P. A. Sillard]). 8vo. Pp. xiii. 297. [*Brit. Mus.*]   Dublin, 1893

LIFE (the) and letters of St Paul. ... Arranged [by J. S. H. *i.e.* John Saul Howson]. ... 12mo. Pp. x. 83. [*Brit. Mus.*]   Liverpool [1845]

LIFE and nature in the light of evolution. By a Quidnunc [Harford J. Lowe]. 8vo. Pp. 64. [*Brit. Mus.*]
                                 Torquay [1924]
Signed : H. J. L.

LIFE (the) and perambulation of a mouse. By M. P. [Dorothy Kilner]. 8vo. 2 vols. [*Brit. Mus.*]   London [1775 ?]
M. P. are the initials of her pseudonym, " Mary Pelham."

LIFE and select writings of . . . Louis Marie Grignon de Montfort. Translated . . . by a Secular Priest [Alexander F. J. Cruikshank]. ... 8vo. Pp. lxxxiv. 482. [*Brit. Mus.*]
                                 London, 1870

LIFE (the) and teaching of Jesus Christ. ... By N. Avancino. [Translated from the German. Edited by H. J. C. *i.e.* Henry James Coleridge.] 8vo. 2 vols. [*Brit. Mus.*]   London, 1883
" Quarterly Series," vols. 41, 42.

LIFE (the) and times of Alexander I., Emperor of all the Russias. By C. Joyneville [Catherine Laura Johnstone]. 8vo. 3 vols. [*Brit. Mus.*] London, 1875

LIFE (the) and works of Alfred Aloysius Horn [Alfred Aloysius Smith] an old visiter. . . . Edited by Ethelreda Lewis. ... 8vo. 3 vols. [*Amer. Cat.*]   London, 1927-29

LIFE in America ; or, the wigwam and the cabin. [Tales.] By the author of *The Yemassee*, etc. [William Gilmore Simms]. 12mo.   Aberdeen, 1848

*LIFE in Mexico. . . . By Madame C—— de la B—— [Frances Erskine Inglis Calderon de la Barca]. 8vo. [Sabin's *Dictionary.*]
Republished in 1872 with the author's name.

LIFE (the) in the law of Sir Henry Hawkins, Baron Brampton, as related by him to the writer. By E. [Ernest B. B. Rowlands]. 8vo. Pp. 64. [*Brit. Mus.*]   London [1907 ?]

LIFE insurance ; its nature and progress. . . . [By C. B. Norton ?] 12mo. [*Brit. Mus.*]   New York, 1852

LIFE, love and light ; practical morality for men and women. [By Alfred William Pollard.] 8vo. Pp. viii. 177. [*Who's Who.*]   London, 1911
Preface signed : Z.

LIFE of Alexander II., Emperor of all the Russias. By the author of *Science, art, and literature in Russia*, etc. [Catherine Laura Johnstone]. 8vo. Pp. xii. 329. [*Brit. Mus.*] London, 1883

LIFE (the) of Ali Pacha of Jannina. [Translated from the French of Alphonse de Beauchamp.] ... 8vo. [*Brit. Mus.*]   London, 1823

LIFE (the) of Anne Catharine Emmerick. By Helen Ram. [Edited by H. J. C. *i.e.* Henry James Coleridge.] 8vo. Pp. xvi. 231. [*Brit. Mus.*] London, 1874
" Quarterly Series," vol. 10.

LIFE (the) of B. Father Ignatius of Loyola. [By P. de Ribadeneira.] Translated out of Spanish . . . by W. M. [Michael Walpole]. 8vo. Pp. 358. [*Brit. Mus.*]   N.P. 1616
The author's name is given in the Epistle Dedicatory.

LIFE (the) of . . . Benedict Joseph Labre, who died at Rome . . . 1783. Trans. from the French. Together with an account of several miracles. ... [By Giuseppe Loreto Marconi.] 12mo. Pp. xxviii. 232. [Hawkes' *Lancashire Books*, p. 152.]   Wigan, 1786
The original Italian edition, *Vita del Servo di Dio B. G. Labre francese scritta dal suo medesimo confessore*, in the same year was also anonymous. The French translation was by Maximilian Marie Harel. [*Brit. Mus.*]

LIFE (the) of Dr J. Barwick, translated into English by the editor of the Latin life [Hilkiah Bedford], with notes. . . . [*Brit. Mus.*] London, 1724

*LIFE (the) of Haydn . . .
For Thomas Gardiner, *read* William Gardiner. [*Brit. Mus.*]

LIFE (the) of John Mitchel; with an historical sketch of the '48 movement in Ireland. By P. A. S. [P. A. Sillard]. 8vo. Pp. xviii. 286. [*Brit. Mus.*] Dublin, 1889

*LIFE (the) of Lady Warner . . .
For the correct title see " The Life of the Lady Warner."

LIFE (the) of Lamenther; a true history written by herself. In five parts. Containing a just account of the many misfortunes she underwent occasioned by the ill-treatment of an unnatural father. [By Anne Wall.] 8vo. [*Brit. Mus.*] London, 1771
A letter on p. 94 is signed " Anne W—."

LIFE (the) of Margaret Mostyn. . . . By . . . Edmund Bedingfield. [Edited by H. J. C. *i.e.* Henry James Coleridge.] 8vo. Pp. xv. 275. [*Brit. Mus.*] London, 1878
" Quarterly Series," vol. 25.

LIFE of Mother Margaret Mary Hallahan, foundress of the English Congregation of St Catherine of Sienna of the third order of St Dominic. By her religious children. [Edited by Augusta Theodosia Drane.] 8vo. Pp. xv. 539. [*Brit. Mus.*] London, 1869
The second edition (1862) is " Edited by the author of *Christian schools and scholars,*" and an edition in 1930 bears the editor's full name.

LIFE (the) of Mr James Sharp, from his birth to his instalment in the archbishoprick of St Andrews: written in the time of his life; with a short digression touching the rise and progress of Mr Andrew Honyman, Bishop of Orkney: with an appendix, containing an account of some of Mr Sharp's actions during the time of his being archbishop, and the manner and circumstances of his death, by one of the persons concerned in it. [By Alexander Hamilton, laird of Kinkell?] 12mo. Pp. 174.   1719
Another title is usually prefixed: see " The life and death of Mr James Sharp . . ."

*LIFE of Robert Rudolf Suffield. . . .
For Rev. C. Hargrave, *read* Rev. Charles Hargrove. [*D. N. B.* vol. 55, p. 152.]

LIFE (the) of Saint Edward, King and Confessor. . . . By the Rev. F. Jerome Porter. Revised . . . by a priest (C. J. B.) [Charles J. Bowen?]. 16mo. Pp. xii. 114. [*Brit. Mus.*] London, 1868

LIFE (the) of St Francis de Sales. . . . By Robert Ornsby. . . . [With a preface signed: J. M. C. *i.e.* John Moore Capes.] 8vo. [*Brit. Mus.*] London, 1856

L I F E (the) of Saint Monica. . . . [Translated and abridged from the Life by L. E. Bougaud.] By Lady Herbert. 8vo. Pp. viii. 114. [*Brit. Mus.*] London, 1894
Another translation, by Mrs E. Hazeland, of the full work was published earlier [in 1886], and a new edition in 1892.

L I F E of Sir Edward Widdrington, Knt., and Baronet of Cartington, in Northumberland. . . . By a Catholic gentleman [Francis John Angus Skeet]. 8vo. Pp. 32. [*Brit.Mus.*] London, 1923

LIFE (the) of the blessed Peter Favre . . . From the Italian of Father G. Boero [by Henry James Coleridge]. 8vo. Pp. xiv. 397. [*Brit. Mus.*] London, 1873
" Quarterly Series," vol. 8.

*LIFE (the) of the Lady Warner . . .
Signed: N. N.

*LIFE (the) of the late Hon. Robert Price . . .
Now definitely known to be by Edmund Curll. See R. Straus' *The Unspeakable Curll*, p. 297.

LIFE (the) of the most reverend father in God, John Tillotson, Archbishop of Canterbury, compiled from the minutes of . . . Mr Young . . . Dean of Salisbury. By F. H., M.A. [F. Hutchinson?] . . . 8vo. [R. Straus' *The Unspeakable Curll*, p. 243.] London, 1717

LIFE (the) of the ocean waifs. [Verses.] By Dowie [G. Dowsmith]. 8vo. [*Brit. Mus.*] London [1927]

LIFE (the) of the reverend Fa. Angel of Joyeuse, Capucin Preacher . . . [by Jacques Brousse]. Together with the lives of Father Bennet, and Father Archangell, of the same Order [by Faustinus Diestensis]. Written first in the Frenche tongue, and now translated into Englishe by R. R., Catholique priest. 8vo. 3 parts. [*Pollard and Redgrave.*] Douay, 1623

LIFE (the) of the venerable father Claude de la Colombière. . . . By Eugene Seguin. [Edited by H. J. C. *i.e.* Henry James Coleridge.] 8vo. Pp. xiii. 231. [*Brit. Mus.*] London, 1883
" Quarterly Series," vol. 40.

*LIFE (the) of Thomas Pain . . .
"Oldys is said to have been George
Chalmers (1742-1825), then a clerk in the
Council of Trade. The President, Lord
Hawkesbury, afterwards first Lord Liver-
pool, is said by Sherwin to have employed
him and paid him 500 l. for writing it."
[D. N. B. vol. 43, p. 79.]
"This work is usually attributed to
Chalmers ; but, in the year 1864, I sold a
long letter, written by Chalmers, in which
he indignantly denied the statement."
[Sabin's Dictionary, iii. 467.]

LIFE'S edifice. By X. [H. E. Nightin-
gale]. 8vo. Pp. 224. [Brit. Mus.]
London, 1917

LIGHT and shade ; occasional verses
by N. H. M. [N. H. Mason]. 8vo.
Pp. 8. [Brit. Mus.]
[Private print, 1893]

LIGHT (a) bondell of livly discourses
called Churchyardes charge. . . .
[Edited by J. P. C. i.e. John Payne
Collier.] 4to. [Brit. Mus.] [c. 1870]

LIGHTS and shadows. Tales of Karma
and reincarnation. . . . By Aimée
Blech [Lionel Dalsace]. Translation
by Fred Rothwell. 8vo. Pp. 144.
[Brit. Mus.]   London, 1928

LILLIAN and other poems. By W. M.
Praed ; now first collected [by R. W.
G. i.e. Rufus W. Griswold]. 12mo.
Pp. 290. [Brit. Mus.] New York, 1852

LILY (the) of Tiflis ; a sketch from
Georgian church history. [By John
Mason Neale.] 8vo. Pp. 87. [Brit.
Mus.]   London [1859]

LIMANORA, the island of progress.
By Godfrey Sweven [John Macmillan
Brown]. 8vo. Pp. ix. 711. [Brit.
Mus.]   New York, 1903

LIMITED (a) horizon. [A tale. By
Mrs A. C. de la Condamine.] 8vo.
Pp. 143. [Brit. Mus.] London, 1885

*LIMB (the) . . .
For XL., read X. L.

LIMOUSIN folk. By Jean Nesmy
[Henry Surchamp]. Translated by
W. M. Daniels. 8vo. Pp. 282. [Brit.
Mus.]   London, 1930

LINES. [Verses on celebrated men.]
—Stanzas [to Wordsworth, by W. R.
i.e. Sir William Rough]. 12mo. Pp.
12. [Brit. Mus.]   Colombo [c. 1835]
Signed : W. R.

LINES addressed to Lady Byron.   [By
Mrs E. Cockle.] 8vo. [Brit. Mus.]
Newcastle, 1817

L I N E S on Genesis. (The Prophet
Elijah.) By an Orkneyman [William
C. Mainland]. 8vo. Pp. 30, 8. [Brit.
Mus.]   Kirkwall [1911]

LINES on the death of —— [R. B.
Sheridan] from the Morning Chronicle
of . . . August 5, 1816. [By T.
Moore.] . . . Republished, without
note or comment. 8vo. [Brit. Mus.]
London, 1816

LINES on the Psalms. By the author
of Lines on Genesis [William C. Main-
land]. 8vo. Pp. 36. [Brit. Mus.]
Kirkwall, 1924

LINES to a boy pursuing a butterfly.
By a lady [Mrs E. Cockle]. 8vo.
[Brit. Mus.]   Newcastle, 1826

LINES written on the birth of the
young Prince, son of the Emperor and
Empress of the French, March 16,
1856. . . . [By A. Peat.] 12mo.
[Brit. Mus.]   Edinburgh [1856]

LINNET'S (the) life ; twelve poems.
[By Anne and Jane Taylor.] 12mo.
[Brit. Mus.]   London, 1822

LION (the) of Scotland : a tale of 1298
[and other poems. By John Drake].
8vo. Pp. 240. [Brit. Mus.]
Glasgow, 1897

LIP (the) of truth. By the author of
The Lamplighter [Francis Bourdillon].
8vo. [Brit. Mus.]   London [1870]
Signed : F. B.

L I S T (a) of the Archdeacons of
Canterbury. [By Charles Eveleigh
Woodruff.] 4to. Pp. 16. [Brit.
Mus.]   N.P. 1928
Signed : C. E. W.

LIST (a) of the names of the members
of the House of Commons. . . .   The
first centurie.   [By Henry Elsynge ?]
Fol.   S. sh.   [Brit. Mus.]
[London, 1648]
Signed : M. El.

LISTEN and learn ; a short narrative
of a three days' ramble. By the author
of The observing eye [Anne Wright].
12mo. Pp. 141. [Brit. Mus.]
London [1856]

LITERARY pearls strung at random by
R. A. M. [R. A. Mould]. . . . 8vo.
Pp. xi. 266. [Brit. Mus.]
London, 1866

LITHOGRAPHY ; or, the art of taking
impressions from drawings and writing
made on stone. With specimens. . . .
Second edition. . . .   [By ——
Bankes ?] 8vo. [Brit. Mus.]
London, 1816

LITTLE Alice and her sister. [By Mary
Ann Dyson.] 16mo. Pp. 163. [Brit.
Mus.]   1843

LITTLE (the) book of family prayer.
. . . With an introduction on family
prayer [signed : W. L. D. i.e. W. L.
Dickinson]. 12mo. [Brit. Mus.]
London, 1870

LITTLE (a) book on map projection. By Mary Adams [William Garnett]. 8vo. Pp. viii. 108. [*Brit. Mus.*]
London, 1914

LITTLE (the) builders and their voyage to Rangi; a story for children. By R. N. [Philip Alfred Malpas]. . . . 16mo. Pp. 42. [*Brit. Mus.*]
New York [1900]

LITTLE (the) Don of Oxford. [A story.] By Nellie Cornwall [Nellie Sloggett]. 8vo. Pp. 224. [*Brit. Mus.*]
London [1902]

LITTLE (the) garden of the soul. . . . [Abridged from *The garden of the soul* of Richard Challoner, Bishop of Debra.] 16mo. [*Brit. Mus.*]   London, 1873

LITTLE (the) innocent rescued from the hands of a priest. [Verse. By Benjamin Francis.] 4to. S. sh. [*Brit. Mus.*]   London [1798]
Signed: John, the Dipper.

LITTLE (the) maid, and the gentleman; or, we are seven. [By William Wordsworth.] 32mo. Pp. 15. [*Brit. Mus.*]
York [1820?]

LITTLE (a) more nonsense. [Limericks.] The author, R. D. [Randall Davies. With woodcuts from "Specimens of early wood engravings" by W. Dodd]. 8vo. [*Brit. Mus.*]   London, 1923

LITTLE Robinson Crusoe of Paris. Told from the French of Eugénie Foa [Eugénie Rebecca Gradis, *née* Rodrigues] by Julia Olcott. . . . 8vo. Pp. 160. [*Bibl. Nat. Paris.*]
Philadelphia [1925]

LITTLE Tom, the Sailor. 4to.
Lambeth, 1917
One of 100 copies privately printed.
The dedication and colophon imply that the verses as well as the designs are by William Blake. The verses are really by William Hayley. See his *Memoirs*, vol. ii. p. 22, Gilchrist's *Life of Blake*, Keynes' *Bibliography of Blake*, etc.

LITTLE Walter; or, a mother's first lessons on religious subjects. [By Mrs S. Greg.] 18mo. [*Brit. Mus.*]
London, 1855

LITTLE (the) white hag. By Francis Beeding [John Leslie Palmer and Hilary Aidan St George Saunders]. 8vo. Pp. 320. [*Amer. Cat.*]
Boston [1926]

LIVES of Alexander Henderson [by Thomas M'Crie, D.D.] and James Guthrie [by Rev. Thomas Thomson]; with specimens of their writings [edited by Thomas Thomson]. 8vo. [*Brit. Mus.*]   Edinburgh, 1846

*LIVES (the) of all the Roman Emperors . . .
The *D.N.B.* (vol. 6, p. 234) accepts this as Brathwait's, but Pollard and Redgrave (*S. T. C.*) attribute it to Robert Basset.

LIVES (the) of Haydn [by G. Carpani] and Mozart [by A. H. F. von Schlichtegroll]; with observations on Metastasio. . . . Translated from the French of M. Henri Beyle, with notes, by the author of the *Sacred melodies* [William Gardiner]. Second edition. 8vo. Pp. xiv. 496. [*Brit. Mus.*]   London, 1818
The title of the first edition begins "The life of Haydn . . ." *q.v.*

LIVES (the) of holy saints, prophets, patriarchs, apostles and others, contained in Holy Scripture. . . . [By John Marbecke.] 4to. Pp. 328. [*Brit. Mus.*]   London, 1681
Preface signed: R. M. Earlier editions (1574 *et seq.*) bear the author's name.

LIVESTOCK in barracks. By Anthony Armstrong [George Anthony Armstrong Willis]. 8vo. Pp. x. 153. [*Brit. Mus.*]   London, 1929

LIVING waters; a Bible text-book. [With a preface signed: J. E. H. *i.e.* James E. Hawkins.] 16mo. [*Brit. Mus.*]   London [1885]

LOGIC for the young . . . selected from the logic of Isaac Watts, by the author of *Logic for the million* [James William Gilbart]. 12mo. [*Brit. Mus.*]
London, 1855

LOLA of the chocolates. By James James [Arthur Henry Adams]. Second edition. 8vo. Pp. 144. [*Brit. Mus.*]
London [1920]

LONDON (a) girl. [By Harold Begbie.] 8vo. Pp. xii. 172. [*Brit. Mus.*]
London, 1905
One of "Tales from the Great City."

*LONDON, or interesting memorials. . . . By Sholto and Reuben Percy.
The ascription given is inaccurate. Reuben Percy was Thomas Byerley, and Sholto Percy was Joseph Clinton Robertson, not Robinson.

LONDON renovated and England regenerated through justice to Ireland; or, a programme of reform proposed to the new Parliament. By M. O. and I. H. [M. Otway and Iyo Hay] . . . Second edition. . . . 8vo. Pp. 15. [*Brit. Mus.*]   London, 1886

LONDON stories, old and new. Written and edited by John O'London [Wilfred Whitten]. 16mo. Pp. 182. [*Brit. Mus.*]   London [1926]

LONDON'S improvement and the builder's security asserted, by the apparent advantages that will attend their easie charge, in raising such a joint-stock as may assure a re-building of those houses, which shall hereafter be destroyed by . . . fire. [By A. N. *i.e.* A. Newbold?] Fol. [*Brit. Mus.*]
London, 1680

LONDON'S Lord have mercy upon us ; a true relation of five modern plagues . . . in London . . . Written by H. C. [Humfrey Crouch?]. Fol. S. sh. [*Brit. Mus.*]   London [1637]

LONDON'S triumph ; or, the solemn and magnificent reception of . . . R. Tichburn, Lord Mayor, after his return from taking the oath at Westminster. . . . [By John Bulteel.] 4to. [*Brit. Mus.*]   London, 1656
Signed : J. B.

LONDON'S vacation and the countries tearme ; or, a lamentable relation of severall remarkable passages which it hath pleased the Lord to shew on severall persons, both in London, and the country in this present visitation, 1636. . . . By H. C. [Humfrey Crouch?]. 8vo. [*Brit. Mus.*]
London, 1637

LONG (the) trail ; a story of African adventure. By Herbert Strang [George Herbert Ely and C. J. L'Estrange]. 8vo. Pp. 284. [*Brit. Mus.*]
London, 1919

LONG (the) way round. [A novel.] By Michael Maurice [Conrad Arthur Skinner]. 8vo. Pp. 285. [*Brit. Mus.*]   London, 1925

LONGEST (the) shadow. By Jeffery E. Jeffery [Jeffery Eardley Marston]. 8vo. Pp. 325. [*Amer. Cat.*]
Boston, 1927

LONGEVITY ; or, Professor Owen and the Speaker's commentary. By W. F. H. [William Forbes Hobson?]. 8vo. [*Brit. Mus.*]   Oxford, 1872

*"LOOK before you leap." Addresses to the citizens of the Southern States : being a solemn warning against the destructive doctrine of a separation of the Union. By the author of *The Olive Branch* [Matthew Carey]. 8vo. Pp. iv. 24. [*Sabin's Dictionary*, iii. 341.]   Philadelphia, 1835
Signed : Hamilton. *The Olive Branch* is not anonymous.

LOOKING (a) glass for the Nullifiers. [By Matthew Carey.] 8vo. Pp. 4. [*Sabin's Dictionary*, iii. 341.] N.P. 1832

"LOOKING unto Jesus " ; a narrative of a brief race of a young disciple. By her mother [Judith Towers Grant]. 16mo. [*Brit. Mus.*]   Bath [1852]

LOOKING-GLASS (a) for a bad husband ; or, a caveat for a spendthrift. . . . [A ballad.] By T. L. [Thomas Lanfiere?]. Obl. fol. S. sh. B. L. [*Brit. Mus.*]   London [1680?]

LOOKING-GLASS (the) for the mind, or intellectual mirror ; being stories . . . chiefly translated [by W. D. Cooper] from [Arnaud Berquin's] "L'Ami des enfants" : a new edition. . . . 12mo. Pp. 271. [*Brit. Mus.*]
London, 1792

LOOSE-BOX (the) ; a sporting mystery. By Raymond Carew [Frank Victor Hughes Hallett]. 8vo. Pp. 320. [*Brit. Mus.*]   London [1914]

LORD Birkenhead : being an account of the life of F. E. Smith, first Earl of Birkenhead. By Ephesian [Carl Eric Bechhofer Roberts]. 8vo. Pp. 224. [*Brit. Mus.*]   London, 1926

LORD Byron's Farewell to England ; with three other poems, viz. Ode to St Helena, To my daughter, on the morning of her birth, and To the Lily of France. 8vo. Pp. 31. [*Brit. Mus.*]   London, 1816
Purports to be by Lord Byron, but is spurious.

LORD Byron's Pilgrimage to the Holy Land ; a poem. . . . To which is added, The Tempest, a fragment. 8vo. Pp. 72. [*Brit. Mus.*]
London, 1817
Purports to be by Lord Byron, but is spurious.

LORD (the) Lieutenant and High Sheriff. [By C. G. Y., Garter, *i.e.* Sir Charles George Young.] 8vo. [*Brit. Mus.*]   [London] 1860

*LORD (the) Mayor of London . . .
Signed : T. C. N.

LOST (the) Dominion. [An account of British rule in India.] By Al Carthill [Sir John Perronet Thompson]. 8vo. Pp. vi. 351. [*Brit. Mus.*]
Edinburgh, 1924

*LOST (the) father . . .
For Gourand, *read* Gouraud. Julie Gouraud is a *pseud.* for Louise d'Aulnan.

LOTTIE'S silver burden. [A tale.] . . . By E. R. G. [Evelyn R. Garratt]. 8vo. [*Brit. Mus.*]   London, 1879

LOUNGER (the) ; a periodical paper published at Edinburgh in the years 1785 and 1786. By the authors of *The Mirror* [Henry Mackenzie and others]. Second edition. 12mo. 3 vols. [*Brit. Mus.*]   Edinburgh, 1787

*LOVE and valour . . .
For d'Audignier, *read* d'Audiguier.

LOVE conquers all. [A novel.] By A. C. Hertford [Adelaide M. Cameron]. 8vo. Pp. 160. [*Brit. Mus.*]
London [1889]

LOVE frolics of a young scamp. By the author of *Anonyma* [William Stephens Hayward]. 8vo. Pp. iv. 316. [*Brit. Mus.*]
London [1884]

LOVE in letters; illustrated in the correspondence of eminent persons, with biographical sketches of the writers. By Allan Grant [James Grant Wilson]. 8vo. [*Brit. Mus.*]
New York, 1867

LOVE in the dark; or, the man of business: a comedy as it is acted at the Duke's Theatre. [By Sir F. Fane.] 4to. [Arber's *Term Cat.* iii. 227.]
London, 1676

LOVE intrigues; or, the history of the amours of Bosvil and Galesia, as related to Lucasia in St Germain's Garden; a novel. Written by a young lady [Mrs Jane Barker]. 8vo. [R. Straus' *The Unspeakable Curll*, p. 223.] London, 1713
Dedication signed: J. B.
Published as "The amours of Bosvil and Galesia," with the author's name on title-page in a collected edition called "The Entertaining Novels of Mrs Jane Barker" (second edition, 1719).

LOVE lyrics and valentine verses, for young and old. [By Charles Maurice Davies.] 8vo. [*Brit. Mus.*]
London [1875]

LOVE (the) of Prince Raameses. By Anthony Armstrong [George Anthony Armstrong Willis]. 8vo. Pp. 256. [*Brit. Mus.*] London, 1921

LOVE (the) story of a minor poet. By Stellarius [Alfred Starkey]. 8vo. Pp. 31. [*Brit. Mus.*] London, 1907

LOVE-IN-A-MIST; a comedy in three acts. By Amelia Troubetzkoy and Gilbert Emery [Emery Bemstey Pottle]. [*Amer. Cat.*] New York, 1927

LOVE'S a lottery, and a woman the prize. [By Joseph Harris.] . . . 8vo. Pp. 40. [*Lib. of Congress, Cat. of Opera Librettos.*] London, 1699

*LOVE'S contrivance . . .
Signed: R. M.

LOVES fierce desire, and hopes of recovery. . . . [A ballad. Signed: L. P. *i.e.* Laurence Price?] Fol. S. sh. [*Brit. Mus.*] [London, 1670?]

LOVE-TIFF (the). Translated from the stage version of Molière's *Dépit amoureux*—1656—as arranged . . . by Valville [François Bernard] . . . by Frederic Spencer. 8vo. Pp. 48. [*Brit. Mus.*] Oxford, 1930

LOYAL (the) martyr vindicated. [A vindication of John Ashton, the Jacobite conspirator, executed Jan. 28, 1690/1. Said to be by Edward Fowler, Bishop of Gloucester.] 4to. Pp. 52. [*Lincoln's Inn Lib.*] N.P. [1691]
Ascribed also to Hon. R. North.

LOYAL (the) Nonconformist; or, an account what he dare swear and what not. [Signed: R. W. *i.e.* Robert Wild.] Fol. S.sh. [*Brit.Mus.*] N.P.1666

LUCAS redivivus; or, the gospel physitian, prescribing (by way of meditation) divine physic to prevent diseases not yet entered upon the soul. . . . [By John Anthony, M.D.] 4to. [Watt's *Bibl. Brit.*] London, 1654

LUCIA'S marriage; or, the lions of Wady-Araba: a story of the Idumaean desert. [By John Mason Neale.] 8vo. Pp. 102. [*Brit. Mus.*]
London [1860]

LUCK and other stories. By Mary Arden [Mrs Violet Middleton Murry]. 8vo. Pp. 255. [*Times,* 10th April 1931.] London, 1927

LUCKY fool. By L. C. Gould Flemé [Lewis Charles Goldflam]. 8vo. Pp. 328. [*Evening Standard,* 9th July 1931.] London, 1929

LUCKY Spence's last advice. [By Allan Ramsay.] 8vo. Pp. 4. [A. Gibson's *Allan Ramsay,* p. 119.]
[Edinburgh, 1718]
Afterwards (1719) included in a collection without a title-page of works many of which bear Allan Ramsay's name.

LUCY in lion land. By Noel Hope [Sarah L. Morewood]. 8vo. Pp. viii. 154. [*Brit. Mus.*] London [1928]

LURE of the past. [A novel.] By Anthony Armstrong [George Anthony Armstrong Willis]. 8vo. Pp. 256. [*Brit. Mus.*] London, 1920

LURE (the) of Venus; or, a harlot's progress: a heroi-comical poem, in six cantos. By Mr Gay [John Durant de Breval]. Founded on Mr Hogarth's six prints and illustrated with them. 8vo. [*D. N. B.* vol. 6, p. 290.]
London, 1733

LUTHER Wing. [A novel.] By Michael Maurice [Conrad Arthur Skinner]. 8vo. Pp. 280. [*Brit. Mus.*]
London [1930]

LUX e tenebris; or, the testimony of consciousness: a theoretic essay. [By Francis Giles, Surgeon, of Stourbridge.] 8vo. Pp. xi. 361. [*Brit. Mus.*] 1874

LYF (the) of the Mother Teresa of Jesus. . . . Written by herself [or rather by Francesco de Ribera] and now translated . . . out of Spanish by W. M. [Michael Walpole] of the Society of Jesus. 4to. [*Brit. Mus.*] Antwerp, 1611

LYFE of Saynt Radegunde. [By Henry Bradshaw.] 8vo. [*Pollard and Redgrave.*] London [*c.* 1520]
Reprinted by F. Brittain, in 1926.

LYNCH law; or, the hunter's revenge. [A romance.] Translated from the French [of Gustave Aimard] by H. L. Williams. 8vo. [*Brit. Mus.*]
London [1860]

LYRIC (a) ode on the birth of . . . the Prince of Wales. . . . [By Mrs Mary Latter.] 8vo. [*Brit. Mus.*]
London, 1763

LYRICS of the Nile. By an Anglo-Egyptian Civil Servant [Charles Robert Ashbee]. 8vo. Pp. 61.
London, 1919
Acknowledgment by the author.

M

McARDLE (the) peerage. [A novel.] By Evelyn Tempest [Edward W. D. Cuming]. 8vo. Pp. xi. 306. [*Brit. Mus.*] London, 1910

MACBETH. . . . By William Shakespeare. [With remarks by D. G. *i.e.* George Daniel.] 8vo. Pp. 63. [*Brit. Mus.*] London [1864]

*MACCULLOCHS (the) of Glastullich.
For O. M. R. *i.e.* O. Murray Rose, *read* D. M. R. *i.e.* D. Murray Rose.

*MACK-FAUX the mock moralist. [By William Forbes, of Disblair.]
This author appears elsewhere in this dictionary as —— Forbes, of Disblair. We have not been able to find any evidence that his Christian name was William.

MACHIAVIL'S advice to his son. Newly translated out of Italian into English verse [or rather, written] by R. L. Esq. [Roger L'Estrange]. Fol. Pp. 8. [*Brit. Mus.*] London, 1681

MAD (the) cap; a comedy for the digestion, in three acts: from the German of Kotzebue, by R * * * * * H * * * * * [Robert Hunter]. 8vo. [R. Inglis' *Dramatic Writers of Scotland*, p. 145.]
Edinburgh, 1800

MAD (the) man's morrice, etc. [By Humphrey Crouch.] Obl. fol. S. sh. [*Brit. Mus.*] [London, 1690?]
For an earlier edition (1670?) see "The Mad-man's morrice . . ." The original edition (1640?) was not anonymous.

MAD Margrete and little Gumwald; a Norwegian tale. By Nellie Cornwall [Nellie Sloggett]. 8vo. Pp. 256. [*Brit. Mus.*] London, 1889

MAD Tom a Bedlams desires of peace; or, his benedicities for distracted Englands restauration. . . . [Verse. By S F W B, *i.e.* Sir Francis Wortley, Bart.] Fol. S. sh. [*Brit. Mus.*]
London, 1648

*MADAME Gilbert's Cannibal. . . .
For Kitchen, *read* Kitchin.

*MADAM'S ward . . .
For By C. C. Andrews, *read* By C. Andrews. See *Amer. Cat.*, 1884-90.

MADELAINE'S fault; a story of French life: translated [from the French of Pauline Caro] by M. Neale. 8vo. Pp. 183. [*Brit. Mus.*] London, 1882

*MADELINE . . . By Daring Hope.
For Daring Hope, *read* Hope Daring.

MADMAN (the) of St James'; a narrative from the journal of a physician. Translated from the German of Philipp Galen [Ernst P. C. Lange] by T. H. 8vo. 3 vols. [*Brit. Mus.*]
London, 1860

MAD-MAN'S (the) morrice, or a warning for young men to have a care, how they in love intangled are. . . . [A song by Humphrey Crouch.] Fol. S. sh. B. L. [*Brit. Mus.*]
[London, 1670|?]
For a later edition (1690?) see "The Mad man's morice . . ." The original edition (1640?) was not anonymous.

MADRAS. [An account of the various woods, indigenous and imported, used in Madras; with a list of the specimens contained in the Government Central Museum. By Edward Balfour.] 8vo. [*Brit. Mus.*] [Madras, 1855]

MAGIC and Mary Rose. [A novel.] By Faith Baldwin [Faith Baldwin Cuthrell]. 8vo. Pp. 321. [*Amer. Cat.*]
Boston [1924]

MAIDS (the) tragedie. [By Francis Beaumont and John Fletcher.] . . . Second impression. 4to. [*Brit. Mus.*]
London, 1622
For the first edition, see "The Maides Tragedy."

MAINTENANCE (the) of denominational teaching: a note upon section 7 (1) of the Education Act, 1902. By Hakluyt Egerton [Arthur Boutwood]. 8vo. Pp. 109. [*Brit. Mus.*]
London, 1905

MAKESHIFT (the) lover. [A tale.] By Mark Allerton [William Ernest Cameron]. 8vo. Pp. 112. [*Brit. Mus.*]   London, 1923

MAKING a shooting. [By Arthur Hepburn Hastie.] 8vo. Pp. 92. [*Brit. Mus.*]   London, 1894

MAKING (the) of a god ; demonstrating the theory of religion as allegorically conveyed in the Bible. By Roland Saint-Clair [Roland Sinclair Watson]. 8vo. Pp. 31. [*Brit. Mus.*]   London [1920]

MALVAGNA ; a romance of the nineteenth century. [By Edward Cheney.] 8vo. 3 vols. [*Brit. Mus.*]   1835

MALVINA. By Madame C * * * * [Sophie R. Cottin]. Translated from the French by Miss Gunning : second edition. 12mo. 4 vols. [*Brit. Mus.*]   London, 1810

MAN (a) beset. By John Carruthers [John Young Thomson Greig]. 8vo. Pp. 351.   London, 1927

MAN (the) in the car. By Allan Raleigh [Elijah Brown]. 8vo. Pp. 314. [*Brit. Mus.*]   London, 1913

MAN (the) of his time. . . . The story of the life of Napoleon. By J. M. Haswell. . . . [With a preface signed : J. C. H. *i.e.* John Camden Hotten.] 8vo. [*Brit. Mus.*]   London [1871]

MAN (the) of promise : Lord Rosebery. A critical study. By E. T. Raymond [Edward Raymond Thompson]. 8vo. Pp. 263. [*Brit. Mus.*]   London, 1923

MAN (the) of the world ; a comedy in five acts. . . . Written by C— M—, Esq. [Charles Macklin]. 8vo. [*Brit. Mus.*]   Dublin, 1786

MAN (the) of To-morrow, J. Ramsay Macdonald. By Iconoclast [Mary Agnes Hamilton]. 8vo. Pp. 288. [*Brit. Mus.*]   London, 1923
See also " J. Ramsay Macdonald."

MAN (the) who stood alone. By Paul Trent [Edward Platt]. 8vo. Pp. 317. [*Brit. Mus.*]   London, 1926

MAN (the) who was there. By N. A. Temple Ellis [Neville Aldridge Holdaway]. 8vo. Pp. vii. 274. [*Brit. Mus.*]   London, 1930

MAN (the) with the club foot. [A novel.] By Douglas Valentine [Valentine Williams]. 8vo. Pp. viii. 311. [*Brit. Mus.*]   London, 1918

MAN (the) without a necktie. By Arbib-Hauser [Erminia Hauser]. Translated by C. B. Jordan. 8vo. Pp. 287. [*Brit. Mus.*]   London, 1930

MANCHESTER Church questions plainly stated. [By George Hull Bower, D.D.] 8vo. [*Lincoln's Inn Lib.*]   London, 1850

MANIAC (the) of the Pyrenees ; or, the heroic soldier's wife : a melodrama in two acts. [By Lieut. John Shipp.] 8vo. Pp. 35. [*Brit. Mus.*]   Brentford, 1829

MANIFESTATION (a) of prayer in formality, and prayer in the spirit of God. [By William Smith, of Besthorp.] Fol. S. sh. [*Brit. Mus.*]   [London, 1663 ?]
Signed : W. S.

MAN'S (a) belief ; an essay on the facts of religious knowledge. [By Albert Julius Mott.] 8vo. Pp. 103. [*Brit. Mus.*]   London, 1868

MAN'S (a) man ; a novel. By John Strange Winter [Henrietta E. V. Stannard]. 8vo. Pp. 110. [*Brit. Mus.*]   London, 1893

MANTLE (the) of Cæsar. By Friedrich Gundolf [Friedrich Gundelfinger]. Translated from the German by Jacob Wittmer Hartmann. 8vo. Pp. 319. [*Brit. Mus.*]   London [1929]

MANUAL (a) for Christians after confirmation. [By Edward Hawkins, D.D.] 12mo. [*Brit. Mus.*]   [Oxford, 1826]
Signed : E. H.

MANUAL for self-instruction, comprising in one story all the rules of the French language. By V. S. Z. [V. S. Zorawski]. 16mo. [*Brit. Mus.*]   London, 1845

MANUAL (a) for the sick and sorrowful. Arranged by E. S. L. [E. S. Lister]. 8vo. Pp. xii. 157. [*Brit. Mus.*]   London, 1902

MANUAL (a) of criminal law for police, salt, forest, and other magisterial officers. [By P. V. Srinivasacharya.] 8vo. Pp. 278, 90. [*Brit. Mus.*]   Madras, 1899

MANUAL of devotion for Sisters of Mercy. . . . Second edition. [By Thomas Thellusson Carter.] 16mo. 2 vols. [*Brit. Mus.*]   London, 1868
Signed : T. T. C.

MANUAL (a) of light drill. . . . [Based on R. B. Hawley's System of rifle drill. Preface signed : E. T. H. *i.e.* Edward T. H. Hutton.] 32mo. Pp. 76. [*Brit. Mus.*]   Dublin, 1876

MANUAL (a) of prayers for young persons ; or, Bishop Ken's Winchester manual adapted to general use [by W. H. H. *i.e.* William Henry Havergal]. 12mo. Pp. vi. 90. [*Brit. Mus.*]   London, 1832

MANUAL (a) of surgery. . . . By Sir Astley Cooper. . . . Fifth edition. [Reprinted by E. *i.e.* C. C. Egerton.] 12mo. Pp. lx. 542. [*Brit. Mus.*]   Calcutta, 1839

*MANUALL (a) of devout meditations . . .

For By H. M., *read* By a father of the same society. It was edited by I. W. [*i.e.* J. Wilson].

MANUFACTURE (the) of glazed bricks and glazed sanitary ware. . . . [By H. Ansell.] 8vo. Pp. 75. [*Brit. Mus.*]
London, 1894

MAPS and tables of chronology . . . selected and translated from . . . Koch's "Tableau des Revolutions de l'Europe." [By C. T. L. *i.e.* Charles Thomas Longley, afterwards Archbishop of Canterbury.] 4to. [*Brit. Mus.*]
1831

MARCH (the) of the Red Lions—1867. [In verse. By William Pengelly.] 8vo. S. sh. [*Brit. Mus.*] [Dundee? 1867]

Signed with his finials : M. Y.

MARGARET Coryton. By Leigh Cliffe [George Jones]. 8vo. 3 vols. [*Eng. Cat.* 1801-1836, p. 121.] London, 1829

MARIE'S home; or, a glimpse of the past. By Caroline Austin [Mrs —— Whitway]. 8vo. Pp. 190. [*Brit. Mus.*]
London [1885]

MARK (the) of Cain, a tale of the desert. By "Hermann Boscher, Ph.D." [Andrew Lang]. 8vo. Pp. 8.
Bristol, 1886

Edmund Gosse's copy has the following note in his own handwriting :—"By Andrew Lang. Only 5 or 6 copies ever printed. Published to secure copyright in the title, on 26th of March, 1886."

The volume for which the title was desired duly appeared "The Mark of Cain. By Andrew Lang," pp. 86, as part of Arrowsmith's Bristol Library.

MARKET (the) woman ; a true tale : or, honesty is the best policy. [By Hannah More.] Fol. S. sh. [*Brit. Mus.*]
Bath [1795]

Signed : Z.

MARQUERAY'S duel. By the author of *Jenny Essenden* [Agnes Russell Weekes]. 8vo. Pp. 381. [*Who's Who in Lit.*] [1919]

MARQUISE (the) de Vaudreuil. [A play. By Jemima Bullock-Webster.] 8vo. Pp. 148. [*Brit. Mus.*] [*c.* 1885]

MARS ; or, the truth about war. By Alain [E. Chartier]. Translated . . . by Doris Mudie and Elizabeth Hill . . . 8vo. Pp. 318. [*Brit. Mus.*]
London, 1930

MARTHA Maria. In memoriam. By her Uncle Eduard [Edward Lockyer]. 16mo. Pp. 82. [*Brit. Mus.*]
Bristol, private print, 1873

Dedication signed : E. L.

MARTHA Spreull ; being chapters in the life of a single wumman. Edited by Zachary Fleming, writer, with preface by the authoress [but rather written by Henry Johnston, author of *The Dawsons of Glenara*]. 8vo. Pp. 125. [Title-page of H. Johnston's *Chronicles of Glenbuckie.*]
Glasgow, 1887

MARTIN Luther ; reply to his assailants. [By C. H. Collette.] 12mo. [*Lincoln's Inn Lib.*] London, 1883

MARTIN of Old London. By Herbert Strang [George Herbert Ely and C. J. L'Estrange]. 8vo. Pp. 158. [*Brit. Mus.*] London, 1925

MARTYR (the) land ; or, tales of the Vaudois. By the author of *Sunlight through the mist* [Mrs E. Burrows]. 8vo. Pp. 245. [*Brit. Mus.*]
London, 1856

MARUELOUS (a) hystory intitulede, Beware the cat ; conteynyng diuerse wounderfull and incredible matters. [Preface signed : G. B. *i.e.* Gulielmus Baldwin.] . . . 8vo. [*Brit. Mus.*]
London, 1570

MARY Aikenhaid ; her life, her work and her friends. Giving a history of the foundation of the Irish Sisters of Charity. By S. A. [Sarah Aikinson]. Second edition, revised. 8vo. Pp. x. 572. [*Letters of Mary Aikenhaid*, 1914, p. xiii.] Dublin, 1882

*MARY Magdalen's funerall teares . . .

An edition in 1609 was signed : S. W.

MASONIC Union ; an address to His Grace the Duke of Athol on the subject of an union between the Masons that have lately assembled under His Grace's sanction and the regular Masons of England. . . . By a member of that fraternity [Sir Francis Colombine Daniel]. 8vo. [*Memoir of F. C. Daniel*, 1826, p. 12.]
London, 1804

MASQUERADE (the) ; a poem. Inscribed to C - - - T H - - - D - - - G - - - R. By Lemuel Gulliver [Henry Fielding]. 8vo. Pp. 11. [*Brit. Mus.*]
London, 1728

MASSA triumphans ; or, the triumph of the Mass, wherein all the sophistical . . . arguments of Mr de Rodon . . . in his funestuous tract . . . called The funeral of the Mass, are fully . . . answered. . . . [By William Collins.] 12mo. [*Brit. Mus.*] London, 1675

Signed : W. C.

MAST and acorns. Collected by Old Hubert [—— Parkinson]. 8vo. [*Brit. Mus.*] London [1794?]

MASTERDILLO (the) ; a story of youth. [By F. T. Wawn.] 8vo. Pp. 319. [*Brit. Mus.*] London, 1913

MATERIALS for a description of Capri. [By George Norman Douglass.] 8vo. 8 parts. Pp. 333. [*Brit. Mus.*]
London, Napoli, 1904-15
Signed: N. D.

MATILDA; or, the orphans of the Pyrenees. By Father Charles [John Andrew Houban]. 12mo. Pp. 210. [*Brit. Mus.*] Dublin, 1860

MATILDA'S legacy . . . Also a brief sketch of her spiritual career . . . by J. M. [J. Mumford]. 12mo. [*Brit. Mus.*] London, [1850]

MATTHEW Arnold. By Hugh Kingsmill [Hugh Kingsmill Lunn]. With four portraits. 8vo. Pp. xiv. 282. [*Brit. Mus.*] London, 1928

MATTIE and the bluebottle. By Lycaon [Vernon Tracy?]. 8vo. Pp. 112. [*Brit. Mus.*] London [1924]

MAUDIE and the white cat. [A tale.] By H. C. [H. Campbell]. 8vo. Pp. 42. [*Brit. Mus.*] Edinburgh, 1919

MAVIS of Green Hill. [A novel.] By Faith Baldwin [Faith Baldwin Cuthrell]. 8vo. Pp. 272. [*Amer. Cat.*]
Boston [1921]

MAXWELL'S first lessons in geography for the young. By the author of *Home and its duties* [Mrs J. Werner Laurie]. 16mo. [*Brit. Mus.*] London [1869]

*MAY fair. In four cantos.
London, 1827
Also attributed to Henry Luttrell. [O'Donoghue's *Poets of Ireland.*]

*MEADOW (the) queen . . .
For By S. W., *read* By the author of *The Wild Garland.*
The preface is signed: S. W.

MEEKNESS and growth. Colossians, I. By J. N. D. [John Nelson Darby]. 16mo. [*Brit. Mus.*] London [1879]

MELODY (the) of God, and other papers. By Desmond Mountjoy [Wellesley Desmond Mountjoy Chapman-Huston]. 8vo. Pp. x. 262. [*Brit. Mus.*] London, 1923

MEMOIR (a) of Abraham Lincoln. . . . To which is appended an historical sketch on slavery. [By R. B. *i.e.* Robert Black, M.A.] 8vo. Pp. 126. [*Brit. Mus.*] London, 1861

MEMOIR of Charlotte Elliott . . . By her sister E. B. [Mrs E. Babington]. Slightly abridged. 12mo. Pp. 24. [*Brit. Mus.*] London [1875]

MEMOIR of General Sir William Erskine Baker . . . Compiled by two old friends, brother officers and pupils [Sir Henry Yule and Robert Maclagan]. 8vo. Pp. vi. 67. [*Brit. Mus.*] London, 1882
Signed: H. Y., and R. M.

*MEMOIR of H. F. Hallam.
For Meine, *read* Maine.

*MEMOIR of J. G. Children . . .
Attributed by the *Brit. Mus.* to Anne Atkins.

MEMOIRS (the) and history of Prince Titi. Done from the French [of Hyacinthe Cordonnier de Saint Hyacinthe] by a person of quality [James Ralph]. 12mo. Pp. 160. [*Brit. Mus.*] London, 1736
The original "Histoire du Prince Titi, A.R." first published in the same year 1736, was also anonymous. For another translation, see "The History of Prince Titi."

MEMOIRS of a banking house. By Sir William Forbes. [Edited by R. C. *i.e.* Robert Chambers.] 8vo. [*Brit. Mus.*] London, 1860

MEMOIRS of a fox-hunting man. [By Siegfried Sassoon.] 8vo. Pp. 395. [*Arnold Bennett in the Evening Standard*, 11th Oct. 1928.] London, 1928
Later editions (1929, *et seq.*) bear the author's name.

MEMOIRS of a trait in the character of George III. By Johan Horrins [John Harrison, grandson of John Harrison, chronometer maker]. 8vo. Pp. xlviii. 256. [*Brit. Mus.*] London, 1835

MEMOIRS of an Infantry Officer. By the author of *Memoirs of a fox-hunting man* [Siegfried Sassoon]. 8vo. Pp. 334. [*Brit. Mus.*] London, 1930
The author's name occurs on the cover.

MEMOIRS of an unfortunate young nobleman [J. Annesley, calling himself Nephew of Richard, sixth Earl of Anglesey], return'd from a thirteen years slavery in America. 12mo. 2 parts. [*Brit. Mus.*] London, 1743

MEMOIRS of Count Tariff, &c. [Written in whole or part by Daniel Defoe.] 8vo. Pp. 95. [*Brit. Mus.*]
London, 1713

MEMOIRS of F * * * * * * H * * * [Fanny Hill. By John Cleland]. 8vo. [*Brit. Mus.*] London, 1784

MEMOIRS of Madame du Barri. Translated . . . by . . . H. T. Riley [or rather, by W. Maginn?]. 8vo. 4 vols. [*Brit. Mus.*] London, 1896

MEMOIRS of Madame la marquise de Montespan . . . [By Baron Etienne Léon de la Mothe-Langon?] 8vo. [*Brit. Mus.*] 1829

MEMOIRS of the Court of France; in two parts . . . By Madam L. M. D. [Marie Catherine La Mothe, Comtesse d'Aulnoy], author of *The Voyage into Spain.* [Translated by P. B.] 8vo. [*Brit. Mus.*] London, 1692

*MEMOIRS of the Court of Spain . . .
For Done into English [by T. Brown], *read* Done into English by T. Brown.

*MEMOIRS of the late war in Asia . . .
  An edition in the following year (1789) runs, "Memoirs of the war in Asia . . ."

MEMOIRS of the life and writings of Alexander Pope, faithfully collected from authentic authors, original manuscripts, and the testimonies of many persons of credit and honour ; with critical observations. . . . By William Ayre, Esq. [Edmund Curll]. 8vo. 2 vols. [R. Straus' *The Unspeakable Curll*, p. 312.] London, 1745
  A worthless production. For the earliest suggestion that William Ayre, like William Egerton, was really Curll himself, see "Remarks on Squire Ayre's Memoirs " published almost simultaneously.

MEMOIRS of the life and writings of the Right Honourable Lord Byron, with anecdotes of some of his contemporaries. [By John Watkins.] 8vo. Pp. xvi. 428. [*Brit. Mus.*]
London, 1822

MEMOIRS of the life of William Wycherley, Esq. [by Charles Gildon] ; with a character of his writings. By George, Lord Lansdowne . . . 8vo. Pp. 42. [*Brit. Mus.*] London, 1718

MEMOIRS of the life, writings, and amours of W. Congreve, Esq., interspersed with miscellaneous essays, etc., written by him. Also some very curious memoirs of Mr Dryden and his family with a character of him by Mr Congreve. Compiled from their respective originals by Charles Wilson, Esq. [John Oldmixon]. 8vo. Pp. xvi. 156. [R. Straus' *The Unspeakable Curll*, p. 291.]
London, 1730

MEMOIRS (the) of the Marquise de Keroubec, 1781-1858 : being extracts from her diaries . . . [By Henry Baerlein.] 8vo. Pp. 231.
London, 1926
  Acknowledgment by the author.

MEMOIRS of the public life of James Hogg . . . [Edited by A. B. *i.e.* A. Bruce ?] 8vo. [*Brit. Mus.*]
Edinburgh, 1798

MEMOIRS of the war in Asia . . . See " Memoirs of the late war in Asia . . ."

MEMOIRS of Vidocq, principal agent of the French police till 1827 . . . Written by himself [or rather vol. 1 by E. Morice, vol. 2-4 by L. F. L'Heritier]. Translated from the French [by H. T. R. *i.e.* William Maginn ?]. 4 vols. [*Brit. Mus.*]
London, 1828-29
  A reprint, 1866, has the title " Vidocq . . ."

MEMORANDUM on Tintagel Castle. [By Thomas Cornish.] Pp. 8. [*Brit. Mus.*] Penzance [private print, 1870 ?]

MEMORIAL for P. Williamson . . . against W. Fordyce . . . [By John Maclaurin, Lord Dreghorn.] 4to. [*Brit. Mus.*] [1765]

MEMORIAL notices of the Rev. John Davies. [By William Hale Hale.] 12mo. Pp. iv. 76. [*Brit. Mus.*]
Worcester, 1858

MEMORIAL of the citizens of Philadelphia to Congress. [By Matthew Carey.] 12mo. [Sabin's *Dictionary*, iii. 341.] Philadelphia, 1827

MEMORIAL (a) of the life and services of Major-Gen. W. W. H. Greathed, C.B. . . . Compiled by a friend and brother officer [Sir Henry Yule]. 8vo. Pp. 57. [*Brit. Mus.*] London, 1879
  Signed : H. Y.

MEMORIAL (a) of Daniel Webster from the city of Boston. [Edited by G. S. H. *i.e.* George S. Hillard.] 8vo. [*Brit. Mus.*] Boston, 1853

MEMORIAL to Congress of the Pennsylvania Society for the Encouragement of American Manufactures. [By Matthew Carey.] 8vo. [Sabin's *Dictionary*, iii. 341.] Philadelphia, 1820

MEMORIALS for a wife dedicated by her husband [John Hoppus] to their children. 12mo. [*Brit. Mus.*]
London, 1856

*MEMORIALS of Manchester streets.
  This was by Richard Wright Procter, and was not anonymous.

*MEMORIALS of the method and manner of proceedings in Parliament . . .
  An edition of 1658 was issued as By H. S. E. C. P. *i.e.* Henry Scobell, Esq., Clerk of the Parliament.

MEMORIALS of the past. [Poems. By John Henry Newman.] 8vo. Pp. 108. [*Brit. Mus.*] Oxford [private print] 1832
  Dedication signed : J. H. N.

MEMORIALS of the Royal Martyr ; or, a parallel betwixt the Jewes murder of Christ and the English murder of King Charles the First : being a sermon [on Acts ii. 37, 38] preached on the solemnity of His Majestie's Martyrdom . . . 1669. By T. L. [Thomas Lambert ?] . . . 4to. [*Brit. Mus.*]
London, 1670

MEMORIALS of two sisters [Anne C. M. and Emma L. M. *i.e.* A. C. and E. L. Maurice]. Edited [or rather written] by the author of *Aids to developement*, etc.1 [Mary Atkinson Maurice]. 8vo. Pp. 308. [*Brit. Mus.*]
London, 1833

MENTAL amusement ; or, the juvenile moralist. [The preface signed : G. S. *i.e.* G. Sael.] . . . Second edition. 12mo. Pp. viii. 136. [*Brit. Mus.*]
London [1798]

MERCHANT shipping laws and remedies ; Colonial law courts.— St Helena. Owners, captains and men. — Petitions to Parliament for enquiry. [By Charles Nash.] 4to. Pp. 12. [*Brit. Mus.*]   N.P. [1860 ?]

MERCHANTS (the) remonstrance ; wherein is set forth the inevitable miseries which may suddenly befall this kingdome by want of trade . . . By J. B. [John Battie] of London, merchant. 4to. Pp. 10. [*Brit. Mus.*]
London, 1644
An edition of 1648 bears the author's name.

MERLINUS anonymus ; an almanack and no almanack . . . for the year 1653. . . . By Raphael Desmus [Samuel Sheppard], Philologist. 8vo. [*Brit. Mus.*]   London, 1653

MERRY Widow Welcome ; or, the treasure hunters : an Early Victorian frolic. By Edward Percy [Edward Percy Smith]. 8vo. Pp. 27. [*Brit. Mus.*]   London, 1924

MERRY (the) wives of Windsor . . . An introduction and notes are added by the authors of *The Dramatic Censor* [Francis Gentleman]. 12mo. [*Brit. Mus.*]   1773

MERRYLAND displayed ; or, plagiarism, ignorance, and impudence, detected : being observations on a pamphlet intituled A new description of Merryland [by Thomas Stretser]. The second edition. 8vo. Pp. viii. vi.
Bath, 1741
"This peculiar production [The new description of Merryland] had an enormous sale, and went to six or seven editions. The Bath imprint was a bluff. Incidentally its success led Curll [the publisher] to issue a whole series of imitations, all more or less pornographic. It also led him to issue an attack on the original piece, no doubt to stimulate the waning interest in it." [R. Straus' *The Unspeakable Curll*, p. 308.]
This "attack" on Stretser's pamphlet was also Stretser's own production. See R. Straus, p. 314.

MERUAYLOUS (a) straunge deformed swyne. [A ballad. By John Phillip ?] Fol. S. sh. B. L. [*Brit. Mus.*]
London [1570 ?]
Signed : I. P.

MESMERISM & hypnotism ; an epitome of all the best works on the hypnotic phases of psychology in the form of question and answer. By an adept [Caxton Hall]. Illustrated. 8vo. Pp. 71. [*Brit. Mus.*]
Blackpool, 1900
A later edition (1919) bears the author's name.

MESSIAH (the) [and his Kingdom ; the life, sufferings, death, resurrection, and ascension of the Son of God. By John Lavicount Anderdon]. 8vo. Pp. vii. 831. [*Brit. Mus.*]   London, 1861

MESSIANIC (the) idea. By Chilperic Edwards [Edward John Pilcher]. 8vo. Pp. v. 146. [*Brit. Mus.*]
London, 1927

METAMORPHOSIS (the) of Ajax. By Sir John Harington. . . . Edited by Peter Warlock [Philip Heseltine] and Jack Lindsay. 8vo. Pp. xxviii. 143. [*Brit. Mus.*]   London, 1927

METAPHYSICAL (the) basis of "Esoteric Buddhism" ; a letter . . . By C. C. M. [C. C. Massey ?]. . . . 8vo. Pp. 70. [*Brit. Mus.*] [London ? 1883 ?]

METAPHYSICS and mental philosophy. [Edited by James Robert Ballantyne.] 8vo. [*Brit. Mus.*]   Allahabad, 1852
No. 4 of "Reprints for the Pandits."

METEOROLOGICAL account of the weather at Madras from June 1, 1787 to May 31, 1788. [By J. Chamier.] 4to. [*Brit. Mus.*]   Madras, 1788

*METHOD (a) to prevent, without a register, the running of wool . . .
For William Londes *read* Thomas Lowndes. [*D. N. B.* vol. 34, p. 209 ; *Presentation copy in Welbeck Abbey.*]

MID-DAY prayers for use in St Paul's Cathedral. [Compiled by Henry Parry Liddon.] 16mo. [*Brit. Mus.*]   1881
Signed : H. P. L.

MIDDLE (the) parts of fortune. Somme & Ancre, 1916. [By Frederic Manning.] 8vo. Pp. 453. [*Brit. Mus.*]
London, 1929
Previously published as "Her privates we," *q.v.*

MIDNIGHT musings ; being some impressions in verse of a practical idealist. By S. L. L. [S. L. Lloyd]. 8vo. Pp. 95. [*Brit. Mus.*]
London, 1919

MIGHT not right ; or, stories of the discovery and conquest of America. By the author of *Our Eastern Empire*, etc. [Mrs E. Burrows]. 8vo. Pp. viii. 246. [*Brit. Mus.*]   London, 1858

MILES gloriosus, the Spanish braggadocio. . . . Lately written in French [by Jacques Gaultier. Really translated from Rodomuntadas Castellanas], and newly translated into English . . . by I. W. 8vo. 2 parts. [*Brit. Mus.*]
London, 1630

MILK for babes, and meat for strong men. . . . By James Nayler. [With a preface signed : M. B. *i.e.* Mary Booth.] 4to. [*Brit. Mus.*]
London, 1661

MILL (the) and its story ; an abduction and a Gretna Green wedding. [Signed : Northerner, *i.e.* Daniel Scott.] 16mo. [*Brit. Mus.*] N.P. [1898]

MIND and manners ; a diary of occasion. (Reprinted from "The New Age.") [By Acton Reed.] 8vo. Pp. 128. [*Brit. Mus.*] London, 1918

MINE (a) of affection manifested in 31 proposals offer'd to all the sober and freeborn people within this commonwealth. . . . [By Edward Billing or Edward Burrough.] 4to. [*Brit. Mus.*] London, 1659

MINORITIES of one. [Essays.] By Gigadibs [R. E. Crook]. 8vo. Pp. 64. [*Brit. Mus.*] London [1924]

MIRACLES ; a rhapsody. By E. Barton [Sir William Cusack Smith]. 8vo. Pp. 104. [*Brit. Mus.*] London, 1823

*MIRRHA the mother of Adonis. [By William Barksted.] With certain eglogs by L. M. [Lewis Machin]. 8vo. [*Pollard and Redgrave.*] London, 1607

MIRROR (the) in the dusk. By Brinsley Macnamara [A. E. Weldon]. 8vo. Pp. 251. [*Brit. Mus.*] Dublin, 1921

MIRROR of dreams. By Ganpat [Martin Louis Alan Gompertz]. 8vo. Pp. 319. [*Brit. Mus.*] London [1928]

MISCELLANEA Græca dramatica, in scriptis maxime eruditorum virorum varie dispersa, in unum fasciculum collecta. By a graduate of Cambridge [Philip Wentworth Buckham]. [*Brit. Mus.*] Cambridge [1825]

MISCELLANEA Virgiliana, in scriptis maxime eruditorum virorum varie dispersa in unum fasciculum collecta. By a graduate of Cambridge, editor of the *Theatre of the Greeks,* etc. [Philip Wentworth Buckham]. [*Brit. Mus.*] Cambridge, 1825

MISCELLANEOUS (a) essay, concerning the courses pursued by Great Britain, in the affairs of her colonies : with some observations on the great importance of our settlements in America and the trade thereof. [By Henry M'Culloh.] 8vo. Pp. 134. [*Brit. Mus.*] London, 1755
See also " The wisdom and policy of the French . . . "

MISCELLANEOUS poems. [By Ellis Cornelia Knight, W. R. Spencer, Samuel Rogers, and others.] 4to.
Windsor, private print, 1812
From an inscribed copy in the British Museum.

MISCELLANEOUS poems. By several hands, particularly the D— of W—n [Duke of Wharton] . . . Dean S— [Jonathan Swift] . . . Mrs C—r [Mary Chandler] ; publish'd by Mr Ralph. [Other anonymous poems are by Pope, Edward Littleton, Jabez Hughes, and George Jeffreys.] 12mo. Pp. 348. [I. O. Williams in *Bibl. Soc. Trans.,* Dec. 1929.] London, 1729

MISCELLANEOUS poems. By several hands ; published by D. Lewis. [The poems, all anonymous, are by John Dyer, David Mallet, Samuel Wesley the younger, Thomas Fitzgerald, David Lewis, and others.] 8vo. Pp. 320. [I. O. Williams in *Bibl. Soc. Trans.* Dec. 1929.] London, 1726
D. Lewis published a second miscellany, with the same title, in 1730.

MISCELLANEOUS poems and translations. By several hands ; publish'd by Richard Savage. [Includes an anonymous poem by David Mallet.] 8vo. Pp. 312. [I. O. Williams in *Bibl. Soc. Trans.* Dec. 1929.] London, 1726

MISCELLANIES. [By Jonathan Swift.] 8vo. London, 1711
" A manufactured volume made up of such of Swift's pieces as Curll had already printed, including also the *Key to the Tale of a Tub.* It must not be confused with Morphew's *Miscellanies in prose and verse* issued this month." [R. Straus' *The Unspeakable Curll,* p. 215.] See also " Miscellanies in prose and verse," London, 1711.

MISCELLANIES in prose and verse. By Thomas Chatterton. [Edited by J. B. *i.e.* John Broughton ?] 8vo. Pp. xxxiii. 245. [*Brit. Mus.*] London, 1778

MISCELLANIES upon several subjects, occasionally written. By Joseph Gay [John Durant de Breval]. 8vo. [Straus' *The Unspeakable Curll.*] London, 1720

MISCELLANY poems ; containing a new translation of Virgills Eclogues, Ovid's Love Elegies, Odes of Horace, and other authors ; with several original poems. By the most eminent hands [John Dryden and others]. 8vo. 2 parts. [*Brit. Mus.*] London, 1684
Several of the poems have title-pages dated 1683.

MISER (the) ; a catch by W. P. [Walter Pope], author of *The old man's wish,* and set to musick by Mr Michael Wise. . . . [Arber's *Term Cat.* ii. 126.] London, 1685

MISHAP (the) ; a poem. Written by the late Rev. D. J. S. D. D. D. S. P. D. [Dr Jonathan Swift, D.D., Dean of St Patrick's, Dublin]. Fol. S. sh. [*Brit. Mus.*] [Dublin, *c.* 1750]

MISSING girl; a novel. By Berta Onions [Berta Oliver]. 8vo. Pp. viii. 399. [*Brit. Mus.*] London, 1930

MISSING (the) partners. By Henry Wade [Henry Lancelot Aubrey - Fletcher]. 8vo. Pp. 310. [*Amer. Cat.*] London, 1928

*MISSIONARIES (the) arts discovered . . . (A defence of the missionaries arts . . . A plain defence of the Protestant religion . . .) [By —— Wake, Minister of Gray's Inn.]

It is most unfortunate that Dr Kennedy did not note the source of this ascription. The three books have been traditionally associated as the work of one author at least since 1689, when Gee noted them in his Catalogue of discourses against Popery, as being by Mr H—, a divine of the Church of England (the origin of the erroneous ascription to George Hicks). We were for long intrigued by this ascription, and even more so when we found (*D. N. B.*) that the young William Wake (afterwards Archbishop of Canterbury) lately returned from Paris, was appointed Minister of Gray's Inn in 1688, the year in which the Missionaries arts was published. As Wake only held this post until 1696 the ascription has every sign of being nearly contemporary, and may in fact be from an inscribed copy. There would be nothing strange in Wake being the author as he had already been actively engaged in the Romish controversy. At any rate it seems worth noting that Archbishop Wake may have been the author, and if the original source of the ascription is traced we should be glad to hear of it.

*MISSIONARY (a) brotherhood in the Far West . . .
Ascribed by the *Brit. Mus.* to John Hodson Egar.

MISSIONS at home; a true narrative by the author of *The two old men* [César Malan]. Translated from the French. 12mo. [*Brit. Mus.*] London, N.D.
Signed: C. M.

MISSIONS to the heathen. [Preface signed: E. H. *i.e.* Ernest Hawkins.] 16mo. 2 parts. [*Brit. Mus.*] London, 1844-45

"MISTER 44." [A novel.] By E. J. Rath [J. Chauncey Corey Brainerd and Edith Rathbone Brainerd]. 8vo. Pp. v. 236. [*Brit. Mus.*] London, 1917

*MISTERY (the) of iniquity . . .
Not by William Allen. Author not known.

MISTERY (the) of rhetoric unveil'd and abridg'd. . . . By J. H., teacher of geography. [An abridgment of John Smith's *The mysterie of rhetorick unveil'd.*] 4to. [*Brit. Mus.*] London, 1646

MISTERY (the) of the person of Christ, God-man unfolded. . . . With an appendix, concerning the divinity . . . of the spirit. [By Francis Millett?] 8vo. [*Brit. Mus.*] London, 1719

MISTLETOE (the) bough . . . a melodrama. . . . By C. Somerset. [With remarks by D. G. *i.e.* George Daniel.] 12mo. Pp. 36. [*Brit. Mus.*] London [1874]
Lacy's Acting Edition of Plays, vol. 100.

MISTRESS of ceremonies. [A novel.] By Nora K. Strange [Mrs E. Gower Stanley]. 8vo. Pp. 288. [*Brit. Mus.*] London [1930]

MISTRIS Parliament brought to bed of a monstrous childe of Reformation. With her 7 yeers teeming, bitter pangs. . . . By Mercurius Melancholicus [Marchamont Nedham?]. 4to. [*Brit. Mus.*] London, 1648

MISTRIS Parliament, her gossiping. . . . By Mercurius Melancholicus [Marchamont Nedham?]. 4to. [*Brit. Mus.*] London, 1648

MISTRIS Parliament presented in her bed after the sore travaile and hard labour which she endured last week, in the birth of her monstrous offspring, the childe of Deformation, the hopefull fruit of her seven years teeming, and a most precious babe of grace. By Mercurius Melancholicus [Marchamont Nedham?]. 4to. [*Brit. Mus.*] London, 1648

MIXED (a) grill; a medley in retrospect. By the author of *A garden of peace* [Frank Frankfort Moore]. . . . 8vo. Pp. 288. London [1930]

MODEL (a) for a school for the better education of youth. [By A. B. *i.e.* Mark Lewis?] 8vo. [*Brit. Mus.*] [London, *c.* 1675]

MODEL (a) wife; a novel. By G. I. Cervus [William James Roe]. 8vo. [*Amer. Cat.*] Philadelphia, 1885
See the note to "Cut: a story of West Point."

MODERN amours; or, the secret history of the adventures of some persons of the first rank. . . . [By Lydia Grainger.] 12mo. [R. Straus' *The Unspeakable Curll*, p. 295.] London, 1733

MODERN Bridge. By "Slam" [E. Chittenden]. With the laws of Bridge, as approved by the Portland and Turf Clubs, by "Boaz." 8vo. Pp. x. 157. [Jessel's *Bibl. of playing cards*, p. 266.] London, 1901

MODERN (the) pocket Hoyle, containing all the games of skill and chance as played in this country at the present time. Being an authority on all disputed points. By "Trumps" [William Brisbane Dick]. 16mo. Pp. 387. [Jessel's *Bibl. of playing cards*, p. 70.]					New York, 1868

MODERN whist; with complete rules for playing. . . . Compiled from the latest works by "Cavendish" [Henry Jones] on this subject by "Trumps" [William Brisbane Dick]. 8vo. Pp. 72. [*Brit. Mus.*]					New York, 1892

MODEST (a) and true account of the chief points in controversie between the Roman Catholics and the Protestants. . . . By N. C. [Cornelius Nary]. 12mo. [*Brit. Mus.*]			Antwerp, 1696
Attributed also to Nicholas Colson.

*MODEST (a) defence of public stews . . .
Attributed to Bernard de Mandeville as well as to George Ogle.
First published 1724, anonymously, except for "Phil-Porney" at the dedication.
The fourth edition (1740) runs "The natural secret history of both sexes. . . . By Luke Ogle, Esq.," *q.v.*

MOFFATT'S reprint of Pupil Teachers' questions, 1874 . . . with answers . . . by E. N. A. G. [Charles Gane?]. 8vo. [*Brit. Mus.*]					London [1877]

MOGUL (the) tale; a farce. . . . By Mrs Inchbald . . . with remarks . . . by D— G. [George Daniel]. 12mo. Pp. 25. [*Brit. Mus.*]			London [1830]

MOLA asinaria. . . . By William Prynne [or rather by Samuel Butler]. . . . Wherein is demonstrated what slavery the nation must subject itself to, by allowing the lawfulness and usurped authority of the pretended Long Parliament now unlawfully and violently held at Westminster. 4to. Pp. 6. [*Brit. Mus.*]					1659

MON Paul; the private life of a privateer. By A. A. Abbott [Samuel Spewack]. 8vo. Pp. 255. [*Amer. Cat.*]					New York, 1928

MONASTERY (the) and the mountain church. . . . By the author of *Sunlight through the mist* [Mrs E. Burrows]. 8vo. Pp. 277. [*Brit. Mus.*]				London, 1855

*MONASTICON Anglicanum . . .
For John Wright, *read* James Wright.

MONEY and banking; or, their nature and effects considered : together with a plan for the universal diffusion of their legitimate benefits without their evils. By a citizen of Ohio [William Beck]. 12mo. [H. E. Miller's *Banking Theories in the U.S.* p. 228.]
					Cincinnati, 1839

MONIMICS; a new game and a new method of explaining money and teaching elementary economics. By Norman Angell [Ralph Norman Angell Lane]. 8vo. Pp. 15. [*Brit. Mus.*]
					London [1927]
Another issue has the title "The mystery of money . . ."

MONODY (a) on the death of His Royal Highness Frederic-Louis Prince of Wales. [By Richard Rolt.] 8vo. [*Lincoln's Inn Lib.*]			Dublin, 1751

MONSIEUR Tonson. [By John Taylor.] Embellished with . . . coloured engravings. 8vo. [*Brit. Mus.*] [1850?]

MONTH (the) of Mary. By St Alphonsus. [Edited by R. A. C. *i.e.* Robert Astor Coffin.] 16mo. Pp. xii. 260. [*Brit. Mus.*]			London, 1872

MONUMENTA Orcadica; the Norsemen in the Orkneys and the monuments they have left. . . . By L. Dietrichson. . . . [Translated by Jessie Muir.] 8vo. [Pettersen's *Norsk Lexikon*, col. 335.]					Kristiania, 1906

MOON of joy. By Camilla Hope [Grace E. Thompson]. 8vo. Pp. 286. [*Amer. Cat.*]				London, 1927

MOORES (the) baffled; being a discourse concerning Tanger. . . . [By Lancelot Addison, Dean of Lichfield.] 4to. Pp. 27. [*Brit. Mus.*]
					London, 1681
The second edition, 1685, has the author's name and the title "A discourse of Tangier."

MORE cheap riches, or heavenly aphorismes. . . . Faithfully copied out of the manuscripts of Mr H. C. . . . by N. C. [Nathaniel Church]. 12mo. [*Brit. Mus.*]			London, 1660

*MORE fun for our little friends . . .
For By the author of *Great Fun, read* By Harriet Myrtle, the author, etc.

MORE news from Gotham, being a continuation of Gotham in alarm. [By Peter Mackenzie, James Brown, M.D., and others.] 8vo. [R. Inglis' *Dram. Writers of Scotland*, p. 146.]
					Glasgow, 1816
See "Gotham in alarm."

MORE shires and provinces. By Sabretache [A. S. Barrow]. Illustrated by Lionel Edwards. 4to. Pp. xii. 188. [*Brit. Mus.*]			London, 1928
For the first series, see "Shires and provinces."

MORE songs of the glens of Antrim. By Moira O'Neile [Mrs Skrine, *née* Hesta Higginson]. 8vo. Pp. x. 86. [S. J. Brown's *Ireland in Fiction.*]
					Edinburgh, 1921

M O R E verse. By F. S. [Frank Sidgwick]. 8vo. Pp. 63. [*Brit. Mus.*] London, 1921
See also "Some verse . . ."

MORE'S millenium; being the Utopia . . . rendered into modern English by Valerian Paget [Harold and Zoe Paget]. 8vo. Pp. xxiii. 258. [*Brit. Mus.*] London, 1909

MORNING church; or, two meals better than one. [By Francis Bourdillon.] 12mo. [*Brit. Mus.*]
London [1860]
Signed: F. B.

M O S A I C (the) workers; a tale: to which is added The Orco. By George Sand [Mme. Amandine Dudevant]. Translated . . . by E. A. A. [Eliza A. Ashurst]. 16mo. [*Brit. Mus.*]
London, 1844

M O S C O W; or, the grandsire: an historical tale. [By Mrs M. Mainwaring.] 12mo. 3 vols.
London, 1822
From the title-page of her "The Suttee."

M O S E S, the man of God. By the author of *Lines on the prophet Elijah* [William C. Mainland]. 8vo. Pp. 48. [*Brit. Mus.*] Kirkwall, 1930

M O S T (the) delectable history of Clitiphon and Leucippe (of Achilles Tatius). [Translated by William Burton.] 4to. [*Pollard and Redgrave.*]
London, 1597
Signed: W. B.

M O S T (a) excellent sermon of the Lordes Supper, wherein . . . is lively set foorth the matter of the Supper of the Lorde Jesus. . . . Translated out of Frenche into English by I. T. [John Tomkys]. 16mo. B. L. [*Pollard and Redgrave.*] London [1570?]

MOST noble truncheon. [Reflections on modern warfare. By J. T. Griffiths.] 8vo. [*Brit. Mus.*] [1907]

*MOST (a) pleasant description of Benwel Village . . .
The *Brit. Mus.* gives the author's name as Cuthbert Ellison, not John Ellison. Upcott gives simply Dr Ellison.

MOST (the) pleasant history of Bovinian; being an addition [by L. P. *i.e.* Laurence Price?] to that most delightfull history of Crispine and Crispianus [*i.e.* "The Gentle Craft" by T. Delony. With woodcuts]. . . . 4to. Pp. 11. [*Brit. Mus.*] London, 1656
It begins with chapter xvi.

*MOST sacred and divine science of astrology. . . .
The correct title is "Ἀγιαστρολογια. Or, the most sacred . . ." Nor is the book anonymous, the author's name being at the dedication.

MOSUL (the) question. By V. F. M. [V. F. Minorsky]. 8vo. Pp. 44. [*Brit. Mus.*] Paris, 1926

MOTHER'S (a) care rewarded; in the correction of those defects, most general in young people, during their education. [By Mary Robson, later Mrs Hughs?] 12mo. Pp. 108. [*Brit. Mus.*] London [1824]

M O T H E R'S Nell. [A story.] By E. R. G. [Evelyn R. Garratt]. 12mo. [*Brit. Mus.*] London, 1877

MOUNTAIN (the); or, the story of Captain Yevan. By C. K. Munro [Charles W. K. Macmullan]. A symbolic drama. 8vo. Pp. 221. [*Brit. Mus.*] London [1926]

M O U R N E R (the) comforted; an epistle consolatory; written by Hugo Grotius to Monsieur Du Maurier the French Embassadour at the Hague. Translated on a sad occasion, by C. B. [Clement Barksdale]. 12mo. Pp. 31. [*Brit. Mus.*] London, 1652

MOURNFUL (a) lamentation for the sad and deplorable death of Mr Old Tenor, a native of New England. [By Joseph Green.] Fol. S. sh. [*Magazine of History*, extra No. 90.]
[Boston, 1750]

M O U S E (the) trap; or, the Welsh engagement . . .
For the correct title of this book, see "Muscipula . . ."

MOUSE-TRAP (the); or, the Welshmen's scuffle with the mice. [A translation of Edward Holdsworth's Muscipula.] 8vo. Pp. 8. [*Brit. Mus.*]
London, 1709
For other translations, see "Muscipula, sive Cambro-Muo-Machia," and "Taffi's masterpiece . . ."

MR and Mrs Villiers. [A novel.] By Hubert Wales [William Piggott]. 8vo. Pp. 316. [*Brit. Mus.*] London, 1906

MR Balfour; a biography. By E. T. Raymond [Edward Raymond Thompson]. 8vo. Pp. 227. [*Brit. Mus.*]
London, 1920

MR Lloyd George. A biography. . . . By E. T. Raymond [Edward Raymond Thompson]. 8vo. Pp. 368. [*Brit. Mus.*] London, 1922

MR Teedles, the "gland" old man. By Thomas Le Breton [T. Murray Ford]. 8vo. Pp. 188. [*Brit. Mus.*]
London [1928]

MR Thake: his life and letters. By "Beachcomber," of the "Daily Express" [John Bingham Morton]. 8vo. Pp. 285. [*T. L. S.* 19th Dec. 1929.]
London, 1929

MR Woodhouse's correspondence. By G. R. and E. S. [G. W. E. Russell and Edith Sichel]. 8vo. Pp. viii. 277. [*Brit. Mus.*]   London, 1903

*MRS Blackett, her story . . .
    For —— Elliott, *read* Emily Steele Elliott.

MRS Britton's letter touching the Europa troubles. By the author of *A fairy tale for the nineteenth century* [Elizabeth Missing Sewell]. 8vo. [*Brit. Mus.*]   London, 1871
    Signed : Jane Bull.

MRS Finch-Brassey ; a novel. By Mrs Andrew Dean [Mrs Cecily Sidgwick]. 8vo. 3 vols. [*Brit. Mus.*]
                              London, 1893

MRS Gilpin's return from Edmonton ; being the sequel to the Wedding-Day. [By Henry Lemoine.] 8vo. Pp. 15. [*Brit. Mus.*]   London [1784?]

MRS Parliament, her invitation of Mrs London, to a thanksgiving dinner for the . . . victorie, which Mr Horton obtained over Major Powell in Wales. . . . (By Mercurius Melancholicus [Marchamont Nedham?]). 4to. Pp. 8. [*Brit. Mus.*]
                              [London] 1648

MURDER for profit. By William Bolitho [William B. Ryall]. 8vo. Pp. 320. [*Publishers' Weekly*, 1st Sept. 1928.]   London, 1926

MURDER from the grave. By Will Levinrew [William Levine]. 8vo. Pp. 284. [*Brit. Mus.*]   London, 1931

MURDER in the maze. By J. J. Connington [Alfred Walter Stewart]. 8vo. Pp. 287. [*Publishers' Weekly*, 29th Sept. 1928.]   London, 1927

MURTHER will out. [Two letters, relating to the death of the Earl of Essex. By Lawrence Braddon.] 4to. [*Brit. Mus.*]   [London, 1692]
    Signed : L. B.

*MUSÆUS : a monody . . .
    For [By William Mason], *read* By Mr M— [William Mason].

MUSCIPULA sive Cambro-Muo-Machia. The Mouse-trap, or the Welsh engagement with the mice. [By Edward Holdsworth.] 8vo. Pp. 23. [*Brit. Mus.*]   London, 1709
    In Latin and English. The English translation was not by Holdsworth, and the Latin pirated and full of faults. Another translation (1625) is entitled " Muscipula, or the mousetrap." For other translations, see " The Mouse-trap ; or the Welshman's scuffle with the mice " and " Taffi's masterpiece. . . ."

MUSE'S (the) choice ; or, the progress of wit. . . . See " A new collection of miscellanies . . ."

MUSES (the) delight ; an accurate collection of English and Italian songs, cantatas, and duetts, set to music for the harpsichord, violin, german-flute, etc. . . . [Edited by John Sadler, bookseller, of Liverpool.] 8vo. [Hawkes' *Lancashire Printed Books*, p. 33.]   Liverpool, 1754
    Reissued, enlarged, in 1757 under the title " Apollo's Cabinet."

*MY country. . . .
    The *Brit. Mus.* now attributes this to Letitia Willgoss Stone.

MY days and nights on the battlefield ; a book for boys. By " Carleton " [Charles Carleton Coffin]. 8vo. [*Brit. Mus.*]   Boston, 1864

MY first grief ; or, recollections, of a beloved sister. . . . By a provincial surgeon [Charles Beckett]. 12mo. Pp. xi. 134. [*Brit. Mus.*]   [1852]

MY Lady Andros ; a Wharfedale romance. [By M. L. Dawson.] 8vo. Pp. 14. [*Brit. Mus.*]   Frome [1910?]

MY mother. [A poem. By Ann Taylor.] 12mo. [*Brit. Mus.*]   [London, 1856]

MY young wife and my old umbrella ; a farce in one act, in prose adapted from the French [of] (M. Laurincin) [*i.e.* Paul Aimé Chapelle] by B. Webster. 12mo. [*Brit. Mus.*]   1837
    The Acting National Drama, vol. I.

MYRROUR (the) of the Churche. Here followeth a deuout treatyse cŏteynyge many goostly medytacyons ꝗ instruccions to all maner of people. . . . By Saynt Austyn of Abyndon [or rather by St Edmund, Archbishop of Canterbury. Translated by R. Copland]. 8vo. B. L. [*Pollard and Redgrave.*]
                              London, 1521

MYSTERIE (the) of the Lord's Supper. [By Robert Bruce.] 8vo. [*Pollard and Redgrave.*]   London, 1614

MYSTERIES of the old castles of France ; or, secret intrigues of its Kings and Queens, Princes and Princesses, and other great personages of the times. By a Society of Arch Seers, under the direction of A. B. Le François [Alexandre Bailly]. Translated by W. T. Haley. 8vo. [*Brit. Mus.*]   London, 1848

MYSTERY at Lyndon Sands. By J. J. Connington [Alfred Walter Stewart]. 8vo. Pp. 288. [*Publishers' Weekly*, 29th Sept. 1928.]   London, 1928

MYSTERY (the) of Belvoir Mansions. [A tale.] By Ben Bolt [Otwell Binns]. 8vo. Pp. 318. [*Brit. Mus.*]
                              London, 1927

*MYSTERY (the) of godlines . . . By I, the meanest labourer. . . .
> This should read "By I. C., the meanest labourer . . ." Further the author seems to be a Protestant, and to have been licensed by Joseph Caryll, and is therefore very unlikely to have been John Caryl, who was a Catholic.

MYSTERY (the) of money and how to explain it. By Norman Angell [Ralph Norman Angell Lane]. 8vo. Pp. 15. [*Brit. Mus.*]   London [1927]
> Another issue has the title "Monimics . . ."

MYSTERY (the) of the Woman and of the Beast that carrieth her. [By William Tarbet.] 8vo. Pp. 20. [*Brit. Mus.*]   London, 1851

MYSTERY Street. [A novel.] By L. Noel [Leonard Noel Barker]. 8vo. Pp. 288. [*Brit. Mus.*] London [1930]

MYSTIC (a) on the Prussian throne: Frederick-William II. By Gilbert Stanhope [Miss B. M. Ward]. 8vo. Pp. vii. 343. [*Brit. Mus.*]
London, 1912

N

NAMES (the) of the Lord Jesus in the Epistles. [By John Nelson Darby.] 8vo. [*Brit. Mus.*]   London [1879]
> Signed : J. N. D.

NAPOLEON in the other world ; a narrative written by himself, and found near his tomb in the Island of St Helena, by Xongo-Tee-Foh-Tchi, mandarin of the third class. [By Baron Antoine Henry de Jomini? Translated from the French.] 8vo. [*Brit. Mus.*]   London, 1827

NAPOLEON of the Looms. By M. E. Francis [Mary E. Blundell]. 8vo. Pp. 254. [*Brit. Mus.*] London [1925]

NARRATION (a), briefely contayning the history of the French Massacre especially that horrible one at Paris . . . in the yeare 1572. In the passage of which are handled certaine questions both politike and ethike. . . . [Translated from the Latin of Ambrosius de Bruyn.] 4to. [*Pollard and Redgrave.*]
London, 1618

NARRATIVE of a journey through Norway, Sweden and Denmark. By Derwent Conway [Henry David Inglis]. 12mo. [*Eng. Cat.*, 1801-1836, p. 296.]
Edinburgh, 1829

*NARRATIVE of a three years' residence . . .
> Signed : S. M.

NARRATIVE (a) of the voyage of the Argonauts in 1880 ; compiled by the bard [William Mitchell Banks] from the most authentic records, illustrated by the photographer [Richard Caton] . . . 8vo. [Pettersen's *Norsk Lexikon*, col. 342.]   Edinburgh, 1881

NARROW (the) way and the last judgment delivered in two sermons [on Matt. vii. 14]. . . . By G. B. [G. Brian?]. 4to. [*Pollard and Redgrave.*]
London, 1607
> Contains only one sermon.

*NASBY (the) papers. By Petroleum V. Nasby [David Ross Locke. With a preface signed S. O. B. *i.e.* Samuel Orchart Beeton]. 8vo. Pp. 124. [*Brit. Mus.*]   London, 1865

NATHAN the wise ; a dramatic poem. . . . From the German : with an introduction on Lessing and the "Nathan." . . . [By Robert Willis.] 8vo. [*Brit. Mus.*]   London, 1868
> Signed : R. W., M.D.

NATHAN the wise ; dramatic poem from the German of Lessing by the translator of Goethe's Iphigenia and Bürger's Ellenore [William Taylor, of Norwich]. 8vo. [Baker's *Biog. Dram.; Brit. Mus.*]
1805

NATIONAL (the) advocates ; a poem affectionately inscribed to the Honourable Thomas Erskine and Vicary Gibbs, Esquire ; [eulogising their exertions in defence of Hardy, Horne Tooke and others. By William Hayley]. 4to. Pp. 33. [Hayley's *Memoirs*, vol. 1, p. 467.]   London, 1795

NATIONAL song of thanksgiving for the termination of the war in South Africa. [By Henry Longley.] 8vo. S. sh. [*Brit. Mus.*]   London [1902]
> Signed : H. L.

NATION'S (a) manhood ; or, stories of Washington and the American War of Independence. By the author of *Sunlight through the mist* [Mrs E. Burrows]. 8vo. Pp. viii. 358. [*Brit. Mus.*]   London, 1861

NATURAL (the) history of Oxfordshire. . . . By Robert Plot. . . . Second edition, with large additions and . . . a short account of the author [by J. B., M.A., *i.e.* John Burman]. Fol. Pp. 366. [*Brit. Mus.*]   Oxford, 1705

NATURAL (the) history of the Arbor Vitæ, or Tree of Life. [By Thomas Stretzer, Stretser, or Streetser.] Fol. S. sh. [*Brit. Mus.*]   London, 1732

NATURAL (the) secret history of both sexes ; or, a modest defence of public stews ; with an account of the present state of whoring in these kingdoms. By Luke Ogle, Esq. The fourth edition. [Attributed to Bernard de Mandeville, and also to George Ogle.] 8vo. Pp. xv. 119. [*Brit. Mus.*]   London, 1740

First issued as " A modest defence of public stews " *q.v.* (main entry and suppl.).

*NATURALL (the) and morall historie . . .

For Grimestone, *read* Grimstone. [*Pollard and Redgrave.*]

NATURE (the) and design of Christianity ; extracted from a late author. [An abridgment by John Wesley of the first chapter of W. Law's *A practical treatise upon Christian perfection.*] 12mo. Pp. 19. [*Brit. Mus.*]
London, 1740

NATURE and grace ; or, some essential differences between the sentiments of the natural and spiritual man. [By William Cudworth ?] . . . 8vo. Pp. 10. [*Brit. Mus.*]   Salop, 1763

NATURE (the) and unity of the Church of Christ. [By John Nelson Darby.] 12mo. [*Brit. Mus.*]   London [1861]

NATURE (the) of the present excise, and the consequences of its farther extension, examined ; in a letter to a Member of Parliament. [By John Perceval, Second Earl of Egmont.] 8vo.   London, 1733

MS. note in a nearly contemporary hand.

NAUGHTY Nancy ; a musical comedy. By Oliver Bath [Hardinge Coulburn Giffard, Earl of Halsbury]. 8vo. Pp. 31. [*Brit. Mus.*]   London [1902]

NAVAL (a) lieutenant, 1914-1918. By " Etienne " [Stephen King-Hall]. 8vo. Pp. xiv. 260. [*Brit. Mus.*]
London, 1919

NAWORTH. 1643. A new almanacke and prognostication for . . . Durham. By G. Naworth [G. Wharton]. 8vo. [*Brit. Mus.*]   London, 1643

Also published for the year 1644.

NEAPOLITAN (the) ; or, the defender of his mistress. [By —— de Germont.] Done out of French by Mr Ferrand Spence. 12mo. Pp. 80. [*Brit. Mus.*]
London, 1683

NECROMANCER (the) ; or, a tale of the Black Forest. . . . Translated from the German of Lawrence Flammenberg [Carl Friedrich Kahlert] by Peter Teuthold. 8vo. Pp. xv. 232. [*Brit. Mus.*]   London, 1927

*NEEDWOOD Forest. By F. N. C. Mundy. [With commendatory verses signed : E. D. *i.e.* Erasmus Darwin.] 4to. [*Brit. Mus.*]   Lichfield, 1776

An edition of 1779 has verses signed : E. D. jun.

NEMESIS at Raynham Parva. By J. J. Connington [Alfred Walter Stewart]. 8vo. Pp. 286. [*Amer. Cat.*]
London, 1929

NÉOLOGIE ; or, the French of our times : being a collection of more than eleven hundred words. . . . By Mme. Ve D. G. [Mme. F. C. de la Place Gerardin]. 8vo. [*Brit. Mus.*]
London, 1854

*NEREIDES ; or, sea-eclogues.

By William, *not* John Diaper. [*Brit. Mus.*]

NETTIE and Kate ; or, onward to the heights of life. By F. L. M. [F. L. Morse]. 8vo. Pp. 376. [*Brit. Mus.*]
London, 1882

The original (1881) edition is entitled " Onward to the heights of life," *q.v.*

NEW (a) almanack for . . . 1708. . . . By A. C. [Andrew Cumptsy]. 12mo. [*Brit. Mus.*]   Dublin, 1708

NEW (a) argument against Transubstantiation adapted to the Romish controversy at present reviv'd ; in a letter to the author of a book, entitl'd Discourses of religion, between a minister of the Church of England and a country gentleman. . . . To which is added, the Duke of Buckingham's Conference with Father Fitzgerald, an Irish Jesuit sent by King James the II. to convert His Grace in his sickness, to the Romish religion. [By John Henley.] 8vo. [*Lincoln's Inn Lib.*]
London, 1755

NEW (the) attractive ; containing a short discourse of the magnes or loadstone. . . . By Robert Norman. . . . Newly corrected and amended by M. W. B. [Mr William Borough]. 4to. B. L. [*Brit. Mus.*]   London, 1585

NEW (a) ballet of the straunge and cruell whippes which the Spanyards had prepared to whippe and torment English men and women. . . . [By Thomas Deloney ?] Fol. S. sh. B. L. [*Brit. Mus.*]   London, 1588

Signed : T. D.

NEW (a) collection of miscellanies in prose and verse. (The Muse's choice : or, the progress of wit : an elegiac epistle to Major Pack. [By William Bond.] Some remarkable passages in the life of Mr Wycherley. By Mr Dennis.) 8vo. 2 parts. [*Brit. Mus.*]
London, 1725

NEW 405 NEW

NEW (a) collection of original poems, on several occasions. . . . [A re-issue of "A new miscellany of original poems," 1701.] 8vo. [I. O. Williams in *Bibl. Soc. Trans.* Dec. 1929.]
London [*c.* 1720]

NEW Covenant ordinances and order; the Word, sacraments and prayer; practical reflections in rhyme. [By Robert A. Macfie, of Dreghorn.] 8vo. Pp. 79. London [1887]
Presentation copy.

NEW (a) critical review of the public buildings . . . London and Westminster. See "A critical review . . ."

NEW dialogues of the dead; in three parts. [By B. Le Bovier de Fontenelle.] Made English by J. D. [John Dryden?]. 12mo. [*Brit. Mus.*] London, 1683
"Modern Novels," vol. 12.

NEW England's prospect. . . . By W. Wood. [Preface signed: C. D. *i.e.* Charles Deane.] 4to. Pp. xxvi. 131. [*Brit. Mus.*] New York, 1865
Publications of the Prince Society, vol. 3.

NEW English and German word book. By J. B. Richard [J. M. V. Audin] and Kaub. New edition. 16mo. [*Brit. Mus.*] London, 1878

NEW English-German dialogues. By J. B. Richard [J. M. V. Audin] and Kaub. New edition. 16mo. [*Brit. Mus.*] London, 1874

NEW (a) enterlude called Thersytes. [By Nicholas Udall?] 4to. [*Pollard and Redgrave.*] London [1560?]

NEW (a) exposure of the Reverend Leaders of the Voluntary Church Associations. . . . In a letter . . . addressed to them by Anglo-Scotus [John Lockhart?]. Third edition. . . . 8vo. Pp. 69. [*Brit. Mus.*]
Newcastle-upon-Tyne, 1834

NEW (the) fiction; a protest against sex mania and other papers. By the Philistine (J. A. S. [*i.e.* J. A. Sterry?]). 8vo. Pp. vii. 122. London, 1895
Westminster Gazette Library, vol. 3.

*NEW Form of Process before the Court of Session . . .
The *Brit. Mus.* ascription is to John Russell, Clerk to the Signet.

NEW (a) guide to the English tongue. By Edward Baldwin, Esq. [William Godwin]. [F. K. Brown's *Godwin.*] London, 1809

NEW (a) letter of notable contents. . . . [By Gabriel Harvey. The introduction signed: J. P. C. *i.e.* John Payne Collier.] 4to. Pp. xii. 32. [*Brit. Mus.*]
[London, 1870]

*NEW light on old truths . . .
For By I. O., and M. T. *read* By I. O., M.T. and M. A., M.T. [G. R. J. Ouseley].

VOL. VI.

NEW (a) method of curing without internal medicines, that degree of the venereal disease called gonorrhœa or clap . . .
The first edition was issued in 1709 as "by E. N. Surgeon": the second edition, 1711, as "by G. Warren, Surgeon," an imposture meant to cause confusion with George Warren, Surgeon in Cambridge. [*Watt, Brit. Mus., Surgeon-General's Lib.*] R. Straus' *The Unspeakable Curll,* pp. 31, 32, 210, suggests that it may be the work of John Marten, Surgeon, author of "A treatise of all the degrees and symptoms of the venereal disease" (1706, 1708, 1711), who wrote quack medical books for Curll. See "The charitable surgeon" and "The generous surgeon."

NEW (a) miscellany; being a collection of pieces of poetry from Bath, Tunbridge, Oxford, Epsom and other places, in the year 1725. [Contains a poem attributed to Jabez Earle.] 8vo. Pp. 90. [I. O. Williams in *Bibl. Soc. Trans.* Dec. 1929.] London [1725]

*NEW (a) miscellany of original poems on several occasions. Written by the E. of D. [Earl of Dorset] . . . and several other eminent hands. 8vo. Pp. 341. [I. O. Williams in *Bibl. Soc. Trans.* Dec. 1929.] London, 1701
There are other anonymous poems in this miscellany, edited by Charles Gilston, by Lady Winchelsea and John Philips.

NEW (a) miscellany of original poems, translations and imitations. By the most eminent hands, Mr Prior . . . Lady M. W. M— [Lady Mary Wortley Montague]. . . . [Preface signed: A. H. *i.e.* Anthony Hammond, who contributed poems.] 8vo. Pp. 371. [I. O. Williams in *Bibl. Soc. Trans.* Dec. 1929.] London, 1720
Second edition, 1740.

*NEW (the) ordeal . . .
For Charles C. Chesney, *read* George Tomkins Chesney.

NEW (the) parsonage; or, the great importance of a good foundation. By the author of *The lamplighter* [Francis Bourdillon]. 12mo. [*Brit. Mus.*] London, 1860
Signed: F. B.

NEW (a) poem on the . . . Society of Journey-men Taylors. . . . By H. N., Bricklayer, one of the brethren [H. Nelson]. Fol. S. sh. [*Brit. Mus.*] Dublin, 1725
See also "A poem in the honour of the Antient and loyal Society . . ."

NEW poems. By J. Marjoram [Ralph Hale Mottram]. 8vo. Pp. viii. 69. [*Brit. Mus.*] London, 1909

NEW (the) Pope ; or, a true account of the ceremonies . . . at Rome . . . for the election of a new Pope. . . . Translated out of the French by J. D. [John Davies?]. 8vo. Pp. 102. [*Brit. Mus.*]
London, 1677

NEW (the) precept upon precept. . . . By the author of *Line upon line* [Mrs Favel Lee Mortimer]. . . . 8vo. Pp. 236. [*Brit. Mus.*]   London, 1926

NEW (a) selection from the poems of Lionel Johnson. [Edited by H. V. M. *i.e.* H. V. Marrot.] 8vo. [*Brit. Mus.*]
London, 1897

NEW (a) solution of the mystery of Edwin Drood. By Mary Kavanagh [Margaret M. Spain]. 8vo. Pp. 32. [*Innisfail, a quarterly magazine*, No. 1.]
London, 1919

NEW songs, and poems, A-la-mode both at court, and theatres now extant. Never before printed. By P. W. Gent. [Thomas Duffett]. 8vo. Pp. 120. [*Brit. Mus.*]   London, 1677

A duplicate, with new engraved title-page, and without the two leaves of dedicatory verses of Duffett's "New poems, songs, prologues and epilogues" (1676).

*NEW test of the Church of England's loyalty . . .

This was by Defoe. See *Camb. Hist. of English Lit.* and Dottin's *Defoe.*

NEW (the) Testament . . . with . . . expositions of Theod. Beza . . . placed in due order by J. C. [John Canne]. Fol. [*Brit. Mus.*]   London, 1642

NEW (a) trial of the ladies. Hide park, May day. . . . [Signed : W. B. *i.e.* William Blake, of Highgate.] 4to. Pp. 48. [*Brit. Mus.*]   London, 1658

See also "The trial of the ladies . . .", " A serious letter sent by a private Christian . . ." and "The Yellow book."

NEW (a) vocabulary of modern Billingsgate phrases, for the use of clergymen and others. . . .   By the Rev. Mr A . . G—b [Adam Gib]. 8vo. [*Brit. Mus.*]   Perth, 1782

NEW (a) way in apologetic. [A review of "Reason and Revelation" by J. R. Illingworth.] . . . By Hakluyt Egerton [Arthur Boutwood]. 8vo. Pp. 56. [*Brit. Mus.*]   London [1907]

NEWEL (a), which may turn out to be anything but a jewel. Suggested by J. O. H. [James Orchard Halliwell]. 16mo. [*Brit. Mus.*]
[London] private print, 1865
10 copies only printed.

NEW-ENGLAND freemen warned and warmed. Election sermon, 1671. By Rev. J. O. [John Oxenbridge]. 16mo. Pp. 48. [Sabin's *Dictionary.*]
N.P. 1673

NEW-ENGLAND (a) tale ; or, sketches of New-England character and manners. [By Catherine Maria Sedgwick.] 8vo. [*Allibone's Dict.*]
New York, 1822

*NEWES from Italy of a second Moses . . .

For other editions with different titles, see "A president to the nobilitie . . ." (1612) and "The Italian convert . . ." (1635).

NEW-YEARS-GIFT (a) for the Anti-Prerogative - Men ; or, a lawyer's opinion, in defence of His Majesties Power-Royal of granting pardons as he pleases. [By John Brydall.] 4to. [*Lincoln's Inn Lib.*]   London, 1682

NEW-YEAR'S (a) gift ; meditations miscellaneous, holy and humane. By J. H. [Joseph Henshaw], D.D. . . . 12mo. [*Brit. Mus.*]   London, 1704

NEXT (the) chapter ; the war against the moon. By André Maurois [Emile Herzog]. 8vo. Pp. 74. [*Observer*, 1st Feb. 1931.]   London [1927]

NIGHTFALL. By the author of *Marqueray's duel* and *Jenny Essenden* [Agnes Russell Weekes]. 8vo. Pp. 336. [*Who's Who in Lit.*]   London, 1921

NINE historical letters of the reign of Henry VIII. ; written by Reginald Pole [and others]. . . . Copied from the originals [by John Payne Collier]. 4to. [*Brit. Mus.*]
London, private print, 1871

NINETEEN beautiful years ; or, sketches of a girl's (Mary E. W. [*i.e.* Mary E. Willard]) life. Written by her sister [Frances E. Willard]. With an introduction by . . . R. S. Foster. 8vo. [*Brit. Mus.*]   New York, 1864

*NIPOTISMO (il) di Roma . . .

W. A., Fellow of the Royal Society, the translator, is William Aglionby. See Arber's *Term Cat.* i. 2. The 1669 and 1673 editions are as by W. A., without epithet.

NISI Dominus . . . Rimes : H. D. C. P. [Hilary D. C. Pepler]. . . . 8vo. Pp. 56. [*Brit. Mus.*]   Ditchling, 1919

NO song, no supper ; a musical entertainment. By P. Hoare. . . . With . . . remarks by D. G. [George Daniel]. 12mo. Pp. 26. [*Brit. Mus.*]
London [1871]
Lacy's Acting Edition of Plays, vol. 89.

NO ;—this is the truth : a poem. [By Edward Chicken?] Fol. Pp. 11.
Newcastle-upon-Tyne [1750?]

NO Union ! but unite and fall. By Paddy Whack, of Dyott Street, London [John Fitzgibbon, Earl of Clare] ; in a loving letter to his dear mother Sheelah, of Dame Street, Dublin. . . . Second edition. 12mo. [*Brit. Mus.*]
London, 1799

*NOBLENESSE (the) of the asse . . .
1595.
  The Christie-Miller attribution to Daniel
Heinsius is incorrect, and is a confusion with
" Laus asini " by Heinsius, first published
in 1623. " The Noblenesse of the asse " is
by Adriano Banchieri. See *Brit. Mus.;
Pollard and Redgrave.*

NOBLES (the) ; or, of nobilitye : the
original nature, dutyes, right, and
Christian institution thereof three
bookes. Fyrste eloquentlye writtē in
Latine by Laurence Humphrey . . .
late Englished [by Nicholas Grimald
or Grimbald?] . . . 8vo. [*D. N. B.*
vol. 23, p. 250.]   London, 1563

NOBODY'S daughter ; a play in four
acts. By George Paston [Emily Morse
Symonds]. 8vo. Pp. 127. [*Brit.
Mus.*]   London, 1924

NOMQUA, a Zulu maid. By Noel
Hope [Sarah L. Morewood]. . . . 8vo.
Pp. vi. 176. [*Brit. Mus.*]
                           London, 1923

NOLI me tangere ; the young student's
letter to the old lawyer in the country
containing several other authenticks
to corroborate . . . that royal maxim,
The King can do no wrong ; to which
is added a post-script consisting of
some words of the Royal Martyr. [By
John Brydall.] 4to. [*Lincoln's Inn
Lib.*]   London, 1703

NONSENSCORSHIP. . . . Edited by
G. P. P. [George Palmer Putnam].
Sundry observations concerning pro-
hibitions, inhibitions, and illegalities.
. . . 8vo. Pp. xiii. 181. [*Brit. Mus.*]
                           New York, 1922

NORDENHOLT'S million. By J. J.
Connington [Alfred Walter Stewart].
8vo. Pp. vii. 303. [*Publishers' Weekly*,
29th Sept. 1928.]   London, 1923

NORFOLKES furies ; or, a view of Kett's
campe : necessary for the malecontents
of our time, for their instruction, or
terror ; and profitable for every good
subject, to incourage him upon the
undoubted hope of the victorie. . . .
With a table of the maiors and sheriffes
of . . . Norwich . . . set forth first in
Latin by Alexander Neville. Translated into English . . . by R. W.
Minister at Frettenham in Norfolk
[Richard Woods]. 4to. [*Brit. Mus.*]
                           London, 1615

NORTH and south ; or, scenes and
adventures in Mexico. By Seatsfield
[Karl Anton Postl, afterwards Charles
Sealsfield]. Translated from the
German by J. T. H. [Joel Tyler
Headley?]. 8vo. Pp. 118. [*Brit.
Mus.* ; Sabin's *Dictionary*].
                           New York [*c.* 1845]

NORTH American rock writing. . . . By
Thomas Ewbank. [Edited by H. B. D.
i.e. Henry Barton Dawson.] 8vo. Pp.
49. [*Brit. Mus.*]   Morrisania, 1866

NORTH (the) Georgia Gazette and
Winter chronicle. [Edited by Edward
Sabine.] 4to.   London, 1821
  Presentation copy from the editor.

NORTH Sea Bubbles. [By Sir Robert
Grimshaw Dunville.] [O'Donoghue's
Poets of Ireland, p. 497.] Belfast, N.D.

NORTHERN (the) Atalantis ; or, York
Spy. Displaying the secret intrigues
and adventures of the Yorkshire gentry;
more particularly the amours of
Melissa. . . . [By Capt. Bland.] The
second edition, corrected. 8vo. Pp. 73.
[R. Straus' *The Unspeakable Curll*,
p. 222.]   London, 1713

NORTHERN garlands. . . . Edited
by . . . J. Ritson [and republished by
J. H. *i.e.* Joseph Haslewood]. 8vo.
4 parts. [*Brit. Mus.*]   London, 1810

NORTHERN (the) lights, and other
poems. By Violet Jacob [Lady Helena
Mariota Carnegie and Mrs Arthur
Jacob]. 8vo. Pp. 43. [*Brit. Mus.*]
                           London, 1927

NORWAY ; a few facts from Norwegian
history and politics, addressed to the
International Council of women by the
Norwegian National Council of women.
[By Gina Krog.] 8vo. [Pettersen's
Norsk Lexikon, col. 369.]
                           Christiania, 1905

NORWAY (the) wood carrier or reduction of Norway deals. By the author
of the Danish and English Dictionary
[Ernst Wolff]. The third edition.
8vo. [Pettersen's *Norsk Lexikon*, col.
369.]   London, 1785

NORWEGIAN (a) ramble among the
fjörds, fjelds, mountains and glaciers.
By one of the ramblers [John Bishop
Putnam]. 8vo. [Pettersen's *Norsk
Lexikon*, col. 369.]   New York, 1904

NORWEGIAN (the) sailor ; a sketch of
the life of George Noscoe [Jørgen
Nøstø]. Written by himself. With
an introductory note by Thos. Raffles.
. . . 8vo. [Pettersen's *Norsk Lexikon*,
col. 370.]   London, 1850

NOSE (the) ; a poem, in six stanzas . . .
dedicated to all unmarried ladies, who
may profit by the example . . . of
Dorothy Spriggins. [Written and
illustrated by Frances Parker, Countess
of Morley?] 8vo. Pp. 8. [*Brit. Mus.*]
                           [London] 1831

NOSE-GAY (a) for the House of
Commons ; made up of the stincking
flowers of their seven yeares labours.
. . . By Mercurius Melancholicus
[Marchamont Nedham?]. 4to. [*Brit.
Mus.*]   London, 1648

NOT in our stars. [A novel.] By Michael Maurice [Conrad Arthur Skinner]. 8vo. Pp. 288. [*Brit. Mus.*]
London, 1923
First Novel Library.

NOTABLE (a) historye of Nastagio and Traversari. Translated [from the Italian of Boccaccio] by C. T. [Christopher Tye]. 8vo. [*D. N. B.* vol. 57, p. 413.] London, 1569

NOTE book of observations in practical physics. Compiled by C. E. A. [Cyril Ernest Ashford]. 4to. Pp. 54. [*Brit. Mus.*] Harrow, 1903

NOTES of a reading on I. and II. Corinthians. By J. N. D. [John Nelson Darby]. 8vo. [*Brit. Mus.*]
London [1879]

NOTES of lectures. [Religious tracts.] By F. E. R. [F. E. Raven]. 8vo. [*Brit. Mus.*] 1891, etc.

NOTES of readings and addresses at Newcastle, September 1895. [By J. B. S. *i.e.* J. B. Stoney, and others.] 8vo. [*Brit. Mus.*] [London, 1895]

NOTES on Arlington and its churches. [By Charles E. Powell.] 8vo. [*Brit. Mus.*] Eastbourne [1931]

NOTES on Mr William Fowler of Winterton, and his works. [By Henry William Ball.] 8vo. Pp. 16. [*Brit. Mus.*] Hull, 1869
Signed : H. W. B.

NOTES on so much of the catalogue of the present exhibition of the Royal Academy as relates to the works of the members. [In verse. By Richard James Lane.] 8vo. Pp. 61. [*Brit. Mus.*] London [1855]

NOTES on the campaign of the Army of Reserve in the Year 1800. By an officer of artillery [John Hambly Humfrey]. 8vo. Pp. 57. [*Brit. Mus.*] 1827
Preface signed : J. H. H.

NOTES on the church of St Nicholas, Rattlesden, Suffolk. With illustrations. Edited by J. R. O. [J. R. Olorenshaw]. Fol. Pp. 12. [*Brit. Mus.*]
Coventry, 1910

NOTES on the family of Spreull; collected and arranged by J. M. S. [J. M. Spreull] and G. J. S. [G. J. Spreull]. 8vo. Pp. 63. [*Brit. Mus.*] Glasgow, 1915

NOTES on the months; a book of "feasts, fasts, saints and sundries." [By Eliza Gutch.] 8vo. Pp. xi. 428. [*Brit. Mus.*] London, 1866

NOTES on the postscript to a pamphlet entitled "Observations anatomical and physiological" . . . by A. Monro. . . . [By Mark Akenside.] 8vo. [*Edinb. Univ. Lib.*] London, 1758

NOTES on the Rye elections. [By Dr —— Edwards.] 8vo. [*Lincoln's Inn Lib.*] London, 1830

NOTES on the Scottish family of Playfair. Compiled by A. G. P. [A. G. Playfair]. 8vo. Pp. 44. [*Brit. Mus.*]
Tunbridge Wells, 1906

NOTES on the state of Virginia ; written [by Thomas Jefferson] in . . . 1781 . . . enlarged in . . . 1782 for the use of a foreigner of distinction. . . . 8vo. Pp. 391, 14. [*Brit. Mus.*]
[Paris] 1782 [for 1784]
The *Brit. Mus.* copy has the author's autograph. An edition (London, 1787) bears the author's name.

NOTES on the tesselated pavement at Woodchester. [By William George.] Reprinted from *Bristol Times and Mirror*. 8vo. Pp. 4. [*Brit. Mus.*]
[Bristol, 1880]

NOTES on un-natural history ; being a selection of fictions accounting for facts. By the author of *Notes on the months* [Eliza Gutch]. 8vo. Pp. viii. 152. [*Brit. Mus.*] London, 1868

NOTES on W. Bromfield's two volumes of chirurgical observations and cases. With an appendix addressed to Doctor Laurence. By D. A. S - - -, M.D. and Professor of Surgery [D. A. Smith]. 8vo. Pp. 72. [*Brit. Mus.*]
London, 1773

NOTICE of tertiary fossils from Labrador, Maine . . . and remarks on the climate of Canada, in the newer Pliocene or Pleistocene period. [By Sir John William Dawson.] 8vo. [*Brit. Mus.*] [Montreal? 1860?]

NOTICE of the botanical writings of the late C. S. Rafinesque. [By Asa Gray.] 8vo. [*Brit. Mus.*] [New York, 1841]
Signed : A. G. Off-print from the *American Journal of Science and Art*.

NOTICE of William Thaddeus Harris, Esq. [By Francis James Child.] 16mo. [*Brit. Mus.*] Pp. 14.
Boston, 1855
Signed : F. J. C. The preface is signed : S. G. D. *i.e.* S. G. Drake. Six copies only printed.

NOTITIA historicorum selectorum ; or, animadversions upon the antient . . . historians. Written in French by . . . Francis La Mothe le Vayer ; translated . . . by W. D., B.A. [William Davenant]. 8vo. Pp. 256. [*Brit. Mus.*]
Oxford, 1678

NOVANGLUS and Massachusettensis ; or, political essays . . . the former by John Adams . . . the latter by Jonathan Sewell [or rather Daniel Leonard]. 8vo. [*Brit. Mus.*]
Boston, 1819

*NOVELS (the) of Elizabeth . . .
  The last (2nd) part, 1681, bears the author's name.

NOVUS annus luni-solaris, sive ratio temporis emendato. A rectified account of time, by a new luni-solar year. [By Robert Wood, LL.D.] 4to. S. sh. [Brit. Mus.]   [1680?]
  Signed : R. W.

*NUGÆ. By W. S. Y.
  For Siddon, read Siddons.

NUGÆ derelictæ quas colligerunt J. M. [James Maidment] et R. P. [Robert Pitcairn]. L. P. 8vo. [Brit. Mus.]
          Edinburgi, private print, 1832
  Eighteen rare tracts relating to the history of Scotland.

*NUGAE Scoticae . . .
  In addition to Maidment and Kinloch, Charles Baxter was editor. [T. G. Stevenson's Maidment Bibl.]

NUN of Heaven. [Poems. By] T. L. P. [T. L. Paton]. 8vo. Pp. 42. [Brit. Mus.]   Richmond, 1928

NUNNS (the) complaint against the Fryars ; being the charge given in to the court of France by the Nunns of St Katherine near Provins. [By Alexandre Varet.]. . . . Now faithfully done into English. 8vo. Pp. 192. [Arber's Term Cat.]   London, 1676

NURSES' (the) "Enquire within" ; a pocket encyclopædia of diseases, their symptoms, nursing, treatment, and much other valuable information. . . . By C. O. M. [E. M. Clarke]. 16mo. Pp. viii. 166.   London [1906]
  Later editions bear the author's name.

NUTSHELLS. (A Death-day book.) By M. K. M. [M. K. Moore]. 8vo. Pp. vi. 279. [Brit. Mus.]
          London, 1909

O

OBSERVATIONS and strictures on the conduct of Mrs Clarke, etc. etc. By a lady [Olivia Wilmot Serres?]. 4to. Pp. 37. [Brit. Mus.]   London, 1809

OBSERVATIONS, moral and political, particularly respecting the necessity of good order . . . in our prisons ; occasioned by Fidelio's letters . . . By J. H. [John Howard?]. 8vo. [Brit. Mus.]   London, 1784

*OBSERVATIONS on the amalgamation of the Royal and Indian Artillery.
  For Col. George Chesney, read Frances Rawdon Chesney.

OBSERVATIONS on the expedition of General Buonaparte to the East, and the probability of its success considered ; to which is added a brief sketch of the present state of Egypt ; an historical account of Alexandria. . . . By the editor of the History of Peter III. and Catharine II. of Russia [W. Tooke]. 8vo. [Brit. Mus.]   London, 1798

OBSERVATIONS on the judgements of the High Court in the Rent case by a member of the British Indian Association [John Cochrane]. 8vo. [Lincoln's Inn Lib.]   Calcutta, 1865

OBSERVATIONS on the present state and future prospects of Scandinavia. By a Swede [S. G. Lallerstedt]. 8vo. [Pettersen's Norsk Lexikon, col. 381.]
          Paris, 1856

OBSERVATIONS on the proposition for increasing the means of theological education at the University in Cambridge. [By William Ellery Channing.] 8vo. [Sabin's Dictionary.]
          Cambridge [Mass.] 1815

*OBSERVATIONS on the Revised Version of the Bible. . . .
  For John Harrison, read John Harris.

OBSERVATIONS on the scheme for Screw Ships evolutions. [By Sir William Fanshawe Martin.] 8vo. Pp. 20. [Brit. Mus.]   Valletta, 1863

OBSERVATIONS on the use and abuse of red tape, for the juniors in the Eastern, Western, and American Departments [of the Foreign Office. By T. H. Sanderson]. 8vo. Pp. 14. [Brit. Mus.]   [London, 1891]

OBSERVATIONS upon the lives of Alexander, Cæsar, Scipio. Newly Englished. [By Giovanni Botero.] 8vo. [Pollard and Redgrave.]
          London, 1602
  Signed : J. B. B.

*OCCASIONAL papers by the late William Dodd, LL.D. . . .

These papers were written almost entirely by Dr Samuel Johnson. Dodd, once a chaplain to George III. and an eloquent and popular preacher, forged the name of his friend and ex-pupil, Lord Chesterfield, on a bond, and although he repaid the money, he was sentenced to be hanged. Strenuous but futile efforts in which Johnson joined were made to get the sentence commuted. For the benefit of Mrs Dodd, Johnson was about to publish these "Occasional papers," but at her earnest desire the book was suppressed.

OCCASIONAL poems, fables and translations from Filicaja and other Italian poets. By C. T. W. [Charlotte Theresa Wheler]. 8vo. Pp. 159. [*Brit. Mus.*]
Leamington, 1865

OCTAVE (an). By Jeffery E. Jeffery [Jeffery Eardley Marston]. 8vo. Pp. 320. [*Amer. Cat.*] London, 1925

ODE (an) addressed to the author of the Conquered Duchess. In answer to that celebrated performance. [By Sir Charles Hanbury Williams.] Fol. Pp. 8. [*Brit. Mus.*] London, 1746

ODE for the Encœnia at Oxford, July 1810. [By Edward Copleston, Bishop of Llandaff.] 4to. Pp. 4. [*Brit. Mus.*]
Oxford [1810]

ODE (an), humbly inscribed to the Queen, on the late glorious success of Her Majesty's Arms. [By Matthew Prior.] [*Brit. Mus.*] London, 1706

ODE on His Majesty's recovery. By the author of *Sympathy* and *Humanity* [Samuel Jackson Pratt]. 4to. [*Brit. Mus.*] London, 1789

ODE to dawn and other poems. By John Doe [Victor Sampson]. 8vo. Pp. 55. [*Brit. Mus.*] London, 1923

ODE (an) to His Royal Highness [Frederick, Prince of Wales] on his birth-day. [By Robert Craggs Nugent, Earl Nugent.] Fol. Pp. 7. [*Brit. Mus.*] London, 1739

ODE (an) to the Honourable H - - - y F - - x [Henry Fox, afterwards Lord Holland], on the marriage of the Du - - - s of M - - - - - - r [Duchess of Manchester] to H - - - s - - - y [Hussey], Esq. [By Sir Charles Hanbury Williams.] Fol. Pp. 8. [*Brit. Mus.*] London, 1746

OEDIPUS ; or, the resolver ; being a clew that leads to the chiefe secrets and true resolution of amorous, naturall, morall, and politicall problemes. . . . By G. M. [Gervase Markham?]. 12mo. Pp. 307. [*Brit. Mus.*]
London, 1650

OF mariage and wiving ; an excellent, pleasant and philosophicall controversie between the two famous Tassi now living, the one Hercules the philosopher, the other Torquato the poet. Done into English by R. T., Gentleman [Robert Tofte]. 4to. B. L. [*Brit. Mus.*] London, 1599

OF smoking ; four poems in praise of tobacco ; an imitation of the style of four modern poets [Pope, Ambrose Philips, Young and Thomson. By Isaac Hawkins Browne]. 8vo. [R. Straus' *The Unspeakable Curll*, p. 305.]
London, 1736

*OF the circumference of the earth . . .

This is another edition of "Fata mihi totum mea sunt agitanda per orbem," (1611) also anonymous, *q.v.*

OF the Divinity of Christ. (Of the union of the divine and human nature in the person of Christ.) [Two sermons on John i. 1 and 14 by Richard Taylor, dissenting minister.] 8vo. Pp. 95. [*Brit. Mus.*] N.P. [1730]

OF the eternal felicity of the saints. By R. Bellarmine. Translated into English by A. B. [Thomas Everard or Everett]. 12mo. Pp. 441. [*Pollard and Redgrave.*] [St Omer] 1638

OF the imitation of Christ. By Thomas à Kempis. [Translated by Frederick Apthorp Paley.] 8vo. [*Brit. Mus.*]
London, 1881

OF the imitation of Christ. . . . By Thomas A'Kempis. With an . . . essay on the authorship [signed : F. S. A. *i.e.* Edmund Waterton]. 8vo. Pp. xxxvi. 256. [*Brit. Mus.*] London, 1883

OF the interchangeable course, or variety of things. [By Robert Ashley.] Fol. [*Huntington Lib. Checklist.*]
London, 1594

*OF the laws of chance ; or, a method of calculation of the hazards of game . . .

Mainly translated by Dr John Arbuthnot from the *De ratiociniis in ludo aleae* by Christiaan Huygens. [*Brit. Mus.*]

*OF the progress of the soule . . .

This is part two of "An anatomie of the world . . .", *q.v.*

OF the visible sacrifice of the Church of God. By Anonymus Eremita [Simon Stock, or in religion, Simon a S. Maria]. 4to. 2 parts. [*Brit. Mus.*] Bruxelles, 1637, 38

OF trade . . . also, of coyn. bullion. . . . By J. P., Esq. [J. Pollexfen ?]. To which is annexed, The argument of the late Lord Chief Justice Pollexphen, upon an action of the case, brought by the East India Company. . . . 8vo. 2 parts. [*Brit. Mus.*] London, 1700

OFFICIA anglicana ; or, a manual of daily devotion, for members of the Church of England compiled from the Prayers of Bp. Andrewes, Dr Cosin, and Bp. Wilson. . . . [Compiled by Sir George Prevost.] 32mo. Pp. 68. [*Brit. Mus.*] London, 1847

Preface signed : G. P.

OHIO Valley historical series miscellanies. [Edited by R. C. *i.e.* Robert Clarke?] 8vo. 3 parts. [*Brit. Mus.*] Cincinnati, 1869-71

*'ΟΙΝΟΣ Κρίθινος. . . .

Not by Rolleston but by Benjamin Buckler. Information from a descendant of Buckler's who produced the author's own copy, with MS. notes, etc. See also "A philosophical dialogue concerning decency . . . "

OLD (the) and New Testaments ; being the English version of the Polyglott Bible. . . . [Edited by T. C. *i.e.* Thomas Chevalier.] 8vo. [*Brit. Mus.*] London, 1819

OLD (Ye) Brum and ye New, from a humorous point of view : a complete history of the town. . . . By Jayhay [John Anderton]. . . . Illustrated. 8vo. Pp. 88. [*Birm. Cent. Lib.*] Birmingham, 1878-9

OLD Bumble's art of whist. By F. R. D. [Francis Robert Drew]. 8vo. [Jessel's *Bibl. of playing cards.*] Malvern, 1870

OLD (the) churches of the Province of Quebec, 1647-1800. [By Pierre Georges Roy.] 8vo. Pp. viii. 323. [*Brit. Mus.*] Quebec, 1925

*OLD [fox, *i.e.* John Lauderyou] . . .

For By John Wilson, Grocer, of Truro, *read* By John Williams, Grocer, of Truro.

OLD Humphrey's [George Mogridge's] walks in London and its neighbourhood. 12mo. [*Brit. Mus.*] London [1843?]

OLD (the) man ; or, ravings and ramblings round Conistone. [By Alexander C. Gibson.] 16mo. Pp. vi. 146. [*Brit. Mus.*] London, 1849

Signed : A. C. G.

OLD (the) man's wish. [A song. By Walter Pope.] Fol. [*Brit. Mus.*] [1685?]

A later edition (1697) entitled "The Wish" bears the author's name.

OLD (the) orthodox foundation of religion ; left for a patterne to a new reformation. Collected long since by Mr Henry Ainsworth . . . and now republished . . . by S. W. [Samuel White, of Polsholt]. 4to. [*Edinb. Univ. Lib.*] London, 1653

See also "The orthodox foundation of religion."

OLD (the) Testament. By Chilperic Edwards [Edward John Pilcher]. 8vo. Pp. vi. 154. [*Brit. Mus.*] London, 1913

The Inquirer's Library, No. 3.

OLD (the) year and the new ; a midnight reverie, 1895-96. [By A. D. Phelp.] 8vo. Pp. 3. [*Brit. Mus.*] [Leyton, 1895]

Signed : A. D. P.

ON building a church for divine worship ; a discourse. [By J. P. Knight.] 8vo. Pp. 23. [*Brit. Mus.*] London, 1850

ON cholera. By Medicus [Forbes Winslow]. 8vo. [*Eng. Cat.*, 1801-1836, p. 111.] 1803

ON common and perfect magic squares. With examples constructed by the author also with his sections of the simple and compound perfect square of the mystic number 666 (1 to 443556). By F. Latoon [William Shaw]. London, 1895

On the authority of the author's son, Mr Plato E. Shaw. F. Latoon is from the Turkish "Eflatoon," meaning " Plato."

ON division among the churches ; a letter to . . . the Earl of Derby. By Medicus Cantabrigiensis [John Spurgin, M.D.]. Second edition. 8vo. [*Brit. Mus.*] London, 1858

ON Free Trade. [An address. By Sir Thomas Phillipps.] Fol. S. sh. [*Brit. Mus.*] Broadway, 1851

Signed : T. P.

ON lots. [A letter to the editor of the Secession Magazine, signed : A. G. *i.e.* Alexander Gardner.] 12mo. [*Brit. Mus.*] Paisley, 1851

ON notes and note books. [By David B. Muir.] 8vo. Pp. 27. [*Brit. Mus.*] London [1927]

ON persecution and a persecuting temper. Matt. x. 34-36. [A sermon. By G. A. Poole.] 8vo. [*Brit. Mus.*] [N.P. 1840?]

Signed : G. A. P.

ON repentance. By J. N. D. [John Nelson Darby]. 12mo. [*Brit. Mus.*] London [1865]

ON , symbols in worship. [By Thomas Carlyle, advocate.] 8vo. Pp. 22. [*Brit. Mus.*] London, 1853

ON the amusements of clergymen and Christians in general ; in three dialogues between a dean and a curate. By Edward Stillingfleet [or rather Rev. William Gilpin]. 8vo. Pp. 224. [*Brit. Mus.*] London, 1796

The title does not begin " Three dialogues . . ." as sometimes quoted. Cf. *Gent. Mag.* xci. i. 53 ; *N. and Q.* 18th Dec. 1869, p. 530.

*ON the conduct of the war in the East ;
the Crimean expedition. . . . By a
General Officer. . . . Attributed by
the Belgian newspapers to the pen of
Prince Napoleon. [By —— Tavernier.]
8vo. [*Brit. Mus.*] London, 1855

ON the immediate and glorious advent
of our Lord Jesus Christ. . . . By
a clergyman, J. A., P. E. [Joseph
Amesbury]. 12mo. Pp. 66. [*Brit.
Mus.*] London, 1849

*ON the landscape architecture of the
great painters of Italy . . .
For By G. L. M., *read* G. L. M. Esq.
For 1838, *read* 1828.

ON the law of libel : with strictures on
the self-styled Constitutional Association. [By Francis Place.] 8vo. Pp.
73. [*Brit. Mus.*] London, 1823

ON the meeting of three schoolfellows
and friends after a separation of forty
years. [In verse. By Sir William
Norris.] 8vo. Pp. 16. [*Brit. Mus.*]
[London] private print, 1850

ON the moral state and political union
of Sweden and Norway in answer
to Mr S. Laing's statement. [By
Magnus Björnstjerna.] 8vo. [Petter-
sen's *Norsk Lexikon*, col. 401.]
London, 1840

ON the sixth day. [A novel.] By
Giuseppe Bianco [Joseph White]. 8vo.
Pp. 312. [*Brit.Mus.*] Indianapolis [1928]

ON the Tarshish of the second book of
Chronicles. [By William Aloysius
Clavering.] 4to. London, 1849

ON the use and abuse of satire.
[By Charles Abbot, afterwards Lord
Tenterden.] 8vo. [*Gent. Mag.* Aug.
1839, p. 157.] Oxford, 1786

ON the white horse mentioned in the
Apocalypse. . . . From the Latin of
Emanuel Swedenborg. [Edited by
T. M. G. *i.e.* Thomas Murray Gorman.]
8vo. Pp. vi. 62. [*Brit. Mus.*]
London, 1871

ON this great eclipse : a poem. By
A. R. [Allan Ramsay]. See above, "A
forecast of the sun's eclipse . . . "

ONE dreamer who awakes. [A novel.]
By E. Shaw Cowley [Elsie Mary
Boulton]. 8vo. Pp. 314. [*Brit.Mus.*]
London, 1905

ONE good turn. By Valentine [Arthur
Valentine Peachey]. 8vo. Pp. 256.
[*Brit. Mus.*] London, 1928

ONE (the) hope of all believers, as set
forth in the Holy Scriptures. . . . From
the German [of C. J. T. Boehm]. By
C. P. P. 12mo. Pp. 24. [*Brit. Mus.*]
London, 1856

100 Books to read and enjoy, with
reasons for their selection. By . . .
"Amicus" [Charles Joseph Palmer].
8vo. [*Brit. Mus.*] Ipswich [1922]

ONE million of comic anecdotes . . .
Collected by Dr Merryman and Hilaire
le Gai [Pierre Alexandre Gratet-
Duplessis]. 32mo. [*Brit. Mus.*] 1853
A translation. The original French (1848)
was by Hilaire le Gai alone.

ONE sheet against the Quakers, detecting
their errour and mis-practice in refusing
to reverence men outwardly. . . . By
J. C. [John Cheney]. 4to. Pp. 8.
[*Brit. Mus.*] London, 1677

1489 Cartæ antiquæ in the Tower. . . .
Index of those which are printed.
Second edition. . . . T. P. [Sir Thomas
Phillipps]. Fol. Pp. 4. [*Brit. Mus.*]
[Middle Hill] private print, 1846

OPEN (the) road to Bethlehem. [Verse.
Signed : J. S. *i.e.* John Sammes.]
16mo. [*Brit. Mus.*] Reigate [1929]

*OPTICKS ; or, a treatise . . .
Preface signed : I. N.

OPTIMYSTICA. [Poems. By Eglan-
tyne L. Jebb.] 4to.
Letchworth, 1925, *etc.*
Only Part I. is anonymous.

ORACLE (the) ; or, a short panegyric
[in verse] on Mr Peter Edwards's . . .
Defence of infant sprinkling. By
John, of Eton [Benjamin Francis ?].
8vo. Pp. 22. [*Brit. Mus.*]
London [1799 ?]
A satire.

ORACLES (the) of the dissenters containing forty-five relations of pretended
judgments, prodigies and apparitions
in behalf of the Non-Conformists : in
opposition to the Establish'd Church.
By an impartial hand. Part I. [By
John Brydall.] 4to. [*Lincoln's Inn
Lib.*] London, 1707

ORATION on the influence of Italian
works of imagination on the same
class of compositions in England ;
delivered in Trinity College Chapel,
December 16, 1831. [By Arthur
Hallam.] 8vo. [*Lincoln's Inn Lib.*]
Cambridge, 1832

ORATION on the influence of the
political movements of the last half-
century on the literature of the same
period ; delivered in Trinity College
Hall, Dec. 13, 1842. [By Frederick
Waymouth Gibbs.] 8vo.
Cambridge, 1843
Ascription by the Librarian of Trinity
College, Cambridge.

ORATIONNE (ane) in favouris of all
thais of the Congregation . . . set
furth be Master Quintine Kennedy. . . .
[Edited by Sir Alexander Boswell.]
4to. Pp. vii. 20. [*Brit. Mus.*]
Edinburgh, 1812

ORDER in the family and in the church. [By William Tarbet.] 8vo. Pp. 8. [*Brit. Mus.*]   1862
> Signed : A minister of the Catholic Apostolic Church.

ORGANIC remains, Kirkdale, near Kirbymoorside. [A letter signed : J. G. *i.e.* J. Gibson of Stratford. Extracted from *The Yorkshire Gazette*, March 9, 1822.] 4to. S. sh. [*Brit. Mus.*]   [York, 1822]

ORIGIN (the) and progress of language. [By G. Smith, minister of Trinity Chapel, Poplar.] 16mo.
                              London [1848]

ORIGIN (the) of every miracle of the Bible separately considered. By Ben De Monkton [Benjamin Walker]. 4to. No. 1. [*Brit. Mus.*]
                         Manchester [1876]
> No more published.

ORPHAN'S (the) home. By the author of *Hymns and scenes of childhood* [Jane Euphemia Leeson]. 32mo. [Julian's *Dict.*]   1849
> Signed : J. E. L.

ORTHODOX (the) foundation of religion long since collected by Henry Ainsworth ; and now divulged by S. W. [Samuel White, of Polsholt]. 4to. [*Brit. Mus.*]   London, 1641
> See also, " The old orthodox foundation of religion."

*OTHER (the) side of the Herring-pond . . .
> *For* side of, *read* side.

OUR childhood's pattern ; being tales based upon incidents in the life of the Holy Child Jesus. [By Cecilia Anne Jones.] 16mo. [*Brit. Mus.*]
                              London [1870]

OUR Eastern Empire ; or, stories from the history of British India. By the author of *The Martyr land* [Mrs E. Burrows]. . . . 8vo. Pp. xii. 236. [*Brit. Mus.*]   London, 1857

OUR fighting sea men. By Lionel Yexley [James Woode]. 8vo. Pp. 345. [*Brit. Mus.*]   London [1911]

OUR future hope. (A Bible study of the past, present and future of the Israel of God.) By E. E. M. [E. E. Marshall]. 8vo. Pp. v. 18. [*Brit. Mus.*]
                              London, 1889

OUR Library. By a Reader [Catherine Cooper Hopley. On the Library of the British Museum]. 4to. Pp. 19. [*Brit. Mus.*]   London [*c.* 1880]

"OUR neighbourhood ;" or, sketches in the suburbs of Yedo. By T. A. P. [T. A. Purcell]. 8vo. Pp. 124. [*Brit. Mus.*]   Yokohama, 1874

OUT of school at Eton ; being a collection of poetry and prose writing. By some present Etonians, [Largely the work of George Nathaniel Curzon, Marquis Curzon.] 8vo. [Ronaldshay's *Curzon.*]   London, 1877

OUTLINE (an) of the Epistle to the Romans. By C. A. C. [C. A. Coates]. 8vo. Pp. 245. [*Brit. Mus.*]
                              London [1927]

OUTLINE (an) of the history of the Botanical Department of University College, London . . . [By Francis Wall Oliver.] 8vo. Pp. 23. [*Brit. Mus.*]   London, 1927

OUTLINES of a plan for promoting the art of painting in Ireland . . . [By Joseph Cooper Walker.] 12mo. Pp. 36. [*Brit. Mus.*]   Dublin, 1790

OUTLINES of English grammar ; partly abridged from Mr Hazlitt's New and improved grammar. By Edward Baldwin, Esq. [William Godwin]. [F. K. Brown's *Godwin.*]
                              London, 1810

OUTLINES of geography for junior classes. [By Robert Sullivan, LL.D.] 12mo. Pp. 84. [*Brit. Mus.*]   1878

OUTLINES of the history of England and Great Britain, B.C. 55 to A.D. 1890. [By J. M. D. Meiklejohn.] 8vo. Pp. 82. [*Brit. Mus.*]   London, 1890
> Preface signed : J. M. D. M.

OUTPOST (an) wooing. By Norah K. Strange [Mrs E. Gower Stanley]. 8vo. Pp. 250. [*Brit. Mus.*] London [1924]

OVID in masquerade ; being a burlesque upon the xiii. book of his Metamorphoses. By Joseph Gay [John Durant de Breval]. 8vo. [*Brit. Mus.*]
                              London, 1719

*OWD Jem un his five daughters . . .
> *For* Jem, *read* Yem.

OXFORD and Cambridge miscellany ; poems. [Contains anonymous poems attributed to Matthew Prior, Sir Richard Steele and Edward Fenton.] 8vo. Pp. 400. [I. O. Williams in *Bibl. Soc. Trans.*, Dec. 1929.] London [1707]

OXFORD and Flanders. [Poems.] By "Observer, R.F.C." [Gordon Alchin]. 8vo. Pp. 40. [*Brit. Mus.*]
                              Oxford, 1916

OXFORD (the) ars poetica ; or, how to write a Newdigate. [By George Murray, of Magdalen Hall, Oxford.] 8vo. [*Brit. Mus.*]   Oxford, 1853

OXFORD (the) Methodists ; being some account of a society of young gentlemen in that city, so denominated. . . . In a letter from a gentleman near Oxford [William Law, author of *A serious call*]. . . . 8vo. Pp. 32. [*Brit. Mus.*]
                              London, 1733

P

P. W.'s [Peter Walsh's] reply to the Person of Quality's Answer : dedicated to His Grace the Duke of Ormond. 4to. Pp. 151. [*Brit. Mus.*] Paris, 1654

PACKET (a) of letters which lately passed between . . . and the Rev. Dr Waterland. 8vo. [By William Staunton.] [Straus' *The Unspeakable Curll.*] London, 1722

PAGAN Rome . . . Translated from the French [by A. G. *i.e.* Alexander Gordon?]. 12mo. [*Brit. Mus.*] London, 1838

PAGE (a) from the life of Brevet-Colonel Peter Nemo . . . extracted by his friend, Timothy Scribbler . . . (By W. S. Y. [William Siddons Young].) 8vo. Pp. 26. [*Brit. Mus.*] Malvern, private print, 1897

PALACE (the) martyr! [*i.e.* Lady F. E. R. Hastings]. A satire [in verse]. By the Honourable * * * [*i.e.* Hon. —— Osborn?]. 8vo. Pp. 15. [*Brit. Mus.*] London, 1839

PALACE (the) of silence ; a philosophic tale : translated from the French [of Cadmus the Milesian, *i.e.* Philippe Auguste de Sainte Foix] by a lady. 12mo. Pp. lix. 215. [*Brit. Mus.*] London, 1775

PALÄOPHRON and Neoterpe. From . . . the German of Goethe, by the translator of Goethe's *Herrmann and Dorothea* [Joseph Charles Mellish]. 4to. [*Brit. Mus.*] 1801

PALESTINE and the British taxpayer. [By Israel Cohen.] 8vo. Pp. 12. [*Brit. Mus.*] 1929

PALMS of Elim . . . By the author of *Morning and night watches* [James R. Macduff]. 8vo. [*Brit. Mus.*] London, 1879

PAMPHLETEERS (the) ; a satyr. [By Bernard de Mandeville.] Fol. 1703
It is indicated in an advertisement in *The Flying Post*, 17th June 1703, that it was " by the author of Some Fables after the familiar method of Mr De la Fontaine."

ΠΑΝΑΛΕΘΑ Πλαστολογα. Or, the deplumation of Mrs Anne Gibbs . . . deplored by . . . R. W. [Richard Walden]. (Παλινοδια, sive, fama vapulans. . . .) 8vo. Pp. 3, 7. [*Brit. Mus.*] [Oxford?] 1662

PANAMA. . . . By Albert Edwards [Arthur Bullard]. 8vo. Pp. x. 585. [*Brit. Mus.*] New York, 1912
Macmillan's Travel Series.

PANEGYRICK (a) upon Oates. [By Richard Duke.] Fol. S. sh. [*D. N. B.* vol. 4, p. 117.] [London, 1678 ?]

PANEGYRICAL poem on the horn-book. With a surprising satire upon a very surprising Lord. [By Jonathan Swift?] 8vo. [R. Straus' *The Unspeakable Curll*, p. 295.] London, 1733

PANEGYRIQUE (a) humbly addrest to the King's Most Excellent Majesty : on his auspicious meeting his two houses of Parliament, February the 4th, 5th, 1672/3, and his most gratious speech . . . on that occasion. [In verse.] By R. W. [Robert Wild]. Fol. Pp. 6. [*Brit. Mus.*] London, 1673

PANGS of jealousy ; an Anglo-Spanish drama in the Pyrenees. By Prudens Futuri [Nelly Davidson]. 8vo. Pp. 180. [*Brit. Mus.*] Antwerp, 1926

PAPER (the) chase. By Hearnden Balfour [Beryl Hearnden and Eva Balfour]. 8vo. Pp. 320. [*Amer. Cat.*] London [1927]

*PAPIST (a) misrepresented, not represented . . .
The original edition is dated 1665, a misprint for 1685. An edition in 1686 continues "to which is added a book entituled The doctrines and practices of the Church of Rome truly represented in answer to the aforesaid book. By a Protestant of the Church of England [Edward Stillingfleet]." This was also published independently in the same year.

PARACELSUS his archidoxes; englished and published by J. H. [James Howell?] Oxon. 8vo. [*Brit. Mus.*] London, 1661

PARACELSUS his Aurora, & Treasure of the philosophers, as also the Waterstone . . . Englished . . . by J. H. [James Howell?] Oxon. 12mo. [*Brit. Mus.*] London, 1659

*PARADISE lost; a poem in two books . . .
For two, *read* ten.

PARADISE (the) of delights ; or, the B. Virgin's Garden of Loreto : with briefe discourses upon her divine Letanies. . . . By I. S. of the Society of Jesus [John Sweetnam]. 8vo. Pp. 217. [*Brit. Mus.*] [St Omer] 1620

*PARADISE (the) of the soule. . . .
This translation was not by Francis Walsingham. All authorities (*Gillow, De Backer, D.N.B., S.T.C.*) are agreed that it was by Thomas Everard or Everett, S.J.

PARADISE regain'd . . . a poem. [By John Lawrence, Rector of Yelvertoft.] 8vo. [*Brit. Mus.*]   1728

*PARADOXES of state relating to the present government. . . .
> Not by John Toland, but by Anthony Ashley Cooper, third earl of Shaftesbury. See *D. N. B.* vol. 12, p. 131.

PARAGRAPHS on the subject of judicial reform in Maryland. . . . [Signed : Ina *i.e.* William Price.] 8vo. [*Brit. Mus.*]   Baltimore, 1846

PARALLEL (the) ; or, an account of the growth of knavery under the pretext of arbitrary government and popery. . . . [By Sir Roger L'Estrange.] Fol. Pp. 12. [*Brit. Mus.*]   London, 1679
> With reference to "An account of the growth of popery " [by Andrew Marvell], *q.v.* For an earlier edition, see "An account of the growth of knavery. . . ."

PARAPHRASTICALL (a) explication of the prophecie of Habakkuk. [By Dr Stokes.] 4to. [*Lincoln's Inn Lib.*]
Oxford, 1646

PARCEL (a) for heaven, and other stories. . . . By Jean Nesmy [Henry Surchamp]. . . . Translated by E. M. Walker. 8vo. Pp. 120. [*Brit. Mus.*]
London [1917]

PARIS by day and night, a book for the exhibition. By Anglo-Parisian [Walter Francis Lonergan]. 8vo. Pp. 256. [*Brit. Mus.*]   London, 1889

PARIS (the) Estafette ; or, pilferings from the Paris and Dover post-bag. . . . Embellished with portraits and woodcuts. [By F. Lloyd?] 12mo. Pp. xii. 430. [*Brit. Mus.*] London [1842]
> Dedication signed : F. L.

PARISH churches turned into conventicles, by serving God therein. . . . By Rich. Hart. 4to.   London, 1683
> In an answer published later in the same year this is alleged to have been " pretended to be written by Rich. Hart ; but really penn'd by Mr T. A., barrister-at-law. . . . By O. U." T. A. is unknown.

PARLIAMENT (the) arraigned, convicted ; wants nothing but execution. . . . By Tom Tyranno-Mastix ; *alias* Mercurius Melancholicus [Marchamont Nedham ?] . . . 8vo. Pp. 24. [*Brit. Mus.*]   [London ?] 1648

PARLIAMENTS (the) reformation ; or, a worke for presbyters, elders and deacons. . . . By S. H. [Samuel Hartlib], a friend of the Commonwealth. 4to. Pp. 6. [*Brit. Mus.*]
London, 1646

PARLOUR (the) menagerie ; wherein are exhibited the habits, the resources and the mysterious instincts of the . . . animal creation. . . . [Edited by J. H. *i.e.* John Hogg.] 8vo. [*Brit. Mus.*]
London, 1875
> Second edition, 1878.

PARNASSUS aboriens : or, some sparkes of poesie. By R. W. Philomus [Richard Walden]. 8vo. Pp. 30. [*Brit. Mus.*]
London, 1664

PARSON'S (the) daughter ; a tale : for the use of pretty girls with small fortunes. [By Christopher Wyvill.] To which are added Epigrams, and the Court Ballad, by Mr Pope. 8vo. [R. Straus' *The Unspeakable Curll,* p. 264.]   London, 1717
> Signed : C. W.

*PARTHENIA sacra . . .
> For Parthenia, *read* Partheneia.

PARTICULAR (a) account of the last siege of Mastricht. [By William Carr.] [*Brit. Mus.*]   London, 1676
> Signed : W. C.
> There was an earlier edition in the same year : " A particular account of the present siege . . .", *q.v.*

PARTNERSHIP law. [By Edward Westby Nunn.] Second edition. . . . 8vo. Pp. 156. [*Brit. Mus.*]
London [1930]

PASQUIL'S mistresse ; or, the worthie and unworthie woman. [By Nicholas Breton.] 4to. [*Christie-Miller Cat.*]
1600

*PASSAGES from the autobiography of a " Man of Kent " . . .
> Reginald Fitz-Roy Stanley is also a pseudonym, and = John Collyer Knight. [*Brit. Mus.*]

PASSING (the) of Guto, and other poems. By Huw Menai [Huw Menai Williams]. 8vo. Pp. 99. [*Brit. Mus.*]
London, 1929

PAST feeling. By the author of *The lamplighter* [Francis Bourdillon]. 12mo. [*Brit. Mus.*] London [1860]
> Signed : F. B.

PASTOR Sang ; being the Norwegian drama Over Aevne by Björnstjerne Björnson. Translated . . . by William Wilson [More Adey]. 8vo. [Pettersen's *Norsk Lexikon,* col. 417.]
London, 1893

PASTORAL counsels. . . . By the Rev. John Robertson. . . . Third edition. [With a preface signed A. K. H. B. *i.e.* Andrew K. H. Boyd.] 8vo. Pp. xxxiii. 327. [*Brit. Mus.*]
London, 1867

PASTORAL (a) poem, sacred to the memory of . . . Lord Basil Hamiltoun. By A. P. [Alexander Pennecuik]. 4to. Pp. 8. [*Brit. Mus.*] Edinburgh, 1701

PASTORALS (the) and other workes of William Basse. [Introduction signed : J. P. C. *i.e.* John Payne Collier.] 4to. Pp. iv. 130. [*Brit. Mus.*]
London [1870]

PASTOR'S (the) daughter ; a memoir of Susan Amelia W. . . . written by her father. With an introduction by the author of *The anxious inquirer* [John Angell James]. 32mo. [*Brit. Mus.*]
London [1844]
Introduction signed : J. A. J.

PATCH (the) ; an heroi-comical poem. [By Francis Hauksbee.] 8vo. [R. Straus' *The Unspeakable Curll*, p. 273.]
London, 1723

*PATHWAY (the) to knowledge. . . .
W. B. in the text is a mistake repeated from Watt's *Bibl. Brit.* and gave rise to the error that the translation was by William Barley who was in fact only the printer. The correct text is "by W. P." and the British Museum gives this as William Peters, *Mathematician* ? or William Phillip ? Pollard and Redgrave, *S.T.C.*, say that the Dutch text was by Nicholaus Peters and the English translation by William Philipp.

PATIE and Roger ; a pastoral inscribed to Josiah Burchet, Esq., Secretary to the Admiralty. [By Allan Ramsay.] 8vo. Pp. 12. [A. Gibson's *Allan Ramsay*, p. 131.] [Edinburgh, 1720]
The last stanza of the Inscription in verse on pp. 1-3 ends : "Devoted Allan." This pastoral subsequently formed the first scene of *The Gentle Shepherd*.

PATIENCE. By Perseverance [William Henry Cremer]. 8vo. Pp. 28. [F. Jessell's *Bibl. of playing cards*, p. 58.]
London, 1860

PATRIARCHAL longevity reattainable. By Parallax [Samuel Birley Rowbotham]. Part I. 8vo. [*Brit. Mus.*]
London, 1883
See also " Zetetic philosophy."

PATRICIA Brent, spinster. By the author of ? [Herbert George Jenkins]. 8vo. Pp. vii. 312. [*Brit. Mus.*]
London, 1918

PATRICIA Pendragon. By E. Ward [Evelyn Everett-Green]. 8vo Pp. 311. [*Brit. Mus.*]
London, 1911

PATRICK, undergraduate. [A novel.] By Anthony Armstrong [George Anthony Armstrong Willis]. 8vo. Pp. 224. [*Brit. Mus.*] London, 1926

PATRIOT (the) ; an epistle to . . . Philip Earl of Chesterfield. . . . By H. Stanhope [William Bond?]. 8vo. Pp. 8. [R. Straus' *The Unspeakable Curll*, p. 133.] London, 1733

PATRIOT (the) chief : a tragedy. By a Native of Algiers [Peter Markoe]. [Flitcroft's *Outline Studies in Amer. Lit.* p. 29.] 1784

PATRIOTISM ; an essay towards a constructive theory of politics. By Hakluyt Egerton [Arthur Boutwood]. 8vo. Pp. viii. 343. [*Brit. Mus.*]
London, 1905

PAUL and Virginia ; a musical drama. [By James Cobb.] 12mo. Pp. 36. [*Brit. Mus.*] Dublin, 1817
An earlier edition (Dublin, 1801) bears the author's name.

PAUL & Virginia and The Indian cottage. [Translated from the French of J. H. B. de Saint-Pierre.] 24mo. Pp. 200. [*Brit. Mus.*] London, 1837

PAUL, the Jew. [A novel.] By the author of *By an unknown disciple* [Cecily Phillimore]. 8vo. Pp. 271. [*Brit. Mus.*] London, 1927

PAULINE (the) doctrine of the righteousness of faith, in reply to an article in "The British and Foreign Evangelical Review." [By John Nelson Darby.] 12mo. [*Brit. Mus.*] London [1862]
Signed : J. N. D.

*PAUSANIAS and Aurora . . .
For Hon. Mrs Stanley, *read* Hon. Mrs Eliza Stanley.

PAX animæ ; a short treatise declaring how necessary the tranquillity . . . of the soul . . . is. [Here attributed to Saint Peter of Alcantara, but really by Joannes de Bonilla.] From an old English translation [by T. W.] of 1665. . . . 32mo. Pp. 85. [*Brit. Mus.*] London [1876]

PEACE and Dunkirk ; being an excellent new song upon the surrender of Dunkirk to General Hill. [By Jonathan Swift.] Fol. S. sh. [*Brit. Mus.*]
London, 1712

PEACE be with you. [By William Tarbet.] 12mo. Pp. 4. [*Brit. Mus.*]
[1870 ?]

PEACE in Europe. By Augur [V. Poliakoff]. 12mo. Pp. 96. [*Publishers' Weekly*, 28th January 1928.]
New York, 1928

PEACH blossom. By Hugo Wast [G. Martinez Zuviria]. Translated . . . by Herman and Miriam Hespelt. 8vo. Pp. 300. [*Brit. Mus.*] New York, 1929

PEACE ode written on the conclusion of the Three Years' War. By R. B. [Robert Bridges]. . . . 4to. [*Brit. Mus.*] [Oxford] 1902

PEARLS cast before swine, by Edmund Burke. Scraped together by Old Hubert [—— Parkinson]. 8vo. Pp. 8. [*Brit. Mus.*] London [1793 ?]

PEBBLES on the shore. Alpha of the plough [Alfred George Gardiner]. 8vo. Pp. 254. [*Brit. Mus.*] London [1916]

PEDIGREE of Goddard of Swindon, Clive-Pipard and Purton. [By Sir Thomas Phillipps.] Fol. [*Brit. Mus.*] [1830?]

PEEP (a) into Alfred Crowquill's [A. H. Forrester's] folio. 8vo. [*Eng. Cat.*, 1801-1836, p. 146.] London, 1833

*PEEP (a) into the principal seats and gardens in and about Twickenham. . . .

Not by Lady Pembroke and not strictly anonymous, since on A 4 verso there occurs ten lines of verse headed "Lines by Dr Campbell on reading the following journal written by Mrs Hampden Pye" [J. Henrietta Pye]. There were two previous editions: 1760, "A short account of the principal seats . . . " completely anonymous, and 1767, "A short view of the principal seats . . . " which on A 4 recto contains some verses headed "To Mrs Pye, on her account of Twickenham."

PEEPER (the); being a sequel to *The Curious Maid.* [By Matthew Prior.] [*Brit. Mus.*] London, 1721

PEER (the) and the paper girl. By Edward Percy [Edward Percy Smith]. 8vo. Pp. 16. [*Brit. Mus.*] London [1924]

*PEGASUS. . . .
The second part is signed: Basilius Philomus. [*Brit. Mus.*]

PEGGIE gets the sack. [A novel.] By Paul Gwynne [Ernest Slater]. 8vo. Pp. 284. [*Brit. Mus.*] London [1926]

PEGGY; a love romance. By Seamark [Austin J. Small]. 8vo. Pp. 320. [*Brit. Mus.*] London [1925]

PEGGY makes good. By Elsie Jeanette Oxenham [Elsie Jeanette Dunkerley]. 8vo. Pp. 160. [*Brit. Mus.*] London [1927]

PENCHANT; a game of cards for two players. By Jack Smarte [John Smith M'Tear]. 8vo. Pp. 111. [*Brit. Mus.*] London, 1893

PENMARK Abbey; a nautical melodrama in three acts. By W. M. Thackeray [or rather, by Thomas James Thackeray and Pierre Tournemine]. Translated from the original French by H. L. Williams. . . . 12mo. [*Brit. Mus.*] [1884]

PENNY packet. [Tracts on phonetic spelling by A. J. E. *i.e.* Alexander John Ellis.] 16mo. 6 parts. [*Brit. Mus.*] Bath [1849]

PENNY reprints. [Edited by A. H. H. *i.e.* Alsager Hay Hill.] 8vo. No. 1. [*Brit. Mus.*] London, 1872

*PENTAMERON (the) and Pentalogia.
The preface to the former is signed: D. Grige, and the dedication to the latter is signed: W. S. L.

VOL. VI.

PEPPER. [A novel.] By Holworthy Hall [Harold Everett Porter]. 8vo. Pp. 316. [*Brit. Mus.*] New York, 1915

PERCIVAL and I. By Anthony Armstrong [George Anthony Armstrong Willis]. 8vo. Pp. viii. 152. [*Brit. Mus.*] London, 1927

PERFECT (a) little fool; a comedietta in one act. By Edward Percy [Edward Percy Smith]. 8vo. Pp. 22. [*Brit. Mus.*] London [1930]

PERFVMING of tabacco, and the great abvse committed in it; with many other auncient and moderne perfumings; and the exposition of the chapter of the true odoriferous cane of Dioscorides. Taken out of the new Historie or illustration of plants, written by Matth. de l'Obel, Botanographer of the King his most excellent maiesty. Translated out of Latin by I. N. G. [John Nasmith?] 1610. [*Jerome E. Brooks.*] London, 1611

*PERIPATETIC (the) philosopher. By Q.
Not by Quiller-Couch, who was six years old when this was published. This earlier Q is unknown.

PERMANENCY (the) of the Apostolic Office, as distinct from that of Bishops, with reasons for believing that it is now revived in the Church. By a presbyter of the Protestant Episcopal Church [John Sidney Davenport]. 8vo. Pp. 61. [*Brit. Mus.*] 1853

PERMANENT (the) settlement imperelled; or, Act X. of 1859 in its true colours, by a lover of Justice [John Cochrane]. 8vo. [*Lincoln's Inn Lib.*] Calcutta, 1865

PERPETUAL calendar of Cornish saints, with selections of poetry and prose relating to Cornwall. By Sarah L. Enys [Nellie Sloggett]. 16mo. [*Brit. Mus.*] Truro, 1923

PERSIAN Poppy; a one-act play for one woman. By Gilbert Emery [Emery Bernsley Pottle]. 8vo. [*Amer. Cat.*] New York, 1926

PERSONATION . . . a comic interlude. . . . By Mrs Charles Kemble . . . with remarks . . . by D. G. [George Daniel]. 12mo. Pp. 19. [*Brit. Mus.*] London [1835]

PERSPECTIVE (the); or, Callista dissected: to which are prefixed a lock and key to the late opera of Callista. [A poem, by Peter Chamberlen?] 4to. [*Brit. Mus.*] London, 1731

*PERSWASIVE (a) to peace . . .
Not by William Allen, D.D., but William Allen, tradesman of London. See his *Works*, 1707.

2 D

PERTINENT & impertinent; an assortment of verse. [By the author of *Nisi Dominus, i.e.* Hilary D. C. Pepler.] 8vo. Pp. 69. [*Brit. Mus.*]
Ditchling, 1926

PESSIMIST (the); a confession. [A novel.] By A. Newman [Herbert Moore Pim]. 8vo. Pp. 312. [*Brit. Mus.*]   London, 1914

PETER Palette's [Thomas Onwhyn's] tales and pictures, in short words, for young folk. 4to. 2 parts. [*Brit. Mus.*]   London [1856]

PETER Parley's [William Tegg's] tales about Christmas. 12mo. [*Allibone's Dict.*]   London, 1839

PETER Parley's [Samuel Griswold Goodrich's] tales about Great Britain and Ireland. 12mo. [*Brit. Mus.*]
London, 1834

PETER'S repentance . . . a sermon. . . . By a godly pastor [John Hart, D.D.]. 12mo. [*Brit. Mus.*]   1776

A reprint. The contemporary editions were published as "A godly sermon of Peter's repentance . . ." *q.v.*

*PETTICOAT (the); an heroi-comical poem . . .

Not by John Durant de Breval, but by his predecessor in this pseudonym Francis Chute. This is one of Edmund Curll the publisher's scandalous impostures on the public. The title-page bears the words "By Mr Gay." The preface is signed Joseph Gay, but many copies were bought under the impression that it was by the author of the much discussed *Trivia* which had appeared at the beginning of this year. This and its second edition "The Hoop-Petticoat" were Chute's only works under this pseudonym. Curll's subsequent productions under the name of Gay or Joseph Gay were written for him by John Durant de Breval. See R. Straus' *The Unspeakable Curll*, p. 78 *et seq.*, p. 133.

PEVERIL of the Peak; a melo-dramatic play, founded on the celebrated romance of the same name, by the author of *Waverley* . . . performed at the Theatre-Royal, Edinburgh. [By Isaac Pocock.] 12mo. Pp. 55. [*D. N. B.* vol. 46, p. 4.]   [Edinburgh, 1823]

PHIL and the farm; a story of the Orkneys. By H. C. [H. Campbell]. 8vo. Pp. 77. [*Brit. Mus.*]
Edinburgh, 1920

PHILARGYRIE of great Britayne. [In verse.] 8vo. B. L. London, 1551

Robert Crowley, whose name occurs in the colophon as the printer of this fable, is now held to have been the author as well. [*T. L. S.*, 3rd December 1931.]

PHILIP Quarll. (The adventures of Philip Quarll.) [A chapbook, abridged from *The Hermit,* by Peter Longueville.] 12mo. Pp. 8. [*Brit. Mus.*]
1840

See also "The adventures of Philip Quarll . . .", "The English Hermit," "The Hermit," and "The surprising adventures of Philip Quarll."

PHILOLOGICAL (the) museum. Edited by J. C. H. [Julius Charles Hare]. 8vo. [*Brit. Mus.*]   Cambridge, 1832

PHILOPATRIA'S remarks, I. On the dear times and decay of trade. II. On the courts of justice. III. On the revenues of the clergy. [By J. C. Bie.] Translated from the original. 8vo. [Pettersen's *Norsk Lexikon.*]
St Croix, 1771

*PHILOSOPHICAL (a) dialogue concerning decency. . . .

The author of the Dissertation on barley wine ('Οινος κριθινος) is now known to be Benjamin Buckler. See the note to 'Οινος κριθινος in the Supplement.

PHILOSOPHICAL (a) endeavour towards the defence of the being of witches and apparitions; in a letter to . . . R. Hunt, Esq. By a member of the Royal Society [James Glanvil]. 4to. [*Brit. Mus.*]   London, 1666

Signed: J. G. The title of another edition begins: "Some philosophical considerations . . ."

PHILOSOPHY (the) of healthe. . . . By T. Southwood Smith. [Edited by G. H. *i.e.* Miss Georgiana Hill.] Eleventh edition. 8vo. Pp. xiii. 395. [*Brit. Mus.*]   London, 1865

PHILOSOPHY (the) of history and other essays. By the author of *Prisoners of the Lord* [R. F. Norman]. 8vo. Pp. 29. [*Brit. Mus.*]
Cardiff, 1925

Reissued in 1928 as part of *Word Pictures,* which bears the author's name.

PHILOTHEA; or, an introduction to a devout life. By St Francis de Sales; newly translated . . . by R. C. [Richard Challoner?]. 12mo. Pp. 311. [*Brit. Mus.*]   London, 1770

PHYLLIS in Bohemia. . . . By L. H. Bickford and Richard Stillman Powell [Ralph Henry Barbour]. 8vo. Pp. 233. [*Amer. Cat.*]   London, 1897

PHYRNE; a drama, in four acts . . . (originally published in the Italian language). By Democritus, Castelvecchio [*i.e.* translated by Democritus, *pseud. for* Frederick Allan Laidlaw, from the Italian of Riccardo Castelvecchio, *pseud. for* Count Giulio Cesare B. L. Pullè]. 8vo. Pp. 78. [*Brit. Mus.*]   London, 1900

PHYSICK is a jest, a whim, an humour, a fancy, a mere fashion, even full as much as dress or dancing : to which is added, A discourse or letter on the degree of doctor in this profession. [By Dennis de Coetlogon.] 8vo. [*Lincoln's Inn Lib.*]   London, 1739

PICCADILLY (the) murder. By Anthony Berkeley [Anthony Berkeley Cox]. 8vo. Pp. 287. [*Brit. Mus.*]
                                 London [1929]

PIERCE Penilesse his supplication to the Diuell . . . By Tho. Nash. [The introduction signed : J. P. C. *i.e.* John Payne Collier.] 4to. Pp. 101. [*Brit. Mus.*]   [London, 1870]

PIERCES supererogation ; or, a new prayse of the old asse . . . [By] Gabriel Harvey. [The introduction signed : J. P. C. *i.e.* John Payne Collier.] 4to. Pp. ii. 237. [*Brit. Mus.*]   [London, 1870]

PIETATIS in parentes disquisitio ; or, the duty of children towards their parents : truly examined and stated. [By John Brydall.] 4to. [*Lincoln's Inn Lib.*]   London, 1700

*PIL (a) for pork-eaters. . . .
    The *Brit. Mus.* attributes this to Alexander Pennecuik.

PILGRIM'S (the) progress ; with notes by a Bachelor of Arts of . . . Oxford [John Bradford]. 8vo.   London, 1792
    Preface signed : I. B.

PINDARIC (a) epistle addressed to Lord Buckhorse. . . . A new edition. By C. A., Esq. [Christopher Anstey]. 4to. Pp. 67. [*Brit. Mus.*]
                                 London, 1779

PINDARIQUE (a) ode, describing the excellency of true virtue ; with reflexions on the Satyr against virtue. [By John Oldham.] 4to. Pp. 6. [*Brit. Mus.*]   London, 1679

PIP, Squeak and Wilfred ; their luvly adventures. By Uncle Dick [Bertram John Lamb]. 8vo. Pp. 62. [*Amer. Cat.*]   New York, 1921

PIPES (the) of Pan. [A novel.] By Julia Tregenna [F. Britten Austin]. 8vo. Pp. 296. [*Ashley Library*, vol. 9.]
                                 London [1926]

'PISCOPADE (the) ; a panegyri-satiri-serio-comical poem. By Porcupinus Pelagius [Macnamara Morgan]. 4to. [*D. N. B.* vol. 39, p. 23.]
                                 London, 1748

PISO'S conspiracy ; a tragedy. [Altered from Nathaniel Lee's *Nero*.] 4to. [*Brit. Mus.*]   London, 1676

PLACE (the) and state of the departed. [By Jasper Peck.] 8vo. Pp. 8. [*Brit. Mus.*]   N.P. [1880 ?]
    Signed : J. P.

PLACE (the) of the damn'd.   By J. S. D. D., D.S.P.D. [Jonathan Swift, Dean of St Patrick's, Dublin. In verse]. Fol. S. sh. [*Brit. Mus.*]
                                 [Dublin] 1731

*PLAIN (a) defence of the Protestant religion . . .
    See the note to " The Missionaries arts discovered. . . ." in this supplement.

PLAIN (a) guide to peace with God ; for the use of members of the Church of England who have little leisure time. By the author of *First steps to faith and piety* [J. F. Laing]. 16mo. Pp. 29. [*Brit. Mus.*]   London, 1876
    Signed : J. F. L.

PLAIN (the) man's reply to the Catholick missionaries. [By William Assheton.] 24mo. Pp. 35. [*Brit. Mus.*]
                                 London, 1686

PLAIN sailing ; a novel. By a gentleman with a duster [Harold Begbie]. 8vo. Pp. 285. [*Brit. Mus.*]
                                 London, 1929

*PLAIN truth . . .   By Candidus [Charles Inglis].
    This entry should be deleted. It is the same book as the following entry and the author was undoubtedly Dr William Smith, of Philadelphia.

PLAIN truths about the soul and salvation. By the author of *The lamplighter* [Francis Bourdillon]. 12mo. [*Brit. Mus.*]   London [1860]
    Signed : F. B.

PLAIN words about our Lord's life ; or, how to follow Christ. By the author of *How to come to Christ*. Edited by a parish priest [Hon. Charles Leslie Courtenay]. 8vo. [*Brit. Mus.*]
                                 London, 1875

PLAINE (a) description of the Bermudas, now called sommer ilands, with the manner of their discouerie anno 1609. [By Silvester Jourdan.] . . .   4to. B. L. [*Brit. Mus.*]   London, 1613
    No pagination. The first part is a reprint of S. Jourdan's "A discovery of the Bermudas. . . ." 1610.

PLAINE (a) pathway to heaven ; meditations upon the ghospells. . . . By T. Buckland [Edmund Thomas Hill]. 12mo. [*Pollard and Redgrave*.]
                                 [St Omer] 1637

PLANE tales from the skies. By "Wing Adjutant" [Wilfred Theodore Blake]. 8vo. Pp. 123. [*Brit. Mus.*]   1918
    Signed : W. T. B.

*PLANTAGANET'S tragicall story. . . . By T. W. Gent.
    T. W. is Thomas Wincoll, not Weaver [see *D. N. B.*] nor Whichcot which is a confusion for Wincoll, see *Stationers Register* i. 318.

PLEA (a) for church schools. By Hakluyt Egerton [Arthur Boutwood]. 8vo. Pp. 45. [*Brit. Mus.*]
London, 1906

PLEA (a) for the pardoning part of the sovereignty of the Kings of England. [By Fabian Phillipps.] 4to. [*Lincoln's Inn Lib.*] London, 1682

PLEA (a) for the reall-presence; wherein the preface of Syr Humfrey Linde, concerning the booke of Bertram, is examined and censured. Written by I. O. [John Floyd]. . . . 8vo. Pp. 62. [*Brit. Mus.*] [St Omer] 1624

*PLEASANT (a) comedie of Faire Em . . .
Mr W. W. Greg considers that there is some plausibility in Fleay's ascription of Fair Em to Robert Wilson, and that no other attribution is worth consideration. [*Fair Em*, ed. W. W. Greg, pp. viii., ix.]

PLEASANT (a) description of the Fortunate Ilandes, called the Ilands of Canaria. . . . Composed by the poore Pilgrime [Thomas Nicols]. 8vo. B. L. [*Brit. Mus.*] London, 1583

PLEASANT (a) disport of divers noble personages; written in Italian by M. J. Bocace . . . in his book which is entitled Philocopo and nowe Englished by H. G. [H. Granthum]. 4to. Pp. 58. B. L. [*Pollard and Redgrave.*] [London, 1566?]
For another edition see "Thirteene most pleasaunt . . ."

PLEASANT (the) land despised. Numbers xiii. xiv. By J. N. D. [John Nelson Darby]. 16mo. Pp. 16. [*Brit. Mus.*] London [1880]

PLEASANT (a) new dialogue; or, the discourse between the serving-man and the husband-man. . . . [A ballad, by Richard Climsell?] Fol. S. sh. B. L. [*Brit. Mus.*] London [*c.* 1635]
Signed: R. C.

PLOTS (the) of Jesuites (viz. of R. Parsons . . . A. Coutzen . . . T. Campanella): how to bring England to the Romane Religion without tumult. Translated out of the original copies. [Compiled by Michael Spark? who published it.] 4to. Pp. 12. [*Brit. Mus.*] London, 1653

*PLOTTERS (the) doom . . .
This cannot have been by Samuel Palmer, who did not join the Church of England, until 25 or 30 years later. There is a copy with an MS. note in a contemporary hand, "By Mr Conyers of Peterhouse" and Tobias Conyers may be supposed to have been the author. See *M'Alpin Coll. Cat.* and Gerould's *Sources of Eng. Hist.*

PLOUGHMAN'S (the) tale; shewing by the doctrine and lives of the Romish clergie that the Pope is Antichrist. [By Thomas Brampton?] 4to. [*Pollard and Redgrave.*] London, 1606

POCKET (the) Birkenhead: being selections . . . edited, with an introduction, by Ephesian [Carl Eric Bechhofer Roberts]. 8vo. [*Brit. Mus.*] London, 1927

POEM (a) in honour of the birthday of . . . King George. . . . [By Henry Nevil.] Fol. [*Brit. Mus.*]
London, 1720

POEM (a) in praise of tea. [By Pierre Antoine Motteux.] Fol. [*Brit. Mus.*] [London, 1712?]
An edition entitled "A poem upon tea" (London, 1712) bears the author's name.

POEM (a) in the honour of the antient and loyal Society of the Journey-Men-Taylors. . . . Written by H. N., Brick-layer, one of the brethren [H. Nelson]. Fol. S. sh. [*Brit. Mus.*]
Dublin [1726]
See also "A new poem on the . . . Society . . ."

POEM on a tour to North Cape. By A. L. T. [a lady tourist *i.e.* Lavinia King]. 8vo. [Pettersen's *Norsk Lexikon*, p. 427.] Dublin, 1885

POEM (a) on birth. By S. E. B. [Sir Samuel Egerton Brydges]. 8vo. [*Brit. Mus.*] [Geneva, 1831?]

POEM (a) on the anniversary of His Majesty's birthday. . . . [By Henry Nevil.] Fol. [*Brit. Mus.*]
London, 1718

POEM (a) on the birthday of . . . King George. . . . [By Henry Nevil.] Fol. [*Brit. Mus.*] London, 1717

POEM (a) to the memory of the famous Archibald Pitcairn, M.D. By a member of the Easy Club in Edinburgh [Allan Ramsay]. 4to. [A. Gibson's *Allan Ramsay*, p. 99.]
[Edinburgh, 1713]
Dedication signed: Gawin Douglass.

POEMS. By a Gallowa' Lass [Miss Madge Black]. Pp. 22. 8vo. [*Brit. Mus.*] Dumfries, 1928

POEMS. By George Forester [Sir Granville George Greenwood]. 8vo. Pp. 47. [*Brit. Mus.*] London, 1912

POEMS. By J. S. [James Stirling]. 12mo. Pp. 92. Newcastle, 1829
From an inscribed copy.

POEMS. By K. H. D. [K. H. D. Cecil]. 8vo. Pp. xv. 270. [*Brit. Mus.*]
London, 1902

POEMS. By W. H. [William Hammond]. 8vo. [*Brit. Mus.*]
London, 1655

POEMS and sonnets of Percy Bysshe Shelley. Edited by Charles Alfred Seymour [Thomas James Wise and Edward Dowden]. 4to. Pp. 74. [*Ashley Library.*]
Philadelphia, private print, 1887

POEMS from the English Bijou Alma-
nack . . . by L. E. L. [Letitia Elizabeth
Landon]. . . . 4to. [*Brit. Mus.*]
　　　　　　　　London, 1835, *et seq.*
POEMS, fugitive pieces and hymns. By
F. W. [F. Woodhouse]. 12mo. Pp.
126. [*Brit. Mus.*]
　　　　　　　　N.P. private print, 1884
POEMS, occasioned by several circum-
stances and occurrences in the present
grand contest of America for liberty.
[By Rev. Wheeler Case.] 8vo.
Pp. 41. [Sabin's *Dictionary*.]
　　　　　　　　New Haven, 1778
　　Republished with his name in *Revolu-
tionary memories* (1852).
POEMS on several occasions. [By
Thomas Gibbons, D.D.] 8vo. Pp. iv.
36. [Watt's *Bibl. Brit.*] London, 1743
POEMS on several occasions. By a
lady [Mrs —— Letches?]. 4to. [*Brit.
Mus.*]　　　　　　　Bristol, 1792
POETICAL miscellanies consisting of
original poems and translations. By
the best hands. Publish'd by Mr Steele.
[Contains anonymous poems by George
Jeffreys and others.] 8vo. Pp. 318.
[I. O. Williams in *Bibl. Soc. Trans.*
Dec. 1929.]　　　　　London, 1714
POETICAL (the) works of James Ham-
mond and Lord Hervey, with bio-
graphical sketches of the authors
[signed G. D. *i.e.* George Dyer?]. 12mo.
[*Brit. Mus.*]　　　　　London, 1818
POETICAL (the) works of John Milton
. . with . . . notes on each book of the
Paradise Lost [by P. H. *i.e.* Patrick
Hume]. Fol. 5 parts. [*Brit. Mus.*]
　　　　　　　　London, 1695
POETICAL (the) works of Robert Burns.
. . . To which is prefixed a sketch of
his life [signed : A. C. *i.e.* Archibald
Constable]. 8vo. [*Brit. Mus.*]
　　　　　　　　Edinburgh, 1823
POETICAL (the) works of the author of
the *Heroick epistle to Sir William
Chambers* [Rev. William Mason].
8vo. Pp. vi. 127. [*Brit. Mus.*]
　　　　　　　　London, 1805
POETRY (the) and prose of J. H. M.
[J. H. Merridew]. 12mo. [*Brit. Mus.*]
　　　　　　　　Private print, 1841
POETS' (the) birthday book ; being brief
biographies . . . of the popular poets of
the period. Edited by Clarence Sinclair
[Charles Frederick Forsham]. 16mo.
Pp. 413. [*Brit. Mus.*] London, 1907
POKER. By A. B. Lougher [Charles
Frederick Pardon]. Edited by Rawdon
Crawley, Bart., of Queen's Crawley,
Hants. 32mo. Pp. 28. [Jessel's *Bibl.
of playing cards*.]　　　London, 1889
　　Rawdon Crawley, Bart., of Queen's
Crawley, Hants, is also a *pseud.* used by
C. F. Pardon. See "Cribbage."

POKER ; how to play it : a sketch of the
great American game, with its laws
and rules and some of its amusing
incidents. By one of its victims
[Charles Welsh]. 8vo. Pp. 109.
[F. Jessel's *Bibl. of playing cards*,
p. 290.]　　　　　　London, 1882
POKER ; its laws and practice. By
Cyper Redalf [Alfred Percy]. 8vo.
Pp. iv. 43. [F. Jessel's *Bibl. of playing
cards*, p. 228.]　　　Allahabad, 1879
POLICIE unueiled ; wherein may be
learned the order of true policie in
kingdomes and common-wealths. . . .
Written in Spanish [by Juan de Santa
Maria]. . . . Translated into English
by J. M. [James Mabbe]. 4to. Pp.
481. [*Brit. Mus.*]　　London, 1632
　　The Epistle Dedicatorie is signed by the
author.
　　The title of another issue begins "Christian
policie . . ."
POLITICAL poems. [By Nicholas
Amherst.] 8vo. [R. Straus' *The Unspeakable Curll*, p. 256.] London, 1719
　　A made-up volume by Curll of such of
Amherst's pieces as he had previously
printed.
POLITICK (the) maid ; or, a dainty new
ditty, both pleasant and witty. . . . [By
Richard Climsell?] Fol. S. sh. B. L.
[*Brit. Mus.*]　　London [*c.* 1640]
　　Signed : R. C.
P O L I T I C S for American farmers ;
being a series of tracts exhibiting the
blessings of free government, as it is
administered in the United States,
compared with the boasted stupendous
fabric of British Monarchy. . . . [By
William Duane.] 8vo. Pp. 96. [*Brit.
Mus.*]　　　　Washington City, 1807
POMANDER (the) of prayer. [By
Thomas Becon.] Wherein is contained
many godly prayers. . . . (The XV.
Ooes. The Letanie.) 8vo. B. L.
[*Brit. Mus.*]　　　[London] 1558
POMPS and vanities. By a Gentleman
with a duster [Harold Begbie]. 8vo.
Pp. 153. [*Brit. Mus.*] London, 1927
POOL (the) of Shcrc and other poems.
By Stephen Reid Heyman [Lydia
Dorothy Parsons]. 16mo. Pp. vii.
76. [*Brit. Mus.*]　　　London, 1918
POOR Emma. By Evelyn Tempest
[Edward W. D. Cuming]. 8vo. Pp.
xii. 340. [*Brit. Mus.*] London [1911]
POOR (the) gentleman. [A novel.] By
Ian Hay [John Hay Beith]. 8vo.
Pp. 312. [*Brit. Mus.*] London [1928]
POPE Alexander's supremacy and in-
fallibility examin'd. . . . [An attack
on the Dunciad. By George Duckett
and John Dennis.] 4to. [*Brit. Mus.*]
　　　　　　　　London, 1729

POPE (the) in his fury doth answer returne to a lettei ye which to Rome is late come. . . . [A ballad. By Stephen Peele.] Fol. S. sh. [*Brit. Mus.*]   London, 1570
Signed : S. P.

POPERY and hypocrisy detected and opened from the Holy Scriptures . . . in a sermon upon the occasion of a general fast, kept Decemb. 22, 1680. By the author of *The Plotter's Doom*, a true son of the Church of England [Tobias Conyers].   London, 1680
There is a copy of *The Plotter's Doom* with an MS. note in a contemporary hand, " By Mr Conyers of Peterhouse." See *M'Alpin Coll. Cat.* and Gerould's *Sources of Eng. Hist.*

POPES (the) canons. (By Theodore Beza.) Translated by T. S. G. [T. Stocker, Gent.]. 8vo. [*Pollard and Redgrave.*]   London, 1584

POPISH (the) damnable plot . . . laid open . . . in the breviats of threescore and four letters . . . past between the Pope, Duke of York, Cardinal Norfolk, Cardinal Cibo. . . . [By Ezerel Tonge.] Fol. Pp. 31. [*Brit. Mus.*]
London, 1680

POPULAR lectures on commercial law. By George Sharswood. [Edited by S. W. C. *i.e.* S. W. Crittenden.] 8vo. [*Brit. Mus.*]   1856

POPULAR rhymes, proverbs, sayings, etc., peculiar to the Isle of Man and the Manx people. [By Michael Aislabie Denham.] 12mo. [*Brit. Mus.*]
[Durham, 1850]
Signed : M. A. D.

POPULAR stories and legends. In two series. By Leo Tolstoy. (Translated by N - - - [*i.e.* —— Kosnakova], A. C. Fifield and Aylmer Maude.) 8vo. Pp. 158. [*Brit. Mus.*]
London [1921]

PORT Royal and its harbour. . . . [By] M. M.—R. P. K. [R. P. Kitson ?]—St L. M.—F. Mc. I. R. 8vo. Pp. 56.
[Port Royal] 1893

PORTRAITS of the New Century—the first ten years. By E. T. Raymond [Edward Raymond Thompson]. 8vo. Pp. 336. [*Brit. Mus.*]   London, 1928

PORTRAITS of the Nineties. . . . By E. T. Raymond [Edward Raymond Thompson]. 8vo. Pp. 319. [*Brit. Mus.*]   London, 1921

*PORTRAITURES of persons in public and private life . . .
This was by Richard Dearman. See *Barnsley Chronicle*, 25th March 1882.

*POST-CAPTAIN (the) ; or, the wooden walls well manned . . .
This is by John Davis, of Salisbury. See *Athenæum*, 9th December 1843, and R. H. Case's edition (1928). The 4th edition was issued as by the author of " Edward " and " A view of Society in France." These works were by John Moore, M.D. Hence the attribution to Moore. This was presumably deliberate dishonesty on the part of the author.

POSTHUMOUS works of the Rev. Thomas Adam, Rector of Wintringham. . . . To which is prefixed . . . a sketch of his life and character [signed : J. S. *i.e.* James Stillingfleet]. 8vo. 3 vols. [*Brit. Mus.*]   York, 1786

POSTSCRIPT (a) [signed: J. M., D.D. *i.e.* John Milner, Bishop of Castabala] to the second edition of the Address to the . . . Bishop of St David's [T. Burgess] occasioned by his Lordship's " One word to . . . Dr Milner." 8vo. [*Brit. Mus.*]   London, 1819
See also, " The end of religious controversy . . ."

POSTSCRIPTS. [Papers written for The Post, Houston.] By O. Henry [William Sydney Porter]. . . . 8vo. Pp. xix. 202. [*Amer. Cat.*]
New York, 1923

PRACTICAL directions for the construction and fixing of sun-dials. By W. R. [John Wigham Richardson]. 8vo. [*Brit. Mus.*]   London, 1889

*PRACTICAL (a) discourse of humility . . .
Not by William Allen, D.D., but by William Allen, tradesman of London. See his *Works*, 1707.

PRACTICAL (a) French course. By Chrysostôme Dagobert [J. B. A. Led'huy]. 8vo. 2 parts. [*Brit. Mus.*]
London, 1859

PRACTICAL (a) French grammar and book of reference. By Chrysostôme Dagobert [J. B. A. Led'huy]. 8vo. [*Brit. Mus.*]   London, 1859

PRACTICAL (a) guide to the Greek Testament. [By Edward Burton, D.D.] 16mo. [*Brit. Mus.*]   London [1849]
Signed : E. B., D.D.

PRACTICAL politics ; on free land. [By R. S. *i.e.* R. Swiney.] 8vo. Pp. 10. [*Brit. Mus.*]   Cheltenham [1886]

PRACTICAL politics ; the great national question or the Home Rule catechism; for the people of Great Britain. [By R. S. *i.e.* R. Swiney.] 8vo. Pp. 7. [*Brit. Mus.*]   Cheltenham, 1894

PRACTICAL (a) programme for working men. [By Edmond Kelly.] 8vo. Pp. xiii. 227. [*Brit. Mus.*]
London, 1906

PRACTICE (the) of salivating vindicated ; in answer to Dr Willoughby's translation of Mons. Chicoyneau's pamphlet against mercurial salivations. . . . By J. C., M.D. [Joseph Cam]. 8vo. [*Brit. Mus.*] London, 1724

PRACTICE register and comments for teacher and student, including a reference to musical terms and a chronological chart of the great composers. [By Ernest Haywood.] 8vo. Pp. 31. [*Brit. Mus.*] London [1929]

*PRAIRIE Chickens. By Chanticleer.
> Not by Ralph Nisbet, who wrote a book on Poultry under this *pseud.* in 1878, but by the writer of verses, G. F. Joy.

PRAISE (the) and blame of love, with other verse. [By Robert Kemp, Minister of Blairgowrie and John Wellwood.] 8vo. Pp. viii. 154. [*Brit. Mus.*] Glasgow, 1882

*PRAISES (the) of heroes. By T. B. A.
> The attribution to Thomas Bailey Aldrich is removed in the new edition of the *Brit. Mus. Catalogue.* It is not mentioned in F. Greenslet's bibliography (*Life of T. B. Aldrich*, 1908). Author not known.

*PRAYSE (the) of nothing . . .
> Mr Ralph M. Sargent considers that this was the work of Edward Daunce. See *The Library*, Dec. 1931.

PRAZIMENE ; a romance. [By —— Le Maire.] Translated into English by R. B. 12mo. Pp. 258. [*Brit. Mus.*] London, 1707

PREDICTIONS concerning the raising the dead body of Mr T. Emes . . . who . . . died on the 23rd day of December 1707. . . . [By John Lacy, and others.] 4to. [*Brit. Mus.*] London [1708 ?]

P R E F A C E (offered as a solemn warning) for a new edition of M. Renan's "Life of Jesus." [By David Walther.] 8vo. [*Brit. Mus.*] London, 1864
> Signed : Mnason.

PREPARING for the press, from an ancient MS. De fucorum ordinibus, continued by a modern hand ; a complete history of the Mallardians [*i.e.* the Warden and fellows of All-Souls College, Oxford ; being a satire by —— Bilson and Edward Rowe Mores on B. Buckler's "Complete vindication of the Mallard of All-Souls College"]. . . . Fol. Pp. iv. [*Brit. Mus.*] London, 1752

PREPOSITAS his practise, a worke . . . for the better preservation of the health of man. . . . Translated out of Latin into English by L. M. [Leonard Mascall ?]. . . . 4to. Pp. 111. B. L. [*Brit. Mus.*] London, 1588

PRESBYTERIANISM ; a reply to [Dr Steele's] "The Church and the pulpit." [By John Nelson Darby.] 12mo. London [1868]
> Signed : J. N. D.

PRESENCE (the) of the Holy Ghost, and the coming of the Lord . . . the true hope of the Church of God. By J. N. D. [John Nelson Darby]. 8vo. [*Brit. Mus.*] London [1878]

PRESENT (the) state of chyrurgery, with some remarks on the abuses committed . . . in a letter [signed : T. D. *i.e.* Dr Turner ?] to C. Bernard [or written by him ?]. 4to. [*Brit. Mus.*] London, 1703

*P R E S E N T (the) state of Great Britain . . .
> Now ascribed in the *Brit. Mus.* to John Mitchell, botanist.

*PRESENT (the) state of North America.
> Not by John Huske, but by his younger brother Ellis Huske. See the *D. N. B.* and *Brit. Mus. Cat.* (New ed.)

PRESENT (the) state of physick in the Island of Cajamai [*i.e.* Jamaica]. To the members of the R[oyal] S[ociety]. No. 1. [A satire on Sir Hans Sloane. By William King, LL.D. ?] 4to. [*Brit. Mus.*] [London, 1710 ?]

PRESENT (the) state of the parties in Great Britain ; particularly an enquiry into the state of the dissenters in England and the Presbyterians in Scotland. [By Daniel Defoe.] 8vo. Pp. 352. [*Brit. Mus.*] London, 1712

PRESIDENT Joseph Reed of Pennsylvania ; a correspondence between . . . W. B. Reed and J. C. Hamilton. [Preface signed : H. B. D. *i.e.* Henry Barton Dawson.] 4to. [*Brit. Mus.*] Morrisania, 1867

*PRESIDENT (a) to the nobilitie . . .
> For other editions with different titles, see "Newes from Italy of a second Moses . . ." (1608) and "The Italian convert . . ." (1635).

PRETTY (the) gentleman ; or, softness of manners vindicated from the false ridicule exhibited, under the character of William Fribble, Esq. [in Garrick's farce "Miss in her Teens." By Nathaniel Lancaster]. 8vo. [*Brit. Mus.*] London, 1747
> Dedication signed : Philautus.

PRETTY Nannie; or, a dainty new ditty, fit for the contry, town or citty. . . . [By Richard Climsell ?] Fol. S. sh. B. L. [*Brit. Mus.*] London [c. 1640]
> Signed : R. C.

PRETTY sinister. By Francis Beeding [John Leslie Palmer and Hilary Aidan St George Saunders]. 8vo. Pp. 320. [*Amer. Cat.*] London [1929]

PRIEST (the) of Isis, and other poems. By Ethna Kavanagh [Sara Spain]. 8vo. Pp. 45. London, 1920
　　Authorship revealed in No. 1 of *Innisfail*, *a quarterly magazine*.

PRIESTANITY; or, a view of the disparity between the apostles and the modern inferior clergy. By the author of *The creed of an independent Whig* [Conyers Place]. 8vo. [R. Straus' *The Unspeakable Curll*, p. 265.]
　　　　　　　　　　　London, 1720
　　The creed of an independent Whig has sometimes been attributed (see vol. 1) to Thomas Gordon of Kirkcudbright, on the ground that he was author of the tract called the "Independent Whig," joint editor of the periodical of the same name, and author of the *Character of an independent Whig*.

PRIESTHOOD. [By William Tarbet.] 12mo. Pp. 4. [*Brit. Mus.*] [1870?]

PRIESTHOOD (the) of Christ. [By William Kelly, of Guernsey.] 8vo. [*Brit. Mus.*] [1875]

PRIEST'S (the) book of private devotion. Compiled . . . by two priests [J. Oldknow and Augustine David Crake]. Second edition. 16mo. Pp. xiii. 292. [*Brit. Mus.*] Oxford, 1877
　　Preface signed: A. D. C.

*PRIEST'S (the) prayer-book . . .
　　For edited by two clergymen, *read* edited by two clergymen, R. F. L. and J. E. V.

PRINCE Dorus; or, the romance of the nose of which the most striking feature is borrowed from the Countess d'Aulnois. . . . By the author of *Diogenes and his lantern* [Tom Taylor]. 12mo. [*Brit. Mus.*] London, 1850
　　Lacy's Acting Edition, vol. 3.

PRINCESS Pirlipatine and the nutcracker. By Alexandre Dumas [or rather Dumas' version of the story by E. T. W. Hoffmann]. Translated . . . by O. Eliphaz Keat [P. B. M. Allan]. 4to. Pp. 146. [*Brit. Mus.*] London, 1919
　　In a later edition (1924) entitled "The delectable story of Princess Pirlipatine . . ." the translator signs himself: P. B. M. A.

PRINCIPLES (the) and practice of whist. By Lennard Leigh [Charles Harcourt Forbes-Lindsay] and Ernest Bergholt. Including an essay on probabilities by W. H. Whitfeld. 8vo. Pp. xv. 511. [*Brit. Mus.*]
　　　　　　　　Philadelphia, 1902
PRINCIPLES (the) of assessment; a concise and practical guide to the valuation of property for rating purposes. By a solicitor [J. J. Hitchings]. 8vo. [*Lincoln's Inn Lib.*] London [1890]

PRISCIANUS embryo et nascens; being a key to the grammar-school . . . [By Anthony Huish.] The fourth edition, with . . . additions. 8vo. 2 parts. [*Brit. Mus.*] 1670, 69
　　The preface signed: A. H.
　　The title of the first edition (1660) runs "Priscianus nascens; or a key . . ."

*PRISON amusements . . .
　　For By Peter Positive, *read* By Paul Positive.

PRISONER (the) and his dream. A ballad. [By Walter White.] 12mo. Pp. 31. [*Brit. Mus.*]
　　　　　　　　　　London [1885?]
　　Signed: W. W.

PRISONER'S (the) advocate; or, caveat against under sheriffs and their officers; jayl keepers and their agents. [By Edmund Curll.] 8vo. [R. Straus' *The Unspeakable Curll*, p. 279.]
　　　　　　　　　　　London, 1726
PRISONERS of state. [A novel.] By E. Shaw Cowley [Elsie Mary Boulton]. 8vo. Pp. 310. [*Brit. Mus.*]
　　　　　　　　　　New York, 1921
PRISONERS of the Lord. . . . By a business man [R. F. Norman]. 8vo. Pp. 62. [*Brit. Mus.*] Cardiff, 1924
　　Re-issued in 1928 as part of "Word pictures," which bears the author's name.

PRISONERS (the) of the Temple. . . . By M. C. O'C. Morris. [With a preface by H. J. C. *i.e.* Henry James Coleridge.] 8vo. Pp. xii. 209. [*Brit. Mus.*]
　　　　　　　　　　　London, 1874
　　"Quarterly Series," vol. 11.

PRISONERS of war. By A. Boyson Weekes [*i.e.* Agnes Russell Weekes and a collaborator or collaborators]. 8vo. Pp. 128. [*Who's Who in Lit.*]
　　　　　　　　　　　London, 1899
PRISONERS of war in Germany; a personal note. By E. F. O. [Ernest F. Oppé]. 8vo. Pp. 15. [*Brit. Mus.*]
　　　　　　　　　　Aldershot, 1919
PRIVATE Dowding; a plain record of the after-death experiences of a soldier killed in battle. . . . With notes [or rather written] by W. T. P. [W. Tudor Pole]. 8vo. Pp. xi. 108. [*Brit. Mus.*]
　　　　　　　　　　　London, 1917
PRIVATE journal of a visit to Egypt and Palestine by way of Italy and the Mediterranean. [By Lady Judith Montefiore.] 8vo. [*Brit. Mus.*]
　　　　　London, private print, 1836
　　See above, "Notes from a private journal . . ."

PRIVATE (the) papers of a bankrupt bookseller. [By William Young Darling.] 8vo. Pp. 306. Edinburgh, 1931
　　Information from the publishers.

PRIVATE virtue and publick spirit display'd ; in a succinct essay on the character of Capt. Thomas Coram. . . . [By Richard Brocklesby, M.D. ?] 8vo. [*Brit. Mus.*] London, 1751

PRIZE sermons on the Sabbath. . . . [The introduction signed : J. G. *i.e.* John Gritton.] 8vo. [*Brit. Mus.*] London, 1883

PRO Presbytero Joanne, ac omnibus ejus Regibus & Principibus subordinati [*sic*]. A Populo Dei in Anglia, vocato Anglice Quakers. For Presbyter John and all his subordinate Kings and Princes. Fkom [*sic*] the People of God in England, in English called Quakers. H. F[ell]. J. S[tubs]. 4to. Pp. 6. [*Brit. Mus.*] London, 1660

PROCEEDINGS (the) and transactions of the Bethune Society from November 10th, 1859 to April 20th, 1869. [Edited by J. L. *i.e.* James Long.] 8vo. [*Brit. Mus.*] Calcutta, 1870

PROCEEDINGS of the late Railroad Commission. . . . By a citizen of Burlington [Henry C. Carey]. 8vo. Pp. 8. [Sabin's *Dictionary*, iii. 329.] Philadelphia, 1850

*PROCEEDINGS (the) of the Vice-chancellor and University of Cambridge against Dr Bentley . . . By Thomas Sherlock. [*Brit. Mus.*]

PROCESSIONADE (the); in panegyri-satiri-serio-comi-baladical versicles. By Porcupinus Pelagius [Macnamara Morgan]. 4to. [*D. N. B.* vol. 39, p. 23.] London, 1745
A satire on William Murray, afterwards Earl of Mansfield.

PROFESSION (a) of the Catholic faith, extracted out of the Council of Trent by Pope Pius IV. With the chief grounds of the controverted articles. By way of question and answer. [By Bishop Richard Challoner.] 8vo. [*D. N. B.* vol. 9, p. 442.] London, 1732
Reprinted under the title : " The grounds of the Catholick doctrine."

PROFESSOR Max Müller on Durga. [By K. S. MacDonald.] 8vo. Pp. 8. [*Brit. Mus.*] Calcutta [1890]
Signed : K. S. M.

PROFITABLE (a) adventure to the fortunate, and can be unfortunate to none. Being a proposal for raising one million of money. . . . [By Thomas Neale.] Fol. S. sh. [*Brit. Mus.*] London, 1693/4
See also " The best way of disposing . . .", " A proposal concerning the coin," and " A way to make plenty of money . . ."

PROFITABLENESS (the) of Scripture. By the author of *The lamplighter* [Francis Bourdillon]. 12mo. [*Brit. Mus.*] London [1862]
Signed : F. B.

PROGRESS (the) of Catholic work in and around Guildford. [By G. C. Williamson.] 12mo. Pp. 39. [*Brit. Mus.*] Guildford, private print, 1901
Signed : G. C. W.

PROGRESS (the) of dulness. By an eminent hand (H. Stanhope [William Bond?]) which will serve for an explanation of the Dunciad. 8vo. [R. Straus' *The Unspeakable Curll*, p. 285.] London, 1728

PROGRESS (the) of science, art and literature in Russia. By F. R. Grahame [Catherine Laura Johnstone]. 8vo. Pp. 480. [*Brit. Mus.*] London [1865]

PROLOGUE ; spoke by one of the young gentlemen who for their improvement and diversion, acted The Orphan, and Cheats of Scapin, the last night of the year 1719. [By Allan Ramsay.] 8vo. Pp. 2. [A. Gibson's *Allan Ramsay*, p. 128.] [Edinburgh, 1720]

PROPER (a) dyalogue between a gentill-man and a husbandman, eche complanynge to other their miserable calamite through the ambicion of the clergye. [By William Roy.] 8vo. B. L. [*Brit. Mus.*] [Antwerp] 1530

PROPER leads in whist. Compiled by F. H. C. [F. H. Culver]. 8vo. Pp. 8. [F. Jessel's *Bibl. of playing cards*.] Chicago, 1887

PROPER spirit. By the author of *Margaret Whyte* [Mrs Lucy Lyttelton Cameron]. 8vo. [*Brit. Mus.*] Wellington, Salop [1830?]

PROPHET (the) Elisha. By the author of *Lines on the Prophet Elijah* [William C. Mainland]. 8vo. Pp. 16. [*Brit. Mus.*] Kirkwall, 1927

PROPHETE (the) Jonas with an intro-duccio before teachinge to vnderstöde him and the right vse also of all the scripture . . . [By W. T. *i.e.* William Tyndale.] 8vo. B. L. [*Brit. Mus.*] [Antwerp, 1531 ?]

PROPOSAL (a) concerning the coin. [By Thomas Neale.] Fol. S. sh. [*Brit. Mus.*] [London ? 1696 ?]
Signed : T. N.
See also " The best way of disposing . . .", " A way to make plenty of money . . . ", and " A profitable adventure . . ."

PROPOSAL (the) for sending back the nobility and gentry of Ireland, with a vindication of the same. . . . By R. B. [Sir Richard Buckley]. 4to. [*Brit. Mus.*] London, 1690

PROPOSALS for printing an English dictionary, in two volumes, in folio. [By Ambrose Philips.] 8vo. [*Brit. Mus.*]   [*c.* 1720]

PROPOSALS for the reformation of schools & universities, in order to the better education of youth ; humbly offered to the serious consideration of the High Court of Parliament. [By Andrew Fletcher, of Saltoun?] 4to. [R. A. Scott Macfie's *Bibl. of Fletcher*, p. 25.]   [Edinburgh?] 1704

PROPOSALS for uniting the English Colonies on the Continent of America so as to enable them to act with force and vigour against their enemies. [By Henry McCulloh.] 8vo. Pp. vi. 38. [*Brit. Mus.*]   London, 1757
There is a reference on p. 1 to his previous book, " The Wisdom and Policy of the French . . ." *q.v.*

PROPOSITIONS and principles of diuinitie . . . disputed in the universitie of Geneva, by certaine students of divinitie . . . under T. Beza and A. Faius, wherein is contained a . . . summarie . . . of the common places of divinitie. Translated out of Latine . . . [by John Penry]. . . . 4to. [*Brit. Mus.*]   Edinburgh, 1591

PROPOSITIONS as to Chancery reform. [By Edgar Taylor.] 8vo. [*Lincoln's Inn Lib.*]   London, 1830

PROPRIETORS (the) of the Northern Neck ; chapters of Culpeper genealogy. [Preface signed : F. H. *i.e.* Fairfax Harrison.] 8vo. Pp. 178. [*Brit. Mus.*]   Richmond, Va., private print, 1926

PROS and cons ; a magazine for every county. Edited by James Cassidy [Mrs E. M. Story]. 8vo. 3 nos. [*Brit. Mus.*]   London, 1903

PROSPECT (a) from the Congress Gallery during the session begun December 7, 1795. . . . By Peter Porcupine [William Cobbett]. Second edition. 8vo. [*Brit. Mus.*]
Philadelphia, 1796

PROSPECTIVE (a) glasse wherein the child in understanding is enabled to see what the wicked Counsellours did above twenty yeares ago to maintaine the Protestant religion. [By Hezekiah Woodward.] . . . 4to. [*Brit. Mus.*]
N.P. [1644]
An addition to " A good souldier maintaining his militia."

PROSPECTS beyond the Rubicon ; a gratuitous exhibition of the Great Southern War Horse, yclept Nullification, alias Separation, alias Dissolution of the Union. [By Matthew Carey.] 8vo. Pp. 8. [Sabin's *Dictionary*, iii. 342.]   Philadelphia, 1833
Signed : Hamilton.

*PROSPEROUS (a) kingdom . . .
The *Brit. Mus.* gives the author's name as —— Meares.

*PROTECTING (the) system ; nos. 1-9. Signed : Hamilton. [Sabin's *Dictionary*.]

PROTESTANT orders. " Are clergymen of the English Church rightly ordained ? " [By H. P. L. *i.e.* H. P. Liddon and W. B. *i.e.* W. Bright.] A reply to this inquiry, by an English catholic. 16mo. [*Brit. Mus.*]
Derby, 1872

PROTESTANT songs for troublous times. By B. M. N. [Thomas O. Beeman?]. 16mo. [*Brit. Mus.*]
London, 1891

PROTESTANT - DISSENTER'S (the) catechism, containing I. A brief history of the Nonconformists. II. The reasons of the dissent from the National Church . . . [By Samuel Palmer, minister at Hackney.] Tenth edition. [*Brit. Mus.*]   London, 1794
First published 1773. The tenth edition contains an advt. of works (by the same author) which includes " A vindication of the Modern Dissenters " (1790, with Palmer's name on the title-page). One edition at least of this catechism was issued under the initials : S. P.

PROTOCOLS (the) and world revolution ; including a translation and analysis of the Protocols of the meetings of the Zionist men of wisdom [adapted from Maurice Joly's *Dialogue aux enfers* and published in a work by S. A. Nilus]. 8vo. Pp. 149. [*Brit. Mus.*]   Boston [1920]

PROVERBS ; with glossary. By M. L. M. [M. L. Miln?]. 16mo. [*Brit. Mus.*]
Arbroath, private print, 1895

PSALMS and hymns as sung in the Parish Church, Rugby. . . . [Compiled by John Moultrie.] 24mo. Pp. iv. 140. [*Brit. Mus.*]   Rugby, 1851
Signed : J. M.

PSALTER (the) of Jesus, contayninge very devoute and godlie petitions. Newlie imprinted and amplified with enrichement of figures. [Ascribed to Richard Whitford.] [*D. N. B.* vol. 61, p. 128 ; *Pollard and Redgrave*.]
Doway, 1618
For other editions, see " An invocacyon glorious . . ." (1529) and " Certaine devout and godly petition . . ." (1545).

PSYCHIC (a) vigil ; in three watches. By " X-Rays " [Alexander Bell Filson Young]. 8vo. Pp. viii. 167. [*Brit. Mus.*]   London [1896]

PTE-SKA, the white buffalo. [Verse.] By To-ka-ni-ya [Howard Clark Brown]. 12mo. Pp. 136. [*Publishers' Weekly*, 26th May 1928.] Charles City, Iowa, 1927

PUBLIC companies tracts. No. 8. Railway management, illustrated by the judgment in "Hare versus The London and North-Western." . . . By a journalist [Charles Nash]. Second edition. 8vo. [*Brit. Mus.*]   1861

PUBLIC good; being an examination into the claim of Virginia to the vacant western territory, and of the right of the United States to the same; to which is added, Proposals for laying off a new state, to be applied as a fund for carrying on the war, or redeeming the National Debt. By the author of *Common sense* [Thomas Paine]. 8vo. Pp. 38. [*Sabin's Dictionary.*]   Philadelphia, 1780

An edition of London, 1819, bears Paine's name.

PUBLIC schools and the Great War, 1914-19: some figures; with a list of all officers, public school and otherwise, who received orders of knighthood or higher distinctions for their military services. By A. H. H. M. [Alick Henry Herbert Maclean]. 8vo. Pp. 20. [*Brit. Mus.*]   London [1923]

PUBLIC villainy exposed; or, a discovery of the different adulterations and poison in bread. By Dr M****** of Bath. [An extract from *The nature of bread,* by James Manning.] Fol. S. sh. [*Brit. Mus.*]   Bristol [1800]

PULPIT-LUNATICKS (the); or, a mad answer to the mad report made by a Committee of mad priests against Benjamin, Lord Bishop of Bangor. . . . Also a mad speech to the Convocation . . . [By John Dunton.] 8vo. Pp. 32. [*Brit. Mus.*]   London [1717]

PUNCTUALITY. [A tract. By William Morgan, B.D.?] 12mo. Pp. 8. [*Brit. Mus.*]   Bradford [1835?]

PUPPET'S (the) dallying. By Louis Marlow [Louis Wilkinson]. 8vo. Pp. 306. [Millard's *Cat.* 16, 1927.]
London, 1905

*PURITANE (the) set forth. . . .

Attributed to William Chamberlayne, Shaftesbury, in Murphy's *Characters*.

PURPLE (the) pearl. By Anthony Pryde [Agnes Russell Weekes] and Rose K. Weekes. 8vo. Pp. 288. [*Who's Who in Lit.*]   London, 1923

PURPOSE (the); reflections and digressions. By Hubert Wales [William Piggott]. 8vo. Pp. 255. [*Brit. Mus.*]
London [1913]

PUSEY (the) memorial . . . or, moral rectitude and integrity as exemplified in the character of the late . . . E. B. Pusey. A letter addressed to the Marquis of Salisbury . . . by a Nottinghamshire rector [Alfred Hensley?]. 8vo. Pp. 20. [*Brit. Mus.*]
Market Rasen, 1883

Signed: A. H.

PUTNAM'S Homemaker Series. By Olive Green [Myrtle Reed, afterwards MacCullough]. 8vo. [*Amer. Cat.*]
New York, 1905, etc.

*PYGMAÏOGERANOMACHIA . . .

Not by Lectius. The ascription is due to a confusion with Lectius' *Certaminis Pygmæorum cum gruibus descriptio* (1613). The *Pygmaïogeranomachia* is not anonymous and is a translation of the Latin Poem of Joseph Addison.

Q

QUAKER (the) boy; a tale of the outgoing generation as it appears chronicled in the autobiography of Robert Barclay Dillingham. [By William Dudley Foulke.] 8vo. Pp. 258. [*Brit. Mus.*]   New York, 1910

QUARTER (a) of an hour's amusement. [Prose and verse.] By W. N. H. [William Nevile Hart]. 8vo. [*Brit. Mus.*]   Reading, 1798

QUARTERBACK Reckless. By Hawley Williams [William Heyliger]. 8vo. Pp. 239. [*Amer. Cat.*]
New York, 1912

QUEEN (the) of Sheba. . . . By S. M. A. [Sister Mary Agnes]. 8vo. [*Brit. Mus.*]   Winnipeg, [1915]

QUEENES (the) visiting of the campe at Tilsburie with her entertainment there. [A ballad signed: T. D. *i.e.* Thomas Deloney?] Fol. S. sh. B. L. [*Brit. Mus.*]   London, 1588

QUEEN'S (the) masque; a satirical sketch [on the ball given by Queen Victoria at Buckingham Palace]. By the author of *The Palace martyr* [Hon. —— Osborn?]. 8vo. Pp. 16. [*Brit. Mus.*]   London, 1842

QUEEN'S (the) voyage ; or, the follies of Scotland : a satire : with notes. By the Honble * * * * *, author of *The Palace martyr* [Hon. —— Osborn ?]. 8vo. Pp. 24. [*Brit. Mus.*]   1842

QUESTION (the). What is an Arminian? Answered by a lover of free grace [John Wesley]. 8vo. [*Brit. Mus.*]   London, 1770

QUESTIONS and answers on the reigns of the four Georges, deduced principally from *Exercises in English history.* [By Mary Poole Hastings.] 16mo. [*Brit. Mus.*]   Chester, 1835
   Signed : M. P. H.

QUESTIONS (the) between the conformist and non-conformist truly stated and discussed. Dr Falkner, the "friendly debate," etc., examined and answered. Together with a discourse about separation and some animadversions upon Dr Stillingfleet's book entituled, "The unreasonableness of separation " . . . [By G. F. *i.e.* Giles Firmin.] 4to. [*D. N. B.* vol. 36, p. 247.]   London, 1681

QUIP (a) for an upstart courtier. [By Robert Greene. The introduction signed : J. P. C. *i.e.* John Payne Collier.] 4to. Pp. 70. [*Brit. Mus.*]
[London, 1870]

R

RACCOLTA (the) ; or, collection of indulgenced prayers. By Ambrose St John [or rather, translated by him from the work by Telesphorus Galli] . . . Fifth edition. 8vo. Pp. 384.
London, 1880
   The first edition (1857) bears Galli's name.

RAILROAD (the) monopoly. . . . By a Citizen of Burlington [Henry C. Carey]. 8vo. [Sabin's *Dictionary*, iii. 329.]   Philadelphia, 1849

RAILWAY tracts. [Signed : C. S. *i.e.* Charles Stanley, Sheffield.] 24mo. 16 nos. [*Brit. Mus.*]   London [1893]

RAMBLER (the) papers. By Jeffery C. Jeffery [Jeffery Charles Marston]. 8vo. Pp. 253. [*Brit. Mus.*]   London, 1889

RANDOM recollections of some of my schoolfellows. [By W. G. Fretton.] 8vo. Pp. 4. [*Brit. Mus.*]
[Coventry? private print, 1860?]
   Signed : W.

RAOKIN (the) lino-cuts of Malta. (Designed, engraved and printed by Raokin [Harold Frederick Weaver Hawkins]). [*Brit. Mus.*]
Notabile [1929, *etc.*]

RAPALLO, past and present ; walks and excursions. By P. I. A. [Phyllis Innocent Alt]. 8vo. Pp. xv. 158. [*Brit. Mus.*]   London, 1904

RA-REE (a) show. To the tune of I am a senseless thing. [A political ballad. By Stephen College.] Obl. fol. S. sh. [*Brit. Mus.*]   1681

*RASMIN and Ezzelina . . .
   For A. M. Adie *read* C. M. Adie. The work is signed : C. M. A.

RATIONALIST (the). By Hubert Wales [William Piggott]. 8vo. Pp. 320. [*Brit. Mus.*]   London, 1917

REASON humbly offered by the Governour, assistants, and fellowship of Eastland-Merchants, against the giving of a general liberty . . . to export the English woollen manufacture. . . . [By Nathaniel Tenche.] 4to. Pp. 15. [*Brit. Mus.*]   1689

*REASONS for a modification of the Act of Anne respecting the delivery of books and copyright.
   Also ascribed to Edward Christian. [Watt's *Bibl. Brit.*]

REASONS for establishing a Marine Insurance Company in Liverpool. [By John Towne Danson.] 8vo. [*Brit. Mus.*]   1859

REASONS humbly offer'd why the name of W. Lenthall should be left out of the exception in the Act of Oblivion. [By William Lenthall, himself.] Fol. S. sh. [*Brit. Mus.*]
[London, 1660]

REASONS humbly offered for the liberty of unlicens'd printing ; to which is subjoin'd, The just and true character of Edmund Bohun, the licenser of the press : in a letter from a gentleman in the country [signing himself J. M. *i.e.* Charles Blount], to a member of Parliament. 4to. Pp. 32. [*Brit. Mus.*]   London, 1693

REASONS (the) which induced His Majesty to create Sir Thomas Parker . . . a peer. [By Joseph Addison ?] 4to. [R. Straus' *The Unspeakable Curll*, p. 239.]   London, 1716

REASONS why D. Garrick should not appear on the stage ; in a letter to J. Rich, Esq. [By David Garrick?] 8vo. [*Brit. Mus.*] London, 1759

Signed : Y. Z.

*RECENT recollections of the Anglo-American Church . . .

This could not have been by Henry Caswall, who was not a layman, and had been resident for many more than five years in 1861. There is a copy in the library of the General Theological Seminary, New York, which was presented by "the author" to the Rev. David A. Bonnar, upon whose attestation it is there credited to a certain Thomas Ramsay, otherwise unknown.

RECOLLECTIONS of an eventful life, chiefly passed in the army. [By Joseph Donaldson, sergeant in the ninety-fourth Scots Brigade.] 8vo.
Glasgow, 1824

Republished with its continuations, "The War in the Peninsula" and "Scenes and Sketches of a soldier's life in Ireland" in 1856 as "Recollections of the eventful life of a soldier," and bearing the author's name.

RECOLLECTIONS of the two St Mary Winton Colleges (Winchester College —New College, Oxford). By an old Wykehamist [Edward John George Henry Rich]. 8vo. Pp. viii. 199. [*Brit. Mus.*] Walsall, 1883

RECORD of the death-bed of C. M. W. [C. M. Walter. By I. Walter]. 12mo. Pp. 33. [*Brit. Mus.*] London [1844]

Signed : I. W.

RECORDS (the) of love ; or weekly amusements for the fair. [Compiled by Henry Carey.] Vol. i. nos. 1-12. 8vo. [*T. L. S.* 25th Dec. 1930.]
London, 1710

RECORDS of Salem Witchcraft, copied from the original documents. [By W. E. Woodward.] 4to. 2 vols. [*Brit. Mus.*] 1864

Signed : W.

RECORDS of the Council for New England. . . . [Edited by C. D. *i.e.* Charles Deane.] 8vo. [*Brit. Mus.*]
Cambridge, Mass., 1867

*RECORDS of the ministry of the Rev. E. T. March Phillipps . . .

The title continues "By the author of *My life and what shall I do with it.*" The introduction is signed : L.

*RED-SHANKES (the) sermon . . .

For James Low, *read* James Row.

REED (the) of Egypt piercing the hand that leans upon it ; or, a demonstration that the arguments of the Right Reverend the Lord Bishop of London [Edmund Gibson] in his second pastoral letter against the Deists, are inconsistent with his principles as Bishop of London, destroy his own local religion, and therefore subvert the cause of the Church of England. Submitted in a discourse deliver'd, at Rumford in the County of Essex, May 2, 1730. By Simon Croxeall, D.D. [John Henley]. 8vo. [*Lincoln's Inn Lib.*]
London, 1730

REFLECTIONS on shipboard. By Lord Byron. 8vo. Pp. 16. [*Brit. Mus.*] London, 1816

A spurious work. Not by Lord Byron.

REFLECTIONS on spiritual subjects . . . Translated from the Italian of St Alphonsus. [Preface signed : J. M. C. *i.e.* John Moore Capes.] 16mo. Pp. xv. 240. [*Brit. Mus.*] London, 1849

*REFLECTIONS on the state of parties . . .

The date MDCCXLVI is in error for 1776, the reference being to the War of Independence. The second edition, in the same year, but also misdated, bears the author's name.

REFLECTIONS upon Coll. Sidney's Arcadia ; the old cause, being some observations upon his last paper, given to the sheriffs at his execution. [By Dr John Nalson.] Fol. [*Lincoln's Inn Lib.*] London, 1684

REFLECTIONS upon the eloquence of these times ; particularly of the barr and pulpit. [Translated from the French of R. Rapin.] 8vo. [*Brit. Mus.*] London, 1672

Signed : N. N.

*REFLECTOR (the) ; representing human affairs . . .

The same sheets were reissued in 1762 with a different title-page, and title, "The Tablet, or picture of real life . . ." also anonymous, *q.v.*

REIVER'S (the) penance ; ane ballad of the bishoppricke. [By Robert Surtees of Mainsforth.] 8vo. Pp. 8. [*Brit. Mus.*] [Edinburgh] 1848

Signed : R. S. of M.

RELIC (a) of Dr Johnson [viz. his copy of the works of Bacon. By Roger Ingpen and Charles A. Stonehill]. 8vo. Pp. 10. [*Brit. Mus.*] London [1929]

*RELIGION (the) of Jesus delineated. . . . [By —— Reynolds.]

This was by John Reynolds, of Pembroke College, Oxford. See "Memoirs of the life of John Reynolds" (3rd ed., 1735), p. 168.

RELIQUIÆ Britannico-Romanæ; containing figures of Roman antiquities. [By Samuel Lysons.] 8vo. 2 vols. [Gross' *Sources of Engl. Hist.* p. 164.]
London, 1801-17

REMAINS of the late Rev. Henry Francis Lyte . . . with a prefatory memoir by the editor [A. M. M. H. *i.e.* Anna Maria Maxwell Hogg]. 12mo. Pp. cxii. 292. [*Brit. Mus.*]
London, 1850

REMARKS on "Christianity and modern progress, by . . . A. Raleigh." . . . [By John Nelson Darby.] 8vo. [*Brit. Mus.*]   London [1869]
Signed: J. N. D.

REMARKS on Dr [William] Wake's want of temper in his writings about Convocation, as also upon Dr Kennet, etc., from their own words. [By George Smallridge, Bishop of Bristol.] Second edition. [Arber's *Term Cat.* iii. 318.]   London, 1702
Also attributed to Francis Atterbury.

REMARKS on light and conscience. [With reference to Dr Wardlaw's "Friendly letters."] By J. N. D. [John Nelson Darby]. 8vo. [*Brit. Mus.*]
London [1867]

REMARKS on Squire Ayre's Memoirs on the life and writings of Mr Pope. In a letter to Edmund Curl, bookseller. [By John Henley, Orator Henley? or John Hill?] 8vo. [R. Straus' *The Unspeakable Curll*, p. 312.]
London, 1745
Signed: J. H. See "Memoirs on the life and writings of Mr Pope. . . . By William Ayre, Esq."

REMARKS on "The Church and the world." By J. N. D. [John Nelson Darby]. 8vo. [*Brit. Mus.*]
London [1874]

REMARKS on the practicability of establishing a railroad from Boston to the Connecticut river. [By Nathan Hale.] 8vo. [R. A. Peddie's *Railway Literature*.]   Boston, 1827

REMARKS on the present aspect of the Turkish question. By a member of the University of Oxford who visited Constantinople in . . . 1850 and 1851 (W. P. [*i.e.* William Parry]). 8vo. Pp. 24. [*Brit. Mus.*]   London, 1853

REMARKS on the recent ordination at Beverly. By "Another Layman" [Warwick Palfray]. 8vo. Pp. 24. [Sabin's *Dictionary*.]   Salem, 1824

REMARKS upon the *London Gazette* relating to the Streights Fleet, and the battle of Landen in Flanders. [By Jeremy Collier.] 4to.   1693
Reprinted in Somers' *Third Collection of Tracts*, vol. 3.

REMARKS with reference to the Land-Laws of England, on some passages in Mr John Stuart Mill's "Principles of political economy," and M. Louis Blanc's "Letters on England." [By William Hayes.] 8vo. [*Lincoln's Inn Lib.*]   London, 1867

REMEMBER Louvain ! a little book of liberty and war. [A collection of verse. Edited by E. V. L. *i.e.* E. V. Lucas.] 8vo. Pp. viii. 86.   London, 1914

REMEMBRANCES (the) of a Polish exile. [The dedication signed : A. J— *i.e.* A. A. Jakubowski.] 12mo. Pp. 72. [*Brit. Mus.*]   London, 1835

REMEMBRANCES of some methods, orders and proceedings : . . used . . . in the House of Lords, extracted out of the journals of that house by H. S. E. C. P. [Henry Scobell, Esq., Clericus Parliamenti]. 12mo. [*Brit. Mus.*]   London, 1657

REMINISCENCES of forty years. By an hereditary High Churchman [James Hicks Smith]. Reprinted with additions from the "Ecclesiastic." . . . 8vo. Pp. iv. 51. [Brilioth's *The Anglican Revival*, p. 22.]
London, 1868

REMINISCENCES of persons and places in Kendal, sixty years ago. By D. K. K. [Henry W. Duncan]. 8vo. [*Bibliotheca Jacksoniana*, p. 66.]
Kendal, 1890

REPLY (a) to Dr [Thomas] Morton's particular defence of three nocent ceremonies. . . . [By William Ames.] 4to. [*Pollard and Redgrave*.]
N.P. 1623
See also "A reply to Dr Morton's generall defence . . ."

*REPLY (a) to General Joseph Reed's remarks. . . .
Reprinted with Gen. Cadwallader's name on the title-page in 1846. The real authorship, however, has been attributed to Dr Benjamin Rush. See Sabin's *Dictionary*.

REPLY to Lord Byron's *Fare thee well*. [A poem, signed : C. *i.e.* Mrs E. Cockle.] 8vo. [*Brit. Mus.*]
Newcastle, 1817

REPLY to the Observations of the *Quarterly Review* on the autobiography of Admiral the Earl of Dundonald. By Marcus [John Cochrane]. 8vo. [*Lincoln's Inn Lib.*]   London, 1861

REPORT of the Juanpur mission in connexion with the Church Missionary Society, 1847-48. [By R. Hawes.] 8vo. [*Brit. Mus.*]   Calcutta, 1848
Signed : R. H.

REPOSE, and other verses. By J. Marjoram [Ralph Hale Mottram]. 8vo. Pp. xliii. [*Brit. Mus.*]
London, 1907
Contemporary Poets Series.

REST (the) cottage. By Adam Lilburn [Lillias Wassermann]. 8vo. Pp. 346. [*Brit. Mus.*]   London [1923]
Title-page of her " Road of life."

REST days ; or, the rambler of the country side. [In verse.] By A. E. P. [A. E. Pearson]. 8vo. Pp. 15. [*Brit. Mus.*]   Nottingham, 1923

RESURGAM and lyrics. By J. Cave Winscombe [John Cave]. 8vo. Pp. 32. [*Brit. Mus.*]   London [1898]

REVELATION (a) of the secret spirit, declaring the most concealed secret of alchymie. Written first in Latine by an unknown author . . . lately translated into English by R. N. E. Gentleman [Robert Napier, Esq., of Edinburgh ?]. 16mo. Pp. 80. [*Brit. Mus.*]   London, 1623

REVELATION (a) or charact. [An Anglo-Saxon charm copied from a MS., with notes by M. A. D. *i.e.* Michael Aislabie Denham.] 8vo. [*Brit. Mus.*]   [Durham, 1854]

REV. (the) Mr Gill's book, call'd Truth defended, examined by scripture and reason. . . . By a sufferer for truth [Ebenezer Hewlett]. 8vo. Pp. 24. [*Brit. Mus.*]   1738

R E V E R S I and go bang. By " Berkeley " [W. H. Peel]. . . . 8vo. Pp. 71. [Jessel's *Bibl. of playing cards.*]   London, 1890
One of " The Club Series."

REVIEW (a) of an address of the Joint Board of Directors of the Delaware and Raritan Canal and Camden and Amboy Railroad Companies. By a Citizen of Burlington [Henry C. Carey]. 8vo. Pp. 83. [Sabin's *Dictionary*, iii. 329.]   Philadelphia, 1848

REVIEW (a) of " Niti-niganduwa " and the caste-system in Ceylon by W. W. [W. D. S. Vikramasekara]. . . . 8vo. Pp. xix. 38. [*Brit. Mus.*]   Colombo, 1885

R E V I E W (a) of the affairs of the Austrian Netherlands. [By James Shaw, author of *Sketches of the history of the Austrian Netherlands ?*] 8vo. [*Brit. Mus.*]   London, 1788

REVIEW of the " Remarks on Dr Channing's Slavery by a Citizen of Massachusetts." [By G. F. Simmons.] 8vo. Pp. 48. [Sabin's *Dictionary*, iii. 493.]   Boston, 1836
See " Remarks on Dr Channing's slavery . . ."

REVIEW of the Report of the late Commissioners for investigating the affairs of the Joint Companies. . . . By a Citizen of Burlington [Henry C. Carey]. 8vo. Pp. 78. [Sabin's *Dictionary*, iii. 329.]   Philadelphia, 1850

REVIEW of the Rev. Dr Channing's Letter to Jonathan Phillips, Esq., on the slavery question. [By James Trecothick Austin.] 12mo. Pp. 77. [Sabin's *Dictionary*, iii. 491.]   1839

REVIEW of three pamphlets lately published by the Rev. W. V. Harold. . . . By a Catholic Layman [Matthew Carey]. Second edition, corrected. 8vo. Pp. 40. [Sabin's *Dictionary*, iii. 341.]   Philadelphia, 1822

REVISION of the Lectionary ; a letter. . . . By J. M. Neale. [With an introductory note signed : J. H. *i.e.* Joseph Haskoll.] 8vo. Pp. 30. [*Brit. Mus.*]   London [1868]

REVIVALS (the) of the Latter Day. [By William Tarbet.] 8vo. Pp. 8. [*Brit. Mus.*]   [1860 ?]

RHYMES for Harry and his nursemaid. [Preface signed : A. M. *i.e.* Maria Arthington.] 8vo. Pp. 36. [*Brit. Mus.*]   London [*c.* 1850]
Later editions bear the author's name.

RIALLARO, the archipelago of exiles. By Godfrey Sweven [John Macmillan Brown]. 8vo. Pp. iv. 420. [*Brit. Mus.*]   New York, 1901

RIENZI : a tragedy. . . . By Mary R. Mitford. [With remarks by D— G. *i.e.* George Daniel.] 12mo. Pp. 66. [*Brit. Mus.*]   London [1871]
Lacy's Acting Edition of Plays, vol. 90.

RIGHT (a) pleasant historie of the mylner of Abingdon. [Sometimes ascribed to Andrew Borde.] 4to. [*Pollard and Redgrave.*]   London, N.D.
Another edition begins " Here is a merry jest . . ." *q.v.*

RIGHT (the) way of learning, pronouncing . . . and writing French . . . Second edition. . . . By Chrysostôme Dagobert [J. B. A. Led'huy]. 16mo. [*Brit. Mus.*]   London, 1855

RIGHTEOUSNESS (the) of God. By J. N. D. [John Nelson Darby]. 12mo. [*Brit. Mus.*]   London [1861]

RIGHTS (the) of industry ; addressed to the working men of the United Kingdom. By the author of *The results of machinery* [Charles Knight]. I. Capital and labour. 12mo. Pp. 213. [*Brit. Mus.*]   London, 1831
Part of " The Working Man's Companion."

RIGORDANS (the) ; a play in three acts. By Edward Percy [Edward Percy Smith]. 8vo. Pp. 100. [*Brit. Mus.*]   London, 1924

ROAD (a) to Fairyland. By Erica Fay [Marie Charlotte Carmichael Stopes]. 8vo. Pp. 219. [*Brit. Mus.*]   London, 1926

ROBBER (the) of the Rhine ; a melodrama. . . . By G. Almar. [With
remarks by D— G. *i.e.* George Daniel.]
12mo. Pp. 40. [*Brit. Mus.*]
London [1871]
Lacy's Acting Edition of Plays, vol. 87.

ROBERT Bridges. [A bibliography of
his works. By Iolo A. Williams.]
8vo. Pp. 8. [O'Leary's *Eng. Lit.
Hist.* p. 149.]   London, 1921
Bibliographies of Modern Authors, vol. 8.

ROBERT White. [A biographical sketch,
reprinted from the *Hawick Advertiser*,
signed : J. H. *i.e.* John Hilson.] 12mo.
[*Brit. Mus.*]   [Hawick, 1869]

ROCKLITZ (the). By George R. Preedy
[Gabrielle Margaret Vere Long]. 8vo.
Pp. vi. 362. [*Daily Mail*, 3rd Feb.
1931.]   London, 1930

RODS and axes. [On government.]
By Al Carthill [Sir John Perronet
Thompson]. 8vo. Pp. 309. [*Brit.
Mus.*]   Edinburgh, 1928

ROGER Sheringham and the Vane
mystery. By Anthony Berkeley
[Anthony Berkeley Cox]. 8vo. Pp.
viii. 306. [*Amer. Cat.*] London, 1927

ROGUISH (the) miller ; or, nothing got
by cheating : a true ballad. [By
Hannah More.] Fol. S. sh. [*Brit.
Mus.*]   Bath [1795 ?]
Signed : Z.

ROLL (the) of the house of Lacy ;
pedigrees, military memoirs and
synoptical history of the . . . family
of De Lacy . . . and a memoir of
the Brownes, Camas. Collected and
compiled by De Lacy-Bellingari [Edy
Harnett]. Pp. viii. 409. 8vo. [*Brit.
Mus.*]   Baltimore, 1928

*ROMAN Catholic morality . . .
For Maynooth, *read* Maynooth College.

ROMANCE (the) of Ali. By Eleanor
Stuart [Eleanor Stuart Childs]. 8vo.
Pp. 333. [*Brit. Mus.*]
New York, 1913

ROMANCE of the Strangford power
scheme ; a historical narrative. By
Maurice Fitzgerald [Thomas M'Cormac
Adair]. 8vo. [*Brit. Mus.*]
Belfast, 1930

ROMANCES of Gretna Green and its
runaway marriages. By Lochinvar
[Richard P. MacDougall]. Fifth
edition. 8vo. Pp. 68. [*Brit. Mus.*]
Newcastle, 1929
Previously published as " Guide to Gretna
Green."

ROME exactly describ'd, as to the
present state of it, under Pope
Alexandre the seventh ; in two curious
discourses. A new relation of Rome,
as to the government of the city. . . .
English'd by G. Torriano [from the
" Relatione di Roma del Almaden "]
— A relation of the state of the Court
of Rome, made in the year 1661 . . .
by . . . A. Corraro . . . translated
by J. B. Gent. [John Bulteel]. 8vo.
2 parts. [*Brit. Mus.*]   London, 1664

ROMISH (the) mass and the English
Church. By an English presbyter
[Rev. Nathaniel Dimock]. 8vo.
[*Lincoln's Inn Lib.*]   London, 1874

ROMULUS and Tarquin. First written
in Italian by V. Malvezzi and now
taught English by [H. C. L. *i.e.* Henry
Carey, Earl of Monmouth]. 12mo.
[*Brit. Mus.*]   London, 1637

ROSE Campion's platonic. By Adam
Lilburn [Lillias Wasserman]. 8vo.
Pp. viii. 308. [*Brit. Mus.*]
London, 1908
Title-page of her " Road of life."

ROUGE et noir ; roulette, hazard and
faro. By " Berkeley " [W. H. Peel].
8vo. Pp. 30. [Jessel's *Bibl. of playing
cards.*]   [London ? 1892 ?]

ROUGH catalogue of a geological
collection at Villa Syracusa, Torquay.
[By John Edward Lee.] 8vo. [*Brit.
Mus.*]   Private print, 1880
Preface signed : J. E. L.

ROYAL (the) merchant ; a sermon. [By
Robert Wilkinson, D.D., Pastor of
St Olave's, Southwark.] 8vo. [*Brit.
Mus.*]   [1700 ?]

ROYAL (the) pastime of cock-fighting ;
or, the art of breeding, feeding, fighting
and curing cocks of the game. . . .
By R. H., a lover of the sport [Robert
Howlett]. 8vo. Pp. 92. [*Brit. Mus.*]
London, 1709
" ROYAL Sussex " (a) hero ; memorials of
Lieutenant Anson Lloyd Silvester. . . .
Portrait and illustrations. Edited by
J. S. [James Silvester]. . . . 8vo. Pp.
vii. 137. [*Brit. Mus.*] London, 1920

ROYALL (the) law, and covenant of
God. What and where it is, and who
are in it. . . . [By James Nayler.]
4to. Pp. 8. [*Brit. Mus.*]
London, 1655

ROYALL (the) oake ; or, a crown's
worth of loyalty for a tester. [A
genealogy of the Kings of Scotland.
By John Shambothie ?] 8vo. Pp. 24.
[*Brit. Mus.*]   Edinburgh, 1682

RUBBER estate values. Reprinted from the " Straits Times." [By A. W. S. i.e. A. W. Still.] 8vo. Pp. vii. 94. [Brit. Mus.]   Singapore [1911]

RUBRIC (the) as to ornaments; remarks on its legal operation. By J. M. D. [J. M. Dale]. 8vo. [Lincoln's Inn Lib.]   London, 1867

RUDIMENTS of the Latin language. . . . For the use of Charterhouse schools. [By John Russell, D.D.] 8vo. 4 parts. [Brit. Mus.] London, 1813-14

*RULES and customs which by . . .
     For H. S. E., C.P., read H.S.E.C.P.

RULES (the) and directions for playing the new garden game of Lawn, or Line Hockey. . . . By J. H. M. [J. H. Matthews]. 8vo. [Brit. Mus.]
     London [1901]

RULES (the) of the Candlewick Ward Club ; with a short review of its history [by William Blades]. 8vo. [Brit. Mus.]   London, 1876

RUNNER (the). By Ralph Connor [Charles William Gordon]. 8vo. Pp. 478. [Brit. Mus.]   London [1930]

RURAL economy ; or, essays on the practical parts of husbandry. . . . By the author of the Farmer's letters [Arthur Young]. 8vo. [Brit. Mus.]
     London, 1770

RUSKIN (the) birthday book . . . arranged by M. A. B. [Maud A. Bateman] and G. A. [Grace Allen]. 4to. [Brit. Mus.]   Orpington, 1883

RYGHT (a) notable sermon. [By Richard Argentine, alias Sexten.] 8vo. [Huntington Lib. Checklist.]
     Ippeswich, 1548

S

SACRED (the) bee, and other poems. By Caroline Nash. [Edited by F. C. i.e. F. Clemence.] 12mo. Pp. 96. [Brit. Mus.]   London, 1850

SACRIFICE (the). By Wilmot Kaye [Edward Platt]. 8vo. Pp. 313. [Brit. Mus.]   London, 1911

SAFE (a) and sure method of acquiring a practical knowledge of French. By Chrysostôme Dagobert [J. B. A. Led'huy]. 12mo. [Brit. Mus.]
     London, 1857

SAILING directions for the Baltic sea. . . . By Admiral Gustaf Klint. [Edited by F. B. i.e. Sir Francis Beaufort.] 8vo. Pp. x. 157. [Brit. Mus.]
     London, 1854

SAILING directions for the Bristol Channel. [Advertisement signed: F. J. E. i.e. Sir Frederick J. O. Evans.] 8vo. [Brit. Mus.] London, 1879

SAILING directions for the West coasts of France, Spain, and Portugal. . . . [Advertisement signed: F. J. E. i.e. Sir Frederick J. O. Evans.] 8vo. [Brit. Mus.]   London, 1881

ST Cyprian Bishop and Martyr . . . of discipline, prayer, patience. . . . Translated by C. B. [Clement Barksdale]. 12mo. [Brit. Mus.] London, 1675

S. John's Cathedral, Hongkong. Anthem book : compiled by C. F. A. S. [C. F. A. Sangster]. 8vo. Pp. 66. [Brit. Mus.]   Hongkong, 1892

S. Mary, Lewisham Church Lads Brigade, 1892-1929. [By F. G. Marshall.] 8vo. Pp. 39. [Brit. Mus.] London [1930]

ST Patrick; a national tale of the 5th century. By an antiquary [——— Rennie]. 12mo. 3 vols. [Watt's Bibl. Brit.]   Edinburgh, 1819, 18
     It has been suggested that the author was James Rennie, of Sorn, Ayrshire, Professor of Natural History at King's College, London.

SALTMARSH returned from the dead . . . or, the resurrection of James the Apostle. . . . [By Samuel Gorton.] 4to. Pp. 198. [Brit. Mus.]
     London, 1655
     The Epistle dedicatory signed : S. G.

SALUTEM in Christo ; good men and evill delyght in contraries. . . . [A letter concerning the commitment of the Duke of Norfolk to the Tower, dated 13th Oct. 1571, and signed : R. G. i.e. Richard Grafton ? It is attributed to William Cecil, Lord Burleigh.] 8vo. B. L. [Brit. Mus.]
     [London, 1571]

SALVATION by Jesus Christ. [By J. Backhouse.] 12mo. Pp. 24. [Brit. Mus.]   Cape Town, 1838

SALVATION : what it is, and, what it is for : a word for the new year. By J. E. H. [James E. Hawkins]. 16mo. [Brit. Mus.]   London [1875]

SANCTIFICATION. [By William Kelly, of Guernsey.] 8vo. [Brit. Mus.]   [1875?]

SANITARY and social questions of the day. By an observer [Guy Cadogan Rothery]. 8vo. Pp. 92. [Brit. Mus.]
     London [1897]

SAYONARA — good - bye. By John Paris [Frank Trelawny Arthur Ashton-Gwatkin]. 8vo. Pp. viii. 370. [*Brit. Mus.*] London [1924]

SCALE for changing statute measure of $5\frac{1}{2}$ into the customary of Lancashire, being 7 yards to the perch. [By H. H. Fishwick?] Fol. S. sh. [*Brit. Mus.*] Rochdale [1830?]

SCANDAL. By the biographer of Anacreon [Joshua Smith? Introduction signed: A.]. 12mo. Pp. 48. [*Brit. Mus.*] Holt, Norfolk, 1827

SCATTERED gems, or weekly meditations; consisting of gleanings from various authors, with a scripture text and a verse of a hymn attached to each meditation. By a lady [Mary Judith Fellowes]. Second edition. 8vo. Pp. 262. [*Brit. Mus.*] London, 1853
Signed: M. J. F.

SCELERA aquarum; or, a supplement to Mr Graunt on the bills of mortality. . . . [By James Harvey?] 4to. Pp. 30. [*Brit. Mus.*] London, 1701
Signed: J. H., M.D.

SCENES and narratives from German history. [By M. A. Donne.] 16mo. [*Brit. Mus.*] London [1861]

*SCENES and sketches of a soldier's life in Ireland . . .
The attribution given is incorrect. The author was Joseph Donaldson, sergeant in the ninety-fourth Scots Brigade. This is the third of a series of army sketches (see also "Recollections of an eventful life" and "The War in the Peninsula") which were published anonymously, and published posthumously in one volume as "Recollections of the eventful life of a soldier" in 1856 with the author's name.

SCEPTIC (the) and other poems. By Leigh Cliffe [George Jones]. 12mo. [*Eng. Cat.* 1801-1836, p. 121.] London, 1836

SCEPTICAL (the) muse; or, a paradox on humane understanding: a poem. [By William Dove, of St Catharine's Hall, Cambridge.] Fol. Pp. 10. [*Brit. Mus.*] London, 1699

SCHEME (the) of God's eternal great designe in the world for Christ and his elect Saints, given to him by the father upon the performance of his great work of mediatorship. . . . [By William Sherwin.] Fol. [*Brit. Mus.*] [London? 1675?]

*SCHISM of the Church of England . . .
Attributed in the *M'Alpin Collection Catalogue* to John Spencer.

*SCHOOL (the) for fathers . . .
For Gulston, *read* Galston.

SCHOOLMASTERS (the) auxiliaries to remove the Barbarians Siege from Athens: advanced under two guides: the first leading by rule and reason to read and write English dexterously: the second asserting the Latine tongue in prose and verse to its just inlargement, splendor and elegancy. The industry of neer thirty years by R. L. [Richard Lloyd]. 12mo. 3 vols. [*Brit. Mus.*] London, 1659

SCIENCE gossip for young and old. By "Gossip" [Robert McMillan]. 8vo. Pp. 182. [*Brit. Mus.*] Sydney, 1907

SCIENCE (the) of religious truth . . . elucidated in theory and practice; a guide to the peculiar . . . knowledge . . . needful to compose an adequate . . . biography of . . . W. Law . . . [By Christopher Walton.] 8vo. Pp. xvi.-xxxiv. [*Brit. Mus.*] London, 1856
A reprint from the preface of his "Notes and materials for an adequate biography of . . . W. Law," which was itself anonymous.

SCOPE (the) of the Gospel; being notes of addresses by J. B. S. [J. B. Stoney]. 8vo. Pp. 187. [*Brit. Mus.*] London [1897]

SCOTIA'S noblest son; a concise account of the life and labours of David Livingstone. [By Henry Pickering.] 8vo. [*Brit. Mus.*] Glasgow [1916]
Signed: Hy. P.

SCOTISH elegiac verses on the principal nobility and gentry from 1629 to 1729. With . . . notes and an appendix of illustrative papers. [Edited by J. M. *i.e.* James Maidment.] 8vo. [*Brit. Mus.*] Edinburgh, 1842
Only ninety copies printed.

*SCOTLAND'S interest . . . 1704.
R. A. Scott-Macfie (*Bibliography of Andrew Fletcher*, p. 23) considers that on internal evidence this cannot be by Fletcher, although the style resembles his.

SCOTTISH (a) anthology. By A. H. S. [Annie H. Small]. 8vo. Pp. 66. [*Brit. Mus.*] London, 1912
No. 3 of the Iona Books.

SCOTTISH (the) national dances; their origin, nature and history. By R. H. C. [Robert Hogg Calder, M.A.]. 8vo. Pp. 21. [*Brit. Mus.*] Aberdeen, 1928
From an inscribed copy.

*SCOURGE (the) of Venus; or, the wanton lady . . . Written by A. H. [Henry Austin. A verse translation of part of Ovid's *Metamorphoses*, lib. x.]. 8vo. [*Brit. Mus.*] London, 1620
The edition of 1614 bears the initials: H. A.

SCRIPTURAL (the) faith of the young churchman, shown by the Church's own teaching. By E. S. A. [Letitia Willgoss Stone]. Second edition. 8vo. Pp. 48. [*Brit. Mus.*]
London [1874]

SCRIPTURE (the) accounts of the attributes and worship of God . . . By Hopton Haynes. [Edited by R. A. *i.e.* Richard Aspland.] 12mo. Pp. xii. 272. [*Brit. Mus.*]
London, 1815

SEARCH the Scriptures. By the author of *The lamplighter* [Francis Bourdillon]. 8vo. [*Brit. Mus.*]
London [1867]
Signed: F. B.

SEASONABLE (a) warning to Protestants ; from the cruelty and treachery of the Parisian Massacre, August the 24th, 1572. [By Vincent Alsop.] 4to.
London, 1680
Publisher's advertisement in Vincent Alsop's *Melius Inquirendum*, 1681 ed.

SEA-TIGER (the) ; a tale of mediæval Nestorianism. [By John Mason Neale.] 8vo. Pp. iv. 91. [*Brit. Mus.*]
London [1860]

SECESSION resisted. [By Joseph Reed Ingersoll, LL.D.] 8vo. Pp. 38. [Sabin's *Dictionary*.]
Philadelphia, 1861
See above, "Secession, a folly and a crime."

SECOND (the) booke of the English husbandmen . . . See "Cheape and good husbandry . . ."

SECOND (the) coming of the Lord Jesus Christ. [By Henry Drummond.] 12mo. Pp. 32. [*Brit. Mus.*]
London, 1829

SECOND (a) holiday for John Gilpin ; or a voyage to Vauxhall. . . . [In verse. By John Oakman.] Fol. S. sh. [*Brit. Mus.*]
London, 1785

SECOND (a) (-fourth) letter from a friend to the Right Honourable [Chief Justice W. Whitshed, on his discharging the Grand-Jury that refused to find the bill against J. Harding, the printer of the Draper's *i.e.* Dean Swift's letters. Subscribed N. N. *i.e.* R. Lindsay?] Fol. [*Brit. Mus.*]
Dublin, 1724-25
The third letter is entitled, "A third letter from —— to the ——.

*SECOND (a) letter to Dr M. . . .
Preceded by "An extract from the case of the electors . . ." and "A letter to the Rev. Dr M." All three were republished in the same year under the title "The election of aliens . . .", *q.v.*

SECOND (a) manuduction for Mr Robinson ; or, a confirmation of the former, in an answer to his manumission. [By William Ames.] 4to. Pp. 35. [*Brit. Mus.*]   N.P. 1615
"A Manuduction for Mr Robinson" forms the second part of "The unreasonableness of the separation . . . " *q.v.* It has been wrongly attributed to William Bradshaw, the author of "The unreasonableness of the separation . . ."

SECOND (the) part of Pasquils madcap intituled the fooles - cap. [By Nicholas Breton.] 4to. [*Christie-Miller Cat.*]
London, 1600
Signed : N. B.

SECOND (the) representation of the loyal subjects of Albinia [Queen Anne]. [By William Wagstaffe, M.D.] 8vo. [*D. N. B.* vol. 58, p. 436.] London, 1712
See above, "The representation . . ."

SECRET (the) history of Pythagoras. Part I. Translated from the original lately found at Otranto [or rather, written by J. W., M.D. *i.e.* Samuel Croxall?]. 8vo. [*Brit. Mus.*]
London, 1721

*SECRET memoirs of the late Mr Duncan Campbel . . .
Not by Defoe. The author is unknown.

SECRET (the) of the Curé d'Ars [Jean-Marie-Baptiste Vianney]. By Henri Ghéon [—— Vanglon]. (Translated by F. J. Sheed.) 8vo. Pp. 217. [Lorenz's *Catalogue générale; Brit. Mus.*]
London, 1929

SECRET (the) of the road. By Margaret Stuart Lane [Margaret Ashworth]. 8vo. Pp. 96. [*Brit. Mus.*] London, 1929

SECRET (the) of the Weird Sisters. By Mary Kavanagh [Margaret M. Spain]. 8vo. Pp. 64. [*Innisfail, a quarterly magazine*, No. 1.]
London [1924]

SECRET (the) room. By Anthony Pryde [Agnes Russell Weekes]. 8vo. Pp. 342. [*Who's Who in Lit.*]
New York, 1929

SECRETES (the) of . . . Alexis of Piemont [Girolamo Ruscelli] containyng excellente remedies against divers diseases, woundes and other accidents. . . . Translated out of Frenche . . . by W. Warde. 4to. 4 parts. [*Pollard and Redgrave*.]
London, 1558-69
A later edition (1614-15) begins, "The secrets . . ."

SELECT hymns ; a supplement to Dr Watts's psalms and hymns for the use of the congregation assembling in the Chapel, Hoxton Academy, London. [By Thomas Wilson.] 24mo. [*Brit. Mus.*]
London, 1807

SELECTED modern English essays. [Chosen by H. S. M. *i.e.* H. S. Milford.] 8vo. Pp. x. 414. [*Brit. Mus.*]
London, 1925

SELECTION (a) of curious and entertaining games at chess, that have been actually played. [By J. Cazenove.] 8vo. [*Brit. Mus.*]   London, 1817

SELECTION (a) of hymns, arranged as a companion to Horne's Manual of parochial psalmody. [By Frederick Edward Gretton.] 12mo. [*Brit. Mus.*]   London, 1859
Signed: F. E. G.

SELECTION (a) of hymns, designed principally for the use of prisoners. By the author of *Facts . . . respecting climbing boys* [Ann Alexander]. 24mo. Pp. 120. [*Brit. Mus.*]   York, 1819
Signed: A. A.

SELECTION (a) of hymns for public and private worship. [Compiled by S. M. *i.e.* Rev. Samuel Martin.] 8vo. Pp. 38. [*Brit. Mus.*] Falmouth [1824]

SELECTION (a) of hymns for the festivals of the Church of England, designed as an appendix to the New version of Psalms. . . . Second edition. . . . Printed . . . for the use of St Marks, Myddelton Square, Pentonville. [By T. M. *i.e.* Thomas Mortimer.] 24mo. [*Brit. Mus.*]
London, 1831

SELECTION (a) of passages from "Mind" . . . "Nature" . . . "Natural Science" . . . bearing on changes and defects in the significance of terms and in the theory and practice of logic. [Compiled by V. W. *i.e.* the Hon. Victoria A. M. L., Lady Welby Gregory.] 8vo. Pp. ii. 42. [*Brit. Mus.*]   Grantham, 1893

SELECTION (a) of psalms and hymns, chiefly adapted for public worship. [Edited by E. D. and J. A. B. *i.e.* Edward Davies and J. A. Baxter.] 12mo. Pp. xiii. 240. [*Brit. Mus.*]
Birmingham, 1830

SELECTIONS from Les recherches philosophiques sur les Americains of M. Pauw by Mr W * * * [Daniel Webb]. 8vo. [*Brit. Mus.*]   1789

SELECTIONS from the poems and letters of Bernard Barton. . . . [With a memoir of the author signed: E. F. G. *i.e.* Edward Fitzgerald.] 8vo. [*Brit. Mus.*]   London, 1849

SELECTIONS from the poems of Charlotte Elliott. . . . With a memoir . . . by E. B. [Mrs E. Babington?]. 8vo. [*Brit. Mus.*]   London [1873]

SELECTIONS from the poetical literature of the West. [Edited by W. D. G. *i.e.* William D. Gallagher.] 12mo. [*Brit. Mus.*]   Cincinnati, 1841

SELECTIONS from the versions of the Psalms. . . . [Edited by P. P. G. *i.e.* Philip Parker Gilbert.] Fifth edition. 12mo. [*Brit. Mus.*]   London, 1851

SELF culture; a course of lessons on developing the physical, unfolding the soul, attaining unto the spiritual. By Levi [Levi H. Dowling]. 8vo. Pp. 92. [*Brit. Mus.*]   Los Angeles, 1912

SENTIMENTAL excursions to Windsor and other places. . . . [By Leonard MacNally]. 12mo. London, 1781
Disclosed in an advt. at the end of his *Tristram Shandy* (1783).

SEPARATION and sedition inseparable, whilst Dissenters and Commonswealthsmen are permitted to controll in all publick administrations of Church and State: being a farther prosecution of the Dutch toleration. [By —— M—n *i.e.* W. Baron, Chaplain to the Earl of Clarendon.] 4to. Pp. 29. [*Brit. Mus.*]   London, 1703

SEPARATION (the) of mother and child by the law of "Custody of infants" considered. [By Sir Thomas Noon Talfourd.] 8vo. [*Lincoln's Inn Lib.*]   London, 1838

SERIES (a) of letters addressed to Sir William Fordyce . . . containing a voyage and journey from England to Smyrna, from thence to Constantinople, and from that place over land to England. Translated from the original into English by the author. To which is prefixed a short answer to Volney's Contradictions on Ali-Bey's History and revolt. . . . By S. L. Κοσμοπολίτης [S. Lusignan]. 8vo. 2 vols. [*Brit. Mus.*]   London, 1788
See "A history of the revolt of Ali Bey . . ."

*SERIES (a) of letters on the circulating medium . . .
The letters are signed: Y. Z.

*SERIOUS (a) and friendly address . . .
Not by William Allen, Vicar of Bridgewater, but by William Allen, Tradesman of London. See his *Works*, 1707.

SERIOUS (a) and seasonable warning unto all people; occasioned by two . . . epistles to a late book [*i.e.* the "new impression" of "Quakerism no Christianity"] of John Falldoe's, subscribed by Richard Baxter, Tho. Manton [and others]. By C. P. [Caleb Pusey]. 4to. Pp. 22. [*Brit. Mus.*]
[London, 1675]

SERIOUS (a) call to the Quakers inviting them to return to Christianity. [By George Keith.] 4to. S. sh. [*Brit. Mus.*]   London, 1700
An edition in the same year bears the author's name.

SERIOUS (a) letter [signed W. B. *i.e.* William Blake, Housekeeper to the Ladies Charity School, Highgate] sent by a private Christian to the Lady Consideration . . . 1 May 1655, which she is desired to communicate in Hide Park to the gallants of the times a little after sunset. . . . 4to. Pp. 22. [*Brit. Mus.*]   London, 1655
    For a later edition (1656) with a variant title, see " The Yellow book ; or a serious letter . . ." See also " The Trial of the ladies . . ." and " A new trial of the ladies . . ."

SERMON (a) lately preached on 1 Corinth. 3, 15, by a reverend divine of the Church of England [John Tillotson, Abp. of Canterbury]. 8vo. [*Lincoln's Inn Lib.*]   London, 1673

SERMON (a) [on John i. 1] on the supreme Godhead of Christ. [By Thomas Cooke, LL.D. ?] 8vo. Pp. 19. [*Brit. Mus.*]   London, 1810

SERMON (a) preached at Flitton Bedford at the funeral of Henrie E. of Kent. [By John Bowle, Bishop.] 4to. [*Pollard and Redgrave.*] London, 1615
    Signed: I. B.

SERMON (a) preach'd before the King and Queen . . . October 24, 1686. By . . . Dom W. M. [William Marsh], Monk of the Holy Order of St Benedict . . . Chaplain in Ordinary to His Majesty. 4to. Pp. 48. [*Brit. Mus.*]   London, 1687

SERMON (a) [on Joel ii. 15-17] preached upon the 30th of January S.V. 1684/5 at Paris. . . . [By William Wake.] 4to. Pp. 46. [*Brit. Mus.*] London, 1685
    The Epistle dedicatory is signed : W. W.

SERMONS for children. . . . By J. M. Neale. [Edited by J. H. *i.e.* Joseph Haskoll.] 8vo. [*Brit. Mus.*]   London, 1867

SERMONS for the Black Letter days. . . . By J. M. Neale. [Edited by J. H. *i.e.* Joseph Haskoll.] 8vo. Pp. xx. 299. [*Brit. Mus.*]   London, 1868

SERMONS of John Calvin upon the songe that Ezechias made after he had bene sicke . . . Translated out of Frenche into English [by A. L. *i.e.* A. Lock?]. 8vo. [*Brit. Mus.*] [1574]
    See also " Foure sermons . . ."

SERMONS on the Song of songs. By J. M. Neale. [Edited by J. H. *i.e.* Joseph Haskoll.] 8vo. [*Brit. Mus.*] London [1867]

SERMONS preached before His Maiestie. . . . By . . . John Preston. [The Epistle to the reader signed : T. G. and T. B. *i.e.* Thomas Goodwin and Thomas Ball.] 4to. Pp. 150. [*Brit. Mus.*]   London, 1631

SERMONS preached in a Religious House. By . . . J. M. Neale. [Edited by J. H. *i.e.* Joseph Haskoll.] 8vo. 2 vols. [*Brit. Mus.*]   London, 1869

SERPENT (the) of Devision ; wherein is conteined the true history or mappe of Romes overthrowe . . . [Written or translated by J. Lydgate.] . . . 4to. 2 parts. [*Brit. Mus.*] London, 1590

SERVANTS of the guns. [Tales.] By Jeffery E. Jeffery [Jeffery Eardley Marston]. 8vo. Pp. 263. [*Amer. Cat.*]   London, 1917

*SETONS (the) . . .
    For By Olivia Douglas [Ann Buchan], *read* By O. Douglas [Anna Buchan].

SEVEN gardens and a palace. By E. V. B. [Hon. Mrs Eleanor Vere Boyle]. 8vo. [*Who's Who in Lit.*]   London, 1900

SEVEN (the) sleepers. By Francis Beeding [John Leslie Palmer and Hilary Aidan St George Saunders]. 8vo. Pp. 317. [*Amer. Cat.*] Boston, 1925

SEVEN summers: an Eton medley. By the editors of the *Parachute* and *Present Etonian* [Robert Carr Bosanquet and others]. 8vo. Pp. 189. [M. Baring's *The Puppet Show of Memory.*]   Eton, 1890

SEVERAL grounds, reasons . . . and propositions offered to the King's . . . Majesty for the improvement of his revenue. . . . [By George Carew?] Fol. S. sh. [*Brit. Mus.*]   [1660]
    Signed : G. C.

SEVERAL letters between two ladies ; wherein the lawfulness and unlawfulness of artificial beauty in point of conscience are nicely debated. . . . [By Jeremy Taylor?] 12mo. [*Brit. Mus.*]   London, 1701

SEVERAL occasions for poems by persons of quality. Edited by R. D. [Randall Davies]. 4to. [*Brit. Mus.*]   London, 1928

SEVERAL orations of Demosthenes. . . . English'd . . . by several hands. . . . [The Second Philippic by K. C. *i.e.* Knightley Chetwood.] 12mo. Pp. 222. [*Brit. Mus.*]   London, 1702

SEVERAL papers ; some of them given forth by George Fox ; others by Jane Nayler. . . . Gathered together and published by A. P. [Alexander Parker] . . . with . . . a few queries propounded to Tho. Ledgard. . . . 4to. Pp. 40. [*Brit. Mus.*]   N.P. 1654

SEVERAL seats in Parliament to be had gratis ; or, the only method of securing the best election : being . . . a letter to a gentleman in Shrewsbury. [By Sir Richard Hill.] 8vo. Pp. 7. [*Brit. Mus.*]   Bath [1768]
    Signed : R. H.

SHADE (the) of the Balkans ; being a collection of Bulgarian folk-songs and proverbs [compiled by Pencho Rachev Slaveikov] . . . rendered into English (by Henry Bernard [Henry Baerlein]) . . . 8vo. Pp. 328. [*Brit. Mus.*]
London, 1904

SHAKESPEARE (the) birthday book. [Selected by M. F. P. D. *i.e.* Mary F. P. Dunbar.] 8vo. Pp. 277. [*Brit. Mus.*]   London, 1875

SHAKESPEARE (the) problem: a paper for students [ascribing the authorship of "Pedantius" to Francis Bacon]. By E. A. [Edward George Harman]. 8vo. Pp. 24. [*Brit. Mus.*]   London, 1909

SHAKESPEARE'S chair. [An account of a chair, formerly belonging to Shakespeare, now preserved at Lewes. By Kate Lintott.] 16mo. Pp. 8. [*Brit. Mus.*]   Uckfield [1908]
Signed : K. L.

*SHAW'S manual . . .
For J. Lithiby, *read* J. Letheby.

SHEEN Hall. By W. Dane Bank [William Henry Williamson]. 8vo. Pp. 287. [*Brit. Mus.*] London [1926]

SHEPHEARD'S (the) oracle delivered in an eclogue. [By Francis Quarles.] 4to. [*Brit. Mus.*]   Oxford, 1644

SHEPHERD (the) of Derwent Valley ; a drama. . . . By J. Lunn. . . . With . . . remarks by D. G. [George Daniel]. 12mo. Pp. 42. [*Brit. Mus.*]
London [1871]
Lacy's Acting Edition of Plays, vol. 89.

SHEPHERD (the) of Salisbury Plain, etc. [By Hannah More.] 12mo. [*Brit. Mus.*]   London, 1831
Signed : Z.

SHEPHERD (a) tale, and other verses. By G. H. F. N. [G. H. F. Norris]. 8vo. Pp. viii. 79. [*Brit. Mus.*] London, 1914

*SHETLAND fireside tales . . .
The title-page continues . . . By G. S. L. [*i.e.* George Stewart, of Lerwick].

SHIP (the) of hell. [A play.] By Gil Vicente. English version by A. F. Gerald [Aubrey Fitzgerald Bell]. 4to. Pp. 98. [*Brit. Mus.*]   Watford, 1929
Only 35 copies printed.

SHIPWRECKS and tales of the sea. [Edited by W. and R. C. *i.e.* William and Robert Chambers.] 8vo. [*Brit. Mus.*]   London, 1860

SHIRES and provinces. By Sabretache [A. S. Barrow]. Illustrated by Lionel Edwards. 4to. Pp. xiv. 195. [*Brit. Mus.*]   London, 1926
For a second series, see " More shires and provinces."

SHOOTER'S (the) diary ; or, forms for registering game killed during the year. . . . By I. E. B. C. [Irvine E. B. Cox]. 4to. [*Brit. Mus.*]
London [1866]

*SHORT (a) account of the city of Aberdeen. . . .
Mitchell and Cash attribute this to both Moir and Robertson.

SHORT (a) account of the office of the King's Remembrancer. [By Sir George Albert Bonner.] 8vo. [*Lincoln's Inn Lib.*]   London, 1928

*SHORT (a) account of the principal seats and gardens . . .
See also "A short view of the principal . . ."

SHORT (a) and private discourse betweene Mr Bolton and one M. S. concerning usury, published by E. B. [Edward Bagshawe]. 4to. [*Pollard and Redgrave.*]   London, 1637

SHORT (a) catechisme ; containing the principles of religion : very profitable for all sorts of people. [By John Ball.] 12mo. [*M'Alpin Coll. Cat.*]
London, 1637
Attribution by Dr Charles A. Briggs. See "A short treatise, contayning all the principall . . ."

SHORT (a) Christian doctrine (the manner how to help a priest to say Masse). . . . Translated into English [by Richard Gibbons]. 24mo. Pp. 72. [*Pollard and Redgrave.*]
[St Omer] 1633

SHORT (a) direction for the performance of Cathedrall service. . . . By E. L. [Edward Lowe]. 8vo. [*Brit. Mus.*]
Oxford, 1661

SHORT discourses of the late attemptat against His Maiesties person. [By William Alexander, Earl of Stirling.] 8vo. [*Pollard and Redgrave.*]
Edinburgh, 1600

SHORT (a) grammar of the English tongue, with . . . exercises. [By J. M. D. Meiklejohn.] 8vo. Pp. iv. 176. [*Brit. Mus.*]   London, 1890
Preface signed : J. M. D. M.

SHORT (a) historical account of the Public Library at Port Elizabeth. . . . [By P. E. Lewin.] 8vo. Pp. 17. [*Brit. Mus.*]   Port Elizabeth, 1906
Signed : P. E. L.

*SHORT (a) history of insects . . .
For By E. Fenn, *read* By Eleanor, Lady Fenn.

SHORT (a) history of the 3rd Volunteer Battalion of the Devonshire Regiment, 1859 to 1908. . . . By a Retired Officer of the 3rd Devon [William Hardinge Hastings]. 8vo. Pp. 51. [*Brit. Mus.*]   1908
From an inscribed copy.

SHORT (a) history, with notes and references, of the ancient and honourable family of Ancketill or Anketell. Compiled by one of its members [Augusta Anketell]. 8vo. Pp. 60. [*Brit. Mus.*] Belfast, 1902

SHORT (a) introduction to grammar. Compiled for the instruction of youth. [By David Wedderburn.] 12mo. Pp. 94. [*Pollard and Redgrave.*]
Aberdene, 1637
An earlier edition (1632) bears the author's name.

SHORT (a) life of the Apostle Paul, with a summary of Christian doctrine as unfolded in his epistles : in Sanskrit verse. [By J. M. *i.e.* John Muir.] With an English version. . . . 8vo. [*Brit. Mus.*] Calcutta, 1850

SHORT (a) manifestation of the main end of outward government. [By William Smith, of Besthorp.] Fol. S. sh. [*Brit. Mus.*] [1664]
Signed : W. S.

SHORT notes on Isaiah, chap. v.-xii. [By George Montagu, Duke of Manchester.] 8vo. [*Brit. Mus.*]
[London] private print, 1852
Signed : M.

SHORT (a) reply to "Landmarks," No. 6, of the S.P.C.K. By J. N. D. [John Nelson Darby]. 8vo. Pp. 32. [*Brit. Mus.*] London [1880]

SHORT sermons preached in the chapel of St Mary's College, Oscott. Collected and edited by the President (J. S. N. [*i.e.* James Spencer Northcote]). 8vo. [*Brit. Mus.*] London, 1876

SHORT stories of to-day and yesterday. [With introductory notes by Francis Henry Pritchard.] 8vo. [*Brit. Mus.*]
London, 1928
Signed : F. H. P.

*SHORT (a) treatise on harmony, containing . . . rules for composing in two, three and four parts. [By J. C. Pepusch.] Dedicated to all lovers of musick, by an admirer of this agreeable science [James Abercorn, seventh Earl of Abercorn, the translator]. Obl. 8vo. London, 1730

SHORT (a) treatise, shewing the causes and remedies of that general disease . . . commonly termed by many the plague of the guts. . . . Published by N. H. of Dorchester in the County of Dorset [Nathaniel Highmore]. . . . 8vo. Pp. 15. [*Brit. Mus.*]
London, 1658

*SHORT (a) view of the principal seats and gardens . . .
See also "A short account of the principal . . ."
For Miss J. H. Pye, *read* Mrs J. H. Pye.

SHOT-GUN (the) and its uses. By "East Sussex" [Frank Bonnett]. 8vo. Pp. xix. 179. London, 1914
Authorship disclosed in his "Mixed and rough shooting."

SHYPPE (the) of fooles. (By Sebastian Brant.) [Translated by Thomas Watson.] 4to. [*Pollard and Redgrave.*] [London] 1509
Another edition, 1517.

*SI mihi ! By Egomet. . . .
Not by W. T. Shore but by Henry Watson Fowler, author of *The King's English.* Revealed in an edition published under Fowler's own name in 1929 with the altered title "If wishes were horses."

SIBILLA Odaleta ; an historical romance, and episode of the wars of Italy, during the 15th century. Translated from the original Italian [of Carlo Varese]. [*Brit. Mus.*] London, 1852

SIDE issues. [Short stories.] By Jeffery E. Jeffery [Jeffery Eardley Marston]. 8vo. Pp. 256. [*Brit. Mus.*]
London, 1920

*SIDERO-THRIAMBOS . . .
For By A. M., *read* By A. M., citizen and draper of London.

SIEGE (t') o' Brou'lton. [By J. P. Morris.] [*Bibliotheca Jacksoniana*, p. 24.] 1867

SIEGE (the) of Mentz ; or, the German heroin : a novel. [Translated by P. B. *i.e.* Peter Bellon.] 12mo. [*Brit. Mus.*]
London, 1692

SIGNALS to be made by one man, without flags, haulyards, or any previous preparation, by day or at night, to be understood by all nations : 3rd Oct. 1812. [Signed : R. N. *i.e.* William Pringle Green.] Fol. S. sh. [*Brit. Mus.*] [London, 1812]

SIGNOR Topsy-Turvy's wonderful magic-lantern ; or, the world turned upside down. By the author of *My Mother* and other verses. [By Ann and Jane Taylor.] 16mo. Pp. 71. [*D. N. B.* vol. 55, p. 421.] London, 1811
Ann Taylor alone was the author of "My Mother."

SILENCE in life and forgiveness in death ; from the Spanish of Fernan Caballero [Cecilia F. J. Arrom de Ayala] . . . by J. J. Kelly. 8vo. [*Brit. Mus.*] London, 1883

SILENCE (the) of Colonel Bramble. By André Maurois [Emile Herzog]. Translated from the French [by Thurfrida Wake]. . . . 8vo. Pp. 207. [*Observer,* 1st Feb. 1931.]
London, 1919

SILK (the) stocking murders . . . By Anthony Berkeley [Anthony Berkeley Cox]. 8vo. Pp. vii. 276. [*Amer. Cat.*] London [1928]

SILVER linings. By Wilhelmina Stitch [Ruth Collie]. 8vo. Pp. 63. [*Brit. Mus.*]   London, 1928

SINS of the tongue, lying and other fraud ; a sermon [on Eph. iv. 25] preached in South Lambeth Chapel. [By C. P. Shepherd ?] 8vo. [*Brit. Mus.*]   [London] 1858

*SIR Humphry Davy's monument . . .
Signed : V.

SIR Joseph Wilson Swan, F.R.S. A memoir by M. E. S. and K. R. S. [Mary Edmonds Swan and Kenneth Raydon Swan]. 8vo. Pp. 183. [*Brit. Mus.*]   London, 1929

SIRENICA. By W. Compton Leith [Ormonde Maddock Dalton]. 8vo. Pp. 178.   London, 1913

SIX (the) proud walkers. By Francis Beeding [John Leslie Palmer and Hilary Aidan St George Saunders]. 8vo. Pp. 311. [*Amer. Cat.*]
London [1928]

SIXTEEN Irish sermons, in an easy and familiar style. . . . By J. G. [James O'Gallagher, Bishop of Raphoe]. 8vo. [*Brit. Mus.*]   Dublin, 1736

SIXTH (the) speed. By E. J. Rath [J. Chauncey Corey Brainerd and Edith Rathbone Brainerd]. 8vo. Pp. v. 236. [*Brit. Mus.*]   London, 1917

*SKETCH of a plan for settling in Upper Canada . . .
The second edition begins " Sketches of a plan . . . ", *q.v.*

SKETCH of operations in the Benares Sanskrit College. [By James Robert Ballantyne.] 8vo. [*Brit. Mus.*]
Mirzapore, 1852
Signed : J. R. B.

SKETCH (a) of some parts of the county of Carnarvon. By M. L. L. [M. L. Louis ?]. 12mo. Pp. 32. [*Brit. Mus.*]
Llanrwst, 1837

SKETCH of the history of Scots Law. [By Professor —— Mackay.] 8vo.
N.P., N.D.
Presentation copy from the author.

*SKETCH (a) of the internal condition of the United States . . .
For M. Poletika, *read* Peter Ivanovich Poletika. [Sabin's *Dict.* ; *Brit. Mus.*]

SKETCH (a) of the life of Linnæus ; in a series of letters : designed for young persons. [By Miss S. Waring.] 12mo. [Smith's *Cat. of Friends' Books*, ii. 860.]   London, 1827

SKETCHES of Newport and its vicinity ; with notices respecting the history, settlement, and geography of Rhode Island. . . . [By Sarah S. Cahoone.] 12mo. Pp. 213. [Sabin's *Dictionary.*]
New York, 1842
Issued earlier (1840) as "A visit to grandpa . . .", *q.v.*

SKETCHES of plans for settling in Upper Canada a portion of the unemployed labourers of Great Britain and Ireland. Second edition. . . . By a settler [John William Bannister]. 8vo. [Sabin's *Dictionary.*]
London, 1822
The first edition begins "Sketch of a plan . . .", *q.v.*

SKETCHES of Society and manners in Portugal ; in a series of letters from Arthur William Costigan to his brother. [By Major James Ferrier ?] 8vo. 2 vols.
London [1787]
From an inscribed copy.

SKIALETHEIA. . . . [By Edward Guilpin. The introduction signed : J. P. C. *i.e.* John Payne Collier.] 4to. Pp. 56. [*Brit. Mus.*]   London [1870]

SKITTLES . . . [A novel. By William Stephens Hayward.] 8vo. Pp. iv. 316. [*Brit. Mus.*]   London [1884]

SKITTLES in Paris . . . [A novel. By William Stephens Hayward.] 8vo. Pp. iv. 311. [*Brit. Mus.*]
London [1884]

SKYSCRAPER Murder. By A. A. Abbott [Samuel Spewack]. 8vo. Pp. 279. [*Amer. Cat.*]   New York, 1928

SLIP-CARRIAGE (the) mystery. (Colonel Gore's cases, No. 4.) By Lynn Brock [Alister M'Allister]. 8vo. Pp. 304. [*Brit. Mus.*]   London [1928]

*SMALL (a) handfull of fragrant flowers . . .
Pollard and Redgrave, giving the title as "A smale handfull . . .", attribute this to Nicholas Breton. In any case Nicholas Baxter would seem to be an error for Nathaniel Baxter.

SMILING (the) faces, and other stories. By Brinsley Macnamara [A. E. Weldon]. 16mo. Pp. 163. [*Brit. Mus.*]
London, 1929

SMOKE in the flame. [A novel.] By " Iota " [Mrs Mannington Caffyn]. 8vo. Pp. 346. [*Brit. Mus.*]
London, 1906

*SOCIAL life and manners in Australia . . .
For Massey, *read* Massary.

SOILED (the) dove ; a biography of a fast young lady known as " The Kitten." [By William Stephens Hayward.] 12mo. Pp. 316. [*Brit. Mus.*]
London, 1865

S O L E M N E (a) joviall disputation, theoreticke and practicke; briefly shadowing the Law of Drinking . . . fully discussed according to the Civill Law. Which . . . Blasius Multibibus [Richard Brathwait] . . . hath publicly expounded. . . . Faithfully rendered according to the originall Latine copie. (The smoaking age; or, the man in the mist: with the life and death of tobacco.) 8vo. 2 parts. [Brit. Mus.]
At the sign of Red Eyes: OENOZΨTHO-POLIS [London] 1617

*SOLO-WHIST . . .
There is another edition which continues ". . . a new edition, revised by his son, Rawdon Crawley, Bart., of Queen's Crawley, Hants." [Charles Frederick Pardon]. [Jessel's Bibl. of playing cards.]

S O M E account of General Robert Venables . . . By L. P. Townsend. [Edited by J. C. i.e. James Crossley.] 4to. Pp. iv. 28.   Manchester, 1871
"Chetham Miscellany," vol. 4.

*SOME account of the life and writings of the late Rev. Thomas Rennell . . .
Signed : J. L.

SOME account of the third Provincial Synod of Westminster; with the sermons of . . . the Cardinal President. . . . [Compiled by W. R. G. i.e. W. R. Francis Gawthorn?] 8vo. [Brit. Mus.]   London, 1859

SOME better thing for us. By A. S. L. [Mrs A. S. Jones]. 8vo. [Brit. Mus.]
London, 1905

SOME considerations on the reasonableness and necessity of increasing and encouraging the seamen. . . . [By Daniel Defoe.] 8vo. Pp. 51. [Brit. Mus.]   London, 1728

SOME considerations upon pluralities, non-residence, and salaries of curates. [By Dr Sherlock, Bishop of Salisbury.] 8vo. [Lincoln's Inn Lib.]
London, 1737

*SOME married fellows. . . .
For Fenn, read Venn.

SOME memoirs of the life of Dr Nathan Alcock, lately deceased. [By Thomas Alcock, his brother, vicar of Runcorn.] 8vo. [Brit. Mus.]   London, 1780
The authorship is clear from internal evidence.

SOME observations. I. On the antiquity of the present United Brethren, called Moravians; II. On some of the extracts of their General Synods; and III. On the doctrine of the Trinity and Person of Christ. [By William Cudworth.] 8vo. Pp. 22. [Brit. Mus.]
London, 1751

SOME observations on the Rev. R. Williams' preface to his Lexicon Cornu-Britannicum. [By Louis Lucien Bonaparte.] 4to. S. sh. [Brit. Mus.]
[London, 1865]
Signed : L. L. B.

SOME portions of essays contributed to The Spectator. By Mr Joseph Addison . . . [Edited by J. D. C. i.e. John David Chambers.] 4to. Pp. 46. [Brit. Mus.]   Glasgow, 1864

SOME reasons offered by the late ministry in defence of their administration. [By Daniel Defoe.] 8vo. Pp. 78. [P. Dottin's Daniel De Foe.]
London, 1715

SOME reflections on 1928 conferences, and other matters. [By Edgar London.] 8vo. Pp. 11.   Bridport [1928]
Signed : E. L.

SOME sacramentall instructions; or, an explanation of the principles of religion. . . . By T. B., B.D. [Thomas Bedford], Pastor of M. O. [Martin Outwich]. 16mo. [Brit. Mus.]
London, 1649

SOME short and useful reflections upon duelling, which should be in the hands of every person who is liable to receive a challenge or an offence. By a Christian patriot [Joseph Hamilton, of Dublin]. Second edition. 12mo. [Levi and Gelli's Bibl. del Duello, p. 179.]   Dublin, 1823

SOME thoughts concerning the affairs of this session of parliament, 1700. [By Andrew Fletcher, of Saltoun?] 8vo. Pp. 30. [R. A. Scott Macfie's Bibl. of Fletcher, p. 25.]
[Edinburgh?] 1700

SOME worthy proverbs left behind by Judith Zins-Penninck . . . Translated . . . by . . . W. C. [William Caton]. 4to. Pp. 10. [Brit. Mus.]
London, 1683

SOMETHING for everybody. [Religious addresses.] By Charles Lambert [Lambert Gore]. 4to. [Brit. Mus.]
Portsmouth [1867]

SOMETHING written concerning the world's creed, or what they teach their children to believe; for a belief of words cannot save the soul, but a belief in the light, Christ Jesus the word of God . . . [By William Smith, of Besthorp.] 4to. Pp. 8. [Brit. Mus.]
London, 1660

SONG (the) of the drains. [By] Libra [William Scales]. 8vo. S. sh. [Brit. Mus.]   London [1874]

SONGS from the glens of Antrim. By Moira O'Neill [Mrs Skrine, née Nesta Higginson]. 8vo. Pp. x. 61. [S. J. Brown's Ireland in Fiction.]
Edinburgh, 1900

SONGS of a crazy poet. By Stephen Reid Heyman[Lydia Dorothy Parsons]. 8vo. Pp. 108. [*Brit. Mus.*]
Oxford, 1929

SONGS of the red rose. By Alpha [Mrs A. Mackereth]. 16mo. Pp. 27. [*Brit. Mus.*] [Manchester] 1915

SONGS of the sailor men. By T. B. D. [William Milbourne James]. 8vo. Pp. 127. [*Brit. Mus.*] 1916

SONNETS. By the author of *Specimens of sonnets from the most celebrated Italian poets, with translations* [Charles Strong]. 8vo. Pp. 42. [*Brit. Mus.*]
Torquay, private print, 1829

SONNETS. [By] Zoemé [Alice Wills]. 8vo. [*Brit. Mus.*] [London, 1927]

SONNETS (the) of the Lady of the Garden. By Ethna Kavanagh [Sara Spain]. 8vo. [*Innisfail, a quarterly magazine*, No. 1.] London [1920]

SOULES (the) immortall crowne consisting of seaven glorious graces. . . . Divided into seaven dayes workes. [By Nicholas Breton.] 4to. [*Brit. Mus.*] London, 1605
Dedication signed: Ber. N., Gent.

SOULES (the) life; exercising it selfe in the sweet fields of divine meditation. Written by R. P. [Richard Portman]. 12mo. Pp. 138, 264. [*Brit. Mus.*]
London, 1645

SOUL'S (the) journey. [A sonnet sequence.] By A. F. Gerald [Aubrey Fitzgerald Bell]. 8vo. Pp. 29. [*Brit. Mus.*] Watford, 1928

SOUL'S (the) looking-glasse lively representing its estate before God. . . . By . . . William Fenner. [Edited by Edm. C. *i.e.* Edmund Calamy.] 8vo. Pp. 323. [*Brit. Mus.*]
Cambridge, 1640

SOUVENIR of H.M.S. *Victory;* specially designed for the Naval Exhibition, 1891. [By L. de Lautour Wells.] Obl. 8vo. Pp. 9. [*Brit. Mus.*] [London] 1891
Signed: L. de L. W.

SOUVENIR (a) of sympathy. Compiled by H. S. [Helen Simpson], Banff. With illustrations. 8vo. Pp. 198. [*Brit. Mus.*] Aberdeen, 1900

SOVEREIGNS (the) of England from the Norman Conquest, in rhyme. By J. B. B. [Sir John Bernard Burke]. 8vo. [O'Donoghue's *Poets of Ireland*, p. 16.] Dublin, 1876

SOVIET versus Civilization. By Augur [Vladimir Polyakov]. 8vo. Pp. 95. [*Amer. Cat.*] London, 1927

*SPANISH (the) bawd . . .
The original "Tragicomedia de Calisto y Melibea" was first published in Seville in 1501, and could not therefore have been by J. Perez de Montalban who lived in the next century. The traditional attributions are to Fernando de Rojas, Rodrigo de Cota, and Juan de Mena. In the first edition, and many subsequent ones, the attribution to Fernando de Rojas is contained in an acrostic, "El bachiller fernando de rojas acabo la comedia de calysto y melybea e fue nascido en la puebla de montavan."

SPARROW (the) and the primrose. By Y. S. N. [Mary Dutton]. 16mo. [*Brit. Mus.*] London [1862]

SPECIAL studies of cultivated rubber companies, by the editor of the *Rubber Investor* [W. G. Tarbet]. 8vo. [*Brit. Mus.*] 1908, *et seq.*

SPECIALL (a) remedie against the furious force of lawlesse loue. [By William Averell.] 4to. [*Pollard and Redgrave.*] London, 1579
Signed: W. A.

SPECIMENS of African languages spoken in the colony of Sierra Leone. [By Mrs Hannah Kilham.] 12mo. 3 parts. [*Brit. Mus.*] 1828

SPECIMENS of translation from Horace and other ancient poets; with some additional poems. By the author of *Poetical epistles*, etc. [Robert Morehead, D.D.]. 8vo. Pp. 133. [*Brit. Mus.*] Edinburgh, 1814

*SPECULUM ecclesiasticum . . .
This is signed: Per T. W.

SPECULUM nauticum; a looking-glasse for sea-men: first set forth by John Aspley. The sixth edition . . . by H. P. [H. Phillips] and W. L. [William Leybourn]. 4to. [*Brit. Mus.*] 1662

SPEECH (a) against continuing the army, spoken the 4th of December, 1717. By W— S—, Esq. [William Shippen]. 8vo. [*Brit. Mus.*]
London, 1718

SPEECHES and toasts; how to make and propose them. . . . By the author of the *Letter Writer's handbook* [Henry Frith]. 8vo. Pp. 136. [*Brit. Mus.*] London [1883]

SPEECHES of M. Dupin Ainé at the Bar. [By Abraham Hayward.] 8vo. [*Brit. Mus.*] [London, 1834]
Signed: H. An extract from the *Law Magazine*, vol. 9.

SPINSTER (the). By Hubert Wales [William Piggott]. 8vo. Pp. 319. [*Brit. Mus.*] London, 1912

SPINSTER'S (a) tour in France, the states of Genoa, etc., during the year 1827. [By Elizabeth Frost, later Mrs Byron, then Mrs Strutt.] 12mo. Pp. iv. 427. [*Brit. Mus.*]   London, 1828

*SPIRIT (the) of detraction . . .
For William Vaughan, *read* Sir William Vaughan.

SPIRIT (the) of our laws. [By Herman Joseph Cohen.] 8vo. Pp. xi. 299. [*Brit. Mus.*]   London, 1906

SPIRIT rapping and spiritual manifestations. [By William Tarbet.] 8vo. Pp. 11. [*Brit. Mus.*] London [1855?]
Signed: A member of the Catholic Apostolic Church.

SPIRITUAL (the) conflict in five treatises . . . See "The Christian pilgrim in his spirituall conflict . . ."

SPIRITUAL manifestations in the present day. [By William Tarbet.] 8vo. Pp. 12. [*Brit. Mus.*]   1855

SPIRITUALISM a sign and prelude of the coming judgments. [By William Tarbet.] 8vo. Pp. 8. [*Brit. Mus.*]
                                                     [1862]
SPLENDID (a) cousin. By Mrs Andrew Dean [Mrs Cecily Sidgwick]. 8vo. Pp. 201. [*Brit. Mus.*]
                                    London, 1892
*SPLENDID sins; a letter addressed to . . . the Duke of Wellington [on the observance of Sunday]. By Latimer Redivivus [John Davies, D.D.]. Second edition. 8vo. [*Brit. Mus.*]
                                    London, 1820
SQUATTERS at Dabchick Lake; a Western story. By Emart Kinsburn [Arthur Preston Hankins]. 8vo. Pp. 288. [*Brit. Mus.*]   London [1926]

SQUATTER'S treasure. . . . By Emart Kinsburn [Arthur Preston Hankins]. 8vo. Pp. 287. [*Brit. Mus.*]
                                    London [1929]
STAGE struck . . . Adapted from [James Cobb's] *Love in the East* by W. Dimond. 12mo. Pp. 22. [*Brit. Mus.*]
                                    London [1853]
Lacy's Acting Edition of Plays, vol. 10.

STANLEY Spencer. [A monograph. By R. H. Wilenski.] 4to. Pp. 30. Pl. 35. [*Brit. Mus.*]   London, 1924
Signed: R. H. W.

STANZAS to Queen Victoria and other poems. By Sennoia Rubek [John Burke.] 8vo. Pp. 208. [Sabin's *Dictionary*.]   New York, 1866
Sennoia Rubek is an anagram for Joannes Burke.

STANZAS written by an unfortunate schoolmaster [Samuel Lines]. S. sh. [*Brit. Mus.*]   [Woodbridge? 1840?]
Signed: S. L.

STATE (the) and interest of the nation, with respect to His Royal Highness the Duke of York. [By Sir Roger L'Estrange.] 4to. [*Lincoln's Inn Lib.*]
                                    London, 1680
STATE (the) remedy for poverty. By a doctor of medicine, author of *The elements of social science* [George Drysdale]. . . . Second edition. Pp. 14. 8vo. [*Brit. Mus.*] London, 1904

STATEMENT of the constitution of the Belfast Academy; with an account of the history and present state of the system of education pursued in that seminary. [By Reuben John Bryce.] 8vo. Pp. 30. [*Brit. Mus.*]
                                    Belfast, 1829
STATION life in New Zealand. By Lady Barker. [Edited by F. N. B. *i.e.* Sir Frederick Napier Broome.] 8vo. Pp. xi. 238. [*Brit. Mus.*]
                                    London, 1870
STATISTICS of Protestant Missionary Societies, 1872-3. [Compiled by W. B. B. *i.e.* William Binnington Boyce.] 8vo. [*Brit. Mus.*]
                        London, private print, 1874
STELLA Nash. By Ganpat [Martin Louis Alan Gompertz]. 8vo. Pp. viii. 351. [*Brit. Mus.*]   Edinburgh, 1924

STEPPING stones; a book for the young. By the author of *Village Missionaries* [Emily Steele Elliott]. 8vo. Pp. 193. [*Brit. Mus.*]
                                    London, 1862
STONE desert. By Hugo Wast [G. Martínez Zuviria]. Translated . . . by Louis Imbert and Jacques Le Clercq. 8vo. Pp. v. 302. [*Brit. Mus.*]
                                    New York, 1928
STONE preachers. By the author of *The lamplighter* [Francis Bourdillon]. 12mo. [*Brit. Mus.*]   London [1869]
Signed: F. B.

STONEPASTURES. By Eleanor Stuart [Eleanor Stuart Childs]. 8vo. Pp. 178. [*Brit. Mus.*]
                                    New York, 1895
"STOPS"; or, how to punctuate . . . By Paul Allardyce [George Paul Macdonell]. [*Amer. Cat.*]   London, 1884

STORIES for workers. By the author of *Copsley annals* [Emily Steele Elliott]. 8vo. [*Brit. Mus.*]   London, 1873

*STORIES from Church history . . .
For Banbury, *read* Bunbury.

STORM-BOUND. [A novel.] By J. G. Sarasin [Geraldine Gordon Salmon]. 8vo. Pp. 288. [*Brit. Mus.*]
London [1930]

STORY (the) of Aston-on-Trent Church. [Signed: R. L. F. *i.e.* Robert Lethbridge Farmer.] 8vo. [*Brit. Mus.*]
N.P. [1930]

STORY (the) of Elize Marcel. By Madame J. de Lambert [Jules Rostaing. Translated from the French]. 16mo. [*Brit. Mus.*]   London, 1874

STORY (the) of Florence Nightingale. By W. J. W. [W. J. Wintle]. 8vo. Pp. 157. [*Brit. Mus.*] London [1928]

STORY (the) of Hamlet and Horatio. [By Sir Robert Rice, K.C.M.G.] 8vo. Pp. 722.   London, 1924
Information received by Mr John Grant from Lady Rice.

STORY (the) of his love; the journal and early correspondence of A. M. Ampère. . . . Edited by Madame H. C. [Henriette Chevreux]. 8vo. [*Brit. Mus.*]   London, 1873

STORY (the) of Orford Castle; told briefly by the Chamberlain of the Orford Town Trust [Richard A. Roberts]. 8vo. Pp. 16. [*Brit. Mus.*]
Ipswich [1930]

STORY (the) of our British ancestors. By M. C. [M. Cooke]. 12mo. Pp. 85. [*Brit. Mus.*]   London, 1927

STORY (the) of our days; an Empire birthday book. [By R. M. Leonard.] 12mo. Pp. 255. [*Brit. Mus.*]
London [1915]
Preface signed: R. M. L.

STORY (the) of the Jubilee singers, with their songs. [Compiled by J. B. T. Marsh.] 8vo. [*Brit. Mus.*]
London, 1875
Signed: J. B. T. M.

STOWE: the gardens of . . . Richard Lord Viscount Cobham. Addressed to Mr Pope. [A poem. By Gilbert West.] Fol. [Gough's *Bibl. Buckingham*, p. 43.]   London, 1732
There was an 8vo edition in the same year. It has been wrongly ascribed to George Bickham the younger.

STRANGE (a) but true relation how Mr Edmund Curll . . . out of an extraordinary desire of lucre went into Change Alley, and was converted from the Christian religion by certain eminent Jews; and how he was circumcised and initiated into their mysteries. [By Alexander Pope.]
London [1717]
See the note to "A full and true account of a horrid . . . revenge by poison . . ."

STRANGE (the) case of Mary Page. By Frederick Lewis [Frederick Lewis Collins]. 8vo. Pp. 188. [*Brit. Mus.*]
London [1916]

STRANGE (a) history; a dramatic tale, in eight chapters. By Slingsby Lawrence [George Henry Lewes] and Charles James Mathews. 12mo. [*Brit. Mus.*]   London [1853]
Lacy's Acting Edition of Plays, vol. 10.

STRANGE (the) inheritance. By Paul Trent [Edward Platt]. 8vo. Pp. 303. [*Brit. Mus.*]   London, 1921

STRANGE (the) little girl; a story for children. By V. M. [Philip Alfred Malpas]. . . . 8vo. Pp. 74. [*Brit. Mus.*]   Point Loma [1911]

STRANGE (the) search. Told from the French of Eugénie Foa [Eugénie Rebecca Gradis, *née* Rodrigues] by Amena Pendleton. . . . 8vo. Pp. 202. [*Bibl. Nat. Paris.*] Philadelphia [1929]

STRANGE (the) story of Ahrinziman. By A. F. S. [Anita F. Silvani]. 8vo. Pp. iv. 284. [*Brit. Mus.*]
London, 1906

STRANGE tales from the Fleet. By "Etienne" [Stephen King-Hall]. 8vo. Pp. 145. [*Brit. Mus.*] London, 1919

STRENGTH (the) of lovers. By Hugo Wast [G. Martínez Zuviria]. Translated by Louis Imbert and Jacques Le Clercq. 8vo. Pp. 315. [*Brit. Mus.*]   London, 1930

*STRICTURES on the abolition of the slave trade . . .
Signed: J. S.

STRICTURES on the Friendly address [by Myles Cooper] examined, and a refutation of its principles attempted: addressed to the people of America. [By Thomas Bradbury Chandler.] [Evans' *Amer. Bibl.*] 8vo.
[New York] 1775

STUDENTS (the); or, biography of Grecian philosophers. By the author of *Wars of the Jews*, etc. [Christian Isobel Johnstone]. 12mo. Pp. 217. [*Brit. Mus.*]   London [1827]

STUDIES and translations from the Tamil. By P. A. [P. Arunāchalam]. 8vo. Pp. 62. [*Brit. Mus.*]
Madras, 1898

STUDY (a) of the prologue and epilogue in English literature, from Shakespeare to Dryden. By G. S. B. [George Spencer Bower]. 8vo. Pp. xi. 187. [*Brit. Mus.*]   London, 1884

SUBALTERN'S (a) war; being a memoir of the Great War from the point of view of a romantic young man. . . . By Charles Edmonds [Charles Edmonds Carrington]. 8vo. Pp. 224. [*Brit. Mus.*] London, 1929

*SUBPOENA (a) from the high Imperiall Court . . .

A writer in *T.L.S.*, 31st July 1930, points out that in the 1623 title an acrostic is formed by the initials of each line which, read upwards, gives John Andrewes; this being John Andrews, of Trinity College, Oxford. The 1623 title starts: "A subpaena . . ."

SUBSIDIA primaria. I(-III). Steps to Latin : First (-fourth) course : being a . . . companion book to "The Public School Latin Primer." By the editor of the "Primer" [Benjamin H. Kennedy]. 12mo. 3 vols. [*Brit. Mus.*] London, 1868-73

SUGGESTED (a) history course for the elementary school. Standards I.-VII. [By E. H. Spalding.] 8vo. Pp. 24. [*Brit. Mus.*] New Cross, 1909

Signed : E. H. S. The second edition, 1915, "Suggestions for a history course . . .", was by E. H. S. and R. H. S., the latter unidentified.

SUGGESTIONS for thought to the searchers after truth among the artizans of England. [By Florence Nightingale.] 8vo. 3 vols. [*Brit. Mus.*]
London, 1860

ΣΥΓΚΡΗΤΙΣΜΟΣ; or, dissatisfaction satisfied : in seventeen sober and serious queries tending to allay the discontents of persons dis-satisfied about the late revolution of government. . . . Proposed by J. G. [John Goodwin]. 4to. [*Brit. Mus.*] London, 1654

SUMMARY (a) of the arguments for the new grammatical arrangement of the Latin verb. . . . [By W. Belcher.] 8vo. [*Brit. Mus.*] Canterbury, 1817

*SUMMUS Angliae Seneschallus . . .

According to the *D. N. B.* (vol. 7, p. 160) the author was John Brydall, and in the Brydall Collection in Lincoln's Inn Library there is a copy to which Brydall has put his name as author.

SUNDAY (a) evening's conversation at Benwell ; or, a pastoral between Corydon and Thyrsis ; occasioned by a book [by Q. Z. *i.e.* Cuthbert Ellison] lately published intituled "A Sunday's trip to Benwell : by a lover of the clergy [—— Thirkeld, Curate of Whicham]. Fol. Pp. x. [*Brit. Mus.*]
Newcastle upon Tyne, 1726

SUNLIGHT through shadows. By F. M. S. With a preface by the author of *English hearts and English hands* [signed C. M. *i.e.* Miss C. M. Marsh]. 8vo. [*Brit. Mus.*]   1877

*SUNLIGHT through the mist . . .

For Mrs —— Burrows, *read* Mrs E. Burrows.

SUPPLICATIONS and prayers for the coming again of the Lord Jesus Christ as the only deliverer. [By W. F. Pitcairn.] 16mo. Pp. 14. [*Brit. Mus.*]   Edinburgh [1875 ?]

SUPPLY (a) to a draught of an act or system proposed by the Committee for regulations concerning the law . . . To which is added a short treatise of tithes . . . Published by divers officers and souldiers of the Commonwealth . . . being the second part of their antidote. [By Edward Leach ?] 4to. [*Brit. Mus.*]   [London] 1653

Subscribed : E. L. T. P. H. W. S. G., etc.

SURRENDER (the) of Calais ; an historical drama. [By George Colman the younger.] 8vo. [*Brit. Mus.*]
York, 1801

SURSUM corda ; a defence of idealism. [By Edmond Gore Alexander Holmes.] 8vo. Pp. vi. 212. [*Brit. Mus.*]   1898

SURVEY (the) of London . . . Begunne first by . . . John Stowe . . . finished by . . . H. D. [Henry Dyson] and others. . . . Fol. [*Brit. Mus.*]
London, 1633

SWEDEN'S rights and her present political position. By Anders Svenske [Anna Wallenberg]. 8vo. Pp. 118. [Pettersen's *Norsk Lexikon.*]
London, 1907

SWISS (the) peasant. By J. Rickle. [Translated by J. Y. *i.e.* John Yardley ?] 12mo. [*Brit. Mus.*]   1856

SYMPHONIES. [In verse.] By E. H. W. M. [E. H. W. Meyerstein]. 8vo. Pp. 79. [*Brit. Mus.*]
Oxford, 1915

T

*TALES of the dead . . .

Mrs Utterson was only the translator of this volume. The original was entitled "Fantasmagoriana, ou recueil d'histoires d'apparitions. . . . Traduit de l'Allemand par un amateur." This was also anonymous. The compiler was J. B. B. Eyriès. [Barbier.]

TEACHINGS (the) of Freemasonry. By "Essex Master" [George Edward Roebuck]. 8vo. Pp. 175. [*Brit. Mus.*] London, 1928
Signed : G. E. R.
Acknowledgment by the author.

TESTIMONY (a) of antiquity ; shewing the ancient faith of the Church of England, touching the sacrament of the body and blood of the Lord, here publickly preached, and also received in the Saxons time, above seven hundred years ago. [By William Lisle.] 8vo. [*Camb. Univ. Lib.*] Oxford, 1675
An extract from Lisle's edition (1623) of Aelfric's Saxon Treatise.

TEXTS (the) examined which Papists cite out of the Bible for the proof of their doctrine of auricular confession. [By Thomas Lynford.] [*M'Alpin Coll. Cat.*] London, 1688
The author is named in the table of contents.

*TEXTS which Papists cite . . .
The author, Edward Fowler, is named in the table of contents.

THAT all might see who they were that had a command, and did pay tythes, and who they were that had a law to receive them : and also them that witnessed in spirit and life the law fulfilled, the substance and end of the law, and that priesthood that took tythes . . . [By] G. F. [George Fox]. [*Smith's Cat. of Friends' Books*, i. 653.] London, 1657

THREE (the) Kerry pearls. [By Annie MacInlay-Jamieson.] 8vo.
Kingston, Jamaica, N.D.
From an inscribed copy.

TREATISE of prayer ; two quaeries resolved touching formes of prayer, and six quaeries relating specially to the Lord's Prayer. [By Hezekiah Woodward.] London, 1656
See the note at the end of his Law-Power, 1656.

TREATISE of the confession of sinne, and chiefly as it is made unto the priests and ministers of the Gospel : together with the power of the keys, and of absolution. [By Thomas Ailesbury.] [*D. N. B.* vol. 2, p. 278.]
London, 1657

TRIUMPHS (the) of steam ; or stories from the lives of Watt, Arkwright and Stephenson. By the author of *Might not right*, etc. [Mrs E. Burrows]. 8vo. Pp. 263. [*Brit. Mus.*] London, 1859

*TRUE (a) and impartial narrative of the most material debates . . .
The *D. N. B.* supports the attribution to Bethel. Dr Charles A. Briggs ascribes it to James Harrington [*M'Alpin Coll. Cat.*]

TRUE (the) chronicle historie of the whole life and death of Thomas Lord Cromwell . . . written by W. S. 4to.
London, 1613
To Wentworth Smith have been unwarrantably ascribed the three plays "Locrine," "The Puritan" and "Cromwell." . . . There is no clue to the authorship. [*D. N. B.* vol. 53, p. 138.]

TRUE (the) news of the good new world shortly to come [Heb. 2, 5] for all such as then shall be found real saints. . . . [By William Sherwin.] [*Brit. Mus.*] N.P. [1675 ?]

TWO (the) Americas ; Great Britain and the Holy Alliance. [By William Duane.] Second edition. 8vo. Pp. 40. [*Brit. Mus.*] Washington, 1824
Signed : W. D.

TWO points of great moment, the obligation of humane laws, and the authority of the magistrate about religion discussed ; together with the case which gave occasion to the first point. In opposition to the two authors of the Friendly debate, and of the preface to a late book of Bishop Bramhalls. By J. H. [John Humfrey]. [*D. N. B.* vol. 28, p. 236.] 1672
The "Obligation of Human laws discussed" appeared separately in the previous year.

TWO treatises and an appendix to them concerning infant-baptisme. . . . [By John Tombes.] 8vo.
London, Dec. 15, 1646
This is the second edition. The previous impression, dated December 15, 1645, is identical but bears the author's name.

U

UNTO the questions sent me last night I pray accept of the ensuing answer, under the title of two questions concerning the power of the supream magistrate about religion, and the worship of God : with one about tythes proposed and resolved. [By John Owen.] 4to. Pp. 8. [*M'Alpin Coll. Cat.*] London, 1659
No title-page. Signed : J. O.

UPON the late storm and death of the Protector ensuing the same. [By Edmund Waller.] [*D. N. B.* vol. 59, p. 127.] London, 1659

V

VAGABOND'S (a) wallet. By Stephen Reid Heyman [Lydia Dorothy Parsons]. 8vo. Pp. 76. [*Brit. Mus.*] London, 1916

*VANITY (the) of humane inventions . . .
This was by the author of *Nehushtan*, traditionally John Wilson, but more probably Joseph Wilson of Beverley, in Yorkshire. See the note to *Nehushtan*.

VERONIQUE ; a comic opera in three acts. By A. Vanloo and G. Duval. Translated by Lilian Eldée [Mrs Lilian Bertha Duncombe]. 8vo. Pp. 53. [*Brit. Mus.*] London, 1903

VERSES from the Grand Fleet. By Etienne [Stephen King-Hall]. 8vo. Pp. 45. [*Brit. Mus.*] London, 1917
One of the Malory Booklets.

VERY (a) heroical epistle from my Lord All-Pride to Dol-Common, etc. (Epigram upon my Lord All-Pride). [Satirical verses on the Duke of Buckingham. By Sir Carr Scrope?] Fol. S. sh. [*Brit. Mus.*] [London] 1679

VIKING (the) and other poems. By Hugh M'Nab [Hugh M'Nab Humphry, barrister]. 8vo. Pp. vi. 115. London, 1906
From an inscribed copy.

VINDICATION of that prudent and honourable knight, Sir Henry Vane, from the lyes and calumnies of Mr Richard Baxter, minister of Kidderminster. In a monitory letter to the said Mr Baxter. By a true friend and servant of the Commonwealth of England . . . [Henry Stubbe]. 8vo. [*D. N. B.* vol. 55, p. 117.] London, 1659

VINDICATION of the Unitarians against a late Reverend author on the Trinity ; in a letter : second edition corrected and enlarged. [By William Freke.] [M'Lachlan's *Nonconf. Lib.*, p. 64.] London, 1690

VINDICIÆ Ecclesiæ Anglicanæ ; or, a iustification of the religion now professed in England. . . . By W. T. [Walter Travers]. 4to. [*Pollard and Redgrave*]. London, 1630

VINDICIÆ vindiciarum ; or, a further manifestation of M. J. C., his contradictions instanced in Vindiciæ clavium. Part 2. By D. C. [Daniel Cawdrey]. 4to. [*M'Alpin Coll. Cat.*] London, 1651
The author's name was on the title-page of Part I.

VISION (a) of immortality. By Stephen Reid Heyman [Lydia Dorothy Parsons]. 8vo. Pp. 77. [*Brit. Mus.*] Oxford, 1917

VOICE (the) of liberty ; or a British Philippic. A poem in Miltonic verse. [Subscribed Britannicus, *i.e.* Mark Akenside.] Fol. [*Brit. Mus.*] London, 1738
For another edition in the same year, see "A British Philippic . . . "

VOX clamantis ; or an essay for the honour, happiness and prosperity of the English gentry, and the whole nation ; in the promoting religion and vertue, and the peace both of Church and State. By P. A., Gent. [Philip Ayres]. 8vo. Pp. 110. [*D. N. B.* vol. 2, p. 292.] London, 1684

W

WALTER Graham, statesman; an American romance. By an American [Thomas Whitson]. 8vo. Pp. 602. [Appleton's *Dict. of Amer. Biog.*]
Lancaster, Pa., 1891

WAR (the) in the Peninsula. A continuation of the "Recollections of an eventful life," etc. [By Joseph Donaldson, sergeant in the ninety-fourth Scots Brigade.] 8vo.
Glasgow, 1825

The second of a series of three works, "Recollections, etc.," "The war in the Peninsula," and "Scenes and sketches of a soldier's life in Ireland," which were later (1856) republished in one volume as "Recollections of the eventful life of a soldier" and bearing the author's name.

WARS (the) of the Jews [of Josephus] ... Adapted to young persons ... [by Christina Jane Johnstone]. 12mo. [*Brit. Mus.*]   London, 1832
Preface signed : Aunt Jane.

WAY (the) to the peace and settlement of these nations, fully discovered in two letters, delivered to his late Highness the Lord Protector, and one to the present Parliament, wherein the liberty of speaking (which every one desires for himself) is opposed against Antichrist. . . . By Peter Cornelius, van Zurick-Zee [Hugh Peters]. 4to. Pp. 30. [*D. N. B.* vol. 45, p. 77.]   London [1659]

WEEK'S (a) entertainment at a wedding; containing six surprising and diverting adventures. . . . Written in Spanish by the author of Don Quixot, and now first translated into English. 8vo. Pp. xii. 232.   1710

This is a reissue with a different title-page only of "The diverting works of the famous Miguel de Cervantes" (1709) *q.v.* It is not the work of Cervantes but is a translation by Edward Ward of the "Para todos" of Juan Perez de Montalban.

WEEPERS (the); or the bed of snakes broken; wit vitiated and made a pander to wickednesse; instanced in a pack of knaves. . . . By S. S. [Samuel Sheppard]. [*D. N. B.* vol. 52, p. 63.]   London, 1652

WEIRD (the) of the wanderer; being the papyrus records of some incidents in one of the previous lives of Mr Nicholas Crabbe. Here produced by Prospero and Caliban [Frederick William Rolfe]. 8vo. Pp. xxii. 298. [*Brit. Mus.*]   London, 1912

WEST (the) of Scotland Arch-Voluntary; or the Rev. Andrew Marshall . . . called to account for his mendacious, dishonest and impertinent lucubrations in the 24th number of the *United Secession Magazine*. By Anglo-Scotus [John Lockhart ?]. 8vo. Pp. 26. [*Brit. Mus.*]   Newcastle, 1835

WHAT saith the Scripture ; an exposition of Bible prophecies, concerning the Covenant people, the latter days, and the second advent. By Discipulus [Basil Stewart]. 8vo. Pp. xv. 287. [*Brit. Mus.*]   London, 1922

WHERE freedom falters. By the author of *The Pomp of Power* [Laurance Lyon]. 8vo. Pp. xxiii. 355. [*Brit. Mus.*]
London, 1927

The authorship is, however, disclosed on p. xix.

WHERE is the wise? Where is the scribe? Where is the disputer of this world? Hath not God made foolish the wisdome of this world? 1 Cor. i. 20. [By Isaac Pennington.] [Smith's *Cat. of Friends' Books*, ii. 342.]   1660
Signed: I. P. No title-page.

WHITE (the) blackbird. By Hudson Douglas [Robert Aitken]. 8vo. Pp. viii. 366. [*Brit. Mus.*]   Boston, 1912

WHO told you that? The story-teller's vademecum. Compiled by Quex, of the *Evening News* [George Herbert Fosdike Nichols]. 16mo. 2 parts. [*Brit. Mus.*]   London, 1921, 22

"WHOOPS, Dearie !" By Peter Arno [Curtis Arno Peters]. Pp. 176. [*Sat. Review of Lit.*, 21st May 1927.]
New York, 1927

WINCHESTER College Hall windows ; a note by H. C. [Herbert Chitty] and R. G. [Reginald Morier Yorke Gleadowe]. 8vo. Pp. 6, pl. 4. [*Brit. Mus.*]   Winchester, 1931

WINCHESTER College notions. By three Beetleites (W. H. L[awson], J. F. R. H[ope], A. H. S. C[ripps]). 8vo. Pp. viii. 161. [*Brit. Mus.*]
Winchester, 1901

WISDOME crying out to sinners to returne from their evill wayes. . . . Now published for the generall good. [By William Milbourne.] 8vo. Pp. 319. [*Pollard and Redgrave.*]
London, 1639

An edition of the previous year, entitled "Sapientia clamitans : wisdom calling out to sinners . . . ", bears the author's name.

WISDOM'S better than money ; or the whole art of knowledge, and the art to know men ; in four hundred sententious essays, political and moral. Written by a late person of quality [Francis Quarles]. 12mo. Pp. 286. [*Brit. Mus.*]   London, 1698

This is an edition of Quarles' "Enchiridion" with an altered title. See also "Institutions, essays and maxims. . . ."

WIT and fancy in a maze ; or the incomparable champion of love and beautie ; a mock romance . . . written originally in the British tongue and now made English [or rather written] by a person of much honor [Samuel Holland]. 8vo. Pp. 211. [*Brit. Mus.*]
                    London, 1656

Another edition in the same year bears the title "Don Zara del Fogo . . . ", and a later edition (1719), "The Spaniards ; or Don Zara del Fogo. . . ." An edition of 1660 with the title "Romancio-Mastix" bears Holland's name.

WITH the R.A.M.C. in Egypt. By "Sergeant-Major, R.A.M.C." [Edward Tickner Edwardes]. 8vo. Pp. 315. [*Brit. Mus.*]   London, 1918

WOE (the) of scandal ; or, scandal in its general nature and effects ; discours'd, as one strongest argument against impositions in religious things acknowledged to be indifferent. [By Thomas Beverley.] [*M'Alpin Coll. Cat.*]
                    London, 1682

Included in his "Principles of Protestant Truth and Peace" (1683), with separate register and pagination.

WORD (a) in season ; or, motives to peace, accomodation, and unity, 'twixt Presbyterian and Independent Brethren. Drawn from necessity of duty, necessity of expediency, and from the possibility of atchieving. [By William Walwyn.] 8vo. Pp. 8. [*D.N.B.* vol. 59, p. 285.]   London, 1646

Y

YARN (the) of a Yankee privateer. [By Benjamin Frederick Browne]. Edited by Nathaniel Hawthorne. Introduction by Clifford Smyth. 8vo. Pp. 308. [*New York Times Book Review*, 20th March 1927.]   New York, 1926

Originally published serially in the *Democratic Review* as "Papers of an old Dartmoor prisoner."

YELLOW (the) book ; or a serious letter [signed W. B. *i.e.* William Blake, Housekeeper to the Ladies Charity School, Highgate], sent by a private Christian to the Lady Consideration 1st May 1656, which she is desired to communicate in Hide Park to the gallants of the time. . . . 4to. Pp. 21. [*Brit. Mus.*]   London, 1656

For an earlier edition (1655) with variant title see "A serious letter . . ." See also "The trial of the ladies . . ." and "A new trial of the ladies . . ."

YES and No. [By Sir Henry Rich.] 8vo. Pp. 13. [*Brit. Mus.*]
                    London, 1852

YOUNG (a) autocrat. By Cecil Adair [Evelyn Everett-Green]. 8vo. Pp. 220.
                    London, 1923

YOUNG Jemmy ; or the princely Shepherd [*i.e.* James Fitzroy, Duke of Monmouth]. Being a most pleasant new song. [By Mrs Aphra Behn.] Fol. S. sh. B. L. [*Brit. Mus.*]
                    [London, 1683 ?]

YOUNG (a) traveller's Journal of a tour in North and South America during the year 1850. With numerous illustrations by the authoress. [By Victoria Stuart Wortley, afterwards Lady Welby-Gregory.] Pp. xi. 260. [*Brit. Mus.*]   London, 1852

The illustrations are signed : V. S. W.

YOUR luck's in your hand. [A palmistry chart. By Eurica Twiss.] Fol. S. sh. [*Brit. Mus.*]
                    [London, 1917]

YOUTH (the) of Jefferson ; or, a chronicle of College scrapes at Williamsburg in Virginia, A.D. 1764. [By John Esten Cooke.] 12mo. Pp. 249. [Wegelin's *Bibl. of J. E. Cooke.*]
                    New York, 1854

PRINTED BY
OLIVER AND BOYD LTD.
EDINBURGH